800

mon 908
I act - 961
2no 2 act
wed 3 act

# Patterns for
# LIVING

THE MACMILLAN COMPANY
NEW YORK · BOSTON · CHICAGO · DALLAS
ATLANTA · SAN FRANCISCO

MACMILLAN AND CO., Limited
LONDON · BOMBAY · CALCUTTA · MADRAS
MELBOURNE

THE MACMILLAN COMPANY
OF CANADA, Limited
TORONTO

# Patterns for
# LIVING

### Edited by

OSCAR JAMES CAMPBELL   *Columbia University*

JUSTINE VAN GUNDY   *University of Wisconsin*

CAROLINE SHRODES   *Stockton Junior College*

## THE MACMILLAN COMPANY

*New York*

# FOREWORD

The though analyzing the second main division of this anthology is the relation of the individual to his social milieu. The first section examines the problems of a three conditions to significance and science consideration of our ideas of liberty and democracy; the struggle for peace; problems of war and peace; and visions of a better world.

Since we wished above all to capture the interest of our readers we have chosen most of our material from contemporary literature, which commands

THE EDITORS have designed this anthology for college students of English as a foundation for a closely coördinated course in reading and writing. It expresses our belief that only when a person has something to say can he write lucidly and vigorously. A page of manuscript can be no more interesting than the mind from which it comes. It is true that an undergraduate's personal experience is limited, but nevertheless it can be enlarged and clarified through his reading. For it is in books that he will find many problems and situations like those he has already met, and many more like those which life will thrust upon him. Literary experience may be relatively pale; but if one learns how to absorb it, it often drives one to put into words the thoughts and feelings which it arouses. Only books which give a student something that he needs will jostle his ideas out of stale inertia into articulate expression. The serious undergraduate is therefore justified in insisting that every course which he elects be in some sense practical. He demands that it contribute to the sense of security without which he cannot find any sure footing in our wildly careening world. No wonder that he asks with deepening earnestness, "What will this course do for me? How will it help me to understand life and to find my place in it? How will it teach me to solve the problems, personal, social, and economic, which crowd in upon me?"

English can probably give an undergraduate better guidance for his living than any other subject in his curriculum. Therefore teachers of the subject, far from resenting his utilitarian attitude, should seize the opportunity to make clear even to the most sceptical of their students the profoundly practical values to be found in literature. To do so they need not treat the books they read with their classes as essays in social adjustment or as bibles of moral instruction. They need only emphasize the fact that literature is the very stuff of life. These are the considerations which have led the editors of this volume to choose materials dealing with questions of immediate interest to students who are eager above all else to understand the dominant forces of the world in which they live.

The first section of the book deals with problems which the student is certain to meet in his search for personal satisfaction. It begins with selections which present simple sense experience and continues with those which illustrate the more complex satisfactions sought by the individual in his personal relationships, in the arts, in science, in religion, and in living philosophies which present a synthesis of the various personal quests.

The theme unifying the second main division of this anthology is the relation of the individual to the social group. The first section examines the problems of college education; the sections following introduce the student to significant social issues—consideration of our ideas of liberty and democracy, the struggle for justice, problems of war and peace, and visions of a better world.

Since we wished above all to capture the interest of our readers, we have chosen most of our material from contemporary literature which comments upon the world in which we all live. However, we have included a number of classics in order to remind the student that experience has remained much the same throughout the ages, and that his most persistent problems have attracted the best minds of many generations. We have excluded the selections from literature of the past which are ordinarily studied in the senior year of high school or in the sophomore survey course.

We have not adopted a chronological arrangement of our material. Instead, we have put the selections in the order which we believed would be most likely to stimulate active thinking. We have usually tried to follow the presentation of a theory or a concept with its concrete illustration and to present together affirmative and negative views of the same problem. Although within the various topical divisions we have grouped the selections according to literary types, in general we have avoided formal or academic methods of organization. In choosing our material our first interest has been to represent a wide range of human experience.

The brief prefaces to each division point out the many variations played upon the ideas to be found in it. We hope that they may induce a questioning attitude of mind and lead the student to vigorous and independent thought and expression. To this end the suggestions for reading and writing may also contribute. Throughout this anthology it has been our wish to arouse in the student a sense of his relationship with thinkers and artists of past and present who may lead him to an enrichment of his own life.

In the reprint of December, 1941, at the request of users of this book, the date of publication has been added to each selection and appears opposite the author's name, in the only available space.

# ACKNOWLEDGMENTS

FOR PERMISSION to reprint material in copyright, acknowledgment is hereby made to the following publishing houses and individuals:

MAXWELL ANDERSON: For *The Arts as Motive Power*.

ANDERSON HOUSE: For *Winterset*. Copyright, 1935, by Anderson House. Reprinted by permission of author and publisher.

ATLANTIC MONTHLY: For *Sweetness and Light—Fifty Years Afterward*, by James Truslow Adams.
    For *The Influence of My Father on My Son*, by Lincoln Steffens.
    For *Lord of Marutea*, by James Norman Hall.
    For *Aggression, Savage and Domesticated*, by Gregory Zilboorg.
    For *Science and the Money Minded*, by T. Swann Harding.
    For *A Novelist Begins*, by James T. Farrell. Originally this essay appeared in *The Atlantic Monthly* and subsequently it was printed as the introduction to The Modern Library edition of *Studs Lonigan*.
    These selections are reprinted by permission of the authors and *The Atlantic Monthly*.

STEPHEN VINCENT BENÉT: For *The Devil and Daniel Webster*, from *Thirteen o'Clock*, published by Farrar and Rinehart, Inc. Copyright, 1936, 1937, by Stephen Vincent Benét.

EDWIN BORCHARD: For the Bronson M. Cutting Lecture of Feb. 7, 1938, on *Democracy and Foreign Policy*.

PEARL S. BUCK: For *America's Medieval Women*, first published in *Harper's Magazine* for August, 1938.

COVICI, FRIEDE, INC.: For the selections from *Chorus for Survival*, by Horace Gregory.

F. S. CROFTS AND COMPANY: For *The Marxian View of History*, by Carl Becker, from *Every Man His Own Historian*. Copyright by F. S. Crofts and Co.

DODD, MEAD AND COMPANY, INC.: For *The Great Lover*, by Rupert Brooke, from *The Collected Poems of Rupert Brooke*. Copyright, 1915, by Dodd, Mead and Company, Inc.

DOUBLEDAY, DORAN AND COMPANY, INC.: For the *Epilogue at the Core of Earth*, from *Break the Heart's Anger*, by Paul Engle. Copyright, 1935, 1936, by Doubleday, Doran and Company, Inc.
    For *Memory of the Witness*, from *On the Witness Stand*, by Hugo Münsterberg. Copyright, 1923, by Doubleday, Doran and Company, Inc.
    For *Seeing Life*, from *The Author's Craft*, by Arnold Bennett. Copyright, 1914, by Doubleday, Doran and Company, Inc.
    For the selection from *Typhoon*, by Joseph Conrad. Copyright, 1902, 1903, 1921, by Doubleday, Doran and Company, Inc.

For the *Preface* from *The Nigger of the Narcissus,* by Joseph Conrad. Copyright, 1897, 1914, by Doubleday, Doran and Company, Inc.

For *Four Years in a Shed,* from *Madame Curie,* by Eve Curie. Copyright, 1937, by Doubleday, Doran and Company, Inc.

For *Young Man Axelbrod,* from *Selected Short Stories of Sinclair Lewis,* by Sinclair Lewis. Copyright, 1931, reprinted by permission of Doubleday, Doran and Company, Inc.

For *Enjoying Life,* by W. N. P. Barbellion. Copyright, 1920, by Doubleday, Doran and Company, Inc.

For the selections from *Leaves of Grass,* by Walt Whitman. Copyright, 1924, by Doubleday, Doran and Company, Inc.

THE ENGLISH JOURNAL: For *Poetry in a Machine Age,* by Paul Engle.
For *The Second Lost Generation,* by Harlan Hatcher.
Reprinted by permission of the authors and *The English Journal.*

FARRAR AND RINEHART: For *A Visit to Sacco,* from *A Footnote to Folly,* by Mary Heaton Vorse. Copyright, 1935, and reprinted by permission of Farrar and Rinehart, Inc., Publishers.

For *No More Peace,* a play by Ernst Toller. Copyright, 1937, and reprinted by permission of Farrar and Rinehart, Inc., Publishers.

For *Speech to Those Who Say Comrade, Speech to The Detractors, Speech to a Crowd, Dover Beach—A Note to That Poem,* from *Public Speech:* Poems by Archibald MacLeish. Copyright, 1936, and reprinted by permission of Farrar and Rinehart, Inc., Publishers.

For *The Music Lover,* from *Toscanini and Great Music,* by Lawrence Gilman. Copyright, 1938, and reprinted by permission of Farrar and Rinehart, Inc., Publishers.

For *The Preacher,* from *Jasbo Brown and Selected Poems,* by DuBose Heyward. Copyright, 1931, and reprinted by permission of Farrar and Rinehart, Inc., Publishers.

JOHN GOULD FLETCHER: For *Down the Mississippi* and *Skyscrapers,* published by Farrar and Rinehart, Inc., Publishers.

FOREIGN AFFAIRS: For *Education under the Nazis,* by Charles A. Beard.

THE FORTNIGHTLY: For *Return to Religion,* by Gilbert Keith Chesterton.

FORTUNE: For *Youth in College,* by the Editors of *Fortune.*

THE FORUM: For *Apology for Man,* by E. A. Hooton.

WILLIAM HARLAN HALE: For *Mr. Minnow in Trouble,* published by *Story.*

HARCOURT, BRACE AND COMPANY, INC.: For *Abe at 37,* from *Abraham Lincoln: The Prairie Years,* by Carl Sandburg. Copyright, 1926, by Harcourt, Brace and Company, Inc.

For *Love: or the Life and Death of a Value,* from *The Modern Temper,* by Joseph Wood Krutch. Copyright, 1929, by Harcourt, Brace and Company, Inc.

For *I Go To College* and *I Become a Student,* from *The Autobiography of Lincoln Steffens.* Copyright, 1931, by Harcourt, Brace and Company, Inc.

For *The Love Song of J. Alfred Prufrock,* from *Collected Poems,* by T. S. Eliot. Reprinted by permission of Harcourt, Brace and Company, Inc.

For the selection from *The People, Yes,* by Carl Sandburg. Copyright, 1936, by Harcourt, Brace and Company, Inc.

For *Lament of the Normal Child,* from *One More Manhattan,* by Phyllis McGinley. Copyright, 1937, by Harcourt, Brace and Company, Inc.

For *Boy and Father* from *Smoke and Steel*, by Carl Sandburg. Copyright, 1920, by Harcourt, Brace and Company, Inc.

For *The Plain Reader* from *The Modern Novel*, by Elizabeth A. Drew. Copyright, 1926, by Harcourt, Brace and Company, Inc.

For *Hyman Kaplan Cuts a Gordian Knot*, by Leonard Q. Ross. Copyright, 1937, by Harcourt, Brace and Company, Inc.

For *A College Laboratory* from *Arrowsmith*, by Sinclair Lewis. Copyright, 1935, by Harcourt, Brace and Company, Inc.

HARPER AND BROTHERS: For the selection from *Brave New World*, by Aldous Huxley, published by Harper and Brothers.

For the selection from *Autobiography*, by Mark Twain.

For *Life of the Mind, 1935* from *Collected Poems*, by Genevieve Taggard.

For *First Philosopher's Song* from *Leda*, by Aldous Huxley.

HARPER'S MAGAZINE: For *Chemistry Wrecks the Farm*, by W. W. Parrish and H. F. Clark.

For *A College for One*, by Philip Curtiss.

For *Socrates Crosses the Delaware*, by Milton S. Mayer.

For *Collective Living*, by John Hyde Preston.

For *The Man with a Tractor*, by M. Mayo.

For *His Autumn Colored Face*, by Jesse Stuart.

GRANVILLE HICKS: On behalf of the Harvard Alumni John Reed Committee for *Almost Thirty*, by John Reed.

HENRY HOLT AND COMPANY: For *The Tools for Life* from *I Change Worlds*, by Anna Louise Strong. Copyright by Henry Holt and Company.

For *Prairie*, by Carl Sandburg. Copyright by Henry Holt and Company.

For *Prayers of Steel* from *Cornhuskers*, by Carl Sandburg. Copyright by Henry Holt and Company.

For *Birches* from *Mountain Interval*, by Robert Frost. Copyright by Henry Holt and Company.

HOUGHTON MIFFLIN COMPANY: For *You, Andrew Marvell* and *"Not Marble Nor the Gilded Monuments"* from *Collected Poems*, by Archibald MacLeish, by permission of Houghton Mifflin Company.

For the selection from *Looking Backward*, by Edward Bellamy, by permission of Houghton Mifflin Company.

For *The Father* by Björnstjerne Björnson. Translated by Professor R. B. Anderson. Copyright by Houghton Mifflin Company, authorized publishers.

HOWARD MUMFORD JONES: For *The American Scholar Once More*, published in *The Harvard Alumni Bulletin*.

FREDA KIRCHWEY: For *A Plea for Democracy*, published in *The Journal of the American Association of University Women*.

ALFRED A. KNOPF, INC.: For *The Fly*, reprinted from *The Collected Stories of Katharine Mansfield*, by Katharine Mansfield, by permission of and special arrangement with Alfred A. Knopf, Inc., authorized publishers.

For *Letter to a Teacher of English*, reprinted from *Letter to Robert Frost, and Others*, by Robert Hillyer, by permission of and special arrangement with Alfred A. Knopf, Inc., authorized publishers.

For *Castilian* and *Nonsense Rhyme*, reprinted from *Collected Poems*, by Elinor Wylie, by permission of and special arrangement with Alfred A. Knopf, Inc., authorized publishers.

For *My Father's Religion*, reprinted from *Life with Father*, by Clarence Day, by permission of and special arrangement with Alfred A. Knopf, Inc., authorized publishers.

For *Paul's Case*, reprinted from *Youth and The Bright Medusa*, by Willa Cather, by permission of and special arrangement with Alfred A. Knopf, Inc., authorized publishers.

LIVERIGHT PUBLISHING CORPORATION: For the selection from *Story of Utopias*, by Lewis Mumford, published by Liveright Publishing Corporation.

LONGMANS, GREEN AND COMPANY: For *The New Age and The New Man*, by R. E. Flanders from Charles A. Beard's *Towards Civilization*. Copyright by Longmans, Green and Company.

THE MACMILLAN COMPANY: For *Color* and *Sight* from *Poems*, by Wilfred Gibson.

For *God Forgotten*, *At Tea*, *At the Drapers*, *The Man He Killed*, *In Time of the Breaking of Nations*, and *Lausanne* from *Collected Poems*, by Thomas Hardy.

For the selection from *Tristram*, by E. A. Robinson.

For the selection from *Dauber*, *A Consecration*, and *Laugh and Be Merry* from *Poems*, by John Masefield.

For *Eyewitness* from *Hesperides*, by Ridgely Torrence.

For *Prayer for My Daughter* and *The Scholars* from *Poems*, by William Butler Yeats.

For *On the Building of Springfield* and *Abe Lincoln Walks at Midnight* from *Poems*, by Vachel Lindsay.

For *Evolution of the Physical World* from *Science and the Unseen World*, by Arthur Stanley Eddington.

For *Is Man an Absurdity?* from *Patterns for Survival*, by John Hodgdon Bradley.

For the selection from *The Method of Freedom*, by Walter Lippmann.

For *The Bet* from *The Schoolmistress*, by Anton Chekhov, translated by Constance Garnett.

For *The Struggle for Existence* from *On the Origin of Species*, by Charles Darwin.

The above selections are all used by permission of The Macmillan Company.

ALBERT MALTZ: For *Man on the Road*, published by *The New Masses*.

EDGAR LEE MASTERS: For *Seth Compton* from *The Spoon River Anthology*, published by The Macmillan Company.

EDNA ST. VINCENT MILLAY: For *When We That Wore the Myrtle* and *Love Is Not All*, from *Fatal Interview*, published by Harper and Bros. Copyright, 1931, by Edna St. Vincent Millay.

For *Justice Denied in Massachusetts*, from *The Buck in the Snow*, published by Harper and Bros. Copyright, 1928, by Edna St. Vincent Millay.

A. A. MILNE: For *Mr. Pim Passes By*, from *Second Plays*, by A. A. Milne, published by Alfred A. Knopf, Inc. Reprinted by permission of the author. Copyright, 1922, by Alfred A. Knopf, Inc.

WILLIAM MORROW AND COMPANY, INC.: For the selection from *Lost Horizon*, by James Hilton. Copyright, 1933, 1936, by William Morrow and Company, Inc., by permission of William Morrow and Company, Inc.

For *Mrs. Maddison* from *The Trouble I've Seen*, by Martha Gellhorn, by permission of William Morrow and Company, Inc.

THE NATION: For *Pacifism Means Suicide,* by Aurel Kolnai.
For *Munich Rather than War,* by Bertrand Russell.
For *A Very Private Utopia,* by Stuart Chase.
For *What Is a Poet?* by Mark Van Doren.
The above selections are reprinted by permission of the authors and *The Nation,* original publishers.

NEW MASSES: For *The Tide,* by William Rose Benét.
For *To My Students, Autumn Song for Anti-Fascists,* and *Definition of Song,* by Genevieve Taggard.
For *The Democratic Idea,* by Joseph Freeman.
For *Man on the Road,* by Albert Maltz.
The above selections are reprinted by permission of the authors and *New Masses,* original publishers.

THE NEW REPUBLIC: For *Joe Louis Never Smiles,* by Jonathan Mitchell.
For *Diary of a Worrier,* by Bruce Bliven.
For *Gulliver's Grandson,* by Hamilton Basso.
The above selections are reprinted by permission of the authors and *The New Republic.*

JOSEPHINE K. NEWTON: For *Youth Challenges the Church,* published by *Scribner's Magazine.*

THE NEW YORKER: For *City Rhythms.*
For *Wake Up and Live,* by James Thurber.
For *The Lament of the Normal Child,* by Phyllis McGinley.
For *Midwifery of Ideas,* by Morris Bishop.
The above selections are reprinted by permission of the authors and *The New Yorker.*

W. W. NORTON AND COMPANY, INC.: For *A Free Man's Worship* from *Mysticism and Logic,* by Bertrand Russell. Copyright by W. W. Norton and Company, Inc., Publishers.

OXFORD UNIVERSITY PRESS: For *Sonnet* and *God's Grandeur,* by Gerard Manley Hopkins.
By permission of the Oxford University Press and the poet's family.

JO PAGANO: For *The Disinherited,* published by *Scribner's Magazine.*

RANDOM HOUSE: For the poems by Stephen Spender.
For the selection from *The Magnetic Mountain,* by C. Day Lewis.
For *To the Stone-Cutters,* by Robinson Jeffers.
For *The Cup of Tea* from *Swann's Way,* by Marcel Proust.
For *Shadow and Substance,* by Paul Vincent Carroll.
Reprinted by permission of Random House, Inc., N. Y.

VIRGINIA RICE: For *The Ballad of the Goodly Fere,* by Ezra Pound.

TESS SLESINGER: For *A Life in the Day of a Writer,* published by *Story.*

SIEGFRIED SASSOON: For *Dreamers* and *Aftermath.*

THE SATURDAY REVIEW: For *No More of the Moon,* by Morris Bishop, reprinted by permission of the author and *The Saturday Review,* original publishers.
For *Try Tropic,* by Genevieve Taggard, reprinted by permission of the author and *The Saturday Review,* original publishers.

SCRIBNER'S MAGAZINE: For *Our Hypnotized World*, by V. F. Calverton, reprinted by permission of the author and publisher.

CHARLES SCRIBNER'S SONS: For *Flammonde, Dear Friends*, and *Sonnet*, by Edwin Arlington Robinson.
For *Old Man at the Bridge* from *the Fifth Column and the First Forty-nine Stories*, by Ernest Hemingway.
For *Apology for Idlers* and *Walking Tours*, by Robert Louis Stevenson.

SIMON AND SCHUSTER, INC.: For *Leonardo da Vinci* from *Men of Art*, by Thomas Craven. Copyright by Simon and Schuster, Inc.
For *The Coming Humanism*, by Thomas Mann, from *I Believe*, edited by Clifton Fadiman. Copyright by Simon and Schuster, Inc.
For *Why I am a Marxist*, by Harold Laski, from *I Believe*, edited by Clifton Fadiman. Copyright by Simon and Schuster, Inc.
For *What I Believe*, by Lewis Mumford, from *Living Philosophies*. Copyright by Simon and Schuster, Inc.

JOHN STEINBECK: For *The Chrysanthemums*, from *The Long Valley*, by John Steinbeck, published by the Viking Press, 1938.

STORY AND THE STORY PRESS: For *If This Be Treason*, by Walter Gilkyson.
For *Boy in the Summer Sun*, by Mark Schorer.
For *David, I've Told Them*, by Mary Jonathan.
For *A Life in the Day of a Writer*, by Tess Slesinger.
For *Mr. Minnow in Trouble*, by William Harlan Hale.
For *$595 F. O. B.*, by George Corey.
By permission of the authors and *Story* and The Story Press.

THEATRE ARTS MONTHLY: For *Katharine Cornell: The Actor Attacks His Part*, by Morton Eustis. Copyright by *Theatre Arts Monthly*.

THE VIKING PRESS, INC.: For *Young Writer Remembering Chicago* from *On the Shore*, by Albert Halper. Copyright, 1934. By permission of The Viking Press, Inc., New York.
For *The New Wasteland* from *It Is Later than You Think*, by Max Lerner. Copyright, 1938, by Max Lerner. By permission of The Viking Press, Inc., New York.
For Chapter V from *The Grapes of Wrath*, by John Steinbeck. Copyright, 1939, by John Steinbeck. By permission of The Viking Press, Inc., New York.
For *Strange Meeting* from *The Poems of Wilfred Owen*. By permission of The Viking Press, Inc., New York.
For *The Old Agitator* and *Resolve* from *A Son of Earth*, by W. E. Leonard. Copyright, 1928. By permission of The Viking Press, Inc., New York.

THE VIRGINIA QUARTERLY REVIEW: For *Much Could Be Done*, by Ernestine Evans. Copyright by *The Virginia Quarterly Review*.

YALE UNIVERSITY PRESS: For the selections from *Theory of Flight*, by Muriel Rukeyser. Copyright by Yale University Press.

# CONTENTS

### PART ONE

## *The Quest of the Individual for Personal Satisfaction*

## 3. THE ARTS 253

*Essays*

*Biography*

*Fiction*

PART TWO

## The Quest of the Individual for Adjustment to the Social Group

## 2. IDEAS OF LIBERTY AND DEMOCRACY

### Essays

## 3. THE STRUGGLE FOR JUSTICE

## 4. WAR AND PEACE

### *Essays*

### *Fiction*

### *Drama*

### *Poetry*

## 5. THE WORLD OF TOMORROW

### *Essays*

# PART ONE

## The Quest of the Individual for Personal Satisfaction

# THE WORLD OF THE SENSES AND NATURE

To our great-grandparents, used to the muffled noises of a century ago, the brutal din of a modern city would be a kind of anguish. Five minutes of the Chicago that Halper describes would exhaust Browning's Person of Quality. The blessed church bells that used to peal in "Up at a Villa—Down in the City" or even the bang-whang-whang of the drum on the square would not have prepared his ears for the hum of motorcars, the roar of trucks and the shrieking of ambulances and fire engines. He would be astonished to see the quiet stars and the drifting clouds hidden by a fleet of airplanes or perhaps a blimp advertising in fiery scrolls the virtues of an automobile tire. Indoors he would find himself sitting either before a radio, listening to the blare of a swing band or in a movie theatre gazing at pictures which flashed out news of a turbulent world. We who live every day in this confusion are in danger of being imprisoned by our senses.

Neither villages nor remote farms offer a safe refuge from the sights and sounds of our machine age. Our lives move restlessly forward on a continuous stream of sensation. We are so busy looking and listening that we seldom search beneath the surface of things. Yet mere sensations have a profound effect upon everyone. They fix, to a large extent, the character of our emotions, which, in turn, determine the quality of our personalities. The objects that assail our ears and eyes should therefore be of the sort to give our lives elevation and stability.

Sensations also coöperate with the memory to bring to life the most precious moments of the past. The process is a simple one. It begins with a vivid and joyous moment of excitement. This experience may come from the mere touch of smooth sheets or of woolly blankets or, as Marcel Proust tells us, from the taste of a piece of cake. Or the ecstasy may be awakened by the sight of a cherry tree "hung with snow" and the pungent odor of the blossoms. The intense delight which we feel calls out of the past into present life another adventure written in the same emotional key. This becomes a focus for other related memories until the present and the past unite to form one intense experience, which may become a permanent source of power and happiness.

Our knowledge of the world about us and the nature of the relations we establish with it depends upon just such adventures as these. Indeed, the quality of our inner life is greatly affected by the way we respond to the appeals of the ever-changing world of natural objects. Many of the authors represented in this volume can teach us how to make our relations to nature constant and vivid. Wordsworth said of his sister Dorothy that she gave him eyes and ears. Poets also can do this service for us. They can quicken our interest in the world of eye and ear, in its gray skies, its mists and autumn woods and also in the people whom we meet either one by one or as they are part of the pageantry of a football game or a prize fight.

Moreover, it is safe to say that all great writers pass on to their readers more than the bare reports of their senses. They are likely to discover in nature more than appears on the surface. At least they search for something of deeper human import than their joy in the vast pageant of creation. And they may find it as they contemplate the brave, unbroken life of plants, of animals, of the moon and of the stars. There, they may realize, are the peace and security which their inner world of feeling and aspirations must possess.

The advance of biological knowledge has forced man to acknowledge a close relationship between himself and other creatures of the earth. In some writers this realization has awakened only despair. They see no hope for the development of man's finest impulses in a world of relentless struggle for survival. Other thinkers are less pessimistic. The realization that they form a part of a great chain of beings brings them a feeling of elation. Their joy is perhaps like that which stirred the most sensitive of pagans when their imagination showed them Proteus rising from the sea and let them hear "old Triton blow his wreathed horn."

Some imaginative writers appeal to still deeper impulses. They may, like Wordsworth, lead us to find behind all appearance a mysterious presence, the soul of all things that are. Other authors less mystical than he, finding design in nature, see in this order evidence of the existence of a Supreme Power who has imposed on man patterns for his life. Philosophical speculation of this sort shows how short and straight is the way from the world of the senses to deep religious convictions. Even in the uproar of our world we can find in simple natural objects the guide and guardian of our better selves.

## SEEING LIFE

### *Arnold Bennett* (*1914*)

### I

A young dog, inexperienced, sadly lacking in even primary education, ambles and frisks along the footpath of Fulham Road, near the mysterious gates of a Marist convent. He is a large puppy, on the way to be a dog of much dignity, but at present he has little to recommend him but that gawky elegance, and that bounding gratitude for the gift of life, which distinguish the normal puppy. He is an ignorant fool. He might have entered the convent of nuns and had a fine time, but instead he steps off the pavement into the road, the road being a vast and interesting continent imperfectly explored. His confidence in his nose, in his agility, and in the goodness of God is touching, absolutely painful to witness. He glances casually at a huge, towering vermilion construction that is whizzing towards him on four wheels, preceded by a glint of brass and a wisp of steam; and then with disdain he ignores it as less important than a speck of odorous matter in the mud. The next instant he is lying inert in the mud. His confidence in the goodness of God had been misplaced. Since the beginning of time God had ordained him a victim.

An impressive thing happens. The motor-bus reluctantly slackens and stops. Not the differential brake, nor the footbrake, has arrested the motor-bus, but the invisible brake of public opinion, acting by administrative transmission. There is not a policeman in sight. Theoretically, the motor-bus is free to whiz onward in its flight to the paradise of Shoreditch, but in practice it is paralysed by dread. A man in brass buttons and a stylish cap leaps down from it, and the blackened demon who sits on its neck also leaps down from it, and they move gingerly towards the puppy. A little while ago the motor-bus might have overturned a human cyclist or so, and proceeded nonchalantly on its way. But now even a puppy requires a post-mortem: such is the force of public opinion aroused. Two policemen appear in the distance.

"A street accident" is now in being, and a crowd gathers with calm joy and stares, passive and determined. The puppy offers no sign whatever; just lies in the road. Then a boy, destined probably to a great future by reason of his singular faculty of initiative, goes to the puppy and carries him by the scruff of the neck, to the shelter of the gutter. Relinquished by the boy, the lithe puppy falls into an easy horizontal attitude, and seems bent upon repose. The boy lifts the puppy's head to examine it, and the head drops back wearily. The puppy is dead. No cry, no blood, no disfigurement! Even no perceptible jolt of the wheel as it climbed over the obstacle of the puppy's body! A wonderfully clean and perfect accident!

The increasing crowd stares with beatific placidity. People emerge impatiently from the bowels of the throbbing motor-bus and slip down from its back, and either join the crowd or vanish. The two policemen and the crew of the motor-bus have now met in parley. The conductor and the driver have an air at once nervous and resigned; their gestures are quick and vivacious. The policemen, on the other hand, indicate by their slow and huge movements that eternity is theirs. And they could not be more sure of the conductor and the driver if they had them manacled and leashed. The conductor and the driver admit the absolute dominion of the elephantine policemen; they admit that before the simple will of the policemen inconvenience, lost minutes, shortened leisure, docked wages, count as less than naught. And the policemen are carelessly sublime, well knowing that magistrates, jails, and the very Home Secretary on his throne—yes, and a whole system of conspiracy and perjury and brutality—are at their beck in case of need. And yet occasionally in the demeanour of the policemen towards the conductor and the driver there is a silent message that says: "After all, we, too, are working men like you, overworked and under-paid and bursting with grievances in the service of the pitiless and dishonest public. We, too, have wives and children and privations and frightful apprehensions. We, too, have to struggle desperately. Only the awful magic of these garments and of the garter which we wear on our wrists sets an abyss between us and you." And the conductor writes and one of the policemen writes, and they keep on writing while the traffic makes beautiful curves to avoid them.

The still increasing crowd continues to stare in the pure blankness of pleasure. A close-shaved, well-dressed, middle-aged man, with a copy of *The Sportsman* in his podgy hand, who has descended from the motor-bus, starts stamping his feet. "I was knocked down by a taxi last year," he says fiercely. "But nobody took no notice of *that*! Are they going to stop here all the blank morning for a blank tyke?" And for all his respectable appearance, his features become debased, and he emits a jet of disgusting profanity and brings most of the Trinity into the thunderous assertion that he has paid his fare. Then a man passes wheeling a muck-cart. And he stops and talks a long time with the other uniforms, because he, too, wears vestiges of a uniform. And the crowd never moves nor ceases to stare. Then the new arrival stoops and picks up the unclaimed, masterless puppy, and flings it, all soft and yielding, into the horrid mess of the cart, and passes on. And only that which is immortal and divine of the puppy remains behind, floating perhaps like an invisible vapour over the scene of the tragedy.

The crowd is tireless, all eyes. The four principals still converse and write. Nobody in the crowd comprehends what they are about. At length the driver separates himself, but is drawn back, and a new parley is commenced. But everything ends. The policemen turn on their immense heels. The driver and conductor race towards the motor-bus. The bell rings, the motor-bus, quite empty, disappears snorting round the corner into Walham Green. The crowd is now lessening. But it separates with reluctance, many of its members continuing to stare with intense absorption at the place where the puppy lay or the place where the policemen stood. An appreciable interval elapses before the "street accident" has entirely ceased to exist as a phenomenon.

The members of the crowd follow their noses, and during the course of the day remark to acquaintances:

"Saw a dog run over by a motor-bus in the Fulham Road this morning! Killed dead!"

And that is all they do remark. That is all they have witnessed. They will not, and could not, give intelligible and interesting particulars of the affair (unless it were as to the breed of the dog or the number of the bus-service). They have watched a dog run over. They analyse neither their sensations nor the phenomenon. They have witnessed it whole, as a bad writer uses a *cliché*. They have observed—that is to say, they have really seen—nothing.

## II

It will be well for us not to assume an attitude of condescension towards the crowd. Because in the matter of looking without seeing we are all about equal. We all go to and fro in a state of the observing faculties which somewhat resembles coma. We are all content to look and not see.

And if and when, having comprehended that the role of observer is not passive but active, we determine by an effort to rouse ourselves from the coma and really to see the spectacle of the world (a spectacle surpassing circuses and even street accidents in sustained dramatic interest), we shall discover, slowly in the course of time, that the act of seeing, which seems so easy, is not so easy as it seems. Let a man resolve: "I will keep my eyes open on the way to the office of a morning," and the probability is that for many mornings he will see naught that is not trivial, and that his system of perspective will be absurdly distorted. The unusual, the unaccustomed, will infallibly attract him, to the exclusion of what is fundamental and universal. Travel makes observers of us all, but the things which as travellers we observe generally show how unskilled we are in the new activity.

A man went to Paris for the first time, and observed right off that the carriages of suburban trains had seats on the roof like a tram-car. He was so thrilled by the remarkable discovery that he observed almost nothing else. This enormous fact occupied the whole foreground of his perspective. He returned home and announced that Paris was a place where people rode on the tops of trains. A Frenchwoman came to London for the first time—and no English person would ever guess the phenomenon which vanquished all others in her mind on the opening day. She saw a cat walking across a street. The vision excited her. For in Paris cats do not roam in thoroughfares, because there are practically no houses with gardens or "areas"; the flat system is unfavourable to the enlargement of cats. I remember once, in the days when observation had first presented itself to me as a beautiful pastime, getting up very early and making the circuit of inner London before summer dawn in quest of interesting material. And the one note I gathered was that the ground in front of the all-night coffee-stalls was white with eggshells! What I needed then was an operation for cataract. I also remember taking a man to the opera who had never seen an opera. The work was *Lohengrin*. When we came out he said: "That swan's neck was rather stiff." And it was all he did say. We went and had a drink. He was not mistaken. His observation was most just; but his perspective was that of those literary critics who give ten lines to pointing out three slips of syntax, and three lines to an ungrammatical admission that the novel under survey is not wholly tedious.

But a man may acquire the ability to observe even a large number of facts, and still remain in the infantile stage of observation. I have read, in some work of literary criticism, that Dickens could walk up one side of a long, busy street and down the other, and then tell you in their order the names on all the shop-signs; the fact was alleged as an illustration of his great powers of observation. Dickens was a great observer, but he would assuredly have been a still greater observer had he been a little less pre-occupied with trivial and uncoördinated details. Good observation consists not in multiplicity of detail, but in coördination of detail according to a true perspective of relative importance, so that a finally just general impression may be reached in the shortest possible time. The skilled observer is he who does not have to change his mind. One has only to compare one's present adjusted impression of an intimate friend with one's first impression of him to perceive the astounding inadequacy of one's powers of observation. The man as one has learnt to see him is simply not the same who walked into one's drawing-room on the day of introduction.

There are, by the way, three sorts of created beings who are sentimentally supposed to be able to judge individuals at the first glance: women, children, and dogs. By virtue of a mystic gift with which rumour credits them, they are never mistaken. It is merely not true. Women are constantly quite wrong in the estimates based on their "feminine instinct"; they sometimes even admit it; and the matrimonial courts prove it *passim*. Children are more often wrong than women. And as for dogs, it is notorious that they are for ever being taken in by plausible scoundrels; the perspective of dogs is grotesque. Not seldom have I grimly watched the gradual disillusion of deceived dogs. Nevertheless, the sentimental legend of the infallibility of women, children, and dogs, will persist in Anglo-Saxon countries.

### III

One is curious about one's fellow-creatures: therefore one watches them. And generally the more intelligent one is, the more curious one is, and the more one observes. The mere satisfaction of this curiosity is in itself a worthy end, and would alone justify the business of systematised observation. But the aim of observation may, and should, be expressed in terms more grandiose. Human curiosity counts among the highest social virtues (as indifference counts among the basest defects), because it leads to the disclosure of the causes of character and temperament and thereby to a better understanding of the springs of human conduct. Observation is not practised directly with this high end in view (save by prigs and other futile souls); nevertheless it is a moral act and must inevitably promote kindliness—whether we like it or not. It also sharpens the sense of beauty. An ugly deed—such as a deed of cruelty —takes on artistic beauty when its origin and hence its fitness in the general scheme begin to be comprehended. In the perspective of history we can derive an æsthetic pleasure from the tranquil scrutiny of all kinds of conduct— as well, for example, of a Renaissance Pope as of a Savonarola. Observation endows our day and our street with the romantic charm of history, and stimulates charity—not the charity which signs cheques, but the more precious charity which puts itself to the trouble of understanding. The one condition is that the observer must never lose sight of the fact that what he is trying to see is life, is the woman next door, is the man in the train—and not a concourse of abstractions. To appreciate all this is the first inspiring preliminary to sound observation.

## IV

The second preliminary is to realise that all physical phenomena are interrelated, that there is nothing which does not bear on everything else. The whole spectacular and sensual show—what the eye sees, the ear hears, the nose scents, the tongue tastes and the skin touches—is a cause or an effect of human conduct. Naught can be ruled out as negligible, as not forming part of the equation. Hence he who would beyond all others see life for himself—I naturally mean the novelist and playwright—ought to embrace all phenomena in his curiosity. Being finite, he cannot. Of course he cannot! But he can, by obtaining a broad notion of the whole, determine with some accuracy the position and relative importance of the particular series of phenomena to which his instinct draws him. If he does not thus envisage the immense background of his special interests, he will lose the most precious feeling for interplay and proportion without which all specialism becomes distorted and positively darkened.

Now, the main factor in life on this planet is the planet itself. Any logically conceived survey of existence must begin with geographical and climatic phenomena. This is surely obvious. If you say that you are not interested in meteorology or the configurations of the earth, I say that you deceive yourself. You are. For an east wind may upset your liver and cause you to insult your wife. Beyond question the most important fact about, for example, Great Britain is that it is an island. We sail amid the Hebrides, and then talk of the fine qualities and the distressing limitations of those islanders; it ought to occur to us English that we are talking of ourselves in little. In moments of journalistic vainglory we are apt to refer to the "sturdy island race," meaning us. But that we are insular in the full significance of the horrid word is certain. Why not? A genuine observation of the supreme phenomenon that Great Britain is surrounded by water—an effort to keep it always at the back of the consciousness—will help to explain all the minor phenomena of British existence. Geographical knowledge is the mother of discernment, for the varying physical characteristics of the earth are the sole direct terrestrial influence determining the evolution of original vital energy.

All other influences are secondary, and have been effects of character and temperament before becoming causes. Perhaps the greatest of them are roads and architecture. Nothing could be more English than English roads, or more French than French roads. Enter England from France, let us say through the gate of Folkestone, and the architectural illustration which greets you (if you can look and see) is absolutely dramatic in its spectacular force. You say that there is no architecture in Folkestone. But Folkestone, like other towns, is just as full of architecture as a wood is full of trees. As the train winds on its causeway over the sloping town you perceive below you thousands of squat little homes, neat, tended, respectable, comfortable, prim, at once unostentatious and conceited. Each a separate, clearly defined entity. Each saying to the others: "Don't look over my wall, and I won't look over yours!" Each with a ferocious jealousy bent on guarding its own individuality! Each a stronghold—an island! And all careless of the general effect, but making a very impressive general effect. The English race is below you. Your own son is below you insisting on the inviolability of his own den of a bedroom! . . . And contrast all that with the immense communistic and splendid façades of a French town, and work out the implications. If you really intend to see life you cannot afford to be blind to such thrilling phenomena.

Yet an inexperienced, unguided curiosity would be capable of walking through a French street and through an English street, and noting chiefly that whereas English lamp-posts spring from the kerb, French lamp-posts cling to the side of the house! Not that that detail is not worth noting. It is—in its place. French lamp-posts are part of what we call the "interesting character" of a French street. We say of a French street that it is "full of character." As if an English street was not! Such is blindness—to be cured by travel and the exercise of the logical faculty, most properly termed common sense. If one is struck by the magnificence of the great towns of the Continent, one should ratiocinate, and conclude that a major characteristic of the great towns of England is their shabby and higgledy-piggledy slovenliness. It is so. But there are people who have lived fifty years in Manchester, Leeds, Hull, and Hanley without noticing it. The English idiosyncrasy is in that awful external slovenliness too, causing it, and being caused by it. Every street is a mirror, an illustration, an exposition, an explanation, of the human beings who live in it. Nothing in it is to be neglected. Everything in it is valuable, if the perspective is maintained. Nevertheless, in the narrow individualistic novels of English literature—and in some of the best—you will find a domestic organism described as though it existed in a vacuum, or in the Sahara, or between Heaven and earth; as though it reacted on nothing and was reacted on by nothing; and as though it could be adequately rendered without reference to anything exterior to itself. How can such novels satisfy a reader who has acquired or wants to acquire the faculty of seeing life?

## V

The net result of the interplay of instincts and influences which determine the existence of a community is shown in the general expression on the faces of the people. This is an index which cannot lie and cannot be gainsaid. It is fairly easy, and extremely interesting, to decipher. It is so open, shameless, and universal, that not to look at it is impossible. Yet the majority of persons fail to see it. We hear of inquirers standing on London Bridge and counting the number of motor-buses, foot-passengers, lorries, and white horses that pass over the bridge in an hour. But we never hear of anybody counting the number of faces happy or unhappy, honest or rascally, shrewd or ingenuous, kind or cruel, that pass over the bridge. Perhaps the public may be surprised to hear that the general expression on the faces of Londoners of all ranks varies from the sad to the morose; and that their general mien is one of haste and gloomy preoccupation. Such a staring face is paramount in sociological evidence. And the observer of it would be justified in summoning Heaven, the legislature, the county council, the churches, and the ruling classes, and saying to them: "Glance at these faces, and don't boast too much about what you have accomplished. The climate and the industrial system have so far triumphed over you all."

## VI

When we come to the observing of the individual—to which all human observing does finally come if there is any right reason in it—the aforesaid general considerations ought to be ever present in the hinterland of the consciousness, aiding and influencing, perhaps vaguely, perhaps almost imperceptibly, the formation of judgments. If they do nothing else, they will at any rate accustom the observer to the highly important idea of the correlation of all phenomena. Especially in England a haphazard particularity is the chief vitiating element in the operations of the mind.

In estimating the individual we are apt not only to forget his environment, but—really strange!—to ignore much of the evidence visible in the individual himself. The inexperienced and ardent observer will, for example, be astonishingly blind to everything in an individual except his face. Telling himself that the face must be the reflection of the soul, and that every thought and emotion leaves inevitably its mark there, he will concentrate on the face, singling it out as a phenomenon apart and self-complete. Were he a god and infallible, he could no doubt learn the whole truth from the face. But he is bound to fall into errors, and by limiting the field of vision he minimises the opportunity for correction. The face is, after all, quite a small part of the individual's physical organism. An Englishman will look at a woman's face and say she is a beautiful woman or a plain woman. But a woman may have a plain face, and yet by her form be entitled to be called beautiful, and (perhaps) *vice versa*. It is true that the face is the reflection of the soul. It is equally true that the carriage and gestures are the reflection of the soul. Had one eyes, the tying of a bootlace is the reflection of the soul. One piece of evidence can be used to correct every other piece of evidence. A refined face may be refuted by clumsy finger-ends; the eyes may contradict the voice; the gait may nullify the smile. None of the phenomena which every individual carelessly and brazenly displays in every motor-bus terrorising the streets of London is meaningless or negligible.

Again, in observing we are generally guilty of that particularity which results from sluggishness of the imagination. We may see the phenomenon at the moment of looking at it, but we particularise in that moment, making no effort to conceive what the phenomenon is likely to be at other moments.

For example, a male human creature wakes up in the morning and rises with reluctance. Being a big man, and existing with his wife and children in a very confined space, he has to adapt himself to his environment as he goes through the various functions incident to preparing for his day's work. He is just like you or me. He wants his breakfast, he very much wants to know where his boots are, and he has the usually sinister preoccupations about health and finance. Whatever the force of his egoism, he must more or less harmonise his individuality with those of his wife and children. Having laid down the law, or accepted it, he sets forth to his daily duties, just a fraction of a minute late. He arrives at his office, resumes life with his colleagues sympathetic and antipathetic, and then leaves the office for an expedition extending over several hours. In the course of his expedition he encounters the corpse of a young dog run down by a motor-bus. Now you also have encountered that corpse and are gazing at it; and what do you say to yourself when he comes along? You say: "Oh! Here's a policeman." For he happens to be a policeman. You stare at him, and you never see anything but a policeman—an indivisible phenomenon of blue cloth, steel buttons, flesh resembling a face, and a helmet; "a stalwart guardian of the law"; to you little more human than an algebraic symbol: in a word—a policeman.

Only, that word actually conveys almost nothing to you of the reality which it stands for. You are satisfied with it as you are satisfied with the description of a disease. A friend tells you his eyesight is failing. You sympathise. "What is it?" you ask. "Glaucoma." "Ah! Glaucoma!" You don't know what glaucoma is. You are no wiser than you were before. But you are content. A name has contented you. Similarly the name of policeman contents you, seems to absolve you from further curiosity as to the phenomenon. You have looked at tens of thousands of policemen, and perhaps never seen the hundredth part of the reality of a single one. Your imagination has not truly worked on the phenomenon.

There may be some excuse for not seeing the reality of a policeman, because a uniform is always a thick veil. But you—I mean you, I, any of us—are oddly dim-sighted also in regard to the civil population. For instance, we get into the empty motor-bus as it leaves the scene of the street accident, and examine the men and women who gradually fill it. Probably we vaunt ourselves as being interested in the spectacle of life. All the persons in the motor-bus have come out of a past and are moving towards a future. But how often does our imagination put itself to the trouble of realising this? We may observe with some care, yet owing to a fundamental defect of attitude we are observing not the human individuals, but a peculiar race of beings who pass their whole lives in motor-buses, who exist only in motor-buses and only in the present! No human phenomenon is adequately seen until the imagination has placed it back into its past and forward into its future. And this is the final process of observation of the individual.

## VII

Seeing life, as I have tried to show, does not begin with seeing the individual. Neither does it end with seeing the individual. Particular and unsystematised observation cannot go on for ever, aimless, formless. Just as individuals are singled out from systems, in the earlier process of observation, so in the later processes individuals will be formed into new groups, which formation will depend upon the personal bent of the observer. The predominant interests of the observer will ultimately direct his observing activities to their own advantage. If he is excited by the phenomena of organisation—as I happen to be—he will see individuals in new groups that are the result of organisation, and will insist on the variations from type due to that grouping. If he is convinced—as numbers of people appear to be—that society is just now in an extremely critical pass, and that if something mysterious is not forthwith done the structure of it will crumble to atoms—he will see mankind grouped under the different reforms which, according to him, the human dilemma demands. And so on! These tendencies, while they should not be resisted too much, since they give character to observation and redeem it from the frigidity of mechanics, should be resisted to a certain extent. For, whatever they may be, they favour the growth of sentimentality, the protean and indescribably subtle enemy of common sense.

## YOUNG WRITER REMEMBERING CHICAGO

### *Albert Halper*   (*1934*)

#### I. FALL

STARK days these. Stark nights too. In the parks the trees stand firm, the bare boughs creaking in the wind. The gravel paths, clean from many rains, are neat against the dead brown of faded grass. The wind blows, the leaves fall, and smoke rolls up from factories.

Through the South Side the trains come in at night, long gray metal monsters, racing from off the plains, thundering over viaducts, small squares of light glittering from their windowed steel bodies.

And mist hangs over the lake, drifting to the shore. Tugs creep up the river like water beetles, blunt-nosed, going under bridges, chugging. Fog hangs over the Loop all night. The empty iron streets are gray and dead.

Rearing themselves in the morning, big buildings go up, the steel framework clear against a dirty sky. The chatter of pneumatic hammers, the coarse casual language of men who earn two dollars an hour and like hot beans, drop from the height, but never reach the street.

The nights are blue and chill, with foggy air to breathe. The Elevated goes west, south, north, spanning the miles, returning to the Loop, the crowded Loop, where big buildings stand lank, showing their thin sides, their flat buttocks. Cool shadows fall against the walls and the bricks are pressed down hard for strength.

Well, what about the town, what about the Windy City, the tough burg with the bad reputation? What about Chicago in the fall? Who knows Chicago? There's no wind. No answer.

A sprawl of shacks nibbling at the prairie, then came the smokestacks and the noise. A blare, a crash, and the hum of turbines all day long.

Fall comes, the hurly-burly season, the windy-shrieking season. The freights roll in from Texas, loaded to the doors with fat steers who stamp upon the flooring, rubbing sides, grunting in the swaying, roaring trains. Everything comes into Chicago. The long-legged cowboys in charge of the cattle, lads who are fond of plug tobacco, walk through the Loop on high-heeled boots, see the classy legs on Michigan Avenue, feel their bluish chins, and swallow. Oh, you Panhandle boys, how do you like the Windy City? What do you think of the big noisy town?

And after harvest the farm boys come in, big lanky fellers in overalls, with wide mouths and great brown hands, all eager to bite into Chicago, all hoping to get a job. They walk south along State Street, reach Harrison, stare at the photos in front of the cheap burlesque shows, see the penny arcades, the pimps standing in the doorways. They walk slowly under the lamps at night. Chicago has enough women to go around, women whose job it is to make big awkward farm boys happy, women with hard eyes and tight mouths, sloppy dames with loose breasts. The cops say nothing, look the other way, twirl their clubs, and think about getting on the day shift.

Oh, you farm boys, what do you think of the tough town by the lake? Corn sways when the wind blows over the prairie, but the wind in Chicago howls down the street; it howls over the rooftops of factories and office buildings; and during lunch hour the young fellers stand on the corners with toothpicks in their mouths and watch the girls waiting for the traffic signal, watch the wind act naughty-naughty. Why go to a burlesque show, folks, when you live in the Windy City? Why? You see, my friends, I am a booster for Chicago, I want my town to become the biggest in the land.

And now, folks, my own people, let me tell you my story. I was born on the West Side near the Northeastern tracks; there were factories and big livery stables in the neighborhood. My old man ran a grocery and once a week I sprinkled sawdust on the floor, throwing out the grains like golden seeds. That was before the chain-stores were popular, that was a long time ago. In those days my old man carried a lot of book-trade customers who paid every Saturday; but if the wage-earner of the family came home drunk, why of course my old man had to wait until the next Saturday. He marked down the items in his big book, then marked them in duplicate in the customer's. Everybody was satisfied, it was fair enough, fair enough.

I remember the Polish janitress who lived on Lake Street near St. John's Place. She bought a half-dozen rolls every morning; she used to pinch my cheeks and feel my buttocks and say it was too bad I was only nine years old. I remember she had a rosy face and dark eyes and was always walking fast, always out of breath. Her husband was a plumber's helper; he was tall and skinny and had the piles. One day she ran away with a husky shipping clerk.

We kids used to make fun of Lumpy Louie, the old cracked gent who had three bumps on his head that looked like three small eggs. He used to stand in front of the wooden Indian in front of Sutton's candy store, arguing and lifting his cane at it; sometimes he scolded the Indian for not keeping his appointment the evening before. He would rap the fire-plugs sharply too and grow angry, and once in a while, when we hit him in the back with stones, he cried.

I used to go swimming in Union Park, in the old lagoon with the cement bottom, that bottom that got slippery because the water wasn't changed often enough. There was a stone bridge over the neck of the pond and people used to toss pennies down into the water on Saturday afternoons and we dived for them. There was quite a scramble. When we got a few we stuck them in our mouths, took a breath and dived for some more. One day a husky girl, a good diver, pushed us little fellers aside and got almost all the pennies. I remember she didn't wear a bathing suit, but an old dirty suit of clinging underwear; she was about twelve years old. We ducked her and kicked her, but she wouldn't go away, and the men on the bridge tossed pennies near her all the time.

George Hurrel, the kid who turned out to be an artist, the short, strong kid who was always drawing pictures on the sidewalk, was my buddy. Every night we went up the alley, crept near the rear window of Healy's, and looked into the back room. The window had a coat of black paint, but there were a few scratches that allowed us to see fairly well. We saw two women showing a few men a good time, and though the men changed from night to night, the women were always the same ones—the tall stout one and the one with black hair; they sat on the laps of the men, squeezed the boys hard, and made them dance to the tune of the old mechanical piano. We watched them drinking, saw old hunch-backed Paddy Curley bring in the bottles, and when the women started smoking our eyes popped. That was the first time I had ever seen ladies smoke, that was when I was a kid. Sometimes the dancing looked like wrestling; and when I told my mother about it, she slapped my face, telling me not to go back in that alley any more.

Yes, folks, I know many stories. And once I was acquainted with a very clever fellow. He told me that if you place a chair upon a table you create a new height. The world is full of clever folk, and I'm not so bad myself. Only I am too modest, I am not aggressive enough.

I go away to a town, a big strange town, and try to hammer out a good book. The days come, the days go, and big ships sail into the harbor. . . .

Speed is in the wind, all right, but the world rolls dead and heavy. Here in this Manhattan rooming-house, a thousand miles from home, it's hell to stare at brown bare walls, with your money almost gone. The place is chilly, and two limp towels hang from a rod. My arms are heavy, I've got the blues; there's a locomotive in my chest, and that's a fact.

Rain falls upon the asphalt and in Central Park the rocks are wet. Autos hurry over bridges, skimming along, while cops swear, mud is dashed onto the sidewalk, and a guy doesn't feel heroic when he gets some in the eye.

"For every shout upon the mountain top there's a million miles of wailing wind." This is from the book of Success, from the wide open door of Opportunity. Panes of glass rattle in their sockets, a roomer from the third floor goes tramping down the stairs, turns the knob, and slams the door, while outside the street lamps throw their cold white glare.

## II. Winter

In the winter all things do not die. The waves leap up along a cold shore and the wind blows hard. The gulls band in flocks, swerving, wheeling to the right, and the bright sunlight glances from their bellies.

Oh, the iron streets are cold, cold. The raw wind whistles over buildings, rattles the laundry signs, swirls the snow into high drifts in the alleys, and long, blue sparks fly from the third rail as the Elevated goes over the frosty tracks.

Jake Bowers, coming from down-state, walks along Madison Street, stands on the corner of Clinton, takes his hands from his pockets and begins blowing on his fists. Jake is broke. His overalls are getting frayed, his hair is long, and he's getting thin. He shuffles in the cold, bucks the wind, thinks about the big wheat-cakes he has eaten all summer, thinks about the farmer's big stout wife, and when he reaches the Salvation Army headquarters his mind is warm all right, but his legs are like wood. He sees the long line of broken men, all anxious to get a bed, and, when he blows on his fists again, his chapped lips split open in several places and he begins sucking the blood coming from the cracks.

When the wind blows over the prairie, the cornstalks make a dry rustling sound, but in Chicago the wind whistles through your pants and you shiver plenty. Ask Jake Bowers, the tall, lanky boy from down-state. Hey, Jake, how do you like Chicago? Tell the folks about it. Jake doesn't answer; he wets his dry, cracked lips, stands in line with the others, and thinks about a bed for the night.

At dawn the day breaks, the cold, dark sky cracks slowly. Now the iron streets are noisy, the trucks pound hard, teamsters swing their heavy whips through the frosty air, and long columns of vapor come from the nostrils of the horses.

Hey, hey, my buckos. Go on, you bastards. Drag your loads, pull them through the streets, pull them along the shiny car tracks. At night I'll turn you toward the barn, I'll give you hay and water, I'll whack your steamy rumps. Hey, hey, my buckos. Go on, you big fat bastards.

And the long whips swing through the frosty air while the Elevated booms by overhead. The rear legs of the horse bulge with strength.

When I was a small kid, only a few autos were on the streets. I saw the big horses leaning forward, pulling; I heard the swearing teamsters swaying on their seats. Race-horses are nice to look at and pretty nice to write about, but what of the brutes who pull heavy loads, what of the animals that fall and break their legs on slippery streets, kicking weakly until a cop comes running with a gun in his hand? Hey, hey, my buckos. What about those poor bastards, pulling?

At noon the cracked sky is wide open. Small-faced flappers hurry in the cold, their long thin legs moving very fast. They head for the drug-stores, the long narrow stores lined with high stools. They crowd at the counters where prim sandwiches are sold, nicely decorated, good stuff to nibble at with small teeth. Some gals smoke now, swing their legs, and eye the soda-jerker, a tall slick lad with a turned-up shiny nose. The gals look from the windows, hoping for a rich feller, hoping the boss won't have too many letters to dictate.

I once worked in a factory. There were punch-presses near the wall. One noon I sat talking to a man who spoke broken English, but had good jaws. It was snowing outside and we watched the big flakes floating down. Next to me another fellow, a big Swede, yawned, closed his mouth slowly, sighted at the factory cat like at a target, then spat a good stream of rich brown tobacco juice. The cat was white. But it was half brown as it sprang away. The Swede did not laugh; he yawned again, hoping the snow would stop at half-past five.

And I once had a job as order-picker for a mail-order house, my first job after graduating from high school, when I was eager to conquer the world, to advance with the times, as it were. I went along aisles of merchandise and picked the orders, reading the sheets sent in by customers from Arkansas and Minnesota. There were many items to pick, cheap work shirts, rubber collars, corduroy pants, fedora hats that the firm picked up at auction. I used to stand in the aisles when the supervisor wasn't looking and read the letters accompanying the orders. Some of the customers couldn't spell properly; they had scrawly handwriting and wrote in the personal vein; they told the firm that the last pair of pants was a bit too small for Tom—Tom liked more room around the seat. Yes, folks, those were the days. Another fellow worked with me, a huge Hollander, and his name was Big Bill Mesland; he had to leave Holland because of a girl there. Big Bill was fiery when the boss was not around, but as soon as Kerton walked by Bill became meek in manner. He used to coax the packing girls into the darker aisles, and none of them hollered very much. And at Christmas, when the orders grew heavy, when we had to work overtime until our eyes were so red we could hardly read the customers' writing, Big Bill cursed the firm, standing in the aisle. He shot off all the high-pressure oratory at his command. And one night, a clear starry night, as the poets say, after we had checked out, he and I walked toward the car-line and at the corner Bill wheeled around, raised his big fist in the air, and cursed the building behind us, cursed it in his broken English. I laughed at him. But one year later, while I was working at another job, I heard that the firm of Philipsborn had gone bankrupt. Well, maybe Bill was a medicine man after all. Who knows? He went away to California and wrote me a letter, but I didn't answer it and I don't know why.

And I once had another good friend, but he left town, left his job at the Post Office and is now working as a seaman; he once wrote me from Brussels. Before he left, he told me this: he said big hills are not small mountains. We had a long argument, but I don't recall who won. I told him he was a fathead, called him a mystic, but now I'm beginning to understand what he meant.

The point is, never go to New York, my friends. Stick in Chicago where you belong. They say New York is a great town, that it's the greatest thing in America, but that's all a lie, and a bloody lie at that.

Let the subways roar on, let them rumble underground, let the big boats sail into the harbor bringing freight and people. But the wide mouth of the continent can swallow it whole for all I care. Folks, if you'll please step closer, I'll tell you something; I want to tell you that New York is just a big small town, a burg full of suckers, swollen with yokels. Dear old Manhattan, sweet papa Knickerbocker. Eighty black years on you and yours.

But now it's winter, good old winter in Chicago. The wind howls and snow is whirled into drifts back in the alleys. A strong boat goes up the Chicago River, breaking the ice, keeping the way clear. And every Saturday afternoon races are held in the parks, the bands play on platforms, a few cops on skates keep the crowds back, and sometimes the favorite falls on the last lap and the people feel sorry for him. The wide oval pond glitters dully under the sun and the wind blows fine snow over the ice. People stamp to keep warm, some slap their sides. . . .

Here in New York the gusts blow in from the Battery; and sirens howl, and the bells of the Greek Catholic church over on Twelfth Street go bong-bong-bong all day long. When the air grows raw and damp here, the keys of my typewriter stick a little and I have to pound a bit harder; so hard in fact that some folks will say, "Too raw and awkward, too unfinished and slangy."

But I was born in a raw slangy city, in a raw slangy neighborhood. I lived near railroads, and on warm nights I could smell the strong odor from the stockyards rolling in heavy waves all the way from the South Side. Just try to write in the classic tradition with that stink in your nostrils, sit down and spin out smooth poetic sentences with the roar of railroads in your ears.

When I was a kid I saw sluggers pull down teamsters from the seats of wagons during the big strikes. I watched the bloody brawls at the polls at election time, and some of my old buddies are now successful gangsters. I was an errand-boy working after school when the race riots broke out on the South Side, and, coming from a home where I had just delivered a package, I saw five whites chasing a Negro up the street. The Negro was howling, waving his arms. He ran so hard his shirt worked loose from his pants and flapped in the summer wind. They chased him up an alley off Indiana Avenue, cornered him near a shed, and one white kicked the coon in the mouth as the dark boy got down on his knees to beg for mercy. The nigger begged hard. He said he had never done harm to any white man; he howled and then stopped, and for a while it looked as if he was trying to swallow his own lips. That was when one of the whites pulled out a gun, a shiny revolver that caught the sun. It took two shots to finish the business. The whites stood grim. The coon, his arms spread out as if nailed to a cross, lay quiet near a pile of horse manure. The whites chased me out of the alley, told me to beat it, to keep my mouth shut. Then the cops came, didn't ask me a question, and forced me to ride in the patrol wagon until we passed the danger zone. Soldiers of the National Guard stood on the corners. Many papers were sold.

I'm not a snooper, I don't go around looking for stories, but I know what I know, I know what I have seen. If I was born in a raw slangy town, if I happened to see raw slangy things, why shouldn't my stuff be raw slangy?

The wind shrieks and howls, and there's no answer, folks.

And meanwhile it's winter back in Chicago. Cold air blows over the frozen lagoons, whirls thin fine snow toward the pavilion, and out on the ice a small man wearing a fur cap tries to perform fancy turns on dull skates.

And the weeks slip by, with two limp towels hanging from a rod. The windows rattle. I've got a locomotive in my chest, and that's a fact. It's a gray day, my friends, and the traffic pounds down Eighth Avenue. Across the way, level with my window, a woman sticks a mop out and shakes it hard; but she's not much to look at, no shape at all, kind of middle-aged and her hair is hidden in an old house-cap.

Now a few peeps of steam come up, thin and faint, a drawn-out whistling sound. The landlady's heart has melted, she's a good sport after all. When I become famous, in forty years or so, when I learn to write that slick tricky stuff, I'll type her a nice letter, a letter that will make her proud. "Dear Madam," I will say, and I'll say plenty of nice things. She's a tall thin old lady, and once upon a time a young writer from Kentucky beat her out of two weeks' rent. A few more peeps come up, drearily, like lost pieces of fog drifting down a river on a sunny day.

### III. Spring

The wind blows, but it is not so cold now; its howling mood is gone, gone down that twining river which disappears into the trees. On the left bank lies a rowboat, bottom up, like a fat man's belly. The paint is peeling, small worms crawl along the seams.

The wind is warm now, a little wet too, and small buds, hanging from the branches, tremble there like heavy drops of water.

When the damp air blows over the prairie, the tall new grass nods in the breeze, but in Chicago people sniff the air, begin walking through the parks again, and a few married young fellers hit the bosses for a raise.

And it's nice to walk up a street late at night when the warm wind blows. There goes the Windy City Kid, coming from work on the night shift down at the Post Office. It's four o'clock in the morning, folks, the street is quiet. He takes his time, walks with his hands in his pockets, and when he sees a police squad whiz around the corner he pretends he's in a hurry, luring them on, smiling a little to himself. Ah, Windy City Kid, you're no greenhorn, you know your onions. The police car bears down, swings over toward the curb, the cops leaning out. And then they call halt! The Windy City Kid halts; he recognizes the voice of authority. He stands firm but feels frisky, and has a mocking look around the eyes. The cops get out heavily, slap his body to feel for weapons, maybe he's a dangerous guy, they question him, tell him to talk up, threaten to run him in. But the Windy City Kid holds a trump card; he works nights, sleeps days, and he's got to have his little joke now and then. When the cops grow ugly he pulls out his government Post Office badge, flashes it under their noses, tells them he works on the night shift, dares them to call up the supervisor if they doubt it. The cops swear. They get into their auto and drive away. And the Windy City Kid stands on the curb grinning. He calls himself a crazy nut, but he feels pretty good. Then he resumes walking up the dark silent street toward home. He has turned this trick a few times; he works nights, he's got to have his little joke once in a while.

And so spring comes to Chicago. The lake boats sail away like ocean liners, cruise a few hundred miles along Lake Michigan and bring back a load. Smoke trails them, hangs in the air, follows them over the water, and on clear days the horizon seems as boundless as the open sea.

And the warm wind blows, whirling dust along the street, into the public's eyes, into the eyes of those young fellers who stand on the corners during lunch hour, chewing on their toothpicks and looking for a free show.

Yes, folks, it's spring. The curbs along Madison are lined with men, husky fellers and broken geezers. It's spring and they also taste the warm wind. They stand east of Halsted Street, where the cheap employment agencies, with their signs posted outside, are doing a big business. Men are wanted, big raw fellers for the railroad gangs, men for road building, men to go north to the lumber mills. Forty dollars a month, board free. Well, bohunks, what do you say? Come on, what do you say? Take it or leave it. Hey, you, the big guy with the high shoulders, do you want a job? Your fists are big, you've got small angry eyes, maybe you've had a tough time this winter, eh? Want a job, want work? Here we are, forty bucks a month up north in the camps, or forty-five with the road gang. Hey, bohunks, what do you say? Hurry, hurry, hurry, men, the train pulls out when the sun stands in the sky like a fried egg on high.

But Jake Bowers from down-state says nothing. There he stands, his eyes half-sunken, pretty thin now, his country color gone, his big brown hands a dirty white. Hey, Jake, what do you think of Chicago? Tell the folks about it. Send your story singing against the wind. The breeze blows gently over the prairie, but in Chicago a man's got to think about a job. Hey, Jake, how about a job up north? Forty bucks a month and cheap booze every other Saturday. How about it? Jake says nothing. He stands lank, shoves his hands in his pockets, then shuffles away. Jake wants to go back home on the farm. Jake wants his wheat-cakes every morning and the sight of the farmer's tall stout wife. Jake wants to go home. He has had a tough winter, the raw lake wind has whistled through his pants for a long time. Now he wants to go back to the soil. He has been going to a quack doctor, trying to get cured of a dose, and he wants to go back awfully bad.

Spring comes. The brisk wind flaps the colored signs of the employment agencies, and the men walk by. Merchants wash their windows, advertise bargains, hire extra clerks, and stand behind the counters waiting for business.

Oh, blow, wind, go on blowing. Whistle through their Danish whiskers, blow the black smoke away from factories, sweep it out upon the lake.

The hard spring rains go drumming down the street, and wooden men and women go walking on their wooden feet. The water gurgles in the gutters, and on the corner the fat cop mutters.

And this is what I say, yes, this is what I say:

If you have seen pigeons wheeling in the sky, if you have looked at heavy sunlight warming the naked branches of trees, if all the sounds of a city merge, swelling into one great tone, if after you come back to your room, that room with the two towels hanging from a rod, if after all this has come about and you sit on your chair, your arms heavy, the keys of the typewriter staring at you—if you've gone as far as this, I want to tell you that in the winter all things do not die, but death takes many things in the spring. I want to tell you that if warm wind is sticky with new life, it also suffocates the old. It drives the young writers home, the brave boys, the heroic lads with epics in their chests, who came to New York. The young lads pack their grips, pay the landladies, take the subway to the station, and stand waiting for their trains. Youth does not always win, it rides home and tells the folks nothing, gets a job and lets the days go by.

Spring comes. The wharves along the coast lose their hard lines. Ferry boats plow away like dumpy washer-women, and the heights of Jersey City are blue-gray in the distance. But the hard shiny railroad tracks go grinning west, mile after mile. The tank towns and the jerk-water towns, the junctions and the sidings blur, while the locomotive, like a bullet in a groove, whistles along the rails.

Folks, please listen. Once upon a time I thought that sincerity and simplicity were all that mattered, that if a young writer was honest and had a little talent, that was enough. In my high school days our composition teacher, a tall strong woman of Scotch descent, was always talking to us of honesty. That's how I got a bum steer, that's how I learned out-dated stuff. Like all young fools who lived away from the racket of Manhattan, I thought the wise men of the East were a noble group, and with my sweat I brought them every gift I had. When I crept up to the manger, there was no pure or holy thing in sight; the feed-trough was overturned and the wise boys were slapping down cards, a poker game was going strong. "It's a tough racket," one of them said. "War novels are going good this season, but I'll place a few chips on mystery books for the spring."

In the Sahara there's a sand storm, and in Chicago Hymie Katz gets taken for a ride for squealing on his pals. Women in back yards hang clothes out to dry and old man Sutton thinks about painting his wooden Indian.

I do not believe in heroes, I do not believe in valorous deeds. But why must death take so many things in the spring, why must the young grow weak fighting the old? The walls of New York are high and thick, and many lads have fired their loads of buckshot at them. Out of the west they come, up from the south, but they all go back, they all go back to where they belong.

And upon the upturned manger the wise men of the East slap their cards down. One guy moves a small pile of chips and another spits into the hay.

Roar, New York, keep on roaring. Some day I'll write a book that'll interrupt the poker game—a big raw slangy piece of work that'll set the chips to flying. So roar, New York, go on and roar. Your rumbling dies over the harbor, fades away in Brooklyn, disappears in Astoria.

And all the while the wind blows toward Chicago. People come home from work and eat big meals; roast beef and fried potatoes are washed down with strong coffee. Eat, Chicago, sock it in your belly. You'll need plenty of meat, lots of coffee in the spring.

For in the winter all things do not die, but death takes many things in the spring.

## IV. SUMMER

Now the days are hot, the sunlight is intense. Heat quivers upward from the asphalt in crinkly lines. The tin roofs of garages glitter in the light. When the sun goes down, women take their clothes from the lines and the windows in the east are blood-red. The street cars during late rush hours are jammed to the doors, boxcars for human freight, swaying packing cases made of steel and glass.

The days are hot in Chicago, even though a breeze blows off the lake. The green grass in the parks is short and thick, and oars dip slowly as the rowboats go along.

And every evening pop-corn venders take their stands near the parks, draw their small white wagons toward the curb, and send their little whistling sounds into the hot dark night. Pop, kernels, keep on popping. The Greek puts another scoop of kernels over the gas-flame, gazes at it vaguely, shakes the pan a bit, then begins twisting his big mustaches very slowly.

Folks, did you ever go strolling with a gal through the park? Did you ever stop with her at the curb, hand the Greek a nickel, sit on the bench under those thickly set bushes where it was dark, and have your girl shake small handfuls of pop-corn and give them to you? When the bag was empty, you blew it up, then smashed it with your fist; there was a great noise. Your girl laughed. She gave you a shove and, when you kissed her, you tasted the butter from the pop-corn on her lips. The night was dark, brethren, and warm.

Oh, pop, kernels, keep on popping. Pop in the summer for dear old Chicago.

And there's outdoor public dancing in the West Side parks. Workmen have laid a cement floor and built a little platform, and a small peppy orchestra spurts hot music. Hey, hey, sister, let's go.

And around the wire enclosure stand the middle-aged men, eyeing the young gals dancing, those fifteen- and sixteen-year-old gals. The middle-aged men have their cars parked a short distance away, those men who take the kids for long rides past the city limits, those men who know their onions. Yes, folks, such is life in a big city. Lift your glass and drain it down, the sour with the sweet, the good with the not-so-good.

And a few yards away from the dance floor boys and girls get together, hold hands as they sit on benches, make a little progress in the humanities. Then they walk along empty streets, thinking things over. Insects swarm about the arc lamps. And they reach her home.

"Farewell, farewell," he tells her mournfully.

"Good night, good night," she answers softly, then climbs the stairs, going around the back way, tells the little doggie not to bark, not even to make a squeal, then up to her room to undress, takes off her clothes, gazes at herself in the cracked mirror, feeling her breasts meanwhile, and so to bed, alone.

Yes, folks, that's the way things go in the summer, in the good old summer-time.

When I was a kid band-concerts were held in Union Park. That was when Flo Jacobson had a reputation as a sweet singer, that was when music publishers hired her to plug their numbers at the concerts. She wore a big white floppy hat, stood on the platform, and sang the new songs. I copped a handful of navy beans from the store when my father wasn't looking, and at the concert George Hurrel and I tossed the beans at the band, aiming for the brass instruments. When the music was soft you could hear those hard navy beans hit the cornets and trombones, then go rattling to the wooden floor. One night a cop caught us, but that's another story, and a long sad one at that.

Oh, grow, navy beans, keep on growing. Grow hard and firm for dear old Chicago.

And one summer I worked nights in the Post Office, that great gray building wherein are many stories. I sweated with the others, tossed mail hour on hour, my body swaying, my arms moving, my mind going dead, my eyes reading the addresses. We were supposed to sort fifty letters a minute. Figure that out, folks. I must have tossed a few billion while I was there, and where those letters went I did not care, and if the letters had black borders, if they carried sad news, I didn't care either; I kept on tossing them into the small squares. It was some job, and it taught me plenty. It taught me how to stand on one spot until the bell rang. There were long lines of mail-cases and a thousand men on the floor, and the hard chatter of over a hundred canceling machines went on all night. Who knows big business? Who knows all the big mail-order firms, those houses that dump loads and loads of mail into the Post Office? The belts rumbled on, carrying the mail away, and merchandise rattled down the chutes. Some music, folks, a symphony in the blues: the Negroes humming as they tossed the mail, the sweat rolling down their faces, the dust whirling under the lights. Can a man dance standing still? He can. He can if he's a Negro, if he's throwing mail down at the Post Office. He stands at the case, hums and sways, and pretty soon it's dancing.

Oh, dance, dark boys, go on dancing. Dance on the night shift for dear old Chicago.

The windows were opened, but no wind came inside. At eleven o'clock we ate, went across the street for a big hamburger on rye, told the Greek to hurry up, folded the bread over a big slice of onion, then sank our fangs into onion, hamburger, and bread. The cashier, an old guy with three teeth in his mouth, grinned at us, showing his caved-in gums. "Is the meat juicy, is the onion strong enough?" he asked.

Ha-ha, folks, I have to laugh when I remember that old boy, that ancient guy who sat behind the register grinning at us, no hair on his head. That was a long time ago, that was a thousand years ago. We left the lunchroom, crossed the street again, sat on the wide stone stairs at the Jackson Boulevard entrance, and felt the hot wind blowing up the street. We wore short aprons to protect our clothes, and Christ knows why; they flapped in the hot wind. We waved at autos going by, whistled to a few whores coming from the cheap hotel on Clark Street, and smoked a cigarette or two. There we sat on the cool stone stairs, whites, Negroes, and Filipinos, all in the same boat, our hands moist, our shirts sticking to our backs, all waiting for the bell to ring. And it rang. It rang on time too. We dribbled through the small doorway, showed our badges to the watchman, checked in again at the desk, got another tray of mail, and our arms began tossing letters again. We worked up a swaying movement. Our legs, restless at first, grew steady, and our arms seemed to flow on forever. And under the lights, those strong glaring bulbs, the dust from the dirty mail-sacks whirled in the air.

Yes, folks, I've held down some mighty fine jobs; you've got to hand it to me.

I once worked for an electrotype foundry, stood in the office, checking cuts, making out statements. When work was slack, I went into the shop, near the big twin dynamos where I could hear the whir of power, the deep hum of current. Back in the rear the hydraulic presses were making wax molds for printing plates, and up in front, along the windows, the air hammers were smoothening out the casts. The gang of workmen were a swell bunch. I worked in the office, wore a white collar, but they treated me as an equal. Sometimes we talked about baseball. But back in the rear was a man who didn't give a hang about the game. He stood over the pots of boiling lead, pouring the hot liquid upon the copper shells. He was Pete the caster, and he had hair on his chest. All the men liked him; they called him the bloody barstard. Pete was blind on one side, he had only one eye, but that optic was so sharp that few men would sit down with him at a game of cards during lunch hour. And you couldn't blame them. He was lucky in cards and love, a tall lean man with wide shoulders, and there was hair on his chest. Every Saturday he got shaved at the lady barber's around the corner, the shop near Polk Street.

And he always sat in Kitty's chair. She was the first barber, the big stout one, the one whose hair was dyed so red it knocked your eye out. She shaved Pete. She swung the chair back, and as the razor went over his face her big breasts nuzzled his shoulder. Every Monday morning Pete told me about it. He was a married man, had grown children, but he worked mighty hard and had to have a change once in a while. He stood half-naked over the pots, and the muscles stood out on his lean powerful arms.

And in the office were three bosses, men who fought among themselves. One was a woman-hound, he used to tell me dirty stories and watch me narrowly; another was impotent; and the third was absent-minded and had five grown daughters. This third one looked over my shoulder as I stood checking the cuts, to make sure I wasn't making mistakes.

And that's not all the jobs I've had.

I was a salesman representing a southern tobacco house, doing pioneer work, as it were. I sold a brand of chewing tobacco that the public didn't want to buy, a brand I pushed onto the dealers. When I came around to take re-orders, I was thrown out of the stores. The plug tobacco tasted like sour apples mixed with dried oatmeal. I tried it once just for fun; that was the time I went into a candy store run by a widow. She dared me to chew it, and I told her the Irish never say die. We had a good laugh together.

And I was once a salesman for a house selling beauty parlor supplies. Cripes, what a racket. Plenty life, plenty hot stuff in that game, folks. I sold supplies to the little manicure gals, to the hair-dressers, the big stout women who had tasted everything in life there was to be tasted, who had been married three or four times and were still game, who were good sports for all that. In those days I knew all about mud-packs, astringent lotions, permanent waves, and skin rejuvenator. In those days I met a hair-dresser, a handsome German girl whose father ran a farm in Iowa. She lived in a strict rooming-house and had to meet me on the corner. Sometimes I think she was the finest kid I ever knew. Her name was Thelma.

That was a long time ago. . . .

Folks, I'm going strong, mighty strong indeed. I'd like to tell you more, like to go on forever. But here we are in Chicago and it's summer. The heat is terrific. When a gal dances with you, her dress sticks to her back. And the small excursion boats ply between Navy Pier and Lincoln Park, twenty-five cents one way, a half a dollar up and back. Hurry, hurry, hurry, folks, the big steamer leaves in three minutes, takes you out upon the ample bosom of the lake. Kids free, madam, take 'em along. The sea air is good for their tummies, it's good for their constitutions, too.

If you stand on the Pier, you hear the dinky orchestra playing as the whistle blows, you hear the banjos strummin', the darkies hummin', and once I saw a nigger gal shake her Swedish movement to get the customers on board. Then another boat docks, more playin', and the whistle blows, the boat plows away, short and heavy toward the breakwater, and a few more Chicago souls are made happy.

Oh, sail, boats, sail away. Sail out upon the lake and buck the wind. Let the dinky music hit the water sharply with a sweet smack, sail away for dear old Chicago. . . .

And what about Jake Bowers, you say, the farm boy from down-state? Well, Jake went home, got his old job back, now eats big wheat-cakes and gazes at the farmer's fat wife, but his stare is rather empty. Hey, Jake, how did you like Chicago? Tell the folks about it, tell them how you stood in line, waiting for a bed while the wind went whistling through your pants. Go on, Jake, tell the folks. Jake doesn't answer. He shoves his plate away, gets up, walks behind the barn, and gulps down a pink pill. He has to take two pills a day, that's what the quack doctor back in Chicago said, the doc who has his office in back of the dental parlors.

And the summer wind tosses the new corn playfully about, bends it slightly so that it curves golden in the sun, but in Chicago the wind is damn hot and folks walk up the street wiping their faces.

Well, folks, I won't keep you any longer. I am sorry, very sorry that my time is up. I've got a lot more to say, many stories to tell, but there's no time, and so I'm sorry. Believe me, I am sorry.

I am sorry for many things in life. I am sorry for the small folk who live thin twisted lives, who have to hold onto their jobs and look alive when the big chief passes by. I am sorry for the broken men who stand against buildings when the wind howls down the street and the snow whirls past the arc lamps. I am sorry for the clerks working in big stockrooms, for all my old buddies down at the Post Office—the whites, the Negroes, and the Filipinos, who stand hour on hour tossing mail, their armpits stinking, going to the whorehouses every payday, walking down the stairs after being with the girls, going slowly, thinking things over.

I tell you I am sorry for many things. I am sorry for all the dead jobs I have held, for lonely days in a big strange town, for long walks at night past the blazing signs of Broadway, for the dark side streets near the river. I am sorry too for the men who jam the burlesque houses in the afternoons, who lean forward as the girls kick their powdered legs, those girls who are always worrying about future bookings, who sing songs of happiness so loudly that big veins stand out in their necks. I tell you I am sorry. I have slept alone in a narrow bed in a small New York room many nights and have tried to think a few things out.

And now it is summer and I am sorry in the summer for many things, for those hot nights of open-air dancing that had to fade, for the fall that is coming. And for all the gray dead things in life, the things that drag themselves slowly along, I am sorry.

Folks, please listen. I would like to close this little piece with a grand flourish, with a blare of bugles, but I've got a locomotive in my chest, and that's a fact. . . .

When I was a kid, I went camping alone in the pine woods of upper Michigan. I was sixteen years old and carried a heavy pack upon my shoulder blades. Down past an old sawmill I hit a crooked trail that didn't seem to have any ending, and now all my years seem to be going down that trail. There were short bushes on either side, like the stunted lives of small folk, the branches warped and crooked, no buds showing, though it was already midsummer.

When I reached the bottom of the hill, I struck an old railroad spur that curved away, then straightened out into a direct line. The shiny steel tracks, giving off a harsh glitter in the sun, grew small and taut, meeting at the horizon; and as I began walking over the wooden ties I heard the faint sound of a train. I didn't see the locomotive for a long time, but heard it coming closer and closer. Finally it showed at the end of the tracks, a small black beetle against the horizon. I stepped off to one side to let it pass, hearing the sound increase, seeing the far-off smoke.

It whirled past me, shot around the curve, and went out of sight, but I still heard it. I can hear it yet.

*Chug-chug-chug. Chug-chug-chug.*

Listen to it.

# JOE LOUIS NEVER SMILES
### *Jonathan Mitchell* (1935)

THESE people are here, 95,000 of them, because they have money. Down there on the field, men have paid $150 and more for a pair of tickets. Twenty thousand seats were stamped "ringside," and the customers out beyond third base were bilked. They should have known that Mike Jacobs, who is running this fight, is a smart man. No one can do anything to him because he has the support of Hearst.

It feels good to have money again. Everyone in this crowd has money. The people who were swindled by Jacobs can afford it. Happy days are here again. Of course, things aren't so good, with twenty millions on relief. A man can be fired, and next morning there are ten men in line waiting for his job. But the unemployed have been around for a long time. No one can expect us to sit home and be sympathetic indefinitely.

It is a cold, clear night. The Stadium rises steeply around one-half of the field. The floodlights on its upper edge are directed on the field and the bleachers, and the Stadium itself is black except for a steady row of red exit signs. Almost the whole of the immense field is covered with chairs. Jacobs has pushed the customers so closely together that all that can be seen of them, under the floodlights, is their microscopic, bright faces. They form neat rows, divided into plots by the aisles, like commercial Dutch tulip beds. There are acres of them, shining pinkly. Men in white, with high cardboard signs in their caps, move gravely about selling pop, like gardeners. The ring is at second base, and the movie operators' metal cage, high on a pole, that you used to see at fights, is missing. The only movement comes from white tobacco smoke, rising in heavy waves. Through it you can see the American flags along the top of the Stadium, after the fashion of the opening verse of "The Star Spangled Banner."

Near at hand the crowd is a respectable, bridge-playing one. About a fifth are Negroes, more carefully dressed and more mannerly than the whites. The little drunk with the long, woolen muffler is certainly a Bronx dentist. He thinks correctly that the preliminary match now going on is poor, and keeps screaming, "Lousy." He brandishes a handful of crumpled bills, and will give odds to anyone. There seems to be something painful in his past that he would like to explain, but the woolen muffler keeps blowing in his face, and communication between him and us is eternally frustrated.

There is a stirring in the aisles near the ring. The people who amount to something, and who are bowed through the police lines outside the Stadium, are entering. There are five state Governors, the Republican National Committee, important business figures and a large number of people whose press agents made them come so that their names would be in tomorrow's papers. Max Baer and his attendants are now at home plate. A dozen little pushing figures open up the crowd for him, and another dozen follow behind. Baer wears a white bathrobe, and has his hands on the shoulders of the state trooper in front of him. He nods to his many friends. Joe Louis, with another state trooper and other attendants, pushes in from third base. We learn afterwards that his bride, Marva Trotter, is in the first row in a bright green dress and orchids. Louis seems to see no one.

The floodlights are extinguished. Nothing exists except the brightly glowing ring. That is old Joe Humphries being lifted through the ropes, the man who announced fights before the depression. Since then he has been sick, and had a bad time. We have all been having a bad time, for that matter. Jack Dempsey squats in Baer's corner, but no one notices him. Humphries' assistant is bawling into the microphones: "Although Joe Louis is colored, he is a great fighter, in the class of Jack Johnson and the giants of the past." His voice fades away, and returns: "American sportsmanship, without regard to race, creed or color, is the talk of the world. Behave like gentlemen, whoever wins." Nearly two thousand police at the entrances of the Stadium are there to break up a possible race riot.

Baer has stripped. He has made a lot of money, Baer has. From all reports, he has spent a lot. He has played Broadway, Miami and the other hot spots. Why shouldn't he have done so? Joe Louis takes off his flashing silk bathrobe, blue with a vermilion lining. It is the only extravagant gesture he makes. For all his youth, he is thick under the jaws, thick around the waist. His face is earnest, thoughtful, unsmiling.

Max Baer hasn't been, I suppose, what you would call a good boy. Joe Louis has, though. This is his greatest advantage. He once was taken to a night club, and it is reported that within ten minutes he wanted to go home. He said he was sleepy. He is supposed to have saved his money. Louis' father died when he was only two years old, down in Alabama. Until she married again, his mother had a hard struggle to support the children, and they were very dear to her. Louis is fond of his mother. She is a Lily of the Valley at her church in Detroit, where the family now lives. The Lilies are having a supper, or some such event, in a few days. She wants him there, and he is going with his new wife.

We are too far away to hear the gong. They are out in the middle of the ring, with a stubby little man in a white sweater moving softly around them. Baer holds both hands, open, clumsily in front of him. Look at Joe

Louis. He is leading with a straight left arm, his right hand before his face ready to block, and his right elbow tucked in to his ribs. That is scientific. That is what they teach in correspondence courses, or the night gymnasium classes of the Y.M.C.A. In the first thirty seconds you can tell that he reeks of study, practice, study. Any romantic white person who believes that the Negro possesses a distinctive quality ought to see Louis. He suggests a gorilla or a jungle lion about as much as would an assistant professor at the Massachusetts Institute of Technology.

Baer stands flatfooted, with his great death-dealing right fist doubled by his side. He swings, and you can almost count three while the fist sails through the air. Louis moves sidewise and back, because he has been taught that if you move with a blow it can never hurt you. Baer's glove slides up the side of Louis's head harmlessly. He swings again and again, and, carefully and unhurriedly, Louis slips away. Look! Louis at last is going in. A left, a right and another left in close. Louis has pulled in his head, and, with both arms up before him, he looks like a brown crayfish. All you can see is the twitching of his shoulders. So incredibly fast he is that the blows themselves are almost invisible. His hands cannot possibly move more than a few inches. Look! Baer is backing into a neutral corner. Louis is raining down blows. Baer's nose spurts blood, his lower lip bleeds, his face is red pulp.

Baer must have meant something to many people. He made wisecracks and went to parties and was a harbinger of the return of the old days. He was Broadway, he was California and Florida, he represented the possession of money once more and spending it. This saddle-colored, dour-faced, tongue-tied, studious youth, who is punishing Baer, punishing him more cruelly than human flesh and bones can endure, what does he represent? Baer stands with his hands hanging at his sides. He is helpless. He cannot hit the dissolving form before him, and he has never learned to protect himself. He holds his fine head, with its sweep of tightly curled hair and its great, brooding nose, high above his torturer. Pride alone keeps his head up, pride that has no tangible justification whatever. It was the same pride that kept Colonel Baratieri at Adowa, twenty years before Joe Louis was born.

It is the first round, and the fight is as good as over. Maybe it was foolish to spend money going to a fight. There must be many people, even down there in the ringside seats, who couldn't afford to spend what they did on tickets. No one can be sure of his job with twenty millions on relief. This is a crazy country, with people handing out a million dollars to Mike Jacobs and Hearst, while families right here in New York City are without enough to eat.

Round one is ended. Jack Dempsey vaults into the ring in a single, startling leap. Perhaps it is a trick. He must have vaulted from the ground to the edge of the ring platform, and from there into the ring itself. But from a distance, it seems one motion, and it is beautiful. Beside the man that Dempsey was, Baer and Louis and Schmeling are phonies. Nowadays everything, including men, is somehow different.

The next three rounds are slaughter. In the second, Baer makes a wild, swinging, purposeless attack. For probably fifteen seconds, he appears formidable, but his attack has no substance inside it. With the third round, he is beaten, but Louis does not rush in, as Dempsey would have, to kill. Deliberately he circles Baer, with his earnest, thoughtful face, seeking an opening through which to strike without possible risk of injury. He takes no chance of a last, desperate fling of Baer's prodigious right hand. He is a planner. He is a person who studies the basic aspects of a problem and formulates a program. Apparently his studies are satisfactory, for he carefully steps up and knocks Baer down twice. Baer is on the canvas when time is called. Dempsey slides across the ring, picks Baer up like a mother, fusses over him until the fourth, and final, round. Baer once more is down. When the stubby referee, swinging his arm, reaches seven, he tries to rouse himself. This turns out later to have been a fortunate gesture. The customers who suspected the honesty of the fight, and were unconvinced that a man could be half-killed by fifty blows full on the jaw, were reassured as they watched Baer struggling to his feet. Had he been trying to throw the fight, they reasoned, he would have lain still. At the count of ten, Baer is on one knee, his swollen face wearing a comical expression of surprise.

The floodlights return us to time and space. Near at hand, there is remarkably little cheering, even from Negroes. They act as if, despite the police, they think it more prudent to restrain their feelings. There in the ring, placing his hand on Baer's shoulder in a stiff gesture, is the best fighter living, and the first Negro whose backers and trainer are men of his race. No white man shares in Louis' winnings. If the whites of the Boxing Commission will permit the match, he will be champion of the world.

All across the Stadium, the neat tulip beds are being broken up as tiny figures push into the aisles and toward the exits. A man with a small blonde mustache is sobbing: "Maxie, why didn't you hit him?" Downtown in the Forties and Fifties, redecorated speakeasies will quickly be crammed to the doors and customers turned away. In Lenox Avenue in Harlem, Negroes will be tap-dancing from curb to curb, and singing: "The Baer goes over the mountain," and "Who won the fight?" Tomorrow the financial sections of the newspapers will report that business leaders regard the fight as final proof that the country's economic worries are past, and a comfortable and prosperous future is assured.

## WALKING TOURS
### *Robert Louis Stevenson* (*1881*)

It must not be imagined that a walking tour, as some would have us fancy, is merely a better or worse way of seeing the country. There are many ways of seeing landscape quite as good; and none more vivid, in spite of canting dilettantes, than from a railway train. But landscape on a walking tour is quite accessory. He who is indeed of the brotherhood does not voyage in quest of the picturesque, but of certain jolly humors—of the hope and spirit with which the march begins at morning, and the peace and spiritual repletion of the evening's rest. He cannot tell whether he puts his knapsack on, or takes it off, with more delight. The excitement of the departure puts him in key for that of the arrival. Whatever he does is not only a reward in itself, but will be further rewarded in the sequel; and so pleasure leads on to pleasure in an end-less chain. It is this that so few can understand; they will either be always lounging or always at five miles an hour; they do not play off the one against the other, prepare all day for the evening, and all evening for the next day. And, above all, it is here that your overwalker fails of comprehension. His heart rises against those who drink their curaçoa in liqueur glasses, when he himself can swill it in a brown john. He will not believe that to walk this unconscionable distance is merely to stupefy and brutalize himself, and come to his inn, at night, with a sort of frost on his five wits, and a starless night of darkness in his spirit. Not for him the mild luminous evening of the temperate walker! He has nothing left of man but a physical need for bedtime and a double night-cap; and even his pipe, if he be a smoker, will be savorless and disenchanted. It is the fate of such an one to take twice as much trouble as is needed to obtain happiness, and miss the happiness in the end; he is the man of the proverb, in short, who goes further and fares worse.

Now, to be properly enjoyed, a walking tour should be gone upon alone. If you go in a company, or even in pairs, it is no longer a walking tour in any-thing but name; it is something else and more in the nature of a picnic. A walking tour should be gone upon alone, because freedom is of the essence; because you should be able to stop and go on, and follow this way or that, as the freak takes you; and because you must have your own pace, and neither trot alongside a champion walker, nor mince in time with a girl. And then you must be open to all impressions and let your thoughts take color from what you see. You should be as a pipe for any wind to play upon. "I cannot see the wit," says Hazlitt, "of walking and talking at the same time. When I am in the country, I wish to vegetate like the country,"—which is the gist of all that can be said upon the matter. There should be no cackle of voices at your elbow, to jar on the meditative silence of the morning. And so long as a man is reasoning he cannot surrender himself to that fine intoxication that comes of much motion in the open air, that begins in a sort of dazzle and slug-gishness of the brain, and ends in a peace that passes comprehension.

During the first day or so of any tour there are moments of bitterness, when the traveler feels more than coldly towards his knapsack, when he is half in a mind to throw it bodily over the hedge and, like Christian on a similar occasion, "give three leaps and go on singing." And yet it soon acquires a property of easiness. It becomes magnetic; the spirit of the journey enters into it. And no sooner have you passed the strap over your shoulder than the lees of sleep are cleared from you, you pull yourself together with a shake, and fall at once into your stride. And surely, of all possible moods, this, in which a man takes the road, is the best. Of course, if he *will* keep thinking of his anxieties, if he *will* open the merchant Abudah's chest and walk arm-in-arm with the hag—why, wherever he is, and whether he walk fast or slow, the chances are that he will not be happy. And so much the more shame to himself! There are perhaps thirty men setting forth at that same hour, and I would lay a large wager there is not another dull face among the thirty. It would be a fine thing to follow, in a coat of darkness, one after another of these wayfarers, some summer morning, for the first few miles upon the road. This one, who walks fast, with a keen look in his eyes, is all concentrated in his own mind; he is up at his loom, weaving and weaving, to set the landscape to words. This one peers about, as he goes, among the grasses; he waits by the canal to watch the dragon-flies; he leans on the gate of the pasture, and cannot look enough upon the complacent kine. And here comes another, talking, laughing, and gesticulating to himself. His face changes from time to time, as indignation flashes from his eyes or anger clouds his forehead. He is composing articles, delivering orations, and conducting the most impassioned interviews, by the way. A little farther on, and it is as like as not he will begin to sing. And well for him, supposing him to be no great master in that art, if he stumble across no stolid peasant at a corner; for on such an occasion, I scarcely know which is the more troubled, or whether it is worse to suffer the confusion of your troubadour, or the unfeigned alarm of your clown. A sedentary population, accustomed, besides, to the strange mechanical bearing of the common tramp, can in no wise explain to itself the gaiety of these passers-by. I knew one man who was arrested as a runaway lunatic, because, although a full-grown person with a red beard, he skipped as he went like a child. And you would be astonished if I were to tell you all the grave and learned heads who have confessed to me that, when on walking tours, they sang—and sang very ill—and had a pair of red ears when, as described above, the inauspicious peasant plumped into their arms from around a corner. And here, lest you should think I am exaggerating, is Hazlitt's own confession, from his essay *On Going a Journey*, which is so good that there should be a tax levied on all who have not read it:

"Give me the blue sky over my head," says he, "and the green turf beneath my feet, a winding road before me, and a three hours' march to dinner—and then to thinking! It is hard if I cannot start some game on these lone heaths. I laugh, I run, I leap, I sing for joy."

Bravo! After that adventure of my friend with the policeman, you would not have cared, would you, to publish that in the first person? But we have no bravery nowadays, and, even in books, must pretend to be as dull and foolish as our neighbors. It was not so with Hazlitt. And notice how learned he is (as, indeed, throughout the essay) in the theory of walking tours. He is none of your athletic men in purple stockings, who walk their fifty miles a day:

three hours' march is his ideal. And then he must have a winding road, the epicure!

Yet there is one thing I object to in these words of his, one thing in the great master's practice that seems to me not wholly wise. I do not approve of that leaping and running. Both of these hurry the respiration; they both shake up the brain out of its glorious open-air confusion; and they both break the pace. Uneven walking is not so agreeable to the body, and it distracts and irritates the mind. Whereas, when once you have fallen into an equable stride, it requires no conscious thought from you to keep it up, and yet it prevents you from thinking earnestly of anything else. Like knitting, like the work of a copying clerk, it gradually neutralizes and sets to sleep the serious activity of the mind. We can think of this or that, lightly and laughingly, as a child thinks, or as we think in a morning doze; we can make puns or puzzle out acrostics, and trifle in a thousand ways with words and rhymes; but when it comes to honest work, when we come to gather ourselves together for an effort, we may sound the trumpet as loud and long as we please; the great barons of the mind will not rally to the standard, but sit, each one, at home, warming his hands over his own fire and brooding on his own private thought!

In the course of a day's walk, you see, there is much variance in the mood. From the exhilaration of the start to the happy phlegm of the arrival, the change is certainly great. As the day goes on, the traveler moves from the one extreme towards the other. He becomes more and more incorporated with the material landscape, and the open-air drunkenness grows upon him with great strides, until he posts along the road, and sees everything about him, as in a cheerful dream. The first is certainly brighter, but the second stage is the more peaceful. A man does not make so many articles towards the end, nor does he laugh aloud; but the purely animal pleasures, the sense of physical well-being, the delight of every inhalation, of every time the muscles tighten down the thigh, console him for the absence of the others, and bring him to his destination still content.

Nor must I forget to say a word on bivouacs. You come to a milestone on a hill, or some place where deep ways meet under trees; and off goes the knapsack, and down you sit to smoke a pipe in the shade. You sink into yourself, and the birds come round and look at you; and your smoke dissipates upon the afternoon under the blue dome of heaven; and the sun lies warm upon your feet, and the cool air visits your neck and turns aside your open shirt. If you are not happy, you must have an evil conscience. You may dally as long as you like by the roadside. It is almost as if the millennium were arrived, when we shall throw our clocks and watches over the housetop, and remember time and seasons no more. Not to keep hours for a lifetime is, I was going to say, to live forever. You have no idea, unless you have tried it, how endlessly long is a summer's day, that you measure out only by hunger, and bring to an end only when you are drowsy. I know a village where there are hardly any clocks, where no one knows more of the days of the week than by a sort of instinct for the *fête* on Sundays, and where only one person can tell you the day of the month, and she is generally wrong; and if people were aware how slow Time journeyed in that village, and what armfuls of spare hours he gives, over and above the bargain, to its wise inhabitants, I believe there would be a stampede out of London, Liverpool, Paris, and a variety of large towns, where the clocks lose their heads, and shake the hours out each one faster than the other, as though they were all in a wager. And all these foolish pilgrims would each bring his own misery with him, in a watch-pocket! It is to be noticed, there were no clocks and no watches in the much-vaunted days before the flood. It follows, of course, there were no appointments, and punctuality was not yet thought upon. "Though ye take from a covetous man all his treasure," says Milton, "he has yet one jewel left; ye cannot deprive him of his covetousness." And so I would say of a modern man of business, you may do what you will for him, put him in Eden, give him the elixir of life—he has still a flaw at heart, he still has his business habits. Now, there is no time when business habits are more mitigated than on a walking tour. And so during these halts, as I say, you will feel almost free.

But it is at night, and after dinner, that the best hour comes. There are no such pipes to be smoked as those that follow a good day's march; the flavor of the tobacco is a thing to be remembered, it is so dry and aromatic, so full and fine. If you wind up the evening with grog, you will own there was never such grog; at every sip a jocund tranquillity spreads about your limbs, and sits easily in your heart. If you read a book—and you never do so save by fits and starts—you find the language strangely racy and harmonious; words take a new meaning; single sentences possess the ear for half an hour together; and the writer endears himself to you, at every page, by the nicest coincidence of sentiment. It seems as if it were a book you had written yourself in a dream. To all we have read on such occasions we look back with special favor. "It was on the 10th of April, 1798," says Hazlitt, with amorous precision, "that I sat down to a volume of the *New Héloïse*, at the Inn at Llangollen, over a bottle of sherry and a cold chicken." I should wish to quote more, for though we are mighty fine fellows nowadays, we cannot write like Hazlitt. And, talking of that, a volume of Hazlitt's essays would be a capital pocket-book on such a journey; so would a volume of Heine's songs; and for *Tristram Shandy* I can pledge a fair experience.

If the evening be fine and warm, there is nothing better in life than to lounge before the inn door in the sunset, or lean over the parapet of the bridge, to watch the weeds and the quick fishes. It is then, if ever, that you taste Joviality to the full significance of that audacious word. Your muscles are so agreeably slack, you feel so clean and so strong and so idle, that whether you move or sit still, whatever you do is done with pride and a kingly sort of pleasure. You fall in talk with any one, wise or foolish, drunk or sober. And it seems as if a hot walk purged you, more than of anything else, of all narrowness and pride, and left curiosity to play its part freely, as in a child or a man of science. You lay aside all your own hobbies, to watch provincial humors develop themselves before you, now as a laughable farce, and now grave and beautiful like an old tale.

Or perhaps you are left to your own company for the night, and surly weather imprisons you by the fire. You may remember how Burns, numbering past pleasures, dwells upon the hours when he has been "happy thinking." It is a phrase that may well perplex a poor modern, girt about on every side by clocks and chimes, and haunted, even at night, by flaming dial-plates. For we are all so busy, and have so many far-off projects to realize, and castles in the fire to turn into solid, habitable mansions on a gravel soil, that we can find no time for pleasure trips into the Land of Thought and among the Hills of Vanity. Changed times, indeed, when we must sit all night, beside the fire, with folded hands; and a changed world for most of us, when we can pass the hours without discontent, and be happy thinking. We are in such haste to be doing, to be writing, to be gathering gear, to make our voice audible a moment in the derisive silence of eternity, that we forget that one thing, of which these are but the parts—namely, to live. We fall in love, we drink hard, we run to and fro upon the earth like frightened sheep. And now you are to ask yourself if, when all is done, you would not have been better to sit by the fire at home, and be happy thinking. To sit still and contemplate,—to remember the faces of women without desire, to be pleased by the great deeds of men without envy, to be everything and everywhere in sympathy, and yet content to remain where and what you are—is not this to know both wisdom and virtue, and to dwell with happiness? After all, it is not they who carry flags, but they who look upon it from a private chamber, who have the fun of the procession. And once you are at that, you are in the very humor of all social heresy. It is no time for shuffling, or for big, empty words. If you ask yourself what you mean by fame, riches or learning, the answer is far to seek; and you go back into that kingdom of light imaginations, which seem so vain in the eyes of Philistines perspiring after wealth, and so momentous to those who are stricken with the disproportions of the world, and, in the face of the gigantic stars, cannot stop to split differences between the two degrees of the infinitesimally small, such as a tobacco pipe or the Roman Empire, a million of money or a fiddlestick's end.

You lean from your window, your last pipe reeking whitely into the darkness, your body full of delicious pains, your mind enthroned in the seventh circle of content; when suddenly the mood changes, the weather-cock goes about, and you ask yourself one question more: whether, for the interval, you have been the wisest philosopher or the most egregious of donkeys? Human experience is not yet able to reply; but at least you have had a fine moment, and looked down upon all the kingdoms of the earth. And whether it was wise or foolish, tomorrow's travel will carry you, body and mind, into some different parish of the infinite.

## CITY RHYTHMS
### *The New Yorkers* (*1934*)

THE lament for the past and for dead things runs like a strong, sweet weed through literature today. Sensitive writers, in this nervous and cranky period, find relief in nostalgia and in recapturing their childhood; their recollections are at once enormously affecting and acutely discouraging, in books like Dr. Canby's *The Age of Confidence,* in which he recalls with longing his safe and conventional boyhood in Wilmington, or like the beautiful novel *Mary Peters,* through whose pages Mary Ellen Chase revisits the quiet streets of a seacoast village and sighs for its once noble character. This wave of affectionate regret which sets in motion so great a body of good writing today is, of course, no mere fad but the consequence of a long, sad period of economic sickness and of blood thinned by carbon monoxide. It has resulted in some of the most excellent stuff to be found between covers, for when an author writes of his childhood, his pen discovers a double skill; not only does time, sifting the memory, cast out all but the picturesque and the pertinent details, but there is something about reminiscence which induces literary sincerity, from which comes literary greatness.

Yet these backward-glancing books, accenting the rhythm and the strength of the home and immortalizing a kindlier day, have an insidious vein of poison in them. Returning with Dr. Canby to a brick house on a cobbled Delaware street, revisiting Blue Hill, Maine, with Miss Chase, are adventures which both feed and destroy one's moral tissue. In their detail and mood the books do not exaggerate the change that has come over life in America and over such institutions as the home; yet in effect they carry an insinuation which is demoralizing. They imply, quite innocently, a permanent decadence which seems to us (by nature and circumstance a somewhat hopeful individual in the midst of a distraught society) only partially justified. Life this morning in Wilmington admittedly lacks the stable, well-appointed security that gave Dr. Canby his gracious childhood; and if we should return to Blue Hill this morning, we would find a harbor with no masts, a village tightening its belt after the departure of the summer people, and a storekeeper overstocked with Birdseye Frosted Clams. Yet, despite the changing times, we believe that the cumulative effect of these wistful books in some degree aggravates the national pessimism and disillusion. Just now we are as thoroughly disheartened a race as ever breathed, and unquestionably some of our dispirit (particularly among those of us who are not in want) is a sort of mental habit nourished on a literature of regret.

Can it be true that all graciousness went out of life when "Alexander's Ragtime Band" came in, or all nobility and rhythm with the arrival of the Pope Toledo? To take the idea of rhythm: we suspect that even a New York City apartment, with its electric accoutrements and its quick-time beat and its motorcar at the door, is for a modern child not wholly devoid of that sustaining and comforting rhythm which Dr. Canby celebrates as of the past alone. Even in these horrid nineteen-thirties, an apartment moves with a cadence through a child's long, safe day. Our children, though they have been unsettled, are not utter transients, and they may conceivably retain and cherish memories of a life which has both form and meaning. At any rate we like to think that a New York child experiences a vaguely rhythmical existence, that he hears—perhaps more than we realize—the early morning: the distinct and isolated whistles from the river, the milkman banging a door in the court. We suspect that he is rhythmically affected by the gradual infiltration of light and sound—the dark living-room before the curtains are pulled, the plaid shadows on the steps of the fire-escape, the hum of the refrigerator, like a cicada in the apartment. He must, we are sure, feel and know the steady progress of the morning: a crosstown car establishing its characteristic crescendo, a hose being played in a doorway after a hot summer night, the eight-o'clock greeting of a saw in a picture-framer's shop nearby. There is a rhythm even in our day: there are carpenters' hammers, colored maids humming at their dusting, the death rattle in the throat of the dumbwaiter, the buzz of a vacuum cleaner at the crest of the morning, chimes from a clock tower at lunch, and a piano in the slow hours of mid-afternoon. Before supper the tinkle and startle of guests; and later, the quiet rooms, and the dog that must go around the block before grownups go to bed. And even though the whole apartment shakes and trembles whenever a truck passes in the street outside, it must seem somehow safe and good, and perhaps rhythmical, to a child. We hope it does, anyway.

# THE MEMORY OF THE WITNESS

### (*From* On the Witness Stand)

### *Hugo Münsterberg* (*1923*)

LAST summer I had to face a jury as witness in a trial. While I was with my family at the seashore my city house had been burglarised and I was called upon to give an account of my findings against the culprit whom they had caught with a part of the booty. I reported under oath that the burglars had entered through a cellar window, and then described what rooms they had visited. To prove, in answer to a direct question, that they had been there at night, I told that I had found drops of candle wax on the second floor. To show that they intended to return, I reported that they had left a large mantel clock, packed in wrapping paper, on the dining-room table. Finally, as to the amount of clothes which they had taken, I asserted that the burglars did not get more than a specified list which I had given the police.

Only a few days later I found that every one of these statements was wrong. They had not entered through the window, but had broken the lock of the cellar door; the clock was not packed by them in wrapping paper, but in a tablecloth; the candle droppings were not on the second floor, but in the attic; the list of lost garments was to be increased by seven more pieces; and while my story under oath spoke always of two burglars, I do not know that there was more than one. How did all these mistakes occur? I have no right to excuse myself on the plea of a bad memory. During the last eighteen years I have delivered about three thousand university lectures. For those three thousand coherent addresses I had not once a single written or printed line or any notes whatever on the platform; and yet there has never been a moment when I have had to stop for a name or for the connection of the thought. My memory serves me therefore rather generously. I stood there, also, without prejudice against the defendant. Inasmuch as he expects to spend the next twelve years at a place of residence where he will have little chance to read my writings, I may confess frankly that I liked the man. I was thus under the most favorable conditions for speaking the whole truth and nothing but the truth, and, as there is probably no need for the assurance of my best intentions, I felt myself somewhat alarmed in seeing how many illusions had come in.

Of course, I had not made any careful examination of the house. I had rushed in from the seashore as soon as the police notified me, in the fear that valuable contents of the house might have been destroyed or plundered. When I saw that they had treated me mildly, inasmuch as they had started in the wine cellar and had forgotten under its genial influence, on the whole, what they had come for, I had taken only a superficial survey. That a clock was lying on the table, packed ready to be taken away, had impressed itself clearly on my memory; but that it was packed in a tablecloth had made evidently too slight an impression on my consciousness. My imagination gradually substituted the more usual method of packing with wrapping paper, and I was ready to take an oath on it until I went back later, at the end of the summer vacation. In the same way I got a vivid image of the candle droppings on the floor, but as, at the moment of the perception, no interest was attached to the peculiar place where I saw them, I slowly substituted in my memory the second floor for the attic, knowing surely from strewn papers and other disorder that they had ransacked both places. As to the clothes, I had simply forgotten that I had put several suits in a remote wardrobe; only later did I find it empty. My other two blunders clearly arose under the influence of suggestion. The police and every one about the house had always taken as a matter of course that the entrance was made by a cellar window, as it would have been much more difficult to use the locked doors. I had thus never examined the other hypothesis, and yet it was found later that they did succeed in removing the lock of a door. And finally, my whole story under oath referred to two burglars, without any doubt at the moment. The fact is, they had caught the gentleman in question when he, a few days later, plundered another house. He then shot a policeman, but was arrested, and in his room they found a jacket with my name written in it by the tailor. That alone gave a hint that my house also had been entered; but from the first moment he insisted that there had been two in this burglary and that the other man had the remainder of the booty. The other has not been found, and he probably still wears my badges; but I never heard any doubt as to his existence, and thus, in mere imitation, I never doubted that there was a companion, in spite of the fact that every part of the performance might just as well have been carried out by one man alone; and, after all, it is not impossible that he should lie as well as shoot and steal.

In this way, in spite of my best intentions, in spite of good memory and calm mood, a whole series of confusions, of illusions, of forgetting, of wrong conclusions, and of yielding to suggestions were mingled with what I had to report under oath, and my only consolation is the fact that in a thousand courts at a thousand places all over the world, witnesses every day affirm by oath in exactly the same way much worse mixtures of truth and untruth, combinations of memory and of illusion, of knowledge and of suggestion, of experience and wrong conclusions. Not one of my mistakes was of the slightest consequence. But is it probable that this is always so? Is it not more natural to suppose that every day errors creep into the work of justice through wrong evidence which has the outer marks of truth and trustworthiness? Of course, judge and jury and, later, the newspaper reader try their best to weigh the evidence. Not every sworn statement is accepted as absolute reality. Contradictions between witnesses are too familiar. But the instinctive doubt refers primarily to veracity. The public in the main suspects that the witness lies, while taking for granted that if he is normal and conscious of responsibility he may forget a thing, but it would not believe that he could remember the wrong thing. The confidence in the reliability of memory is so general that the suspicion of memory illusions evidently plays a small role in the mind of the juryman, and even the cross-examining lawyer is mostly dominated by the idea that a false statement is the product of intentional falsehood.

All this is a popular illusion against which modern psychology must seriously protest. Justice would less often miscarry if all who are to weigh evidence were more conscious of the treachery of human memory. Yes, it can be said that, while the court makes the fullest use of all the modern scientific methods when, for instance, a drop of dried blood is to be examined in a murder case, the same court is completely satisfied with the most unscientific and haphazard methods of common prejudice and ignorance when a mental product, especially the memory report of a witness, is to be examined. No juryman would be expected to follow his general impressions in the question as to whether the blood on the murderer's shirt is human or animal. But he is expected to make up his mind as to whether the memory ideas of a witness are objective reproductions of earlier experience or are mixed up with associations and suggestions. The court proceeds as if the physiological chemistry of blood examination had made wonderful progress, while experimental psychology, with its efforts to analyze the mental faculties, still stood where it stood two thousand years ago.

The fact is that experimental psychology has not only in general experienced a wonderful progress during the last decades, but has also given in recent years an unusual amount of attention to just those problems which are involved on the witness stand. It is perhaps no exaggeration to say that a new special science has even grown up which deals exclusively with the reliability of memory. It started in Germany and has had there for some years even a magazine of its own. But many investigations in France and the United States tended from the start in the same direction, and the work spread rapidly over the psychological laboratories of the world. Rich material has been gathered, and yet practical jurisprudence is, on the whole, still unaware of it; and while the alienist is always a welcome guest in the court room, the psychologist is still a stranger there. The Court would rather listen for whole days to the "science" of the handwriting experts than allow a witness to be examined with regard to his memory and his power of perception, his attention and his associations, his volition and his suggestibility, with methods which are in accord with the exact work of experimental psychology. It is so much easier everywhere to be satisfied with sharp demarcation lines and to listen only to a yes or no; the man is sane or insane, and if he is sane, he speaks the truth or he lies. The psychologist would upset this satisfaction completely.

The administration of an oath is partly responsible for the wrong valuation of the evidence. Its seriousness and solemnity suggest that the conditions for complete truth are given if the witness is ready not to lie. We are too easily inclined to confuse the idea of truth in a subjective and in an objective sense. A German proverb says, "Children and fools speak the truth," and with it goes the old "In vino veritas." Of course, no one can suppose that children, fools, and tipsy men have a deeper insight into true relations than the sober and grown-up remainder of mankind. What is meant is only that all the motives are lacking which, in our social turmoil, may lead others to the intentional hiding of the truth. Children do not suppress the truth, because they are naïve; the fools do not suppress it, because they are reckless; and the mind under the influence of wine does not suppress it, because the suppressing mechanism of inhibition is temporarily paralysed by alcohol. The subjective truth may thus be secured, and yet the idle talk of the drunkard and the child and the fool may be objectively untrue from beginning to end. It is in this way only that the oath by its religious background and by its connection with threatened punishment can work for truth. It can and will remove to a high degree the intention to hide the truth, but it may be an open question to what degree it can increase the objective truthfulness.

Of course, everyone knows that the oath helps in at least one more direction in curbing misstatements. It not only suppresses the intentional lie, but it focusses the attention on the details of the statement. It excludes the careless, hasty, chance recollection, and stirs the deliberate attention of the witness. He feels the duty of putting his best will into the effort to reproduce the whole truth and nothing but the truth. No psychologist will deny this effect. He will ask only whether the intention alone is sufficient for success and whether the memory is really improved in every respect by increased attention. We are not always sure that our functions run best when we concentrate our effort on them and turn the full light of attention on the details. We may speak fluently, but the moment we begin to give attention to the special movements of our lips and of our tongue in speaking and make a special effort to produce the movements correctly, we are badly hampered. Is it so sure that our memory works faultlessly simply because we earnestly want it to behave well? We may try hard to think of a name and it will not appear in consciousness; and when we have thought of something else for a long time, the desired name suddenly slips into our mind. May it not be in a similar way that the effort for correct recollection under oath may prove powerless to a degree which public opinion underestimates? And no subjective feeling of certainty can be an objective criterion for the desired truth.

A few years ago a painful scene occurred in Berlin, in the University Seminary of Professor von Liszt, the famous criminologist. The Professor had spoken about a book. One of the older students suddenly shouts, "I wanted to throw light on the matter from the standpoint of Christian morality!" Another student throws in, "I cannot stand that!" The first starts up, exclaiming, "You have insulted me!" The second clenches his fist and cries, "If you say another word—" The first draws a revolver. The second rushes madly upon him. The Professor steps between them and, as he grasps the man's arm, the revolver goes off. General uproar. In that moment Professor Liszt secures order and asks a part of the students to write an exact account of all that has happened. The whole had been a comedy, carefully planned and rehearsed by the three actors for the purpose of studying the exactitude of observation and recollection. Those who did not write the report at once were, part of them, asked to write it the next day or a week later; and others had to depose their observations under cross-examination. The whole objective performance was cut up into fourteen little parts which referred partly to actions, partly to words. As mistakes there were counted the omissions, the wrong additions and the alterations. The smallest number of mistakes gave twenty-six per cent. of erroneous statements; the largest was eighty per cent. The reports with reference to the second half of the performance, which was more strongly emotional, gave an average of fifteen per cent. more mistakes than those of the first half. Words were put into the mouths of men who had been silent spectators during the whole short episode; actions were attributed to the chief participants of which not the slightest trace existed; and essential parts of the tragi-comedy were completely eliminated from the memory of a number of witnesses.

This dramatic psychological experiment of six years ago opened up a long series of similar tests in a variety of places, with a steady effort to improve the conditions. The most essential condition remained, of course, always the complete naïveté of the witnesses, as the slightest suspicion on their part would destroy the value of the experiment. It seems desirable even that the writing of the protocol should still be done in a state of belief. There was, for instance, two years ago in Göttingen a meeting of a scientific association, made up of jurists, psychologists, and physicians, all, therefore, men well trained in careful observation. Somewhere in the same street there was that evening a public festivity of the carnival. Suddenly, in the midst of the scholarly meeting, the doors open, a clown in highly coloured costume rushes in in mad excitement, and a negro with a revolver in hand follows him. In the middle of the hall first the one, then the other, shouts wild phrases; then the one falls to the ground, the other jumps on him; then a shot, and suddenly both are out of the room. The whole affair took less than twenty seconds. All were completely taken by surprise, and no one, with the exception of the President, had the slightest idea that every word and action had been rehearsed beforehand, or that photographs had been taken of the scene. It seemed most natural that the President should beg the members to write down individually an exact report, inasmuch as he felt that the matter would come before the courts. Of the forty reports handed in, there was only one whose omissions were calculated as amounting to less than twenty per cent. of the characteristic acts; fourteen had twenty to forty per cent. of the facts omitted; twelve omitted forty to fifty per cent., and thirteen still more than fifty per cent. But besides the omissions there were only six among the forty which did not contain positively wrong statements; in twenty-four papers up to ten per cent. of the statements were free inventions, and in ten answers—that is, in one-fourth of the papers—more than ten per cent. of the statements were absolutely false, in spite of the fact that they all came from scientifically trained observers. Only four persons, for instance, among forty noticed that the negro had nothing on his head; the others gave him a derby, or a high hat, and so on. In addition to this, a red suit, a brown one, a striped one, a coffee-coloured jacket, shirt sleeves, and similar costumes were invented for him. He wore in reality white trousers and a black jacket with a large red necktie. The scientific commission which reported the details of the inquiry came to the general statement that the majority of the observers omitted or falsified about half of the processes which occurred completely in their field of vision. As was to be expected, the judgment as to the time duration of the act varied between a few seconds and several minutes.

It is not necessary to tell more of these dramatic experiments, which have recently become the fashion and almost a sport, and which will still have to be continued with a great variety of conditions if the psychological laws involved are really to be cleared up. There are many points, for instance, in which the results seem still contradictory. In some cases it was shown that the mistakes made after a week were hardly more frequent than those made after a day. Other experiments seemed to indicate that the number of mistakes steadily increases with the length of time which has elapsed. Again, some experiments suggest that the memory of the two sexes is not essentially different, while the majority of the tests seems to speak for very considerable difference. Experiments with school children, especially, seem to show that the girls have a better memory than the boys as far as omissions are concerned; they forget less. But they have a worse memory than the boys as far as correctness is concerned; they unintentionally falsify more.

We may consider here still another point which is more directly connected with our purpose. A well-known psychologist showed three pictures, rich in detail, but well adapted to the interest of children, to a large number of boys and girls. They looked at each picture for fifteen seconds and then wrote a full report of everything they could remember. After that they were asked to underline those parts of their reports of which they felt so absolutely certain that they would be ready to take an oath before court on the underlined words. The young people put forth their best efforts, and yet the results showed that there were almost as many mistakes in the underlined sentences as in the rest. This experiment has been often repeated and the results make clear that this happens in a smaller and yet still surprising degree in the case of adults also. The grown-up students of my laboratory commit this kind of perjury all the time.

Subtler experiments which were carried on in my laboratory for a long time showed that this subjective feeling of certainty cannot only obtain in different degrees, but has, with different individuals, quite different mental structure and meaning. We found that there were, above all, two distinct classes. For one of those types certainty in the recollection of an experience would rest very largely upon the vividness of the image. For the other type it would depend upon the congruity of an image with other previously accepted images; that is, on the absence of conflicts, when the experience judged about is imagined as part of a wide setting of past experiences. But the most surprising result of those studies was perhaps that the feeling of certainty stands in no definite relation to the attention with which the objects are observed. If we turn our attention with strongest effort to certain parts of a complex impression, we may yet feel in our recollection more certain about those parts of which we hardly took notice than about those to which we devoted our attention. The correlations between attention, recollection, and feeling of certainty become the more complex the more we carefully study them. Not only the self-made psychology of the average juryman, but also the scanty psychological statements which judge and attorney find in the large compendiums on Evidence fall to pieces if a careful examination approaches the mental facts.

The sources of error begin, of course, before the recollection sets in. The observation itself may be defective and illusory; wrong associations may make it imperfect; judgments may misinterpret the experience; and suggestive influences may falsify the data of the senses. Everyone knows the almost unlimited individual differences in the power of correct observation and judgment. Everyone knows that there are persons who, under favourable conditions, see what they are expected to see. The prestidigitateurs, the fakirs, the spiritualists could not play their tricks if they could not rely on associations and suggestions, and it would not be so difficult to read proofs if we did not usually see the letters which we expect. But we can abstract here from the distortions which enter into the perception itself; we have discussed them before. The mistakes of recollection alone are now the object of our inquiry and we may throw light on them from still another side.

Many of us remember minutes in which we passed through an experience with a distinct and almost uncanny feeling of having passed through it once before. The words which we hear, the actions which we see, we remember exactly that we experienced them a long time ago. The case is rare with men, but with women extremely frequent, and there are few women who do not know the state. An idea is there distinctly coupled with the feeling of remembrance and recognition, and yet it is only an associated sensation, resulting from fatigue or excitement, and without the slightest objective basis in the past. The psychologist feels no difficulty in explaining it, but it ought to stand as a great warning signal before the minds of those who believe that the feeling of certainty in recollection secures objective truth. There is no new principle involved, of course, when the ideas which stream into consciousness spring from one's own imagination instead of being produced by the outer impressions of our surroundings. Any imaginative thought may slip into our consciousness and may carry with it in the same way that curious feeling that it is merely the repetition of something we have experienced before.

A striking illustration is well known to those who have ever taken the trouble to approach the depressing literature of modern mysticism. There we find an abundance of cases reported which seem to prove that either prophetic fortune tellers or inspired dreams have anticipated the real future of a man's life with the subtlest details and with the most uncanny foresight. But as soon as we examine these wonderful stories, we find that the coincidences are surprising only in those cases in which the dreams and the prophecies have been written down after the realisation. Whenever the visions were given to the protocol beforehand, the percentage of true realisations remains completely within the narrow limits of chance coincidents and natural probability. In other words, there cannot be any doubt that the reports of such prophecies which are communicated after having been realised are falsified. That does not reflect in the least on the subjective veracity; our satisfied client of the clever fortune teller would feel ready to take oath to his illusions of memory; but illusions they remain. He also, in most cases, feels sure that he told the dream to the whole family the next morning exactly as it happened; only when it is possible to call the members of the family to a scientific witness stand, does it become evident that the essentials of the dream varied in all directions from the real later occurrence. The real present occurrence completely transforms the reminiscences of the past prophecy and every happening is apperceived with the illusory overtone of having been foreseen.

We must always keep in mind that a content of consciousness is in itself independent of its relation to the past and has thus in itself no mark which can indicate whether it was experienced once before or not. The feeling of belonging to our past life may associate itself thus just as well with a perfectly new idea of our imagination as with a real reproduction of an earlier state of mind. As a matter of course, the opposite can thus happen, too; that is, an earlier experience may come to our memory stripped of every reference to the past, standing before our mind like a completely new product of imagination. To point again to an apparently mysterious experience: the crystal gazer feels in his half hypnotic state a free play of inspired imagination, and yet in reality he experiences only a stirring up of the deeper layers of memory pictures. They rush to his mind without any reference to their past origin, picturing a timeless truth which is surprisingly correct only because it is the result of a sharpened memory. Yes, we fill the blanks of our perceptions constantly with bits of reproduced memory material and take those reproductions for immediate impressions. In short, we never know from the material itself whether we remember, perceive, or imagine, and in the borderland regions there must result plenty of confusion which cannot always remain without dangerous consequences in the court room.

Still another phenomenon is fairly familiar to everyone, and only the courts have not yet discovered it. There are different types of memory, which in a very crude and superficial classification might be grouped as visual, acoustical, and motor types. There are persons who can reproduce a landscape or a painting in full vivid colours and with sharp outlines throughout the field, while they would be unable to hear internally a melody or the sound of a voice. There are others with whom every tune can easily resound in recollection and who can hardly read a letter of a friend without hearing his voice in every word, while they are utterly unable to awake an optical image. There are others again whose sensorial reproduction is poor in both respects; they feel intentions of movement, as of speaking, of writing, of acting, whenever they reconstruct past experience. In reality the number of types is much larger. Scores of memory variations can be discriminated. Let your friends describe how they have before their minds yesterday's dinner table and the conversation around it, and there will not be two whose memory shows the same scheme and method. Now we should not ask a short-sighted man for the slight visual details of a far distant scene, yet it cannot be safer to ask a man of the acoustical memory type for strictly optical recollections. No one on the witness stand is today examined to ascertain in what directions his memory is probably trustworthy and reliable; he may be asked what he has seen, what he has heard, what he has spoken, how he has acted, and yet even a most superficial test might show that the mechanism of his memory would be excellent for one of these four groups of questions and utterly useless for the others, however solemnly he might keep his oath.

The courts will have to learn, sooner or later, that the individual differences of men can be tested today by the methods of experimental psychology far beyond anything which common sense and social experience suggest. Modern law welcomes, for instance, for identification of criminals all the discoveries of anatomists and physiologists as to the individual differences; even the different play of lines in the thumb is carefully registered in wax. But no one asks for the striking differences as to those mental details which the psychological experiments on memory and attention, on feeling and imagination, on perception and discrimination, on judgment and suggestion, on emotion and volition, have brought out in the last decade. Other sciences are less slow to learn. It has been found, for instance, that the psychological speech impulse has for every individual a special character as to intonation and melody. At once the philologists came and made the most brilliant use of this psychological discovery. They have taken, for instance, whole epic texts and examined those lines as to which it was doubtful whether they belonged originally to the poem or were later interpolations. Wherever the speech intonation agreed with that of the whole song, they acknowledged the authentic origin, and where it did not agree they recognised an interpolation of the text. Yet the lawyers might learn endlessly more from the psychologists about individual differences than the philologians have done. They must only understand that the working of the mental mechanism in a personality depends on the constant coöperation of simple and elementary functions which the modern laboratory experiment can isolate and test. If those simplest elements are understood, their complex combination becomes necessary; just as the whole of a geometrical curve becomes necessary as soon as its analytical formula is understood for the smallest part.

But the psychological assistance ought not to be confined to the discrimination of memory types and other individual differences. The experimentalist cannot forget how abundant are the new facts of memory variations which have come out of experiments on attention and inhibition. We know and can test with the subtlest means the waves of fluctuating attention through which ideas become reinforced and weakened. We know, above all, the inhibitory influences which result from excitements and emotions which may completely change the products of an otherwise faithful memory.

A concrete illustration may indicate the method of the experimenters. The judge has to make up his mind as soon as there is any doubt on which side the evidence on an issue of fact preponderates. If it can be presupposed that both sides intend to speak the truth, he is ready to consider that the one side had, perhaps, a more frequent opportunity to watch the facts in question, the other side, perhaps, saw them more recently; the one saw them, perhaps, under especially impressive circumstances, the other, perhaps with further knowledge of the whole situation, and so on. Of course, his buckram-bound volumes of old decisions guide him, but those decisions report again only that the one or the other judge, relying on his common-sense, thought recency more weighty than frequency, or frequency more important than impressiveness, or perhaps the opposite. It is the same way in which common-sense tells a man what kind of diet is most nourishing. Yet what responsible physician would ignore the painstaking experiments of the physiological laboratory, determining exactly the quantitative results as to the nourishing value of eggs or milk or meat or bread? The judges ignore the fact that with the same accuracy their common-sense can be transformed into careful measurements the results of which may widely differ from haphazard opinion. The psychologist, of course, has to reduce the complex facts to simple principles and elements. An investigation, devoted to this problem of the relative effectiveness of recency, frequency, and vividness was carried on in my psychological laboratory. Here we used simple pairs of coloured papers and printed figures, or colours and words, or words and figures, or colours and forms, and so on. A series of ten such pairs may be exposed successively in a lighted field, each time one colour and one figure of two digits. But one pair, perhaps the third, is repeated as the seventh, and thus impresses itself by its frequency; another pair, perhaps the fifth, comes with impressive vividness, from the fact that instead of two digits, suddenly three are used. The last pair has, of course, the advantage in that it sticks to the mind from its position at the end; it remains the most recent, which is not inhibited by any following pair. After a pause the colours are shown again and every one of the subjects has to write down the figures together with which he believes himself to have seen the particular colours. Is the vivid pair, or the frequently repeated pair, or the recent pair better remembered? Of course, the experiment was made under most different conditions, with different pauses, different material, different length of the series, different influences, different distribution, different subjects, but after some years of work, facts showed themselves which can stand as facts. The relative value of the various conditions for exact recollection became really measurable. They may and must be corrected by further experiments, but they are raised from the first above the level of the chance opinions of the lawyer-psychologist.

All this remains entirely within the limits of the normal healthy individuality. Nothing of all that we have mentioned belongs to the domain of the physician. Where the alienist has to speak, that is, where pathological amnesia destroys the memory of the witness, or where hallucinations of disease, or fixed ideas deprive the witness's remembrance of its value, there the psychologist is not needed. It is in normal mental life and its borderland regions that the progress of psychological science cannot be further ignored. No railroad or ship company would appoint to a responsible post in its service men whose eyesight had not been tested for colour blindness. There may be only one among thirty or forty who cannot distinguish at a distance the red from the green lantern. Yet if he slips into the service without being tested, his slight defect, which does not disturb him in practical life and which he may never have noticed if he was not just picking red strawberries among green leaves, may be sufficient to bring about the most disastrous wrecking of two trains or the most horrible collision of steamers. In the life of justice trains are wrecked and ships are colliding too often, simply because the law does not care to examine the mental colour blindness of the witness's memory. And yet we have not even touched one factor which, more than anything else, devastates memory and plays havoc with our best intended recollections: that is, the power of suggestion.

## EARLY DAYS

### (*From* Mark Twain's Autobiography) (*1898*)

It was a heavenly place for a boy, that farm of my uncle John's. The house was a double log one, with a spacious floor (roofed in) connecting it with the kitchen. In the summer the table was set in the middle of that shady and breezy floor, and the sumptuous meals—well, it makes me cry to think of them. Fried chicken, roast pig; wild and tame turkeys, ducks, and geese; venison just killed; squirrels, rabbits, pheasants, partridges, prairie-chickens; biscuits, hot batter cakes, hot buckwheat cakes, hot "wheat bread," hot rolls, hot corn pone; fresh corn boiled on the ear, succotash, butter-beans, string-beans, tomatoes, peas, Irish potatoes, sweet potatoes; buttermilk, sweet milk, "clabber"; watermelons, muskmelons, cantaloupes—all fresh from the garden; apple pie, peach pie, pumpkin pie, apple dumplings, peach cobbler—I can't remember the rest. The way that the things were cooked was perhaps the main splendor—particularly a certain few of the dishes. For instance, the corn bread, the hot biscuits and wheat bread, and the fried chicken. These things have never been properly cooked in the North—in fact, no one there is able to learn the art, so far as my experience goes. The North thinks it knows how to make corn bread, but this is mere superstition. Perhaps no bread in the world is quite so good as Southern corn bread, and perhaps no bread in the world is quite so bad as the Northern imitation of it. The North seldom tries to fry chicken, and this is well; the art cannot be learned north of the line of Mason and Dixon, nor anywhere in Europe. This is not hearsay; it is experience that is speaking. In Europe it is imagined that the custom of serving various kinds of bread blazing hot is "American," but that is too broad a spread; it is custom in the South, but is much less than that in the North. In the North and in Europe hot bread is considered unhealthy. This is probably another fussy superstition, like the European superstition that ice-water is unhealthy. Europe does not need ice-water and does not drink it; and yet, notwithstanding this, its word for it is better than ours, because it describes it, whereas ours doesn't. Europe calls it "iced" water. Our word describes water made from melted ice—a drink which has a characterless taste and which we have but little acquaintance with.

It seems a pity that the world should throw away so many good things merely because they are unwholesome. I doubt if God has given us any refreshment which, taken in moderation, is unwholesome, except microbes. Yet there are people who strictly deprive themselves of each and every eatable, drinkable, and smokable which has in any way acquired a shady reputation. They pay this price for health. And health is all they get for it. How strange it is! It is like paying out your whole fortune for a cow that has gone dry.

The farmhouse stood in the middle of a very large yard, and the yard was fenced on three sides with rails and on the rear side with high palings; against these stood the smoke-house; beyond the palings was the orchard; beyond the orchard were the negro quarters and the tobacco fields. The front yard was entered over a stile made of sawed-off logs of graduated heights; I do not remember any gate. In a corner of the front yard were a dozen lofty hickory trees and a dozen black walnuts, and in the nutting season riches were to be gathered there.

Down a piece, abreast the house, stood a little log cabin against the rail fence; and there the woody hill fell sharply away, past the barns, the corn-crib, the stables, and the tobacco-curing house, to a limpid brook which sang along over its gravelly bed and curved and frisked in and out and here and there and yonder in the deep shade of overhanging foliage and vines—a divine place for wading, and it had swimming pools, too, which were forbidden to us and therefore much frequented by us. For we were little Christian children and had early been taught the value of forbidden fruit.

.    .    .    .    .    .    .

I can see the farm yet, with perfect clearness. I can see all its belongings, all its details; the family room of the house, with a "trundle" bed in one corner and a spinning-wheel in another—a wheel whose rising and falling wail, heard from a distance, was the mournfullest of all sounds to me, and made me homesick and low spirited, and filled my atmosphere with the wandering spirits of the dead; the vast fireplace, piled high, on winter nights, with flaming hickory logs from whose ends a sugary sap bubbled out, but did not go to waste, for we scraped it off and ate it; the lazy cat spread out on the rough hearthstones; the drowsy dogs braced against the jambs and blinking; my aunt in one chimney corner, knitting; my uncle in the other, smoking his corn-cob pipe; the slick and carpetless oak floor faintly mirroring the dancing flame tongues and freckled with black indentations where fire coals had popped out and died a leisurely death; half a dozen children romping in the background twilight; "split"-bottomed chairs here and there, some with rockers; a cradle— out of service, but waiting, with confidence; in the early cold mornings a snuggle of children, in shirts and chemises, occupying the hearthstone and procrastinating—they could not bear to leave that comfortable place and go out on the wind-swept floor space between the house and kitchen where the general tin basin stood, and wash.

Along outside of the front fence ran the country road, dusty in the summertime, and a good place for snakes—they liked to lie in it and sun themselves; when they were rattlesnakes or puff adders, we killed them; when they were black snakes, or racers, or belonged to the fabled "hoop" breed, we fled, without shame; when they were "house snakes," or "garters," we carried them home and put them in Aunt Patsy's work basket for a surprise; for she was prejudiced against snakes, and always when she took the basket in her lap and they began to climb out of it it disordered her mind. She never could seem to get used to them; her opportunities went for nothing. And she was always cold toward bats, too, and could not bear them; and yet I think a bat is as friendly a bird as there is. My mother was Aunt Patsy's sister and had the same wild superstitions. A bat is beautifully soft and silky; I do not know any creature that is pleasanter to the touch or is more grateful for caressings, if offered in the right spirit. I know all about these coleoptera, because our great cave, three miles below Hannibal, was multitudinously stocked with them, and often I brought them home to amuse my mother with. It was easy to manage if it was a school day, because then I had ostensibly been to school and hadn't any bats. She was not a suspicious person, but full of trust and confidence; and when I said, "There's something in my coat pocket for you," she would put her hand in. But she always took it out again, herself; I didn't have to tell her. It was remarkable, the way she couldn't learn to like private bats. The more experience she had, the more she could not change her views.

. . . . . .

As I have said, I spent some part of every year at the farm until I was twelve or thirteen years old. The life which I led there with my cousins was full of charm, and so is the memory of it yet. I can call back the solemn twilight and mystery of the deep woods, the earthy smells, the faint odors of the wild flowers, the sheen of rain-washed foliage, the rattling clatter of drops when the wind shook the trees, the far-off hammering of woodpeckers and the muffled drumming of wood pheasants in the remoteness of the forest, the snapshot glimpses of disturbed wild creatures scurrying through the grass—I can call it all back and make it as real as it ever was, and as blessed. I can call back the prairie, and its loneliness and peace, and a vast hawk hanging motionless in the sky, with his wings spread wide and the blue of the vault showing through the fringe of their end feathers. I can see the woods in their autumn dress, the oaks purple, the hickories washed with gold, the maples and the sumachs luminous with crimson fires, and I can hear the rustle made by the fallen leaves as we plowed through them. I can see the blue clusters of wild grapes hanging among the foliage of the saplings, and I remember the taste of them and the smell. I know how the wild blackberries looked, and how they tasted, and the same with the pawpaws, the hazelnuts, and the persimmons; and I can feel the thumping rain, upon my head, of hickory nuts and walnuts when we were out in the frosty dawn to scramble for them with the pigs, and the gusts of wind loosed them and sent them down. I know the stain of blackberries, and how pretty it is, and I know the stain of walnut hulls, and how little it minds soap and water, also what grudged experience it had of either of them. I know the taste of maple sap, and when to gather it, and how to arrange the troughs and the delivery tubes, and how to boil down the juice, and how to hook the sugar after it is made, also how much better hooked sugar tastes than any that is honestly come by, let bigots say what they will. I know how a prize watermelon looks when it is sunning its fat rotundity among pumpkin vines and "simblins"; I know how to tell when it is ripe without "plugging" it; I know how inviting it looks when it is cooling itself in a tub of water under the bed, waiting; I know how it looks when it lies on the table in the sheltered great floor space between house and kitchen, and the children gathered for the sacrifice and their mouths watering; I know the crackling sound it makes when the carving knife enters its end, and I can see the split fly along in front of the blade as the knife cleaves its way to the other end; I can see its halves fall apart and display the rich red meat and the black seeds, and the heart standing up, a luxury fit for the elect; I know how a boy looks behind a yard-long slice of that melon, and I know how he feels; for I have been there. I know the taste of the watermelon which has been honestly come by, and I know the taste of the watermelon which has been acquired by art. Both taste good, but the experienced know which tastes best. I know the look of green apples and peaches and pears on the trees, and I know how entertaining they are when they are inside of a person. I know how ripe ones look when they are piled in pyramids under the trees, and how pretty they are and how vivid their colors. I know how a frozen apple looks, in a barrel down cellar in the wintertime, and how hard it is to bite, and how the frost makes the teeth ache, and yet how good it is, notwithstanding. I know the disposition of elderly people to select the specked apples for the children, and I once knew ways to beat the game. I know the look of an apple that is roasting and sizzling on a hearth on a winter's evening, and I know the comfort that comes of eating it hot, along with some sugar and drenched in cream. I know the delicate art and mystery of so cracking hickory nuts and walnuts on a flatiron with a hammer that the kernels will be delivered whole, and I know how the nuts, taken in conjunction with winter apples, cider, and doughnuts, make old people's old tales and old jokes sound fresh and crisp and enchanting, and juggle an evening away before you know what went with the time. I know the look of Uncle Dan'l's kitchen as it was on the privileged nights, when I was a child, and I can see the white and black children grouped on the hearth, with the firelight playing on their faces and the shadows flickering upon the walls, clear back toward the cavernous gloom of the rear, and I can hear Uncle

Dan'l telling the immortal tales which Uncle Remus Harris was to gather into his book and charm the world with, by and by; and I can feel again the creepy joy which quivered through me when the time for the ghost story was reached —and the sense of regret, too, which came over me, for it was always the last story of the evening and there was nothing between it and the unwelcome bed.

I can remember the bare wooden stairway in my uncle's house, and the turn to the left above the landing, and the rafters and the slanting roof over my bed, and the squares of moonlight on the floor, and the white cold world of snow outside, seen through the curtainless window. I can remember the howling of the wind and the quaking of the house on stormy nights, and how snug and cozy one felt, under the blankets, listening; and how the powdery snow used to sift in, around the sashes, and lie in little ridges on the floor and make the place look chilly in the morning and curb the wild desire to get up— in case there was any. I can remember how very dark that room was, in the dark of the moon, and how packed it was with ghostly stillness when one woke up by accident away in the night, and forgotten sins came flocking out of the secret chambers of the memory and wanted a hearing; and how ill chosen the time seemed for this kind of business; and how dismal was the hoo-hooing of the owl and the wailing of the wolf, sent mourning by on the night wind.

I remember the raging of the rain on that roof, summer nights, and how pleasant it was to lie and listen to it, and enjoy the white splendor of the lightning and the majestic booming and crashing of the thunder. It was a very satisfactory room, and there was a lightning rod which was reachable from the window, an adorable and skittish thing to climb up and down, summer nights, when there were duties on hand of a sort to make privacy desirable.

I remember the 'coon and 'possum hunts, nights, with the negroes, and the long marches through the black gloom of the woods, and the excitement which fired everybody when the distant bay of an experienced dog announced that the game was treed; then the wild scramblings and stumblings through briers and bushes and over roots to get to the spot; then the lighting of a fire and the felling of the tree, the joyful frenzy of the dogs and the negroes, and the weird picture it all made in the red glare—I remember it all well, and the delight that everyone got out of it, except the 'coon.

I remember the pigeon seasons, when the birds would come in millions and cover the trees and by their weight break down the branches. They were clubbed to death with sticks; guns were not necessary and were not used. I remember the squirrel hunts, and prairie-chicken hunts, and wild-turkey hunts, and all that; and how we turned out, mornings, while it was still dark, to go on these expeditions, and how chilly and dismal it was, and how often I regretted that I was well enough to go. A toot on a tin horn brought twice as many dogs as were needed, and in their happiness they raced and scampered about, and knocked small people down, and made no end of unnecessary noise. At the word, they vanished away toward the woods, and we drifted silently after them in the melancholy gloom. But presently the gray dawn stole over the world, the birds piped up, then the sun rose and poured light and comfort all around, everything was fresh and dewy and fragrant, and life was a boon again. After three hours of tramping we arrived back wholesomely tired, overladen with game, very hungry, and just in time for breakfast.

# A CUP OF TEA

(*From* Swann's Way)

*Marcel Proust* (*1919*)

I FEEL that there is much to be said for the Celtic belief that the souls of those whom we have lost are held captive in some inferior being, in an animal, in a plant, in some inanimate object, and so effectively lost to us until the day (which to many never comes) when we happen to pass by the tree or to obtain possession of the object which forms their prison. Then they start and tremble, they call us by our name, and as soon as we have recognized their voice the spell is broken. We have delivered them: they have overcome death and return to share our life.

And so it is with our own past. It is a labour in vain to attempt to recapture it: all the efforts of our intellect must prove futile. The past is hidden somewhere outside the realm, beyond the reach of intellect, in some material object (in the sensation which that material object will give us) which we do not suspect. And as for that object, it depends on chance whether we come upon it or not before we ourselves must die.

Many years had elapsed during which nothing of Combray, save what was comprised in the theatre and the drama of my going to bed there, had any existence for me, when one day in winter, as I came home, my mother, seeing that I was cold, offered me some tea, a thing I did not ordinarily take. I declined at first, and then, for no particular reason, changed my mind. She sent out for one of those short, plump little cakes called *petites madeleines*, which look as though they had been moulded in the fluted scallop of a pilgrim's shell. And soon, mechanically, weary after a dull day with the prospect of a depressing morrow, I raised to my lips a spoonful of the tea in which I had soaked a morsel of the cake. No sooner had the warm liquid, and the crumbs with it, touched my palate than a shudder ran through my whole body, and I stopped, intent upon the extraordinary changes that were taking place. An exquisite pleasure had invaded my senses, but individual, detached, with no suggestion of its origin. And at once the vicissitudes of life had become indifferent to me, its disasters innocuous, its brevity illusory—this new sensation having had on me the effect which love has of filling me with a precious essence; or rather this essence was not in me, it was myself. I had ceased now to feel mediocre, accidental, mortal. Whence could it have come to me, this all-powerful joy?

I was conscious that it was connected with the taste of tea and cake, but that it infinitely transcended those savours, could not, indeed, be of the same nature as theirs. Whence did it come? What did it signify? How could I seize upon and define it?

I drink a second mouthful, in which I find nothing more than in the first, a third, which gives me rather less than the second. It is time to stop; the potion is losing its magic. It is plain that the object of my quest, the truth, lies not in the cup but in myself. The tea has called up in me, but does not itself understand, and can only repeat indefinitely, with a gradual loss of strength, the same testimony; which I, too, cannot interpret, though I hope at least to be able to call upon the tea for it again and to find it there presently, intact and at my disposal, for my final enlightenment. I put down my cup and examine my own mind. It is for it to discover the truth. But how? What an abyss of uncertainty whenever the mind feels that some part of it has strayed beyond its own borders; when it, the seeker, is at once the dark region through which it must go seeking, where all its equipment will avail it nothing. Seek? More than that: create. It is face to face with something which does not so far exist, to which it alone can give reality and substance, which it alone can bring into the light of day.

And I begin again to ask myself what it could have been, this unremembered state which brought with it no logical proof of its existence, but only the sense that it was a happy, that it was a real state in whose presence other states of consciousness melted and vanished. I decide to attempt to make it reappear. I retrace my thoughts to the moment at which I drank the first spoonful of tea. I find again the same state, illumined by no fresh light. I compel my mind to make one further effort, to follow and recapture once again the fleeting sensation. And that nothing may interrupt it in its course I shut out every obstacle, every extraneous idea, I stop my ears and inhibit all attention to the sounds which come from the next room. And then, feeling that my mind is growing fatigued without having any success to report, I compel it for a change to enjoy that distraction which I have just denied it, to think of other things, to rest and refresh itself before the supreme attempt. And then for the second time I clear an empty space in front of it. I place in position before my mind's eye the still recent taste of that first mouthful, and I feel something start within me, something that leaves its resting-place and attempts to rise, something that has been embedded like an anchor at a great depth; I do not know yet what it is, but I can feel it mounting slowly; I can measure the resistance, I can hear the echo of great spaces traversed.

Undoubtedly what is thus palpitating in the depths of my being must be the image, the visual memory which, being linked to that taste, has tried to follow it into my conscious mind. But its struggles are too far off, too much confused; scarcely can I perceive the colourless reflection in which are blended the uncapturable whirling medley of radiant hues, and I cannot distinguish its form, cannot invite it, as the one possible interpreter, to translate to me the evidence of its contemporary, its inseparable paramour, the taste of cake soaked in tea; cannot ask it to inform me what special circumstance is in question, of what period in my past life.

Will it ultimately reach the clear surface of my consciousness, this memory, this old, dead moment which the magnetism of an identical moment has travelled so far to importune, to disturb, to raise up out of the very depths of my being? I cannot tell. Now that I feel nothing, it has stopped, has perhaps gone down again into its darkness, from which who can say whether it will ever rise? Ten times over I must essay the task, must lean down over the abyss. And each time the natural laziness which deters us from every difficult enterprise, every work of importance, has urged me to leave the thing alone, to drink my tea and to think merely of the worries of today and of my hopes for tomorrow, which let themselves be pondered over without effort or distress of mind.

And suddenly the memory returns. The taste was that of the little crumb of madeleine which on Sunday mornings at Combray (because on those mornings I did not go out before churchtime), when I went to say good day to her in her bedroom, my aunt Léonie used to give me, dipping it first in her own cup of real or of lime-flower tea. The sight of the little madeleine had recalled nothing to my mind before I tasted it; perhaps because I had so often seen such things in the interval, without tasting them, on the trays in pastry-cooks' windows, that their image had dissociated itself from those Combray days to take its place among others more recent; perhaps because of those memories, so long abandoned and put out of mind, nothing now survived, everything was scattered; the forms of things, including that of the little scallop-shell of pastry, so richly sensual under its severe, religious folds, were either obliterated or had been so long dormant as to have lost the power of expansion which would have allowed them to resume their place in my consciousness. But when from a long-distant past nothing subsists, after the people are dead, after the things are broken and scattered, still, alone, more fragile, but with more vitality, more unsubstantial, more persistent, more faithful, the smell and taste of things remain poised a long time, like souls, ready to remind us, waiting and hoping for their moment, amid the ruins of all the rest; and bear unfaltering, in the tiny and almost impalpable drop of their essence, the vast structure of recollection.

And once I had recognised the taste of the crumb of madeleine soaked in her decoction of lime-flowers which my aunt used to give me (although I did not yet know and must long postpone the discovery of why this memory made me so happy) immediately the old grey house upon the street, where her room was, rose up like the scenery of a theatre to attach itself to the little pavilion, opening on to the garden, which had been built out behind it for my parents (the isolated panel which until that moment had been all that I could see); and with the house the town, from morning to night and in all weathers, the Square where I was sent before luncheon, the streets along which I used to run errands, the country roads we took when it was fine. And just as the Japanese amuse themselves by filling a porcelain bowl with water and steeping in it little crumbs of paper which until then are without character or form, but, the moment they become wet, stretch themselves and bend, take on colour and distinctive shape, become flowers or houses or people permanent and recognisable, so in that moment all the flowers in our garden and in M. Swann's park, and the water-lilies on the Vivonne and the good folk of the village and their little dwellings and the parish church and the whole of Combray and of its surroundings, taking their proper shapes and growing solid, sprang into being, town and gardens alike, from my cup of tea.

## PAUL'S CASE

### *Willa Cather* (*1920*)

It was Paul's afternoon to appear before the faculty of the Pittsburgh High School to account for his various misdemeanors. He had been suspended a week ago, and his father had called at the Principal's office and confessed his perplexity about his son. Paul entered the faculty room suave and smiling. His clothes were a trifle out-grown, and the tan velvet on the collar of his open overcoat was frayed and worn; but for all that there was something of the dandy about him, and he wore an opal pin in his neatly knotted black four-in-hand, and a red carnation in his button-hole. This latter adornment the faculty somehow felt was not properly significant of the contrite spirit befitting a boy under the ban of suspension.

Paul was tall for his age and very thin, with high, cramped shoulders and a narrow chest. His eyes were remarkable for a certain hysterical brilliancy, and he continually used them in a conscious, theatrical sort of way, peculiarly offensive in a boy. The pupils were abnormally large, as though he were addicted to belladonna, but there was a glassy glitter about them which that drug does not produce.

When questioned by the Principal as to why he was there, Paul stated, politely enough, that he wanted to come back to school. This was a lie, but Paul was quite accustomed to lying; found it, indeed, indispensable for over-coming friction. His teachers were asked to state their respective charges against him, which they did with such a rancor and aggrievedness as evinced that this was not a usual case. Disorder and impertinence were among the offences named, yet each of his instructors felt that it was scarcely possible to put into words the real cause of the trouble, which lay in a sort of hysterically defiant manner of the boy's; in the contempt which they all knew he felt for them, and which he seemingly made not the least effort to conceal. Once, when he had been making a synopsis of a paragraph at the blackboard, his English teacher had stepped to his side and attempted to guide his hand. Paul had started back with a shudder and thrust his hands violently behind him. The astonished woman could scarcely have been more hurt and embarrassed had he struck at her. The insult was so involuntary and definitely personal as to be unforgettable. In one way and another, he had made all his teachers, men and women alike, conscious of the same feeling of physical aversion. In one class he habitually sat with his hand shading his eyes; in another he always looked out of the window during the recitation; in another he made a running commentary on the lecture, with humorous intent.

His teachers felt this afternoon that his whole attitude was symbolized by his shrug and his flippantly red carnation flower, and they fell upon him without mercy, his English teacher leading the pack. He stood through it smiling, his pale lips parted over his white teeth. (His lips were continually twitching, and he had a habit of raising his eyebrows that was contemptuous and irritating to the last degree.) Older boys than Paul had broken down and shed tears under that ordeal, but his set smile did not once desert him, and his only sign of discomfort was the nervous trembling of the fingers that toyed with the buttons of his overcoat, and an occasional jerking of the other hand which held his hat. Paul was always smiling, always glancing about him, seeming to feel that people might be watching him and trying to detect something. This conscious expression, since it was as far as possible from boyish mirthfulness, was usually attributed to insolence or "smartness."

As the inquisition proceeded, one of his instructors repeated an impertinent remark of the boy's, and the Principal asked him whether he thought that a courteous speech to make to a woman. Paul shrugged his shoulders slightly and his eyebrows twitched.

"I don't know," he replied. "I didn't mean to be polite or impolite, either. I guess it's a sort of way I have of saying things regardless."

The Principal asked him whether he didn't think that a way it would be well to get rid of. Paul grinned and said he guessed so. When he was told that he could go, he bowed gracefully and went out. His bow was like a repetition of the scandalous red carnation.

His teachers were in despair, and his drawing master voiced the feeling of them all when he declared there was something about the boy which none of them understood. He added: "I don't really believe that smile of his comes altogether from insolence; there's something sort of haunted about it: The boy is not strong, for one thing. There is something wrong about the fellow."

The drawing master had come to realize that, in looking at Paul, one saw only his white teeth and the forced animation of his eyes. One warm afternoon the boy had gone to sleep at his drawing-board, and his master had noted with amazement what a white, blue-veined face it was; drawn and wrinkled like an old man's about the eyes, the lips twitching even in his sleep.

His teachers left the building dissatisfied and unhappy; humiliated to have felt so vindictive toward a mere boy, to have uttered this feeling in cutting terms, and to have set each other on, as it were, in the gruesome game of intemperate reproach. One of them remembered having seen a miserable street cat set at bay by a ring of tormentors.

As for Paul, he ran down the hill whistling the Soldiers' Chorus from *Faust*, looking wildly behind him now and then to see whether some of his teachers were not there to witness his light-heartedness. As it was now late in the afternoon and Paul was on duty that evening as usher at Carnegie Hall, he decided that he would not go home to supper.

When he reached the concert hall the doors were not yet open. It was chilly outside, and he decided to go up into the picture gallery—always deserted at this hour—where there were some of Raffelli's gay studies of Paris streets and an airy blue Venetian scene or two that always exhilarated him. He was delighted to find no one in the gallery but the old guard, who sat in the corner, a newspaper on his knee, a black patch over one eye and the other closed. Paul possessed himself of the place and walked confidently up and down, whistling under his breath. After a while he sat down before a blue Rico and lost himself. When he bethought him to look at his watch, it was after seven o'clock, and he rose with a start and ran downstairs, making a face at Augustus Cæsar, peering out from the cast-room, and an evil gesture at the Venus of Milo as he passed her on the stairway.

When Paul reached the ushers' dressing-room half-a-dozen boys were there already, and he began excitedly to tumble into his uniform. It was one of the few that at all approached fitting, and Paul thought it very becoming— though he knew the tight, straight coat accentuated his narrow chest, about which he was exceedingly sensitive. He was always excited while he dressed, twanging all over to the tuning of the strings and the preliminary flourishes of the horns in the music-room; but tonight he seemed quite beside himself, and he teased and plagued the boys until, telling him that he was crazy, they put him down on the floor and sat on him.

Somewhat calmed by his suppression, Paul dashed out to the front of the house to seat the early comers. He was a model usher. Gracious and smiling he ran up and down the aisles. Nothing was too much trouble for him; he carried messages and brought programs as though it were his greatest pleasure in life, and all the people in his section thought him a charming boy, feeling that he remembered and admired them. As the house filled, he grew more and more vivacious and animated, and the color came to his cheeks and lips. It was very much as though this were a great reception and Paul were the host. Just as the musicians came out to take their places, his English teacher arrived with checks for the seats which a prominent manufacturer had taken for the season. She betrayed some embarrassment when she handed Paul the tickets, and a *hauteur* which subsequently made her feel very foolish. Paul was startled for a moment, and had the feeling of wanting to put her out; what business had she here among all these fine people and gay colors? He looked her over and decided that she was not appropriately dressed and must be a fool to sit downstairs in such togs. The tickets had probably been sent her out of kindness, he reflected, as he put down a seat for her, and she had about as much right to sit there as he had.

When the symphony began Paul sank into one of the rear seats with a long sigh of relief, and lost himself as he had done before the Rico. It was not that symphonies, as such, meant anything in particular to Paul, but the first sigh of the instruments seemed to free some hilarious spirit within him; something that struggled there like the Genius in the bottle found by the Arab fisherman. He felt a sudden zest of life; the lights danced before his eyes and the concert hall blazed into unimaginable splendor. When the soprano soloist came on, Paul forgot even the nastiness of his teacher's being there, and gave himself up to the peculiar intoxication such personages always had for him. The soloist chanced to be a German woman, by no means in her first youth, and the mother of many children; but she wore a satin gown and a tiara, and she had that indefinable air of achievement, that world-shine upon her, which always blinded Paul to any possible defects.

After a concert was over, Paul was often irritable and wretched until he got to sleep,—and tonight he was even more than usually restless. He had the feeling of not being able to let down; of its being impossible to give up this delicious excitement which was the only thing that could be called living at all. During the last number he withdrew and, after hastily changing his clothes in the dressing-room, slipped out to the side door where the singer's carriage stood. Here he began pacing rapidly up and down the walk, waiting to see her come out.

Over yonder the Schenley, in its vacant stretch, loomed big and square through the fine rain, the windows of its twelve stories glowing like those of a lighted cardboard house under a Christmas tree. All the actors and singers of any importance stayed there when they were in the city, and a number of the big manufacturers of the place lived there in the winter. Paul had often hung about the hotel, watching the people go in and out, longing to enter and leave school-masters and dull care behind him forever.

At last the singer came out, accompanied by the conductor, who helped her into her carriage and closed the door with a cordial *auf wiedersehen,*—which set Paul to wondering whether she were not an old sweetheart of his. Paul followed the carriage over to the hotel, walking so rapidly as not to be far from the entrance when the singer alighted and disappeared behind the swinging glass doors which were opened by a negro in a tall hat and a long coat. In the moment that the door was ajar, it seemed to Paul that he, too, entered. He seemed to feel himself go after her up the steps, into the warm, lighted building, into an exotic, a tropical world of shiny, glistening surfaces and basking ease. He reflected upon the mysterious dishes that were brought into the dining-room, the green bottles in buckets of ice, as he had seen them in the supper party pictures of the Sunday supplement. A quick gust of wind brought the rain down with sudden vehemence, and Paul was startled to find that he was still outside in the slush of the gravel driveway; that his boots were letting in the water and his scanty overcoat was clinging wet about him; that the lights in front of the concert hall were out, and that the rain was driving in sheets between him and the orange glow of the windows above him. There it was, what he wanted—tangibly before him like the fairy world of a Christmas pantomime; as the rain beat in his face, Paul wondered whether he were destined always to shiver in the black night outside, looking up at it.

He turned and walked reluctantly toward the car tracks. The end had to come some time; his father in his night-clothes at the top of the stairs, explanations that did not explain, hastily improvised fictions that were forever tripping him up, his upstairs room and its horrible yellow wall-paper, the creaking bureau with the greasy plush collar-box, and over his painted wooden bed the pictures of George Washington and John Calvin, and the framed motto, "Feed my Lambs," which had been worked in red worsted by his mother, whom Paul could not remember.

Half an hour later Paul alighted from the Negley Avenue car and went slowly down one of the side streets off the main thoroughfare. It was a highly respectable street, where all the houses were exactly alike, and where business men of moderate means begot and reared large families of children, all of whom went to Sabbath-school and learned the shorter catechism, and were interested in arithmetic; all of whom were as exactly alike as their homes, and of a piece with the monotony in which they lived. Paul never went up Cordelia Street without a shudder of loathing. His home was next the house of the Cumberland minister. He approached it tonight with the nerveless sense of defeat, the hopeless feeling of sinking back forever into ugliness and commonness that he had always had when he came home. The moment he turned into Cordelia Street he felt the waters close above his head. After each of these orgies of living, he experienced all the physical depression which follows a debauch; the loathing of respectable beds, of common food, of a house permeated by kitchen odours; a shuddering repulsion for the flavourless, colourless mass of every-day existence; a morbid desire for cool things and soft lights and fresh flowers.

The nearer he approached the house, the more absolutely unequal Paul felt to the sight of it all; his ugly sleeping chamber; the cold bath-room with the grimy zinc tub, the cracked mirror, the dripping spigots; his father, at the top of the stairs, his hairy legs sticking out from his night-shirt, his feet thrust into carpet slippers. He was so much later than usual that there would certainly be inquiries and reproaches. Paul stopped short before the door. He felt that he could not be accosted by his father tonight; that he could not toss again on that miserable bed. He would not go in. He would tell his father that he had no car-fare, and it was raining so hard he had gone home with one of the boys and stayed all night.

Meanwhile, he was wet and cold. He went around to the back of the house and tried one of the basement windows, found it open, raised it cautiously, and scrambled down the cellar wall to the floor. There he stood, holding his breath, terrified by the noise he had made; but the floor above him was silent, and there was no creak on the stairs. He found a soap-box, and carried it over to the soft ring of light that streamed from the furnace door, and sat down. He was horribly afraid of rats, so he did not try to sleep, but sat looking distrustfully at the dark, still terrified lest he might have awakened his father. In such reactions, after one of the experiences which made days and nights out of the dreary blanks of the calendar, when his senses were deadened, Paul's head was always singularly clear. Suppose his father had heard him getting in at the window and had come down and shot him for a burglar? Then, again, suppose his father had come down, pistol in hand, and he had cried out in time to save himself, and his father had been horrified to think how nearly he had killed him? Then, again, suppose a day should come when his father would remember that night, and wish there had been no warning cry to stay his hand? With this last supposition Paul entertained himself until daybreak.

The following Sunday was fine; the sodden November chill was broken by the last flash of autumnal summer. In the morning Paul had to go to church and Sabbath-school, as always. On seasonable Sunday afternoons the burghers of Cordelia Street usually sat out on their front "stoops," and talked to their neighbors on the next stoop, or called to those across the street in neighborly fashion. The men sat placidly on gay cushions placed upon the steps that led down to the sidewalk, while the women, in their Sunday "waists," sat in rockers on the cramped porches, pretending to be greatly at their ease. The children played in the streets; there were so many of them that the place resembled the recreation grounds of a kindergarten. The men on the steps— all in their shirt sleeves, their vests unbuttoned—sat with their legs well apart, their stomachs comfortably protruding, and talked of the prices of things, or told anecdotes of the sagacity of their various chiefs and overlords. They occasionally looked over the multitude of squabbling children, listened affectionately to their high-pitched, nasal voices, smiling to see their own proclivities reproduced in their offspring, and interspersed their legends of the iron kings with remarks about their sons' progress at school, their grades in arithmetic, and the amounts they had saved in their toy banks.

On this last Sunday of November, Paul sat all the afternoon on the lowest step of his "stoop," staring into the street, while his sisters, in their rockers, were talking to the minister's daughters next door about how many shirtwaists they had made in the last week, and how many waffles some one had eaten at the last church supper. When the weather was warm, and his father was in a particularly jovial frame of mind, the girls made lemonade, which was always brought out in a red-glass pitcher, ornamented with forget-me-nots in blue enamel. This the girls thought very fine, and the neighbors joked about the suspicious colour of the pitcher.

Today Paul's father, on the top step, was talking to a young man who shifted a restless baby from knee to knee. He happened to be the young man who was daily held up to Paul as a model, and after whom it was his father's dearest hope that he would pattern. This young man was of a ruddy complexion, with a compressed, red mouth, and faded, near-sighted eyes, over which he wore thick spectacles, with gold bows that curved about his ears. He was clerk to one of the magnates of a great steel corporation, and was looked upon in Cordelia Street as a young man with a future. There was a story that, some five years ago—he was now barely twenty-six—he had been a trifle "dissipated," but in order to curb his appetites and save the loss of time and strength that a sowing of wild oats might have entailed, he had taken his chief's advice, oft reiterated to his employes, and at twenty-one had married the first woman whom he could persuade to share his fortunes. She happened to be an angular schoolmistress, much older than he, who also wore thick glasses, and who had now borne him four children, all near-sighted, like herself.

The young man was relating how his chief, now cruising in the Mediterranean, kept in touch with all the details of the business, arranging his office hours on his yacht just as though he were at home, and "knocking off work enough to keep two stenographers busy." His father told, in turn, the plan his corporation was considering, of putting in an electric railway plant at Cairo. Paul snapped his teeth; he had an awful apprehension that they might spoil it all before he got there. Yet he rather liked to hear these legends of the iron kings, that were told and retold on Sundays and holidays; these stories of palaces in Venice, yachts on the Mediterranean, and high play at Monte Carlo appealed to his fancy, and he was interested in the triumphs of cash boys who had become famous, though he had no mind for the cash-boy stage.

After supper was over, and he had helped to dry the dishes, Paul nervously asked his father whether he could go to George's to get some help in his geometry, and still more nervously asked for carfare. This latter request he had to repeat, as his father, on principle, did not like to hear requests for money, whether much or little. He asked Paul whether he could not go to some boy who lived nearer, and told him that he ought not to leave his school work until Sunday; but he gave him the dime. He was not a poor man, but he had a worthy ambition to come up in the world. His only reason for allowing Paul to usher was that he thought a boy ought to be earning a little.

Paul bounded upstairs, scrubbed the greasy odor of the dish-water from his hands with the ill-smelling soap he hated, and then shook over his fingers a few drops of violet water from the bottle he kept hidden in his drawer. He left the house with his geometry conspicuously under his arm, and the moment he got out of Cordelia Street and boarded a downtown car, he shook off the lethargy of two deadening days, and began to live again.

The leading juvenile of the permanent stock company which played at one of the downtown theatres was an acquaintance of Paul's, and the boy had been invited to drop in at the Sunday-night rehearsals whenever he could. For more than a year Paul had spent every available moment loitering about

Charley Edwards's dressing-room. He had won a place among Edwards's following not only because the young actor, who could not afford to employ a dresser, often found him useful, but because he recognized in Paul something akin to what churchmen term "vocation."

It was at the theatre and at Carnegie Hall that Paul really lived; the rest was but a sleep and a forgetting. This was Paul's fairy tale, and it had for him all the allurement of a secret love. The moment he inhaled the gassy, painty, dusty odor behind the scenes, he breathed like a prisoner set free, and felt within him the possibility of doing or saying splendid, brilliant things. The moment the cracked orchestra beat out the overture from *Martha*, or jerked at the serenade from *Rigoletto,* all stupid and ugly things slid from him, and his senses were deliciously, yet delicately fired.

Perhaps it was because, in Paul's world, the natural nearly always wore the guise of ugliness, that a certain element of artificiality seemed to him necessary in beauty. Perhaps it was because his experience of life elsewhere was so full of Sabbath-school picnics, petty economies, wholesome advice as to how to succeed in life, and the unescapable odors of cooking, that he found this existence so alluring, these smartly clad men and women so attractive, that he was so moved by these starry apple orchards that bloomed perennially under the lime-light.

It would be difficult to put it strongly enough how convincingly the stage entrance of that theatre was for Paul the actual portal of Romance. Certainly none of the company ever suspected it, least of all Charley Edwards. It was very like the old stories that used to float about London of fabulously rich Jews, who had subterranean halls, with palms, and fountains, and soft lamps and richly apparelled women who never saw the disenchanting light of London day. So, in the midst of that smoke-palled city, enamoured of figures and grimy toil, Paul had his secret temple, his wishing-carpet, his bit of blue-and-white Mediterranean shore bathed in perpetual sunshine.

Several of Paul's teachers had a theory that his imagination had been perverted by garish fiction; but the truth was, he scarcely ever read at all. The books at home were not such as would either tempt or corrupt a youthful mind, and as for reading the novels that some of his friends urged upon him—well, he got what he wanted much more quickly from music; any sort of music, from an orchestra to a barrel organ. He needed only the spark, the indescribable thrill that made his imagination master of his senses, and he could make plots and pictures enough of his own. It was equally true that he was not stage-struck—not, at any rate, in the usual acceptation of that expression. He had no desire to become an actor, any more than he had to become a musician. He felt no necessity to do any of these things; what he wanted was to see, to be in the atmosphere, float on the wave of it, to be carried out, blue league after blue league, away from everything.

After a night behind the scenes, Paul found the school-room more than ever repulsive; the hard floors and naked walls; the prosy men who never wore frock coats, or violets in their button-holes; the women with their dull gowns, shrill voices, and pitiful seriousness about prepositions that govern the dative. He could not bear to have the other pupils think, for a moment, that he took these people seriously; he must convey to them that he considered it all trivial, and was there only by way of a joke, anyway. He had autographed pictures of all the members of the stock company which he showed his class-mates, telling them the most incredible stories of his familiarity with these people, of his acquaintance with the soloists who came to Carnegie Hall, his suppers with them and the flowers he sent them. When these stories lost their effect, and his audience grew listless, he would bid all the boys good-bye, an-nouncing that he was going to travel for a while; going to Naples, to California, to Egypt. Then, next Monday, he would slip back, conscious and nervously smiling; his sister was ill, and he would have to defer his voyage until spring.

Matters went steadily worse with Paul at school. In the itch to let his instructors know how heartily he despised them, and how thoroughly he was appreciated elsewhere, he mentioned once or twice that he had no time to fool with theorems; adding—with a twitch of the eyebrows and a touch of that nervous bravado which so perplexed them—that he was helping the people down at the stock company; they were old friends of his.

The upshot of the matter was that the Principal went to Paul's father, and Paul was taken out of school and put to work. The manager at Carnegie Hall was told to get another usher in his stead; the doorkeeper at the theatre was warned not to admit him to the house; and Charley Edwards remorsefully promised the boy's father not to see him again.

The members of the stock company were vastly amused when some of Paul's stories reached them—especially the women. They were hard-working women, most of them supporting indolent husbands or brothers, and they laughed rather bitterly at having stirred the boy to such fervid and florid inven-tions. They agreed with the faculty and with his father, that Paul's was a bad case.

The east-bound train was ploughing through a January snow-storm; the dull dawn was beginning to show gray when the engine whistled a mile out of Newark. Paul started up from the seat where he had lain curled in uneasy slumber, rubbed the breath-misted window glass with his hand, and peered out. The snow was whirling in curling eddies above the white bottom lands, and the drifts lay already deep in the fields and along the fences, while here and there the long dead grass and dried weed stalks protruded black above it. Lights shone from the scattered houses, and a gang of laborers who stood beside the track waved their lanterns.

Paul had slept very little, and he felt grimy and uncomfortable. He had made the all-night journey in a day coach because he was afraid if he took a Pullman he might be seen by some Pittsburgh business man who had noticed him in Denny & Carson's office. When the whistle woke him, he clutched quickly at his breast pocket, glancing about him with an uncertain smile. But the little, clay-bespattered Italians were still sleeping, the slatternly women across the aisle were in open-mouthed oblivion, and even the crumby, crying babies were for the nonce stilled. Paul settled back to struggle with his impatience as best he could.

When he arrived at the Jersey City Station, he hurried through his breakfast, manifestly ill at ease and keeping a sharp eye about him. After he reached the Twenty-third Street Station, he consulted a cabman, and had himself driven to a men's furnishing establishment which was just opening for the day. He spent upward of two hours there, buying with endless reconsidering and great care. His new street suit he put on in the fitting-room; the frock coat and dress clothes he had bundled into the cab with his new shirts. Then he drove to a hatter's and a shoe house. His next errand was at Tiffany's, where he selected silver-mounted brushes and a scarf-pin. He would not wait to have his silver marked, he said. Lastly, he stopped at a trunk shop on Broadway, and had his purchases packed into various travelling bags.

It was a little after one o'clock when he drove up to the Waldorf, and, after settling with the cabman, went into the office. He registered from Washington; said his mother and father had been abroad, and that he had come down to await the arrival of their steamer. He told his story plausibly and had no trouble, since he offered to pay for them in advance, in engaging his rooms; a sleeping-room, sitting-room and bath.

Not once, but a hundred times Paul had planned this entry into New York. He had gone over every detail of it with Charley Edwards, and in his scrap book at home there were pages of description about New York hotels, cut from the Sunday papers.

When he was shown to his sitting-room on the eighth floor, he saw at a glance that everything was as it should be; there was but one detail in his mental picture that the place did not realize, so he rang for the bell boy and sent him down for flowers. He moved about nervously until the boy returned, putting away his new linen and fingering it delightedly as he did so. When the flowers came, he put them hastily into water, and then tumbled into a hot bath. Presently he came out of his white bath-room, resplendent in his new silk underwear, and playing with the tassels of his red robe. The snow was whirling so fiercely outside his windows that he could scarcely see across the street; but within, the air was deliciously soft and fragrant. He put the violets and jonquils on the taboret beside the couch, and threw himself down with a long sigh, covering himself with a Roman blanket. He was thoroughly tired; he had been in such haste, he had stood up to such a strain, covered so much ground in the last twenty-four hours, that he wanted to think how it had all come about. Lulled by the sound of the wind, the warm air, and the cool fragrance of the flowers, he sank into deep, drowsy retrospection.

It had been wonderfully simple; when they had shut him out of the theatre and concert hall, when they had taken away his bone, the whole thing was virtually determined. The rest was a mere matter of opportunity. The only thing that at all surprised him was his own courage—for he realized well enough that he had always been tormented by fear, a sort of apprehensive dread that, of late years, as the meshes of the lies he had told closed about him, had been pulling the muscles of his body tighter and tighter. Until now, he could not remember a time when he had not been dreading something. Even when he was a little boy, it was always there—behind him, or before, or on either side. There had always been the shadowed corner, the dark place into which he dared not look, but from which something seemed always to be watching him—and Paul had done things that were not pretty to watch, he knew.

But now he had a curious sense of relief, as though he had at last thrown down the gauntlet to the thing in the corner.

Yet it was but a day since he had been sulking in the traces; but yesterday afternoon that he had been sent to the bank with Denny & Carson's deposit as usual—but this time he was instructed to leave the book to be balanced. There was above two thousand dollars in checks, and nearly a thousand in the bank notes which he had taken from the book and quietly transferred to his pocket. At the bank he had made out a new deposit slip. His nerves had been steady enough to permit of his returning to the office, where he had finished his work and asked for a full day's holiday tomorrow, Saturday, giving a perfectly reasonable pretext. The bank book, he knew, would not be returned before Monday or Tuesday, and his father would be out of town for the next week. From the time he slipped the bank notes into his pocket until he boarded the night train for New York, he had not known a moment's hesitation.

How astonishingly easy it had all been; here he was, the thing done; and this time there would be no awakening, no figure at the top of the stairs. He watched the snow flakes whirling by his window until he fell asleep.

When he awoke, it was four o'clock in the afternoon. He bounded up with a start; one of his precious days gone already! He spent nearly an hour in dressing, watching every stage of his toilet carefully in the mirror. Everything was quite perfect; he was exactly the kind of boy he had always wanted to be.

When he went downstairs, Paul took a carriage and drove up Fifth Avenue toward the Park. The snow had somewhat abated; carriages and tradesmen's wagons were hurrying soundlessly to and fro in the winter twilight; boys in woollen mufflers were shovelling off the doorsteps; the avenue stages made fine spots of color against the white street. Here and there on the corners were stands, with whole flower gardens blooming behind glass windows, against which the snow flakes stuck and melted; violets, roses, carnations, lilies of the valley—somehow vastly more lovely and alluring that they blossomed thus unnaturally in the snow. The Park itself was a wonderful stage winterpiece.

When he returned, the pause of the twilight had ceased, and the tune of the streets had changed. The snow was falling faster, lights streamed from the hotels that reared their many stories fearlessly up into the storm, defying the raging Atlantic winds. A long, black stream of carriages poured down the avenue, intersected here and there by other streams, tending horizontally. There were a score of cabs about the entrance of his hotel, and his driver had to wait. Boys in livery were running in and out of the awning stretched across the sidewalk, up and down the red velvet carpet laid from the door to the street. Above, about, within it all, was the rumble and roar, the hurry and toss of thousands of human beings as hot for pleasure as himself, and on every side of him towered the glaring affirmation of the omnipotence of wealth.

The boy set his teeth and drew his shoulders together in a spasm of realization; the plot of all dramas, the text of all romances, the nerve-stuff of all sensations were whirling about him like the snow flakes. He burnt like a faggot in a tempest.

When Paul came down to dinner, the music of the orchestra floated up the elevator shaft to greet him. As he stepped into the thronged corridor, he sank back into one of the chairs against the wall to get his breath. The lights, the chatter, the perfumes, the bewildering medley of color—he had, for a moment, the feeling of not being able to stand it. But only for a moment; these were his own people, he told himself. He went slowly about the corridors, through the writing-rooms, smoking-rooms, reception-rooms, as though he were exploring the chambers of an enchanted palace, built and peopled for him alone.

When he reached the dining-room he sat down at a table near a window. The flowers, the white linen, the many-colored wine glasses, the gay toilettes of the women, the low popping of corks, the undulating repetitions of the *Blue Danube* from the orchestra, all flooded Paul's dream with bewildering radiance. When the roseate tinge of his champagne was added—that cold, precious bubbling stuff that creamed and foamed in his glass—Paul wondered that there were honest men in the world at all. This was what all the world was fighting for, he reflected; this was what all the struggle was about. He doubted the reality of his past. Had he ever known a place called Cordelia Street, a place where fagged looking business men boarded the early car? Mere rivets in a machine they seemed to Paul,—sickening men, with combings of children's hair always hanging to their coats, and the smell of cooking in their clothes. Cordelia Street—Ah, that belonged to another time and country! Had he not always been thus, had he not sat here night after night, from as far back as he could remember, looking pensively over just such shimmering textures, and slowly twirling the stem of a glass like this one between his thumb and middle finger? He rather thought he had.

He was not in the least abashed or lonely. He had no especial desire to meet or to know any of these people; all he demanded was the right to look on and conjecture, to watch the pageant. The mere stage properties were all he contended for. Nor was he lonely later in the evening, in his loge at the Opera. He was entirely rid of his nervous misgivings, of his forced aggressiveness, of the imperative desire to show himself different from his surroundings. He felt now that his surroundings explained him. Nobody questioned his purple; he had only to wear it passively. He had only to glance down at his dress coat to reassure himself that here it would be impossible for any one to humiliate him.

He found it hard to leave his beautiful sitting-room to go to bed that night, and sat long watching the raging storm from his turret window. When he went to sleep, it was with the lights turned on in his bedroom; partly because of his old timidity, and partly so that, if he should wake in the night, there would be no wretched moment of doubt, no horrible suspicion of yellow wall-paper, or of Washington and Calvin above his bed.

On Sunday morning the city was practically snow-bound. Paul breakfasted late, and in the afternoon he fell in with a wild San Francisco boy, a freshman at Yale, who said he had run down for a "little flyer" over Sunday. The young man offered to show Paul the night side of the town, and the two boys went off together after dinner, not returning to the hotel until seven o'clock the next morning. They had started out in the confiding warmth of a champagne friendship, but their parting in the elevator was singularly cool. The freshman pulled himself together to make his train, and Paul went to bed. He awoke at two o'clock in the afternoon, very thirsty and dizzy, and rang for ice-water, coffee, and the Pittsburgh papers.

On the part of the hotel management, Paul excited no suspicion. There was this to be said for him, that he wore his spoils with dignity and in no way made himself conspicuous. His chief greediness lay in his ears and eyes, and his excesses were not offensive ones. His dearest pleasures were the gray winter twilights in his sitting-room; his quiet enjoyment of his flowers, his clothes, his wide divan, his cigarette and his sense of power. He could not remember a time when he had felt so at peace with himself. The mere release from the necessity of petty lying, lying every day and every day, restored his self-respect. He had never lied for pleasure, even at school; but to make himself noticed and admired, to assert his difference from other Cordelia Street boys; and he felt a good deal more manly, more honest, even, now that he had no need for boastful pretensions, now that he could, as his actor friends used to say, "dress the part." It was characteristic that remorse did not occur to him. His golden days went by without a shadow, and he made each as perfect as he could.

On the eighth day after his arrival in New York, he found the whole affair exploited in the Pittsburgh papers, exploited with a wealth of detail which indicated that local news of a sensational nature was at a low ebb. The firm of Denny & Carson announced that the boy's father had refunded the full amount of his theft, and that they had no intention of prosecuting. The Cumberland minister had been interviewed, and expressed his hope of yet reclaiming the motherless lad, and Paul's Sabbath-school teacher declared that she would spare no effort to that end. The rumor had reached Pittsburgh that the boy had been seen in a New York hotel, and his father had gone East to find him and bring him home.

Paul had just come in to dress for dinner; he sank into a chair, weak in the knees, and clasped his head in his hands. It was to be worse than jail, even; the tepid waters of Cordelia Street were to close over him finally and forever. The gray monotony stretched before him in hopeless, unrelieved years; Sabbath-school, Young People's Meeting, the yellow-papered room, the damp dish-towels; it all rushed back upon him with sickening vividness. He had the old feeling that the orchestra had suddenly stopped, the sinking sensation that the play was over. The sweat broke out on his face, and he sprang to his feet, looked about him with his white, conscious smile, and winked at himself in the mirror. With something of the childish belief in miracles with which he had so often gone to class, all his lessons unlearned, Paul dressed and dashed whistling down the corridor to the elevator.

He had no sooner entered the dining-room and caught the measure of the music, than his remembrance was lightened by his old elastic power of claiming the moment, mounting with it, and finding it all sufficient. The glare and glitter about him, the mere scenic accessories had again, and for the last time, their old potency. He would show himself that he was game, he would finish the thing splendidly. He doubted, more than ever, the existence of Cordelia Street, and for the first time he drank his wine recklessly. Was he not, after all, one of these fortunate beings? Was he not still himself, and in his own place? He drummed a nervous accompaniment to the music and looked about him, telling himself over and over that it had paid.

He reflected drowsily, to the swell of the violin and the chill sweetness of his wine, that he might have done it more wisely. He might have caught an outbound steamer and been well out of their clutches before now. But the other side of the world had seemed too far away and too uncertain then; he could not have waited for it; his need had been too sharp. If he had to choose over again, he would do the same thing tomorrow. He looked affectionately about the dining-room, now gilded with a soft mist. Ah, it had paid indeed!

Paul was awakened next morning by a painful throbbing in his head and feet. He had thrown himself across the bed without undressing, and had slept with his shoes on. His limbs and hands were lead heavy, and his tongue and throat were parched. There came upon him one of those fateful attacks of clear-headedness that never occurred except when he was physically exhausted and his nerves hung loose. He lay still and closed his eyes and let the tide of realities wash over him.

His father was in New York; "stopping at some joint or other," he told himself. The memory of successive summers on the front stoop fell upon him like a weight of black water. He had not a hundred dollars left; and he knew now, more than ever, that money was everything, the wall that stood between all he loathed and all he wanted. The thing was winding itself up; he had thought of that on his first glorious day in New York, and had even provided a way to snap the thread. It lay on his dressing-table now; he had got it out last night when he came blindly up from dinner,—but the shiny metal hurt his eyes, and he disliked the look of it, anyway.

He rose and moved about with a painful effort, succumbing now and again to attacks of nausea. It was the old depression exaggerated; all the world had become Cordelia Street. Yet somehow he was not afraid of anything, was absolutely calm; perhaps because he had looked into the dark corner at last, and knew. It was bad enough, what he saw there; but somehow not so bad as his long fear of it had been. He saw everything clearly now. He had a feeling that he had made the best of it, that he had lived the sort of life he was meant to live, and for half an hour he sat staring at the revolver. But he told himself that was not the way, so he went downstairs and took a cab to the ferry.

When Paul arrived at Newark, he got off the train and took another cab, directing the driver to follow the Pennsylvania tracks out of the town. The snow lay heavy on the roadways and had drifted deep in the open fields. Only here and there the dead grass or dried weed stalks projected, singularly black, above it. Once well into the country, Paul dismissed the carriage and walked, floundering along the tracks, his mind a medley of irrelevant things. He seemed to hold in his brain an actual picture of everything he had seen that morning. He remembered every feature of both his drivers, the toothless old woman from whom he had bought the red flowers in his coat, the agent from whom he had got his ticket, and all of his fellow-passengers on the ferry. His mind, unable to cope with vital matters near at hand, worked feverishly and deftly at sorting and grouping these images. They made for him a part of the ugliness of the world, of the ache in his head, and the bitter burning on his tongue. He stooped and put a handful of snow into his mouth as he walked, but that, too, seemed hot. When he reached a little hillside, where the tracks ran through a cut some twenty feet below him, he stopped and sat down.

The carnations in his coat were drooping with the cold, he noticed; all their red glory over. It occurred to him that all the flowers he had seen in the show windows that first night must have gone the same way, long before this. It was only one splendid breath they had, in spite of their brave mockery at the winter outside the glass. It was a losing game in the end, it seemed, this revolt against the homilies by which the world is run. Paul took one of the blossoms carefully from his coat and scooped a little hole in the snow, where he covered it up. Then he dozed a while, from his weak condition, seeming insensible to the cold.

The sound of an approaching train woke him, and he started to his feet, remembering only his resolution, and afraid lest he should be too late. He stood watching the approaching locomotive, his teeth chattering, his lips drawn away from them in a frightened smile; once or twice he glanced nervously sidewise, as though he were being watched. When the right moment came, he jumped. As he fell, the folly of his haste occurred to him with merciless clearness, the vastness of what he had left undone. There flashed through his brain, clearer than ever before, the blue of Adriatic water, the yellow of Algerian sands.

He felt something strike his chest,—his body was being thrown swiftly through the air, on and on, immeasurably far and fast, while his limbs gently relaxed. Then, because the picture-making mechanism was crushed, the disturbing visions flashed into black, and Paul dropped back into the immense design of things.

## MAN AGAINST THE SEA

### (*From* Typhoon)

#### Joseph Conrad　(*1902*)

JUKES was as ready a man as any half-dozen young mates that may be caught by casting a net upon the waters; and though he had been somewhat taken aback by the startling viciousness of the first squall, he had pulled himself together on the instant, had called out the hands and had rushed them along to secure such openings about the deck as had not been already battened down earlier in the evening. Shouting in his fresh, stentorian voice, "Jump, boys, and bear a hand!" he led in the work, telling himself the while that he had "just expected this."

But at the same time he was growing aware that this was rather more than he had expected. From the first stir of the air felt on his cheek the gale seemed to take upon itself the accumulated impetus of an avalanche. Heavy sprays enveloped the *Nan-Shan* from stem to stern, and instantly, in the midst of her regular rolling, she began to jerk and plunge as though she had gone mad with fright.

Jukes thought, "This is no joke." While he was exchanging explanatory yells with his captain, a sudden lowering of the darkness came upon the night, falling before their vision like something palpable. It was as if the masked lights of the world had been turned down. Jukes was uncritically glad to have his captain at hand. It relieved him as though that man had, by simply coming on deck, taken most of the gale's weight upon his shoulders. Such is the prestige, the privilege, and the burden of command.

Captain MacWhirr could expect no relief of that sort from any one on earth. Such is the loneliness of command. He was trying to see, with that watchful manner of a seaman who stares into the wind's eye as if into the eye of an adversary, to penetrate the hidden intention and guess the aim and force of the thrust. The strong wind swept at him out of a vast obscurity; he felt under his feet the uneasiness of his ship, and he could not even discern the shadow of her shape. He wished it were not so; and very still he waited, feeling stricken by a blind man's helplessness.

To be silent was natural to him, dark or shine. Jukes, at his elbow, made himself heard yelling cheerily in the gusts, "We must have got the worst of it at once, sir." A faint burst of lightning quivered all round, as if flashed into a cavern—into a black and secret chamber of the sea, with a floor of foaming crests.

It unveiled for a sinister, fluttering moment a ragged mass of clouds hanging low, the lurch of the long outlines of the ship, the black figures of men caught on the bridge, heads forward, as if petrified in the act of butting. The darkness palpitated down upon all this, and then the real thing came at last.

It was something formidable and swift, like the sudden smashing of a vial of wrath. It seemed to explode all round the ship with an overpowering concussion and a rush of great waters, as if an immense dam had been blown up to windward. In an instant the men lost touch of each other. This is the disintegrating power of a great wind: it isolates one from one's kind. An earthquake, a landslip, an avalanche, overtake a man incidentally, as it were—without passion. A furious gale attacks him like a personal enemy, tries to grasp his limbs, fastens upon his mind, seeks to rout his very spirit out of him.

Jukes was driven away from his commander. He fancied himself whirled a great distance through the air. Everything disappeared—even, for a moment, his power of thinking; but his hand had found one of the rail-stanchions. His distress was by no means alleviated by an inclination to disbelieve the reality of this experience. Though young, he had seen some bad weather, and had never doubted his ability to imagine the worst; but this was so much beyond his powers of fancy that it appeared incompatible with the existence of any ship whatever. He would have been incredulous about himself in the same way, perhaps, had he not been so harassed by the necessity of exerting a wrestling effort against a force trying to tear him away from his hold. Moreover, the conviction of not being utterly destroyed returned to him through the sensations of being half-drowned, bestially shaken, and partly choked.

It seemed to him he remained there precariously alone with the stanchion for a long, long time. The rain poured on him, flowed, drove in sheets. He breathed in gasps; and sometimes the water he swallowed was fresh and sometimes it was salt. For the most part he kept his eyes shut tight, as if suspecting his sight might be destroyed in the immense flurry of the elements. When he ventured to blink hastily, he derived some moral support from the green gleam of the starboard light shining feebly upon the flight of rain and sprays. He was actually looking at it when its ray fell upon the uprearing sea which put it out. He saw the head of the wave topple over, adding the mite of its crash to the tremendous uproar raging around him, and almost at the same instant the stanchion was wrenched away from his embracing arms. After a crushing thump on his back he found himself suddenly afloat and borne upwards. His first irresistible notion was that the whole China Sea had climbed on the bridge. Then, more sanely, he concluded himself gone overboard. All the time he was being tossed, flung, and rolled in great volumes of water, he kept on repeating mentally, with the utmost precipitation, the words: "My God! My God! My God! My God!"

All at once, in a revolt of misery and despair, he formed the crazy resolution to get out of that. And he began to thresh about with his arms and legs. But as soon as he commenced his wretched struggles he discovered that he had become somehow mixed up with a face, an oilskin coat, somebody's boots. He clawed ferociously all these things in turn, lost them, found them again, lost them once more, and finally was himself caught in the firm clasp of a pair of stout arms. He returned the embrace closely round a thick solid body. He had found his captain.

They tumbled over and over, tightening their hug. Suddenly the water let them down with a brutal bang; and, stranded against the side of the wheelhouse, out of breath and bruised, they were left to stagger up in the wind and hold on where they could.

Jukes came out of it rather horrified, as though he had escaped some unparalleled outrage directed at his feelings. It weakened his faith in himself. He started shouting aimlessly to the man he could feel near him in that fiendish blackness. "Is it you, sir? Is it you, sir?" till his temples seemed ready to burst. And he heard in answer a voice, as if crying far away, as if screaming to him fretfully from a very great distance, the one word "Yes!" Other seas swept again over the bridge. He received them defencelessly right over his bare head, with both his hands engaged in holding.

The motion of the ship was extravagant. Her lurches had an appalling helplessness: she pitched as if taking a header into a void, and seemed to find a wall to hit every time. When she rolled she fell on her side headlong, and she would be righted back by such a demolishing blow that Jukes felt her reeling as a clubbed man reels before he collapses. The gale howled and scuffled about gigantically in the darkness, as though the entire world were one black gully. At certain moments the air streamed against the ship as if sucked through a tunnel with a concentrated solid force of impact that seemed to lift her clean out of the water and keep her up for an instant with only a quiver running through her from end to end. And then she would begin her tumbling again as if dropped back into a boiling caldron. Jukes tried hard to compose his mind and judge things coolly.

The sea, flattened down in the heavier gusts, would uprise and overwhelm both ends of the *Nan-Shan* in snowy rushes of foam, expanding wide, beyond both rails, into the night. And on this dazzling sheet, spread under the blackness of the clouds and emitting a bluish glow, Captain MacWhirr could catch a desolate glimpse of a few tiny specks black as ebony, the tops of the hatches, the battened companions, the heads of all the covered winches, the foot of a mast. This was all he could see of his ship. Her middle structure, covered by the bridge which bore him, his mate, the closed wheelhouse where a man was steering shut up with the fear of being swept overboard together with the whole thing in one great crash—her middle structure was like a half-tide rock awash upon a coast. It was like an outlying rock with the water boiling up, streaming over, pouring off, beating round—like a rock in the surf to which shipwrecked people cling before they let go—only it rose, it sank, it rolled continuously, without respite and rest, like a rock that should have miraculously struck adrift from a coat and gone wallowing upon the sea.

The *Nan-Shan* was being looted by the storm with a senseless, destructive fury: trysails torn out of the extra gaskets, double-lashed awnings blown away, bridge swept clean, weather-cloths burst, rails twisted, light-screens smashed—and two of the boats had gone already. They had gone unheard and unseen, melting, as it were, in the shock and smother of the wave. It was only later, when, upon the white flash of another high sea hurling itself amidships, Jukes had a vision of two pairs of davits leaping black and empty out of the solid blackness, with one overhauled fall flying and an iron-bound block capering in the air, that he became aware of what had happened within about three yards of his back.

He poked his head forward, groping for the ear of his commander. His lips touched it—big, fleshy, very wet. He cried in an agitated tone, "Our boats are going now, sir."

And again he heard that voice, forced and ringing feebly, but with a penetrating effect of quietness in the enormous discord of noises, as if sent out from some remote spot of peace beyond the black wastes of the gale; again he heard a man's voice—the frail and indomitable sound that can be made to carry an infinity of thought, resolution and purpose, that shall be pronouncing confident words on the last day, when heavens fall, and justice is done—again he heard it, and it was crying to him, as if from very, very far—"All right."

He thought he had not managed to make himself understood. "Our boats —I say boats—the boats, sir! Two gone!"

The same voice, within a foot of him and yet so remote, yelled sensibly, "Can't be helped."

Captain MacWhirr had never turned his face, but Jukes caught some more words on the wind.

"What can—expect—when hammering through—such—— Bound to leave—something behind—stands to reason."

Watchfully Jukes listened for more. No more came. This was all Captain MacWhirr had to say; and Jukes could picture to himself rather than see the broad squat back before him. An impenetrable obscurity pressed down upon the ghostly glimmers of the sea. A dull conviction seized upon Jukes that there was nothing to be done.

If the steering-gear did not give way, if the immense volumes of water did not burst the deck in or smash one of the hatches, if the engines did not give up, if way could be kept on the ship against this terrific wind, and she did not bury herself in one of these awful seas, of whose white crests alone, topping high above her bows, he could now and then get a sickening glimpse—then there was a chance of her coming out of it. Something within him seemed to turn over, bringing uppermost the feeling that the *Nan-Shan* was lost.

"She's done for," he said to himself, with a surprising mental agitation, as though he had discovered an unexpected meaning in this thought. One of these things was bound to happen. Nothing could be prevented now, and nothing could be remedied. The men on board did not count, and the ship could not last. This weather was too impossible.

Jukes felt an arm thrown heavily over his shoulders; and to this overture he responded with great intelligence by catching hold of his captain round the waist.

They stood clasped thus in the blind night, bracing each other against the wind, cheek to cheek and lip to ear, in the manner of two hulks lashed stem to stern together.

## THE GREAT LOVER
### *Rupert Brooke* (*1915*)

I HAVE been so great a lover: filled my days
So proudly with the splendor of Love's praise,
The pain, the calm, the astonishment,
Desire illimitable, and still content,
And all dear names men use, to cheat despair,          5
For the perplexed and viewless streams that bear
Our hearts at random down the dark of life.
Now, ere the unthinking silence on that strife
Steals down, I would cheat drowsy Death so far,
My night shall be remembered for a star          10
That outshone all the suns of all men's days.
Shall I not crown them with immortal praise
Whom I have loved, who have given me, dared with me
High secrets, and in darkness knelt to see
The inenarrable godhead of delight?          15
Love is a flame—we have beaconed the world's night;
A city—and we have built it, these and I;
An emperor—we have taught the world to die.
So, for their sakes I loved, ere I go hence,
And the high cause of Love's magnificence,          20
And to keep loyalties young, I'll write those names
Golden forever, eagles, crying flames,
And set them as a banner, that men may know,
To dare the generations, burn, and blow
Out on the wind of Time, shining and streaming.          25
These I have loved:
                    White plates and cups, clean-gleaming,
Ringed with blue lines; and feathery, faëry dust;
Wet roofs, beneath the lamp-light; the strong crust

Of friendly bread; and many-tasting food;
Rainbows; and the blue bitter smoke of wood;                           30
And radiant raindrops couching in cool flowers;
And flowers themselves, that sway through sunny hours,
Dreaming of moths that drink them under the moon;
Then, the cool kindliness of sheets, that soon
Smooth away trouble; and the rough male kiss                          35
Of blankets; grainy wood; live hair that is
Shining and free; blue-massing clouds; the keen
Unpassioned beauty of a great machine;
The benison of hot water; furs to touch;
The good smell of old clothes; and other such—                        40
The comfortable smell of friendly fingers,
Hair's fragrance, and the musty reek that lingers
About dead leaves and last year's ferns—
                        Dear names,
And thousand others throng to me! Royal flames;
Sweet water's dimpling laugh from tap or spring;                      45
Holes in the ground; and voices that do sing—
Voices in laughter, too; and body's pain,
Soon turned to peace; and the deep-panting train;
Firm sands; the little dulling edge of foam
That browns and dwindles as the wave goes home;                      50
And washen stones, gay for an hour; the cold
Graveness of iron; moist black earthen mold;
Sleep; and high places; footprints in the dew;
And oaks; and brown horse-chestnuts, glossy-new;
And new-peeled sticks; and shining pools on grass—                   55
All these have been my loves. And these shall pass.
Whatever passes not, in the great hour,
Nor all my passion, all my prayers, have power
To hold them with me through the gate of Death.
They'll play deserter, turn with the traitor breath,                 60
Break the high bond we made, and sell Love's trust
And sacramented covenant to the dust.
—Oh, never a doubt but, somewhere, I shall wake,
And give what's left of Love again, and make
New friends, new strangers—
                        But the best I've known,        65
Stays here, and changes, breaks, grows old, is blown
About the winds of the world, and fades from brains
Of living men, and dies.
                Nothing remains.

O dear my loves, O faithless, once again
This one last gift I give: that after men                             70
Shall know, and later lovers, far-removed,
Praise you, "All these were lovely"; say, "He loved."

## PROEM TO ENDYMION

*John Keats*  (*1818*)

A thing of beauty is a joy forever:
Its loveliness increases; it will never
Pass into nothingness; but still will keep
A bower quiet for us, and a sleep
Full of sweet dreams, and health, and quiet breathing.          5
Therefore, on every morrow, are we wreathing
A flowery band to bind us to the earth,
Spite of despondence, of the inhuman dearth
Of noble natures, of the gloomy days,
Of all the unhealthy and o'er-darkened ways          10
Made for our searching: yes, in spite of all,
Some shape of beauty moves away the pall
From our dark spirits.  Such the sun, the moon,
Trees old, and young, sprouting a shady boon
For simple sheep; and such are daffodils          15
With the green world they live in; and clear rills
That for themselves a cooling covert make
'Gainst the hot season; the mid-forest brake,
Rich with a sprinkling of fair musk-rose blooms:
And such too is the grandeur of the dooms          20
We have imagined for the mighty dead;
All lovely tales that we have heard or read:
An endless fountain of immortal drink,
Pouring unto us from the heaven's brink.

Nor do we merely feel these essences          25
For one short hour; no, even as the trees
That whisper round a temple become soon
Dear as the temple's self, so does the moon,
The passion Poesy, glories infinite,
Haunt us till they become a cheering light          30
Unto our souls, and bound to us so fast,
That, whether there be shine, or gloom o'ercast,
They always must be with us, or we die.

## DOWN THE MISSISSIPPI

*John Gould Fletcher*  (*1921*)

### EMBARKATION

Dull masses of dense green,
The forests range their sombre platforms.
Between them silently, like a spirit,
The river finds its own mysterious path.

Loosely the river sways out, backward, forward,                                    5
Always fretting the outer side;
Shunning the invisible focus of each crescent,
Seeking to spread into shining loops over fields:

Like an enormous serpent, dilating, uncoiling,
Displaying a broad scaly back of earth-smeared gold;              10
Swaying out sinuously between the dull motionless forests,
As molten metal might glide down the lip of a vase of dark bronze.

### HEAT

As if the sun had trodden down the sky,
Until no more it holds air for us, but only humid vapor,
The heat, pressing upon earth with irresistible languor,              15
Turns all the solid forest into half-liquid smudge.

The heavy clouds, like cargo-boats, strain slowly up 'gainst its current;
And the flickering of the heat haze is like the churning of ten thousand paddles
Against the heavy horizon, pale blue and utterly windless,
Whereon the sun hangs motionless, a brassy disk of flame.              20

### FULL MOON

Flinging its arc of silver bubbles, quickly shifts the moon
From side to side of us as we go down its path;
I sit on the deck at midnight, and watch it slipping and sliding,
Under my tilted chair, like a thin film of spilt water.

It is weaving a river of light to take the place of this river—              25
A river where we shall drift all night, then come to rest in its shallows.
And then I shall wake from my drowsiness and look down from some dim
    tree-top
Over white lakes of cotton, like moon-fields on every side.

### THE MOON'S ORCHESTRA

When the moon lights up
Its dull red camp-fire through the trees;
And floats out, like a white balloon,              30
Into the blue cup of the night, borne by a casual breeze;
The moon-orchestra then begins to stir:
Jiggle of fiddles commence their crazy dance in the darkness;
Crickets churr              35
Against the stark reiteration of the rusty flutes which frogs
Puff at from rotted logs
In the swamp.
And the moon begins her dance of frozen pomp
Over the lightly quivering floor of the flat and mournful river.              40
Her white feet slightly twist and swirl—
She is a mad girl

In an old unlit ball-room,
Whose walls, half-guessed-at through the gloom,
Are hung with the rusty crape of stark black cypresses,                45
Which show, through gaps and tatters, red stains half hidden away.

### THE STEVEDORES

Frieze of warm bronze that glides with cat-like movements
Over the gang-plank poised and yet awaiting—
The sinewy thudding rhythms of forty shuffling feet
Falling like muffled drum-beats on the stillness:                      50

> *Oh, roll the cotton down—*
> *Roll, roll, the cotton down!*
> *From the further side of Jordan,*
> *Oh, roll the cotton down!*

And the river waits,                                                    55
The river listens,
Chuckling with little banjo-notes that break with a plop on the stillness.
And by the low dark shed that holds the heavy freights,
Two lonely cypress trees stand up and point with stiffened fingers
Far southward where a single chimney stands aloof in the sky.          60

### NIGHT LANDING

After the whistle's roar has bellowed and shuddered,
Shaking the sleeping town and the somnolent river,
The deep-toned floating of the pilot's bell
Suddenly warns the engines.

They pause like heart-beats that abruptly stop:                        65
The shore glides to us, in a wide low curve.

And then—supreme revelation of the river—
The tackle is loosed, the long gang-plank swings outwards;
And poised at the end of it, half naked beneath the search-light,
A blue-black negro with gleaming teeth waits for his chance to leap.   70

### THE SILENCE

There is a silence which I carry about with me always—
A silence perpetual, for it is self-created;
A silence of heat, of water, of unchecked fruitfulness,
Through which each year the heavy harvests bloom, and burst, and fall.

Deep, matted green silence of my South,                                75
Often, within the push and the scorn of great cities,
I have seen that mile-wide waste of water swaying out to you,
And on its current glimmering I am going to the sea.

There is a silence I have achieved—I have walked beyond its threshold.
I know it is without horizons, boundless, fathomless, perfect.          80
And some day maybe, far away,
I shall curl up in it at last and sleep an endless sleep.


## COLOR

*Wilfrid Wilson Gibson   (1915)*

A blue-black Nubian plucking
    oranges
At Jaffa by a sea of malachite,
In red tarboosh, green sash, and flow-
    ing white
Burnous—among the shadowy mem-
    ories
That haunt me yet by these bleak
    northern seas                        5
He lives for ever in my eyes' delight,
Bizarre, superb in young immortal
    might—
A god of old barbaric mysteries.

Maybe he lived a life of lies and lust,
Maybe his bones are now but scat-
    tered dust;                          10
Yet, for a moment he was life su-
    preme
Exultant and unchallenged: and my
    rhyme
Would set him safely out of reach of
    time
In that old heaven where things are
    what they seem.


## SIGHT

*Wilfrid Wilson Gibson   (1914)*

By the lamplit stall I loitered, feasting
    my eyes
On colors ripe and rich for the
    heart's desire—
Tomatoes, redder than Krakatoa's
    fire,
Oranges like old sunsets over Tyre,
And apples golden-green as the glades
    of Paradise.                         5

And as I lingered, lost in divine de-
    light,
My heart thanked God for the goodly
    gift of sight
And all youth's lively senses keen and
    quick . . .
When suddenly, behind me in the
    night,
I heard the tapping of a blind man's
    stick.                               10


## LOVELIEST OF TREES

*A. E. Housman   (1896)*

Loveliest of trees, the cherry now
Is hung with bloom along the bough,
And stands about the woodland ride
Wearing white for Eastertide.

Now, of my threescore years and ten,
Twenty will not come again,             6
And take from seventy springs a
    score,
It only leaves me fifty more.

And since to look at things in bloom
Fifty springs are little room,          10
About the woodlands I will go
To see the cherry hung with snow.


## REVEILLE

*A. E. Housman   (1896)*

Wake: the silver dusk returning
    Up the beach of darkness brims,
And the ship of sunrise burning
    Strands upon the eastern rims.

Wake: the vaulted shadow shatters, 5
　Trampled to the floor it spanned,
And the tent of night in tatters
　Straws the sky-pavilioned land.

Up, lad, up, 'tis late for lying:
　Hear the drums of morning play; 10
Hark, the empty highways crying
　"Who'll beyond the hills away?"

Towns and countries woo together,
　Forelands beacon, belfries call;
Never lad that trod on leather　　15
　Lived to feast his heart with all.

Up, lad: thews that lie and cumber
　Sunlit pallets never thrive;
Morns abed and daylight slumber
　Were not meant for man alive.　20

Clay lies still, but blood's a rover;
　Breath's a ware that will not keep.
Up, lad: when the journey's over
　There'll be time enough to sleep.

## CORINNA'S GOING
## A-MAYING

### *Robert Herrick* (1648)

Get up, get up for shame! The bloom-
　ing morn
Upon her wings presents the god un-
　shorn.
　See how Aurora throws her fair,
　Fresh-quilted colors through the
　air.
　Get up, sweet slug-a-bed, and see 5
　The dew bespangling herb and
　tree!
Each flower has wept and bowed to-
　ward the east
Above an hour since, yet you not
　drest;
　Nay! not so much as out of bed? 9
　When all the birds have matins said

And sung their thankful hymns, 'tis
　sin,
　Nay, profanation, to keep in,
Whereas a thousand virgins on this
　day
Spring sooner than the lark, to fetch
　in May.

Rise and put on your foliage, and be
　seen
To come forth, like the springtime,
　fresh and green,　　　　　　　15
　And sweet as Flora. Take no care
　For jewels for your gown or hair.
　Fear not; the leaves will strew
　Gems in abundance upon you.　20
Besides, the childhood of the day has
　kept
Against you come, some orient pearls
　unwept.
　Come, and receive them while the
　light
　Hangs on the dew-locks of the
　night;
　And Titan on the eastern hill　25
　Retires himself, or else stands still
Till you come forth! Wash, dress,
　be brief in praying;
Few beads are best when once we go
　a-Maying.

Come, my Corinna, come; and com-
　ing, mark
How each field turns a street, each
　street a park,　　　　　　　　30
　Made green and trimmed with
　trees! see how
　Devotion gives each house a bough
　Or branch! each porch, each door,
　ere this,
　An ark, a tabernacle is,
Made up of whitethorn neatly inter-
　wove,　　　　　　　　　　　35
As if here were those cooler shades
　of love.
　Can such delights be in the street
　And open fields, and we not see't?

Come, we'll abroad; and let's obey
The proclamation made for May,
And sin no more, as we have done, by
    staying;                          41
But, my Corinna, come, let's go
    a-Maying.


There's not a budding boy or girl this
    day
But is got up and gone to bring in
    May.
    A deal of youth ere this is come  45
    Back, and with whitethorn laden
    home.
    Some have dispatched their cakes
    and cream,
    Before that we have left to dream;
And some have wept and wooed, and
    plighted troth,
And chose their priest, ere we can
    cast off sloth.                   50
    Many a green-gown has been
    given,
    Many a kiss, both odd and even;
    Many a glance, too, has been sent
    From out the eye, love's firma-
    ment;
Many a jest told of the keys betray-
    ing                               55
This night, and locks picked; yet
    we're not a-Maying!


Come, let us go, while we are in our
    prime,
And take the harmless folly of the
    time!
    We shall grow old apace, and die
    Before we know our liberty.       60
    Our life is short, and our days run
    As fast away as does the sun.
And, as a vapor or a drop of rain,
Once lost, can ne'er be found again,
    So when or you or I are made      65
    A fable, song, or fleeting shade,
    All love, all liking, all delight
    Lies drowned with us in endless
    night.

Then, while time serves, and we are
    but decaying,
Come, my Corinna, come, let's go
    a-Maying.                         70


## TO HIS COY MISTRESS

### Andrew Marvell  (1650)

Had we but world enough, and time,
This coyness, lady, were no crime.
We would sit down, and think which
    way
To walk, and pass our long love's day.
Thou by the Indian Ganges' side   5
Shouldst rubies find: I by the tide
Of Humber would complain. I would
Love you ten years before the flood,
And you should, if you please, refuse
Till the conversion of the Jews;    10
My vegetable love should grow
Vaster than empires and more slow;
An hundred years should go to praise
Thine eyes, and on thy forehead
    gaze;
Two hundred to adore each breast, 15
But thirty thousand to the rest;
An age at least to every part,
And the last age should show your
    heart.
For, lady, you deserve this state,
Nor would I love at lower rate.    20
    But at my back I always hear
Time's wingèd chariot hurrying near,
And yonder all before us lie
Deserts of vast eternity.             24
Thy beauty shall no more be found,
Nor, in thy marble vault, shall sound
My echoing song; then worms shall
    try
That long preserved virginity,
And your quaint honour turn to dust,
And into ashes all my lust:         30
The grave's a fine and private place,
But none, I think, do there embrace.
    Now therefore, while the youthful
    hue
Sits on thy skin like morning dew,

And while thy willing soul transpires
At every pore with instant fires,   36
Now let us sport us while we may,
And now, like amorous birds of prey,
Rather at once our time devour,
Than languish in his slow-chapt
    power.                            40
Let us roll all our strength and all
Our sweetness up into one ball,
And tear our pleasures with rough
    strife,
Thorough the iron gates of life;
Thus, though we cannot make our
    sun                               45
Stand still, yet we will make him run.

## YOU, ANDREW MARVELL

### *Archibald MacLeish*   (*1930*)

And here face down beneath the sun
And here upon earth's noonward
    height
To feel the always coming on
The always rising of the night

To feel creep up, the curving east   5
The earthy chill of dusk and slow
Upon those under lands the vast
And ever climbing shadow grow

And strange at Ecbatan the trees
Take leaf. by leaf the evening
    strange                          10

Take flooding dark about their knees
The mountains over Persia change

And now at Kermanshah the gate
Dark empty and the withered grass
And through the twilight now the
    late                             15
Few travellers in the westward pass

And Baghdad darken and the bridge
Across the silent river gone
And through Arabia the edge
Of evening widen and steal on        20

And deepen on Palmyra's street
The wheel rut in the ruined stone
And Lebanon fade out and Crete
High through the clouds and over-
    blown

And over Sicily the air              25
Still flashing with the landward gulls
And loom and slowly disappear
The sails above the shadowy hulls

And Spain go under and the shore
Of Africa the gilded sand            30
And evening vanish and no more
The low pale light across that land

Nor now the long light on the sea
And here face downward in the sun
To feel how swift how secretly       35
The shadow of the night comes
    on . . . .

## THE LOTOS-EATERS

### *Alfred Lord Tennyson*   (*1832*)

"Courage!" he said, and pointed toward the land,
"This mounting wave will roll us shoreward soon."
In the afternoon they came unto a land
In which it seeméd always afternoon.
All round the coast the languid air did swoon,        5

Breathing like one that hath a weary dream.
Full-faced above the valley stood the moon;
And, like a downward smoke, the slender stream
Along the cliff to fall and pause and fall did seem.

A land of streams! some, like a downward smoke,          10
Slow-dropping veils of thinnest lawn, did go;
And some through wavering lights and shadows broke,
Rolling a slumbrous sheet of foam below.
They saw the gleaming river seaward flow
From the inner land; far off, three mountain-tops,        15
Three silent pinnacles of aged snow,
Stood sunset-flushed; and, dewed with showery drops,
Up-clomb the shadowy pine above the woven copse.
The charméd sunset lingered low adown
In the red west; through mountain clefts the dale         20
Was seen far inland, and the yellow down
Bordered with palm, and many a winding vale
And meadow, set with slender galingale;
A land where all things always seemed the same!
And round about the keel with faces pale,                 25
Dark faces pale against that rosy flame,
The mild-eyed melancholy Lotos-eaters came.

Branches they bore of that enchanted stem,
Laden with flower and fruit, whereof they gave
To each, but whoso did receive of them                    30
And taste, to him the gushing of the wave
Far, far away did seem to mourn and rave
On alien shores; and if his fellow spake,
His voice was thin, as voices from the grave;
And deep-asleep he seemed, yet all awake,                 35
And music in his ears his beating heart did make.

They sat them down upon the yellow sand,
Between the sun and moon upon the shore;
And sweet it was to dream of fatherland,
Of child, and wife and slave; but evermore                40
Most weary seemed the sea, weary the oar,
Weary the wandering fields of barren foam.
Then someone said, "We will return no more";
And all at once they sang, "Our island home
Is far beyond the wave; we will no longer roam."          45

CHORIC SONG

I

There is sweet music here that softer falls
Than petals from blown roses on the grass,
Or night-dews on still waters between walls
Of shadowy granite, in a gleaming pass;
Music that gentlier on the spirit lies,                   50
Than tired eyelids upon tired eyes;

Music that brings sweet sleep down from the blissful skies.
Here are cool mosses deep,
And through the moss the ivies creep,
And in the stream the long-leaved flowers weep,                55
And from the craggy ledge the poppy hangs in sleep.

### II

Why are we weighed upon with heaviness,
And utterly consumed with sharp distress,
While all things else have rest from weariness?
All things have rest; why should we toil alone,              60
We only toil, who are the first of things,
And make perpetual moan,
Still from one sorrow to another thrown;
Nor ever fold our wings,
And cease from wanderings,                                    65
Nor steep our brows in slumber's holy balm;
Nor harken what the inner spirit sings,
"There is no joy but calm!"—
Why should we only toil, the roof and crown of things?

### III

Lo! in the middle of the wood,                               70
The folded leaf is wooed from out the bud
With winds upon the branch, and there
Grows green and broad, and takes no care,
Sun-steeped at noon, and in the moon
Nightly dew-fed; and turning yellow                          75
Falls, and floats adown the air.
Lo! sweetened with the summer light,
The full-juiced apple, waxing overmellow,
Drops in a silent autumn night.
All its allotted length of days                              80
The flower ripens in its place,
Ripens and fades, and falls, and hath no toil,
Fast-rooted in the fruitful soil.

### IV

Hateful is the dark-blue sky,
Vaulted o'er the dark-blue sea.                              85
Death is the end of life; ah, why
Should life all labor be?
Let us alone. Time driveth onward fast,
And in a little while our lips are dumb.
Let us alone. What is it that will last?                     90

All things are taken from us, and become
Portions and parcels of the dreadful past.
Let us alone. What pleasure can we have
To war with evil? Is there any peace
In ever climbing up the climbing wave?                          95
All things have rest, and ripen toward the grave
In silence—ripen, fall, and cease.
Give us long rest or death, dark death, or dreamful ease.


V

How sweet it were, hearing the downward-stream,
With half-shut eyes ever to seem                                100
Falling asleep in a half-dream!
To dream and dream, like yonder amber light,
Which will not leave the myrrh-bush on the height;
To hear each other's whispered speech;
Eating the Lotos day by day,                                    105
To watch the crisping ripples on the beach,
And tender curving lines of creamy spray;
To lend our hearts and spirits wholly
To the influence of mild-minded melancholy;
To muse and brood and live again in memory,                    110
With those old faces of our infancy
Heaped over with a mound of grass,
Two handfuls of white dust, shut in an urn of brass!


VI

Dear is the memory of our wedded lives,
And dear the last embraces of our wives                         115
And their warm tears; but all hath suffered change;
For surely now our household hearths are cold,
Our sons inherit us, our looks are strange,
And we should come like ghosts to trouble joy.
Or else the island princes over-bold                           120
Have eat our substance, and the minstrel sings
Before them of the ten years' war in Troy,
And our great deeds, as half-forgotten things.
Is there confusion in the little isle?
Let what is broken so remain.                                   125
The gods are hard to reconcile;
'Tis hard to settle order once again.
There *is* confusion worse than death,
Trouble on trouble, pain on pain,
Long labor unto agéd breath,                                    130
Sore task to hearts worn out by many wars
And eyes grown dim with gazing on the pilot-stars.

VII

But, propped on beds of amaranth and moly,
How sweet—while warm airs lull us, blowing lowly—
With half-dropped eyelid still,                                        135
Beneath a heaven dark and holy,
To watch the long bright river drawing slowly
His waters from the purple hill—
To hear the dewy echoes calling
From cave to cave through the thick-twined vine—                       140
To watch the emerald-colored water falling
Through many a woven acanthus-wreath divine!
Only to hear and see the far-off sparkling brine,
Only to hear were sweet, stretched out beneath the pine.

VIII

The Lotos blooms below the barren peak,                                145
The Lotos blows by every winding creek;
All day the wind breathes low with mellower tone;
Through every hollow cave and alley lone
Round and round the spicy downs the yellow Lotos-dust is blown.
We have had enough of action, and of motion we,                       150
Rolled to starboard, rolled to larboard, when the surge was seething
      free,
Where the wallowing monster spouted his foam-fountains in the sea.
Let us swear an oath, and keep it with an equal mind,
In the hollow Lotos-land to live and lie reclined
On the hills like gods together, careless of mankind.                  155
For they lie beside their nectar, and the bolts are hurled
Far below them in the valleys, and the clouds are lightly curled
Round their golden houses, girdled with the gleaming world;
Where they smile in secret, looking over wasted lands,
Blight and famine, plague and earthquake, roaring deeps and fiery
      sands,                                                           160
Clanging fights, and flaming towns, and sinking ships, and praying
      hands.
But they smile, they find a music centered in a doleful song
Steaming up, a lamentation and an ancient tale of wrong,
Like a tale of little meaning though the words are strong;
Chanted from an ill-used race of men that cleave the soil,            165
Sow the seed, and reap the harvest with enduring toil,
Storing yearly little dues of wheat, and wine and oil;
Till they perish and they suffer—some, 'tis whispered—down in hell
Suffer endless anguish, others in Elysian valleys dwell,
Resting weary limbs at last on beds of asphodel.                      170
Surely, surely, slumber is more sweet than toil, the shore
Than labor in the deep mid-ocean, wind and wave and oar;
Oh, rest ye, brother mariners, we will not wander more.

## CHILDHOOD AND SCHOOL-TIME

(*From* The Prelude, Book I)

*William Wordsworth* (*1850*)

Fair seed-time had my soul, and I grew up
Fostered alike by beauty and by fear:
Much favored in my birthplace, and no less
In that belovèd Vale to which erelong
We were transplanted—there were we let loose          5
For sports of wider range. Ere I had told
Ten birthdays, when among the mountain slopes
Frost, and the breath of frosty wind, had snapped
The last autumnal crocus, 'twas my joy
With store of springes o'er my shoulder hung          10
To range the open heights where woodcocks run
Among the smooth green turf. Through half the night,
Scudding away from snare to snare, I plied
That anxious visitation;—moon and stars
Were shining o'er my head. I was alone,          15
And seemed to be a trouble to the peace
That dwelt among them. Sometimes it befell
In these night wanderings, that a strong desire
O'erpowered my better reason, and the bird
Which was the captive of another's toil          20
Became my prey; and when the deed was done
I heard among the solitary hills
Low breathings coming after me, and sounds
Of undistinguishable motion, steps
Almost as silent as the turf they trod.          25

Nor less when spring had warmed the cultured Vale,
Moved we as plunderers where the mother-bird
Had in high places built her lodge; though mean
Our object and inglorious, yet the end
Was not ignoble. Oh! when I have hung          30
Above the raven's nest, by knots of grass
And half-inch fissures in the slippery rock
But ill-sustained, and almost (so it seemed)
Suspended by the blast that blew amain,
Shouldering the naked crag, oh, at that time          35
While on the perilous ridge I hung alone,
With what strange utterance did the loud dry wind
Blow through my ear! the sky seemed not a sky
Of earth—and with what motion moved the clouds!

Dust as we are, the immortal spirit grows          40
Like harmony in music; there is a dark

Inscrutable workmanship that reconciles
Discordant elements, makes them cling together
In one society.  How strange that all
The terrors, pains, and early miseries,                              45
Regrets, vexations, lassitudes interfused
Within my mind, should e'er have borne a part,
And that a needful part, in making up
The calm existence that is mine when I
Am worthy of myself!  Praise to the end!                            50
Thanks to the means which Nature deigned to employ;
Whether her fearless visitings, or those
That came with soft alarm, like hurtless light
Opening the peaceful clouds; or she may use
Severer interventions, ministry                                     55
More palpable, as best might suit her aim.

   One summer evening (led by her) I found
A little boat tied to a willow tree
Within a rocky cove, its usual home.
Straight I unloosed her chain, and stepping in                      60
Pushed from the shore.  It was an act of stealth
And troubled pleasure, nor without the voice
Of mountain echoes did my boat move on;
Leaving behind her still, on either side,
Small circles glittering idly in the moon,                          65
Until they melted all into one track
Of sparkling light.  But now, like one who rows,
Proud of his skill, to reach a chosen point
With an unswerving line, I fixed my view
Upon the summit of a craggy ridge,                                  70
The horizon's utmost boundary; far above
Was nothing but the stars and the gray sky.
She was an elfin pinnace; lustily
I dipped my oars into the silent lake,
And, as I rose upon the stroke, my boat                             75
Went heaving through the water like a swan;
When, from behind that craggy steep till then
The horizon's bound, a huge peak, black and huge,
As if with voluntary power instinct
Upreared its head.  I struck and struck again,                      80
And growing still in stature the grim shape
Towered up between me and the stars, and still,
For so it seemed, with purpose of its own
And measured motion like a living thing,
Strode after me.  With trembling oars I turned,                     85
And through the silent water stole my way
Back to the covert of the willow tree;

There in her mooring-place I left my bark,—
And through the meadows homeward went, in grave
And serious mood; but after I had seen                              90
That spectacle, for many days, my brain
Worked with a dim and undetermined sense
Of unknown modes of being; o'er my thoughts
There hung a darkness, call it solitude
Or blank desertion. No familiar shapes                              95
Remained, no pleasant images of trees,
Of sea or sky, no colors of green fields;
But huge and mighty forms, that do not live
Like living men, moved slowly through the mind
By day, and were a trouble to my dreams.                           100

    Wisdom and Spirit of the universe!
Thou Soul that art the eternity of thought,
That givest to forms and images a breath
And everlasting motion, not in vain
By day or star-light thus from my first dawn                       105
Of childhood didst thou intertwine for me
The passions that build up our human soul;
Not with the mean and vulgar works of man,
But with high objects, with enduring things—
With life and nature—purifying thus                                110
The elements of feeling and of thought,
And sanctifying, by such discipline,
Both pain and fear, until we recognize
A grandeur in the beatings of the heart.
Nor was this fellowship vouchsafed to me                           115
With stinted kindness. In November days,
When vapors rolling down the valley made
A lonely scene more lonesome, among woods,
At noon and 'mid the calm of summer nights,
When, by the margin of the trembling lake,                         120
Beneath the gloomy hills homeward I went
In solitude, such intercourse was mine;
Mine was it in the fields both day and night,
And by the waters, all the summer long.

    And in the frosty season, when the sun                    125
Was set, and visible for many a mile
The cottage windows blazed through twilight gloom,
I heeded not their summons: happy time
It was indeed for all of us—for me
It was a time of rapture! Clear and loud                           130
The village clock tolled six,—I wheeled about,
Proud and exulting like an untired horse
That cares not for his home. All shod with steel,

We hissed along the polished ice in games
Confederate, imitative of the chase                                    135
And woodland pleasures,—the resounding horn,
The pack loud chiming, and the hunted hare.
So through the darkness and the cold we flew,
And not a voice was idle; with the din
Smitten, the precipices rang aloud;                                    140
The leafless trees and every icy crag
Tinkled like iron; while far distant hills
Into the tumult sent an alien sound
Of melancholy not unnoticed, while the stars
Eastward were sparkling clear, and in the west                        145
The orange sky of evening died away.
Not seldom from the uproar I retired
Into a silent bay, or sportively
Glanced sideway, leaving the tumultuous throng,
To cut across the reflex of a star                                    150
That fled, and, flying still before me, gleamed
Upon the glassy plain; and oftentimes,
When we had given our bodies to the wind,
And all the shadowy banks on either side
Came sweeping through the darkness, spinning still                    155
The rapid line of motion, then at once
Have I, reclining back upon my heels,
Stopped short; yet still the solitary cliffs
Wheeled by me—even as if the earth had rolled
With visible motion her diurnal round!                                160
Behind me did they stretch in solemn train,
Feebler and feebler, and I stood and watched
Till all was tranquil as a dreamless sleep.

    Ye Presences of Nature in the sky
And on the earth!  Ye Visions of the hills!                           165
And Souls of lonely places! can I think
A vulgar hope was yours when ye employed
Such ministry, when ye through many a year
Haunting me thus among my boyish sports,
On caves and trees, upon the woods and hills,                        170
Impressed upon all forms the characters
Of danger or desire; and thus did make
The surface of the universal earth
With triumph and delight, with hope and fear,
Work like a sea?
                    Not uselessly employed,                          175
Might I pursue this theme through every change
Of exercise and play, to which the year
Did summon us in his delightful round.

## EXPOSTULATION AND REPLY

*William Wordsworth* *(1798)*

"Why, William, on that old gray stone,
Thus for the length of half a day,
Why, William, sit you thus alone,
And dream your time away?

"Where are your books?—that light bequeathed 5
To Beings else forlorn and blind!
Up! up! and drink the spirit breathed
From dead men to their kind.

"You look round on your Mother Earth, 9
As if she for no purpose bore you;
As if you were her first-born birth,
And none had lived before you!"

One morning thus, by Esthwaite lake,
When life was sweet, I knew not why,
To me my good friend Matthew spake, 15
And thus I made reply:

"The eye—it cannot choose but see;
We cannot bid the ear be still;
Our bodies feel, wher'er they be,
Against or with our will. 20

"Nor less I deem that there are Powers
Which of themselves our minds impress;
That we can feed this mind of ours
In a wise passiveness.

"Think you, 'mid all this mighty sum
Of things for ever speaking, 26
That nothing of itself will come,
But we must still be seeking?

"—Then ask not wherefore, here, alone,
Conversing as I may, 30
I sit upon this old gray stone,
And dream my time away."

## THE TABLES TURNED

### AN EVENING SCENE ON THE SAME SUBJECT

*William Wordsworth* *(1798)*

Up! up! my Friend, and quit your books;
Or surely you'll grow double:
Up! up! my Friend, and clear your looks;
Why all this toil and trouble?

The sun, above the mountain's head, 5
A freshening luster mellow
Through all the long green fields has spread,
His first sweet evening yellow.

Books! 'tis a dull and endless strife:
Come, hear the woodland linnet, 10
How sweet his music! on my life,
There's more of wisdom in it.

And hark! how blithe the throstle sings!
He, too, is no mean preacher:
Come forth into the light of things, 15
Let Nature be your Teacher.

She has a world of ready wealth,
Our minds and hearts to bless—
Spontaneous wisdom breathed by health,
Truth breathed by cheerfulness. 20

One impulse from a vernal wood
May teach you more of man,
Of moral evil and of good,
Than all the sages can.

Sweet is the lore which Nature
  brings;             25
Our meddling intellect
Mis-shapes the beauteous forms of
  things:—
We murder to dissect.

Enough of Science and of Art;
Close up those barren leaves;     30
Come forth, and bring with you a
  heart
That watches and receives.

## THE WORLD IS TOO MUCH WITH US

### *William Wordsworth* (*1806*)

The world is too much with us; late and soon,
Getting and spending, we lay waste our powers;
Little we see in Nature that is ours;
We have given our hearts away, a sordid boon!
This sea that bares her bosom to the moon;                5
The winds that will be howling at all hours,
And are up-gathered now like sleeping flowers;
For this, for everything, we are out of tune;
It moves us not.—Great God! I'd rather be
A Pagan suckled in a creed outworn;                10
So might I, standing on this pleasant lea,
Have glimpses that would make me less forlorn;
Have sight of Proteus rising from the sea;
Or hear old Triton blow his wreathèd horn.

## BIRCHES

### *Robert Frost* (*1916*)

When I see birches bend to left and right
Across the lines of straighter darker trees,
I like to think some boy's been swinging them.
But swinging doesn't bend them down to stay.
Ice-storms do that. Often you must have seen them      5
Loaded with ice a sunny winter morning
After a rain. They click upon themselves
As the breeze rises, and turn many-colored
As the stir cracks and crazes their enamel.
Soon the sun's warmth makes them shed crystal shells     10
Shattering and avalanching on the snow-crust—
Such heaps of broken glass to sweep away
You'd think the inner dome of heaven had fallen.
They are dragged to the withered bracken by the load,

And they seem not to break; though once they are bowed          15
So low for long, they never right themselves:
You may see their trunks arching in the woods
Years afterwards, trailing their leaves on the ground
Like girls on hands and knees that throw their hair
Before them over their heads to dry in the sun.          20
But I was going to say when Truth broke in
With all her matter-of-fact about the ice-storm
(Now am I free to be poetical?)
I should prefer to have some boy bend them
As he went out and in to fetch the cows—          25
Some boy too far from town to learn baseball,
Whose only play was what he found himself,
Summer or winter, and could play alone.
One by one he subdued his father's trees
By riding them down over and over again          30
Until he took the stiffness out of them,
And not one but hung limp, not one was left
For him to conquer. He learned all there was
To learn about not launching out too soon
And so not carrying the tree away          35
Clear to the ground. He always kept his poise
To the top branches, climbing carefully
With the same pains you use to fill a cup
Up to the brim, and even above the brim.
Then he flung outward, feet first, with a swish,          40
Kicking his way down through the air to the ground.
So was I once myself a swinger of birches.
And so I dream of going back to be.
It's when I'm weary of considerations,
And life is too much like a pathless wood          45
Where your face burns and tickles with the cobwebs
Broken across it, and one eye is weeping
From a twig's having lashed across it open.
I'd like to get away from earth awhile
And then come back to it and begin over.          50
May no fate willfully misunderstand me
And half grant what I wish and snatch me away
Not to return. Earth's the right place for love:
I don't know where it's likely to go better.
I'd like to go by climbing a birch tree,          55
And climb black branches up a snow-white trunk
*Toward* heaven, till the tree could bear no more,
But dipped its top and set me down again.
That would be good both going and coming back.
One could do worse than be a swinger of birches.          60

## UP AT A VILLA—DOWN IN THE CITY
### AS DISTINGUISHED BY AN ITALIAN PERSON OF QUALITY

*Robert Browning*   *(1855)*

Had I but plenty of money, money enough and to spare,
The house for me, no doubt, were a house in the city-square;
Ah, such a life, such a life, as one leads at the window there!

Something to see, by Bacchus, something to hear, at least!
There, the whole day long, one's life is a perfect feast;                      5
While up at a villa one lives, I maintain it, no more than a beast.

Well now, look at our villa! stuck like the horn of a bull
Just on a mountain-edge as bare as the creature's skull,
Save a mere shag of a bush with hardly a leaf to pull!
—I scratch my own, sometimes, to see if the hair's turned wool.              10

But the city, oh, the city—the square with the houses! Why?
They are stone-faced, white as a curd, there's something to take the eye!
Houses in four straight lines, not a single front awry;
You watch who crosses and gossips, who saunters, who hurries by;
Green blinds, as a matter of course, to draw when the sun gets high;          15
And the shops with fanciful signs which are painted properly.

What of a villa? Though winter be over in March by rights,
'Tis May perhaps ere the snow shall have withered well off the heights.
You've the brown plowed land before, where the oxen steam and wheeze,
And the hills over-smoked behind by the faint gray olive trees.              20

Is it better in May, I ask you? You've summer all at once;
In a day he leaps complete with a few strong April suns.
'Mid the sharp short emerald wheat, scarce risen three fingers well,
The wild tulip, at end of its tube, blows out its great red bell
Like a thin clear bubble of blood, for the children to pick and sell.        25

Is it ever hot in the square? There's a fountain to spout and splash!
In the shade it sings and springs; in the shine such foam-bows flash
On the horses with curling fish-tails, that prance and paddle and pash
Round the lady atop in her conch—fifty gazers do not abash,
Though all that she wears is some weeds round her waist in a sort of sash.   30

All the year long at the villa, nothing to see though you linger,
Except yon cypress that points like death's lean lifted forefinger.
Some think fireflies pretty, when they mix i' the corn and mingle,
Or thrid the stinking hemp till the stalks of it seem a-tingle.
Late August or early September, the stunning cicala is shrill,              35
And the bees keep their tiresome whine round the resinous firs on the hill.
Enough of the seasons—I spare you the months of the fever and chill.

Ere you open your eyes in the city, the blessed church-bells begin;
No sooner the bells leave off than the diligence rattles in;
You get the pick of the news, and it costs you never a pin.    40
By and by there's the traveling doctor gives pills, lets blood, draws teeth;
Or the Pulcinello-trumpet breaks up the market beneath.

At the post office such a scene-picture—the new play, piping hot!
And a notice how, only this morning, three liberal thieves were shot.
Above it, behold the Archbishop's most fatherly of rebukes,    45
And beneath with his crown and his lion, some little new law of the Duke's!
Or a sonnet with flowery marge, to the Reverend Don So-and-So,
Who is Dante, Boccaccio, Petrarca, Saint Jerome, and Cicero;
"And moreover"—the sonnet goes riming—"the skirts of Saint Paul has
     reached,
Having preached us those six Lent-lectures more unctuous than ever he
     preached."    50

Noon strikes—here sweeps the procession! our Lady borne smiling and smart,
With a pink gauze gown all spangles, and seven swords stuck in her heart!
*Bang-whang-whang* goes the drum, *tootle-te-tootle* the fife;
No keeping one's haunches still; it's the greatest pleasure in life.

But bless you, it's dear—it's dear! fowls, wine, at double the rate.    55
They have clapped a new tax upon salt, and what oil pays passing the gate
It's a horror to think of. And so, the villa for me, not the city!
Beggars can scarcely be choosers; but still—ah, the pity, the pity!
Look, two and two go the priests, then the monks with cowls and sandals,
And the penitents dressed in white shirts, a-holding the yellow candles;    60
One, he carries a flag up straight, and another a cross with handles,
And the Duke's guard brings up the rear, for the better prevention of scandals;
*Bang-whang-whang* goes the drum, *tootle-te-tootle* the fife.
Oh, a day in the city-square, there is no such pleasure in life!

## GIVE ME THE SPLENDID SILENT SUN

### *Walt Whitman* (*1855*)

I

Give me the splendid silent sun with all his beams full-dazzling,
Give me juicy autumnal fruit ripe and red from the orchard,
Give me a field where the unmow'd grass grows,
Give me an arbor, give me the trellis'd grape,
Give me fresh corn and wheat, give me serene-moving animals teaching
     content,    5
Give me nights perfectly quiet as on high plateaus west of the Mississippi, and
     I looking up at the stars,
Give me odorous at sunrise a garden of beautiful flowers where I can walk
     undisturb'd,

Give me for marriage a sweet-breath'd woman of whom I should never tire,
Give me a perfect child, give me away aside from the noise of the world a
    rural domestic life,
Give me to warble spontaneous songs recluse by myself, for my own ears
    only,       10
Give me solitude, give me Nature, give me again O Nature your primal
    sanities!

These demanding to have them, (tired with ceaseless excitement, and rack'd
    by the war-strife,)
These to procure incessantly asking, rising in cries from my heart,
While yet incessantly asking still I adhere to my city,
Day upon day and year upon year O city, walking your streets,    15
Where you hold me enchain'd a certain time refusing to give me up,
Yet giving to make me glutted, enrich'd of soul, you give me forever faces;
(O I see what I sought to escape, confronting, reversing my cries,
I see my own soul trampling down what it ask'd for.)

2

Keep your splendid silent sun,    20
Keep your woods O Nature, and the quiet places by the woods,
Keep your fields of clover and timothy, and your corn-fields and orchards,
Keep the blossoming buckwheat fields where the Ninth-month bees hum;
Give me faces and streets—give me these phantoms incessant and endless along
    the trottoirs!
Give me interminable eyes—give me women—give me comrades and lovers
    by the thousand!    25
Let me see new ones every day—let me hold new ones by the hand every day!
Give me such shows—give me the streets of Manhattan!
Give me Broadway, with the soldiers marching—give me the sound of the
    trumpets and drums!
(The soldiers in companies or regiments—some starting away, flush'd and
    reckless,
Some, their time up, returning with thinn'd ranks, young, yet very old, worn,
    marching, noticing nothing;)    30
Give me the shores and wharves heavy-fringed with black ships!
O such for me!  O an intense life, full to repletion and varied!
The life of the theatre, bar-room, huge hotel, for me!
The saloon of the steamer! the crowded excursion for me! the torchlight
    procession!
The dense brigade bound for the war, with high piled military wagons fol-
    lowing;    35
People, endless, streaming, with strong voices, passions, pageants,
Manhattan streets with their powerful throbs, with beating drums as now,
The endless and noisy chorus, the rustle and clank of muskets, (even the sight
    of the wounded,)
Manhattan crowds, with their turbulent musical chorus!
Manhattan faces and eyes forever for me.    40

## IN HARMONY WITH NATURE

### TO A PREACHER

*Matthew Arnold   (1849)*

"In harmony with Nature?" Restless
fool,
Who with such heat dost preach
what were to thee,
When true, the last impossibility—
To be like Nature strong, like Nature
cool!
Know, man hath all which Nature
hath, but more,                    5
And in that *more* lie all his hopes of
good.
Nature is cruel, man is sick of blood;
Nature is stubborn, man would fain
adore;
Nature is fickle, man hath need of
rest;
Nature forgives no debt, and fears no
grave;                             10
Man would be mild, and with safe
conscience blest.
Man must begin, know this, where
Nature ends;
Nature and man can never be fast
friends.
Fool, if thou canst not pass her, rest
her slave!

## TRY TROPIC

### OF THE PROPERTIES OF NATURE
### FOR HEALING AN ILLNESS

*Genevieve Taggard   (1928)*

Try tropic for your balm,
Try storm,
And after storm, calm.
Try snow of heaven, heavy, soft and
slow,
Brilliant and warm.                5
Nothing will help, and nothing do
much harm.

Drink iron from rare springs; follow
the sun;
Go far
To get the beam of some medicinal
star;
Or in your anguish run            10
The gauntlet of all zones to an ulti-
mate one.
Fever and chill
Punish you still,
Earth has no zone to work against
your ill.

Burn in the jewelled desert with the
toad.                             15
Catch lace
Of evening mist across your haunted
face;
Or walk in upper air, the slanted
road.
It will not lift that load;
Nor will large seas undo your subtle
ill.                             20

Nothing can cure and nothing kill
What ails your eyes, what cuts your
pulse in two
And not kill you.

## I HEAR THE CRIES OF EVENING

*Stephen Spender   (1934)*

I hear the cries of evening, while the
paw
Of dark creeps up the turf;
Sheep's bleating, swaying gulls' cry,
the rock's caw,
The hammering surf.

I am inconstant yet this constancy   5
Of natural rest twangs at my heart;
Town-bred, I feel the roots of each
earth-cry
Tear me apart.

These are the creakings of the dusty
    day
When the dog night bites sharp,    10
These fingers grip my soul and tear
    away
And pluck me like a harp.

I feel this huge sphere turn, the great
    wheel sing
While beasts move to their ease:
Sheep's love, gulls' peace—I feel my
    chattering    15
Uncared by these.

## PRAIRIE

### *Carl Sandburg* (*1918*)

I was born on the prairie and the milk of its wheat, the red of its clover, the
    eyes of its women, gave me a song and a slogan.

Here the water went down, the icebergs slid with gravel, the gaps and the
    valleys hissed, and the black loam came, and the yellow sandy loam.
Here between the sheds of the Rocky Mountains and the Appalachians, here
    now a morning star fixes a fire sign over the timber claims and cow pas-
    tures, the corn belt, the cotton belt, the cattle ranches.
Here the gray geese go five hundred miles and back with a wind under their
    wings honking the cry for a new home.
Here I know I will hanker after nothing so much as one more sunrise or a
    sky moon of fire doubled to a river moon of water.    5
The prairie sings to me in the forenoon and I know in the night I rest easy in
    the prairie arms, on the prairie heart.

.     .     .

    After the sunburn of the day
    handling a pitchfork at a hayrack,
    after the eggs and biscuit and coffee,
    the pearl-gray haystacks    10
    in the gloaming
    are cool prayers
    to the harvest hands.

In the city among the walls the overland passenger train is choked and the
    pistons hiss and the wheels curse.
On the prairie the overland flits on phantom wheels and the sky and the soil
    between them muffle the pistons and cheer the wheels.    15

.     .     .     .

    I am here when the cities are gone.
    I am here before the cities come.
    I nourished the lonely men on horses.
    I will keep the laughing men who ride iron.
    I am dust of men.    20

The running water babbled to the deer, the cottontail, the gopher.
You came in wagons, making streets and schools,
Kin of the ax and rifle, kin of the plow and horse,
Singing *Yankee Doodle, Old Dan Tucker, Turkey in the Straw,*
You in the coonskin cap at a log house door hearing a lone wolf howl,      25
You at a sod house door reading the blizzards and chinooks let loose from
    Medicine Hat,
I am dust of your dust, as I am brother and mother
To the copper faces, the worker in flint and clay,
The singing women and their sons a thousand years ago
Marching single file the timber and the plain.                              30

I hold the dust of these amid changing stars.
I last while old wars are fought, while peace broods mother-like,
While new wars arise and the fresh killings of young men.
I fed the boys who went to France in great dark days.
Appomattox is a beautiful word to me and so is Valley Forge and the Marne
    and Verdun,                                                             35
I who have seen the red births and the red deaths
Of sons and daughters, I take peace or war, I say nothing and wait.

Have you seen a red sunset drip over one of my cornfields, the shore of night
    stars, the wave lines of dawn up a wheat valley?
Have you heard my threshing crews yelling in the chaff of a strawpile and
    the running wheat of the wagonboards, my cornhuskers, my harvest
    hands hauling crops, singing dreams of women, worlds, horizons?

> Rivers cut a path on flat lands.                 40
> The mountains stand up.
> The salt oceans press in
> And push on the coast lines.
> The sun, the wind, bring rain
> And I know what the rainbow writes
>     across the east or west in a half circle:    45
> A love-letter pledge to come again.

.        .        .

> Towns on the Soo Line,
> Towns on the Big Muddy,
> Laugh at each other for cubs
> And tease as children.                           50

Omaha and Kansas City, Minneapolis and St. Paul, sisters in a house together,
    throwing slang, growing up.
Towns in the Ozarks, Dakota wheat towns, Wichita, Peoria, Buffalo, sisters
    throwing slang, growing up.

.      .      .      .      .      .

Out of the prairie-brown grass crossed with a streamer of wigwam smoke—
out of a smoke pillar, a blue promise—out of wild ducks woven in greens
and purples—
Here I saw a city rise and say to the peoples round the world: Listen, I am
strong, I know what I want.
Out of log houses and stumps—canoes stripped from tree-sides—flatboats
coaxed with an ax from the timber claims—in the years when the red
and the white men met—the houses and streets rose.       55

A thousand red men cried and went away to new places for corn and women:
a million white men came and put up skyscrapers, threw out rails and
wires, feelers to the salt sea: now the smokestacks bite the skyline with
stub teeth.

In an early year the call of a wild duck woven in greens and purples: now the
riveter's chatter, the police patrol, the song-whistle of the steamboat.

To a man across a thousand years I offer a handshake.
I say to him: Brother, make the story short, for the stretch of a thousand
years is short.

          .          .          .          .

What brothers these in the dark?                          60
What eaves of skyscrapers against a smoke moon?
These chimneys shaking on the lumber shanties
When the coal boats plow by on the river—
The hunched shoulders of the grain elevators—
The flame sprockets of the sheet steel mills                65
And the men in the rolling mills with their shirts off
Playing their flesh arms against the twisting wrists of steel:

                    what brothers these
                    in the dark
                    of a thousand years?                    70

               .          .          .

A headlight searches a snowstorm.
A funnel of white light shoots from the pilot of the Pioneer Limited crossing
Wisconsin.

In the morning hours, in the dawn,
The sun puts out the stars of the sky
And the headlight of the Limited train.                    75

The fireman waves his hand to a country schoolteacher on a bobsled.
A boy, yellow hair, red scarf and mittens, on the bobsled, in his lunch box a
pork chop sandwich and a V of gooseberry pie.
The horses fathom a snow to their knees.
Snow hats are on the rolling prairie hills.
The Mississippi bluffs wear snow hats.                     80

          .          .          .          .

Keep your hogs on changing corn and mashes of grain,
    O farmerman.
    Cram their insides till they waddle on short legs
    Under the drums of bellies, hams of fat.
    Kill your hogs with a knife slit under the ear.    85
    Hack them with cleavers.
    Hang them with hooks in the hind legs.

. . . . .

A wagonload of radishes on a summer morning.
Sprinkles of dew on the crimson-purple balls.    89
The farmer on the seat dangles the reins on the rumps of dapple-gray horses.
The farmer's daughter with a basket of eggs dreams of a new hat to wear to
    the county fair.

On the left- and right-hand side of the road,
                    Marching corn—
I saw it knee high weeks ago—now it is head high—tassels of red silk creep
    at the ends of the ears.

. . . .

I am the prairie, mother of men, waiting.
They are mine, the threshing crews eating beefsteak, the farmboys driving
    steers to the railroad cattle pens.    95
They are mine, the crowds of people at a Fourth of July basket picnic, listen-
    ing to a lawyer read the Declaration of Independence, watching the
    pinwheels and Roman candles at night, the young men and women two
    by two hunting the bypaths and kissing bridges.
They are mine, the horses looking over a fence in the frost of late October
    saying good-morning to the horses hauling wagons of rutabaga to market.
They are mine, the old zigzag rail fences, the new barb wire.

The cornhuskers wear leather on their hands.
There is no let-up to the wind.    100
Blue bandannas are knotted at the ruddy chins.

Falltime and winter apples take on the smolder of the five o'clock November
    sunset: falltime, leaves, bonfires, stubble, the old things go, and the earth
    is grizzled.
The land and the people hold memories, even among the anthills and the
    angleworms, among the toads and woodroaches—among gravestone
    writings rubbed out by the rain—they keep old things that never grow
    old.

The frost loosens corn husks.
The sun, the rain, the wind loosens cornhusks.    105
The men and women are helpers.

They are all cornhuskers together.
I see them late in the western evening in a smoke-red dusk.

. . . . .

The phantom of a yellow rooster flaunting a scarlet comb, on top of a dung
    pile crying hallelujah to the streaks of daylight,
The phantom of an old hunting dog nosing in the underbrush for muskrats,
    barking at a coon in a treetop at midnight, chewing a bone, chasing his
    tail round a corncrib,                                                    110
The phantom of an old workhorse taking the steel point of a plow across a
    forty-acre field in spring, hitched to a harrow in summer, hitched to a
    wagon among cornshocks in fall,
These phantoms come into the talk and wonder of people on the front porch
    of a farmhouse late summer nights.
"The shapes that are gone are here," said an old man with a cob pipe in his
    teeth one night in Kansas with a hot wind on the alfalfa.

. . . . .

               Look at six eggs
               In a mockingbird's nest.                                      115
               Listen to six mockingbirds
               Flinging follies of O-be-joyful
               Over the marshes and uplands.

               Look at songs
               Hidden in eggs.                                              120

. . . . .

When the morning sun is on the trumpet-vine blossoms, sing at the kitchen
    pans: Shout All Over God's Heaven.
When the rain slants on the potato hills and the sun plays a silver shaft on the
    last shower, sing to the bush at the backyard fence: Mighty Lak a Rose.
When the icy sleet pounds on the storm windows and the house lifts to a
    great breath, sing for the outside hills: The Ole Sheep Done Know the
    Road, the Young Lambs Must Find the Way.

. . . . .

Spring slips back with a girl face calling always: "Any new songs for me?
    Any new songs?"
O prairie girl, be lonely, singing, dreaming, waiting—your lover comes—your
    child comes—the years creep with toes of April rain on new-turned
    sod.                                                                       125
O prairie girl, whoever leaves you only crimson poppies to talk with, whoever
    puts a good-by kiss on your lips and never comes back—
There is a song deep as the falltime red haws, long as the layer of black loam
    we go to, the shine of the morning star over the corn belt, the wave line
    of dawn up a wheat valley.

. . . . .

O prairie mother, I am one of your boys.
I have loved the prairie as a man with a heart shot full of pain over love.
Here I know I will hanker after nothing so much as one more sunrise or a
    sky moon of fire doubled to a river moon of water.     130

. . . . . . .

I speak of new cities and new people.
I tell you the past is a bucket of ashes.
I tell you yesterday is a wind gone down, a sun dropped in the west.
I tell you there is nothing in the world, only an ocean of to-morrows, a sky of
    to-morrows.

I am a brother of the cornhuskers who say at sundown:
                  To-morrow is a day.     135

## TO AUTUMN

### *John Keats*  (*1819*)

    Season of mists and mellow fruitfulness,
        Close bosom-friend of the maturing sun:
    Conspiring with him how to load and bless
        With fruit the vines that round the thatch-eves run;
    To bend with apples the mossed cottage-trees,     5
        And fill all fruit with ripeness to the core;
            To swell the gourd, and plump the hazel shells
    With a sweet kernel; to set budding more,
    And still more, later flowers for the bees,
    Until they think warm days will never cease,     10
        For Summer has o'er-brimmed their clammy cells.

    Who hath not seen thee oft amid thy store?
        Sometimes whoever seeks abroad may find
    Thee sitting careless on a granary floor,
        Thy hair soft-lifted by the winnowing wind;     15
    Or on a half-reaped furrow sound asleep,
        Drowsed with the fume of poppies, while thy hook
            Spares the next swath and all its twinèd flowers:
    And sometimes like a gleaner thou dost keep
        Steady thy laden head across a brook;     20
        Or by a cider-press, with patient look,
        Thou watchest the last oozings hours by hours.

    Where are the songs of Spring?  Ay, where are they?
        Think not of them, thou hast thy music too,—
    While barrèd clouds bloom the soft-dying day,     25
        And touch the stubble-plains with rosy hue;

Then in a wailful choir the small gnats mourn
   Among the river sallows, borne aloft
   Or sinking as the light wind lives or dies;
And full-grown lambs loud bleat from hilly bourn;         30
   Hedge-crickets sing; and now with treble soft
   The red-breast whistles from a garden-croft;
   And gathering swallows twitter in the skies.

# PERSONAL RELATIONSHIPS

OUR HAPPINESS depends largely on the character of the relationships which we establish with other people. Many of the most important are not of our choosing. We acquire parents, brothers and sisters, and other relatives at birth. Yet all of these persons, so we are told, profoundly influence our natures even before we can talk. Except in our infancy the quality of such close associations is partly of our own making. And the older we grow, the greater our freedom in the choice of friends and intimates and the greater our opportunities to create from all our personal relationships more and more satisfying experience.

The opportunity for applying wisdom to the effective direction of our lives was never better than it is now. For the relations of parents to children, husbands to wives, brothers to sisters, masters to servants, teachers to pupils, are all changing with bewildering rapidity. Nothing about them is now settled or sure. Not long ago all the members of a family were bound closely together in work and play. Today most of the bonds which used to draw them together have been loosened. No member of the group exercises as much of the old-fashioned authority and control over the others as he formerly did. Wise parents advise their children instead of giving them orders. Fewer women now devote all their attention to their families and their housekeeping. They are often themselves wage-earners, and more frequently, leaders in many enterprises of their communities. Such women regard their homes more as nurseries for the development of self-reliant individuals than as harsh schools of discipline.

Many regret the disintegration of the old-fashioned family. Aldous Huxley in his satiric picture of the future, *Brave New World*, shows what might happen if these disruptive tendencies were all carried to their logical conclusion. In the fantastic world of his imagination babies will be created and developed in test tubes. Then they will be taken to laboratories where they will be conditioned for the positions in society which they are expected to fill. Naturally, products of this sort of scientific magic will not belong to any family group. We can see the point of Huxley's satire without following him into this grotesque future. We know that the loosening of domestic ties need not destroy the really valuable aspects of family life. It may have the contrary effect of placing the relationships of the home on a sounder basis than ever.

Many husbands and wives are now trying to establish a richer and happier marriage relationship than the older, more rigid one. They regard their union less as a legal contract binding them, perhaps unwillingly, to certain prescribed duties, and more as an opportunity for a genuine companionship and devotion. When persons with such ideas realize that their life together is destroying rather than fostering these high ideals, they may feel justified in seeking divorce. Others, finding themselves in the same unhappy situation, may ask the advice of a psychiatrist; and still others, the aid of a clergyman or priest. Almost all husbands and wives today share the belief that they need not be doomed to perpetual maladjustment. All hope to find a way of recapturing the happiness which they anticipated. Do these new attitudes necessarily mean, as Joseph Wood Krutch implies, that love has lost its idealism or that the permanence of marriage is at the mercy of whim? On the contrary, may not the new situation show each individual how he can retain all that was good in this relationship and at the same time develop new values even more fruitful?

In the work of preservation and reconstruction great writers offer us valuable guidance. Their books give memorable expression to those ideals which never change no matter how great the alterations in social custom. No one who has felt the power of Shakespeare's lines:

> Let me not to the marriage of true minds
> Admit impediments. Love is not love
> Which alters when it alteration finds
> Or bends with the remover to remove.

can ever take a flippant attitude toward infidelity or regard marriage as mere legalized sensuality.

Other authors have treated with similar insight the joys and sorrows of human friendship or the beauty, tedium, or sheer horror which the various relationships within the home may produce. Acquaintance with the large family described in Galsworthy's *Forsyte Saga* or with Thomas Mann's *Buddenbrooks* may suggest how we can get rid of many of the tensions which have developed in our own households and how we may avoid similar complications in the future. Men of letters not only report the life with which they are acquainted, but through the power of their imagination they also furnish us with new patterns of social behavior. Poets who lived in the late Middle Ages at the courts of Provence and Sicily probably created the sentiment of romantic love which men and women ever since have been able to feel in some form or other. In a similar way a group of American novelists who wrote during the nineteen-twenties apparently suggested to the post-war generation much of the dissipation which made it notorious. They may even have created the scatter-brained girl whom countless "flappers" used to imitate. Literature, then, may unravel for us the complexities of human behavior and lead to the enrichment of our own lives through a better understanding of others.

# THE INFLUENCE OF MY FATHER ON MY SON

*Lincoln Steffens* (*1937*)

## I

IF MY father could watch my son for a while, he might realize his own immortality. A glance would not suffice. My brown-eyed, brown-haired son does not look like my red-headed, blue-eyed father. Not a bit. And the immortality I speak of has not taken on the angelic form my good father expected. The child is more like his grandfather than that. My father would invite me sweetly to come and sit on a stool at his feet, and, as I let myself trustingly down, he would gently kick the seat from under me—and laugh. I should like to have had him see his little grandson plant his sled on the basement door mat and call me out to stumble over the trap—and laugh. In both cases the victim, the devilish spirit, and the laugh were the same. So I say that if my father had the time to give to the observation of my son he might realize, if not his immortality, then the partial continuity of his character, disposition, and certainly his influence upon his line, and be—not satisfied, perhaps, but convinced, surprised, and—let me guess—amused or embarrassed.

He would be amused to see Pete, a child of six, who did not know his grandfather, wave his hand in the identical gesture my father used to make to indicate that a questionable assertion of his was obvious or final and decisive. I was highly pleased myself when I first noticed it and recognized my father. I called it an inheritance direct from him till my matter-of-fact wife showed me that I had the same wave and used it in saying I didn't.

My son's mother, by the way, spoils many of our most wonderful fancies, Pete's and mine, and that's why he and I have agreed upon a sentiment which we say in unison behind her back, and sometimes in her presence. We sing: "Pete and Papa are wonderful. Mama and Anna [the maid] are ab-surd."

My father would be amused at that, anyhow. He would say, "S-s-s-h! Don't say such things," but he would recognize in it himself and his son and his wife and my mother. He and I were often in cahoots against my mother, affectionately, on the side. Mothers do not always understand a fellow.

He would have been surprised and he might have been embarrassed when I did not rebuke my son, as he would have rebuked his son, for tripping his father over that sled. This I'll call indirect inheritance. My father, the practical joker, did not care for practical jokes on himself; he did not encourage the practice in me. I saw and I have reacted against this inconsistency with my son. I tease, too; I don't approve of it, but my father and my grandfather in me make me play tricks on my boy, so I have to let him have some fun with me. But my son inherits the benefit of at least one half of my father's fault.

My father required me to honor my father and my mother too much to put up games on them. I did on occasion. (That's how I know that my son can't help it.) I let my father mount my pony one afternoon in time to ride past the neighboring brewery just as the engineer let off steam, and my father was pitched off; and I laughed behind a tree, where, however, my father found me and—Well, I don't do to my little boy what he did to his little boy. I feel my father in me want to, but I remember him and my feelings, and I laugh. The family laugh at the family trait.

My son "honors" his mother, as I did mine. He would not plant a sled for his mother, as I would not for mine. On the other hand, if my son breaks something, he will run to tell me about it first, and then, when his mother discovers the wreck, he backs into my arms and bids her not to speak of it. "Daddy minded that," he says.

I asked him once why it was that he respected his mother and had no fear of me.

"Oh," he said, "you are a funny man. You can get mad, like Mama, but you laugh. And—and anybody that laughs can't—can't do—what Mama does."

My father would have been surprised to hear this, as I was. My father was slower but he was severer than my mother, who was quick but light and irregular in discipline. It is just so in my son's family. My mother would thump me sharply on the head with a thimble or a spoon if I became too noisy with the whistle when I was playing I was a steamboat captain. She had no sense of the dignity of command. My father seemed always to know not only what I was doing, but what I was being. He had too much respect for a steamboat captain to humiliate me before my crew. If I committed a crime, he would not break into the scene and spoil it; he would say quietly, as between him and me, "I'll see you to-morrow morning right after breakfast about this." Now I find that I preferred my father's way and I take it with his grandson, who likewise prefers it. His mother will call suddenly: "Pete! It's bedtime," when she thinks of it, and off he must go, regardless of his occupation. I look first, to see that he is busy with, say, an important building operation, and I would no more interrupt him than I would a crooked contractor. If it's late, I join my builder, we finish the job, and then he goes satisfied to bed, the day's work done.

One improvement I have learned from my childhood experience with my father; I do not threaten punishment in the morning. That was awful. Late into the night I would lie awake tossing and wondering what he was going to do to me. Usually he did nothing. A quiet, impressive "talking to" was all I got. And no doubt his idea was that the postponement of penalty—to save himself from acting in anger—would set me to thinking and be punishment enough, but my father did not visualize the anxiety, the agony of my sleepless hours of anticipation. Hence it is that I do visualize a bad night, and so we go to bed in Pete's house with a clean slate and a happy morrow to wake up to. No hang-overs for us, and I am pretty sure Pete feels this benefit he has from my correction of my father's error. At the end of a "serious talk" the boy and I had one day, he rested a moment, then got up and said: "Well, that's all over, isn't it?" and I assured him it was. "We'll forget it now, Pete, and never mention it again."

## II

Dealing with my son makes me recall my father so clearly that I think now that I could state his policy with me and his philosophy, if he had one. Of the philosophy I am not sure. His acts and his sayings to me were all in the direction of freedom and independence. I let my boy go and do and say pretty much as he likes, as, and perhaps because, my father kept no string on me. I could roam as a child far afield; he gave me my pony to widen my range; and I am sure that I went where my parents did not know I went. My mother would ask where I had been, rarely my father, and he backed me up if I did not want to tell—at the time.

"No, don't ask him that now," he would say to my mother. "He will tell us if he goes anywhere he shouldn't." And later, some time when the pressure was off, I would tell him that, say, I had gone down to the dangerous one of our two rivers. That was forbidden. I was afraid myself of that river; it looked cruel, snarling, grasping, but my mother's fear was excited and unreasonable. I could not tell her I had been there. My father, when I told him, would become very quiet, thoughtful, till, looking up inquiringly, he would say:—

"You have been told not to go to that river?"

"Yes."

A pause, "You don't often disobey us, do you?"

"No."

"You must have wanted very much to go there if you disregarded our command that way. What was it that made you do it?"

I gave him my boy's reason, straight: a man had been drowned and I wanted to see them drag for the body.

"Did you?" he asked, interested.

"Yes, we saw them drag, but they didn't get the body." And, because he was so keen, I described all that we boys saw, and did, and said, just as I would to "another fellow." We had a long, equal talk about the day's work on the river and I had forgotten all about my disobedience when my father said:—

"I should have liked to see that myself. I wish you had come by my office and taken me with you. Do that next time. Give me a chance. And say, I wouldn't again disobey directly like that any of the few rules we lay down for you." That was all, except that at the next meal my father told my mother before me the story of my day without any reference to the disobedience part. He told it well, too; to my satisfaction, but not to my mother's. She kept saying, "But—but—"

I loved my mother, but—but—my father respected me. He respected, as you see, my disobedience; he respected my bunk, my lies, my crimes. When I was a fireman, my mother made me clothes of red stuff that were suitable to a firefighter—sure; and she let me ride my pony to fires; but when one day there was an alarm during dinner and I leaped up so quick that I nearly upset the table, she remonstrated and forbade me to go to that fire. I wasn't really a fireman to her. To my father I was. He sprang up too, put out a hand to stay my mother's indignation, and he shouted: "Go it, boy! Get there—first!" I did. I got first to that fire, and when I came back I found that it had been settled in the family that I could go, fast, to any fire that occurred any time when I was on duty, any time of day except when I was in school or in bed.

This I have passed on intact to Pete, with a smile added. When the boy was in the so-called lying period (he was about five years old) he learned to tell his big stories to me rather than his mother. She was patient with them, but they were whoppers just the same. I joined in his fiction, as I did in his building or business operations. We ran a garage, I as owner, he as manager; we had a taxi and baggage service, which met all trains and responded, fast, to all private calls. It was real and pretty strenuous to us all,—his mother, too— but the test came when there was a train to meet at mealtimes. Then it appeared pretty plainly that Pete's mother really regarded the garage business as bunk, or at any rate it was not as serious as his dinner!

Well, we business men held a directors' meeting and decided and announced that, hereafter, our garage would close from one to two P.M. But we sang our little song: "Pete and Papa are wonderful, Mama and Anna are absurd."

Mama, Anna, and many of our neighbors disapproved of this song. When we sang it together at a tea, women were shocked and some men wagged their funny old heads. "How can you teach your son such nonsense!" they exclaimed—and if I explained that it doesn't matter what you *teach* a child, that all that matters is what he *learns*, they did not understand me. My father and my grandfather would have understood perfectly, as their grandson and great-grandson did. Maybe the following incident will clear it all up.

One day Pete came to my study door and said that he had just killed a bear.

"Where?" I asked.

"Over there," he waved.

"That's wonderful," I said. "A coincidence. I just killed ten bears." He looked a bit dashed, but he inquired:—

"Where?"

"Over there," I waved.

He looked so beaten that I rose and said: "Come on, Pete, let's go and tell Mama."

"Oh, no," he protested, "not Mama."

"Ah, come on," I urged, offering to take his hand. "I'll do the talking."

Very reluctantly, he put his hand in mine and we went into the house, up to his mother, who was busy (writing fiction).

"Mama," I said, "Pete killed a bear."

Annoyed, she looked up at me and demanded why I encouraged the boy to lie like that.

"Oh, that's nothing," I said. "I just killed ten bears."

"Oh, go away!" she exclaimed, in real irritation. "You are both liars and I don't think it's funny." And she actually pushed us.

We took hands again; we bear-killers, we liars, we slunk out of the house and sat down on the front steps, he at one side, I at the other, and we were silent a long time. I was wondering what was going on in the boy's head. At last he spoke.

"Daddy."

"Yes, Pete."

"Daddy, Pete and Papa are not wonderful."

"No?"

"No. Mama is wonderful. Pete and Papa are absurd."

Well, I took that. We got up, hand in hand; we walked about a bit in the garden till we were called to luncheon. Seated at table, I wanted to break the strain, so I said: "Come on, Pete, let's say it," and, with his grandfather's twinkle of the eye, he joined me in saying: "Pete and Papa are wonderful," and so forth.

He knew. You don't have to be careful with children, unless you have taken a pose and have to remember to keep it up; and even then . . .

## III

My father made with me one serious mistake which I see parents about me making. He got himself somehow into the awkward position of an authority; I thought he knew and was right on everything—for a while. He did not pretend to righteousness or omniscience. He seemed to me as a boy to be fair, and he seems to me now, as a man, to have been either very modest or well aware of the danger there is of exposure for a father who has been idealized. Just the same, he was idealized. I suppose that he did what I see these other parents do; he probably answered impatiently and, therefore, thoughtlessly and positively the prattling questions of my early childhood, of that impressionable period of the first seven years. Anyway, when I became conscious and my father took me and my problems seriously, he was already my household god. And then—and then—

Among the many places out in the world to which I rode off alone on the pony he had given me was the State Fair grounds. Happening to turn in there of a spring morning, I saw some jockeys exercising a string of race horses. I joined them; they objected at first to the kid, but one of them—a colored boy named Smoke—said I could stay, and by and by I was accepted. The trainers found a use for me: to ride bareback their trotting horses. I decided to become a jockey. My mother discovered the secret first. I did not eat—not regularly. I would fast for a day or two, then break down and gobble. She complained, scolded, questioned. Mothers are awful. My father saved me. He bade her leave me alone and he observed me for a day or two, then he took me aside and asked me quietly. "What is all this fasting for?" He was so "nice and easy" about it that I told him about me and the jockeys and the trainers; and how they said that "if I kept my weight down I might be a winner."

My father sat reflecting a long time, his way, before he answered, and his speech showed that he accepted my career on the turf absolutely. He began by advising me about fasting. I wasn't to do it as I had been doing it: going without food, then eating too much. A better way was to eat moderately, choosing foods that I did not like and usually avoided, like vegetables, for instance, and holding to what he called my "diet." He talked about horses and horse racing, which he named the king of sports and the sport of kings. What struck me was that he knew all about the turf, as he knew all about everything. Also he spoke to my mother, so that she entered into the game—not enthusiastically; she made faces and tended to utter protests, but my daddy "minded" them. He stopped her with that immortal wave of the hand which I see his grandson wave.

So I went on as a jockey apprentice to learn all about horses, racing, and riding, till the spring meets. We knew the horses entered for those races, which were good, which were best, and we had our favorites. Smoke had one in his stable that could beat anything in sight. Smoke loved, we all respected, I adored that horse, and when he ran, sure to win, he lost. Smoke "pulled" him. I saw it from my perch under the wire. I saw the horse fight for the bit with Smoke, who fought back. I saw it all, and I learned that horse racing wasn't on the level, that some races were "fixed" to catch the "suckers" and give the racing men and jockeys a chance to make some money. Smoke blamed the suckers—"they spoil everything." I blamed and I hated the suckers who spoiled everything.

I quit the track, I gave up the turf as a career, I ate my fill. My father noticed it, asked me why, but I could not tell him right away. Too painful. And besides, he must know what racing was. He invited me to go with him to several races, but I refused till some big business friends came to town and joined in asking me to "Come on, boy, and see the sport." It was too humiliating to enter with them at the main gate. I went in "free" through the stable door the jockeys used, joined them on the grandstand where the despised public sat, the suckers. They were betting on the favorite in the next race and talking wisely about his condition and past performances. It seemed to me they were pretending to know some things that they did not know. I got up, ran down to the stables and my friend, Smoke and the rest. They were laughing about this race. It was fixed; the favorite was to lose, and I heard the name of the horse that was to win. Darting back to my father's party of superior grown-ups, I said, not too loud, that the favorite they were betting on would not win and I named the winner—who won. I knew, they didn't. Astonished, they asked me how I knew. I refused to tell them then. They were suckers.

Of course most of them were; but my father? He asked me afterwards how I picked the winner and I told him then—all about horse racing. He was all right; he listened, reflected, believed, and he tried to save some of my illusions.

But—the tragedy of this little comedy, repeated in other departments of life as I was seeing it, was the discovery that my father did not know everything; he was not always right.

## IV

Now, I recovered from this, from all these experiences. I saw that he did not pretend to know all, that he felt and could admit that he was often wrong and in doubt. It was only my infant idol that suffered, my idealization of my father, and—*and* myself. But that was enough.

When my son appeared on the scene, when he was a baby, I remembered the disappointment and distress of my young disillusionment and I determined to save him and *his* father from any such experience. The first time my father's grandson asked me a question, I said I did not know; and the next time, and the next. I have never known the answer. Sometimes I say, "I don't know. Let's go and see." So we find out things together. If that is not possible, if we can't see with our eyes what we want to know, I may say: "I don't know, Pete, but I think it's—so." Or I say, "Grown-ups say it's so, but we don't really know." Indeed, we have a saying, the boy and I, which we repeat often in unison: "I think so, but I don't know," or "I don't know, but I think so."

The theory of this skepticism is that the child has everything to learn for himself and, for us, not only what we don't know, but also—all over again—what we think we do know. And to enforce his self-reliance I seek cases where he and I can differ. He thinks his ball went over there where I saw it go; I think it went over here. We look here first, and Daddy is wrong. We look over there, and there it is. Pete was right—often.

I think that my father if he could observe us might wag his head over these exercises that have gone on for six years—during the unconscious, most sensitive period of his grandson's life. I don't know what my father would have thought when his grandson said the other day:—

"My daddy is always wrong. My mama is always right. And Pete? I am half right and half wrong."

I don't know, but I think that my father would have sat silent a long time, reflecting, remembering, and then seen that his influence upon his grandson—through me—was both directly and indirectly his very own, his immortal self. And he would have been convinced if he saw what I saw: that Pete thought that on the whole, humanly and socially speaking, it was rather better to be wrong than right, or, at any rate, more amusing.

# DREAM-CHILDREN: A REVERIE
## *Charles Lamb* (*1822*)

CHILDREN love to listen to stories about their elders, when *they* were children; to stretch their imagination to the conception of a traditionary greatuncle or grandame, whom they never saw. It was in this spirit that my little ones crept about me the other evening to hear about their great-grandmother Field, who lived in a great house in Norfolk (a hundred times bigger than that in which they and papa lived), which had been the scene—so at least it was generally believed in that part of the country—of the tragic incidents which they had lately become familiar with from the ballad of the Children in the Wood. Certain it is that the whole story of the children and their cruel uncle was to be seen fairly carved out in wood upon the chimney-piece of the great hall, the whole story down to the Robin Redbreasts, till a foolish rich person pulled it down to set up a marble one of modern invention in its stead, with no story upon it. Here Alice put out one of her dear mother's looks, too tender to be called upbraiding.

Then I went on to say how religious and how good their great-grand-mother Field was, how beloved and respected by everybody, though she was not indeed the mistress of this great house, but had only the charge of it (and yet in some respects she might be said to be the mistress of it too), committed to her by the owner, who preferred living in a newer and more fashionable mansion which he had purchased somewhere in the adjoining county; but still she lived in it in a manner as if it had been her own, and kept up the dignity of the great house in a sort while she lived, which afterwards came to decay, and was nearly pulled down, and all its old ornaments stripped and carried away to the owner's other house, where they were set up, and looked as awkward as if some one were to carry away the old tombs they had seen lately at the Abbey, and stick them up in Lady C.'s tawdry gilt draw-ing-room. Here John smiled, as much as to say, "that would be foolish indeed." And then I told how, when she came to die, her funeral was attended by a concourse of all the poor, and some of the gentry too, of the neighborhood for many miles round, to show their respect for her memory, because she had been such a good and religious woman; so good indeed that she knew all the Psaltery by heart, ay, and a great part of the Testament besides. Here little Alice spread her hands.

Then I told what a tall, upright, graceful person their great-grandmother Field once was; and how in her youth she was esteemed the best dancer—here Alice's little right foot played an involuntary movement, till, upon my looking grave, it desisted—the best dancer, I was saying, in the county, till a cruel disease, called a cancer, came, and bowed her down with pain; but it could never bend her good spirits, or make them stoop, but they were still upright, because she was so good and religious. Then I told how she was used to sleep by herself in a lone chamber of the great lone house; and how she believed that an apparition of two infants was to be seen at midnight gliding up and down the great staircase near where she slept, but she said "those innocents would do her no harm"; and how frightened I used to be, though in those days I had my maid to sleep with me, because I was never half so good or religious as she—and yet I never saw the infants. Here John expanded all his eyebrows and tried to look courageous. Then I told how good she was to all her grandchildren, having us to the great house in the holidays, where I in particular used to spend many hours by myself, in gazing upon the old busts of the Twelve Cæsars, that had been Emperors of Rome, till the old marble heads would seem to live again, or I to be turned into marble with them; how I never could be tired with roaming about that huge mansion, with its vast empty rooms, with their worn-out hangings, fluttering tapestry, and carved oaken panels, with the gilding almost rubbed out—sometimes in the spacious old-fashioned gardens, which I had almost to myself, unless when now and then a solitary gardening man would cross me—and how the nectarines and peaches hung upon the walls, without my ever offering to pluck them, because they were forbidden fruit, unless now and then,—and because I had more pleasure in strolling about among the old melancholy-looking yew-trees, or the firs, and picking up the red berries, and the fir apples, which were good for nothing but to look at—or in lying about upon the fresh grass, with all the fine garden smells around me—or basking in the orangery, till I could almost fancy myself ripening too along with the oranges and the limes in that grateful warmth—or in watching the dace that darted to and fro in the fish-pond, at the bottom of the garden, with here and there a great sulky pike hanging midway down the water in silent state, as if it mocked at their impertinent friskings,—I had more pleasure in these busy-idle diversions than in all the sweet flavors of peaches, nectarines, oranges, and such-like common baits of children. Here John slyly deposited back upon the plate a bunch of grapes, which, not unobserved by Alice, he had meditated dividing with her, and both seemed willing to relinquish them for the present as irrelevant.

Then in somewhat a more heightened tone, I told how, though their great-grandmother Field loved all her grandchildren, yet in an especial manner she might be said to love their uncle, John L——, because he was so handsome and spirited a youth, and a king to the rest of us; and, instead of moping about in solitary corners, like some of us, he would mount the most mettlesome horse he could get, when but an imp no bigger than themselves, and make it carry him half over the county in a morning, and join the hunters when there were any out—and yet he loved the old great house and gardens, too, but had too much spirit to be always pent up within their boundaries—and how their uncle grew up to man's estate as brave as he was handsome, to the admiration of everybody, but of their great-grandmother Field most especially; and how he used to carry me upon his back when I was a lame-footed boy—for he was a good bit older than me—many a mile when I could not walk for pain;—and how in after life he became lame-footed, too, and I did not always (I fear) make allowances enough for him when he was impatient, and in pain, nor remember sufficiently how considerate he had been to me when I was lame-footed; and how when he died, though he had not been dead an hour, it seemed as if he had died a great while ago, such a distance there is betwixt life and death; and how I bore his death as I thought pretty well at first, but afterwards it haunted and haunted me; and though I did not cry or take it to heart as some do, and as I think he would have done if I had died, yet I missed him all day long, and knew not till then how much I had loved him. I missed his kindness, and I missed his crossness, and wished him to be alive again, to be quarreling with him (for we quarreled sometimes), rather than not have him again, and was as uneasy without him, as he their poor uncle must have been when the doctor took off his limb. Here the children fell a-crying, and asked if their little mourning which they had on was not for uncle John, and they looked up, and prayed me not to go on about their uncle, but to tell them some stories about their pretty dead mother.

Then I told how for seven long years, in hope sometimes, sometimes in despair, yet persisting ever, I courted the fair Alice W——n; and, as much as children could understand, I explained to them what coyness, and difficulty, and denial meant in maidens—when suddenly, turning to Alice, the soul of the first Alice looked out at her eyes with such a reality of re-presentment, that I became in doubt which of them stood there before me, or whose that bright hair was; and while I stood gazing, both the children gradually grew fainter to my view, receding, and still receding till nothing at last but two mournful features were seen in the uttermost distance, which, without speech, strangely impressed upon me the effects of speech; "We are not of Alice, nor of thee, nor are we children at all. The children of Alice call Bartrum father. We are nothing; less than nothing, and dreams. We are only what might have been, and must wait upon the tedious shores of Lethe millions of ages before we have existence, and a name"—and immediately awaking, I found myself quietly seated in my bachelor armchair, where I had fallen asleep, with the faithful Bridget unchanged by my side—but John L. (or James Elia) was gone forever.

## LOVE—OR THE LIFE AND DEATH OF A VALUE

### *Joseph Wood Krutch* (*1929*)

### I

In one of these popular phrases too generally current to be attributed to any particular person, and hence seeming to have been uttered by a whole and united folk, our Victorian ancestors were accustomed to say that "love is best." Perhaps no other cultural group had ever set itself more resolutely to discipline this most unruly of passions by laying down the conditions under which one might permissibly indulge in it, and perhaps no other had expressed a more inflexible disapproval of any violation of the taboos with which it was surrounded; but, for all the strictness of its definition, it gave to "virtuous love" the highest place in its hierarchy of values.

The age was, though we sometimes forget the fact, an age of many skepticisms, during which many things were called in question, but it never doubted the worth of that which we are accustomed to call, in a phrase whose downrightness would have shocked it profoundly, "sublimated sex." It looked with loathing and fear at any of the cruder manifestations of the sexual instincts, but when those instincts had been adorned with poetry, and submitted to the discipline of society, it regarded them as the source not only of the most admirable virtues, but of the most intrinsically valuable of human experiences as well. In theory, at least, a successful love crowned all other successes and obliterated all other failures. It made all men equal because all men were capable of it, and it stood between man and any ultimate pessimism because, so long as love was possible, life could not be either meaningless or not worth the living. Nor was this evaluation questioned by the leaders in any school of thought, for upon this point even Gladstone and Huxley would have agreed. Whether man were son of God or great-grandson of the ape, it was in love that he fulfilled himself. If he were the former, then love brought him nearer than anything else to the divine state from which he had fallen; if he were the latter, then at least love carried him to the highest level of which he was capable.

Now faiths such as this lie deeper than religious or political creeds. The Christian knows that he is a Christian and that other people are not; the Democrat is aware of theories of government other than his; but such tacit evaluations as that set upon love are accepted as matters of fact, almost as something established by the scheme of nature. These Victorians knew that they were, in the literal sense of the word, puritans here as elsewhere. They knew, that is to say, that they had insisted upon a soberness in love as well as in religion, and that they looked upon the antisocial tendencies of extravagant passion in the same way that they looked upon the antisocial tendencies of extravagant religion; but that it was in love that the meaning of life must inevitably be sought they never stopped to doubt. They did not much consider the fact that the ability to live for love in any form was a relatively recent accomplishment on the part of the human race; that the tacit assumption which lay behind all their literature and all their thinking was not, after all, part of the unchangeable nature of man, but merely an assumption, seemingly inevitable because it had been handed on and accepted by one generation after another, which had changed the rules of the game, but never doubted that it was worth the playing. And it was in part because love seemed to them so inevitably valuable that they were able to hold so firmly to their belief in its supreme importance.

We, however, have specialized in origins, and it requires no more than a glance at the past to show that the high values set upon love are not inevitable. Certainly the savage—the American Indian, for example—knows little of what we call romance. When he sings his songs or addresses his gods, when, that is to say, his consciousness reaches the intensest level of which he is capable, it is upon thoughts of agriculture and of war that he dwells. These are the activities which seem to him to be most worthy to be realized or adorned in contemplation, because they are the ones which seem to bring him closest to the meaning of life; and when he thinks of wooing he does so chiefly not because he regards love as the most significant of human emotions, but because his wife will bear him sons to help guide the destiny of the tribe or to slay its enemies. Like all human beings, the savage considers certain experiences as ends in themselves, but he still regards the act of sexual union as a relatively simple process, important chiefly because of its biological function; it is only somewhere between savagery and civilization that love is born.

At first it holds, no doubt, a relatively low place in the hierarchy of values. The stories which deal with it are at first fewer than those which deal with the struggle against the elements and warfare with neighboring tribes; the lover is still far less than the warrior the type of the hero; and soft emotions are still a matter for surprise, almost for shame. But, once these emotions have been accepted into song and story, they reveal an amazing capacity to elaborate and complicate themselves. They come to be regarded with respect and awe; a mythology quite as elaborate as that concerning the combats of warriors grows up around them; and tacitly it is assumed that a great love is a subject hardly less worthy, hardly less near the divine, than a great heroism.

Perhaps the sterner members of the society set themselves up against it and shake their heads when amorous songs or poems win more applause than warlike ones, but at least the romantic view of life has come to set itself against what, for want of a better name, we must call the heroic one, and a value is born.

Love is, then, not a fact in nature of which we become aware, but rather a creation of the human imagination; and this is true not only when we think of the word as implying some complicated system of attitudes like that of the Victorians, but even when we think of it as referring to no more than a mere physical act to which considerable importance is attached. The very singling out of this particular desire as one more significant than others must precede any attribution of transcendental values to it, and even this singling out took place recently enough for us to be aware of it. If mere lust cannot play any very large part in human life until the imagination has created it, how much more conspicuously is it true that we must regard as purely a creation of the human mind so complex a system of emotional attitudes—interwoven with all sorts of æsthetic, sociological and mystical conceptions—as that which was implied by the Victorian in the word "love." Behind the simple phrase "love is best" lies a history—half of social organization, half of human imagination—which volumes could not adequately trace.

Yet, artificial as is this system of values, and fundamentally illogical as are the associations which lead us to centre the chief human experiences around love, they tend strongly to perpetuate themselves, both because the young of a nation become habituated to an acceptance of them long before any critical sense is developed and because, so far as they are the result of any biologically transmutable evolution, the development of the race is recapitulated in that of the individual. As a child, the normal individual is, like the savage on all but special occasions, either almost unaware of sex or inclined to regard it as something between the ludicrous, the forbidden, and the obscene. He is ashamed of any unexpected emotion which he feels in the presence of his complement, and he is inclined to jeer at those slightly older than himself who show any tendency to abandon the—to him—rational preoccupations of childhood. But then, as he reaches adolescence, a change no less surprising to himself than to others takes place. Much that, as a child, he had heard without understanding becomes suddenly meaningful to him, and he realizes that he is capable of participating in experiences which have hitherto been known to him only by the words applied to them. All his daydreams now centre around exploits which a little before would have seemed to him silly, and if he happens to have been born into one of those highly developed societies, like our own, where love is often regarded as the supreme human privilege, he will invest thoughts of that which had been, a short time before, both ridiculous and obscene, with a religious awe.

Not only will his thoughts be constantly busy with it, but he will tend to centre around it even those of his aspirations which do not seem to be actually related. He will plan to become virtuous, brave, and successful in order to please some member of the opposite sex; he will achieve wealth, power, or fame in order to lay them at her feet. Even those things which earlier—and perhaps also later—seem to him quite worth having for themselves must now borrow their value from her. The ramifications of a simple biological act have come to fill the universe, and it, with all that it involves, has come to be not merely one of the things which make life worth while, but *the* thing which at all justifies or makes it meaningful. For him, as for his race, love has, in a word, become a value,—perhaps the supreme one,—something indubitably worth while in itself and something capable by its own magic of making other things valuable either as means or as adornments.

Such a youth has come into an inheritance of illusions as important and perhaps as valuable as anything else which his ancestors have transmitted to him. He accepts it as part of nature, but it is, as surely as the government under which he lives or the house which shelters him, a human creation, and one which is more fundamental than any other, because it is not something which enables him to live, but something which endows living with a meaning and a purpose. It is an illusion to which centuries of existence have been necessary before it could assume the form and the apparent solidity with which to him it seems endowed, a value which was gradually created while other values faded away.

To the savage who knew nothing of romantic love the world was not so barren without it as it would seem under similar circumstances to the average Latin or Teuton of our day. The experiences of the hunt, still lingeringly delightful to many, were to him passionately absorbing and intrinsically as worth while as love-making later came to be. In the celebration of the spring festival he had as ecstatic a sense of a mystical initiation into the meaning of the universe as the modern young romantic for the first time in the arms of his mistress. But the possibility of these experiences has passed away.

While love was gradually being created, other values vanished; for such, for all their apparent inevitability to those who feel them, is their way; and to know this is to know that even the complex of illusions called "love" is one which might also, under certain circumstances, pass away. Certain peoples, it is obvious, have never had it. Consider, for example, the mental and social organization not only of the savage, but of, let us say, the Chinese, whose entire spiritual life is fundamentally incomprehensible to us, largely because of the fact that, having always regarded sexual passion as a relatively trivial thing, they have set the highest value upon filial rather than upon marital love, and about this latter have centred not only their social structure, but the most important of their moral and emotional groupings, as well, so that, for example, they would not be, like us, inclined to think of love as the chief source of virtue or the chief reward of fortitude.

Nor do we need, in order to get some faint idea how love might come to be less for us than it was for our ancestors, go so far afield as savagery or China, since we may observe in the lives of our own not too remote forefathers how certain self-justifying and intrinsically worth-while activities came to lose their magic. From certain pursuits—war, for example—they got satisfactions which, at least so far as the more advanced part of mankind is concerned, we find it difficult to understand. Of it, of chivalric honor, of national glory, of noble birth, and of various other things, they spoke in a way which indicates that these things had for them an emotional content which is rapidly becoming as nearly extinct as that which is embodied for the savage in the spring festival, and which it is almost as hard for us to understand as it would be for a Chinese sage to understand what we mean when we speak of a "world well lost for love."

Values of this kind seem so inevitably natural to those who accept them, and pass so insensibly away, that their rise and fall are only imperfectly recorded, but the changes which take place in their status are, perhaps, the most momentous events in the life of the human race. They have a far more profound effect upon man than any mere changes of government, for they are, in effect, changes of God, and they involve a change both in his whole conception of the meaning of the universe and in the thing for which he lives. Every time a value is born, existence takes on a new meaning; every time one dies, some part of that meaning passes away.

## II

Most of the faiths which we received from the Victorians had already by then been shaken. Certainly the Church which they left us was already weakened and despoiled, and the majority of their dogmas had become gradually so much attenuated that it needed only the resolute "Pooh!" uttered by the new generation to make them vanish away. Yet their religion of love, or at least the value which they attached to that passion, reached us almost intact. With no subject has the contemporary mind been more persistently busy, but it did not, in the beginning, think of questioning the fundamental premise.

If one reads the novels of H. G. Wells—which will stand as perhaps the best expression of the minds of the "liberal" mass—one will see that, for all their social iconoclasm, they imply a tacit acceptance of the assumption that "love is best" quite as complete as that of any Victorian novel; and if one reads the six volumes of Havelock Ellis's *Studies in the Psychology of Sex*— which will stand perhaps as the completest and most characteristic of those works which made a rationalist attitude toward sex an important feature of the spirit of the age—one will see that to Ellis, too, love has its element of transcendental value. Neither the scientist nor the romancer dreamed of questioning the fact that love was the most significant of human experiences and that in it men might find the ultimate justification of life. If both were frequently concerned with an attack upon what were beginning to be called, even in popular language, the "taboos" which surround the theory and the practice of love, both were so concerned because they thought of love as too obviously the supreme privilege of man to be burdened with irrational proscriptions; and their ultimate purpose was, in a word, not to cheapen or tarnish, but merely to free it.

The Victorians, for all their romantic system of values, had accepted the frustrations and the sacrifices entailed by their social code with a complacency which seemed to the new generation hardly less than heartless. They had seemed to take even a sort of perverse satisfaction in contemplating the bowed head with which people were supposed to acknowledge the inviolability of the rules and which Matthew Arnold had celebrated in two of his most characteristic stanzas:—

> Each in his own strict line we move,
> And some find death ere they find love;
> So far apart their lives are thrown
> From the twin soul that halves their own.

And sometimes, by still harder fate,
The lovers meet, but meet too late
—Thy heart is mine; *True, true. Ah, true,*
—Then, love, thy hand; *Ah, no! Adieu!*

They had, moreover, visited their punishments mercilessly, and they had even—witness George Eliot in *Adam Bede*—persuaded themselves that the punishments visited by society upon those who violated its taboos were the result of a law of nature, and the new generation was merely anxious to avoid the commoner tragedies of love which it regarded as avoidable. It looked forward to an individual who, free from a corroding sense of sin, should live in a society which placed no unnecessary restrictions upon emotional fulfillment, and, far from anticipating any cynical devaluation of love itself, it hoped only for an age in which men should love more freely, more fully, and more perfectly.

Yet it requires no more than a casual acquaintance with either contemporary life or its reflection in contemporary literature to enable one to perceive that this life hardly corresponds to the anticipation.

Freedom has come, but with it a certain lessened sense of the importance of the passions that are thus freely indulged; and, if love has come to be less often a sin, it has come also to be less often a supreme privilege. If one turns to the smarter of those novelists who describe the doings of the more advanced set of those who are experimenting with life,—to, for example, Mr. Aldous Huxley or Mr. Ernest Hemingway,—one will discover in their tragic farces the picture of a society which is at bottom in despair because, though it is more completely absorbed in the pursuit of love than in anything else, it has lost the sense of any ultimate importance inherent in the experience which preoccupies it; and if one turns to the graver of the intellectual writers,— to, for example, Mr. D. H. Lawrence, Mr. T. S. Eliot, or Mr. James Joyce,— one will find both explicitly and implicitly a similar sense that the transcendental value of love has become somehow attenuated, and that, to take a perfectly concrete example, a conclusion which does no more than bring a man and woman into complete possession of one another is a mere bathos which does nothing except legitimately provoke the comment, "Well, what of it?" One can hardly imagine them concerned with what used to be called, in a phrase which they have helped to make faintly ridiculous, "the right to love." Individual freedom they have inherited and assumed as a right, but they are concerned with something which their more restricted forefathers assumed— with, that is to say, the value of love itself. No inhibitions either within or without restrain them, but they are asking themselves, "What is it worth?" and they are certainly no longer feeling that it is obviously and in itself something which makes life worth the living.

To Huxley and Hemingway—I take them as the most conspicuous exemplars of a whole school—love is at times only a sort of obscene joke. The former in particular has delighted to mock sentiment with physiology, to place the emotions of the lover in comic juxtaposition with quaint biological lore, and to picture a romantic pair "quietly sweating palm to palm." But the joke is one which turns quickly bitter upon the tongue, for a great and gratifying illusion has passed away, leaving the need for it still there. His characters still feel the physiological urge, and, since they have no sense of sin in connection with it, they yield easily and continually to that urge; but they have also the human need to respect their chief preoccupation, and it is the capacity to do this that they have lost. Absorbed in the pursuit of sexual satisfaction, they never find love and they are scarcely aware that they are seeking it, but they are far from content with themselves. In a generally devaluated world they are eagerly endeavoring to get what they can in the pursuit of satisfactions which are sufficiently instinctive to retain inevitably a modicum of animal pleasure, but they cannot transmute that simple animal pleasure into anything else. They themselves not infrequently share the contempt with which their creator regards them, and nothing could be less seductive, because nothing could be less glamorous, than the description of the debaucheries born of nothing except a sense of the emptiness of life.

Now it is gratifyingly appropriate that this Huxley should be the grandson of the great Victorian exponent of life rationally conducted in the light of natural knowledge, since the predicament which he recognizes is a direct result of the application of the principles advocated by the grandfather. It is true, of course, that Thomas Henry Huxley felt too strongly the influence of Victorian taboos ever to indulge in any extended naturalistic consideration of the problems of sex, but the Ellises and the Wellses, whom we have taken as the type of those who have concerned themselves with such an effort, did little more than apply the principles which he laid down. They used analysis in an effort to clarify an illusion, and the result, which now seems as though it might have been foretold, was to destroy that illusion.

They were, to be sure, successful in the immediate objects which they proposed to themselves; they did, that is to say, succeed in freeing love, both by relaxing somewhat the ferocity with which society had punished conduct which deviated from even the mere letter of its code and by lifting from mankind the burden of that sense of guilt which had oppressed so many and not infrequently poisoned what would have been otherwise a mighty and perfect experience. But when the consequences of love were made less momentous, then love itself became less momentous too, and we have discovered that the now-lifted veil of mystery was that which made it potentially important as well as potentially terrible. Sex, we learned, was not so awesome as once we had thought; God does not care so much about it as we had formerly been led to suppose; but neither, as a result, do we. Love is becoming gradually so accessible, so unmysterious, and so free that its value is trivial.

That which the Victorians regarded as possessed of a supreme and mystical value was, as we have already pointed out, a group of related ideas and emotional aptitudes whose elements had, during a long period of time, been associated by means of connections not always logical. Analysis can dissociate them and has indeed done so, but in so doing it destroys the importance which only as a group they possessed. We know that the social consequences which once followed a surrender to love need no longer do so, and hence the nexus between the sexual act and those elements of the love complex which are predominantly social has disappeared. More important yet, we know, or rather we feel, that this act is a simple biological one which sends no reverberations through a spiritual universe, and so it no longer has any transcendental implications. With vertiginous rapidity it is being reduced to that which it was in savage or prehuman society, and threatens to become again no more than a simple physiological act with no more than a simple physiological act's importance or value.

For many generations the adolescence of the individual has repeated the miracle achieved in the first place by the human race as a whole; it has, that is to say, associated the new impulses suddenly discovered in itself with various duties to society and with all the other aspirations of which it is capable; but this miracle is one which is becoming constantly more difficult of performance. Certain individuals have always and for different reasons failed to achieve it, and they have been compelled in consequence to lead jangled lives; but more and more people find themselves victims of a disharmony which results from the fact that they cannot escape a continual preoccupation with a passion which seems to their intellect trivial, and it would not be wholly fanciful to say that this sense of disharmony, of the unworthiness of their aims, is the modern equivalent of the conviction of sin.

It is not to be supposed, I take it, that any mood so disrupted as this is destined to endure. It represents an unstable equilibrium of forces in which one or the other is bound sooner or later to yield; for if the passion of love is to be devaluated, then it must be made to play in human life a part as small as our slight estimate of its importance makes appropriate. Such was the position to which the early Church Fathers attempted to reduce it, and they were unsuccessful because the conflict which they felt between their instincts and their intellectual convictions was resolved in the religion of love; but the modern consciousness is surely destined either to evolve some equally mighty fiction or, while surrendering the erotic instinct as a source of important values, to dispose of it in some fashion involving a minimum of inconvenience and distraction. Nor is the fact that the ferocious and deliberate nastiness of some current writers suggests that of the Fathers, that, for example, Huxley has even in the midst of one of his novels quoted in the Latin from which he hardly dared translate it one of the most brutally scornful of their comments upon the flesh, merely an accident, since there is a certain similarity between the early saint and the contemporary sophisticate which is due to the fact that, however different their experiences may be, each rejects love for the same reason—each, that is to say, has refused to surround it with mystical implications, and each, looking at it as a mere biological fact, has found it ridiculous and disgusting. Certainly the nastiness of, let us say, James Joyce's *Ulysses* is the nastiness of an ascetic reviling the flesh in order that he may be free of it.

Now, if we set aside the ascetic ideal which in the past, at least, has generally proved itself radically impracticable, and if we set aside also the romantic ideal which the rationalizing tendencies of the human mind seem certain to destroy, there is only one way in which the artist—by which term is here meant whoever is distinctly human enough to have a plan for his life which he sets up in opposition to the simple plan of nature—may deal with sex, and that way is the one in which it is accepted as something ineluctable, perhaps, but nevertheless uncomplex and trivial. The man who follows it may feel no need to battle against the flesh; he may have no desire to waste his energies in a futile struggle against the inclinations of the natural man, and he may preach no stern denials; but he makes of love a game, a joke, a ribaldry even, in order that, since it no longer seems really significant, it may be reduced to a mere incident.

And if, leaving the Huxleys and the Hemingways, who are concerned with characters still in the midst of confusion, we turn to certain other novelists, poets, and critics, we shall find them at least adumbrating such a solution, as may be illustrated by the words put into the mouth of a by no means ascetic painter in one of the most powerful of contemporary novels. "The tendency of my work," he remarks, "is, as you may have noticed, that of an invariable severity. Apart from its being good or bad, its character is ascetic rather than sensuous, and divorced from immediate life. There is no slop of sex in *that*."

Such a character is merely the novelist's projection of a type which logically results from the effort to think one's way through the confusions just outlined. This painter—Tarr is his name—represents the direction in which we are moving, and he explains the growing popularity of abstract design in the plastic arts and of pure intellectualism in literature, since both represent a reaction from that diffusion of sublimated sex through all the arts which is one of the chief characteristics of romanticism. But however logical and inevitable such a tendency may be, and however preferable it is to an absorption in things which can no longer be respected, it must be remembered that it is, nevertheless, based upon a complete surrender of something which we have been accustomed to regard as one of the chief values in human life, and that it leaves a mighty blank in existence.

Whatever else love may still be,—game, puerility, or wry joke played by the senses and the imagination upon the intellect,—it no longer is the ultimate self-justifying value which once it was. We may still on occasion surrender to it, but surrender is no longer a paradoxical victory and the world is no longer well lost for love. Many other things we have come to doubt,— patriotism, self-sacrifice, respectability, honor,—but in the general wreck the wreck of love is conspicuous and typical. Rationalism having destroyed the taboos which surrounded it, and physiology having rudely investigated its phenomena upon the same level as other biological processes, it has been stripped of the mystical penumbra in whose shadow its transcendental value seemed real, though hid; and somehow, in the course of the very process of winning the right to love, love itself has been deprived of its value.

Such, in outline, is the process by which is accomplished what has here been called the death of a value. Many of us, not yet old, were born at a time when the religion of love was all but unquestioned, when it seemed to stand more firmly than even the religion of the Church, whose foundations science was already known to have slowly undermined. But if we have followed the course of modern thought we have seen it rapidly disintegrate. We have seen how works, of which Havelock Ellis's *magnum opus* is a type, claimed love as a legitimate subject for rationalistic consideration, and how, though Ellis himself believed that the superstructure of poetry would remain after its foundations had been subject to rational examination, just as Thomas Huxley believed that the superstructure of Christian morality would stand after the supernatural props had been removed from under it, the mystical values lingered as ghosts for only one generation after rationalism had attacked the mythology upon which they rested.

We have seen the rise of an atheism quite as significant in the history of the human soul as that which has regard to religion in the more conventional sense, and one whose result may be summed up by a consideration of the fact that, though the phrase "love is best" meant to our grandfathers more things than a volume could describe, it is to us so completely denuded that we can only repeat it as we repeat one of those formulæ of theology which, though once rich with meaning, are to us only words, words, words.

## III

Others who have described, though perhaps in somewhat different terms, the disintegration of the love complex have been concerned chiefly with its effect upon human society. They have stressed their fear that, for example, the progressive tendency to dissociate love from family life would involve the most thoroughgoing reconstruction of our social organization, even if it did not destroy the possibility of any stable society, and in general they have thought of modified sexual customs in terms of their effect upon the race. We, however, are here concerned with the individual and with the consequences which the process we have been describing may have for the intimate emotional life of the separate soul—with, in a word, the changes involved by the death of love in the character of what we may call the experience of living.

We will, if we must, give up the illusion of love. The time may come when it will mean to us even less than it now means to the philosophical Chinese and no more than it did to the savage; when, to state the case somewhat differently, romance will be, either as a motive in art or an aim in living, as fundamentally incomprehensible to us as it is to the American Indian, and when it will be so, not because we have not yet developed the complex system of associations upon which it depends, but because the analytical tendencies of our intelligence forbid our imagination to create the values once deemed so precious.

We may realize now that the effort to develop the possibilities of love as an adornment of life by understanding it more completely wrecks itself upon the fact that to understand any of the illusions upon which the values of life depend inevitably destroys them; but we realize that fact too late, and even if we should convince ourselves that we have paid too high a price for our rationality, that we should willingly reassume all the taboos of the Victorian if we could feel again his buoyant sense that the meaning of life had been revealed to him through love, we could no more recapture his illusions by means of an intellectual conviction than we could return to the passionate faith of the Middle Ages merely because, having read Ruskin, we should like to build a cathedral.

Nor is human life so rich in values as to justify us in surrendering any one of them complacently. At bottom, life is worth living only because certain of our conscious activities allowed themselves to be regarded as though they were possessed of some importance or significance in themselves, and even the number of such conscious activities is too strictly limited to permit us to accept without foreboding the reduction of so important a one as that of sexual union to the status of a mere triviality. Many of the life processes—and by no means the least important—are carried on without the accompaniment of any awareness whatsoever. The beating of the heart and the slow churning of the stomach, to say nothing of the infinitely complicated activities with which the glands are busy, are as little a part of that consciousness which we know of as ourselves as is the shifting of the earth upon its axis or the explosive disintegration of an atom of radium. In one sense man cannot either "know himself" or "live completely," for the simple reason that only a fragment of his total organism is connected with that part of the brain wherein resides all that he is accustomed to call his ego or self. The body keeps itself alive by processes which we neither will nor recognize, and death may be preparing itself for months before a warning finally bursts its way into that relatively small mass of cells to which our awareness and hence our emotions confine themselves. When the life of any individual rises above the dim level of the mere toiler whose existence is scarcely more than a round of duties, and reaches that distinctly human level upon which contemplation in some form or other furnishes the motive for living, it does so because he has attributed a meaningfulness to some aspect of consciousness, but the possibilities for such attribution are limited.

Eating, because it is a conscious and not an unconscious process, because the taste buds of the tongue happen to be connected by nerves with the cerebrum and not the cerebellum, can be made into one of the ceremonies by which life is elaborated and can pass as a symbol into poetry and philosophy. So, for the same reason, can the act of sexual union; but both digestion and gestation, because they are controlled without the intervention of consciousness, are destined to remain merely unadorned processes of nature. Man has wanted to live in order to love or even in order to eat, but hardly in order either to gestate or to digest. Yet it is merely an accident of our nervous organization that this is so.

Thus it is that of the infinitely complicated processes of life, in the biological sense, only a few are subject to that elaboration and poetization which make them even potentially a part of significant human experience. Just as the ears can hear only a certain limited class of the innumerable kinds of waves which roll incessantly through the air, and the eyes can see only a certain few of those vibrations in the ether which, after ranging from red to violet, pass on into invisibility, so, too, only a few of the processes of life furnish materials available to the mind. From a limited number of colors we must paint our pictures, from a limited number of sounds compose our symphonies, and from a limited number of conscious processes construct our "good life." But we are no more aware through our minds of the totality of what living involves than we are through our sense of the entire natural world. To ultra-violet light we are as blind as a man without eyes, and, similarly, most of our biological existence is as meaningless to us as the life of an insect is to it. Whatever does not happen within a few square inches upon the surface of our forebrain does not, so far as we are concerned, happen at all. It cannot be made the source of any human value, because it is a part of us which lives as the plant lives, without any knowledge of itself.

Nature, then, has imposed a certain rigid selection upon us. Grudgingly, perhaps, she has permitted us to be aware of certain of her activities, and has bid us do what we may by way of contemplating or elaborating them until they seem to become not, as to her all things are, merely the means by which life is kept going, but ends to be enjoyed or valued in themselves. Within the limits which she has set we have, moreover, made certain choices of our own. Certain of the available conscious processes have seemed to us more suitable than others for this contemplation or elaboration, and we have devoted ourselves to them, leaving the others merely upon the fringe of awareness. Thus we made mere animal combativeness into chivalry, surrounded lair-making with all the association which belongs to the idea of home, and created a sense of the presence of God out of the fears for our security; but the greatest and most elaborate of our creations was love, and the process by which it is stripped of its meaning is a process by which man is dehumanized and life is made to sink back to a level nearer that of the animal, for whom life is a phenomenon in which there is no meaning except the biological urge.

At the very least it means that a color has faded from our palette, a whole range of effects dropped out of our symphony. Intellectually we may find romantic people and romantic literature only ridiculous, intellectually we may convince ourselves that we regret the passing of love no more than the passing of the spring festival or even the disappearance of those passionate convictions which made civil war seem to the Middle Ages intrinsically worth while; but we cannot deny that life is made paler and that we are carried one step nearer to that state in which existence is seen as a vast emptiness which the imagination can no longer people with fascinating illusions.

For the more skeptical of the Victorians, love performed some of the functions of the God whom they had lost. Faced with it, many of even the most hard-headed turned, for the moment, mystical. They found themselves in the presence of something which awoke in them that sense of reverence which nothing else claimed, and something to which they felt, even in the very depths of their being, that an unquestioning loyalty was due. For them love, like God, demanded all sacrifices; but like Him, also, it rewarded the believer by investing all the phenomena of life with a meaning not yet analyzed away. We have grown used—more than they—to a Godless universe, but we are not yet accustomed to one which is loveless as well, and only when we have so become shall we realize what atheism really means.

## AMERICA'S MEDIEVAL WOMEN
### *Pearl S. Buck* (*1928*)

I AM AN American woman but I had no opportunity until a few years ago to know women in America. Living as I did in China, it is true that I saw a few American women; but that is not the same thing. One was still not able to draw many conclusions from them about American women. I gathered, however, that they felt that girls in China had a hard time of it, because there every family liked sons better than daughters, and, in the average family, did not give them the same education or treatment. In America, however, they said people welcomed sons and daughters equally and treated them the same. This, after years in a country which defines a woman's limitations very clearly, seemed nothing short of heaven—if true.

When I came to America to live therefore I was interested particularly in her women. And during these immediate past years I have come to know a good many of them—women in business, artists, housewives in city and country, women young and old. I have taken pains to know them. More than that, I have made my own place as a woman in America. And I find that what I anticipated before I came here is quite wrong. It seems to me that women are very badly treated in America. A few of them know it, more of them dimly suspect it, and most of them, though they know they ought to be glad they live in a Christian country where women are given an education, do not feel as happy in their lonely hearts as they wish they did. The reason for this unhappiness is a secret sense of failure, and this sense of failure comes from a feeling of inferiority, and the feeling of inferiority comes from a realization that actually women are not much respected in America.

I know quite well that any American man hearing this will laugh his usual tolerant laughter, though tolerant laughter is the cruelest form of contempt. He always laughs tolerantly when the subject of women is broached, for that is the attitude in which he has been bred. And immaturely, he judges the whole world of women by the only woman he knows at all—his wife. Nor does he want the sort of wife at whom he cannot laugh tolerantly. I was once amazed to see a certain American man, intelligent, learned, and cultivated, prepare to marry for his second wife a woman as silly and unfit for him as the first one had been, whom he had just divorced. I had to exclaim before it was too late, "Why do you do the same thing over again? She's merely younger and prettier than the other one—that's all. And even those differences are only temporary." To which he growled, "I do not want a damned intelligent woman in the house when I come home at night. I want my mind to rest."

What he did not see of course—though he found it out later—was that there could be no rest for him of any kind. He was irritated by a thousand stupidities and follies and beaten in the end by his own cowardice. He died a score of years too soon, exhausted not by work but by nervous worry. His two wives go hardly on, headed for a hundred, since he left them what is called "well provided for." Neither of them has ever done an honest day's work in her life, and he literally sacrificed his valuable life to keep them alive.

And yet, going home that day from his funeral and wondering how it could have been helped, I knew it could not have been helped. He was doomed to the unhappiness, or at least to the mediocre happiness, with which many if not most American men must be satisfied in their relationships with their women. For if he had been married to an intelligent superior woman he would have been yet more unhappy, since, with all his brilliance as a scientist, he belonged to that vast majority of American men who still repeat to-day the cry of traditional male pride, "I don't want *my* wife to work."

That is, he wanted a woman who would contain herself docilely within four walls. And he could not have seen that an intelligent, energetic, educated woman cannot be kept in four walls—even satin-lined, diamond-studded walls —without discovering sooner or later that they are still a prison cell. No home offers scope enough to-day for the trained energies of an intelligent modern woman. Even children are not enough. She may want them, need them and have them, love them and enjoy them, but they are not enough for her, even during the short time they preoccupy her. Nor is her husband, however dear and congenial, enough for her. He may supply all her needs for human companionship, but there is still more to life than that. There is the individual life. She must feel herself growing and becoming more and more complete as an individual, as well as a wife and mother, before she can even be a good wife and mother. I heard a smug little gray-haired woman say last week, "No, I don't know anything about politics. It takes all my time to be a good wife and mother. I haven't time to keep up with other things." Unfortunately her husband, successful doctor that he is, has time to keep up not only with his business and with being what she calls a "wonderful husband and father," but with another woman as well. But that too is one of the things she knows nothing about. . . . Yet who can blame him? He is clever and full of interest in many things, and his wife is dulled with years of living in the four walls he put round her. It is a little unfair that he so encouraged her to stay in the walls that she came to believe in them completely as her place.

But tradition is very strong in this backward country of ours. We Americans are a backward nation in everything except in the making and using of machines. And we are nowhere more backward than we are in our attitude toward our women. We still, morally, shut the door of her home on a woman. We say to her, "Your home ought to be enough for you if you are a nice woman. Your husband ought to be enough—and your children." If she says, "But they aren't enough—what shall I do?", we say, "Go and have a good time, that's a nice girl. Get yourself a new hat or something, or go to the matinée or join a bridge club. Don't worry your pretty head about what is not your business."

If she persists in being interested in things beyond her home we insist that she must be neglecting her home. If she still persists and makes a success through incredible dogged persistence we laugh at her. We even sneer at her and sometimes we treat her with unbelievable rudeness. I do not know the Secretary of Labor in our government, but I have seen her. She looks a quiet, serious, unassuming woman. I have taken pains to inquire of people who know, and it seems her home is not neglected. She has done at least as good a job in Washington as a number of men there in leading positions. But the slurs that have been cast upon her, the rudenesses of private and public talk, the injustices that have been done her merely because she is a woman in a place heretofore occupied by a man, have been amazing to a person unaccustomed to the American attitude toward women. It seems nothing short of barbarous.

And yet, vicious circle that it is, I cannot blame Americans for distrusting the ability of their women. For if the intelligent woman obeys the voice of tradition and limits herself to the traditional four walls she joins the vast ranks of the nervous, restless, average American women whose whimsies torture their families, who spoil the good name of all women because they are often flighty, unreliable, without good judgment in affairs, and given to self-pity. In short, she becomes a neurotic, if not all the time, a good deal of the time. Without knowing it or meaning it she falls too often to being a petty dictator in the home, a nag to her husband and children, and a gossip among her women friends. Too often too she takes no interest in any matters of social importance and refuses all responsibility in the community which she can avoid. She may be either a gadabout and extravagant or she may turn into a recluse and pride herself on being a "home woman." Neither of these escapes deceives the discerning. When will American men learn that they cannot expect happiness with a wife who is not her whole self? A restless unfulfilled woman is not going to be a satisfied wife or satisfactory lover. It is not that "women are like that." Anyone would be "like that" if he were put into such circumstances—that is, trained and developed for opportunity later denied.

"Plenty of men like that too nowadays," someone may murmur.

Yes, but the times have done it, and not tradition. There is a difference. And one man has as good a chance as another to win or lose, even in hard times. But no woman has a man's chance in hard times, or in any times.

## II

I am not so naïve, however, as to believe that one sex is responsible for this unfortunate plight of the American woman. I am not a feminist, but I am an individualist. I do not believe there is any important difference between men and women—certainly not as much as there may be between one woman and another or one man and another. There are plenty of women—and men, for that matter—who would be completely fulfilled in being allowed to be as lazy as possible. If someone will ensconce them in a pleasant home and pay their bills they ask no more of life. It is quite all right for these men and women to live thus so long as fools can be found who will pay so much for nothing much in return. Gigolos, male and female, are to be found in every class and in the best of homes. But when a man does not want to be a gigolo he has the freedom to go out and work and create as well as he can. But a woman has not. Even if her individual husband lets her, tradition in society is against her.

For another thing we Americans cannot seem to believe or understand is that women—some women, any woman, or as I believe, most women—are able to be good wives, ardent lovers, excellent mothers, and yet be themselves too. This seems strange, for as a nation we have fitted woman to be an individual as well as a woman by giving her a physical and mental education and a training superior to that of women in any other nation. But when she comes eagerly to life, ready to contribute her share, not only to home, but to government, sciences, and arts, we raise the old sickening cry of tradition, "This isn't your business! Woman's place is in the home—" and we shut the door in her face.

I am aware that at this point American men will be swearing and shouting, "You don't know what you're talking about! Why, we give our women more than any women on earth have!" With that I perfectly agree. American women are the most privileged in the world. They have all the privileges—far too many. They have so many privileges that a good many of them are utterly spoiled. They have privileges but they have no equality. "Nobody keeps them back," the American man declares. Ah, nobody, but everybody! For they are kept back by tradition expressed through the prejudices not only of men but of stupid, unthinking, tradition-bound women. Here is what I heard a few days ago.

A young woman wanted a new book to read and her father offered to send it to her. "What do you want?" he asked.

"Anything, only not one by a woman," she said carelessly. "I have a prejudice against books written by women."

Ignoring the rudeness, I asked, "Why?"

"Oh, I dislike women," she said. What she really meant was she despised women so much that she actually disliked women who did anything beyond the traditional jobs that the average women do. There are thousands of women who uphold medieval tradition in America more heartily than do men —just as in China it is the ignorant tradition-bound women who have clung to foot binding for themselves and their daughters. . . . No, women have many enemies among women. It goes back of course to the old jealous sense of general female inferiority. Tradition, if it binds one, should bind all, they feel.

Sometimes, I confess, I do not see how American men can endure some of their women—their imperiousness, their peevishness, their headstrongness, their utter selfishness, their smallness of mind and outlook, their lack of any sense of responsibility toward society, even to be pleasant. And their laziness —look at the motion-picture houses, the theaters, the lecture halls—crowded all day with women! The average house, even with no servant, can be no full-time job or they wouldn't be there in such hordes—they couldn't be there. But children go to school as soon as they stop being babies, and electricity cleans and washes the house and clothing, and husbands are away all day. So what is there for the restless woman to do? She goes to the show—and comes home, if she has any sense, to wonder what life is for, and to think that marriage isn't so much after all, though if she hadn't been married she would have been ashamed of herself. For tradition is there too, and it would have made her seem, if unmarried, unsuccessful as a female.

"But what are we going to do?" the harassed American man cries. "There aren't enough jobs now to go round. And women are getting into industries more and more."

This is nonsense and a masculine bugaboo, though merely getting a job is not what I mean. The truth is the number of women in industries is increasing at so slow a rate that it is shocking when one considers how long they have had an equal chance with men for education and training. In the past fifty years—that is, half a century, during which education for women has enormously increased—the percentage of women in industry and the professions has increased from fourteen per cent only to twenty-two per cent. That means millions of women have been made ready for work they either had no chance to do or never wanted to do.

As to what men are going to do with women, I do not pretend to know. But I know I have never seen in any country—and I have seen most of the countries of the world—such unsatisfactory personal relationships between men and women as are in America—no, not even in Japan, where women as a class are depressed. For the Japanese are wiser in their treatment of women than we Americans are. They keep them down from the beginning so that they never hope for or expect more than life is to give them. They are not restless or neurotic or despotic, nor are they spoiled children. They have not been trained for equality and they do not expect it. They know they are upper servants, and they fulfil their duties gracefully and ably, and are happier on the whole than women in American. To know what one can have and to do with it, being prepared for no more, is the basis of equilibrium.

III

No, what is wrong in America is this matter of educating women. Life for the American woman is still controlled by old traditions. Men think of women, if at all, in the old simple traditional ways. Then women ought to be prepared for this sort of life and shaped through childhood and girlhood for what is to come. The root of the discontent in American women is that they are too well educated. What is the use of it? They do not need college educations nor even high school educations. What they ought to have is a simple course in reading, writing, and arithmetic—and advanced courses in cosmetics, bridge, sports, how to conduct a club meeting gracefully, how to be an attractive hostess, with or without servants, and how to deal with very young children in the home. This last course, obviously, should be purely optional.

But all this higher present education is unfortunate. It has led American women into having ideas which they can never realize when they come to maturity. A college education may, for instance, persuade a girl to become interested in biology, which may lead her into wanting to become a doctor. And yet she will never have the chance to become a first-rate doctor, however gifted she is by birth. People will not allow it—not only men, but women will not allow it. They will look at her tentative little shingle and shrug their shoulders and say, "I don't feel I'd *trust* a woman doctor as I would a man." So after a while, since she has to earn something, she takes her shingle down and accepts a secondary position in a hospital or a school or goes into baby-clinic work, supplemented by magazine articles on child care—or she just marries a doctor. But inside herself she knows she still wants to *be* a doctor, only she cannot. Tradition does not allow it.

Or a college education may lead a girl into wanting to be a banker. It is natural for women to be interested in finance since they own about seventy per cent of America's money. But it is unfortunate if a woman thinks she can be a real banker. I have talked with a good many women who work in our American banking system. Not one is where she hoped to be when she began, and a fair percentage are not where they should be with their high executive ability, or where they would be if they were men. As one of the most brilliant of them said to me bitterly, "I know if I were a man I should now, at the age of fifty, and after thirty years of experience, be a bank president. But I'll never be anything but an assistant to a vice-president. I reached the top—for a woman—years ago. I'll never be allowed to go on."

"Why can't you?" I inquired, being then too innocent.

"They say no one would want to put money in a bank run by a woman," she said.

I pondered this. I had then just come from Shanghai, where one of the best modern banks was run and controlled entirely by modern Chinese women. It was a prosperous bank because most people there thought women were probably more honest than men and more practical in the handling of money. So the Chinese women bankers did very well.

A good deal is said too about the profession of teaching for women. There are a great many women teachers in America—many more in proportion to men than in other countries. Men here, it seems, allow women to teach in lower schools because they themselves do not want to teach in anything less than a college. And even the best men do not like to teach in women's colleges nor in co-educational colleges. The finest teaching in America, I am told, is done by men for men.

As for the arts, I know very well that the odds are strongly against the woman. Granted an equally good product, the man is given the favor always. Women artists in any field are not often taken seriously, however serious their work. It is true that they often achieve high popular success. But this counts against them as artists. American men critics may show respect to a foreign woman artist, feeling that perhaps the foreign women are better than their own. But they cannot believe that the fools they see in department stores, in the subways and buses, or running to the movies and lectures, or even in their own homes, can amount to anything in the arts. Indeed they cannot think of a woman at all, but only of "women." And the pathetic efforts of American women to improve their minds by reading and clubs have only heightened the ridicule and contempt in which their men hold them. To educate women, therefore, to think, so that they need the personal fulfillment of activity and participation in all parts of life is acute cruelty, for they are not allowed this fulfillment. They should be educated not to think beyond the demands of simple household affairs or beyond the small arts and graces of pleasing men who seem always to want mental rest. The present method is not only cruel; it is extremely wasteful. Good money is spent teaching women to do things for which there will be no need. Men strain themselves to furnish educations for their daughters which they would be happier without, and not only happier but better women because they would be more contented women.

It is not only wasteful but dangerous. To educate women as we do for our present state of traditionalism is to put new wine into old bottles. A good deal of ferment is going on. And if we keep this up more will come of it. No one knows the effect upon children, for instance, of so many discontented women as mothers. Amiable, ignorant, bovine women make much better mothers than neurotic college graduates. And a woman does not need to complain aloud to let her children know she is unhappy. The atmosphere about her is gray with her secret discontent and children live deprived of that essential gayety in which they thrive as in sunshine. So few American women are really gay. This must have an effect.

## IV

So, though I am impressed with the fact that American women do not, as a group, seem happy, privileged as they are, I am not surprised. I know that happiness comes to an individual only as a result of personal fulfillment through complete functioning of all the energies and capabilities with which one is born. I do not for a moment mean that all women must go out and find jobs and "do something" outside the home. That would be as silly and general a mistake as our present general clinging to tradition. I simply mean let us be realistic. Let us face the fact that as a nation we are in a medieval state of mind about the place of women in society. Let each man ask himself—he need not answer aloud—where he really wants his woman. The majority, if they are honest, must acknowledge that they would like contented adoring women who want no more than their homes. I do not quarrel with that. What is, is. All I say is, let us realize facts. Tradition rules the relation of the sexes in America. Women are not welcome outside the home except in subsidiary positions, doing, on the whole, things men do not want to do. The great injustice to women is in not recognizing this frankly and in not preparing them for it.

Of course there is the chimeralike possibility that we might change tradition. But I do not see anyone capable of changing it. Men certainly will not. They do not even want to talk about it. They do not want the woman question stirred up, having as they say, "enough on their hands already." To them, of course, women "stirred up" simply means nervous, illogical, clamoring children who must be placated in one way or another. They cannot conceive of woman as a rational being, equal to themselves and not always fundamentally connected with sex. Emotionally, as it has been truly said, many American men are adolescents—kind, delightful, charming adolescents. "He's just like a boy" seems to be considered a compliment to a man in America. It ought to be an insult. This horrible boyishness lingering in persons who should be adult is as dismaying as mental retardation. It is responsible for our childish tendencies to "jazz things up," to make "whoopee," to think of being drunk, of removing "inhibitions," of playing the clown, as the only way to have a good time, to the complete destruction of adult conversation and real wit and subtler humor. It certainly is responsible for wanting women to be nothing but wives, mothers, or leggy relaxations for tired business men. Even a pretty college girl said despairingly not long ago in my presence, "You can't get anywhere with men if you show any brains. I have to make myself a nitwit if I want dates. Oh, well, that's the way they are!" There are too many nice and rather sad American women who patiently accept even their middle-aged and old men as perennial "boys." "Men are like that," they say, at least as often as men say, "women are like that."

Nothing could show a greater misunderstanding between the sexes than this frequent fatalistic remark. Neither men nor women are like that if "that" means what they now seem to each other. It is a strange fact that in new America, as in old India or China, the real life of each sex is not with each other but away from each other. Men and women in America meet stiffly for social functions, drink together in an earnest effort to feel less inhibited, play the fool guardedly and feel queer about it afterward. Or they meet for physical sex, in the home or out. And they jog along in family life. Of the delight of exploring each other's differing but equally important personalities and points of view, of the pleasure of real mutual comprehension and appreciation and companionship, there is almost none, inside the home or out. Tradition decrees that after marriage real companionship between persons of opposite sex must cease except between husband and wife. Tradition decrees that all companionship indeed between men and women is tinged with sex. Such an idea as interest in each other as persons, aside from sex, is almost unknown. Women, talking of this among themselves, say, "Men don't want anything else." I am inclined to think they are right. The average American man demands amazingly little from his women—nothing much except to look as pretty as possible on as little money as possible, to run the home economically with as little trouble as possible to the man when he comes home tired. What educated, intelligent, clever, gifted woman is going to be satisfied with that? What average woman would be satisfied even? Ask the average man if he would change places with a woman—any woman. The idea horrifies him. Yet women are far more like him than he knows or wants to know, and modern times have done everything to make her more so.

No, our men, perennial boys, most of them, will not do anything about changing tradition. They do not know how, absorbed as they are in the game of business, abashed as they are in the presence of sex as anything except simply physical, and afraid as they are of women. They are, naturally, afraid of women or they would not cling so to tradition. They were afraid of their mothers when they were children, their imperious, discontented mothers, and that fear carries over into fear of their wives and fear of all women, in industry as well as at home. It leads to the attitude of petty deception which so many perennially boyish men maintain toward their women.

So, naturally enough, men do not want women "getting too smart." I heard a carpenter working in my home say pontifically to his assistant about to be married, "And why would you want a woman eddicated? Says I, if I want eddication I can go to the public library. A woman should know just so much as when it rains she stands on the sheltered side of the street. It's enough." And after a moment he added solemnly, "You don't want a woman what can talk smart. You want one what can keep quiet smart."

The voice of America's perennial boys, I thought—speaking out in a carpenter, but heard as clearly in the embarrassed reserves of an after-dinner circle in a drawing-room. And yet, I do not blame them. There are so many women who chatter without thought, who stop all attempts at conversation with continual commonplaces uttered with all the petty authority of ignorance. And the fetters of another tradition—that of chivalry—still hang upon American men. Foolish, haughty women, standing in crowded buses, staring at a tired man in a seat, accepting favors as their right; peevish, idle women, wasting their husbands' money; dogmatic women talking ignorantly about practical important matters—men must try to be polite to them all alike. I do not blame American men, except for not seeing that not all women are the same.

We are so clever with machines, we Americans. But we have done a silly thing with our women. We have put modern high-powered engines into old antiquated vehicles. It is no wonder the thing is not working. And there are only two courses to follow if we do want it to work. We must go back to the old simple one-horse-power engine or else we must change the body to suit the engine—one or the other. If the first, then tradition must be held to from the moment a woman is born, not, as it now is, clamped upon her when, after a free and extraordinarily equal childhood and girlhood with boys, she attempts to enter into a free and equal adult life with men and finds it denied her, to discover then that her education has had nothing to do with her life.

Or else we must be willing to let her go on as she began. This means that American men must cease being "sweet boys" and grow up emotionally as well as physically and face women as adult men. But they, poor things, have not been fitted for that either! Besides of course they are afraid of what women might do. And women, inexperienced and eager, will probably do as many foolish things as men have until they have had as much practice.

Of one thing I am sure, however. There will be no real content among American women unless they are made and kept more ignorant or unless they are given equal opportunity with men to use what they have been taught. And American men will not be really happy until their women are.

## LIFE AT HERNE HILL

### (*From* Praeterita)

#### John Ruskin (*1889*)

WHEN I was about four years old my father found himself able to buy the lease of a house on Herne Hill, a rustic eminence four miles south of the "Standard in Cornhill"; of which the leafy seclusion remains, in all essential points of character, unchanged to this day: certain Gothic splendours, lately indulged in by our wealthier neighbours, being the only serious innovations;

and these are so graciously concealed by the fine trees of their grounds, that the passing viator remains unappalled by them; and I can still walk up and down the piece of road between the Fox tavern and the Herne Hill station, imagining myself four years old.

Our house was the northernmost of a group which stand accurately on the top or dome of the hill, where the ground is for a small space level, as the snows are (I understand), on the dome of Mont Blanc; presently falling, however, in what may be, in the London clay formation, considered a precipitous slope, to our valley of Chamouni (or of Dulwich) on the east; and with a softer descent into Cold Harbor lane on the west: on the south, no less beautifully declining to the dale of the Effra (doubtless shortened from Effrena, signifying the "Unbridled" river; recently, I regret to say, bricked over for the convenience of Mr. Biffin, chemist, and others); while on the north, prolonged indeed with slight depression some half mile or so, and receiving, in the parish of Lambeth, the chivalric title of "Champion Hill," it plunges down at last to efface itself in the plains of Peckham, and the rural barbarism of Goose Green.

The group, of which our house was the quarter, consisted of two precisely similar partner-couples of houses, gardens and all to match; still the two highest blocks of buildings seen from Norwood on the crest of the ridge; so that the house itself, three-storied, with garrets above, commanded, in those comparatively smokeless days, a very notable view from its garret windows, of the Norwood hills on one side, and the winter sunrise over them; and of the valley of the Thames on the other, with Windsor telescopically clear in the distance, and Harrow, conspicuous always in fine weather to open vision against the summer sunset. It had front and back gardens in sufficient proportion to its size; the front, richly set with old evergreens, and well-grown lilac and laburnum; the back, seventy yards long by twenty wide, renowned over all the hill for its pears and apples, which had been chosen with extreme care by our predecessor (shame on me to forget the name of a man to whom I owe so much!)—and possessing also a strong old mulberry tree, a tall white-heart cherry tree, a black Kentish one, and an almost unbroken hedge, all round, of alternate gooseberry and currant bush; decked, in due season (for the ground was wholly beneficent), with magical splendour of abundant fruit: fresh green, soft amber, and rough-bristled crimson bending the spinous branches; clustered pearl and pendent ruby joyfully discoverable under the large leaves that looked like vine.

The differences of primal importance which I observed between the nature of this garden, and that of Eden, as I had imagined it, were, that, in this one, *all* the fruit was forbidden; and there were no companionable beasts: in other respect the little domain answered every purpose of paradise to me; and the climate, in that cycle of our years, allowed me to pass most of my life in it. My mother never gave me more to learn than she knew I could easily get learnt, if I set myself honestly to work, by twelve o'clock. She never allowed anything to disturb me when my task was set; if it was not said rightly by twelve o'clock, I was kept in till I knew it, and in general, even when Latin Grammar came to supplement the Psalms, I was my own master for at least an hour before half-past one dinner, and for the rest of the afternoon.

My mother, herself finding her chief personal pleasure in her flowers, was often planting or pruning beside me, at least if I chose to stay beside *her*. I never thought of doing anything behind her back which I would not have done before her face; and her presence was therefore no restraint to me; but, also, no particular pleasure, for, from having always been left so much alone, I had generally my own little affairs to see after; and, on the whole, by the time I was seven years old, was already getting too independent, mentally, even of my father and mother; and, having nobody else to be dependent upon, began to lead a very small, perky, contented, conceited, Cock-Robinson-Crusoe sort of life, in the central point which it appeared to me (as it must naturally appear to geometrical animals) that I occupied in the universe.

This was partly the fault of my father's modesty; and partly of his pride. He had so much more confidence in my mother's judgment as to such matters than in his own, that he never ventured even to help, much less to cross her, in the conduct of my education; on the other hand, in the fixed purpose of making an ecclesiastical gentleman of me, with the superfinest of manners, and access to the highest circles of fleshy and spiritual society, the visits to Croydon, where I entirely loved my aunt, and young baker-cousins, became rarer and more rare: the society of our neighbours on the hill could not be had without breaking up our regular and sweetly selfish manner of living; and on the whole, I had nothing animate to care for, in a childish way, but myself, some nests of ants, which the gardener would never leave undisturbed for me, and a sociable bird or two; though I never had the sense or perseverance to make one really tame. But that was partly because, if ever I managed to bring one to be the least trustful of me, the cats got it.

Under these circumstances, what powers of imagination I possessed, either fastened themselves on inanimate things—the sky, the leaves, and pebbles, observable within the walls of Eden,—or caught at any opportunity of flight into regions of romance, compatible with the objective realities of existence in the nineteenth century, within a mile and a quarter of Camberwell Green.

Herein my father, happily, though with no definite intention other than of pleasing me, when he found he could do so without infringing any of my mother's rules, became my guide. I was particularly fond of watching him shave; and was always allowed to come into his room in the morning (under the one in which I am now writing), to be the motionless witness of that operation. Over his dressing-table hung one of his own water-colour drawings, made under the teaching of the elder Nasmyth, I believe, at the High School of Edinburgh. It was done in the early manner of tinting, which, just about the time when my father was at the High School, Dr. Munro was teaching Turner; namely, in gray under-tints of Prussian blue and British ink, washed with warm colour afterwards on the lights. It represented Conway Castle, with its Firth, and, in the foreground, a cottage, a fisherman, and a boat at the water's edge.

When my father had finished shaving, he always told me a story about this picture. The custom began without any initial purpose of his, in consequence of my troublesome curiosity whether the fisherman lived in the cottage, and where he was going to in the boat. It being settled, for peace' sake, that he *did* live in the cottage, and was going in the boat to fish near the castle, the plot of the drama afterwards gradually thickened; and became, I believe, involved with that of the tragedy of Douglas, and of the Castle Specter, in both of which pieces my father had performed in private theatricals, before my mother, and a select Edinburgh audience, when he was a boy of sixteen, and she, at grave twenty, a model housekeeper, and very scornful and religiously suspicious of theatricals. But she was never weary of telling me, in later years, how beautiful my father looked in his Highland dress, with the high black feathers.

In the afternoons, when my father returned (always punctually) from his business, he dined, at half-past four, in the front parlour, my mother sitting beside him to hear the events of the day, and give counsel and encouragement with respect to the same;—chiefly the last, for my father was apt to be vexed if orders for sherry fell the least short of their due standard, even for a day or two. I was never present at this time, however, and only avouch what I relate by hearsay and probable conjecture; for between four and six it would have been a grave misdemeanour in me if I so much as approached the parlour door. After that, in summer time, we were all in the garden as long as the day lasted; tea under the white-heart cherry tree; or in winter and rough weather, at six o'clock in the drawing-room,—I having my cup of milk, and slice of bread-and-butter, in a little recess, with a table in front of it, wholly sacred to me; and in which I remained in the evenings as an Idol in a niche, while my mother knitted, and my father read to her,—and to me, so far as I chose to listen.

The series of the Waverley novels, then drawing towards its close, was still the chief source of delight in all households caring for literature; and I can no more recollect the time when I did not know them than when I did not know the Bible; but I have still a vivid remembrance of my father's intense expression of sorrow mixed with scorn, as he threw down *Count Robert of Paris*, after reading three or four pages; and knew that the life of Scott was ended: the scorn being a very complex and bitter feeling in him,—partly, indeed, of the book itself, but chiefly of the wretches who were tormenting and selling the wrecked intellect, and not a little, deep down, of the subtle dishonesty which had essentially caused the ruin. My father never could forgive Scott his concealment of the Ballantyne partnership.

Such being the salutary pleasures of Herne Hill, I have next with deeper gratitude to chronicle what I owe to my mother for the resolutely consistent lessons which so exercised me in the Scriptures as to make every word of them familiar to my ear in habitual music,—yet in that familiarity reverenced, as transcending all thought, and ordaining all conduct.

This she effected, not by her own sayings or personal authority; but simply by compelling me to read the book thoroughly, for myself. As soon as I was able to read with fluency, she began a course of Bible work with me, which never ceased till I went to Oxford. She read alternate verses with me, watching, at first, every intonation of my voice, and correcting the false ones, till she made me understand the verse, if within my reach, rightly, and energetically. It might be beyond me altogether; that she did not care about; but she made sure that as soon as I got hold of it at all, I should get hold of it by the right end.

In this way she began with the first verse of Genesis, and went straight through, to the last verse of the Apocalypse; hard names, numbers, Levitical law, and all; and began again at Genesis the next day. If a name was hard, the better the exercise in pronunciation,—if the chapter was tiresome, the better lesson in patience,—if loathsome, the better lesson in faith that there was some use in its being so outspoken. After our chapters (from two to three a day, according to their length, the first thing after breakfast, and no interruption from servants allowed,—none from visitors, who either joined in the reading or had to stay upstairs,—and none from any visitings or excursions, except real travelling), I had to learn a few verses by heart, or repeat, to make sure I had not lost, something of what was already known; and, with the chapters thus gradually possessed from the first word to the last, I had to learn the whole body of the fine old Scottish paraphrases, which are good, melodious, and forceful verse; and to which, together with the Bible itself, I owe the first cultivation of my ear in sound.

It is strange that of all the pieces of the Bible which my mother thus taught me, that which cost me most to learn, and which was, to my child's mind, chiefly repulsive—the 119th Psalm—has now become of all the most precious to me, in its overflowing and glorious passion of love for the Law of God, in opposition to the abuse of it by modern preachers of what they imagine to be His gospel.

But it is only by deliberate effort that I recall the long morning hours of toil, as regular as sunrise,—toil on both sides equal—by which, year after year, my mother forced me to learn these paraphrases, and chapters (the eighth of 1st Kings being one—try it, good reader, in a leisure hour!), allowing not so much as a syllable to be missed or misplaced; while every sentence was required to be said over and over again till she was satisfied with the accent of it. I recollect a struggle between us of about three weeks, concerning the accent of the "of" in the lines

"Shall any following spring revive
The ashes of the urn?"—

I insisting, partly in childish obstinacy, and partly in true instinct for rhythm (being wholly careless on the subject both of urns and their contents), on reciting it with an accented *of*. It was not, I say, till after three weeks' labor, that my mother got the accent lightened on the "of" and laid on the "ashes," to her mind. But had it taken three years she would have done it, having once undertaken to do it. And, assuredly, had she not done it,—well, there's no knowing what would have happened; but I'm very thankful she *did*.

I have just opened my oldest (in use) Bible—a small, closely, and very neatly printed volume it is, printed in Edinburgh by Sir D. Hunter Blair and J. Bruce, Printers to the King's Most Excellent Majesty, in 1816. Yellow, now, with age, and flexible, but not unclean, with much use, except that the lower corners of the pages at 8th and 1st Kings, and 32d Deuteronomy, are worn somewhat thin and dark, the learning of these two chapters having cost me much pains. My mother's list of the chapters with which, thus learned, she established my soul in life, has just fallen out of it. I will take what indulgence the incurious reader can give me, for printing the list thus accidentally occurrent:

| Exodus, | chapters | 15th and 20th. |
|---|---|---|
| 2 Samuel, | " | 1st, from 17th verse to end. |
| 1 Kings, | " | 8th. |
| Psalms, | " | 23d, 32d, 90th, 91st, 103rd, 112th, 119th, 139th. |
| Proverbs, | " | 2d, 3rd, 8th, 12th. |
| Isaiah, | " | 58th. |
| Matthew, | " | 5th, 6th, 7th. |
| Acts, | " | 26th. |
| 1 Corinthians | " | 13th, 15th. |
| James, | " | 4th. |
| Revelation, | " | 5th, 6th. |

And, truly, though I have picked up the elements of a little further knowledge—in mathematics, meteorology, and the like, in after-life,—and owe not a little to the teaching of many people, this maternal installation of my mind in that property of chapters, I count very confidently the most precious, and, on the whole, the one *essential* part of all my education.

And it is perhaps already time to mark what advantage and mischief, by the chances of life up to seven years old, had been irrevocably determined for me.

I will first count my blessings (as a not unwise friend once recommended me to do, continually; whereas I have a bad trick of always numbering the thorns in my fingers and not the bones in them).

And for best and truest beginning of all blessings, I had been taught the perfect meaning of Peace, in thought, act, and word.

I never had heard my father's or mother's voice once raised in any question with each other; nor seen an angry, or even slightly hurt or offended, glance in the eyes of either. I had never heard a servant scolded; nor even suddenly, passionately, or in any severe manner, blamed. I had never seen a moment's trouble or disorder in any household matter; nor anything whatever either done in a hurry, or undone in due time. I had no conception of such a feeling as anxiety; my father's occasional vexation in the afternoons, when he had only got an order for twelve butts after expecting one for fifteen, as I have just stated, was never manifested to *me;* and itself related only to the question whether his name would be a step higher or lower in the year's list of sherry exporters; for he never spent more than half his income, and therefore found himself little incommoded by occasional variations in the total of it. I had never done any wrong that I knew of—beyond occasionally delaying the commitment to heart of some improving sentence, that I might watch a wasp on the window pane, or a bird in the cherry tree; and I had never seen any grief.

Next to this quite priceless gift of Peace, I had received the perfect understanding of the natures of Obedience and Faith. I obeyed word, or lifted finger, of father or mother, simply as a ship her helm; not only without idea of resistance, but receiving the direction as a part of my own life and force, a helpful law, as necessary to me in every moral action as the law of gravity in leaping. And my practice in Faith was soon complete: nothing ever threatened me that was not inflicted, and nothing ever told me that was not true.

Peace, obedience, faith; these three for chief good; next to these, the habit of fixed attention with both eyes and mind—on which I will not further enlarge at this moment, this being the main practical faculty of my life, causing Mazzini to say to me, in conversation authentically reported, a year or two before his death, that I had "the most analytic mind in Europe." An opinion in which, so far as I am acquainted with Europe, I am myself entirely disposed to concur.

Lastly, an extreme perfection in palate and all other bodily senses, given by the utter prohibition of cake, wine, comfits, or, except in carefulest restriction, fruit; and by fine preparation of what food was given me. Such I esteem the main blessings of my childhood;—next, let me count the equally dominant calamities.

First, that I had nothing to love.

My parents were—in a sort—visible powers of nature to me, no more loved than the sun and the moon: only I should have been annoyed and puzzled if either of them had gone out; (how much, now, when both are darkened!)—still less did I love God; not that I had any quarrel with Him, or fear of Him; but simply found what people told me was His service, disagreeable; and what people told me was His book, not entertaining. I had no companions to quarrel with, neither; nobody to assist, and nobody to thank. Not a servant was ever allowed to do anything for me, but what it was their duty to do; and why should I have been grateful to the cook for cooking, or the gardener for gardening,—when the one dared not give me a baked potato without asking leave, and the other would not let my ants' nests alone, because they made the walks untidy? The evil consequence of all this was not, however, what might perhaps have been expected, that I grew up selfish or unaffectionate; but that, when affection did come, it came with violence utterly rampant and unmanageable, at least by me, who never before had anything to manage.

For (second of chief calamities) I had nothing to endure. Danger or pain of any kind I knew not: my strength was never exercised, my patience never tried, and my courage never fortified. Not that I was ever afraid of anything, —either ghosts, thunder, or beasts; and one of the nearest approaches of insubordination which I was ever tempted into as a child, was in passionate effort to get leave to play with the lion's cubs in Wombwell's menagerie.

Thirdly, I was taught no precision nor etiquette of manners; it was enough if, in the little society we saw, I remained unobtrusive, and replied to a question without shyness: but the shyness came later, and increased as I grew conscious of the rudeness arising from the want of social discipline, and found it impossible to acquire, in advanced life, dexterity in any bodily exercise, skill in any pleasing accomplishment, or ease and tact in ordinary behaviour.

Lastly, and chief of evils. My judgment of right and wrong, and powers of independent action, were left entirely undeveloped; because the bridle and blinkers were never taken off me. Children should have their times of being off duty, like soldiers; and when once the obedience, if required, is certain, the little creature should be very early put for periods of practice in complete command of itself; set on the barebacked horse of its own will, and left to break it by its own strength. But the ceaseless authority exercised over my youth left me, when cast out at last into the world, unable for some time to do more than drift with its vortices.

My present verdict, therefore, on the general tenor of my education at that time, must be, that it was at once too formal and too luxurious; leaving my character, at the most important moment for its construction, cramped indeed, but not disciplined; and only by protection innocent, instead of by practice virtuous.

## THE FLY

### *Katharine Mansfield* (*1922*)

"Y'ARE very snug in here," piped old Mr. Woodifield, and he peered out of the great, green leather armchair by his friend the boss's desk as a baby peers out of its pram. His talk was over; it was time for him to be off. But he did not want to go. Since he had retired, since his . . . stroke, the wife and the girls kept him boxed up in the house every day of the week except Tuesday. On Tuesday he was dressed up and brushed and allowed to cut back to the City for the day. Though what he did there the wife and girls couldn't imagine. Made a nuisance of himself to his friends, they supposed. . . . Well, perhaps so. All the same, we cling to our last pleasures as the tree clings to its last leaves. So there sat old Woodifield, smoking a cigar and staring almost greedily at the boss, who rolled in his office chair, stout, rosy, five years older than he, and still going strong, still at the helm. It did one good to see him.

Wistfully, admiringly, the old voice added, "It's snug in here, upon my word!"

"Yes, it's comfortable enough," agreed the boss, and he flipped the *Financial Times* with a paper-knife. As a matter of fact he was proud of his room; he liked to have it admired, especially by old Woodifield. It gave him a feeling of deep, solid satisfaction to be planted there in the midst of it in full view of that frail old figure in the muffler.

"I've had it done up lately," he explained, as he had explained for the past—how many?—weeks. "New carpet," and he pointed to the bright red carpet with a pattern of large white rings. "New furniture," and he nodded towards the massive bookcase and the table with legs like twisted treacle. "Electric heating!" He waved almost exultantly towards the five transparent, pearly sausages glowing so softly in the tilted copper pan.

But he did not draw old Woodifield's attention to the photograph over the table of a grave-looking boy in uniform standing in one of those spectral photographers' parks with photographers' storm-clouds behind him. It was not new. It had been there for over six years.

"There was something I wanted to tell you," said old Woodifield, and his eyes grew dim remembering. "Now what was it? I had it in my mind when I started out this morning." His hands began to tremble, and patches of red showed above his beard.

Poor old chap, he's on his last pins, thought the boss. And, feeling kindly, he winked at the old man, and said jokingly, "I tell you what. I've got a little drop of something here that'll do you good before you go out into the cold again. It's beautiful stuff. It wouldn't hurt a child." He took a key off his watch-chain, unlocked a cupboard below his desk, and drew forth a dark, squat bottle. "That's the medicine," said he. "And the man from whom I got it told me on the strict Q. T. it came from the cellars at Windsor Cassel."

Old Woodifield's mouth fell open at the sight. He couldn't have looked more surprised if the boss had produced a rabbit.

"It's whisky, ain't it?" he piped, feebly.

The boss turned the bottle and lovingly showed him the label. Whisky it was.

"D'you know," said he, peering up at the boss wonderingly, "they won't let me touch it at home." And he looked as though he was going to cry.

"Ah, that's where we know a bit more than the ladies," cried the boss, swooping across for two tumblers that stood on the table with the water-bottle, and pouring a generous finger into each. "Drink it down. It'll do you good. And don't put any water with it. It's sacrilege to tamper with stuff like this. Ah!" He tossed off his, pulled out his handkerchief, hastily wiped his moustaches, and cocked an eye at old Woodifield, who was rolling his in his chaps.

The old man swallowed, was silent a moment, and then said faintly, "It's nutty!"

But it warmed him; it crept into his chill old brain—he remembered.

"That was it," he said, heaving himself out of his chair. "I thought you'd like to know. The girls were in Belgium last week having a look at poor Reggie's grave, and they happened to come across your boy's. They're quite near each other, it seems."

Old Woodifield paused, but the boss made no reply. Only a quiver in his eyelids showed that he heard.

"The girls were delighted with the way the place is kept," piped the old voice. "Beautifully looked after. Couldn't be better if they were at home. You've not been across, have yer?"

"No, no!" For various reasons the boss had not been across.

"There's miles of it," quavered old Woodifield, "and it's as neat as a garden. Flowers growing on all the graves. Nice broad paths." It was plain from his voice how much he liked a nice broad path.

The pause came again. Then the old man brightened wonderfully.

"D'you know what the hotel made the girls pay for a pot of jam?" he piped. "Ten francs! Robbery, I call it. It was a little pot, so Gertrude says, no bigger than a half-crown. And she hadn't taken more than a spoonful when they charged her ten francs. Gertrude brought the pot away with her to teach 'em a lesson. Quite right, too; it's trading on our feelings. They think because we're over there having a look around we're ready to pay anything. That's what it is." And he turned towards the door.

"Quite right, quite right!" cried the boss, though what was quite right he hadn't the least idea. He came round by his desk, followed the shuffling footsteps to the door, and saw the old fellow out. Woodifield was gone.

For a long moment the boss stayed, staring at nothing, while the grey-haired office messenger, watching him, dodged in and out of his cubby-hole like a dog that expects to be taken for a run. Then: "I'll see nobody for half an hour, Macey," said the boss. "Understand? Nobody at all."

"Very good, sir."

The door shut, the firm heavy steps recrossed the bright carpet, the fat body plumped down in the spring chair, and leaning forward, the boss covered his face with his hands. He wanted, he intended, he had arranged to weep. . . .

It had been a terrible shock to him when old Woodifield sprang that remark upon him about the boy's grave. It was exactly as though the earth had opened and he had seen the boy lying there with Woodifield's girls staring down at him. For it was strange. Although over six years had passed away, the boss never thought of the boy except as lying unchanged, unblemished in his uniform, asleep for ever. "My son!" groaned the boss. But no tears came yet. In the past, in the first months and even years after the boy's death, he had only to say those words to be overcome by such grief that nothing short of a violent fit of weeping could relieve him. Time, he had declared then, he had told everybody, could make no difference. Other men perhaps might recover, might live their loss down, but not he. How was it possible? His boy was an only son. Ever since his birth the boss had worked at building up this business for him; it had no other meaning if it was not for the boy. Life itself had come to have no other meaning. How on earth could he have slaved, denied himself, kept going all those years without the promise for ever before him of the boy's stepping into his shoes and carrying on where he left off?

And that promise had been so near being fulfilled. The boy had been in the office learning the ropes for a year before the war. Every morning they had started off together; they had come back by the same train. And what congratulations he had received as the boy's father! No wonder; he had taken to it marvellously. As to his popularity with the staff, every man jack of them down to old Macey couldn't make enough of the boy. And he wasn't in the least spoilt. No, he was just his bright, natural self, with the right word for everybody, with that boyish look and his habit of saying, "Simply splendid!"

But all that was over and done with as though it never had been. The day had come when Macey had handed him the telegram that brought the whole place crashing about his head. "Deeply regret to inform you . . ." And he had left the office a broken man with his life in ruins.

Six years ago, six years . . . How quickly time passed! It might have happened yesterday. The boss took his hands from his face; he was puzzled. Something seemed to be wrong with him. He wasn't feeling as he wanted to feel. He decided to get up and have a look at the boy's photograph. But it wasn't a favorite photograph of his; the expression was unnatural. It was cold, even stern-looking. The boy had never looked like that.

At that moment the boss noticed that a fly had fallen into his broad inkpot, and was trying feebly but desperately to clamber out again. Help! help! said those struggling legs. But the sides of the inkpot were wet and slippery; it fell back again and began to swim. The boss took up a pen, picked the fly out of the ink, and shook it on to a piece of blotting-paper. For a fraction of a second it lay still on the dark patch that oozed round it. Then the front legs waved, took hold, and, pulling its small sodden body up it began the immense task of cleaning the ink from its wings. Over and under, over and under, went a leg along a wing, as the stone goes over and under the scythe. Then there was a pause, while the fly, seeming to stand on the tip of its toes, tried to expand first one wing and then the other. It succeeded at last, and sitting down, it began, like a minute cat, to clean its face. Now one could imagine that the little front legs rubbed against each other lightly, joyfully. The horrible danger was over; it had escaped; it was ready for life again.

But just then the boss had an idea. He plunged his pen back into the ink, leaned his thick wrist on the blotting paper, and as the fly tried its wings down came a great heavy blot. What would it make of that? What indeed! The little beggar seemed absolutely cowed, stunned, and afraid to move because of what would happen next. But then, as if painfully, it dragged itself forward. The front legs waved, caught hold, and, more slowly this time, the task began from the beginning.

He's a plucky little devil, thought the boss, and he felt a real admiration for the fly's courage. That was the way to tackle things; that was the right spirit. Never say die; it was only a question of . . . But the fly had again finished its laborious task, and the boss had just time to refill his pen, to shake fair and square on the new-cleaned body yet another dark drop. What about it this time? A painful moment of suspense followed. But behold, the front legs were again waving; the boss felt a rush of relief. He leaned over the fly and said to it tenderly. "You artful little b . . ." And he actually had the brilliant notion of breathing on it to help the drying process. All the same, there was something timid and weak about its efforts now, and the boss decided that this time should be the last, as he dipped the pen into the inkpot.

It was. The last blot fell on the soaked blotting-paper, and the draggled fly lay in it and did not stir. The black legs were stuck to the body; the front legs were not to be seen.

"Come on," said the boss. "Look sharp!" And he stirred it with his pen— in vain. Nothing happened or was likely to happen. The fly was dead.

The boss lifted the corpse on the end of the paper-knife and flung it into the waste-paper basket. But such a grinding feeling of wretchedness seized him that he felt positively frightened. He started forward and pressed the bell for Macey.

"Bring me some fresh blotting-paper," he said, sternly, "and look sharp about it." And while the old dog padded away he fell to wondering what it was he had been thinking about before. What was it? It was . . . He took out his handkerchief and passed it inside his collar. For the life of him he could not remember.

# A FATHER

## *Björnstjerne Björnson*   (*1881*)

THE MAN whose story is here to be told was the wealthiest and most influential person in his parish; his name was Thord Överaas. He appeared in the priest's study one day, tall and earnest.

"I have gotten a son," said he, "and I wish to present him for baptism."

"What shall his name be?"

"Finn—after my father."

"And the sponsors?"

They were mentioned and proved to be the best men and women of Thord's relations in the parish.

"Is there anything else?" inquired the priest, and looked up.

The peasant hesitated a little.

"I should like very much to have him baptized by himself," said he, finally.

"That is to say on a week-day?"

"Next Saturday, at twelve o'clock noon."

"Is there anything else?" inquired the priest.

"There is nothing else," and the peasant twirled his cap as though he were about to go.

Then the priest rose. "There is yet this, however," said he, and walking toward Thord, he took him by the hand and looked gravely into his eyes: "God grant that the child may become a blessing to you!"

One day sixteen years later, Thord stood once more in the priest's study.

"Really, you carry your age astonishingly well, Thord," said the priest; for he saw no change whatever in the man.

"That is because I have no troubles," replied Thord.

To this the priest said nothing, but after a while he asked: "What is your pleasure this evening?"

"I have come this evening about that son of mine who is to be confirmed to-morrow."

"He is a bright boy."

"I did not wish to pay the priest until I heard what number the boy would have when he takes his place in church to-morrow."

"He will stand number one."

"So I have heard; and here are ten dollars for the priest."

"Is there anything else I can do for you?" inquired the priest, fixing his eyes on Thord.

"There is nothing else."

Thord went out.

Eight years more rolled by, and then one day a noise was heard outside the priest's study, for many men were approaching, and at their head was Thord, who entered first.

The priest looked up and recognized him.

"You come well attended this evening, Thord," said he.

"I am here to request that the banns may be published for my son; he is about to marry Karen Storliden, daughter of Gudmund, who stands here beside me."

"Why, that is the richest girl in the parish."

"So they say," replied the peasant, stroking back his hair with one hand.

The priest sat a while as if in deep thought, then entered the names in his book, without making any comments, and the men wrote their signatures underneath. Thord laid three dollars on the table.

"One is all I am to have," said the priest.

"I know that very well; but he is my only child; I want to do it handsomely."

The priest took the money.

"This is now the third time, Thord, that you have come here on your son's account."

"But now I am through with him," said Thord, and folding up his pocketbook he said farewell and walked away.

The men slowly followed him.

A fortnight later, the father and son were rowing across the lake, one calm, still day, to Storliden to make arrangements for the wedding.

"This thwart is not secure," said the son, and stood up to straighten the seat on which he was sitting.

At the same moment the board he was standing on slipped from under him; he threw out his arms, uttered a shriek, and fell overboard.

"Take hold of the oar!" shouted the father, springing to his feet and holding out the oar.

But when the son had made a couple of efforts he grew stiff.

"Wait a moment!" cried the father, and began to row toward his son. Then the son rolled over on his back, gave his father one long look, and sank.

Thord could scarcely believe it; he held the boat still, and stared at the spot where his son had gone down, as though he must surely come to the surface again. There rose some bubbles, then some more, and finally one large one that burst; and the lake lay there as smooth and bright as a mirror again.

For three days and three nights people saw the father rowing round and round the spot, without taking either food or sleep; he was dragging the lake for the body of his son. And toward morning of the third day he found it, and carried it in his arms up over the hills to his farm.

It might have been about a year from that day, when the priest, late one autumn evening, heard some one in the passage outside the door, carefully trying to find the latch. The priest opened the door, and in walked a tall, thin man, with bowed form and white hair. The priest looked long at him before he recognized him. It was Thord.

"Are you out walking so late?" said the priest, and stood still in front of him.

"Ah, yes! it is late," said Thord, and took a seat.

The priest sat down also, as though waiting. A long, long silence followed. At last Thord said:

"I have something with me that I should like to give to the poor; I want it to be invested as a legacy in my son's name."

He rose, laid some money on the table, and sat down again. The priest counted it.

"It is a great deal of money," said he.

"It is half the price of my farm. I sold it to-day."

The priest sat long in silence. At last he said, but gently:

"What do you propose to do now, Thord?"

"Something better."

They sat there for a while, Thord with downcast eyes, the priest with his eyes fixed on Thord. Presently the priest said slowly and softly:

"I think your son has at last brought you a true blessing."

"Yes, I think so myself," said Thord, looking up, while two big tears coursed slowly down his cheeks.

# BOY IN THE SUMMER SUN
## *Mark Schorer* (*1937*)

UNALLOYED, summer had lingered miraculously into late September without a suggestion that autumn was at hand. Leaves and grass were green still, smoke had not yet come into the air, and the lake was calm, almost sapphire blue. Mid-mornings were hot, like mornings in July. So they walked where the woods were thickest, where the air was always slightly damp and the cool of night never quite gone. They did not speak much but went silently along the path, almost shoulder to shoulder, their hands touching, or their arms, as they moved. Now and then the girl spoke, quietly, briefly pointed out a bird, a flower, once a green snake gliding through the grass, and the boy answered with a nod or a monosyllable, his face touched with abstraction and a slight worry. After they came to a place in the wood where they stretched out now with their arms about each other lightly as if the place and this gesture were habitual, they did not speak at all until at last the girl, Rachel, asked suddenly, "Why are you so quiet? Is it Max? Are you angry because he's coming, Will?"

The boy started and looked into her face. "Angry? No, I'm not angry . . . I was just thinking about that lousy job. When I'm out here it's hard to believe that a job like that can be waiting for me when I get back. It's foul."

The girl looked away into the depth of the wood. "Is it, Will?" she asked. "Or is it just that four years of school pretty well spoiled us for anything else? That we never learn there that for most people life finally comes down to work?"

"Maybe that's it."

"Or is it foul, Will? Is it worse than most jobs in the city, in summer?"

"Maybe not. But it's still foul."

They were quiet again, and it seemed a long time later, to him, when Rachel said, "Anyway, I'm glad it isn't Max."

His arms tightened around her shoulders. Then he sat up, his eyes narrowed in the shade, and he asked, "Why should it be?"

She said, "It shouldn't."

He lay down beside her again. He stared up into the lacework of green leaves arched above them, and at the rare patches of blue sky that the leaves did not cover. Why should it be Max? Or why should she think it might be?

He had been awakened that morning by the ringing telephone, and lay sleepily in bed listening to Rachel's voice talking to someone in a way that did disturb him vaguely then, although now it seemed only mildly irritating that this week end should be intruded upon. "But darling!" her voice had cried over the telephone. "What are you doing here? Come over at once! Mind? Of course not! We'll love it! In two hours? Good!"

When he came to breakfast, she smiled brightly and cried, "Guess who's coming, Will! Max Garey! He got bored and started out early this morning, and just now called from the village. Isn't it grand? Mother's so fond of him —she'll take care of him."

"Does your mother know him? I didn't know she did."

"Oh yes, that last week at school, when she came to help me pack, you know . . ."

"No, I didn't," he said. And now he wondered why she had not told him.

Then Mrs. Harley came out on the porch. "Good morning, Will," she said brightly as she patted her white hair. "Isn't it *nice* that Mr. Garey can come! I'm so fond of Mr. Garey!"

"Yes, isn't it?" Will said into his coffee, and looked across the table into Rachel's eyes, which were shining with pleasure and were quite heedless of the question in his.

"Did you have any work with Mr. Garey, Will? Rachel thought him such a splendid teacher."

"No, I didn't," Will said. "His classes were always filled with girls."

Rachel looked at him quickly. "Now you're being unfair, Will. He's not one of those. Everybody thinks he's a good teacher."

"I'm sorry," he said, and felt suddenly sad, lonely in the bright morning with Rachel only across the table from him.

He felt that loneliness again now. "Maybe it is more than the job," he said. "Everything's different since June. I don't know why."

"What do you mean, Will?"

"Just that feeling that everything's breaking up, smashing."

They were quiet then until Rachel said, "I know. I'm different, too. Something's changed in me. There's something sad, some ache. . . ."

Will knew that something had changed in her. She was older than she had been in June. There was something about her now that bewildered him, the feeling that she lived without him, an aloofness, a self-sufficiency which was new. She was like a woman, sometimes, putting up with a boy. He had felt it almost every week end, and this and the more general sadness of the summer had darkened otherwise golden hours. And yet there was that in her kisses still, in her sweet arms around him, in her yielding body that belied his feeling. And, with him, there still came from her throat a little moan of pain and passion which he knew no one else had ever heard. And yet, now in the deep cool wood as she lay in his arms, he felt that she had forgotten him beside her.

She spoke at last as with an effort, as if recalling herself from a dream. "You know, Will, after you left school, in that week I stayed on, I saw Max rather often. Then mother met him. She invited him to come up. He was here earlier in the summer. Didn't I tell you?"

"No," he said, his throat contracting. "You must have forgotten."

His sadness knotted in his throat suddenly, intensely, and he remembered then very clearly, almost as if she were saying it again now, something she had said before he left her in June. "Sometimes I wonder if this can last, Will, if it mustn't end. It's been almost too lovely, too complete. We've *realized* each other. We know each other as I think people almost never do. Now it begins to seem a little unreal, perhaps because it's been too lovely, part of this unreal life we're leaving. I wonder if that sometimes happens, Will."

Then he had laughed; but now, as he remembered, his arms tightened around her suddenly, as if from fright, and he leaned down and kissed her. Her lips were quiet, without response. He opened his eyes then to look at her and saw that her eyes were fixed on some remote object in the arch of trees or beyond, some dream, something far from him. He stood up and moved away. "Let's go back," he said, and without waiting for her started quickly up the path, toward the house.

All the afternoon they lay on the raft, Rachel between them. Max talked, his voice reflective and lazy, mixing with the sun of that afternoon and the endless laziness in the sounds that insects made in the woods and in the long grass along the shore, his voice spinning itself out, pausing now and then to listen to itself, and going on again, with Rachel lying quiet between them, her eyes closed and the oil gleaming on her brown skin. Will's head was turned toward her, his eyes wandering back and forth from her parted lips and her gleaming lashes to the swell of her breasts under her white swimming suit, to her long browned legs and her crossed feet at the end of the raft.

All the time Max's voice went on, the lazy, professor's voice. Will could tell as he heard it that it was a voice that always talked and that always had listeners, and yet, now, it did not irritate him. He was almost content to lie in the sun with the sensation of burning on his skin, and a soft warm glow of skin absorbing bright sun enough in the afternoon to allay for the moment the morning's inarticulate fears, even though it was Max who was lying stretched out beyond Rachel, who was talking, pausing, talking, sometimes falling silent and no word coming from Rachel or himself, and then starting up again, the voice spinning itself out softly in the afternoon sun, with all the laziness of the afternoon in his slow words.

" . . . and so in Donne the central factor is death . . . death, of course . . . he, more than any of the poets, built what he wrote upon what may be called a metaphysic of death . . . death as the great leveller on the one hand, the great destroyer of everything, beauty, love . . . and death as the figure at the gate of Heaven . . . these two, this one . . . the central factor, always present . . ."

His voice was slow, modulated, a little affected, quite soft, and in it, Will knew as he looked at Rachel's face, there was some magic, a magic of wisdom and experience that enthralled her.

Rachel's voice began, slow and soft as if infected by Max's voice, as warm as the sun, and speaking lines that Max doubtless first spoke to her, perhaps— only perhaps—in the classroom:

> "*When I dyed last, and, Deare, I dye*
> *As often as from thee I goe,*
> *Though it be but an houre agoe,*

> *And Lovers houres be full eternity,*
> *I can remember yet, that I*
> *Something did say, and something did bestow . . ."*

Max laughed. "But darling," he said, "that's still another kind of death, not so serious."

Rachel said nothing. And the sun wove around them its bright and golden web, and the whole world then as they lay there had slipped away and left the three of them stranded together in an unreality of sunlight on burning skin and closed eyelids, and nothing more. And Will, too, felt out of the world of fact, was empty of feeling, as if pure sensation had replaced it. And only slowly did a faint jangling come into his mind, the jangle of Max's word *darling*, like something shaken in a metal box, some harsh sound, or a feeling perhaps, shaking him abruptly from the web. He stirred. He turned. And in turning the web was broken, and he was free of it again, his hand plunged in the cold blue water of the lake and left to dangle there, his eyes turned from Rachel and Max for the moment but seeing nothing in the indeterminable depths of the blue water that gently lapped his hand.

"Not nearly so serious," Max said. "Only a metaphor, a way of speaking . . ."

Will turned toward them again, and now he saw in Rachel's face how serious it was, for she looked suddenly ill for all the glow of her skin, her face turned away from him and her lips fallen apart, and every line in her face and body taut suddenly, yearning, aching suddenly with sharp longing, sharp pain, she quite sick for love. Will's hands closed at his sides and opened again, turned empty to the sun.

"Poetry is full of such conventions, formalized short cuts to express familiar sentiments," Max was saying. "In Donne, of course, there's enough fire, usually, to vitalize them, but in others . . . mere metaphors . . ."

Something in Will's mind snapped, then seemed to shout, *Who cares? For God's sake, who cares?* He was enraged beyond endurance by the man's pompous classroom manner, his easy presence, his way of excluding Will, as if he were alone with Rachel and no one else existed. He hated him, and the very presence of Rachel there made his throat ache with something like the pressure of tears coming. The sun had lost its spell. The buzz of insects on the shore seemed for a moment unbearably loud, and the sun no longer warm, but hot, searing, parching his throat and mouth, blinding him. For now he hated Max, and he knew as he remembered Rachel's voice speaking those lines, that she was lost to him, that he had nothing more for her, that Max had all. And there Max lay, as if he belonged there, had every right to be there, talking and priding himself in his talk, delighting to hear his own words, lecturing there as though he were in the classroom and Rachel in the front row looking up at him with wide eyes, lecturing as though Rachel and he were alone in the room, and he, Will, did not exist.

Will's eyes clouded in anger as he stared down into the water disturbed by his hand. He tried not to hear what their low voices said, and only when they were silent did he turn suddenly on the raft again to see how their bodies had moved together, so that their legs touched, and Max's hand lay quite near Rachel's hair. He stood up abruptly, stirring the raft in the water, and then dived deep, swam quickly out and away from them, his arms beating the water in his anger, in a frantic effort to forget the hurt which came from Rachel's willing reception of the man's intolerable arrogance.

He struck out into the lake. The water was cold on his skin, and as he swam, his anger cooled. But when his anger was gone, he felt sad and futile again, swam more slowly, felt helpless and wounded, felt almost weak in the water, so that he grew angry with himself instead and wished that he could hold that other anger. When he turned back and swam slowly toward the shore, only the hurt remained, and he did not go to the raft. There Max's words would still be spinning themselves out in the sunlight, catching Rachel's mind in their spell, catching her heart firmly and her whole mind and life, and holding them there, as if the words were really magic.

He walked up the beach and stretched out on the sand. He lay on his back and looked up into the blue sky, and as he lay there he felt suddenly that this was the last time in his life that he would be doing quite this. All summer he had been coming from the sweltering, grimy city, and in seeing Rachel in the country, in living in her mother's friendly house, in swimming and dancing and drinking and finding cool spots in the woods where the moss was thick and only the trees and birds made sound—in all of this it had seemed that nothing had changed or was ending. And this in spite of the fact that when they parted in June, when they walked for the last time along familiar walks between familiar buildings, they had vaguely felt that an end had come to a period, that a new life was waiting for both of them, and that (Rachel felt) somehow they were therefore ending for one another. But then Max was nothing to him, only a professor whom she liked; so for him nothing really ended.

Now the golden day was unbearable. He turned over on his stomach and put his face in his arms. Almost at once he could feel the sun burning his neck, his back. But it alleviated nothing. There was the dull ache in his chest and throat, the constant feeling that at any moment he would cry out like a child in sobs. It was a pressure in his body that he could not put into thoughts, only the feeling that something was ending, inevitably ending. He thought of his past and it was all gold, all brightness and gold, all magic landscape, all love, all an idyl, all a bright day, and all ending.

He thought he must cry. All his youth was gathered into a knot of pain that choked him, a youth that had been like gold but that pressed against his heart now, dull and heavy. He thought of going back to the city, to the hot office, to the dull and stupid work, sweating over accounts, of the years he had ahead of him in which to slave there. And he knew as he lay in the sand, really *knew*, for the first time, that all of that was no mere interlude, that golden days must end, gold vanish.

He felt a touch on his shoulder, turned, and looked up. It was Rachel, brown in the sun, saying, "Darling, don't be rude."

He sat up. "Am I being rude?"

"Does he bore you?"

"Yes. I don't like him much."

"Well, I'm sorry he came, Will, but I couldn't help it. Come back and try to bear him. He's not bad, you know."

"No?" Will asked as he got up.

She looked at him swiftly, then smiled. "Don't be silly, darling."

"No, *darling*."

"Good."

Then they went up the shore, back to the raft where Max still lay in the lessening glare of the sun.

Then finally he could put up with him no longer. The whole thing, suddenly, was impossible, too foul, too much for him. He sat at the table for a minute more and fought against the impulse to leave. But Mrs. Harley, cooing in a voice that almost made him ill ("But how *interesting*, Mr. Garey. *Do* go on! Do you *really* believe that?") and Max, toying with his fork and smiling with what Will supposed was great "charm" before continuing his monologue, decided him. He looked quickly at Rachel. She sat at the end of the table, opposite her mother. She looked very cool in a white dress, brown throat and arms cool and lovely, her lips slightly parted, her eyes fixed—lost to him.

Then he rose quickly to his feet. "Excuse me, please," he said, and went quickly to the porch, and then outside, down the steps, stumbled down toward the shore under the pines. He sat down in the grass. His fingers fumbled for a cigarette and a match in his pocket. Then he stared out at the water and the new moon hanging close over the opposite shore. In the reeds the frogs sang. From above came the ring of silver on china. He bit hard into his lower lip when he knew suddenly that the salt he tasted was of tears.

Then everything broke, collapsed in him like a sail when the wind dies. He wept as he had not wept since he was a small boy; and there, for a time in the night, he felt that he was a small boy still, alone in the dark and lonely night. He lay on the grass and sobbed, and there was a violence in his weeping as of a body tortured. He smothered the sound in the grass.

But he could not smother the pain in his chest. It was like a live thing in his heart, heavy and pressing, torturing, not relieved by sobs. It came over him in waves of torment, and now it was no longer anything of the mind, but of the body alone, a physical pressure, wracking and violent, eruptive and convulsive, as if his very life, well-loved, were ending in the torment.

He did not feel Rachel's hand on his shoulder. It was her voice that recalled him: "Will—darling—please!"

Even then he could not prevent his sobs from coming. It was as if they were something separate from him, separate from his will, as if they had their own life, must come to their own slow end. He felt no shame before her, had no feelings at all, no thoughts, was given over entirely to what seemed wholly a physical act. Then slowly, at last, his shoulders grew quieter. Slowly his breathing quieted. Slowly his eyes dried. And it was over at last. He felt empty, weak, desolate as he turned slowly over on his back to look at her.

The moon was almost in the water. He could see it, touching the opposite shore. The sky was dark, sprinkled with cold stars. These too he saw, blurred and faint, unsteady in the darkness. Beside him knelt Rachel, her white dress a vague lightness, her face above him a vague blur. She spoke again; "Darling, what is it, what's *wrong*?"

He swallowed hard but could not speak. He lay on his back and looked at the blur of her face. His hand reached out and seized hers, held it tightly. Then she lay down beside him suddenly, put her arms around him, and her cheek to his mouth. He sensed the familiar perfume of her hair and moved away from her a little. Now he could see the stars more clearly; their light was brighter, harder, they were steadier in the sky, fixed and remote. Then, although Rachel's arms were around him and her face so close that he could feel her warm breath sweet on his face, he was alone, desolate, empty, alone on the shore under the stars. He did not say this then, nor did he even quite feel it, but he knew it, his body, empty and quiet, knew it—the cold loneliness of the stars even on a summer night. He lay still and looked up. He knew that something momentous had happened, something momentous changed.

"I felt sick," he said at last, though Rachel had not spoken again.

She said nothing for a while, then whispered, "I'm sorry."

"It's all right now."

As if startled by the deadly quiet of his voice, she sat up and looked closely into his face. "*Are* you all right now, Will?"

"Yes, it's all right now." He said it clearly, calmly, his eyes on the distant stars.

"What was it, though?" she asked.

"You know."

"No."

"Yes, you do."

"Not *Max*, Will?"

"What else?"

"Oh, but *darling*—"

"It doesn't matter, Rachel."

"What do you mean—doesn't matter? Do you think—?"

"I know, Rachel. I knew it this morning. But only tonight, suddenly, at the table, when I saw your face while he was talking—it took that long until I really could believe it. But it doesn't matter now."

"You think I love him?"

"You do love him."

Then she did not answer.

"Yesterday I wouldn't have believed that things like this happen. For over a year . . ." He paused. Then, "Nothing will ever be the same again—love, or anything."

"Please, Will. Nothing's happened."

"Everything's happened. Now it's over."

She looked at him closely. Then she said, "I've never heard you talk like that. You're different. Your voice—it's . . ."

"What?"

"You're different. Your voice frightens me. It's so quiet and cold and far away, so different—" She spoke jerkily. "So dead!"

He sat up, leaned back on his elbows. The moon was gone, sunk under the water. The sky was darker, and the stars seemed brighter still, separate, and farther away. Then he lay down again and she beside him. They were both very quiet. Finally she said, "Do you hate me?"

He turned to her. "No," he answered. He watched her face. He saw her eyes sparkling with tears. He said, "What are you crying for?"

"I can't tell you why, I can't say, I don't know. I'm afraid. I do love you, Will. Only now I'm afraid, because I do love someone else—more. I don't want to. But I do. It frightens me!"

Now she was no longer older than he. She was a girl again, her woman's poise, given her briefly by this new love, taken from her again by that same love because, in the face of it, she was afraid. She was afraid of its swiftness, of what it might hold, of her own heart, turning. Now he felt older than she, felt that he could tell her something. He said, "I know what it is. It isn't just that we've been in love. We've had such a swell time. I don't know if I can say this, but it's something like this anyway—you weren't just yourself for me, and I wasn't just myself for you. We were both in love with much more than each other. You were all of that life for me, and maybe I was that for you, too. We were that whole life for each other, and we didn't want to lose it, but we couldn't help ourselves, couldn't keep it any longer."

She was crying. She put her face on his shoulder and he felt her tears on his neck. Then he put his arms around her and held her close. But he felt no less alone. And he thought then that this aloneness would never entirely leave him again, but that when he got back to the city next day, after he had been there a while, working in the office, after a week or two or perhaps a whole year, finally anyway, it would have left him somewhat less empty, less deadly calm. Then this day and this summer and all the golden days would have become the dream; and the other life would be real.

"How did your poem go, Rachel? When I last died, and, dear, I die whenever you go from me . . . ?"

"Please—don't," she said.

He began to stroke her hair. She was quiet now, no longer crying, held close in his arms. He said, "Maybe it's always like this. Maybe the end of every love is a kind of little death, when you have to put behind more than just the love itself, but all the life, too, in which the love was wrapped. Maybe that's what living is—a lot of little dyings. I don't know—I can't say it very well. Maybe I don't even know."

For a moment more they sat together and then she said, "We have to go back. They'll wonder . . ."

"All right," he said.

Then, clinging together, helping each other up the slope, they went up to the house, where the lights were, and the sounds of voices, clinging together like children still, under the stars.

## DAVID, I'VE TOLD THEM

### *Mary Jonathan* (*1939*)

DEAREST, it's done now. I've told them we're married. I know it's only a week until graduation and I should have waited, but I'm so tired, so unbearably tired of waiting and hiding. I told the girls at lunch. Anna Wembly asked about my boy friend at Yale and I said, "You mean my husband." It was as simple as that.

Janey Colby dropped her fork and said, "You mean you've actually married that Jew?" and then got up and left the table. The others hurried to wish me happiness, in a dubious sort of way. All except Judy Miller. She didn't say anything, just looked at me with the expression that people in movies get watching a newsreel of the bombing of Madrid.

Lil Porter said half under her breath, "How does it feel to love a man like that?" and for a moment she looked awfully old and tired.

The moment lunch was over I left them to tear it to pieces and ran down to the dam. I wanted a moment alone to have a cigarette and talk to you (or is it to myself?). The water in the pond was quiet, looking up at the sun and dozing. I remembered how hot it was in the sun the day I met you. It was almost a whole year ago, in August, a day of city heat, defenseless, unshaded streets. I was so restless, packing to go up to Maine, I just had to get out, so I went down to the Workers Bookshop on 13th Street just to be among fellow-travelers for a moment, to hear a record played, see an etching or a Gropper cartoon, maybe to buy a three-cent pamphlet and feel myself a part of that vital throbbing thing, the Labor movement.

You came up to me there because (you told me much later) I looked as cool as icing on a cake in my big-brimmed hat and lacy gloves.

We can tell our grandchildren that your first words to me were, "Did you mistake the Bookshop for Longchamps?"

Nor did I take that one lying down. I looked at your unwrinkled white linen suit, screaming of Rogers Peet and returned with all my sweetness, "Oh, no, I recognized the place by the horny-handed son of toil lounging in the corner."

You had enough grace to look embarrassed, and you offered to help me select some books. Imagine your surprise and pleasure to find that I too had heard of Michael Gold, leghorn hat notwithstanding. We were still bickering, still amused at each other when we left, you carrying my package of books out into the hot street. There were old men sitting in the shade of the park when we got to Union Square. Tired women pushed their baby carriages home, grateful for an hour's parole from their breathless apartments. Children, dirty and sweating, ran through the little oasis.

We didn't speak to each other, feeling ashamed when we came to your yellow roadster and drove away in it. You put it into words for both of us when you said, "It doesn't seem fair, does it?" and I answered "No." So for an hour we drove through the streets of lower Manhattan, seeing our city together like strangers on their first trip to town. We said very little to each other, if you count only spoken words. But I knew that you saw the familiar Fifth Avenue shops and the feet that shuffle along Sixth Avenue around the agencies still hoping for the miracle of a job. We didn't have to say very much, we just looked at things and neither pointed the reproachful finger at the other to say, "Your class has done this."

We had supper that night at a little Italian restaurant where the phonograph had a bad sinusitis, and played Italian opera through its nose. You taught me to wind spaghetti around my fork from a soup spoon. It got all over my face and we laughed and laughed.

We watched the daylight go, over red wine and fruit. We fell in love that night, although we didn't know it until long after. When you took me home I thought I'd had a very pleasant evening, made a new friend, perhaps. I didn't think of love in connection with a big dark-eyed Jewish boy, however Yale in manner. The next day I went up to my Aunt Henrietta in Maine and sometimes I thought of you, but not always.

Dick Colby took me to the Yale-Dartmouth game early in the season. Dick is a swell date and we might have had a grand time. We might have if I hadn't seen you with Judy Miller. You met her at the station and drove away with her in the yellow roadster and it came over me that I'd been looking for that roadster for months, watching the roads without knowing why for a fresh-painted Buick with New York plates.

And of course, although there were thousands of people in the Bowl, I had to see you. I resented Judy because she was having such a good time and because she had a softly-irregular Semitic profile and I felt shut out. I cheered too loudly during that game, and waved and yelled. There was no reason for acting like that. I wouldn't have gone to that game with you had you asked me, not then I wouldn't.

There would be that business of what house we'd dance in, and what my friends would have to say about it, or if they'd pick that time to be funny.

I could just see Janey Colby arching the patrician eyebrow and saying, "I'm afraid I didn't get that last name," while I prayed you missed the inflection. That would have bothered me, then.

No, David, I wouldn't have gone to the Yale-Dartmouth game with you, but I knew you'd seen me there and when you wrote to me I knew I'd been waiting for the letter. Even though it was a very formal and unrevealing invitation for the Williams-Union game, I knew what you meant . . . we'd gone to games with other people, you wanted to take me to one.

This afternoon I also remembered, while I was sitting down by the dam, that day in October when you and I set out over the Mohawk Trail for Williamstown. The Trail exerted itself to be beautiful and succeeded. We went around each curve impatient to find what glory of red and gold and green leaves waited for us beyond. There's a brook that cuts through beside the road. The same brook about which the New England poets wrote a century ago. We stopped to walk along there, you in your brown polo coat and I in my tan polo coat, looking like every other college date.

We never got to the game because we talked so long. You told me about your brother who's studying for the rabbinate and won't play handball with you on Saturday mornings any more. You were telling me about your first doubts of God, when he didn't punish you for eating on the fast day and how you came from that inexorably to materialism, then to an understanding of man's struggle to work out scientific laws in human society. It was only from there that you went on to an emotional interest in the sicknesses of society, to wonder about your father and his factories and the trade-unions.

With me it was so different. I hated the uglinesses first. It bothered me that there were children with running noses and chilblained hands and old ladies peddling pencils on cold street corners. I told you that day about my prep-school roommate Janey Colby who cares more for horses than for people and who is "nauseated by the smell of Jews."

We never got to the game because we walked so slowly back to the car and drove so slowly on to Williamstown. We had dinner there and walked along the streets, kicking the fallen leaves and listening to the fun pouring out of the fraternity houses, streaming across the lawns, in and out of the autos in the early twilight.

We discovered that day how precious time is when we do anything together and we relished each moment as a child savors a candystick.

We came back over the Trail that night, remembering lines from the poets we love. Not the ones we'd laboriously copied in school but the new fighting poets of the faith we share. I think I began it with Langston Hughes' "To make a poet black and bid him sing."

And you went on with "Move over, Comrade Lenin, and give me room."

Then Millay's sonnets after Sacco and Vanzetti, "So have we loved sweet justice to the last, that now lies here in this unseemly place."

You were surprised to find that I too had wept over the shoemaker and the fish-peddler, not silly girlish tears, but I had wept that men in our age still die fighting for what they know is right.

The dead leaves blew into the car as we drove along, and I snuggled under the car robe, in perfect contentment. Every discovery we made about each other was RIGHT. You did not think my ideas "unsuitable for a young lady." I did not need to apologize to you for my beliefs.

That was the first of our many Saturdays together in Collegetown walking through the November-stripped woods around the pond, in New York Thanksgiving time when we saw "Waiting for Lefty," held hands in the darkness and believed. We talked ourselves inside out. We laughed over the cartoons in the *New Yorker* and argued hotly over the Party Line and Class Collaboration.

Remember the Friday night you took me to Temple so I might hear Hebrew spoken? The service was beautiful. It raised no more of a barrier between us than hearing you tell of a trip you'd made before you met me, or a hobby you'd enjoyed for years. It was no more painful than that. The faith we now share is so all-embracing it does not shut out. It's a living, growing faith that can be questioned and that works itself out as the need arises for it to change and grow. There is no name that fits it; it is softer than Marxism, it is stronger than the easy liberalism of our campus discussions. It is more emotional than an economic philosophy and more scientific than a blind acceptance of God. We might call it socialism, but that is the name of a party; we might call it communism, but that too needs to be defined.

Whatever you want to call what we believe in, dearest, we and our comrades are the only people in our generation who have a valid reason for living and hoping. We alone have reason to believe in the possibility of peace and of plenty. With what other conviction could I, a descendant of the Hudson River patroons, marry a second-generation Russian Jew? With what other inner fortification could you tear yourself away from your home, give up the comfortable customs and friendships of your people to live out your life with me, a stranger and an alien?

And what other belief could give us such unity that enables us always to know what the other is thinking? It is that above all else that binds me to you, David. Oh, I love you because of your good looks, as any woman would, because you are big and shut out the world when you put your arms around me. But that pride and satisfaction in you came as a result of the other feeling. It was Christmas time before you even kissed me . . . and after that it seemed clear to both of us that our spiritual union was incomplete without the complete union of mind and body. So we got married.

I'm glad we waited. Sex is after all such a coldly impersonal thing; it can happen to anybody. But a true marriage is a union between two who are already united by every other bond.

And how we celebrated our wedding day by buying armfuls of ten-cent toys to give to the Salvation Army girl on the corner? When she protested we kissed her, one on each cheek and said WE JUST GOT MARRIED and ran away. We looked in the shop windows and there were bells in the streets and everyone was in such a hurry to get home. The park was decorated in icicles, just for us; it was a big municipal Wedding Cake Project. We stood at the window of our room in the Park Central, breathing in great gulps of cold air, and tracing our names on the frosted window glass and giggling.

But the next morning we had to tell our parents. Even now, writing to you, I hate to remember it. It was easier to bear your mother's tears than my mother's half-smile and that poisonous way she said, "Well, David, I really must learn to pronounce your last name."

Your father kept saying, "Hannah, she looks like a nice girl. It isn't as if she were a nurse or something."

But my father, when we went to him, said, "This will make a fine story at my Club."

I sometimes remember that I'll never again be invited to Aunt Henrietta's, and I do like Maine. It's harder, sweet, to remember your grandfather mourns you as though you were dead, because you married me.

It was with that in our teeth that we came back to school. It seemed to me that you were with me in class, in the library, even when I write to you it seems superfluous to tell you the news; you were with me when it happened.

Sometimes your nearness is almost a physical sensation, as when you went with me to the Peace Strike in April. I came out of class (cutting the exam the prof gave to cripple the Strike) and went toward the chapel. It was raining and we held the meeting indoors. All the way along more and more students fell into the group and we had half the college there in the end. We stood jammed together in the back, when the seats were all gone and our raincoats steamed and water trickled off our hat brims and down our necks. Some were there out of curiosity; some to scoff; and some to pray.

After the speakers finished, about half of the crowd stood up and the Chairman began the Oxford Pledge. Slowly and quietly, aware of what they were saying, those on their feet murmured, "I swear that I will not support my country in any war it may conduct."

Standing along the side wall, Professor Quinn of the Music Department turned his face away to hide the tears. He lost his only son, a young fellow your age, who went away full of enthusiasm and came back full of syphilis. When he found out what he had he put a bullet in his head.

I cried a little, too, hidden by the mackintosh in front of me. I believed with all my heart that if enough young people all over the world would take that oath. . . .

This has been too long a spring, David. I know better than to say that I miss you. That does not describe the ache of separation that throbs like a physical torment. I want you all the time. I find myself talking to you alone in my room and I have to strain against my desire to bring your name into the conversation everywhere I go. I imagine you can hear my love, as if it made a sound.

And what is so wonderful to me is that I dare write these things to you . . . and you will not laugh or try to play me for a fool. I was brought up, and you were too, on the barter and trade system of romance, in which a man and woman cannot be honest with each other any more than business men can . . . they dare not trust each other. Lil Porter has had great success in this line. She would never write these things, lest you come to take her for granted. It must be a poverty-stricken sort of love that has to live on the emotional garbage of pretty speeches and innuendoes. All the flowers and the phone calls and the special-delivery letters from men who don't believe what they're saying, to girls who weigh and measure each little token, deciding just what it's worth on the scale of future attentions and . . . possibly . . . marriage. I would rather lose you than have to flutter my eyelashes at you, and play little tricks to make you love me. I have no time to practice being charming. There is so much to do, and so little time for it all.

Yes, David dearest. I've told them. And I heard all their doubts and their misgivings and I want to say right out loud to all of them, "You don't even know what it is to be alive, and you give me advice on living!" Overconfidence? I don't think so. I don't think anything could separate us now, not if we are always too busy to quarrel, so caught up in the main stream of life that the little bits of rubbish floating along will only touch us, will be swept away by the current.

And now goodnight.

## THE CHRYSANTHEMUMS
### *John Steinbeck* (*1938*)

THE HIGH gray-flannel fog of winter closed the Salinas Valley from the sky and from all the rest of the world. On every side it sat like a lid on the mountains and made of the great valley a closed pot. On the broad, level land floor the gang plows bit deep and left the black earth shining like metal where the shares had cut. On the foot-hill ranches across the Salinas River the yellow stubble fields seemed to be bathed in pale cold sunshine; but there was no sunshine in the valley now in December. The thick willow scrub along the river flamed with sharp and positive yellow leaves.

It was a time of quiet and of waiting. The air was cold and tender. A light wind blew up from the southwest so that the farmers were mildly hopeful of a good rain before long; but fog and rain do not go together.

Across the river, on Henry Allen's foot-hill ranch there was little work to be done, for the hay was cut and stored and the orchards were plowed up to receive the rain deeply when it should come. The cattle on the higher slopes were becoming shaggy and rough-coated.

Elisa Allen, working in her flower garden, looked down across the yard and saw Henry, her husband, talking to two men in business suits. The three of them stood by the tractor shed, each man with one foot on the side of the Little Fordson. They smoked cigarettes and studied the machine as they talked.

Elisa watched them for a moment and then went back to her work. She was thirty-five. Her face was lean and strong and her eyes were as clear as water. Her figure looked blocked and heavy in her gardening costume, a man's black hat pulled low down over her eyes, clodhopper shoes, a figured print dress almost completely covered by a big corduroy apron with four big pockets to hold the snips, the trowel and scratcher, the seeds and the knife she worked with. She wore heavy leather gloves to protect her hands while she worked.

She was cutting down the old year's chrysanthemum stalks with a pair of short and powerful scissors. She looked down toward the men by the tractor shed now and then. Her face was eager and mature and handsome; even her work with the scissors was over-eager, over-powerful. The chrysanthemum stems seemed too small and easy for her energy.

She brushed a cloud of hair out of her eyes with the back of her glove, and left a smudge of earth on her cheek in doing it. Behind her stood the neat white farmhouse with red geraniums close-banked round it as high as the windows. It was a hard-swept looking little house, with hard-polished windows, and a clean mat on the front steps.

Elisa cast another glance toward the tractor shed. The stranger men were getting into their Ford Coupé. She took off a glove and put her strong fingers down into the forest of new green chrysanthemum sprouts that were growing round the old roots. She spread the leaves and looked down among the close-growing stems. No aphids were there, no sow bugs nor snails nor cut worms. Her terrier fingers destroyed such pests before they could get started.

Elisa started at the sound of her husband's voice. He had come near quietly and he leaned over the wire fence that protected her flower garden from cattle and dogs and chickens.

"At it again," he said. "You've got a strong new crop coming."

Elisa straightened her back and pulled on the gardening glove again. "Yes. They'll be strong this coming year." In her tone and on her face there was a little smugness.

"You've got a gift with things," Henry observed. "Some of those yellow chrysanthemums you had last year were ten inches across. I wish you'd work out in the orchard and raise some apples that big."

Her eyes sharpened. "Maybe I could do it too. I've a gift with things all right. My mother had it. She could stick anything in the ground and make it grow. She said it was having planter's hands that knew how to do it."

"Well, it sure works with flowers," he said.

"Henry, who were those men you were talking to?"

"Why, sure, that's what I came to tell you. They were from the Western Meat Company. I sold those thirty head of three-year-old steers. Got nearly my own price too."

"Good," she said. "Good for you."

"And I thought," he continued, "I thought how it's Saturday afternoon, and we might go into Salinas for dinner at a restaurant and then to a picture show—to celebrate, you see."

"Good," she repeated. "Oh, yes. That will be good."

Henry put on his joking tone. "There's fights to-night. How'd you like to go to the fights?"

"Oh, no," she said breathlessly. "No, I wouldn't like fights."

"Just fooling, Elisa. We'll go to a movie. Let's see. It's two now. I'm going to take Scotty and bring down those steers from the hill. It'll take us maybe two hours. We'll go in town about five and have dinner at the Cominos Hotel. Like that?"

"Of course I'll like it. It's good to eat away from home."

"All right then. I'll go get up a couple of horses."

She said, "I'll have plenty of time to transplant some of these sets, I guess."

She heard her husband calling Scotty down by the barn. And a little later she saw the two men ride up the pale-yellow hillside in search of the steers.

There was a little square sandy bed kept for rooting the chrysanthemums. With her trowel she turned the soil over and over and smoothed it and patted it firm. Then she dug ten parallel trenches to receive the sets. Back at the chrysanthemum bed she pulled out the little crisp shoots, trimmed off the leaves of each one with her scissors, and laid it on a small orderly pile.

A squeak of wheels and plod of hoofs came from the road. Elisa looked up. The country road ran along the dense bank of willows and cottonwoods that bordered the river, and up this road came a curious vehicle, curiously drawn. It was an old spring-wagon, with a round canvas top on it like the cover of a prairie schooner. It was drawn by an old bay horse and a little gray-and-white burro. A big stubble-bearded man sat between the cover flaps and drove the crawling team. Underneath the wagon, between the hind wheels, a lean and rangy mongrel dog walked sedately. Words were painted on the canvas in clumsy, crooked letters. "Pots, pans, knives, scissors, lawn mowers, Fixed." Two rows of articles, and the triumphantly definitive "Fixed" below. The black paint had run down in little sharp points beneath each letter.

Elisa, squatting on the ground, watched to see the crazy loose-jointed wagon pass by. But it didn't pass. It turned into the farm road in front of her house, crooked old wheels skirling and squeaking. The rangy dog darted from beneath the wheels and ran ahead. Instantly the two ranch shepherds flew out at him. Then all three stopped, and with stiff and quivering tails, with taut straight legs, with ambassadorial dignity, they slowly circled, sniffing daintily. The caravan pulled up to Elisa's wire fence and stopped. Now the newcomer dog, feeling outnumbered, lowered his tail and retired under the wagon with raised hackles and bared teeth.

The man on the wagon seat called out, "That's a bad dog in a fight when he gets started."

Elisa laughed. "I see he is. How soon does he generally get started?"

The man caught up her laughter and echoed it heartily. "Sometimes not for weeks and weeks," he said. He climbed stiffly down over the wheel. The horse and the donkey dropped like unwatered flowers.

Elisa saw that he was a very big man. Although his hair and beard were graying, he did not look old. His worn black suit was wrinkled and spotted with grease. The laughter had disappeared from his face and eyes the moment his laughing voice ceased. His eyes were dark and they were full of the brooding that gets in the eyes of teamsters and of sailors. The calloused hands he rested on the fence were cracked, and every crack was a black line. He took off his battered hat.

"I'm off my general road, ma'am," he said. "Does this dirt road cut over across the river to the Los Angeles highway?"

Elisa stood up and shoved the thick scissors in her apron pocket. "Well, yes, it does, but it winds around and then fords the river. I don't think your team could pull through the sand."

He replied with some asperity, "It might surprise you what them beasts can pull through."

"When they get started?" she asked.

He smiled for a second. "Yes. When they get started."

"Well," said Elisa, "I think you'll save time if you go back to the Salinas road and pick up the highway there."

He drew a big finger down the chicken wire and made it sing. "I ain't in any hurry, ma'am. I go from Seattle to San Diego and back every year. Takes all my time. About six months each way. I aim to follow nice weather."

Elisa took off her gloves and stuffed them in the apron pocket with the scissors. She touched the under edge of her man's hat, searching for fugitive hairs. "That sounds like a nice kind of a way to live," she said.

He leaned confidentially over the fence. "Maybe you noticed the writing on my wagon. I mend pots and sharpen knives and scissors. You got any of them things to do?"

"Oh, no," she said quickly. "Nothing like that." Her eyes hardened with resistance.

"Scissors is the worst thing," he explained. "Most people just ruin scissors trying to sharpen 'em, but I know how. I got a special tool. It's a little bobbit kind of thing and patented. But it sure does the trick."

"No. My scissors are all sharp."

"All right then. Take a pot," he continued earnestly, "a bent pot or a pot with a hole. I can make it like new so you don't have to buy no new ones. That's a saving for you."

"No," she said shortly. "I tell you I have nothing like that for you to do."

His face fell to an exaggerated sadness. His voice took on a whining undertone. "I ain't had a thing to do to-day. Maybe I won't have no supper to-night. You see I'm off my regular road. I know folks on the highway clear from Seattle to San Diego. They save their things for me to sharpen up because they know I do it so good and save them money."

"I'm sorry," Elisa said irritably. "I haven't anything for you to do."

His eyes left her face and fell to searching the ground. They roamed about until they came to the chrysanthemum bed where she had been working. "What's them plants, ma'am?"

The irritation and resistance melted from Elisa's face. "Oh, those are chrysanthemums, giant whites and yellows. I raise them every year, bigger than anybody around here."

"Kind of a long-stemmed flower? Looks like a quick puff of colored smoke?" he asked.

"That's it. What a nice way to describe them."

"They smell kind of nasty till you get used to them," he said.

"It's a good bitter smell," she retorted, "not nasty at all."

He changed his tone quickly. "I like the smell myself."

"I had ten-inch blooms this year," she said.

The man leaned farther over the fence. "Look. I know a lady down the road a piece has got the nicest garden you ever seen. Got nearly every kind of flower but no chrysanthemums. Last time I was mending a copper-bottom wash tub for her (that's a hard job but I do it good), she said to me, 'If you ever run acrost some nice chrysanthemums I wish you'd try to get me a few seeds.' That's what she told me."

Elisa's eyes grew alert and eager. "She couldn't have known much about chrysanthemums. You *can* raise them from seed, but it's much easier to root the little sprouts you see there."

"Oh," he said. "I s'pose I can't take none to her then."

"Why yes, you can," Elisa cried. "I can put some in damp sand, and you can carry them right along with you. They'll take root in the pot if you keep them damp. And then she can transplant them."

"She'd sure like to have some, ma'am. You say they're nice ones?"

"Beautiful," she said. "Oh, beautiful." Her eyes shone. She tore off the battered hat and shook out her dark pretty hair. "I'll put them in a flower pot, and you can take them right with you. Come into the yard."

While the man came through the picket gate Elisa ran excitedly along the geranium-bordered path to the back of the house. And she returned carrying a big red flower pot. The gloves were forgotten now. She kneeled on the ground by the starting bed and dug up the sandy soil with her fingers and scooped it into the bright new flower pot. Then she picked up the little pile of shoots she had prepared. With her strong fingers she pressed them into the sand and tamped round them with her knuckles. The man stood over her. "I'll tell you what to do," she said. "You remember so you can tell the lady."

"Yes, I'll try to remember."

"Well, look. These will take root in about a month. Then she must set them out, about a foot apart in good rich earth like this, see?" She lifted a handful of dark soil for him to look at. "They'll grow fast and tall. Now remember this. In July tell her to cut them down, about eight inches from the ground."

"Before they bloom?" he asked.

"Yes, before they bloom." Her face was tight with eagerness. "They'll grow right up again. About the last of September the buds will start."

She stopped and seemed perplexed. "It's the budding that takes the most care," she said hesitantly. "I don't know how to tell you." She looked deep into his eyes searchingly. Her mouth opened a little, and she seemed to be listening. "I'll try to tell you," she said. "Did you ever hear of planting hands?"

"Can't say I have, ma'am."

"Well, I can only tell you what it feels like. It's when you're picking off the buds you don't want. Everything goes right down into your fingertips. You watch your fingers work. They do it themselves. You can feel how it is. They pick and pick the buds. They never make a mistake. They're with the plant. Do you see? Your fingers and the plant. You can feel that, right up your arm. They know. They never make a mistake. You can feel it. When you're like that you can't do anything wrong. Do you see that? Can you understand that?"

She was kneeling on the ground looking up at him. Her breast swelled passionately.

The man's eyes narrowed. He looked away self-consciously. "Maybe I know," he said. "Sometimes in the night in the wagon there—"

Elisa's voice grew husky. She broke in on him. "I've never lived as you do, but I know what you mean. When the night is dark—the stars are sharp-pointed, and there's quiet. Why, you rise up and up!"

Kneeling there, her hand went out toward his legs in the greasy black trousers. Her hesitant fingers almost touched the cloth. Then her hand dropped to the ground.

He said, "It's nice, just like you say. Only when you don't have no dinner it ain't."

She stood up then, very straight, and her face was ashamed. She held the flower pot out to him and placed it gently in his arms. "Here. Put it in your wagon, on the seat, where you can watch it. Maybe I can find something for you to do."

At the back of the house she dug in the can pile and found two old and battered aluminum sauce pans. She carried them back and gave them to him. "Here, maybe you can fix these."

His manner changed. He became professional. "Good as new I can fix them." At the back of his wagon he set a little anvil, and out of an oily tool box dug a small machine hammer. Elisa came through the gate to watch him while he pounded out the dents in the kettles. His mouth grew sure and knowing. At a difficult part of the work he sucked his under-lip.

"You sleep right in the wagon?" Elisa asked.

"Right in the wagon, ma'am. Rain or shine I'm dry as a cow in there."

"It must be nice," she said. "It must be very nice. I wish women could do such things."

"It ain't the right kind of a life for a woman."

Her upper lip raised a little, showing her teeth. "How do you know? How can you tell?" she said.

"I don't know, ma'am," he protested. "Of course I don't know. Now here's your kettles, done. You don't have to buy no new ones."

"How much?"

"Oh, fifty cents'll do. I keep my prices down and my work good. That's why I have all them satisfied customers up and down the highway."

Elisa brought him a fifty-cent piece from the house and dropped it in his hand. "You might be surprised to have a rival sometime. I can sharpen scissors too. And I can beat the dents out of little pots. I could show you what a woman might do."

He put his hammer back in the oily box and shoved the little anvil out of sight. "It would be a lonely life for a woman, ma'am, and a scary life, too, with animals creeping under the wagon all night." He climbed over the singletree, steadying himself with a hand on the burro's white rump. He settled himself in the seat, picked up the lines. "Thank you kindly, ma'am," he said. "I'll do like you told me; I'll go back and catch the Salinas road."

"Mind," she called, "if you're long in getting there, keep the sand damp."

"Sand, ma'am—Sand? Oh, sure. You mean around the chrysanthemums. Sure I will." He clucked his tongue. The beasts leaned luxuriously into their collars. The mongrel dog took his place between the back wheels. The wagon turned and crawled out the entrance road and back the way it had come, along the river.

Elisa stood in front of her wire fence watching the slow progress of the caravan. Her shoulders were straight, her head thrown back, her eyes half-closed, so that the scene came vaguely into them. Her lips moved silently, forming the words "Good-by—good-by." Then she whispered, "That's a bright direction. There's a glowing there." The sound of her whisper startled her. She shook herself free and looked about to see whether anyone had been listening. Only the dogs had heard. They lifted their heads toward her from their sleeping in the dust, and then stretched out their chins and settled asleep again. Elisa turned and ran hurriedly into the house.

In the kitchen she reached behind the stove and felt the water tank. It was full of hot water from the noonday cooking. In the bathroom she tore off her soiled clothes and flung them into the corner. And then she scrubbed herself with a little block of pumice, legs and thighs, loins and chest and arms, until her skin was scratched and red. When she had dried herself she stood in front of a mirror in her bedroom and looked at her body. She tightened her stomach and threw out her chest. She turned and looked over her shoulder at her back.

After a while she began to dress slowly. She put on her newest underclothing and her nicest stockings and the dress which was the symbol of her prettiness. She worked carefully on her hair, pencilled her eyebrows, and rouged her lips.

Before she was finished she heard the little thunder of hoofs and the shouts of Henry and his helper as they drove the red steers into the corral. She heard the gate bang shut and set herself for Henry's arrival.

His step sounded on the porch. He entered the house calling, "Elisa, where are you?"

"In my room, dressing. I'm not ready. There's hot water for your bath. Hurry up. It's getting late."

When she heard him splashing in the tub, Elisa laid his dark suit on the bed, and shirt and socks and tie beside it. She stood his polished shoes on the floor beside the bed. Then she went to the porch and sat primly and stiffly down. She looked toward the river road where the willow-line was still yellow with frosted leaves so that under the high gray fog they seemed a thin band of sunshine. This was the only color in the gray afternoon. She sat unmoving for a long time.

Henry came banging out of the door, shoving his tie inside his vest as he came. Elisa stiffened and her face grew tight. Henry stopped short and looked at her. "Why—why, Elisa. You look so nice!"

"Nice? You think I look nice? What do you mean by 'nice'?"

Henry blundered on. "I don't know. I mean you look different, strong and happy."

"I am strong? Yes, strong. What do you mean 'strong'?"

He looked bewildered. "You're playing some kind of a game," he said helplessly. "It's a kind of a play. You look strong enough to break a calf over your knee, happy enough to eat it like a watermelon."

For a second she lost her rigidity. "Henry! Don't talk like that. You didn't know what you said." She grew complete again. "I am strong," she boasted. "I never knew before how strong."

Henry looked down toward the tractor shed, and when he brought his eyes back to her, they were his own again. "I'll get out the car. You can put on your coat while I'm starting."

Elisa went into the house. She heard him drive to the gate and idle down his motor, and then she took a long time to put on her hat. She pulled it here and pressed it there. When Henry turned the motor off she slipped into her coat and went out.

The little roadster bounced along on the dirt road by the river, raising the birds and driving the rabbits into the brush. Two cranes flapped heavily over the willow-line and dropped into the river-bed.

Far ahead on the road Elisa saw a dark speck in the dust. She suddenly felt empty. She did not hear Henry's talk. She tried not to look; she did not want to see the little heap of sand and green shoots, but she could not help herself. The chrysanthemums lay in the road close to the wagon tracks. But not the pot; he had kept that. As the car passed them she remembered the good bitter smell, and a little shudder went through her. She felt ashamed of her strong planter's hands, that were no use, lying palms up in her lap.

The roadster turned a bend and she saw the caravan ahead. She swung full round toward her husband so that she could not see the little covered wagon and the mismatched team as the car passed.

In a moment they had left behind them the man who had not known or needed to know what she said, the bargainer. She did not look back.

To Henry she said loudly, to be heard above the motor, "It will be good, to-night, a good dinner."

"Now you're changed again," Henry complained. He took one hand from the wheel and patted her knee. "I ought to take you in to dinner oftener. It would be good for both of us. We get so heavy out on the ranch."

"Henry," she asked, "could we have wine at dinner?"

"Sure. Say! That will be fine."

She was silent for a while; then she said, "Henry, at those prize fights do the men hurt each other very much?"

"Sometimes a little, not often. Why?"

"Well, I've read how they break noses, and blood runs down their chests. I've read how the fighting gloves get heavy and soggy with blood."

He looked round at her. "What's the matter, Elisa? I didn't know you read things like that." He brought the car to a stop, then turned to the right over the Salinas River bridge.

"Do any women ever go to the fights?" she asked.

"Oh, sure, some. What's the matter, Elisa? Do you want to go? I don't think you'd like it, but I'll take you if you really want to go."

She relaxed limply in the seat. "Oh, no. No. I don't want to go. I'm sure I don't." Her face was turned away from him. "It will be enough if we can have wine. It will be plenty." She turned up her coat collar so he could not see that she was crying weakly—like an old woman.

# MR. PIM PASSES BY

### A COMEDY IN THREE ACTS

### *A. A. Milne* (*1922*)

#### CHARACTERS

GEORGE MARDEN, J.P.  
OLIVIA, *his wife*  
DINAH, *his niece*  
LADY MARDEN, *his aunt*

BRIAN STRANGE  
CARRAWAY PIM  
ANNE

## ACT I

THE *morning-room at Marden House (Buckinghamshire) decided more than a hundred years ago that it was all right, and has not bothered about itself since. Visitors to the house have called the result such different adjectives as "mellow," "old-fashioned," "charming"—even "baronial" and "antique"; but nobody ever said it was "exciting." Sometimes* OLIVIA *wants it to be more exciting, and last week she let herself go over some new curtains. At present they are folded up and waiting for her; she still has the rings to put on. It is obvious that the curtains alone will overdo the excitement; they will have to be harmonized with a new carpet and cushions.* OLIVIA *has her eye on just the things, but one has to go carefully with* GEORGE. *What was good enough for his great-great-grandfather is good enough for him. However, we can trust* OLIVIA *to see him through it, although it may take time.*

*There are two ways of coming into the room; by the open windows leading from the terrace or by the door. On this pleasant July morning* MR. PIM *chooses the latter way—or rather* ANNE *chooses it for him; and old* MR. PIM, *wistful, kindly, gentle, little* MR. PIM, *living in some world of his own whither we cannot follow, ambles after her.*

ANNE. I'll tell Mr. Marden you're here, sir. Mr. Pim, isn't it?

PIM [*coming back to this world*]. Yes—er—Mr. Carraway Pim. He doesn't know me, you understand, but if he could just see me for a moment —er— [*He fumbles in his pockets*] I gave you that letter?

ANNE. Yes, sir, I'll give it to him.

PIM [*bringing out a letter which is not the one he was looking for, but which reminds him of something else he has forgotten*]. Dear me!

ANNE. Yes, sir?

PIM. I ought to have sent a telegram, but I can do it on my way back. You have a telegraph office in the village?

ANNE. Oh, yes, sir. If you turn to the left when you get outside the gates, it isn't more than a hundred yards down the hill.

PIM. Thank you, thank you. Very stupid of me to have forgotten. [ANNE *goes out.* MR. PIM *wanders about the room humming to himself, and looking vaguely at the pictures. He has his back to the door as* DINAH *comes in. She is nineteen, very pretty, very happy, and full of boyish high spirits and conversation*]

DINAH. Hullo!

PIM [*turning round*]. Ah, good morning, Mrs. Marden. You must forgive my—er—

DINAH. Oh, I say, I'm not Mrs. Marden. I'm Dinah.

PIM [*with a bow*]. Then I will say, Good morning, Miss Diana.

DINAH [*reproachfully*]. Now, look here, if you and I are going to be friends you mustn't do that. Dinah *not* Diana. Do remember it, there's a good man, because I get so tired of correcting people. Have you come to stay with us?

PIM. Well, no, Miss—er—Dinah.

DINAH [*nodding*]. That's right. I can see I shan't have to speak to *you* again. Now tell me *your* name, and I bet you I get it right first time. And do sit down.

PIM [*sitting down*]. Thank you. My name is—er—Pim, Carraway Pim—

DINAH. Pim, that's easy.

PIM. And I have a letter of introduction to your father—

DINAH. Oh, no; now you're going wrong again, Mr. Pim. George isn't my father; he's my uncle. *Uncle* George—he doesn't like me calling him George. Olivia doesn't mind—I mean she doesn't mind being called Olivia, but George is rather touchy. You see, he's been my guardian since I was about two, and then about five years ago he married a widow called Mrs. Telworthy—that's Olivia—so she became my Aunt Olivia, only she lets me drop the Aunt. Got that?

PIM [*a little alarmed*]. I—I think so, Miss Marden.

DINAH [*admiringly*]. I say, you *are* quick, Mr. Pim. Well, if you take my advice, when you've finished your business with George, you will hang about a bit and see if you can't see Olivia. She's simply devastating. I don't wonder George fell in love with her.

PIM. It's only the merest matter of business—just a few minutes with your uncle—I'm afraid I shall hardly—

DINAH. Well, you must please yourself, Mr. Pim. I'm just giving you a friendly word of advice. Naturally, I was awfully glad to get such a magnificent aunt, because, of course, marriage *is* rather a toss up, isn't it, and George might have gone off with anybody. It's different on the stage, where guardians always marry their wards, but George couldn't marry *me* because I'm his niece. Mind you, I don't say that I should have had him, because between ourselves he's a little bit old-fashioned.

PIM. So he married—er—Mrs. Marden instead.

DINAH. Mrs. Telworthy—don't say you've forgotten already, just when you were getting so good at names. Mrs. Telworthy. You see, Olivia married the Telworthy man and went to Australia with him, and he drank himself to death in the bush, or wherever you drink yourself to death out there, and Olivia came home to England, and met my uncle, and he fell in love with her and proposed to her, and he came into my room that night—I was about fourteen—and turned on the light and said, "Dinah, how would you like to have a beautiful aunt of your very own?" And I said: "Congratulations, George." That was the first time I called him George. Of course, I'd seen it coming for *weeks*. Telworthy, isn't it a funny name?

PIM. Very singular. From Australia, you say?

DINAH. Yes, I always say that he's probably still alive, and will turn up here one morning and annoy George, because that's what first husbands always do in books, but I'm afraid there's not much chance.

PIM [*shocked*]. Miss Marden!

DINAH. Well, of course, I don't really *want* it to happen, but it *would* be rather exciting, wouldn't it? However, things like that never seem to occur down here, somehow. There was a hay-rick burnt last year about a mile away, but that isn't quite the same thing, is it?

PIM. No, I should say that that was certainly different.

DINAH. Of course, something very, very wonderful did happen last night, but I'm not sure if I know you well enough— [*She looks at him hesitatingly*]

PIM [*uncomfortably*]. Really, Miss Marden, I am only a—a passer-by, here today and gone tomorrow. You really mustn't—

DINAH. And yet there's something about you, Mr. Pim, which inspires confidence. The fact is—[*in a stage whisper*]—I got engaged last night!

PIM. Dear me, let me congratulate you.

DINAH. I expect that's why George is keeping you such a long time. Brian, my young man, the well-known painter—only nobody has ever heard of him—he's smoking a pipe with George in the library and asking for his niece's hand. Isn't it exciting? You're really rather lucky, Mr. Pim—I mean being told so soon. Even Olivia doesn't know yet.

PIM [*getting up*]. Yes, yes. I congratulate you, Miss Marden. Perhaps it would be better— [ANNE *comes in*]

ANNE. Mr. Marden is out at the moment, sir— Oh, I didn't see you, Miss Dinah.

DINAH. It's all right, Anne. *I'm* looking after Mr. Pim.

ANNE. Yes, Miss. [*She goes out*]

DINAH [*excitedly*]. That's me. They can't discuss me in the library without breaking down, so they're walking up and down outside, and slashing at the thistles in order to conceal their emotion. *You* know. I expect Brian—

PIM [*looking at his watch*]. Yes, I think, Miss Marden, I had better go now and return a little later. I have a telegram which I want to send, and perhaps by the time I came back—

DINAH. Oh, but how disappointing of you, when we were getting on together so nicely. And it was just going to be your turn to tell me all about *your*self.

PIM. I have really nothing to tell, Miss Marden. I have a letter of introduction to Mr. Marden, who in turn will give me, I hope, a letter to a certain distinguished man whom it is necessary for me to meet. That is all. [*Holding out his hand*] And now, Miss Marden—

DINAH. Oh, I'll start you on your way to the post office. I want to know if you're married, and all that sort of thing. You've got heaps to tell me, Mr. Pim. Have you got your hat? That's right. Then we'll—hullo, here's Brian. [BRIAN STRANGE *comes in at the windows. He is what* GEORGE *calls a damned futuristic painter-chap, aged twenty-four. To look at, he is a very pleasant boy, rather untidily dressed*]

BRIAN [*nodding*]. How do you do?

DINAH [*seizing him*]. Brian, this is Mr. Pim. Mr. Carraway Pim. He's been telling me all about himself. It's so interesting. He's just going to send a telegram, and then he's coming back again. Mr. Pim, this is Brian—*you* know.

BRIAN [*smiling and shaking hands*]. How do you do?

DINAH [*pleadingly*]. You *won't* mind going to the post office by yourself, will you, because, you see, Brian and I—[*she looks lovingly at* BRIAN].

PIM [*because they are so young*]. Miss Dinah and Mr.—er—Brian, I have only come into your lives for a moment, and it is probable that I shall now pass out of them for ever, but you will allow an old man—

DINAH. Oh, not old!

PIM [*chuckling happily*]. Well, a middle-aged man—to wish you both every happiness in the years that you have before you. Good-by, good-by. [*He disappears gently through the windows*]

DINAH. Brian, he'll get lost if he goes that way.

BRIAN [*going to the windows and calling after him*]. Round to the left, sir. . . . That's right. [*He comes back into the room*] Rum old bird. Who is he?

DINAH. Darling, you haven't kissed me yet.

BRIAN [*taking her in his arms*]. I oughtn't to, but then one never ought to do the nice things.

DINAH. Why oughtn't you? [*They sit on the sofa together*]

BRIAN. Well, we said we'd be good until we'd told your uncle and aunt all about it. You see, being a guest in their house—

DINAH. But, darling child, what *have* you been doing all this morning *except* telling George?

BRIAN. *Trying* to tell George.

DINAH [*nodding*]. Yes, of course, there's a difference.

BRIAN. I think he guessed there was something up, and he took me down to see the pigs—he said he had to see the pigs at once—I don't know why; an appointment perhaps. And we talked about pigs all the way, and I couldn't say, "Talking about pigs, I want to marry your niece—"

DINAH [*with mock indignation*]. Of course you couldn't.

BRIAN. No. Well you see how it was. And then when we'd finished talking about pigs, we started talking *to* the pigs—

DINAH [*eagerly*]. Oh, *how* is Arnold?

BRIAN. The little black-and-white one? He's very jolly, I believe, but naturally I wasn't thinking about him much. I was wondering how to begin. And then Lumsden came up, and wanted to talk pig-food, and the atmosphere grew less and less romantic, and—and I gradually drifted away.

DINAH. Poor darling. Well, we shall have to approach him through Olivia.

BRIAN. But I always wanted to tell her first; she's so much easier. Only you wouldn't let me.

DINAH. That's your fault, Brian. You would tell Olivia that she ought to have orange-and-black curtains.

BRIAN. But she *wants* orange-and-black curtains.

DINAH. Yes, but George says he's not going to have any futuristic nonsense in an honest English country house, which has been good enough for his father and his grandfather and his great-grandfather, and—and all the rest of them. So there's a sort of strained feeling between Olivia and George just now, and if Olivia were to—sort of recommend you, well, it wouldn't do you much good.

BRIAN [*looking at her*]. I see. Of course I know what *you* want, Dinah.

DINAH. What do I want?

BRIAN. You want a secret engagement, and notes left under door-mats, and meetings by the withered thorn, when all the household is asleep. *I* know you.

DINAH. Oh, but it is such fun! I love meeting people by withered thorns.

BRIAN. Well, I'm not going to have it.

DINAH [*childishly*]. Oh, George! Look at us being husbandy!

BRIAN. You babe! I adore you. [*He kisses her and holds her away from him and looks at her*] You know, you're rather throwing yourself away on me. Do you mind?

DINAH. Not a bit.

BRIAN. We shall never be rich, but we shall have lots of fun, and meet interesting people, and feel that we're doing something worth doing, and not getting paid nearly enough for it, and we can curse the Academy together and the British Public, and—oh, it's an exciting life.

DINAH [*seeing it*]. I shall love it.

BRIAN. I'll make you love it. You shan't be sorry, Dinah.

DINAH. You shan't be sorry either, Brian.

BRIAN [*looking at her lovingly*]. Oh, I know I shan't. . . . What will Olivia think about it? Will she be surprised?

DINAH. She's never surprised. She always seems to have thought of things about a week before they happen. George just begins to get hold of them about a week *after* they've happened. [*Considering him*] After all, there's no reason why George *shouldn't* like you, darling.

BRIAN. I'm not his sort, you know.

DINAH. You're more Olivia's sort. Well, we'll tell Olivia this morning.

OLIVIA [*coming in*]. And what are you going to tell Olivia this morning? [*She looks at them with a smile*] Oh, well, I think I can guess.

[*Shall we describe* OLIVIA? *But you will know all about her before the day is over*]

DINAH [*jumping up*]. Olivia, darling!

BRIAN [*following*]. Say you understand, Mrs. Marden.

OLIVIA. Mrs. Marden, I am afraid, is a very dense person, Brian, but I think if you asked Olivia if she understood—

BRIAN. Bless you, Olivia. I knew you'd be on our side.

DINAH. Of course she would.

OLIVIA. I don't know if it's usual to kiss an aunt-in-law, Brian, but Dinah is such a very special sort of niece that— [*She inclines her cheek and* BRIAN *kisses it*]

DINAH. I say, you *are* in luck today, Brian.

OLIVIA [*going over to her chair by the work-table and getting to business with the curtains*]. And how many people have been told the good news?

BRIAN. Nobody yet.

DINAH. Except Mr. Pim.

BRIAN. Oh, does *he*—

OLIVIA. Who's Mr. Pim?

DINAH. Oh, he just happened—I say, are those *the* curtains? Then you're going to have them after all?

OLIVIA [*with an air of surprise*]. After all what? But I decided on them long ago. [*To* BRIAN] You haven't told George yet?

BRIAN. I began to, you know, but I never got any farther than "Er—there's just—er—"

DINAH. George *would* talk about pigs all the time.

OLIVIA. Well, I suppose you want me to help you.

DINAH. Do, darling.

BRIAN. It would be awfully decent of you. Of course, I'm not quite his sort really—

DINAH. You're *my* sort.

BRIAN. But I don't think he objects to me, and— [GEORGE *comes in, a typical, narrow-minded, honest country gentleman of forty-odd*]

GEORGE [*at the windows*]. What's all this about a Mr. Pim? [*He kicks some of the mud off his boots*] Who is he? Where is he? I had most important business with Lumsden, and the girl comes down and cackles about a Mr. Pim, or Ping, or something. Where did I put his card? [*Bringing it out*] Carraway Pim. Never heard of him in my life.

DINAH. He said he had a letter of introduction, Uncle George.

GEORGE. Oh, *you* saw him, did you? Yes, that reminds me, there *was* a letter— [*He brings it out and reads it*]

DINAH. He had to send a telegram. He's coming back.

OLIVIA. Pass me those scissors, Brian.

BRIAN. These? [*He picks them up and comes close to her*]

OLIVIA. Thank you. [*She indicates* GEORGE's *back. "Now?" says* BRIAN *with his eyebrows. She nods*]

GEORGE [*reading*]. Ah, well, a friend of Brymer's. Glad to oblige him. Yes, I know the man he wants. Coming back, you say, Dinah? Then I'll be going back. Send him down to the farm, Olivia, when he comes. [*To* BRIAN] Hallo, what happened to *you?*

OLIVIA. Don't go, George, there's something we want to talk about.

GEORGE. Hallo, what's this?

BRIAN [*to* OLIVIA]. Shall I—?

OLIVIA. Yes.

BRIAN [*stepping out*]. I've been wanting to tell you all this morning, sir, only I didn't seem to have an opportunity of getting it out.

GEORGE. Well, what is it?

BRIAN. I want to marry Dinah, sir.

GEORGE. You want to marry Dinah? God bless my soul!

DINAH [*rushing to him and putting her cheek against his coat*]. Oh, do say you like the idea, Uncle George.

GEORGE. Like the idea! Have you heard of this nonsense, Olivia?

OLIVIA. They've just this moment told me, George. I think they would be happy together.

GEORGE [*to* BRIAN]. And what do you propose to be happy together *on?*

BRIAN. Well, of course, it doesn't amount to much at present, but we shan't starve.

DINAH. Brian got fifty pounds for a picture last March!

GEORGE [*a little upset by this*]. Oh! [*Recovering gamely*] And how many pictures have you sold since?

BRIAN. Well, none, but—

GEORGE. None! And I don't wonder. Who the devil is going to buy pictures with triangular clouds and square sheep? And they call that art nowadays! Good God, man [*waving him to the windows*], go outside and *look* at the clouds!

OLIVIA. If he draws round clouds in future, George, will you let him marry Dinah?

GEORGE. What—what? Yes, of course, you *would* be on his side—all this Futuristic nonsense. I'm just taking these clouds as an example. I suppose I can see as well as any man in the county, and I say that clouds *aren't* triangular.

BRIAN. After all, sir, at my age one is naturally experimenting and trying to find one's [*with a laugh*]—well, it sounds priggish, but one's medium of expression. I shall find out what I want to do directly, but I think I shall always be able to earn enough to live on. Well, I have for the last three years.

GEORGE. I see, and now you want to experiment with a wife, and you propose to start experimenting with *my* niece?

BRIAN [*with a shrug*]. Well, of course, if you—

OLIVIA. You could help the experiment, darling, by giving Dinah a good allowance until she's twenty-one.

GEORGE. Help the experiment! I don't *want* to help the experiment.

OLIVIA [*apologetically*]. Oh, I thought you did.

GEORGE. You will talk as if I was made of money. What with taxes always going up and rents always going down, it's as much as we can do to rub along as we are, without making allowances to everybody who thinks she wants to get married. [*To* BRIAN] And that's thanks to you, my friend.

BRIAN [*surprised*]. To me?

OLIVIA. You never told me, darling. What's Brian been doing?

DINAH [*indignantly*]. He hasn't been doing anything.

GEORGE. He's one of your Socialists who go turning the country upside down.

OLIVIA. But even Socialists must get married sometimes.

GEORGE. I don't see any necessity.

OLIVIA. But you'd have nobody to damn after dinner, darling, if they all died out.

BRIAN. Really, sir, I don't see what my politics and my art have got to do with it. I'm perfectly ready not to talk about either when I'm in your house, and as Dinah doesn't seem to object to them—

DINAH. I should think she doesn't.

GEORGE. Oh, you can get round the women, I daresay.

BRIAN. Well, it's Dinah I want to marry and live with. So what it really comes to is that you don't think I can support a wife.

GEORGE. Well, if you're going to do it by selling pictures, I don't think you can.

BRIAN. All right, tell me how much you want me to earn in a year, and I'll earn it.

GEORGE [*hedging*]. It isn't merely a question of money. I just mention that as one thing—one of the important things. In addition to that, I think you are both too young to marry. I don't think you know your own minds, and I am not at all persuaded that, with what I venture to call your outrageous tastes, you and my niece will live happily together. Just because she thinks she loves you, Dinah may persuade herself now that she agrees with all you say and do, but she has been properly brought up in an honest English country household, and—er—she—well, in short, I cannot at all approve of any engagement between you. [*Getting up*] Olivia, if this Mr.—er—Pim comes, I shall be down at the farm. You might send him along to me. [*He walks towards the windows*]

BRIAN [*indignantly*]. Is there any reason why I shouldn't marry a girl who has been properly brought up?

GEORGE. I think you know my views, Strange.

OLIVIA. George, wait a moment, dear. We can't quite leave it like this.

GEORGE. I have said all I want to say on the subject.

OLIVIA. Yes, darling, but I haven't begun to say all that *I* want to say on the subject.

GEORGE. Of course, if you have anything to say, Olivia, I will listen to it; but I don't know that this is quite the time, or that you have chosen—[*looking darkly at the curtains*]—quite the occupation likely to—er—endear your views to me.

DINAH [*mutinously*]. I may as well tell you, Uncle George, that *I* have got a good deal to say, too.

OLIVIA. I can guess what you are going to say, Dinah, and I think you had better keep it for the moment.

DINAH [*meekly*]. Yes, Aunt Olivia.

OLIVIA. Brian, you might take her outside for a walk. I expect you have plenty to talk about.

GEORGE. Now mind, Strange, no love-making. I put you on your honor about that.

BRIAN. I'll do my best to avoid it, sir.

DINAH [*cheekily*]. May I take his arm if we go up a hill?

OLIVIA. I'm sure you'll know how to behave—both of you.

BRIAN. Come on, then, Dinah.

DINAH. Righto.

GEORGE [*as they go*]. And if you do see any clouds, Strange, take a good look at them. [*He chuckles to himself*] Triangular clouds—I never heard of such nonsense. [*He goes back to his chair at the writing-table*] Futuristic rubbish. . . . Well, Olivia?

OLIVIA. Well, George?

GEORGE. What are you doing?

OLIVIA. Making curtains, George. Won't they be rather sweet? Oh, but I forgot—you don't like them.

GEORGE. I don't like them, and what is more, I don't mean to have them in my house. As I told you yesterday, this is the house of a simple country gentleman, and I don't want any of these new-fangled ideas in it.

OLIVIA. Is marrying for love a new-fangled idea?

GEORGE. We'll come to that directly. None of you women can keep to the point. What I am saying now is that the house of my fathers and fore-fathers is good enough for me.

OLIVIA. Do you know, George, I can hear one of your ancestors saying that to his wife in their smelly old cave, when the new-fangled idea of build-ing houses was first suggested. "The Cave of my Fathers is—"

GEORGE. That's ridiculous. Naturally we must have progress. But that's

just the point. [*Indicating the curtains*] I don't call this sort of thing progress. It's—ah—retrogression.

OLIVIA. Well, anyhow, it's pretty.

GEORGE. There I disagree with you. And I must say once more that I will
not have them hanging in my house.

OLIVIA. Very well, George. [*But she goes on working*]

GEORGE. That being so, I don't see the necessity of going on with them.

OLIVIA. Well, I must do something with them now I've got the material.
I thought perhaps I could sell them when they're finished—as we're so poor.

GEORGE. What do you mean—so poor?

OLIVIA. Well, you said just now that you couldn't give Dinah an allowance because rents had gone down.

GEORGE [*annoyed*]. Confound it, Olivia! Keep to the point! We'll talk
about Dinah's affairs directly. We're discussing our own affairs at the
moment.

OLIVIA. But what is there to discuss?

GEORGE. Those ridiculous things.

OLIVIA. But we've finished that. You've said you wouldn't have them
hanging in your house, and I've said, "Very well, George." Now we can go
on to Dinah and Brian.

GEORGE [*shouting*]. But put these beastly things away.

OLIVIA [*rising and gathering up the curtains*]. Very well, George. [*She
puts them away, slowly, gracefully. There is an uncomfortable silence.
Evidently somebody ought to apologize*]

GEORGE [*realizing that he is the one*]. Er—look here, Olivia, old girl,
you've been a jolly good wife to me, and we don't often have rows, and if
I've been rude to you about this—lost my temper a bit perhaps, what?—
I'll say I'm sorry. May I have a kiss?

OLIVIA [*holding up her face*]. George, darling! [*He kisses her*] Do you
love me?

GEORGE. You know I do, old girl.

OLIVIA. As much as Brian loves Dinah?

GEORGE [*stiffly*]. I've said all I want to say about that. [*He goes away
from her*]

OLIVIA. Oh, but there must be lots you want to say—and perhaps don't
like to. Do tell me, darling.

GEORGE. What it comes to is this. I consider that Dinah is too young to
choose a husband for herself, and that Strange isn't the husband I should
choose for her.

OLIVIA. You were calling him Brian yesterday.

GEORGE. Yesterday I regarded him as a boy, now he wants me to look
upon him as a man.

OLIVIA. He's twenty-four.

GEORGE. And Dinah's nineteen. Ridiculous!

OLIVIA. If he'd been a Conservative, and thought that clouds were round, I suppose he'd have seemed older, somehow.

GEORGE. That's a different point altogether. That has nothing to do with his age.

OLIVIA [*innocently*]. Oh, I thought it had.

GEORGE. What I am objecting to is these ridiculously early marriages before either party knows its own mind, much less the mind of the other party. Such marriages invariably lead to unhappiness.

OLIVIA. Of course, *my* marriage wasn't a happy one.

GEORGE. As you know, Olivia, I dislike speaking about your first marriage at all, and I had no intention of bringing it up now, but since you mention it— well, that is a case in point.

OLIVIA [*looking back at it*]. When I was eighteen, I was in love. Or perhaps I only thought I was, and I don't know if I should have been happy or not if I had married him. But my father made me marry a man called Jacob Telworthy; and when things were too hot for him in England—"too hot for him"—I think that was the expression we used in those days—then we went to Australia, and I left him there, and the only happy moment I had in all my married life was on the morning when I saw in the papers that he was dead.

GEORGE [*very uncomfortable*]. Yes, yes, my dear, I know. You must have had a terrible time. I can hardly bear to think about it. My only hope is that I have made up to you for it in some degree. But I don't see what bearing it has upon Dinah's case.

OLIVIA. Oh, none, except that *my* father *liked* Jacob's political opinions and his views on art. I expect that that was why he chose him for me.

GEORGE. You seem to think that I wish to choose a husband for Dinah. I don't at all. Let her choose whom she likes as long as he can support her and there's a chance of their being happy together. Now, with regard to this fellow—

OLIVIA. You mean Brian?

GEORGE. He's got no money, and he's been brought up in quite a different way from Dinah. Dinah may be prepared to believe that—er—all cows are blue, and that—er—waves are square, but she won't go on believing it forever.

OLIVIA. Neither will Brian.

GEORGE. Well, that's what I keep telling him, only he won't see it. Just as I keep telling you about those ridiculous curtains. It seems to me that I am the only person in the house with any eyesight left.

OLIVIA. Perhaps you are, darling; but you must let us find out our own mistakes for ourselves. At any rate, Brian is a gentleman; he loves Dinah, Dinah loves him; he's earning enough to support himself, and you are earning enough to support Dinah. I think it's worth risking, George.

GEORGE [*stiffly*]. I can only say the whole question demands much more anxious thought than you seem to have given it. You say that he is a gentleman. He knows how to behave, I admit; but if his morals are as topsy-turvy as his tastes and—er—politics, as I've no doubt they are, then—er— In short, I do *not* approve of Brian Strange as a husband for my niece and ward.

OLIVIA [*looking at him thoughtfully*]. You *are* a curious mixture, George. You were so very unconventional when you married me, and you're so very conventional when Brian wants to marry Dinah. . . . George Marden to marry the widow of a convict!

GEORGE. Convict! What do you mean?

OLIVIA. Jacob Telworthy, convict—I forget his number—surely I told you all this, dear, when we got engaged?

GEORGE. Never!

OLIVIA. I told you how he carelessly put the wrong signature to a check for a thousand pounds in England; how he made a little mistake about two or three companies he'd promoted in Australia; and how—

GEORGE. Yes, yes, but you never told me he was *convicted!*

OLIVIA. What difference does it make?

GEORGE. My dear Olivia, if you can't see that—a convict!

OLIVIA. So, you see, we needn't be too particular about our niece, need we?

GEORGE. I think we had better leave your first husband out of the conversation altogether. I never wished to refer to him; I never wish to hear about him again. I certainly had not realized that he was actually—er—*convicted* for his—er—

OLIVIA. Mistakes.

GEORGE. Well, we needn't go into that. As for this other matter, I don't for a moment take it seriously. Dinah is an exceptionally pretty girl, and young Strange is a good-looking boy. If they are attracted to each other, it is a mere outward attraction which I am convinced will not lead to any lasting happiness. That must be regarded as my last word in the matter, Olivia. If this Mr.—er—what was his name, comes, I shall be down at the farm. [*He goes out by the door. Left alone,* OLIVIA *brings out her curtains again, and gets calmly to work upon them.* DINAH *and* BRIAN *come in by the windows*]

DINAH. Finished?

OLIVIA. Oh, no, I've got all these rings to put on.

DINAH. I meant talking to George.

BRIAN. We walked about outside—

DINAH. Until we heard him *not* talking to you any more—

BRIAN. And we didn't kiss each other once.

DINAH. Brian was very George-like. He wouldn't even let me tickle the back of his neck. [*She goes up suddenly to* OLIVIA *and kneels by her and kisses her*] Darling, being George-like is a very nice thing to be—I mean a nice thing for other people to be—I mean—oh, you know what I mean. But say that he's going to be decent about it.

OLIVIA. Of course he is, Dinah.

BRIAN. You mean he'll let me come here as—as—

DINAH. As my young man?

OLIVIA. Oh, I think so.

DINAH. Olivia, you're a wonder. Have you really talked him round?

OLIVIA. I haven't said anything yet. But I daresay I shall think of something.

DINAH [*disappointedly*]. Oh!

BRIAN [*making the best of it*]. After all, Dinah, I'm going back to London tomorrow—

OLIVIA. You can be good for one more day, Dinah, and then when Brian isn't here, we'll see what we can do.

DINAH. Yes, but I didn't want him to go back tomorrow.

BRIAN [*sternly*]. Must. Hard work before me. Earn thousands a year. Paint the Mayor and Corporation of Pudsey, life-size, including chains of office; paint slice of haddock on plate. Copy Landseer for old gentleman in Bayswater. Design antimacassar for middle-aged sofa in Streatham. Earn a living for you, Dinah.

DINAH [*giggling*]. Oh, Brian, you're heavenly. What fun we shall have when we're married.

BRIAN [*stiffly*]. Sir Brian Strange, R.A., if you please, Miss Marden. Sir Brian Strange, R.A., writes: "Your Sanogene has proved a most excellent tonic. After completing the third acre of my Academy picture 'The Mayor and Corporation of Pudsey' I was completely exhausted, but one bottle of Sanogene revived me, and I finished the remaining seven acres at a single sitting."

OLIVIA [*looking about her*]. Brian, find my scissors for me.

BRIAN. Scissors. [*Looking for them*] Sir Brian Strange, R.A., looks for scissors. [*Finding them*] Aha! Once more we must record an unqualified success for the eminent Academician. Your scissors.

OLIVIA. Thank you so much.

DINAH. Come on, Brian, let's go out. I feel open-airy.

OLIVIA. Don't be late for lunch, there's good people. Lady Marden is coming.

DINAH. Aunt Juli-ah! *Help!* [*She faints in* BRIAN's *arms*] That means a clean pinafore. Brian, you'll jolly well have to brush your hair.

BRIAN [*feeling it*]. I suppose there's no time now to go up to London and get it cut? [*Enter* ANNE, *followed by* PIM]

ANNE. Mr. Pim!

DINAH [*delighted*]. Hullo, Mr. Pim! Here we are again! You can't get rid of us so easily, you see.

PIM. I—er—dear Miss Marden—

OLIVIA. How do you, Mr. Pim? I can't get up, but do come and sit down. My husband will be here in a minute. Anne. send somebody down to the farm—

ANNE. I think I heard the Master in the library, madam.

OLIVIA. Oh, will you tell him then?

ANNE. Yes, madam. [ANNE *goes out*]

OLIVIA. You'll stay to lunch, of course, Mr. Pim?

DINAH. Oh, do!

PIM. It's very kind of you, Mrs. Marden, but—

DINAH. Oh, you simply must, Mr. Pim. You haven't told us half enough about yourself yet. I want to hear all about your early life.

OLIVIA. Dinah!

PIM. Oh, we are almost, I might say, old friends, Mrs. Marden.

DINAH. Of course we are. He knows Brian, too. There's more in Mr. Pim than you think. You *will* stay to lunch, won't you?

PIM. It's very kind of you to ask me, Mrs. Marden, but I am lunching with the Trevors.

OLIVIA. Oh, well, you must come to lunch another day.

DINAH. The reason why we like Mr. Pim so much is that he was the first person to congratulate us. We feel that he is going to have a great influence on our lives.

PIM [*to* OLIVIA]. I, so to speak, stumbled on the engagement this morning and—er—

OLIVIA. I see. Children, you must go and tidy yourselves up. Run along.

BRIAN. Sir Brian and Lady Strange never run; they walk. [*Offering his arm*] Madam!

DINAH [*taking it*]. Au revoir, Mr. Pim. [*Dramatically*] We—shall—meet—*again!*

PIM [*chuckling*]. Good morning, Miss Dinah.

BRIAN. Good morning. [*He and* DINAH *go out*]

OLIVIA. You must forgive them, Mr. Pim. They're such children. And naturally they're rather excited just now.

PIM. Oh, not at all, Mrs. Marden.

OLIVIA. Of course you won't say anything about their engagement. We only heard about it five minutes ago, and nothing has been settled yet.

PIM. Of course, of course! [*Enter* GEORGE]

GEORGE. Ah, Mr. Pim, we meet at last. Sorry to have kept you waiting before.

PIM. The apology should come from me, Mr. Marden for having—er—

GEORGE. Not at all. Very glad to meet you now. Any friend of Brymer's. You want a letter to this man Fanshawe?

OLIVIA. Shall I be in your way at all?

PIM. Oh, no, no, please don't.

GEORGE. It's only just a question of a letter. [*Going to his desk*] Fanshawe will put you in the way of seeing all that you want to see. He's a very old friend of mine. [*Taking a sheet of notepaper*] You'll stay to lunch, of course?

PIM. I'm afraid I am lunching with the Trevors—

GEORGE. Oh, well, they'll look after you all right. Good chap, Trevor.

PIM [*to* OLIVIA]. You see, Mrs. Marden, I have only recently arrived from Australia after traveling about the world for some years, and I'm rather out of touch with my—er—fellow-workers in London.

OLIVIA. Oh, yes. You've been in Australia, Mr. Pim?

GEORGE [*disliking Australia*]. I shan't be a moment, Mr. Pim. [*He frowns at* OLIVIA]

PIM. Oh, that's all right, thank you. [*To* OLIVIA] Oh, yes, I have been in Australia more than once in the last few years.

OLIVIA. Really? I used to live at Sydney many years ago. Do you know Sydney at all?

GEORGE [*detesting Sydney*]. H'r'm! Perhaps I'd better mention that you are a friend of the Trevors?

PIM. Thank you, thank you. [*To* OLIVIA] Indeed yes, I spent several months in Sydney.

OLIVIA. How curious. I wonder if we have any friends in common there.

GEORGE [*hastily*]. Extremely unlikely, I should think. Sydney is a very big place.

PIM. True, but the world is a very small place, Mr. Marden. I had a remarkable instance of that, coming over on the boat this last time.

GEORGE. Ah! [*Feeling that the conversation is now safe, he resumes his letter*]

PIM. Yes. There was a man I used to employ in Sydney some years ago, a bad fellow, I'm afraid, Mrs. Marden, who had been in prison for some kind of fraudulent company-promoting and had taken to drink and—and so on.

OLIVIA. Yes, yes, I understand.

PIM. Drinking himself to death I should have said. I gave him at the most another year to live. Yet to my amazement the first person I saw as I stepped on board the boat that brought me to England last week was this fellow. There was no mistaking him. I spoke to him, in fact; we recognized each other.

OLIVIA. Really?

PIM. He was traveling steerage; we didn't meet again on board, and as it happened at Marseilles, this poor fellow—er—now what *was* his name? A very unusual one. Began with a—a T, I think.

OLIVIA [*with suppressed feeling*]. Yes, Mr. Pim, yes? [*She puts out a hand to* GEORGE]

GEORGE [*in an undertone*]. Nonsense, dear!

PIM [*triumphantly*]. I've got it! Telworthy!

OLIVIA. Telworthy!

GEORGE. Good God!

PIM [*a little surprised at the success of his story*]. An unusual name, is it not? Not a name you could forget when once you had heard it.

OLIVIA [*with feeling*]. No, it is not a name you could forget when once you had heard it.

GEORGE [*hastily coming over to* PIM]. Quite so, Mr. Pim, a most remarkable name, a most odd story altogether. Well, well, here's your letter, and if you're sure you won't stay to lunch—

PIM. I'm afraid not, thank you. You see, I—

GEORGE. The Trevors, yes. I'll just see you on your way—[*To* OLIVIA] Er—my dear—

OLIVIA [*holding out her hand, but not looking at him*]. Good-by, Mr. Pim.

PIM. Good-by, good-by!

GEORGE [*leading the way through the windows*]. This way, this way. Quicker for you.

PIM. Thank you, thank you. [GEORGE *hurries* MR. PIM *out.* OLIVIA *sits there and looks into the past. Now and then she shudders.* GEORGE *comes back*]

GEORGE. Good God! Telworthy! Is it possible? [*Before* OLIVIA *can answer,* LADY MARDEN *is announced. They pull themselves together and greet her*]

## ACT II

*Lunch is over and coffee has been served on the terrace. Conversation drags on, to the satisfaction of* LADY MARDEN, *but of nobody else.* GEORGE *and* OLIVIA *want to be alone; so do* BRIAN *and* DINAH. *At last* BRIAN *murmurs something about a cigarette-case; and, catching* DINAH's *eye, comes into the house. He leans against the sofa and waits for* DINAH.

DINAH [*loudly as she comes in*]. Have you found it?

BRIAN. Found what?

DINAH [*in her ordinary voice*]. That was just for *their* benefit. I said I'd help you find it. It *is* your cigarette-case we're looking for, isn't it?

BRIAN [*taking it out*]. Yes. Have one?

DINAH. No, thank you, darling. Aunt Juli-ah still thinks it's unladylike. . . . Have you ever seen her beagling?

BRIAN. No. Is that very ladylike?

DINAH. Very. . . . I say, what has happened, do you think?

BRIAN. Everything. I love you, and you love me.

DINAH. Silly! I meant between George and Olivia. Didn't you notice them at lunch?

BRIAN. I noticed that you seemed to be doing most of the talking. But then I've noticed that before sometimes. Do you think Olivia and your uncle have quarreled because of *us?*

DINAH. Of course not. George may *think* he has quarreled, but I'm quite sure Olivia hasn't. No, I believe Mr. Pim's at the bottom of it. He's brought some terribly sad news about George's investments. The old home will have to be sold up.

BRIAN. Good. Then your uncle won't mind your marrying me.

DINAH. Yes, darling, but you must be more dramatic about it than that. "George," you must say, with tears in your eyes, "I cannot pay off the whole of the mortgage for you. I have only two and ninepence; but at least let me take your niece off your hands." Then George will thump you on the back and say gruffly, "You're a good fellow, Brian, a damn good fellow," and he'll blow his nose very loudly, and say, "Confound this cigar, it won't draw properly." [*She gives us a rough impression of* GEORGE *doing it*]

BRIAN. Dinah, you're a heavenly idiot. And you've simply got to marry me, uncles or no uncles.

DINAH. It will have to be "uncles," I'm afraid, because, you see, I'm his ward, and I can get sent to Chancery or Coventry or somewhere beastly, if I marry without his consent. Haven't *you* got anybody who objects to your marrying *me?*

BRIAN. Nobody, thank Heaven.

DINAH. Well, that's rather disappointing of you. I saw myself fascinating your aged father at the same time that you were fascinating George. I should have done it much better than you. As a George-fascinator you aren't very successful, sweetheart.

BRIAN. What am I like as a Dinah-fascinator?

DINAH. Plus six, darling.

BRIAN. Then I'll stick to that and leave George to Olivia.

DINAH. I expect she'll manage him all right. I have great faith in Olivia. But you'll marry me, anyhow, won't you, Brian?

BRIAN. I will.

DINAH. Even if we have to wait till I'm twenty-one?

BRIAN. Even if we have to wait till you're fifty-one.

DINAH [*holding out her hands to him*]. Darling!

BRIAN [*uneasily*]. I say, don't do that.

DINAH. Why not?

BRIAN. Well, I promised I wouldn't kiss you.

DINAH. Oh! . . . Well, you might just *send* me a kiss. You can look the other way as if you didn't know I was here.

BRIAN. Like this? [*He looks the other way, kisses the tips of his fingers, and flicks it carelessly in her direction*]

DINAH. That was a lovely one. Now here's one coming for you. [*He catches it gracefully and conveys it to his mouth*]

BRIAN [*with a low bow*]. Madam, I thank you.

DINAH [*curtseying*]. Your servant, Mr. Strange.

OLIVIA [*from outside*]. Dinah!

DINAH [*jumping up*]. Hullo! [OLIVIA *comes in through the windows, followed by* GEORGE *and* LADY MARDEN, *the latter a vigorous young woman of sixty-odd, who always looks as if she were beagling*]

OLIVIA. Aunt Julia wants to see the pigs, dear. I wish you'd take her down. I'm rather tired, and your uncle has some business to attend to.

LADY MARDEN. I've always said that you don't take enough exercise, Olivia. Look at me—sixty-five and proud of it.

OLIVIA. Yes, Aunt Julia, you're wonderful.

DINAH. How old would Olivia be if she took exercise?

GEORGE. Don't stand about asking silly questions, Dinah. Your aunt hasn't much time.

BRIAN. May I come, too, Lady Marden?

LADY MARDEN. Well, a little exercise wouldn't do *you* any harm, Mr. Strange. You're an artist, ain't you?

BRIAN. Well, I try to paint.

DINAH. He sold a picture last March for—

GEORGE. Yes, yes, never mind that now.

LADY MARDEN. Unhealthy life. Well, come along. [*She strides out, followed by* DINAH *and* BRIAN. GEORGE *sits down at his desk with his head in his hand, and stabs the blotting-paper with a pen.* OLIVIA *takes the curtains with her to the sofa and begins to work on them*]

GEORGE [*looking up and seeing them*]. Really, Olivia, we've got something more important, more vital to us than curtains, to discuss, now that we *are* alone at last.

OLIVIA. I wasn't going to discuss them, dear.

GEORGE. I'm always glad to see Aunt Julia in my house, but I wish she hadn't chosen this day of all days to come to lunch.

OLIVIA. It wasn't Aunt Julia's fault. It was really Mr. Pim who chose the wrong day.

GEORGE [*fiercely*]. Good Heavens, is it true?

OLIVIA. About Jacob Telworthy?

GEORGE. You told me he was dead. You always said that he was dead. You—you—

OLIVIA. Well, I always thought that he was dead. He was as dead as anybody could be. All the papers said he was dead.

GEORGE [*scornfully*]. The papers!

OLIVIA [*as if this would settle it for* GEORGE]. The *Times* said he was dead. There was a paragraph about him. Apparently even his death was fraudulent.

GEORGE. Yes, yes. I'm not blaming you, Olivia, but what are we going to do, that's the question, what are we going to do? My God, it's horrible! You've never been married to me at all! You don't seem to understand.

OLIVIA. It is a little difficult to realize. You see, it doesn't seem to have made any difference to our happiness.

GEORGE. No, that's what's so terrible. I mean—well, of course, we were quite innocent in the matter. But, at the same time, nothing can get over the fact that we—we had no right to—to be happy.

OLIVIA. Would you rather we had been miserable?

GEORGE. You're Telworthy's wife, that's what you don't seem to understand. You're Telworthy's wife. You—er—forgive me, Olivia, but it's the horrible truth—you committed bigamy when you married me. [*In horror*] Bigamy!

OLIVIA. It is an ugly word, isn't it?

GEORGE. Yes, but don't you understand— [*He jumps up and comes over to her*] Look here, Olivia, old girl, the whole thing is nonsense, eh? It isn't your husband, it's some other Telworthy that this fellow met. That's right, isn't it? Some other shady swindler who turned up on the boat, eh? This sort of thing doesn't happen to people like *us*—committing bigamy and all that. Some other fellow.

OLIVIA [*shaking her head*]. I knew all the shady swindlers in Sydney, George. . . . They came to dinner. . . . There were no others called Telworthy. [GEORGE *goes back despondently to his seat*]

GEORGE. Well, what are we going to do?

OLIVIA. You sent Mr. Pim away so quickly. He might have told us things. Telworthy's plans. Where he is now. You hurried him away so quickly.

GEORGE. I've sent a note round to ask him to come back. My one idea at the moment was to get him out of the house—to hush things up.

OLIVIA. You can't hush up two husbands.

GEORGE [*in despair*]. You can't. Everybody will know. Everybody!

OLIVIA. The children, Aunt Julia, they may as well know now as later. Mr. Pim must, of course.

GEORGE. I do not propose to discuss my private affairs with Mr. Pim—

OLIVIA. But he's mixed himself up in them rather, hasn't he, and if you're going to ask him questions—

GEORGE. I only propose to ask him one question. I shall ask him if he is absolutely certain of the man's name. I can do that quite easily without letting him know the reason for my inquiry.

OLIVIA. You couldn't make a mistake about a name like Telworthy. But he might tell us something about Telworthy's plans. Perhaps he's going back to Australia at once. Perhaps he thinks I'm dead, too. Perhaps—oh, there are so many things I want to know.

GEORGE. Yes, yes, dear. It would be interesting to—that is, one naturally wants to know these things, but of course it doesn't make any real difference.

OLIVIA [*surprised*]. No difference?

GEORGE. Well, that is to say, you're as much his wife if he's in Australia as you are if he's in England.

OLIVIA. I am not his wife at all.

GEORGE. But, Olivia, surely you understand the position—

OLIVIA [*shaking her head*]. Jacob Telworthy may be alive, but I am not his wife. I ceased to be his wife when I became yours.

GEORGE. You never *were* my wife. That is the terrible part of it. Our union—you make me say it, Olivia—has been unhallowed by the Church. Unhallowed even by the Law. Legally, we have been living in—living in— well, the point is, how does the Law stand? I imagine that Telworthy could get a—a divorce. . . . Oh, it seems impossible that things like this can be happening to *us*.

OLIVIA [*joyfully*]. A divorce?

GEORGE. I—I imagine so.

OLIVIA. But then we could *really* get married, and we shouldn't be living in—living in—whatever we were living in before.

GEORGE. I can't understand you, Olivia. You talk about it so calmly, as if there was nothing blameworthy in being divorced, as if there was nothing unusual in my marrying a divorced woman, as if there was nothing wrong in our having lived together for years without having been married.

OLIVIA. What seems wrong to me is that I lived for five years with a bad man whom I hated. What seems right to me is that I lived for five years with a good man whom I love.

GEORGE. Yes, yes, my dear, I know. But right and wrong don't settle themselves as easily as that. We've been living together when you were Telworthy's wife. That's *wrong*.

OLIVIA. Do you mean wicked?

GEORGE. Well, no doubt the Court would consider that we acted in perfect innocence—

OLIVIA. What Court?

GEORGE. These things have to be done legally, of course. I believe the proper method is a nullity suit, declaring our marriage null and—er—void. It would, so to speak, wipe out these years of—er—

OLIVIA. Wickedness?

GEORGE. Of irregular union, and—er—then—

OLIVIA. Then I could go back to Jacob. . . . Do you really mean that, George?

GEORGE [*uneasily*]. Well, dear, you see—that's how things are—one can't get away from—er—

OLIVIA. What you feel is that Telworthy has the greater claim? You are prepared to—make way for him?

GEORGE. Both the Church and the Law would say that I had no claim at all, I'm afraid. I—I suppose I haven't.

OLIVIA. I see. [*She looks at him curiously*] Thank you for making it so clear, George.

GEORGE. Of course, whether or not you go back to—er—Telworthy is another matter altogether. That would naturally be for you to decide.

OLIVIA [*cheerfully*]. For me and Jacko to decide.

GEORGE. Er—Jacko?

OLIVIA. I used to call my first husband—I mean my only husband—Jacko. I didn't like the name of Jacob, and Jacko seemed to suit him somehow. . . . He had very long arms. Dear Jacko.

GEORGE [*annoyed*]. You don't seem to realize that this is not a joke, Olivia.

OLIVIA [*a trifle hysterically*]. It may not be a joke, but it *is* funny, isn't it?

GEORGE. I must say I don't see anything funny in a tragedy that has wrecked two lives.

OLIVIA. Two? Oh, but Jacko's life isn't wrecked. It has just been miraculously restored to him. And a wife, too. There's nothing tragic for Jacko in it.

GEORGE [*stiffly*]. I was referring to *our* two lives—yours and mine.

OLIVIA. Yours, George? Your life isn't wrecked. The Court will absolve you of all blame; your friends will sympathize with you, and tell you that I was a designing woman who deliberately took you in; your Aunt Julia—

GEORGE [*overwrought*]. Stop it! What do you mean? Have you no heart? Do you think I *want* to lose you, Olivia? Do you think I *want* my home broken up like this? Haven't you been happy with me these last five years?

OLIVIA. Very happy.

GEORGE. Well then, how can you talk like that?

OLIVIA [*pathetically*]. But you want to send me away.

GEORGE. There you go again. I don't *want* to. I have hardly had time to realize just what it will mean to me when you go. The fact is I simply daren't realize it. I daren't think about it.

OLIVIA [*earnestly*]. Try thinking about it, George.

GEORGE. And you talk as if I *wanted* to send you away!

OLIVIA. Try thinking about it, George.

GEORGE. You don't seem to understand that I'm not *sending* you away. You simply aren't mine to keep.

OLIVIA. Whose am I?

GEORGE. Your husband's. Telworthy's.

OLIVIA [*gently*]. If I belong to anybody but myself, I think I belong to you.

GEORGE. Not in the eyes of the Law. Not in the eyes of the Church. Not even in the eyes of—er—

OLIVIA. The County?

GEORGE [*annoyed*]. I was about to say "Heaven."

OLIVIA [*unimpressed*]. Oh!

GEORGE. That this should happen to *us!* [*He gets up and walks about the room, wondering when he will wake up from this impossible dream.* OLIVIA *works in silence. Then she stands up and shakes out her curtains*]

OLIVIA [*looking at them*]. I do hope Jacko will like these.

GEORGE. What! You— [*Going up to her*] Olivia, Olivia, have you no heart?

OLIVIA. Ought you to talk like that to another man's wife?

GEORGE. Confound it, is this just a joke to you?

OLIVIA. You must forgive me, George; I am a little over-excited—at the thought of returning to Jacob, I suppose.

GEORGE. Do you *want* to return to him?

OLIVIA. One wants to do what is right. In the eyes of—er—Heaven.

GEORGE. Seeing what sort of man he is, I have no doubt that you could get a separation, supposing that he didn't—er—divorce you. I don't know *what* is best. I must consult my solicitor. The whole position has been sprung on us, and [*miserably*] I don't know, I don't know. I can't take it all in.

OLIVIA. Wouldn't you like to consult your Aunt Julia too? She could tell you what the County—I mean what Heaven really thought about it.

GEORGE. Yes, yes. Aunt Julia has plenty of common sense. You're quite right, Olivia. This isn't a thing we can keep from the family.

OLIVIA. Do I still call her *Aunt* Julia?

GEORGE [*looking up from his pacings*]. What? What? [ANNE *comes in*] Well, what is it?

ANNE. Mr. Pim says he will come down at once, sir.

GEORGE. Oh, thank you, thank you. [ANNE *goes out*]

OLIVIA. George, Mr. Pim has got to know.

GEORGE. I don't see the necessity.

OLIVIA. Not even for me? When a woman suddenly hears that her long-lost husband is restored to her, don't you think she wants to ask questions? Where is he living, and how is he looking, and—

GEORGE [*coldly*]. Of course, if you are interested in these things—

OLIVIA. How can I help being? Don't be so silly, George. We *must* know what Jacko—

GEORGE [*annoyed*]. I wish you wouldn't call him by that ridiculous name.

OLIVIA. My husband—

GEORGE [*wincing*]. Yes, well—your husband?

OLIVIA. Well, we must know his plans—where we can communicate with him, and so on.

GEORGE. I have no wish to communicate with him.

OLIVIA. I'm afraid you'll have to, dear.

GEORGE. I don't see the necessity.

OLIVIA. Well, you'll want to—to apologize to him for living with his wife for so long. And as I belong to him, he ought to be told where he can—call for me.

GEORGE [*after a struggle*]. You put it in a very peculiar way, but I see your point. [*With a shudder*] Oh, the horrible publicity of it all!

OLIVIA [*going up to him and comforting him*]. Poor George. Dear, don't think I don't sympathize with you. I understand so exactly what you are feeling. The publicity! It's terrible.

GEORGE [*miserably*]. I want to do what's right, Olivia. You believe that?

OLIVIA. Of course I do. It's only that we don't quite agree as to what is right and what is wrong.

GEORGE. It isn't a question of agreeing. Right is right, and wrong is wrong, all the world over.

OLIVIA [*with a sad little smile*]. But more particularly in Buckingham-shire, I think.

GEORGE. If I only considered myself, I should say: "Let us pack this man Telworthy back to Australia. He would make no claim. He would accept money to go away and say nothing about it." If I consulted simply my own happiness, Olivia, that is what I should say. But when I consult—er—

OLIVIA. [*surprised*]. Mine?

GEORGE. My conscience—

OLIVIA. Oh!

GEORGE. Then I can't do it. It's wrong. [*He is at the windows as he says this*]

OLIVIA [*making her first and last appeal*]. George, aren't I worth a little—

GEORGE [*turning round*]. H'sh! Dinah! [*Loudly for* DINAH's *benefit*] Well, then I'll write to him and— Ah, Dinah, where's Aunt Julia?

DINAH [*coming in*]. We've seen the pigs, and now she's discussing the Art of Landseer with Brian. I just came to ask—

OLIVIA. Dinah, dear, bring Aunt Julia here. And Brian too. We have things we want to talk about with you all.

GEORGE [*outraged*]. Olivia!

DINAH. Righto. What fun! [*Exit* DINAH]

GEORGE. Olivia, you don't seriously suggest that we should discuss these things with a child like Dinah and a young man like Strange, a mere acquaintance.

OLIVIA. Dinah will have to know. I'm very fond of her, George. You can't send me away without telling Dinah. And Brian is my friend. You have your solicitor and your aunt and your conscience to consult—mayn't I even have Brian?

GEORGE [*forgetting*]. I should have thought that your *husband*—

OLIVIA. Yes, but we don't know where Jacko is.

GEORGE. I was not referring to—er—Telworthy.

OLIVIA. Well then?

GEORGE. Well, naturally I—you mustn't— Oh, this is horrible! [*He comes back to his desk as the others come in*]

OLIVIA [*getting up*]. George and I have had some rather bad news, Aunt Julia. We wanted your advice. Where will you sit?

LADY MARDEN. Thank you, Olivia. I can sit down by myself. [*She does* so, *near* GEORGE. DINAH *sits on the sofa with* OLIVIA, *and* BRIAN *half leans against the back of it. There is a hush of expectation. . . .*] What is it? Money, I suppose. Nobody's safe nowadays.

GEORGE [*signaling for help*]. Olivia—

OLIVIA. We've just heard that my first husband is still alive.

DINAH. Telworthy!

BRIAN. Good Lord!

LADY MARDEN. George!

DINAH [*excitedly*]. And only this morning I was saying that nothing ever happened in this house! [*Remorsefully to* OLIVIA] Darling, I don't mean that. Darling one!

LADY MARDEN. What does this mean, George? I leave you for ten minutes—barely ten minutes—to go and look at the pigs, and when I come back you tell me that Olivia is a bigamist.

BRIAN [*indignantly*]. I say—

OLIVIA [*restraining him*]. H'sh!

BRIAN [*to* OLIVIA]. If this is a row, I'm on your side.

LADY MARDEN. Well, George?

GEORGE. I'm afraid it's true. Aunt Julia. We heard the news just before lunch—just before you came. We've only this moment had an opportunity of talking about it, of wondering what to do.

LADY MARDEN. What was his name—Tel—something—

OLIVIA. Jacob Telworthy.

LADY MARDEN. So he's alive still?

GEORGE. Apparently. There seems to be no doubt about it.

LADY MARDEN [*to* OLIVIA]. Didn't you see him die? I should always want to *see* my husband die before I married again. Not that I approve of second marriages, anyhow. I told you so at the time, George.

OLIVIA. *And* me, Aunt Julia.

LADY MARDEN. Did I? Well, I generally say what I think.

GEORGE. I ought to tell you, Aunt Julia, that no blame attaches to Olivia over this. Of that I am perfectly satisfied. It's nobody's fault, except—

LADY MARDEN. Except Telworthy's. *He* seems to have been rather careless. Well, what are you going to do about it?

GEORGE. That's just it. It's a terrible situation. There's bound to be so much publicity. Not only all this, but—but Telworthy's past and—and everything.

LADY MARDEN. I should have said that it was Telworthy's present which was the trouble. Had he a past as well?

OLIVIA. He was a fraudulent company promoter. He went to prison a good deal.

LADY MARDEN. George, you never told me this!

GEORGE. I—er—

OLIVIA. I don't see why he should want to talk about it.

DINAH [*indignantly*]. What's it got to do with Olivia, anyhow? It's not *her* fault.

LADY MARDEN [*sarcastically*]. Oh, no, I daresay it's mine.

OLIVIA [*to* GEORGE]. You wanted to ask Aunt Julia what was the right thing to do.

BRIAN [*bursting out*]. Good Heavens, what *is* there to do except the one and only thing? [*They all look at him and he becomes embarrassed*] I'm sorry. You don't want *me* to—

OLIVIA. *I* do, Brian.

LADY MARDEN. Well, go on, Mr. Strange. What would *you* do in George's position?

BRIAN. Do? Say to the woman I loved, "You're *mine*, and let this other damned fellow come and take you from me if he can!" And he couldn't—how could he?—not if the woman chose *me*. [LADY MARDEN *gazes at* BRIAN *in amazement*, GEORGE *in anger*. OLIVIA *presses his hand gratefully. He has said what she has been waiting—oh, so eagerly—for* GEORGE *to say*]

DINAH [*adoringly*]. Oh, Brian! [*In a whisper*] It is me, isn't it, and not Olivia?

BRIAN. You baby, of course!

LADY MARDEN. I'm afraid, Mr. Strange, your morals are as peculiar as your views on art. If you had led a more healthy life—

BRIAN. This is not a question of morals or of art, it's a question of love.

DINAH. Hear, hear!

LADY MARDEN [*to* GEORGE]. Isn't it that girl's bed-time yet?

OLIVIA [*to* DINAH]. We'll let her sit up a little longer if she's good.

DINAH. I will be good, Olivia, only I thought anybody, however important a debate was, was allowed to say "Hear, hear!"

GEORGE [*coldly*]. I really think we could discuss this better if Mr. Strange took Dinah out for a walk. Strange, if you—er—

OLIVIA. Tell them what you have settled first, George.

LADY MARDEN. Settled? What is there to be settled? It settles itself.

GEORGE [*sadly*]. That's just it.

LADY MARDEN. The marriage must be annulled—is that the word, George?

GEORGE. I presume so.

LADY MARDEN. One's solicitor will know all about that of course.

BRIAN. And when the marriage has been annulled, what then?

LADY MARDEN. Presumably Olivia will return to her husband.

BRIAN [*bitterly*]. And that's morality! As expounded by Bishop Landseer!

GEORGE [*angered*]. I don't know what you mean by Bishop Landseer. Morality is acting in accordance with the Laws of the Land and the Laws of the Church. I am quite prepared to believe that *your* creed embraces neither marriage nor monogamy, but my creed is different.

BRIAN [*fiercely*]. My creed includes both marriage *and* monogamy, and monogamy means sticking to the woman you love, as long as she wants you.

LADY MARDEN [*calmly*]. You suggest that George and Olivia should go on living together, although they have never been legally married, and wait for this Telworthy man to divorce her, and then—bless the man, what do you think the County would say?

BRIAN [*scornfully*]. Does it matter?

DINAH. Well, if you really want to know, the men would say, "Gad, she's a fine woman; I don't wonder he sticks to her," and the women would say, "I can't *think* what he sees in her to stick to her like that," and they'd both say, "After all, he may be a damn fool, but you can't deny he's a sportsman." That's what the County would say.

GEORGE [*indignantly*]. Was it for this sort of thing, Olivia, that you insisted on having Dinah and Mr. Strange in here? To insult me in my own house?

LADY MARDEN. I can't think what young people are coming to nowadays.

OLIVIA. I think, dear, you and Brian had better go.

DINAH [*getting up*]. We will go. But I'm just going to say one thing, Uncle George. Brian and I *are* going to marry each other, and when we are married we'll stick to each other, how*ever* many of our dead husbands and wives turn up! [*She goes out indignantly, followed by* BRIAN]

GEORGE. Upon my word, this is a pleasant discussion.

OLIVIA. I think the discussion is over, George. It is only a question of where I shall go, while you are bringing your—what sort of suit did you call it?

LADY MARDEN [*to* GEORGE]. Nullity suit. I suppose that *is* the best thing?

GEORGE. It's horrible. The awful publicity. That it should be happening to us, that's what I can't get over.

LADY MARDEN. I don't remember anything of the sort in the Marden Family before, ever.

GEORGE [*absently*]. Lady Fanny.

LADY MARDEN [*recollecting*]. Yes, of course; but that was two hundred years ago. The standards were different then. Besides, it wasn't quite the same, anyhow.

GEORGE [*absently*]. No, it wasn't quite the same.

LADY MARDEN. No. We shall all feel it. Terribly.

GEORGE [*his apology*]. If there were any other way! Olivia, what *can* I do? It *is* the only way, isn't it? All that that fellow said—of course, it sounds very well—but as things are. . . . *Is* there anything in marriage, or isn't there? You believe that there is, don't you? You aren't one of these Socialists. Well, then, can we go on living together when you're another man's wife? It isn't only what people will say, but it *is* wrong, isn't it? . . . And supposing he doesn't divorce you, are we to go on living together, unmarried, for *ever?* Olivia, you seem to think that I'm just thinking of the publicity—what people will say. I'm not. I'm not. That comes in any way. But I want to do what's right, what's best. I don't mean what's best for *us*, what makes us happiest, I mean what's really best, what's rightest. What anybody else would do in my place. *I* don't know. It's so unfair. You're not my wife at all, but I want to do what's right. . . . Oh, Olivia, Olivia, you do understand, don't you? [*They have both forgotten* LADY MARDEN. OLIVIA *has never taken her eyes off him as he makes his last attempt to convince himself*]

OLIVIA [*almost tenderly*]. So very, very well, George. Oh, I understand just what you are feeling. And oh, I do so wish that you could—[*with a little sigh*]—but then it wouldn't be George, not the George I married—[*with a rueful little laugh*]—or didn't quite marry.

LADY MARDEN. I must say, I think you are both talking a little wildly.

OLIVIA [*repeating it, oh, so tenderly*]. Or didn't—quite—marry. [*She looks at him with all her heart in her eyes. She is giving him his last chance to say, "Damn Telworthy; you're mine!" He struggles desperately with himself. . . . Will he?—will he? . . . But we shall never know, for at that moment* ANNE *comes in*]

ANNE. Mr. Pim is here, sir.

GEORGE [*emerging from the struggle with an effort*]. Pim? Pim? Oh, ah yes, of course. Mr. Pim. [*Looking up.*] Where have you put him?

OLIVIA. I want to see Mr. Pim, too, George.

LADY MARDEN. Who on earth is Mr. Pim?

OLIVIA. Show him in here, Anne.

ANNE. Yes, madam. [*She goes out*]

OLIVIA. It was Mr. Pim who told us about my husband. He came across with him in the boat, recognized him as the Telworthy he knew in Australia.

LADY MARDEN. Oh! Shall I be in the way?

GEORGE. No, no. It doesn't matter, does it, Olivia?

OLIVIA. Please stay. [ANNE *enters followed by* MR. PIM]

ANNE. Mr. Pim.

GEORGE [*pulling himself together*]. Ah, Mr. Pim! Very good of you to have come. The fact is—er— [*It is too much for him; he looks despairingly at* OLIVIA]

OLIVIA. We're so sorry to trouble you, Mr. Pim. By the way, do you know Lady Marden? [MR. PIM *and* LADY MARDEN *bow to each other*] Do come and sit down, won't you? [*She makes room for him on the sofa next to her*] The fact is, Mr. Pim, you gave us rather a surprise this morning, and before we had time to realize what it all meant, you had gone.

MR. PIM. A surprise, Mrs. Marden? Dear me, not an unpleasant one, I hope?

OLIVIA. Well, rather a—surprising one.

GEORGE. Olivia, allow me a moment. Mr. Pim, you mentioned a man called Telworthy this morning. My wife used to—that is to say, I used to— that is, there are reasons—

OLIVIA. I think we had better be perfectly frank, George.

LADY MARDEN. I am sixty-five years of age, Mr. Pim, and I can say that I've never had a moment's uneasiness by telling the truth.

MR. PIM [*after a desperate effort to keep up with the conversation*]. Oh! . . . I—er—I'm afraid I am rather at sea. Have I—er—left anything unsaid in presenting my credentials to you this morning? This Telworthy whom you mention—I seem to remember the name—

OLIVIA. Mr. Pim, you told us this morning of a man whom you had met on the boat, a man who had come down in the world, whom you had known in Sydney. A man called Telworthy.

MR. PIM [*relieved*]. Ah yes, yes, of course. I did say Telworthy, didn't I? Most curious coincidence, Lady Marden. Poor man, poor man! Let me see, it must have been ten years ago—

GEORGE. Just a moment, Mr. Pim. You're quite sure that his name was Telworthy?

MR. PIM. Telworthy—Telworthy—didn't I say Telworthy? Yes, that was it—Telworthy. Poor fellow!

OLIVIA. I'm going to be perfectly frank with you, Mr. Pim. I feel quite sure that I can trust you. This man Telworthy whom you met is my husband.

MR. PIM. Your husband? [*He looks in mild surprise at* GEORGE] But—er—

OLIVIA. My first husband. His death was announced six years ago. I had left him some years before that, but there seems no doubt from your story that he's still alive. His record—the country he comes from—above all, the very unusual name—Telworthy.

MR. PIM. Telworthy—yes—certainly a most peculiar name. I remember saying so. Your first husband? Dear me! Dear me!

GEORGE. You understand, Mr. Pim, that all this is in absolute confidence.

MR. PIM. Of course, of course.

OLIVIA. Well, since he is my husband, we naturally want to know something about him. Where is he now, for instance?

MR. PIM [*surprised*]. Where is he now? But surely I told you? I told you what happened at Marseilles?

GEORGE. At Marseilles?

MR. PIM. Yes, yes, poor fellow, it was most unfortunate. [*Quite happy again*] You must understand, Lady Marden, that although I had met the poor fellow before in Australia, I was never in any way intimate—

GEORGE [*thumping the desk*]. Where is he *now*, that's what we want to know? [MR. PIM *turns to him with a start*]

OLIVIA. *Please*, Mr. Pim!

PIM. Where is he now? But—but didn't I tell you of the curious fatality at Marseilles—poor fellow—the fish-bone?

ALL. Fish-bone?

MR. PIM. Yes, yes, a herring, I understand.

OLIVIA [*understanding first*]. Do you mean he's dead?

MR. PIM. Dead—of course—didn't I—

OLIVIA [*laughing hysterically*]. Oh, Mr. Pim, you—oh, what a husband to have—oh, I— [*But that is all she can say for the moment*]

LADY MARDEN. Pull yourself together, Olivia. This is so unhealthy for you. [*To* PIM] So he really *is* dead this time?

MR. PIM. Oh, undoubtedly, undoubtedly. A fish-bone lodged in his throat.

GEORGE [*trying to realize it*]. Dead!

OLIVIA [*struggling with her laughter*]. I think you must excuse me, Mr. Pim—I can never thank you enough—a—herring—there's something about a herring—morality depends on such little things—George, you— [*Shaking her head at him in a weak state of laughter, she hurries out of the room*]

MR. PIM. Dear me! Dear me!

GEORGE. Now, let us have this quite clear, Mr. Pim. You say that the man, Telworthy, Jacob Telworthy, is dead?

MR. PIM. Telworthy, yes—didn't I say Telworthy? This man I was telling you about—

GEORGE. He's dead?

MR. PIM. Yes, yes, he died at Marseilles.

LADY MARDEN. A dispensation of Providence, George. One can look at it in no other light.

GEORGE. Dead! [*Suddenly annoyed*] Really, Mr. Pim, I think you might have told us before.

MR. PIM. But I—I *was* telling you—I—

GEORGE. If you had only told us the whole story at once, instead of in two—two installments like this, you would have saved us all a good deal of anxiety.

MR. PIM. Really, I—

LADY MARDEN. I am sure Mr. Pim meant well, George, but it seems a pity he couldn't have said so before. If the man was dead, *why* try to hush it up?

MR. PIM [*lost again*]. Really, Lady Marden, I—

GEORGE [*getting up*]. Well, well, at any rate, I am much obliged to you, Mr. Pim, for having come down to us this afternoon. Dead! *De mortuis*, and so forth, but the situation would have been impossible had he lived. Good-by! [*Holding out his hand*] Good-by!

LADY MARDEN. Good-by, Mr. Pim.

MR. PIM. Good-by, good-by! [GEORGE *takes him to the door*] Of course, if I had— [*to himself*] Telworthy—I *think* that was the name. [*He goes out, still wondering*]

GEORGE [*with a sigh of thankfulness*]. Well! This is wonderful news, Aunt Julia.

LADY MARDEN. Most providential! . . . You understand, of course, that you are not married to Olivia?

GEORGE [*who didn't*]. Not married?

LADY MARDEN. If her first husband only died at Marseilles a few days ago—

GEORGE. Good Heavens!

LADY MARDEN. Not that it matters. You can get married quietly again. Nobody need know.

GEORGE [*considering it*]. Yes . . . yes. Then all these years we have been —er— Yes.

LADY MARDEN. Who's going to know?

GEORGE. Yes, yes, that's true. . . . And in perfect innocence, too.

LADY MARDEN. I should suggest a Registry Office in London.

GEORGE. A Registry Office, yes.

LADY MARDEN. Better go up to town this afternoon. Can't do it too quickly.

GEORGE. Yes, yes. We can stay at an hotel—

LADY MARDEN [*surprised*]. George.

GEORGE. What?

LADY MARDEN. *You* will stay at your club.

GEORGE. Oh—ah—yes, of course, Aunt Julia.

LADY MARDEN. Better take your solicitor with you to be on the safe side. . . . To the Registry Office, I mean.

GEORGE. Yes.

LADY MARDEN [*getting up*]. Well, I must be getting along, George. Say good-by to Olivia for me. And those children. Of course, you won't allow this absurd love-business between them to come to anything?

GEORGE. Most certainly not. Good-by, Aunt Julia!

LADY MARDEN [*indicating the windows*]. I'll go *this* way. [*As she goes*] And get Olivia out more, George. I don't like these hysterics. You want to be firm with her.

GEORGE [*firmly*]. Yes, yes! Good-by! [*He waves to her and then goes back to his seat.* OLIVIA *comes in, and stands in the middle of the room looking at him. He comes to her eagerly, holding out his hands*] Olivia! Olivia! [*But it is not so easy as that*]

OLIVIA [*drawing herself up proudly*]. Mrs. Telworthy!

## ACT III

OLIVIA *is standing where we left her at the end of the last act.*

GEORGE [*taken aback*]. Olivia, I—I don't understand.

OLIVIA [*leaving melodrama with a little laugh and coming down to him*]. Poor George! Did I frighten you rather?

GEORGE. You're so strange today. I don't understand you. You're not like the Olivia I know. [*They sit down on the sofa together*]

OLIVIA. Perhaps you don't know me very well after all.

GEORGE [*affectionately*]. Oh, that's nonsense, old girl. You're just my Olivia.

OLIVIA. And yet it seemed as though I wasn't going to be your Olivia half an hour ago.

GEORGE [*with a shudder*]. Don't talk about it. It doesn't bear thinking about. Well, thank Heaven that's over. Now we can get married again quietly and nobody will be any the wiser.

OLIVIA. Married again?

GEORGE. Yes, dear. As you—er—[*he laughs uneasily*] said just now, you are Mrs. Telworthy. Just for the moment. But we can soon put that right. My idea was to go up this evening and—er—make arrangements, and if you come up tomorrow morning, if we can manage it by then, we could get quietly married at a Registry Office, and—er—nobody any the wiser.

OLIVIA. Yes, I see. You want me to marry you at a Registry Office tomorrow?

GEORGE. If we can arrange it by then. I don't know how long these things take, but I should imagine there would be no difficulty.

OLIVIA. Oh, no, that part ought to be quite easy. But— [*She hesitates*]

GEORGE. But what?

OLIVIA. Well, if you want to marry me tomorrow, George, oughtn't you to propose to me first?

GEORGE [*amazed*]. Propose?

OLIVIA. Yes. It is usual, isn't it, to propose to a person before you marry her, and—and we want to do the usual thing, don't we?

GEORGE [*upset*]. But you— but we . . .

OLIVIA. You see, dear, you're George Marden, and I'm Olivia Telworthy, and you—you're attracted by me, and think I would make you a good wife, and you want to marry me. Well, naturally you propose to me first, and—tell me how much you are attracted by me, and what a good wife you think I shall make, and how badly you want to marry me.

GEORGE [*falling into the humor of it, as he thinks*]. The baby! Did she want to be proposed to all over again?

OLIVIA. Well, she did rather.

GEORGE [*rather fancying himself as an actor*]. She shall then. [*He adopts what he considers to be an appropriate attitude*] Mrs. Telworthy, I have long admired you in silence, and the time has now come to put my admiration into words. Er— [*But apparently he finds a difficulty*]

OLIVIA [*hopefully*]. Into words.

GEORGE. Er—

OLIVIA [*with the idea of helping*]. Oh, Mr. Marden!

GEORGE. Er—may I call you Olivia?

OLIVIA. Yes, George.

GEORGE [*taking her hand*]. Olivia—I— [*He hesitates*]

OLIVIA. I don't want to interrupt, but oughtn't you to be on your knees?

It is—usual, I believe. If one of the servants came in, you could say you were looking for my scissors.

GEORGE. Really, Olivia, you must allow me to manage my own proposal in my own way.

OLIVIA [*meekly*]. I'm sorry. Do go on.

GEORGE. Well, er—confound it, Olivia, I love you. Will you marry me?

OLIVIA. Thank you, George, I will think it over.

GEORGE [*laughing*]. Silly girl! Well then, tomorrow morning. No wedding-cake, I'm afraid, Olivia. [*He laughs again*] But we'll go and have a good lunch somewhere.

OLIVIA. I will think it over, George.

GEORGE [*good-humoredly*]. Well, give us a kiss while you're thinking.

OLIVIA. I'm afraid you mustn't kiss me until we are actually engaged.

GEORGE [*laughing uneasily*]. Oh, we needn't take it as seriously as all that.

OLIVIA. But a woman must take a proposal seriously.

GEORGE [*alarmed at last*]. What do you mean?

OLIVIA. I mean that the whole question, as I heard somebody say once, demands much more anxious thought than either of us has given it. These hasty marriages—

GEORGE. Hasty!

OLIVIA. Well, you've only just proposed to me, and you want to marry me tomorrow.

GEORGE. Now you're talking perfect nonsense, Olivia. You know quite well that our case is utterly different from—from any other.

OLIVIA. All the same, one has to ask oneself questions. With a young girl like—well, with a young girl, love may well seem to be all that matters. But with a woman of my age, it is different. I have to ask myself if you can afford to support a wife.

GEORGE [*coldly*]. Fortunately that is a question that you can very easily answer for yourself.

OLIVIA. Well, but I have been hearing rather bad reports lately. What with taxes always going up, and rents always going down, some of our land-owners are getting into rather straitened circumstances. At least, so I'm told.

GEORGE. I don't know what you're talking about.

OLIVIA [*surprised*]. Oh, isn't it true? I heard of a case only this morning—a landowner who always seemed to be very comfortably off, but who couldn't afford an allowance for his only niece when she wanted to get married. It made me think that one oughtn't to judge by appearances.

GEORGE. You know perfectly well that I can afford to support a wife as my wife *should* be supported.

OLIVIA. I'm so glad, dear. Then your income—you aren't getting anxious at all?

GEORGE [*stiffly*]. You know perfectly well what my income is. I see no reason for anxiety in the future.

OLIVIA. Ah, well, then we needn't think about that any more. Well, then, there is another thing to be considered.

GEORGE. I can't make out what you're up to. Don't you want to get married; to—er—legalize this extraordinary situation in which we are placed?

OLIVIA. I want to be sure that I am going to be happy, George. I can't just jump at the very first offer I have had since my husband died, without considering the whole question very carefully.

GEORGE. So I'm under consideration, eh?

OLIVIA. Every suitor is.

GEORGE [*sarcastically, as he thinks*]. Well, go on.

OLIVIA. Well, then, there's your niece. You have a niece who lives with you. Of course Dinah is a delightful girl, but one doesn't like marrying into a household in which there is another grown-up woman. But perhaps she will be getting married herself soon?

GEORGE. I see no prospect of it.

OLIVIA. I think it would make it much easier if she did.

GEORGE. Is this a threat, Olivia? Are you telling me that if I do not allow young Strange to marry Dinah, you will not marry me?

OLIVIA. A threat? Oh, no, George.

GEORGE. Then what does it mean?

OLIVIA. I'm just wondering if you love me as much as Brian loves Dinah. You *do* love me?

GEORGE [*from his heart*]. You know I do, old girl. [*He comes to her*]

OLIVIA. You're not just attracted by my pretty face? . . . *Is* it a pretty face?

GEORGE. It's an adorable one. [*He tries to kiss it, but she turns away*]

OLIVIA. How can I be sure that it is not *only* my face which makes you think that you care for me? Love which rests upon a mere outward attraction cannot lead to any lasting happiness—as one of our thinkers has observed.

GEORGE. What's come over you, Olivia? I don't understand what you're driving at. Why should you doubt my love?

OLIVIA. Ah!—Why?

GEORGE. You can't pretend that we haven't been happy together. I've— I've been a good pal to you, eh? We—we suit each other, old girl.

OLIVIA. Do we?

GEORGE. Of course we do.

OLIVIA. I wonder. When two people of our age think of getting married, one wants to be very sure that there is real community of ideas between them. Whether it is a comparatively trivial matter, like the right color for a curtain, or some very much more serious question of conduct which arises, one wants to feel that there is some chance of agreement between husband and wife.

GEORGE. We—we love each other, old girl.

OLIVIA. We do now, yes. But what shall we be like in five years' time? Supposing that after we have been married five years, we found ourselves estranged from each other upon such questions as Dinah's future, or the decorations of the drawing-room, or even the advice to give to a friend who had innocently contracted a bigamous marriage? How bitterly we should regret then our hasty plunge into a matrimony which was no true partnership, whether of tastes, or of ideas, or even of consciences– [*With a sigh*] Ah, me!

GEORGE [*nastily*]. Unfortunately for your argument, Olivia, I can answer you out of your own mouth. You seem to have forgotten what you said this morning in the case of—er— young Strange.

OLIVIA [*reproachfully*]. Is it quite fair, George to drag up what was said this morning?

GEORGE. You've brought it on yourself.

OLIVIA. I? . . . Well, and what did I say this morning?

GEORGE. You said that it was quite enough that Strange was a gentleman and in love with Dinah for me to let them marry each other.

OLIVIA. Oh! . . . *Is* that enough, George?

GEORGE [*triumphantly*]. You said so.

OLIVIA [*meekly*]. Well, if you think so, too, I—I don't mind risking it.

GEORGE [*kindly*]. Aha, my dear! You see!

OLIVIA. Then you do think it's enough?

GEORGE. I—er— Yes, yes, I—I think so.

OLIVIA [*going to him*]. My darling one! Then we can have a double wedding. How jolly!

GEORGE [*astounded*]. A double one!

OLIVIA. Yes. You and me, Brian and Dinah.

GEORGE [*firmly*]. Now look here, Olivia, understand once and for all, I am not to be blackmailed into giving my consent to Dinah's engagement. Neither blackmailed nor tricked. Our marriage has nothing whatever to do with Dinah's.

OLIVIA. No, dear. I quite understand. They may take place about the same time, but they have nothing to do with each other.

GEORGE. I see no prospect of Dinah's marriage taking place for many years.

OLIVIA. No, dear, that was what I said.

GEORGE [*not understanding for the moment*]. You said . . . ? I see. Now, Olivia, let us have this perfectly clear. You apparently insist on treating my—er—proposal as serious.

OLIVIA [*surprised*]. Wasn't it serious? Were you trifling with me?

GEORGE. You know quite well what I mean. You treat it as an ordinary proposal from a man to a woman who have never been more than acquaintances before. Very well then. Will you tell me what you propose to do, if you decide to—ah—refuse me? You do not suggest that we should go on living together—unmarried?

OLIVIA [*shocked*]. Of course not, George! What would the County—I mean Heaven—I mean the Law—I mean, of *course* not! Besides, it's so unnecessary. If I decide to accept you, of *course* I shall marry you.

GEORGE. Quite so. And if you—ah—decide to refuse me? What will you do?

OLIVIA. Nothing.

GEORGE. Meaning by that?

OLIVIA. Just that, George. I shall stay here—just as before. I like this house. It wants a little re-decorating perhaps, but I do like it, George. . . . Yes, I shall be quite happy here.

GEORGE. I see. You will continue to live down here—in spite of what you said just now about the immorality of it.

OLIVIA [*surprised*]. But there's nothing immoral in a widow living alone in a big country house, with perhaps the niece of a friend of hers staying with her, just to keep her company.

GEORGE [*sarcastic*]. And what shall *I* be doing, when you've so very kindly taken possession of my house for me?

OLIVIA. I don't know, George. Traveling, I expect. You could come down sometimes with a chaperon. I suppose there would be nothing wrong in that.

GEORGE [*indignant*]. Thank you! And what if I refuse to be turned out of my house?

OLIVIA. Then, seeing that we can't *both* be in it, it looks as though you'd have to turn *me* out. [*Casually*] I suppose there are legal ways of doing these things. You'd have to consult your solicitor again.

GEORGE [*amazed*]. Legal ways?

OLIVIA. Well, you couldn't *throw* me out, could you? You'd have to get an injunction against me—or prosecute me for trespass—or something. It would make an awfully unusual case, wouldn't it? The papers would be full of it.

GEORGE. You must be mad!

OLIVIA [*dreamily*]. Widow of well-known ex-convict takes possession of J. P.'s house. Popular country gentleman denied entrance to his own home. Doomed to travel.

GEORGE [*angrily*]. I've had enough of this. Do you mean all this nonsense?

OLIVIA. I do mean, George, that I am in no hurry to go up to London and get married. I love the country just now, and [*with a sigh*] after this morning, I'm—rather tired of husbands.

GEORGE [*in a rage*]. I've never heard so much—damned nonsense in my life. I will leave you to come to your senses. [*He goes out indignantly.* OLIVIA, *who has forgiven him already, throws a loving kiss after him, and then turns triumphantly to her dear curtains. She takes them, smiling, to the sofa, and has just got to work again, when* MR. PIM *appears at the open windows*]

PIM [*in a whisper*]. Er, may I come in, Mrs. Marden?

OLIVIA [*turning round in surprise*]. Mr. Pim!

PIM [*anxiously*]. Mr. Marden is—er—not here?

OLIVIA [*getting up*]. Do you want to see him? I will tell him.

PIM. No, no, no! Not for the world! [*He comes in and looks anxiously at the door*] There is no immediate danger of his returning, Mrs. Marden?

OLIVIA [*surprised*]. No, I don't think so. What is it? You—

PIM. I took the liberty of returning by the window in the hope of—er—coming upon you alone, Mrs. Marden.

OLIVIA. Yes?

PIM [*still rather nervous*]. I—er—Mr. Marden will be very angry with me. Quite rightly. I blame myself entirely. I do not know how I can have been so stupid.

OLIVIA. What is it, Mr. Pim? Has my husband come to life again?

PIM. Mrs. Marden, I throw myself on your mercy entirely. The fact is—his name was Polwittle.

OLIVIA [*at a loss*]. Whose? My husband's?

PIM. Yes, yes. The name came back to me suddenly, just as I reached the gate. Polwittle, poor fellow.

OLIVIA. But, Mr. Pim, my husband's name was Telworthy.

PIM. No, no, Polwittle.

OLIVIA. But, really I ought to . . .

PIM [*firmly*]. Polwittle. It came back to me suddenly just as I reached the gate. For the moment, I had thoughts of conveying the news by letter. I was naturally disinclined to return in person, and— Polwittle. [*Proudly*] If you remember, I always said it was a curious name.

OLIVIA. But who *is* Polwittle?

PIM [*in surprise at her stupidity*]. The man I have been telling you about, who met with the sad fatality at Marseilles. Henry Polwittle—or was it Ernest? No, Henry, I think. Poor fellow.

OLIVIA [*indignantly*]. But you said his name was Telworthy! How *could* you?

PIM. Yes, yes, I blame myself entirely.

OLIVIA. But how could you *think* of a name like Telworthy, if it wasn't Telworthy?

PIM [*eagerly*]. Ah, that is the really interesting thing about the whole matter.

OLIVIA. Mr. Pim, all your visits here today have been interesting.

PIM. Yes, but you see, on my first appearance here this morning, I was received by—er—Miss Diana.

OLIVIA. Dinah.

PIM. Miss Dinah, yes. She was in—er—rather a communicative mood, and she happened to mention, by way of passing the time, that before your marriage to Mr. Marden you had been a Mrs.—er—

OLIVIA. Telworthy.

PIM. Yes, yes, Telworthy, of course. She mentioned also Australia. By some process of the brain—which strikes me as decidedly curious—when I was trying to recollect the name of the poor fellow on the boat, whom you remember I had also met in Australia, the fact that this other name was also stored in my memory, a name equally peculiar—this fact I say . . .

OLIVIA [*seeing that the sentence is rapidly going to pieces*]. Yes, I understand.

PIM. I blame myself, I blame myself entirely.

OLIVIA. Oh, you mustn't do that, Mr. Pim. It was really Dinah's fault for inflicting all our family history on you.

PIM. Oh, but a charming young woman. I assure you I was very much interested in all that she told me. [*Getting up*] Well, Mrs.—er—Marden, I can only hope that you will forgive me for the needless distress I have caused you today.

OLIVIA. Oh, you mustn't worry about that—please.

PIM. And you will tell your husband—you will break the news to him?

OLIVIA [*smiling to herself*]. I will—break the news to him.

PIM. You understand how it is that I thought it better to come to you in the first place?

OLIVIA. I am very glad you did.

PIM [*holding out his hand*]. Then I will say good-by, and—er—

OLIVIA. Just a moment, Mr. Pim. Let us have it quite clear this time. You never knew my husband, Jacob Telworthy, you never met him in Australia, you never saw him on the boat, and nothing whatever happened to him at Marseilles. Is that right?

PIM. Yes, yes, that is so.

OLIVIA. So that, since he was supposed to have died in Australia six years ago, he is presumably still dead?

PIM. Yes, yes, undoubtedly.

OLIVIA [*holding out her hand with a charming smile*]. Then good-by, Mr. Pim, and thank you so much for—for all your trouble.

PIM. Not at all, Mrs. Marden. I can only assure you I—

DINAH [*from the window*]. Hullo, here's Mr. Pim! [*She comes in, followed by* BRIAN]

PIM [*anxiously looking at the door in case* MR. MARDEN *should come in*]. Yes, yes, I—er—

DINAH. Oh, Mr. Pim, you mustn't run away without even saying how do you do! Such old friends as we are. Why, it is ages since I saw you! Are you staying to tea?

PIM. I'm afraid I—

OLIVIA. Mr. Pim has to hurry away, Dinah. You musn't keep him.

DINAH. Well, but you'll come back again?

PIM. I fear that I am only a passer-by, Miss—er—Dinah.

OLIVIA. You can walk with him to the gate, dear.

PIM [*gratefully to* OLIVIA]. Thank you. [*He edges towards the window*] If you would be so kind, Miss Dinah—

BRIAN. I'll catch you up.

DINAH. Come along then, Mr. Pim. [*As they go out*] I want to hear all about your *first* wife. You haven't really told me anything yet. [OLIVIA *resumes her work, and* BRIAN *sits on the back of the sofa looking at her*]

BRIAN [*awkwardly*]. I just wanted to say, if you don't think it cheek, that I'm—I'm on your side, if I may be, and if I can help you at all I should be very proud of being allowed to.

OLIVIA [*looking up at him*]. Brian, you dear. That's sweet of you. . . . But it's quite all right now, you know.

BRIAN. Oh, I'm so glad.

OLIVIA. Yes, that's what Mr. Pim came back to say. He'd made a mistake about the name. [*Smiling*] George is the only husband I have.

BRIAN [*surprised*]. What? You mean that the whole thing—that Pim— [*With conviction*] Silly ass!

OLIVIA [*kindly*]. Oh, well, he didn't mean to be. [*After a pause*] Brian, do you know anything about the Law?

BRIAN. I'm afraid not. I hate the Law. Why?

OLIVIA [*casually*]. Oh, I just—I was wondering—thinking about all the shocks we've been through today. Second marriages, and all that.

BRIAN. Oh! It's a rotten business.

OLIVIA. I suppose there's nothing wrong in getting married to the *same* person twice?

BRIAN. A hundred times if you like, I should think.

OLIVIA. Oh?

BRIAN. After all, in France, they always go through it twice, don't they? Once before the Mayor or somebody, and once in church.

OLIVIA. Of course they do! How silly of me. . . . I think it's rather a nice idea. They ought to do it in England more.

BRIAN. Well, once will be enough for Dinah and me, if you can work it. [*Anxiously*] D'you think there's any chance, Olivia?

OLIVIA [*smiling*]. Every chance, dear.

BRIAN [*jumping up*]. I say, do you really? Have you squared him? I mean, has he—

OLIVIA. Go and catch them up now. We'll talk about it later on.

BRIAN. Bless you. Righto. [*As he goes out by the windows,* GEORGE *comes in at the door.* GEORGE *stands looking after him, and then turns to* OLIVIA, *who is absorbed in her curtains. He walks up and down the room, fidgeting with things, waiting for her to speak. As she says nothing, he begins to talk himself, but in an obviously* **unconcerned** *way. There is a pause after each answer of hers, before he gets out his next remark*]

GEORGE [*casually*]. Good-looking fellow, Strange.

OLIVIA [*equally casually*]. Brian—yes, isn't he? And such a nice boy. . . .

GEORGE. Got fifty pounds for a picture the other day, didn't he? Hey?

OLIVIA. Yes. Of course he has only just begun. . . .

GEORGE. Critics think well of him, what?

OLIVIA. They all say he has genius. Oh, I don't think there's any doubt about it. . . .

GEORGE. Of course, I don't profess to know anything about painting.

OLIVIA. You've never had time to take it up, dear.

GEORGE. I know what I like, of course. Can't say I see much in this new-fangled stuff. If a man can paint, why can't he paint like—like Rubens or—or Reynolds?

OLIVIA. I suppose we all have our own styles. Brian will find his directly. Of course, he's only just beginning. . . .

GEORGE. But they think a lot of him, what?

OLIVIA. Oh, yes!

GEORGE. H'm! . . . Good-looking fellow. [*There is rather a longer silence this time.* GEORGE *continues to hope that he is appearing casual and unconcerned. He stands looking at* OLIVIA'*s work for a moment*] Nearly finished 'em?

OLIVIA. Very nearly. Are my scissors there?

GEORGE [*looking round*]. Scissors?

OLIVIA. Ah, here they are. . . .

GEORGE. Where are you going to put 'em?

OLIVIA [*as if really wondering*]. I don't quite know. . . . I *had* thought of this room, but—I'm not quite sure.

GEORGE. Brighten the room up a bit.

OLIVIA. Yes. . . .

GEORGE [*walking over to the present curtains*]. H'm. They *are* a bit faded.

OLIVIA [*shaking out hers, and looking at them critically*]. Sometimes I think I love them, and sometimes I'm not quite sure.

GEORGE. Best way is to hang 'em up and see how you like 'em then. Always take 'em down again.

OLIVIA. That's rather a good idea, George!

GEORGE. Best way.

OLIVIA. Yes. . . . I think we might do that. . . . The only thing is— [*she hesitates*]

GEORGE. What?

OLIVIA. Well, the carpet and the chairs, and the cushions and things—

GEORGE. What about 'em?

OLIVIA. Well, if we had new curtains—

GEORGE. You'd want a new carpet, eh?

OLIVIA [*doubtfully*]. Y-yes. Well, new chair-covers anyhow.

GEORGE. H'm. . . . Well, why not?

OLIVIA. Oh, but—

GEORGE [*with an awkward laugh*]. We're not so hard up as all that, you know.

OLIVIA. No, I suppose not. [*Thoughtfully*] I suppose it would mean that I should have to go up to London for them. That's rather a nuisance.

GEORGE [*extremely casual*]. Oh, I don't know. We might go up together one day.

OLIVIA. Well, of course if we *were* up—for anything else—we could just look about us, and see if we could find what we want.

GEORGE. That's what I meant. [*There is another silence.* GEORGE *is wondering whether to come to closer quarters with the great question*]

OLIVIA. Oh, by the way, George—

GEORGE. Yes?

OLIVIA [*innocently*]. I told Brian, and I expect he'll tell Dinah, that Mr. Pim had made a mistake about the name.

GEORGE [*astonished*]. You told Brian that Mr. Pim—

OLIVIA. Yes—I told him that the whole thing was a mistake. It seemed the simplest way.

GEORGE. Olivia! Then you mean that Brian and Dinah think that—that we have been married all the time?

OLIVIA. Yes. . . . They both think so now.

GEORGE [*coming close to her*]. Olivia, does that mean that you *are* thinking of marrying me?

OLIVIA. At your old Registry Office?

GEORGE [*eagerly*]. Yes!

OLIVIA. Tomorrow?

GEORGE. Yes!

OLIVIA. Do you want me to *very* much?

GEORGE. My darling, you know I do!

OLIVIA [*a little apprehensive*]. We should have to do it very quietly.

GEORGE. Of course, darling. Nobody need know at all. We don't *want* anybody to know. And now that you've put Brian and Dinah off the scent, by telling them that Mr. Pim made a mistake— [*He breaks off, and says admiringly*] That was very clever of you, Olivia. I should never have thought of that.

OLIVIA [*innocently*]. No, darling. . . . You don't think it was wrong, George?

GEORGE [*his verdict*]. An innocent deception . . . perfectly harmless.

OLIVIA. Yes, dear, that was what I thought about—about what I was doing.

GEORGE. Then you will come tomorrow? [*She nods*] And if we happen to see the carpet, or anything that you want—

OLIVIA. Oh, what fun!

GEORGE [*beaming*]. And a wedding lunch at the Carlton, what? [*She nods eagerly*] And—and a bit of a honeymoon in Paris?

OLIVIA. Oh, George!

GEORGE [*hungrily*]. Give us a kiss, old girl.

OLIVIA [*lovingly*]. George! [*She holds up her cheek to him. He kisses it, and then suddenly takes her in his arms*]

GEORGE. Don't ever leave me, old girl.

OLIVIA [*affectionately*]. Don't ever send me away, old boy.

GEORGE [*fervently*]. I won't. . . . [*Awkwardly*] I—I don't think I would have, you know. I—I— [DINAH *and* BRIAN *appear at the windows, having seen* MR. PIM *safely off*]

DINAH [*surprised*]. Oo, I say! [GEORGE *hastily moves away*]

GEORGE. Hallo!

DINAH [*going up impetuously to him*]. Give *me* one, too, George; Brian won't mind.

BRIAN. Really, Dinah, you are the limit.

GEORGE [*formally, but enjoying it*]. Do you mind, Mr. Strange?

BRIAN [*a little uncomfortably*]. Oh, I say, sir—

GEORGE. We'll risk it, Dinah. [*He kisses her*]

DINAH [*triumphantly to* BRIAN]. Did you notice that one? That wasn't just an ordinary affectionate kiss. It was a special bless-you-my-children one. [*To* GEORGE] Wasn't it?

OLIVIA. You do talk nonsense, darling.

DINAH. Well, I'm so happy, now that Mr. Pim has relented about your first husband— [GEORGE *catches* OLIVIA's *eye and smiles; she smiles back; but they are different smiles*]

GEORGE [*the actor*[. Yes, yes, stupid fellow Pim, what?

BRIAN. Absolute idiot.

DINAH. And now that George has relented about *my* first husband.

GEORGE. You get on much too quickly, young woman. [*To* BRIAN]. So you want to marry my Dinah, eh?

BRIAN [*with a smile*]. Well, I do rather, sir.

DINAH [*hastily*]. Not at once, of course, George. We want to be engaged for a long time first, and write letters to each other, and tell each other how much we love each other, and sit next to each other when we go out to dinner.

GEORGE [*to* OLIVIA]. Well, *that* sounds fairly harmless, I think.

OLIVIA [*smiling*]. I think so. . . .

GEORGE [*to* BRIAN]. Then you'd better have a talk with me—er—Brian.

BRIAN. Thank you very much, sir.

GEORGE. Well, come along then. [*Looking at his watch*] I am going up to town after tea, so we'd better—

DINAH. I say! Are you going to London?

GEORGE [*with the smile of the conspirator*]. A little business. Never you mind, young lady.

DINAH [*calmly*]. All right. Only, bring me back something nice.

GEORGE [*to* BRIAN]. Shall we walk down and look at the pigs?

BRIAN. Righto!

OLIVIA. Don't go far, dear. I may want you in a moment.

GEORGE. All right, darling, we'll be on the terrace. [*They go out together*]

DINAH. Brian and George always try to discuss me in front of the pigs. So tactless of them. Are you going to London, too, darling?

OLIVIA. Tomorrow morning.

DINAH. What are you going to do in London?

OLIVIA. Oh, shopping, and—one or two little things.

DINAH. With George?

OLIVIA. Yes. . . .

DINAH. I say, wasn't it lovely about Pim?

OLIVIA. Lovely?

DINAH. Yes; he told me all about it. Making such a hash of things, I mean.

OLIVIA [*innocently*]. Did he make a hash of things?

DINAH. Well, I mean keeping on coming like that. And if you look at it all round—well, for all he had to say, he needn't really have come at all.

OLIVIA [*smiling to herself*]. I shouldn't quite say that, Dinah. [*She stands up and shakes out the curtains*]

DINAH. I say, aren't they jolly?

OLIVIA [*demurely*]. I'm so glad everybody likes them. Tell George I'm ready, will you?

DINAH. I say, is *he* going to hang them up for you?

OLIVIA. Well, I thought he could reach best.

DINAH. Righto! What fun! [*At the windows*] George! George! [*To* OLIVIA] Brian is just telling George about the five shillings he's got in the Post Office. . . . George!

GEORGE [*from the terrace*]. Coming! [*He hurries in, the model husband.* BRIAN *follows*]

OLIVIA. Oh, George, just hang these up for me, will you?

GEORGE. Of course, darling. I'll get the steps from the library. [*He hurries out.* BRIAN *takes out his sketching block. It is obvious that his five shillings has turned the scale. He bows to* DINAH. *He kisses* OLIVIA'S *hand with an air. He motions to* DINAH *to be seated*]

DINAH [*impressed*]. What is it?

BRIAN [*beginning to draw*]. Portrait of Lady Strange. [GEORGE *hurries in with the steps and gets to work. There is a great deal of curtain, and for the moment he becomes slightly involved in it. However, by draping it over his head and shoulders, he manages to get successfully up the steps. There we may leave him.*

> *But we have not quite finished with* MR. PIM. *It is a matter of honor with him now that he should get his little story quite accurate before passing out of the* MARDENS' *life for ever. So he comes*

*back for the last time; for the last time we see his head at the*
*window. He whispers to* OLIVIA]

MR. PIM. Mrs. Marden! I've just remembered. His name was *Ernest*
Polwittle—*not* Henry. [*He goes off happily. A curious family the* MARDENS.
*Perhaps somebody else would have committed bigamy if he had not remem-*
*bered in time that it was Ernest. . . . Ernest. . . . Yes. . . . Now he can go*
*back with an easy conscience to the Trevors'*]


## LOVE IS NOT ALL

### *Edna St. Vincent Millay   (1931)*

LOVE is not all; it is not meat nor drink
Nor slumber nor a roof against the rain,
Nor yet a floating spar to men that sink
And rise and sink and rise and sink again;
Love cannot fill the thickened lung with breath,          5
Nor clean the blood, nor set the fractured bone;
Yet many a man is making friends with death
Even as I speak, for lack of love alone.
It well may be that in a difficult hour,
Pinned down by pain and moaning for release,          10
Or nagged by want past resolution's power,
I might be driven to sell your love for peace,
Or trade the memory of this night for food.
It well may be. I do not think I would.


## WHEN WE THAT WORE THE MYRTLE

### *Edna St. Vincent Millay   (1931)*

When we that wore the myrtle wear the dust,
And years of darkness cover up our eyes,
And all our arrogant laughter and sweet lust
Keep counsel with the scruples of the wise;
When boys and girls that now are in the loins          5
Of croaking lads, dip oar into the sea,—
And who are these that dive for copper coins?
No longer we, my love, no longer we—
Then let the fortunate breathers of the air,
When we lie speechless in the muffling mould,          10
Tease not our ghosts with slander, pause not there
To say that love is false and soon grows cold,
But pass in silence the mute grave of two
Who lived and died believing love was true.

# EFFORT AT SPEECH BETWEEN TWO PEOPLE

## *Muriel Rukeyser* (*1935*)

: Speak to me. Take my hand. What are you now?
I will tell you all. I will conceal nothing.
When I was three, a little child read a story about a rabbit
who died, in the story, and I crawled under a chair :
a pink rabbit : it was my birthday, and a candle                    5
burnt a sore spot on my finger, and I was told to be happy.

: Oh, grow to know me. I am not happy. I will be open:
Now I am thinking of white sails against a sky like music,
like glad horns blowing, and birds tilting, and an arm about me.
There was one I loved, who wanted to live, sailing.                 10

: Speak to me. Take my hand. What are you now?
When I was nine, I was fruitily sentimental,
fluid : and my widowed aunt played Chopin,
and I bent my head on the painted woodwork, and wept.
I want now to be close to you. I would                              15
link the minutes of my days close, somehow, to your days.

: I am not happy. I will be open.
I have liked lamps in evening corners, and quiet poems.
There has been fear in my life. Sometimes I speculate
On what a tragedy his life was, really.                             20

: Take my hand. First my mind in your hand. What are you now?
When I was fourteen, I had dreams of suicide,
and I stood at a steep window, at sunset, hoping toward death :
if the light had not melted clouds and plains to beauty,
if light had not transformed that day, I would have leapt.         25
I am unhappy. I am lonely. Speak to me.

: I will be open. I think he never loved me:
he loved the bright beaches, the little lips of foam
that ride small waves, he loved the veer of gulls:
he said with a gay mouth: I love you. Grow to know me.             30

: What are you now? If we could touch one another,
if these our separate entities could come to grips,
clenched like a Chinese puzzle . . . yesterday
I stood in a crowded street that was live with people,
and no one spoke a word, and the morning shone.                    35
Everyone silent, moving. . . . Take my hand. Speak to me.

# FOUR IN A FAMILY

### Muriel Rukeyser  (1935)

The father and mother sat, and the sister beside her.
I faced the two women across the table's width,
speaking, and all the time he looked at me,
sorrowing, saying nothing, with his hard tired breath.

Their faces said : This is your home; and I :    5
I never come home, I never go away.
And they all answered : Stay.

All day the city turned about this room,
and silence had remained between our faces,
divisions outside to concentrate a world    10
tally here only to dead profits and losses.

We follow barrier voices, and we go fast,
unknown to each other, they race, I turn away.
No voice is strong enough to cry me Stay.

 My sister, I wished upon you those delights   15
 time never buries,
 more precious than heroes.

 Strange father, strange mother, who are you, who are you?
 Where have I come,
 how shall I prosper home?     20


# REMEMBER

### Christina Rossetti  (1847)

Remember me when I am gone away,
Gone far away into the silent land;
When you can no more hold me by the hand,
Nor I half turn to go, yet turning stay.
Remember me when no more, day by day,    5
You tell me of our future that you planned:
Only remember me; you understand
It will be late to counsel then or pray.
Yet if you should forget me for a while
And afterwards remember, do not grieve:    10
For if the darkness and corruption leave
A vestige of the thoughts that once I had,
Better by far you should forget and smile
Than that you should remember and be sad.

## SONNETS FROM THE PORTUGUESE
### *Elizabeth Barrett Browning*  (*1847*)

#### VI

Go from me. Yet I feel that I shall stand
Henceforward in thy shadow. Nevermore,
Alone upon the threshold of my door
Of individual life I shall command
The uses of my soul, nor lift my hand                          5
Serenely in the sunshine as before,
Without the sense of that which I forbore—
Thy touch upon the palm. The widest land
Doom takes to part us, leaves thy heart in mine
With pulses that beat double. What I do                       10
And what I dream include thee, as the wine
Must taste of its own grapes. And when I sue
God for myself, he hears that name of thine,
And sees within my eyes the tears of two.

#### VII

The face of all the world is changed, I think,
Since first I heard the footsteps of thy soul
Move still, oh, still, beside me, as they stole
Betwixt me and the dreadful outer brink
Of obvious death, where I, who thought to sink,              5
Was caught up into love, and taught the whole
Of life in a new rhythm. The cup of dole
God gave for baptism, I am fain to drink,
And praise its sweetness, Sweet, with thee anear.
The names of country, heaven, are changed away             10
For where thou art or shalt be, there or here;
And this . . . this lute and song . . . loved yesterday,
(The singing angels know) are only dear
Because thy name moves right in what they say.

#### XIV

If thou must love me, let it be for nought
Except for love's sake only. Do not say,
"I love her for her smile—her look—her way
Of speaking gently,—for a trick of thought
That falls in well with mine, and certes brought            5
A sense of pleasant ease on such a day"—
For these things in themselves, Belovèd, may
Be changed, or change for thee,—and love, so wrought,
May be unwrought so. Neither love me for
Thine own dear pity's wiping my cheeks dry,—               10
A creature might forget to weep, who bore
Thy comfort long, and lose thy love thereby!
But love me for love's sake, that evermore
Thou may'st love on, through love's eternity.

### XX

Belovèd, my Belovèd, when I think
That thou wast in the world a year ago,
What time I sat alone here in the snow
And saw no footprint, heard the silence sink
No moment at thy voice, but, link by link,                                5
Went counting all my chains as if that so
They never could fall off at any blow
Struck by thy possible hand,—why, thus I drink
Of life's great cup of wonder! Wonderful,
Never to feel thee thrill the day or night                                10
With personal act or speech,—nor ever cull
Some prescience of thee with the blossoms white
Thou sawest growing! Atheists are as dull,
Who cannot guess God's presence out of sight.

### XLIII

How do I love thee? Let me count the ways.
I love thee to the depth and breadth and height
My soul can reach, when feeling out of sight
For the ends of Being and ideal Grace.
I love thee to the level of every day's                                   5
Most quiet need, by sun and candlelight.
I love thee freely, as men strive for Right;
I love thee purely, as they turn from Praise.
I love thee with the passion put to use
In my old griefs, and with my childhood's faith.                          10
I love thee with a love I seemed to lose
With my lost saints—I love thee with the breath,
Smiles, tears, of all my life—and, if God choose,
I shall but love thee better after death.

## SONNETS

*William Shakespeare* (*1593–98*)

### XXIX

When, in disgrace with fortune and men's eyes,
I all alone beweep my outcast state
And trouble deaf heaven with my bootless cries
And look upon myself and curse my fate,
Wishing me like to one more rich in hope,                                 5
Featured like him, like him with friends possessed,
Desiring this man's art and that man's scope,
With what I most enjoy contented least;

Yet in these thoughts myself almost despising,
Haply I think on thee, and then my state,      10
Like to the lark at break of day arising
From sullen earth, sings hymns at heaven's gate;
     For thy sweet love remembered such wealth brings
     That then I scorn to change my state with kings.

### XXX

When to the sessions of sweet silent thought
I summon up remembrance of things past,
I sigh the lack of many a thing I sought,
And with old woes new wail my dear time's waste,
Then can I drown an eye, unused to flow,      5
For precious friends hid in death's dateless night,
And weep afresh love's long since cancelled woe,
And moan the expense of many a vanished sight—
Then can I grieve at grievances foregone,
And heavily from woe to woe tell o'er      10
The sad account of fore-bemoanéd moan,
Which I new pay as if not paid before.
     But if the while I think on thee, dear friend,
     All losses are restored and sorrows end.

### LXXIII

That time of year thou mayst in me behold
When yellow leaves, or none, or few, do hang
Upon those boughs which shake against the cold,
Bare ruined choirs, where late the sweet birds sang.
In me thou see'st the twilight of such day      5
As after sunset fadeth in the west,
Which by and by black night doth take away,
Death's second self, that seals up all in rest.
In me thou see'st the glowing of such fire
That on the ashes of his youth doth lie,      10
As the deathbed whereon it must expire,
Consumed with that which it was nourished by.
     This thou perceivest, which makes thy love more strong,
     To love that well which thou must leave ere long.

### CXVI

Let me not to the marriage of true minds
Admit impediments. Love is not love
Which alters when it alteration finds,
Or bends with the remover to remove.
O, no! it is an ever-fixéd mark      5
That looks on tempests and is never shaken;
It is the star to every wand'ring bark,
Whose worth's unknown, although his height be taken.

Love's not Time's fool, though rosy lips and cheeks
Within his bending sickle's compass come;                                10
Love alters not with his brief hours and weeks,
But bears it out even to the edge of doom.
　　　If this be error and upon me proved,
　　　I never writ, nor no man ever loved.

### CXXX

My mistress' eyes are nothing like the sun;
Coral is far more red than her lips' red;
If snow be white, why then her breasts are dun;
If hairs be wires, black wires grow on her head.
I have seen roses damasked, red and white,                               5
But no such roses see I in her cheeks;
And in some perfumes is there more delight
Than in the breath that from my mistress reeks.
I love to hear her speak, yet well I know
That music hath a far more pleasing sound;                               10
I grant I never saw a goddess go;
My mistress, when she walks, treads on the ground:
　　　And yet, by heaven, I think my love as rare
　　　As any she belied with false compare.

# SONNETS

### (*From* The House of Life)

## Dante Gabriel Rossetti   (*1881*)

#### IV.  LOVESIGHT

When do I see thee most, belovéd one?
When in the light the spirits of mine eyes
Before thy face, their altar, solemnize
The worship of that Love through thee made known?
Or when in the dusk hours, (we two alone,)                               5
Close-kissed and eloquent of still replies
Thy twilight-hidden glimmering visage lies,
And my soul only sees thy soul its own?
O love, my love! if I no more should see
Thyself, nor on the earth the shadow of thee,                            10
Nor image of thine eyes in any spring,—
How then should sound upon Life's darkening slope
The ground-whirl of the perished leaves of Hope,
The wind of Death's imperishable wing?

### V. HEART'S HOPE

By what word's power, the key of paths untrod,
Shall I the difficult deeps of Love explore,
Till parted waves of Song yield up the shore
Even as that sea which Israel crossed dryshod?
For lo! in some poor rhythmic period,      5
Lady, I fain would tell how evermore
Thy soul I know not from thy body, nor
Thee from myself, neither our love from God.
Yea, in God's name, and Love's, and thine, would I
Draw from one loving heart such evidence      10
As to all hearts all things shall signify;
Tender as dawn's first hill-fire, and intense
As instantaneous penetrating sense,
In Spring's birth-hour, of other Springs gone by.

### XIII. YOUTH'S ANTIPHONY

"I love you, sweet: how can you ever learn
How much I love you?" "You I love even so,
And so I learn it." "Sweet, you cannot know
How fair you are." "If fair enough to earn
Your love, so much is all my love's concern."      5
"My love grows hourly, sweet." "Mine too doth grow,
Yet love seemed full so many hours ago!"
Thus lovers speak, till kisses claim their turn.
Ah! happy they to whom such words as these
In youth have served for speech the whole day long,      10
Hour after hour, remote from the world's throng,
Work, contest, fame, all life's confederate pleas,—
What while Love breathed in sighs and silences
Through two blent souls one rapturous undersong.

### XIX. SILENT NOON

Your hands lie open in the long, fresh grass,—
The finger-points look through like rosy blooms:
Your eyes smile peace. The pasture gleams and glooms
'Neath billowing skies that scatter and amass.
All round our nest, far as the eye can pass,      5
Are golden kingcup-fields with silver edge
Where the cow-parsley skirts the hawthorn hedge.
'T is visible silence, still as the hour-glass.
Deep in the sun-searched growths the dragon-fly
Hangs like a blue thread loosened from the sky,—      10
So this wing'd hour is dropped to us from above.
Oh! clasp we to our hearts, for deathless dower,
This close-companioned inarticulate hour
When twofold silence was the song of love.

### XXVI. MID-RAPTURE

Thou lovely and belovéd, thou my love;
   Whose kiss seems still the first; whose summoning eyes,
   Even now, as for our love-world's new sunrise,
Shed very dawn; whose voice, attuned above
All modulation of the deep-bowered dove,                    5
   Is like a hand laid softly on the soul;
   Whose hand is like a sweet voice to control
Those worn tired brows it hath the keeping of:—
What word can answer to thy word,—what gaze
   To thine, which now absorbs within its sphere        10
   My worshiping face, till I am mirrored there
Light-circled in a heaven of deep-drawn rays?
What clasp, what kiss mine inmost heart can prove,
O lovely and belovéd, O my love?

### XXXIV. THE DARK GLASS

Not I myself know all my love for thee:
How should I reach so far, who cannot weigh
To-morrow's dower by gage of yesterday?
Shall birth and death, and all dark names that be
As doors and windows bared to some loud sea,              5
Lash deaf mine ears and blind my face with spray;
And shall my sense pierce love,—the last relay
And ultimate outpost of eternity?
Lo! what am I to Love, the lord of all?
One murmuring shell he gathers from the sand,            10
One little heart-flame sheltered in his hand.
Yet through thine eyes he grants me clearest call
And veriest touch of powers primordial
That any hour-girt life may understand.

### LXX. THE HILL SUMMIT

This feast-day of the sun, his altar there
In the broad west has blazed for vesper-song;
And I have loitered in the vale too long
And gaze now a belated worshiper.
Yet may I not forget that I was ware,                      5
So journeying, of his face at intervals
Transfigured where the fringed horizon falls,—
A fiery bush with coruscating hair.
And now that I have climbed and won this height,
I must tread downward through the sloping shade          10
And travel the bewildered tracks till night.
Yet for this hour I still may here be stayed
And see the gold air and the silver fade
And the last bird fly into the last light.

# SONG

## *John Donne*  (*1633*)

Go and catch a falling star,
  Get with child a mandrake root,
Tell me where all past years are,
  Or who cleft the devil's foot;
Teach me to hear mermaids singing, 5
Or to keep off envy's stinging,
    And find
    What wind
Serves to advance an honest mind.

If thou be'st born to strange sights, 10
  Things invisible go see,
Ride ten thousand days and nights
  Till Age snow white hairs on thee;
Thou, when thou return'st, wilt tell
me

All strange wonders that befell thee,
  And swear    16
  Nowhere
Lives a woman true and fair.

If thou find'st one, let me know;
  Such a pilgrimage were sweet. 20
Yet do not; I would not go,
  Though at next door we might
    meet.
Though she were true when you met
    her,
And last till you write your letter,
    Yet she    25
    Will be
False, ere I come, to two or three.

# THE INDIFFERENT

## *John Donne*  (*1633*)

I can love both fair and brown;
  Her whom abundance melts, and her whom want betrays;
  Her who loves loneness best, and her who masks and plays;
  Her whom the country formed, and whom the town;
  Her who believes, and her who tries;    5
  Her who still weeps with spongy eyes,
  And her who is dry cork and never cries.
I can love her, and her, and you, and you;
I can love any, so she be not true.

Will no other vice content you?    10
Will it not serve your turn to do as did your mothers?
Or have you all old vices spent and now would find out others?
Or doth a fear that men are true torment you?
  O we are not, be not you so;
  Let me—and do you—twenty know;    15
  Rob me, but bind me not, and let me go.
Must I, who came to travel thorough you,
Grow your fixed subject, because you are true?

Venus heard me sigh this song;
  And by love's sweetest part, variety, she swore    20
She heard not this till now; it should be so no more.
  She went, examined, and returned ere long,

And said, "Alas! some two or three
Poor heretics in love there be,
    Which think to stablish dangerous constancy.                    25
But I have told them, 'Since you will be true,
You shall be true to them who're false to you'."

## THE DREAM

### *John Donne*   *(1633)*

Dear love, for nothing less than thee
Would I have broke this happy dream;
    It was a theme
For reason, much too strong for fantasy.
Therefore thou waked'st me wisely; yet                              5
My dream thou brok'st not, but continued'st it.
Thou art so true that thoughts of thee suffice
To make dreams truths and fables histories;
Enter these arms, for since thou thought'st it best
Not to dream all my dream, let's act the rest.                     10

As lightning, or a taper's light,
Thine eyes, and not thy noise, waked me;
    Yet I thought thee—
For thou lov'st truth—an angel, at first sight;
But when I saw thou saw'st my heart,                               15
And knew'st my thoughts beyond an angel's art,
When thou knew'st what I dreamt, when thou knew'st when
Excess of joy would wake me, and cam'st then,
I must confess it could not choose but be
Profane to think thee anything but thee.                           20

Coming and staying showed thee thee,
But rising makes me doubt that now
    Thou art not thou.
That Love is weak where Fear's as strong as he;
'Tis not all spirit pure and brave                                25
If mixture it of fear, shame, honor have.
Perchance as torches, which must ready be,
Men light and put out, so thou deal'st with me.
Thou cam'st to kindle, go'st to come; then I
Will dream that hope again, but else would die.                   30

# MY LAST DUCHESS

## *Robert Browning*   (*1842*)

### FERRARA

That's my last Duchess painted on the wall,
Looking as if she were alive. I call
That piece a wonder, now: Fra Pandolf's hands
Worked busily a day, and there she stands.
Will't please you sit and look at her? I said      5
"Fra Pandolf" by design, for never read
Strangers like you that pictured countenance,
The depth and passion of its earnest glance,
But to myself they turned (since none puts by
The curtain I have drawn for you, but I)      10
And seemed as they would ask me, if they durst,
How such a glance came there; so, not the first
Are you to turn and ask thus. Sir, 't was not
Her husband's presence only, called that spot
Of joy into the Duchess' cheek: perhaps      15
Fra Pandolf chanced to say, "Her mantle laps
Over my lady's wrist too much," or "Paint
Must never hope to reproduce the faint
Half-flush that dies along her throat": such stuff
Was courtesy, she thought, and cause enough      20
For calling up that spot of joy. She had
A heart—how shall I say?—too soon made glad,
Too easily impressed: she liked whate'er
She looked on, and her looks went everywhere.
Sir, 'twas all one! My favor at her breast,      25
The dropping of the daylight in the West,
The bough of cherries some officious fool
Broke in the orchard for her, the white mule
She rode with round the terrace—all and each
Would draw from her alike the approving speech,      30
Or blush, at least. She thanked men,—good! but thanked
Somehow—I know not how—as if she ranked
My gift of a nine-hundred-years-old name
With anybody's gift. Who'd stoop to blame
This sort of trifling? Even had you skill      35
In speech—(which I have not)—to make your will
Quite clear to such an one, and say, "Just this
Or that in you disgusts me; here you miss,
Or there exceed the mark"—and if she let
Herself be lessoned so, nor plainly set      40
Her wits to yours, forsooth, and made excuse,

—E'en then would be some stooping; and I choose
Never to stoop. Oh sir, she smiled, no doubt,
Whene'er I passed her; but who passed without
Much the same smile? This grew; I gave commands;                    45
Then all smiles stopped together. There she stands
As if alive. Will 't please you rise? We'll meet
The company below, then. I repeat
The Count your master's known munificence
Is ample warrant that no just pretense                              50
Of mine for dowry will be disallowed;
Though his fair daughter's self, as I avowed
At starting, is my object. Nay, we'll go
Together down, sir. Notice Neptune, though,
Taming a sea-horse, thought a rarity,                               55
Which Claus of Innsbruck cast in bronze for me!


# ANDREA DEL SARTO

### CALLED "THE FAULTLESS PAINTER"

### *Robert Browning*   (*1855*)

But do not let us quarrel any more,
No, my Lucrezia; bear with me for once:
Sit down and all shall happen as you wish.
You turn your face, but does it bring your heart?
I'll work then for your friend's friend, never fear,                 5
Treat his own subject after his own way,
Fix his own time, accept too his own price,
And shut the money into this small hand
When next it takes mine. Will it? tenderly?
Oh, I'll content him,—but to-morrow, Love!                          10
I often am much wearier than you think,
This evening more than usual, and it seems
As if—forgive now—should you let me sit
Here by the window with your hand in mine
And look a half-hour forth on Fiesolé,                              15
Both of one mind, as married people use,
Quietly, quietly the evening through,
I might get up to-morrow to my work
Cheerful and fresh as ever. Let us try.
To-morrow, how you shall be glad for this!                          20
Your soft hand is a woman of itself,
And mine the man's bared breast she curls inside.
Don't count the time lost, neither; you must serve
For each of the five pictures we require:
It saves a model. So! keep looking so—                             25

My serpentining beauty, rounds on rounds!
—How could you ever prick those perfect ears,
Even to put the pearl there! oh, so sweet—
My face, my moon, my everybody's moon,
Which everybody looks on and calls his,                    30
And, I suppose, is looked on by in turn
While she looks—no one's: very dear, no less.
You smile? why, there's my picture ready made,
There's what we painters call our harmony!
A common grayness silvers everything,—                      35
All in a twilight, you and I alike
—You, at the point of your first pride in me
(That's gone you know),—but I, at every point;
My youth, my hope, my art, being all toned down
To yonder sober pleasant Fiesolé.                           40
There's the bell clinking from the chapel-top;
That length of convent-wall across the way
Holds the trees safer, huddled more inside;
The last monk leaves the garden; days decrease,
And autumn grows, autumn in everything.                     45
Eh? the whole seems to fall into a shape
As if I saw alike my work and self
And all that I was born to be and do,
A twilight-piece. Love, we are in God's hand.
How strange now looks the life he makes us lead;            50
So free we seem, so fettered fast we are!
I feel he laid the fetter: let it lie!
This chamber for example—turn your head—
All that's behind us! You don't understand
Nor care to understand about my art,                        55
But you can hear at least when people speak:
And that cartoon, the second from the door
—It is the thing, Love! so such thing should be—
Behold Madonna!—I am bold to say.
I can do with my pencil what I know,                        60
What I see, what at bottom of my heart
I wish for, if I ever wish so deep—
Do easily, too—when I say, perfectly,
I do not boast, perhaps: yourself are judge,
Who listened to the Legate's talk last week,               65
And just as much they used to say in France.
At any rate, 'tis easy, all of it!
No sketches first, no studies, that's long past:
I do what many dream of all their lives,
—Dream? strive to do, and agonize to do,                    70
And fail in doing. I could count twenty such
On twice your fingers, and not leave this town,
Who strive—you don't know how the others strive

To paint a little thing like that you smeared
Carelessly passing with your robes afloat,—                      75
Yet do much less, so much less, Someone says,
(I know his name, no matter)—so much less!
Well, less is more, Lucrezia: I am judged.
There burns a truer light of God in them,
In their vexed beating stuffed and stopped-up brain,             80
Heart, or whate'er else, than goes on to prompt
This low-pulsed forthright craftsman's hand of mine.
Their works drop groundward, but themselves, I know,
Reach many a time a heaven that's shut to me,
Enter and take their place there sure enough,                    85
Though they come back and cannot tell the world.
My works are nearer heaven, but I sit here.
The sudden blood of these men! at a word—
Praise them, it boils, or blame them, it boils too.
I, painting from myself and to myself,                           90
Know what I do, am unmoved by men's blame
Or their praise either. Somebody remarks
Morello's outline there is wrongly traced,
His hue mistaken; what of that? or else,
Rightly traced and well ordered; what of that?                   95
Speak as they please, what does the mountain care?
Ah, but a man's reach should exceed his grasp,
Or what's a heaven for? All is silver-gray
Placid and perfect with my art: the worse!
I know both what I want and what might gain,                      100
And yet how profitless to know, to sigh
"Had I been two, another and myself,
Our head would have o'erlooked the world!" No doubt.
Yonder's a work now, of that famous youth
The Urbinate who died five years ago.                            105
('Tis copied, George Vasari sent it me.)
Well, I can fancy how he did it all,
Pouring his soul, with kings and popes to see,
Reaching, that heaven might so replenish him,
Above and through his art—for it gives way;                      110
That arm is wrongly put—and there again—
A fault to pardon in the drawing's lines,
Its body, so to speak: its soul is right,
He means right—that, a child may understand.
Still, what an arm! and I could alter it:                        115
But all the play, the insight and the stretch—
Out of me, out of me! And wherefore out?
Had you enjoined them on me, given me soul,
We might have risen to Rafael, I and you!
Nay, Love, you did give all I asked, I think—                    120
More than I merit, yes, by many times.
But had you—oh, with the same perfect brow,

And perfect eyes, and more than perfect mouth,
And the low voice my soul hears, as a bird
The fowler's pipe, and follows to the snare—    125
Had you, with these the same, but brought a mind!
Some women do so. Had the mouth there urged
"God and the glory! never care for gain.
The present by the future, what is that?
Live for fame, side by side with Agnolo!    130
Rafael is waiting: up to God, all three!"
I might have done it for you. So it seems:
Perhaps not. All is as God overrules.
Beside, incentives come from the soul's self;
The rest avail not. Why do I need you?    135
What wife had Rafael, or has Agnolo?
In this world, who can do a thing, will not;
And who would do it, cannot, I perceive:
Yet the will's somewhat—somewhat, too, the power—
And thus we half-men struggle. At the end,    140
God, I conclude, compensates, punishes.
'Tis safer for me, if the award be strict,
That I am something underrated here,
Poor this long while, despised, to speak the truth.
I dared not, do you know, leave home all day,    145
For fear of chancing on the Paris lords.
The best is when they pass and look aside;
But they speak sometimes; I must bear it all.
Well may they speak! That Francis, that first time,
And that long festal year at Fontainebleau!    150
I surely then could sometimes leave the ground,
Put on the glory, Rafael's daily wear,
In that humane great monarch's golden look,—
One finger in his beard or twisted curl
Over his mouth's good mark that made the smile,    155
One arm about my shoulder, round my neck,
The jingle of his gold chain in my ear,
I painting proudly with his breath on me,
All his court round him, seeing with his eyes,
Such frank French eyes, and such a fire of souls    160
Profuse, my hand kept plying by those hearts,—
And, best of all, this, this, this face beyond,
This in the background, waiting on my work,
To crown the issue with a last reward!
A good time, was it not, my kingly days?    165
And had you not grown restless . . . but I know—
'T is done and past; 't was right, my instinct said;
Too live the life grew, golden and not gray,
And I'm the weak-eyed bat no sun should tempt
Out of the grange whose four walls make his world.    170
How could it end in any other way?

You called me, and I came home to your heart.
The triumph was—to reach and stay there; since
I reached it ere the triumph, what is lost?
Let my hands frame your face in your hair's gold, 175
You beautiful Lucrezia that are mine!
　　"Rafael did this, Andrea painted that;
The Roman's is the better when you pray,
But still the other's Virgin was his wife—"
Men will excuse me. I am glad to judge 180
Both pictures in your presence; clearer grows
My better fortune, I resolve to think.
For, do you know, Lucrezia, as God lives,
Said one day Agnolo, his very self,
To Rafael . . . I have known it all these years . . . 185
(When the young man was flaming out his thoughts
Upon a palace-wall for Rome to see,
Too lifted up in heart because of it)
"Friend, there's a certain sorry little scrub
Goes up and down our Florence, none cares how, 190
Who, were he set to plan and execute
As you are, pricked on by your popes and kings,
Would bring the sweat into that brow of yours!"
To Rafael's!—And indeed the arm is wrong.
I hardly dare . . . yet, only you to see, 195
Give the chalk here—quick, thus the line should go!
Ay, but the soul! he's Rafael! rub it out!
Still, all I care for, if he spoke the truth
(What he? why, who but Michel Agnolo?
Do you forget already words like those?), 200
If really there was such a chance, so lost,—
Is, whether you're—not grateful—but more pleased.
Well, let me think so. And you smile indeed!
This hour has been an hour! Another smile?
If you would sit thus by me every night 205
I should work better, do you comprehend?
I mean that I should earn more, give you more.
See, it is settled dusk now; there's a star;
Morello's gone, the watch-lights show the wall,
The cue-owls speak the name we call them by. 210
Come from the window, love—come in, at last,
Inside the melancholy little house
We built to be so gay with. God is just.
King Francis may forgive me; oft at nights,
When I look up from painting, eyes tired out, 215
The walls become illumined, brick from brick
Distinct, instead of mortar, fierce bright gold,
That gold of his I did cement them with!
Let us but love each other. Must you go?
That Cousin here again? he waits outside? 220

Must see you—you, and not with me? Those loans?
More gaming debts to pay? you smiled for that?
Well, let smiles buy me! have you more to spend?
While hand and eye and something of a heart
Are left me, work's my ware, and what's it worth?          225
I'll pay my fancy. Only let me sit
The gray remainder of the evening out,
Idle, you call it, and muse perfectly
How I could paint, were I but back in France,
One picture, just one more—the Virgin's face,          230
Not yours this time! I want you at my side
To hear them—that is, Michel Agnolo—
Judge all I do and tell you of its worth.
Will you? To-morrow, satisfy your friend.
I take the subjects for his corridor,          235
Finish the portrait out of hand—there, there,
And throw him in another thing or two
If he demurs; the whole should prove enough
To pay for this same Cousin's freak. Beside,
What's better and what's all I care about,          240
Get you the thirteen scudi for the ruff!
Love, does that please you? Ah, but what does he,
The Cousin! what does he to please you more?

I am grown peaceful as old age to-night.
I regret little, I would change still less.          245
Since there my past life lies, why alter it?
The very wrong to Francis!—it is true
I took his coin, was tempted and complied,
And built this house and sinned, and all is said.
My father and my mother died of want.          250
Well, had I riches of my own? you see
How one gets rich! Let each one bear his lot.
They were born poor, lived poor, and poor they died:
And I have labored somewhat in my time
And not been paid profusely. Some good son          255
Paint my two hundred pictures—let him try!
No doubt, there's something strikes a balance. Yes,
You loved me quite enough, it seems to-night.
This must suffice me here. What would one have?
In heaven, perhaps, new chances, one more chance—          260
Four great walls in the New Jerusalem,
Meted on each side by the angel's reed,
For Leonard, Rafael, Agnolo and me
To cover—the three first without a wife,
While I have mine! So—still they overcome          265
Because there's still Lucrezia,—as I choose.

Again the Cousin's whistle! Go, my Love.

# THE LAST RIDE TOGETHER

## *Robert Browning* (*1855*)

I said—Then, dearest, since 'tis so,
Since now at length my fate I know,
Since nothing all my love avails,
Since all, my life seemed meant for, fails,
   Since this was written and needs
   must be—     5
My whole heart rises up to bless
Your name in pride and thankfulness!
Take back the hope you gave,—I claim
Only a memory of the same,
—And this beside, if you will not blame,   10
   Your leave for one more last ride
   with me.

My mistress bent that brow of hers;
Those deep dark eyes where pride demurs
When pity would be softening through,
Fixed me a breathing-while or two  15
   With life or death in the balance: right!
The blood replenished me again;
My last thought was at least not vain:
I and my mistress, side by side
Shall be together, breathe and ride, 20
So, one day more am I deified.
   Who knows but the world may end
   to-night?

Hush! if you saw some western cloud
All billowy-bosomed, over-bowed
By many benedictions—sun's  25
And moon's and evening-star's at once—
   And so, you, looking and loving best,
Conscious grew, your passion drew
Cloud, sunset, moonrise, star-shine too,
Down on you, near and yet more near,  30

Till flesh must fade for heaven was here!—
Thus leant she and lingered—joy and fear!
   Thus lay she a moment on my breast.

Then we began to ride. My soul
Smoothed itself out, a long-cramped scroll  35
Freshening and fluttering in the wind.
Past hopes already lay behind.
   What need to strive with a life awry?
Had I said that, had I done this,
So might I gain, so might I miss.  40
Might she have loved me? just as well
She might have hated, who can tell!
Where had I been now if the worst befell?
   And here we are riding, she and I.

Fail I alone, in words and deeds?  45
Why, all men strive, and who succeeds?
We rode; it seemed my spirit flew,
Saw other regions, cities new,
   As the world rushed by on either side.
I thought,—All labor, yet no less  50
Bear up beneath their unsuccess.
Look at the end of work, contrast
The petty done, the undone vast,
This present of theirs with the hopeful past!
   I hoped she would love me; here
   we ride.  55

What hand and brain went ever paired?
What heart alike conceived and dared?
What act proved all its thought had been?

What will but felt the fleshly screen?
  We ride and I see her bosom heave.
There's many a crown for who can
    reach.                               61
Ten lines, a statesman's life in each!
The flag stuck on a heap of bones,
A soldier's doing! what atones?
They scratch his name on the Abbey-
    stones.                             65
  My riding is better, by their leave.

What does it all mean, poet? Well,
Your brains beat into rhythm, you tell
What we felt only; you expressed
You hold things beautiful the best, 70
  And place them in rime so, side by
  side.
'Tis something, nay 'tis much: but
    then,
Have you yourself what's best for
    men?
Are you—poor, sick, old ere your
    time—
Nearer one whit your own sublime 75
Than we who never have turned a
    rime?
  Sing, riding's a joy! For me, I ride.

And you, great sculptor—so, you
    gave
A score of years to Art, her slave,
And that's your Venus, whence we
    turn                                80
To yonder girl that fords the burn!
  You acquiesce, and shall I repine?
What, man of music, you grown gray
With notes and nothing else to say,

Is this your sole praise from a friend,
"Greatly his opera's strains intend, 86
But in music we know how fashions
    end!"
  I gave my youth; but we ride, in
  fine.

Who knows what's fit for us? Had
    fate
Proposed bliss here should sublimate
My being—had I signed the bond— 91
Still one must lead some life beyond,
  Have a bliss to die with, dim-
  descried.
This foot once planted on the goal,
This glory-garland round my soul, 95
Could I descry such? Try and test!
I sink back shuddering from the quest.
Earth being so good, would heaven
    seem best?
  Now, heaven and she are beyond
  this ride.

And yet—she has not spoke so long!
What if heaven be that, fair and
    strong                             101
At life's best, with our eyes upturned
Whither life's flower is first dis-
    cerned,
  We, fixed so, ever should so abide?
What if we still ride on, we two, 105
With life for ever old yet new,
Changed not in kind but in degree,
The instant made eternity,—
And heaven just prove that I and she
  Ride, ride together, for ever
  ride?                                110

## SOLILOQUY OF THE SPANISH CLOISTER

### *Robert Browning* (*1843*)

Gr-r-r—there go, my heart's abhor-
    rence!
  Water your damned flower-pots,
  do!
If hate killed men, Brother Lawrence,

God's blood, would not mine kill
    you!
What? your myrtle-bush wants trim-
    ming?                               5
  Oh, that rose has prior claims—

Needs its leaden vase filled brimming?
  Hell dry you up with its flames!

At the meal we sit together:
  *Salve tibi!* I must hear                    10
Wise talk of the kind of weather,
  Sort of season, time of year:
*Not a plenteous cork-crop: scarcely
  Dare we hope oak-galls, I doubt:
What's the Latin name for "parsley"?*
  What's the Greek name for Swine's
    Snout?                                     16

Whew! We'll have our platter bur-
    nished,
  Laid with care on our own shelf!
With a fire-new spoon we're fur-
    nished,
  And a goblet for ourself,                    20

Rinsed like something sacrificial
  Ere 'tis fit to touch our chaps—
Marked with L for our initial!
  (He-he! There his lily snaps!)

*Saint*, forsooth! While brown Dolo-
    res                                        25
  Squats outside the Convent bank
With Sanchicha, telling stories,
  Steeping tresses in the tank,
Blue-black, lustrous, thick like horse-
    hairs,
  —Can't I see his dead eye glow,  30
Bright, as 'twere a Barbary corsair's?
  (That is, if he'd let it show!)

When he finishes refection,
  Knife and fork he never lays
Cross-wise, to my recollection,               35
  As do I, in Jesu's praise.
I the Trinity illustrate,
  Drinking watered orange-pulp—

In three sips the Arian frustrate;
  While he drains his at one gulp.  40

Oh, those melons! If he's able
  We're to have a feast! so nice!
One goes to the Abbot's table,
  All of us get each a slice.
How go on your flowers? None
    double?                                    45
  Not one fruit-sort can you spy?
Strange!—And I, too, at such trouble
  Keep them close-nipped on the sly!

There's a great text in Galatians,
  Once you trip on it, entails    50
Twenty-nine distinct damnations
  One sure, if another fails:
If I trip him just a-dying,
  Sure of heaven as sure can be,
Spin him round and send him flying 55
  Off to hell, a Manichee?

Or, my scrofulous French novel
  On gray paper with blunt type!
Simply glance at it, you grovel
  Hand and foot in Belial's gripe:  60
If I double down its pages
  At the woeful sixteenth print,
When he gathers his greengages,
  Ope a sieve and slip it in't?

Or, there's Satan! one might venture
  Pledge one's soul to him, yet leave
Such a flaw in the indenture         67
  As he'd miss till, past retrieve,
Blasted lay that rose-acacia
  We're so proud of! *Hy, Zy,
    Hine* . . .                                70
'St, there's Vespers! *Plena gratiâ,
    Ave, Virgo!* Gr-r-r—you swine!

# THE LOVE SONG OF J. ALFRED PRUFROCK

## *T. S. Eliot* (*1917*)

*S'io credesse che mia risposta fosse*
*A persona che mai tornasse al mondo,*
*Questa fiamma staria senza piu scosse.*
*Ma perciocche giammai di questo fondo*
*Non torno vivo alcun, s'i'odo il vero,*
*Senza tema d'infamia ti rispondo.*

Let us go then, you and I,
When the evening is spread out against the sky
Like a patient etherized upon a table;
Let us go, through certain half-deserted streets,
The muttering retreats                                                    5
Of restless nights in one-night cheap hotels
And sawdust restaurants with oyster-shells:
Streets that follow like a tedious argument
Of insidious intent
To lead you to an overwhelming question. . . .                           10
Oh, do not ask, "What is it?"
Let us go and make our visit.

In the room the women come and go
Talking of Michelangelo.

The yellow fog that rubs its back upon the window-panes,                  15
The yellow smoke that rubs its muzzle on the window-panes,
Licked its tongue into the corners of the evening,
Lingered upon the pools that stand in drains,
Let fall upon its back the soot that falls from chimneys,
Slipped by the terrace, made a sudden leap,                               20
And seeing that it was a soft October night,
Curled once about the house, and fell asleep.

And indeed there will be time
For the yellow smoke that slides along the street,
Rubbing its back upon the window panes;                                   25
There will be time, there will be time
To prepare a face to meet the faces that you meet;
There will be time to murder and create,
And time for all the works and days of hands
That lift and drop a question on your plate;                              30
Time for you and time for me,
And time yet for a hundred indecisions,
And for a hundred visions and revisions,
Before the taking of a toast and tea.

In the room the women come and go                                         35
Talking of Michelangelo.

And indeed there will be time
To wonder, "Do I dare?" and, "Do I dare?"
Time to turn back and descend the stair,
With a bald spot in the middle of my hair—                              40
(They will say: "How his hair is growing thin!")
My morning coat, my collar mounting firmly to the chin,
My necktie rich and modest, but asserted by a simple pin—
(They will say: "But how his arms and legs are thin!")
Do I dare                                                              45
Disturb the universe?
In a minute there is time
For decisions and revisions which a minute will reverse.

For I have known them all already, known them all:
Have known the evenings, mornings, afternoons,                          50
I have measured out my life with coffee spoons;
I know the voices dying with a dying fall
Beneath the music from a farther room.
         So how should I presume?

And I have known the eyes already, known them all—                      55
The eyes that fix you in a formulated phrase,
And when I am formulated, sprawling on a pin,
When I am pinned and wriggling on the wall,
Then how should I begin
To spit out all the butt-ends of my days and ways?                      60
         And how should I presume?

And I have known the arms already, known them all—
Arms that are braceleted and white and bare
(But in the lamplight, downed with light brown hair!)
Is it perfume from a dress                                              65
That makes me so digress?
Arms that lie along a table, or wrap about a shawl.
         And should I then presume?
         And how should I begin?

                    .         .         .

Shall I say, I have gone at dusk through narrow streets                  70
And watched the smoke that rises from the pipes
Of lonely men in shirt-sleeves, leaning out of windows? . . .

I should have been a pair of ragged claws
Scuttling across the floors of silent seas.

          .         .         .         .         .

And the afternoon, the evening, sleeps so peacefully!                    75
Smoothed by long·fingers,
Asleep . . . tired . . . or it malingers,
Stretched on the floor, here beside you and me.
Should I, after tea and cakes and ices,
Have the strength to force the moment to its crisis?                      80
But though I have wept and fasted, wept and prayed,
Though I have seen my head (grown slightly bald) brought in upon a
    platter,
I am no prophet—and here's no great matter;
I have seen the moment of my greatness flicker,
And I have seen the eternal Footman hold my coat, and snicker,           85
And in short, I was afraid.

And would it have been worth it, after all,
After the cups, the marmalade, the tea,
Among the porcelain, among some talk of you and me,
Would it have been worth while,                                          90

To have bitten off the matter with a smile,
To have squeezed the universe into a ball
To roll it toward some overwhelming question,
To say: "I am Lazarus, come from the dead,
Come back to tell you all, I shall tell you all"—                       95
If one, settling a pillow by her head,
    Should say: "That is not what I meant at all;
    That is not it, at all."

And would it have been worth it, after all,
Would it have been worth while,                                         100
After the sunsets and the dooryards and the sprinkled streets,
After the novels, after the teacups, after the skirts that trail along the floor—
And this, and so much more?—
It is impossible to say just what I mean!
But as if a magic lantern threw the nerves in patterns on a screen      105
Would it have been worth while
If one, settling a pillow or throwing off a shawl,
And turning toward the window, should say:
    "That is not it at all,
    That is not what I meant, at all."                110

No! I am not Prince Hamlet, nor was meant to be;
Am an attendant lord, one that will do
To swell a progress, start a scene or two,
Advise the prince; no doubt, an easy tool,
Deferential, glad to be of use,                                         115

Politic, cautious, and meticulous;
Full of high sentence, but a bit obtuse;
At times, indeed, almost ridiculous—
Almost, at times, the Fool.

I grow old. . . . I grow old. . . .                                    120
I shall wear the bottoms of my trousers rolled.

Shall I part my hair behind? Do I dare to eat a peach?
I shall wear white flannel trousers, and walk upon the beach.
I have heard the mermaids singing, each to each.

I do not think that they will sing to me.                              125

I have seen them riding seaward on the waves
Combing the white hair of the waves blown back
When the wind blows the water white and black.

We have lingered in the chambers of the sea
By sea-girls wreathed with seaweed red and brown                       130
Till human voices wake us, and we drown.


## ISOLT OF BRITTANY

### (*From* Tristram)

### *Edwin Arlington Robinson*  (*1927*)

#### I

Isolt of the white hands, in Brittany,
Could see no longer northward anywhere
A picture more alive or less familiar
Than a blank ocean and the same white birds
Flying, and always flying, and still flying,                           5
Yet never bringing any news of him
That she remembered, who had sailed away
The spring before—saying he would come back,
Although not saying when. Not one of them,
For all their flying, she thought, had heard the name    10
Of Tristram, or of him beside her there
That was the King, her father. The last ship
Was out of sight, and there was nothing now
For her to see before the night came down
Except her father's face. She looked at him              15
And found him smiling in the way she feared,
And loved the while she feared it. The King took
One of her small still hands in one of his
That were so large and hard to be so kind,
And weighed a question, not for the first time:          20

"Why should it be that I must have a child
Whose eyes are wandering always to the north?
The north is a bad region full of wolves
And bears and hairy men that have no manners.
Why should her eyes be always on the north,     25
I wonder, when all's here that one requires
Of comfort, love, and of expediency?
You are not cheered, I see, or satisfied
Entirely by the sound of what I say.
You are too young, may be, to make yourself     30
A nest of comfort and expediency."

"I may be that," she said, and a quick flush
Made a pink forage of her laughing face,
At which he smiled again. "But not so young
As to be told for ever how young I am.     35
I have been growing for these eighteen years,
And waiting here, for one thing and another.
Besides, his manners are as good as yours,
And he's not half so hairy as you are,
Even though you be the King of Brittany,     40
Or the great Jove himself, and then my father."
With that she threw her arms around his neck,
Throbbing as if she were a child indeed.

"You are no heavier than a cat," said he,
"But otherwise you are somewhat like a tiger.     45
Relinquish your commendable affection
A little, and tell me why it is you dream
Of someone coming always from the north.
Are there no proper knights or princes else
Than one whose eyes, wherever they may be fixed,     50
Are surely not fixed hard on Brittany?
You are a sort of child, or many sorts,
Yet also are too high and too essential
To be much longer the quaint sport and food
Of shadowy fancies. For a time I've laughed     55
And let you dream, but I may not laugh always.
Because he praised you as a child one day,
And may have liked you as a child one day,
Why do you stare for ever into the north,
Over that water, where the good God placed     60
A land known only to your small white ears?"

"Only because the good God, I suppose,
Placed England somewhere north of Brittany—
Though not so far but one may come and go
As many a time as twice before he dies.     65
I know that's true, having been told about it.

I have been told so much about this world
That I have wondered why men stay in it.
I have been told of devils that are in it,
And some right here in Brittany.  Griffon                    70
Is one of them; and if he ever gets me,
I'll pray for the best way to kill myself."


King Howel held his daughter closer to him,
As if a buried and forgotten fear
Had come to life and was confronting him                     75
With a new face.  "Never you mind the devils,"
He said, "be they in Brittany or elsewhere.
They are for my attention, if need be.
You will affright me and amuse me less
By saying, if you are ready, how much longer                 80
You are to starve yourself with your delusion
Of Tristram coming back.  He may come back,
Or Mark, his uncle, who tonight is making
Another Isolt his queen—the dark Isolt,
Isolt of Ireland—may be coming back,                         85
Though I'd as lief he would remain at home
In Cornwall, with his new queen—if he keeps her."


"And who is this far-off Isolt of Ireland?"
She said, like a thing waiting to be hurt:
"A creature that one hears of constantly,                     90
And one that no man sees, or none to say so,
Must be unusual—if she be at all."


"The few men who have told of her to me
Have told of silence and of Irish pride,
Inhabiting too much beauty for one woman.                     95
My eyes have never seen her; and as for beauty,
My eyes would rather look on yours, my child.
And as for Tristram coming back, what then—
One of these days?  Any one may come back.
King Arthur may come back; and as for that,                  100
Our Lord and Saviour may come back some time,
Though hardly all for you.  Have you kept hid
Some promise or protestation heretofore,
That you may shape a thought into a reason
For making always of a distant wish                          105
A dim belief?  You are too old for that—
If it will make you happy to be told so.
You have been told so much."  King Howel smiled,
And waited, holding her white hands in his.

"I have been told that Tristram will come back," 110
She said; "and it was he who told me so.
Also I have this agate that he gave me;
And I believe his eyes."

                       "Believe his agate,"
The king said, "for as long as you may save it. 115
An agate's a fair plaything for a child,
Though not so boundless and immovable
In magnitude but that a child may lose it.
Since you esteem it such an acquisition,
Treasure it more securely, and believe it 120
As a bright piece of earth, and nothing more.
Believe his agate, and forget his eyes;
And go to bed.  You are not young enough,
I see, to stay awake and entertain
Much longer your exaggerated fancies. 125
And if he should come back?  Would you prepare
Upon the ruinous day of his departure
To drown yourself, and with yourself his agate?"

Isolt, now on a cushion at his feet,
Finding the King's hard knees a meagre pillow, 130
Sat upright, thinking.  "No I should not do that;
Though I should never trust another man
So far that I should go away with him.
King's daughters, I suppose, are bought and sold,
But you would not sell me." 135

                       "You seize a question
As if it were an agate—or a fact,"
The King said, laughing at the calm gray eyes
That were so large in the small face before him.
"I might sell you, perhaps, at a fair bargain. 140
To play with an illustrious example,
If Modred were to overthrow King Arthur—
And there are prophets who see Arthur's end
In Modred, who's an able sort of reptile—
And come for you to go away with him, 145
And to be Queen of Britain, I might sell you,
Perhaps.  You might say prayers that you be sold."

"I may say prayers that you be reasonable
And serious, and that you believe me so."
There was a light now in his daughter's eyes 150
Like none that he remembered having seen
In eyes before, whereat he paused and heard,
Not all amused.  "He will come back," she said,
"And I shall wait.  If he should not come back,

I shall have been but one poor woman more          155
Whose punishment for being born a woman
Was to believe and wait. You are my King,
My father, and of all men anywhere,
Save one, you are the world of men to me.
When I say this of him you must believe me,         160
As I believe his eyes. He will come back;
And what comes then I leave to him, and God."

Slowly the King arose, and with his hands
He lifted up Isolt, so frail, so light,
And yet, with all, mysteriously so strong.          165
He raised her patient face between his hands,
Observing it as if it were some white
And foreign flower, not certain in his garden
To thrive, nor like to die. Then with a vague
And wavering effect of shaking her                   170
Affectionately back to his own world,
Which never would be hers, he smiled once more
And set her free. "You should have gone to bed
When first I told you. You had best go now,
And while you are still dreaming. In the morning     175
Your dreams, if you remember them, will all
Be less than one bird singing in a tree."

Isolt of the white hands, unchangeable,
Half childlike and half womanly, looked up
Into her father's eyes and shook her head,           180
Smiling, but less for joy than certainty:
"There's a bird then that I have never seen
In Brittany; and I have never heard him.
Good night, my father." She went slowly out,
Leaving him in the gloom.                            185

                              "Good night, my child,
Good night," he said, scarce hearing his own voice
For crowded thoughts that were unseizable
And unforeseen within him. Like Isolt,
He stood now in the window looking north             190
Over the misty sea. A seven days' moon
Was in the sky, and there were a few stars
That had no fire. "I have no more a child,"
He thought, "and what she is I do not know.
It may be fancy and fantastic youth                  195
That ails her now; it may be the sick touch
Of prophecy concealing disillusion.
If there were not inwoven so much power
And poise of sense with all her seeming folly,

I might assume a concord with her faith 200
As that of one elected soon to die.
But surely no infringement of the grave
In her conceits and her appearances
Encourages a fear that still is fear;
And what she is to know, I cannot say. 205
A changeling down from one of those white stars
Were more like her than like a child of mine."

Nothing in the cold glimmer of a moon
Over a still, cold ocean there before him
Would answer for him in the silent voice 210
Of time an idle question. So the King,
With only time for company, stood waiting
Alone there in the window, looking off
At the still sea between his eyes and England.

# SATIRES OF CIRCUMSTANCE

## *Thomas Hardy* (*1911*)

### AT TEA

The kettle descants in a cosy drone,
And the young wife looks in her husband's face,
And then at her guest's, and shows in her own
Her sense that she fills an envied place;
And the visiting lady is all abloom, 5
And says there was never so sweet a room.

And the happy young housewife does not know
That the woman beside her was first his choice,
Till the fates ordained it could not be so . . .
Betraying nothing in look or voice, 10
The guest sits smiling and sips her tea,
And he throws her a stray glance yearningly.

### AT THE DRAPER'S

"I stood at the back of the shop, my dear,
But you did not perceive me.
Well, when they deliver what you were shown
I shall know nothing of it, believe me!"

And he coughed and coughed as she paled and said, 5
"Oh, I didn't see you come in there—
Why couldn't you speak?"—"Well, I didn't. I left
That you should not notice I'd been there."

"You were viewing some lovely things.                                       10
'*Soon required for a widow of latest fashion*';
And I knew 'twould upset you to meet the man
Who had to be cold and ashen,

"And screwed in a box before they could dress you
'*In the last new note in mourning*,'                                       15
As they defined it. So, not to distress you,
I left you to your adorning."


## BOY AND FATHER

(*From* Smoke and Steel)

*Carl Sandburg* (*1920*)

The boy Alexander understands his father to be a famous lawyer.
The leather law books of Alexander's father fill a room like hay in a barn.
Alexander has asked his father to let him build a house like bricklayers build,
    a house with walls and roofs made of big leather law books.

The rain beats on the windows
And the raindrops run down the window glass                                 5
And the raindrops slide off the green blinds down the siding.
The boy Alexander dreams of Napoleon in John C. Abbott's history, Napo-
    leon the grand and lonely man wronged, Napoleon in his life wronged
    and in his memory wronged.
The boy Alexander dreams of the cat Alice saw, the cat fading off into the
    dark and leaving the teeth of its Cheshire smile lighting the gloom.

Buffaloes, blizzards, way down in Texas, in the panhandle of Texas snuggling
    close to New Mexico,
These creep into Alexander's dreaming by the window when his father talks
    with strange men about land down in Deaf Smith County.                  10
Alexander's father tells the strange men: Five years ago we ran a Ford out
    on the prairie and chased antelopes.

Only once or twice in a long while has Alexander heard his father say "my
    first wife" so-and-so and such-and-such.
A few times softly the father has told Alexander, "Your mother . . . was a
    beautiful woman . . . but we won't talk about her."
Always Alexander listens with a keen listen when he hears his father mention
    "my first wife" or "Alexander's mother."

Alexander's father smokes a cigar and the Episcopal rector smokes a cigar
    and the words come often: mystery of life, mystery of life.             15
These two come into Alexander's head blurry and gray while the rain beats
    on the windows and the raindrops run down the window glass and the
    raindrops slide off the green blinds and down the siding.

These and: There is a God, there must be a God, how can there be rain or sun unless there is a God?

> So from the wrongs of Napoleon and the Cheshire cat smile on to the buffaloes and blizzards of Texas and on to his mother and to God, so the blurry gray rain dreams of Alexander have gone on five minutes, maybe ten, keeping slow easy time to the raindrops on the window glass and the raindrops sliding off the green blinds and down the siding.

## A POISON TREE

### *William Blake* (*1794*)

I was angry with my friend:
I told my wrath, my wrath did end.
I was angry with my foe:
I told it not, my wrath did grow.

And I watered it in fears          5
Night and morning with my tears,
And I sunnèd it with smiles
And with soft deceitful wiles.

And it grew both day and night,
Till it bore an apple bright,          10
And my foe beheld it shine,
And he knew that it was mine,—

And into my garden stole
When the night had veiled the pole;
In the morning, glad, I see          15
My foe outstretched beneath the tree.

## THE CLOD AND THE PEBBLE

### *William Blake* (*1794*)

"Love seeketh not itself to please,
    Nor for itself hath any care,
But for another gives its ease,
    And builds a heaven in hell's despair."

So sung a little clod of clay,          5
    Trodden with the cattle's feet.
But a pebble of the brook
    Warbled out these metres meet:

"Love seeketh only self to please,
    To bind another to its delight,          10
Joys in another's loss of ease,
    And builds a hell in heaven's despite."

## JOHN ANDERSON MY JO

### *Robert Burns* (*1789*)

John Anderson my jo, John,
    When we were first acquent,
Your locks were like the raven,
    Your bonnie brow was brent;
But now your brow is beld, John,          5
    Your locks are like the snow;
But blessings on your frosty pow,
    John Anderson, my jo.

John Anderson my jo, John,
    We clamb the hill thegither;          10
And mony a canty day, John,
    We've had wi' ane anither:
Now we maun totter down, John,
    And hand in hand we'll go,
And sleep thegither at the foot,          15
    John Anderson, my jo.

## SHE WAS A PHANTOM OF DELIGHT

*William Wordsworth*  (*1804*)

She was a Phantom of delight
When first she gleamed upon my
    sight;
A lovely Apparition, sent
To be a moment's ornament;
Her eyes as stars of Twilight fair;  5
Like Twilight's too, her dusky hair;
But all things else about her drawn
From May-time and the cheerful
    Dawn;
A dancing Shape, an Image gay,
To haunt, to startle, and waylay.  10

I saw her upon nearer view,
A Spirit, yet a Woman too!
Her household motions light and free,
And steps of virgin liberty;
A countenance in which did meet  15
Sweet records, promises as sweet;
A Creature not too bright or good
For human nature's daily food;
For transient sorrows, simple wiles,
Praise, blame, love, kisses, tears, and
    smiles.  20

And now I see with eye serene
The very pulse of the machine;
A Being breathing thoughtful breath,
A Traveler between life and death;
The reason firm, the temperate will,
Endurance, foresight, strength, and
    skill;  26
A perfect Woman, nobly planned,
To warn, to comfort, and command;
And yet a Spirit still, and bright
With something of angelic light.  30

## SHE DWELT AMONG THE UNTRODDEN WAYS

*William Wordsworth*  (*1799*)

She dwelt among the untrodden ways
    Beside the springs of Dove,

A maid whom there were none to
    praise
And very few to love:

A violet by a mossy stone            5
    Half hidden from the eye!
—Fair as a star, when only one
    Is shining in the sky.

She lived unknown, and few could
    know
    When Lucy ceased to be;          10
But she is in her grave, and, oh,
    The difference to me!

## SHE WALKS IN BEAUTY

*George Gordon, Lord Byron*
(*1814*)

She walks in beauty, like the night
    Of cloudless climes and starry
    skies;
And all that's best of dark and bright
    Meet in her aspect and her eyes:
Thus mellowed to that tender light  5
    Which heaven to gaudy day de-
    nies.

One shade the more, one ray the less,
    Had half impaired the nameless
    grace
Which waves in every raven tress,
    Or softly lightens o'er her face;  10
Where thoughts serenely sweet ex-
    press
    How pure, how dear their dwell-
    ing-place.

And on that cheek, and o'er that
    brow,
So soft, so calm, yet eloquent,
The smiles that win, the tints that
    glow,                            15
    But tell of days in goodness spent,
A mind at peace with all below,
    A heart whose love is innocent!

## MAID OF ATHENS

*George Gordon, Lord Byron*
(*1810*)

Ζώη μοῦ, σᾶς ἀγαπῶ

Maid of Athens, ere we part,
Give, oh, give me back my heart!
Or, since that has left my breast,
Keep it now, and take the rest!
Hear my vow before I go, 5

Ζώη μοῦ, σᾶς ἀγαπῶ

By those tresses unconfined,
Wooed by each Aegean wind;
By those lids whose jetty fringe
Kiss thy soft cheeks' blooming tinge;
By those wild eyes like the roe, 11

Ζώη μοῦ, σᾶς ἀγαπῶ

By that lip I long to taste;
By that zone-encircled waist;
By all the token-flowers that tell 15
What words can never speak so well;
By love's alternate joy and woe,

Ζώη μοῦ, σᾶς ἀγαπῶ

Maid of Athens! I am gone;
Think of me, sweet! when alone. 20
Though I fly to Istambol,
Athens holds my heart and soul;
Can I cease to love thee? No!

Ζώη μοῦ, σᾶς ἀγαπῶ

## TO———

*Percy Bysshe Shelley* (*1821*)

One word is too often profaned
For me to profane it,
One feeling too falsely disdained
For thee to disdain it;
One hope is too like despair 5
For prudence to smother,
And pity from thee more dear
Than that from another.

I can give not what men call love,
But wilt thou accept not 10
The worship the heart lifts above
And the Heavens reject not,—
The desire of the moth for the star,
Of the night for the morrow,
The devotion to something afar 15
From the sphere of our sorrow?

## LOVE'S PHILOSOPHY

*Percy Bysshe Shelley* (*1819*)

The fountains mingle with the river
And the rivers with the ocean,
The winds of heaven mix for ever
With a sweet emotion;
Nothing in the world is single, 5
All things by a law divine
In one another's being mingle—
Why not I with thine?

See the mountains kiss high heaven,
And the waves clasp one another; 10
No sister-flower would be forgiven
If it disdained its brother:
And the sunlight clasps the earth,
And the moonbeams kiss the sea—
What are all these kissings worth, 15
If thou kiss not me?

## BRIGHT STAR! WOULD I WERE STEADFAST AS THOU ART

*John Keats* (*1820*)

Bright star! would I were steadfast
as thou art—
Not in lone splendor hung aloft the
night,
And watching, with eternal lids apart,
Like Nature's patient, sleepless Ere-
mite,
The moving waters at their priestlike
task 5
Of pure ablution round earth's human
shores,
Or gazing on the new soft-fallen mask

Of snow upon the mountains and the
    moors—
No—yet still steadfast, still unchange-
    able,
Pillowed upon my fair love's ripening
    breast,                             10

To feel for ever its soft fall and swell,
Awake for ever in a sweet unrest,
Still, still to hear her tender-taken
    breath,
And so live ever—or else swoon to
    death.

## THE CONSTANT LOVER

### *Sir John Suckling*   (*1646*)

Out upon it, I have loved
    Three whole days together!
And am like to love three more,
    If it prove fair weather.

Time shall moult away his wings 5
    Ere he shall discover
In the whole wide world again
    Such a constant lover.

But the spite on't is, no praise
    Is due at all to me:                10
Love with me had made no stays,
    Had it any been but she.

Had it any been but she
    And that very face,
There had been at least ere this      15
    A dozen dozen in her place.

# THE ARTS

Most of us do not easily discover for ourselves the beauty that lies all around us. We depend upon artists to open our eyes and ears. As Browning says, they teach us to love many things which we have passed again and again without noticing. How many people who used to be completely indifferent to a wayside sunflower have been made aware of its glowing color and the beauty of its design by the painting of Van Gogh! Almost no one thought a red barn worth looking at until Grant Wood returned from Paris to paint scenes of the Iowa farm country that he knew best. His stern courageous farmers of the middle-west seen against a background of their barns, fences, and farm implements assume an importance that few had before recognized. Ruth Suckow in her stories of ordinary people arouses in a similar way a fresh understanding and sympathy in us. Artists like these by enabling us to see the beauty latent in humble men and women may encourage us to express the meaning that we have discovered in the small tragedies and comedies of everyday life. Thus in a modest way some of us may ourselves become artists.

Others may think themselves quite without artistic talent of any kind and feel utterly incapable of expressing in words, in music, in painting, or in acting their sense of the wonder, the terror, or the joy in human experience. Yet the principles of art play a part in the life of almost everyone. Many times a day we make choices or pass judgments that express our taste. When we buy our clothes, we consider the effect of color, line, form, and general harmony upon our appearance. We may not be able to tell why one combination of shirt and tie pleases us and another offends, or why the new hat with the snood adds charm to one woman and makes another unfortunate creature look like a figure in a comic strip. But in each case our judgment has been guided, perhaps misguided, by our taste. When we arrange the pictures and furniture in our rooms, we depend upon a feeling for what looks well and what does not. Every time we see a movie we express an opinion which is often an artistic judgment, uncertain and inarticulate though it may be. We may be puzzled to know why we approved Leslie Howard's portrayal of the smug English professor in *Pygmalion* or we may be unable to decide what was the secret of Katharine Cornell's appeal as a Malay princess in the stage play, *The Wingless Victory*. Above all we may wonder why people's opinions differ so much in these matters. One reason is that many of our aesthetic preferences are prejudices, having no sound artistic basis whatever. Life becomes much more interesting when we learn to understand such judgments and to know what the principles are that we have applied in arriving at our decisions.

In this section of the book various types of artists describe the satisfactions that they have found in their work. Critics and lovers of art suggest what we must look for if we are thoroughly to enjoy a concert, an art gallery, a book or a play. They may help us to dispel some of the mystery which too often surrounds the work of a musician, a painter, a poet or an actor. Then we, like Wordsworth, can see that a great artist is not a queer person or even a remote genius, but simply a man speaking with peculiar directness and eloquence to other men like himself. Once we have grasped this important truth, we shall be able to look upon art not as an escape from life, but as the best of all ways to enrich the routine of daily living.

## THE PLAIN READER

(*From* The Modern Novel)

*Elizabeth A. Drew*   (*1926*)

If all the good people were clever
And all the clever people were good,
The world would be better than ever
We thought that it possibly could;

But somehow 'tis seldom or never
The two hit it off as they should,
The good are so harsh to the clever
The clever so rude to the good.
                                 *Elizabeth Wordsworth*

AND THE rudeness of the clever to the good is expressed nowhere more caustically than when the æsthetes address the general public on the subject of literary appreciation. "Anyone who has anything to say cannot fail to be misunderstood," says Mr. Cardan in *Those Barren Leaves*. "The public only understands the things with which it is perfectly familiar. Something new makes it lose its orientation." Or we can hear Mr. Mencken cackling triumphantly as he scores hit upon palpable hit on the subject of the Nordic incapacity to comprehend art and the artist. It is all quite true. The vast majority of the public are in the position of Florence in *The Constant Nymph* as she argues with her artist husband.

"You put the wrong things first. Music, all art— What is it for? What is its justification? After all . . ."

"It's not for anything. It has no justification."

"It's only part of the supreme art, the business of living beautifully. You can't put it on a pedestal above decency and humanity and civilization."

"I know. You want to use it like electric light . . . I've seen it; my father's cultured——"

"That is a much abused word, but it means an important thing which we can't do without."

"Can't we?  I can!  By God, I can!"

The pure artist claims, as Lewis Dodd claims here, to be creator and nothing else, and demands to be judged as such.  Literature, however, with the possible exception of what Mr. George Moore calls pure poetry, differs from the other major arts by its far closer approach to the terms of actual life. In a sense this makes it easier for the general public to appreciate, but in another sense it complicates the outlook.  It has led to the unending strife among the critics as to the plane on which the enjoyment of literature should function, and the poor reading public, sincerely anxious to know what books to read, and what to look for in the books it reads, finds itself confused and fuddled by the contradictory advices of the experts.  It knows, from the rude things which the superior intellectuals say about it, that its natural instinct to regard literary values exactly as if they were moral values, and to judge books as it would judge human conduct, is inadequate and misleading; but how is it to choose an alternative?  It reads books in a straightforward way, and wants to criticize them in a straightforward way, but there are the Art for Art's sakers who demand a purely æsthetic standard, making of literature, as of the fine arts, an exclusive cult for exclusive people.  The intellectual theorists are not very much more helpful, even though Matthew Arnold and Pater, the literary philosophers, with their somewhat vague talk of abstractions like Beauty and Good and Sweetness and Light and hard gemlike flames of the mind, have been followed by the newer race of literary psychologists; then there are the social historians like Taine, generalizing all individuality into a national and social significance, with the anatomists to whom technique means everything, and finally the mere gossips who deal in nothing but the froth of personalities.

It is no wonder if the patient dies while all these doctors disagree, yet the holding of some standard of appreciation is essential to the intelligent enjoyment of reading, even of novel reading.  The novel may be an amusement for an idle hour, but it may equally be, as Jane Austen claims for it, "a work in which the greatest powers of the mind are displayed: in which the most thorough knowledge of human nature, the happiest delineations of its varieties, the liveliest effusions of wit and humour, are conveyed to the world in the best chosen language."  It is worth considering, therefore, how a novel which is a serious work of literature should be approached, for it is an inquiry which is of importance to all readers and to all writers of novels, that is, to a majority of the inhabitants of the English-speaking world.

It may, I think, be of some help if, before arguing further about literary appreciation, we go back another step, to the root of the matter, and ask the basic question what literature *is*.  Sir Arthur Quiller-Couch has defined it, "what sundry men and women have said memorably concerning life," which is, perhaps, as good a working definition as it is possible to find.  As modern scholarship enables us to see further and further into past civilizations and "the dark backward and abyss of time," the more apparent does it become that human nature remains essentially unchanged. Egyptian, Greek, Chinese, Hindu, medieval, Renaissance or modern European thinkers and creators, tell the same stories, and distil the same comments from them as to the nature of life and of mankind. Men and women all down the ages have faced the same eternal human problems and have asked the same eternal human questions as they found themselves confronted by the same harsh interplay of human venture and event, the same clash of opposites which forever thwart and jar each other in human existence: aspiration and achievement, physical and spiritual, actual and ideal, good and evil, life and death. Meanwhile, all those who have had what we vaguely call the gift of expression, have always striven to describe in words something of what they have seen, something of what they have heard, something of what they have thought, something of what they have felt, in this eternal and unchanging drama, the author of the Book of Job crying with the same voice as Oedipus or Milton's Samson, "God of our Fathers, what is Man?" No writer can ever solve the riddle: the characters he creates are but comments suggested by his own mind, the stories he tells are but illustrations evolved by his own mind, and these comments and illustrations vary with every age and nationality and individual. But the aim of each in turn is always and eternally the same: to give some created vision of what life is; it may be to fall into the baffling fascination of attempting to explain its why; and the unfading interest for the reader is to compare epochs and peoples and personalities as they practise this single aim: to watch each one, from Confucius to Conrad, from Sophocles to Shaw, as he illustrates and interprets human existence in the terms of his own times and his own temperament. We are all, as Galsworthy says, little bits of continuity, and "the still sad music of humanity" remains the same melody, whether we listen to it as the Song of Solomon or in the latest jazz tempo, interpreted through shawm or lyre, spinet or saxophone.

All art, since it cannot use as its material anything but what already exists in the universe, must in some degree be a comment and interpretation of that universe, but literature has a relationship to life far more close than that of any of the other arts, since it uses the same medium by whose help we carry on our human intercourse, the medium of language. The media of colour, sound, mass or line are not used as natural bases for human communication except in the world of cinema, where the art of miming and making faces must perforce replace human speech. Average human beings live their lives with the help of words, conveying their experiences, expressing their thoughts, and interpreting their emotions through them. The literary artist uses exactly the same material, hence the impossibility of detaching the experiences of literature entirely from those of actual living. Oscar Wilde declares that, to the elect, beautiful things mean only Beauty, but I think we can safely say that there is no human being to whom *Hamlet* or the *Odyssey* means only Beauty.

The artistic emotion the most cultivated and sensitive mind experiences on reading them is complicated by direct emotional, intellectual, and moral impressions which it inevitably receives at the same time.

More than ever is this so with the novel, since the novel is almost entirely concerned with problems and situations common to all men, so that it is more than ever inevitable that questions of content alone should intrude in our judgment of it, as well as the æsthetic questions of the fusion of subject matter and form. The novel, dealing as it does with the actions and passions of human beings whom we think of in the terms of fellow living creatures, and telling of crisis, incident, character and circumstance within the observation of us all, is bound to express certain of the moral values men live by, and by implication, if not directly, the attitude of the author towards those values, so that it is almost as difficult to divorce a discussion of the novel from questions of conduct as for a blind man with one arm to get out of a bunker with a toothpick— as Mr. P. G. Wodehouse would say!

But this brings us at once to the central difficulty of intelligent appreciation of the modern English and American novel, and the ground of attack by the intellectuals and the æsthetes. Human life, as all experiencers of it are agreed, is a sorry scheme. We are all comrades in distress and dissatisfaction, united in a tragic community of longing to lighten "the weary weight of all this unintelligible world.". Hence, since the novel portrays so many of the riddles of life as we meet them in life itself, great numbers of readers go to the novel in much the same spirit in which they would go to a fortune teller. They do not really want to be told the truth about life, or to listen to speculation about life, they want to be reassured about it: to get some comforting "message." There is a certain American magazine which sends out slips for its contributors' guidance, stating: "Humour, tragedy and pathos are acceptable, but not stories that are morbid or that leave the reader uncomfortable." The editor of this magazine reads the average reader aright. Hence the inanities of the ordinary magazine story and the glut of popular love romances, where, in place of the pessimism "more black than ash buds in the front of March" (which is so popular among the intellectuals, but which leaves the average reader uncomfortable), we find a sincere sentimentalism more sticky than chestnut buds in the front of April, which apparently somehow convinces him, and still more, her, that she herself some day will be clothed with the heavens and crowned with the stars.

This craving for a certain emotional effect in fiction goes deeper than the demand for sentimental romance, and involves the whole matter of "uplift." There is, says Mr. Edwin Muir, one great orthodox heresy about the universe which makes it such a dull place to live in, and that is the dogma that if a thing is not useful it cannot be important. It is a heresy imbedded with peculiar tenacity in the Anglo-Saxon mind, which makes it demand perpetually that the meaning of life and the message of art shall lie in its own especial code of conduct, and which makes it distrust any manifestation of human energy unless a definite lesson can be drawn from it. Readers who hold this heresy seem to regard literature as the Polonius of life, a sort of mine of useful and helpful and improving maxims and truisms, whose sole purpose is to be the mouthpiece of established order and the bourgeois virtues: the missing link between God and suburbia. It arises from a failure to distinguish between literary and moral values, between conduct in life and the representation of conduct in writing. Now this *is* difficult for the general reader, because as I have already said it is not possible entirely to divorce literature from moral questions. There is, of course, always the extreme logical position of Plato, the first Puritan, who argued that since art is imitation, and of bad no less than good, therefore there must be evil in it: that the same person cannot at the same time devote himself to the development of pure good and be creating characters of evil. Hence his ideal republic must banish entirely all art and all artists. But if we accept the Aristotelian view that the universe is rationally organized, and that the existence of art in it as one of the natural functions of human nature proves that it has a proper place in life and a part in the ultimate perfection of life, we must decide what that place is. "You confuse two things," says Tchekov, "solving a problem, and stating it correctly. It is only the second that is obligatory for the artist." This is the whole kernel of the matter. When the artist is creating he no more thinks of the purely moral qualities of his creation than passionate lovers think of the moral qualities of the child that may spring from their ecstatic union. Creation is creation, not something else. The artist takes as much pains and is as much absorbed in his creation of evil as of good, of ugliness as of beauty. He lavishes as much work and care, and exactly the same *sort* of work and care, on Iago as on Othello, on Medea as on Alcestis, on a gargoyle as on the Venus of Milo. He looks on experience as an end in itself, while the moralist regards it as a symptom which must be treated in relation to some general manifestation of truth, and requires that a book shall conform to some special ethical formula. We might illustrate the point from that very brilliant recent novel, from which I have already quoted, *The Constant Nymph*. The implacable reporter of human experience who is the creator of that book chooses a group of human beings to play her story, notes the inevitable outcome of the clashes of character and circumstance she has planned, and is concerned only to present that interplay of character and circumstance with all the intensity of realization, clarity of outline and economy of language of which she is capable. *She has no other aim.* Were she a sentimentalist we should be presented with an Ethel M. Dell or a Maud Diver solution and Florence would have a convenient railway accident so that Teresa could marry Lewis Dodd and live happily ever afterwards. Sentimental readers, no doubt, wished this had happened. Or again, if she were a social moralist, like the late Mrs. Humphry Ward, Lewis would conform his music to the immediate claims of his environment, and we should have an end typifying Art rendering Service to Humanity through the Sacrifice of Selfish Aims. And social moralists, no doubt, wish *that* had happened.

But as it is the book stands as a piece of literature and must be discussed as such. It is neither a dream nor a tract.

To say that a serious novel must be discussed as a piece of creative art and not as a piece of life is to contradict what we have already said as to the impossibility of divorcing the discussion of literature from questions of conduct. The novel is concerned with the statement of human truths and problems and cannot get away from them, but the point always to be remembered is that the author is concerned with the *creation* of those truths and problems and not primarily with any *comment* on them. The illustrations of conduct which he creates concern us (in our character as critics of literature) only in so far as they involve a criticism of the *literary* treatment of such conduct, and an understanding of the author's mind. It is just as much a sin against *literature* to read a book for nothing but a useful moral lesson, as to read it for nothing but a sensual thrill, and to judge a work to be defective *as literature* because it leaves no helpful message and encouragement for living, is as stupid as to judge a chrysanthemum to be defective because it does not eat as well as a cauliflower.

Perhaps the point will be clearer if we again look for a moment at the past and consider some accepted masterpieces and our attitude to them. We shall then be aware at once that our enjoyment of them depends not at all on our agreement or disagreement with their ethical standards. Since public opinion is now agreed about the artistic value of these works, we instinctively leave any personal view of their morality out of account in reading them and concentrate our attention on feeling their literary qualities. For example, suppose we found this paragraph in the police news of a daily paper:

## MIXED MARRIAGE
## MURDER AND SUICIDE
### Finds Truth Too Late, Says Colored Husband

An inquest was held on Wednesday last to investigate the circumstances attending the deaths of a Moor and his wife (a white woman) which took place Monday night last under tragic circumstances. It appeared from the evidence of the deceased man's secretary, Michael Cassio, that the couple, who had only recently been married, had lived together very happily, until his employer had come under the influence of his manager, a man of the name of Iago. This man, who was now in hospital as a result of wounds received on the night of the murder, had convinced his employer of his wife's improper intimacy with himself (the witness). Inflamed by jealousy, and without waiting to carefully investigate the charge, the Moor had suffocated his wife in bed, and on discovering from her maid that his suspicions had been groundless, had stabbed himself to death in the presence of the police who were about to take him into custody.

On reading this sordid tale of lust and jealousy we should probably comment on the problems of marriages of mixed races, and the baseness of human instincts, and so on: if it appeared as a modern novel, the American Society for the Suppression of Vice would certainly try to get it suppressed, and a great number of readers would say that they didn't want to hear about that sort of people and that life was unpleasant enough without meeting that sort of thing in fiction. But when we read the play of *Othello* we are not concerned to discuss the facts of the plot as such, because we allow ourselves to be concerned with the validity of Shakespeare's imagination in dealing with them: the literary and not the moral question. Or again, the fact that there are very few people nowadays who would agree with Milton's theology or believe literally the story of *Paradise Lost* does not impair our literary enjoyment of the epic. In the same way Shelley's *Prometheus Unbound* can be fully appreciated by someone who is neither a Socialist nor a pantheist: Burns's *Jolly Beggars* can be read with pleasure by a member of the Charity Organization Society, and Cowley's delightful lines on drinking not only by any citizen of the United States in general, but I believe by even the strictest inhabitant of Kansas! It will be found, indeed, that none of us demands standards of use from accepted works of art: we do not ask the cubic contents of Keats's Grecian Urn, or require that Shelley's West Wind shall grind corn.

It is time, though, to leave the negative discussion of what intelligent criticism is not, and to attempt to form some standard of what it is: to try to answer that continually recurring and teasing question of what to look for in a book, and how the average man and woman can get all that can be got out of his or her general reading.

Appreciation depends on partnership, on the establishment of understanding between writer and reader. "What is a book?" says Anatole France. "A series of little printed signs, essentially only that. It is for the reader himself to supply the forms and colors and sentiments to which these signs correspond. It will depend on him whether the book be dull or brilliant, hot with passion or cold as ice." It is true that the reader gets what he deserves out of a book. As we have seen, the writer of a novel is trying to interpret something of human existence as it appears to his temperament, to give some created vision of what life seems to him to be. At the same time the reader unconsciously contributes his own view and his own personality, and the result of the fusion is criticism. And there are always two main positions from which criticism springs. On the one hand the reader's view of his partnership with the writer may be that it should merely supply a duplication of his own ideas. He may desire, not a stimulus to further thought, but certainty, and assurance about his own pre-established codes of decision, which shall make any further search for reality unnecessary to him. Or, on the other hand, he may possess the experiencing faculty, the love of mental and emotional adventure for its own sake, the knowledge that there is always something to be discovered about the world we live in, that it must necessarily be larger than any one view of it, and that to have an ardor for such discovery is to make life full of an inexhaustible interest. Such a reader will not be concerned only with the sort of people and the sort of conventions and codes to which he is accustomed and of which he approves. He is not a Puritan, but he loves *The Pilgrim's Progress,* not a sentimentalist, but he delights in the analysis of *Clarissa;* not a libertine, but a happy reader of Byron; not a Catholic, but enraptured by *The Hound of Heaven;* not a Jew, but profoundly stirred by the drama of Job and Jehovah. And although he has likes and dislikes, he makes them give an account of themselves; using his intellectual faculties to make his criticism self-conscious, aware of itself, and of the reason for its pleasures and rebellions. "A good hater" if need be, but not a mere helpless victim of prejudice.

From this latter position springs Taste. In other words, to have a gusto for life is its essential root. To be able, with Fielding, to address humanity as "thou jolly substance." Art is communication of experience; the novel is direct communication of human experience, and the fascination of its study lies first of all in an unquenchable and detached curiosity to meet and appraise as many as possible of the multitudinous existing varieties of character, situation, action and opinion. It follows, then, that from the emotional and intellectual point of view, the matter of supreme importance in criticizing a novel is the answer to the question: from what kind of mind does this writing come? Out of how deep and wide an experience was it born? This, and not the mere question of the subject matter, is the all-important starting point for discussion. Here again, perhaps, illustrations are best first from literary classics. Let us take Shakespeare's tragedies. Judged merely as a picture of human existence, nothing could be more ghastly than the spectacle of the cosmos they present. We see innocence murdered and trust betrayed, cruelty torturing old age and treachery triumphing over honesty. Nobility, courage, generosity, truth, are dashed to pieces under the wheels of Fate. Man, struggling in the grip of circumstance and character, is beaten in that struggle every time. Evil always triumphs over good: Iago is proved stronger than Othello and Desdemona, Goneril and Regan vanquish Lear, Hamlet is overthrown, so is Brutus, so is Antony, so is poor young Romeo. Yet the flavor of life which is left on the mental palate after reading Shakespeare is not that of the despair which a play like Galsworthy's *Justice,* for instance, leaves, but something much nearer exaltation—a very strange effect to be produced by the spectacle of the world's illusion! Shakespeare's mind being rich, sure, intense, powerful and comprehensive, it is the impress of the qualities of richness, sureness, intensity, power and understanding which is left upon the mind of the reader. The same magic is achieved by Hardy, whose mind is such that his treatment of the mockery of life and the ignoble bludgeonings of Fate, his picture of this "show God ought surely to shut up soon," becomes a thing of grandeur, its pettiness transmuted into dignity, its baseness ennobled. If again, we look at the world with the eyes and mind of George Moore, we see it as a place for little more than varied opportunities for various kinds of sensation; if we look at it with Shaw, we see it from the point of view of inspired common sense; if we look at it with Dickens, from that of inspired common sensibility. Coming to the modern novel, we can illustrate the same truth by seeing the various ways in which one theme can be treated by different personalities. Let us take that ever-popular situation in fiction, the theme of illicit love. The moralist will simply disapprove of any novel dealing with an "unpleasant theme," and dismiss it at that. The possessor of taste, very well aware that it is a part of life and cannot be ignored so easily, is interested to mark all the tones and degrees of its representation in the terms of various mentalities. He can see it handled by a detached artistic mind like Arnold Bennett or Rose Macaulay or Willa Cather; or by a pictorial mind like Hergesheimer; or by a scientific, analytic mind like Shaw or Wells; or a pitiful, gentle mind, like Galsworthy; or a sincerely sentimental mind, like A. S. M. Hutchinson, or a cynically sentimental mind like Michael Arlen; or a commonplace and rather base mind, as is usual in any of the Legs and Lingerie School; or perhaps one might say, by a vacuum in place of a mind, as is usual in any of the writers of sentimental romances.

Individual preferences must always exist, in literature as in life, and they have to be accepted in the same spirit. Just as sometimes we simply cannot understand how our friends choose their mates as they do, so, maybe, we cannot understand what they see in, say Miss Dorothy Richardson. It does not really help matters, however, to echo Dr. Johnson as he discussed a book with Boswell, and to bellow as if it were a convincing argument, "You, Sir, may think it excellent, but that does not make it so." Tastes differ, and if you are all for steak and onions, caviar and peaches are unsatisfying. Beyond opinion about the merits of individual writers, there are always the two great types of mind which we label Romantic and Realistic. When all the recent criticism which argues against the academic exactitude of the labels has been accepted, there still remain two types of mind, and most readers have a bias towards one or the other. Some naturally prefer looking "through" magic casements opening on the foam of perilous seas in faëry lands forlorn: their Pegasus is like that of Edward Lear's old Person of Bazing,

> Whose presence of mind was amazing,
> He purchased a steed,
> Which he rode at full speed
> And escaped from the people of Bazing.

(A poem which might stand as a symbolist rendering of that literature of escape the psychologists tell us so much about.) This class of readers generally regards the novels of Jane Austen or of Ethel Sidgwick or of Trollope or of Arnold Bennett, much as du Maurier's Frenchman regarded the fox-hunt, "no promenade, no band of music, nossing," while to those who enjoy that kind of thing the commonplace brings its own excitement and thrill, and a book like Walter de la Mare's *Memoirs of a Midget*, or Cabell's tales of romance, and stories in general of "elves, fairies and such like mummery," as

Fielding would say, are about as comforting as a cold crumpet. It is useless to argue about it, because the extremists on either side cannot understand each other, just as the mystic cannot understand the cynic's profound indifference to inner realities, and the intellectual ironist cannot understand anyone really bothering much about the soul. The critic can only follow that excellent advice, "Do not call the tortoise unworthy, because she is not something else," and recognize the fact, true again in literature as in life, that it is quite possible to have a detached admiration without affection and complete sympathy.

So much for the human appeal of the novel and its capacity to satisfy the human curiosity of its readers. That curiosity is the essential basis of all enjoyment of fiction, but it is not possible fully to appreciate it without a further quality—the sense of craftsmanship and style. The difference between art and life is one of Form. Every day of our existence we meet, and realize quite well that we meet, both in our own lives and in those of others, the materials for drama or fiction. But the experiences of living are blurred and confused by a mass of superfluous detail and dialogue, by a bewildering medley of extraneous character and action, which interfere constantly with the development and statement of any single situation. To try to report the thoughts, speech, and activities of one single day in a man's life has spread over nearly a thousand pages of print in *Ulysses*. The function of art is to select, clarify and isolate the experiences of life within a certain form. "Life is like a blind and limitless expanse of sky, forever dividing into tiny drops of circumstance that rain down, thick and fast, a ceaseless, meaningless drip. Art is like the dauntless plastic force that builds up stubborn, amorphous substance, cell by cell, into the frail geometry of a cell." This subject will be treated at greater length in a later chapter, and now it is enough to say that in the novel this means bringing character, situation, point of view, setting and background under the discipline of outline, enclosing both the raw material and the creative vision of the artist towards his material in a certain structure of expression. Critics of the novel in textbooks which profess to teach novel-writing in twelve lessons (or words to that effect), often speak as if there were a right or a wrong form for the novel. This cannot be. The purpose of the serious novel (I mean a novel which is a serious piece of literary work, though it may be a pure comedy) is to give interest and enjoyment to the reader—not the merely superficial enjoyment and interest of something which amuses him when he is tired, but the true enjoyment of having his faculties energized and vitalized by being called into play in a comparison of the experience of another mind with that of his own. That novel is a good novel which succeeds in communicating vividly the writer's experience, and there can be no rules for what form succeeds in doing that—except the rule of success! We might quote Mr. Kipling on tribal lays, and apply the same remark to the novel:

> There are nine and sixty ways of constructing tribal lays.
> And every single one of them is right.

The novelist may convey his effects by the rambling, enormously patient reporting of James Joyce in *Ulysses*, or by the rigid selection of Willa Cather in *A Lost Lady*, by the architectural massiveness of Arnold Bennett's *The Old Wives' Tale* or by the brilliant impressionism of Aldous Huxley's *Antic Hay*. He may be as direct as Wells or as elusive as Virginia Woolf: he may set chronology at defiance, as in *Lord Jim*, or he may make the lives of a group of characters centre in one night as in *Nocturne*: he may make his action live at four removes from the teller of the tale, as when, in *Chance*, we listen to what Marlow said that Mrs. Fyne said that Flora said the governess said, or he may be as frankly autobiographical as Samuel Butler in *The Way of All Flesh*. Provided that the reader feels that he simply must finish the book, the novelist has succeeded in his aim and his form has justified itself.

## PREFACE TO THE NIGGER OF THE NARCISSUS
### *Joseph Conrad*   (*1897*)

A WORK that aspires, however humbly, to the condition of art should carry its justification in every line. And art itself may be defined as a single-minded attempt to render the highest kind of justice to the visible universe, by bringing to light the truth, manifold and one, underlying its every aspect. It is an attempt to find in its forms, in its colours, in its light, in its shadows, in the aspects of matter and in the facts of life what of each is fundamental, what is enduring and essential—their one illuminating and convincing quality—the very truth of their existence. The artist, then, like the thinker or the scientist, seeks the truth and makes his appeal. Impressed by the aspect of the world the thinker plunges into ideas, the scientist into facts—whence, presently, emerging they make their appeal to those qualities of our being that fit us best for the hazardous enterprise of living. They speak authoritatively to our common-sense, to our intelligence, to our desire of peace or to our desire of unrest; not seldom to our prejudices, sometimes to our fears, often to our egoism—but always to our credulity. And their words are heard with reverence, for their concern is with weighty matters: with the cultivation of our minds and the proper care of our bodies, with the attainment of our ambitions, with the perfection of the means and the glorification of our precious aims.

It is otherwise with the artist.

Confronted by the same enigmatical spectacle the artist descends within himself, and in that lonely region of stress and strife, if he be deserving and fortunate, he finds the terms of his appeal. His appeal is made to our less obvious capacities: to that part of our nature which, because of the warlike conditions of existence, is necessarily kept out of sight within the more resisting and hard qualities—like the vulnerable body within a steel armour. His appeal is less loud, more profound, less distinct, more stirring—and sooner forgotten. Yet its effect endures forever. The changing wisdom of successive generations discards ideas, questions facts, demolishes theories. But the artist appeals to that part of our being which is not dependent on wisdom; to that in us which is a gift and not an acquisition—and, therefore, more permanently enduring. He speaks to our capacity for delight and wonder, to the sense of mystery surrounding our lives; to our sense of pity, and beauty, and pain; to the latent feeling of fellowship with all creation—and to the subtle but invincible conviction of solidarity that knits together the loneliness of innumerable hearts, to the solidarity in dreams, in joy, in sorrow, in aspirations, in illusions, in hope, in fear, which binds men to each other, which binds together all humanity—the dead to the living and the living to the unborn.

It is only some such train of thought, or rather of feeling, that can in a measure explain the aim of the attempt, made in the tale which follows, to present an unrestful episode in the obscure lives of a few individuals out of all the disregarded multitude of the bewildered, the simple and the voiceless. For, if any part of truth dwells in the belief confessed above, it becomes evident that there is not a place of splendour or a dark corner of the earth that does not deserve, if only a passing glance of wonder and pity. The motive then, may be held to justify the matter of the work; but this preface, which is simply an avowal of endeavour, cannot end here—for the avowal is not yet complete.

Fiction—if it at all aspires to be art—appeals to temperament. And in truth it must be, like painting, like music, like all art, the appeal of one temperament to all the other innumerable temperaments whose subtle and resistless power endows passing events with their true meaning, and creates the moral, the emotional atmosphere of the place and time. Such an appeal to be effective must be an impression conveyed through the senses; and, in fact, it cannot be made in any other way, because temperament, whether individual or collective, is not amenable to persuasion. All art, therefore, appeals primarily to the senses, and the artistic aim when expressing itself in written words must also make its appeal through the senses, if its high desire is to reach the secret spring of responsive emotions. It must strenuously aspire to the plasticity of sculpture, to the colour of painting, and to the magic suggestiveness of music—which is the art of arts. And it is only through complete, unswerving devotion to the perfect blending of form and substance; it is only through an unremitting never-discouraged care for the shape and ring of sentences that an approach can be made to plasticity, to colour, and that the light of magic suggestiveness may be brought to play for an evanescent instant over the commonplace surface of words: of the old, old words, worn thin, defaced by ages of careless usage.

The sincere endeavour to accomplish that creative task, to go as far on that road as his strength will carry him, to go undeterred by faltering, weariness or reproach, is the only valid justification for the worker in prose. And if his conscience is clear, his answer to those who in the fulness of a wisdom which looks for immediate profit, demand specifically to be edified, consoled, amused; who demand to be promptly improved, or encouraged, or frightened, or shocked, or charmed, must run thus:—My task which I am trying to achieve is, by the power of the written word to make you hear, to make you feel—it is, before all, to make you *see*. That—and no more, and it is everything. If I succeed, you shall find there according to your deserts: encouragement, consolation, fear, charm—all you demand—and, perhaps, also that glimpse of truth for which you have forgotten to ask.

To snatch in a moment of courage, from the remorseless rush of time, a passing phase of life, is only the beginning of the task. The task approached in tenderness and faith is to hold up unquestioningly, without choice and without fear, the rescued fragment before all eyes in the light of a sincere mood. It is to show its vibration, its colour, its form; and through its movement, its form, and its colour, reveal the substance of its truth—disclose its inspiring secret: the stress and passion within the core of each convincing moment. In a single-minded attempt of that kind, if one be deserving and fortunate, one may perchance attain to such clearness of sincerity that at last the presented vision of regret or pity, of terror or birth, shall awaken in the hearts of the beholders that feeling of unavoidable solidarity; of the solidarity in mysterious origin, in toil, in joy, in hope, in uncertain fate, which binds men to each other and all mankind to the visible world.

It is evident that he who, rightly or wrongly, holds by the convictions expressed above cannot be faithful to any one of the temporary formulas of his craft. The enduring part of them—the truth which each only imperfectly veils—should abide with him as the most precious of his possessions, but they all: Realism, Romanticism, Naturalism, even the unofficial sentimentalism (which like the poor, is exceedingly difficult to get rid of), all these gods must, after a short period of fellowship, abandon him—even on the very threshold of the temple—to the stammerings of his conscience and to the outspoken consciousness of the difficulties of his work. In that uneasy solitude the supreme cry of Art for Art itself, loses the exciting ring of its apparent immorality. It sounds far off. It has ceased to be a cry, and is heard only as a whisper, often incomprehensible, but at times and faintly encouraging.

Sometimes, stretched at ease in the shade of a roadside tree, we watch the motions of a labourer in a distant field, and after a time, begin to wonder languidly as to what the fellow may be at. We watch the movements of his body, the waving of his arms, we see him bend down, stand up, hesitate, begin again. It may add to the charm of an idle hour to be told the purpose of his exertions. If we know he is trying to lift a stone, to dig a ditch, to uproot a stump, we look with a more real interest at his efforts; we are disposed to condone the jar of his agitation upon the restfulness of the landscape; and even, if in a brotherly frame of mind, we may bring ourselves to forgive his failure. We understood his object, and, after all, the fellow has tried, and perhaps he had not the strength—and perhaps he had not the knowledge. We forgive, go on our way—and forget.

And so it is with the workman of art. Art is long and life is short, and success is very far off. And thus, doubtful of strength to travel so far, we talk a little about the aim—the aim of art, which, like life itself, is inspiring, difficult—obscured by mists. It is not in the clear logic of a triumphant conclusion; it is not in the unveiling of one of those heartless secrets which are called the Laws of Nature. It is not less great, but only more difficult.

To arrest, for the space of a breath, the hands busy about the work of the earth, and compel men entranced by the sight of distant goals to glance for a moment at the surrounding vision of form and colour, of sunshine and shadows; to make them pause for a look, for a sigh, for a smile—such is the aim, difficult and evanescent, and reserved only for a few to achieve. But sometimes, by the deserving and the fortunate, even that task is accomplished. And when it is accomplished—behold!—all the truth of life is there: a moment of vision, a sigh, a smile—and the return to an eternal rest.

# A NOVELIST BEGINS

## *James T. Farrell*  (*1938*)

### I

I BEGAN writing what has developed into the trilogy, *Studs Lonigan*, in June 1929. *Judgment Day* was finally completed at the end of January 1935. In June 1929, I was a young man who had burned other bridges behind me with the determination to write whether my efforts brought success or failure. I was then finishing what happened to be the last quarter in which I was a student at the University of Chicago.

Three times before, I had dropped out of classes because I was restless and dissatisfied. I resolved to devote my time to writing and to educating myself in my own haphazard manner. For a fourth and last time I had matriculated and I managed to finish out the quarter. Although I read continuously and rather broadly, I could not, after my sophomore year, maintain a steady interest in any of my courses except composition, where I could write as much as I pleased. I would cut other classes, day after day, finally dropping out, heedless of the loss of credit and the waste of money I had spent in tuition.

My mood or state of mind in those days was, I believe, one which most young writers will recognize. To be a young man with literary aspirations is not to be particularly happy. At first, the desire to write is more strong than is a clear perception of what one wants to write and how one will write it. There are surprising oscillations of mood. One moment the young writer is energetic and hopeful. The next, he is catapulted into a fit of despair with his faith in himself infirm, his self-confidence shattered and broken, his view of the future one in which he sees futile self-sacrifices ending only in dismal failure. There are times when he cannot look his friends in the eye. There are moments when he feels himself to be set against the opposition of the entire world. There are occasions when he turns a caustic wit, a brutal sarcasm, and a savage arrogance on others only because he is defending himself from himself.

Suddenly he will be devastated by an image of himself in which he sees a nobody who has had the temerity and egotism to want to call himself a writer. He measures himself, with his few unpublished manuscripts, against the accomplishments of great writers, and his ambition suddenly seems like insanity. Even though he is not particularly conscious of clothes, there are periods when he gazes upon his own shabbiness—his unshined shoes, his worn and unpressed suit, his frayed overcoat, his uncut hair—and sees this all as a badge of his own miserable mediocrity. A sense of failure dogs his steps. Living with himself becomes almost unendurable.

Writing is one of the cruelest of professions. The sense of possible failure in a literary career can torment one pitilessly. And failure in a literary career cannot be measured in dollars and cents. Poverty and the struggle for bread are not the only features of a literary career which can make it so cruel. There is the self-imposed loneliness. There is the endless struggle to perceive freshly and clearly, to realize and re-create a sense of life on paper. There is more than economic competition involved. The writer feels frequently that he is competing with time and with life itself. His hopes will sometimes ride high. His ambitions will soar until they have become so grandiose that they cannot be realized within the space of a single lifetime.

The world opens up before the young writer as a grand and glorious adventure in feeling and in understanding. Nothing human is unimportant to him. Everything that he sees is germane to his purpose. Every word that he hears uttered is of potential use to him. Every mood, every passing fancy, every trivial thought, can have its meaning and its place in the store of experience which he accumulates. The opportunities for assimilation are enormous, endless. And there is only one single short life of struggle in which to assimilate.

A melancholy sense of time becomes a torment. One's whole spirit rebels against a truism which all men must realize because it applies to all men. One seethes in rebellion against the realization that the human being must accept limitations, that he can develop in one line of effort only at the cost of making many sacrifices in other lines. Time becomes for the writer the most precious good in all the world. And how often will he not feel that he is squandering this precious good? His life then seems like a sieve through which his days are filtering, leaving behind only a few, a very few, miserable grains of experience. If he is wasting time to-day, what assurance can he give himself that he will not be doing likewise to-morrow? He is struggling with himself to attain self-discipline. He weighs every failure in his struggle. He begins to find a sense of death—death before he has fulfilled any of his potentialities—like a dark shadow cast constantly close to his awareness.

Such were some of the components of my own state of mind when *Studs Lonigan* was begun.

## II

In the spring of 1929, I took a course in advanced composition conducted by Professor James Weber Linn. And Professor Linn—with whom I was constantly at loggerheads concerning literary questions—was encouraging. His encouragement, as well as my arguments with him and with the majority of the class, assisted me in maintaining my own self-confidence. For his course I wrote thousands of words. I wrote stories, sketches, book reviews, essays, impressions, anecdotes.

Most of these manuscripts related to death, disintegration, human indignity, poverty, drunkenness, ignorance, human cruelty. They attempted to describe dusty and deserted streets, street corners, miserable homes, poolrooms, brothels, dance halls, taxi dances, bohemian sections, express offices, gasoline filling stations, scenes laid in slum districts. The characters were boys, boys' gangs, drunkards, Negroes, expressmen, homosexuals, immigrants and immigrant landlords, filling-station attendants, straw bosses, hitch-hikers, bums, bewildered parents. Most of the manuscripts were written with the ideal of objectivity in mind. I realized then that the writer should submit himself to an objective discipline. These early manuscripts of mine were written, in the main, out of such an intention.

One of the stories which I wrote for Professor Linn's course was titled "Studs." It was originally published in *This Quarter*. "Studs" is the story of a wake, written in the first person. The corpse is a lad from the Fifty-eighth Street neighborhood who died suddenly at the age of twenty-six. The story describes his background and his friends. They have come to the wake, and they sit in the rear of the apartment discussing the mysteries of death in banalities, nostalgically remembering the good old days, contentedly describing dull details of their current life. The author of the story sits there, half-heartedly trying to join in the conversation, recollecting the past vividly, remembering how these fellows who are now corpulent and sunk in the trivialities of day-to-day living were once adventurous boys.

Professor Linn read this story in class and praised it most enthusiastically. I had no genuine opinion concerning it. I had tried to write it as honestly, as clearly, and as well as I could. I did not know what I thought of it. The praise which the story received in class greatly encouraged me. I asked Professor Robert Morss Lovett to read it. He kindly consented, and after doing so he called me to his office and suggested that the story should be developed at greater length, and the milieu described in it put down in greater detail. I had already begun to think of doing this, and Professor Lovett's advice clinched the matter for me.

In a sense, Professor Linn and Professor Lovett are the spiritual godfathers of *Studs Lonigan*.

When I began working on this material, I envisaged one long novel, ending in a scene similar to that described in the story, "Studs." I saw in the character of Studs Lonigan, who was growing in my mind, a number of tendencies at work in a section of American life which I happened to know because it had been part of my own education in living. I began to see Studs not only as a character in imaginative fiction but also as a social manifestation. In the early stages of writing this work, I analyzed my character as I considered him in his relations to his own world, his own milieu. I set as my aim that of unfolding the destiny of Studs Lonigan in his own words, his own actions, his own patterns of thought and feeling. I decided that my task was not to state formally what life meant to me, but to try to re-create a sense of what life meant to Studs Lonigan.

I worked on with this project, setting up as an ideal the strictest possible objectivity. As I wrote, the book enlarged and expanded. It grew into two novels, and finally into three. There were numberless changes and expansions of the original conception, alterations in emphasis, reconstructions of the structure of events, from the time that the project was first conceived until the last line was written. However, to go into this phase of the work would be dull, and it would sound too much like a pretentious effort to bring one's laboratory out in public. All works of imaginative fiction go through such a process of change and expansion.

## III

Studs Lonigan was conceived as a normal American boy of Irish Catholic extraction. The social milieu in which he lived and was educated was one of spiritual poverty. It was not, contrary to some misconceptions, a slum neighborhood. Had I written *Studs Lonigan* as a story of the slums, it would have been easy for the reader falsely to place the motivation and causation of the story directly in immediate economic roots. Such a placing of motivation would have obscured one of the most important meanings which I wanted to infuse into my story—my desire to reveal the concrete effects of spiritual poverty.

It is readily known that poverty and slums cause spiritual poverty in many lives. One of the important meanings which I perceived in this story was that here was a neighborhood several steps removed from the slums and dire economic want, and here was manifested a pervasive spiritual poverty.

The fathers, grandfathers, great-grandfathers of boys like Studs Lonigan came to America as to a new world. They came from the shores of that island whose history is one of the most bitter of all time. Most of them were poor immigrants. Some of them could not read or write. They belonged at the bottom of the American social and economic ladder. Many of them did menial work, and the lives which they led were hard. They struggled upward in American society just as have other immigrant groups and races before and after them.

Their lives constituted a process in which they were assimilated into the American petty bourgeoisie and the American labor aristocracy. Their lives were dedicated to work, to advancing themselves, to saving and thrift, to raising their families. They rose socially and economically. Ultimately many of them owned buildings and conducted their own small business enterprises. They became politicians, straw bosses, salesmen, boss craftsmen, and the like. And they became tired.

Their spiritual resources were meagre. They believed in the American myths of success and advancement. They believed in the teachings and dogma of their faith. They believed that with homilies, platitudes about faith and work, and little fables about good example they could educate their children. They believed that thus their children would start off in the race of life with greater advantages than they had had, and that their children would advance so much the farther, so many more rungs on the economic and social ladder.

The story of Studs Lonigan opens on the day that Woodrow Wilson is renominated to run for a second term as President of the United States. It closes in the depths of the Hoover era.

It was during the period of the Wilsonian Administration that this nation reached upward toward the zenith of its power and became, perhaps, the richest and the most powerful nation in all history. The story of Studs Lonigan was conceived as the story of the education of a normal American boy in this period. The important institutions in the education of Studs Lonigan are the home and the family, the church, the school, and the playground. These institutions break down, and do not serve their desired function. The streets become a potent educative factor in the boy's life. In time, the poolroom becomes an important institution in his life. When Studs reaches his young-manhood, this nation is moving headlong into one of the most insane eras of our history—the Prohibition era.

A word here is necessary concerning the drinking of Studs and his companions. This drinking has a definite social character. When Studs and his companions drink, they do so as a gesture of defiance which is in the spirit of the times. Drinking in those days became a social ritual. Furthermore, when Studs and his companions began drinking, the worst liquor of the Prohibition era was being sold. Those were the days when the newspapers published daily death lists of the number of persons who had died from bootleg liquor and wood alcohol. That was the time when men and boys would take one or two drinks, pass out into unconsciousness, and come to their senses later to learn that they would never again have their eyesight.

All generations drink more or less in the period of young-manhood. But all generations do not drink the kind of bootleg liquor which Studs Lonigan and his companions drank. The health of Studs and many of his friends is impaired and permanently ruined in this story. That very loss of health has, it can be seen now, a social character.

Studs Lonigan is neither a tough nor a gangster. He is not really a hard guy. He is a normal young American of his time and his class. His values become the values of his world. He has as many good impulses as normal human beings have. In time, because of defeat, of frustration, of a total situation which is characterized by spiritual poverty, these good impulses go more and more into the stream of his revery. Here we find the source of Studs's constant dream of himself.

His dream of himself changes in character as the story progresses. In the beginning, it is a vision of what he is going to be. He is a boy waiting at the threshold of life. His dream of himself is a romantic projection of his future, conceived in the terms and the values of his milieu. In time, this dream of himself turns backward. It is no longer a romantic projection of things to come. More and more it becomes a nostalgic image turned toward the past. Does this not happen in greater or lesser degree to all of us?

Shortly after I began working on *Studs Lonigan*, I happened to be reading John Dewey's *Human Nature and Conduct*, and I came upon the following sentence which I used as a frontispiece quotation in *Young Lonigan*: "The poignancy of situations which evoke reflection lies in the fact that we do not know the meaning of the tendencies that are pressing for action." This observation crystallized for me what I was seeking to do. This work grew out of a situation which evoked reflection. The situation revealed to me the final meaning of tendencies which had been pressing for action. And that final situation became death, turning poignancy into tragedy.

*Studs Lonigan* was conceived as the story of an American destiny in our time. It deals with the making and the education of an American boy. My attitude toward it and toward my character here is essentially a simple one. "There, but for the grace of God, go I.". . . There, but for the grace of God, go many others.

## WHAT IS A POET?

### Mark Van Doren (*1932*)

Poetry speaks for itself. But poets, curiously enough, do not; and so it is time that someone speak for them and say what they would say if they spoke in prose. It is time that they be defended against the silent charge—all the more damning because it is so silent—that they are a special race of men and women, different from all other creatures of their kind and possessed of faculties which would make them, if we knew them, only too wonderful to live with, not to say too embarrassing. I should like to relieve them from the burden of being queer. Poets are supposed to be a suffering race, but the only thing they suffer from is the misapprehension that they are endowed with a peculiar set of thoughts and feelings—particularly feelings—and that these endowments are of the romantic sort. It consists, to speak for the moment historically, in the notion that the poet has always and must always cut the same figure he has cut during the past hundred years or so. It consists in expecting him to be a Shelley, a Keats, a Byron, a Poe, a Verlaine, a Swinburne, a Dowson. He may be another one of those, to be sure; but he also may be any kind of person under the sun. My only conception of the poet is that he is a person who writes poetry. That may sound absurdly simple, but it is arrived at after reflection upon the innumerable kinds of poetry which poets have written, and upon the baffling variety of temperaments which these poets have revealed.

Here is the figure we have set up. A pale, lost man with long, soft hair. Tapering fingers at the ends of furtively fluttering arms. An air of abstraction in the delicate face, but more often a look of shy pain as some aspect of reality —a real man or woman, a grocer's bill, a train, a load of bricks, a newspaper, a noise from the street—makes itself manifest. He is generally incompetent. He cannot find his way in a city, he forgets where he is going, he has no aptitude for business, he is childishly gullible and so the prey of human sharks, he cares nothing for money, he is probably poor, he will sacrifice his welfare for a whim, he stops to pet homeless cats, he is especially knowing where children are concerned (being a child himself), he sighs, he sleeps, he wakes to sigh again. The one great assumption from which the foregoing portrait is drawn is an assumption which thousands of otherwise intelligent citizens go on. It is the assumption that the poet is more sensitive than any other kind of man, that he feels more than the rest of us and is more definitely the victim of his feeling.

I am tempted to assert that the poet is as a matter of fact less sensitive than other men. I shall make no such assertion for the simple reason that to do so would be to imply that I knew what kind of man the poet necessarily was. My whole point is that the poet is not anything necessarily. He may be sensitive, and he may not; the question has nothing directly to do with his being a poet. Certainly there have been poets with very thick hides. We have to account for the fact that Browning looked more like a business man than he did like a poet—whatever a poet is supposed to look like; that Horace was plump, phlegmatic, easy-going, shrewd, and sensible; that Dryden was an excellent trader in literary affairs; that Pope was so insensitive, at least to the sufferings of others, that he poured an emetic into the tea of a publisher with whom he had quarreled; that Li Po and most of the other great Chinese poets were government officials; that Robert Frost is to all outward appearances—and what other appearances are there?—a New England farmer.

There is reason for supposing that no artist is as sensitive in one respect as the man who is not an artist. He is not so likely, that is, to be overwhelmed by his own feelings. Consider what he does with his feelings. He uses them, deliberately, for the purposes of his art. The ordinary man—meaning for the moment the man who is not an artist—may be so affected by the death of a parent, for instance, that he becomes dumb. There was Daudet, however, who at the funeral of his mother could not help composing the room where he stood into a room that would be the setting of a new story. He was using his feelings, together with the scene which called them forth, for an ulterior purpose. The artist is callous, and must be so in order to keep his mind clear for the work he has before him. So also the poet must be sensitive to words, rhythms, ideas, and moods; but in the very act of perceiving them clearly, in realizing them for what they are worth, he distinguishes himself from the race of men who feel and only feel. When we read the poetry of a man like Pope, who was extraordinarily, almost abnormally, susceptible to the charms of verbal music, we can have no doubt that he was, in that one department of his existence, all sense. We are not justified, however, in going on, as a recent biographer of the little man has done, to attribute to him a sensitive heart. As a matter of fact he had another kind, and in the ordinary man it would be denounced as an ugly one.

From the notion that the poet is deeply affected by life we often proceed to the notion that he cannot stand a great deal of it; we say he dies young. To be sure there are the English romantic poets—Shelley, Keats, and Byron—to support our error, and to be sure they are always conspicuously present in spirit when poetry is under discussion, since it was their generation that gave us our conception of poetry and the poet; we still are in the romantic period. But even as we talk this way we seem to forget their contemporary Wordsworth, who lived in perfect peace till he was eighty. We forget that Dryden lived to seventy, Shakespeare to fifty-two, Browning to seventy-seven, Tennyson to eighty-three, Milton to sixty-six, Herrick to eighty-three, Spenser to almost fifty, and Chaucer to an even sixty. We disregard the great age of Homer when he died, at least if the traditions be true. And anyway the ancient traditions about poets have their significance. For one of them was that poets die old; hence the bust of Homer, wrinkled, composed, resigned, with sunken eyes. The three great tragic poets of Greece died old indeed; Aeschylus at sixty-nine, Sophocles at ninety, and Euripides at seventy-five. Vergil and Horace gave up the struggle in their fifties, Lucretius committed suicide, it is said, at forty-three or forty-four, and Catullus, like Shelley, was extinguished at thirty; but Ovid, for all his banishment to a cold, uncomfortable part of the world, and his probable suffering there, lived into his sixtieth year; and Ennius, first of all the known Roman poets, saw seventy. Dante had a hard life, but it lasted fifty-six years. Racine went on to sixty; Goethe expired peacefully, calling for more light, at eighty-three. And what of the greatest English poet in recent times? Thomas Hardy, who did not even begin to be a professional poet until he was more than fifty-five, wrote ten volumes of verse after that, and when he died at eighty-eight was busy with the preparation of a new volume, which appeared posthumously!

Another burden of which I should like to relieve poets is the burden of being strangely wise. They have been called prophets, I believe, and seers; clairvoyants, informers, transformers, and what not. All this, too, in spite of the impracticality attributed to them. Indeed, there seems to be a connection between the two attributes. The poets know nothing of the world, but they may tell us a good deal about life; not life as we live it, but life—shall we say?—as we ought to live it. Simply by virtue of their stupidity in ordinary affairs they somehow become conversant with extraordinary affairs which we ourselves shall never experience but which it might be rather nice to hear about. So runs another legend, and one as romantic as the rest. For it has no foundation whatever if the whole history of poetry be taken into account. In a primitive tribe the poet is also the medicine man, the priest, and the foreteller of future events, since it is in verse that these functionaries speak. Among savages, then, the poet is a prophet. But nowhere else. The division of labor has gone on; the prophet is the prophet, in verse or in prose as the occasion may be; the poet is the poet, and always in verse. The poet is a sayer, not a seer. Wordsworth brought on a considerable confusion by insisting that the poet is one who goes to Nature for her secrets, which are substantially the secrets of existence, and then comes back with the dew of knowledge on his lips. The poet, in other words, is equipped with a peculiar mind which enables him to plumb—or fathom, or penetrate, or see through, or pierce; the phrase matters not—the world's appearances. For us the mere appearances, for him the reality behind. Thus he not only cursed his successors with the responsibility of being prophets; he cursed them also with the duty of being acquainted with Nature, and of pretending to some sort of mastery over her. The truth, I suspect, is that the poet is no more of a magician in this respect than the scientist is. And think of the poets, long ago and since, who have never been the least bit interested in the out-of-doors. Dr. Johnson said that he was unable to tell the difference between one green field and another. Milton got his flowers and mountains out of old books; Spenser got his landscapes out of sixteenth-century woodcuts; Dante read Nature as a work in theology; Horace was comfortable in the presence of his hills only when a few friends from Rome were with him to drink wine and make remarks about life; Vergil in the country was concerned with husbandry and the diseases of sheep; Ovid would not look at a tree unless it had once contained a nymph.

The poet may think anything, feel anything, do anything; he may or may not be a wanderer; he may or may not love his home better than any other plot of ground; he may love children; he may hate them; he may be restless under the pressure of a domestic establishment; he may get his chief joy out of a wife and kitchen; he may inhabit a palace; he may shiver in a garret; he may be noble; he may be mean. He is not limited, in other words, more than other men. Yet we go on limiting him. And to what? To a simpering, humorless, pious, nervous existence which for all the world we should be unwilling to share with him. No wonder we don't like him, and no wonder we don't really enjoy reading poetry.

# WHAT IS A POET?

## (*From* Preface to the Lyrical Ballads)

### *William Wordsworth*  (*1800*)

WHAT is a Poet? To whom does he address himself? And what language is to be expected from him?—He is a man speaking to men; a man, it is true, endowed with more lively sensibility, more enthusiasm and tenderness, who has a greater knowledge of human nature, and a more comprehensive soul, than are supposed to be common among mankind; a man pleased with his own passions and volitions, and who rejoices more than other men in the spirit of life that is in him; delighting to contemplate similar volitions and passions as manifested in the goings-on of the Universe, and habitually impelled to create them where he does not find them. To these qualities he has added a disposition to be affected more than any other men by absent things as if they were present; an ability of conjuring up in himself passions, which are indeed far from being the same as those produced by real events, yet (especially in those parts of the general sympathy which are pleasing and delightful) do more nearly resemble the passions produced by real events than anything which, from the motions of their own minds merely, other men are accustomed to feel in themselves:—whence, and from practice, he has acquired a greater readiness and power in expressing what he thinks and feels, and especially those thoughts and feelings which, by his own choice, or from the structure of his own mind, arise in him without immediate external excitement.

·      ·      ·      ·      ·      ·      ·

To this knowledge which all men carry about with them, and to these sympathies in which, without any other discipline than that of our daily life, we are fitted to take delight, the Poet principally directs his attention. He considers man and nature as essentially adapted to each other, and the mind of man as naturally the mirror of the fairest and most interesting properties of nature. And thus the Poet, prompted by this feeling of pleasure, which accompanies him through the whole course of his studies, converses with general nature, with affections akin to those which, through labor and length of time, the Man of science has raised up in himself, by conversing with those particular parts of nature which are the objects of his studies. The knowledge both of the Poet and the Man of science is pleasure; but the knowledge of the one cleaves to us as a necessary part of our existence, or natural and unalien-able·inheritance; the other is a personal and individual acquisition, slow to come to us, and by no habitual and direct sympathy connecting us with our fellow-beings. The Man of science seeks truth as a remote and unknown bene-factor; he cherishes and loves it in his solitude: the Poet, singing a song in which all human beings join with him, rejoices in the presence of truth as our visible friend and hourly companion. Poetry is the breath and finer spirit of all knowledge; it is the impassioned expression which is in the countenance of all Science. Emphatically may it be said of the Poet, as Shakespeare hath said of man, "that he looks before and after." He is the rock of defense for human nature; an upholder and preserver, carrying everywhere with him relationship and love. In spite of difference of soil and climate, of language and manners, of laws and customs: in spite of things silently gone out of mind, and things violently destroyed; the Poet binds together by passion and knowledge the vast empire of human society, as it is spread over the whole earth and over all time. The objects of the Poet's thoughts are everywhere; though the eyes and senses of man are, it is true, his favorite guides, yet he will follow wheresoever he can find an atmosphere of sensation in which to move his wings. Poetry is the first and last of all knowledge—it is as immortal as the heart of man. If the labors of Men of science should ever create any material revolution, direct or indirect, in our condition, and in the impressions which we habitually receive, the Poet will sleep then no more than at present; he will be ready to follow the steps of the Man of science, not only in those general indirect effects, but he will be at his side, carrying sensation into the midst of the objects of the science itself. The remotest discoveries of the Chemist, the Botanist, or Mineralogist, will be as proper objects of the Poet's art as any upon which it can be employed, if the time should ever come when these things shall be familiar to us, and the relations under which they are contemplated by the followers of these respective sciences shall be manifestly and palpably material to us as enjoying and suffering beings. If the time should ever come when what is now called science, thus familiarized to men, shall be ready to put on, as it were, a form of flesh and blood, the Poet will lend his divine spirit to aid the transfiguration, and will welcome the Being thus produced as a dear and genuine inmate of the household of man.

## POETRY IN A MACHINE AGE

### *Paul Engle* (*1937*)

THE MOST evident quality of poetry is intensity—a certain verbal exaggeration. It is that which distinguishes it from prose and from plain speech. It is that which emphasizes what is being said. It is the basis of the pleasure afforded by verse. This intensity is not elaborate description or the piling-up of adjectives. It may be the opposite—a reducing of what is said to its simplest terms, as in the following couplet from Robert Frost:

> I often see flowers from a passing car
> That are gone before I can tell what they are.

Or it may be the bare statement of a fact which, although it has nothing at all added, expresses the fact imaginatively, as does MacLeish's calling of the ocean "that endless silence, edged with unending sound." Or the intensification may be achieved by symbol and figurative language. In these lines from *John Brown's Body* the image is completely obvious and clear:

> Jack Ellyat turned away from the window now,
> The frosty sleighbell of winter was in his ears,
> He saw the new year, a child in a buffalo-robe.

The image may be far more subtle, as the lines from the German poet Rilke in which he describes a visit to a small church in pre-revolutionary Russia where he found God crouching in a corner like a wounded and captured animal. Whatever the means of intensification may be, it is always a heightening of the voice, although that may involve a lowering of its sound. It is a lifting of the words like a hand's gesture.

When the vowels and consonants of a line of verse are so skilfully arranged in relation to the sense and to each other that the line seems to vibrate like a taut wire, it is the contribution that this tautness makes to the transference of a certain feeling from one mind into another mind which is important. The sound of the line considered by itself is of less value, however pleasant it may be, than the function it has of emphasizing the meaning through the force of its sound. In this passage from *Conquistador* the swing of the lines makes clearer the feeling in the mind of the writer, thinking of the armored Spaniards who came in their pride and were killed by stone and arrow:

> Those with the glaze in their eyes and the fine bearing:
> The born leaders of men: the resonant voices:
> They give them the lands for their tombs: they call it *America*.

It is the mood of the mind, and the accuracy with which the verse reproduces it—the attitude toward a thing and not the thing itself—which is the real concern of poetry. Bettors on horse races call this attitude a hunch because it has not been reached rationally, but intuitively. It is for the telling about these hunches that rhythms and forms of verse exist. It is Carl Sandburg writing "See the trees lean to the wind's way of learning" instead of "See the wind bend the trees."

If a poet's business, then, is to communicate his own mind in an intelligible and intensified language, how is the saying that a poet is "representative of his times" to be explained? What is a man like who is, in his verse, representative of today? How has living in a machine age affected the position of a poet who is trying to tell about the excitements in his head?

A poet cannot repudiate his age. If he tries to do so, even his repudiation will belong to it. He is a part of all his environment, both that which he unconsciously takes in, as his eyes automatically acknowledge what confronts them, and that which he consciously acquires, as in the study of folklore and psychiatry. Being so integrated to his age, when he comes to talk about his own character in verse, what he says has not only the individual accent of his own voice but also the larger intonation of his times.

Three forces which belong particularly to the twentieth century have altered the conditions of writing poetry: machinery, psychology, and sociology.

The change that machinery has brought is more than a new collection of sights and sounds and smells, although these are relevant. It is partly the mechanizing of daily acts—the substitution of button-pushing and switch-throwing for acquired skills. But it is far more the revelation of new worlds of power and movement. It is the hands extended, in making an article, to elaborate machines, the nimble fingers losing their genius to the thousand-times more nimble parts of loom and drill press. It is the eye magnified by intricately cut glass, and the ear amplified by the radio, made more sensitive than that of any forest-living creature.

A poet today, seeking for a way to express a great force, will think as readily of compressed steam in a cylinder as of the tides; of an electrical current rather than the strength of an animal. The fact of a human voice thrown out through the air by a machine and being made audible half the world away by another machine is exciting to the imagination. The purring cat's-head of a dynamo has as great possibilities for becoming as familiarly used in verse as the traditional plow, itself a machine. One of the largest conceptions possible in poetry now is the airplane—man catapulted through space by his own creation.

The machine must not be worshiped as god or devil, nor must it be damned, save when it is misused as in the deadly instruments of war. The poet must accept it as part of his world in the way that the author of *John Brown's Body* has urged:

> Out of John Brown's strong sinews the tall skyscrapers grow,
> Out of his heart the chanting buildings rise,
> Rivet and girder, motor and dynamo,
> Pillar of smoke by day and fire by night,
> The steel-faced cities reaching at the skies,
> The whole enormous and rotating cage
> Hung with hard jewels of electric light. . . .
> If you at last must have a word to say,
> Say neither, in their way,
> "It is a deadly magic and accursed,"
> Nor "It is blest," but only, "It is here."

The necessary thing is to combine the new machinery with the old—plows, spinning wheels, ships, and wagons. The new is an immensely speeded-up addition to these. Poetry has previously drawn most of its images from nature. It must now draw a greater number from machines, as they displace part of nature in our experience. This is not to imply that poetry must be filled with the whir and clatter of a factory, although it should be at times. The autumnal flight of birds and the turn and pound of a driving wheel should both move through the verse of our time.

Equally with the aspects of nature, machines may be merely described or their relation to men indicated. Or they may be converted into symbols and images as MacKnight Black does in "Reciprocating Engine" from his book of poems, *Machinery:*

> The arc of a balance-wheel
> Flows like a curved rush of swallows, come over a hill. . . .
> Things lost come again in sudden new beauty.
> Look long on an engine. It is sweet to the eyes.

In these lines from "Smoke and Steel" Sandburg describes the union of the blood of men and the smoke of fires in the making of steel:

> A bar of steel—it is only
> Smoke at the heart of it, smoke and the blood of a man.
> A runner of fire ran in, ran out, ran somewhere else,
> And left—smoke and the blood of a man
> And the finished steel, chilled and blue.

Ultimately the machine must be transformed into a generalized term, as in Auden's looking at something: "As the hawk sees it or the helmeted airman." In these lines from Stephen Spender the machine no longer stands outside the inner motivation of the poem, nor is it merely described. It is an integral part of the original mood and the writing.

> More beautiful and soft than any moth
> With burring furred antennae feeling its huge path
> Through dusk, the air-liner with shut-off engines
> Glides over suburbs and the sleeves set trailing tall
> To point the wind. Gently, broadly, she falls,
> Scarcely disturbing charted currents of air.

The poem convinces you that it was as natural for Spender to write so sympathetically of an airplane as it was for Keats to write of a Grecian urn, or Shelley of the west wind.

The knowledge that the air around him swarms with words and music on radio waves, with the sun's energy and an infinitude of light-waves bearing the appearances of objects, is as important to a poet as it is fascinating. The roaring flame of blast furnaces at night may have for him the same burning terror that the sun has by day. The problem of using science and machines in verse has so far been their impersonality, their lack of human association. We were accustomed to windmills but not to dynamos. We were familiar with a horse-drawn plow but not with tractors, and besides there was an ancient tradition for using the plow and the windmill in poetry. But this is changing. It begins with the child. He plays now with miniature airplanes, streamlined trains, and a multitude of mechanical devices. He sees them represented in the funnies. They will not be strange to him when he grows up. He may have his childhood recalled by the sight, not of a certain flower remembered from his mother's garden, but by the sight of a certain airplane with a distinctive wing—if any model will last that long.

It is often complained that machines, being inanimate, can never even partly displace animate nature in poetry. They say that such a nature image as that in the line "But thine eternal summer shall not fade" can never be replaced by an image from science or machinery. There are two replies to this.

In the first place, much of the nature used in poetry is just as non-living as machines; a season's change is weather as well as plants; and Wordsworth's "something far more deeply interfused" was actually fused with rock and sun as well as daffodils. The traditional comparison of a man's old age to the setting sun shows how an inanimate object may, by long association, acquire the aspect of life. And yet surely the running-down and disrepair of an old machine are more definite images of a man's age, and far more contemporary ones. In the second place, as with the example of the sun above, machines may by constant familiarity acquire that semblance of a life which inanimate objects of nature have long had.

There are many city dwellers today for whom a machine and impersonal environment are far more real and understandable than a nature environment. Nature for them is something kept behind cages in parks or used as an escape from city heat; a place where empty beer cans are thrown on Sunday. The nature tradition of poetry will in time seem for them unreal and irrelevant—as lifeless as machine poetry now seems to many. Their life will have to be expressed in its hard and daily terms, in steel and motor. The clouds are there, over the city, but they are bringers of gutter-streams and coolers of hot apartment-house roofs rather than nourishers of crops and growing things.

There is one further consideration. Machinery may not serve precisely the same purpose in poetry that nature does, and therefore will not be substituted directly for it. Its function may be to reveal a portion of human life which thus far the use of nature has not been able to reveal, in doing which it will not compete with nature but rather complement and complete it. One specific example of this is the difficulty of expressing man's social relationships in verse by means of the traditional forms and images. It may be that the highly complex and perfectly unified parts of machines, the relationship between separate but interacting machines, and the power that operates through all of them will express social terms and the unity and interaction of social life far better than can anything drawn from nature. With that increasing sympathy for society which will come with understanding, there will rise a stronger motivation to write poetry which deals with specific social and political questions. Anything that affects the lives of men is fit subject for poetry. If the life of this century is going to be one of social unrest and profound efforts to

adjust the machine to society, or our social and economic system to a machine age, then poetry will be unavoidably concerned, at least in part, with that unrest. This will not be strange to him when he grows
~~soured at the injustice. This will not be strange to him when he grows~~

Modern psychology has altered the position of a poet today less obviously than machinery, and yet as deeply. It has entirely eliminated the inspiration theory of writing by showing that poems derive not from some external source but from such immediate and internal influences as a childhood memory unconsciously retained, last night's supper, a forgotten conversation, and the terrible directness of dreams. It has proved that the condition of mind from which a poet writes is not isolated, separate from his complete person or even a unique and entirely single feeling, but rather the fulfilment of the total person—the end-result of nerve, muscle, emotion, idea—twisted by the imagination into a unified form. However humiliating to the poet, it can be said of some poetry that it comes not from the mind alone but from the glands.

As much understanding of the intricate working of the human mind as possible is necessary to the poet. Until now this has come largely through the qualities of sympathy and intuition. But these can be supplemented today by all that psychology has contributed to opening the dark area of the mind. Not only has it enlarged our comprehension of past literature, as of the characters in Shakespeare, but it has expanded our belief about what should go into future literature. What we know of the sex impulse may not give us a deeper sense of the power of love in human affairs, but it will surely give us increased understanding in writing about it. Inhibition and repression have been the cause and source of much verse. A true knowledge of them may be able to make them subjects, however indirectly, of verse.

It must not be thought that poems will become case histories. The poet can use the analyses of a psychiatrist without simply versifying them. He will use them to help interpret the actions of men. As with machinery, psychology is something to be added to our customary ways of thinking and of writing. It is not intended to replace them. Its purpose is to increase the capacity of poetry to express the time in which it is written, and the men who live in that time.

Just as science and its creation machinery have advanced knowledge of our material environment, and psychology knowledge of personality, so has sociology increased knowledge of our social environment. We realize now the multitude of forces working on the individual that come not from nature or from within himself but from society. The daily dependence of every man on legions of other men he has never seen, and the existence of a vast social structure, greater than the sum of all its living parts, are important to the poet—as important as the fact of the earth turning in day and night.

As a poet better understands his social being, he will turn with greater interest toward it. Social phenomena and feeling may suffuse his verse as natural phenomena have. It may be that society will become as compelling and dominant for some poet as nature was for Wordsworth; that the energy running through all men and connecting them in one organic whole will charge his mind with as strong an electric current as that sense of a natural power in all things charged the mind of Wordsworth, producing in each a mood of mingling with a will and a being greater than himself. The difference between the two conditions is that a man can associate himself with nature but not alter it, passively letting his personality respond to its impulses; but a man is able to merge himself with society and yet move actively to change it, in which he has the amazing and human faculty of changing himself.

Certainly poetry will as a whole become more "social-minded." It will react instinctively to social movements as it once did to the moving wind. Poetry has already come out of the tower to talk with men and women on the street, and it can never go back. In these days of universal conscription a poet must be interested in an armament bill in Washington or Westminster and in the foreign policy of his own and all other nations, for they may affect his own life deeply or end it. He must be aware, in a time when so many millions of lives depend on an industrial system's working smoothly, of economic changes and forces which control these millions. A wage rise or fall has as strong and immediate an impact on factory workers as ever rainfall or good and bad crops had on an agricultural people.

One result of this awareness will be the desire to use common speech and contemporary images, and new verse forms and cadences to fit them. Mac-Leish, in a note to his verse-play *Panic*, has argued that modern dramatic verse must be the opposite of Elizabethan; that today the American voice drops away toward the end of its sentence or its speaking, and so the line of verse must fall away. Elizabethan verse rose toward the end because men spoke with a rising inflection. Hence the strong endings in plays of that time and the weak endings of MacLeish's verse. I do not agree with this, but it is such a searching for a form to match the speech that we need. In America our verse has tended more and more to match the rhythms of speech. With this tendency, and our enormous facilities for communication by radio, book, and newspaper, verse may come to be written for the medium in which it will appear. As the ballads were written for singing, so may a new kind of verse be written for the radio. The movies should produce a highly rhythmic and onomatopoeic verse to be spoken with music, which was written inseparably for the verse. I have heard a poem of the young English poet W. H. Auden, written especially for the occasion, read during the showing of a film depicting the passage of a night mail train to the north of England. The verse, like the film, followed the progress and speed of the train through village and valley, both in its details and in its sounds. It was very exciting to watch dawn moving over the dark northern hills and to hear it carefully described in strong verse.

This concern with social life has already produced one result—an increase of politics in verse that is almost an invasion. It is not new. Milton was moved to write a sonnet on the late massacre in Piedmont. Shelley, far away in Italy, wrote a long poem condemning the "Peterloo massacre" in 1819, when a huge crowd of people, meeting outside Manchester to protest certain policies of the government, was fired upon by soldiers. Shelley wrote numerous poems directly dealing with the politics of his time and with republicanism in a time when to be a republican was far more dangerous than to be a communist in England now. The Russian Revolution has moved many poets, especially in France and England, as deeply as the French Revolution moved Wordsworth.

One of the most curious means of enlarging our expression both of contemporary life and of the ancient human instincts has been the utilization of one of the newest sciences, anthropology. What has been discovered about prehistoric and primitive peoples is used to interpret the most civilized of men. T. S. Eliot acknowledges his debt, in writing *The Waste Land*, to Frazer's *Golden Bough*, especially the Adonis and Osiris volumes, and to Jessie L. Weston's *From Ritual to Romance*. MacLeish's *Pot of Earth* is filled with the study of fertility legends and rites. Auden has written of the primitivism of music:

> The string's excitement, the applauding drum
> Are but the initiating ceremony
> That out of cloud the ancestral face may come.

And of the personality's urge to assure its own nature:

> And all emotions to expression came,
> Recovering the archaic imagery;
> This longing for assurance takes the form
> Of a hawk's vertical swooping at the sky. . . .

Should the facilities for understanding the nature of personality increase as rapidly in this century as the facilities for understanding the nature of matter increased in the last, we shall have the possibility of putting into verse such a comprehension of the character and motivations of men as has not been thought of. One result has already been the struggle of the ego to maintain its validity in face of the annihilating knowledge both of it and of society and of the world of energy and matter which this century has revealed. Poetry was for a while in the twenties a chant of the unimportance of the self. *The Love Song of J. Alfred Prufrock* is a type of utter self-flagellation in verse— an assertion that the individual, in spite of his preoccupation with his own mind, is meaningless before the huge complexities of modern life. Here is the complete statement of man as petty, valueless, and doomed:

> No! I am not Prince Hamlet, nor was meant to be,
> Am an attendant Lord, one that will do
> To swell a progress, start a scene or two,
> Advise the Prince, no doubt an easy tool,
> Deferential, glad to be of use. . . .

I do not wish to repudiate all poetry which comes from the self and is entirely about it. Surely poets will use their new knowledge and understanding to interpret not only other men and social groups but themselves. They may be led to an examination of their minds so deep that it is terrifying. But those with courage will use their new material and not be used by it, although it involves stretching their minds out on a board like a pinned moth. John Lehmann wrote of this:

> To penetrate that room is my desire,
> The extreme attic of the mind that lies
> Just beyond the last bend in the corridor.

Some poets have tried to solve the problem of the self by going beyond it in historical or social poetry, where the self is concealed in objective action or in a political movement. The individual is merged in something so much bigger than himself that he disappears, losing his identity, save in so far as the whole external action may be an image of his mind. These poets seek a way in which the immense awareness of our time can be asserted on a broader scale than one man. Men may say of the self what Stephen Spender said:

> What I had not foreseen
> Was the gradual day
> Weakening the will
> Leaking the brightness away. . . .

But others will say that there is a vaster will than the self's own which works through that gradual day, and a brightness which burns when the small flame goes out.

This finding of the individual inadequate, and his private feelings insufficient for all the poetry a man writes, does not mean that the individuality of men will be destroyed. It may, on the contrary, be the salvation of the individual today. If a man stands out in solitary aloofness from his time he may drown in it. But in losing his lone self he may find it in a more powerful and daring state of being. Some find it in the necessity of faith, some in the exhilarating purge of action, and some in a belief demanding action. C. Day Lewis has praised this man who has solved his private fate by mingling with a public one:

> For those who had the power,
> Unhesitating whether to kill or cure:
> Those who were not afraid
> To dam the estuary or start the forest fire:
> Whose hearts were filled
> With enthusiasm as with a constant wind . . .
> There need be no obituary nor wreath,
> Accomplices of death . . .
> Their spirit shall be blowing out of the sunrise,
> Their veins our rivers, their bones our bread.

That spirit blowing out of the sunrise is the moving force toward which men, whose way of talking is that high and tense speech called "poetry," will more and more turn their waiting faces.

## MUCH COULD BE DONE

### *Ernestine Evans* (*1938*)

WE ARE a picture-craving people. We go on our own steam to see the movies, as few of us go to books, once school is over. We are Hollywood almost as much as we are Washington, and there are Afghans and even Irish who think Hollywood *is* our capital. The great inclusive audience in America is the crowd that sees the pictures, not the crowd that goes to church. The great listening audience is in the front room, the back room, the bed room, listening to the more than seven hundred privately owned radio stations in the United States, or to the short waves of all the world. It isn't at the New England town meeting—God rest its give and take—or really getting its money's worth about its own interests and its own affairs from the daily press. Should we not, then, use the pictures, still and moving, to build up common knowledge and common feeling, the broad bases of democratic living? Hollywood having got the voters out and assembled, open-minded and starry-eyed at Shirley Temple and Clark Gable, it seems a pity not to let Washington communicate some solid facts about how the ninety per cent do live as addenda to what is going on amongst the stars.

All this I set down because only this morning I had a letter from my Republican friend in Minnesota who is very much upset at the news that the United States government has set up a film unit, to make films for the purpose of recording government work and communicating government policy. I cannot quite make out whether she is galled that a Democratic administration proposes to make good films (I doubt if bad films would trouble her), or whether she is still angry at "The River." For that film, which Pare Lorentz made for the Farm Security Administration as part of the campaign for flood control of the Mississippi, said plainly that we the citizens of the United States had been worse than Esau—that we had sold our birthright of forest for a mess of pottage, and had not even collected the pottage. My friend is the inheriting kin of timber barons, and is loath to be, as they say, "objective" about the good old days.

We are too accustomed to think of the movies as the great escape diversion, the place to go now that there is no frontier with free land and easy money (was it ever easy?) beyond the blue horizon. I am not ungrateful to Hollywood for these movie houses and palaces where at the end of a farm or factory, an office or kitchen, or even a drawing-room day, the cost is so little to get to Broadway, China, or Paris; and in the dark, to mountains and deserts and battlefields, boudoirs, beaches, and Scotland a hundred years ago. I like machine guns and horses; wisecracks and croonings do less for me.

Of news reels, even in the days when the navy putting out to sea was a safe one-quarter of every program, I am never tired. And until "The March of Time" began to use its immensely dramatic and plastic technique to make films like its recent one on social medicine, which was no better than a fixed fight, with Dr. Fishbein of the American Medical Association warning the audience against government control, and one of those appendicitis operations with a vast display of shiny instruments and a stage doctor, you could get me to give up dinner and go through sleet to see their snatches of the world.

But we have been tardy, I think, in seeing what a means of communication we had, between classes and regions, and finally between the people and the leaders, whether their leaders are dictators or duly elected and conscientious representatives of the masses.

It is a two-way line of communication. Never before has an audience of this size been assembled to look and listen. Never before have leaders been able to send out any instrument or agent comparable with this one, to note conditions, causes, and effects, at home and abroad. The camera, to be sure, can distort, omit, avoid the very point of a matter; it can be obsequious to taboos and it can make fiction; but by and large, it is the great new instrument of record and communication. The Department of Agriculture, for many years the largest manufacturer of "educational" motion pictures in the United States (the use of films was started in a Republican administration), has long been making pictures of country problems, grasshopper plagues, the feeding of pigs, the identification of the Japanese beetle, et cetera; and county agents all over the country have been grateful to have films, as well as eight- and ten-point bulletins from the Government Printing Office, in their effort to get the scientist's information to the layman, the often illiterate owner or cropper. But even Department of Agriculture officials would admit that the films they have made, on the whole, lack zest and talent, any camera art, and emotion. They have little dynamic quality.

At one time or another, several other departments of the government have had a shot at the movies: the Department of Commerce, the National Parks, the Works Progress Administration, and the Tennessee Valley Authority. The War Department (in whose Signal Corps files the Brady stills of the Civil War are one of the priceless possessions) was quick to follow the French military college of St. Cyr in using the camera both for recording all engines of war and for teaching. And the head of the Signal Corps, by special arrangement, always has carte blanche to keep an inspector in Hollywood who examines every new lens and development of technique. The Labor Department, perhaps because Secretary Perkins does not like the movies, is miles behind the Department of Labor in France, which has documented most of the historic handicraft and machine techniques of the past and present, and has put them at the service of the French schools to assist teachers of history and geography, and to be used in vocational guidance.

Hollywood, of course, has kept an eye on government and some of its activities. G-Men, and an Annapolis that left doubt in people's minds whether the navy had time for anything but love, and plenty of aviators, have figured in Hollywood films. But on the whole, few of the facts of government life, certainly not in the sense of showing what a united and wilful people could do to create a commonwealth, have been part of the Hollywood statement.

Other countries and other governments have made other uses of films. From the Soviet Union, from Italy, from Nazi Germany, but most of all from Great Britain, we can learn what to do and what not to do. All four are concerned with a broad base of homogeneous common knowledge for their people; all four have embarked on policies of film reporting and film exposition of government achievement and apparatus. When the Soviet government built the Turk-Sib railway, it was as much a part of the plan of its building to have a film record of the achievement and its relation to the economy of the whole country, as the very laying of the tracks. In Russia, films have been of incalculable power in convincing the people that they themselves are making history. T.V.A. and the Coulee Dam are not less important for us than the Turk-Sib was for the Russians, but no films of the epic quality of those contemporary achievements are under way to galvanize the people to fresh effort. Engineers on both jobs, of course, have thousands of feet of progress recorded. But I am talking about something else—about films that would be works of art, to make us both feel the achievement and begin to understand the possibilities of our engineering age. We have plenty of scientists doing the people's work; and the politicians in their way were supposed to be the artists who carried the people with them, but what we need now is the dramatization of the job. We need a new patriotism that harmonizes and realizes regional relations and obligations, and gives us again what we seem to have lost—that continental consciousness that once made us so cheerful and so envied. The continent is still ours to husband, though no longer ours to pursue in the old way. But even that statement is inaccurate. Once we were a people continually on the move to free land; we are a hundred times more on the move than ever before, but we understand less the forces that push us and the dreams that guide us. We need artists. And we have them.

The two films made by Pare Lorentz have attracted world-wide attention —criticism too—but each has tackled a great social theme; and both of them, by their experimental technique and by their success in telling a story, opened our eyes to national tasks in a way that no speech could do. "The Plough That Broke the Plains" told the story of the Dust Bowl in such a way that even Vermont farmers, hearing and seeing that story in a damp and lush summer, joined in the tragedy of mistaken policy and hideous weather and were in some measure willing, as tax payers, to tide their brothers over. They may not have liked the Resettlement Administration, but they understood that some sort of doctor was needed, and they saw what the sickness of their fellow citizens was. They were drawn out of the circle of too local politics.

"The River" has had even more success, and of course more criticism, too. Where is the school book that could give children such a sense of the waters of that river and the valleys which it drains? I agree with the critics who want a more exact account of what the engineers are going to do about the problem; I would like to know if any domesday book of land titles in that valley will ever be made; I know that the story is told in broad sweeps and not in precise pictures of individual relationships to the big story. But "The River" is memorable not alone for its pictures, but for its poetic narration. A querulous photographer I know scoffed at the verse Lorentz wrote for his picture— "ham singsong," he called it. I laughed, because on that very day I had a letter from Paris from someone who had taken the nearly blind James Joyce to listen to the film, and Joyce had asked to have the film over and over again. "What poetry," he said, "the epic of this century." But he had brought to the film an Irish ear accustomed from aforetime to hear the troubles of a people from the lips of a bard.

> From as far West as Idaho—
>     Down from the glacier peaks of the Rockies—
> From as far East as New York—
>     Down from the turkey ridges of the Alleghenies—
> Down from Minnesota, twenty-five hundred miles,
>     The Mississippi River runs to the Gulf.
> Carrying every drop of water that flows down two-thirds
>         the continent—
>     Carrying every brook and rill—
>     Rivulet and creek—
> Carrying all the rivers that run down two-thirds the continent.
>     The Mississippi runs to the Gulf of Mexico.

No, I like it. It tells the people, it tells me something. Whitman would have liked it. The hired man can get it, and the method will last a long time, in spite of the inevitable maudlin imitations that have already begun to whine on other screens.

The British, too, are beginning to use verse in their documentary films, and a new line of communication is opened. Poets and narrators on the radio too often, almost always, are wraiths of the old bards chanting to the people. Too much modern poetry is written for the eye and not the ear, and is stopped at the head before it ever reaches the pulse and heart. Not so the waggish verses of Wystan Auden, jerked out to the rhythm of the Postal Special hurrying from the Euston Station, up through Crewe, through the night, to Aberdeen.

> This is the night mail crossing the border
> Bringing the check and the postal order
> Letters for the rich, letters for the poor
> The shop at the corner and the girl next door;
> Pulling up Beattock, a steady climb—
> The gradient's against her, but she's on time.
>
> Past cotton grass and moorland boulder,
> Shovelling white steam over her shoulder,
> Snorting noisily as she passes
> Silent miles of wind-bent grasses;
> Birds turn their heads as she approaches,
> Stare from the bushes at her blank-faced coaches;
> Sheepdogs cannot turn her course
> They slumber on with paws across,
> In the farm she passes, no one wakes
> But a jug in a bed room gently shakes.

Auden's verses are on the sound track of my favorite British documentary, made by the film unit of the General Post Office. "Documentary" is a word that Americans will have to learn. The British crowd who established the word, and who have half discarded it in favor of "realist," are a cheerful group, going new places; they define their field as picturing "the world of men and women at work and at leisure; their responsibilities and commitments to the world in which they live." They reproduce cross sections of British life on the screen.

As a group, under the leadership of John Grierson, the British makers of "documentary" films have fought to keep clear of the British commercial film companies, which are less talented and just as commercial as Hollywood, and whose financing has been one of the greatest British rackets. The group gained its foothold when Sir Stephen Tallents was head of the government body, the Empire Marketing Board. American audiences served by the Film Library of the Museum of Modern Art may have seen one film sponsored by that agency, Basil Wright's "Song of Ceylon," a lyric film into which was woven the story of the tea plantations. In "Drifters" was told the story of the men of the herring fleet. From the Empire Marketing Board Sir Stephen and John Grierson moved to a second acre on the public domain, the General Post Office. They worked within a not too generous budget. Their business was to make the people aware of the Post Office—its functions, its services, the character of its devoted personnel. Not a little of the confusion of modern life is that so many simple services have grown to immense size and developed complicated relationships. The Post Office is a great administrative staff running an intricate piece of machinery, touching the lives of men and women in war and peace, in their personal and working lives. I forget who said that advertising was of two sorts, the loud reiterant statement of the powers of the article, or the proving of the pudding. The Post Office film unit set out to convey to the public what the Post Office did in the public service, and as they have exhibited, picture by picture, the wonders of the Post Office technique and dramatized the daily services of its enormous staff, they have proved that it was worth every shilling of its budget. Englishmen know vastly more than they did, not merely about the Post Office, but about the British Isles, about the civil servants who work in all branches of the Postal service, the Savings Banks, and the British Broadcasting Corporation. They know how the telephone book is printed and how the Empire air mail is carried. The Post Office film workers have not always made successful films: good camera work, expert cutting, and the perfect sound track are not always easily come by. But as a group they have held together, and to one end: to build up the use of film to mirror the real world, and to socialize our life by making the public aware, not of cabinet ministers and stars, but of daily work and public policy. They see in the use of film not merely a great technique of reportage, but a dazzling way to propose change, the moving blueprint of possibilities, for a world bogged down in precedent—a world forever moving if we would only let it.

The zest (with a dash, of course, of factional theorizing) of the British documentary group is like that which I recall in the Mexican mural painters in the early days of the Mexican revolution. There has been the same willingness to work at any price, the same anxiety to recruit talent and to build for a team. They were the first in London to shout for the enormous vitality of the technique of "The March of Time," and the first to show their disappointment when its subject matter became shallow. They have influenced British broadcasting, and they know themselves as the fathers of many a regional broadcast and of the fresh use of the people of England on the air. They have played the game of trying to get as much commercial money as possible for their crowd—which they use to make films that are not "commercial." For example, they have made films on nutrition, on crowded schools, and on British slums, backed by the Gas Light and Coke Company, a corporation accepting the principle that to promote a good work is to lay a brick toward an edifice of good name. (Coca Cola, please note. Mr. Ford, why not make a film about fifty million more cows the children need?)

Grierson has now embarked on another job. The empire will be only "the empire," and not a commonwealth of nations, until its parts behold each other at daily living. The Empire Fair at Glasgow was the occasion for the making of a covey of documentaries, but those who see them do not see merely more travel films, picturesque scenes, but the dramatization of relationships, of trade, of industry. The speech in these films, instead of being ironed out to some synthetic semi-Oxford norm, is kept in all its rich diversity. Words on a page lose much of their cadence. Sound tracks of the people speaking (even in Brooklyn maybe) remind us of infinite variety.

One question interests me. What about the "propaganda" in these films, and of what use in international exchange are films made for internal consumption? To hear people wince at the very word, you would think that propaganda always worked, or that it was illegitimate. It may be true, as Mr. Dooley said when he tried to explain pragmatism, that "if a lie works, it's so." But frank knowledge of the source of any statement and any picture is like vaccination against a polluted message. And then, what *does* capture the heart of the beholder? I remain dazzled but unrecruited by Hitler's pageants and by Mussolini shouting that he has raised Rome from the dead. "Half phoney," I mutter, and accept that part of their message which says that whole peoples can be bamboozled to die for a place in the sun. But envy and irritation often follow on the heels of the other fellow's grandest displays. That is human. Certainly, the Coronation Parade down the Mall last May did not kindle in me the amount of affection for Great Britain that I got from "Night Mail," which left me so beholden to the workers of England who brought my daily letters.

And I think it fair to say that, abroad, "The River" has engendered more affection for and understanding of the United States than any other single circumstance in the last five years. It was, to be sure, a grand album, with the sweep of a continent in it; but it was also a confession of a sorry problem, of neglect, of stupid waywardness with the good earth. And the effect? I have had a dozen letters about it from London, and it was as if the ice had gone out in the spring. It was wonderful to them to hear of our troubles. We became not the envied lost colony, but a clumsy, strong people, strong enough to take hold of a terrific problem, admitting failure, preparing for something new. Old M.P.'s, men up from the city, workmen, all sorts of Britishers, loving the narration for the beauty in it, catching the emotion in the film, were in communication with their fellow men. They too have exploited peoples and places. Perhaps that is why they were moved.

A good film surpasses, in this day, any book's possibility of building common knowledge and common feeling. The film-makers must have the books, to carry on to the larger circle. There is no competition here, but enlargement.

The United States government is going to have a film unit. It will have a thimbleful of backing compared to the Government Printing Office; but by far more than a thimbleful will the government print be enhanced by its operation. The experiment is worth watching; and one wonders which cabinet officer will see in the unit his chance to make plain to the people what he has never been able to show before. First, the people must see what is going on; then will come mandates to act. Suppose the sorry story of the migratory workers who, homeless or housed like refugees, follow the sun and endure the rain for the sake of the American standard of living they do not share, were put upon the screen? Suppose the history of housing in the past, or the ownership of land as we left New England and moved across the plains, were really to be shown to us?

If with four men and their still cameras Dr. Roy Stryker of the Farm Security Administration has been able to create, for the public and for students, a vast documentation of the condition of the people in the South and in the Dust Bowl, what presentation of facts and revelation of the flow of our national life, region by region, occupation by occupation, can we not hope for from a film director who throws his report on the screen? Hollywood has made us rich in technicians; the audience is organized; why shouldn't the government catch us between Valentino and Hepburn, for an hour of reality?

## KATHARINE CORNELL:

### THE ACTOR ATTACKS HIS PART

### *Morton Eustis* (*1937*)

THE YEAR was 1919. The place, London. The scene, the stalls of a playhouse during the matinee of a current hit . . . Katharine Cornell, a young American actress who had come to London to achieve her first success as Jo in *Little Women*, was seated in the darkened auditorium watching a tense drama unfold on the stage before her. At the climax of a highly emotional scene, tears welled up in the eyes of the leading lady; they fell slowly, drop by drop, down her fair cheeks. Instantly a woman sitting in front of Miss Cornell in the audience nudged her companion: "Look," she whispered admiringly, "real tears." Through the entire house ran the same electric consciousness. "*Real tears!* The actress is so overcome by emotion that she is crying. She is *actually* crying!" The curtain, like the tears, fell slowly. It rose again. The star, still in the throes of emotion, took her bow. Her face was streaked with mascara where the tears had coursed. She wiped her eyes. A salvo of applause ran through the auditorium.

Miss Cornell was not among those to applaud. A season of trouping, the year before, in a small part in the tear-jerker, *The Man Who Came Back*, had made her realize that tears, real or glycerine, could easily be induced into an actor's eyes. How the actress in this play made herself cry, even the fact that she did cry, did not concern Miss Cornell as she walked out of the theatre. What did affect her was this: the moment the actress dramatized her own tears, held them on show, as it were, for all observers to see, *the character lost her audience.* Every person in the theatre thought only of the fact that the actress, herself, was crying. At the one time, of all others, when the audience should have been hypnotized into forgetting it was in a theatre watching a play, its thoughts had been diverted from the character to the actor, from illusion to reality.

Then and there, Miss Cornell made up her mind that when she had a "big scene" to play, she would use her authority as an actress to melt the eyes of her audience rather than her own. How much better, she thought—looking into the future, perhaps, to parts like Candida, Juliet, Joan of Arc—for the spectators to believe that a character on the stage is moved to laughter or tears and, believing it, to laugh or cry themselves, and for the actor, conscious every moment of what he is doing, always a step ahead of his part, to use his powers to create, sustain and heighten that illusion! "Acting is only the creation of an illusion of reality," Miss Cornell insists. *"The essential thing is to make the audience believe all the time."*

Although any form of personal exhibitionism on the part of the player at once destroys illusion, every actor is, on the other hand, faced with the necessity of building each role within the framework of his own personal presence. His body, his voice, and his ego are the scaffolding around the edifice of character which he creates. For Katharine Cornell this problem was made more than usually difficult by the very distinction of her presence. When a young assistant stage manager, named Guthrie McClintic, saw her act with the Washington Square Players during her first season on the stage, he scribbled on his program the words: "Interesting, monotonous, worth watching." Yet his comment at that time was kinder than that of other critics and friends. Miss Cornell was told, variously, that she was too tall; she looked awkward, gawky; her features were striking but far from beautiful; her voice musical but uninteresting; her whole presence was *wrong* for the theatre—too marked, perhaps; she should never consider a stage career. Two seasons of minor roles with the Washington Square Players, an arduous year with the Jessie Bonstelle Stock Company in Buffalo (playing parts of maids, scrub ladies and the like) and the road season with the *Man Who Came Back* company endowed Miss Cornell with the technical facility and poise to confound her former critics with a gracious and charming performance in *Little Women*. But the actress had not yet solved the problem of relating her own uncommon presence to a theatre's stage. The special radiance and grandeur that was to add lustre to many insignificant plays and enrich fine plays—qualities that must have been hers even then—still shone but fitfully in the actress' performance.

The task of "making audiences believe" is made doubly hard for the young actor by the fact that he is compelled, through inexperience and lack of opportunity, to play many unimportant roles in mediocre plays. He has to make the audience accept not only a playwright's character but often a story essentially false. Miss Cornell's career, in this respect, was no exception to the general rule. Despite her success in London, she could not get a part in New York. After a brief tour in *The Man Outside,* she rejoined Miss Bonstelle's stock company, then in Detroit, playing the leading roles in works no better or worse than the usual stock fare. Her early critic, McClintic, happened to be a stage director for the company and he not only displayed a personal interest in Miss Cornell—they were married the following year—but he coached the actress in her roles—a new one each week. "Don't play down your height, your peculiarities of presence," he must have told her. "Use them. . . . Attack each part as if it were new and vital. Learn to project character *through* your own personality. Use your God-given gift of glamour to make audiences believe even the silly parts. When the good parts come along, half your work will be done for you, and through them you will mature."

The role of Sydney Fairfield in *A Bill of Divorcement*, the next year, offered Miss Cornell her first chance to enact a believable characterization on Broadway. (She was engaged for this part, against the judgment of the producer, on the insistence of the British actor in the lead who had seen her play Jo in London.) The play and the characterization were an instantaneous hit. And, even today, people who have entirely forgotten the drama still remember the feeling of sympathy evoked for the young girl who remained faithful to her father, shell-shocked and mentally injured in the War. A lovely character-portrait of Mary Fitton the next year (she impersonated Juliet for one scene) in the Winthrop Ames production of *Will Shakespeare* proved that Miss Cornell was not simply a one-part or a "modern-play" actress. Years of less fruitful appearances were to follow in melodramas like *Tiger Cats, The Green Hat, The Letter* and *Dishonored Lady*—*Candida* alone, in 1924, breaking the spell of tawdry parts, giving true scope to the actress' powers and receiving, in grateful return, a glowing impersonation. Yet such was Miss Cornell's determination to make the audience care that she made Iris March, and the other murderesses and adulteresses she depicted, seem vibrant people and she built, for the moment, some universal truth out of the unreal stories these plays told. Not entirely incidental, too, was the fact that she made enough money out of these portrayals to enable her to set herself up under her own management.

Her own best development as an actress grew—as McClintic had told her years earlier that it would—out of the good parts in good plays that she then selected for production. The changing elements of character in the roles provided by *The Barretts, Lucrece* (the first classic role), *Romeo and Juliet, Saint Joan* and, this year, *The Wingless Victory* gave the actress the chance to create something more than excitement. And the presence and technique— in speech, timing and projection—used to such good effect in the trashy roles, found their ultimate expression in genuine characterization.

How Miss Cornell attacks a part—more specifically, how she adapts her own presence to contrasting characterizations—is, she says, "very hard to describe." Where Nazimova, with the Russian background of training, approaches a role with a complete sense of detachment—feeling that she, herself, is "nothing, nobody"—Miss Cornell quite consciously attempts to relate a part to herself. "Every character," she feels, "is both near and far from an actor's own personality. The player must understand the person, have a cerebral as well as an emotional sympathy with the role, to act it. Then he has to present it through his own qualities of mind and physique.

"There may be actors who completely disguise themselves. But if the process is absolute, I doubt if the desired effect is produced. Every part must mirror something of the actor, himself, just as every book, every painting, every piece of music, reflects something of its creator. If an actor lost his personality, the public would lose interest in him, just as it would in a Rembrandt or Whistler painting that bore no trace of the style or personality of the artist. A good actor can play diverse roles, be a distinctly different character in each one of them, and yet retain his own personality all the time. I believe, for instance, that my Elizabeth Barrett, my Juliet and my Joan were three different people. You could not imagine Elizabeth, as I acted her, behaving as I did as Juliet or as Joan—at least, I hope you couldn't. . . . The three characters, even with contrasting make-up, all looked like Katharine Cornell. But each was—perhaps I should say, was *intended* to be—a person with distinct individual reality."

Acting technique, Miss Cornell believes, can never be reduced to formula. In every art, there is "much that is instinctive, much that is subconscious." In acting, these qualities are observed especially in the relation of the character, and the actor, to the other characters, the other actors in a cast. "To understand one's own character thoroughly one must see it in relation not only to itself but to the other characters in the play." For this reason, Miss Cornell always tries to hold her impressions of a play "in a state of fluidity" until rehearsals commence. Reading a play for the first time, she concentrates principally on her own role, to determine whether the part is suitable for her, one to which she can—"perhaps"—do justice. Once she has decided that she likes the part, she studies the play as a whole, examines the relation of all the roles, the reactions of one character on another, the influences and emotional disturbances of the play. Then she re-studies her own part in relation to the play and to the other roles. *The Barretts of Wimpole Street,* her first production as an actress-manager, was one of the few plays she visualized at once, not in terms of the central part but as an entity. This, she confesses, may have been because it never occurred to her then that she could portray the frail poetess. (Perhaps the Iris March influence was still too fresh.) It was only later, through the suggestion of Guthrie McClintic (who had, and has subsequently, directed all her plays since *The Green Hat*), that she undertook to essay the role.

Although certain moments in every play immediately stand out in imagination as scenes played by actors, Miss Cornell spends a long time studying the character as a character before she attempts to project herself as an actress into the role. The actual development of the part is "a slow, cumulative process". Certain details—of gesture, speech, costume and manner—communicate themselves the moment the actor reads the play. Working out the part, in terms of a stage and of herself, Miss Cornell "develops, refines and heightens these automatic suggestions".

As soon as the "sides" are delivered to her (her part typed out in full, with only the first and last lines of the other speeches included), she begins to "break" the part. She reads the lines aloud, over and over, without any expression, without giving any thought to their meaning, in order to have them tabled in the back of her mind by the time rehearsals start. She deliberately leaves them "suspended" for the first week of rehearsals and reads her part with the other players in order that her reading should not become set and conflict or jar with other voices or personalities. Listening to the other actors, concentrating on their interpretations more than on her own, she is apt to read very poorly herself for the first few days. In the first day's rehearsal of *Saint Joan*, in fact, she gave such "a stumbling, frightened reading" that Maurice Evans, the Dauphin, confided to a friend that Miss Cornell could never play the part. At the end of the first week, she will try out the role without sides to help her, and this time will draw on her reservoir of memory. With the lines "out of the way" she can devote her whole attention to character development.

The finest hair line, in Miss Cornell's opinion, separates the good actor from the so-called "ham". The difference, nine times out of ten, lies in "the power of selection, *the ability to seize upon essentials* and throw away the alluring temptations that clutter up a performance. Almost every imaginative person has a certain instinct for acting. But few have the power to execute, to put into practice, *to make real to an audience*, what they see or feel. . . . Lines, situations, character, all suggest an infinite number of things to 'do'. The artist is the one who has the ability to select, and select accurately, the right and significant things. . . . I have seen promising actors go wrong because they could not choose. They could not resist the impulse to 'do, do, do'."

Rehearsals are the period during which the actor must edit his performance. After the opening night, except for minor readjustments, it is too late. Miss Cornell as a rule works out the details of stage business by herself and then lets the director "add and subtract". The director, Miss Cornell feels—and by "director" she means Guthrie McClintic—"is the editor, the critic, the eye of a production. He is like a conductor who, with a fine, or poor, instrument to play upon, is able to lead his men so that he obtains the best out of them. He does not set the part or impose the conception. He draws the reins or hastens the outflow, guides the actor in the direction he is taking. When the goal is false, when the actor is getting away from the play, he sets him on the right path."

Although Miss Cornell plays the dual role of actress and manager, she is probably less concerned with the physical routine of production than most managers. Having worked for so many years with Mr. McClintic and his associates, she is able to "throw off" all the production details onto their shoulders, convinced, through long experience, that they will be handled with sagacity. Her faith in Mr. McClintic is so implicit that she will let him, even, engage a Romeo and a Mercutio in London whom she has never seen. Her main concern, as a manager, lies in seeing that the play receives the best possible production, in engaging the best available actors for all the roles. Her chief responsibility as an actress is to give the best rendition she can of her own role *in relation to the play and the other players.* "And, obviously, one acts best when one is surrounded by the best actors, for the give and take brings life not only to the play but to the players."

All the productions under Miss Cornell's management have reflected—in the quality of presentation, the "give and take" between the actors, the lack of emphasis upon the star—her conviction that "the play's the thing!" The increasing excellence of the Cornell productions, however, has been due not alone to Miss Cornell's ambition and Mr. McClintic's flair for presentation but to the fact that Miss Cornell, working toward an ultimate repertory company, has gradually set up the nucleus of such a troupe—a permanent director and technical staff, and actors who have played together in many of her productions, both on Broadway and on the road. She has in that way been able to start work on each production well ahead of other Broadway "hit or miss" producing units; to take short cuts and spend her energy on fine points instead of on routine work.

Once the performance is "set" in rehearsals, Miss Cornell changes her acting little. The receptiveness, apathy or antagonism of an individual audience have their effect. But, in the main, she follows the one pattern, though striving, always, to improve the part. "The actor," she says, "is always conscious of whether he is making his points or not. He may give a good account of himself in character and yet realize that he is not making the audience understand, or feel, all that he finds in the part. Certain scenes will always worry and vex him. Instinctively, he will feel that they have not come across as well as they should. This may be due to faulty writing, bad casting, the wrong tempo, lighting or scenery, as well as the playing. Whatever the reason, the actor always struggles with such a scene. He will try different readings, gestures and movements on different nights, but only after he has thoroughly considered, and practiced, each in turn. Often it takes long playing to make a characterization satisfying to an actor. It took many months to break through the shell of Juliet. And if I played the part until I was ninety—which I shan't—I am convinced I would still find things to do, or, more likely, *not to do.*"

When a playgoer says to an actor, "You *lived* the part!", he thinks he has paid the player the highest possible compliment. But the good actor, Miss Cornell declares, "does not live the part; he *cannot* live the part. All the actor does is to *recognize* the emotion of the character and endeavor to transmit the illusion of that emotion across the footlights." Emotion in acting, Miss Cornell believes, is a subject which should only be debated in private among players. Nevertheless, she is willing to state—"flatly"—that she never loses herself in a role. Nor does she believe it is necessary for an actor to have experienced an emotion, or its equivalent, in real life to be able to portray it effectively on the stage. "The truth of that is shown clearly in the other arts." She agrees wholeheartedly with George Arliss, who once said: "If the actor really feels an emotion, there is no sensible reason why he should continue his performance on a confined stage. He should rush into the public square and play out the scene there!"

"Spontaneous or inspired acting—meaning that something which drops from the sky at the moment when the player, Heaven help him, is on the grill in front of an audience—is equally unreliable. By a miracle it might save an actor once. But it would be unfair to tempt fate twice. Inspiration can be of real and lasting value to an actor when he is *studying* a role. But, even then, the actor must be careful to see that it has its roots in his work and is not a misleading flash. . . . *The actor should know, at all times, what he intends to do* and he should practice each bit most carefully before he puts himself in front of spectators. If the actor does live the role at all, it is only in the sense of concentrating on it, and it alone, from the moment he reads a script until the last night of a play's run."

Audiences often wonder how an actor can play the same role, night after night, without going stale, without losing interest in the part. One reason he can is because "each performance is a challenge. No two audiences are alike and each audience has to be convinced. Audiences, moreover, teach a player a great deal. Their reaction is the thermometer. They cannot show an actor how to act, but they can—and do—register whether the actor is ringing true." Miss Cornell loves trouping not only because she believes that the salvation of the theatre lies in building up a theatre-minded audience outside of New York, but because the road audiences can often teach the actor more than the sophisticated New York public. "Their reaction is less consciously analytical, more spontaneous." The longer an actor plays a part, too, the better he is bound to be. "I know that after over seven hundred performances of Elizabeth Barrett, I more nearly approached Mr. Besier's characterization than I did the first one hundred times, and Juliet at my last performance was nearer to Shakespeare than at any time before. The value of repertory is great, for alternating roles gives variety and freshness. But I know that I need a continuous spell at a part to get well into it, perhaps because of my training. The important thing, as William Gillette once said, is to give on the one-hundredth or the one-thousandth night the same illusion of freshness as at the premiere. . . . Oh, it's very difficult to make it all clear!"

The hardest role Miss Cornell ever played was in *Tiger Cats*, not because the role itself was unusually difficult, but because she was expected by the leading man to play it in the same style that Edith Evans had used in London. The most difficult role, in another sense, was Leslie Crosby in *The Letter* because, as an avowed murderess, she had to fight every minute against the antagonism of the audience. Joan—"without any question"—was the most rewarding part, "for I feel that the audience got a tremendous lift out of Shaw's play and this exaltation reacted on the actors." The most valuable training a young actor can get is—"banally enough"—the chance to act. "*We need stock companies and touring companies.* Young people must learn their craft with seasoned actors, not novices like themselves."

"All this," Miss Cornell says, "is a groping and very personal viewpoint, subject to change. Opinions alter and methods grow. We all know actors who are perfect technicians but who can never interest the public. We know people on the stage who, truly, are not expert and yet enchant hosts of admirers. . . . The final answer—if there is any final answer—rests with the gallery gods."

# THE ARTS AS MOTIVE POWER
## *Maxwell Anderson* (*1939*)

THERE is always something slightly embarrassing about the public statements of writers and artists, for they should be able to say whatever they have to say in their work, and let it go at that. Moreover, the writer or artist who brings a message of any importance to his generation will find it impossible to reduce that message to a bald statement, or even a clearly scientific statement, because the things an artist has to communicate can be said only in symbols, in the symbols of his art. The work of art is a hieroglyph, and the artist's endeavor is to set forth his vision of the world in a series of picture writings which convey meanings beyond the scope of direct statement. There is reason for believing that there is no other way of communicating new concepts save the artist's way, no other way save the artist's way of illuminating new pathways in the mind. Even the mathematician leaves the solid plane of the multiplication table and treads precariously among symbols when he advances toward ideas previously unattained.

It may be that I am trying, at this moment, to reduce to plain statement an intuitive faith of my own which cannot be justified by logic and which may lose, even for me, some of its iridescence when examined under a strong light by many searching eyes. For though the question I meant to take up was only the utility of prizes for artistic excellence, I can find no approach to that question save through a definition of the artist's faith as I see it, and no definition of that faith without an examination of the artist's place in his universe, his relation to the national culture and the dependence of a nation on its culture for coherence and enduring significance.

Let me begin then, quite simply and honestly, even naïvely, with a picture of the earth as I see it. The human race, some two billion strong, finds itself embarked on a curious voyage among the stars, riding a planet which must have set out from somewhere, and must be going somewhere, but which was cut adrift so long ago that its origin is a matter of speculation and its future beyond prophecy. Our planet is of limited area, and our race is divided into rival nations and cultures that grow and press on one another, fighting for space and the products of the ground.

We are ruled by men like ourselves, men of limited intelligence, with no foreknowledge of what is to come, and hampered by the constant necessity of maintaining themselves in power by placating our immediate selfish demands. There have been men among us from time to time who had more wisdom than the majority, and who laid down precepts for the conduct of a man's brief life. Some of them claimed inspiration from beyond our earth, from spirits or forces which we cannot apprehend with our five senses. Some of them speak of gods that govern our destinies, but no one of them has had proof of his inspiration or of the existence of a god. Nevertheless, there have been wise men among them, and we have taken their precepts to heart and taken their gods and their inspiration for granted.

Each man and woman among us, with a short and harried life to live, must decide for himself what attitude he will take toward what they have said, and toward the shifting patterns of government, justice, religion, business, morals and personal conduct. We are hampered as well as helped in these decisions by every prejudice of ancestry and race, but no man's life is ready-made for him. Whether he chooses to conform or not to conform, every man's religion is his own, every man's politics is his own, every man's vice or virtue is his own, for he alone makes decisions for himself. Every other freedom in this world is restricted, but the individual mind is free according to its strength and desire. The mind has no master save the master it chooses.

Yet it must make its choices, now as always, without sufficient knowledge and without sufficient wisdom, without certainty of our origin, without certainty of what undiscovered forces lie beyond known scientific data, without certainty of the meaning of life, if it has a meaning, and without an inkling of our racial destiny. In matters of daily and yearly living, we have a few, often fallible, rules of thumb to guide us, but on all larger questions the darkness and silence about us is complete.

Or almost complete. Complete save for an occasional prophetic voice, an occasional gleam of scientific light, an occasional extraordinary action which may make us doubt that we are utterly alone and completely futile in this incomprehensible journey among the constellations. From the beginning of our story men have insisted that they had a destiny to fulfill—that they were part of a gigantic scheme which was understood somewhere, though they themselves might never understand it.

There are no proofs of this. There are only indications—in the idealism of children and young men, in the sayings of such teachers as Christ and Buddha, in the vision of the world we glimpse in the hieroglyphics of the masters of the great arts and in the discoveries of pure science, itself an art, as it pushes away the veils of fact to reveal new powers, new laws, new mysteries, new goals for the eternal dream. The dream of the race is that it may make itself better and wiser than it is, and every great philosopher or artist who has ever appeared among us has turned his face away from what man is toward whatever seems to him most godlike that man may become.

Whether the steps proposed are immediate or distant, whether he speaks in the simple parables of the New Testament or the complex musical symbols of Bach and Beethoven, the message is always to the effect that men are not essentially as they are but as they imagine and as they wish to be. The geologists and anthropologists, working hand in hand, tracing our ancestry to a humble little animal with a rudimentary forebrain which grew with use and need, reinforce the constant faith of prophet and artist. We need more intelligence and more sensitivity if ever an animal needed anything. Without them we are caught in a trap of selfish interest, international butchery, and a creed of survival that periodically sacrifices the best to the worst, and the only way out that I can see is a race with a better brain and superior inner control. The artist's faith is simply a faith in the human race and its gradual acquisition of wisdom.

Now it is always possible that he is mistaken or deluded in what he believes about his race, but I myself accept his creed as my own. I make my spiritual code out of my limited knowledge of great music, great poetry and great plastic and graphic arts, including with these, not above them, such wisdom as the Sermon on the Mount and the last chapter of Ecclesiastes. The test of a man's inspiration for me is not whether he spoke from a temple or the stage of a theatre, from a martyr's fire or a garden in Hampstead. The test of a message is its continuing effect on the minds of men over a period of generations.

The world we live in is given meaning and dignity, is made an endurable habitation, by the great spirits who have preceded us and set down their records of nobility or torture or defeat in blazons and symbols which we can understand. I accept these not only as prophecy, but as direct motivation toward some far goal of racial aspiration. He who meditates with Plato, or finds himself shaken by Lear's "five-fold never" over Cordelia, or climbs the steep and tragic stairway of symphonic music, is certain to be better, both intellectually and morally, for the experience.

The nobler a man's interests the better citizen he is. And if you ask me to define nobility, I can answer only by opposites, that it is not buying and selling, or betting on the races. It might be symbolized by such a figure as a farmer boy in Western Pennsylvania plowing corn through a long afternoon and saying over and over to himself certain musical passages out of Marlowe's "Doctor Faustus." He might plow his corn none too well, he might be full of what we used to call original sin, but he carries in his brain a catalytic agent the presence of which fosters ripening and growth. It may be an impetus that will advance him or his sons an infinitesimal step along the interminable ascent.

The ascent, if we do climb, is so slow, so gradual, so broken, that we can see little or no evidence of it between the age of Homer and our own time. The evidence we have consists in a few mountain peaks of achievement, the age of Pericles, the centuries of Dante and Michelangelo, the reign of Elizabeth in England, the century and a half of music in Germany, peaks and highlands from which the masters seem to have looked forward into the distance far beyond our plodding progress. Between these heights lie long valleys of mediocrity and desolation, and, artistically, at least, we appear to be miles beneath the upper levels traversed behind us. It must be our hope as a nation that either in pure art or in pure science we may arrive at our own peak of achievement, and earn a place in human history by making one more climb above the clouds.

The individual, the nation and the race are all involved together in this effort. Even in our disillusioned era, when fixed stars of belief fall from our sky like a rain of meteors, we find that men cling to what central verities they can rescue or manufacture, because without a core of belief neither man nor nation has courage to go on. This is no figure of speech, no sanctimonious adjuration—it is a practical, demonstrable fact which all men realize as they add to their years. We must have a personal, a national and a racial faith, or we are dry bones in a death valley, waiting for the word that will bring us life.

Mere rationalism is mere death. Mere scientific advance without purpose is an advance toward the waterless mirage and the cosmic scavengers. The doctrine of Machiavelli is a fatal disease to the citizen or the State. The national conscience is the sum of personal conscience, the national culture the sum of personal culture—and the lack of conscience is an invitation to destruction, the lack of culture an assurance that we shall not even be remembered.

No doubt I shall be accused of talking a cloudy philosophy, of mixed metaphors and fantasy, but unless I misread my history, the artist has usually been wiser even about immediate aims than the materialist or the enthusiast for sweeping political reform. The artist is aware that man is not perfect, but that he seeks perfection. The materialist sees that men are not perfect, and erects his philosophy on their desire for selfish advantage. He fails quickly, always, because men refuse to live by bread alone.

The utopian sees that men seek perfection and sets out to achieve it or legislate it for them. He fails because he cannot build an unselfish state out of selfish citizens, and he who asks the impossible gets nothing. The concepts of truth and justice are variables approaching an imaginary limit which we shall never see; nevertheless, those who have lost their belief in truth and justice and no longer try for them are traitors to the race, traitors to themselves, advocates of the dust.

To my mind a love of truth and justice is bound up in men with a belief in their destiny; and the belief in their destiny is of one piece with national and international culture. The glimpse of the godlike in man occasionally vouchsafed in a work of art or prophecy is the vital spark in a world that would otherwise stand stock still or slip backward down the grade, devoid of motive power.

For national growth and unity the artist's vision is the essential lodestone without which there is no coherence. A nation is not a nation until it has a culture which deserves and receives affection and reverence from the people themselves. Our culture in this country has been largely borrowed or sectional or local; what we need now to draw us together and make us a nation is a flowering of the national arts, a flowering of the old forms in this new soil, a renaissance of our own.

How much the gardeners may contribute to the making of such a new garden we can only guess, for genius is not readily producible, cannot be forced or anticipated, cannot be bred from known varieties. It is our hope that it can be encouraged, and the prizes that are given for excellence in the theatre, in music and in painting do seem to have a kind of effectiveness. A prize is more effective than mere monetary success, for it confers leadership, lends a sense of direction and imparts a dignity to the attempt which is not bestowed by popular acclaim or ready sales.

Let us remember always that no award is final, and that current opinion is subject to the veto of next year, next decade and next century. Sophocles did not win first place in the annual competition with his "Oedipus Tyrannus," though it seems to us now the best of the Greek tragedies. We can only judge honestly for ourselves, give what encouragement we can to what seems to us the best in our generation, and hope that some of the work produced by our contemporaries will grow and not disintegrate with the passing of time.

Looking ahead, myself, I still have no more than a hope that our nation will some time take as great a place in the cultural history of the world as has been taken by Greece or Italy or England. So far we have, perhaps, hardly justified even the hope. But let us do what we can to encourage our nascent arts, for if we are to be remembered as more than a mass of people who lived and fought wars and died, it is for our arts that we will be remembered. The captains and the kings depart; the great fortunes wither, leaving no trace; the multitudes blow away like locusts, the records and barriers go down. The rulers, too, are forgotten unless they have had the forethought to surround themselves with singers and makers, poets and artificers in things of the mind.

This is not immortality, of course. So far as I know there is no immortality. But the arts make the longest reach toward permanence, create the most enduring monuments, project the farthest, widest, deepest influence of which human prescience and effort are capable. The Greek religion is gone, but Aeschylus remains. Catholicism shrinks back toward the Papal State, but the best of medieval art perishes only where its pigments were perishable. The Lutheranism of Bach retains little content for us, but his music is indispensable. And there is only one condition that makes possible a Bach, an Aeschylus or a Michelangelo—it is a national interest in and enthusiasm for the art he practices.

The supreme artist is only the apex of a pyramid; the pyramid itself must be built of artists and art lovers, apprentices and craftsmen so deeply imbued with a love for the art they follow or practice that it has become for them a means of communication with whatever has been found highest and most admirable in the human spirit. To the young people of this country I wish to say, if you now hesitate on the threshold of your maturity, wondering what rewards you should seek, wondering perhaps whether there are any rewards beyond the opportunity to feed and sleep and breed, turn to the art which has moved you most readily, take what part in it you can, as participant, spectator, secret practitioner or hanger-on and waiter at the door. Make your living any way you can, but neglect no sacrifice at your chosen altar.

It may break your heart, it may drive you half mad, it may betray you into unrealizable ambitions or blind you to mercantile opportunities with its wandering fires. But it will fill your heart before it breaks it; it will make you a person in your own right; it will open the temple doors to you and enable you to walk with those who have come nearest among men to what men may sometimes be. If the time arrives when our young men and women lose their extravagant faith in the dollar and turn to the arts we may then become a great nation, nurturing great artists of our own, proud of our own culture and unified by that culture into a civilization worthy of our unique place on this rich and lucky continent between its protecting seas.

## LEONARDO DA VINCI

### (*From* Men of Art)

#### *Thomas Craven* (*1931*)

O wretched mortals, open your eyes!
*Leonardo's Notebooks*

Leonardo da vinci is perhaps the most resplendent figure in the history of the human race. In person, distinguished and strong; in bearing, generous and gentle; in intellect, a giant; in art, the most perfect painter who ever held a brush, he stands so far above the ordinary mortal that his name, for centuries, has signified less a man than a legend, less an artist than a magician. During his lifetime his presence stirred people to wonder and admiration, and to uncomfortable conjectures on his marvellous powers. When he walked through the streets of Milan, his long fair hair crowned with a black cap, and his blond beard flowing down over his favorite rose-colored tunic, passers-by drew aside, and whispered to one another, "There he goes to paint *The Last Supper!*" He would travel from his house across the whole length of the city to work on the picture, mount the scaffold, add two or three touches of color, and then go away; at other times he would paint in the deepest concentration from morning till night, without food or drink. Kings and cities bid for him, as if he were, himself, a work of art; commissions were thrust upon him by public opinion; and when one of his cartoons was exhibited at Florence "a vast crowd of men and women, old and young—a concourse such as one sees flocking to the most solemn festivals—hastened to behold the wonders produced by Leonardo." The loveliest woman in Italy, a duchess whose habit it was to dictate to artists the pictures she fancied, implored him again and again to paint for her a little twelve-year-old Christ, or "at least a little picture of the Madonna, devout and sweet." The picture was never painted. Leonardo was also an artist in warfare, and pressed by all sorts of demands, entered the service of Cesare Borgia as chief military engineer. It is no wonder that such a figure should have passed so swiftly into legend.

The legend was not of Leonardo's making. No man ever labored so stead-fastly and scientifically to destroy mysteries and to enlighten the world by discoveries proceeding from observation and experiment. Profoundly religious, he was the enemy of superstition and magic; disillusioned and skeptical, cease-lessly inquiring into the operations of all phenomena, he was at the same time, a poet who loved all outward shapes and forms—children, stern old men, enchanting women, horses, flowers, mountains and moving waters—and who tracked every outward manifestation of life down to the secret source of its energy. "O marvellous necessity," he declared, "thou with supreme reason constrainest all effects to issue from their causes in the briefest possible way!" This law burned in his mind, colored his ambitions, provided him with a scien-tific basis for his investigations, determined the nature of all his performances. He saw no essential difference between art and science; his mind was serene, strikingly deliberate, realistic, and endlessly experimental, and yet filled with the artist's delight in the making of new things. Whatever he applied himself to—and we shall see that he attempted everything under the sun—he consid-ered as a problem in construction. He put no trust in inspiration or momen-tary impulses; he was a master of calculations, a thoroughly modern man, superbly conscious in his methods and perfectly balanced in his procedures. He believed with Blake that "if the doors of perception were cleansed, every-thing would appear to man, as it is, infinite"; and to the end that he might understand the connection of all things, he trained his faculties consciously and with the utmost rigor, and with immense toil and no small amount of pain. He believed that all the laws of structure are within the scope of the human mind, and that once these laws have been grasped, then all things become of equal importance, and man can create spontaneously, like God himself. It scarcely needs to be said that his passion for omniscience was not realized. After all, he was mortal, a Florentine susceptible to human influences and predisposed to certain forms, gestures and scenes. And he was never able to create spontaneously. He painted but few pictures, and those after infinite reflections and readjustments. He struggled for sixteen years with an eques-trian statue that was never finished. But in the completeness of his knowledge and in his conception of the world and the whole celestial system as one vast design, he came closer to universality than any other man.

When Leonardo was fifty-two years old, he entered the following item in his notebook:

"On July 6, 1504, Wednesday, at seven in the morning, died Ser Piero da

Vinci, notary to the Palazzo del Podestá, my father. He was eighty years of age and left ten sons and two daughters." There is no further comment. His relations with his father had been pleasant and honorable, but he had freed himself from fears and lamentations and had learned to accept events with excellent composure. His mind contained the whole of the past and the beginning of everything that was to come. "In rivers," he said, "the water that you touch is the last of what has passed and the first of that which comes: so with time present." His father's family rose from the soil, produced four generations of notaries, and by accident, an artist, and then reverted to the land again. It was a virile stock: Ser Piero's youngest child appeared fifty years after his first born, Leonardo; recently a genealogist, exploring the ancestral properties of the family, discovered a direct descendant of one of the artist's brothers. The man was a peasant, crushed and silent and overworked, but not without memorable dignity as he drove his oxen over the steep hillsides—and his name was Leonardo da Vinci!

Leonardo was born in the village of Vinci, a few miles west of Florence. He was an illegitimate, his mother being a peasant girl of sixteen who, for a consideration, surrendered her child and became the wife of a craftsman. His first years were spent among the mountains of his grandfather's country estate; at the age of thirteen he was received in his father's house at Florence. As a youth he saw the shining Tuscan city rise to the height of her physical power and artistic grandeur. The Prince of the Medici, Lorenzo the Magnificent, the most civilized scoundrel of the Renaissance, was engaged in strangling the commonwealth with despotic bonds forged by an unexampled mastery of statecraft, and to cajole the favor of the populace kept the city riotous with festivals and tournaments worthy of his splendid title. Always the politician, Lorenzo was as well a lavish patron of the arts, a poet and classical scholar, and his villa was the meeting place of the most brilliant minds in Italy. But the old austerity of Florence was gone forever. The masses, incapable of genuine gaiety and relaxation, yielded to organized frivolity and subtle tyranny, and at length, ashamed of their silly levity and softness, hearkened to the ravings of the Puritan spellbinder, Savonarola. The artists, debilitated by culture, substituted taste for strength, and affected the ideals and unseemly refinements of the old Greeks and Romans. The glory of the city lingered on in the genius of Leonardo and Michelangelo.

Leonardo was never at ease in Florence. Though it has, with reason, been urged and echoed that he is the matchless composite of all that the Renaissance contributed to civilization, he was a lonely figure in the center of culture. He was above the coarse mercantile spirit of his age; he was lacking in the push and harsh aggressiveness necessary to material success; he would not be hurried or commanded; he did not venerate the past—he studied it only to be delivered from it; he had a wise contempt for book-learning and declared that "whoever in discussion adduces authority uses not intellect but rather memory"; he was suspicious of the wholesale worship of Greek and Latin—

a fetish the world has not yet shaken off; his decency and self-respect made it impossible for him to solicit favors from corrupt prelates—"friars," he wrote down, "that is to say, Pharisees"—and to find a convenient outlet for his comprehensive energies. Thus he was, for all his delight in life, and his social graces, a man of few friendships. Very early he learned to keep his own counsel, and depend on his own resources. His solitary habits were enhanced by his position in the Vinci family. There was no particular dishonor attached to illegitimacy, but his half-brothers and sisters—his father married four times— a swinish lot, jealous of his superior gifts, seized upon his irregular birth as an excuse to get rid of him. But it did not matter. The world was bigger than a quarrelsome family circle. He avoided and forgave them, and in his will left them some money.

The young Leonardo was extraordinarily precocious. When a boy he displayed his ability in many directions, in mathematics, music and every branch of design. He played the lute, "singing to that instrument most divinely," as Vasari fondly relates, and improvising both words and music; he modelled figures in bas-relief and made drawings of faces, animals and flowers. His father, a fashionable lawyer but a man of sense, showed some of the drawings to his friend, Verrocchio, and so astonished was that master at the quality of the work that he accepted the boy immediately as his pupil. No better teacher could have been found in Florence. Verrocchio was a bachelor whose life was devoted entirely to intellectual pursuits. He was not the greatest painter in the world, but in sculpture he was unsurpassed, and he was also renowned for his skill in goldsmithing, geometry, music and wood-inlaying. Leonardo's loyalty to his master was the only personal tie formed in his youth. He remained in Verrocchio's workshop from his thirteenth to his twenty-fifth year, probably the most purely enjoyable period of his career. It was the time of learning rather than accomplishment. Here he found support in his scientific researches; here he met Botticelli, Perugino, and Lorenzo di Credi; close by were the brothers Pollaiuolo whose studies of the nude were among the latest marvels of art. He lived soberly in his master's house; his fame was rising and he was by common consent the most richly gifted and enviable young man in Italy. Reluctantly, five or six years after he had become a licensed painter, he set up his own shop, for he had little interest in art as a physical exercise or a means to a livelihood, and disliked having to finish a work within a specified time. Nor was he, like Michelangelo, possessed of a mad competitive fury which drove him to impossible commissions and bound him to the service of thankless popes.

During Leonardo's first residence at Florence his mind was enormously active. He was continually experimenting—striving to perfect new methods of expression. Art absorbed only a part of his attention, or, as he would have said, he encompassed the union of art and science, analyzing natural forces and phenomena empirically and co-ordinating them with creative vision. It was not, of course, a new thing for an artist to concern himself with scientific problems: his master was a mathematician and an engineer, and most of his distinguished predecessors had studied anatomy, perspective and light and shade—but only so far as such matters had a practical bearing upon art. Leonardo was the first modern man of science. He observed life minutely and patiently, testing his theories by laboratory methods; he was the founder of the science of geology; he was a botanist with a classified herbarium; he formulated the law of the parallelogram of forces and invented deadly engines of warfare; he dissected corpses to ascertain the relation between function and structure and ascribed the deaths of persons of advanced age to hardening of the arteries. And he went further. He believed that all substances are inherently connected, mutually dependent, and in the final analysis, as modern chemistry insists, interchangeable. Hence he regarded every fact as sacred and every form as a symbol of universal significance. He conceived the world as a living organism warmed by the sun and nourished by the circulation of rivers just as the human body is maintained by the movement of the blood. But his view did not lead him into quack metaphysics or astrology. He conceded the supernatural but did not invoke it, confining himself to observable issues. His universe, as Paul Valéry has aptly pointed out, was entered by a well-devised perspective.

Applying his ideas to art, he scorned the specialists, avowing that no man is so big a fool that he cannot succeed in one thing, if he persists in it, and calling attention to the infinite diversity of nature, "the various kinds of animals there are, the different trees, herbs, and flowers, mountains and plains, springs, rivers and towns." Occasionally, when he felt he was ripe for the task, he painted a picture, and his pictures are, structurally, so perfectly put together that every part takes its position in space with scientific inevitability. And all the components—the rocks, trees, fingers and faces—are painted with equal tenderness and care, with the devotion of one who said, "we have no right to love or hate anything unless we have full knowledge of it."

Naturally, with this unlimited range of interests, Leonardo painted less than the average artist, but it is certain that he painted, at least in his early years, a great deal more than has been preserved. His reputation among his contemporaries, though fabulous and somewhat sinister because of his inventive powers, was primarily that of an artist. It was the general opinion that whenever Leonardo undertook a commission, he would produce something wonderful to behold—and he generally did. But from 1478 to 1483, his first years as an independent artist, we have only three authenticated pictures, the *St. Jerome* in the Vatican, the *Adoration* in the Uffizi, and the *Virgin of the Rocks* in the Louvre. None of these brought him any money, and the first and second are unfinished. Yet he contrived to live, not sumptuously, but well, keeping servants and horses. The conclusion is that he supported himself by painting, and that a number of canvases from this period are still in existence.

In his apprenticeship Leonardo seems to have been a faithful assistant to his master. Precocious as he was, he was obliged to learn the essentials of art.

It is a fact not sufficiently recognized that the painter leans heavily on tradition and that his originality asserts itself slowly, after laborious study of past developments. The reason is clear enough. The writer has the advantage of a medium which is shaped and cultivated and enriched by conversation, and it is not necessary for him to read anything—many authors apparently have not —to produce a sophisticated and moving work. But the language of painting is limited to a few practitioners, and the artist, without instruction and without examples to guide his initial efforts, would be as helpless as a child. Leonardo's first work was in sculpture: Vasari mentions certain heads of "smiling women and children, done in his first youth, which might be supposed to have come from the hand of a master." He likewise "formed models of different figures in clay on which he would arrange fragments of soft drapery dipped in plaster, and from these he would then set himself patiently to draw on very fine cambric or linen with the point of a pencil in the most admirable manner." He must have seen specimens of Greek sculpture; he studied the men who had founded the great tradition of Florentine art, especially Masaccio; he journeyed to Arezzo to examine the frescoes of Piero della Francesca, another painter who worked from clay models, and incidentally to make drawings of stratified rocks.

From the scanty records dealing with his early years we might infer that Leonardo was shadowy and mysterious and something of a dilettante. Nothing could be more false. His personality was vivid and ingenuous, his intentions definite and consistent. But his contemporaries could not fathom his complex mind—and he did not turn out pictures with the regularity expected of one so magnificently endowed. Stories went round of his exceptional strength: how he could mount unbroken stallions and how he could bend a horseshoe as if it were a coil of lead; he was left-handed or ambidextrous, as has been fairly well proved, drawing with his left hand and painting with his right; he was fond of animals, "treating them with infinite kindness and consideration," a singular thing in an Italian, and when he passed shops where birds were sold, so Vasari tells us, "he would frequently take them from their cages, pay the price demanded, and let them fly away." It has been suggested that Leonardo's kindness to birds arose from another motive—his interest in flying-machines and aerial problems. He made models and drawings of mechanical appliances of every description, demonstrating by diagrams to the city magistrates, who could not refute him and could not believe, how the church of San Giovanni might be raised and steps placed beneath it without injury. He consorted with mutes to observe the expression of feelings by gesticulations; extraordinarily receptive to visual impressions, he adorned his notebooks with sketches, done from memory, of unusual types he had encountered, handsome or hideous— heads as delicately proportioned as the finest Greek sculptures, faces as repulsive as Savonarola and "The Ugly Duchess"; he invited peasants to his house, entertained them with stories, marked their peculiarities, and threw them into fits of laughter by caricaturing their queer faces.

At the age of seventeen, if we are to judge by the angel and the landscape which he painted in Verrocchio's *Baptism,* Leonardo was a remarkably mature artist commanding a style of his own. With such a beginning, most painters would have rushed into a fervent career of profitable commissions and popular acclaim. Not so Leonardo. The modelling of forms by the subtle flow of light into dark; the scientific analysis of atmospheric effects; the psychology of emotions and the relation of gestures and facial expressions to the deepest feelings: such things possessed him, and hundreds of others. He was indifferent to the hero-worshipping of a populace which boasted so loudly and understood so little. And, as I have said, he would not be hurried. We need not vex ourselves over the pictures done in collaboration with his master: the quarreling micrologists will never agree upon these joint products. Of more importance are his innumerable drawings. In his *Treatise on Painting,* he places the graphic arts at the top of all forms of expression, arguing, among other things, that the visual image is much more explicit and convincing than any image evoked by words. Accordingly, when he describes a machine, engages to prove a theory, or record an observation, he supplements his text with drawings. There are literally thousands of these sketches, some purely expository, others elaborate studies for paintings or memories of scenes and figures. It would be difficult to exaggerate the radiant animation of Leonardo's work in black and white, but let us not fall into the error frequently committed by cranks and connoisseurs and set his drawings above his finished pictures. All drawings, in a certain small sense, are more satisfactory than paintings for the reason that they fulfil more perfectly a specific purpose. But how much more limited the purpose! Artists know this, if the critics do not. A drawing is essentially a framework, a study in structure. In most cases it is simply a preliminary sketch. Even the etching, a work complete in itself, is a pale thing of slight, suggestive charm when compared to a painting with its full-bodied splendor of color and mass.

Corot called Leonardo "the father of modern landscape." In a drawing dating from his twenty-first year, the first work entirely by his own hand to come down to us, we have the earliest independent landscape in western art. It was, however, probably intended for a background. Despite his universal interests, his major concern, as a painter, was with the figure. The sketch is remarkable for its dramatic distribution of lights and darks, the beginnings of *chiaroscuro,* a technical method practically invented by Leonardo and destined to exert a tremendous influence on painting, for good and ill. He employed this method to accentuate modelling, that is, to give his forms greater bulk and relief. The richest effects in *chiaroscuro* are, of course, to be had in paint, but he obtains in black-and-white, by the simplest means imaginable, results almost equally astonishing. He has a series of madonna studies—a fine Florentine mother holding in her lap a child who is playing with a cat—which fairly glow with life. It is impossible to analyze the incomparable vitality of these diminutive sketches.

We may say that his elastic outlines swell and recede with a wavy motion, that his knowledge of anatomy and muscular action enabled him to twist the figure into positions of exquisite movement, that, with his subtle power over light and shade, "he had only to stroke the surface with parallel hatchings in order to bring out relief, and to give an inestimable homogeneity of effect to his sheets." Such comments are true but largely technical, and they do not explain—nor can it be explained—how his figures reflect his own ideas, and how he caught and clarified within the mesh of a few lines, certain smiles and movements and attitudes which reveal the workings of the spirit.

In Florence, when important malefactors had been apprehended and hanged, the magistrates appointed a prominent artist to paint the portraits of the rascals, head downward, on the walls of the town-hall, an excellent custom, and one which, I think, might be advantageously revived in modern America. It would probably have no deterrent effect upon crime, but it would be a great boon to art. Every city would have an annual exhibition of genuine social significance, and Washington would be the center of American art! After the infamous Pazzi conspiracy to extinguish the Medici, eighty criminals were lynched and thrown down to a rejoicing mob, and Botticelli was honored with the job of painting the leaders. The chief man of blood, Bandino, escaped to the East, was extradited by the Turks, and five days after he arrived at Florence was swinging from a rope. On a cold day in December, Leonardo, aged twenty-seven, notebook in hand, viewed the spectacle at close range and calmly sketched the victim, emphasizing the peculiar spinal stiffness and gaping terror of one whose neck had been suddenly broken, and jotting down for reasons known only to himself the various details and colors of Bandino's last costume. Another opportunity to observe the behavior of man under unusual circumstances. But he did not share the common hunger of the Florentines for slaughter; he believed that fighting and killing were senseless and uncivilized. Towards the end of his life he became a vegetarian.

About a year later he began his first great painting. The work was ordered by the monks of San Donato; the subject was the *Adoration of the Magi*, and he agreed to finish it in thirty months for a sum equivalent to $3000. The picture was never finished. It never, in fact, got beyond the greenish-red monochrome of the under-painting, and it remains a colossal sketch of the greatest complexity. Apart from its position in the development of Renaissance art, the chief claim of the *Adoration* on modern interest lies in its constructive transformations. It shows us that a work of art is never preconceived, that it begins simply, grows resolutely, and suffers endless alterations. The subject was dear to Leonardo's heart. Long before he accepted the commission he had experimented with it. He made drawings for the principal characters —dozens of them, nude and draped; he plotted out a marvellous perspective graph; three times he elaborated the idea into a tentative composition and as many times was dissatisfied; finally, he found, by trial and error, what he wanted and the actual painting was begun. But his newly discovered *chiaro-*

*scuro* defeated him. Determined to achieve the maximum of relief—the very perfection of modelling—by the use of strong lights and shadows gradually deepening into the densest blacks, he worked the picture into so low a key that he could no longer control it. Whereupon the monks lost patience and appealed to that handy manufacturer, Filippino Lippi, who, in short order, gave them exactly what their tastes required, a pretty thing of small artistic merit.

Leonardo abandoned the project with few regrets. The fundamental brain-work was done, the problem solved. Design, he said, was for the master, execution for servants. He had completely severed painting from ecclesiastical authority; to his own satisfaction he had proved that a multiplicity of forms could be put together with geometrical clarity. From the studies, Michael Angelo derived his idea for his slaves; Raphael imitated the central figures, the Madonna and Child; before the design modern artists stare and gasp. There is nothing to be gained by considering the work as a philosophical criticism of Christianity. I do not believe Leonardo intended anything of the kind: the painting must be regarded as an experiment. Notwithstanding the sweeping movement, the intense characterizations and significant gestures, and the flowing unity, it is, as a subject picture, unconvincing: the entire background —the galloping horsemen, the architectural ruins, and the broken landscape— though structurally related to, is emotionally isolated from, the rest of the drama. More convincing is the *Virgin of the Rocks*, the Louvre version, painted a year or so afterward. Here again he departed from the conventional treatment and stationed an enchanting and youthful Florentine woman, an angel, and two naked children in a grotto reminiscent of the caves of the Arno which fascinated him in his geological studies. But the idea is devoid of all incongruity. Science and observation and sentiment are perfectly fused; the design is flawless; the faces are refined to the last degree—carried further by Raphael, the type becomes, not more spiritual but vacuous, and with Luini, sickening; and the flesh painting has never been equalled—the children seem to have been fashioned in heaven by a creator who was a plastic artist.

Leonardo did not thrive at Florence and in his thirtieth year entered the service of the Duke of Milan. The occasion of his departure for the North is unknown. It seems that he made a certain musical instrument, a lute of silver in the shape of a horse's skull, and that Lorenzo de' Medici, greatly pleased with the invention, despatched him to Milan to play before the Duke for whom music had especial charms. At all events, he was only too glad to leave Florence, and aware of the wealth of Milan and the prodigality of the unlawful Duke, wrote a letter to his Excellency enumerating the various capacities in which he might be useful—if attached to the court. The letter is one of the most amazing documents on record. Coming from any one else, we might dismiss it as egregious bounce; in reality it is an application for employment from a man whose vast powers had never received more than passing consideration. In part Leonardo wrote:

"I have a method of constructing very light and portable bridges, to be used in pursuit of, or in retreat from, the enemy, with others of a stronger sort, proof against fire, and easy to fix or remove.

"For the service of sieges, I am prepared to remove the water from the ditches, and to make an infinite variety of scaling-ladders and other engines proper to such purposes.

"I have also most convenient and portable bombs, proper for throwing showers of small missiles, and with the smoke thereof causing great terror to the enemy.

"By means of excavations made without noise, and forming tortuous and narrow ways, I have means of reaching any given point, even though it be necessary to pass beneath rivers.

"I can also construct covered wagons, secure and indestructible, which, entering among the enemy, will break the strongest bodies of men; and behind these the infantry can follow in safety and without impediment.

"I can make mortars and field-pieces of beautiful and useful shape, entirely different from those in common use.

"For naval conflicts, I have methods for making numerous instruments, offensive and defensive . . . and I can also make powders or vapors for the offense of the enemy.

"In time of peace, I believe that I could equal any other as regards works in architecture. I can prepare designs for buildings, whether public or private, and also conduct water from one place to another.

"Furthermore, I can execute works in sculpture, marble, bronze, or terra-cotta. In painting also I can do what may be done, as well as any other, whosoever he may be.

"I can likewise undertake the execution of the bronze horse which is a monument that will be to the perpetual glory of my lord your father of happy memory, and of the illustrious house of Sforza.

"And if any of the above-named things shall seem to any man impossible or impracticable, I am perfectly ready to make trial of them in whatever place you shall be pleased to command, commending myself to you with all possible humility."

The Duke did not hesitate, and Leonardo was engaged forthwith as general constructionist and court utilitarian; and remembering that he remained with his Excellency for sixteen years, we may conclude that he made good his claims. The records of his life at Milan are confused and sparse, and in our ignorance we must be content with a few details. Besides a substantial salary, his position carried with it a house and vineyard and numerous perquisites. He lived unostentatiously with his pupils and apprentices, avoiding the princely splendor of Raphael and the squalid loneliness of Michelangelo, kept strict accounts and saved a little money. "It is only those who have too much who cannot bear vicissitudes and losses," he said. He painted the Duke's mistresses, designed costumes, organized festivals and supervised weddings—

in a word, supplied the court with an artistic background. Whether these minor exactions bored Leonardo we do not know. Probably not. He had what most Florentine artists lacked—the ability to play and to enjoy life. Also, he looked upon his ceremonial duties as the price paid for his freedom. He had an assured living; was free to come and go as he pleased; and his obligations to the Duke did not interrupt his scientific studies. In a more serious vein, he assisted in the completion of the Cathedral, acted as hydraulic engineer, built canals with wonderfully improved locks, drained marshes, and invented the machine gun and breech-loading cannon. His intellectual activities at Milan fall into three divisions: the equestrian statue; the notebooks; and *The Last Supper*.

The Duke, Ludovico Sforza, known as Il Moro because of his swarthy skin, desired to honor the memory of his father with a bronze monument and gave out that "there was only one man capable of the task, Leonardo, the Florentine; he alone was equal to it—and even he might not be able to finish it, inasmuch as it was the work of a lifetime." Leonardo entered into the plan with characteristic thoroughness, having in mind a horse that would throw the monuments of Donatello and Verrocchio into the shade and indeed surpass the efforts of the Greeks. He knew more about the subject than any man of his time—had he not outlined a book on the anatomy of the horse? For six years he fought with the idea of a horse in violent action—something unheard of in sculpture—making countless designs and studies of animal movement, then abandoning the scheme as too pictorial. At length he fixed upon a more restrained attitude, and at the end of ten more years of intermittent labor, constructed a clay model twenty-six feet high, devising a new kind of armature to support the beast. It must have been a stupendous sight—but alas, it was never cast! He needed eighty tons of bronze for the horse alone—and the ducal exchequer was empty. Shortly afterward the French invaded Milan, Il Moro was captured, and the model was used as a target by Gascon bowmen. Soon it crumbled into the earth again—one of the greatest tragedies in art. Some years later, in Florence, Leonardo was arguing a passage from Dante with a friend when Michelangelo, an authority on the Inferno, happened to pass by. On being asked civilly to expound the quotation, Michelangelo, who envied the composure and freedom of Leonardo, turned upon his rival savagely. "You're the one who made an equestrian model that was never finished—to your eternal shame! You couldn't cast it!" As a parting shot: "And those castrated Milanese believed in your ability to do it!" Leonardo, in his fifties, smiled at the impudence of youth and said nothing.

The notebooks of Leonardo constitute a repository of incalculable scientific research and speculative inquiry. From boyhood it was his habit to record his theories and observations; the habit grew with years, and at the age of thirty-seven, in Milan, he began to revise and collate his papers, and to keep his notes on a more extended scale with a view to complete formulation. But other duties continually interfered; his experiments multiplied; his writings piled up, and he was never able to give them anything like systematic arrangement. As a consequence, we have today, dispersed in European libraries, 5,000 manuscript pages of unclassified reflections set down in reversed, or mirror writing, and embellished with drawings of the highest value. Let us make no mistake about the notebooks. They are not the maunderings of a metaphysician nor the pompous effusions of the professional hemlock-drinker. In method and in terminology, in magnitude and limpidity, they reveal one of the finest brains ever put in a human head, the brain of the artist-scientist, or shall we say, the universal artist? Havelock Ellis, examining these documents from a scientific point of view, credits Leonardo with being the founder of engineering and the study of anatomy and geology, a biologist in every field of mechanism, an hydrographer, geometrician, master of optics, and inventor of innumerable varieties of ballistic machines and ordnance. And these were only a fraction of the man! But unfortunately he did not give many of his discoveries to the world. Possibly he feared the Church and "the timid friends of God," as he called them, his ideas being so greatly at variance from orthodox Christianity, and including the belief that the soul, though divine, does not exist apart from the body. For whatever cause, the manuscripts lay concealed for centuries, and science in the meantime had produced Bacon, Newton, and Watt. In geology he established the laws of petrifaction; he was aware of the circulation of the blood; he invented the military tank, hydrophonic devices for communication among ships, roller bearings, and the wheelbarrow; he described the flight of birds and made drawings of a "bird-man" and of aeroplanes driven by a propeller attached to a spring motor; he worked out every possible type of domed architecture and designed a cupola for St. Peter's sixty years before Michelangelo; he planned hygienic cities with underground avenues flushed by canals, and houses limited in height to the width of the streets, complaining that "people should not be packed together like goats and pollute the air for one another"; he had a cure for seasickness—the list is endless.

In all the 5000 pages there is but one reference to women, a certain "Catarina who worked in a hospital—and had a fantastic face"; in the whole life of Leonardo there is no record of a single love affair, or indeed of a distant Platonic friendship. He who dissected the human body, studied its proportions and movements, and made cross sections of embryos, who penetrated the soul of woman and painted madonnas of divine serenity and charm, declared that "intellectual passion drives out sensuality," and that "the act of procreation and everything connected with it is so disgusting that the human race would soon die out if there were no pretty faces and sensual dispositions."

In the section devoted to painting, Leonardo deals with the fundamental values of art, presenting the subject both scientifically and in the universal terms of God and man. He defines painting technically as modelling, "the task of giving corporeal shape of the three dimensions on a flat surface," spiritually as the rendering of emotions, or states of the soul, by means of appropriate postures and movements. He advises the artist to acquaint himself with all phases of life and to subject its details to the severest criticism—to go directly to nature and experience for his materials and not to make pictures out of other pictures. On the other hand, he counsels against imitation, emphasizing repeatedly the necessity for synthesis and organization. "The painter," he points out, "who draws merely by practice and by eye, without any vision, is like a mirror which copies all the objects placed before it, without being conscious of their existence." The treatise contains, besides directions for depicting everything imaginable from draperies to deluges, an intricate and exhaustive analysis of optical phenomena accompanied by illustrations of the most searching and portentous character. It is not too much to say that Leonardo's knowledge of light and atmospheric effects is equal to that of the modern Impressionists, or even superior. He describes at length the division of tones, the color of shadows—particularly the variable blues and violets—and the vivid illumination obtained by the use of complementaries, but he rejects the methods of the Impressionists on the ground that they dissolve form and wreck design. Though he said that "the eye is the window of the soul," he could not think of art as a chromatic formula or the mechanical imitation of visual appearances.

The illustrations to the notebooks afford us beautiful proof of the difference between artistic drawing and photography. Here we have sketches of scientific apparatus, interiors of gun foundries, cannon, hydraulic engines, median sections of the skull, muscles, bones, fossils, leaves, trees, and cloud formations, all of which are a joy to behold. None but Leonardo could have made these drawings. They are separated from the photograph by a gulf as wide as that which separates the poetry of Shelley from the tabulated reports of the New York Stock Exchange. Did he, as a scientist, merely attempt to represent and describe with cold-blooded accuracy the object before him? Obviously not. The artistic impulse, co-existent and predominant, incited him to reconstruct his materials, to add himself to them, to make infinitesimal alterations of contour, to introduce light and shade and subtle variations of natural appearances for the sake of harmony. Thus a dead skull or a cogwheel becomes a living organism—a creature of Leonardo's brain, a dynamic part of the world remade.

With such a brain a man should be capable of anything. But there is, let me explain, an idea that will not down, a superstition widespread, mischievous and nonsensical, that a painter should not have any brains, that he is, when really artistic, a sensitive instrument through which God's will automatically functions, a gilded harp upon which the winds of life play tremulously, plucking out divine melodies. And if, perchance, a painter does possess a brain, the sensitive numskulls who faint before a shapely bosom or a bowl of fruit, snuffle with fear and sigh contemptuously, "He thinks too much!" They cry "He has no feeling, no inspiration! He works by formula!" Now if ever a man were able to paint by formula, surely Leonardo would be the man. But the more he studied, the deeper his wisdom, the sharper his experiences, the more troublesome did the making of pictures become. Each new undertaking implied a new and unique design. Inspiration meant nothing to him except the choice of subject-matter which he could mould to his own ends. In the popular sense, he was not sensitive at all: he was calculating, penetrative, and rational. It took him three years to paint *The Last Supper*.

This masterpiece was finished in the year 1497. It was painted in the damp refectory of Saint Mary of the Graces, at the command of the Duke of Milan, who wished to erect a memorial to his deceased wife in the church that had been her favorite place of worship. The theme was common property and had been conventionalized by many treatments. It had been in Leonardo's mind for years, and long before he received the commission he had made provisional studies for the work. It was a challenge to his highest powers, a stimulus to perfection. The painting immediately lifted him above his contemporaries, and throughout the ages has remained not only the most famous picture in the world but the supreme exemplification of monumental design. Of the grandeur of the undamaged original we can only guess. Leonardo, impatient of fresco, painted in tempera on a ground prepared to resist the clamminess of the wall. The medium was a disastrous choice. The ground began to contract and flake, and within fifty years the picture was covered with spots; deterioration went ahead slowly; dreadful restorations were made by heavy-handed meddlers; some imbecile Dominican monks cut a door through the lower central part; Napoleon's dragoons stabled their horses in the refectory and threw their boots at Judas Iscariot; more restorations and more disfigurements. About twenty years ago an Italian of genius completely removed the unsightly smears laid on by alien retouchers and found a way to prevent further decay. Today *The Last Supper* is in fair conditon. What we see is genuine Leonardo, and it is enough to warrant an appraisal based on the fact itself and not on historical panegyrics or misleading copies. The popularity of the picture may be attributed, in a large measure, to the engraving made by Raphael Morghen in 1800, an engraving that resembles a Sunday School chromo. Morghen copied, not the original, but a drawing executed by a nondescript Florentine, diluted Leonardo's stern conception into pervasive sentimentality, and substituted for the noble figure of Christ, a nice lymphatic gentleman, sleepy and a little sad.

The greatness of a work is not an indeterminate quality. Without reciting the theories propounded in behalf of a pure æsthetic, or talking the language of abstractions, it is possible, I think, to specify one or two things which those who have trained themselves to look at pictures acknowledge to be implicit in a great painting. In the first place, the conception must not be mawkish, sentimental or eccentric. It must be apparent that what the artist has to say is worthy of his best efforts. He must show us that he has good reason for the selection of his theme, that he knows vastly more about it than we do, and he must illuminate it with the sympathy born of closest intimacy and the gusto that comes from exceptional wisdom. If the idea is old—and what idea is not?—he must bring to it new evaluations and fresh considerations. Second, the purpose must be transcendently certain and definite. The artist must express his meaning with clarity and power, throwing aside all needless accessories, disturbing flourishes, and exhibitions of virtuosity. What we experience vaguely and with mixed emotions he must present with singleness and undivided emphasis. Third, the picture must give us something to think about; it must have many avenues of interest, many sources of appeal. Avoiding merely physical seductiveness, it must ask for the cooperation of our noblest faculties, emancipating our emotions and stimulating us to feel and live deeply and liberally. In short, it must act upon the spirit and lift us out of our daily round of mean preoccupations into a realm of purging tragedy, exhilarating joy, profound human pity, dramatic power.

Does *The Last Supper* fulfil these requirements? We may say that it does, without question and without reserve. The picture is too well known to call for description. The subject was consummately suited to test his theory that in painting the "facial expressions must vary according to the emotional state of the person, and that the attitudes of the figures must correspond to the emotions reflected in the faces." He prepared his studies with extraordinary care, giving minute attention to detailed characterizations—to hands, beards, and costumes—roving the Ghetto for a model to serve as Judas, and experimenting with the design. He has left us, in his notebooks, an eloquent account of the psychological action which he regarded as the mainspring of the drama. At first he adhered to the conventional arrangement, with St. John asleep by the side of Christ, and Judas by himself in the foreground, but the actual work of construction changed his plans. At last, with a stroke of genius, he found the one and only way to tell the story. Christ sits in the middle of the table with the apostles in groups of three on either side: He has said, "One among you shall betray me." The utterance is a proclamation of tragedy, and to reveal the tragedy, Leonardo portrays the effects of the word as it pierces the souls of the twelve men. Everything in the picture conspires to this end: the lighting; the architecture; the bare walls stripped of distracting ornament and converging to carry us directly into the scene; the perspective plan; the heads, gestures and faces. Never was a painting so perfectly put together. Structurally, all the lines focus in the right eye of Christ, the movement beginning slowly in the distant figures and increasing in agitation as it approaches the center; emotionally, the prophetic word of the Lord reverberates among the two groups of His followers, provoking horror, consternation and curiosity, and binding the groups together by the force of spiritual tension.

It is an undeniable fact that every one comes to a picture of *The Last Supper* in a peculiarly receptive mood, with a mind preattuned to the tragic situation and eager to participate in the religious sentiment. Hence the subject, if only tolerably presented, is more moving and impressive to the average person than the magnificent mythological compositions of Rubens, which as illustrations have lost their significance. Theoretically one art should not be dependent upon another; it should express itself fully in its own language.

Painting should be self-revealing and not rely upon literature to complete its meaning. Acting on this premise, certain critics advocate a "pure approach" to art, that is to say, they tell us, in all seriousness, that when they look at a picture they judge it as the only thing of its kind in existence, suppressing all associatory elements, and responding like infants with eyes and souls but no experiences, to the emotional appeal of lines, colors and volumes. Perhaps they are able to behave in this fashion when looking at the utterly negative and empty nudes and still-lifes—pictures done by artists who seem to have no connection with life whatever—comprising most exhibitions, but when confronted with Leonardo's *The Last Supper* they cannot overlook the sub-ject-matter. Despite their anæsthetic theories, something irritatingly human and eternally sad gets under their skins. So they say, "It is not art. It is exaggerated illustration."

I mention these unpleasant matters only to remind the reader that all art partakes of illustration. The moment an artist contrives a unit of form, a fig-ure, let us say, he makes a representation clothed with habitual associations and memories from which the beholder cannot remove himself by an act of will. Leonardo did not consider it vulgar to tell a story in paint. Nor did he imagine that to create a spiritual type one had merely to represent an effemi-nate figure with the traditional blond beard and label it Christ. *The Last Supper* is illustration in that it brings before us with convincing reality a situa-tion first described in the medium of words. But we cannot say that it is the counterpart of the Biblical story. It is Leonardo's *The Last Supper*, a part of his mind, containing his science, his understanding, and his preferences. It is more than illustration: on one side of a table large enough to accommodate only six or seven guests he has placed thirteen figures, but we are not conscious of any crowding; the disciples are Italians, and no one seems to notice that they have no legs; his Christ is beardless; there is, in truth, nothing oriental in the conception. The psychological import is conveyed with such absolute precision and dramatic force that the meaning of the picture would not, I think, be lost on any one ignorant of the Christian legend. Into these excited and gesticulating apostles Leonardo has infused his immense fund of human experiences; he has indeed so thoroughly filled his characters with their appro-priate emotions that they become, not Italians posing as vehement Jews, but living symbols of grief, terror, bewilderment, and woe. And the Christ has the grandeur, the imperturbable grace and tranquillity characteristic of Leonardo himself in his noblest moods.

I have watched painters go into ecstasies over this picture—over the plastic form, the marvellous composition, the distribution of the figures, apparently so simply ordered yet, on analysis, so complexly balanced and inextricably united; the rushing, involute rhythms, the expressive hands,—and I have won-dered what Leonardo would have done, had he wished to represent, not a group of men bound together by a community of tragic purpose, but merely an assemblage of plastic forms. He would, I fancy, have produced something analogous to those compositions of Picasso, so astonishing and yet so meaningless; for Picasso is a man who has tried to learn the secrets of art from other art and not from life. It was the subject that released Leonardo's creative activity and inspired him to incorporate a great idea into a great design. And I have also fancied, in moments when I permit myself a little indulgence in the more esoteric meanings of art, that Leonardo, having finished *The Last Supper*, must have surveyed the work with a smile of satisfaction, seeing that he had represented once and for all time how men of ordinary clay are appalled by the presence of supreme intelligence.

The following year the French crossed the Alps and captured the swarthy tyrant of Milan. Leonardo noted the event succinctly. "This day the Duke lost his state, his possessions and his liberty—and none of his works is completed." By unfinished works he probably meant "the horse" and certain enterprises in engineering, and with the hope of carrying them out under the new regime, he tarried a while in the North. It is told that on being entreated to make something extraordinary for the reception of the foreign monarch, he constructed a mechanical toy in the shape of a golden lion which, after advancing a few steps, opened its huge jaws, and disgorged a bundle of lilies. We next hear of him in Venice where he invented a diving-bell and swimming-belt, and at the opening of the new century he is in Florence again, deep in geometry and anatomy, and painting little. As field engineer for Cesare Borgia, he explored central Italy from coast to coast and proved himself a cartographer of immense skill. These maps are still useful, showing mountains, roads, rivers and towns that have changed but slightly since the sixteenth century—all accurate in configuration and drawn in relief with as much care as he bestowed upon his madonnas. The political manoeuvres of the Borgias did not concern him, and after Cesare's collapse, he returned to Florence and prepared for one of the monasteries a cartoon of the *Virgin and St. Anne*, a study which caused great commotion in the greedy city, reviving for a moment the ancient custom of celebrating the appearance of a new masterpiece with processions and ecclesiastical extravagance. At the same date he made his only venture in mythology, a drawing of *Leda and the Swan*. More than likely he painted the subject as well, for there are half a dozen Ledas in the European galleries, all springing from a common ancestor and imitative of Leonardo's style.

Finally it occurred to one of the burghers to remind his fellow citizens that Leonardo was beginning to look like an old man, that he was much given to wandering, and that if the people desired to wring from him something to the eternal lustre of the commonwealth, they had best lay hands on him while he was residing among them. It was therefore decreed that the Grand Council chamber, speedily completed after the expulsion of the Medici, should be decorated with martial scenes witnessing the power of Florentine arms, one wall being entrusted to Leonardo da Vinci, and the other to Michelangelo, a young man of unlimited promise. With her usual malice and to humiliate an errant son, the city imposed on Leonardo the Battle of Anghiari, an encounter in which the Milanese were conquered by the warriors of Florence. But war to him was an exhibition of energy and he had no faith in patriotic motives. He chose a cavalry episode, a number of horsemen fighting for a lost standard, intending to paint the personification of bestial frenzy—the diametrical opposite of *The Last Supper*. The cartoon raised a tumult of applause. Such cyclonic fury, such concentrated energy and rhythm had never before been even suggested in art. But the painting itself came to grief. Leonardo, always trying new things, used an encaustic medium and the colors, instead of fusing with the plaster under the action of heat, ran down the wall. The picture was ruined. Nothing that relates to it has survived except some wonderful drawings and two or three copies of part of the design, one by Rubens. Leonardo abandoned the work without more ado, and the Florentine council, naturally, was plunged in gloom. The artist, however, does not appear to have been troubled by the catastrophe: he was interested in Mona Lisa.

The *Mona Lisa* shines out among the portraits of the world like a star. Though time has appreciably impaired the color of the picture, the glory of it increases with the passing years. The canvas hangs in the Louvre, a veritable shrine attracting pilgrims from every land, all of whom gaze upon it with a liquid reverence not accorded to any of the more essentially sacred pieces in that gigantic morgue. Fable and gossip have made the famous lady a strange and uncanny charmer, a sphinx whose smile entrapped the soul of a great artist and impelled him, bit by bit, to build up an image of unfathomable mystery. The image lives on, but the legend also endures—and the soul of the artist is buried in the mystery of a woman's smile!

The story is that in the year 1502, Leonardo looked upon Mona Lisa, the third wife of Francesco del Giocondo, and found her fascinating, for she was, according to contemporary opinion, "exceedingly beautiful," and he was by no means insensitive to feminine charms. She was young and her husband was old and impotent and unkind. He had pawned her jewels and forced her to put on mourning so that the absence of personal ornaments might not be suspected. When Leonardo desired to paint her portrait, she assented eagerly, cast a spell upon him, and became his mistress. She had lost her only daughter and was chronically sad, and it is told that he hired an orchestra to lighten her melancholy and jesters to make her smile. And it was the smile that held him in her toils and called up the secrets of his soul.

The legend is damaged by several inconsistencies. Leonardo was not a youth at this time: he was in his fifties and fearfully venerable, appearing indeed in a portrait sketch made three years later, an octogenarian. He worked on the picture for four years, but not merely to preserve the features of a striking woman—likenesses came easy to him and he had no use for them as such. Nor was much of the period devoted to Mona Lisa. Florentine artists did not paint directly from models but from black and white studies. Furthermore, we know that Mona Lisa posed for the head alone—the torso and hands were drawn from other sitters, a fact which may account for the rather stiff joining of the neck and shoulders—and that Leonardo, the most painstaking of painters, in solitude, undisturbed by music and a beautiful woman, slowly created a figure of imperishable vitality. Whatever he may have thought of the sitter, he prized the picture more, as an artist should, keeping it in his possession to the end of his days. All things considered, it would seem that his interest in the model was neither protracted nor sentimental, and that he found in nature a face which helped him to realize in paint an ideal type towards which he had constantly moved from his earliest efforts. His concessions to portraiture only served to enhance this ideal: Mona Lisa was a lady and he gave her the sensitive hands of an aristocrat; he observed the mourner's costume but turned it into living drapery; the high forehead and the plucked eyebrows, current marks of distinction, facilitated the modelling of the features. But Mona Lisa, the woman, the mistress, the Neapolitan, has vanished from the picture forever. It may fairly be questioned whether the work is a portrait at all, that is, as we understand the term today. Certainly the head resembles all the other heads that he painted, male or female, and might be substituted for any one of his madonnas. Mona Lisa is the sister to his other forms, only more exquisitely embodied.

She is purely a devotional creation, devotional in the largest sense; the incarnation of Leonardo's love for life, and women, and all perfect forms, the nexus between the world of memories, experiments and disappointments, and the flawlessly appointed world of his imagination. Into this picture he has projected all of himself and all his arts—his subtlety, his elaborate and dazzling refinement; his scientific perfection, his psychological penetration, his puzzling serenity, his infallible knowledge of structure. In comparison most of the paintings of the world seem flat and lifeless. Like it you may not, but you cannot escape its reality. It stops you and holds you with confounding directness. Many other canvases are perhaps corporeally as substantial and convincing; other figures are even more truthful representations of flesh and blood, but this, you feel, is more than flesh and blood. The face is that of a more sentient being, a more highly organized intelligence. You are not conscious of paint, of color, or of canvas. Lifeless material has been shaped into a human face, and the face, as Leonardo said and intended, becomes "the mirror of the soul." Your spirit is somehow touched by another spirit, and for a moment you may be repelled—repelled by a figure that is made in the form of a human being and yet made without weaknesses or imperfections. To apprehend the *Mona Lisa*, you must remain with the picture, see it again and again, for it contains, like all works of art, the history of its creator, and you cannot, at a single glance, enter into the mind of Leonardo da Vinci.

The figure is a solid and as permanently established as the rocks behind it, yet plastic, and free to bend and breathe and move, and brought into fullest relief by the purposely strange background of dwindling rivers and shadowy peaks; the landscape, wrought out with as much affection as the face of the woman, is a living thing; the smile is achieved by imperceptible variations in the lines of the eyes and mouth—so delicately modelled, in fact, that it is lost in coarsely screened reproductions. The smile is not peculiar to Mona Lisa; it was not original with Leonardo. It is written in the faces of the archaic goddesses of Greece; we find it in the sculptures of his master, Verrocchio, and in other paintings of the time. If Leonardo was prepossessed with it, then so is every artist with certain expressions and attitudes. Why he so loved the smile we cannot say, but we do know that by means of it he made his faces conclusively real and emblematic of the deepest emotional states. The mystery of the *Mona Lisa* arises from the romantic gossip attaching to the model and to repeated misconceptions of the artist's purpose. The emotional life of art is, in the final analysis, like all life, insoluble. We can no more explain it than we can explain a tree or a woman or any organic thing, and when we attempt to do so, we are driven into dreams and mysteries. Leonardo's aim was to dispel mysteries, not to create them. His purpose was to create a form which should be neither vague nor enigmatical—not a stimulus to reveries, but actually and in all its parts, an articulate and convincing expression of the spirit. He succeeded, and that, I think, is enough.

His business with the city of Florence having ended in monumental disaster, Leonardo departed for Milan again, taking the *Mona Lisa* along with him. The Republic granted him a leave of absence, but with an ill grace, strongly bent on forcing him to attend to the unfortunate battle picture. He never returned. From time to time he received angry protests and sarcastic communications from the Florentine magistrates reminding him that he had made "only a little beginning on a great work," but these he calmly disregarded. In the employ of the French viceroy, he superintended the building of canals and other public utilities, and prepared designs for an equestrian statue. His second venture in heroic sculpture, like his first, was never to be cast. His painting was limited to two pictures, both religious, both of the highest importance. One, the London version of the *Madonna of the Rocks*, was executed with the help of a colleague to appease an unforgetting group of Franciscans who compelled him by legal action to live up to a contract made twenty years before; the other, *St. Anne with the Virgin and the Infant Christ*, now in the Louvre, though faded and unfinished, is a marvellous reconstruction of an old subject. Disregarding the inflexible arrangements of his predecessors, he poured into a recalcitrant theme all his wisdom and all his skill, and developed a group of human forms which, for expressive power, plastic richness, and intricacy of design, cannot be too lavishly extolled. It was his last great picture. The French were expelled from Milan, and he travelled to Rome to work for the Pope.

His visit to Rome was a mistake. Leo X, sleek and superficial, was busy exploiting Raphael's fresco factory, and could not understand a man of Leonardo's leisurely habits and interminable ponderings. At the end of two unprofitable years he journeyed to France, invited thither by Francis I, one of his warmest admirers. Comfortably lodged in a chateau in Touraine, exempt from creative toil, he was eminently at peace with the world. His hands were paralyzed and he could not paint, but nothing could interrupt his speculations, his desire to discover the connection between all things so that he might create spontaneously, like God himself. One day he wrote in his notebook, "When I thought I had been learning how to live, I had only been learning how to die." In his will he commended his soul "to our Lord Almighty God and to the glorious Virgin Mary, to all the blessed Angels and Saints, male and female, in Paradise." He died on the first of May, 1519, in his sixty-seventh year.

## THE MUSIC LOVER

(*From* Toscanini and Great Music)

### *Lawrence Gilman* (*1938*)

WHAT is it that Toscanini chiefly means to those who cherish and revere him?

He is first of all and obviously, of course, a genius, and a consummate craftsman. But there are many geniuses, many consummate craftsmen. When you have the craftsman of genius plus the fanatically pure of heart, the dedicated celebrant, you have the phenomenon that is Toscanini.

It was a modern artist of exquisite authenticity and profound discernment, the late Katherine Mansfield, who observed that "one reason for the poverty of art today is that artists have no religion. . . . For artists," she added, "are priests after all." With few exceptions, the greatest creative artists, at least in music, have been religious—not in the narrow and doctrinal sense of the word, but in its free and ultimate and sublimating sense. Today, is it not rather the great interpreters who are religious in that unconfined and ultimate and dedicatory sense—is it not to them that the custody of the Grail has passed? Is it not they, the few who are truly consecrated and elect, the priests and guardians of immortal beauty, who are filled with that mystical power of creative faith which can turn an act of service into a miracle of resurrection?

Who of us can forget the fathomless serenity, the rapt loveliness of mood and pace and accent, that Toscanini draws from the slow movement of the Ninth Symphony? Or the epic mourning of the Dirge from *Götterdämmerung?* Or the magically recovered innocence of the *Pastoral* Symphony? Or the startling glory of the music of the resurrection in the *Missa Solemnis?* Hearing such feats of realization, one knows what it means when an artist of piercing and creative vision sets himself to this task of imaginative identification and fulfillment: when the interpreter becomes merged with that which is interpreted. We seem to be listening for the first time to the essential reality that lies behind the music, so that we find ourselves saying, in amazement: "This *is* the dreamer rapt and transfigured; this *is* the mourning voice of heroes; this *is* the wisdom of the hills and of sunlight and quiet valleys and free winds; this *is* the glory of the risen dead gathered up to Paradise."

.        .        .        .        .        .

One cannot say that such things are the issue of genius alone: for many of those artists who transmit music eloquently to the listener have indisputable genius, yet lack that mysterious quality which makes a Toscanini what he is. Perhaps it has nothing essentially to do with genius—though the rare interpreter cannot, of course, dispense with genius, any more than the inspired prophet can dispense with speech, though it is not in speech that his prophetic power lies.

Given, then, the interpreter of genius, what is it that must be added in order to set him among those transcendent and lonely artists who appear but once or twice in a generation, and whom we recognize at once as chosen and apart? Is it aesthetic integrity? Or humility? Or selflessness? Or completeness of dedication? Or intensity of belief? Or faith? Or is it a kind of love— a love so incandescent and transforming that the one possessed of it reminds us of that luminous, enraptured being of whom Dante speaks as "enamored, so that he seems made of fire"?

Perhaps it is no one of these qualities, but all of them, that must be added to the artist of genius before he is fit to stand with the elect; for the sum of them is unqualified devotion, a kind of worship; and that, it may be, gives us a hint of the truth. We shall find, I think, that the supreme interpreter is not commanding music: instead, it is commanding him—filling him with a divine humility, a divine ecstasy of revelation, a divine excess of love.

Of all the musicians one has observed and studied as interpretative artists, there has been none who loved music with the undivided intensity that is characteristic of Toscanini. As Shelley, one might say, is the perfect type of the poet, the poet *in excelsis*, so Toscanini is the music lover *in excelsis*.

Toscanini has many qualities as an interpreting musician. But the one that integrates them all is a passion for music so imperious and ungovernable that it will not let him rest until he has shared with us, through the medium of the instruments that he commands and inspires, his image of the ideal beauty that possesses him.

A scholastic philosopher of an earlier century said that the influence of inspired men is to be explained in four ways. First, he said, because they have an undistorted vision of reality. Second, because they are receptacles of light. Third, because they know, and make us know, that the reality which they perceive is identical with beauty. Fourth, because they are distinguished by what he called "an excess of love," which is "an inextinguishable radiance, illuminating others."

I think that this describes all men, all artists, who are vehicles of what we call, for want of a better name, inspiration. Their perception is undistorted; they receive illumination; they see beauty as the supreme reality of the spirit; and their love of it is boundless, irradiating, and creative.

．　　．　　．　　．　　．

That supreme quality of love belongs to the great re-creative artists. Yet it is shared in humbler measure by all those of us for whom music is indispensable. I have sometimes wondered what proportion of those whom we call music lovers would come within this classification. Are they relatively few, or relatively many, those to whom music is indispensable?

For many persons, music is only an amenity, something to which one resorts after the crossword puzzle has been solved and other diversions are exhausted. That is one way of enjoying music. There is another way, which one might illustrate by quoting the apocryphal remarks of Lucullus to Caesar on the subject of music, as they are found in Landor's brilliant collection of character studies called *Imaginary Conversations*.

This is Lucullus speaking:

"I listen to music willingly at all times, but most willingly while I am reading. At such times, a voice or even a whisper disturbs me: but music refreshes my brain when I have read long. I find also that if I write poetry, listening to music gives rapidity and variety and brightness to my ideas. Sometimes, I command a fresh instrument or another voice; which is to the mind like a change of posture or of air to the body. My health is benefited by the gentle play of sounds thus opened to the most delicate of the fibres."

．　　．　　．　　．　　．

Well, that way of listening to music has its merit, and no one need say a word against it. But it is a way that implies the use of music as a means, as an aid to something else—an aid to thinking, or daydreaming, or relaxing, or recuperating. It is not the way of the music lover. It is not the way of those who are possessed by music, either as listeners or as interpreters. For them, music is something imperious and tyrannical—not soothing, not refreshing, not diverting; but often exhausting and almost unendurable, as terrible as flame or revelation. But always it possesses.

We sometimes say of a friend or an acquaintance, "He is passionately fond of music." Is he? The pertinent question has been asked, "What will he do for it? Will he forego leisure, forget to eat, face poverty? Will the blood leave his face as he listens to the Third *Leonore* Overture or the Finale of Schubert's C major Symphony?" That is a fair question and a searching one.

In Karel Capek's inimitable book, *The Gardener's Year*, one may read about the kind of lover that I have in mind: one for whom the thing he loves is despotic and possessing—though the object of Capek's love is not music, but a garden.

"I will tell you," writes Capek, "how to recognize a true gardener."

" 'You must come to see me,' he says: 'I will show you my garden.' Then, when you go (just to please him), you will find him busy somewhere among the perennials. 'I will come in a moment,' he shouts to you, over his shoulder. 'Just wait till I have planted this rose.'

" 'Please don't worry,' you say kindly to him.

"After a while he must have planted it; for he gets up, shakes your hand, and covers it with damp earth. Then, beaming with hospitality, he says: 'Come and have a look: It's a small garden, but—wait a moment!' and he bends over a bed to weed some tiny grass. 'Come along. I will show you my Dianthus Musalae—it will open your eyes. . . . Great Scott! I forgot to loosen it here!' he says, and begins to poke in the soil, forgetting you entirely.

"A quarter of an hour later he straightens up again. 'Ah!' he says, 'I wanted to show you that bellflower, Campanula Wilsonae. That is the best campanula which—Wait a moment; I must tie up this delphinium.'

"After he has tied it up, he remembers: 'Oh, I see, you have come to look at that erodium. Just a moment!' he murmurs. 'I must transplant this aster; it hasn't enough room here!'

"After that, you go away on tiptoe, leaving him absorbed among the perennials.

"When you meet him again, he will say: 'You must come to see me; I have one rose in flower, a pernetiana; you have not seen that before. Will you come? Do!'

"Very well; you will go and see him again as the year passes by, when you have plenty of time. Meanwhile, you depart, leaving the gardener to his inexhaustible desires."

.　　.　　.　　.　　.　　.　　.

That is Capek's picture of his equivalent of the music lover, the insatiable gardener. It helps us, I think, to recognize that cultivator of spiritual soils and seeds to whom music is indispensable. We shall know what music means in his life by the degree to which it possesses him. The test is as simple and as certain as that. We shall find that the music lover is not commanding music, after the manner of Lucullus, for his benefit and ease. Instead, music is commanding him, wreaking itself upon him, and—if he be one of the elect among its ministers—filling him with an impassioned humility and devoutness, a consuming ecstasy of revelation, a divine excess of love. If he be artist and music lover at once, we shall recognize that he must perforce achieve his act of re-creation in his own image; and we can but repeat the wondering words of Dante as he saw in Beatrice's eyes the changing image of the Truth unchanged:

> ". . . within myself I marvelled,
> When I beheld the thing itself stand still,
> And in its image it transformed itself."

We shall realize that the artist, this music lover *in excelsis*, is continually refreshed with the waters of that living fountain of Dante's Everlasting Garden; and that he has become, like every human instrument of a beauty passionately understood, part of that radiant energy "which moves the sun and the other stars."

. . . . .

Toscanini is that kind of music lover. Music is unspeakably dear to him, a wonderful and sacred thing; and by some mysterious and inexplicable power of communication he makes it so for those of us who also love and cherish it.

A poet has told us that the truth and rapture of man are holy things, not lightly to be scorned, Toscanini is constantly reminding us that this holiness of the truth and rapture of man exists in the memorials of created art. His sense of the inviolability of great music, the priestly quality of his attitude toward its revelation, will always remain, for those who have been aware of them, among the major validations of one's occasionally wavering belief that man is worthy of the stewardship of everlasting things.

"The Golden Age has not its name from those who lived in it," remarked Dr. Burney somewhat caustically many years ago. There are several things less likely than that musical historians of the future will give that name to the age in which Toscanini once wrought his miracles of transubstantiating beauty, in the presence of awed believers who can no longer tell of them only because they have fallen silent among the forgotten, happy dead.

Now and again, unpredictably, in the course of the generations, an artist such as this appears—some rare and luminous apparition emerges out of time and space, burns for a while with valor and swift flame among the chaos and the murk, and finally departs, leaving untarnishable memories. Those moments are of inestimable price, for it is then that the content of life seems fullest and most rich—as when we meet "the friend of friends," or pause suddenly, face to face with beauty, and know that life, for all its frustration and its treachery, is full of wonder, beneficence, and grace.

## LORD OF MARUTEA

### THE DIRECTOR'S STORY

#### *James Norman Hall* (*1933*)

### I

BEFORE the war there were a number of Germans scattered among the islands of French Polynesia. Afterward they were gathered in and sent back to Germany, and their property confiscated. Herr Müller was an exception; he was left on Marutea. I don't know why, unless it was that he had lived there for so many years. I shouldn't wonder if they were afraid to molest him. Whatever the reason, there he was when I went to his island in 1923.

I was employed by a European syndicate at that time, under contract to produce one picture a year for a term of three years, each of them to be concerned with the life of primitive people in remote corners of the world. That is how I came to be interested in Marutea in the first place. I was attracted by its name almost as much as by its isolated position. As a matter of fact, it proved to be precisely the island I was searching for.

"His island" I have called it, and so it was, although he didn't own a square foot of land outside his trading compound; but he had lived there for so long that he had come to look upon it as his own property. "My island," he would say: "my copra," "my pearls," "my pearl shell," "my people." He was right about it, too. The very fish in the lagoon and in the sea beyond belonged to him, and could only be caught and eaten by his authority. Mussolini himself might have been envious of this man's power. It was confined to the one island, but absolute within that limit.

He did own one piece of property in addition to his trading station—the *Turia*, an ancient, leaky, sixty-ton schooner used to bring his copra and pearl shell to the Tahiti market and to carry back his supplies of trade goods. When I arrived at Tahiti the vessel was in port there, on one of her annual calls. Her skipper was a huge man of forty-odd years, with mild brown eyes and a gentle, engaging manner of speech. He was Otto Müller, Jr., the oldest of his father's large family of half-caste children.

Otto Müller was shocked, almost incredulous, at my request for passage to Marutea for myself and my two cameramen. I can think of no other words with which to express his attitude.

"I couldn't possibly take you, sir," he said.

"Why not?" I asked.

"My father would never permit it. He will have no visitors on the island. He would be very angry with me if I brought any."

He regarded me with an awed, frightened expression, like that of a small boy asked by another boy to rifle his father's desk, or to commit some other unheard-of depredation.

Well, the more he objected, the more I urged. No other vessel called at Marutea; it was the *Turia* or nothing, and I was determined to go. At last I gained Otto's reluctant consent. I agreed to take full responsibility, and to explain to his father, if it should be necessary, how I had forced myself aboard the schooner with all my goods and chattels. Otto was of the opinion that we should not be permitted to land. I told him that I was willing to take a chance on that and, if permission were not given, would pay whatever his father asked for passage in the *Turia* to another island I had in reserve, one hundred and fifty miles from Marutea.

## II

At the outset of the voyage I put Herr Müller out of mind; I would worry about him when the time came. Meanwhile, we had to reach his island in a vessel that leaked like a wicker basket. We must have pumped half the Pacific through her before we reached Marutea. We had calms and head winds day after day, and once we were hove to in a gale that I thought would founder us. My two cameramen, George Crossland and Karl Zimmerman, thought it a great lark. Fine lads, both of them. As for myself, it seemed to me that we had been born on that vessel; that we had traveled beyond the limits of the known world. Not a sail, not a smudge of smoke on the horizon— nothing but empty sea and the tired old schooner, her belly half full of salt water, trudging along in the centre of it, under an empty sky.

We got there at last, and from the moment of sighting land all the anxieties and discomforts of the voyage were forgotten. I shall not attempt to give you an idea of the beauty of the place. Words can't do it, pictures can't do it. Music could, and only music. If you were to see Marutea, you would understand why I think so.

Through my binoculars I saw Herr Müller from afar; he was standing on the beach near the landing place with a telescope on a tripod before him. He leveled it at us from time to time as we approached, searching the schooner carefully, from stem to stern. Several times the glass was directed at me, long and steadily. I confess that I felt uncomfortable under that long-range scrutiny. An influence decidedly hostile seemed to be making itself felt. A large crowd of natives stood or sat in a circle around him. They made a glorious picture against the background of dazzling white beach, coconut palms, and blue sky. I saw no buildings except a sort of warehouse at one side, near the beach. Even that was beautiful with the shadows of palm fronds moving over its whitewashed walls. One would have said it had been built for that purpose.

The schooner was brought into the wind a quarter of a mile offshore and the whaleboat lowered. Otto Müller was very uneasy and apprehensive. He could not go ashore with us, and he warned me to be careful what I should say to his father.

"Have you any suggestions as to how to begin?" I asked.

"No; only let him speak first, Mr. Forrest. I'm afraid there's no hope of his letting you stay. I shouldn't have brought you; I really shouldn't have!"

"Nonsense, Otto!" I said, jokingly. "He won't shoot me, will he?"

Otto was silent for a moment, as though seriously considering this possibility.

"No, he wouldn't do that, but he might strike you with his walking stick. It is an ironwood stick, and he might hurt you badly. It wouldn't be the first time he has used it. He would be very sorry afterward, but then it would be too late."

Crossland and Zimmerman came ashore with me. With four native boys at the oars and one at the steering sweep, we approached the reef. It was an ugly-looking landing place, and the heavy onshore swell made it uglier still. We got across without mishap, but my heart was in my mouth for a few seconds. The boat grounded in the shallows twenty yards or so from the beach, and the sailors started to carry the three of us, pickaback, to dry ground. Herr Müller strode forward and shouted something to them in the native tongue. They dropped us so abruptly that I lost my balance and sat down in two feet of water. Crossland and Zimmerman were as surprised as I was, but they had not fallen and they whooped with joy at my plight. They were the only ones who laughed. The crowd of natives looked on in silence, gazing from Herr Müller to me and back again. He stood with his hands clasped over his cane, which looked more like a war club than a walking stick.

He was a magnificent figure of a man, with thick white hair and a snow-white beard reaching nearly to his waist. I had seen many an island trader in my wanderings, but never one like this. It was inconceivable to me that he could belong to that fraternity. Race and character were written all over him; he looked like some old German baron who had strayed out of the feudal system. Vitality radiated from him—from his beard, from the tips of his strong brown fingers, most of all from his blazing blue eyes. You felt it as you feel the heat of tropical sunlight, and it seemed to come from as inexhaustible a reservoir. He folded his hands across his chest, one hand still grasping the stick, and waited for us to approach.

We all have our pride, and I could imagine what a ridiculous figure I presented as I waded, dripping, to the beach. Inwardly, I was boiling with rage, but I took care to conceal it. Remembering Otto's advice, I waited for his father to speak. He looked from one to another of us for a moment; then he said, in English, "Why have you come here?"

His voice was deep and powerful, and he spoke with only a slight accent. I suppose I should have been prepared for that question, but the fact was that I stood there, tongue-tied, like a small boy caught stealing cookies in his mother's pantry.

"Why have you come here?" he repeated. The knuckles of his huge fists were white, and I more than half expected him to swing his club without giving me a further chance to reply. He took a quick stride forward, and I needed all my presence of mind to keep from ducking. He didn't offer to strike me, however. With his stick he drew a line in the sand. "You will go no farther than that from where you stand," he said. Then he raised his arms horizontally and glanced back over his shoulder. Two husky young men sprang forward, ducked under his arms, picked him up, and staggered out with him to the whaleboat. A moment later they were across the reef and on their way out to the schooner.

### III

Never in my life before had I been so taken at a disadvantage. After the showing I had made before all those people, I felt that I must do something to reassert my manhood, so I walked across Herr Müller's boundary line and sat down in the shade at the upper slope of the beach. Crossland and Zimmerman came too. A murmur ran through the crowd at this defiant action, but whether of surprise or approval or apprehension it was impossible to say. Soon the hum of talk became general, but I noticed that the natives kept their voices under, as though they were afraid that Herr Müller might hear them even at that distance.

I glanced over the gathering, sick at heart at the thought that we should not, in all probability, be permitted to stay on Marutea. Nature has developed no finer race than the Polynesian. Here was the company for my picture, from the children to the great-grandparents. They had intelligent mobile faces, their teeth were flawless, as white as coconut milk, and their bodies were a delight to the eye. There was not a deformed or sickly-looking person among them. I picked out my principals there and then, and in the imagination I was already at work, the film, "Marutea," taking shape.

The buzz of conversation died away; the whaleboat was returning. Herr Müller was now at the steering sweep. He had removed his shoes and his white coat, rolled up his trousers to the knee, and was standing with his bare feet braced on the gunwales. In the intervals between the thunder of the surf we could hear him urging the oarsmen on, but, instead of coming to the usual boat passage, he steered to a point where the surf piled up in an awe-inspiring manner.

"Good Lord!" Crossland said. "Surely he won't try crossing there!" It looked like a mad attempt, but there was no doubt of Herr Müller's purpose. Immense coral boulders were scattered there, the wreckage, evidently, of some old hurricane, and the surf piling in among them spouted high in fountains of spray and solid water. All the natives were now on their feet, talking excitedly. Old Müller stood in an easy, careless posture, his head turned over his shoulder as he watched the following seas. I wanted to cheer at the noble picture he made. At last, far out, he saw the wave he was waiting for, lifting its back slowly and majestically as it swept in. He shouted his order and the men made their oars crack. Involuntarily I closed my eyes for an instant. When I opened them again the whaleboat was gliding down an appalling slope of surf between two boulders that dwarfed the little craft, and the great volume of water hurled over the reef carried them across the shallows and grounded their boat high up on the sand.

Herr Müller sprang out and came toward us in great strides, his arms outstretched, his face beaming. He seized both my hands and shook them warmly.

"Mr. Forrest!" he exclaimed. "You are welcome to my island! Forgive me, my friend! What a beast I am! I lose my temper like that—for nothing! But why did you not speak? And you have with you a countryman of mine, *nicht wahr*? It is this young man!" And he turned to Zimmerman and grasped him by the shoulders. "Not since ten years have I met a German!" He spoke rapidly and eagerly to Zimmerman, and a moment later turned again to me, laughing delightedly.

"Do you know what this young man say to me, Mr. Forrest? He thinks I am a wonderful boat steerer. Never has he seen anyone cross the reef like I do it. No, and you will never see another, my young friend! Ask these men, born on the island, who live in the sea half the time. Not one of them has the courage, or the strength, or the quick eye, like mine. I am seventy years old, Mr. Forrest, and I am the best man on this island, old or young!"

Of a sudden his eyes filled with tears.

"And I treat you like dogs! But why have you not told me? You are an artist! I too am an artist, Mr. Forrest. Yes, in this lonely place you find a brother artist."

"It is kind of you to call me that, Herr Müller," I replied; "but the truth is, I am only a maker of motion pictures."

"Well, that too may be art," he replied. "Never have I seen a motion picture, but I keep in touch with the world. I have my books from Germany, my reviews and illustrated journals. I know a little of what is being done in this new form of art. It is not great, perhaps, like music, but I give it my sympathy, my respect."

To say that I was relieved is to say little. He was simply charming. I could hardly believe this the same man who had stood, grasping his club, half an hour before.

"Otto has told me," he went on. "You are employed by a German company. You wish to make a picture of our island life?"

"I should like to very much, Herr Müller. Will you let us stay?"

"Stay? Of course you shall stay!" he replied, warmly. "You shall have everything you want. You have only to ask me."

## IV

With the natives following, we crossed the island to the lagoon beach where the village lay. The houses were scattered along the curve of the beach for a distance of half a mile on either side of Herr Müller's trading station, and before them stretched the great lagoon, as placid as a mountain lake, shimmering in the morning sunlight. The native dwellings were of palm-frond thatch, and stood on clean coral sand that looked as though it were swept every morning; and so it was, as I found later. Every leaf, every twig, every fallen palm frond, was gathered up daily and burned by Herr Müller's orders. For all his many years of exile he had not lost his German passion for order and cleanliness.

His trading station was a two-story building of coral cement, with wide verandahs both upstairs and down. It stood at a distance of fifty yards from the beach, and the intervening space was like the military parade grounds one sees in German provincial towns—except that it was beautifully shaded with coconut palms, and fine old puka trees that must have been growing there from heathen times. The store and warerooms occupied most of the lower floor. Upstairs were his living quarters, cool, spacious, high-ceilinged rooms furnished with richly carved and massive beds, wardrobes, tables, chairs, and sofas. On the walls were mirrors in heavy gilded frames, and paintings of German landscapes in the romantic style of fifty years ago. There was even a grand piano. You can imagine our astonishment at finding one on a coral island seven hundred miles from the nearest steamship route.

I heard the piano played a few evenings later. It was a strange and memorable experience. We had had dinner with Herr Müller, served in his spacious dining room at a table that would have accommodated a dozen guests. Shortly after the meal he excused Crossland and Zimmerman, but it was plain that he wished me to remain. We smoked in silence for a few minutes; then he said, "Tell me, Mr. Forrest; you have recently come from Germany?"

"Not six months ago," I replied.

"You have been in Hanover, perhaps?" And, without waiting for a reply: "That was my home, and I have not seen it for fifty years!"

His eyes filled with tears and he leaned his head on his hands, gazing at the table in front of him. Not knowing what to say, I said nothing. I was surprised at this sudden change in mood; not five minutes earlier his light-hearted laughter had made the walls ring. Presently he raised his head, with such a look of desolation in his eyes that I was deeply touched.

"Forgive me. I cry this way—like a child. But it is not for nothing, believe me!" He drew a handkerchief from his pocket and blew a blast on his nose that must have been heard all over the village, but somehow there was nothing comical in the action.

"I have told you that I am an artist," he went on. "You have wondered about that, perhaps? You have said to yourself: 'An artist? *Was für ein* artist in such a place?' . . . I keep it locked up—so long—so long—here!" He struck his chest a heavy blow. "Sometimes, Mr. Forrest, I think I go mad! I am more than forty years in this savage place, and now my life is over. When I think what it might have been . . . And I have been ruined by my own father!"

He straightened up in his chair and his eyes blazed with anger. "A beast of a man! But no . . . what am I saying? He is dead. Yes, I have forgiven him, but it has been hard . . . hard. Listen, my friend. You shall judge."

## V

And then he told me his story. I wish that I could tell it as he did—with his voice, his words, his passionate intensity. He gave me the history of his life. Briefly, these were the facts of it.

He was the fourth of eight sons. His father was a wealthy and influential manufacturer of surgical instruments. He had definite plans for all his boys. Four were to go into the army, two into the diplomatic service, and two into his own business. When the fourth son gave promise of having remarkable musical ability, his father encouraged him to develop it. He was supplied with the best teachers that could be found, in both voice and piano, but it was no part of his father's plan that any of his children should follow a musical career. Music was well enough as an accomplishment, as an amusement for leisure hours, but this son was destined for the army, and into the army he must go.

Young Müller had his father's iron will and passionate nature. Music was the breath of life to him, and he determined to carve out a career for himself. In his eighteenth year came the trial of strength. His father commanded him to return home from Munich, where he was studying, prepared to enter an officers' training school. Müller refused. His father cut off his funds and the son was compelled to work for his living. No matter. He worked ten hours a day and continued his musical studies at night. In his twenty-first year he was given a place in the Hanover opera company. He joined it secretly, living in lodgings hidden away from his family, and studied and rehearsed his parts without his father knowing that he was in the city. Then came the opening night of the opera season. It was the great event of his life. He had a triumph, he said, and was called repeatedly before the curtain with the principals. His father was present, and young Müller thought he had vindicated his right to direct his own life. The father thought otherwise. Being a man of great influence, he compelled the directors of the company to discharge his son.

"Then, Mr. Forrest, I am like a crazy man. You cannot know what this chance to sing means to me. In my dreams I have seen how splendid my future will be. Everyone is astonished at my voice, and my teachers have all said that I shall be one of the great singers of Germany, perhaps the greatest of my time. When I am told, 'You can no longer sing in this company; your father will not permit it,' I am like a man who has lost everything. If only I could be patient, and work, and say nothing! Hanover is not the only city in Germany. But no, in my grief, my great madness, I forgot everything. Think of it! I destroy my life to shame my father! Yes, that is what I do. I say to myself: 'I will sing no more! Never! Never! I will be like a dog, a homeless dog! I will throw dirt on the name of Müller!'"

For three years, so he told me, he held fast to this resolution. He wandered far and wide over the earth, and all the time his one desire was to degrade himself and disgrace the name of Müller. At last he came to Marutea, still planning some revenge that would break his father's heart. Then came the inspiration. He married an island woman, daughter of the chief of Marutea, but still a native, and when he had two children by her he sent all the way to Tahiti for a photographer to come to the island. He dressed himself, his wife, and their two children like the lowest of savages. They were photographed in this fashion before a palm-thatched hovel. He then sent home his marriage certificate and one of these photographs, inscribed, "To my father, from Otto Müller and his family."

"Then, Mr. Forrest, I wake up . . . like that!" and he snapped his fingers. "I am a man who has been mad, who has had an evil dream. Now it is gone; I am a Müller again, and my good German blood speaks to me. I have taken a terrible revenge; but it is too late now—the harm is done. I killed my father— that I was told by one of my brothers. His pride was broken forever. The anger I have kept so long leave me, and I again wish to make something of my life. I have a wife. I have children I love; they are of the best Polynesian blood; I have no need to be ashamed. I see that I must build up my life here, on this island. When I come out of my bad dream I begin to plan, to create. This island shall be a kingdom for me, and all of these people shall be my children. I see how I can make them happy and prosperous, and I take charge of their affairs."

Then returned his great love and longing for music. He had sworn never to play or sing again, but with the first money he earned as a trader he sent for a piano. Gradually he sent for other things, so that he might live like a self-respecting German.

## VI

That, in the barest outline, is the story he told me. When he had finished he rose, and I thought I was to be dismissed; but no—this was to be one of his musical evenings. One night in every week, he said, his people came to hear him play and sing. "One must have music, *nicht wahr?* You will see, my friend, how my people love this music. It is necessary. No longer can they live without it."

Sure enough, when we walked out to the upstairs verandah, the whole village was gathering in the open space before his house. A chair was placed for me at one side of the crowd. The natives sat cross-legged on the ground, at a distance of twenty or thirty yards from the house. The piano was rolled out on the upstairs verandah and so placed that, while playing, Herr Müller would sit sidewise to his audience. Over it was suspended a gasoline vapor lamp, provided with a shade that threw the clear white light directly upon him. It was the nearest thing to a spotlight, I imagine, that he was able to devise.

Presently a bell was struck—three sonorous clangs. The latecomers seated themselves hurriedly and the hum of conversation died away. There must have been well over two hundred people in the audience. We waited in deep silence for some little time; then Herr Müller appeared, in full evening dress, as he might have appeared on the concert stage in Hanover. A fine figure he made as he came forward to the verandah railing and stood, resting his hands upon it, looking down at us. At the moment of his appearance the audience started a vigorous clapping of hands, and Herr Müller bowed gravely to right and left; then he seated himself at the piano.

Picture, if you can, that strange scene. It was a perfect tropic night, windless and clear. From the far side of the island came the faint thunder of the surf, giving a voice to mid-ocean solitude, and behind us lay the lagoon with the stems of the palms outlined in silhouette against it. Herr Müller's audience was all but invisible in the deep shade of the puka trees, but here and there a gleam of moonlight outlined a bare brown leg, the contour of a cheek, or the curve of a naked shoulder. The intense light of the vapor lamp fell full upon him, deepening the gloom outside.

I wish that I might have known his thoughts at that moment. One thing seemed quite certain: he was no longer at Marutea. He was in Germany—in Munich, perhaps, or Berlin, before a vast audience of his fellow countrymen. He was at the summit of his career, the great singer he had so often dreamed of being. He sat for a moment with his head bowed, his fingers resting lightly on the keys. Then he sang Wagner's "Evening Star."

*"Oh, du mein holder Abendstern . . ."* I can hear the words at this moment, sung, and powerfully sung, in his deep and splendid voice. I admit that I was stirred. I had not known what to expect of this performance. In outlining his story, I have said little of his superb self-confidence, his unshakable belief that his father had wrecked the career of one of the most promising singers in the whole of Germany. As I listened, I could easily believe that this might have been true. His voice had great range and flexibility, as well as power; it was one that a much younger singer might well have been proud of.

At the close of the song, prolonged and hearty applause broke out. He rose and bowed in his courtly manner to right and left. I could see tears trickling down his great white beard, and gleaming in the lamplight. There was something inexpressibly pathetic, to me, in this makeshift of an audience, of a setting, that circumstances had forced him to accept and be content with; and yet it seemed to serve his purpose. Make-believe, if indulged in long enough by a man passionately eager to delude himself, may become almost as good as reality. So it was here, I think. What Herr Müller needed was an audience, the heartening sound of two hundred pairs of hands clapping vigorously at the close of each of his numbers. The rest he could himself provide. He had only to close his eyes to believe, for the moment at least, that all of his dreams had come true.

Naturally the thought came to me: How spontaneous is this applause? Remembering that these concerts had been taking place over a period of many years, I could imagine that his audience might have become bored with them. Furthermore, Polynesian music differs vastly from ours, and it was hard to believe that the Maruteans had ever cared greatly for Brahms, or Wagner, or Schubert, or Chopin. I watched with interest the faces of those near me, and, whatever the song or the instrumental number, they remained as placid and seemingly unmoved as the coconut palms. I observed that the applause was always started by the same old man. As long as he clapped, the others clapped; when he stopped, they stopped. Herr Müller saw nothing of this, of course, and he may have known nothing of it. These weekly concerts were given by his royal command, but in my opinion he truly believed that the natives attended for the pleasure they derived from them and not because of the fear which his dominating character inspired.

## VII

I shall pass quickly over the events of the following month. It was a busy, anxious, and happy time for me. Herr Müller had given us the use of one of his coral-cement copra houses for a studio. It stood on the lagoon beach, half a mile from his dwelling. There I installed my small electrical plant, my film driers, and the rest of our gear.

Herr Müller was kindness itself in helping us to get comfortably settled. At first he was like a child in his eagerness to see us at work; but as the days passed I became conscious of a change in his attitude. He tried hard not to show it, but I could see that he resented the new interest we had brought into the lives of his people. It deprived him, not of any of his authority, to be sure, but of the position he had held for so long in the very centre of the Marutea stage. I did everything possible to keep him there. Never did we miss attendance at his weekly concerts, and I saw to it that there should be no distractions for which we were responsible on those particular evenings. Nevertheless, I was not easy in mind, and worked as never before to complete the filming of the picture in the briefest possible time. With a host of such violent and capricious moods, anything was possible. What I feared, of course, was that he might command us to leave the island before the work was finished.

Days passed, and everything went smoothly. We had splendid luck. The weather—everything—was in our favor. As for the company, they surpassed my most hopeful expectations. Half a dozen rehearsals sufficed to show the natives what we wanted: simply a pictorial story of their life as they lived it from day to day,—fishing, pearl diving, housebuilding, dancing,—all their individual and communal activities strung on the thread of a story concerning one family. They were wholly unselfconscious before the camera; not once in a dozen times was a retake necessary. I saw little of our host during working hours, but I passed more than one pleasant evening in his company. One day he sent me word that he was going on one of his periodical vists to another smaller village on an island fifteen miles distant across the lagoon. He was to be absent for ten days or longer.

In the midst of our work, while he was away, I all but forgot his existence.

His son Otto acted as my interpreter and general factotum. Otto and I had struck up a warm friendship during the long voyage to Marutea, and it had grown since that time. It was interesting to see how he expanded and throve during his father's absence, and the effect was equally noticeable upon the rest of the people. They were like children who had been granted an unexpected holiday. Nearly everyone in the village belonged to my company, and by this time their interest in the picture was enormous.

Meanwhile, Crossland and Zimmerman had been working late every evening developing film. I was looking forward to projecting the pictures. I wanted to show the company the results of our work, and I knew that I could better explain what remained to be done by letting them see themselves in the shots already taken. At last we were ready, and I informed the village that if they would come to the studio that evening I would show them what they had been doing all this while.

We rigged up our screen out of doors, against one of the walls of the copra house. The whole village came. Otto and perhaps half a dozen others had seen motion pictures at Tahiti when they had gone there with Herr Müller's schooner. The others had little conception of what would be forthcoming.

At first their astonishment was so great that they sat in complete silence; then they went half crazy with delight. They laughed, they yelled, they rushed up to the screen to convince themselves that those moving figures were merely pictures and not their own flesh and blood. I had to stop the show until we could quiet them down a little. Otto explained that they must remain seated and not throw their shadows on the screen.

We were in the midst of the performance when I heard, or thought I heard, the ringing of the bell at Herr Müller's house. I had a decidedly uneasy moment. I remembered that this was the usual evening for the weekly concert, but I had heard nothing of his return and knew that he was not expected back for several days. Zimmerman was at the camera. I strolled a little way down the beach and listened again for the bell. Not hearing it, I decided that I must have been mistaken. Certainly none of the audience had heard it, which was not strange, considering the noise they were making.

When the performance was over they begged to see it again. I was glad to comply, and while repeating it I explained to them, through Otto, the work yet to be done, and how the various scenes would fit into place when all had been taken. We were getting on famously. Otto was in the midst of one of his explanations when he stopped short as though he had been smitten dumb. Following his awe-struck glance, I saw his father standing at the rear of the crowd. He was in evening dress, his concert costume, and stood drawn up to his full height, his arms folded across his mighty chest. In one hand he grasped his ironwood walking stick.

Not a word was said. Otto began to move backward as though some mysterious force were pushing him away. He melted into the darkness. Every member of the audience followed him. They neither walked nor ran—they simply vanished, without a sound. Within thirty seconds the place was deserted except for Zimmerman at the camera, Herr Müller, and myself.

I was prepared for anything. I was prepared to see him step forward and smash our precious camera to bits. Had he offered to do so, I doubt whether Zimmerman or I would have lifted a finger to prevent him. I have spoken of his immense vitality. It was more than that; what, precisely, I cannot explain, but the influence, whatever it was, seemed to rob us, for the moment, of everything but the capacity to feel it. He came forward two or three paces, breathing heavily, as though he had run all the way from his house. He raised his ironwood stick and pointed it at me, and opened his mouth as though about to speak; but instead of doing so he turned and strode off into the darkness.

## VIII

I passed a sleepless night. My first impulse had been to follow him, but upon second thought it seemed best to allow time for his anger to cool before making any attempt to explain. I was certain that no one had been informed of his return. Had it been known, Otto would have told me. We were to have started work at daylight the next morning. No one came—not a soul. I waited for an hour, and then went along to the village.

A few children were playing about in the dooryards; otherwise the village street was deserted, but I saw faces peeping concernedly out at me as I went along. I found Otto and a younger brother, Walter, at the store. They greeted me in subdued, anxious voices. They had not dared speak to their father. He had forbidden the people to leave their houses without his permission. While they were telling me this we heard his tread on the staircase. The two sons, with frightened apologetic glances at me, disappeared into a back room.

I was ready to bring into play all the tact and diplomacy learned in twenty years of motion-picture directing. Fortunately they were not needed. All that I had to do was to point out that he himself was responsible for the failure of his people to attend his concert. He had returned home several days before he was expected, and late in the evening, after everyone had left the village to come to our picture show. I assured him that no one had heard the ringing of the bell. Strangely enough, this simple explanation had not even occurred to him.

"Mr. Forrest! What a fool I am!" he said. "Yes, it is so! I am like my father. I lose my temper and then I remember nothing, not even why I have lost it! You will not be angry with me? You are working so hard to do a beautiful thing. You wish to show people in the great cities this lonely island and the life of my people, so strange, so romantic, and I . . ." He shook his head, ruefully. "You will forgive me? Tell me, what can I do to show you how deeply I am sorry?"

Forgive him? Indeed I did, what little there was to forgive. When truly himself, he had the most charming manners—a gracious, old-world courtesy rarely met with anywhere. The difficult thing for me to realize, in all my dealings with him, was that I had to do with a man who, in many respects, had never grown up. Intellectually he was splendidly mature, and yet he had the capacity for intense suffering of a sensitive, imaginative child. With him a slight, however small, and whether fancied or real, grew in a moment to enormous proportions, completely overshadowing the light of his day. I almost envied him that virginity of spirit. Had it not been for his fearful temper, how wholly lovable he would have been!

Nothing would do then but we must have one of our long talks. I excused myself as delicately as possible.

"I was rather hoping to go on with a scene we started filming yesterday, Herr Müller, if the people could come . . . ?"

He slapped his forehead.

"*Donnerwetter!* I forget! Of course! You wish to work, and I have told them . . . *Ach, du lieber Gott,* what a man I am! Otto! Walter! Come! Come quickly!"

They appeared from the back room, and their father galvanized them into action at once. Walter ran up to ring the bell which hung at the end of the upper verandah. The natives came thronging from their houses on to the village recreation ground in front of the store. I wish that you might have heard him address them. He was now in his happiest mood; he laughed with them, joked with them, and the effect was immediate. If they feared him, it was very plain to me that they loved him as well.

"Now, Mr. Forrest, what will you have them do? *Ach,* how can you forgive me who make you waste so much of this beautiful morning? Along with you, Otto! No, wait! You shall stay at home. It is I who shall go with Mr. Forrest to-day. I shall work hard, hard! You will see. Come, my children, all of you!"

What a day it was! We accomplished more than in any four days previously. We filmed two scenes in particular that removed any doubts I may have had as to the ultimate success of the picture. I am prouder of that afternoon's work than of all my years of directing, either before or since, and the credit belongs to Herr Müller. He could have made a success of a dozen different careers, motion-picture directing among them. He knew by instinct what I wanted done; and with his knowledge of island life, and his deep insight into native character, he offered suggestions that were priceless to me.

## IX

If only I could have let well enough alone! Well enough? It was vastly better than well enough. I had a feeling of deep obligation toward him, and in my desire to show it I blundered. My intentions were of the best, but I don't excuse myself. The consequences of that blunder were tragic.

You see, there was something more than pathetic, to me, in the immense need he had for his people's admiration and respect, not as a man and a leader, —that he could and did take for granted,—but as a musician, a singer of genius. He had brooded so long over his ruined career; his spiritual pain at the thought of it was, I am convinced, all but unbearable at times. It was softened somewhat by his belief that his gifts had not been entirely wasted; that even here, among children of nature whom most people would regard as little above savages, he could give pleasure by his singing. I realized more clearly every day how vital it was to his happiness that he should believe the Maruteans deeply loved his music. I wanted him to keep that illusion, if it was an illusion. It seemed to me that if I could help him keep it I should be doing as great a service as it is possible for one man to perform for another.

Well, I encouraged him to believe that our picture was nothing to his people in comparison with his music. He could not help seeing their interest, but I made light of it, and convinced him that it was merely the interest in novelty and would quickly pass. He was wistfully eager to believe me.

"You feel that, Mr. Forrest?" he said earnestly. His eyes lighted up with pleasure and he laid a hand affectionately on my shoulder. "One sees that you are truly an artist! We know, you and I, that music stands first, *nicht wahr?* Yes, it is so, in all lands, with all peoples. It will always be so. Even here, among these Polynesians, there is this great passion for music."

We were walking back through the groves, from the studio to his house. He halted and faced me. "You know, we can prove that," he said.

"How?" I asked.

"I tell you what we do," he went on, eagerly. "Some evening soon you will again show the pictures? . . . Good! Well, I will say to my people. 'Mr. Forrest will show the new scenes he has been making with you. Do you wish to see them?' And they will say, 'Yes.' 'Very well, my children,' I will say; 'those who wish to go may do so. I shall have my concert on this evening, but no matter; I wish you to do as you like. You shall see the pictures if that pleases you better, and I shall sing and play for myself.' "

I at once realized the danger of this plan; but I tried not to show my alarm.

"Herr Müller," I said, "we should have not one spectator at our picture show."

"*Gewiss!*" he said, laughing delightedly. "I believe that, too, so much they love the music."

"Then why prove what we both already know?"

"To make a little more sure. We have this wonderful chance; never again, perhaps, will it happen, anywhere. There are ignorant men, Mr. Forrest, who think these island people are savages who care only to eat and sleep. We know how wrong is their idea; and you can say, after you leave my island, when you hear their foolish talk, 'But let me tell you what I *know.*' "

There was no dissuading him. I tried in every possible way, only to increase his enthusiasm for the plan. He pressed me to set an evening for the double attraction. I delayed day after day, made excuse after excuse until further ones would not serve. He was not to be turned from his purpose, and at last I was compelled to comply. I had a possible resource in Otto. Although we had never spoken of the native attitude toward his father's music, I knew how he felt about it in his heart: that it was both fear and love that compelled attendance at the weekly concerts. I told him that he must warn the people, secretly, not to come to the studio on that evening, promising them another showing of pictures the following night.

Otto shook his head. "My father would be sure to hear of it, Mr. Forrest, and he would be very angry. He would think you did not believe in the love of our people for his music, and wished to save him from being disappointed. He is a proud man; he would never forgive you for that. No, there is nothing we can do. It must be as he wishes."

## X

I made my preparations with a heavy heart. My hope was that the people would not take him at his word, or that a sense of loyalty to him would prevent their attendance. That hope soon faded. They came in twos and threes, in family groups, the girls and young men, the middle-aged. Only the Müller children and a few of the old people were missing; otherwise all the natives were seated on the ground before the screen, eagerly waiting for us to begin. If they were at all worried as to what Herr Müller would think, it was not apparent in their manner. For the moment, at least, they seemed to have quite forgotten him. At another time I should have enjoyed the animation of that scene, but my heart was with Herr Müller. I recalled his words: "On that evening, Mr. Forrest, I shall have a great emotion, a very great emotion. I shall sing as never before." I dared not think of the great empty square before his house. But the harm was done, now. There was nothing for it but to proceed with our show.

Crossland was at the camera; I had sent Zimmerman to attend the concert. I remained at the studio only long enough to inspect one bit of film I had been particularly anxious to see; then I set out for the village as fast as I could walk. We had the same wildly appreciative audience. I could hear their shouts of delight long after I had left the studio.

Herr Müller was singing when I arrived; the song was "Heilige Nacht." It was only then that I remembered we were in Christmas week; there were no seasonable reminders at Marutea. I forgot the tropics as I listened to that timeless old song. I had never before heard it sung by a man; I didn't suppose that it could be. Now I know that only a man—if he be German, with the voice of a Müller—can sing it as it should be sung. It was lovely, unspeakably so. It seemed to me that I was hearing it for the first time. As I listened I forgot time and place, and all my anxieties.

When it was finished I came back with an effort to the little world of

Marutea lost in the wastes of the Pacific. The great square before Herr Müller's house was all but empty. The Müller children were present, and a dozen or fifteen of the old people. All applauded heartily, and I clapped till the palms of my hands burned, but the effect, in volume, was nothing compared to what was customary at these concerts. Herr Müller rose and bowed, but he seemed scarcely aware of our presence at the moment. He was deeply stirred; the spell he had cast upon one, at least, of his audience was upon him as well.

I sought out Zimmerman immediately. In a rapidly whispered conference he told me that Herr Müller had given no indication that he was aware of the smallness of his audience. As a matter of fact, they had spread themselves over a wide area in an effort to make their numbers appear much larger than they were. That was Otto's doing, undoubtedly. The moon was again in its second quarter and the light fell in pools and splashes among the trees. It would have been easy for Herr Müller to be deceived as to the numbers of his audience, the more so because his eyes were accustomed to the brilliant light from his vapor lamp. I tried to persuade myself that he was deceived. Believing that the situation might yet be saved, I asked Zimmerman to hurry back to the studio and stop our performance, telling the people to come at once to the concert. However, thinking of the distance, I was apprehensive. Twenty minutes at least would pass before any of them could appear.

Meanwhile, Herr Müller proceeded with the concert. He sang next one of Heine's lyrics set to music by himself. It was as fragrant of a northern spring as an apple tree in blossom. I tell you, the man *was* a genius! I could easily imagine him in Carnegie Hall in New York, the place filled with sophisticated music lovers, and every one of them deeply moved, as the human heart will always be moved by simple and beautiful things. Again I applauded like a dozen men, and so did the others. The applause was genuine, too; at least mine was. A tenderness welled up in my heart, a deep longing to please the fine old fellow; to make good to him, somehow, all his years of loneliness, of homesickness, of unrealized dreams. This time he did not rise from his stool; he seemed to be in a deep reverie. Then he played the Moonlight Sonata.

Ghosts of old memories, of places, people, evoked by associations the music had for me, came thronging back. It was strange indeed to think that there could be no such memories for the others of that tiny gathering. I thought: "Never shall I forget this! Never! From this night on, the Moonlight Sonata will mean Marutea to me." And so it does; so it always will. If ever my memories of the island grow dim, I shall know how to conjure up again all its loneliness and beauty.

Of a sudden the music was broken off, in the middle of a bar. I looked up quickly. Herr Müller had risen from his stool. He came to the verandah railing and stood looking down at us. Then, in a low dead voice, he said, "Go home. I shall play no more"; and, without waiting to see his command obeyed, he disappeared through a doorway.

## XI

The little gathering dispersed; they seemed to float away rather than to walk. There were a dozen Müller children, married and unmarried, from the ages of forty-odd to eighteen. Two of the younger ones lived with their father; the others had homes of their own near by. They stood for a moment, conversing in whispers, looking toward the house. The intense white light from the vapor lamp seemed to spill like water over the piano keys to the floor, and the instrument cast a block of impenetrable shadow on the other side. I felt suddenly weary, emptied of the desire or the capacity for thought. I rose and made my way slowly to the beach, walking on for a hundred yards or so; there I sat down facing the lagoon, with my back to a tree. A few moments later I saw someone approaching. It was Otto. He sat down beside me. Presently he said, "He is in his bedroom, Mr. Forrest, walking up and down. I am afraid when he is like this."

"What do you think we should do, Otto?"

"Nothing. We must wait and see."

From far down the beach we heard a murmur of voices. The people were returning from our picture show. Otto hurried along to meet them, to tell them to go very quietly to their houses. They separated in silence among the groves; those who lived on the farther side of the village kept to the beach as they passed Herr Müller's house. Within five minutes the last of them had gone.

It was useless to think of sleep. Otto and I wandered away from the house and back to it half a dozen times during the next two hours. The vapor lamp still burned. We were like moths attracted to it again and again.

It must have been well after midnight that we came for the last time, standing in the deep shade, waiting, listening, hearing nothing. We were about to move away for another quarter of an hour of aimless wandering when the curtains at one of the doorways parted and Herr Müller came out. His movements were like those of a sleepwalker. He sat down on the piano stool with his back to the instrument, his elbows on his knees, his chin resting in his hands. He remained motionless for a long time. Suddenly he turned to the piano, squaring his shoulders proudly. I could not see his face, only his magnificent head with its mass of thick snow-white hair, clearly outlined in the brilliant light of the lamp. He let his hands fall lightly on the keys, striking a chord that I can hear to this day. The music of the mingled notes had in it a quality of unutterable loneliness; it was as though some desolate spirit of mid-ocean had uttered a cry of profound despair.

That was all—a single chord. Silence flowed in again; I could hear the faint hiss of the vapor lamp. We waited, and I was hoping that he would play, finding an outlet in music for whatever emotion gripped him. Instead of that he sprang from the stool with an inarticulate cry that froze my blood. He disappeared within doors and returned with an axe in his hand.

How am I to describe what happened next? Have you ever seen and heard a piano being murdered? I am not speaking of piano music done to death by a novice. No—of the instrument itself, beaten, chopped, hacked, splintered, mangled, with an axe wielded by a man with the strength of a giant and the demoniac passion of . . . of nothing human. I doubt whether such a thing had ever happened before, anywhere in the world. With all his enormous strength he swung the axe again, and again, and again, and again—first on the keyboard, then on the beautiful body of the piano whose wood had been so permeated, so mellowed with music through the years. It was as though one were watching a god, who had created order and beauty and harmony, seized of a sudden by the horrible need to destroy all that he had won from chaos and night, himself with it. I leave you to imagine, if you can, the tortured cries that came from the instrument at each blow.

How long its agony lasted I do not know—possibly two or three minutes, though the time seemed endless to me. Then Herr Müller hurled the axe away from him. It flew far out, whirling round and round, and fell not a dozen paces from where Otto and I were standing. When I looked again toward the verandah, Herr Müller had crouched behind what was left of the instrument. The mangled corpse of it was heaved up on two legs, and it was hurled rather than pushed across the verandah. The railings splintered like matchwood at the impact, and the instrument fell with a rending crash to the ground, fifteen feet below.

Otto and I had stood, deprived of the power of thought or movement by the horror of what we saw. Now he cried out, "Oh, Mr. Forrest! To-morrow! To-morrow!" I knew what he meant.

But there was to be no to-morrow for his father. He was mercifully spared the anguish he would have known at the realization of what he had done. He swayed for a second or two at the very edge of the verandah, outlined in silhouette against the light of the vapor lamp. Suddenly he raised his hands to his head, staggered back two or three paces, and fell.

Regaining our power of action, Otto and I ran to the outdoor stairway at the end of the verandah, but we were not the first to reach him. He was lying as he had fallen, but his head was resting in the lap of a lovely old lady who I knew at once must be Mrs. Müller, although I had never seen her before. She paid no attention to us; she was not aware of our presence. She was seated cross-legged on the floor, running her slim brown fingers through his hair. His face looked as peaceful as that of a child asleep.

"*Aué! Aué! Otto iti é! Aué! Aué!*"

I shall never be able to forget that little wailing cry, so tender, so infinitely melancholy, repeated over and over again. "Alas! Alas!" Words other than those were useless. There was nothing more to be said.

He must have burst a blood vessel in his brain. However that may be, he was dead. I remained in the house only long enough to be certain of this. The place was now filling with people; I was neither wanted nor needed there. I made my way down the stairs and through the throng gathered outside, to the beach.

The director of motion pictures ended his story at this point. No one spoke for a moment or two; then someone asked, in a tentative, apologetic voice: "You finished the picture?"

"Yes," he replied, rising. "I was obliged to do that."

## A LIFE IN THE DAY OF A WRITER

### *Tess Slesinger* (*1935*)

O SHINING stupor, O glowing idiocy, O crowded vacuum, O privileged pregnancy, he prayed, morosely pounding X's on his typewriter, I am a writer if I never write another line, I am alive if I never step out of this room again; Christ oh Christ, the problem is not to stretch a feeling, it is to reduce a feeling, *all* feeling, all thought, all ecstasy, tangled and tumbled in the empty crowded head of a writer, to one clear sentence, one clear form, and still preserve the hugeness, the hurtfulness, the enormity, the unbearable all-at-once-ness, of being alive and knowing it too . . .

He had been at it for three hours, an elbow planted on either side of his deaf-mute typewriter, staring like a passionate moron round the walls that framed his life—for a whole night had passed, he had nothing or everything to say, and he awoke each morning in terror of his typewriter until he had roused it and used it and mastered it, he was always afraid it might be dead forever— when the *telephone* screamed like an angry siren across his nerves. It was like being startled out of sleep; like being caught making faces at yourself in the mirror—by an editor or a book-critic; like being called to account again by your wife. His hand on the telephone, a million short miles in time and space from his writing-desk, he discovered that he was shaking. He had spoken to no one all the morning since Louise—shouting that she could put up with being the wife of a non-best-seller, or even the wife of a chronic drunk with a fetich for carrying away coat-hangers for souvenirs, but not by God the duenna of a conceited, adolescent flirt—had slammed the door and gone off cursing to her office. Voices are a proof of life, he explained gently to the angry telephone, and I have not for three hours heard my own; supposing I have lost it? Courage, my self! he said, as he stupidly lifted the receiver and started when nothing jumped out at him. All at once he heard his own voice, unnaturally loud, a little hoarse. "I WISH TO REPORT A FIRE," he wanted to say, but he said instead, roaring it: "HELLO." The answering *Hello, sunshine* came from an immeasurable distance, from America perhaps, or the twentieth century—a rescue party! but he had grown, in three long hours, so used to his solitary island! And though he was a writer and said to be gifted with a fine imagination, it was beyond his uttermost power to imagine that this voice addressing him was really a voice, that since it was a voice it must belong to a person, especially to the person identifying herself as Louise.

"Ho, Louise!" he said, going through with it for the purpose of establishing his sanity, at least in her ears if not actually in his own: he spoke courteously as though her voice were a voice, as though it did belong to her, as though she really were his wife; "now darling, don't go on with—" But then he discovered that she was not going on with anything but being a wife, a voice, an instrument of irrelevant torture. *How goes the work,* she said kindly. What in hell did she think he was, a half-witted baby playing with paper-dolls? "Oh, fine, just fine," he answered deprecatingly. (I'm a writer if I never write another line, he said fiercely to his typewriter, which burst out laughing.) *Well look,* she was saying, *Freddie called up* (who in hell was Freddie?) and then her voice went on, making explanations, and it seemed that he was to put away his paper-dolls and meet her at five at Freddie's, because Freddie was giving a cocktail party. "Cocktail party," he said obediently; "wife; five." Cocktail party, eh—and a dim bell sounded in his brain, for he remembered cocktail parties from some other world, the world of yesterday; a cocktail party meant reprieve from typewriters, rescue from desert islands; and it might also mean Betsey—he cocked a debonair eye at his typewriter to see if it was jealous—Betsey, who, along with half a dozen coat-hangers, had been the cause of this morning's quarrel! *Yes, your wife for a change,* came the off-stage tinkle over the telephone again; *and you might try taking her home for a change too, instead of someone else's—and by the way, my treasure, don't bring those coat-hangers with you, Freddie has plenty of his own.* "Right you are, my pet," he said, feeling smart and cheap and ordinary again, "right you are, my lamb-pie, my song of songs, ace of spades, queen of hearts, capital of Wisconsin, darling of the Vienna press—" But she had got off somewhere about Wisconsin.

He looked, a little self-conscious, about his now twice-empty room; aha, my prison, my lonely four-walled island, someone has seen the smoke from my fire at last, someone has spied the waving of my shirt-tails; at five o'clock today, he said, thumbing his nose at his typewriter, the rescue plane will swoop down to pick me up, see, and for all you know, my black-faced Underwood, my noiseless, portable, publisher's stooge, my conscience, my slave, my master, my mistress—for all you know it may lead to that elegant creature Betsey, whom my rather plump Louise considers a bit too much on the thin side . . . ah, but my good wife is a bit short-sighted there, she doesn't look on the *other* side, the bright side, the sunny side, the side that boasts the little, hidden ripples that it takes imagination, courage, to express; the little hidden ripples that the male eye can't stop looking for. . . .

He seated himself again before his typewriter, like an embarrassed school-boy.

Black anger descended upon him. It was easy enough for her, for Louise, to put out a hand to her telephone where it sat waiting on her office desk, and ring him up and order him to report at a cocktail party—Louise, who sat in a room all day surrounded matter-of-factly by people and their voices and her own voice. But for him it was gravely another matter. Her ring summoned him out of his own world—what if he hadn't written a line all morning except a complicated series of coat-hanger designs in the shape of X's?—and because he couldn't really make the crossing, it left him feeling a little ashamed, a little found-out, caught with his pants down, so to speak—and a little terrified too, to be reminded again that he was not "like other people." He was still shaking. She had no right, damn it, no damn right, to disturb him with that sharp malicious ringing, to present him with the bugbear, the insult, the indignity, of a cocktail party—she, who was proud enough of him in public (Bertram Kyle, author of *Fifty Thousand Lives*, that rather brilliant book), although at home she was inclined to regard him, as his family had when he refused to study banking, as something of a sissy.

Still, when you have accepted an invitation to a party for the afternoon, you have that to think about, to hold over your typewriter's head, you can think of how you will lock it up at half-past four and shave and shower and go out with a collar and a tie around your neck to show people that you can look, talk, drink, like any of them, like the worst of them. But a party! Christ, the faces, the crowds of white faces (like the white keys of the typewriter I had before you, my fine Underwood), and worst of all, the voices. . . . The party became abnormally enlarged in his mind, as though it would take every ounce of ingenious conniving—not to speak of courage!—to get to it at all; and as he fell face downward on his typewriter he gave more thought to the party than even the party's host was likely to do, Freddie, whoever the devil "Freddie" was . . .

O degrading torture, lying on the smug reproachful keys with nothing to convey to them. He remembered how he had once been afraid of every woman he met until he kissed her, beat her, held her captive in his arms; but this typewriter was a thing to master every day, it was a virgin every morning. If I were Thomas Wolfe, he thought, I should start right off: O country of my birth and land I have left behind me, what can I, a youth with insatiable appetite, do to express what there is in me of everlasting hunger, loneliness, nakedness, a hunger that feeds upon hunger and a loneliness that grows in proportion to the hours I lend to strangers . . . If I were Saroyan I should not hesitate either: But I am young, young and hungry (thank God), and why must I listen to the rules the old men make or the rich ones, this is not a story, it is a life, a simple setting down in words of what I see of men upon this earth. No, no, I am not Saroyan (thank God), I am not Thomas Wolfe either, and I am also not Louise's boss (ah, *there's* a man!). And I cannot write an essay; I am a natural liar, I prefer a jumbled order to chronology, and poetry to logic; I don't like facts, I like to imagine their implications. O to get back, get back, to the pre-telephone stupor, the happy mingled pregnancy, the clear confusion of myself only with myself . . .

And so Bertram Kyle opened up his notebooks. He felt again that the story he had outlined so clearly there, of the "lousy guy" who everyone thought was lousy including himself, but who was so only because of a simple happening in his childhood, might be a fine story; but it was one he could not do today. Nor could he do the story (which had occurred to him on a train to Washington) of the old lady, prospective grandmother, who went mad thinking it was her own child to be born. Nor could he do the story—partly because he did not know it yet—which would begin: "He lived alone with a wife who had died and two children who had left him." Perhaps, he thought bitterly, he could never do those stories, for in the eagerness of begetting them he had told them to Louise; too often when he told her a story it was finished then, it was dead, like killing his lust by confiding an infidelity.

And so, desperately, he turned to those thoughtful little flaps in the backs of his notebooks, into which he poured the findings in his pockets each night; out came old menus, the torn-off backs of match books, hotel stationery that he had begged of waiters, ticket-stubs, a time-table, a theatre program, and odd unrecognizable scraps of paper he had picked up anywhere. The writing on these was born of drinking sometimes; of loneliness in the midst of laughing people; of a need to assert himself, perhaps, a desire to remind himself—that he was a writer; but more than anything, he thought, for the sheer love of grasping a pencil and scratching with it on a scrap of paper. "If I were a blind man I should carry a typewriter before me on a tray suspended from my neck by two blue ribbons; I think I *am* blind"—he had written that on a tablecloth once, and Louise was very bored.

"It is always later than you think, said the sundial finding itself in the shade"—from the back of an old match-box, and undoubtedly the relic of an evening on which he had strained to be smart. A night-club menu: "Dear Saroyan: But take a day off from your writing, *mon vieux*, or your writing will get to be a habit . . ." Another menu—and he remembered the evening well, he could still recall the look of tolerance growing into anger on Louise's face as he wrote and wrote and went on writing: "Nostalgia, a nostalgia for all the other nostalgic nights on which nothing would suffice . . . a thing of boredom, of content, of restlessness, *velleities*, in which the sweetness of another person is irrelevant and intolerable, and indifference or even cruelty hurts in the same way . . . linking up with the gray days in childhood when among bewilderingly many things to do one wanted to do none of them, and gray evenings with Louise when everything of the adult gamut of things to do would be the same thing . . ." (At that point Louise had reached down to her anger and said, "All right, sunshine, we come to a place I loathe because you like to see naked women and then, when they come on, you don't even watch them; I wouldn't complain if you were Harold Bell Wright or something . . .") "In order to make friends," he discovered from another match-box, "one need not talk seriously, any more than one needs to make love in French"—and that, he recalled tenderly, was plagiarized from a letter he had written to a very young girl, Betsey's predecessor in his fringe flirtations. "A man's underlying motives are made up of his thwarted, or unrealized, ambitions." "The war between men and women consists of left-overs from their unsatisfactory mating." "But the blinking of the eye"—this on a concert program—"must go on; perhaps one catches the half-face of the player and sees, despite the frenzied waving of his head, a thing smaller than his playing but perhaps the important, the vital thing: like the heart-beat, at once greater and smaller than the thing it accompanies . . ." "We are not so honest as the best of our writing, for to be wholly honest is to be brave, braver than any of us dares to be with another human being, especially with a woman." *"At bottom one is really grave."*

He was pulled up short by that last sentence, which was the only one of the lot that made sense. "At bottom one is really grave."

Suddenly he raised his head and stared wildly round the room. He was terrified, he was elated. Here was his whole life, in these four walls. This year he had a large room with a very high ceiling; he works better in a big room, Louise told people who came in. Last year he had worked in a very small room with a low ceiling; he works better, Louise used to tell people, in a small place. He worked better at night, he worked better in the daytime, he worked better in the country, better in the city, in the winter, in the summer . . . But he was frightened. Here he was all alone with his life until five o'clock in the afternoon. Other people (Louise) went out in the morning, left their life behind them somewhere, or else filed it away in offices and desks; he imagined that Louise only remembered her life and took it up again in the late after-noon when she said good night to her boss and started off for home—or a cocktail party. But he had to live with his life, and work with it; he couldn't leave it alone and it couldn't leave him alone, not for a minute—except when he was drunk, and that, he said, smugly surveying the scattered coat-hangers, relic of last night's debauch, that is why a writer drinks so much. Hell, he thought, proudly, I'm living a life, my own whole life, right there in this room each day; I can still feel the pain I felt last night when I was living part of it and Louise said . . . and I can still feel the joy I felt last week when Betsey said . . . and I can feel the numbness and the excitement of too many scotch-and-sodas, of too perfect dancing, of too many smooth-faced, slick-haired women; I can remember saying *"Listen—listen* to anyone who would or would not, and the truth of it is I had nothing to say anyway because I had too much to say . . . Hell, he thought, my coat-hangers lie on the floor where I flung them at three this morning when Louise persuaded me that it was better not to sleep in my clothes again, I have not hung up my black suit, I have not emptied yesterday's waste-basket nor last week's ashtrays (nor my head of its thirty years' fine accumulation) . . . everything in my room and in my head is testimony to the one important fact, that I am alive, alive as hell, and all I have to do is wait till the whole reeling sum of things adds itself up or boils itself down, to a story . . .

There seemed now to be hunger in his belly, and it was a fact that he had not eaten since breakfast and then only of Louise's anger. But the turmoil in his insides was not, he felt, pure hunger. It came from sitting plunged in symbols of his life, it came because he did not merely have to live with his life each day, but he had to give birth to it over again every morning. Of course, he thought with a fierce joy, I am hungry. I am ravenously hungry, and I have no appetite, I am parched but I am not thirsty, I am dead tired and wide awake and passionately, violently alive.

But he lifted his elbows now from his typewriter, he looked straight before him, and he could feel between his eyes a curious knot, not pain exactly, but tension, as though all of him were focussed on the forefront of his brain, as though his head were a packed box wanting to burst. It was for this moment that, thirty years before, he had been born; for this moment that he had tossed peanuts to an elephant when he was a child; that he had by a miracle escaped pneumonia, dropping from an airplane, death by drowning, concussion from football accidents; that he had fallen desperately and permanently in love with a woman in a yellow hat whose car had been held up by traffic, and whom he never saw again; that he had paused at sight of the blue in Chartres Cathedral and wept, and a moment later slapped angrily at a mosquito; that he had met and married Louise, met and coveted Kitty Braithwaite, Margery, Connie, Sylvia, Elinor, Betsey; for this moment that he had been born and lived, for this moment that he was being born again.

His fingers grew light. The room was changing. Everything in it was integrating; pieces of his life came together like the odd-shaped bits of a puzzle-map, forming a pattern as one assembles fruits and flowers for a still-life. Listen, there is a name, Bettina Gregory. Bettina is a thin girl, wiry, her curves so slight as to be ripples, so hidden that the male eye cannot stop searching for them; she drinks too much; she is nicer when she is sober, a little shy, but less approachable. Bettina Gregory. She is the kind of girl who almost cares about changing the social order, almost cares about people, almost is *at bottom really grave.* She is the kind of girl who would be at a cocktail party when someone named Fr—named Gerry—would call up and say he couldn't come because he was prosecuting a taxi-driver who had robbed him of four dollars. She is the kind of girl who would then toss off another drink and think it funny to take old Carl along up to the night-court to watch old Gerry prosecute a taxi-man. She is the kind of girl who will somehow collect coat-hangers (I give you my coat-hangers, Betsey-Bettina, Bertram Kyle almost shouted in his joy)—and who will then go lilting and looping into the night-court armed to the teeth with coat-hangers and defense mechanisms, who will mock at the whores that have been rounded up, leer at the taxi-driver, ogle the red-faced detective, mimic the rather sheepish Gerry—all the time mocking, leering, ogling, mimicking—nothing but herself. Frankly we are just three people, she explains to the detective, with an arm about Gerry and Carl, who love each other veddy veddy much. She must pretend to be drunker than she is, because she is bitterly and deeply ashamed; she must wave with her coat-hangers and put on a show because she knows it is a rotten show and she cannot stop it. It is not merely the liquor she has drunk; it is the wrong books she has read, the Noel Coward plays she has gone to, the fact that there is a drought in the middlewest, that there was a war when she was a child, that there will be another when she has a child, that she and Carl have something between them but it is not enough, that she is sorry for the taxi-driver and ashamed of being sorry, that *at bottom she is almost grave*. In the end, Bertram Kyle said to anybody or nobody, in the end I think . . .

But there was no reason any more to think. His fingers were clicking, clicking, somehow it developed that Gerry had muddled things because he was drunk, so that the taxi-man must go to jail pending special sessions, and then Bettina and Gerry and Carl take the detective out to a bar some place; explaining frankly to waiters that they are just four people who love each other veddy veddy much . . . and, perhaps because they all hate themselves so veddy veddy much, Carl and Gerry let Bettina carry them all off in her car for a three-day spree, which means that Gerry misses the subpoena and the taxi-driver spends a week in jail, earning himself a fine prison-record because he stole four dollars to which Carl and Gerry and Bettina think him wholly and earnestly entitled, and perhaps in the end they give the four dollars to the Communist Party, or perhaps they just buy another round of drinks, or perhaps they throw it in the river, or perhaps they frankly throw themselves . . .

And is this all, Bertram Kyle, all that will come out today of your living a life by yourself, of your having been born thirty years ago and tossed peanuts to elephants, wept at the Chartres window, slapped at mosquitoes, survived the hells and heavens of adolescence to be born again, today—is this all, this one short story which leaves out so much of life? But neither can a painter crowd all the world's rivers and mountains and railroad tracks onto one canvas, yet if his picture is any good at all it is good because he has seen those rivers and mountains and puts down all that he knows and all that he has felt about them, even if his painting is of a bowl of flowers and a curtain . . . And here, thought that thin layer of consciousness which went on as an undercurrent to his fingers' steady tapping, here is my lust for Betsey, my repentance for Louise, my endless gratitude to the woman who wore a yellow hat, my defeatism, my optimism, the fact that I was born when I was, all of my last night's living and much that has gone before . . .

The room grew clouded with the late afternoon and the cigarettes that he forgot to smoke. His fingers went faster, they ached like the limbs of a tired lover and they wove with delicacy and precision because the story had grown so real to him that it was physical. He knew that his shoulders were hunched, that his feet were cramped, that if he turned his desk about he would have a better light—but all the time he was tearing out sheet after sheet and with an odd accuracy that was not his own at any other time, inserting the next ones with rapidity and ease, he typed almost perfectly, he made few mistakes in spelling, punctuation, or the choice of words, and he swung into a rhythm that was at once uniquely his and yet quite new to him.

Now each idea as he pounded it out on his flying-machine gave birth to three others, and he had to lean over and make little notes with a pencil on little pieces of paper that later on he would figure out and add together and stick in all the gaping stretches of his story. He re-discovered the miracle of something on page twelve tying up with something on page seven which he had not understood when he wrote it, the miracle of watching a shapeless thing come out and in the very act of coming take its own inevitable shape. He could feel his story growing out of the front of his head, under his moving fingers, beneath his searching eye . . . his heart was beating as fast as the keys of his typewriter, he wished that his typewriter were also an easel, a violin, a sculptor's tools, a boat he could sail, a plane he could fly, a woman he could love, he wished it were something he could not only bend over in his passion but lift in his exultation, he wished it could sing for him and paint for him and breathe for him.

And all at once his head swims, he is in a fog, sitting is no longer endurable to him, and he must get up, blind, not looking at his words, and walk about the room, the big room, the small room, whether it is night or day or summer or winter, he must get up and walk it off . . . *Listen, non-writers, I am not boasting when I tell you that writing is not a sublimation of living, but living is a pretty feeble substitute for art. Listen, non-writers, this is passion. I am trembling, I am weak, I am strong, pardon me a moment while I go and make love to the world, it may be indecent, it may be mad—but as I stalk about the room now I am not a man and I am not a woman, I am Bettina Gregory and Gerry and the taxi-driver and all the whores and cops and stooges in the night-court, I am every one of the keys of my typewriter, I am the clean white pages and the word-sprawled used ones, I am the sunlight on my own walls—rip off your dress, life, tear off your clothes, world, let me come closer; for listen: I am a sated, tired, happy writer, and I have to make love to the world.*

Sometimes it was night when this happened and then he must go to bed because even a writer needs sleep, but at those times he went to bed and then lay there stark and wide awake with plots weaving like tunes in his head and characters leaping like mad chess-men, and words, words and their miraculous combinations, floating about on the ceiling above him and burying themselves in the pillow beneath him till he thought that he would never sleep and knew that he was mad . . . till Louise sometimes cried out that she could not sleep beside him, knowing him to be lying there only on sufferance, twitching with his limbs like a madman in the dark . . .

Louise! For it was not night, it was late afternoon, with the dark of coming night stealing in to remind him, to remind him that if he were ever again to make the break from his life's world back to sanity, back to normalcy and Louise, he must make it now, while he remembered to; he must leave this room, stale with his much-lived life, his weary typewriter, he must shake off his ecstasy and his bewilderment, his passion, his love, his hate, his glorious re-birth and his sated daily death—and go to meet Louise; go to a cocktail party . . .

He was shocked and terrified when he met his own face in the mirror because it was not a face, it was a pair of haggard, gleaming eyes, and because like Rip Van Winkle he seemed to have grown heavy with age and yet light with a terrible youth. He managed somehow to get by without letting the elevator man know that he was crazy, that he was afraid of him because he was a face and a voice, because he seemed to be looking at him queerly. On the street Bettina appeared and walked beside him, waving her drunken coat-hangers and announcing "Frankly there is nothing like a coat-hanger," while Gerry leaned across him rather bitterly to say, "If I hear you say frankly again, Bettina, frankly I shall kill you." But they walked along, all of them, very gay and friendly, despite the taxi-driver's slight hostility, and then at the corner they were joined by Carl with the detective's arm about him, and Carl was saying to anybody and nobody that they passed—"Frankly we are veddy veddy mad." And they came at last to Freddie's house, and there Bertram Kyle stood for a moment, deserted by Bettina and Carl and Gerry—even the detective was gone—hiding behind a collar and a tie and frankly panic-stricken. The door opens, he enters mechanically—good God, is it a massacre, a revolution, is it the night-court, a nightmare? . . .

But he pushed in very bravely and began to reel toward all his friends. "Hello, I'm cock-eyed!" he roared at random. "Hell, I've been floating for forty days, where's a coat-hanger, Freddie, frankly, if there's anything I'm nuts about it's coat-hangers, and frankly have you seen my friends, some people I asked along, Bettina Gregory, Gerry, and a detective?" He saw Louise, ominous and tolerant, placing her hands in disgust on her soft hips at sight of him. Frankly, he shouted at her, frankly, Louise, I am just three or four people who love you veddy veddy much, and where's a drink, my pearl, my pet, my bird, my cage, my night-court, my nightmare—for frankly I need a little drink to sober down . . .

## DEAR FRIENDS

### Edwin Arlington Robinson   (1896)

Dear friends, reproach me not for what I do,
Nor counsel me, nor pity me; nor say
That I am wearing half my life away
For bubble-work that only fools pursue.
And if my bubbles be too small for you,                              5
Blow bigger then your own: the games we play
To fill the frittered minutes of a day,
Good glasses are to read the spirit through.

And whoso reads may get him some shrewd skill;
And some unprofitable scorn resign,                         10
To praise the very thing that he deplores;
So, friends (dear friends), remember, if you will,
The shame I win for singing is all mine,
The gold I miss for dreaming is all yours.

## SONNET

### *Edwin Arlington Robinson*   (*1896*)

Oh for a poet—for a beacon bright
To rift this changeless glimmer of dead gray;
To spirit back the muses, long astray,
And flush Parnassus with a newer light;
To put these little sonnet-men to flight                    5
Who fashion, in a shrewd mechanic way,
Songs without souls, that flicker for a day,
To vanish in irrevocable night.

What does it mean, this barren age of ours?
Here are the men, the women, and the flowers,               10
The seasons, and the sunset, as before.
What does it mean?  Shall there not one arise
To wrench one banner from the western skies,
And mark it with his name forevermore?

## CASTILIAN

### *Elinor Wylie*   (*1923*)

Velasquez took a pliant knife
And scraped his palette clean;
He said, "I lead a dog's own life
Painting a king and queen."

He cleaned his palette with oily rags
And oakum from Seville wharves;    6
"I am sick of painting painted hags
And bad ambiguous dwarves.

"The sky is silver, the clouds are
    pearl,
Their locks are looped with rain.   10
I will not paint Maria's girl
For all the money in Spain."

He washed his face in water cold,
His hands in turpentine;

He squeezed out colour like coins of
    gold                              15
And colour like drops of wine.

Each colour lay like a little pool
On the polished cedar wood;
Clear and pale and ivory-cool
Or dark as solitude.                   20

He burnt the rags in the fireplace
And leaned from the window high;
He said, "I like that gentleman's face
Who wears his cap awry."

This is the gentleman, there he stands,
Castilian, sombre-caped,               26
With arrogant eyes, and narrow
    hands
Miraculously shaped.

# THE ARTIST AT WORK
### (*From* Dauber)
### *John Masefield*  (*1913*)

Si talked with Dauber, standing by the side.
"Why did you come to sea, painter?" he said.
"I want to be a painter," he replied,
"And know the sea and ships from A to Z,
And paint great ships at sea before I'm dead;                         5
Ships under skysails running down the Trade—
Ships and the sea; there's nothing finer made.

"But there's so much to learn, with sails and ropes,
And how the sails look, full or being furled,
And how the lights change in the troughs and slopes,                  10
And the sea's colours up and down the world,
And how a storm looks when the sprays are hurled
High as the yard (they say) I want to see;
There's none ashore can teach such things to me.

"And then the men and rigging, and the way                            15
Ships move, running or beating, and the poise
At the roll's end, the checking in the sway—
I want to paint them perfect, short of the noise;
And then the life, the half-decks full of boys,
The fo'c's'les with the men there, dripping wet:                      20
I know the subjects that I want to get.

"It's not been done, the sea, not yet been done,
From the inside, by one who really knows;
I'd give up all if I could be the one,
But art comes dear the way the money goes.                            25
So I have come to sea, and I suppose
Three years will teach me all I want to learn
And make enough to keep me till I earn."

Even as he spoke his busy pencil moved,
Drawing the leap of water off the side                                30
Where the great clipper trampled iron-hooved,
Making the blue hills of the sea divide,
Shearing a glittering scatter in her stride,
And leaping on full tilt with all sails drawing,
Proud as a war-horse, snuffing battle, pawing.                        35

"I cannot get it yet—not yet," he said;
"That leap and light, and sudden change to green,
And all the glittering from the sunset's red,
And the milky colours where the bursts have been,
And then the clipper striding like a queen                            40
Over it all, all beauty to the crown.
I see it all, I cannot put it down.

"It's hard not to be able. There, look there!
I cannot get the movement nor the light;
Sometimes it almost makes a man despair                    45
To try and try and never get it right.
Oh, if I could—oh, if I only might,
I wouldn't mind what hells I'd have to pass,
Not if the whole world called me fool and ass."


## A MUSICAL INSTRUMENT

### *Elizabeth Barrett Browning*  (*1860*)

What was he doing, the great god
    Pan,
  Down in the reeds by the river?
Spreading ruin and scattering ban,
Splashing and paddling with hoofs of
    a goat,
And breaking the golden lilies afloat  5
  With the dragon-fly on the river.

He tore out a reed, the great god Pan,
  From the deep cool bed of the
    river;
The limpid water turbidly ran,
And the broken lilies a-dying lay,    10
And the dragon-fly had fled away,
  Ere he brought it out of the river.

High on the shore sat the great god
    Pan,
  While turbidly flowed the river;
And hacked and hewed as a great god
    can,                                   15
With his hard bleak steel at the pa-
    tient reed,
  Till there was not a sign of the leaf
    indeed
  To prove it fresh from the river.

He cut it short, did the great god Pan,
  (How tall it stood in the river!),  20
Then drew the pith, like the heart of
    a man,

Steadily from the outside ring,
And notched the poor dry empty
    thing
  In holes, as he sat by the river.

"This is the way," laughed the great
    god Pan                                  25
  (Laughed while he sat by the
    river),
"The only way, since gods began
To make sweet music, they could
    succeed."
Then dropping his mouth to a hole
    in the reed,
  He blew in power by the river.   30

Sweet, sweet, sweet, O Pan!
  Piercing sweet by the river!
Blinding sweet, O great god Pan!
The sun on the hill forgot to die,
And the lilies revived, and the dragon-
    fly                                      35
  Came back to dream on the river.

Yet half a beast is the great god Pan,
  To laugh as he sits by the river,
Making a poet out of a man:
The true gods sigh for the cost and
    pain—                                   40
For the reed which grows never more
    again
  As a reed with the reeds in the
    river.

## DEFINITION OF SONG

### *Genevieve Taggard* (*1935*)

Singing is best, it gives right joy to
  speech.
Six years I squandered, studying to
  teach,
Expounding language. Singing it is
  better,
Teaching the joy of the song, not
  teaching the letter.

And of all forms of song surely the
  least                                        5
Is solo. Only the lark in the east
Can say—what no other lone singer
  can say—
The glory, the glory of the arriving
  day.

Singing is the work of many voices.
Only so when choral mass rejoices   10
Is the lock sprung on human isola-
  tion
And all the many welded into one.

Body sings best when feet beat out
  the time.
Translated song, order of bold
  rhyme,—
Swing the great stanza on the pavement,—use                                  15
The public street for publishing good
  news.

Deepest of all, essential to the song
Is common good, grave motive of the
  throng;
Well-spring of affirmation in accord
Beneath the chanting utterance, the
  word.                                       20

Song is not static—joy becomes a
  dance.
In step, vast unison, in step advance.
This is the life of song: that it mean,
  and move,
And state the massive power of our
  love.

## APOLOGY

(Prologue to The Early Paradise)

### *William Morris* (*1868*)

Of Heaven or Hell I have no power to sing,
I cannot ease the burden of your fears,
Or make quick-coming death a little thing,
Or bring again the pleasure of past years,
Nor for my words shall ye forget your tears,          5
Or hope again for aught that I can say,
The idle singer of an empty day.

But rather, when aweary of your mirth,
From full hearts still unsatisfied ye sigh,
And, feeling kindly unto all the earth,                10
Grudge every minute as it passes by,
Made the more mindful that the sweet days die,—
Remember me a little then, I pray,
The idle singer of an empty day.

The heavy trouble, the bewildering care 15
That weighs us down who live and earn our bread,
These idle verses have no power to bear;
So let me sing of names rememberèd,
Because they, living not, can ne'er be dead,
Or long time take their memory quite away 20
From us poor singers of an empty day.

Dreamer of dreams, born out of my due time,
Why should I strive to set the crooked straight?
Let it suffice me that my murmuring rime
Beats with light wing against the ivory gate, 25
Telling a tale not too importunate
To those who in the sleepy region stay,
Lulled by the singer of an empty day.

Folk say, a wizard to a northern king
At Christmas-tide such wondrous things did show, 30
That through one window men beheld the spring,
And through another saw the summer glow,
And through a third the fruited vines arow,
While still, unheard, but in its wonted way,
Piped the drear wind of that December day. 35

So with this Earthly Paradise it is,
If ye will read aright and pardon me,
Who strive to build a shadowy isle of bliss
Midmost the beating of the steely sea,
Where tossed about all hearts of men must be; 40
Whose ravening monsters mighty men shall slay,
Not the poor singer of an empty day.


## WITHOUT THAT ONCE CLEAR AIM

### *Stephen Spender* (*1934*)

Without that once clear aim, the path of flight
To follow for a life-time through white air,
This century chokes me under roots of night
I suffer like history in Dark Ages, where
Truth lies in dungeons, from which drifts no whisper: 5
We hear of towers long broken off from sight
And tortures and war, in dark and smoky rumour,
But on men's buried lives there falls no light.
Watch me who walk through coiling streets where rain
And fog drown every cry: at corners of day 10
Road drills explore new areas of pain,
Nor summer nor light may reach down here to play.
The city builds its horror in my brain,
This writing is my only wings away.

# I THINK CONTINUALLY OF THOSE
# WHO WERE TRULY GREAT

*Stephen Spender* (*1934*)

I think continually of those who were truly great.
Who, from the womb, remembered the soul's history
Through corridors of light where the hours are suns
Endless and singing.  Whose lovely ambition
Was that their lips, still touched with fire,                                  5
Should tell of the Spirit clothed from head to foot in song.
And who hoarded from the Spring branches
The desires falling across their bodies like blossoms.

What is precious is never to forget
The essential delight of the blood drawn from ageless springs        10
Breaking through rocks in worlds before our earth.
Never to deny its pleasure in the morning simple light
Nor its grave evening demand for love.
Never to allow gradually the traffic to smother
With noise and fog the flowering of the spirit.                               15

Near the snow, near the sun, in the highest fields
See how these names are feted by the waving grass
And by the streamers of white cloud
And whispers of wind in the listening sky.
The names of those who in their lives fought for life             20
Who wore at their hearts the fire's centre.
Born of the sun they travelled a short while towards the sun,
And left the vivid air signed with their honour.

# NOTES FOR A POEM

*Muriel Rukeyser* (*1935*)

Here are the long fields inviolate of thought
here are the planted fields raking the sky,
signs in the earth:
water-cast shuttles of light flickering the underside of rock.
These have been shown before; but the fields know new hands,        5
the son's fingers grasp warmly at the father's hoe;
there will be new ways of seeing these ancestral lands.

"In town, the munitions plant has been poor since the war,
And nothing but a war will make it rich again."
Holy, holy, holy, sings the church next door.                                 10

Time-ridden, a man strides the current of a stream's flowing,
stands, flexing the wand curvingly over his head,
tracking the water's prism with the flung line.
Summer becomes productive and mature.
Farmers watch tools like spikes of doom against the sure          15
condemning sky descending upon the hollow lands.

> The water is ridged in muscles on the rock,
> force for the State is planted in the stream-bed.
> Water springs from the stone—the State is fed.

Morning comes, brisk with light,          20
a broom of color over the threshold.
Long flights of shadows escape to the white sky:
a spoon is straightened. Day grows. The sky is blued.

> The water rushes over the shelves of stone
> to anti-climax on the mills below the drop.          25
> The planted fields are bright and rake the sky.
> Power is common. Earth is grown
> and overgrown in unrelated strength, the moral
> rehearsed already, often.
> (There must be the gearing of these facts          30
> into coordination, in a poem or numbers,
> rows of statistics, or the cool iambs.)
> The locked relationships which will be found
> are a design to build these factual timbers—
> a plough of thought to break this stubborn ground.          35

## NOT MARBLE NOR THE GILDED MONUMENTS

### *William Shakespeare* (1593-98)

#### SONNET LV

Not marble, nor the gilded monuments
Of princes, shall outlive this powerful rime;
But you shall shine more bright in these contents
Than unswept stone, besmeared with sluttish time.
When wasteful war shall statutes overturn,          5
And broils root out the work of masonry,
Nor Mars his sword nor war's quick fire shall burn
The living record of your memory.
'Gainst death and all-oblivious enmity
Shall you pace forth; your praise shall still find room          10
Even in the eyes of all posterity
That wear this world out to the ending doom.
    So, till the judgment that yourself arise,
      You live in this, and dwell in lovers' eyes.

## "NOT MARBLE NOR THE GILDED MONUMENTS"

### *Archibald MacLeish*  (*1930*)

The praisers of women in their proud and beautiful poems
Naming the grave mouth and the hair and the eyes
Boasted those they loved should be forever remembered
These were lies

The words sound but the face in the Istrian sun is forgotten            5
The poet speaks but to her dead ears no more
The sleek throat is gone—and the breast that was troubled to listen
Shadow from door

Therefore I will not praise your knees nor your fine walking
Telling you men shall remember your name as long                        10
As lips move or breath is spent or the iron of English
Rings from a tongue

I shall say you were young and your arms straight and your mouth scarlet
I shall say you will die and none will remember you
Your arms change and none remember the swish of your garments           15
Nor the click of your shoe
Not with my hand's strength not with difficult labor
Springing the obstinate words to the bones of your breast
And the stubborn line to your young stride and the breath to your breathing
And the beat to your haste                                              20
Shall I prevail on the hearts of unborn men to remember

(What is a dead girl but a shadowy ghost
Or a dead man's voice but a distant and vain affirmation
Like dream words most)
Therefore I will not speak of the undying glory of women               25
I will say you were young and straight and your skin fair
And you stood in the door and the sun was a shadow of leaves on your
    shoulders
And a leaf on your hair

I will not speak of the famous beauty of dead women                    30
I will say the shape of a leaf lay once on your hair
Till the world ends and the eyes are out and the mouths broken
Look!  It is there!

## ODE ON A GRECIAN URN

### *John Keats* (*1819*)

Thou still unravished bride of quietness,
    Thou foster-child of silence and slow time,
Sylvan historian, who canst thus express
    A flowery tale more sweetly than our rime:
What leaf-fringed legend haunts about thy shape         5
    Of deities or mortals, or of both,
        In Tempe or the dales of Arcady?
    What men or gods are these? What maidens loath?
What mad pursuit? What struggle to escape?
    What pipes and timbrels? What wild ecstasy?         10

Heard melodies are sweet, but those unheard
    Are sweeter; therefore, ye soft pipes, play on;
Not to the sensual ear, but, more endeared,
    Pipe to the spirit ditties of no tone:
Fair youth, beneath the trees, thou canst not leave         15
    Thy song, nor ever can those trees be bare;
        Bold Lover, never, never canst thou kiss,
Though winning near the goal—yet, do not grieve;
        She cannot fade, though thou hast not thy bliss,
    For ever wilt thou love, and she be fair!         20

Ah, happy, happy boughs! that cannot shed
    Your leaves, nor ever bid the Spring adieu;
And, happy melodist, unweariéd,
    For ever piping songs for ever new;
More happy love! more happy, happy love!         25
    For ever warm and still to be enjoyed,
        For ever panting and for ever young;
All breathing human passion far above,
    That leaves a heart high-sorrowful and cloyed,
        A burning forehead, and a parching tongue.         30

Who are these coming to the sacrifice?
    To what green altar, O mysterious priest,
Lead'st thou that heifer lowing at the skies,
    And all her silken flanks with garlands dressed?
What little town by river or sea-shore,         35
    Or mountain-built with peaceful citadel,
        Is emptied of this folk, this pious morn?
And, little town, thy streets for evermore
    Will silent be; and not a soul to tell
        Why thou art desolate, can e'er return.         40

O Attic shape! Fair attitude! with brede
 Of marble men and maidens overwrought,
With forest branches and the trodden weed;
 Thou, silent form, dost tease us out of thought
As doth eternity: Cold Pastoral!        45
 When old age shall this generation waste,
  Thou shalt remain, in midst of other woe
Than ours, a friend to man, to whom thou say'st,
 "Beauty is truth, truth beauty,"—that is all
  Ye know on earth, and all ye need to know.    50

## ON FIRST LOOKING INTO CHAPMAN'S HOMER
### *John Keats* (*1815*)

Much have I traveled in the realms of gold,
 And many goodly states and kingdoms seen;
 Round many western islands have I been
Which bards in fealty to Apollo hold.
Oft of one wide expanse had I been told,      5
 That deep-browed Homer ruled as his demesne:
 Yet did I never breathe its pure serene
Till I heard Chapman speak out loud and bold:
Then felt I like some watcher of the skies
 When a new planet swims into his ken;     10
Or like stout Cortez when with eagle eyes
 He stared at the Pacific—and all his men
Looked at each other with a wild surmise—
 Silent, upon a peak in Darien.

## SONNET
### *John Keats* (*1817*)

When I have fears that I may cease to be
 Before my pen has gleaned my teeming brain,
Before high-pilèd books, in charact'ry,
 Hold like rich garners the full-ripened grain;
When I behold, upon the night's starred face,    5
 Huge cloudy symbols of a high romance,
And think that I may never live to trace
 Their shadows, with the magic hand of chance;
And when I feel, fair creature of an hour,
 That I shall never look upon thee more,     10
Never have relish in the faery power
 Of unreflecting love;—then on the shore
Of the wide world I stand alone, and think,
Till Love and Fame to nothingness do sink.

## TO THE STONE-CUTTERS

*Robinson Jeffers* (*1925*)

Stone-cutters fighting time with marble, you foredefeated
Challengers of oblivion
Eat cynical earnings, knowing rock splits, records go down,
The square-limbed Roman letters
Scale in the thaws, wear in the rain. The poet as well     5
Builds his monument mockingly;
For man will be blotted out, the blithe earth die, the brave sun
Die blind and blacken to the heart;
Yet stones have stood for a thousand years, and strained thoughts found
The honey of peace in old poems.     10

## OZYMANDIAS

*Percy Bysshe Shelley* (*1817*)

I met a traveler from an antique land
Who said: Two vast and trunkless legs of stone
Stand in the desert. Near them, on the sand,
Half sunk, a shattered visage lies, whose frown,
And wrinkled lip, and sneer of cold command,     5
Tell that its sculptor well those passions read
Which yet survive, stamped on these lifeless things,
The hand that mocked them, and the heart that fed:
And on the pedestal these words appear:
"My name is Ozymandias, King of Kings:     10
Look on my works, ye Mighty, and despair!"
Nothing beside remains. Round the decay
     Of that colossal wreck, boundless and bare
The lone and level sands stretch far away.

# THE WORLD OF SCIENCE

SCIENCE is the greatest of modern despots. Within the last hundred years it has remade human life. It has forced upon us a brand-new set of ideas about ourselves and the world in which we live. It has changed our notion of the universe, of the beginnings and growth of human life, of the laws of health and disease, indeed of the very nature of the mind itself. The ceaseless effort to accept and to understand so many strange ideas has set us drifting without a compass on a dangerous and boundless sea.

If science has thus remade the inner world, how much more has it transformed the world around us. Machines work for us and scientific gadgets play for us. By the pressure of a foot in a motor car, the twist of a hand on the knob of a radio, we turn on power which we do not understand to produce results that we cannot really control.

Unfortunately, some of the conquests of science seem to have brought us more evil than good. Machines in the factory or on the farm have stolen the work of many human hands and have turned the few men needed to operate them into mere cogs or belts or pulleys. This has forced unemployment and poverty upon thousands of laborers. Airplanes, although marvels of scientific invention, drop bombs upon panic-stricken women and children and rain fire upon great cities that have been building for centuries. So pressing is the need to protect civilization from such forces of destruction that a few discouraged souls have urged that we declare a moratorium on scientific research and invention for at least ten years. But this is a counsel of despair. Science represents man's most successful attempt to master his environment. No government and no group of individuals can halt or even long impede his efforts to understand the forces of nature and compel them to work for him. But the suggestion, absurd as it may seem, does bring home the truth that scientific knowledge is in itself only raw power and that it is for man to learn how to control this power to promote his own welfare.

The potentialities for good revealed by science have been splendidly realized in many professions. Every year physicians bring more and more diseases under control, until man has been left few sure ways of dying. Architects and engineers have erected in our cities buildings of new splendor and magnificence. Ingenious inventors have added innumerable comforts and conveniences to daily life.

In other fields we have only begun to see what can be done. For example, we recognize that machines have made possible a great increase in the production of goods which man needs for decent living. Yet we have no idea how to distribute the plenty we can pile up. We realize that airplanes and the radio, by annihilating space and time, have knit all the world into a single community. Yet when we try to induce nations to substitute cooperation and negotiation for brutal force we fail. We have not yet made our dreams for a good life come true.

Such reading as the following pages contain will enable us to understand the methods of thinking employed in some of the sciences. It will also present a few of the problems which scientific discovery and invention have created. It is our task to learn how we can compel these powers to work for individual happiness and social betterment.

## THE STRUGGLE FOR EXISTENCE
### *Charles Darwin* (*1859*)

Nothing is easier than to admit in words the truth of the universal struggle for life, or more difficult—at least I have found it so—than constantly to bear this conclusion in mind. Yet unless it be thoroughly engrained in the mind, the whole economy of nature, with every fact on extinction and variation, will be dimly seen or quite misunderstood. We behold the face of nature bright with gladness; we often see superabundance of food; we do not see, or we forget, that the birds which are idly singing round us mostly live on insects or seeds, and are thus constantly destroying life; or we forget how largely these songsters, or their eggs or nestlings, are destroyed by birds and beasts of prey; we do not always bear in mind that food is not abundant at all seasons of each recurring year.

A struggle for existence inevitably follows from the high rate at which all organic beings tend to increase. Every being which during its natural lifetime produces several eggs or seeds must suffer destruction during some period of its life; and during some season or, otherwise, on the principle of geometrical increase, its numbers would quickly become so inordinately great that no country could support the product. Hence, as more individuals are produced than can possibly survive, there must in every case be a struggle for existence—either one individual with another or with the physical conditions of life.

There is no exception to the rule that every organic being naturally increases at so high a rate that, if not destroyed, the earth would soon be covered by the progeny of a single pair. We have better evidence on this subject than mere theoretical calculation,—namely, the numerous recorded cases of the astonishingly rapid increase of various animals in a state of nature when circumstances have been favorable to them during two or three seasons. If the statement of the rate of increase of slow-breeding cattle and horses in South America, and latterly in Australia, had not been well authenticated, they would have been incredible. So it is with plants. Cases could be given of introduced plants which have become common throughout whole islands in a period of less than ten years. Several of the plants which are now the commonest over the whole plains of La Plata have been introduced from Europe. In such cases—and endless others could be given—no one supposes that the fertility of the animals or plants has been suddenly increased. The obvious explanation is that the conditions of life have been highly favorable, and that there has consequently been less destruction of the old and young, and that nearly all the young have been enabled to breed. Their geometrical ratio of increase, the result of which never fails to be surprising, simply explains their extraordinary rapid increase and wide diffusion in their new homes.

In a state of nature almost every full-grown plant annually produces seed, and among animals there are very few which do not annually pair. Hence we may confidently assert that all plants and animals are tending to increase at a geometrical ratio—that all would rapidly stock every station in which they could anyhow exist—and that this geometrical tendency to increase must be checked by destruction at some period of life. In looking at nature it is most necessary to keep the foregoing considerations always in mind—never to forget that every single organic being may be said to be striving to the utmost to increase in numbers, that each lives by a struggle at some period of its life, that heavy destruction inevitably falls either on the young or old during each generation or at recurrent intervals. Lighten any check, mitigate the destruction ever so little, and the number of the species will increase to any amount.

The causes which check the natural tendency of each species to increase are most obscure. I will make only a few remarks, just to recall to the reader's mind some of the chief points. Eggs or very young animals seem generally to suffer most. With plants there is a vast destruction of seeds. Seedlings, also, are destroyed in vast numbers by various enemies; for instance, climate plays an important part in determining the average number of a species, and periodical seasons of extreme cold or drought seem to be the most effective of all checks. I estimated that the winter of 1854–5 destroyed four-fifths of the birds in my own grounds; and this is a tremendous destruction. Climate acts chiefly in reducing food, thus bringing on the most severe struggle between the individuals. Even when extreme cold acts directly, it will be the least vigorous individuals which will suffer most. Each species is constantly suffering enormous destruction at some period of its life from enemies or from competitors for the same place and food; and if these enemies or competitors be in the least degree favored by any slight change of climate they will increase in numbers; and as each area is already fully stocked with inhabitants, the other species must decrease.

What a struggle must have gone on during long centuries between the several kinds of trees, each annually scattering its seeds by the thousand; what war between insect and insect, all striving to increase, all feeding on each other, or on the trees or their seeds and seedlings, or on the other plants which first clothed the ground and thus checked the growth of the trees! Throw up a handful of feathers, and all fall to the ground according to definite laws; but how simple is the problem of where each shall fall, compared to that of the action and reaction of the innumerable plants and animals which have determined, in the course of centuries, the proportional numbers and kinds of trees now growing.

The struggle will almost invariably be most severe between the individuals of the same species, for they frequent the same districts, require the same food, and are exposed to the same dangers. For instance, if several varieties of wheat be sown together, and the mixed seed be resown, some of the varieties which best suit the soil or climate, or are naturally the most fertile, will beat the others and so yield more seed, and will consequently in a few years supplant the other varieties. To keep up a mixed stock of sweet peas they must be each year harvested separately; otherwise the weaker kinds will steadily decrease in number and disappear. It may be doubted whether the varieties of any of our domestic plants or animals could be kept up for half a dozen generations if they were allowed to struggle together in the same manner as beings in a state of nature.

The recent extension over parts of the United States of one species of swallow has caused the decrease of another species. The recent increase of the missel thrush in parts of Scotland has caused the decrease of the song thrush. How frequently we hear of one species of rat taking the place of another species under the most different climates. In Russia the small Asiatic cockroach has everywhere driven before it its great relative. In Australia the imported hive bee is rapidly exterminating the small, stingless native bee. One species of wild mustard has been known to supplant another species.

A corollary of the highest importance may be deduced from the foregoing remarks—namely, that the structure of every organic being is related, in the most essential yet often hidden manner, to that of all the other organic beings with which it comes into competition for food or residence, or from which it has to escape, or on which it preys. This is obvious in the structure of the teeth and talons of the tiger, and in that of the legs and claws of the parasite which clings to the hair on the tiger's body; in the beautifully plumed seed of the dandelion and in the flattened and fringed legs of the water beetle. The advantage of plumed seeds no doubt stands in the closest relation to the land being already clothed with other plants; so that the seeds may be widely distributed and fall on unoccupied ground. In the water beetle the structure of its legs, so well adapted for diving, allows it to compete with other aquatic insects, to hunt for its own prey, and to escape serving as prey to other animals.

The store of nutriment laid up within the seeds of many plants seems at first sight to have no sort of relation to other plants. But from the strong growth of young plants produced from such seeds when sown in the midst of long grass it may be suspected that the chief use of the nutriment in the seed is to favor the growth of the seedlings while struggling with other plants growing vigorously all around.

Look at a plant in the midst of its range. Why does it not double or quadruple its numbers? We know that it can perfectly well withstand a little more heat or cold, dampness or dryness; for elsewhere it ranges into slightly hotter or colder, damper or drier districts. In this case we can clearly see that if we wish, in imagination, to give the plant the power of increasing in number, we should have to give it some advantage over its competitors, or over the animals which prey on it. Not until we reach the extreme confines of life, in the Arctic regions or on the borders of an utter desert, will competition cease. The land may be extremely cold or dry, yet there will be competition between some few species for the warmest or dampest spots.

Hence we can see that when a plant or animal is placed in a new country among new competitors, the conditions of its life will generally be changed in an essential manner, although the climate may be exactly the same as in its former home. If its average numbers are to increase in its new home, we should have to modify it in a different way from what we should have had to do in its native country; for we should have to give it some advantage over a different set of competitors or enemies.

Each organic being is striving to increase in a geometrical ratio; each at some period of its life, during some season of the year, during each generation or at intervals, has to struggle for life and to suffer great destruction. When we reflect on this struggle, we may console ourselves with the full belief that the war of nature is not incessant, that no fear is felt, that death is generally prompt, and that the vigorous, the healthy, and the happy survive and multiply.

## IS MAN AN ABSURDITY?

*John Hodgdon Bradley* (*1936*)

WERE it permissible to speak so of Nature, we might call her a sadist with a sense of humor. We might say that she has perpetrated many a cruel joke upon her children. In an age of meticulously unsentimental agnosticism, however, we may only observe that her ways are scarcely those of propriety and compassion.

The evidence of this fact is more easily found than an appropriate idiom to express it. A man need not go to the sea where so many millions of creatures are born for the few that are permitted to survive; nor to the pond where the May fly liberates her eggs only when her body has rotted. He need not even step into the garden where the successful drone must die as he succeeds, and where the unsuccessful ones pay similarly for failure. He need only remain in the house and look at the mirror to see a creature as capriciously devised as any other.

Seeing, however, does not necessarily involve believing. For so quaintly constructed a thing as man, it almost necessarily does not involve believing. When first he saw in the mirror the unmistakable though altered visage of an ape he howled to heaven that it was not so. Today he is still howling, but not so much in denial of what he sees as in affirmation of what he does not see.

Few modern men are any longer shocked by the compelling evidence of their simian origin and affiliations. Not a few can even be amused by the vulgarities of the monkey house, so similar except in frankness to their own. Those whom these similarities set to thinking may rejoice that above the shoulders men are gods, however bestial they may yet be farther down. Or they may rejoice for the same reason but with emphasis reversed.

Were it possible to formulate the average opinion of civilized man on this matter, or the average opinion of one average man, it would probably disclose a compromise. Man enjoys his ferments and hormones as well as his dreams and aspirations. He is content with being a mongrel blend of god and beast. Indeed, he is more than content. He is proud.

Were he to attempt to examine himself as dispassionately as an entomologist examines a grasshopper, however, he must suspect what a biologically clumsy compromise he is. In the animal pursuits of eating, fighting, and breeding his prowess hardly matches his customary estimation of it. The tapeworm is easily a better feeder, the weasel a better fighter, the rabbit a better lover. The best human swimmers, runners, and fliers are inept amateurs when compared with sharks, horses, and hawks. Except for his brain, man is a generalized and undistinguished animal.

As a god he is scarcely more effective. Though he is the one creature who can significantly alter himself and his environment to suit his private tastes, he is the only one who is obviously maladjusted with himself and his environment. He is the one creature who might possibly obtain the necessities of life without robbing and killing his fellows, yet he is the most selfishly acquisitive and the most ruthlessly murderous of all. He is the one creature who is able to know much about himself and the world, and the only one who is habitually deluded. He is the one creature who can laugh, and the only one who is persistently unhappy. He is the one creature who can dodge many cruel and dangerous exactions of Nature, only to run foul of more cruel and dangerous devices of his own manufacture.

One need be no philosopher, pondering in metaphysical abstractions the problems of human duality, to see that man might be more a god were he less an animal, and vice versa. Between these two stools he falls to the ground, without being either wholly content to crawl over it or wholly able to rise above it. The pterodactyl with the teeth of a reptile, the wings of a bird, and the neck of a mammal, was a somewhat similar hybrid. Without conscious direction the pterodactyl achieved a modicum of success in spite of his incongruities. Will man be able by conscious direction to succeed as well? Or will he go down in history as a mere absurdity?

Before we can attempt any reasonable answers to these questions we must know what we mean by success. Most creatures have little demonstrable capacity for experience beyond the basic routine of nourishment, defense, and reproduction. Success for them as individuals consists in eating and avoiding being eaten until reproduction is achieved. Success for them as species consists in the attainment of a sufficient number of individual successes in each generation to prevent extinction.

Obviously for man the definition must be enlarged. Mere survival is not all of success for a creature with a god in its head. On the other hand, mere survival must be the first concern of a god who chooses to reside in a beast, if the strange cohabitation is to continue. Any sound attempt to foretell the future of man must, therefore, start with an appraisal of his chances for physical survival.

As a genus, man has existed for a relatively short period. The million-odd years of his geologic history are but a moment when compared with the lengthy day of the trilobite or the pterodactyl. Yet in that moment enough changes were recorded to indicate the trend of his physical development. On them must be based any respectable speculations concerning his future as an animal.

Scientists are generally agreed that men and apes were derived from a common ancestor. Though in some quarters it is still necessary to emphasize the fact that this hypothetical creature was not technically an ape, many idealistic and even religious people to-day are able to dispense with the salve of Victorian evasion. They are willing to admit that he was probably not at all like an angel; that should he come in at the door they would doubtless go out at the window. They can believe that men and apes are cousins under their skins, content in the knowledge that with time the relationship has become more distant. Yet they cannot quite escape the feeling that apes are horrible caricatures of themselves. Consequently, they are apt to overlook the fact that not all comparisons of man and ape are to the disadvantage of the ape.

After a million years of reaching for the moon on his hind legs, man's intestines have sagged and his pelvic girdle has narrowed. Constipation and the agony of childbirth, instead of the moon, came down upon him. After a million years of reaching for nothing more lofty than a mate or a cocoanut, the ape has achieved his ambitions, such as they were, without losing any of his capacity to enjoy them.

Reduction in size and power of muzzle, jaw, and teeth brought a refinement to the face of man which no ape enjoys. It also brought the dentist and the specialist on nose and throat, which not even an ape could enjoy. Perfection of hand and head brought man the exquisite pleasure of reason and imagination—and their exquisite pain. The ape suffers neither from the absence of the one nor the presence of the other.

Nevertheless, neither these nor any of the other possible observations in favor of the ape could make a sane man want to change places with him. Men love their own anatomy and physiology as they love their own children and automobiles. Two facts, none the less, are clear. Ever since men and apes definitely parted company in the dawn of the Pleistocene period, men have lost not a few of the physical felicities which apes have retained. By the tokens of geologic history, they will probably lose more in the future.

Fossils neither quibble nor lie. With the customary dispassion of the dead, they tell of humanity's losses as well as its gains. And their story is abundantly corroborated by the flesh of living men. Certain losses of which they speak, to be sure, need not be greatly regretted. That the tail has degenerated in man to a well-hidden bone at the base of the spine is an asset to beauty without being a liability to health. That man no longer has sufficient hair to shed water and to retain warmth matters little so long as he has a house and a suit of clothes. Atrophy of the skin muscles, so useful to his quadruped kin for flicking off flies and for making faces at menacing neighbors, is effectively counterbalanced by the agility of his hands and the resourcefulness of his head. The only real need for these muscles to-day is in the cinema, and more than enough people retain the use of them to supply the grimacing Hollywood requires.

The progressive decadence of more essential organs, however, is a matter of less indifference. Though the safety of modern man does not wholly depend on the perfect functioning of eye and ear, it is fostered not inconsiderably by the ability to tell red from green and to hear the whistle of a locomotive. Though softened by cooking, his food is more nourishing if his jaws can chew and his intestines churn. Whether the inventor will be able to make artificial machines capable of performing such work, or the physician discover ways to stay the degeneration of the natural machines for doing it, is the future's secret.

Not one organ of the human body is surely known to be evolving toward increased effectiveness. Man's hands, which next to his brain have been his most valuable asset, are not destined in the future to be the indispensable adjuncts of the mind that they were in the past. Because modern machinery all but manipulates itself, they can only be expected to degenerate with the rest of the human body. The brain itself seems fated to grow no better. Men know vastly more to-day than the ancients knew, without any demonstrably greater capacity for knowing. There is no reason for believing that this capacity will be any greater to-morrow. Indeed, though learning and possibly wisdom will march ahead, psychoses will probably trail not far behind.

The only reasonable assumption for the future is a continuance of the degenerative trend in the human physique. But it is also only reasonable to assume that man will continue to fight it more or less successfully with his ingenuity. Despite the physical deficiencies of men as individuals, man as a species is quite as successful as most other creatures. Through elaborate care of the young and fervid opposition to any curtailment of their production, man is actually the most rapidly increasing animal on earth. Though the weak and the criminal are too largely responsible for this increase to make us regard it with satisfaction, there is at least no threat of extinction for the immediate future. The gravest dangers for man as a species lie less in the crumbling beast than in the bungling god.

## II

By a strange perversity in the cosmic plan, the biologically good die young. Species are not destroyed for their shortcomings but for their achievements. The tribes that slumber in the graveyards of the past were not the most simple and undistinguished of their day, but the most complicated and conspicuous. The magnificent sharks of the Devonian period passed with the passing of the period, but certain contemporaneous genera of primitive shellfish are still on earth. Similarly, the lizards of the Mesozoic era have long outlived the dinosaurs, which were immeasurably their biologic betters. Illustrations such as these could be endlessly increased. The price of distinction is death.

The reason lies largely in the rigidity with which the progressive species become adjusted to their particular environments. When man bred certain types of horses for the qualities demanded by the racetrack he deprived them of other qualities inherent in the nature of horseflesh. The more brilliantly a horse performs on the track the less patiently and surely will it perform in a harness or on a mountain trail. What man has done to the racehorse Nature has done to innumerable other creatures.

She shapes her darlings for special conditions, and they thrive. Most of them are as automatic in their reactions as adding machines, but they are also as free from self-inspired error. As long as conditions are constant they lead safe and easy lives. But Nature is notoriously fickle. She changes the conditions without any warning or reason. Her erstwhile darlings, too set in their anatomy and their ways to meet the new demands, must die.

Man is one of Nature's darlings, but a darling with a difference. In possessing an organ which is at once his greatest strength and his greatest weakness, he is not unlike the others. When Nature gave him his brain, and with it the unprecedented privilege of contributing to the arrangement of his own life, she included the less enviable capacity of suffering for his own mistakes. By thus being endangered through the flexibility rather than the rigidity of his specialized organ, he is unique.

The human brain, like the feet of an antelope or the claws of a cat, is the outstanding attribute of its owner. Unlike the feet of an antelope or the claws of a cat, it has widened rather than restricted the field of its owner's activities.

Without it man would still be chattering in a Paradise of bananas. With it he has dispersed from the trees to discover weapons, clothing, fire, co-operative living, articulate speech, abstract thought, and a myriad attendant diversities of experience. Without it he would never have gone from the shelter of the forest into the hazards of a wider world. With it he not only accepted the hazards already in this world but he added others of his own invention.

Though man has reached his present position without greatly taxing his power of conscious self-direction, he has obviously passed the turning point of his career. During the more or less civilized last five thousand years, he has increasingly contributed to the arrangement of his own life. This period is scarcely half of one per cent of his sojourn on earth to the present, but it limns the probable pattern of his future evolution.

It shows that the significant changes of the future are apt to come through his mind and spirit, and consequently very largely through his own direction. Through them he can bring happiness and misery upon himself, conditions which for him as a god are equivalent to success and failure. Is it likely that the tackle of civilization will fish up more happiness than misery from the unplumbed deeps of mind and spirit, so that ultimately man may triumph as a god though he fail as a beast?

The answer that history returns is simple enough. Unless he change both his tackle and his tactics it is not.

To be born, to eat, to reproduce, and to die is the most that most creatures can wrench from the world. But they easily accept the narrowness of their lives through the simple device of not being aware of it. Man alone possesses a mechanism of discovery and discontent. Curiosity about himself and the world, and distaste for what his curiosity reveals, are two of his most dominant and distinctive traits. Disguising or altering distasteful conditions have been two of his most dominant and distinctive activities.

Long before the last great ice sheet had begun to recede from the face of Europe some twenty-five thousand years ago, man had already become unique in the animal kingdom. Though far more apelike than any of his living descendants, he already could do what no other creature had ever done before. He could not only strike fire, make tools, and wield weapons with his hands, but he could also dream dreams with his head.

Where the skeletons of these Neanderthal men have been found in their original burial grounds they were accompanied by implements and the remains of food. The only possible interpretation of such facts is that man had already fallen in love with himself; that he had already begun to hope, perhaps even to believe, that death does not kill all; that, in short, the temporal limitations of existence had already grown intolerable to him.

They have been intolerable to him ever since. Men still hope when they cannot believe that, for the spirit at least, death does not exist. But while they dream of an endless eon of bliss beyond the grave, on this side they go on living in the flesh, briefly like other animals. Unfortunately they are not godlike enough to be wholly content with their dreams of an everlasting future, nor bestial enough to be wholly undisturbed by the facts of a fleeting present.

They go on, however, with their dreaming and pretending, dressing up the baseness as well as the briefness of their lives. For each crude exigency of survival they invent a noble motive and a pleasing manner. They are the only creatures who are both moral and polite; but beneath the veneer of evasions is the ancient lust and pain and cruelty of living. And, unhappily, they know it.

Man will doubtless never achieve perfection in self-deception, but he will doubtless continue to try. The fundamentals of existence must continue to shock his sensibilities, and he must continue to protect himself howsoever he may. Though hypocrisy helps him only a little in this endeavor, he prizes it (as he should) for that little. But he will probably never let it replace the other major division of human activity which is concerned rather with changing than with disguising distasteful things.

Most creatures take the world as they find it. They instinctively become partners with their environment. They make working agreements even with such inhospitable places as deserts, hot springs, and subterranean pools of oil. And only rarely in using their surroundings do they abuse them.

Man, on the contrary, is not willing to take the world as he finds it. Only rarely does he use his surroundings without abusing them and without eventually abusing himself. In countless ways he stupidly exploits his environment for immediate gain at the expense of ultimate loss.

He harnesses the rivers for a thousand tasks and repays them in pollution. He builds smelters whose breath, like that of Rappaccini's daughter, is deadly to all it touches. He builds levees to control floods and at the same time destroys the forests without which there can be no effective control. By overgrazing and overplowing, he turns grasslands into deserts where not even sheep can graze nor food plants grow. By transplanting such creatures as the English sparrow and the rabbit, he enables them in the end to become more pestiferous than the pests they were employed to subdue. The net result of such achievements is an increasing unbalance of man and his external environment. Though his genius for maladjustment may never seriously threaten his existence as a species, it considerably weakens his standing as a god.

Internally, man has fared but little better. To be sure, by tampering with himself he has smoothed many stretches on the road from the cradle to the grave. Through medicine he has made himself a little sounder, through plumbing a little cleaner, through education and art a little wiser and finer, through all perhaps a little happier. But he has also made himself immensely complex and confused. He is mentally and spiritually muscle-bound. He stands like Tantalus in the midst of his blessings, unable to assemble them for his own greatest good.

Man is easily the most elaborately organized of all the gregarious and social animals. His society has grown increasingly intricate with the growth of civilization. Yet where to-day is the human state that operates as effectively as a bee-hive? Where is the family as stable and contented as a gorilla and his wives? Even though the answer be "nowhere," man neither envies nor aspires to emulate the bee or the gorilla. Through this attitude he molds his most embarrassing dilemma. The crude simplicity of animals offends him, so he embroiders their simplicity (which is also fundamentally his own) until he is tripped and tied by the strands of the embroidery.

By a strange combination of generosity and greed he protects the weak in asylums and kills the strong in futile wars. By a strange combination of idealism and eroticism he seeks without finding a satisfactory system of inter-sexual relationships. By a strange combination of ingenuity and impotence he multiplies the basic necessities of life far beyond any possible need, only to let millions go hungry and unclothed for lack of efficient distribution.

Man can plumb the immensity of interstellar space and probe the minuteness of the atom. He can invent ingenious devices for his own comfort and entertainment. He can make pictures and music more sublime than any sight or sound in Nature, and poetry more beautiful and just than any she ever conceived. But he has not yet achieved through all these special powers the peace, tranquillity, and general well-being in the world that oysters possess without them.

### III

In view of all this, is not man as a species an absurdity; a hodge-podge of characteristics that will not work together for the good of the whole? In view of all this, he well may be; but, fortunately, all this is not all. His very confusion suggests less that he has definitely failed than that he has not yet taken definite form. He may be the grub of a butterfly to come.

Compared with many another species, man is very young. Though the evolution of his body has probably stopped, the evolution of his mind and spirit may have just begun. The waste and confusion of the past may have been only the bustle of a clumsy start. Nature has always been an inefficient wastrel, and man, however unique, is yet her child.

As a species man can never excel the average of the parts, and the average is still a grub in mind and spirit. Yet individuals of exceptional and varied qualities—scientists, artists, administrators, and saints—are continually appearing. They do for the mental and spiritual evolution of man what mutations do for the physical evolution of lesser creatures. They tend to combat a rigid standardization of type. Though Napoleons and Hitlers will doubtless continue to rise from time to time, and freeze whole nations with fear or greed or desperation, they are ultimately self-defeating. The violence of their actions breeds violent reactions, and the species continues to flux. As long as there is flux there is danger; but there is also hope.

The problem of the future is to discover how the sporadic strength of individual men may be extended to embrace mankind. The need of the future is more knowledge of man, both as an individual and as a species. The folly and heartbreak of prescribing for him without such knowledge has been only too freshly and too clearly shown.

It is odd that the nature of stars and the behavior of gases should have stimulated far more and far abler inquiry than have the nature and behavior of men. To be sure, they are more gratifying subjects for study because they are more simple. But man can live without knowledge of stars and gases, whereas he is finding it increasingly difficult to live without knowledge of himself. Without such knowledge he is finding it increasingly difficult to benefit from his vast and growing knowledge of everything else.

In a recent best-selling compendium, Dr. Carrel has brought to general attention man's appalling ignorance of himself. In a recent article that few have read and possibly none will heed, Dr. Hooton of Harvard has outlined a plan that might help repair the deficiency. It is simply a proposal for an institute of clinical anthropology, where the present status of man as a species might be ascertained, and where guiding principles for the future might just possibly be discovered.

Because the problems of man as a species have never seemed very important to men in their selfish pursuits as individuals, anthropologists and philosophers have been lonely and few. Physicians and priests, though many, have been concerned with the plight of the individual. Innumerable institutions exist whose purpose is human betterment, but presumably not one is devoted to a broad understanding of the creature it is attempting to improve.

Such an institution would be a help without being a panacea. Only fools and charlatans have panaceas for the varied distempers of humanity. When Nature vouchsafed that man might assist at the shaping of his own fate she withheld many automatic safeguards against error which she freely bestowed upon other creatures. No other creature has ever faced sterner problems with fewer guides to workable solutions.

So there seems to be no other way for man but to try and fail and to try again. Quaintly, despite frustration, he remains in love with life and with himself. This is perhaps the crowning absurdity of his present estate. But it is also the greatest hope for his future.

# FORS CLAVIGERA

*John Ruskin* (*1871*)

## Letter 5

"For lo, the winter is past,
The rain is over and gone,
The flowers appear on the earth,
The time of the singing of birds is come
Arise, O my fair one, my dove,
And come."

*Denmark Hill, 1st May, 1871.*

My friends:

It has been asked of me, very justly, why I have hitherto written to you of things you were likely little to care for, in words which it was difficult for you to understand. I have no fear but that you will one day understand all my poor words—the saddest of them perhaps too well. But I have great fear that you may never come to understand these written above, which are a part of a king's love-song, in one sweet May, of many long since gone. I fear that for you the wild winter's rain may never pass, the flowers never appear on the earth; that for you no bird may ever sing; for you no perfect Love arise and fulfil your life in peace. "And why not for us as for others?" Will you answer me so and take my fear for you as an insult? Nay, it is no insult; nor am I happier than you. For me the birds do not sing, nor ever will. But they would for you, if you cared to have it so. When I told you that you would never understand that love-song, I meant only that you would not desire to understand it.

Are you again indignant with me? Do you think, though you should labour and grieve and be trodden down in dishonour, all your days, at least you can keep that one joy of Love, and that one honour of Home? Had you, indeed, kept that, you had kept all. But no men yet, in the history of the race, have lost it so piteously. In many a country and many an age, women have been compelled to labour for their husbands' wealth or bread; but never until now were they so homeless as to say, like the poor Samaritan, "I have no husband." Women of every country and people have sustained without complaint the labour of fellowship; for the women of the latter days in England it has been reserved to claim the privilege of isolation.

This, then, is the end of your universal education and civilization, and contempt of the ignorance of the Middle Ages and of their chivalry. Not only do you declare yourselves too indolent to labour for daughters and wives, and too poor to support them, but you have made the neglected and distracted creatures hold it for an honour to be independent of you and shriek for some hold of the mattock for themselves. Believe it or not, as you may, there has not been so low a level of thought reached by any race since they grew to be male and female out of star-fish, or chickweed, or whatever else they have been made from by natural selection—according to modern science.

That modern science, also, economic and of other kinds, has reached its climax at last. For it seems to be the appointed function of the nineteenth century to exhibit in all things the elect pattern of perfect Folly, for a warning to the farthest future. Thus the statement of principle which I quoted to you in my last letter, from the circular of the Emigration Society, that it is overproduction which is the cause of distress, is accurately the most foolish thing, not only hitherto ever said by men, but which it is possible for men ever to say, respecting their own business. It is a kind of opposite pole (or negative acme of mortal stupidity) to Newton's discovery of gravitation as an acme of mortal wisdom: as no wise being on earth will ever be able to make such another wise discovery, so no foolish being on earth will ever be capable of saying such another foolish thing, through all the ages.

And the same crisis has been exactly reached by our natural science and by our art. It has several times chanced to me, since I began these papers, to have the exact thing shown or brought to me that I wanted for illustration, just in time; and it happened that, on the very day on which I published my last letter, I had to go to the Kensington Museum, and there I saw the most perfectly and roundly ill-done thing which as yet in my whole life I ever saw produced by art. It had a tablet on front of it, bearing this inscription:—

"Statue in black and white marble, a Newfoundland Dog standing on a Serpent, which rests on a marble cushion, the pedestal ornamented with *pietra dura* fruits in relief.—*English, Present Century*. No. I."

It was so very right for me, the Kensington people having been good enough to number it "I.," the thing itself being almost incredible in its one-ness, and, indeed, such a punctual accent over the iota of Miscreation, so absolutely and exquisitely miscreant, that I am not myself capable of conceiving a Number Two or Three, or any rivalship or association with it whatsoever. The extremity of its unvirtue consisted, observe, mainly in the quantity of instruction which was abused in it. It showed that the persons who produced it had seen everything, and practiced everything; and misunderstood every-thing they saw, and misapplied everything they did. They had seen Roman work, and Florentine work, and Byzantine work, and Gothic work; and mis-understanding of everything had passed through them as the mud does through earthworms, and here at last was their worm-cast of a Production.

But the second chance that came to me that day was more significant still. From the Kensington Museum I went to an afternoon tea, at a house where I was sure to meet some nice people. And among the first I met was an old friend who had been hearing some lectures on botany at the Kensington Museum, and been delighted by them. She is the kind of person who gets good out of everything, and she was quite right in being delighted; besides that, as I found by her account of them, the lectures were really interesting, and pleasantly given. She had expected botany to be dull, and had not found it so, and "had learned so much." On hearing this I proceeded naturally to inquire what; for my idea of her was that before she went to the lectures at all she had known more botany than she was likely to learn by them. So she told me that she had learned first of all that "there were seven sorts of leaves." Now I have always a great suspicion of the number Seven; because, when I wrote *The Seven Lamps of Architecture*, it required all the ingenuity I was master of to prevent them from becoming Eight, or even Nine, on my hands. So I thought to myself that it would be very charming if there were only seven sorts of leaves, but that, perhaps, if one looked the woods and forests of the world carefully through, it was just possible that one might discover as many as eight sorts; and then where would my friend's new knowledge of botany be? So I said, "That was very pretty; but what more?" Then my friend told me that the lecturer said "the object of his lectures would be entirely accomplished if he could convince his hearers that there was no such thing as a flower." Now in that sentence you have the most perfect and admirable summary given you of the general temper and purposes of modern science. It gives lectures on Botany, of which the object is to show that there is no such thing as a Flower; on Humanity, to show that there is no such thing as a Man; and on Theology, to show there is no such thing as a God. No such thing as a Man, but only a Mechanism; no such thing as a God, but only a series of Forces. The two faiths are essentially one: if you feel yourself to be only a machine, constructed to be a regulator of minor machinery, you will put your statue of such science on your Holborn Viaduct, and necessarily recognize only major machinery as regulating *you*.

I must explain the real meaning to you, however, of that saying of the botanical lecturer, for it has a wide bearing. Some fifty years ago the poet Goethe discovered that all the parts of plants had a kind of common nature and would change into each other. Now, this was a true discovery and a notable one; and you will find that, in fact, all plants are composed of essentially two parts—the leaf and root; one loving the light, the other darkness; one liking to be clean, the other to be dirty; one liking to grow for the most part up, the other for the most part down; and each having faculties and purposes of its own. But the pure one, which loves the light, has, above all things, the purpose of being married to another leaf, and having child-leaves and children's children of leaves, to make the earth fair forever. And when the leaves marry, they put on wedding-robes and are more glorious than Solomon in all his glory, and they have feasts of honey; and we call them "Flowers."

In a certain sense, therefore, you see the botanical lecturer was quite right. There are no such things as Flowers—there are only gladdened Leaves. Nay, farther than this, there may be a dignity in the less happy but unwithering leaf, which is in some sort, better than the brief lily in its bloom; which the great poets always knew well, Chaucer before Goethe, and the writer of the

First Psalm before Chaucer. The botanical lecturer was, in a deeper sense than he knew, right.

But in the deepest sense of all, the botanical lecturer was, to the extremity of wrongness, wrong; for leaf and root and fruit exist, all of them, only that there may be flowers. He disregarded the life and passion of the creature, which were its essence. Had he looked for these, he would have recognized that in the thought of Nature herself there is in a plant nothing else but its flowers.

Now, in exactly the sense that modern science declares there is no such thing as a Flower, it has declared there is no such thing as a Man, but only a transitional form of Ascidians and apes. It may or may not be true—it is not of the smallest consequence whether it be or not. The real fact is that, rightly seen with human eyes, there is nothing else but Man; that all animals and beings beside him are only made that they may change into him, that the world truly exists only in the presence of Man, acts only in the passion of Man. The essence of Light is in his eyes, the centre of Force in his soul, the pertinence of Action in his deeds. And all true science—which my Savoyard guide rightly scorned me when he thought I had not—all true science is *savoir vivre*. But all your modern science is the contrary of that. It is *savoir mourir*.

And of its very discoveries, such as they are, it cannot make use.

That telegraphic signalling was a discovery, and conceivably, some day, may be a useful one. And there was some excuse for your being a little proud when, about last sixth of April (Cœur de Lion's death-day, and Albert Dürer's), you knotted a copper wire all the way to Bombay, and flashed a message along it, and back. But what was the message, and what the answer? Is India the better for what you said to her? Are you the better for what she replied? If not, you have only wasted an all-round-the-world's length of copper wire—which is, indeed, about the sum of your doing. If you had had, perchance, two words of common sense to say, though you had taken wearisome time and trouble to send them,—though you had written them slowly in gold, and sealed them with a hundred seals, and sent a squadron of ships of the line to carry the scroll, and the squadron had fought its way round the Cape of Good Hope, through a year of storms, with loss of all its ships but one,—the two words of common sense would have been worth the carriage, and more. But you have not anything like so much as that to say, either to India or to any other place.

You think it a great triumph to make the sun draw brown landscapes for you. That was also a discovery, and some day may be useful. But the sun had drawn landscapes before for you, not in brown, but in green and blue and all imaginable colours, here in England. Not one of you ever looked at them then; not one of you cares for the loss of them now, when you have shut the sun out with smoke, so that he can draw nothing more except brown blots through a hole in a box. There was a rocky valley between Buxton and Bakewell, once upon a time, divine as the Vale of Tempe; you might have seen the gods there morning and evening—Apollo and all the sweet Muses of the light—walking in fair procession on the lawns of it and to and fro among the pinnacles of its crags. You cared neither for gods nor grass, but for cash (which you did not know the way to get); you thought you could get it by what the *Times* calls "Railroad Enterprise." You Enterprised a Railroad through the valley—you blasted rocks away, heaped thousands of tons of shale into its lovely stream. The valley is gone, and the gods with it; and now every fool in Buxton can be at Bakewell in half an hour, and every fool in Bakewell at Buxton; which you think a lucrative process of exchange—you Fools Everywhere.

To talk at a distance, when you have nothing to say though you were ever so near; to go fast from this place to that, with nothing to do either at one or the other:—these are powers certainly. Much more, power of increased Production, if you indeed had got it, would be something to boast of. But are you so entirely sure that you *have* got it—that the mortal disease of plenty, and afflictive affluence of good things, are all you have to dread?

Observe. A man and a woman, with their children, properly trained, are able easily to cultivate as much ground as will feed them, to build as much wall and roof as will lodge them, and to spin and weave as much cloth as will clothe them. They can all be perfectly happy and healthy in doing this. Supposing that they invent machinery which will build, plough, thresh, cook, and weave, and that they have none of these things any more to do, but may read, or play croquet or cricket, all day long, I believe myself that they will neither be so good nor so happy as without the machines. But I waive my belief in this matter for the time. I will assume that they become more refined and moral persons, and that idleness is in future to be the mother of all good. But observe, I repeat, the power of your machine is only in enabling them to be idle. It will not enable them to live better than they did before, nor to live in greater numbers. Get your heads quite clear on this matter. Out of so much ground only so much living is to be got, with or without machinery. You may set a million of steam-ploughs to work on an acre, if you like—out of that acre only a given number of grains of corn will grow, scratch or scorch it as you will. So that the question is not at all whether, by having more machines, more of you can live. No machines will increase the possibilities of life. Suppose, for instance, you could get the oxen in your plough driven by a goblin, who would ask for no pay, not even a cream bowl (you have nearly managed to get it driven by an iron goblin, as it is); well, your furrow will take no more seeds than if you had held the stilts yourself. But instead of holding them you sit, I presume, on a bank beside the field, under an eglantine—watch the goblin at his work, and read poetry. Meantime, your wife in the house has also got a goblin to weave and wash for her. And she is lying on the sofa, reading poetry.

Now, as I said, I don't believe you would be happier so, but I am willing to believe it; only, since you are already such brave mechanists, show me at least one or two places where you *are* happier. Let me see one small example of approach to this seraphic condition. *I* can show *you* examples, millions of them, of happy people made happy by their own industry. Farm after farm I can show you, in Bavaria, Switzerland, the Tyrol, and such other places, where men and women are perfectly happy and good, without any iron servants. Show me, therefore, some English family, with its fiery familiar, happier than these. Or bring me—for I am not inconvincible by any kind of evidence—bring me the testimony of an English family or two to their increased felicity. Or if you cannot do so much as that, can you convince even themselves of it? They *are* perhaps happy, if only they knew how happy they were; Virgil thought so, long ago, of simple rustics; but you hear at present your steam-propelled rustics are crying out that they are anything else than happy, and that they regard their boasted progress "in the light of a monstrous Sham." I must tell you one little thing, however, which greatly perplexes my imagination of the relieved ploughman sitting under his rose-bower, reading poetry. I have told it you before, indeed, but I forget where. There was really a great festivity, and expression of satisfaction in the new order of things, down in Cumberland, a little while ago; some first of May, I think it was, a country festival such as the old heathens, who had no iron servants, used to keep with piping and dancing. So I thought, from the liberated country people—their work all done for them by goblins—we should have some extraordinary piping and dancing. But there was no dancing at all, and they could not even provide their own piping. They had their goblin to pipe for them. They walked in procession after their steam-plough, and their steam-plough whistled to them occasionally in the most melodious manner it could. Which seemed to me, indeed, a return to more than Arcadian simplicity; for in old Arcadia ploughboys truly whistled as they went, for want of thought; whereas here was verily a large company walking without thought, but not having any more even the capacity of doing their own whistling.

But next, as to the inside of the house. Before you got your power-looms, a woman could always make herself a chemise and petticoat of bright and pretty appearance. I have seen a Bavarian peasant-woman at church in Munich, looking a much grander creature, and more beautifully dressed, than any of the crossed and embroidered angels in Hesse's high-art frescoes (which happened to be just above her, so that I could look from one to the other). Well, here you are, in England, served by household demons, with five hundred fingers at least, weaving, for one that used to weave in the days of Minerva. You ought to be able to show me five hundred dresses for one that used to be; tidiness ought to have become five-hundred-fold tidier; tapestry should be increased into *cinque-cento*-fold iridescence of tapestry. Not only your peasant-girl ought to be lying on the sofa, reading poetry, but she ought to have in her wardrobe five hundred petticoats instead of one. Is that, indeed, your issue? or are you only on a curiously crooked way to it?

It is just possible, indeed, that you may not have been allowed to get the use of the goblin's work—that other people may have got the use of it, and you none; because, perhaps, you have not been able to evoke goblins wholly for your own personal service, but have been borrowing goblins from the capitalist, and paying interest, in the "position of William," on ghostly self-going planes. But suppose you had laid by capital enough, yourselves, to hire all the demons in the world—nay all that are inside of it; are you quite sure you know what you might best set them to work at, and what "useful things" you should command them to make for you? I told you, last month, that no economist going (whether by steam or ghost) knew what are useful things and what are not. Very few of you know, yourselves, except by bitter experience of the want of them. And no demons, either of iron or spirit, can ever make them.

There are three material things, not only useful but essential to life. No one "knows how to live" till he has got them.

These are Pure Air, Water, and Earth.

There are three immaterial things, not only useful, but essential to life. No one knows how to live till he has got them also.

These are Admiration, Hope, and Love.

Admiration—the power of discerning and taking delight in what is beautiful in visible Form and lovely in human Character, and, necessarily, striving to produce what is beautiful in form and to become what is lovely in character.

Hope—the recognition, by true foresight, of better things to be reached hereafter, whether by ourselves or others; necessarily issuing in the straightforward and undisappointable effort to advance, according to our proper power, the gaining of them.

Love—both of family and neighbour, faithful and satisfied.

These are the six chiefly useful things to be got by Political Economy, when it *has* become a science. I will briefly tell you what modern Political Economy—the great *savoir mourir*—is doing with them.

The first three, I said, are Pure Air, Water, and Earth.

Heaven gives you the main elements of these. You can destroy them at your pleasure, or increase, almost without limit, the available quantities of them.

You can vitiate the air by your manner of life and of death, to any extent. You might easily vitiate it so as to bring such a pestilence on the globe as would end all of you. You, or your fellows, German and French, are at present vitiating it to the best of your power in every direction—chiefly at this moment with corpses, and animal and vegetable ruin in war, changing men, horses, and garden-stuff into noxious gas. But everywhere, and all day long, you are vitiating it with foul chemical exhalations; and the horrible nests, which you call towns, are little more than laboratories for the distillation into heaven of venomous smokes and smells, mixed with effluvia from decaying animal matter and infectious miasmata from purulent disease.

On the other hand, your power of purifying the air, by dealing properly and swiftly with all substances in corruption, by absolutely forbidding noxious manufactures, and by planting in all soils the trees which cleanse and invigorate earth and atmosphere, is literally infinite. You might make every breath of air you draw, food.

Secondly, your power over the rain and river-waters of the earth is infinite. You can bring rain where you will, by planting wisely and tending carefully; drought where you will, by ravage of woods and neglect of the soil. You might have the rivers of England as pure as the crystal of the rock; beautiful in falls, in lakes, in living pools; so full of fish that you might take them out with your hands instead of nets. Or you may do always as you have done now—turn every river of England into a common sewer, so that you cannot so much as baptize an English baby but with filth, unless you hold its face out in the rain; and even *that* falls dirty.

Then for the third, earth, meant to be nourishing for you and blossoming. You have learned about it that there is no such thing as a flower; and as far as your scientific hands and scientific brains, inventive of explosive and deathful instead of blossoming and life-giving dust, can contrive, you have turned the Mother Earth, Demeter, into the Avenger Earth, Tisiphone—with the voice of your brother's blood crying out of it in one wild harmony round all its murderous sphere.

That is what you have done for the Three Material Useful Things.

Then for the Three Immaterial Useful Things. For Admiration, you have learned contempt and conceit. There is no lovely thing ever yet done by man that you care for, or can understand; but you are persuaded you are able to do much finer things yourselves. You gather and exhibit together, as if equally instructive, what is infinitely bad with what is infinitely good. You do not know which is which; you instinctively prefer the Bad, and do more of it. You instinctively hate the Good, and destroy it.

Then, secondly, for Hope. You have not so much spirit of it in you as to begin any plan which will not pay for ten years, nor so much intelligence of it in you (either politicians or workmen) as to be able to form one clear idea of what you would like your country to become.

Then, thirdly, for Love. You were ordered by the Founder of your religion to love your neighbour as yourselves. You have founded an entire science of Political Economy on what you have stated to be the constant instinct of man—the desire to defraud his neighbour. And you have driven your women mad, so that they ask no more for Love nor for fellowship with you, but stand against you, and ask for "justice."

Are there any of you who are tired of all this? Any of you Landlords or Tenants? Employers or Workmen? Are there any landlords, any masters, who would like better to be served by men than by iron devils? Any tenants, any workmen, who can be true to their leaders and to each other? who can vow to work and to live faithfully, for the sake of the joy of their homes?

Will any such give the tenth of what they have, and of what they earn, not to emigrate with, but to stay in England with, and do what is in their hands and hearts to make her a happy England?

I am not rich (as people now estimate riches), and great part of what I have is already engaged in maintaining art-workmen, or for other objects more or less of public utility. The tenth of whatever is left to me, estimated as accurately as I can (you shall see the accounts), I will make over to you in perpetuity, with the best security that English law can give, on Christmas Day of this year, with engagement to add the tithe of whatever I earn after-wards. Who else will help, with little or much? the object of such fund being to begin, and gradually—no matter how slowly—to increase the buying and securing of land in England, which shall not be built upon, but cultivated by Englishmen with their own hands and such help of force as they can find in wind and wave. I do not care with how many or how few this thing is begun, nor on what inconsiderable scale—if it be but in two or three poor men's gardens. So much, at least, I can buy, myself, and give them. If no help come, I have done and said what I could, and there will be an end. If any help come to me, it is to be on the following conditions:—

We will try to make some small piece of English ground beautiful, peace-ful, and fruitful. We will have no steam-engines upon it, and no railroads; we will have no untended or unthought-of-creatures on it; none wretched but the sick; none idle but the dead. We will have no liberty upon it, but instant obedience to known law and appointed persons; no equality upon it, but rec-ognition of every betterness that we can find, and reprobation of every worse-ness. When we want to go anywhere, we will go there quietly and safely, not at forty miles an hour in the risk of our lives; when we want to carry anything anywhere, we will carry it either on the backs of beasts, or on our own, or in carts or boats. We will have plenty of flowers and vegetables in our gardens, plenty of corn and grass in our fields,—and few bricks. We will have some music and poetry; the children shall learn to dance to it and sing it; perhaps some of the old people, in time, may also. We will have some art, moreover; we will at least try if, like the Greeks, we can't make some pots. The Greeks used to paint pictures of gods on their pots. We, probably, cannot do as much; but we may put some pictures of insects on them, and reptiles—butterflies and frogs, if nothing better. There was an excellent old potter in France who used to put frogs and vipers into his dishes, to the admiration of mankind; we can surely put something nicer than that. Little by little, some higher art and imagination may manifest themselves among us, and feeble rays of science may dawn for us:—botany, though too dull to dispute the existence of flowers; and history, though too simple to question the nativity of men; nay, even perhaps an uncalculating and uncovetous wisdom, as of rude Magi, presenting, at such nativity, gifts of gold and frankincense.

Faithfully yours,

JOHN RUSKIN

# THE EVOLUTION OF THE PHYSICAL WORLD

*Arthur Stanley Eddington*   (*1929*)

LOOKING back through the long past we picture the beginning of the world —a primeval chaos which time has fashioned into the universe that we know. Its vastness appals the mind; space boundless though not infinite, according to the strange doctrine of science. The world was without form and almost void. But at the earliest stage we can contemplate the void is sparsely broken by tiny electric particles, the germs of the things that are to be; positive and negative they wander aimlessly in solitude, rarely coming near enough to seek or shun one another. They range everywhere so that all space is filled, and yet so empty that in comparison the most highly exhausted vacuum on earth is a jostling throng. In the beginning was vastness, solitude and the deepest night. Darkness was upon the face of the deep, for as yet there was no light.

The years rolled by, million after million. Slight aggregations occurring casually in one place and another drew to themselves more and more particles. They warred for sovereignty, won and lost their spoil, until the matter was collected round centers of condensation leaving vast empty spaces from which it had ebbed away. Thus gravitation slowly parted the primeval chaos. These first divisions were not the stars but what we should call "island universes" each ultimately to be a system of some thousands of millions of stars. From our own island universe we can discern the other islands as spiral nebulæ lying one beyond another as far as the telescope can fathom. The nearest of them is such that light takes 900,000 years to cross the gulf between us. They acquired rotation (we do not yet understand how) which bulged them into flattened form and made them wreathe themselves in spirals. Their forms, diverse, yet with underlying regularity, make a fascinating spectacle for telescopic study.

As it had divided the original chaos, so gravitation subdivided the island universes. First the star clusters, then the stars themselves were separated. And with the stars came light, born of the fiercer turmoil which ensued when the electrical particles were drawn from their solitude into dense throngs. A star is not just a lump of matter casually thrown together in the general confusion; it is of nicely graded size. There is relatively not much more diversity in the masses of new-born stars than in the masses of new-born babies. Aggregations rather greater than our Sun have a strong tendency to subdivide, but when the mass is reduced a little the danger quickly passes and the impulse to subdivision is satisfied. Here it would seem the work of creation might cease. Having carved chaos into stars, the first evolutionary impulse has reached its goal. For many billions of years the stars may continue to shed their light and heat through the world, feeding on their own matter which disappears bit by bit into ætherial waves.

Not infrequently a star, spinning too fast or strained by the radiant heat imprisoned within it, may divide into two nearly equal stars, which remain yoked together as a double star; apart from this no regular plan of further development is known. For what might be called the second day of creation we turn from the general rule to the exceptions. Amid so many myriads there will be a few which by some rare accident have a fate unlike the rest. In the vast expanse of the heavens the traffic is so thin that a star may reasonably count on travelling for the whole of its long life without serious risk of collision. The risk is negligible for any individual star; but ten thousand million stars in our own system and more in the systems beyond afford a wide playground for chance. If the risk is one in a hundred millions some unlucky victims are doomed to play the role of "one." This rare accident must have happened to our Sun—an accident to the Sun, but to us the cause of our being here. A star journeying through space casually overtook the Sun, not indeed colliding with it, but approaching so close as to raise a great tidal wave. By this disturbance jets of matter spurted out of the Sun; being carried round by their angular momentum they did not fall back again but condensed into small globes—the planets.

By this and similar events there appeared here and there in the universe something outside Nature's regular plan, namely a lump of matter small enough and dense enough to be cool. A temperature of ten million degrees or more prevails through the greater part of the interior of a star; it cannot be otherwise so long as matter remains heaped in immense masses. Thus the design of the first stage of evolution seems to have been that matter should ordinarily be endowed with intense heat. Cool matter appears as an afterthought. It is unlikely that the Sun is the only one of the starry host to possess a system of planets, but it is believed that such development is very rare. In these exceptional formations Nature has tried the experiment of finding what strange effects may ensue if matter is released from its usual temperature of millions of degrees and permitted to be cool.

Out of the electric charges dispersed in the primitive chaos ninety-two different kinds of matter—ninety-two chemical elements—have been built. This building is also a work of evolution, but little or nothing is known as to its history. In the matter which we handle daily we find the original bricks fitted together and cannot but infer that somewhere and somewhen a process of matter-building has occurred. At high temperature this diversity of matter remains as it were latent; little of consequence results from it. But in the cool experimental stations of the universe the differences assert themselves. At root the diversity of the ninety-two elements reflects the diversity of the integers from one to ninety-two; because the chemical characteristics of element No. 11 (sodium) arise from the fact that it has the power at low temperatures of gathering round it eleven negative electric particles; those of No. 12 (magnesium) from its power of gathering twelve particles; and so on.

It is tempting to linger over the development out of this fundamental beginning of the wonders studied in chemistry and physics, but we must hurry on.

The provision of certain cool planetary globes was the second impulse of evolution, and it has exhausted itself in the formation of inorganic rocks and ores and other materials. We must look to a new exception or abnormality if anything further is to be achieved. We can scarcely call it an accident that among the integers there should happen to be the number 6; but I do not know how otherwise to express the fact that organic life would not have begun if Nature's arithmetic had overlooked the number 6. The general plan of ninety-two elements, each embodying in its structural pattern one of the first ninety-two numbers, contemplates a material world of considerable but limited diversity; but the element carbon, embodying the number 6, and because of the peculiarity of the number 6, rebels against limits. The carbon atoms love to string themselves in long chains such as those which give toughness to a soap-film. Whilst other atoms organise themselves in twos and threes or it may be in tens, carbon atoms organise themselves in hundreds and thousands. From this potentiality of carbon to form more and more elaborate structures, a third impulse of evolution arises.

I cannot profess to say whether anything more than this prolific structure-building power of carbon is involved in the beginning of life. The story of evolution here passes into the domain of the biological sciences for which I cannot speak, and I am not ready to take sides in the controversy between the Mechanists and the Vitalists. So far as the earth is concerned the history of development of living forms extending over nearly a thousand million years is recorded (though with many breaks) in fossil remains. Looking back over the geological record it would seem that Nature made nearly every possible mistake before she reached her greatest achievement Man—or perhaps some would say her worst mistake of all. At one time she put her trust in armaments and gigantic size. Frozen in the rock is the evidence of her failures to provide a form fitted to endure and dominate—failures which we are only too ready to imitate. At last she tried a being of no great size, almost defenceless, defective in at least one of the more important sense-organs; one gift she bestowed to save him from threatened extinction—a certain stirring, a restlessness, in the organ called the brain.

And so we come to Man.

## THE MAN WITH A TRACTOR

*Morrow Mayo* (*1938*)

Sank drove into a field that was full of thistles, broom weeds, careless weeds, winter weeds, goat-heads, and blue weeds. The wind was out of the southwest and there were scattering clouds in the east and thunderheads to the north. Despite the rank vegetation, the truck left a trail of dust like a destroyer laying down a smoke screen.

At intervals he got out and bored into the red cat-claw land with a three-foot soil auger. When he unscrewed the auger he pulled the dark, moist earth out of the auger-head, sniffed it, made little balls, and threw them to the ground. He had to drive in low, and twice the truck started to boil. He headed it into the wind, cut off the motor, and let it cool.

He finished in the northwest corner of the field and stood looking out over the woolly land. It was a beautiful half-section, so level that he could see the bottom of the weeds a mile away. There was not a tree, stump, lake, or rock in it. Sank lighted a cigarette, thinking. It was a crime to let land go like that. His hands, face, clothes, shoes, and hat were the same color as the reddish dusty top-soil on which he stood. There was plenty of deep-moisture. It would not be good farming, but a man had to do many things here that he wouldn't do if conditions were different. He got into his truck and drove to the unpainted frame house which stood near the northeast corner of the field.

Sank stopped his tractor in the edge of the field, headed west. He lowered the discs of the one-way plow, socking the levers down to the last notch. He wanted to get all that stuff. In third speed, making three and one-half miles an hour, he took off. The discs cut into the earth like circle saws, throwing the soil one way. The weeds fell as soldiers sometimes fall, going up into the air and pitching forward head first, roots up.

He plowed until dark, walked to the house and ate his supper, rested a little while, and returned to the field. He turned on his lights. One bright eye gleaming on the weeds ahead, one on the plow behind, the tractor lumbered over the land, snorting fire.

It was mighty bleak out there at night. Some wit had called this country the Siberia of America, and he was righter than he knew. There is not much difference between the great wheat lands of the world: between the Siberian steppes and the Australian prairies and the Argentine pampas and the high plains of North America. It is different only in the Danubian countries. All the others are vast uplands—immense, limitless, very similar in appearance, in scenery, in vegetation; very similar nowadays, even down to tractors and implements, and men. Blindfold a man, take him from a tractor on one, put him on a tractor on another, would he know the difference?

At midnight the wind shifted to the west. Going east, the dust blew over Sank; going west, the heat hit him in the face. Horses, no matter how many, got tired eventually. The tractor did not get tired. It was 6½ feet tall, 12 feet long, and 8 feet wide. It weighed 5,300 pounds. The rubber tires on the rear wheels were larger than a woman's body. Sank never wondered what would happen if that monster got out of control, stampeded, or turned on its driver.

It was two o'clock when he stopped. He was asleep by two-thirty, up again before daylight. He plowed eighteen hours a day, and finally he was through. He raised the discs and drove to the house. It was too hot for early September. The windmill was not turning; the sky was clear. No-weather was a weather-breeder. Sank slept ten hours.

A blue norther had struck. The land to the south was a powderhouse. The thin row of young Chinese elms bent low. Sank saw a hawk wheel in the sky in the face of that wind. Across the great level pasture to the east a jackrabbit was loping easily, on four legs, on three. He ran, then coasted. The hawk folded his wings and dropped like a small black bomb tossed from an airplane. The jackrabbit was not coasting now. He was doing forty miles an hour.

The hawk struck, staggered, rose slowly with the weight, great wings flapping. High enough in the air, he opened his talons. The rabbit fell to earth, hit the hard ground, did not move. In slow, triumphant circles the hawk descended to his dinner.

Sank backed his truck into the barn and got down and closed the doors with difficulty. The wind was blowing a young gale. He backed his truck to the other end of the barn, and parked it up close to a mound of seed wheat—pure black hull wheat, strong, high in protein content, one hundred and fifty bushels of it. Near the pile of wheat Sank set up his seed wheat-treating machine.

Before he opened the half-gallon can of chemical Sank put on a gas mask. The can had a skull-and-cross-bones on it. The chemical prevented wheat from becoming infected with smut. In this country smut losses from untreated wheat sometimes run as high as fifty per cent. The fumes from that chemical will kill a man. Sank poured the thick, black, sticky liquid into the seed wheat-treating machine, started the gasoline motor, picked up a scoop, and started scooping the seed wheat into the machine. The wheat ran through the chemical, up the funnel, and poured out of the spout into the truck.

Usually Sank was just an ordinary-looking man, just an average-looking farmer, with arms and legs, a mouth and eyes, a wife and two children. Working there in that barn, the wind howling outside, in the dim half-light, with that gas mask on, and the rats scurrying around, he didn't look like a farmer. He looked like a product of a more advanced civilization. He didn't even look like a man. He looked like some horrible, sightless, anthropoidal thing with a snout.

He scooped the golden grain and it was hard work. He didn't quit until he had put it all through the machine. Then he threw down the scoop, cut off the motor, took off his gas mask, and went to the house. He noticed the thin row of young Chinese elms again. Last year the saplings had bent flat to the ground before the force of the onslaught. This year the Chinese elms were not bowing their heads quite so low. Next year . . .

The wind had subsided as suddenly as it had struck. Sank went out and unhitched his plow, hitched the tractor to the drill, set the sprockets of the drill so that it would sow twenty pounds to the acre, and scooped the seed wheat into the drill-bins until they were level full. He oiled and watered and fueled the tractor and lubricated both tractor and drill. Then he lowered the discs, cranked the tractor, threw it into fourth speed, and took off up the edge of the plowed field, making four miles an hour, sowing wheat.

Wheat is undoubtedly the finest, most courageous thing that grows on the face of the earth. The implement drilled the seed wheat into the earth. If I were called upon to award the first prize to the best thing that grows, I should walk up and hang the gold medal over the head of a stalk of hard winter wheat. The discs made little planting furrows; the drill set down the single grains of wheat in the furrows; the drag-chains covered them over with soil. It was all mechanical. It was different from the days, from Joseph down to not so long ago, when a man dipped into a sack of seed wheat, and sowed it by hand, three scattering throws to the handful.

When Sank put the grains into the soil they were hard as rocks. Twelve hours later they were mealy. Six hours later they were sprouting. This is when the farmers say the earth is moving. Put it in a glass and you can see it grow. Twenty-four hours after Sank put the first hard grains into the soil, the brave, pale green shoots were thrusting themselves up out of the earth. There is nothing petty or knickknacky or clever or obscene about anything connected with wheat. It is clean and strong and vital. Wheat is bread. It is the staff of life.

When Sank came up the east side he saw the Chinese elms. On the west side he looked at a great pasture of Argentine pampa grass. On the south side he passed a sixty-foot border of African sudan grass. Originally it had prevented the Sudan from blowing Egypt off the map. Now they have got it working in the Dust Bowl. And all about Sank were the big green Russian thistles which he had plowed up, and which would become huge tumble-weeds and go galloping over the plains like horses.

Argentine pampa grass, African sudan, Russian thistles, and Chinese elms. From the four corners of the earth. All growing together right in the Panhandle, U. S. A. Nature—if nobody else—was getting international. Nature and machinery. Neither spoke any language, noticed any color, recognized any boundary. So there was still hope for men. . . .

It had better be noted, the metamorphosis of the man with the hoe. Millet, on canvas, caught and held that brutish, hopeless earthpecker leaning on a crude hand-tool. Markham, beholding him, appalled, asked greatly and bitterly, why and how? The tragedy of the world was summed up in that eloquent painting, those awful words. But you can't say :"Bowed by the weight of centuries he leans upon his F-30 tractor."

Driving that tractor Sank didn't look like a humble and degraded tiller of the soil. He didn't look like a hay-chewing rube with chin whiskers, or a dunghill yokel, or a peasant without thought or hope. The tractor had done that. It had changed a farmer from a clod into an operator; from a dumb brute into a mechanic, all over the world. The tractor had done more to make him a self-respecting man than anything that had ever happened in the whole history of agriculture since the invention of the wheel.

The man with the tractor does not gaze on the ground. Unavoidably, by the nature of things, Sank sat and gazed at the distant horizon, which was on a level with his eyes. He gazed at it when the sky was clear and steel-blue, and when the moon set behind clouds that moved slowly in serried masses, and when the sun came up like a ball of fire, a flaming red.

Sank finished sowing his wheat. He raised the discs out of the ground and drove his tractor over the impregnated earth toward his house. It was twilight. The sky was overcast and the air was sultry. But you couldn't say "The ploughman homeward plods his weary way." Sank's eyes, gleaming through caked dirt, were red, but he showed no other signs of fatigue, though he was hot and sweaty and dirty.

He felt a drop of rain on his shoulder. Another. And then a lot more. He watched the big drops strike into the dry, thirsty soil. The rain was wet and cool. And now it began to come down in a slow steady downpour. The wheat, the earth, were drinking it up. Sank had got the job done and now it was raining. It made him feel good. Wet to the skin, water pouring down his dirty face, he sat erect in the tractor-seat, steering the juggernaut to the house.

## SCIENCE AND THE MONEY-MINDED

### T. Swann Harding  (1930)

### I

SOME young men are very fortunate. Even some research workers are very fortunate when they are young. I know one who had a rather remarkable fellowship at a large university. For three years he drew a salary of three thousand dollars annually, including the privilege of working in one of the best-equipped chemical laboratories in the United States, simply to potter around with ephedrine which I may identify for laymen by saying that it seems a drug destined eventually in part to replace adrenalin or epinephrin. The young man could do about what he wanted to do; he was an organic chemist and he had a perfectly ravishing time during the three years—which was unfortunate for reasons that we shall investigate later. His three thousand dollars came from one of the largest and, scientifically, one of the most advanced pharmaceutical manufacturing concerns in this country.

During the three years he was occasionally visited by administrative and technical men employed by the company. They came not to direct him, for they could not do that. He knew more about organic chemistry than the entire company put together and laid length-wise. They came to question him and pick up scraps. They picked up, during the three years, scraps valued commercially at $150,000. In other words, this young man, upon whose time the company expended a total of $9000 (for the university gladly gave him laboratory space and working materials, merely to share the glory of his achievements), found out, quite accidentally, more economically valuable things about ephedrine than all the high-salaried executives of the pharmaceutical company ever found out about anything in their lives. In short, the natural drive of the curiosity of a young man with a talent for organic chemistry brought in a profit of $141,000 to an enterprising group of Babbitts (if we may call them that, with no desire to be derogatory) who happened, by pure chance, to set him the problem. At the end of three years the company had enough information; in short, the law of diminishing returns had begun to apply, the research had become too remotely fundamental to be immediately profitable, and the fellowship ended.

Fortunately, just at that moment certain social scientists who had been studying the narcotic problem decided to drop it. In five years, and after considerable expenditure of money supplied by a rich foundation, they had decided that they did not know how to solve the problem and that a more fundamental science had better be called in. A chemist was needed, and the young man got a new fellowship at the old salary, and he now applies his phenomenal genius, for it is no less, to the problem of discovering narcotic-like substances which will have the same benign qualities as morphine and cocaine, but will lack all of their harmful elements—a very fundamental way to solve a hard social problem.

Should he solve this problem after a further expenditure of $9000, the results would be too tremendous to calculate in economic terms and he would stand ready to accept another $3000 fellowship. Finally, he could honestly and sincerely declare that he had spent six happy years in the laboratory actually getting paid for doing what he most wanted to do anyway.

What have we found out? That some men make fabulous sums of money by the amicable exploitation of other men with better brains, who are so seduced by the idea of being paid a moderate salary for doing exactly what they want to do that the injustice of the situation, if it inheres at all, does not occur to them.

We have also discovered the manner in which knowledge comes into being, and that contributing to the growth and the enhancement of fundamental knowledge is not an activity which has high economic value in our civilization.

Now how could such a man make money if he wished? I can best answer that by the story of a very prominent engineer which was told me yesterday. This man graduated from a university as an engineer and he worked at this profession to some extent. But there came a time when he had the opportunity to help buy some patents and form a company. As an engineer he had been a productive worker adding to the sum total of human knowledge, but he was not well paid. Now he and certain more wealthy men discovered two other men who had devised a method by which ore of a certain type, which had for years been discarded as unprofitable, could be reworked at an enormous profit. He himself happened to know that a large group of abandoned mines supplying this ore existed in a distant country; the other more wealthy men did not know this; the two men who devised the method would not have thought of trying to find out such a thing anyway.

Therefore the engineer and the wealthy men formed a company in which even the inventors of the process were given moderate amounts of stock, for these wealthy men were soft-hearted. The engineer, however, having in mind the distant mines, desired no stock; he asked only the right to use the process. That is about the end of the story. The engineer bought the poor mines and used the process; the wealthy men got a little wealthier; the inventors got much less than the others, but they had enjoyed what they did and probably thought they were overpaid; and the engineer got very rich—no discredit to him. For he and every other member of the group simply did what people do in this civilization of ours in accordance with the social and economic rules by which we contrive so strikingly to misdirect this civilization for the benefit of the few and the degradation of the many. It works for the benefit of men who have the astuteness to know the location of abandoned mines, and to form companies for the friendly exploitation of a small minority of other men who have brains so remarkable that the mere using of them gives a pleasure that money cannot enhance.

## II

Meantime there are voices calling in the wilderness and saying that the research man does not get his just reward. Is this altogether true? It is quite generally admitted that our present civilization rests upon the brains of men of science. It is also admitted that scientists lack power. Finally it is true that, in a democracy, a determined and vociferous minority can, if they set themselves to the task, do about whatever they desire to do. Must research men therefore remain inadequately rewarded?

Again, the scientist gets as the major portion of his reward the same thing the writer and the painter get—that gloriously and deliriously joyous feeling which pervades a man of more than average mental gifts when the machinery is running at high speed. The article produced may or may not sell at a high price. That is secondary. Give such a man a bare living, and the mere joy of feeling the wheels turn will render him so happy that he can conscientiously regard as his benefactors the astute men of very narrowly limited talent who exploit him in the most friendly way imaginable—so long as his incidental by-products have a high market value. He possesses that which could remake civilization; however, the civilization which exists is not only so regulated as to reduce his monetary reward to a minimum, but its very agencies and powers penalize him at every step and tend to restrict or to inhibit the increase and the application of his knowledge.

I know what this means. I have myself been on friendly terms with a man who was enabled to make $50,000 a year in great part by reason of the fact that four men at $2500 a year, of whom I was one, supplied the essential knowledge which enabled the firm of which he was president to pay 19 per cent annual dividends on its mildly watered stock. When I say I was friendly I mean it, and I believe he was sincerely friendly with me. We four enjoyed having our wheels go round; he looked upon us as slightly insane persons whose rather ridiculous gyrations, none the less, happened to produce valuable by-products which he could sell. To say that he was exploiting me would be to talk nonsense; to say that I felt exploited would be equally nonsensical.

That was twelve years ago, and I was well paid and knew it. He was conscious of my value to the company, and that was why he not only paid me well but offered me both his church pew and his seats at the symphony orchestra concerts. (I took the latter gladly!) We were both parts of a great system which had arisen and enabled him to profit from my brains (he admitted he had none of my type of brains, nor did he want any, for he was quite sure they would be both an annoyance and frightfully impractical), but we were honestly friendly, and when our ways parted this fundamental problem between us was ignored. I left largely because my vagrant curiosity led me into fields which were not economically profitable; we both agreed that this would never do in his industry, but I liked those problems, so I cheerfully took less salary to go elsewhere in a publicly supported research laboratory and let my wheels go round.

Now what is the position of the man who undertakes fundamental scientific research for a publicly supported institution? So far as he is a good investigator, he will want to do work which interests him and gives him pleasure. He will be permitted more leeway in state work than in industry. He will have a problem or project; he will be expected to gather facts, formulate conclusions, and these will be published for the direct or indirect benefit of the general public, depending upon the manner in which they are expressed, and whether further simplification is necessary. Yet, so far as he actually accomplishes what he would like to accomplish, either he himself or someone delegated to the task must present his work to laymen who have economic or political minds, whom we shall hereafter call money-minded men, whose sympathy must be aroused in order to permit the research and its publication to continue. That means time wasting; it means that research must be penalized; it means loss to the general public and a brake upon the advance of science, but this again is inherent in the very fundamental organization of our social and economic system—a system, let it be understood, admirably adapted no doubt to certain conditions, but not adapted to the end of making knowledge, and the wealth created by knowledge, available to the greatest possible number.

To be specific. A certain group of scientists wished, among other things, to publish a journal which would contain abstracts of work done in all branches of biology. They had to get $100,000 to do this and they had to get it from men who had no slightest idea what fundamental research in biology was all about, much less why it should be published and then republished in convenient abstract form. That fact came out in the first question put to the scientists by their lay benefactors: "How much do you spend on publishing your results for every one hundred dollars you spend on obtaining them?" No scientist ever thought about the thing that way, so none of them knew the answer. It was useless to stress the great value of having abstracts all over the field of biological research made quickly and regularly available to all research workers everywhere. Money-minded benefactors wanted to know: How many dollars do you usually spend in printing results for each one hundred dollars you spend in obtaining them—that is, on laboratories, equipment, materials, and salaries?

The scientists investigated. The answer was: We normally spend one dollar to make public the amount of knowledge it costs us $3333 to procure, and, come to think of it, that is mighty little, isn't it? Just who was at fault here is a pretty question—the money-minded people for letting such a situation continue, or the scientists for refusing to think like money-minded men just long enough to present the problem to them in such a way that even they could understand it. At any rate it seemed to all of them rather ridiculous to spend only a dollar to disseminate information it took over three thousand dollars to procure, and the funds were made available.

### III

The spectacle of a scientist attempting to defend fundamental research before a Congressional committee makes very interesting reading, and further illustrates what I have in mind. Yet neither of the parties to the spectacle should be blamed except so far as they are mutually responsible for a situation which manifestly should not continue to exist. The gap between their planes of thought should be bridged—or perhaps someone should bring along a ladder.

The scientist says, for instance, that we need money to investigate this beet disease. A member of the committee remarks that the scientist said the same thing last year and also five years ago, and that each time he got ten thousand dollars. The scientist says it is a long piece of fundamental research. Well, is it near an end? He cannot say. Has he ever ended up a piece of research in his life? In fact, isn't it true that if he ever gets a project started it goes on forever?

Well, new problems constantly arise to be subsumed under that project. Then, if he gets the money this time, what does he propose to do? He proposes to study the effect of certain kinds of light in speeding up the growth of beets. And what on earth has that to do with the beet disease? It has this to do with it: the disease advances rapidly; we must quickly develop a beet variety resistant to the disease in order to save a five-million-dollar industry in a certain section; the light will make beets mature and give seed in six months rather than in two years and thus speed up the hunt for a resistant variety. Then he launches into a discussion of light, which rapidly becomes opaque to the committee. Finally the committee chairman says, "That sounds like the Ten Commandments—very fine, but too impractical. Now, what is the next item?"

But one day in a moment of enlightenment a money-minded man asked a scientist: "What value does research in your organization bring back per dollar spent?" The scientist didn't know, of course, for scientists habitually ignore such problems as that. But he decided to find out; he decided it might be convincing if he did find out; so he went through several cubic feet of documents and had trained statisticians make some calculations. He discovered that the return per dollar spent on research by the Department of Agriculture, for that happened to be the organization in this case, was five hundred dollars, or 50,000 per cent, which is not bad outside a public-service corporation, and is impressive even to a money-minded man. It was impressive, and brought agricultural research an earned increment of long-delayed respect and appropriations. The incident also demonstrated that it pays, and does not necessarily demean the scientist, to think like a money-minded man occasionally, and thus accomplish by strategy that which he cannot accomplish by matter-of-fact statement.

There is in history the record of a certain research organization which did very fine work, but which habitually lacked funds to print its findings. Year by year facts accumulated in cold storage simply because certain laymen with money minds could not possibly see the importance of disseminating information which it had cost a great deal to procure. That is very natural. Most lay minds are industrialized, and, as I myself found, an industrial executive sometimes actually objects to the quotation, in a scientific article by one of his technicians, of the work of men who are long since dead and whose publications are actually available to everyone in public libraries. Why? Because he fears the technician may give away some trade or factory secret. While he has spies in every factory similar to his own to send him full information regarding processes developed there, he is somehow insensible to the fact that his competitors have spies in his, and he guards with extreme care the information his men of brains collect. Naturally, when such men become the directors of altruistic scientific foundations, they cannot possibly see the necessity for large funds to make results available in print to everyone; that is not the way of business.

But it is the way of scientists. So, in the case we are describing, the scientists deliberately connived with certain journalists to attack their institute violently in the press as an organization supported by funds set aside for the public good which actually failed to function efficiently simply because it did not rapidly and widely publish its results. These attacks at once drew the attention of industrial men; these men immediately appealed to those in charge of the funds; funds were released for publication, and all was merry once more. But, given the crazy, chaotic social and economic system we now possess, the method taken by the scientists, though a Babbitt method, was the only practicable one.

## IV

This system of ours elaborately rewards the men who, by congenial chance, happen to have the kind of brains which enable them to win in a competitive game which requires an ability of a very narrowly limited character, but it does not commensurately reward the men of brains whose product alone makes the entire game possible and the entire fabric existent. This game tends to bore the artist, the man of literature, and the research investigator, in the same way that it would bore a highly trained engineer if he were compelled to play all day with a toy engine, or the average business executive if he were compelled to read only and exclusively the very best literature in the world.

It is not my intention to be supercilious. I speak from experience, as a personal instance will show. When the depression of 1920 (engineered by the great minds which direct our economic system) occurred, I was working as research chemist in a factory. For some reasons best known to themselves, the money minds decided not to discharge me but to put me into a small department as production foreman. I had never been a foreman in my life, but I had to become one. I took hold, used common sense and the veriest rudiments of my scientific training, applied certainly not one-tenth the mental power I had previously applied to scientific research and decreased the cost of production in my department by one-half. More could easily have been accomplished, but I was called to other fields of endeavor.

Just how was this done? Well, I found that the average foreman or production manager would, when he received a formula from the scientific department, proceed to throw things together before he had read it completely. He would do as seemed right to him, and when the process failed, as it usually did, down the sewer the material went, and a new trial was started. These trials were all on a large scale and they cost money. I, instead, carefully read the formula before I started to make the product, studied it at each step of the process, and, if in grave doubt, tried out a small laboratory lot before I went ahead with a factory batch.

Again, orders came in for chemically pure sucrose. This is common sugar with a college education; it was then selling at about $1.40 a pound with common sugar at 11 cents. The factory manager, being jealous of the scientific departments, decided to make this sucrose himself without consulting research men. He did it by dissolving one hundred pounds of sugar at a time and later crystallizing it out by the use of alcohol. Each time he sent a sample to the analytical laboratory it came back rejected as making a cloudy solution and being more contaminated with dirt than the original sugar he started from. He had thus wasted about five hundred pounds of sugar, plus a great deal of labor, when I entered the factory. I controlled the crystallization with the greatest ease to keep dirt out of the product, and my first lot passed analysis. I next discovered that a certain sugar on the market was chemically pure anyway, so we crushed this, since it was a lump sugar, packaged it, and sold it directly!

These two things were in a way small triumphs to a commercial or money mind; to me they were too silly for words, but I had to make a living. Had I been a true scientist, of course, I would have starved rather than indulge in such antics—but that is my deficiency.

I said I was called to other fields of endeavor. That is not exactly true; I went to them when the president of the firm informed me that reduction of 50 per cent in costs of production did not really interest him enough to increase my salary, because selling price bore no set relation to cost of production anyway, except that the former was so much above the latter that 50 per cent, or even 100 per cent, savings were more or less immaterial.

## V

Let us turn now to what can happen under present circumstances and consider a case or two, in order to show how disorganized our present socio-politico-economic system really is.

Here is a man representing the beet industry. He says that if a single-germed beet could be developed the industry would be saved an enormous amount. The ordinary beet seed sprouts four or five stalks; these have to be painfully thinned down to one (the longest and strongest) by hand. So two scientists set to work on the problem which, if solved, would make beet growing as easy as corn growing. They found about one single-germed seed in five hundred, so they started out by segregating a lot of single-germed seeds. They planted these, and by keeping the line pure they soon had plants which would yield one-half single-germed seeds; a little more selection would have solved the problem. Meantime there had been no publicity—and then something happened.

One of the investigators was offered a better position elsewhere and he took it. The second resigned rather than drop the problem, as a certain lay director requested, but he did not take it elsewhere. The beet man who originally suggested the problem died. The seeds were lost, $60,000 was wasted, and today the industry is about as far from the single-germed seed as ever. Had these scientists been alert to get their results published—but many "pure" scientists somehow often are not—this waste would have been avoided. Publicity is a money-minded method, but it decidedly has its place in the scheme of things as they are.

As a matter of fact it is doubtful whether any scientific organization, even in the field of medicine, should entirely lack lay brains and advice. Absolute control by scientists is often disastrous. Perhaps this is because scientists themselves have inevitably become impregnated with the astute acquisitive ideas of

money-minded men. In the matter of the beets, of course, publicity was woefully neglected; on the other hand, science itself needs sufficient organization
to prevent the permanent sidetracking of important problems so near solution.

Quite recently the chemical director of an important research institute
was offered a position as head of a university department. He went to take this
new position, leaving, at the end of five years, a ten-year programme of fundamental research in physical chemistry. A great deal had been invested in
this programme; the personnel had been very carefully built up, and important
results were just beginning to be recorded. But the new chemical director was
interested in an altogether different line of work, as he was an organic chemist;
he found most of the old personnel and all the old equipment and apparatus
useless. He built up a new personnel, put the expensive apparatus in the cellar,
and started off on ideas of his own. His ideas were valuable and he was a genius,
but science cannot consider itself organized in even a rudimentary way until
such expensive disasters as this cease to occur.

A business man or two on the board might help. The National Academy
of Sciences seems to find such assistance from money-minded men invaluable,
while the biological institute at Woods Hole, controlling a large endowment,
also has a business man Rotarian chairman of its board, the rest all being scientists. On the other hand, too many money-minded men will simply wreck
science altogether, just as their presence, their ownership, and their ideals have
wrecked college and university education in this country. A very, very few
of the very best money minds would be enough to put the needed organization into science. I say this because I remember the president of a company
who, in my industrial days, came to me every so often to weep quietly about
the hundred thousand dollars which, he assured me, went down the sewers of
his concern annually. He was probably right. He felt impotent to stop this
loss. He probably was. The wastage went on, but profits were so high that it
hardly mattered. By this I mean that the returns on knowledge secreted by
brains are so high that you can hobble, inhibit, confine, and abuse it, and yet
make a great deal of money.

Consider soil as an instance. Soil is fundamental, more fundamental than
good roads for pleasure vehicles. We need good roads, of course, to promote
agriculture, which again is fundamental. But we do not need miles of roads
laid out largely to accommodate endless processions of pleasure vehicles,
driven by human automatons with vacuums in their heads, who have been so
long debauched by the machine that they feel uncomfortable unless persisting
in some meaningless mechanical activity. A soil survey is fundamental. The
United States Bureau of Chemistry and Soils assures us that such a survey is
one of the most valuable things economically imaginable and offers an enormous return on the investment. A detailed soil survey of an average county
can be made for less than the cost of one quarter of a mile of state road, and
yet so predominant is the money mind in America that it is easy to get the
state road and very difficult indeed to get funds for the complete soil surveys
we need.

Or, again, Bennett of the United States Bureau of Chemistry and Soils testified in 1929 before the Appropriations Committee of the House of Representatives (money-minded men in the majority—again no discredit to them, things being as they are) that 30,000,000 acres of farm land in the Piedmont Region from New York to Central Alabama had lost the top soil by erosion and that the farmers had to depend on the subsoil. When this washes away, that farm land will be barren and useless. Meantime it requires from four to eight hundred pounds of fertilizer per acre in lieu of a former two hundred pounds. In Fairfield County, South Carolina, 93,000 acres have been destroyed now, and Iowa, Nebraska, Missouri, and other states tell the same story. The soil often washes away at the rate of forty tons per acre per year. Yet this erosion could easily be prevented. The scientist wanted only $80,000 of government funds to spend on the project; he got $19,000. We spent $274,000,000 on cruisers and $57,000 on the prevention of soil erosion in the same three years. Even the most ardent advocate of cruisers should find this rather disproportionate, but it can easily be seen where money minds stand. The soil-erosion program did somewhat better later, after a loud prearranged "bally-hoo" to impress the money minds.

## VI

It is said that we spend approximately two hundred million dollars annually on research in this country. That is a large sum. It is large enough, in fact, to build about five airplane carriers. Our total income is eighty to ninety billion dollars a year. That means that we spend upon research $25 per $10,000 of annual income, which is not so much after all. Of that two hundred millions about twenty millions is devoted to fundamental research in pure science—that is, to the discovery of knowledge and the release of power upon which everything else in our civilization of today builds. That means that we spend only $2.50 per $10,000 of income on fundamental research; the remaining $22.50 goes to practical applications—that is, to such abstruse and difficult things as I told about when I mentioned the pure-sugar incident above. These figures are perhaps not exact, but they are relatively correct as given by Professor A. B. Wolfe.

What do they show? They show that the original source from whence all these magic machines of our modern civilization come to us receives comparatively little attention from the money minds. They show further that preaching to the people the value of research can only be effective when the statement is made in plain economic terms of profits and money value. But there is something deeper than that.

The control of the entire machinery of modern civilization remains in the hands of obsolete types of men who were naturally fitted to be leaders in another age. The popularization of science is a futile and largely impotent gesture so long as the fundamental basis of our social structure naturally gives all direction and power to money minds and practically no power, with scant reward, to productive brains. So long as this condition exists scientists must cry plaintively for funds, must pathetically cultivate money-minded men in order to placate them into making very minor investments in brains.

Furthermore, science is penalized and crippled so long as the production of knowledge must be at the behest and under the direction of men who, however honest, sincere, and good at heart, have narrowly limited minds, entirely unable to think about abstract concepts. Hence it is very doubtful whether all the publicity campaigns undertaken by scientists can ever achieve what they want to achieve, so long as they direct their efforts at superficialities and ignore the root of the problem. To inveigh against the money minds is useless. They are what they are, without the slightest conscious desire to be what they have become. To wheedle funds out of such minds by pathetic beggary demeans the men of brains. For the latter to gain some of the power and control which are rightfully theirs can alone solve the problem.

Of course circumstances occasionally put even a scientist in a position of economic power. During 1917 there came to an industry in this country an English chemist at an annual salary of $25,000. Since we were at war with Germany, he was the only man in the world available who had the knowledge to do a specific thing a rich industrial concern wanted done. But such events are rare, and they are both accidental and incidental. Even when, in the same year, I went to industry as a research chemist at one-tenth that salary, I got a stipend relatively good, for a beginner, because I happened to know more about organic chemistry than any other man available. When that knowledge had been utilized I became both less valuable and less important to my firm.

Implicit, if not explicit, in our entire ethic and philosophy is obeisance to the money mind. James Truslow Adams was perfectly correct when he declared that we educate people to *do*, not to *be*. The men of brains who dispense knowledge to youth do so under such circumstances that they erect in the students' minds a wall. This wall surrounds the Temple of Money. Against it thought beats in vain, save for inconsiderable moments of beneficent generosity. Thus the men of brains who dispense knowledge erect the very barrier against which the fundamental scientists who discover knowledge have later to thrust themselves in order to get meagre funds for their work. The situation is absurd, but so long as it exists we must expect research to occupy the place in our scheme of things which it occupies at present. No amount of popularization of science can ever be really successful until that wall is demolished and men are respected for what they *are* rather than exclusively for what they do.

## VII

We have, then, this situation. The competitive economic system developed at a time when mechanization did not exist, and when success in the system required brains, initiative, and courage. The same qualities were also required at that time to make a good soldier. Science came; it produced knowledge and released power. Scientists enjoyed producing the knowledge and were relatively uninterested in the power released. The best brains gravitated to science as science made the system a thing of chance—depending upon unearned increments, open markets, preëmpted fields, opportune moments, banking and stock-market manipulations, and a certain simple acquisitiveness and astuteness uncomplicated by high mentality or impractical ideals and aspirations. At this time you could be a good soldier with a modicum of brains, initiative, and courage, if you had a machine gun. In short, it became too easy to accumulate power and wealth, and mentally talented individuals naturally entered more difficult fields and drew their reward, as they had even when making money, largely from feeling their own machinery in operation.

Today the old economic system—antiquated, obsolete, anachronistic—still nominally runs things. Centralization increases; production increases; big fortunes increase; skilled workers who are employed (including good scientists) profit more than ever before, but the group of the dispossessed constantly increases. The scientist makes a good living and he has the joy of doing what he wants to do; he is therefore uninclined to be critical of things as they are. Money-minded men succeed better than ever before in history. But the public loses; it loses knowledge, power, and wealth which rightfully belong to it. These things belong to the public both because civilization and wealth are the heritage of humanity today, bequeathed to it by humanity of the past, not the gift of one man nor the right of individuals, and because men who have knowledge, which makes power and wealth, have always freely given since the world began, and it is their nature to give. They give today—but their gifts are at once fenced in, and only reach the general public after the money-minded men have taken just as large a portion of them as they desire.

The relatively complacent self-satisfaction of the scientist is, therefore, unmerited. The situation exists. If any remedy is needed, it is in the hands of one hundred thousand scientific workers of sorts.

## APOLOGY FOR MAN
### *Earnest A. Hooton* (*1937*)

ANTHROPOLOGY is the science of man. However, after nearly a quarter of a century of study of that science, I have decided that the proper function of the anthropologist is to apologize for man. To some, indeed, it may never have occurred that an apology in behalf of man is required; to others, more thoughtful, it may seem that for man no apology is possible. Man usually either considers himself a self-made animal and consequently adores his maker, or he assumes himself to be the creation of a supreme intelligence, for which the latter is alternately congratulated and blamed. An attitude of humility, abasement, contrition, and apology for his shortcomings is thoroughly uncharacteristic of Homo sapiens, except as a manifestation of religion. This most salutary of religious attitudes should be carried over into science. Man should confess his evolutionary deficiencies and resolve that in future he will try to be a better animal.

I propose to offer two apologies for our species, the one defensive, the other penitential. The defensive apology in behalf of man pertains to his appearance, physique, and biological habits. The only proper recipients of such an apology would be the anthropoid apes, whom man sometimes claims as his nearest relatives. The second and penitential apology is offered for man's behavior—for his use of the gift of articulate speech, for his attempts to control nature, for his social habits and his systems of ethics. It is owed to man himself, to Nature, and to the universe.

### APOLOGY FOR MAN'S PHYSIQUE: HIS NAKEDNESS

If you were a respectable anthropoid ape catching your first glimpse of a specimen of man, your modesty would be shocked by the spectacle of his obscene nakedness. Indeed, even to man himself it is a well-nigh insupportable sight, unless he be a savage devoid of culture or a nudist devoid of sensibility. For here is a mammalian anomaly which lacks the customary covering of fur or hair and displays only clumps and tufts disgustingly sprouting from inappropriate areas. What strange capillary blight has afflicted this animal so as to denude his body of the hairy coat which protects the tender skin from bruises and abrasions, insulates the vital organs, and prevents too rapid loss of heat or scorching of the tissues by the actinic rays of the sun? Why has man retained abundant hair only in places where it is relatively useless—such as the brain case, which is already adequately protected by a thick shell of bone, and the face, where whiskers merely interfere with feeding?

· To cover his bodily nakedness, man has been forced to slay more fortunate mammals so that he may array himself in their furs or to weave fabrics from their shorn hair or from vegetable fibers, wherewith to make inconvenient, unhygienic, and generally ridiculous garments. On the other hand, in order to get rid of the superfluous and entangling hair on his face and head, man has been driven to invent many contrivances for eradicating, cutting, and shaving. The adult male White has experimented unhappily through several millennia, trying everything from a flint flake to an electric lawn mower in order to clear his face from hirsute entanglement without flaying himself. Each morning he immolates himself for ten minutes on the altar of evolutionary inefficiency, until, at the age of threescore and ten, he has paid his full tribute of some 3,047 hours of suffering—physical torture, if self-inflicted; both physical and mental, if he has patronized a barber. And even this staggering total is exclusive of haircuts.

We may dismiss summarily the naïve supposition that parts of the body have been denuded of hair by the friction of clothing. The least amount of body hair growth is found, on the one hand, in Negroid stocks which have gone naked for, presumably, at least 30,000 years and, on the other hand, in Mongoloids, who have probably sewed themselves up for the winter during a considerable part of that period. I do not recall the origin of the suggestion that human hairlessness was evolved in the tropics to enable man to rid himself of the external parasites commonly called lice. It need be remarked only that, if such was the case, the evolutionary device has been singularly unsuccessful.

Darwin noted that the female in man and among the anthropoid apes is less hairy than the male and suggested that denudation began earlier in the former sex. He imagined that the process was completed by the incipiently hairless mothers' transmitting the new characteristic to their offspring of both sexes and exercising, both for themselves and for their comparatively naked daughters, a discriminatory choice of mates. The smooth-skinned suitor would be preferred to the shaggy and hirsute. Thus Darwin, like Adam, blamed it on the woman. But abundant body hair in the male is traditionally and probably physiologically associated with an excess of strength and virility, and the prehuman female probably liked her man hairy. In any case, zoological studies of the habits of contemporary subhuman primates indicate that the female is not asked but taken, that she is passive and devoid of aesthetic perception. She does not choose but only stands and waits. There are other theories to account for this deplorably glabrous human condition, but none which would satisfy a critical anthropoid ape.

## His Body Build and Posture

The second aspect of man which would revolt the gazing anthropoid is the monstrous elongation of his legs; his deformed feet, with their misshapen and useless toes; his feeble and abbreviated arms; and his extraordinary posture and gait. Beginning with the juncture of the lower limbs and trunk and avoiding indelicate details, a scrutinizing anthropoid would comment unfavorably on the excessive protrusion of the human buttocks. He would judge the architecture of man's rear elevation to be inept, bizarre, and rococo. The anthropoid gaze, hastily lowered to the thighs, would be further offended by monstrous bulges of muscles; knobby kneepans; razor-crested shinbones, insufficiently covered in front and unduly padded behind; hammer-like heels; humped insteps terminating in vestigial digits—a gross, spatulate great toe devoid of grasping power, lesser toes successively smaller and more misshapen, until the acme of degeneracy is reached in the little toe, a sort of external vermiform appendix.

Planting these mutilated slabs flat on the ground, man advances upon his grotesque hind legs, protruding his thorax, his belly, and those organs which in quadrupeds are modestly suspended beneath a concealing body bulk. It devolves on me to attempt a defense of these human deviations from the norms of mammalian posture and proportions.

Seven millions of years ago the common ancestors of man were already giant primates, perhaps as large as they are today. They were tree dwellers, who progressed from bough to bough by the method of arm swinging. Their arms were elongated and overdeveloped by this method of locomotion. Their legs were comparatively short and weak, equipped with mobile, grasping feet. When on the ground, these generalized anthropoids moved on all fours. At this critical juncture of prehuman and anthropoid affairs, man's forebears seem to have abandoned arboreal life and taken to the ground.

Tree dwelling is advantageous and safe only for small and agile animals. The newly terrestrial protohumans were now confronted with two alternatives of posture and gait: either to go down on all fours like baboons or to attempt an erect stance and progression on the precarious support of their hind limbs. The former offers greater possibilities of speed and stability, but it sentences its users to the fate of earth-bound quadrupeds, nosing through life. Bipedal gait and erect posture, on the contrary, provide the inestimable advantages of increased stature, the ability to see wider horizons, and an emancipated pair of prehensile limbs. Here, forsooth, the ape with human destiny was at the very crossroads of evolution. He took the right turning.

Almost all of man's anomalies of gait and proportion were necessitated by that supremely intelligent choice. The quadruped had to be remade by dint of all sorts of organic shifts and compromises. The axis of the trunk had to be changed from the horizontal to the vertical by a sharp bending of the spine. The pelvis underwent a process of flattening and other changes necessary to adapt it for the transmission of the entire body weight to the legs. The whole lower limb became enormously hypertrophied in response to its amplified function. However, the most profound modifications were effected in the foot—at that time a loose-jointed, prehensile member, with a great toe stuck out like a thumb; long, recurving outer digits; a small heel; and a flat instep. The great toe was brought into line with the long axis of the foot; the lesser toes, no longer needed for grasping, began to shrink; the loose, mobile bones of the instep were consolidated into a strong but elastic vault; the heel was enlarged and extended backward to afford more leverage for the great calf muscles which lift the body weight in walking. Thus a mobile. prehensile foot was transformed into a stable, supporting organ.

Further, the seemingly grotesque abbreviation of man's arms becomes intelligible if one considers the disadvantages of elongated, trailing arms to an animal with upright stance and gait. The creature would be in continual danger of stepping on his own fingers, and, in order to feed himself, would be forced to move the segments of his upper extremity through vast arcs. Lifting his hand to scratch his nose would involve a major gymnastic effort.

## His Face, His Teeth, His Brain

Doubtless, to the superior anthropoid ape, man's most unsightly deformity would be his head. Wherefore the swollen brain case and the dwarfed face receding beneath bulging brows, with a fleshy excrescence protruded in the middle and with degenerative hairy growth pendant from feeble jowls? What of the charnel house exposed when man opens his mouth—the inadequately whited sepulcher of a decaying dentition?

Plausible, if somewhat rationalized, explanations of these features are offered by students of the evolution of the primate brain. The early primates were diminutive, long-snouted, small-brained creatures which ran along the boughs on all fours. The first step toward higher evolution took place when some of the more progressive forms began to sit up in the trees, thus specializing their hind limbs for support and emancipating the upper pair of prehensile limbs. These, equipped with their pentadactyl hands, could be used for plucking food, conveying it to the mouth, bringing objects before the eyes for examination, and general tactile exploration.

The greater the demands made on an organ, the larger it becomes. The movements of the hands are controlled by motor areas in the nervous covering of the forebrain. These areas expand in response to increasing use and complexity of the movements of the members which they direct. Greater use of the brain demands a larger blood supply, which in turn promotes growth. By tactile exploration and visual examination there grow up, adjacent to the respective motor areas in the cortical surface of the brain, areas which picture the movements of the parts concerned, so that the animal is enabled to visualize actions which are to be carried out and to recall those which have been performed. In short, this functional theory of the evolution of the primate brain assumes a sort of physiological perpetual motion, in which emancipated hands continually call for more nervous surface of the brain to govern their increasing movements and to store up their multiplying impressions, while the expanding and active brain, on its part, devises ever more mischief still for idle hands to do.

But what of our shrunken face, the remnant of a once projecting mammalian snout? The elongate muzzle of the lower animals is useful for "feeling," smelling, grazing, and fighting—mainly because the eyes are set well back of the biting or business end, thus allowing the brute to see what it is doing with its jaws. Now the emancipation of the prehensile forelimbs from the duties of support and locomotion permits them to be used for hand feeding and for developing weapons, thus relieving the snout of its grazing and fighting functions.

Just as increased function of a bodily part results in its development, so diminished use causes shrinkage. Consequently, the new utilization of the liberated hands results in a recession of the jaws. The dental arches grow smaller; the outthrust facial skeleton is bent down beneath the expanding brain case; the nose, still a respiratory organ and the seat of the sense of smell, is left—a forlorn, fleshy promontory overhanging the reduced mouth cavity.

However, some doubting Thomases among our ape critics may regard as futile man's attempt to correlate with superior intelligence that vast malignancy which surmounts his spinal cord.

## Apology for Man's Behavior: His Gift of Articulate Speech

For at least 30,000 years, and quite probably for thrice that period of time, man has existed at his modern anatomical status. With this superior evolutionary endowment, what has been the achievement of Homo sapiens?

Man frequently distinguishes himself from other animals by what he proudly calls the gift of articulate speech. To an anthropoid ape the range, quality, and volume of human vocalization would not be remarkable. A gorilla, for example, can both outscream a woman and roar in a deep bass roll, like distant thunder, which can be heard for miles. Even the small gibbon has a voice described by a musician as much more powerful than that of any singer he had ever heard. In fact, one might conclude that an anthropoid ape would regard a Metropolitan opera star as next door to dumb.

The ape, unimpressed with the range and volume of the human voice, would nevertheless be appalled at its incessant utilization. Lacking himself, presumably, the ability to fabricate lofty and complicated thoughts, he would not understand man's unintermittent compulsion to communicate these results of his cerebration to his fellows, whether or not they care to listen. In fact, it would probably not occur to an ape that the ceaseless waves of humanly vocalized sound vibrating against his eardrums are intended to convey thoughts and ideas. Nor would he be altogether wrong. Man's human wants are not radically dissimilar to those of other animals. He wakes and sleeps; eats, digests, and eliminates; makes love and fights; sickens and dies in a thoroughly mammalian fashion. Why, then, does he eternally discuss his animalistic affairs, preserving a decent silence but once a year, for two minutes, on Armistice Day?

"But," I say (in my role of apologist), "human culture is based on the communication of knowledge through the medium of speech." Many competent anatomists who have examined the various fragmentary skulls and brain cases of the earliest known fossil men—undoubtedly the fabricators of some of the more advanced types of Pleistocene stone tools—have questioned their ability to employ articulate speech. I myself disagree with this view and think that man originated from an irrepressibly noisy and babbling type of ape. However, it seems possible that most of the transmission of culture was effected through watching and through imitation, in the early days of human evolution, rather than by language.

Although language is the universal possession of all races of Homo sapiens, the diversification of speech has been so rapid that the world's population from prehistoric times has consisted of many groups whose articulate and written communications are, for the most part, mutually unintelligible. Thus, whereas the common possession of speech might be expected to unite all men, the reverse is the case. Language erects more barriers than bridges. There is in man a deep-rooted tendency to dislike, to distrust, and to adjudge inferior the individual or group speaking a language unintelligible to him, just as he considers the apes lower animals because they have no language at all. Culture is now transmitted largely by language; and, the more groups differ in the former, the further they are likely to be apart in the latter.

Larger and more powerful groups attempt to impose their languages on alien folk with whom they come into contact. The consequent linguistic servitude not only awakens hatred in the vanquished but tends to destroy their native culture without giving them in exchange an understanding of or participation in that of the conquerors. Possibly, then, language has destroyed as much of culture as it has produced.

## His Attempts to Control Nature

Man is pre-eminently an animal good at gadgets. However, there is reason for doubting his good judgment in their utilization.

Perhaps the first chemical process which man employed for his own service was combustion. First utilized to warm naked and chilled bodies, it was then discovered to be effective for scaring off nocturnal beasts of prey and an admirable agent for the preparation and preservation of food. Much later came the discovery that fire could be used in extracting and working metals and last of all that it could be employed to generate power. In ancient times man began to use fire as a weapon, beginning with incendiary torches and arrows and proceeding to explosives, which have been developed principally for the destruction of human beings and their works.

In the control and utilization of gases, the achievements of our species have not been commendable. One might begin with air, which man breathes in common with other terrestrial vertebrates. He differs from other animals in that he seems incapable of selecting the right kind of air for breathing. Man is forever doing things which foul the air and poisoning himself by his own stupidity. He pens himself up in a limited air space and suffocates; he manufactures noxious gases which accidentally or intentionally displace the air and remove him from the ranks of the living; he has been completely unable to filter the air of the disease germs, which he breathes to his detriment; he and all his works are powerless to prevent a hurricane or to withstand its force. Man has indeed been able to utilize the power of moving air currents to a limited extent and to imitate the flight of birds, with the certainty of eventually breaking his neck if he tries it.

Man uses water much in the same way as other animals; he has to drink it constantly, washes in it frequently, and drowns in it occasionally—probably oftener than other terrestrial vertebrates. Without water, he dies as miserably as any other beast and, with too much of it, as in floods, he is equally unable to cope. However, he excels other animals in that he has learned to utilize water power.

But it is rather man's lack of judgment in the exercise of control of natural resources which would disgust critics of higher intelligence, although it would not surprise the apes. Man observes that the wood of trees is serviceable for constructing habitations and other buildings. He straightway and recklessly denudes the earth of forests, in so far as he is able. He finds that the meat and skins of the bison are valuable and immediately goes to work to exterminate the bison. He allows his grazing animals to strip the turf from the soil so that it is blown away and fertile places become deserts. He clears for cultivation and exhausts the rich land by stupid planting. He goes into wholesale production of food, cereals, fruit, and livestock and allows the fruits of his labors to rot or to starve because he has not provided any adequate method of distributing them or because no one can pay for them. He invents machines which do the work of many men, and is perplexed by the many men who are out of work. It would be hard to convince judges of human conduct that man is not an economic fool.

### His Attempts to Control Himself

Man's efforts to control himself, individually and in society, might impel a gorilla to thump his chest and roar with laughter. Let us consider the probable reactions of the chimpanzee to familial functions as performed by modern man.

The ape child begins to fend for itself at an early age. An anthropoid would not understand the domestic custom whereby the young are maintained as economic parasites by their parents for two decades or more of their lives, long after they have reached sexual maturity and adult size.

In ape society a young male does not acquire a mate until he is able to take her by beating off his rivals and to make good his possession. The female is, of course, always self-supporting. The situation of the young man who could not marry his girl because they couldn't live with her folks because her folks were still living with their folks, would not arise in anthropoid society. Apes appear to manage the number of their progeny with such discretion that no mother produces new offspring while she is still burdened with the care of previous infants. Furthermore, the size of any ape group seems to be restricted by the ability of its members to gain a livelihood, whereas, in human society, the less economically capable the group, the more numerous the offspring.

Again, the weak, sickly, and constitutionally unfit among the anthropoid apes are eliminated, either through neglect or deliberately. This is doubtless because our cousins are insufficiently intelligent to have developed those humanitarian sentiments which demand the preservation of life, however painful it is to its possessors and however useless to society.

A critic who had surveyed the great advances which man has made in his material culture might examine with high expectation the extent to which he has applied his intelligence to the improvement of his health and biological status.

The ordinary animal tries to protract his individual existence only by eating, running away, and hiding and his species' existence by breeding and by some exercise of parental care. Primitive man has added another preservative—medical care. The medical science of the savage is, however, compounded of magic and superstition and includes few remedies of actual value. The doctor at the primitive stage of culture kills oftener than he cures. He merely adds to the strain, on a long-suffering organism, exerted by the pressure of a ruthless natural selection.

Medical skill was a negligible factor in the increase of human populations up to the last century, even in the most civilized societies. Now, however, advance in medical knowledge, together with public hygiene and sanitation, has radically reduced the mortality at the beginning of the life span and literally has taken the graves out from under the feet of the aging. In the United States the death rate during the first year of males born alive has been reduced from 12.7 per cent to 6.2 per cent in 30 years, and the expectation of life has increased since the beginning of the century from 48 to 59 years for males and from 51 to 63 years for females. Short of homicide, a man has practically no chance of outliving his wife; females, after attaining a certain age, become almost immortal.

Now it is perfectly obvious to intelligent judges of man's behavior that this preservation and prolongation of life largely increases the proportion among the living population of the constitutionally inferior—the lame, the halt, and the blind. It also makes for a world peopled increasingly with the immature and the senile—those who have not yet developed their mental powers and their judgment and those who are in process of losing both. If medical science were able to make whole the bodies and minds it preserves, one might find little to criticize in the age shift in the composition of the population. But it is unfortunately true that we have succeeded all too well in keeping the engine running but have been quite unable to repair the steering gear. Since the immature are not granted a voice in the government and the decrepit are not denied it, we may expect ever-increasing social ructions, as a result of senile decay dominating dementia praecox in a world of diminishing average intelligence.

One of the human institutions for which apology is required is government. Undoubtedly an anthropoid ape would appreciate and understand government by dictatorship; he might even realize the advantages of a communistic regime. But a superhuman critic of man's affairs would be puzzled by a democracy. He would have to be informed that democracy involves the essential principle that all law-abiding adults have equal rights and privileges and an equal voice in government. Such a democratic government should imply an approximate parity of intelligence in the electorate or a majority of individuals of superior intelligence, if it is to function capably and successfully. There can be no miracle whereby the group intelligence transcends the possibly moronic mean of its constituent members.

Now, on the whole, there is a marked positive association between bodily health and mental health. A ten-year study of American criminals and insane has convinced me that there is an even stronger correlation between mental and social inadequacy and biological inferiority. Since civilized men are preserving the unfit in body, it follows that they are depreciating their intelligence currency.

Judges of human behavior, examining modern warfare, would probably reason as follows "Men are too soft-hearted to keep their populations down to the right numbers by birth control or infanticide. Therefore, when the weak, the unfit, and the useless grow to adult years and become a menace to the common good, nations conspire mutually to start patriotic crusades, whereby their superfluous and inferior populations destroy each other in a high atmosphere of heroism and devotion to public duty."

As the protagonist of the human race, I must admit that in warfare, on the contrary, we select as the victims not the bodily and mentally unfit but those adjudged to be the flower of each nation. Nor do I know how to answer the retort that man's right hand certainly does not know what his left hand is doing, when with the one he preserves the worst of his kind and with the other destroys the best.

I ought probably to try to divert attention from this issue by decanting on the grandeur of human conceptions of justice, the sanctity of the law, and the efficiency of the police systems organized to prevent its infraction; how we regard the criminal not as a vicious brute to be exterminated but as a wayward or sick child to be rehabilitated and cured by patient and loving care. I ought to tell how, at each Christmas season, our wise and noble governors bestow on their happy States the priceless gift of a goodly parcel of liberated murderers, thieves, and other convicted felons.

Such a plea would nauseate an ape. For no animal society tolerates the outlaw. The anti-social animal is killed or driven out. Judges of superior intelligence, however, would put some pertinent questions:

"Is it not true that a liberal education at the public expense has long been extended to nearly every class of person in the United States?

"Is it true that the noble-spirited, who formerly concerned themselves with the salvation of men's souls, are now no longer attempting to prepare men for heaven but rather to rescue them from a very present hell?

"Has not the treatment of the delinquent been improved until now it almost may be said that the convicted felon receives more social consideration than the law-abiding working man?

"Does not crime still increase enormously, and the discharged convict continue to return to his crime like a dog to his vomit?

"Is it not therefore apparent, in the light of the evidence you have presented, that modern man is selling his biological birthright for a mess of morons, that the voice may be the voice of democracy but the hands are the hands of apes?"

# CHEMISTRY WRECKS THE FARM

*Wayne W. Parrish and Harold F. Clark* (1935)

## I

IN THE sense that we have known it in the past, American agriculture is a dying industry. The nation's largest single business still remaining in the hands of private citizens is in the midst of a scientific revolution, and the farm as an individual production unit—the final refuge from a mechanized and goose-stepped civilization—is seeing its last days. For chemistry and technology are bringing agriculture under control.

In broad terms, one may say that the farm is being wrecked by a series of three major frontal attacks, any one of which is deadly enough to have caused a serious crisis:

1. Intensive farming on the soil, with the use of synthetic fertilizers, mechanization, and other control factors, is progressing to such an extent that with even a fifty per cent efficiency in the best farming practices a mere fraction of the present cultivated farm land would suffice to produce all foodstuffs and raiments we need in this country.

2. The whole aim and direction of the chemical revolution in agriculture is to duplicate and to take out of cultivation all staple products of nature and to manufacture them synthetically by automatic processes in factories, thus achieving a uniformity of product unobtainable in nature and eliminating fortuitous elements of chance.

3. The world tendency toward national self-sufficiency is cutting the heart out of world agricultural trade permanently. Foreign markets for agricultural products in any material degree are gone forever. The chemical age gives every highly technical nation a choice between self-sufficiency and trade on whatever barter or bargaining basis it desires, thus upsetting time-honored geographical alignments of monopolies of certain natural products and altering the whole concept of imperialism.

This is an entirely new situation for agriculture. For centuries the threat of eventual scarcity of food and land hung over the world. Within a few decades the march of science has brought about a complete reversal. On the one hand the chemist and the technologist have made possible the production of greater and greater quantities of products on less and less land, resulting in enormous surpluses of acreage, crops, and labor. At the same time, ironically enough, the chemist is removing one product after another from the soil into the laboratory, throwing still more land out of cultivation and further reducing the amount of labor needed.

What has already happened to American agriculture is clearly shown in the statistics of our farm population and production. In 1790, we have carefully estimated from reliable figures, 90 per cent of the population was engaged in agriculture. In 1930 this ratio had fallen to 20 per cent. (The halfway mark, when half the population was engaged in agriculture, occurred in the decade 1870–1880.)

But if anyone thinks that 20 per cent of the population is needed to produce the 1930 production of foodstuffs and raiments, let him not be misled; for the Department of Agriculture in one of its unheralded but significant reports has told the true story without actually saying so. This report shows that 85 per cent of all agricultural products entering trade are produced by half the farmers of the country. Considering the present inefficient stage of agriculture, this means that half of our farm population, by only slightly increasing the efficiency of operation (an extremely simple matter), could produce 100 per cent of all agricultural products now entering trade. We often think of America as still predominantly agricultural, but 10 per cent of the population hardly connotes dominance. The experts know that if the present knowledge of farm operation were properly applied, it would be relatively easy to produce the 1930 crops with only five per cent of the population.

Aside from the inroads of the chemical revolution, several other factors are playing leading roles in this historic transition. One is the decline in the growth of population in the United States, pointing toward a levelling off in half a century or less, and making unnecessary any considerable expansion of enterprise. Mechanization of agriculture and transportation has released from farm labor hundreds of thousands of workers who made meager livelihoods as farm hands. Many of these persons, with no property ties and too inefficient for industry, have become wholly dependent on government relief and odd jobs. Mechanization has not only affected the labor market, but mechanical equipment such as the gasoline engine has released an estimated thirty million acres from cultivation of food consumed by horses. It is estimated that the elimination of the horse reduced the consumption of food as sharply as if forty million persons had stopped eating.

Sociological factors have also played their part. The substitution of motor transportation for walking is estimated to have so reduced the energy requirements of the population that the consumption of meat decreased by 15 per cent during the decade 1920–30. The ten million head of cattle that this reduction represented would have consumed as much food as fifty million persons. The demand for farm products as a whole declined 17 per cent during that decade. All of these factors contribute to the immediate crisis, as well as form an integral part of the long-term problem.

On all sides it is becoming more apparent that agriculture is in the midst of fundamental changes. William J. Hale, a chemist who has portrayed the invasion of chemistry in agriculture in his book, *The Farm Chemurgic*, estimates that chemical research has rendered economically futile twenty-five per cent of the population of Europe and America within the short space of three decades; and Dr. O. W. Willcox, agrobiologist who is concerned solely with intensive agriculture, states in his *Reshaping Agriculture* that it would be relatively easy to eliminate four out of five farmers and four out of five acres in cultivation if the best-known practices of farming were adopted to-day.

## II

The idea that the farmer is a subservient caretaker of God's handiwork, and thus is quite helpless to alter the age-old cycle of the rain, wind, and sun, has persisted through the centuries up into modern times. Only in recent years have there been signs of fundamental changes. Instead of praying for rain, the more progressive of the farmers have decided that it is more practical to control the water supply by storing water for periods of drought. And instead of constantly moving to fresh lands when the old soil is played out, some are discovering that it is more economical to restore fertility by scientific methods.

The agricultural chemist has been the principal disturber of the rustic scene. What is a farm, after all, he asks, but a little factory, a factory that uses an inordinate amount of space and lies idle a good many months out of the year; or, to put it another way, a simple and extremely inefficient chemical laboratory which converts certain organic elements that man can't use into those elements he can use? The farming that has been generally practiced is distinctly savage. The farmer sticks some seeds in the ground, disturbs the soil a little, and does little or nothing until the plants grow up. The whole business has largely been left to God. Lacking pests, drought, floods, tornadoes, hailstorms, and other acts of nature, the farmer has harvested his crops once a year.

But within the past century, and chiefly since the turn of the present century, the chemist has come upon the scene. He discovered what plants are made of, and he found that the soil itself contributes nothing to the growing processes except to act as a reservoir and retainer for the plant, moisture, and the necessary chemical elements that contribute to plant growth. He analyzed the plants themselves, and began his laboratory attempts to duplicate each plant in test tubes by using its chemical components.

The chemist has thus made two vital contributions. By seeking out the secrets of plant composition and growth, he not only learned to "make two blades of grass grow where one grew before," but he learned to duplicate that grass synthetically in numerous forms and varieties in a factory.

On these two fronts fundamental changes have taken place. Production on an acre of land has doubled and trebled; and meanwhile millions of acres of land have gone out of cultivation with the rise of synthetics. Natural dyes, for example, have disappeared over the world with the complete absorption of the industry by synthetic dyes. Manufactured synthetic perfumes eliminated vast areas under cultivation for flowers. An entirely new synthetic fiber, rayon, has transformed the textile world of silk, cotton and wool. With twelve million dollars a year being poured into chemical research—half of this into synthetics alone—it is not difficult to foresee the inroads that the chemist will continue to make into agriculture.

To simplify the revolutionary trends in the entire agricultural enterprise, we have divided the development of farming into four stages. These stages are not chronological; indeed, the revolution has in some instances advanced so swiftly that the fourth and synthetic stage was reached without recourse to the second and third. They are:

1. Primitive stage, still practiced over wide areas of the earth, in which seeds are planted in straight rows in the soil and the whole business is left to nature. A little fertilization is used but mostly unscientifically.

2. Intensive stage, gradually coming into use, in which large quantities of synthetically produced fertilizers are applied to the soil to reap enormous yields. This stage is so perfected that it is known with precision that a specified quantity of the organic chemical matter will yield a specified quantity of crop.

3. Control stage, which eliminates the soil as being unnecessary to plant growth. Plants are grown in a solution of necessary organic substances in trays or cabinets, with a new crop every few weeks. This stage takes agriculture off the farm into factories or kitchens and places it under strict man-made control.

4. Synthetic stage, in which the chemist transfers the whole agricultural enterprise to the factory, eliminating seeds, plant, sun, soil, winds, and rain. He finds out what a plant is made of, duplicates or imitates it, and provides unlimited production of uniform product by automatic processes.

The chemical phase of the agricultural revolution has an analogy in the industrial revolution. Both are identical in effecting ever greater productivity with less and less need for labor. Coupled with this in agriculture is less and less need for land. It was the perfection of the steam engine in the latter part of the eighteenth century that finally culminated in the first installation of automatic mass-production machinery in 1920. Not until the comparatively recent arrival of automatic machinery with straightline production methods did the industrial revolution begin to force a real crisis in the problem of absorbing displaced workers in new fields.

The chemical revolution began much later than the industrial but has not been long in catching up. In one sense the perfection in Germany in 1913 of the Haber-Bosch process of nitrate fixation is analogous to the invention of the steam engine. Indeed, the implications of the nitrogen-fixation process are greater than of the steam engine, for it ended forever the threat of diminishing fertility of the soils.

### III

Of the utmost importance in these days when the Department of Agriculture is tinkering with the problem of taking a few million acres out of, or putting them back into, cultivation is the direction of the second of the four stages listed in the preceding section: intensive farming.

The belief has been prevalent that an acre of land could produce just so much corn or wheat or cotton and no more. It has been believed that God provided good land and bad land, that production of that land was almost static, and that man couldn't do much to change the situation. The agrobiologist is changing this idea by demonstrating that poor land can be turned into the best by the application of intensive farming methods. He has shown that soil itself was not the contributing factor to plant growth. It is what's in the soil—and things can be put into it.

Granted that Dr. Willcox is somewhat visionary when he says that 80 per cent of cultivated farm land can be eliminated by the general introduction of the best practice, it cannot be doubted that the whole farming enterprise is manifestly moving steadily in that direction. And since farming is stimulated by the whip of competition and profits (when and if they come), there is no reason to believe that the trend will be deflected. Intensive farming, despite the increased costs of fertilizers, water control, and other factors, is more economical in the long run than extensive farming, hence the forward trend is toward growing larger crop yields on smaller areas of land.

To illustrate the difference between extensive and intensive farming, suppose Farmer A has ten acres and Farmer B has twenty acres. Farmer A buys fertilizers for intensive farming and thus adds to his initial cost, but he obtains the same crop yield from ten acres that Farmer B obtains from his twenty acres. But Farmer A has less labor cost, for he farms only half the acreage of B, and his taxes, or rent, are less. Further, his crop is likely to be of better quality, and his soil is left in better condition than his neighbor's.

American agriculture, Dr. Willcox says in his *Reshaping Agriculture*, is only 11.3 per cent efficient to-day on the scale of the most efficient methods. If the farmer is now in the midst of a crisis, with ability to produce enormous surpluses, what will happen when the efficiency level is doubled or trebled as in all probability it will be? "Let the coefficient of 11.3 be doubled—brought up to a mere 22.6, which is still below the coefficient of most European agriculture—and the social-economic destruction along the marginal lines of our farmers would be catastrophic," Dr. Willcox asserts.

This threat of catastrophe is not so far-fetched when one examines the present and potential yields of our major crops. The average acre yield of corn in this country, for example, is 25.5 bushels. The agrobiologist maintains that the calculated maximum yield of corn is 225 bushels an acre, and as a matter of record this yield has actually been reached. The average yield of cotton is 0.32 bale an acre; but the agrobiologist says we can raise 4.6 bales an acre by calculation, and he points to the known maximum yield of 3.5 bales an acre to prove his point. Although we raise great surpluses of wheat in non-drought years, the present-day yield is only 8.4 per cent of the calculated possible yield if the best practices were used. And so it goes with all the major crops. Year by year the yield is greater per acre, and yet we are to-day only 11.3 per cent efficient. Raise this to 25 per cent efficiency, or 50 per cent, and then what of the surpluses?

By achieving 100 per cent efficiency in farming methods according to the agrobiologist (a theoretical maximum which has little chance of ever being reached), we could grow on 20,600,000 acres the 1930 actual harvest of eight major crops which required 241,000,000 acres. But eliminating the theoretical maximum and taking the *known* yield per acre as a basis, the total acreage needed for the eight crops is only 27,460,000 acres, an area only a trifle less than the 28,800,000 acres in the farms of Colorado. Dr. Willcox concedes that a 70 per cent efficiency is "reasonable," a level which would require about 40,000,000 acres, which is less than the farm area of Kansas.

Perhaps this 70 per cent level of efficiency is fantasy, but long before the heights of fantasy are reached, the realities of crisis appear. For not only would a mere doubling of efficiency cause a serious disruption of agriculture, but Dr. Willcox and his agrobiologists have not even begun to consider the problem of synthetics and the replacing of natural products by manufactured ones. If intensive farming means increased production on less land with less labor, what is the problem raised by the synthetics which would take this production out of the soil and into the factory?

Controlled agriculture—our third stage—happily avoids all the risks and uncertainties of nature by transferring farming to the factory or the home and placing it under strict supervision and control. More than that, it opens the way to fresh crops every few weeks all the year round. Since soil is almost useless anyway, the plants are grown without it in metal trays in ovenlike cabinets. The plants supply their own heat, and only a few hours of work daily are needed to supply water to the trays in which have been placed a few ounces of chemical food in powder form, there being a different chemical food for each kind of crop.

These cabinets, each containing ten trays providing a fresh crop every day with a ten-day rotation, are finding increased popularity on farms in England, Denmark, and Germany, where they are used for growing fodder crops for cattle and poultry. Only one cabinet has been brought to America and is supplying fodder for cows on a dairy farm near Summit, N. J., while secret tests are being conducted on its efficiency. The crop grows miraculously. A tray of seed corn begins to sprout within a few hours and in ten days is a foot high. The seed germinated is said to produce five times the volume of seed planted in the ground. Dairy farms find the process economical.

Experiments are being conducted in England in the growing of fresh vegetables, with the prediction that the time is not far away when the householder can grow his own year-round supply of greenstuffs in his kitchen or basement in a cabinet resembling an ice-box or electric refrigerator. This stage of agriculture is still in its infancy, but the revolutionary economic and social implications of its intensive development for growing household vegetables are obvious.

## IV

The most amazing strides in the agricultural enterprise have been made in the realm of synthetics, a phase of the rural revolution that has received almost no attention from the standpoint of the farmer and his future. Synthetics mean either an exact reproduction in the laboratory of a natural product heretofore grown in the soil or the creation of an artificial substitute. Sometimes the finished product is a mixture of the synthetic and the natural; but whatever the process, the whole of agriculture is gradually being brought under scientific control. Synthetics assure a uniform product with continuous production the year round, a decided advantage over the more uncertain and slower crop cycle.

Synthetic production of agricultural products began seventy-five years ago, when the chemist found that he could completely eliminate the cultivation of natural dyes by synthetic production in factories. It has been only since the World War, however, that the vast potentialities of synthetics have appeared. For although the synthetic industry moved forward steadily, chemistry has followed rather than preceded the advances of mechanics. Thus the past few decades have brought us such startling new objects from the industrial revolution as the radio, the automobile, the airplane, the moving picture, and a hundred new uses for electric power; the next few decades will bring us developments just as significant, but in the chemically dominated fields of foods, clothing, and plastics. Directly or indirectly, the bulk of these will be concerned with agriculture.

It is necessary to sketch only briefly the growth of synthetics to indicate the trend for the future. The traditional illustration of course is the dye industry; but chemistry is not likely to provide many such altogether devastating examples in the future. More acreage in indigo over the world disappeared than we need to grow cotton in this country today. The growing of vast quantities of madder stopped within the space of a few years. Not only was the dye industry forever lifted from the soil but the chemist was enabled to create by synthesis scores of new dyes that nature had never herself been able to provide.

The second spectacular invasion was in the textile industry. Patient years of research in trying to duplicate a natural fiber were rewarded with the commercial production of rayon—a product, curiously enough, which is not a duplication of natural silk at all but which is an entirely new synthetic fiber. Although rayon has not altogether replaced natural fibers (about 75 per cent of its composition is cotton linters—the short, poor cotton—and 25 per cent is wood pulp), it, nevertheless, has played hob with the textile industry and has critically affected the production of natural silk.

The chemist found that the common base of cellulose for all textiles is obtainable, not only from certain trees and plants, but from virtually all fibrous growth, including even weeds and corn stalks. The laboratories are only now struggling with the cellulose problem, but the strides made in artificial textiles have opened the way for a myriad of other products, for the cellulose base can be used for plastics in housing, interior finishings, enamels, laminated plastic tiling, and a host of other items.

Not only have the chemists made it virtually certain that cotton, silk, and wool will be largely dominated by synthetics in the future, but certain large industrial interests are almost ready to venture into large-scale production of houses and equipment with plastics as the key material. The raw agricultural product of the past thus becomes merely an incidental adjunct of industry. The finest cotton is no longer desirable when poor cotton serves the industrial purpose. Fine lumber becomes unnecessary when any kind of fibrous material, even weeds, is suitable as a base for plastic houses.

Existing industries are always skeptical and scornful when confronted with predictions. The natural-dye industry maintained it could never be abolished by the laboratory, but it is now non-existent. Silk growers said nothing could replace the natural fiber, but the industry is being wrecked by substitutes. Cotton growers scoff at artificial cotton, but synthetic cotton in small quanities is already on the market in this country. The raising of sheep, being a long, tedious job, is destined to go by the board with the development of synthetic wool processes which have already been the subject of extensive experimentation.

The synthetic-rubber industry has moved forward and is bound to supplant the market now occupied by the natural product. Perfumes once supported a vast agricultural population, but today the bulk of perfumes are synthetic. To produce a pound of Bulgarian rose oil requires from 250,000 to 750,000 roses, according to the character of the crop. The chemist produces unlimited quantities of synthetic rose oil at a fraction of the cost of the natural. Natural musk may cost $250 a pound, but the synthetic can be purchased for a few dollars.

The drug industry has been revolutionized by synthetics. Many essential drug products have been removed from agriculture to the synthetic laboratory. Natural leather is disappearing under the strain of competition with substitutes, and the substitutes are almost as good as the raw hides. The paint and varnish industry has been transformed by synthesis, much to the benefit of the industry; for paints and varnishes no longer vary in quality from year to year according to the character of the crops.

Not the least important invasion of chemistry into agriculture is in foodstuffs. Virtually all foods, from wheat and corn to beans, can be made in the laboratory. The problem was merely to break down the natural food into its chemical constituents and rebuild these constituents into new food forms. While this is not strictly a synthetic process, it at least transfers the making of foods from the farm to the factory. One of the outstanding achievements to date has been the manufacture of butter substitutes.

The matter of synthetic foodstuffs is often misunderstood. There will in all likelihood be no change in the present method of eating, and there is little immediate prospect of being served concentrated pellets of chemical elements as our main diet. But there is a prospect that a large variety of new foods will be produced under scientific control of the laboratory. Factory production of milk—a purer and more healthful beverage—is sure to come and at cheaper prices. Milk is 87 per cent water anyway, and it will be relatively easy to substitute a machine for the cow as the agent for converting cullulose (grass) and such into a liquid we call milk.

Only a few months ago the first two "synthetic" sheep in the history of the world were slaughtered with appropriate academic ceremony at Cornell University. These two sheep had never tasted a blade of grass or a kernel of grain. In fact, it was only for the purpose of taking photographs that the hapless sheep were even given the singular thrill of walking on grass. They were weaned from their mothers early and placed on a diet of a synthetic mixture of casein, cellulose, starch, vitamin concentrates, and salts. They grew to maturity rapidly under this curious diet and were killed at the age of a year and a half. They were beautiful sheep, their wool was excellent, and they were free from one of the most common parasites found in almost all sheep of the region. It would seem to be obvious that the chemical revolution is only beginning to open up a new and bewildering world.

The development of synthetics will not necessarily mean complete replacement of natural products, but it will mean sharp adjustments, often affecting millions of acres of land and the livelihood of hundreds of thousands of persons. These adjustments are coming with ever-increasing frequency, causing crises of price, of land values, and of livelihood.

A strong synthetic industry has arisen since the World War, organized into the Synthetic Organic Chemical Manufacturers Association. As spokesman for the industry, C. A. Mace, the association secretary, expresses their ideas in the following significant words: "The greatest advantage of synthetic products lies in the control of manufacturing and uniformity of product, something that is impossible with natural agricultural products. When synthesis keeps out the natural product forever, it is because the synthetic product is uniform. Synthetic vanillin is the same every week and every year, all the time. Natural vanilla beans change from year to year. The nearer you get agriculture to industry, the more you divorce it from the vicissitudes of climate and the like, the more you keep it under control."

## V

A word must be said in passing about the old concepts of agricultural economics. Fundamental changes have come so swiftly with the overcoming of the threat of scarcity and the advancement of chemistry that the academic economist is practically useless. In agriculture, as in many other fields, the economist is a victim of cultural lag, worrying about problems that have already been solved. He continues to discuss the problems of a half-century or two centuries ago, when he should be equipping himself to discuss the changes, shifts, and redistribution of occupations which accompany actual progress.

Incredible as it may seem under existing conditions, Ricardo still sets the pace of agricultural economics. Ricardo, it will be recalled, maintained that land is getting scarcer and scarcer, that land is constant and indestructible and cannot be increased, and that, therefore, the person who owns land will be in control of the economic situation. Poorer and poorer land will have to be used, he said, and that would make a higher and higher rent on good land, and the difference between what the good land and the poor land will produce is the amount of rent to be paid.

It is important that Ricardo's theories of rent be kept in mind, for they are being taught religiously in practically every school in the country (including New York's high school system). There was nothing whatever wrong with Ricardo's theories at the time—over a century ago—when he made a substantial fortune on the Exchange in London and had retired to his estate to write his treatises on economics. His mind was keen and he saw the situation about him beautifully. But changes came almost immediately to upset his theories. He was not to blame for failure to foresee the future; but there is no excuse for the acceptance of his theories today.

The steamboat came almost at once to revolutionize transportation of agricultural products; England could draw food from her wide-flung possessions instead of depending on her own island. Increased mechanization and fertilization were also prime factors in effecting fundamental changes. Yet nearly all economists, up to and including such authorities as E. R. A. Seligman, have persisted in tying up all agricultural economics with the idea that richness is in the soil, that there is good land and poor land, and that man is practically powerless to increase production of foodstuffs except with the use of more land. How distant is this theory from reality when today a farmer can both reduce acreage and double his production!

Only a cursory examination of economic texts being used in schools today reveals their uselessness. As recently as 1929 Professor Seligman wrote that "The time will come in every country when there will be no further supply of fresh lands. When this situation arises the growing difficulty of maintaining the fertility of the soil, not to speak of producing a greater yield per acre, will more than offset the advantages of mechanization and of the application of capital. In the long run agriculture is subject to the law of increasing costs." This statement, amusingly enough, was made by Dr. Seligman in a study for John J. Raskob, then chairman of the National Democratic Committee, who was endeavoring to obtain authentic farm data in the pre-brain trust days. If this had been written in 1900 it would have occasioned no surprise. But by 1929 the threat of scarcity of fresh farm land had been forever removed.

In their widely used book on *Economics with Application to Agriculture,* Dummeir and Heflebower state that "with an increasing demand for products, the increase in the use of land would be to poorer lands," and "the total quantity of land in the world is fixed." It is quite true that the quantity of land is fixed, but this is no longer suitable as a *basis* for economic theory. Production in the future will have little relation whatever to the land itself.

Malthus also had his day and scared the academic world so badly that it has not yet recovered its bearings. He showed that population would some day—and not in a far distant future—overtake the food supply. Some of the academicians, while not abandoning Ricardo, have begun to suspect a fallacy in Malthus' remarks. Certainly the specter which he portrayed has been annihilated, given any reasonable control over the food supply. Both the land and food problems that tormented and harassed the nineteenth-century economists have been solved, and yet almost all of to-day's economic thinking, and many of the sacrificial rites practiced at Washington continue on the assumption that these problems are still foremost.

## VI

This brings us to one of the most curious documents of modern times—the Agricultural Adjustment Act. The historians of the future will at least be able to say that it was a brave and daring measure in time of emergency. It was action in a real political sense, and no one will deny that the millions of dollars in payments to farmers have supported many regions of the country from near collapse.

But what in reality was the AAA? It was based on two utterly false assumptions. The first was that it proceeded from the primitive premise of agriculture, *i.e.*, that the amount of production is dependent upon the amount of land. Naturally any slight reduction in acreage reduced production temporarily; but as we have shown, one can grow 20 per cent more on 20 per cent less acreage by improving his methods (up to a maximum point now distant). The AAA plan of reducing crops by reducing acreage is no real solution.

In the second place—and much more serious over the long term—the AAA set as its goal the achieving of "pre-war parity prices," raising agricultural prices to the relation they bore to industrial prices of five years before the War. Is this what the farmers wanted? It is more logical to assume that what the farmers really wanted was *higher income* for their products. The AAA set out to obtain a higher price for farm products instead of a larger income per family. What value is there in a higher price if the income received is no higher than before? The AAA overlooked the fact that with any sizable increase in agricultural efficiency what was needed was fewer farmers, a larger output, and a larger income per farmer.

It is unlikely that there will be any satisfactory answer to the entire farming problem—at least there is no sound hope for higher incomes for farmers —until Secretary Wallace and his aides are willing to face the question of what is the smallest number of farmers who can raise our own food supply by using the most efficient means possible. This must necessarily involve both a real program for agriculture based upon the latest scientific achievements and controls and a proper re-distribution of the surplus farm population. The AAA was designed to keep a larger number of people on the farms and to reduce the production of all of them, in the vain hope that higher prices will result in higher incomes.

Whatever the AAA's merits as an emergency measure (and it succeeded better than any other New Deal measure in getting dollars into the country), all the scientific evidence at the present time shows that fewer and fewer people can do the job. Instead of paying *all* to reduce acreage, we should *reduce the number of people* in the farming enterprise. The AAA paid people to keep from producing as though they could do nothing else in the world. The aim of any highly civilized nation should be to have the fewest number of people do the job, no matter what the occupation.

The reason for this does not need an extended explanation. When everybody is in agriculture we have a low standard of living, because all we have are agricultural products. This was certainly true when 90 per cent of the population was on the farms. But when the percentage of those on the farms goes down, those released can produce other products and services, contributing toward an increased standard of living. No other argument is valid. For if we are to assume that the AAA was sound then we must also assume that everybody has everything and that we need nothing else. Such a proposition is manifestly fantastic. We should never pay any part of the population to keep from producing when there are unlimited things to be done and when our standard of living is so utterly short of minimum decency.

There are still those in high places who believe the solution to farming lies in foreign trade. Little need be said on this subject. Increasingly, nations will not *have* to have foreign trade. What they will have will depend upon treaties, barter, and such arrangements. Transfers will be made only where they are directly more profitable. This may not mean any great material trade. Any highly technical country to-day may have a choice for the first time. The synthetic industries have already broken numerous monopolies held by one or two countries. Dyes and perfumes have largely been eliminated from foreign trade. Nitrate-fixation processes broke the Chilean monopoly of nitrates. The Japanese monopoly of camphor was broken by German synthetics. Synthetic rubber will break the Dutch and British monopolies.

The fighting point now is not geography, but economic advantage; for the importance of geographical location of natural products has been fast disappearing. Even if synthetic substitutes be inferior to the natural products, or even though they cost more, the price and quality factors become unimportant in a crisis involving war or economic advantage. Germany's present desperate mobilization of her scientific industries to become self-sufficient through synthetics and chemistry is a pertinent illustration of the lessened need of foreign trade. With a battle cry of "irrespective of production costs," Germany is experimenting feverishly with all varieties of fabrics. Through increased fertilization her whole farm program has taken great strides forward.

She still leads the world in scientific research and much of this is being directed toward agricultural self-sufficiency.

Thus any nation that depends on either imports or exports or both is in a precarious situation. With vast areas of land being opened to cotton cultivation in Brazil, as well as in the East, there will be little salvation in exporting American cotton in the coming years. The drive toward national self-sufficiency has gone ahead in almost every country on the globe. Chemistry, particularly since its invasion into agriculture, has practically doomed large foreign trade.

It seems clear from the evidence that, far from being in a temporary crisis which can be adjusted by slight reductions in acreages and manipulation of prices, agriculture has entered a physical revolution of significant proportions. Certain it is that the day of the traditional farmer and his rustic isolation is over. No longer is he an independent entrepreneur. He is becoming more and more an adjunct to industry and dependent on its swift changes and its highly competitive markets. No longer can he profitably expand to new lands except to eke out his life on a subsistence level.

As intensive agriculture advances and as the synthetic industry moves more and more products from soil to the factory, hundreds of millions of acres will have to go out of commercial cultivation. The problem of re-distributing population will increasingly be a paramount task of the central government. The opening up of this marginal land to subsistence homesteading means only a lower standard of living. The threat of scarcity has been overcome but the problem of social control has hardly begun. The AAA will have to move down the alphabet if agriculture is to get on its feet.

# OUR HYPNOTIZED WORLD

## *V. F. Calverton* (*1937*)

THE AVERAGE American thinks of hypnotism as a form of black magic, confined to clandestine chambers, where some long-haired Svengali or turbaned Hindu whirls his circumambient eyes and twines his snakelike fingers about the head of some helpless youth, rendering him subservient to his will. Even highly intelligent people, who are more sophisticated about the matter, view hypnotism merely as a clinical technique valuable in controlling the behavior of dysgenic personalities.

Few people understand that hypnotism today is far more important as a social force than as an individual one. Contemporary society, with its radios, newspapers, films, schools, and churches, all attuned to the minute to what is happening in their respective realms, is more subject to hypnotic compulsion than any society which has ever existed in the past.

Hypnotism is the force which has made possible the reshaping and remaking of the modern world. Without the use of hypnotism, for example, fascism would have been impossible, as well as most of the developments in the modern nationalistic state. Nationalism, in its postwar forms, has become what it is, and what it could never have been otherwise, because of the hypnotic controls effected by the various instruments of mass hypnosis which have been developed by contemporary science. Hypnotism has made it possible to harness the modern nationalist state into a solid, unified entity that was never attainable before. By means of the accelerated contacts of minds rendered possible by the radio, the cinema, the telephone, the telegraph, and the amplifier, people today, within their nationalist orbits, can be made, to an increasing degree, to think as one. In the past, it was religion with its hypnotic appeal which was used to accomplish that end; today the radio, the newspaper, and the cinema can achieve the same hypnotic effects with much more success. In a word, hypnotism, through the invention of modern scientific devices, has been put to work in new fields, where it has become a social force of magnitudinous dimensions.

Hypnotism is described in scientific verbiage as a manifestation of the power of suggestion. Beyond that there is little that science has said or, at the present time, can say on the subject. How suggestion works or what makes it work, still remains a mystery. What is known, however, is that it works, and it is with its workings that this article is concerned.

It is apropos to illustrate just what hypnotism, or *suggestion*, is in practice. An individual is hypnotized by a physician and, while in a hypnotic state, is told that he is going to be given an orange that is sweet and which he will relish to the last bite. Instead of giving him an orange, however, the physician places a tight-skinned lemon in his hands and bids him eat it. What happens is that when the individual bites into it, he smacks his lips, and expresses all those reactions of pleasure which are the concomitants of sweet-tasting stimuli. He devours the whole lemon, manifesting increasing enjoyment with each bite. A minute later, the physician gives the individual a round, succulent orange, telling the latter, however, that it is a lemon. At the first bite, he makes that inevitably wry grimace which everyone does at the taste of a lemon. His mouth continues to screw itself up into a more and more pinched form until he has finally devoured the orange, after which he shakes his head as one does after imbibing a bitter medicine.

But more than changing the behavior and reaction of taste buds and salivary glands, it is possible by hypnosis to control pain reactions, and in recent months this has been demonstrated in most conspicuous fashion in the United States by the several childbirths which have been conducted under posthypnotic suggestion. Only in the United States, where the American Medical Association is, so far as can be discovered, opposed to the practice, would childbirths undertaken in such a manner create such a sensation. In Germany, at the Heidelberg Clinic, for example, thousands of such childbirths have been conducted in the last ten years. In Soviet Russia within the last five years thousands of similar births have occurred. In many other European countries, where hypnosis does not suffer from the stigma which hangs over it in the United States, childbirth by hypnotic procedure has been for some time a familiar procedure.

In the case of the childbirths the physician, in order to achieve his effects, employs the same device used in the case of the orange and lemon experiment. He *suggests* to the prospective mother that she will have no pain at the time of the birth. Because of her trust and faith in him, which really means that she is susceptible to his *suggestion,* she experiences no pain, or at least relatively little. Whereas women under ordinary circumstances suffer excruciatingly during the birth ordeal, women who undergo such posthypnotic suggestion very often suffer little if any pain at all. Of ninety cases of birth delivery undertaken by hypnotic technique within the six months from November, 1935, to April, 1936, Doctor Vassily Zdravosmislov of the First Moscow University reports that "fifty-five per cent were entirely without pain, thirty-three per cent were partly successful, and eleven per cent showed very little result."

Reduced to the lowest common denominator, what such experiments reveal is that there is something about the human being, or about the human mind, which is immediately receptive to influences from the outside, especially to those of a concentrated and incremental variety. If there is anything about the human mind which can be described as an absolute characteristic, it is its universal susceptibility to suggestion. Under the impact of suggestive influences, something happens to the organism which renders it susceptible to alterations in reaction of a profound character. The ordinary patterns of response can be modified, retarded, stopped.

Cures, especially the so-called miraculous ones, are another illustration of hypnotism in individual form. In all these cases, what we are confronted with is not suggestion but autosuggestion; that is, suggestion which is induced by the individual himself as a result of the influence of an outside force powerful enough to awaken the inner potencies of his personality.

A simple experiment, familiar to all those acquainted with such phenomena, will illustrate just how cures of that type are achieved. A physician takes an individual, reduces him to a state of hypnoidal slumber, and suggests to him that he is paralyzed on his right side, and can neither walk nor move any part of that section of his body. The physician thereupon releases the individual from his hypnotic state, and tells him to get up and walk. But he is helpless. He cannot move the hypnotized side of his body at all. He is, to all intents and purposes, paralyzed.

He is allowed to remain in that state for several minutes—in some cases the experiment has been so conducted that he remains in that condition for hours—and then the physician sits him down again, hypnotizes him once more, and tells him that he can move the right side of his body now, that when he gets up he will be able to walk about as ably and agilely as a normal person.

At that point, the physician commands him to get up and walk, which he does with the characteristic nimbleness of a healthy human being. Now what this experiment illustrates is that the man in the case was semiparalyzed by suggestion given him while in a hypnotic state by his physician, and that the moment the suggestion was removed his paralysis disappeared.

In the case of cures what occurs is remarkably similar to the experiment described. The individual is a victim of suggestion, not from a hypnotist or a physician, but *from himself*. He hypnotizes himself, without knowing it, into believing he is paralyzed. Organically, he is no more paralyzed than any normal person; functionally, however, owing to autosuggestion, he is as paralyzed as an authentic paralytic victim. Such cases are so abundant in medical history that they no longer excite comment.

Now the question which immediately arises is: why do people develop such functional paralyses induced by nothing more than a psychological kink or crotchet of personality? In most cases the answer is obvious. The individual, for one reason or another, cannot face the reality which confronts him, or is mentally so dissatisfied with himself that he cannot endure the realization of failure which his life represents.

Examinations of the miraculous cures effected at various shrines, or by various cultists, are almost invariably of cases of individuals whose bodies are functionally but not organically—which means psychologically but not physically—crippled or paralyzed. Any sudden shock, if its impact is sufficient, might release the psychological brake controlling the physical behavior of the individual, and make it possible for him to resume his normal posture. Shrines and cultists of divers stripes, by virtue of the melodramatic challenge they represent, function very often as such releases. Just as certain psychologically paralyzed men have been known to get up and run when the house they are in catches on fire, so such cripples, faced by the overawing presence of something weird and strange, which, like a fire, awakens latent energies within their frames, fling away their crutches and braces and become normal people again.

However, our greatest concern is with the relationship between hypnotism and society, which is a problem in social hypnosis rather than individual hypnosis. When all is said, hypnotism is more important as a social than as an individual fact. It is as a social force that it exercises its greatest influence, achieves its most lasting effects.

The main difference between social and individual hypnosis is that in the case of the former the individuals are unaware of the presence of the hypnotic factor, whereas in the latter they are ineluctably conscious of it. Advertising, for example, is an excellent illustration of social hypnosis in action. As various experiments have shown, people do not buy a special brand of cigarettes because of their special taste, but because of certain mind-sets which they have built up about them. Those mind-sets are created mainly through advertising, which is effective to the degree that it is arresting and repetitive.

All propaganda works by the same principle. The best illustration, and one which has the most disastrous effects, is war, wherein the rulers of a country succeed in whipping up the emotions of a people to a point where the individuals, challenged by the same slogans, the same phrases, the same appeals, think as one. The hypnotic factor involved is central and national; it is a form of mass hypnosis, induced by a combination of all the forms of mass suggestion—newspapers, churches, schools, radio.

It was because of the absence of such forms of mass suggestion, up to several centuries ago, that wars were never fought by any large percentage of the population. Soldiers, in the main, were mercenaries or adventurers. Even as late as the American Revolution, which was a war involving a continent, we find only a small part of the population engaged in it. As Doctor Morison has shown, among a population of 2,500,000 people at the time, it is doubtful if more than 800,000 were concerned with it at all.

The whole psychology of nationalism, which is the most dominant force in modern civilization, could never have developed into the mad juggernaut of impulse which it is, if it were not for the evolution of such forms of mass suggestion as the press, the public school, the telegraph, the telephone, and the radio.

It is only when we analyze religion, however, that we get to the real root of the problem. Religion antedates the press, the public school, the telegraph, the telephone, and the radio. It represents the most ancient and the most persuasive form of social hypnosis. The whole appeal of religion is dependent upon the exploitation of hypnotic technique. The atmosphere of the temple, the church, the synagogue, the mosque, with their dim, awe-inspiring interiors, their strange icons, their swinging censers, could not provide a more ideal setting for the hypnotic approach. The ritual, too, with its simple emotive appeal, combined with its incremental repetitions, pronounced amid music and song, gives to that setting the persuasion and power of magical things.

Because of that background, religion has experienced less difficulty in compelling and inspiring the allegiance of men than any other social force. No absurdity has been too absurd for people to believe under such hypnotic auspices. Hierophants were the first to discover that short cut to the personality which hypnotism affords. Throughout the ages, from ancient times to modern, they have bound their followers to them by means of the hypnotic compulsion.

What all this leads us to is a realization that people are seldom convinced by truth but almost always by suggestion. The mind is far more a suggestible than a logical organ. The full truth of that fact can be seen in politics as well as in religion.

The explanation of the success of Hitler and Mussolini and dozens of other figures in history can be accounted for only on that basis. To begin with, such dictators adopt the assumption, described above, that the mind of the masses is fundamentally open to only one thing—suggestion! Like ecclesiastics, they utilize, in secular instead of religious forms, the same melodramatic hypnoidal technique in their struggle to dominate the populace. Instead of using churches for their medium, they employ open spaces, vast squares, wide circumferential amphitheaters, wherein they succeed in holding their audiences spellbound by virtue of the identical technique which has been employed by religion through the ages. They make their appeals, not to the minds, but to the emotions of their audiences, and like a hypnotist waving a wand over the head of a subject, they manage, by reiterative phrases which grow more compulsive with every reception, to enslave the minds of the populace.

The repetitive emphasis upon the same ideas, encrusted in the same phrases, the same slogans, the same sentiments, theatricalized by parades, demonstrations, and all the pageantry of national display, has always been enough to convert and conscript the masses. The rise of fascism in Europe illustrates how effective such hypnotic technique is in action. In 1921, before Mussolini seized power in Italy, the Italian working class, socialist in its psychology, had succeeded in occupying and controlling approximately 37 per cent of the factories in the country. In 1922 Mussolini marched on Rome, drove the workers out of the factories, suppressed all socialist propaganda, and by co-ordinating and harnessing all the agencies of hypnotic control—the newspapers, the schools, the churches, the radio—succeeded in making over the Italian populace in his own image. Socialist propaganda was forgotten, and fascist propaganda took its place. Within a few years the majority of the workers who had been socialist became fascist. Something of the same thing happened in Germany. Before Hitler took power the majority of the working class was overwhelmingly socialist or communist; after Hitler became dictator, the working class became acquiescently if not belligerently fascist.

The irony of both situations, which is the final proof of the hypnotic fact, is that in both countries, as objective observers and students have shown, the wages of the working class as well as the peasantry have decreased instead of increased under the fascist hegemony. All of which means that the Italian and German masses are willing to support governments whose policies are opposed to their best economic interests because the governments, by their bread and circus hullabaloo, have hypnotized the masses into believing in *the leader* instead of in themselves. There is, of course, nothing new in such technique. By concentrating upon a god instead of upon a leader, religion has thrived for centuries by the same technique.

Such swift shifts in mass psychology are possible only in totalitarian, fascist countries, where control over the agencies of social suggestion is absolute. In democratic countries such as the United States, England, or France, such absolute control does not exist—any more than it did in Italy and Germany before the rise of the fascists to power. In democratic countries the populace is confronted with discordant challenges from the various suggestive instruments of society. The newspapers represent divided attitudes; the schools house teachers of divers opinions, and groups of different philosophies open schools of their own; the churches maintain pastors of different convictions upon social issues; and even the radio, dominated though it is by high finance, proffers opportunity to conflicting groups to voice their programs and platforms. In the face of such divisions and discordances of opinion and sentiment, it is well-nigh impossible to hypnotize the populace into any consolidated support of a single person or policy.

It is only when democratic countries are confronted with an issue of national disaster, such as war, that such consolidation of interests, attitudes, and convictions results. Then the same thing happens that has happened in fascist countries today; the newspapers all take the same stand, the schools all defend the same issues, the churches all support the same program, the radios all proclaim the same ideas and doctrines. Under such conditions, as in the United States during the World War, the whole community is subjected to the same technique of social hypnosis as is practiced in fascist countries today.

If it were possible for those groups opposed to war to stand by their convictions, such a catastrophe might not follow. At the outbreak of hostilities in the United States in 1917 such elements constituted a considerable part of the populace. War, however, because it involves life and death, and galvanizes the life-preservative instinct, individually as well as nationally, tends to destroy such opposition by its very threat. What happens, and what makes the situation so hopeless, is that when a government decides on war, it has only to appeal, in national form, to the self-preservative instinct of the people in order to win their support. With all the agencies of hypnotic control at its disposal, from the radio to the schoolhouse, the government has little difficulty in "selling" war to the masses.

It is that fact which makes the activities of peace societies seem so futile. If the human mind were not so subject to suggestion, peace organizations would not, as they did with but one lone exception in the last war, surrender their convictions without a struggle. The very fact that they do is but an added testimony to the power of mass hypnosis when exercised on a national scale.

The only value that peace organizations can serve is in propagandizing so effectively against war during peacetime that governments may halt and hesitate before venturing to declare war. Once war is declared, however, all such propaganda is nullified by the counterblasts of pro-war propaganda delivered on every side by every agency of the government—and in the case of centralized governments such as exist in every industrial country today the job is simpler and easier than ever before.

But it is not only when democracies are confronted with war that they verge into dictatorships. When the populace becomes sufficiently discontented and restless, and there is a demagogue who can sway it to his support, the danger of dictatorship is imminent. In the United States, for example, democracy can continue only so long as the populace remains acquiescent and no demagogue arises to challenge it to follow him. The existence of the radio alone makes such a possibility all too ominous. The very fact that Roosevelt's recent election, won by such an overwhelming majority, was due in considerable part to his radio magnetism, which means hypnotism, suggests what might readily occur if a new Huey Long, lacking Roosevelt's benevolent vision, should suddenly emerge and, utilizing the radio and exploiting all the other hypnotic devices of contemporary society, take the public by storm. Under such circumstances, democracy can very easily revert to dictatorship, in the same way that Sinclair Lewis described so vividly in his novel *It Can't Happen Here*. The threat of Father Coughlin, Gerald Smith and William Lemke is typical of such a trend. Fortunately, none of these combined in their respective personalities the magic hypnotic appeal of Huey Long, who, in time, might have succeeded wherein they failed.

However, what is a necessary prerequisite for such a catastrophe is a discontented, restless, bellicose populace, already stirred and shaken to the point of social hysteria, where mob reaction replaces individual decision, and individuals become little more than mobsters in their psychology. Just as a physician has to get his patient into an individually receptive state of mind before he hypnotizes him, so a demagogue must have his populace in a socially receptive state of mind before he can victimize it.

The conditions which make a populace receptive to such hypnotic appeal are, in the last analysis, economic. No demagogue has ever been able to stir up a happy, prosperous populace. It is only an unhappy, unprosperous populace which is amenable to his appeal. When a populace is unhappy and unprosperous, as the American populace was during the depths of the depression, and most likely will become with our next "crash," there is the rapid development of the tendency to violence. This tendency existed in all populaces that reverted to fascism. It is when that tendency develops, as Sinclair Lewis describes with such remarkable effectiveness in his novel, and as all European fascisms have borne out, that we can be sure we are on our way to fascism in the United States. This return to the primitive, as it were, to the biological, to the prematurely violent, always marks a breakdown of every civilizational pattern, and opens up the gateways for the triumphal entry of the thieves, the vandals, the gangsters.

*Pari passu* with their advance, develop the tendencies toward suppression. The spirit of tolerance which preceded is succeeded by a spirit of intolerance. Might and right become confused as identical categories. The pacific tenor of rustic as well as urban communities is supplanted by a lynch psychology which crucifies all opposition by terrorism and torture. This change appears first in the economic realm, in the field of labor, where big business employs mercenary forces to beat down the radical labor elements which threaten its hegemony; then it spreads to the psychological realm, where class, group, racial, and national antagonisms are exploited in order to galvanize the populace into violent action. After that, the step to dictatorship is a small one, for by that time the populace has been so browbeaten into submission by the hypnotic appeal of the Führer, the Duce, the demagogue, call him what you will, that it no longer has any decision in the matter. Its social will has been robbed of its independence and virility.

The stability of a government, in the last analysis, depends upon how effective its hypnotic controls are over the populace. In that sense the economic fact is secondary to the psychological. Countries may be economically impoverished, as Germany and Italy today, but if the governments can control the attitudes and convictions of the people, they can maintain themselves without difficulty. Of course, there is a point, as in the case of the French Revolution, where economic distress is so unendurable that it becomes the motive force in igniting the revolt of the people. But such extremes of distress seldom break out into revolutionary violence, unless there is a countergovernment sentiment which has developed a different set of beliefs, with a different set of hypnotic controls to lend them power.

In Spain, for example, the government and the countergovernment forces, owing to the instability of the whole state apparatus, were in a condition of stalemate. The countergovernment forces, fearful that the government, once it was able to solidify its influence over the country, would be able to render all opposition futile, decided to revolt before such controls could be adequately instituted. Given another six months, a revolt might have been practically impossible.

Now that the revolution, or rather civil war, is on in Spain, the future will remain in debate until one side or the other becomes victorious. The side that wins will do what every victorious group does, seize control of all the sources of social suggestion, and within a year or two, or possibly three, win the populace over, by social hypnosis, to accept its position and policy.

The same situation would hold true in any other country in the event of such a crisis. It may be that France will provide the next example of a similar situation. Many competent and experienced observers of European affairs seem to think so. If the Blum government should be overthrown, and the French fascists should seize power, the chances are that a civil war would result, at the end of which a dictatorship of some sort would ensue that would seek to win the populace over by the means I have stated.

What all this proves, by way of conclusion, is that hypnotism is even more powerful as a social device than as an individual therapeutic, and that all those who recognize its powers can turn them to advantage only by directing them toward healthy and progressive social ends. In the hands of individual quacks or social fakers, it can prove as great a menace as, in the hands of scientists and political progressives, it can prove an inestimable boon to the human race.

# FOUR YEARS IN A SHED

### (*From* Madame Curie)

### *Eve Curie* (*1937*)

A MAN chosen at random from a crowd to read an account of the discovery of radium would not have doubted for one moment that radium existed: beings whose critical sense has not been sharpened and simultaneously deformed by specialized culture keep their imaginations fresh. They are ready to accept an unexpected fact, however extraordinary it may appear, and to wonder at it.

The physicist colleagues of the Curies received the news in slightly different fashion. The special properties of polonium and radium upset fundamental theories in which scientists had believed for centuries. How was one to explain the spontaneous radiation of the radioactive bodies? The discovery upset a world of acquired knowledge and contradicted the most firmly established ideas in the composition of matter. Thus the physicist kept on the reserve. He was violently interested in Pierre and Marie's work, he could perceive its infinite developments, but before being convinced he awaited the acquisition of decisive results.

The attitude of the chemist was even more downright. By definition, a chemist only believes in the existence of a new substance when he has seen the substance, touched it, weighed and examined it, confronted it with acids, bottled it, and when he has determined its "atomic weight."

Now, up to the present, nobody had "seen" radium. Nobody knew the atomic weight of radium. And the chemists, faithful to their principles, concluded: "No atomic weight, no radium. Show us some radium and we will believe you."

To show polonium and radium to the incredulous, to prove to the world the existence of their "children," and to complete their own conviction, M. and Mme. Curie were now to labor for four years.

The aim was to obtain pure radium and polonium. In the most strongly radioactive products the scientists had prepared, these substances figured only in imperceptible traces. Pierre and Marie already knew the method by which they could hope to isolate the new metals, but the separation could not be made except by treating very large quantities of crude material.

Here arose three agonizing questions:

How were they to get a sufficient quantity of ore? What premises could they use to effect their treatment? What money was there to pay the inevitable cost of the work?

Pitchblende, in which polonium and radium were hidden, was a costly ore, treated at the St. Joachimsthal mines in Bohemia for the extraction of uranium salts used in the manufacture of glass. Tons of pitchblende would cost a great deal: a great deal too much for the Curie household.

Ingenuity was to make up for wealth. According to the expectation of the two scientists, the extraction of uranium should leave, intact in the ore, such traces of polonium and radium as the ore contains. There was no reason why these traces should not be found in the residue. And, whereas crude pitchblende was costly, its residue after treatment had very slight value. By asking an Austrian colleague for a recommendation to the directors of the mine at St. Joachimsthal would it not be possible to obtain a considerable quantity of such residue for a reasonable price?

It was simple enough: but somebody had to think of it.

It was necessary, of course, to buy this crude material and pay for its transportation to Paris. Pierre and Marie appropriated the required sum from their very slight savings. They were not so foolish as to ask for official credits. . . . If two physicists on the scent of an immense discovery had asked the University of Paris or the French government for a grant to buy pitchblende residue they would have been laughed at. In any case their letter would have been lost in the files of some office, and they would have had to wait months for a reply, probably unfavorable in the end. Out of the traditions and principles of the French Revolution, which had created the metric system, founded the Normal School, and encouraged science in many circumstances, the State seemed to have retained, after more than a century, only the deplorable words pronounced by Fouquier-Tinville at the trial in which Lavoisier was condemned to the guillotine: "The Republic had no need for scientists."

But at least could there not be found, in the numerous buildings attached to the Sorbonne, some kind of suitable workroom to lend to the Curie couple? Apparently not. After vain attempts, Pierre and Marie staggered back to their point of departure, which is to say to the School of Physics where Pierre taught, to the little room where Marie had done her first experiments. The room gave on a courtyard, and on the other side of the yard there was a wooden shack, an abandoned shed, with a skylight roof in such bad condition that it admitted the rain. The Faculty of Medicine had formerly used the place as a dissecting room, but for a long time now it had not even been considered fit to house the cadavers. No floor: an uncertain layer of bitumen covered the earth. It was furnished with some worn kitchen tables, a blackboard which had landed there for no known reason, and an old cast-iron stove with a rusty pipe.

A workman would not willingly have worked in such a place: Marie and Pierre, nevertheless, resigned themselves to it. The shed had one advantage: it was so untempting, so miserable, that nobody thought of refusing them the use of it. Schutzenberger, the director of the school, had always been very kind to Pierre Curie and no doubt regretted that he had nothing better to offer. However that may be, he offered nothing else; and the couple, very pleased at not being put out into the street with their material, thanked him, saying that "this would do" and that they would "make the best of it."

As they were taking possession of the shed, a reply arrived from Austria.

Good news! By extraordinary luck, the residue of recent extractions of uranium had not been scattered. The useless material had been piled up in a no-man's-land planted with pine trees, near the mine of St. Joachimsthal. Thanks to the intercession of Professor Suess and the Academy of Science of Vienna, the Austrian government, which was the proprietor of the State factory there, decided to present a ton of residue to the two French lunatics who thought they needed it. If, later on, they wished to be sent a greater quantity of the material, they could obtain it at the mine on the best terms. For the moment the Curies had to pay only the transportation charges on a ton of ore.

One morning a heavy wagon, like those which deliver coal, drew up in the Rue Lhomond before the School of Physics. Pierre and Marie were notified. They hurried bareheaded into the street in their laboratory gowns. Pierre, who was never agitated, kept his calm; but the more exuberant Marie could not contain her joy at the sight of the sacks that were being unloaded. It was pitchblende, *her* pitchblende, for which she had received a notice some days before from the freight station. Full of curiosity and impatience, she wanted to open one of the sacks and contemplate her treasure without further waiting. She cut the strings, undid the coarse sackcloth and plunged her two hands into the dull brown ore, still mixed with pine needles from Bohemia.

There was where radium was hidden. It was from there that Marie must extract it, even if she had to treat a mountain of this inert stuff like dust on the road.

Marya Sklodovska had lived through the most intoxicating moments of her student life in a garret; Marie Curie was to know wonderful joys again in a dilapidated shed. It was a strange sort of beginning over again, in which a sharp subtle happiness (which probably no woman before Marie had ever experienced) twice elected the most miserable setting.

The shed in the Rue Lhomond surpassed the most pessimistic expectations of discomfort. In summer, because of its skylights, it was as stifling as a hothouse. In winter one did not know whether to wish for rain or frost; if it rained, the water fell drop by drop, with a soft, nerve-racking noise, on the ground or on the work tables, in places which the physicists had to mark in order to avoid putting apparatus there. If it froze, one froze. There was no recourse. The stove, even when it was stoked white, was a complete disappointment. If one went near enough to touch it one received a little heat, but two steps away and one was back in the zone of ice.

It was almost better for Marie and Pierre to get used to the cruelty of the outside temperature, since their technical installation—hardly existent—possessed no chimneys to carry off noxious gases, and the greater part of their treatment had to be made in the open air, in the courtyard. When a shower came the physicists hastily moved their apparatus inside: to keep on working without being suffocated they set up draughts between the opened door and windows.

Marie probably did not boast to Dr. Vauthier of this very peculiar cure for attacks of tuberculosis.

We had no money, no laboratory and no help in the conduct of this important and difficult task (she was to write later). It was like creating something out of nothing, and if Casimir Dluski once called my student years "the heroic years of my sister-in-law's life," I may say without exaggeration that this period was, for my husband and myself, the heroic period of our common existence.

. . . And yet it was in this miserable old shed that the best and happiest years of our life were spent, entirely consecrated to work. I sometimes passed the whole day stirring a mass in ebullition, with an iron rod nearly as big as myself. In the evening I was broken with fatigue.

In such conditions M. and Mme. Curie worked for four years from 1898 to 1902.

During the first year they busied themselves with the chemical separation of radium and polonium and they studied the radiation of the products (more and more active) thus obtained. Before long they considered it more practical to separate their efforts. Pierre Curie tried to determine the properties of radium, and to know the new metal better. Marie continued those chemical treatments which would permit her to obtain salts of pure radium.

In this division of labor Marie had chosen the "man's job." She accomplished the toil of a day laborer. Inside the shed her husband was absorbed by delicate experiments. In the courtyard, dressed in her old dust-covered and acid-stained smock, her hair blown by the wind, surrounded by smoke which stung her eyes and throat, Marie was a sort of factory all by herself.

I came to treat as many as twenty kilograms of matter at a time (she writes), which had the effect of filling the shed with great jars full of precipitates and liquids. It was killing work to carry the receivers, to pour off the liquids and to stir, for hours at a stretch, the boiling matter in a smelting basin.

Radium showed no intention of allowing itself to be known by human creatures. Where were the days when Marie naïvely expected the radium content of pitchblende to be *one per cent?* The radiation of the new substance was so powerful that a tiny quantity of radium, disseminated through the ore, was the source of striking phenomena which could be easily observed and measured. The difficult, the impossible thing, was to isolate this minute quantity, to separate it from the gangue in which it was so intimately mixed.

The days of work became months and years: Pierre and Marie were not discouraged. This material which resisted them, which defended its secrets, fascinated them. United by their tenderness, united by their intellectual passions, they had, in a wooden shack, the "anti-natural" existence for which they had both been made, she as well as he.

At this period we were entirely absorbed by the new realm that was, thanks to an unhoped-for discovery, opening before us (Marie was to write). In spite of the difficulties of our working conditions, we felt very happy. Our days were spent at the laboratory. In our poor shed there reigned a great tranquillity: sometimes, as we watched over some operation, we would walk up and down, talking about work in the present and in the future; when we were cold a cup of hot tea taken near the stove comforted us. We lived in our single preoccupation as if in a dream.

. . . We saw only very few persons at the laboratory; among the physicists and chemists there were a few who came from time to time, either to see our experiments or to ask for advice from Pierre Curie, whose competence in several branches of physics was well-known. Then took place some conversations before the blackboard—the sort of conversation one remembers well because it acts as a stimulant for scientific interest and the ardor for work without interrupting the course of reflection and without troubling that atmosphere of peace and meditation which is the true atmosphere of a laboratory.

Whenever Pierre and Marie, alone in this poor place, left their apparatus for a moment and quietly let their tongues run on, their talk about their beloved radium passed from the transcendent to the childish.

"I wonder what *It* will be like, what *It* will look like," Marie said one day with the feverish curiosity of a child who has been promised a toy. "Pierre, what form do you imagine *It* will take?"

"I don't know," the physicist answered gently. "I should like it to have a very beautiful color. . . ."

It is odd to observe that in Marie Curie's correspondence we find, upon this prodigious effort, none of the sensitive comments, decked out with imagery, which used to flash suddenly amid the familiarity of her letters. Was it because the years of exile had somewhat relaxed the young woman's intimacy with her people? Was she too pressed by work to find time?

The essential reason for this reserve is perhaps to be sought elsewhere. It was not by chance that Mme. Curie's letters ceased to be original at the exact moment when the story of her life became exceptional. As student, teacher or young wife, Marie could tell her story. . . . But now she was isolated by all that was secret and inexpressible in her scientific vocation. Among those she loved there was no longer anybody able to understand, to realize her worries and her difficult design. She could share her obsessions with only one person, Pierre Curie, companion. To him alone could she confide rare thoughts and dreams. Marie, from now on, was to present to all others, however near they might be to her heart, an almost commonplace picture of herself. She was to paint for them only the bourgeois side of her life. She was to find sometimes accents full of contained emotion to express her happiness as a woman. But of her work she was to speak only in laconic, inexpressive little phrases: news in three lines, without even attempting to suggest the wonders that work meant to her.

Here we feel an absolute determination not to illustrate the singular profession she had chosen by literature. Through subtle modesty, and also through horror of vain talk and everything superfluous, Marie concealed herself, dug herself in; or rather, she offered only one of her profiles. Shyness, boredom, or reason, whatever it may have been, the scientist of genius effaced and dissimulated herself behind "a woman like all others."

Marie to Bronya, 1899:

Our life is always the same. We work a lot but we sleep well, so our health does not suffer. The evenings are taken up by caring for the child. In the morning I dress her and give her her food, then I can generally go out at about nine. During the whole of this year we have not been either to the theater or a concert, and we have not paid one visit. For that matter, we feel very well. . . . I miss my family enormously, above all you, my dears, and Father. I often think of my isolation with grief. I cannot complain of anything else, for our health is not bad, the child is growing well, and I have the best husband one could dream of; I could never have imagined finding one like him. He is a true gift of heaven, and the more we live together the more we love each other.

Our work is progressing. I shall soon have a lecture to deliver on the subject. It should have been last Saturday but I was prevented from giving it, so it will no doubt be this Saturday, or else in a fortnight.

This work, which is so dryly mentioned in passing, was in fact progressing magnificently. In the course of the years 1899 and 1900 Pierre and Marie Curie published a report on the discovery of "induced radioactivity" due to radium, another on the effects of radioactivity, and another on the electric charge carried by the rays. And at last they drew up, for the Congress of Physics of 1900, a general report on the radioactive substances, which aroused immense interest among the scientists of Europe.

The development of the new science of radioactivity was rapid, overwhelming—the Curies needed fellow workers. Up to now they had had only the intermittent help of a laboratory assistant named Petit, an honest man who came to work for them outside his hours of service—working out of personal enthusiasm, almost in secret. But they now required technicians of the first order. Their discovery had important extensions in the domain of chemistry, which demanded attentive study. They wished to associate competent research workers with them.

Our work on radioactivity began in solitude (Marie was to write). But before the breadth of the task it became more and more evident that collaboration would be useful. Already in 1898 one of the laboratory chiefs of the school, G. Bemont, had given us some passing help. Toward 1900 Pierre Curie entered into relations with a young chemist, André Debierne, assistant in the laboratory of Professor Friedel, who esteemed him highly. André Debierne willingly accepted work on radioactivity. He undertook especially the research of a new radio element, the existence of which was suspected in the group of iron and rare clays. He discovered this element, named "actinium." Even though he worked in the physico-chemical laboratory at the Sorbonne directed by Jean Perrin, he frequently came to see us in our shed and soon became a very close friend to us, to Dr. Curie and later on to our children.

Thus, even before radium and polonium were isolated, a French scientist, André Debierne, had discovered a "brother," actinium.

At about the same period (Marie tells us), a young physicist, Georges Sagnac, engaged in studying X rays, came frequently to talk to Pierre Curie about the analogies that might exist between these rays, their secondary rays, and the radiation of radioactive bodies. Together they performed a work on the electric charge carried by these secondary rays.

Marie continued to treat, kilogram by kilogram, the tons of pitchblende residue which were sent her on several occasions from St. Joachimsthal. With her terrible patience, she was able to be, every day for four years, a physicist, a chemist, a specialized worker, an engineer and a laboring man all at once. Thanks to her brain and muscle, the old tables in the shed held more and more concentrated products—products more and more rich in radium. Mme. Curie was approaching the end: she no longer stood in the courtyard, enveloped in bitter smoke, to watch the heavy basins of material in fusion. She was now at the stage of purification and of the "fractional crystallization" of strongly radioactive solutions. But the poverty of her haphazard equipment hindered her work more than ever. It was now that she needed a spotlessly clean work-room and apparatus perfectly protected against cold, heat and dirt. In this shed, open to every wind, iron and coal dust was afloat which, to Marie's despair, mixed itself into the products purified with so much care. Her heart sometimes constricted before these little daily accidents, which took so much of her time and her strength.

Pierre was so tired of the interminable struggle that he would have been quite ready to abandon it. Of course, he did not dream of dropping the study of radium and of radioactivity. But he would willingly have renounced, for the time being, the special operation of preparing pure radium. The obstacles seemed insurmountable. Could they not resume this work later on, under better conditions? More attached to the meaning of natural phenomena than to their material reality, Pierre Curie was exasperated to see the paltry results to which Marie's exhausting effort had led. He advised an armistice.

He counted without his wife's character. Marie wanted to isolate radium and she would isolate it. She scorned fatigue and difficulties, and even the gaps in her own knowledge which complicated her task. After all, she was only a very young scientist: she still had not the certainty and great culture Pierre had acquired by twenty years' work, and sometimes she stumbled across phenomena or methods of calculation of which she knew very little, and for which she had to make hasty studies.

So much the worse! With stubborn eyes under her great brow, she clung to her apparatus and her test tubes.

In 1902, forty-five months after the day on which the Curies announced the probable existence of radium, Marie finally carried off the victory in this war of attrition: she succeeded in preparing a decigram of pure radium, and made a first determination of the atomic weight of the new substance, which was 225.

The incredulous chemists—of whom there were still a few—could only bow before the facts, before the superhuman obstinacy of a woman.

Radium officially existed.

It was nine o'clock at night. Pierre and Marie Curie were in their little house at 108 Boulevard Kellermann, where they had been living since 1900. The house suited them well. From the boulevard, where three rows of trees half hid the fortifications, could be seen only a dull wall and a tiny door. But behind the one-story house, hidden from all eyes, there was a narrow provincial garden, rather pretty and very quiet. And from the "barrier" of Gentilly they could escape on their bicycles toward the suburbs and the woods. . . .

Old Dr. Curie, who lived with the couple, had retired to his room. Marie had bathed her child and put it to bed, and had stayed for a long time beside the cot. This was a rite. When Irene did not feel her mother near her at night she would call out for her incessantly, with that "Mé!" which was to be our substitute for "Mamma" always. And Marie, yielding to the implacability of the four-year-old baby, climbed the stairs, seated herself beside the child and stayed there in the darkness until the young voice gave way to light, regular breathing. Only then would she go down again to Pierre, who was growing impatient. In spite of his kindness, he was the most possessive and jealous of husbands. He was so used to the constant presence of his wife that her least eclipse kept him from thinking freely. If Marie delayed too long near her daughter, he received her on her return with a reproach so unjust as to be comic:

"You never think of anything but that child!"

Pierre walked slowly about the room. Marie sat down and made some stitches on the hem of Irene's new apron. One of her principles was never to buy ready-made clothes for the child: she thought them too fancy and impractical. In the days when Bronya was in Paris the two sisters cut out their children's dresses together, according to patterns of their own invention. These patterns still served for Marie.

But this evening she could not fix her attention. Nervous, she got up; then, suddenly:

"Suppose we go down there for a moment?"

There was a note of supplication in her voice—altogether superfluous, for Pierre, like herself, longed to go back to the shed they had left two hours before. Radium, fanciful as a living creature, endearing as a love, called them back to its dwelling, to the wretched laboratory.

The day's work had been hard, and it would have been more reasonable for the couple to rest. But Pierre and Marie were not always reasonable. As soon as they had put on their coats and told Dr. Curie of their flight, they were in the street. They went on foot, arm in arm, exchanging few words. After the crowded streets of this queer district, with its factory buildings, wastelands and poor tenements, they arrived in the Rue Lhomond and crossed the little courtyard. Pierre put the key in the lock. The door squeaked, as it had squeaked thousands of times, and admitted them to their realm, to their dream.

"Don't light the lamps!" Marie said in the darkness. Then she added with a little laugh:

"Do you remember the day when you said to me 'I should like radium to have a beautiful color'?"

The reality was more entrancing than the simple wish of long ago. Radium had something better than "a beautiful color": it was spontaneously luminous. And in the somber shed where, in the absence of cupboards, the precious particles in their tiny glass receivers were placed on tables or on shelves nailed to the wall, their phosphorescent bluish outlines gleamed, suspended in the night.

"Look. . . . Look!" the young woman murmured.

She went forward cautiously, looked for and found a straw-bottomed chair. She sat down in the darkness and silence. Their two faces turned toward the pale glimmering, the mysterious sources of radiation, toward radium—their radium. Her body leaning forward, her head eager, Marie took up again the attitude which had been hers an hour earlier at the bedside of her sleeping child.

Her companion's hand lightly touched her hair.

She was to remember forever this evening of glowworms, this magic.

## IN A COLLEGE LABORATORY

### (*From* Arrowsmith)

### *Sinclair Lewis*   (*1935*)

### I

PROFESSOR MAX GOTTLIEB was about to assassinate a guinea pig with anthrax germs, and the bacteriology class were nervous.

They had studied the forms of bacteria, they had handled Petri dishes and platinum loops, they had proudly grown on potato slices the harmless red cultures of *Bacillus prodigiosus,* and they had come now to pathogenic germs and the inoculation of a living animal with swift disease. These two beady-eyed guinea pigs, chittering in a battery jar, would in two days be stiff and dead.

Martin had an excitement not free from anxiety. He laughed at it, he remembered with professional scorn how foolish were the lay visitors to the laboratory, who believed that sanguinary microbes would leap upon them from the mysterious centrifuge, from the benches, from the air itself. But he was conscious that in the cotton-plugged test-tube between the instrument-bath and the bichloride jar on the demonstrator's desk were millions of fatal anthrax germs.

The class looked respectful and did not stand too close. With the flair of technique, the sure rapidity which dignified the slightest movement of his hands, Dr. Gottlieb clipped the hair on the belly of a guinea pig held by the assistant. He soaped the belly with one flicker of a hand-brush, he shaved it and painted it with iodine.

(And all the while Max Gottlieb was recalling the eagerness of his first students, when he had just returned from working with Koch and Pasteur, when he was fresh from enormous beer seidels and Korpsbrüder and ferocious arguments. Passionate, beautiful days! *Die goldene Zeit!* His first classes in America, at Queen City College, had been awed by the sensational discoveries in bacteriology; they had crowded about him reverently; they had longed to know. Now the class was a mob. He looked at them—Fatty Pfaff in the front row, his face vacant as a doorknob; the co-eds emotional and frightened; only Martin Arrowsmith and Angus Duer visibly intelligent. His memory fumbled for a pale blue twilight in Munich, a bridge and a waiting girl, and the sound of music.)

He dipped his hands in the bichloride solution and shook them—a quick shake, fingers down, like the fingers of a pianist above the keys. He took a hypodermic needle from the instrument-bath and lifted the test-tube. His voice flowed indolently, with German vowels and blurred w's:

"This, gentlemen, iss a twenty-four-hour culture of *Bacillus anthracis.* You will note, I am sure you will have noted already, that in the bottom of the tumbler there was cotton to keep the tube from being broken. I cannot advise breaking tubes of anthrax germs and afterwards getting the hands into the culture. You *might* merely get anthrax boils—"

The class shuddered.

Gottlieb twitched out the cotton plug with his little finger, so neatly that the medical student who had complained, "Bacteriology is junk; urinalysis and blood tests are all the lab stuff we need to know," now gave him something of the respect they had for a man who could do card tricks or remove an appendix in seven minutes. He agitated the mouth of the tube in the Bunsen burner, droning, "Everytime you take the plug from a tube, flame the mouth of the tube. Make that a rule. It is a necessity of the technique, and technique, gentlemen, is the beginning of all science. It iss also the least-known thing in science."

The class was impatient. Why didn't he get on with it, on to the entertainingly dreadful moment of inoculating the pig?

(And Max Gottlieb, glancing at the other guinea pig in the prison of its battery jar, meditated, "Wretched innocent! Why should I murder him, to teach Dummköpfe? It would be better to experiment on that fat young man.")

He thrust the syringe into the tube, he withdrew the piston dextrously with his index finger, and lectured:

"Take one half c.c. of the culture. There are two kinds of M.D.'s—those to whom c.c. means cubic centimeter and those to whom it means compound cathartic. The second kind are more prosperous."

(But one cannot convey the quality of it: the thin drawl, the sardonic amiability, the hiss of the s's, the d's turned into blunt and challenging t's.)

The assistant held the guinea pig close; Gottlieb pinched up the skin of the belly and punctured it with a quick down thrust of the hypodermic needle. The pig gave a little jerk, a little squeak, and the co-eds shuddered. Gottlieb's wise fingers knew when the peritoneal wall was reached. He pushed home the plunger of the syringe. He said quietly, "This poor animal will now soon be dead as Moses." The class glanced at one another uneasily. "Some of you will think that it does not matter; some of you will think, like Bernard Shaw, that I am an executioner and the more monstrous because I am cool about it; and some of you will not think at all. This difference in philosophy iss what makes life interesting."

While the assistant tagged the pig with a tin disk in its ear and restored it to the battery jar, Gottlieb set down its weight in a notebook, with the time of inoculation and the age of the bacterial culture. These notes he reproduced on the blackboard, in his fastidious script, murmuring, "Gentlemen, the most important part of living is not the living but pondering upon it. And the most important part of experimentation is *quantitative* notes—in ink. I am told that a great many clever people feel they can keep notes in their heads. I have often observed with pleasure that such persons do not have heads in which to keep their notes. This iss very good, because thus the world never sees their results and science is not encumbered with them. I shall now inoculate the second guinea pig, and the class will be dismissed. Before the next lab hour I shall be glad if you will read Pater's 'Marius the Epicurean,' to derive from it the calmness which is the secret of laboratory skill."

## II

As they bustled down the hall, Angus Duer observed to a brother Digam, "Gottlieb is an old laboratory plug; he hasn't got any imagination; he sticks here instead of getting out into the world and enjoying the fight. But he certainly is handy. Awfully good technique. He might have been a first-rate surgeon, and made fifty thousand dollars a year. As it is, I don't suppose he gets a cent over four thousand!" ·

Ira Hinkley walked alone, worrying. He was an extraordinarily kindly man, this huge and bumbling parson. He reverently accepted everything, no matter how contradictory to everything else, that his medical instructors told him, but this killing of animals—he hated it. By a connection not evident to him he remembered that the Sunday before, in the slummy chapel where he preached during his medical course, he had exalted the sacrifice of the martyrs and they had sung of the blood of the lamb, the fountain filled with blood drawn from Emmanuel's veins, but this meditation he lost, and he lumbered toward Digamma Pi in a fog of pondering pity.

Clif Clawson, walking with Fatty Pfaff, shouted, "Gosh, ole pig certainly did jerk when Pa Gottlieb rammed that needle home!" and Fatty begged, "Don't! Please!"

But Martin Arrowsmith saw himself doing the same experiment and, as he remembered Gottlieb's unerring fingers, his hands curved in imitation.

### III

The guinea pigs grew drowsier and drowsier. In two days they rolled over, kicked convulsively, and died. Full of dramatic expectation, the class reassembled for the necropsy. On the demonstrator's table was a wooden tray, scarred from the tacks which for years had pinned down the corpses. The guinea pigs were in a glass jar, rigid, their hair ruffled. The class tried to remember how nibbling and alive they had been. The assistant stretched out one of them with thumb-tacks. Gottlieb swabbed its belly with a cotton wad soaked in lysol, slit it from belly to neck, and cauterized the heart with a red-hot spatula—the class quivered as they heard the searing of the flesh. Like a priest of diabolic mysteries, he drew out the blackened blood with a pipette. With the distended lungs, the spleen and kidneys and liver, the assistant made wavy smears on glass slides which were stained and given to the class for examination. The students who had learned to look through the microscope without having to close one eye were proud and professional, and all of them talked of the beauty of identifying the bacillus, as they twiddled the brass thumb-screws to the right focus and the cells rose from cloudiness to sharp distinctness on the slides before them. But they were uneasy, for Gottlieb remained with them that day, stalking behind them, saying nothing, watching them always, watching the disposal of the remains of the guinea pigs, and along the benches ran nervous rumors about a bygone student who had died from anthrax infection in the laboratory.

### IV

There was for Martin in these days a quality of satisfying delight; the zest of a fast hockey game, the serenity of the prairie, the bewilderment of great music, and a feeling of creation. He woke early and thought contentedly of the day; he hurried to his work, devout, unseeing.

The confusion of the bacteriological laboratory was ecstasy to him—the students in shirt-sleeves, filtering nutrient gelatine, their fingers gummed from the crinkly gelatine leaves; or heating media in an autoclave like a silver howitzer. The roaring Bunsen flames beneath the hot-air ovens, the steam from the Arnold sterilizers rolling to the rafters, clouding the windows, were to Martin lovely with activity, and to him the most radiant things in the world were rows of test-tubes filled with watery serum and plugged with cotton singed to a coffee brown, a fine platinum loop leaning in a shiny test-glass, a fantastic hedge of tall glass tubes mysteriously connecting jars, or a bottle rich with gentian violet stain.

He had begun, perhaps in youthful imitation of Gottlieb, to work by him-

self in the laboratory at night. . . . The long room was dark, thick dark, but
for the gas-mantle behind his microscope. The cone of light cast a gloss on the
bright brass tube, a sheen on his black hair, as he bent over the eyepiece. He
was studying trypanosomes from a rat—an eight-branched rosette stained
with polychrome methylene blue; a cluster of organisms delicate as a narcissus,
with their purple nuclei, their light blue cells, and the thin lines of the flagella.
He was excited and a little proud; he had stained the germs perfectly, and it
is not easy to stain a rosette without breaking the petal shape. In the darkness,
a step, the weary step of Max Gottlieb, and a hand on Martin's shoulder.
Silently Martin raised his head, pushed the microscope toward him. Bending
down, a cigarette stub in his mouth—the smoke would have stung the eyes of
any human being—Gottlieb peered at the preparation.

He adjusted the gas light a quarter inch, and mused, "Splendid! You have
craftsmanship. Oh, there is an art in science—for a few. You Americans, so
many of you—all full with ideas, but you are impatient with the beautiful
dullness of long labors. I see already—and I watch you in the lab before—
perhaps you may try the trypanosomes of sleeping sickness. They are very,
very interesting, and very, very ticklish to handle. It is quite a nice disease. In
some villages in Africa, fifty per cent of the people have it, and it is invariably
fatal. Yes, I think you might work on the bugs."

Which, to Martin, was getting his brigade in battle.

"I shall have," said Gottlieb, "a little sandwich in my room at midnight. If
you should happen to work so late, I should be very pleast if you would come
to have a bite."

Diffidently, Martin crossed the hall to Gottlieb's immaculate laboratory at
midnight. On the bench were coffee and sandwiches, curiously small and
excellent sandwiches, foreign to Martin's lunchroom taste.

Gottlieb talked till Clif had faded from existence and Angus Duer seemed
but an absurd climber. He summoned forth London laboratories, dinners on
frosty evenings in Stockholm, walks on the Pincio with sunset behind the
dome of San Pietro, extreme danger and overpowering disgust from excreta-
smeared garments in an epidemic at Marseilles. His reserve slipped from him
and he talked of himself and of his family as though Martin were a contemporary.

The cousin who was a colonel in Uruguay and the cousin, a rabbi, who was
tortured in a pogrom in Moscow. His sick wife—it might be cancer. The
three children—the youngest girl, Miriam, she was a good musician, but the
boy, the fourteen-year-old, he was a worry; he was a saucy, he would not
study. Himself, he had worked for years on the synthesis of antibodies; he
was at present in a blind alley, and at Mohalis there was no one who was interested, no one to stir him, but he was having an agreeable time massacring the
opsonin theory, and that cheered him.

"No, I have done nothing except be unpleasant to people that claim too
much, but I have dreams of real discoveries some day. And— No. Not five

times in five years do I have students who understand craftsmanship and precision and maybe some big imagination in hypotheses. I t'ink perhaps you may have them. If I can help you—So!

"I do not t'ink you will be a good doctor. Good doctors are fine—often they are artists—but their trade, it is not for us lonely ones that work in labs. Once, I took an M.D. label. In Heidelberg that was—Herr Gott, back in 1875! I could not get much interested in bandaging legs and looking at tongues. I was a follower of Helmholtz—what a wild blithering young fellow! I tried to make researches into the physics of sound—I was bad, most unbelievable, but I learned that in this vale of tears there is nothing certain but the quantitative method. And I was a chemist—a fine stink-maker was I. And so into biology and much trouble. It has been good. I have found one or two things. And if sometimes I feel an exile, cold—I had to get out of Germany one time for refusing to sing *Die Wacht am Rhein* and trying to kill a cavalry captain— he was a stout fellow—I had to choke him—you see I am boasting, but I was a lifely *Kerl* thirty years ago! Ah! So!

"There is but one trouble of a philosophical bacteriologist. Why should we destroy these amiable pathogenic germs? Are we too sure, when we regard these oh, most unbeautiful young students attending Y. M. C. A.'s and singing dinkle-songs and wearing hats with initials burned into them—iss it worth while to protect them from the so elegantly functioning *Bacillus typhosus* with its lovely flagella? You know, once I asked Dean Silva would it not be better to let loose the pathogenic germs on the world, and so solve all economic questions. But he did not care for my met'od. Oh, well, he is older than I am; he also gives, I hear, some dinner parties with bishops and judges present, all in nice clothes. He would know more than a German Jew who loves Father Nietzsche and Father Schopenhauer (but damn him, he was teleological-minded!) and Father Koch and Father Pasteur and Brother Jacques Loeb and Brother Arrhenius. Ja! I talk foolishness. Let us go look at your slides and so good-night."

When he had left Gottlieb at his stupid brown little house, his face as reticent as though the midnight supper and all the rambling talk had never happened, Martin ran home, altogether drunk.

# NO MORE OF THE MOON

*Morris Bishop* (*1925*)

OH SING no more of the moon, poets,
No more of the moon,
No more of Diana the sky-huntress
And her silver shoon.

We have measured her round and
   through the middle,      5
We have weighed her mass,
And spectroscopical evidence points
To the absence of gas.

Punctual satellite, she guides
Ships to the dock;       10
The Sea's foreman, she teaches the
   tides
To punch the clock.

So sing no more of the midnight vic-
   tims,
Black goats, black men,
Whose blood on the cross-road made
   Hecate smile      15
And smile again.

Have we not graphed her perturba-
   tions
And mapped her face?

Would you sacrifice to a trolley-car
On the tracks of space?      20

So sing no more of Selene, poets,
That faithless bride
Glimmering in Endymion's dreams
On Latmos-side.

For while you stood moon-bright
   with wonder      25
The scientists came,
Their telescopes outvisioned your
   dreams,
They brought you to shame,
Marvel no more, or we know you play
A child's game.      30

Oh sing no more of the moon, poets,
No more invoke
Pale, wild Cynthia leaping the hills
With her dragon yoke.

And sing no more of the moon, poets,
No more of the moon;      36
But look again on the red world
Under the noon.

# PRAYERS OF STEEL

*Carl Sandburg* (*1918*)

Lay me on an anvil, O God.
Beat me and hammer me into a crowbar.
Let me pry loose old walls;
Let me lift and loosen old foundations.

Lay me on an anvil, O God.      5
Beat me and hammer me into a steel spike.
Drive me into the girders that hold a skyscraper together.
Take red-hot rivets and fasten me into the central girders.
Let me be the great nail holding a skyscraper through blue nights
   into white stars.

## THE EXPRESS

*Stephen Spender* (*1934*)

After the first powerful plain manifesto
The black statement of pistons, without more fuss
But gliding like a queen, she leaves the station.
Without bowing and with restrained unconcern
She passes the houses which humbly crowd outside,     5
The gasworks and at last the heavy page
Of death, printed by gravestones in the cemetery.
Beyond the town there lies the open country
Where, gathering speed, she acquires mystery,
The luminous self-possession of ships on ocean.     10
It is now she begins to sing—at first quite low
Then loud, and at last with a jazzy madness—
The song of her whistle screaming at curves,
Of deafening tunnels, brakes, innumerable bolts.
And always light, aerial, underneath     15
Goes the elate metre of her wheels.
Streaming through metal landscape on her lines
She plunges new eras of wild happiness
Where speed throws up strange shapes, broad curves
And parallels clean like the steel of guns.     20
At last, further than Edinburgh or Rome,
Beyond the crest of the world, she reaches night
Where only a low streamline brightness
Of phosphorus on the tossing hills is white.
Ah, like a comet through flame she moves entranced     25
Wrapt in her music no bird song, no, nor bough
Breaking with honey buds, shall ever equal.

## THE LANDSCAPE NEAR AN AERODROME

*Stephen Spender* (*1934*)

More beautiful and soft than any moth
With burring furred antennae feeling its huge path
Through dusk, the air-liner with shut-off engines
Glides over suburbs and the sleeves set trailing tall
To point the wind. Gently, broadly, she falls     5
Scarce disturbing charted currents of air.

Lulled by descent, the travellers across the sea
And across feminine land indulging its easy limbs
In miles of softness, now let their eyes trained by watching

Penetrate through dusk the outskirts of this town          10
Here where industry shows a fraying edge.
Here they may see what is being done.

Beyond the winking masthead light
And the landing-ground, they observe the outposts
Of work: chimneys like lank black fingers                  15
Or figures frightening and mad: and squat buildings
With their strange air behind trees, like women's faces
Shattered by grief.  Here where few houses
Moan with faint light behind their blinds
They remark the unhomely sense of complaint, like a dog    20
Shut out and shivering at the foreign moon.

In the last sweep of love, they pass over fields
Behind the aerodrome, where boys play all day
Hacking dead grass: whose cries, like wild birds,
Settle upon the nearest roofs                              25
But soon are hid under the loud city.

Then, as they land, they hear the tolling bell
Reaching across the landscape of hysteria
To where, larger than all the charcoaled batteries
And imaged towers against that dying sky,                  30
Religion stands, the church blocking the sun.

## FIRST PHILOSOPHER'S SONG

### *Aldous Huxley*  (*1920*)

A poor degenerate from the ape
Whose hands are four, whose tail's a
  limb,
I contemplate my flaccid shape
And know I may not rival him,

Save with my mind—a nimbler beast
Possessing a thousand sinewy tails,  6
A thousand hands, with which it
  scales,
Greedy of luscious truth, the greased

Poles and the coco palms of thought,
Thrids easily through the mangrove
  maze                                10

Of metaphysics, walks the taut
Frail dangerous liana ways

That link across wide gulfs remote
Analogies between tree and tree;
Outruns the hare, outhops the goat; 15
Mind fabulous, mind sublime and
  free!

But oh, the sound of simian mirth!
Mind, issued from the monkey's
  womb,
Is still umbilical to earth,          20
Earth its home and earth its tomb.

# BY AN EVOLUTIONIST

## Alfred, Lord Tennyson   (1889)

The Lord let the house of a brute to the soul of a man,
  And the man said, "Am I your debtor?"
And the Lord—"Not yet: but make it as clean as you can,
  And then I will let you a better."

### I

If my body come from brutes, my soul uncertain, or a fable,      5
  Why not bask amid the senses while the sun of morning shines,
I, the finer brute rejoicing in my hounds, and in my stable,
  Youth and Health, and birth and wealth, and choice of women and of wines?

### II

What hast thou done for me, grim Old Age, save breaking my bones on the
    rack?
  Would I had past in the morning that looks so bright from afar!      10

#### OLD AGE

Done for thee? starved the wild beast that was linkt with thee eighty years
    back.
  Less weight now for the ladder-of-heaven that hangs on a star.

### I

If my body come from brutes, tho' somewhat finer than their own,
  I am heir, and this my kingdom.  Shall the royal voice be mute?
No, but if the rebel subject seek to drag me from the throne,      15
  Hold the sceptre, Human Soul, and rule thy Province of the brute.

### II

I have climb'd to the snows of Age, and I gaze at a field in the Past,
  Where I sank with the body at times in the sloughs of a low desire,
But I hear no yelp of the beast, and the Man is quiet at last
  As he stands on the heights of his life with a glimpse of a height that is
    higher.      20

# THE APPEAL OF RELIGION

FOR MANY human beings life has always been hard and for all of us it has been mysterious. Where have we come from? What is our purpose in being alive? And what is to happen to us after we die? These are questions that man has asked since the beginning of time. Most of the philosophies and religions in which he has believed have been more or less incomplete answers to these doubts and fears. Today a good many of us do not think of ourselves as being very religious; and yet as we grow older, we realize that we too must take part in this age-old quest of the spirit.

Our first efforts to gain some religious certitude may produce bewilderment and scepticism. Perhaps we have been so much concerned with our everyday occupations and our trivial interests that we have given no serious attention to the church and what it tries to do. If we have thought about religion at all, we may have found it hard to reconcile many of the ideas and doctrines of traditional orthodoxy with the discoveries of science. In any case, the old dogmas seem to contribute nothing to the solution of our immediate problems. In fact the scheme of things appears to be utterly without purpose—to go on its way regardless of our deepest needs and dearest hopes. Then we are tempted to give up all religion, to call ourselves materialists, agnostics or even atheists. Such a state of mind is really a cry for some form of religion or philosophy that can give meaning and direction to our inner lives.

Others have fortunately never fallen into this discouragement and despondency. The faith in which they have been brought up has always remained a source of comfort and peace. Or the simple philosophy of Jesus as revealed in the Gospels has never ceased to seem the most inspiring creed imaginable. Even sceptics, in the long run, are likely to discover that without some positive religious convictions their lives become meaningless. Whatever the state of a man's belief, there are times when he is glad to turn to writers who have considered deeply the problems of religion, in the hope of discovering in their works some satisfactory explanation of his place in the universe and some food for his spirit.

A few will find all that they need in a philosophy of social service, feeling real exaltation in working for the brotherhood of man. Others, believing that they live in a world that is hostile to their dearest hopes and aspirations, make a religion out of heroic endurance lightened only by a sense of companionship with everyone else who is suffering with like courage.

All of these classes of men unite in making one demand of their religion.

It must have a direct effect upon the conduct of those who profess it. Dogma may remain of great importance. Ritual may be the essence of one's worship. But belief and formalism will be justified only when they make individuals better and ennoble their relationships with others. The following selections, while illustrating the truth of these ideas, may enlarge our knowledge of the variety of religious experience and stimulate us to define and express our own deepest convictions.

## YOUTH CHALLENGES THE CHURCH

### *Josephine K. Newton* (*1935*)

WHY HAS the younger generation drifted away from the church? Why do they repudiate the religious leadership accepted as valid by the generation before them? Their attitude is not so much a violent rebellion against the church itself, as a pervasive indifference to any form of organized religion whatsoever. What is the reason for it? The reason may readily be stated. In the opinion of the younger generation, the modern church fails to make contact with the realities of modern life.

Young people today are no more essentially irreligious than young people have always been. As in every generation, there are certain members who are both radical and atheistical. They boast of their "spiritual integrity." They analyze religion, in accordance with the dictates of psychology and biology, by reference to impulses, mental opiates, and escape mechanisms. In method and approach they are unassailably modern. Yet they differ little from similar groups in previous generations, unless it be in the wider range of training and influence that their attitude represents. For it is unquestionably true, without any intention of impugning their sincerity as a group, that an appreciable number of those who flaunt a noisy atheism before the world do so because it is expected of them, because it is fashionable to appear skeptical and intolerant.

This attitude may be traced not simply to the influence of the universities, but more directly to that considerable section of American homes where golf and cocktails have extensively replaced Sabbath observance, and where the subject of religion, if not entirely ignored, is regarded more often than not with a kind of humorous indifference. It has long been customary to blame the colleges for the increasing indifference to religion among the young people. This may have been true before the war. But today a definite proportion of young people matriculate from homes where an intolerance to religion has already been fixed in their minds. If college training with its emphasis upon dialectic develops a number of these into the more violent type of radical, it is hardly surprising.

Yet this extreme element of the younger generation, while the most spectacular and best advertised, does not in the least represent the majority. It is undoubtedly true that to this generation religion is not the driving, motivating force that it perhaps was to the generation that attained maturity before the war. It is a negative rather than a positive force in our lives. But this is not due to any inherent attitude of cynicism or defeatism on the part of the young people. Religious thought, in common with artistic and literary expression, is apt to mirror the shifting moods and perplexities of its social and economic environment. The greater number of young people today talk very little about religion. But they remain silent, not because they are militant or atheistical, certainly not because they are indifferent . . . but simply because they are profoundly bewildered.

Life today is swift and startling. It is no longer the sane, predictable thing it used to be. The world is changing, not sedately but madly, not year by year, nor even day by day, but hourly. To the generation before the war, life presented itself in a direct and ordered pattern. They accepted certain philosophical and social conceptions as irrevocable, and from them derived mental stimulus and stability.

They believed, for instance, in an ordered Newtonian universe, in a divine causality emphasizing the importance of the individual. They believed in science, in the harnessing of natural forces as the means to universal happiness and security. They believed in progress, in big business and private profit, in an evolution upward, in universal education and representative democracy as the ultimate in civilized achievement. They had faith in the stability of marriage, in the near possibility of international peace, in the final merging of nationalism into a World State. Perhaps more indicative than anything else, they believed implicitly in the ultimate, if not inevitable, perfectibility of mankind.

In the swift moving events of the past years, we have seen most of these faiths challenged, many of them definitely falsified. We have seen representative democracies demonstrate their weakness and dictatorships supplant them. We have seen collectivism replace the doctrine of individualism; Einstein challenge Newton; and Spengler, Darwin. We have seen the growth of a virulent nationalistic spirit throughout the world. We know that at this very moment, night and day, the nations of Europe are arming for another war. We have seen the failure of an economic structure based upon big business and competitive individualism. We know that the idealization of science, and the frantic rush for mechanical supremacy have resulted only in the hunger and desperation of millions.

And so we have been forced to discard the majority of the truisms of the generation before us. But we have not as yet discovered anything to take their place. In the confusion of a post-war depression world, we have lost what more than anything else is essential to our significance as a generation, the sense of any Divine Providence overarching our lives, the belief in any meaning or direction to human affairs. This is neither a cheap cynicism, nor yet the braggadocio of youth trying to call attention to itself. It is a very deep and profound conviction, and a conviction that has resulted in a gaping spiritual void. Our attempts to ignore this void by an assumption of indifference or skepticism, our efforts to fill it with speed and gin, with jazz and movies and material success, have resulted only in an overwhelming sense of futility. We realize that if we are to integrate ourselves, we must find for ourselves a direct and positive philosophy of life. We must have something to sweep us up and out of ourselves, something to give color and purpose to our existence. This is what we need, and we need it desperately. It is the fundamental condition upon which our very survival depends.

We do not find it in the church. In our opinion, the church of today ignores the vital problems of this generation. It clings to the past. It is more interested in preserving its minutiæ of dogma and ritual and observance, than in meeting the challenge of a changing world. Its very terminology falls strangely upon our ears. Its symbolism is alien to our minds. Its mode of expression belongs not to the crowding necessities of this era, but to another day and another generation.

Such words as "sin," "salvation," and "damnation," for instance, mean nothing to us. From what are we to be "saved," and by whom? Is there any one of the clergymen who use that term so freely who can give us an understandable definition of what it means? Are we to be saved from our "sins"? We do not recognize a state of "sin" in the sense that our parents defined it. We are apt to consider that whatever we do is the concern solely of ourselves and of the "still small voice" within us, and that it is wrong only as it betrays that voice and as it brings harm to other people. We are apt to think, also, that our sins are the least interesting things about us. Nor can we accept the idea, redolent of barbarism, of eternal damnation. It is far easier to believe in annihilation than in a benevolent deity twisting his victims on a spitting fork.

Our criticism of the church, however, is not that it does not speak our particular language, but that its own language has long lost its vitality and meaning. It is not the past in itself that we discredit. We have a deep respect for the history of the church, for its dignity and splendor, for the men who have walked in sunlight through its pages. Nor would we criticize the ritual of worship. There is beauty in the order of the liturgy, a dim-lit and ancient beauty, rich in symbolism, mellow in the reverence of generations. To some of us it may have little direct or personal meaning, but there are few who do not feel its color and cadence, who do not respond to its age-old majestic beauty.

It is not the past in this sense that we criticize. It is not the glory of a great history nor the use of things old and well worn, not the tradition of beauty, but the tradition of bigotry. We criticize what appears to us the slavish adherence to modes of expression and thought for the sake of the modes themselves without regard to the vitality of what they express. For the significance of theology lies, after all, only in its function as the crystallization of a living faith. In our eyes, the theology of the modern pulpit is sterile and dead.

Why are the churches today empty of youth? Because the average sermon preached in the average pulpit makes no contact with reality. It is as a rule either a stale repetition of some controversial sectarianism, or else a sticky sentimentalism that by its very insignificance irritates us to desperation. We look to the pulpit for spiritual guidance. We are impressed by its reliance upon doctrine, and above all by its great complacency. Indeed, from the quality of thought prevalent in the church today, one wonders whether some of the clergy enter the ministry because of the call of God, or because it offers them an easy berth from which they cannot be discharged for incompetence. It is the more disheartening since a clergy that is capable both of adhering to an outworn theology and of employing publicity stunts to attract attention, cannot hope to lure into the ministry the vital minds of the oncoming generation.

A few preachers there are whose voices sing through the land, whose words flash color in the pervading drabness, a note of melody in the monotone of mediocrity. They are men of deep insight, of high courage, and rich humanity. But they alone cannot counterbalance the appalling mental lethargy of the rest. Yet we make no impossible demands for intellect or scholarship or personal charm. We lay down no criteria of word or thought. We would listen to anything the pulpit might have to say, no matter how alien to our manner of thinking, no matter how poorly presented . . . if it rang true.

But even the clergy do not seem convinced of the reality of what they preach. They do not make us feel it. Their sermons are either vague or stereotyped. They lack both the power and the drive of profound conviction. We feel that they are preaching not from any compelling inner certainty, but from the compulsion of habit and precedent. That they are merely repeating by rote something that they have been taught to accept, but which is no more real to them, no more a part of their vivid personal experience than it is a part of ours. And it is this more than anything else that alienates the young people from the church. We resent its implied insincerity, its indirect hypocrisy. We resent the fact that it fails to demonstrate one of its most fundamental doctrines.

For the modern church, while it professes to expound a single religious faith, is not a single organized church. It is a body divided against itself. Its forces are dissipated into insignificant sects, some of them small enough to be insects, each one more dogmatic, more inflexible, more stubbornly narrow-minded than the last. At a time when the world cries out for religious leadership, the church is absorbed in petty bickering. It argues over "high" church and "low," over liberalism and fundamentalism. It wages mighty battles concerning the punctuation of the prayer book.

How can the young people respect such a church? We are sickened by its pettiness, disgusted with its unreality, its microscopic differences. What we want from the church is a vital religious leadership. And by this we mean an interpretation of life as we see it in the world today. For it is unquestionably the tragedy of this generation that we are oppressed by a conviction of the meaninglessness of our existence. It has been said of modern science that, in contrast with the science of Newton and Darwin, its besetting difficulty is an overabundance of physical data without any great theory to give it cohesion. To a great many of the younger generation, the same statement might be made of contemporary life. It appears to us little more than a confusion of contradictions.

What we ask of the church, therefore, is an interpretation of life that will fuse it into meaning, that will sweep away its drabness and flood it with color and light. We want conviction of the purposefulness of our existence, since it is only through such a conviction that it is possible to work and find fulfillment of personality. It is unquestionably due to the fact that it does to a certain extent manage to fill this demand, that the Oxford Group Movement owes its increasing popularity. So compelling is the need, in fact, that it must in some manner be satisfied, whether within the church or elsewhere.

It is obvious that religious leadership such as this cannot be achieved by the reiteration of traditional theology, by "revealed religion," or by biblical interpretation and criticism, however clever and enlightened. It is not enough to tell us that "God so loved the world that He gave it His Only Begotten Son." We need to be convinced that today He does indeed love it at all. Nor will a purely theosophical interpretation of life meet our demands. We are not, as a whole, either a mystically minded or yet a philosophical generation. We are apt to boast of being hard-boiled, and more than anything else, persistently materialistic. To what extent this attitude is sincere or even representative, it is impossible to say. Yet the fact remains that to a great majority of this generation, a religious interpretation of life implies, not primarily the consideration of such eternal problems as the nature of the Divinity, the logic of immortality, the incidence of evil or the amorality of nature . . . but rather the formulation of a code of ethics, a standard of values, by which to guide our lives in the world today.

It is of course impossible to formulate ethical standards without in some manner making reference to these metaphysical questions and one must sympathize with a clergy of whom such a demand is made. At the same time, however, it is of little purpose to deal with the problems of today by standards of the past. It is of no constructive value, for instance, merely to assert the sanctity of marriage to a generation to whom an increasing divorce rate would seem to imply the failure rather than the inevitability of the marriage system. It would be of more avail to help us discover the reason for the increasing divorce rate in order that we might be better prepared to make a success of our own marriages. Some such attempts have been made in various colleges. But we have yet to find them in the church.

Nor is it possible to apply traditional Christian morality to modern problems of sex. The younger generation has been accused of over-emphasizing the importance of sex. If the current trend in literature, in moving pictures, and to a certain extent in art, be taken into consideration, this is perhaps not

an exclusive characteristic of the young people. In comparison with the pre-
war generation, however, it is undoubtedly true. And it may be laid very
largely to the fact that economic pressure, with its drastic curtailment of
marriage and family life, has resulted in new conceptions of personal morality
and sexual relationship concerning which the young people are profoundly
puzzled. The church, if it deals with this question at all, is still apt to dwell
upon the essential evil of sex, upon sex as the reason for man's Fall, rather than
upon its place in modern life.

It will be said that to expect the church to deal with questions such as these,
is to reveal a conception of religion that is both superficial and materialistic.
The more immediate issues of this generation, however, are apt to be materialistic. The relation of religion to the present trend in world affairs, the possibility of our economic disinheritance as a generation, the reconciliation of
the Christian doctrine of humility with the competitivism of modern life . . .
all these are questions concerning which the church, if it is to be the religious
leader of this generation, should take cognizance.

By religious leadership, therefore, we mean a constructive consideration
of the vital problems of this day and generation. As to the means by which
this leadership can be achieved, perhaps only the future will reveal them. It is
obvious that at present the church has not as yet discovered them. The
younger generation, however, has no desire to abolish the church. Not only
are revolutionary methods fundamentally alien to the American mind, but we
realize that in the church we have the one body corporate that represents and
has represented unswervingly throughout history, the highest idealism of mankind. Its function and value in civilization are unique. And it is for the very
reason that we recognize so clearly the necessity in society for the organized
church, or for some body closely paralleling it, that we criticize it so strin-
gently. For it is manifestly true that unless the church does awaken from its
present torpor and does deal constructively, humanly, with the problems of
this day and generation, it cannot demand the allegiance either of this generation or of the generations following. Religious leadership is the vested right
and responsibility of the church. Will the church assume this responsibility?

## THE RETURN TO RELIGION
### *Gilbert K. Chesterton* (*1931*)

In the days when Huxley and Herbert Spencer and the Victorian agnostics
were trumpeting as a final truth the famous hypothesis of Darwin, it seemed
to thousands of simple people almost impossible that Christianity should survive. It is all the more ironic that it has not only survived them all, but it is
a perfect example, perhaps the only real example, of what they called the
Survival of the Fittest.

It so happens that it does really and truly fit in with the theory offered by Darwin; which was something totally different from most of the theories accepted by Darwinians. This real original theory of Darwin has since very largely broken down in the general field of biology and botany; but it does actually apply to this particular argument in the field of religious history. The recent reëmergence of our religion is a survival of the fittest as Darwin meant it, and not as popular Darwinism meant it; so far as it meant anything. Among the innumerable muddles, which mere materialistic fashion made out of the famous theory, there was in many quarters a queer idea that the Struggle for Existence was of necessity an actual struggle between the candidates for survival; literally a cutthroat competition. There was a vague idea that the strongest creature violently triumphed over and trampled on the others. And the notion that this was the one method of improvement came everywhere as good news to bad men; to bad rulers, to bad employers, to swindlers and sweaters and the rest. The brisk owner of a bucket shop compared himself modestly to a mammoth, trampling down other mammoths in the primeval jungle. The business man destroyed other business men, under the extraordinary delusion that the eohippic horse had devoured other eohippic horses. The rich man suddenly discovered that it was not only convenient but cosmic to starve or pillage the poor; because pterodactyls may have used their little hands to tear each other's eyes. Science, that nameless being, declared that the weakest must go to the wall; especially in Wall Street. There was a rapid decline and degradation in the sense of responsibility in the rich, from the merely rationalistic eighteenth century to the purely scientific nineteenth. The great Jefferson, when he reluctantly legalized slavery, said he trembled for his country, knowing that God is just. The profiteer of later times, when he legalized usury or financial trickery, was satisfied with himself, knowing that Nature is unjust.

But, however that may be (and of course the moral malady has survived the scientific mistake), the people who talked thus of cannibal horses and competitive oysters, did not understand what Darwin's thesis was. If later biologists have condemned it, it should not be condemned without being understood, widely as it has been accepted without being understood. The point of Darwinism was not that a bird with a longer beak (let us say) thrust it into other birds, and had the advantage of a duelist with a longer sword. The point of Darwinism was that the bird with the longer beak could reach worms (let us say) at the bottom of a deeper hole; that the birds who could not do so would die; and he alone would remain to found a race of long-beaked birds. Darwinism suggested that if this happened a vast number of times, in a vast series of ages, it might account for the difference between the beaks of a sparrow and a stork. But the point was that the fittest did not need to *struggle* against the unfit. The survivor had nothing to do except to survive when the others could not survive. He survived because he alone had the features and organs necessary for survival. And, whatever be the truth about mammoths or monkeys, that is the exact truth about the present survival of Christianity. It is surviving because nothing else can survive.

Religion has returned; because all the various forms of scepticism that tried to take its place, and do its work, have by this time tied themselves into such knots that they cannot do anything. That chain of causation of which they were fond of talking (a chain which the first physicist of the age has just burst into bits of scrap iron) seems really to have served them after the fashion of the proverbial rope; and when modern discussion gave them rope enough, they quite rapidly hanged themselves. For there is not a single one of the fashionable forms of scientific scepticism, or determinism, that does not end in stark paralysis, touching the practical conduct of human life. Take any three of the normal and necessary ideas on which civilisation and even society depend. First, let us say, a scientific man of the old normal nineteenth-century sort would remark, "We can at least have common sense, in its proper meaning of a sense of reality common to all; we can have common morals, for without them we cannot even have a community; a man must in the ordinary sense obey the law, and especially the moral law." But the newer sceptic, who is progressive and has gone further and fared worse, will immediately say, "Why should you worship the taboo of your particular tribe? Why should you accept prejudices that are the product of a blind herd instinct? Why is there any authority in the unanimity of a flock of frightened sheep?" Suppose the normal man falls back on the deeper argument: "I am not terrorised by the tribe; I do keep my independent judgment; I have a conscience and a light of justice within which judges the world." And the stronger sceptic will answer: "If the light in your body be darkness—and it is darkness because it is only in your body, what are your judgments but the incurable twist and bias of your particular heredity and accidental environment? What can we know about judgments, except that they must all be equally unjust? For they are all equally conditioned by defects and individual ignorances, all of them different and none of them distinguishable; for there exists no single man so sane and separate as to be able to distinguish them justly. Why should your conscience be any more reliable than your rotting teeth or your quite special defect of eyesight? God bless us all, one would think you believed in God!" Then perhaps the normal person will get annoyed and say rather snappishly: "At least, I suppose we are men of science; there is science to appeal to and she will always answer; the evidential and experimental discovery of real things." And the other sceptic will answer, if he has any sense of humour: "Why, certainly. Sir Arthur Eddington is Science; and he will tell you that man really has free will and ought to hang on to religion for his life. Sir Bertram Windle was Science; and he would tell you that the scientific mind is completely satisfied in the Roman Catholic Church. For that matter, Sir Oliver Lodge is Science; and he has reached by purely experimental and evidential methods to a solid belief in ghosts. But I admit that there are men of science who cannot get to a solid belief in anything; even in science; even in themselves. There is the crystallographer of Cambridge who writes in the *Spectator* the lucid sentence: 'We know that most of what we know is probably untrue.' Does that help you on a bit, in founding your sane and solid society?"

It is the perishing of the other things, at least as much as the persistence of one thing, that has left us at last face to face with the ancient religion of our fathers. The thing once called free thought has come finally to threaten everything that is free. It denies personal freedom in denying free will and the human power of choice. It threatens civic freedom with a plague of hygienic and psychological quackeries, spreading over the land such a network of pseudo-scientific nonsense as free citizens have never yet endured in history. It is quite likely to reverse religious freedom, in the name of some barbarous nostrum or other, such as constitutes the crude and ill-cultured creed of Russia. It is perfectly capable of imposing silence and impotence from without. But there is no doubt whatever that it imposes silence and impotence from within. The whole trend of it, which began as a drive and has ended in a drift, is towards some form of the theory that a man cannot help himself; that a man cannot mend himself; above all, that a man cannot free himself. In all its novels and most of its newspaper articles it takes for granted that men are stamped and fixed in certain types of abnormality or anarchical weakness; that they are pinned and labelled in a museum of morality or immorality; or of that sort of unmorality which is more priggish than the one and more hoggish than the other. We are practically told that we might as well ask a fossil to reform itself. We are told that we are asking a stuffed bird to repent. We are all dead, and the only comfort is that we are all classified. For by this philosophy, which is the same as that of the blackest of Puritan heresies, we all died before we were born. But as it is Kismet without Allah, so also it is Calvinism without God.

The agnostics will be gratified to learn that it is entirely due to their own energy and enterprise, to their own activity in pursuing their own antics, that the world has at last tired of their antics and told them so. We have done very little against them; *non nobis, Domine;* the glory of their final overthrow is all their own. We have done far less than we should have done to explain all that balance of subtlety and sanity which is meant by a Christian civilization. Our thanks are due to those who have so generously helped us, by giving a glimpse of what might be meant by a Pagan civilization. And what is lost in that society is not so much religion as reason; the ordinary common daylight of intellectual instinct that has guided the children of men. A world in which men know that most of what they know is probably untrue cannot be dignified with the name of a sceptical world; it is simply an impotent and abject world, not attacking anything, but accepting everything while trusting nothing, accepting even its own incapacity to attack, accepting its own lack of authority to accept, doubting its very right to doubt. We are grateful for this public experiment and demonstration; it has taught us much. We did not believe that rationalists were so utterly mad until they made it quite clear to us.

We did not ourselves think that the mere denial of our dogmas could end in such dehumanised and demented anarchy. It might have taken the world a long time to understand that what it had been taught to dismiss as mediæval theology was often mere common sense; although the very term common sense or *communis sententia* was a mediæval conception. But it took the world very little time to understand that the talk on the other side was most uncommon nonsense. It was nonsense that could not be made the basis of any common system, such as has been founded upon common sense.

To take one example out of many: the whole question of Marriage has been turned into a question of Mood. The enemies of marriage did not have the patience to remain in their relatively strong position; that marriage could not be proved to be sacramental; and that some exceptions must be treated as exceptions, so long as it was merely social. They could not be content to say that it is not a sacrament but a contract; and that exceptional legal action might break a contract. They brought objections against it that would be quite as facile and quite as futile, if brought against any other contract. They said that a man is never in the same mood for ten minutes together; that he must not be asked to admire in a red daybreak what he admired in a yellow sunset; that no man can say he will even be the same man by the next month or the next minute; that new and nameless tortures may afflict him if his wife wears a different hat; or that he may plunge her into hell by putting on a pair of socks that does not harmonise with somebody else's carpet. It is quite obvious that this sort of sensitive insanity applies as much to any other human relation as to this relation. A man cannot choose a profession because, long before he has qualified as an architect, he may have mystically changed into an aviator, or been convulsed in rapid suggestion by the emotions of a ticket-collector, a trombone-player, and a professional harpooner of whales. A man dare not buy a house, for fear a fatal stranger with the wrong sort of socks should come into it, or for fear his own mind should be utterly changed in the matter of carpets or cornices. A man may suddenly decline to do any business with his own business partner, because he also, like the cruel husband, wears the wrong necktie. And I saw a serious printed appeal for sympathy for a wife who deserted her family because her psychology was incompatible with orange neckties. This is only one application, as I say, but it exactly illustrates how the sceptical principle is now applied, and how scepticism has recently changed from apparent sense to quite self-evident nonsense. The heresies not only decay but destroy themselves—in any case they perish without a blow.

For the reply, not merely of religion but of reason and the rooted sanity of mankind, is obvious enough. "If you feel like that, why certainly you will not found families, or found anything else. You will not build houses; you will not make partnerships; you will not in any fashion do the business of the world. You will never plant a tree lest you wish next week you had planted it somewhere else; you will never put a potato into a pot or stew, because it will be too late to take it out again; your whole mood is stricken and riddled with cowardice and sterility; your whole way of attacking any problem is to think of excuses for not attacking it at all. Very well, so be it; the Lord be with you. You may be respected for being sincere; you may be pitied for being sensitive; you may retain some of the corrective qualities which make it useful on occasion to be sceptical. But if you are too sceptical to do these things, you must stand out of the way of those who can do them; you must hand over the world to those who believe that the world is workable, to those who believe that men can make houses, make partnerships, make appointments, make promises—and keep them. And, if it is necessary to believe in God making Man, in God being made Man, or in God made Man coming in the clouds in glory, in order to keep a promise or boil a potato or behave like a human being—well, then you must at least give a chance to these credulous fanatics, who can believe the one and who can do the other." That is what I mean by the spiritual Survival of the Fittest. That is why the old phrase, which is probably a mistake in natural history, is a truth in supernatural history. The organic thing called religion has, in fact, the organs that take hold on life. It can feed where the fastidious doubter finds no food; it can reproduce where the solitary sceptic boasts of being barren. It may be accepting miracles to believe in free will; but it is accepting madness, sooner or later, to disbelieve in it. It may be a wild risk to make a vow; but it is a quiet, crawling, and inevitable ruin to refuse to make a vow. It may be incredible that one creed is the truth and the others are relatively false; but it is not only incredible, but also intolerable, that there is no truth either in or out of creeds, and all are equally false. For nobody can ever set anything right, if everybody is equally wrong. The intense interest of the moment is that the Man of Science, the hero of the modern world and the latest of the great servants of humanity, has suddenly and dramatically refused to have anything more to do with this dreary business of nibbling negation, and blind scratching and scraping away of the very foundations of the mastery of man. For the work of the sceptic for the past hundred years has indeed been very like the fruitless fury of some primeval monster; eyeless, mindless, merely destructive and devouring; a giant worm wasting away a world that he could not even see; a benighted and bestial life, unconscious of its own cause and of its own consequences. But Man has taken to himself again his own weapons—will, and worship, and reason, and the vision of the plan in things; and we are once more in the morning of the world.

## MY FATHER'S RELIGION

### *Clarence Day*  (*1935*)

My father's ideas of religion seemed straightforward and simple. He had noticed when he was a boy that there were buildings called churches; he had accepted them as a natural part of the surroundings in which he had been born.

He would never have invented such things himself. Nevertheless they were here. As he grew up he regarded them as unquestioningly as he did banks. They were substantial old structures, they were respectable, decent, and venerable. They were frequented by the right sort of people. Well, that was enough.

On the other hand he never allowed churches—or banks—to dictate to him. He gave each the respect that was due to it from his point of view; but he also expected from each of them the respect he felt due to him.

As to creeds, he knew nothing about them, and cared nothing either; yet he seemed to know which sect he belonged with. It had to be a sect with the minimum of nonsense about it; no total immersion, no exhorters, no holy confession. He would have been a Unitarian, naturally, if he'd lived in Boston. Since he was a respectable New Yorker, he belonged in the Episcopal Church.

As to living a spiritual life, he never tackled that problem. Some men who accept spiritual beliefs try to live up to them daily: other men, who reject such beliefs, try sometimes to smash them. My father would have disagreed with both kinds entirely. He took a more distant attitude. It disgusted him when atheists attacked religion: he thought they were vulgar. But he also objected to have religion make demands upon him—he felt that religion too was vulgar, when it tried to stir up men's feelings. It had its own proper field of activity, and it was all right there, of course; but there was one place religion should let alone, and that was a man's soul. He especially loathed any talk of walking hand in hand with his Saviour. And if he had ever found the Holy Ghost trying to soften his heart, he would have regarded Its behavior as distinctly uncalled for; even ungentlemanly.

The only religious leader or prophet I can think of who might have suited my father was Confucius—though even Confucius would have struck him as addled. Confucius was an advocate of peace, and of finding the path; and he enjoined the Golden Rule on his followers long before Christ. My father would not have been his follower in any of these. Finding "the path"? Not even Confucius could have made him see what that meant. He was too busy for that, too hot-tempered for peace, and the Golden Rule he regarded as claptrap; how could things work both ways? Whatever he did unto others he was sure was all right, but that didn't mean that he would have allowed them to do the same things to him. He saw other men as disorderly troops, and himself as a general; and the Golden Rule was plainly too mushy to apply in such circumstances. He disciplined himself quite as firmly as he tried to discipline others, but it wasn't necessarily by any means the same kind of discipline. There was one saying of Confucius', however, with which he would have agreed: "Respect spiritual beings—if there are any—but keep aloof from them." My father would have regarded that principle as thoroughly sound.

When Confucius was asked about the rule to return good for evil, he said: "What then will you return for good? No: return good for good; for evil, return justice." If my father had been asked to return good for evil he would have been even more pithy—his response would have consisted of a hearty and full-throated "Bah!"

If he had been let alone, he would have brought up his sons in this spirit. But my mother's feelings and teachings were different, and this complicated things for us. Like my father, she had accepted religion without any doubtings, but she had accepted more of it. She was far more devout. And she loved best the kind of faith that comforted her and sweetened her thoughts. My father didn't object to this at all—it was all right enough—for a woman: but it led to her giving us instructions that battled with his.

They both insisted strongly, for example, on our going to church, but they didn't agree in their reasons. It was the right thing to do, Father said. "But why do we have to go, Father?" "Because I wish to bring you up properly. Men who neglect going to church are a lazy, disreputable lot." A few might be good fellows, he would admit, but they were the exceptions. As a rule, non-churchgoers were not solid, respectable citizens. All respectable citizens owed it to themselves to attend.

My mother put it differently to us. She said we owed it to God. Church to her was a place where you worshiped, and learned to be good. My father never dreamed of attending for any such reason. In his moral instructions to us he never once mentioned God. What he dwelt on was integrity. My mother once wrote in my plush-covered autograph album, "Fear God and keep His commandments"; but the motto that Father had written on the preceding page, over his bolder signature, was: "Do your duty and fear no one."

And nobody could tell him his duty—he knew it without that, it seemed. It wasn't written down in any book, certainly not in the Bible, but it was a perfectly definite and indisputable thing nevertheless. It was a code, a tradition. It was to be upright and fearless and honorable, and to brush your clothes properly; and in general always to do the right thing in every department of life. The right thing to do for religion was to go to some good church on Sundays. When Father went to church and sat in his pew, he felt he was doing enough. Any further spiritual work ought to be done by the clergy.

When hymns were sung he sometimes joined in mechanically, for the mere sake of singing; but usually he stood as silent as an eagle among canaries and doves, leaving others to abase themselves in sentiments that he didn't share. The hymns inculcated meekness and submission, and dependence on God; but Father was quick to resent an injury, and he had no meekness in him.

> Jesus, lover of my soul,
> Let me to Thy bosom fly,
> While the nearer waters roll,
> While the tempest still is nigh.

How could Father sing that? He had no desire to fly to that bosom.

> Hide me, O my Saviour, hide,
>   Till the storm of life be past;
> Safe into the haven guide,
>   Oh receive my soul at last . . .
> All my trust on Thee is stayed;
>   All my help from thee I bring;
> Cover my defenseless head
>   With the shadow of thy wing.

But Father's head was far from defenseless, and he would have scorned to hide, or ask shelter. As he stood there, looking critically about him, high-spirited, resolute, I could imagine him marching with that same independence through space—a tiny speck masterfully dealing with death and infinity.

When our rector talked of imitating the saints, it seemed drivel to Father. What! imitate persons who gave their whole lives to religion, and took only a perfunctory interest in the affairs of this world? Father regarded himself as a more all-round man than the saints. They had neglected nine-tenths of their duties from his point of view—they had no business connections, no families, they hadn't even paid taxes. In a word, saints were freaks. If a freak spent an abnormal amount of time being religious, what of it?

The clergy were a kind of freaks also. A queer lot. Father liked Bishop Greer and a few others, but he hadn't much respect for the rest of them. He thought of most clergymen as any busy man of action thinks of philosophers, or of those scholars who discuss the fourth dimension, which is beyond human knowing. He regarded the self-alleged intimacy of our rector with that fourth dimension most skeptically. He himself neither was nor wished to be intimate with a thing of that sort. But this didn't mean that he doubted the existence of God. On the contrary, God and Father had somehow contrived to achieve a serene and harmonious relation that the clergy themselves might have envied.

How did Father think God felt towards my mother? Why, about the way he did. God probably knew she had faults, but He saw she was lovely and good; and—in spite of some mistaken ideas that she had about money—He doubtless looked on her most affectionately. Father didn't expect God to regard *him* affectionately—they stood up man to man—but naturally God loved my mother, as everyone must. At the gate of Heaven, if there was any misunderstanding about his own ticket, Father counted on Mother to get him in. That was her affair.

This idea runs far back, or down, into old human thoughts. "The unbelieving husband is sanctified by the wife." (First Corinthians, vii, 14.) Medical missionaries report that today, in some primitive tribes, a healthy woman will propose to swallow medicine in behalf of her sick husband. This plan seems to her husband quite reasonable. It seemed so—in religion—to Father.

As to his mental picture of God, I suppose that Father was vague, but in a general way he seemed to envisage a God in his own image. A God who had small use for emotionalism and who prized strength and dignity. A God who probably found the clergy as hard to bear as did Father himself. In short, Father and God, as I said, usually saw eye to eye. They seldom met, or even sought a meeting, their spheres were so different; but they had perfect confidence in each other—at least at most moments. The only exceptions were when God seemed to be neglecting His job—Father's confidence in Him was then withdrawn, instantly. But I'll come to this later.

As to the nature of God's sphere, namely Heaven, compared to Father's, the earth, Heaven wasn't nearly so solid and substantial. Father had all the best of it. Life here on earth was trying, but it shouldn't be—it was all right intrinsically—he felt it was only people's damned carelessness that upset things so much. Heaven on the other hand had a more serious and fundamental defect: the whole place was thin and peculiar. It didn't inspire much confidence. Father saw glumly that the time would come when he'd have to go there, but he didn't at all relish the prospect. He clung to his own battered realm.

Yet its faults and stupidities weighed on his spirit at times; all the chuckle-headed talk and rascality in business and politics. He was always getting indignant about them, and demanding that they be stamped out; and when he saw them continually spreading everywhere, it was maddening. Nature too, though in general sound and wholesome, had a treacherous streak. He hated and resented decay, and failing powers. He hated to see little children or animals suffer. His own aches and pains were an outrage; he faced them with anger. And aside from these treacheries, there was a spirit of rebellion in things. He would come in from a walk over his fields—which to me had seemed pleasant—oppressed by the balky disposition both of his field and his farmer. He would get up from an inspection of his account books with the same irritation: there were always some bonds in his box that hadn't behaved as they should. And twice a day, regularly, he would have a collision, or bout, with the newspaper: it was hard to see why God had made so many damned fools and Democrats.

I would try to persuade him sometimes—in my argumentative years—that it would be better for him to accept the world as it was and adapt himself to it, since he could scarcely expect to make the planet over, and change the whole earth single-handed. Father listened to this talk with suspicion, as to an *advocatus diaboli*. If he ever was tempted to give in, it was only in his weak moments; a minute later he was again on the war-path, like a materialistic Don Quixote.

There was one kind of depression that afflicted Mother which Father was free from: he never once had any moments of feeling "unworthy." This was a puzzle to Mother, and it made her look at Father with a mixture of awe and annoyance. Other people went to church to be made better, she told him. Why didn't he? He replied in astonishment that he had no need to be better—he was all right as he was. Mother couldn't get over his taking this stand, but she never could get him to see what the matter was with it. It wasn't at all easy for Father to see that he had any faults; and if he did, it didn't even occur to him to ask God to forgive them. He forgave them himself. In his moments of prayer, when he and God tried to commune with each other, it wasn't his own shortcomings that were brought on the carpet, but God's.

He expected a good deal of God, apparently. Not that he wanted God's help, of course; or far less His guidance. No, but it seemed that God—like the rest of us—spoiled Father's plans. He, Father, was always trying to bring this or that good thing to pass, only to find that there were obstacles in the way. These of course roused his wrath. He would call God's attention to such things. They should not have been there. He didn't actually accuse God of gross inefficiency, but when he prayed his tone was loud and angry, like that of a dissatisfied guest in a carelessly managed hotel.

I never saw Father kneel in supplication on such occasions. On the contrary he usually talked with God lying in bed. My room was just above Father's, and he could easily be heard through the floor. On those rare nights when he failed to sleep well, the sound of damns would float up—at first deep and tragic and low, then more loud and exasperated. Fragments of thoughts and strong feelings came next, or meditations on current bothers. At the peak of these, God would be summoned. I would hear him call "Oh God?" over and over, with a rising inflection, as though he were demanding that God should present himself instantly, and sit in the fat green chair in the corner, and be duly admonished. Then when Father seemed to feel that God was listening, he would begin to expostulate. He would moan in a discouraged but strong voice: "Oh God, it's too much. Amen. . . . I say it's too damned much . . . No, no, I can't stand it. Amen." After a pause, if he didn't feel better, he would seem to suspect that God might be trying to sneak back to Heaven without doing anything, and I would hear him shout warningly: "Oh God! I *won't* stand it! Amen. Oh damnation! A-a-men." Sometimes he would ferociously bark a few extra Amens, and then, soothed and satisfied, peacefully go back to sleep . . . And one night in the country, when the caretaker of our house in town telephoned to Father that the rain was pouring in through a hole in the roof, I heard so much noise that I got out of bed and looked over the banisters, and saw Father standing alone in the hall, shaking his fist at the ceiling, and shouting in hot indignation to Heaven, "What next?"

But Father was patient with God after all. If he didn't forgive, he forgot. His wrath didn't last—he had other things to think of—and he was genial at heart. The very next Sunday after an outburst he would be back in church. Not perhaps as a worshiper or a devotee, but at least as a patron.

## SIR ROGER AT CHURCH

### *Joseph Addison* (1711)

I AM ALWAYS very well pleased with a country Sunday, and think, if keeping holy the seventh day were only a human institution, it would be the best method that could have been thought of for the polishing and civilizing of mankind. It is certain the country people would soon degenerate into a kind of savages and barbarians were there not such frequent returns of a stated time, in which the whole village meet together with their best faces, and in their cleanliest habits, to converse with one another upon indifferent subjects, hear their duties explained to them, and join together in adoration of the Supreme Being. Sunday clears away the rust of the whole week, not only as it refreshes in their minds the notions of religion, but as it puts both the sexes upon appearing in their most agreeable forms, and exerting all such qualities as are apt to give them a figure in the eye of the village. A country fellow distinguishes himself as much in the churchyard as a citizen does upon the 'Change, the whole parish politics being generally discussed in that place either after sermon or before the bell rings.

My friend Sir Roger, being a good churchman, has beautified the inside of his church with several texts of his own choosing; he has likewise given a handsome pulpit-cloth, and railed in the communion-table at his own expense. He has often told me that, at his coming to his estate, he found his parishioners very irregular; and that, in order to make them kneel and join in the responses, he gave every one of them a hassock and a common-prayer-book, and at the same time employed an itinerant singing-master, who goes about the country for that purpose, to instruct them rightly in the tunes of the Psalms; upon which they now very much value themselves, and indeed outdo most of the country churches that I have ever heard.

As Sir Roger is landlord to the whole congregation, he keeps them in very good order, and will suffer nobody to sleep in it besides himself; for, if by chance he has been surprised into a short nap at sermon, upon recovering out of it he stands up and looks about him, and, if he sees anybody else nodding, either wakes them himself, or sends his servant to them. Several other of the old knight's particularities break out upon these occasions; sometimes he will be lengthening out a verse in the Singing-Psalms half a minute after the rest of the congregation have done with it; sometimes, when he is pleased with the matter of his devotion, he pronounces "Amen" three or four times to the same prayer; and sometimes stands up when everybody else is upon their knees, to count the congregation, or see if any of his tenants are missing.

I was yesterday very much surprised to hear my old friend, in the midst of the service, calling out to one John Matthews to mind what he was about, and not disturb the congregation. This John Matthews, it seems, is remarkable for being an idle fellow, and at that time was kicking his heels for his diversion. This authority of the knight, though exerted in that odd manner which accompanies him in all circumstances of life, has a very good effect upon the parish, who are not polite enough to see anything ridiculous in his behavior; besides that the general good sense and worthiness of his character makes his friends observe these little singularities as foils that rather set off than blemish his good qualities.

As soon as the sermon is finished, nobody presumes to stir till Sir Roger is gone out of the church. The knight walks down from his seat in the chancel between a double row of his tenants, that stand bowing to him on each side, and every now and then inquires how such an one's wife, or mother, or son, or father do, whom he does not see at church,—which is understood as a secret reprimand to the person that is absent.

The chaplain has often told me that, upon a catechizing day, when Sir Roger had been pleased with a boy that answers well, he has ordered a Bible to be given him next day for his encouragement, and sometimes accompanies it with a flitch of bacon to his mother. Sir Roger has likewise added five pounds a year to the clerk's place; and, that he may encourage the young fellows to make themselves perfect in the church service, has promised, upon the death of the present incumbent, who is very old, to bestow it according to merit.

The fair understanding between Sir Roger and his chaplain, and their mutual concurrence in doing good, is the more remarkable because the very next village is famous for the differences and contentions that rise between the parson and the squire, who live in a perpetual state of war. The parson is always preaching at the squire, and the squire, to be revenged on the parson, never comes to church. The squire has made all his tenants atheists and tithe-stealers; while the parson instructs them every Sunday in the dignity of his order, and insinuates to them in almost every sermon that he is a better man than his patron. In short, matters are come to such an extremity that the squire has not said his prayers either in public or private this half year; and that the parson threatens him, if he does not mend his manners, to pray for him in the face of the whole congregation.

Feuds of this nature, though too frequent in the country, are very fatal to the ordinary people, who are so used to be dazzled with riches that they pay as much deference to the understanding of a man of an estate as of a man of learning; and are very hardly brought to regard any truth, how important soever it may be, that is preached to them, when they know there are several men of five hundred a year who do not believe it.

## A FREE MAN'S WORSHIP

*Bertrand Russell  (1918)*

To DR. FAUSTUS in his study Mephistopheles told the history of the Creation, saying:

"The endless praises of the choirs of angels had begun to grow wearisome; for, after all, did he not deserve their praise? Had he not given them endless joy? Would it not be more amusing to obtain undeserved praise, to be worshipped by beings whom he tortured? He smiled inwardly, and resolved that the great drama should be performed.

"For countless ages the hot nebula whirled aimlessly through space. At length it began to take shape, the central mass threw off planets, the planets cooled, boiling seas and burning mountains heaved and tossed, from black masses of cloud hot sheets of rain deluged the barely solid crust. And now the first germ of life grew in the depths of the ocean, and developed rapidly in the fructifying warmth into vast forest trees, huge ferns springing from the damp mould, sea monsters breeding, fighting, devouring, and passing away. And from the monsters, as the play unfolded itself, Man was born, with the power of thought, the knowledge of good and evil, and the cruel thirst for worship. And Man saw that all is passing in this mad, monstrous world, that all is struggling to snatch, at any cost, a few brief moments of life before Death's inexorable decree. And Man said: 'There is a hidden purpose, could we but fathom it, and the purpose is good; for we must reverence something, and in the visible world there is nothing worthy of reverence.' And Man stood aside from the struggle, resolving that God intended harmony to come out of chaos by human efforts. And when he followed the instincts which God had transmitted to him from his ancestry of beasts of prey, he called it Sin, and asked God to forgive him. But he doubted whether he could be justly forgiven, until he invented a Divine Plan by which God's wrath was to have been appeased. And seeing the present was bad, he made it yet worse, that thereby the future might be better. And he gave God thanks for the strength that enabled him to forgo even the joys that were possible. And God smiled; and when he saw that Man had become perfect in renunciation and worship, he sent another sun through the sky, which crashed into Man's sun; and all returned again to nebula.

" 'Yes,' he murmured, 'it was a good play; I will have it performed again.' "

Such, in outline, but even more purposeless, more void of meaning is the world which Science presents for our belief. Amid such a world, if anywhere, our ideals henceforward must find a home. That Man is the product of causes which had no prevision of the end they were achieving; that his origin, his growth, his hopes and fears, his loves and his beliefs, are but the outcome of accidental collocations of atoms; that no fire, no heroism, no intensity of thought and feeling, can preserve an individual life beyond the grave; that all the labours of the ages, all the devotion, all the inspiration, all the noonday brightness of human genius, are destined to extinction in the vast death of the solar system, and that the whole temple of Man's achievement must inevitably be buried beneath the débris of a universe in ruins—all these things, if not quite beyond dispute, are yet so nearly certain, that no philosophy which rejects them can hope to stand. Only within the scaffolding of these truths, only on the firm foundation of unyielding despair, can the soul's habitation henceforth be safely built.

How, in such an alien and inhuman world, can so powerless a creature as Man preserve his aspirations untarnished? A strange mystery it is that Nature, omnipotent but blind, in the revolutions of her secular hurryings through the abysses of space, has brought forth at last a child, subject still to her power, but gifted with sight, with knowledge of good and evil, with the capacity of judging all the works of his unthinking Mother. In spite of Death, the mark and seal of the parental control, Man is yet free, during his brief years, to examine, to criticise, to know, and in imagination to create. To him alone, in the world with which he is acquainted, this freedom belongs; and in this lies his superiority to the resistless forces that control his outward life.

The savage, like ourselves, feels the oppression of his impotence before the powers of Nature; but having in himself nothing that he respects more than Power, he is willing to prostrate himself before his gods, without inquiring whether they are worthy of his worship. Pathetic and very terrible is the long history of cruelty and torture, of degradation and human sacrifice endured in the hope of placating the jealous gods: surely, the trembling believer thinks, when what is most precious has been freely given, their lust for blood must be appeased, and more will not be required. The religion of Moloch—as such creeds may be generically called—is in essence the cringing submission of the slave, who dare not, even in his heart, allow the thought that his master deserves no adulation. Since the independence of ideals is not yet acknowledged, Power may be freely worshipped, and receive an unlimited respect, despite its wanton infliction of pain.

But gradually, as morality grows bolder, the claim of the ideal world begins to be felt; and worship, if it is not to cease, must be given to gods of another kind than those created by the savage. Some, though they feel the demands of the ideal, will still consciously reject them, still urging that naked Power is worthy of worship. Such is the attitude inculcated in God's answer to Job out of the whirlwind: the divine power and knowledge are paraded, but of the divine goodness there is no hint. Such also is the attitude of those who, in our own day, base their morality upon the struggle for survival, maintaining that the survivors are necessarily the fittest. But others, not content with an answer so repugnant to the moral sense, will adopt the position which we have become accustomed to regard as specially religious, maintaining that, in some hidden manner, the world of fact is really harmonious with the world of ideals. Thus Man creates God, all-powerful and all-good, the mystic unity of what is and what should be.

But the world of fact, after all, is not good; and, in submitting our judgment to it, there is an element of slavishness from which our thoughts must be purged. For in all things it is well to exalt the dignity of Man, by freeing him as far as possible from the tyranny of non-human Power. When we have realised that Power is largely bad, that man, with his knowledge of good and evil, is but a helpless atom in a world which has no such knowledge, the choice is again presented to us: Shall we worship Force, or shall we worship Goodness? Shall our God exist and be evil, or shall he be recognised as the creation of our own conscience?

The answer to this question is very momentous, and affects profoundly our whole morality. The worship of Force, to which Carlyle and Nietzsche and the creed of Militarism have accustomed us, is the result of failure to maintain our own ideals against a hostile universe: it is itself a prostrate submission to evil, a sacrifice of our best to Moloch. If strength indeed is to be respected, let us respect rather the strength of those who refuse that false "recognition of facts" which fails to recognise that facts are often bad. Let us admit that, in the world we know, there are many things that would be better otherwise, and that the ideals to which we do and must adhere are not realised in the realm of matter. Let us preserve our respect for truth, for beauty, for the ideal of perfection which life does not permit us to attain, though none of these things meet with the approval of the unconscious universe. If Power is bad, as it seems to be, let us reject it from our hearts. In this lies Man's true freedom: in determination to worship only the God created by our own love of the good, to respect only the heaven which inspires the insight of our best moments. In action, in desire, we must submit perpetually to the tyranny of outside forces; but in thought, in aspiration, we are free, free from our fellow-men, free from the petty planet on which our bodies impotently crawl, free even, while we live, from the tyranny of death. Let us learn, then, that energy of faith which enables us to live constantly in the vision of the good; and let us descend in action, into the world of fact, with that vision always before us.

When first the opposition of fact and ideal grows fully visible, a spirit of fiery revolt, of fierce hatred of the gods, seems necessary to the assertion of freedom. To defy with Promethean constancy a hostile universe, to keep its evil always in view, always actively hated, to refuse no pain that the malice of Power can invent, appears to be the duty of all who will not bow before the inevitable. But indignation is still a bondage, for it compels our thoughts to be occupied with an evil world; and in the fierceness of desire from which rebellion springs there is a kind of self-assertion which it is necessary for the wise to overcome. Indignation is a submission of our thoughts, but not of our desires; the Stoic freedom in which wisdom consists is found in the submission of our desires, but not of our thoughts. From the submission of our desires springs the virtue of resignation; from the freedom of our thoughts springs the whole world of art and philosophy, and the vision of beauty by which, at last, we half reconquer the reluctant world. But the vision of beauty is possible only to unfettered contemplation, to thoughts not weighted by the load of eager wishes; and thus Freedom comes only to those who no longer ask of life that it shall yield them any of those personal goods that are subject to the mutations of Time.

Although the necessity of renunciation is evidence of the existence of evil, yet Christianity, in preaching it, has shown a wisdom exceeding that of the Promethean philosophy of rebellion. It must be admitted that, of the things we desire, some, though they prove impossible, are yet real goods; others, however, as ardently longed for, do not form part of a fully purified ideal. The belief that what must be renounced is bad, though sometimes false, is far less often false than untamed passion supposes; and the creed of religion, by providing a reason for proving that it is never false, has been the means of purifying our hopes by the discovery of many austere truths.

But there is in resignation a further good element: even real goods, when they are unattainable, ought not to be fretfully desired. To every man comes, sooner or later, the great renunciation. For the young, there is nothing unattainable; a good thing desired with the whole force of a passionate will, and yet impossible, is to them not credible. Yet, by death, by illness, by poverty, or by the voice of duty, we must learn, each one of us, that the world was not made for us, and that, however beautiful may be the things we crave, Fate may nevertheless forbid them. It is the part of courage, when misfortune comes, to bear without repining the ruin of our hopes, to turn away our thoughts from vain regrets. This degree of submission to Power is not only just and right: it is the very gate of wisdom.

But passive renunciation is not the whole of wisdom; for not by renunciation alone can we build a temple for the worship of our own ideals. Haunting foreshadowings of the temple appear in the realm of imagination, in music, in architecture, in the untroubled kingdom of reason, and in the golden sunset magic of lyrics, where beauty shines and glows, remote from the touch of sorrow, remote from the fear of change, remote from the failures and disenchantments of the world of fact. In the contemplation of these things the vision of heaven will shape itself in our hearts, giving at once a touchstone to judge the world about us, and an inspiration by which to fashion to our needs whatever is not incapable of serving as a stone in the sacred temple.

Except for those rare spirits that are born without sin, there is a cavern of darkness to be traversed before that temple can be entered. The gate of the cavern is despair, and its floor is paved with the gravestones of abandoned hopes. There Self must die; there the eagerness, the greed of untamed desire must be slain, for only so can the soul be freed from the empire of Fate. But out of the cavern the Gate of Renunciation leads again to the daylight of wisdom, by whose radiance a new insight, a new joy, a new tenderness, shine forth to gladden the pilgrim's heart.

When, without the bitterness of impotent rebellion, we have learnt both to resign ourselves to the outward rule of Fate and to recognise that the non-human world is unworthy of our worship, it becomes possible at last so to transform and refashion the unconscious universe, so to transmute it in the crucible of the imagination, that a new image of shining gold replaces the old idol of clay. In all the multiform facts of the world—in the visual shapes of trees and mountains and clouds, in the events of the life of man, even in the very omnipotence of Death—the insight of creative idealism can find the reflection of a beauty which its own thoughts first made. In this way mind asserts its subtle mastery over the thoughtless forces of Nature. The more evil the material with which it deals, the more thwarting to untrained desire, the greater is its achievement in inducing the reluctant rock to yield up its

hidden treasures, the prouder its victory in compelling the opposing forces
to swell the pageant of its triumph. Of all the arts, Tragedy is the proudest,
the most triumphant; for it builds its shining citadel in the very centre of the
enemy's country, on the very summit of his highest mountain; from its impreg-
nable watch-towers, his camps and arsenals, his columns and forts, are all
revealed; within its walls the free life continues, while the legions of Death
and Pain and Despair, and all the servile captains of tyrant Fate, afford the
burghers of that dauntless city new spectacles of beauty. Happy those sacred
ramparts, thrice happy the dwellers on that all-seeing eminence. Honour to
those brave warriors who, through countless ages of warfare, have preserved
for us the priceless heritage of liberty, and have kept undefiled by sacrilegious
invaders the home of the unsubdued.

But the beauty of Tragedy does but make visible a quality which, in more
or less obvious shapes, is present always and everywhere in life. In the spectacle of Death, in the endurance of intolerable pain, and in the irrevocableness
of a vanished past, there is a sacredness, an overpowering awe, a feeling of the
vastness, the depth, the inexhaustible mystery of existence, in which, as by
some strange marriage of pain, the sufferer is bound to the world by bonds of
sorrow. In these moments of insight, we lose all eagerness of temporary desire,
all struggling and striving for petty ends, all care for the little trivial things
that, to a superficial view, make up the common life of day by day; we see,
surrounding the narrow raft illumined by the flickering light of human com-
radeship, the dark ocean on whose rolling waves we toss for a brief hour;
from the great night without, a chill blast breaks in upon our refuge; all the
loneliness of humanity amid hostile forces is concentrated upon the individual
soul, which must struggle alone, with what of courage it can command, against
the whole weight of a universe that cares nothing for its hopes and fears. Victory, in this struggle with the powers of darkness, is the true baptism into
the glorious company of heroes, the true initiation into the overmastering
beauty of human existence. From that awful encounter of the soul with the
outer world, renunciation, wisdom, and charity are born; and with their birth
a new life begins. To take into the inmost shrine of the soul the irresistible
forces whose puppets we seem to be—Death and change, the irrevocableness
of the past, and the powerlessness of man before the blind hurry of the universe from vanity to vanity—to feel these things and know them is to conquer
them.

This is the reason why the Past has such magical power. The beauty of its
motionless and silent pictures is like the enchanted purity of late autumn, when
the leaves, though one breath would make them fall, still glow against the sky
in golden glory. The Past does not change or strive; like Duncan, after life's
fitful fever it sleeps well; what was eager and grasping, what was petty and
transitory, has faded away, the things that were beautiful and eternal shine
out of it like stars in the night. Its beauty, to a soul not worthy of it, is unendurable; but to a soul which has conquered Fate it is the key of religion.

The life of Man, viewed outwardly, is but a small thing in comparison with the forces of Nature. The slave is doomed to worship Time and Fate and Death, because they are greater than anything he finds in himself, and because all his thoughts are of things which they devour. But, great as they are, to think of them greatly, to feel their passionless splendour, is greater still. And such thought makes us free men; we no longer bow before the inevitable in Oriental subjection, but we absorb it, and make it a part of ourselves. To abandon the struggle for private happiness, to expel all eagerness of temporary desire, to burn with passion for eternal things—this is emancipation, and this is the free man's worship. And this liberation is effected by a contemplation of Fate; for Fate itself is subdued by the mind which leaves nothing to be purged by the purifying fire of Time.

United with his fellow-men by the strongest of all ties, the tie of a common doom, the free man finds that a new vision is with him always, shedding over every daily task the light of love. The life of Man is a long march through the night, surrounded by invisible foes, tortured by weariness and pain, towards a goal that few can hope to reach, and where none may tarry long. One by one, as they march, our comrades vanish from our sight, seized by the silent orders of omnipotent Death. Very brief is the time in which we can help them, in which their happiness or misery is decided. Be it ours to shed sunshine on their path, to lighten their sorrows by the balm of sympathy, to give them the pure joy of a never-tiring affection, to strengthen failing courage, to instil faith in hours of despair. Let us not weigh in grudging scales their merits and demerits, but let us think only of their need—of the sorrows, the difficulties perhaps the blindnesses, that make the misery of their lives; let us remember that they are fellow-sufferers in the same darkness, actors in the same tragedy with ourselves. And so, when their day is over, when their good and their evil have become eternal by the immortality of the past, be it ours to feel that, where they suffered, where they failed, no deed of ours was the cause; but wherever a spark of the divine fire kindled in their hearts, we were ready with encouragement, with sympathy, with brave words in which high courage glowed.

Brief and powerless is Man's life; on him and all his race the slow, sure doom falls pitiless and dark. Blind to good and evil, reckless of destruction, omnipotent matter rolls on its relentless way; for Man, condemned to-day to lose his dearest, to-morrow himself to pass through the gate of darkness, it remains only to cherish, ere yet the blow falls, the lofty thoughts that ennoble his little day; disdaining the coward terrors of the slave of Fate, to worship at the shrine that his own hands have built; undismayed by the empire of chance, to preserve a mind free from the wanton tyranny that rules his outward life; proudly defiant of the irresistible forces that tolerate, for a moment, his knowledge and his condemnation, to sustain alone, a weary but unyielding Atlas, the world that his own ideals have fashioned despite the trampling march of unconscious Power.

## KNOWLEDGE AND FAITH

*John Henry Newman* (1852)

PEOPLE say to me that it is but a dream to suppose that Christianity should regain the organic power in human society which once it possessed. I cannot help that; I never said it could. I am not a politician; I am proposing no measures, but exposing a fallacy, and resisting a pretence. Let Benthamism reign, if men have no aspirations; but do not tell them to be romantic, and then solace them with glory; do not attempt by philosophy what once was done by religion. The ascendancy of Faith may be impracticable, but the reign of Knowledge is incomprehensible. The problem for statesmen of this age is how to educate the masses, and literature and science cannot give the solution.

Not so deems Sir Robert Peel; his firm belief and hope is "that an increased sagacity will administer to an exalted faith; that it will make men not merely believe in the cold doctrines of Natural Religion, but that it will so prepare and temper the spirit and understanding, that they will be better qualified to comprehend the great scheme of human redemption." He certainly thinks that scientific pursuits have some considerable power of impressing religion upon the mind of the multitude. I think not, and will now say why.

Science gives us the grounds of premises from which religious truths are to be inferred; but it does not set about inferring them, much less does it reach the inference;—that is not its province. It brings before us phenomena, and it leaves us, if we will, to call them works of design, wisdom, or benevolence; and further still, if we will, to proceed to confess an Intelligent Creator. We have to take its facts, and to give them a meaning, and to draw our own conclusions from them. First comes Knowledge, then a view, then reasoning, and then belief. This is why Science has so little of a religious tendency; deductions have no power of persuasion. The heart is commonly reached, not through the reason, but through the imagination, by means of direct impressions, by the testimony of facts and events, by history, by description. Persons influence us, voices melt us, looks subdue us, deeds inflame us. Many a man will live and die upon a dogma: no man will be a martyr for a conclusion. A conclusion is but an opinion; it is not a thing which *is*, but which *we are* "*certain about*"; and it has often been observed, that we never say we are certain without implying that we doubt. To say that a thing *must* be, is to admit that it *may not* be. No one, I say, will die for his own calculations; he dies for realities. This is why a literary religion is so little to be depended upon; it looks well in fair weather, but its doctrines are opinions, and, when called to suffer for them, it slips them between its folios, or burns them at its hearth. And this again is the secret of the distrust and raillery with which moralists have been so commonly visited. They say and do not. Why? Because they are contemplating the fitness of things, and they live by the square, when they should be realizing their high maxims in the concrete. Now

Sir Robert thinks better of natural history, chemistry, and astronomy, than of such ethics; but they too, what are they more than divinity *in posse?* He protests against "controversial divinity": is *inferential* much better?

I have no confidence, then, in philosophers who cannot help being religious, and are Christians by implication. They sit at home, and reach forward to distances which astonish us; but they hit without grasping, and are sometimes as confident about shadows as about realities. They have worked out by a calculation the lie of a country which they never saw, and mapped it by means of a gazetteer; and like blind men, though they can put a stranger on his way, they cannot walk straight themselves, and do not feel it quite their business to walk at all.

Logic makes but a sorry rhetoric with the multitude; first shoot round corners, and you may not despair of converting by a syllogism. Tell men to gain notions of a Creator from His works, and, if they were to set about it (which nobody does), they would be jaded and wearied by the labyrinth they were tracing. Their minds would be gorged and surfeited by the logical operation. Logicians are more set upon concluding rightly, than on right conclusions. They cannot see the end for the process. Few men have that power of mind which may hold fast and firmly a variety of thoughts. We ridicule "men of one idea"; but a great many of us are born to be such, and we should be happier if we knew it. To most men argument makes the point in hand only more doubtful, and considerably less impressive. After all, man is *not* a reasoning animal; he is a seeing, feeling, contemplating, acting animal. He is influenced by what is direct and precise. It is very well to freshen our impressions and convictions from physics, but to create them we must go elsewhere. Sir Robert Peel "never can think it possible that a mind can be so constituted, that, after being familiarized with the wonderful discoveries which have been made in every part of experimental science, it can retire from such contemplations without more enlarged conceptions of God's providence, and a higher reverence for His name." If he speaks of religious minds, he perpetrates a truism; if of irreligious, he insinuates a paradox.

Life is not long enough for a religion of inferences; we shall never have done beginning, if we determine to begin with proof. We shall ever be laying our foundations; we shall turn theology into evidences, and divines into textuaries. We shall never get at our first principles. Resolve to believe nothing, and you must prove your proofs and analyze your elements, sinking further and further, and finding "in the lowest depth a lower deep," till you come to the broad bosom of skepticism. I would rather be bound to defend the reasonableness of assuming that Christianity is true, than to demonstrate a moral governance from the physical world. Life is for action. If we insist on proofs for everything, we shall never come to action: to act you must assume, and that assumption is faith.

Let no one suppose that in saying this I am maintaining that all proofs are equally difficult, and all propositions equally debatable. Some assumptions are greater than others, and some doctrines involve postulates larger than others, and more numerous. I only say that impressions lead to action, and that reasonings lead from it. Knowledge of premises, and inferences upon them,—this is not to *live*. It is very well as a matter of liberal curiosity and of philosophy to analyze our modes of thought; but let this come second, and when there is leisure for it, and then our examinations will in many ways even be subservient to action. But if we commence with scientific knowledge and argumentative proof, or lay any great stress upon it as the basis of personal Christianity, or attempt to make man moral and religious by Libraries and Museums, let us in consistency take chemists for our cooks, and mineralogists for our masons.

Now I wish to state all this as matter of fact, to be judged by the candid testimony of any persons whatever. Why we are so constituted that Faith, not Knowledge or Argument, is our principle of action, is a question with which I have nothing to do; but I think it is a fact, and if it be such, we must resign ourselves to it as best we may, unless we take refuge in the intolerable paradox that the mass of men are created for nothing, and are meant to leave life as they entered it. So well has this practically been understood in all ages of the world, that no Religion has yet been a Religion of physics or of philosophy. It has ever been synonymous with Revelation. It never has been a deduction from what we know: it has ever been an assertion of what we are to believe. It has never lived in a conclusion; it has ever been a message, or a history, or a vision. No legislator or priest ever dreamed of educating our moral nature by science or by argument. There is no difference here between true religions and pretended. Moses was instructed, not to reason from the creation, but to work miracles. Christianity is a history, supernatural, and almost scenic: it tells us what its Author is, by telling us what He has done. . . .

When Sir Robert Peel assures us from the Town Hall at Tamworth that physical science must lead to religion, it is no bad compliment to him to say that he is unreal. He speaks of what he knows nothing about. To a religious man like him, Science has ever suggested religious thoughts; he colours the phenomena of physics with the hues of his own mind, and mistakes an interpretation for a deduction. "I am sanguine enough to believe," he says, "that that superior sagacity which is most conversant with the course and constitution of Nature will be first to turn a deaf ear to objections and presumptions against revealed religion, and to acknowledge the harmony of the Christian dispensation with all that reason, assisted by revelation, tells us of the course and constitution of Nature." Now, considering that we are all of us educated as Christians from infancy, it is not easy to decide at this day whether science creates faith, or only confirms it; but we have this remarkable fact in the history of heathen Greece against the former supposition, that her most eminent empirical philosophers were atheists, and that it was their atheism which was the cause of their eminence. "The natural philosophies of Democritus and others," says Lord Bacon, "*who allow no God or mind* in the frame of things, but attribute the structure of the universe to infinite essays and trials of nature, or what they call fate or fortune, and assigned the causes of particular things to the necessity of matter, *without any intermixture of final causes*, seem, as far as we can judge from the remains of their philosophy, *much more solid*, and to have *gone deeper into nature*, with regard to physical causes, than the philosophies of Aristotle or Plato: and this only because they *never meddled with final causes*, which the others were perpetually inculcating."

Lord Bacon gives us both the fact and the reason for it. Physical philosophers are ever inquiring *whence* things are, not *why;* referring them to nature, not to mind; and thus they tend to make a system a substitute for a God. Each pursuit or calling has its own dangers, and each numbers among its professors men who rise superior to them. As the soldier is tempted to dissipation, and the merchant to acquisitiveness, and the lawyer to the sophistical, and the statesman to the expedient, and the country clergyman to ease and comfort, yet there are good clergymen, statesmen, lawyers, merchants, and soldiers, notwithstanding; so there are religious experimentalists, though physics, taken by themselves, tend to infidelity; but to have recourse to physics to *make* men religious is like recommending a canonry as a cure for the gout, or giving a youngster a commission as a penance for irregularities.

The whole framework of Nature is confessedly a tissue of antecedents and consequents; we may refer all things forwards to design, or backwards on a physical cause. La Place is said to have considered he had a formula which solved all the motions of the solar system; shall we say that those motions came from this formula or from a Divine Fiat? Shall we have recourse for our theory to physics or to theology? Shall we assume Matter and its necessary properties to be eternal, or Mind with its divine attributes? Does the sun shine to warm the earth, or is the earth warmed because the sun shines? The one hypothesis will solve the phenomena as well as the other. Say not it is but a puzzle in argument, and that no one ever felt it in fact. So far from it, I believe that the study of Nature, when religious feeling is away, leads the mind, rightly or wrongly, to acquiesce in the atheistic theory, as the simplest and easiest. It is but parallel to that tendency in anatomical studies, which no one will deny, to solve all the phenomena of the human frame into material elements and powers, and to dispense with the soul. To those who are conscious of matter, but not conscious of mind, it seems more rational to refer all things to one origin, such as they know, than to assume the existence of a second origin such as they know not. It is Religion, then, which suggests to Science its true conclusions; the facts come from Knowledge, but the principles come of Faith.

There are two ways, then, of reading Nature—as a machine and as a work. If we come to it with the assumption that it is a creation, we shall study it with awe; if assuming it to be a system, with mere curiosity. . . . The truth is that the system of Nature is just as much connected with religion, where minds are not religious, as a watch or a steam-carriage. The material world, indeed, is infinitely more wonderful than any human contrivance; but wonder is not

religion, or we should be worshipping our railroads. What the physical creation presents to us in itself is a piece of machinery, and when men speak of a
Divine Intelligence as its Author, this god of theirs is not the Living and True,
unless the spring is the god of a watch, or steam the creator of the engine.
Their idol, taken at advantage (though it is *not* an idol, for they do not worship
it), is the animating principle of a vast and complicated system; it is subjected
to laws, and it is connatural and co-extensive with matter. Well does Lord
Brougham call it "the great architect of nature"; it is an instinct, or a soul of
the world, or a vital power; it is not the Almighty God. . . .

I consider, then, that intrinsically excellent and noble as are scientific pursuits, and worthy of a place in a liberal education, and fruitful in temporal
benefits to the community, still they are not, and cannot be, *the instrument*
of an ethical training; that physics do not supply the basis, but only materials,
for religious sentiment; that knowledge does but occupy, does not form, the
mind; that apprehension of the unseen is the only known principle capable
of subduing moral evil, educating the multitude, and organizing society; and
that, whereas man is born for action, action flows not from inferences, but
from impressions,—not from reasonings, but from Faith. . . .

## SHADOW AND SUBSTANCE

### *Paul Vincent Carroll* (*1937*)

Oh, what a power has white Simplicity!
*Keats*

TO M. P. L. AND THE LITTLE WHITE DOG

### CHARACTERS

VERY REV. THOMAS CANON SKERRITT
BRIGID, *his servant, about 18*
FATHER CORR } *two curates, in their*
FATHER KIRWAN } *twenties*
DERMOT FRANCIS O'FLINGSLEY, *the local schoolmaster, thirty-two years old*

THOMASINA CONCANNON, *Canon Sker-ritt's step-niece*
MISS JEMIMA COONEY, *a local spinster*
FRANCIS IGNATIUS O'CONNOR, *her nephew*
MARTIN MULLAHONE, *middle-aged*
ROSEY VIOLET, *his wife, in the thirties*

### SCENES

Act I. Mid-day, late in January.
Act II. Evening of the following day.
Act III. Morning. A few days later.
Act IV. The following morning: February 1st.

The time is the present.

The action passes in the living room of Canon Skerritt's parochial house in
"Ardmahone," one of the small towns lying round the feet of the Mourne hills in
County Louth, Ireland.

*Shadow and Substance* was first produced at the Abbey Theatre, Dublin, on January 25th, 1937.

*A legend connected with St. Brigid relates how; in order to escape the attentions of persistent suitors, she disfigured the loveliness of her face at Fanghart, her birthplace, near Dundalk, Ireland.*

## ACT ONE

SCENE: *The living room in the Parochial House of the Very Rev. Thomas Canon Skerritt in Ardmahone, one of the small towns lying round the feet of Mourne, on the borders of Louth.*

*The room is excellently furnished, and gives evidence in its accoutrements, its beautiful leaded bookcases, its pictures and other tasteful details, of the refined character of the Canon.*

*The one incongruous note in the harmony of the whole design is a large gaudy oleograph of the Sacred Heart over the door, left.*

*A window, back, in French manner, very tastefully curtained to the ground with crimson art brocade, and giving access to the gardens. Through the window, a view of Mourne's rugged peaks. The walls are hung with small Spanish and Roman reproductions of very good quality, including Velasquez, Murillo, El Greco, Da Vinci and Raphael.*

*As the curtain rises,* BRIGID *is ushering in* DERMOT FRANCIS O'FLINGSLEY, *the schoolmaster, a young man, very alert, alive, and intelligent, obviously capable of feeling things acutely, and of passion and pride. He is bright in manner, and has a pleasing sense of humor.* BRIGID *is small, possibly a little stupid-looking, with large eyes; neat, but not to any degree Quakerish. She is obviously not mentally outstanding, but capable of deep affection, and pleasing in her person.*

*A table is laid, very carefully and very completely, for lunch, and both it and the chairs, and the table-ware are of excellent quality. There is no sign of tawdriness or of slipshod carelessness about the room.*

BRIGID. He said, Master, he might be home for lunch and he mightn't. It's to Dublin he went, I think. It'll be maybe to see one of them Spanish gentlemen that writes to him since the time he was in Spain. Sure just rest a wee while, Master, seein' he's not here yet.

O'FLINGSLEY [*entering carelessly, hands in jacket pocket*]. Thanks, Brigid. It's not often I get this far into the great one's privacy. Such privileges are not for schoolmasters.

BRIGID. Ach, sure it's just his way. Are ye goin' to quarrel with him again?

O'FLINGSLEY. No, Brigid, definitely no. But I will, all the same.

BRIGID. Yous hate one another. Sure I know, be now . . .

O'FLINGSLEY. I suppose we do.

BRIGID. Isn't it funny now that I think there's no one like aythur of yous. Would that not mean that the two of yous are maybe the one? Or am I blatherin'?

O'FLINGSLEY. You certainly *are* blatherin', Brigid. If you love him, you hate *me*, and if you love *me*, you hate *him*.

BRIGID [*slowly*]. That's maybe the way it would show on paper, but in the mind it's not maybe as true. [*Pause*] St. Brigid wouldn't deceive me like that.

O'FLINGSLEY [*regarding her half-seriously, half-humorously*]. Are you still on that nonsense, Brigid?

BRIGID [*hurt*]. Don't say it's nonsense, Master.

O'FLINGSLEY. Have you told anyone about this—the Canon or the curates?

BRIGID. No. [*Secretively*] No one only you.

O'FLINGSLEY. Why just me?

BRIGID. I don't know. . . . Didn't you tell me yourself, one time, that there's no words at all for some of the things we think and feel?

O'FLINGSLEY [*touched*]. I am not worth all this trust, Brigid. Suppose, some night when I'd have a spree, I'd tell it in a snug.

BRIGID [*catching at his arm, tensely*]. You—wouldn't do that. . . . [*He smiles at her*] Sure, don't I know. . . . You have the fine thing in you—the same thing that the Canon has.

O'FLINGSLEY [*laughing*]. Don't you dare compare me with *him*. [*Pause*] Why don't you tell *him* about—this secret of yours? Or the curates?

BRIGID. Sure, they'd question and cross-question, and then make me promise never to see her again. That would be somethin' too terrible for me to bear—the same as you could bear the burn of a hot poker or of scaldin' water.

O'FLINGSLEY. Then—you *do* see her actually?

BRIGID [*rapt*]. Yes . . . often. I'm used to her now. She is always smilin', smilin' and in great humor, as if she was enjoyin' makin' me happy. It's lovely that she's not sour like a nun, at the convent school, or like a priest in the box.

O'FLINGSLEY [*seriously*]. I don't want to hurt you, Brigid, but if you're a wise girl, you'll put this thing absolutely away from you. Some day, maybe she or it, whatever it is, will desert you, and you'll go crazy with despair. Are you listenin' to me?

BRIGID [*softly*]. Yes . . . but she promised . . .

O'FLINGSLEY. Supposing she's an evil thing? It could well be.

BRIGID. If she was evil, I would feel the fear in me. Doesn't God make us like that?

O'FLINGSLEY. Why don't you ask her for a proof, as I told you?

BRIGID. I did. I asked her one night to make the bed-chair move. Wasn't that what you said?

O'FLINGSLEY. And did she?

BRIGID. No. . . . She just smiled, and her eyes laughed the way she was amused at me.

O'FLINGSLEY. Maybe it was at me she was amused—O'Flingsley, the idiot.

BRIGID. It was never that. She loves you too. I can see it. She told me you had a secret.

O'FLINGSLEY [*startled*]. What sort of a secret?

BRIGID. She said—a dark secret, and that you were a blunderer, but that God loved blunderers because they were the children of Peter.

O'FLINGSLEY [*concerned*]. Brigid, you dreamed this! You *did!*

BRIGID [*slowly*]. No. . . . Sure I know I didn't. . . . She told me about the Canon too.

O'FLINGSLEY. *Him?* What did she say about him?

BRIGID. She said that there was great holiness in him, but that his pride would need the tears of a hundred just men and the soul of a child, to soften it.

O'FLINGSLEY [*tensely*]. Did she say—what child?

BRIGID. She only smiled and went away.

O'FLINGSLEY. Good God! What creature is this at all? I'm warning you, Brigid. I'm warning you, mind.

BRIGID. I love her too much now to be afraid. . . . [*Pause*] *Have* you a secret?

O'FLINGSLEY [*secretively*]. I have written a book and published it. No one knows it's mine.

BRIGID. Is it a *good* book?

O'FLINGSLEY. It might be. It's a *bitter* book.

BRIGID. She will not be pleased. Why could you not make it full of love?

O'FLINGSLEY [*tensely*]. I don't believe in love.

BRIGID. St. Brigid does. She stood near me at the bed last night when the new moon was in it. I said, "There's the new moon, God bless it," and I blessed meself, and she laughed without any noise, and her eyes had the moon in them like a mirror. She stood lookin' out at the big boulders of the hills, and her speakin' low. Then she said when I came close to her that the hills were just like that long long ago, and that they were God's hint to man to build in the heart forever and ever, instead of with stone and mortar and the pride that puts a stone on another stone without meanin'. And a lot more that the words will not come to me for. I fell asleep listenin' to her— her voice was sinkin' me all the time into sleep. [*She looks up at* O'FLINGSLEY. *A shadow of fear crosses her face suddenly. She grips him*] I'm a fool to be tellin' you—a fool, a fool. You'll put it in a bitter book and laugh at it.

O'FLINGSLEY [*touched*]. No, Brigid . . . not in a book. . . . [*Pause— He catches her arm*] Are you—lying to me, Brigid?

BRIGID [*pathetically*]. No, Master. . . . How could I lie?

O'FLINGSLEY. But how do you remember it all like this?

BRIGID. Remember it? Sure how could I *forget* it? [*She looks at him in pain. He soothes her*]

O'FLINGSLEY. There! There! I don't mean to hurt you. I'm just nervous about you. I think you'd better tell the Canon about this.

BRIGID. Not—not yet. I won't be separated from her. I love her. Some day I shall come to her, she said.

O'FLINGSLEY [*worried*]. You must keep your mind off that now. You must first live your life here.

BRIGID. She told me that too.

O'FLINGSLEY [*after a pause*]. You're a funny little customer, Brigid. There's times when I'd like to pull your hair, and give you a smack on the jaw.

BRIGID. Sure I would never feel it. . . .

O'FLINGSLEY. There's tears for you, and I'm warning you. But you won't heed. Well, I'd better be getting back to the school. I'll come back later and see if he's home.

BRIGID. Will you lave a message?

O'FLINGSLEY. Anything to oblige, Brigid. Ask him when is the school going to get any coal, when I can have the new maps I asked for last year, when the windows are going to be repaired, and if he'll supply me with two pails to catch the raindrops from the ceiling on wet days. And when is he going to relieve *me* of the job of brushing and cleaning out the place?

BRIGID [*breathless*]. I'll never remember all of them.

O'FLINGSLEY. Oh, don't let that worry you. *He'll* not remember any of them anyway.

BRIGID [*disconsolately*]. I can see another fight comin', and you bein' ordered out again. Yous are never done.

O'FLINGSLEY. Well, what can *I* do? What could anyone do? If only I had enough guts in me, I'd clap on my hat, and walk right out of this place. But I haven't. Actually, Brigid, I'm afraid I'd have no money and be hungry. Amn't I a miserable creature?

BRIGID. If you could have somethin' grand and lovely to rise for, every day, like me with St. Brigid.

O'FLINGSLEY [*tensely*]. Maybe I have.

BRIGID. Tell me about it, Master.

O'FLINGSLEY. No. . . . It's all—fire and smoke . . . and things falling.

BRIGID [*reprovingly*]. Sure isn't that just like you! [*She laughs*] I'll bet St. Brigid would know.

O'FLINGSLEY. Will you ask her?

BRIGID. I will, if you promise to obey her.

O'FLINGSLEY. I'll—try. [*He is crossing, and looking back whimsically at* BRIGID *when* THOMASINA CONCANNON *enters briskly. She is a very "bunty" girl of about 22, with full animal spirits, round fat face, all dimples, given to giggling laughter, and eternally sucking sweetmeats*]

THOMASINA [*as she rushes in*]. Is me uncle back yet, Bridgie?

BRIGID. No, miss. But I'm expectin' him any minute. The Master's waitin' on him too.

THOMASINA [*to* O'FLINGSLEY]. Oh, you're Mr. O'Flingsley. I'm a school teacher too—just finished a few months, and was doing substitute to Dunaree. I'm pleased to meet you. [*She giggles*]

O'FLINGSLEY. So am I. How do you do, Miss—

BRIGID. Miss Concannon her name is, Master.

THOMASINA. I'm the Canon's niece, you know. Me mother says I'm a bit like him round the nose. [*She giggles*] Do *you* think so?

O'FLINGSLEY. On the contrary, I think you have a very nice nose.

BRIGID. Oh, Master! [THOMASINA *and* O'FLINGSLEY *laugh together.* BRIGID *goes, quickly*]

THOMASINA. Well, I have another hold on him anyway. I'm called after him. You see, they thought I'd be a boy, and the name was ready and all.

O'FLINGSLEY [*entering the fun*]. And you weren't?

THOMASINA. Why of course I wasn't, stupid! [*She giggles heartily*] So me mother, who lets nothin' bate her, said: "She'll be Thomasina." Wasn't it awful cute of her?

O'FLINGSLEY. It certainly was a great idea, Miss Concannon.

THOMASINA [*holding up poke of sweets*]. Do have a liquorice-all-sort, Mr. O'Flingsley, and you may call me Thomasina.

O'FLINGSLEY [*taking sweet*]. Th-thanks. *You* can call me anything you like, and quote your uncle as a precedent.

BRIGID [*entering hastily*]. The Canon's back on the train. He's in the Post Office below, writin' a postcard. The milkman's after tellin' me.

O'FLINGSLEY [*to go*]. I'll come back later when he settles, Brigid.

THOMASINA. Wait till he hears I slept in his room last night:

O'FLINGSLEY. Slept in his room!

THOMASINA. The bed in the spare room has bronchitis. [*With a gasp*] Oh, dear God! I believe I left *Love's Purple Passions* under his pilla. Ex-excuse *me*, Mr. O'Flingsley. [*She rushes off breathlessly.* O'FLINGSLEY *looks at* BRIGID *in a bewildered way*]

O'FLINGSLEY. Is that the one that's trying to get in here as my Assistant?

BRIGID. Yis, Master.

O'FLINGSLEY. Good God! The mists thicken, O, Israel. . . . [*He goes, worried.* BRIGID *looks after him softly, then runs to table, and in a scared way begins rearranging things on the dining table.* FATHER CORR *enters, left. He is a young man, small and round-shouldered with a face easily affected by fervor or sentiment. His mood is melancholic and introspective*]

FATHER CORR [*kindly*]. Well, Bridgie, me heartie, and how's the bones today? [*Flings hat on chair*]

BRIGID. Oh, Father Corr, do *you* see anythin' missin' on that table? The Canon's back. He's in the Post Office.

FATHER CORR [*careless glance*]. Ach sure, isn't it fine?

BRIGID. Oh, but the Canon! If there's a single spot . . . (FATHER KIRWAN *enters, left, wearing motor goggles and gloves. Athletic, good-humored and well-meaning. Neatly lands his hat on a bookcase, takes off goggles, etc., and then turns very severely to* FATHER CORR—*obviously mimicking the Canon*]

FATHER KIRWAN. Father Corr, may I ask who owns this—er—motor machine I observe at the front entrance?

FATHER CORR [*with a wave*]. Cut out that coddin' and get a shave. The Canon's back.

FATHER KIRWAN [*incredibly*]. He's *not*?

FATHER CORR. He is.

FATHER KIRWAN. Heavens! [*Feeling hairy cheek*] Am I bad? Brigid, tell me like a decent woman, do I need a shave, or do I not?

BRIGID. Indeed you do, Father. And I sent you up shavin' water this mornin'.

FATHER KIRWAN. So you did, but seein' the Canon was—not in residence, I used it for softenin' a corn. God made feet, but an enemy came and over-sowed corns. . . .

BRIGID. Do *you* see anythin' missin' there, Father Kirwan?

FATHER KIRWAN [*wistfully*]. Sure and I do, Bridgie. A whippin' good plate o' cabbage and bacon.

BRIGID. Ah, Father! And the Canon always sayin' we know nothin' about food in Ireland.

FATHER KIRWAN [*mimicking again*]. When I was in Spain, my excellent friend, Don Miguel Del Fuego . . . [*All start laughing*]

BRIGID [*looking from window, suddenly*]. Oh, here's the Canon comin' up the lawn. [*All flurried*] Oh, dear me, I hope everythin's right. And I wish I had him told about Thomasina. [*She runs off, scared. The two curates laugh rather nervously*]

FATHER KIRWAN. Wait till you see his face when he sees that niece of his! She always sends him off the deep end!

FATHER CORR. The girl's a bit of an ass right enough, but there's no harm in her. Now remember we're to tackle him about that filthy book that's on the rounds. I expect you to back me up and not let the confraternity down.

FATHER KIRWAN. I'll do my best. But you know the dry way he can bottle you up. And be Heavens I left the wee car at the gate. He'll have a fit when he sees it!

FATHER CORR. Well, aren't all the curates everywhere gettin' cars? And it's a free country. Come on into the garden and give him time to settle. [*They go out by the window*]

FATHER KIRWAN [*as they go, dubiously*]. I wish that niece had stayed at home, and—I wish I had shaved. . . . [BRIGID *comes in quickly, and nervously*

*sets glasses on table. She stands over the table counting and calculating.* CANON
THOMAS SKERRITT *enters, left. Finely built, but a little too full in the stomach,
fine face, but a little too red. His eyes are vividly living always, and at times
his whole being concentrates in them. He has a perfect bow, his voice is cultured, he can be very charming and courteous, can quickly adapt himself to
suit people, and has a kingly walk and dignity. He is excellently dressed. He
is wearing a tall silk hat, and carries an umbrella*]

CANON [*benignly*]. Ah, Brigid, you're there!

BRIGID [*soothingly*]. Yis, Canon. Your hat and umbrella, Canon. [*She
takes them with great care, and looks up at him with childish simplicity combined with womanly prudence*] I hope, Canon, you're grand and well after
the week-end.

CANON. You will be pleased to know, Brigid, that the Canon feels excellently.

BRIGID. And did you meet your great friend from Spain, Canon?

CANON. I met him, Brigid. My friend Don Miguel Barzan y Perdito. It
was good, Brigid. It was very good. I mentioned you, Brigid. [*Clapping her
patronizingly*] I said to Don Miguel, "My truest friend in this fallen land is
Brigid." And he smiled in his excellent way, and said, "Donde esta la verdad
esta Dios."

BRIGID. Wasn't that lovely of you, Canon! And what did Don Miguel
mean be that?

CANON [*deprecating*]. He meant, Brigid, in the crude language of the—
Saxon: "Where we have truth we have God."

BRIGID. It's lovely. It's like what a saint—I mean a gentleman, would say.

CANON. A saint *and* a gentleman, you mean, Brigid. That is the classic
equivalent to the—the odious Northern Officer and gentleman. But go,
Brigid, see to lunch immediately.

BRIGID. Yis, Canon. [*She crosses*]

CANON. Stay, Brigid. There is no news—I hope?

BRIGID. No, Canon, except that—that your niece is here.

CANON [*immediately on edge*]. My step-niece, Brigid. I insist on the
distinction. What evil brings her here?

BRIGID. It's to see you, special, she said—about the school, I think. She
insisted on stayin' last night. She said her mother said it.

CANON [*with suppressed venom*]. Her mother! That barbarian who links
me by law to a—cattle-jobber. It burns me, Brigid,—it *burns* me.

BRIGID. Please now, Canon, don't make yourself ill again.

CANON. You are wise, child. I forget myself. I always forget myself in
the face of this recurring decimal of relationship. [*Holding* BRIGID'S *arm*]
Consider, Brigid! My name—grave and classical—purloined—that's the word
for it—to gain a—nomenclature for a human dumpling who reeks eternally
of peppermints.

BRIGID. Sure, you're angerin' yourself, Canon. Sure, maybe if she got married, it would settle her down, and you wouldn't be pestered with her no more.

CANON. There is wisdom there, Brigid. I will consider that. I shall turn that over carefully.

BRIGID. Sure, I try to help ye, Canon.

CANON. As you say, Brigid, you try to help me, and as I say, there is wisdom in you. Let it be written of you, Brigid. You are a good child—an excellent child. Go, Brigid!

BRIGID [*going*]. Yis, Canon.

CANON. Wait, Brigid. Where did she stay last night?

BRIGID [*in fear*]. She—she said the spare room was draughty and there was a mouse in the wardrobe, and she—she—

CANON. She what?

BRIGID. She took *your* room, Canon.

CANON [*fuming*]. Eh? She—she what? Brigid! I am incensed beyond words. You are arraigned! You are in the dock!

BRIGID. But I could do nothin', Canon. Says she to me, "I'm the Canon's niece, and the place for his servant is at me footstool."

CANON. The Canon's niece! That Irish matrimonial luggage label! That ecclesiastical buckle on a female shoe! Go, Brigid! Restore my room to its—austerity.

BRIGID. Yis, Canon. Sure it'll be lovely and grand for you now, if you'll not be vexin' yourself.

CANON [*softening*]. There, child, I do not blame you. We are thwarted. We shall die outwitted by boobs and idiots. Mark it, Brigid, mark it! Go, Brigid!

THOMASINA [*calling offstage*]. Cooee, Brigid! Did my uncle come?

CANON. God! Must I suffer this?

BRIGID [*fearfully*]. Yis, Miss. He's—here. [THOMASINA *bounds in, and runs as if to embrace the* CANON. *He skillfully counters this by blowing his nose with one hand and holding out a defensive other hand.* BRIGID *slips out, scared*]

THOMASINA [*gurglingly*]. Oh, Uncle Thomas! I thought you'd never come. Oh, isn't it lovely you're back?

CANON [*vaguely, staring at her*]. Ah, it's you. Of course it's you. I was expecting you. You wrote, of course. I remember. You are a good child—an excellent child. . . .

THOMASINA. But I never wrote, Uncle.

CANON. Ah, you never wrote. Of course you didn't. I remember distinctly. It was the last time you wrote.

THOMASINA. I came down, Uncle Thomas, to tell you I finished in Dunaree School on Friday. The teacher is better now.

CANON. Very creditable, very creditable.

THOMASINA. And Father Crone, the parish priest, said to say to you, do you remember Crone, your old crony in Maynooth before you went to Spain. [*She giggles loudly*]

CANON [*gravely*]. Never heard of him.

THOMASINA. But he swears him and you used to keep a pot o' jam in the dormitory against the rules. [*She giggles explosively*]

CANON [*outraged*]. Come, come! I dislike levity in young people.

THOMASINA [*pouting ponderously*]. I'm sorry, Uncle Thomas. Sure it was only to show you the great man Father Crone is for jokes. Do you think they'll make a Canon of him, Uncle? I think he'd make a lovely Canon—and it would go so grand with his name too—Kevin Canon Crone.

CANON [*ironic*]. No doubt the accumulated wisdom of the Church will endorse your conclusions. [*He sniffs and blows his nose meaningly*] In future, my dear, when seeking a—a—an audience with me, I wish you would compose yourself with some degree of mental sobriety, and in addition fast from peppermints for at least one hour.

THOMASINA [*pouting*]. You're not glad to see me, Uncle Thomas. Well, it was me mother kept *at* me, Uncle. "There y'are," she kept girnin', "walkin' about idle for three whole days and nights, and you Canon Thomas Skerritt's niece be law and be blood. A fine state this country's comin' to." That's *her* all the time.

CANON [*with calm brutality*]. Your mother, my dear, I regret to say, is, and has ever been, a woman berefit—that's the word, berefit—of one iota of sound sense or dignity. The fact burns me. But it is—irrefutable. [THOMASINA *giggles involuntarily, and then dabs her face with a mint-reeking handkerchief*]

THOMASINA. Sure, maybe you're right, Uncle. The talk and blatherin' of her—you'd think I had no name o' me own—I'm the Canon's niece to everyone we meet.

CANON [*grimly*]. I am well aware of it. But it is a national disease, and I am no surgeon. You must leave me now, and I shall let you know in a few days about the school. [*Consulting watch*]

THOMASINA. But sure it's the bus I go by always, Canon.

CANON [*countering*]. There is a bus back in *six* minutes.

THOMASINA [*as she is moved off*]. Will you appoint me to the school, Uncle, when Miss Driscoll goes to her training next week?

CANON. Possibly.

THOMASINA. I'll just say "yes," instead of "possibly" to me mother. Let me play a wee tune for you on the piano before I go.

CANON. Certainly not!

THOMASINA. But it's a lovely wee thing, Canon. Father Crone sang it at a wee tea-party before I left Dunaree School. It begins, "When first I saw your face of virgin kew."

CANON [*evenly*]. You will go now, my dear.

THOMASINA. All right then, Uncle, but I'll come again.

CANON. So you will. [*Almost sotto voce*] *Est Natura rerum*. . . . [*As he moves her on*]

THOMASINA. What does that mean, Canon?

CANON. You would not appreciate it. [*They go out together.* BRIGID *comes in and lays serving dishes on table. The two curates,* FATHER CORR *and* FATHER KIRWIN, *come in from garden by window*]

BRIGID. Lunch is ready, Fathers, and the Canon's ready. Will you please sit down?

FATHER CORR. Grand news, Bridgie. What are you going to give us?

FATHER KIRWAN [*as they both sit*]. Nothin' Spanish, I hope.

BRIGID [*half secretively*]. It's another of them dishes the Canon used to love in Spain. [*She smiles secretively at them and goes*]

FATHER KIRWAN. *In Nomine De*, when is this goin' to stop?

FATHER CORR [*tired*]. Ach, just take it for your sins, and hope for the best.

FATHER KIRWAN. I wish to God I could get a transfer to some old P.P. that loves cabbage and eats peas with his knife, and snores after his dinner.

FATHER CORR. Sssh! [*The* CANON *re-enters. The curates rise respectfully. The* CANON *comes slowly to the table, with dignity. He stands at the head of the table*]

CANON [*courteously, with a slight bow*]. Good morning, Fathers.

CURATES [*together*]. Good mornin', Canon.

CANON [*acidly*]. I didn't quite catch the final "g" in "morning," Fathers. [*Pause. They silently say grace. Further pause*] May I ask, Fathers, who owns that motor-car at the gate?

FATHER CORR. It's ours, Canon.

FATHER KIRWAN. It killed a man, Canon, and the owner wanted rid of it. We got it dirt cheap.

CANON. I am glad to hear it has such excellent capabilities. But—is it necessary?

FATHER CORR. It will come in useful I'm sure. Father Kirwan and I do a lot of running about. And besides we feel entitled to contribute in any way we can to our happiness here.

CANON. You mean it will make your job more comfortable.

FATHER KIRWAN. Job, Canon?

CANON. Yes . . . a word that Columkille and Columbanus knew in another sense. However, there is no Canon law against—owner-driver clerics. You may be seated. [*All sit.* BRIGID *enters and starts serving*] Well, Brigid, did the experiment work again?

BRIGID [*as she serves*]. Sure, it's lovely, Canon, and it was easy follyin' your directions.

CANON. Very creditable, Brigid. You have today, Fathers, an extremely delicious Spanish dish, given me some years ago by the chatelaine of my friend Don Juan Almeria y Fernandez. [CURATES *taste dish gingerly and nod to the* CANON]

FATHER CORR. Very good indeed, Canon.

FATHER KIRWAN. Grand, Canon. [BRIGID *moves about and on and off.* CANON *notices a newspaper sticking out of* FATHER KIRWAN'S *pocket*]

CANON. The development of a sensitive palate, Fathers, is not the most unimportant of legitimate activities. Father Kirwin, may I ask what—litter is that protruding from the outer pocket of your attire?

FATHER KIRWAN [*touching paper*]. Sure it's just the—the *Ballyedminstown Courier*, Canon.

CANON [*suavely*]. Would you please adjust the—the—*Ballyelphinstown Courier*, Father, so that it will not detract from the dignity of your person?

FATHER KIRWAN [*pushing paper right into pocket*]. Sorry, Canon. [*Pause*] There's a very strong leader in it this week, Canon, on that outrageous book that's just after comin' out. It's called *I Am Sir Oracle*.

FATHER CORR. I was just goin' to mention that, Canon. It's a very grave matter altogether, and I think it calls for action. The people's demandin' it.

FATHER KIRWAN. They say, Canon, the author is a schoolmaster with a spite agin the local P.P. He calls himself Eugene Gibney.

FATHER CORR. Are *you* prepared to take anny action, Canon?

CANON [*acidly*]. There is no such word as "anny," except of course the female appellation, and the verb agrees with its subject, always—even in Ireland. [*As* BRIGID *enters*] You may serve the coffee black, Brigid. [*The two curates look very abject*]

BRIGID. Yis, Canon. It's ready.

FATHER CORR [*apologetically*]. If you don't mind, Canon, I'll have tea instead.

CANON [*with withering suavity*]. You may serve Father Corr with—tea.

FATHER KIRWAN. And me too, Canon, if you please.

CANON. You are at liberty to poison Father Kirwan also.

BRIGID. Yis, Canon. [*She crosses*]

CANON. And, Brigid. [*Takes key from pocket and gives it to her*] You know the one, Brigid. It is marked "Vino de Amontillado."

BRIGID. Is that the one, Canon, with the gold silver-paper on it that Don Miguel sent you from Spain?

CANON. Exactly, Brigid. My friend, Don Miguel Barzan y Perdito. [*As* BRIGID *unlocks cupboard under the bookshelves*] Are you having a little wine, Fathers?

FATHER CORR. I'll take a thimbleful, Canon.

FATHER KIRWAN. And I too, thanks. [BRIGID *brings small flagon of rich golden wine, expensively wrapped, which the* CANON *handles with great delicacy*]

CANON. I'm afraid there are no—thimbles reasonably convenient, Father. Better take a wineglassful. [*As he receives bottle*] Excellent, Brigid. You may bring Fathers Corr and Kirwan the bottle of Empire wine that's on the left-hand side. [*With a sardonic curve of lip*]

BRIGID. Is it the one, Canon, that Martin Reilly sent up last Christmas for a present?

CANON. Precisely, Brigid. [*Ironically*] It should be considerably matured by this. [*As* BRIGID *gets it*] You were speaking, gentlemen, of the proposed suppression of a book, entitled, *I Am Sir Oracle.*

FATHER KIRWAN. The editor of this paper, from my home town, Canon, calls for it to be burned on every market square in Ireland.

FATHER CORR. It demands action too from the Board of Censors.

CANON [*lifting glass and examining golden wine carefully*]. And on what grounds are we to have this extensive series of rural bonfires?

FATHER CORR [*with fire*]. Why, the whole book is a dastardly attack on the Catholicism of Ireland, Canon! [BRIGID *pours out the red port for curates, and then goes softly*]

CANON [*looking closely at bubbling wine*]. Grave news surely out of Bally—Ballyeffelstown. A seamew blunders against a lighthouse and the keeper sends up distress rockets. [*With suave irony*] Your health, Fathers. [*He drinks delicately and with great relish. The curates fling back their port and cough into napkins. As he lies back, enjoying the wine on his tongue*] May I ask if the writer attacks any specific doctrine of the Church?

FATHER CORR. He evades that, Canon. In a Catholic country like this, a fellow like that should be hung.

CANON [*imperturbably*]. Hanged, Father Corr. [*Pause.* BRIGID *serves coffee and tea, etc.*] Were *you* about to make some observation, Father Kirwan?

FATHER KIRWAN. I was goin' to say, Canon, that the men of the football team I run, are up in arms agin it. And Father Corr can tell you about the Sacred Heart Confraternity.

FATHER CORR. Martin Reilly's wife, Canon, had the book home from Dublin, and it's got round the people. The whole men and women of the Sacred Heart are anxious to burn it in public. And Father Kirwan and myself agree with them. We'd like your advice.

CANON. You mean my—direction.

BRIGID [*as she goes*]. If you please, Canon, when you want me to clear away, will you shout?

CANON [*eyelids raised*]. Shout, Brigid? Certainly not. I shall ring.

BRIGID. Yis, Canon. And if you please, Canon, the schoolmaster is back again wantin' to see you, and he says he's in a hurry.

CANON. Dear me! Even the school teachers are becoming presumptuous. We live, Brigid, in an incongruous age. Tell him, I shall possibly see him when his hurry is more in keeping with his status.

BRIGID. Yis, Canon. And if you please, Canon, are ye rememberin' that Miss Jemima Cooney and her nephew Francis Ignatius is waitin' since before lunch to show you Francis' new teachin' certificate?

CANON. Brigid, I fear you fret yourself unduly. Tell them both to go round into the Church, and say the Rosary, and by that time I may possibly be in a position to receive them.

BRIGID. But you see, Canon—

CANON. Go, Brigid!

BRIGID. Yis, Canon. [*She goes. The* CURATES *now make to rise. The* CANON *detains them with a finger*]

CANON. One moment, Fathers. An observation or two is—imperative. [*They settle stiffly*] Father Corr, I am given to understand that since your arrival here you have attained quite an inordinate amount of popularity mixed with a particularly abhorrent form of sentimentality, and that this copious bathing—shall we say—springs from your antics with bouncing babies, and such like, the prescribing of cures for old ladies' rheumatics and for carious diseases in horses and cows. I suggest to you, that since Catholicism rests on a classical, almost abstract, love of God, rather than on the frothy swirl of stirred emotionalism that these popular heroics of yours are not, canonically speaking, the duties of a Catholic curate.

FATHER CORR [*blushing and abashed*]. I—I was only tryin' to be kind, Canon.

CANON. *I* call it hunting after popular glory—an Irish clerical disease.

FATHER CORR [*rising, with fire*]. I'm a farmer's son, Canon, and I'm not ashamed of it.

CANON. I am not interested in your antecedents. I am interested instead in the behavior of my curate. You may be seated. [FATHER CORR *sits down, crushed.* FATHER KIRWAN *shifts uneasily in his seat, with one eye on the* CANON *who presently regards him with calm brutality*]

CANON [*with slight cough*]. Father Kirwan, may I ask if it is the custom in *your* part of the country for the curate to don football-regalia, and—er— kick ball?

FATHER KIRWAN. Sure it's quite common down in Ballyedminstown, Canon. The curate in me father's place is a very noted center-half.

CANON [*cruelly, leading him on, hand to ear*]. I—I didn't quite catch that word, Father Kirwan. Center—what?

FATHER KIRWAN. Center-half, Canon. The fellow, Canon, that the team most depends on when the enemy makes an onslaught.

CANON [*suavely*]. Incongruous as it may seem, Father Kirwan, it is *not* the custom here for the curate to be the fellow that—er—does what you say he does.

FATHER KIRWAN. But you misunderstand me, Canon. I strip and play with the men to entice them all into the Sacred Heart Confraternity. Sure, Canon, that's a grand motive for a grand end!

CANON. I see . . . And since when has the Sacred Heart of our Redeemer, that kings and emperors and queens like Violante and Don John of Austria and the great Charles V, and the soldier Ignatius, walked barefooted for the love of—since when has it become a sort of snap door chamber where dolts and boobs come to—to kick ball and find themselves tripped up on an altar step instead of a goal post?

FATHER KIRWAN [*aghast*]. I—I never looked at it that way, Canon. Doesn't it justify itself if it brings people to the Sacred Heart?

CANON. Am I justified then, in staging amateur theatricals on the high altar to coax boobs along the Latin way of salvation? [*There are awesome ejaculations from the two* CURATES]

FATHER KIRWAN AND FATHER CORR. God forbid, Canon! There is no comparison, surely!

CANON. To my thinking, there is a parallel. As a consequence, Brigid will be instructed that—er—football regalia is barred from the parochial clothes line.

FATHER KIRWAN. As you wish, Canon.

CANON. There is just one other matter. Is it the custom also in Bally— Bally—eskerstown, to sit down to lunch unshaven?

FATHER KIRWAN. I'm afraid it's not, Canon.

CANON. Interesting to compare the topographical similarities. It is *not* the custom in *this* part of the country either. [*With a sardonic smile and a slight bow, he waves a finger and rises. The* CURATES *rise also.* CANON *now rings bell with dignity.* BRIGID *enters to clear away.* FATHERS CORR *and* KIRWAN *are crossing to go out. The* CANON's *eye lights on the gaudy German oleograph. He almost explodes*] Wait, all! Stay! What—what incongruity is this? [*Points to picture. All look at it*]

FATHER CORR. The Women's Confraternity presented it to Father Kirwan and meself yesterday. [BRIGID *is very perturbed*]

CANON. And does it follow that I am to suffer it?

FATHER KIRWAN. But sure it's the—Sacred Heart, Canon.

CANON [*ironically*]. I should never have believed it, Father Kirwan. I could have sworn it was the nightmarish conception of some uncouth vulgarian. [CURATES *regard each other, nonplussed.* BRIGID *is all "at sea." She fears the* CANON *is ill*]

BRIGID [*emotionally, her face in pain*]. Please, Canon, are ye not well again?

CANON. I am very well, child.

BRIGID. But—it's the Sacred Heart, Canon.

CANON. No. [*Pause*]

FATHER CORR. We thought, Canon, it would give a deeper religious tone to this room. The pictures are nearly all secular.

CANON. Secular? What word is that? [*Pointing*] There is a beautiful reproduction of Velasquez's "Philip IV Entering Lerida," and *there* another of Murillo's "Immaculate Conception," and *there* is Raphael's bitter "Dispute of the Sacrament." Could any picture in this room be called secular if we know anything of the might of the thing that has given us birth?

FATHER CORR. I was just followin' the pious custom, Canon, of havin' colored pictures of religious subjects near us to give a feeling of sanctity.

CANON. A feeling of sanctity from that! [*He points to the oleograph. A pause. When he speaks again, it is with great quietness*] I am a man, Fathers, who by study, travel and observation, has seen the decline and decay of the great classic ideals and the steady vulgarization of our life by that tributaried stream of barbarians who have taken all that was royal in conception, and given nothing but their vulgar deluge in return. Their achievement is the Nordic civilization, in which the passport to fame is financial scoundrelism, and the scholar of taste is ever the avowed "enemy of the people." They have vulgarized our reading, our music, our art, our very privacy. They have thrust books into the hands of herds who are forever misreading them; they have reduced us all to the lowest social class by teaching us how to get from excess the same emotionalism the classicist used to get from music and art; they have taken away our aesthetic sense and given us in exchange a rather spurious ethical sense, and as you can see here—[*he points to picture*] they deal with a whitewash brush in terms of the divine. Yet you stand aghast when I point it out to you—when I refuse to allow barbarians to impose on me their vulgar conception of Christ and His Saints. If, for a moment, I felt our Redeemer's heart was akin to that monstrosity on the wall, I should go back to Socrates, and be a pagan. [*The two* CURATES *look at him dumbfounded and mystified.* BRIGID *is very worried*]

BRIGID. Please, Canon, you are not well again.

CANON [*gently*]. I am very well, child. Go, Brigid, and have Dave Dooley remove this—this caricature from my room.

BRIGID. I'll get him from the garden, Canon. [*She goes, left*]

FATHER CORR [*lamely*]. It's this funny sort of way you have of looking at things, Canon. It's maybe you being abroad so much.

CANON [*dryly*]. Maybe. . . .

FATHER CORR. I'm sorry you don't like it.

FATHER KIRWAN. Sure we'll just hang it up in the church hall, **Canon,** if you have no objection.

CANON [*tiredly, with veiled contempt*]. Where you wish—but not here. Hang it at the crossroads where a people who at least had a classic past, can see their Nordic God, and forget about the Royal Christ of the Renaissance. [*He turns tiredly away. The* CURATES, *nonplussed, look at each other, and go out quietly.* BRIGID *re-enters. She looks at him, very worried*]

BRIGID [*appeasingly*]. Dave Dooley will take it away, Canon, when he comes back from his dinner.

CANON. Dinner! Must there be this delay, Brigid?

BRIGID. Just a little delay, Canon. He'll be here any minute now.

CANON. It is the way of things, Brigid. An important issue confused and involved by the dinner of a boob! You may go, Brigid!

BRIGID. Yis, Canon.

CANON [*softly*]. But no, Brigid. Stay! It is good, child, you are here with me. You are not nauseous to me, Brigid, you are clean and simple. Oh, my child, this wilderness. . . . Knaves, fools, spirit-grocers and their women . . . clerical football-kickers . . . palavering C.C.'s . . . and only one scoundrel. . . . Come here to me, Brigid.

BRIGID [*coming, almost in tears*]. Yis, Canon.

CANON. Do you smell it?

BRIGID. What, Canon? [*She sniffs*]

CANON. The vulgarity of it all.

BRIGID [*not understanding*]. Will I open the window, Canon?

CANON. Yes . . . [*She goes and opens it*] . . . and the walls . . . But it will not matter . . .

BRIGID [*returning from window*]. I'm terrible sorry, Canon, you're not well again. You're lonely.

CANON [*wearily*]. As you say, Brigid, I'm lonely.

BRIGID. It'll be after your friend, Don Miguel, you'll be lonely.

CANON. Yes . . . my friend . . . Don Miguel Barzano y Perdito . . . [*As in a reverie*] I can see the stone tables in the sun where we used to sit . . . and the grave courtesy and grace of the people and their walk—that heartbreak of these Northern cripples . . . oh, these Northerners, morally afraid, mentally bereft, physically fatigued and hoof-footed. They have touched us, Brigid—we who should be great—and given us humps like a dromedary. Go, Brigid.

BRIGID. Yis, Canon. [*She goes*]

CANON. Come back, Brigid.

BRIGID. Yis, Canon.

CANON. Do you know what I'm saying to you?

BRIGID [*afraid*]. N-n-no, Canon. [*She shrinks*]

CANON. Then I can safely make you my friend. You are the Canon's friend, Brigid.

BRIGID. Yis, Canon. Thank you, Canon. [*A pause. She looks at him timidly*] Can—can I speak to you, Canon?

CANON. You can always speak to me, Brigid. It is your privilege.

BRIGID. Thank you, Canon. I—I— [*She looks at him and then stops*] It's nothin', Canon.

CANON. Are you sure, Brigid?

BRIGID. Yis . . . no . . . I'll not tell you now, Canon. I'll—go, Canon. [*She tries to go, but he holds her with his look*]

CANON. You are hiding something from me, Brigid.

BRIGID. Yis, Canon.

CANON. Is it something I should know?

BRIGID [*pathetically*]. Yis . . . No . . . I—I don't know . . .

CANON. If it's a matter of your soul, Brigid, I must know it.

BRIGID. Please Canon, not—not now. I'll tell you when I'm—able. I—I don't want it taken away from—from me yet.

CANON [*rising*]. This is a serious matter, Brigid. I insist. The Canon insists.

BRIGID [*hands to face*]. N-no, Canon. I want it. I want it.

CANON. Did I say that I insist, Brigid?

BRIGID [*backing against wall*]. Not for a while yet, Canon. Not—not now.

CANON [*coming to her*]. I will dismiss you, Brigid, for this disobedience.

BRIGID [*hands to face, back to wall*]. Yis, Canon.

CANON. I will cast you down—down!

BRIGID [*pathetically*]. Yis, Canon.

CANON. You will be the Canon's friend no longer.

BRIGID. Yis, Canon.

CANON. You will tell me then?

BRIGID. N-no, Canon.

CANON. You will suffer all these things?

BRIGID. Yis, Canon.

CANON [*terribly*]. The Canon commands it.

BRIGID. N-no, no, Canon. N-no. I—I couldn't! Not—now . . .

CANON. Put down those hands and look at me. [*She puts down her hands. Head is held up, but tears in her eyes. She is firmly against the wall like one at bay. An incongruous pride sits upon her. The* CANON *observes her strangely, as if deeply moved at a discovery*]

CANON. You defy me!

BRIGID. N-no, Canon.

CANON. But you—refuse to tell me!

BRIGID. [*pathetically but proudly*]. Y-yis, Canon. [*Long pause. He stands watching her as if fascinated*]

CANON [*as if to himself*]. My God, my God, that—that is what we have come from . . . Pride . . . loyalty . . . a classic race . . . a royal conception . . . A thousand years ago, someone with that brow and face held up His head and died like a prince. . . . It was that . . . [*He stares at her, his face working visibly*] Come here to me, Brigid.

BRIGID [*as she comes slowly and looks humbly up at him*]. Yis, Canon.

CANON. I shall ask you—nothing.

BRIGID. Th-thank you, Canon. [*She looks gratefully at him*]

CANON [*slowly*]. You are the Canon's friend, Brigid. Let it be written of you. Let it be written of both of us. [*They are looking at each other, the* CANON *with deep emotions stirred, and* BRIGID *with the tears glistening in her eyes, as the curtain falls*]

**CURTAIN**

# ACT TWO

SCENE: *Following day.*

*The* CANON *is discovered reading the castigated novel,* I Am Sir Oracle. *Now and again he smiles sardonically, and sips from a glass of wine.*

*The picture of the Sacred Heart is removed.* BRIGID *knocks and enters. Lays evening paper on table.*

BRIGID. That's the *Evenin' Herald,* Canon.

CANON. Very good, Brigid. [*He reads on*]

BRIGID. And if you please, Canon, are ye not forgettin' about them two in the waitin' room?

CANON [*tolerantly*]. Which two, Brigid? You are always a little vague lately.

BRIGID. The two I told you about, after dinner. Miss Cooney and her nephew with his new teacher's certificate. I told him you'd see them after you were done readin' the Bishop's Pastoral.

CANON [*remembering*]. Of course, of course, Brigid. I remember now. I distinctly remember saying to you, "Brigid, I'll see them presently."

BRIGID. That's just what you said, Canon.

CANON. To be sure it was. Tell them, Brigid—tell them to come back tomorrow.

BRIGID. But they've spent the whole day between waitin' on you here, Canon, and follyin' ye about the streets.

CANON. But my dear child, they like doing that. It is a corporate part of our national life. Tell them, Brigid, that the Canon—no, no—say, "His reverence presents his compliments to Miss Cooney and his heartiest congratulations to Francis Xavier—"

BRIGID. Francis Ignatius, Canon.

CANON. Thank you, Brigid. Let us have accuracy at all costs in these important matters. But be careful of the exact wording. Wording, Brigid, is an art. [*Repeating*] "His reverence presents his compliments." [*He reads on*]

BRIGID. Yis, Canon, but sure they're in and out o' the kitchen every minute pesterin' me. Is the Canon here? Is the Canon there? Where is the Canon? What hat has he on? Sure you could get rid of them in a minute, Canon, with a grand word and a clap on the back.

CANON [*rising*]. Excellent, Brigid. An answer and a suggestion at once plausible and philosophic. The Canon, Brigid—the Canon shall do exactly as you say.

BRIGID. Will I show them in then, Canon?

CANON. By all means, Brigid. And Brigid, if by any ill chance, they weary me beyond their time— [*He raises a finger meaningly*]

BRIGID. Sure, you needn't tell me, Canon. [*She goes.* CANON *lays down the book resignedly, and mutters in Latin.* BRIGID *re-enters followed by* MISS JEMIMA COONEY *and her nephew* FRANCIS O'CONNOR. FRANCIS *is a sheepish, obsequious youth, his whole being in the grip of an inferiority complex. He is awkward and without confidence.* JEMIMA *is a thin, gaunt spinster, secretly vicious but very virtuous before the* CANON. *The storm of "Yis, Canons" and "No, Canons" should be played very rapidly]* This is them, Canon. *[She goes.* JEMIMA *and* FRANCIS *advance awkwardly gesticulating and very obsequious. The* CANON *rises with calm dignity, embraces his nose with a silk handkerchief, and gives them a curt bow, tempered with a quite unreadable smile]*

JEMIMA. Sure, Lord, Canon, are we disturbin' ye?

FRANCIS. Sure, now, Canon, anny time would do!

JEMIMA. Sure, now, Canon, are ye after leavin' off sayin' your office for us?

FRANCIS. Sure, Lord, Canon, we could have come back anny time at all.

JEMIMA. Sure, Heavens, Canon, Francis is that up in the air about his new certificate!

FRANCIS. Sure, Canon, you'll be thinkin' me a nuisance!

CANON *[in a lull, dignified]*. You may be seated. *[Silence while they sit.* CANON *heroically contains himself, again embraces his nose, and seats himself opposite them. With scoundrel grace]* And now, Miss Cooney, I hope I see you well. And you too, Francis, none the less, mark! In short, I hope I see you *both* well. *[He smiles sardonically]*

JEMIMA. Sure, Lord, Canon, I'm lovely now. Sure I never felt so well since I came home from the hospital.

FRANCIS. And I'm like a two-year-old, Canon, ready to attack me work.

CANON *[with bow]*. Excellent. I assure you this news is a *great* satisfaction to me.

JEMIMA *[exploding]*. Sure, you're too good, Canon. Run, Francis now, and show His Reverence your teacher's certificate.

FRANCIS *[opening scroll, and going awkwardly to* CANON*]*. . . I just got it from college yisterday mornin', Canon.

CANON *[viewing the certificate without touching it]*. Creditable, Francis. Very creditable. I see in this the seal of—of scholarship, and the beginning of attainment. I congratulate you, Francis. *[*JEMIMA *beams]*

FRANCIS *[explosively]*. Canon, will you please do all you can for me about the school?

JEMIMA *[irascibly]*. Francis, will you mind your manners now? Sure don't you know you don't need to ask the Canon that! *[To the* CANON, *apologetically]* Sure he—he's over-exuberant, Canon.

CANON *[with bow to* JEMIMA*]*. As your Aunt Jemima so wisely observes, Francis, your request is superfluous, since I *must* do my best for you. Is it not written, Francis, in your Penny Catechism that we must all of us come to the aid of each other?

JEMIMA. There now, Francis.

FRANCIS [*backing awkwardly to seat*]. Sure, I'm a—a—an ass, Canon.

CANON. Not a bit, Francis. *Quandoque bonus dormitat Homerus.*

JEMIMA [*impulsively running to the* CANON *with photograph of* FRANCIS]. Look, Canon. A wee surprise. I got it taken in Dublin before we left, in a grand place in Talbot Street. [*Pointing*] That's Francis's certificate in his hand, and the wee book in his waistcoat pocket is the prayer book you gave him yourself for servin' Mass for eight years.

CANON [*benignly regarding photograph as if it were a new uncategoried animal*]. Very good! Uncommonly good! And very farseeing of you, Miss Cooney, to—to have Francis's scholarly achievement—er—permanently recorded.

JEMIMA [*driveling*]. Wouldn't his ma, God rest her, be proud of him there, Canon.

FRANCIS [*blushing and smirking*]. Sure, I'm nothin' at all, Canon.

CANON [*with preliminary grave bow to* JEMIMA]. Your mother, Francis, was a good woman. [*With great gravity*] In fact, a very good woman.

FRANCIS. Thank ye, Canon.

CANON [*gravely*]. In fact, Francis, in the light of my home and foreign experience, I might even say—an excellent woman.

JEMIMA. There now is news for you, Francis!

FRANCIS. It's awful kind of you to say the like of that, Canon.

CANON [*handing back photograph to* JEMIMA]. Very creditable, Miss Cooney. And now, Francis, you must be a little patient. We must *all* be a little patient. Your Aunt Jemima with her invaluable experience of life, as we live it, and of the—the idiosyncrasies of our checkered existence, will have impressed *that* upon you, I feel sure.

JEMIMA. Sure, Lord, Canon, isn't it all now in the will o' God!

CANON [*bowing delightfully*]. Excellent, Miss Cooney. Your Aunt Jemima, Francis, has just made a very wise observation. It is—if I may repeat, Miss Cooney?—in the will of God. Did I say, Francis, that your mother was a good woman?

FRANCIS. You did, indeed, Canon. A very good woman, you said.

CANON. So I did, Francis. I distinctly remember the remark now. I want to add to it, Francis. [*With great gravity*] I want to observe that your Aunt Jemima is a woman, to my knowledge, of incomparable wisdom, piety and virtue.

JEMIMA [*head down, blushing*]. Sure, I'm not worth that, Canon.

FRANCIS. Indeed she's the best in the world, Canon. Sure, I'd be nothin' only for *her.*

CANON. As you say, Francis, you might be nothing but for *her.* And look what you are! *Hoc opus! his labor est!* [CANON *smiles delightfully*]

FRANCIS [*blushing and confused*]. Yis, Canon, indeed yis. I owe her everythin'.

JEMIMA. You didn't happen to see, Canon, the piece in the *Dundalk Sentinel* about him? Sure, the editor was a great college friend of Francis's before he failed for the teachin' and fell back on bein' an editor.

CANON. I regret, Miss Cooney, I missed it. I must inquire from Father Corr. I believe *he* buys the—the *Dundalk Semaphore*.

FRANCIS. *Sentinel*, Canon.

CANON. *Sentinel*, Francis. *Sentinel*, to be sure. Accuracy, Francis, accuracy always.

BRIGID [*entering*]. If you please, Canon, there's a gentleman waitin' with a soft hat and an umbrella.

CANON. Ah, yes, Brigid. Presently, my child, presently. Francis and his aunt are just going. [*They take the tip and rise to go.* CANON *claps* FRANCIS *on back*] And now, Francis, I hope to have excellent news for you shortly. I can say nothing further now. The tongues of none of us are free. But keep within easy call, and employ your waiting time properly.

JEMIMA. Indeed, Canon, he'll spend his time of waitin' your command in makin' a novena.

FRANCIS [*outrageously*]. Sure, Canon, *orare est vigilare*.

JEMIMA. Well, will you listen to that, Canon. And him only a child.

CANON [*beaming*]. Excellent, Francis. I can see you are deeply versed in the profundities of the classics.

JEMIMA. Come on now, we're keepin' the Canon. And he'll pray for you, Canon. We'll both pray for you.

CANON [*bowing repeatedly as they go out*]. Excellent. . . . [*They go. He sinks wearily into chair.* BRIGID *comes in quickly and opens up window*]

BRIGID. I knew you'd want the window open, Canon.

CANON. You are a very understanding child, Brigid. The law of Nature's compensation is not after all a myth. [*He looks up at her as she stands solicitously watching him*] Brigid, promise me you'll never leave me.

BRIBID [*shrinking*]. I—I couldn't do that, Canon.

CANON [*startled*]. What? . . . What is this, Brigid? Are you not happy here?

BRIGID. Oh, yis, Canon. It's not that. I'm always happy.

CANON. Well? . . .

BRIGID. I might want to go away in a little while, Canon.

CANON. For what purpose, Brigid?

BRIGID. I—I don't know how to say it, Canon . . . It's the way I feel.

CANON. You are not well, child. You must take a good rest.

BRIGID. It's not that, Canon.

CANON. Nonsense! It *must* be that. Listen, Brigid. When I die, you will get every penny I have. There now! There's a secret out. Don't breathe it!

BRIGID. But Canon, it's not money I'll be wantin' where I—I think I'm goin'.

CANON. What talk is this? Where are you going?

BRIGID [*faltering*]. Please, Canon, I want to be a nun.

CANON [*flabbergasted*]. Eh? You—you want to be a nun, eh? My God, am I not sufficiently stocked with boobs that *you*, Brigid, *you* must add the final straw.

BRIGID. You're vexed with me, Canon.

CANON. Displeased, Brigid. . . . Displeased that you would go and leave me here alone. And you my friend! You the—the Canon's friend.

BRIGID. It's not just *you*, Canon, but everythin' I'd be leavin'.

CANON [*clapping her affectionately*]. Brigid, you have been doing too much lately, and you are overwrought. Excess in anything is bad, Brigid—in work, in play, in religion—it is not—classical. I am going to send you away for a holiday. And you must have a new hat too—a new hat with—with a feather in it. There now!

BRIGID [*amused*]. But sure, Canon, feathers is not worn anywhere now.

CANON. Do you tell me that, Brigid? That—that—that's astonishing—astonishing, Brigid.

BRIGID. It's a wee white dog at the side they have now and a nose veil.

CANON [*gravely*]. A—a white dog and a nose veil, Brigid? I—I must make a careful note of that, and you must certainly have them both. And it must be size six or seven or whatever you want.

BRIGID. Sure, Canon, with them shallow crowns that's out now, you can't depend on sizes. I'd need a fit-on.

CANON [*gravely*]. You'd need a fit-on, Brigid. So you would. These shallow—shallow crowns are certainly a bit of a problem. We'll arrange that too.

BRIGID. Thank you, Canon.

CANON. There now, you've forgotten already. When you get your holiday you will be again classically simple and quiescent. [*Pause*] Brigid, do you know where we keep the Baptismal Registers in the Cloak Room?

BRIGID. Yis, Canon. In the cupboard behind the door.

CANON. Go, Brigid, and bring me the Register for the year nineteen—nineteen and eight.

BRIGID. Yis, Canon. Nineteen and eight. [*She goes.* CANON *lifts the book again, and looks at the page he left open. He smiles sardonically. He then begins to read aloud. It is near the end of the book*]

CANON [*reading*]. "The Canon lay dying. The mists came white and wraith-like from the bogs to tell him so . . ." [*Puts down book*] Not a bit. On the contrary, the Canon feels well—feels in fact very well. [*As* BRIGID *comes in and hands him Register*] It may interest you to know, Brigid, that the Canon feels—excellently. [*He smiles sardonically*]

BRIGID. Sure, thanks be to God, Canon.

CANON [*as he opens Register*]. Amen, Brigid, amen. . . . Let me see now.

[*Turns pages rapidly*] Mallin, Melling, Nagle, Nolan, O'Brien, O'Connell, O'Kelly . . . ah, here we are,—O'Flingsley. [*He moves his finger along a line of data*] June 8th, 1908, Dermot Francis O'Flingsley.

BRIGID [*looking*]. Is that the Master's birthday, Canon?

CANON. That's it, Brigid. [*Gleefully as he reads on*] His father's name was Francis Eugene O'Flingsley. Mark the princely name, Eugene. Ah, and his mother bore the—storied name of Gibney. Could you credit that now? . . . Incomprehensible in fact. . . . Let me introduce you, Brigid, to Mr. Eugene Gibney,—er—author, amateur theologian, Catholic reformer, public moralist, student of Northern apologetics, erstwhile schoolmaster, ex-peasant and—gentleman.

BRIGID [*sensing fear*]. What does that mean, Canon?

CANON. To you, Brigid, it shall mean—*nothing*. Put that Register back, Brigid, and not a word to any one. [*As he goes*] Did I say a *word*, Brigid?

BRIGID. Yis, Canon.

CANON [*gravely*]. I meant a syllable, Brigid.

BRIGID. Sure, I won't even breathe, Canon.

CANON. Excellent, Brigid.

BRIGID [*turning as she crosses with Register*]. Please, Canon, is there anythin' wrong with the Master?

CANON. You're *breathing*, Brigid.

BRIGID. Yis, Canon. . . . No, Canon. . . . [*She crosses disconsolately*]

CANON. And Brigid. Send Dave Dooley down to the school to tell Mr. O'Flingsley that I wish to see him in the morning.

BRIGID [*almost in tears*]. Y-yis, Canon. [*She looks at him for a moment, as if wishing to speak, then goes off sadly with Register.* FATHER CORR *and* FATHER KIRWAN *enter from the window, carrying their hats*]

FATHER CORR. Father Kirwan and meself, Canon, would like a word with you, if you're not busy.

CANON. I *am* busy.

FATHER CORR. It's about a meeting we've just had of the Confraternity over that scurrilous book. A—a resolution was passed, Canon.

FATHER KIRWAN. Unanimously, Canon.

CANON. Well, what of it? It's a national pastime, isn't it?

FATHER KIRWAN. The members of the Football Club, Canon, are very excited. [*Worriedly*] *They're* the worst. They're gettin' out of hand.

CANON. No doubt, it's the warm weather, Father Kirwan. [*He crosses*] And I note you haven't as yet found time, even between resolutions, to shave. [CANON *goes out slowly.* CURATES *look after him perplexed*]

FATHER CORR. For Heaven's sake, can you not go and shave and not be makin' things harder for us?

FATHER KIRWAN. Ach, can a man not get wearin' his own hair if he wants to! Sure he's so contrary if I shaved every day, he'd grumble because I hadn't a beard like Don-the-Divil's-Father! Is he an Irishman at all?

FATHER CORR. His father was Irish. It's his mother was the Spaniard. They met in Brussels.

FATHER KIRWAN. It's a pity she didn't stay at home instead of gallivantin' about the continent. Sure you'd think he hadn't a drop of Irish Ireland blood in his veins. I'll bet me boots he'll side with that book agin the Confraternity and the Football Club.

FATHER CORR. With a book like that! My God, at least he's a priest.

FATHER KIRWAN. Did you see the schoolmaster?

FATHER CORR. I did, and he was worth seein'. He's all for us burnin' the book in public, and he thinks that the Canon is the proper one to do the actual casting into the flames.

FATHER KIRWAN [*noticing open book*]. Great Scott! Will you look at what's here!

FATHER CORR [*with a start*]. The book!

FATHER KIRWAN. It's open at the last chapter where the P.P. dies miserably. He must have been readin' it.

FATHER CORR [*with passionate aversion*]. I loathe the thing. It's accursed and vile. [*He flings it venomously on the floor*]

FATHER KIRWAN [*"dribbling" with the book with both feet*]. He was certainly no lover of clean sport and the team spirit. [*Still dribbling*] Suppose now yon door was the net. Wait till you see a grand penalty from the touch line. [*He kicks with judgment, and it is hurled against the doorway just as the* CANON *re-enters. He suddenly sees the* CANON *and sinks visibly into himself.* FATHER CORR *is very confused. The* CANON *regards them with extreme frigidity. A definite pause*]

CANON [*tensely*]. You may both be seated. [*They obey silently. With cold hauteur*] My property, Father Corr.

FATHER CORR [*defiantly*]. I—I refuse to touch it. It's—vile.

CANON. My property, Father Corr. [FATHER CORR *is defiant for a definite moment, then emotionally lifts the book and hands it to* CANON. *He then reseats himself. The* CANON *lays the mutilated book on table*] I suppose I am to regard this outbreak of hooliganism in my study, as a typical spasm of—Catholic action.

FATHER CORR [*flashing out*]. Canon, that book is a disgrace and a shame. The Irish Press in Dublin says it's an insult to the Catholic nation.

CANON [*courteously*] Didn't catch that word, Father Corr. [*Hand to ear*] The Irish what?

FATHER CORR. The Irish Press, Canon.

CANON. Never heard of it. [*He pours out a small glass of golden-colored wine at sideboard, and examines it*]

FATHER KIRWAN. Sure, the *Ballyedminstown Courier* quotes whole columns from it every Saturday, Canon.

CANON [*sipping wine*]. In that case, Father Kirwan, I must concede it has a definite claim to our attention.

BRIGID [*entering*]. If you please, Canon, there's four o' the parishioners here wearin' badges, and they'd like a talk with you.

FATHER CORR. I'd like very much, Canon, if you'd receive them. They're a deputation.

FATHER KIRWAN. Sure the whole country's takin' action, Canon.

CANON. Mm . . . I am presumably to agree to a—a descent into Lutheranism and a sort of Kirk Session. Say, Brigid, the Canon says No.

BRIGID [*repeating*]. The Canon says No. [*She makes to go*]

FATHER CORR. Sure, after all if it was only for appearances' sake.

BRIGID. Canon, would you not just give another clap on the back and a grand word?

CANON. What *are* we come to? [*Pause*] Very well then, very well, let the—the neo-theologians come in, but let it be at their peril. I shall ring, Brigid.

BRIGID. Yis, Canon. I'll keep them in the waitin' room. [*She goes*]

CANON. Who are these people, Father Corr?

FATHER CORR. They're all strong confraternity and football club members, Canon. There's Miss Cooney and her nephew Francis—

CANON. Is *he* here? Who are the other two?

FATHER KIRWAN. Martin Mullahone, Canon, the referee of our football team, that has the public house and farm on the Dublin Road, and his wife, Rosey Violet.

CANON. His wife who?

FATHER KIRWAN. He calls her Rosey Violet, Canon.

CANON. I think I recall her, but if my recollection is correct, she was neither rosey nor a violet. [*He rings the bell*] Be seated, Fathers, and offer no comments until these people are gone. [FATHER CORR *and* FATHER KIRWAN *sit at either end of the empty chairs for the deputation. The* CANON *sits magisterially at the large writing desk.* BRIGID *enters with the deputation behind her.* MISS COONEY *and* FRANCIS O'CONNOR *are as obsequious as usual.* MARTIN MULLAHONE, *a large awkward man, with a large stomach and a red nose, is followed by his wife who is typical in dress and voice of the "social status" aspirants in rural Ireland*]

BRIGID. This is them, Canon.

CANON [*curtly*]. Good afternoon, all. You may be seated. [BRIGID *goes. All sit in chairs opposite the* CANON. *They smirk and bow to the* CANON *and look as virtuous as possible. The* CANON's *sardonic eye surveys them pitilessly. They wilt and shift uneasily. His eye on* MARTIN.] Are you the man, Martin Mullahone?

MARTIN. I—I am then, Canon.

ROSEY VIOLET [*chipping in sweetly*]. And I'm his wife, Canon.

CANON. Martin Mullahone, where are your hands? [MARTIN *whips them violently out of his pockets*]

MARTIN. Sure, I—I never thought, Canon. Sure, God's—

ROSEY VIOLET. Sure, I'm always tellin' him, Canon.

CANON. Sit erect and don't loll or sag. Decorum and personal dignity are not by any means the least of the Christian virtues. [*All sit fearfully erect*] And now to the point. You have come—or should I say you have taken it upon yourselves to come—about a certain book.

MARTIN [*explosively*]. Sure, it's a—a terror, Canon. A—a terror and a fright to the world, Canon.

CANON [*with suave irony*]. Having learned from your husband, Mrs. Mullahone, that this book is a—a terror and a fright—two quite incomprehensible epithets to me—do you wish to—er—supplement his observation?

ROSEY VIOLET. If you please, Canon, I agree with what Father Kirwan said when he thumped the table at the meetin', that no clean sportin' man with the team spirit in him could write such a book. [FATHER KIRWAN *is confused*]

CANON [*ironic, with side glance at* FATHER KIRWAN]. An *excellent* observation, Mrs. Mullahone.

ROSEY VIOLET. Sure, if you please, Canon, me eldest son, Dan, is the fullback in Father Kirwan's team.

CANON [*cruelly*]. Didn't catch the word, Mrs. Mullahone. [*Hand to ear*] The—the what? [FATHER KIRWAN *is very confused*]

ROSEY VIOLET. The fullback, Canon.

CANON. Ah! of course. The—the fullback. I must ask Father Kirwan for a glossary of these terms. [*Side glance at* FATHER KIRWAN] And you, Miss Cooney, have *you* any observation?

JEMIMA. Sure, Canon, I only came because Father Corr told me it was me duty to God and Ireland. [*Grasping* FRANCIS's *arm*] Say it in Irish for the Canon, Francis. Go on now! [FATHER CORR *is confused*]

FRANCIS [*rising awkwardly*]. *Do cum gloire De, agus onora na h-Eiremann.*

CANON [*hand to ear*]. Didn't catch that Francis. Cum—cum what?

FRANCIS [*unconscious of cruelty*]. *Do cum gloire De, agus onora na h-Eiremann.*

CANON [*scoundrelishly*]. Excellent, Francis. Excellent! You may be seated. Any other observation, Miss Cooney?

JEMIMA. Sure, I'll just listen now to you, and learn, Canon. Isn't that me duty?

CANON. Very creditable, Miss Cooney. An attitude at once wise, womanly and prudent. And you, Francis?

JEMIMA [*hurriedly*]. He'll just do the same as meself, Canon. Not a word now, Francis, before his reverence.

FRANCIS. Sure, it's for *you* to say, Canon.

CANON. Commendable, Francis. You have a good—a very good counselor.

ROSEY VIOLET [*not to be outdone*]. Sure, if you please, Canon, me brother, Father Jamsie, says it was no one but the divil guided the hand that wrote that book.

CANON [*startled*]. Your who—the what? Speak up, Mrs. Mullahone.

ROSEY VIOLET [*exuberantly*]. Why, me brother, Father Jamsie, Canon, that's up in Dunaree with Father Crone. Sure, Canon, it was Father Jamsie that anointed your sister, Thomasina's mother, when she near died and didn't, last Christmas.

CANON [*shaking head*]. Never heard of him.

ROSEY VIOLET [*sentimentally.*] Ah, sure poor wee Father Jamsie, Canon. Sure, God help him.

CANON. What's the matter with him?

ROSEY VIOLET [*surprised*]. Sure, nothin' at all, Canon. Sure, Lord, what would be the matter with him?

CANON [*with an effort*]. Very well then.

ROSEY VIOLET. Sure, he's happy and lovely in Dunaree, Canon.

CANON [*heroically*]. Very well then.

MARTIN [*blunderingly interposing*]. Sure, will you not be sickenin' the Canon, bargin' in every minute about Father Jamsie because he's your brother.

ROSEY VIOLET [*bursting into tears*]. If you please, Canon, Martin's always insultin' and belittlin' me in public.

CANON [*with great gravity, eyeing* MARTIN *who quails and shifts about*]. Martin Mullahone, what *grave* charge is this I hear as to your conduct and public morals?

MARTIN. Sure—sure, Canon, you'd think by the talk of her mornin' and night that he was a Canon like yourself, and him with the—the cloth on him only a month.

ROSEY VIOLET [*crying*]. Me heart's broke with him, Canon.

CANON. You are a good woman, Mrs. Mullahone, and you have pleased me considerably.

ROSEY VIOLET. Sure, everyone loves me, Canon.

CANON. As for you, Martin Mullahone, I am gravely incensed [MARTIN *squirms*] and not a little pained.

ROSEY VIOLET. Oh, thank you, Canon. Martin badly needed that talkin' to.

CANON. Very well then. We digress. How many of you have read this book? [*Negative murmurs and shaking of heads*]

ROSEY VIOLET. Sure, what Catholic could read a book like that, Canon?

CANON. I take it then that none of you has read this book?

ALL [*shaking heads, murmurs*]. Not a one, Canon.

CANON. And you come here to condemn a book you have not read! What nonsense is this? [*Taps desk*] Preposterous and ridiculous! The deputation is dismissed. [*The* CANON *is just rising when* FATHER CORR *jumps up*]

FATHER CORR. If I may say a word, Canon—

CANON. Be seated, Father Corr. [FATHER CORR *sits*]

FRANCIS [*rising*]. If you please, Canon—

JEMIMA [*seizing him and flinging him down*]. That's enough, you pup! Sit down!

CANON [*sitting back, eyeing* FRANCIS, *benignly*]. We shall allow him the privilege on this occasion, Miss Cooney. Proceed, Francis.

FRANCIS [*awkwardly*]. I was just goin' to say, Canon, that is, as a—a certified teacher, I—I read the book—judiciously.

CANON [*hand to ear, cruelly luring him on*]. What—what word was that, Francis?

FRANCIS. Judiciously, Canon.

CANON. Ah! Enlarge upon that, Francis. It is a little vague.

FRANCIS. Well, Canon, if I—I felt a part was gettin' bad, I skipped.

CANON. You—you skipped, Francis. [*He smiles*]

ROSEY VIOLET [*interposing*]. I done that too, Canon.

JEMIMA. If you please, Canon, when I saw that Francis was determined to—to study it, I felt it me duty to read it before him and turn down some of the pages.

CANON [*face masklike*]. I understand—exactly. And you, Martin Mulla-hone?

MARTIN [*hoarsely*]. I can't read, Canon. It's me wife is the scholar in our family.

ROSEY VIOLET [*interposing, gushingly*]. I was three years in the convent, Canon, before Martin won me.

MARTIN [*hoarsely*]. It was the little fella that has the bike shop, Canon—wee Joey Hardy, that was readin' out bits of it at the counter on Friday, and I—I couldn't help hearin' them, Canon. Out—outrageous and terrible, Canon! A fright to the world!

CANON [*rounding on them*]. I am to take it then that four of my parish-ioners, deliberately—I might even say, wantonly—and without right or lawful authority from me either in person or by proxy, committed themselves to the reading of a book gravely alleged to be pernicious, immoral and—sub-versive. [*He sizes up the four, severely*] Of these, one is the sister of a priest [ROSEY VIOLET *sobs*] another presumptuously aspires to the position of teacher of the young, [JEMIMA *gives* FRANCIS *a vicious elbow dig in the ribs*] a third is or should be a father and a husband [MARTIN *sags visibly*], and a fourth—[JEMIMA *bows her head and sniffs*]—I can find no words to castigate the curiosity that tempted the fourth to this grave indiscretion. [*He rings the bell*] I shall deliver my directions to the two Fathers here who will com-municate them to you for your unswerving acceptance. You will leave imme-diately. I shall contemplate whether it is humanly possible to pardon any or all of you. [CANON *rises, as* BRIGID *appears. The deputation also rises. The* CANON *waves. They go out in confusion following* BRIGID. *The two* CURATES *turn nervously to the* CANON. *Curtly*] Be seated. [*They sit.* CANON *resumes his seat*] I may take it, I suppose, that you two have also presumed to read this book.

FATHER CORR. I frankly considered it my duty, Canon.

FATHER KIRWAN. So did I, Canon.

CANON. Bad theology, Fathers, bad theology. And equally bad theology of course to have any—er—unofficial conflagrations on the public street without my express approval. [*Pause*] The author of this book which I have read, Fathers, is obviously a very young man. I fear his education cannot be more—adequate than that of the average young man of the present, either lay or—er—clerical. [*He coughs*] The theme I take to mean that Ireland has dangerously materialized the outlook of the Church, and that its profound spiritual essence has been stolen by a small band of learned men whom it does not even recognize. A dangerous theme, Fathers, I grant you.

FATHER CORR [*blazing out*]. A blasphemous lie on Catholic Ireland!

CANON [*calmly*]. A theme, Fathers, that in the hands of an abler controversialist with a claim to scholarship or a classic status, might possibly cause alarm amongst us, especially when we have presently no known Irish Catholic scholar with that delicacy of touch, subtlety of culture and profundity of classical knowledge to defend and even rescue the Church intellectually. Coming in contact with such an immaturity as this the insufficiently scholared mind, fed mostly on sentimentalisms in the form of learning, is often shocked, and—vulgarly agitated. Violent emotionalism results, followed by a quite ridiculous hubbub, tawdry heroics, even bigoted physical violence under holy names, and generally a quite ludicrous procedure that the classic dignity of the mind of the Church recoils from. As I have no desire, Fathers, to make a presumptuous young man bogusly important in an age that is itself bogusly important, or to condone a procedure too undignified to be Catholic, I therefore decree that no action of any sort be taken in the case of this book, except such action as I, in my official capacity, shall think fit to perform. [*Pause*] That, I think, Fathers, will be all.

FATHER CORR [*livid*]. Are we then actually to take it that our efforts to deal with this disgraceful libel are banned?

CANON. You are!

FATHER KIRWAN [*touching* FATHER CORR, *as he is about to burst out*]. That's enough now. You'll only be sayin' things you'll be sorry for.

FATHER CORR [*in a temper*]. I'll say what I like.

FATHER KIRWAN. Now, can't you see that's wild talk?

FATHER CORR [*cooling*]. I suppose it is. But he's never done belittlin' and humblin' me. But I'll try not to mind. It's in my nature to be humble.

CANON. Inoculated would be a better word. Inoculated with the prevalent deluge of sentimentalism.

FATHER CORR. I'm afraid, Canon, there's nothin' for me to do but ask the Bishop for a shift and to give my reasons.

CANON. And in spite of your impertinences, Father, I shall be prepared to give his Grace an—adequate report on your work. [FATHER CORR *abruptly leaves the room, left. The* CANON *looks after him quietly and then turns to* FATHER KIRWAN] And you, Father Kirwan? Are you also going to the Bishop?

FATHER KIRWAN [*confused, and crossing*]. I'm goin' for a—for a shave, Canon.

CANON. Dear me! We—progress! [FATHER KIRWAN *goes awkwardly, left. The* CANON *turns away tiredly, goes to the leaded bookcase, unlocks it and extracts a volume. He settles with it in an armchair. But the dusk is falling fast, and in a moment he looks up towards the lamp. He reaches for the bell, and is about to shake it when, with a cry,* BRIGID *runs in*]

BRIGID. Canon! Canon! [*He rises rapidly and goes to her. She tries to recover and looks up at him pathetically*]

CANON. What on earth is the matter, child?

BRIGID [*breathing hard, but trying to recover*]. It's nothin', Canon, nothin' at all. I—I'm all right now.

CANON. Did something frighten you?

BRIGID. Y-yis, Canon. But it's nothin'.

CANON. You should have the lamp lighted in there at this time. There, you are tired and overwrought.

BRIGID. Canon, may I—ask you somethin'?

CANON. Certainly, Brigid.

BRIGID. Do you—do you love St. Brigid?

CANON [*looking at her uncertainly*]. Why, of course I do, child. Sure we *all* love St. Brigid.

BRIGID [*happy*]. Yes . . . I'm glad you do. She'll be pleased.

CANON [*solicitously*]. Brigid, you are ill. You are not well.

BRIGID. Yis, Canon, I'm well.

CANON. I'm afraid not, child.

BRIGID. It's just, Canon, that I—I still want to be a nun.

CANON. There now! I *knew* you weren't well.

BRIGID [*pleadingly*]. But if I could just be a nun, Canon.

CANON. Don't you know, Brigid, that nuns must be very, very strong and brave? They must be cruel to themselves and they must give all.

BRIGID [*tensely*]. I will give all, Canon. I will! I promised her.

CANON. What nonsense is this? Promised whom, child?

BRIGID [*her eyes aglow*]. St. Brigid, Canon. I—I was dryin' the cups in the kitchen when she touched me on the shoulder and says she, "You're holdin' the dish-towel wrong, Brigid." And when I held it right, she whispered to me, "Ask him if he loves me more than the rest." [*The* CANON *stares at her, walks irascibly away, and then turns to her, collected*]

CANON [*gravely*]. Brigid, you are, I fear, stubborn, disobedient, and even defiant, and—I am seriously annoyed and displeased with you.

BRIGID [*simply*]. I—I knew you would, Canon.

CANON. If you were a boob, Brigid, or a footling trifler, I should expel you from my presence. But you are my friend, and I try to bear with you.

BRIGID [*sadly*]. Yis, Canon.

CANON. I have borne all day with fools, Brigid, knowing that at the end you would come to me, and ask my wants and find no fault in me. There now. You see how it is with me.

BRIGID. Yis, Canon. [*Sadly*] I'm a wretch and a villain.

CANON. On the contrary, child, you are a good girl, and you have wisdom and grace. God, Brigid, is not *always* pleased with girls who want to be nuns. Sometimes He expects them to remain at their posts as His soldiers.

BRIGID [*pathetically persistent*]. If only I could just be a nun instead of a soldier! Soldiers make so much noise.

CANON. Brigid, I am afraid your nerves are all shaken. You must go to bed now and on Friday I shall send you to Bray to a friend of mine for a holiday. Miss Cooney will take your place for a few weeks. You must get plenty of sleep and rest. Rest to the body, Brigid, is like prayer to the soul. And you will then forget these imaginings of yours.

BRIGID. But in bed, how can I forget, if her face is there in the curtains and the mark on her cheek where she struck the loveliness out of her face.

CANON [*irascibly*]. Now, now, now! I am trying not to be angry. There is no historical authority for that at all. The Church in its wisdom does not confirm it. It is probably just a myth. A myth, Brigid. Doesn't that show you?

BRIGID [*pathetically*]. What is a myth, Canon?

CANON. A legend, child. [*Pause*]

BRIGID [*venturing*]. And what is a—a legend, Canon?

CANON. Brigid, this is very trying! An old tale, that may or may not be true.

BRIGID. Then—it *could* be true, Canon?

CANON. Now which of us knows best about these things, Brigid?

BRIGID. You, Canon.

CANON. Well now, I say this thing you foolishly think you see is not—not of God. Dismiss it!

BRIGID [*in pain, her head in her hands*]. Canon! . . . oh, Canon! . . . how—how could you be sayin' that?

CANON [*sympathetically*]. There, there! God tempts most those whom He loves best. You should be proud. The soul's great battles are not fought by common boobs. The great Ignatius was tempted like this, and so were Theresa and Augustine and Dominic, but they were not deceived. They rose up and conquered the tempter. So must you conquer this, Brigid.

BRIGID [*tearfully*]. So must you conquer this, Brigid.

CANON. Not more beautiful, Brigid, than the demon that twisted himself round the crucifix St. Ignatius prayed before. He had to lie on his face to save himself. You too, Brigid, must turn away from this thing you think you see. You must be wise. Wise, Brigid, and brave. Promise me, Brigid.

BRIGID [*sobbing*]. I want to die, Canon. . . . I want to—to die. . . .

CANON [*softly*]. Come now, Brigid. That is not being brave! That is being merely heroic, like these modern vulgarians. Say, Brigid, "I want to live and conquer." [*She is silent*] Say it, Brigid. Be proud like a soldier and say it.

BRIGID [*sadly*]. I want to live and—conquer. . . .

CANON [*clapping her on back*]. Ah, Brigid, excellent! Go now, Brigid, to bed and sleep. And none of these dreams, remember, or foolishness. To sleep is safe, to dream is dangerous. I shall go out and send Dave Dooley for Miss Cooney to take your place.

BRIGID [*emotionally*]. Yis, Canon. [*He crosses to window, opens it and passes out, into the garden*]

CANON'S VOICE [*without*]. Dooley! Are you there! Come here, Dooley! [BRIGID'S *emotional stress now visibly shakes her, as she stands undecided and forlorn in the deepening shadows. She sobs pathetically, her head down, like a child. She gives the impression of having lost someone very beloved. She lifts her head suddenly, and stares stealthily over her own shoulders at the slightly swaying curtains, that reach to the ground. Her body shudders, and she covers her face with her hands*]

BRIGID [*sobbing*]. I'm not to look at you. . . . I—I promised him. . . . I'm not to see your face. . . . No, no. I—I mustn't . . . I daren't . . . I must keep my eyes covered from you . . . I must be—be wise and brave . . . I must sleep but not dream . . . but I—I . . . [*She draws her hands from her eyes, shakingly, stretches out her two arms to the curtains, and with a sob, rushes to them as to a loved one*] But I—I love you . . . I love you . . . I love you. . . . [*Her face is buried sobbingly in the great curtains, and her arms are about them pathetically, as the curtain falls slowly*]

CURTAIN

ACT THREE

SCENE: *The same. A few days later.*

*The* CANON *is seated at table finishing breakfast.* FATHER CORR *is standing at the writing-desk, quietly examining a Register of Births.* JEMIMA, *with an apron on, is flitting fearfully about the table, obsequious and uncomfortable in the* CANON'S *presence.*

JEMIMA [*sweetly*]. Is there anythin' else, Canon, if you please?

CANON [*beamingly*]. You leave nothing to be desired, Miss Cooney. Thank·you.

JEMIMA. Thank you, Canon. [*She crosses*]

CANON. One moment, Miss Cooney. Has Brigid had a good night?

JEMIMA. She had, Canon, A wee bit feverish maybe and her eyes are shineyish, but the doctor says it's nothin' to worry about.

CANON. As a good woman, Miss Cooney, what do *you* think yourself?

JEMIMA [*squirming a little under his gaze*]. Sure I'd say, Canon, I'd say nothin' much. I'd put it down, if you'd allow me, Canon, to what—what she came from. Her mother, Canon, was none too strong—[*hoarsely*] in the mind I mean, Canon. They had to—remove her in the end.

CANON. Remove her? Enlarge on that, Miss Cooney.

JEMIMA. Sure—take her away, Canon: to—to Dublin, I mean. It was before your time, sure.

CANON [*understanding*]. Ah! . . . And her father?

JEMIMA [*hoarsely*]. Sure they say, Canon, he didn't die a Christian death in Scotland. But sure God's good, Canon.

CANON. As you say, Miss Cooney. God is good. [*Pause*] I want you to give Brigid very careful attention night and day.

JEMIMA. Sure if it's your wish, Canon.

CANON. Expressly so! That will be all. [*She goes after bowing. The* CANON *watches* FATHER CORR *at the Births' Register, as he finishes his coffee*] I understand you heard Brigid's confession this morning, Father Corr?

FATHER CORR [*raising head from book*]. That's correct, Canon. At eight o'clock. She asked for me.

CANON. Did you—instruct her on these matters we discussed, on the lines I recommended?

FATHER CORR. I carried out your instructions to the letter, Canon, even if I did think myself you were unnecessarily extreme and severe.

CANON. The latter half of your observation, Father Corr, is superfluous.

FATHER CORR. Not so much as you might think, Canon, if you examine this Register of Births.

CANON. I knew from the manner in which you were poring over that book that there was a sort of necromancer's air about you. Well? And what are the—the "signs and wonders"?

FATHER CORR [*impressively*]. Would it surprise you to know, Canon, that Brigid was born on February the first, almost twenty-one years ago? That's St. Brigid's day!

CANON. And you are going to infer vulgarly that there is anything more than mere coincidence in that? [*He sips his coffee slowly*]

FATHER CORR [*coming forward slowly*]. Since I heard of this—contention of Brigid's, Canon, I've been worried and disturbed.

CANON [*sipping*]. I thought you would. The danger with you, Father Corr, is that some trivial happening is always liable to hurl you headlong into violent emotionalism.

FATHER CORR. Sure, I'm doin' nothin' violent, Canon—I'm as calm as any priest could be. I'm only just quietly turnin' over a few things in my mind, such as, for instance the fact that Brigid was born on St. Brigid's day, and that St. Brigid lived and worked in this very locality here in Fanghart.

CANON. I dislike your attitude. If a leaf turns unaccountably in these credulous days ten thousand ferrety nonentities cock their ears and gibber.

FATHER CORR. Suppose, Canon, that Brigid—*did* see this—well, this vision?

CANON. If Brigid saw ten thousand visions, our attitude to the accumulated wisdom of the Church should be unaltered. I wish you, in particular, and this country in general, could digest just *that* much, and cease chasing emotional red-herrings. [*Pause.* FATHER CORR *shifts uneasily*]

FATHER CORR. With all respect to you, Canon, I don't think you understand this country.

CANON [*acidly*]. I understand the mind of the universal Church, and that alone concerns me. [*Pause*] Besides, didn't you hear Miss Cooney just now on the matter of Brigid's antecedents?

FATHER CORR. That might mean nothing.

CANON. It generally means everything. But you *will* strain after miracles, in spite of my previous observations. One can conceivably understand her father dying an unchristian death in a barbarous nation like Scotland, but there is no escaping the significance of the fact that her mother was— removed, as Miss Cooney so Celtically phrased it.

FATHER CORR. That may be, Canon. What worries me, is her insistence that she saw the face and eyes of the Saint. Poor Brigid is not a liar.

CANON. Brigid, as you observe, is not a liar. But the reflections, Father, in an unstable mind are not—shall we say theologically significant? [*As* JEMIMA *enters*] Let us dismiss the subject.

JEMIMA. Please, Canon, you said you wanted to see me nephew, Francis. He's here now.

CANON. Let him come in, Miss Cooney.

JEMIMA. Sure, let him wait till Father Corr is finished with you, Canon.

FATHER CORR [*to* JEMIMA]. You can send him in. I'm going now. [*She bows and goes*] Canon, I've written to the Bishop for a transfer. I don't, and probably never will, understand you. I don't want you to think I'm doin' it behind your back.

CANON [*slowly*]. It is not important. [FRANCIS *comes in awkwardly with his cap in his hand. Neither priest takes the slightest notice of him*]

FATHER CORR. Very well, Canon. [*He bows and goes. Very preoccupied, the* CANON *looks at* FRANCIS *for quite a time, unseeingly.* FRANCIS *sweats*]

FRANCIS. Am I too—too soon, Canon? Sure, I could go back and wait! . . .

CANON [*coming slowly to consciousness*]. Ah, Francis, you've come. Of course. You wanted to see me, Francis?

FRANCIS [*open-mouthed*]. But sure it—was *you* wanted to see *me*, Canon!

CANON. Oh, it was *I* wanted to see *you*, Francis! Why of course it was. I remember now. I distinctly remember. Be seated, Francis. [FRANCIS *sits awkwardly, squeezing cap*]

FRANCIS [*in a typical Irish whisper*]. Is there—anny news, Canon?

CANON. There is, Francis, and there isn't. Contradictory, Francis? But no! I mean by it, there *is* news—relevant news, but there is the necessity for absolute secrecy.

FRANCIS. Sure you can swear me on the book, Canon. [*Magnanimously*] Or if ye lek, Canon, don't tell me a word, if you think fit.

CANON. Excellent, Francis. But—you will be told everything. I trust you. To be exact, moral issues—issues, Francis, of a moral nature, are involved.

FRANCIS [*all at sea*]. I—I see, Canon. . . .

CANON. Your aunt will understand more fully than you, Francis. Moral issues *are* involved, and where such are met with, we must tread warily. We must tread, Francis, with the subtlety of angels. But to proceed. You have met my niece—my step-niece, Thomasina Concannon?

FRANCIS. I—I had the honor, Canon, a good few times, in the hall and at concerts she came down to see.

CANON. As you say, Francis, you've had the honor. A—a gentlemanly expression, Francis. For some time past, I have promised her the first vacancy in the school here. And as Miss Driscoll goes to training next week, I must fulfill that promise, Francis. We must *all* fulfill our promises.

FRANCIS [*very crestfallen*]. Well, sure, thank you annyway, Canon. I know you did your best for me, and sure you can't please everyone.

CANON. Wait, Francis, wait! There is something further. What remains is confidential. But I have your word, Francis.

FRANCIS. Sure me lips is sealed, Canon, and as for me Aunt, sure she's a —a gravestone.

CANON. As you say, Francis, your aunt's a—a gravestone. I may therefore, proceed. I intend, Francis, dismissing the man, O'Flingsley. [FRANCIS *gives a gasp and half rises*] A grave step, Francis—a very grave step, but necessary. We must never hesitate in our duty. That is the sum and the essence of conduct. Note it down, Francis.

FRANCIS. I'll write it in me "Things to Remember" book this very night, Canon.

CANON. Excellent, Francis. That will be another vacancy. Now that position of Principal, Francis, I would give to no one sooner than you.

FRANCIS [*gasping*]. P-principal, Canon!

CANON. But mark what it results in! Mark my problem, Francis, my dilemma, my moral embarrassment. An attractive young man and a comely young girl in the one building all day. Mark it gravely, Francis!

FRANCIS [*wide-eyed, dismayed*]. There—there would be scandal, Canon, and . . . and talk. I see it all.

CANON. Let us say instead, Francis, with the dignity demanded by the phenomenon, that moral issues of grave import are involved.

FRANCIS [*aghast*]. I see it all, Canon. . . .

CANON. You see it all, Francis! You have insight! You inherit it, I have not the *slightest* doubt, from your Aunt Jemima. Now, if my step-niece were a benevolent old lady, the problem would not only solve itself—it would have no existence in fact.

FRANCIS. That's the trouble, Canon, with Thomasina young and—if I may make so bold, Canon—attractive.

CANON. Attractive is the word, Francis, or if you wish—sus-susceptible. An excellent word, Francis. You see my difficulty?

FRANCIS. Sure it's plain, Canon.

CANON. It's plain, Francis. It's more than plain. It's unsurmountable. Unless of course, Francis, you could hit on a way out. Your brain is young and nimble, Francis, not like mine.

FRANCIS. If only I could, Canon! Sure it's grand of you strivin' to help me, and perplexin' yourself.

CANON. Not a bit, Francis. "The labor we delight in physics pain." You remember that great inspirational line, Francis, in your studies.

FRANCIS. Indeed I do, Canon. Sure, I know Lord Macaulay inside out.

CANON. So you do, Francis! I can see that.

FRANCIS. If the two of them was married, Canon?

CANON [*apparently perplexed*]. Which two, Francis?

FRANCIS. The two in the school, Canon.

CANON. Oh, the two in the school, Francis. If they were married. But they're not, Francis. If they *were*, the conditions would be an approximation to the ideal. But we must deal in facts, Francis.

FRANCIS [*uneasily*]. If I could maybe, Canon, ask me aunt to ask Thomasina to—to discuss things. . . .

CANON [*obtusely*]. For—for what purpose, pray, Francis?

FRANCIS. I mean, Canon, that is if *you* have no objection, to see if Thomasina would consider a—a match between us.

CANON [*admirably playacting*]. A—a match! A—match! . . . Francis, what on earth is this? What is that brain of yours propounding?

FRANCIS [*laughing*]. But you asked me to hit on a way out, Canon!

CANON. I asked you to hit on a way out, and you—you bring the house down about my ears without warning! By my soul, Francis, you're a—a scoundrel; a—a desperado! I insist on your Aunt Jemima taking you in hand this instant! [*Goes to door and calls*] Miss Cooney! Come here instantly! [JEMIMA *runs in nervously*]

JEMIMA. You want me, Canon?

CANON [*with mock severity*]. Miss Cooney, take Francis out of my sight, and never let him into my presence again. He's a scoundrel!

JEMIMA [*aghast*]. Did—did he insult ye, Canon? Did he have the—the cheek—! [*Tempestuously, finger up*] Stand before me, Francis, this minute! [CANON *and* FRANCIS *laugh heartily*] Sure is—is it mockin' me yous are, Canon?

CANON [*touching her shoulder*]. No, Miss Cooney. But Francis has mentally, and I might even say morally, winded me. He wants to make a match with my step-niece and take over the school!

JEMIMA [*excitedly*]. Make a match! . . . Take over the school! . . . Canon, if it's takin' liberties he is in your presence, it's your own fault. You're far too kind and free with him, and you don't keep him in his place.

FRANCIS. But you see, Aunt Jemima, O'Flingsley's bein' put out.

JEMIMA. O'Flingsley? Put out! Is that for you to *say*, or the Canon? The cheek of you, Francis. I'll slap your jaw.

CANON. It's true, Miss Cooney. But in strict confidence as yet, remember!

JEMIMA [*involuntarily*]. Praises to God! . . .

CANON. But I can't appoint Francis alongside my step-niece, because of moral issues.

JEMIMA [*awarely*]. You can *not*, Canon. I can see *that*.

FRANCIS. But if we were married, Aunt? The Canon says he has no objection.

JEMIMA [*gravely*]. Did—did you say that, Canon?

CANON. I certainly did, Miss Cooney. But the suggestion is not mine, Miss Cooney. I—wash my hands. [*Laughter*]

JEMIMA. It's God, Canon, that's Who it is! And Thomasina was in the kitchen to see you not three minutes ago.

CANON [*aghast*]. What? She—she's back?

JEMIMA. She came in, Canon. But she left a book she was readin' behind her on the bus, and she's away flyin' down to the Depot to get it.

FRANCIS [*exuberantly*]. I'll go down after her, and help her to get it!

JEMIMA. You'll stay where y'are, till you learn the Canon's wishes. Direct him, Canon.

CANON. I refuse to commit myself by *one* word. Did I not say I had washed my hands?

FRANCIS. I'll go. I—I insist on me independence, in this, Aunt Jemima. [*As he goes, excitedly*] And sure, Canon. *Fortis cadere, cedere non potest!* [CANON *and* JEMIMA *laugh affectedly, as* FRANCIS *goes*]

JEMIMA [*proudly*]. Imagine the nerve of him, Canon, hurlin' the Latin back at you!

CANON. There is no presumption where there is no malice, Miss Cooney. Francis is a good boy. That will be all, Miss Cooney. [*He lifts book and crosses*] I shall be seated at the lower end of the garden if Mr. O'Flingsley calls. I'm expecting him.

JEMIMA. I'll come for you at once, Canon. Sure, it's God's blessin', Canon. You're gettin' rid of him, and him that cheeky and impertinent to you. [*The* CANON *crosses and takes no notice of her remark. She notices this and goes quickly.* CANON *pauses a moment to look out pensively at the hills, then opens the window and with his book passes out. A moment later, the door bell rings and almost immediately* JEMIMA *ushers in* DERMOT O'FLINGSLEY. *Sourly*] Sit there, and I'll run into the garden and see if the Canon will be willin' to see you.

O'FLINGSLEY. I'll stand. And don't *run*. You might break your neck.

JEMIMA [*very sourly*]. Yours is bruck if you only knew it.

O'FLINGSLEY [*squeaking*]. Coo-ee, Jemma! Your petticoat's hangin'! [*She stamps out in a fury.* O'FLINGSLEY *laughs heartily, throws his hat on a chair, and makes a tour of the bookcases and the pictures.* BRIGID, *wrapped in a dressing-gown and bare-footed, comes in left, noiselessly. She crosses until she is right beside him. She looks feverish and frail*] How anyone can have all that beauty about him, and still be a bear! [*He sees* BRIGID *beside him and jumps*] Brigid! Where on earth did *you* drop from? Are you not well?

BRIGID [*softly*]. Yis, Master, I'm well. It's just that the Canon says I'm not.

O'FLINGSLEY [*looking at her*]. I think now, Brigid, that *for once* he's right. Let me feel your hand. [*He takes her hand gently*]

BRIGID. I knew you'd be here.

O'FLINGSLEY [*staring at her*]. Eh? You what?

BRIGID. I knew it. I could—see you. I was dreaming about you. I thought you were going down a long road and waving back to me. So I came down. I—I— [*She suddenly sobs and buries her head in his breast. He is very shaken and tries to control himself by being humorous*]

O'FLINGSLEY. There, silly! I'm not going away. I'm going to stay here and grow a mustache, and play bowls with the Canon.

BRIGID [*looking at him*]. No . . . you're going away . . . You're to— "to take up your bed—"

O'FLINGSLEY [*startled*]. Brigid! Is that the message?

BRIGID [*simply*]. Yis, Master . . . and you're to try to love people when they're dirty because any ass can love them when they're clean.

O'FLINGSLEY [*after a pause, vigorously*]. You dreamt that!

BRIGID. No . . . she said it. She'd have said more only Miss Cooney was annoyin' her dustin' and cleanin'. She went away then . . .

O'FLINGSLEY [*pensively*]. Take up my bed and walk . . . I wonder what exactly that means?

BRIGID. I don't know . . . she said *you'd* know. . . .

O'FLINGSLEY. Yes . . . maybe I do. Brigid, I *am* going away.

BRIGID. I knew . . .

O'FLINGSLEY. If I could just shake this fear off me—this fear of hunger . . . of money . . . of the cold. . . .

BRIGID. It will be terrible, Master, when I see you comin' up the school road, and you not comin' at all. But I'll still have the Canon.

O'FLINGSLEY. The Canon! That man!

BRIGID. Yis, Master . . . Oh, I know you have the dagger for him because he can hurt and say killin' words . . . *You* see him when he's proud, but I see him when he's prayin' in his little place and the tears on his cheeks; *you* see him when he dines but *I* see him when he fasts; *you* see him when his head is up and fiery like a lion, but *I* see his head when it's down low and his words won't come . . . It's because of that, that *you* hate him and *I* love him . . .

St. Brigid says that if we could all see each other all the time in big hangin' mirrors, the whole hate of the world would turn into dust.

O'FLINGSLEY [*touched*]. I'll remember that always, Brigid. And I'll remember you too.

BRIGID. It wouldn't matter not rememberin' *me*, if you'd remember *it*. [*They are staring at each other as the* CANON *appears at the window. His brow clouds. He comes forward into the room and for a moment regards them both*]

CANON [*sharply*]. Brigid, what is this? How dare you leave your bed in your sick state and in this attire? [BRIGID *looks from the* CANON *to* O'FLINGSLEY *and back again. She continues to look at both of them. They are a little uncomfortable, and eye each other surreptitiously*]

BRIGID. I wanted to come down . . . to see—the two of yous.

CANON. For what purpose?

BRIGID. I—I don't know, Canon . . . I just wanted to—to be sure that I loved the two of yous and could serve yous always. [*Pause.* JEMIMA *comes rushing in*]

JEMIMA. Canon! [*She stops short on seeing* BRIGID]

CANON. Preposterous! Miss Cooney, I cannot congratulate you on your care of Brigid.

JEMIMA. It was when I was out findin' you, Canon, that she left her bed.

CANON. Brigid, I am displeased.

BRIGID. Yis, Canon . . . and so is the Master.

CANON [*with glance at* O'FLINGSLEY]. Brigid, go back to bed with Miss Cooney.

JEMIMA [*taking her arm*]. Come on now. Annoyin' the Canon like this.

O'FLINGSLEY. Good-bye, Brigid.

BRIGID [*turning*]. Master! . . . [*She turns to get back, but* JEMIMA *won't let her*]

JEMIMA. Never mind *him*. Come on when you're told.

CANON. Let her come, Miss Cooney. [JEMIMA *releases her. She comes back to* O'FLINGSLEY, *and gives him her hand. She looks up at him*]

BRIGID. Good-bye, Master. And—I love you. [*She looks up at him emotionally. He bends and kisses her hair softly. The* CANON *stands like a statue, his feelings masked completely.* BRIGID *turns and goes with* JEMIMA]

CANON [*as* JEMIMA *takes* BRIGID'S *arm*]. That could have been gentler, Miss Cooney. I will have it so.

JEMIMA. Sure I'm not sayin' a word at all to her, Canon. [*They go.* O'FLINGSLEY *and the* CANON *both regard each other in silence for a moment. One can see them as if shedding their finer feelings and donning their fighting equipment*]

O'FLINGSLEY. Well, Canon? You sent for me.

CANON [*quietly*]. You may be seated, O'Flingsley. [O'FLINGSLEY *sits frankly and without nervousness, in a chair. The* CANON *goes to desk and sits in his large chair. A pause*] O'Flingsley, for some time past, I have had ample grounds for complaint both against your person and your work.

O'FLINGSLEY. *I* have a goodly few complaints also. Perhaps they will cancel each other out.

CANON [*eyebrows raised*]. *You* have complaints, O'Flingsley? I did not think it was considered a—a suitable attitude in a teacher to have complaints.

O'FLINGSLEY [*stung*]. You forget, Canon, that I am "that man O'Flingsley" first, and your schoolmaster second.

CANON [*ironically*]. Very novel, and shall we use that hateful word, modern?

O'FLINGSLEY. If it's something ancient, very ancient you want, here you are:—[*Very rapidly on his fingers*] No coal, no handle on sweeping-brush, no caretaker for the school, no windows that aren't stuck fast; eighteen crumbling desks, six broken panes of glass, no lighting on dark days, and the public highway of the Saorstat Cireann for a playground. And these complaints render my attitude—unsuitable.

CANON [*unperturbed*]. Your enunciation is very imperfect for a teacher, O'Flingsley. I missed quite half of them. Besides, these alleged deficiencies are not complaints. They are officially termed "Recommendations in Writing to the Very Reverend Manager."

O'FLINGSLEY. Or alternately, "Words Scrawled on the Sands by an Innocent."

CANON [*coldly*]. I will not—descend to you, O'Flingsley.

O'FLINGSLEY. You sent for me, Canon, to say something and you haven't said it yet.

CANON. I'll say it now, O'Flingsley. I'll say it now. [*Bending over*] Your mother's name was Gibney.

O'FLINGSLEY [*with a slight start*]. So it was, Canon.

CANON [*grimly*]. Your father's second name was Eugene.

O'FLINGSLEY [*now reckless*]. It was. And if you're as interested as all that in my genealogy, I had a grandmother that was called Poppet, an uncle that could spit over his own shoulder, and a paralyzed aunt that was christened Delia Diana. But I never had a niece that was called after me, thank God.

CANON [*controlling his anger*]. I'll be—calm, O'Flingsley. I'll be—logical. I—I won't descend to you. [*Holding up press cuttings from desk*] I note from these cuttings of *your* book *I Am Sir Oracle*, that the Church of Ireland is controlled by a—a red army of turkey-cocks.

O'FLINGSLEY. If you have, Canon, that's always a big step forward.

CANON [*grimly, his eye gleaming*]. And I see that our educational system is the—the sewage of European culture. I'd never have thought it, O'Flingsley. Could you tell me, on what page of your teacher's Penny Catechism I could find it?

O'FLINGSLEY [*with venom*]. On the page, Canon, the Bishops won't add until they're made.

CANON [*striking desk*]. Damnation! I'll not have—*that!* [*He jumps up fiercely*]

O'FLINGSLEY [*also jumping up*]. And hell and blazes, but you'll have to! [*They face each other on the floor, the masks now off completely. A pause as they regard each other venomously. The* CANON *composes himself with a great effort*]

CANON [*with composure*]. O'Flingsley, do you know Francis Ignatius O'Connor?

O'FLINGSLEY. Who doesn't? [*Imitating* FRANCIS] "Sure, Lord now, Canon!"

CANON [*grimly*]. I—I'm expecting him.

O'FLINGSLEY. I rather thought you were. And his—virgin consort, Aunt Jemima too, of course.

CANON [*fuming*]. In my—my forty years as a priest—

O'FLINGSLEY. You played the turkey-cock with your teachers, and made them your slavish handymen.

CANON [*with some composure*]. No . . . I—I will not stoop! I will not argue. To argue is to assume equality.

O'FLINGSLEY. And equality of course would mean the end of your precious managerial system of education that's the laughing-stock of Europe. That would never do, Canon. By all means, spit on me. [FRANCIS O'CONNOR *comes to the door, left awkwardly. He is rather excited*]

FRANCIS. Can I come in, Canon? I'm back with good news!

CANON. Good news will keep, Francis. Be seated.

FRANCIS [*exuberantly*]. Sure I—I can't keep it, Canon. Your niece has done me the honor of promisin' to be me wife. Everythin's lovely and grand, Canon! [O'FLINGSLEY *chuckles merrily*]

O'FLINGSLEY. Hurrah for the Catholic ideal! A rebel knocked out; a niece married off; and a school made safe for a stagnant tradition all in the one move! Canon, you deserve a seat in Maynooth. [FRANCIS *stares at him goggle-eyed*]

CANON. Take no heed of that man, Francis. He's an occasion of sin. Allow me instead to congratulate you. [*To* O'FLINGSLEY, *grimly turning*] Need I say any more, O'Flingsley? Need I say that Francis will—take over your duties at the end of the month?

O'FLINGSLEY. And I'm—fired?

CANON [*dignifiedly*]. "Dismissed" is the word, O'Flingsley. [*They regard each other grimly*]

O'FLINGSLEY. I somehow feel we'll meet again, we two.

CANON. I trust not.

O'FLINGSLEY [*to* FRANCIS]. And now, O'Connor, you're an Irish schoolmaster! In other words, a clerical handyman, a piece of furniture in a chapel house, a brusher-out of barn schools, a Canon's yesman.

CANON [*as* FRANCIS *goggles*]. You heard that—that man, Francis!

FRANCIS. He'll never have anny luck, Canon. Sure, leave him to God.

CANON. An excellent suggestion, Francis, and it will save me from descending to him. [*To* o'FLINGSLEY] At the end of the month, then, O'Flingsley . . . And that will be all, thank you. [o'FLINGSLEY *crosses*]

O'FLINGSLEY [*turning*]. I'll leave tomorrow, Canon, without pay, and give over the school to your handyman, if you'll answer me one question before I go.

CANON. Your question, O'Flingsley, may have an answer from us if it is —suitable.

O'FLINGSLEY. As a scholar who knows what he won't publicly admit, you loathe and detest the whole miserable fabric of things here. You detest that disgraceful apology for a school down there, even more than *I* do. I know that because I'm not a fool whatever else I am. Why then do you deliberately prepare to perpetuate it through that poor spineless imbecile there beside you?

FRANCIS [*outraged*]. Canon! He's insultin' me. I'd make him take that back. [*The* CANON's *eyes meet* o'FLINGSLEY's *eyes challengingly, in a silent tense duel. Pause*]

CANON [*tensely*]. That will be all, O'Flingsley.

O'FLINGSLEY [*venomously*]. Afraid, Canon? But the heartbreak is there all the same. *You* know it, and I know it. However, I'll always owe you something for taking me by the scruff of the neck out of a mouse's hiding place and putting me back on the high road. Good-bye, Canon, you will be remembered, if at all, not as a classicist, nor as a priest, but for your love for a poor little miserable child.

CANON [*his voice trembling with passion*]. That will—be all, O'Flingsley. [o'FLINGSLEY *turns and snapping up his hat, walks quickly off. The* CANON, *oblivious of* FRANCIS, *stares after him unseeingly.* FRANCIS *is standing flabbergasted and open-mouthed*]

FRANCIS. Is he mad or what, Canon?

CANON [*after a pause*]. Conceivably, Francis . . . conceivably. . . .

CURTAIN

ACT FOUR

SCENE: *The Same. The following morning.*

*On the window, back, there are beautiful long white curtains reaching to the ground, and on the table a great vase of white lilies. The* CANON *rises from the dining table and wipes his mouth with a napkin.* MISS COONEY *enters with a wrapped box.*

JEMIMA. This, Canon, came in from Driscall's of Dundalk. It's the hat and veil you sent in for.

CANON. Just leave it. [*She puts down box*] And undo the string. Are the Fathers finished Mass yet?

JEMIMA. Father Kirwan's takin' off his vestments, Canon. He'll be in for breakfast in a minute. Father Corr had his, this hour since.

CANON. Very well then. And Brigid?

JEMIMA. She was asleep when I riz at seven, Canon. And she didn't call since.

CANON. You should have brought her a cup of tea.

JEMIMA. She was twistin' and fidgettin' durin' the night, Canon, and I thought it best to let her sleep on. It's what the doctor said. [*She suddenly sees the white curtains and starts visibly*] Canon! Who—who changed the curtains? It was the rose-red ones that was on, and I goin' through to your own Mass at seven, and I never noticed nothin' till now. Oh! and them lilies on the table too!

CANON [*staring at flowers and curtains*]. Was it not yourself?

JEMIMA. It was not, then, Canon. I'm sure o' that. They didn't need changin'. [*Pause*] It—it was *her*, I'll bet. [FATHER KIRWAN *comes in bareheaded through the window. He stands and looks on*]

CANON. Who is *her*? Explain yourself.

JEMIMA. Brigid, I mean, Canon. She done it maybe, and I out at Mass.

CANON. What grounds have you for such a statement?

JEMIMA. It was the meanderin' talk of her durin' the night, Canon. She kept sayin' that someone went always in white a long time ago.

CANON. Am I to take it then, that this sick child whom I have placed in your care, has been wandering about in this cold room, bare-footed and undressed?

JEMIMA. But sure, Canon, I had to go to Mass.

CANON. You should have missed Mass in the circumstances.

JEMIMA. But I was makin' a novena for poor Francis.

CANON. I don't care if you were making fifty novenas.

JEMIMA [*sniffing*]. You're wrongin' me, Canon. But sure no matter. I'll not defend myself.

CANON. I want none of this palaver. I want practical wisdom and sound sense. Go to Brigid now and see to her comfort.

JEMIMA. It's what you say, Canon. [*To* FATHER KIRWAN] Will you serve yourself, Father?

FATHER KIRWAN. Sure, and I can. Go ahead and see after Brigie. [MISS COONEY *goes, left.* FATHER KIRWAN *sits and starts his breakfast*]

FATHER KIRWAN. What is it all about, Canon?

CANON. Brigid seems to have risen during my Mass and put up white curtains and decorated the table with flowers. [FATHER KIRWAN *looks at the curtains and flowers*]

FATHER KIRWAN [*smiling*]. She gets the funniest notions. . . . They say her mother, before she was sent away, used to wear her boots on the wrong feet for pure contrariness. [MISS COONEY *re-enters hurriedly*]

JEMIMA [*fearfully*]. Canon! She—she's not there!

CANON [*sharply*]. Not where?

JEMIMA. In the bed, Canon.

CANON [*irascibly*]. What new sort of stupidity is this?

FATHER KIRWAN. Did you try the kitchen?

JEMIMA. I did, Father. She's nowhere about the house.

FATHER KIRWAN. I'll bet she crossed the fields over to St. Brigid's Shrine. This is her feast day—the first of February.

JEMIMA. Sure, it's an Irish mile if it's a yard, Father. Maybe it's down to the schoolmaster she went.

FATHER KIRWAN. That low scum! I hope not, for her own sake.

JEMIMA. Troth, Father, she had a likin' that didn't become her at all for that fella. I was goin' to warn his reverence. . . .

CANON [*irascibly*]. This conjecturing is both ludicrous and undignified. It is obvious that the child's mind is in a very weak state, and that she has wandered aimlessly on to the roads. Miss Cooney, I haven't the slightest hesitation in reprimanding you for neglect of duty.

JEMIMA. It's not for me to answer you back, Canon, but I advised you a few times that she was wake in the mind, as her mother was, and that she needed . . .

CANON [*cutting in*]. I am not concerned with your advice, Miss Cooney. Go out and search for her instead. And you, Father Kirwan, if you are free will also join . . .

FATHER KIRWAN [*rising enthusiasm*]. I'll take the wee car, Canon, and I'll cover the whole parish in a flash. The new gear box, Canon, that . . .

CANON. You will walk! I am averse to cinematic exhibitions on the parochial roads, because our servant has—mislaid herself. And if I may add, Father . . . [*The* CANON *stops abruptly to stare at* BRIGID *who suddenly comes in by the window. She is dressed all in white, is neat and comely, matter-of-fact and practical in manner, and is smiling slightly. She leans against the curtains—a white picture in a white frame. All turn and stare at her*]

CANON. Brigid! What does this mean?

BRIGID. Please, Canon, I had—things to do. So I riz.

CANON. I am incensed and angry.

BRIGID. Not *this* day, Canon, please. Tomorrow maybe . . . [*Pause*] Do you like my white curtains?

FATHER KIRWAN. So it *was* you changed them!

BRIGID. Yes . . . just at dawn and the sky whitenin'. It had to be then.

JEMIMA. The curtains didn't need changin' at all, until Friday, Canon.

CANON. Have you any answer to that?

BRIGID. I just—felt they did. I thought them red ones would be a show before—before anyone comin'. [*She hangs her head*]

CANON. Brigid, I want no nonsense, but sound sense. In leaving your bed you were disobedient.

BRIGID. Yis, Canon. I thought, Canon, that the flowers and me white curtains and me white dress would please you. And—anyone comin' too.

CANON. Instead, you have gravely *dis*pleased me. Where have you been?

BRIGID. In the chapel, Canon. Sure you gave me Communion yourself.

[FATHER CORR *appears back, and comes in through window bareheaded*]

CANON. Eh? I—I what?

BRIGID. Sure, you didn't know me in me white dress. I was near laughin' . . . Father Corr wouldn't have seen me either only he plopped down beside me behind the pillar. [*A pause.* BRIGID *hangs her head*]

BRIGID [*hesitant*]. You—you're angry, Canon.

CANON. I am more than angry. I am disgusted.

JEMIMA. Will I put her back to bed, Canon?

BRIGID. Please no, Canon. I hate bed.

CANON. Very well then, for the present. Take her, Miss Cooney, and give her breakfast. And then, Brigid, I wish to speak to you.

JEMIMA. Come on now, and no nonsense.

BRIGID [*going to* CANON]. *I* want to speak to *you* too, Canon, if you'll let me.

CANON. All of the speaking will be done by me. You will go now.

BRIGID. But—I don't want any breakfast.

CANON. What's that?

FATHER CORR. She specially wants to fast till midday, Canon. I spoke to her against it, but it was no use.

CANON. The Church requires no such penance from a sick child. You will go, Brigid. I forbid this.

BRIGID. But I—I can't, Canon. I promised.

CANON. Miss Cooney, prepare Brigid's breakfast and inform me when it is ready.

JEMIMA. I will, Canon. And that's the right way. Such contrariness and stubbornness! Her mother too—

CANON. You will go, Miss Cooney. [JEMIMA *with a gulp, goes, left.* FATHER KIRWAN *rises from breakfast and crosses*]

FATHER KIRWAN [*apologetically*]. If you'll excuse *me*, I have a meetin' of the football team to attend. [*To* FATHER CORR] Aren't *you* comin', too, Father? It's near ten. We'll take the car.

FATHER CORR. Get the engine started up, and I'll be out after you.

FATHER KIRWAN. Hurry then. We'll have to stop at Ryan's for petrol. [*As he crosses*] Brigie, if you go in and wallop a plate of bacon and eggs, I'll give you a whizz this evenin' in the car. There now!

BRIGID. Not this day, father, but another day.

FATHER KIRWAN. Go on now. You're annoyin' the Canon. And I'll learn you to drive as well.

BRIGID. But, father, I've promised and given me word. . . . Do you think I could bear to break it, and me with a white dress on me too. It would be terrible.

FATHER KIRWAN. Ach, you're a blather! I'll buy you a football jersey.

[*He goes out with a wave.* FATHER CORR *walks uneasily about. He is ill at ease under* BRIGID'S *gaze*]

BRIGID. Please stay—with us here, Father Corr, and—don't go.

FATHER CORR. Brigid, won't you just be a good girl and leave *us* to look after our own business?

CANON. What is going on here that I am not aware of?

FATHER CORR [*evasively*]. Just a meetin' of the football team, Canon. [*A tense pause*]

BRIGID [*bursting out*]. If—if Mr. O'Flingsley done one thing wrong, he'll surely do twinty things right. [*Both turn and stare at her. The* CANON *is mystified.* FATHER CORR *is confused*]

CANON. O'Flingsley? . . . What—what on earth is this?

BRIGID [*in pain*]. The men's havin' a meetin', Canon. There's goin' to be talk and then stones and sticks.

FATHER CORR [*sharply*]. What talk is this *you* have?

CANON. What? . . . What do you know of this, Brigid?

BRIGID. If I told you, Canon, you would say I—I wasn't well.

CANON. Pht! Of course you are not well! You are ill! You are very ill! [*To* FATHER CORR] What truth is there in this, Father Corr?

FATHER CORR [*stiffly*]. Instead of answering that, Canon, might I ask instead why *we* weren't told that that scoundrel, O'Flingsley, was the author of that blasphemous book we read?

CANON. Because it was sufficient for the purposes of the Church that *I* knew of it.

FATHER CORR. These are new times, Canon. Neither we nor the people down there consider that satisfactory.

CANON. There is only one time in God's Church, Father Corr. [*Grimly*] And I expect my rulings to be obeyed.

FATHER CORR. In canonical matters, yes.

CANON. In all matters affecting the dignity of the Church.

FATHER CORR. We made it our business to warn this scoundrel to be clear out of this parish by this morning. If he is still here it is *his* look-out. I will try to moderate the feelings of the people, but I warn you I cannot cork them up in a bottle.

CANON. This is defiance!

FATHER CORR. No, Canon. It is legitimate action, since *you* won't move.

CANON. *Move?* I've dismissed the man summarily.

FATHER CORR. In our opinion, it is not enough.

CANON. It is a most severe sentence in any civilized community. The man's bread and butter.

FATHER CORR. Any bla'guard like *him* can get bread and butter, aye and honey too, in Ireland by slingin' mud at the Church.

CANON. Mud, Father Corr, sticks only to mud. But I would hardly expect that much philosophy from *you*.

FATHER CORR. I'm not here to talk sophistry, Canon. It glosses over unbearable insults. I'm a plain, blunt man.

CANON. Like Luther and Cromwell.

BRIGID. If the Master, Canon, was a bla'guard with terrible things in him, and not just a blunderer the same as Father Corr . . .

FATHER CORR. How dare you, Brigid!

CANON. That will do, Brigid. As usual, Father Corr, you are intemperate in your language, and chaotic in your feelings. I place both you and Father Kirwan under a strict rule of obedience. Any attempt at Dublin's holy hooliganism in *my* parish, will be rigorously met by *me*. Go down and acquaint this meeting of *that*. And in my name, dismiss it.

FATHER CORR. But what do you imagine they will think of me when . . .

CANON [*imperiously*]. I insist, Father Corr!

FATHER CORR. Very well, Canon. I'll—deliver your message. [*Very sulkily he goes, left.* BRIGID *goes close to the* CANON, *and looks at him solicitously*]

BRIGID. It's a mortal sin for us all, Canon, worryin' and annoyin' ye.

CANON [*softly*]. It is a worrying age, child. But what of it? As Don Miguel used to be fond of saying, "*Dios quie da la llaga, da la medicina.*"

BRIGID. And what does that mean, Canon?

CANON. It means, Brigid, that when God sends us evil, He sends with it the weapon to conquer it.

BRIGID. It's lovely. [*Pause*] Is a weapon, Canon, a sword?

CANON. God could make a weapon of anything, child.

BRIGID [*as in a dream*]. Yis. . . . *She* said that too . . . and she was sad. . . . [MISS COONEY *enters, left*]

JEMIMA. Brigid's breakfast is ready, Canon. And this letter's just come in for you. [*She hands* CANON *the letter which he proceeds to open and read.* BRIGID *looks very appealingly at him*]

CANON [*his eyes on the letter*]. Go, Brigid, and have a full meal. [BRIGID *goes dejectedly towards door, and then looks back pathetically at* CANON, *who is immersed in his letter*]

JEMIMA [*at door, waiting*]. Are ye goin' to be all day comin'?

BRIGID [*low*]. I'll be after ye in a minute. Sssh!

JEMIMA. I'll not ssh! at all. It'll be cold. Canon, how much more of her nonsense are we to put up with?

CANON [*finishing letter and looking up*]. You may go, Miss Cooney. Brigid will follow in a moment. [MISS COONEY *goes.* BRIGID *regards the* CANON *wistfully. He looks at her, half-ruffled, half lovingly*] Brigid, are *you* going to be a good girl?

BRIGID. Yis, Canon.

CANON. Excellent, Brigid. Come here! [*She comes to him softly*] This letter will give you a good appetite. It is from a great friend of mine in Bray. You will go up there, Brigid, for an excellent holiday, and I will put a whole five pound note in your bag. There now! And your hat! Why, I was forgetting all about your hat! [*Pointing*] There it is! It has a veil over your ear, Brigid—

BRIGID. My nose, Canon.

CANON. Your nose, Brigid. Your nose to be sure. And an ornament stuck at the side.

BRIGID. Is it a little white dog, Canon?

CANON. A dog? I believe it *is* a dog. I distinctly remember the manageress saying that dogs were the fashion.

BRIGID. So they are, Canon.

CANON. Excellent, Brigid. I consider dogs are in excellent taste myself. But you are not to see the hat now—not till you get your breakfast. Come now, are you pleased?

BRIGID [*softly*]. I—I could cry, Canon. I'll—anger you again and vex you. I—I know it.

CANON. No, Brigid. God will help you not to. You will be my friend instead. It is good to have a friend on a dark day. If anything is ever said of me, child, I want it to be that I found your face always full of grace and comely.

BRIGID. Don't say anythin' nice about me face, Canon, or I would want it to be like St. Brigid's face with the niceness torn out of it with pain.

CANON [*chidingly*]. There! There! Your mind must not dwell on these myths and fancies. What is God's, nothing can destroy. Go now, child, and have a good breakfast, and then we shall fit on your hat and arrange about your train. [BRIGID *moves towards doors, and then comes back pathetically*]

BRIGID [*shrewdly*]. Canon, if—if you made a great promise to—to Don Miguel or Don Pedro, would you keep it in face of everythin'?

CANON. Keep it? Why, most certainly, Brigid. A gentleman *always* keeps his promises, under penalty of dishonor. [*She looks at him pleadingly*]

BRIGID [*after a pause*]. That's why I don't want to—to eat till midday, Canon. I—I promised St. Brigid. [*The* CANON *starts visibly, realizing he is caught. He controls his feelings*]

CANON. Brigid, you are very trying. Will you eat if I, as the Canon, give you a special—a very special dispensation?

BRIGID. But it's for—the love of her, Canon, not as a penance. She asked me to prove I loved her.

CANON. To say she asked you is—inaccurate, Brigid. What you mean is that in praying to St. Brigid, you *told* her you would fast yourself. In that you were harder on yourself than the Church allows. Anything excessive, Brigid, is not classically Catholic.

BRIGID. She *did* ask me, Canon. But you won't believe me.

CANON [*ruffled*]. I thought, Brigid, we finished with this matter long ago!

BRIGID. I tried, Canon. But—she kept pleadin'—as if everythin' else was standin' waitin'. . . . She said I was to offer my Communion this mornin' for *you*, and my fast till midday for *you* too.

CANON [*after a pause*]. Brigid, for offering your Communion for me, I am indeed grateful. It is the act of my friend. But you must not think any *figure told* you to do this. The Church *frowns* at such imaginings, and she is very, very wise.

BRIGID. But there's—somethin' else, Canon. It's—killin' and killin' me. . . .

CANON [*holding himself in*]. I feel you're going to make me angry, Brigid.

BRIGID [*trembling*]. I—I know . . . I'm tremblin'. . . .

CANON [*touching her*]. There! My poor child, there! You are ill, and I will say no word. You may tell me. I will contain myself, Brigid. I will bear with you. Let it be written of me.

BRIGID. She told me to ask you, Canon to—come with me, wearin' your surplice and soutane, and I in this white dress, into the chapel yard today at twelve when the Angelus is ringin' and the people are comin' and goin'. [*The* CANON *is staring at her, holding himself desperately in leash.* BRIGID, *with tearful eyes, is looking up pleadingly at him*] We are to kneel down on the seventh flag from the door and I am to keep sayin' the prayer to St. Brigid. And you are to invoke her three times, and then kiss the stone and say, "Mary of the Gael, show us the way through the dark." And she promises that a stream of water, waitin' there for years, will gush out over the flagstone, and that the fingers of everyone will dip into it forever. [*Pause*] That —that's all, Canon. [*She stands visibly trembling, looking up at the* CANON *whose face is strained and masklike*] Please don't—shout and be angry with me, C-Canon. Just—just say, "G-go, B-Brigid!" [*The* CANON, *his hands clenched to his sides, turns and walks irascibly to the window and stares out. He is fighting desperately to control himself.* BRIGID *keeps watching him— her hand to her trembling mouth. In a few moments, he walks back to her with evident composure*]

CANON [*slowly*]. No, Brigid. I shall not shout or be hard on you. That would be unjust. Even if I am angry. Even if I am *very* angry. But I forgive you, Brigid. You are very ill. You are even more ill than I suspected.

BRIGID [*passionately*]. Canon, believe me! Believe me! I am weak tellin' you. I am not—able.

CANON. Brigid, by the grace of God, I am holding away my anger from you, for you are not deserving of it. If you were not ill, I should be disgusted. I make you my friend, and in return you ask me to be a—boobish sort of conjurer who draws rabbits out of a hat or water out of a stone for the gratification of oafs and idiots.

BRIGID. But sure, Canon, St. Brigid wouldn't belittle *you* and deceive *me*. She—she *couldn't*.

CANON. As you rightly say she couldn't, Brigid. As I explained, child, she wasn't—there.

BRIGID. But I saw her, Canon. And the mark on her face and all.

CANON. I know, Brigid. Our poor sick minds play with terrible pictures.

But *you* know nothing of such things. When you return from your holiday, you will say to me, "Canon, I was a little fool in the wind, and you were a big tree that gave me shelter." [*Enter* MISS COONEY]

JEMIMA. What will I do with Brigid's breakfast, Canon? It's goin' to loss.

CANON. Bring it here to this table, Miss Cooney, on a tray.

JEMIMA [*staring*]. Is it the—the priests' table you mean, Canon?

CANON. Obviously, Miss Cooney. [*With a perplexed bow, she goes*]

CANON. Come and sit down with me, Brigid, till I tell you something. [*He seats her on a couch and seats himself near her*]

BRIGID [*wretchedly*]. I am weak and useless. . . . I am not able. . . . St. Brigid will brush me name off her lips as if it was a piece of soot in the wind.

CANON [*chidingly*]. Brigid! Brigid! These morbid fancies! How now, can I speak to you if you go on giving rein to them like a willful child?

BRIGID. She said she wanted a miracle, Canon, since the world had become so hard. Somethin', she said, that would give us all new life and strength.

CANON [*gently*]. Listen to me, Brigid. When a woman in marriage gives birth to men, she proves herself a mother. Her men are all about her—justifying her. Suppose, Brigid, a fool came along and said, "Prove yourself a mother again," what would happen?

BRIGID. Sure they'd laugh, Canon.

CANON [*touching her shoulder*]. They'd laugh! Excellent, Brigid. You are following me with intelligence. Now, it is just like that with the Church. Her children have justified her eternally. She is venerable with holiness and heavy with the wisdom of ages. And yet, Brigid, you want her to give birth to a new child—to prove herself by a new miracle. St. Brigid would laugh heartily at such a thing. She, Brigid, that redeemed the world, you want her to produce rabbits out of a boob's hat!

BRIGID [*in tears*]. It wasn't like that, that I meant it, Canon.

CANON. You are just very young, Brigid, and your poor mind is ill. If you were as wise and old as me, Brigid, you would know that out there where you cannot see, there is a whole world of spiritual rowdies willing to sell themselves to anything that can produce signs and wonders to please their vanity. And there you are, Brigid, in the center of them, backing them up— you, the Canon's friend who should know better.

BRIGID [*woefully*]. Please, Canon, don't say that to me. . . . It's terrible. . . . I don't know where I am or what to think. It's like people that you love pullin' agin each other. . . . It's hard, Canon, the things that you love goin' crashin' down, as if they were timber fallin'.

CANON. You must learn to laugh, child, at the big shaky things that our poor sick minds build up, and our healthy minds pull down. There is great safety in the right kind of laughter. [MISS COONEY *enters and puts a tray of breakfast things on the dining table*]

JEMIMA. Please, Canon, make her take that now. I had to make fresh tea.

CANON. This very moment, Miss Cooney. [MISS COONEY *goes, left*] Come, Brigid. The Church very wisely tells us that our food is also important. [*He takes her to the table by the arm*] And you will sit at the top in the Canon's chair. [*As she seats herself shyly*] There now!

BRIGID. Please, Canon, *must* I eat?

CANON. Yes, Brigid.

BRIGID. Would you be angry if I didn't?

CANON. *Very* angry. And so would the Church. And St. Brigid too. St. Brigid, if you know anything of her, was a *very* sensible saint indeed.

BRIGID [*resigned*]. I'll—eat, then, Canon.

CANON. Excellent! A good meal now, and then we'll discuss your holiday and—your hat, Brigid. We mustn't forget your hat. That *too* is important. [*As he moves away*] I am going upstairs to attend to—a little matter.

BRIGID. Is it up to the little place off your bedroom that—

CANON [*hand up*]. That will do, Brigid. It is—my affair.

BRIGID. Yis, Canon. Please, Canon, will you—pray for me—too?

CANON [*after a pause*]. I will, child. For both of us. [*He goes out pensively.* BRIGID *lifts the teapot uncertainly, her hand trembles and she puts it down again. She looks towards the door fearfully. She sits a few moments in torment. There is a noise off. She shakingly pours out some tea. She adds sugar and cream in a dazed way. She lifts the cup halfway to her lips, puts it guiltily down, and buries her face in her hands*]

BRIGID. It's not fair . . . after me promisin' . . . and me white dress on me too. . . . [*She rises, her eyes on the curtains, and walks center*] I'm miserable and not able. . . . What name have you for me in your lovely mouth? Soot maybe, or clabber of the ground or maybe dung that smells. . . . [*Pathetically*] Oh, please no, not that! . . . Make it somethin' that has been burned in the fire . . . somethin' burned black with flame. . . . [*She turns sorrowfully back to table.* MISS COONEY *comes to the door*]

JEMIMA. Are ye done there yet? It's near half-eleven already. Why you didn't begin yet! If it's goin' on bein' contrary you are, I'll tell the Canon. [*Looking around*] Where *is* the Canon?

BRIGID. He's not to be disturbed.

JEMIMA. Did he say that?

BRIGID. No, Miss Cooney, but I know he meant it.

JEMIMA. Indeed! And them's *your* orders, are they?

BRIGID [*softly*]. How could I be givin' orders?

JEMIMA. You're daft enough for anythin'. And you're goin' to Dublin, are ye?

BRIGID. It's whatever the Canon says.

JEMIMA. Aye, well you'll not be the first in your family that's seen Nelson's Pillar.

BRIGID [*staring at her, very hurt*]. There's some terrible meanin' in that. You must be wicked and cruel. I can feel it in you.

JEMIMA. You hurry up there, or you'll feel me a good bit more.

BRIGID [*coweringly*]. Yis . . . I'll—eat now—in a minute. If only the Angelus would ring! . . . [THOMASINA CONCANNON *and* FRANCIS O'CONNOR *come in, arm-in-arm, in high spirits*]

THOMASINA. Is me uncle about, Jemima? Francis and meself want a word with him.

FRANCIS. It's about the weddin' arrangements, auntie.

JEMIMA. Sure he was here no time ago. Where did you say he went, Brigid?

BRIGID. He—didn't say.

JEMIMA [*sharply*]. Which way did he go?

BRIGID. He went out into the hall.

JEMIMA. He'll maybe be in his room. Wait now and I'll see.

THOMASINA. We just want to be sure, Jemima, he'll marry us himself, and not push us over to one of the curates. It's never just the same.

JEMIMA. Sure, surely to God, he wouldn't have a curate marryin' his own niece!

FRANCIS [*with a sheet of paper*]. And we want his leave, auntie, to put in the paper, "beloved niece of the Very Rev. Thomas Canon Skerritt. P.P."

JEMIMA. Sure just put it in, and say nothin' till after. Look at the fix you'll be in, if he says no. Have you *my* name in it too?

FRANCIS. Imagine askin' that, auntie!

JEMIMA. And your own middle name, Francis. The scuts o' the country have as many names as ourselves nowadays.

FRANCIS. It's all fireproof, auntie. Lord Macaulay couldn't do better.

JEMIMA. I hope so, after all the schoolin' and collegin' you got. I'll run up and get him for you. [*She goes off, left.* THOMASINA *and* FRANCIS *cross to* BRIGID, *who is moodily sitting with her head in her hands at the table*]

THOMASINA. Well, Brigid, are ye better?

BRIGID. Sure, I wasn't ill, Miss Concannon.

THOMASINA. Not ill? Sure the last time I was in, you were . . . .

FRANCIS [*digging* THOMASINA]. You're dreamin', Thomasina. Brigid wasn't ill.

THOMASINA [*with a giggle*]. Ach, sure of course she wasn't. It's me bein' in love, that's what it is!

BRIGID. Please take some tea, Miss Concannon. It's just fresh wet.

THOMASINA [*eagerly*]. I will in troth. [*Taking cup*] I could eat a cow! It's this love! Are ye finished with the cake there?

BRIGID [*eagerly*]. Yis. Please ate them all. Help her, Francis, if you like. The Canon gets mad when he sees food left over.

FRANCIS. Sure and I will. [*Taking a cake*] I had always a sweet tooth. Make a note o' that, sweetest one! Yum! This is a cocoanut one! [*Both start eating vigorously.* BRIGID *watches them evidently relieved*]

THOMASINA [*munching*]. I wonder if that's true about O'Flingsley—I mean what Dave Dooley was tellin' us below at the bridge, Francis?

FRANCIS. About the people goin' to give him a battherin'? Maybe it is. Anyway, he'll be a good riddance.

BRIGID [*trembling*]. Did—did you hear that? Are the people—sayin' it?

THOMASINA. Ach, behave yourself, Brigid! If they are itself, he deserves it.

BRIGID. But it's cruel and terrible. The Canon wouldn't see that done on him.

FRANCIS [*munching*]. The Canon? Sure, you could ate all the Canon likes of him.

BRIGID [*in pain*]. It's not true. . . . The Canon doesn't hate like that . . . and the Master doesn't hate like that either . . . I know what I'll do. I'll— [*Before the others can restrain her, she passes rapidly like a white vision through the white-curtained window. They stare after her, with pieces of cake in their hands and mouths. Then they look at each other and laugh spontaneously*]

FRANCIS. That one will get hurt if the stones start flyin'.

THOMASINA. The poor thing. It must be terrible to be mad in the head. Is it true, Francis, that they smother mad people in Dublin between blankets? [*Before* FRANCIS *can settle the point, the* CANON *enters, left. He is irascible and ruffled*]

CANON. Who wants me here? And for what purpose?

THOMASINA. Sure, it's just me and Francis, Uncle.

CANON. That much, I observe.

FRANCIS. Did we disturb ye now, Canon? Sure just say the word, Canon, and we'll come back any time.

CANON. I gave orders that I was not to be disturbed.

FRANCIS [*seizing* THOMASINA]. Come on now, Thomasina, and let us not be maddenin' His Reverence. We can come back later by the Canon's leave.

THOMASINA. But me mother's comin' on the two o'clock train, and she'll be mad to know everythin'.

CANON [*acidly*]. You will ask your questions concisely and without superfluity, and I shall answer them in—like manner. Proceed! [MISS COONEY *comes in to collect tea-tray.* THOMASINA *and* FRANCIS *regard each other uncertainly*]

FRANCIS. Sure, Canon, if you'd rather—

CANON. I said, proceed!

THOMASINA [*breathlessly*]. We want to know, uncle, if *you'll* marry us yourself?

CANON [*rapidly*]. No! Next question.

THOMASINA. But me mother will have a fit, uncle, if you don't.

CANON [*acidly*]. Superfluous! I have already suitably defined your mother.

JEMIMA [*at table, obsequiously*]. If I might humbly put in a word, Canon . . .

CANON. You might not, Miss Cooney. [MISS COONEY *goes, humbly*]

FRANCIS. Then I suppose, Canon, you won't allow us to put your name in the marriage notice in the papers?

CANON. Exactly, Francis. And that holds for birth notices too. Where is Brigid?

THOMASINA. She went out through the window, Canon, after we came in.

CANON [*irascibly*]. For what purpose?

FRANCIS. She heard Thomasina and meself, Canon, talkin' about that man O'Flingsley, and the things the people were sayin' down the town.

THOMASINA. And away she went like a madhead.

CANON [*irascibly*]. Why wasn't I told of this immediately instead of wasting time on trivialities? Run both of you instantly, and find her. The child is most unwell. Tell her the Canon wants her this very minute. [*He rushes them out by the window. As he returns,* FATHER KIRWAN *enters hurriedly by the door, wearing gauntlets*]

FATHER KIRWAN. Canon, I flew up in the wee car for you. Father Corr and I want your help.

CANON. Am I to be continually reminding you, Father Kirwan, that I don't give help? I give direction. [*Pause*] What new stupidity is afoot now?

FATHER KIRWAN. It's not our fault really, Canon. It's the men insisted on marching to that O'Flingsley fellow's house.

CANON. For what purpose?

FATHER KIRWAN. To warn him, as was resolved at the meetin', to be gone out of this district.

CANON. On what authority?

FATHER KIRWAN. Sure, Canon, the authority of angry men. [*Loud boohing and cheering from the distance*] Listen! There they're boohin' and shouting. Father Corr is trying to hold them down from anny violence.

CANON. And where might I ask is the Sergeant of police, when a brawl of this nature takes place?

FATHER KIRWAN. His wife's havin' a baby, Canon, and he can't come.

CANON. The sergeant a midwife, and my curates turned American lynchmen! Excellent! [FATHER CORR *enters rapidly by the door. He is excited*]

FATHER CORR. Canon, that fellow O'Flingsley is jeerin' at the people instead of goin' when he's told. He has them as angry as bulls. If you'd just come out and show yourself for a minute . . . [*More boohing and shouting from the distance*]

CANON [*severely*]. Did you and Father Kirwan march this—mob to O'Flingsley's house?

FATHER CORR. We did, Canon. It was—was up to us. But they're no mob, and they were in excellent order, till *he* started jeering.

FATHER KIRWAN. That's the down truth, Canon.

CANON. You are a sentimental youth, Father Corr, or you would know that all men in the mass are barbarians. Every year scores of decent Christians in America sprinkle Negroes with petrol and burn them because they love God and his justice. Yet, you *will* indulge in this—free Presbyterianism, this Lutheran zeal that the Church has never had any nonsense with in history. And in *my* parish too. [*Further bursts of boohing and shouting, and the noise of sticks and stones in the distance.* MISS COONEY *comes in rapidly*]

MISS COONEY [*very scared*]. Canon, did ye ever hear the like! The milkman's after tellin' me about Brigid. She's below holdin' on to the man O'Flingsley on the road, and a crowd peltin' him with sticks and stones.

THE CURATES [*startled*]. Canon!

CANON [*seized with fear*]. Brigid! This—this is defiance! . . . My hat and stick instantly. [MISS COONEY *rushes off. The* CANON *draws himself up to his full height and regards the* CURATES *imperiously*] I have long enough suffered boobs gladly both without and within. Now, I the Canon, will act, and I will have obedience and authority!

FATHER KIRWAN [*boyishly*]. Sure, it wasn't our fault at all, Canon. The men only got out of hand when that fellow, O'Flingsley . . .

CANON [*with a wave*]. Enough! [MISS COONEY *runs in with his stick and two hats, a soft one and a tall silk one. She fumbles nervously*]

MISS COONEY. Is it this one, Canon, or the tall one?

CANON [*Hurling soft hat across room and taking the tall one*]. The tall one. [*He dons it with an awesome sweep of the arm*] I will show these neo-theologians and football kickers of yours that the bulk of the people are not to do but to be done by.

FATHER KIRWAN [*stupidly*]. I'll whip ye down in the wee car in a jiffy, Canon.

CANON [*irascibly*]. Get behind me, fool. I'll walk. [MISS COONEY *and the two* CURATES *cower back as he marches intently towards the window, back. Before he reaches it, there is a commotion.* O'FLINGSLEY *appears in the opening with* BRIGID *lying in his arms. His hair is disheveled and his face streaked with blood and mud.* BRIGID'*s head is almost covered by a large white cloth—in fact, an apron,—and there are bloodstains upon her white dress. She is limp and inert*]

MISS COONEY [*hysterical*]. Canon! It's Brigid! They've kilt her!

FATHER CORR [*in anguish*]. It's not—not true! . . .

FATHER KIRWAN [*hand to face, shakingly*]. No! . . . No, no!

CANON [*hoarsely, doffing hat*]. In the name of God, O'Flingsley . . .

O'FLINGSLEY. I'm not asking protection for myself, Canon. But get a doctor for Brigid at once.

CANON [*controlling himself*]. Rush, Miss Cooney, for Dr. Connell. Say I said instantly. Fly, woman, dash!

MISS COONEY [*rushing out*]. I'll race, Canon. Mother o' God . . .

CANON [*arranging couch*]. Set her here, O'Flingsley.

FATHER KIRWAN [*in pain, bursting out*]. Canon, we didn't mean annythin'. God knows we didn't . . .

CANON [*almost inaudibly*]. Quiet, quiet. [O'FLINGSLEY *gently stretches* BRIGID *on the couch. He stands on one side and the* CANON *on the other. Each is striving desperately to control himself. The* CURATES *stand bowed with fear and remorse*]

CANON [*shakingly*]. God of mercy, do not take this, my one consolation away from me. . . . [*His voice breaks*] Is—is it serious, O'Flingsley?

O'FLINGSLEY. I'm afraid it is. [*They avoid each other's gaze*]

CANON [*as in a dream, huskily*]. What happened? T-tell me. . . .

O'FLINGSLEY [*passionately*]. She got half a brick that one of your hirelings intended for *me*.

CANON [*pathetic*]. They were not *my* hirelings, O'Flingsley. We are surely better enemies than that. [*Pause*] Where is the wound?

O'FLINGSLEY. Side of the head and upper part of the face. I'm afraid of concussion. It was a cruel blow. . . . As I ran with her, a woman poured a bottle of oil over it and tied her apron about her to stop the bleeding.

CANON [*bending, in pain*]. And this in the name of the Communion of Saints . . .

FATHER CORR [*emotionally breaking down*]. Canon, I can't bear it! I can't bear it! . . . God knows I meant no blood or violence . . . that I wouldn't hurt anythin' livin'. . . . I—I never thought . . . I never thought . . .

FATHER KIRWAN [*soothing him*]. There now, there! Let ye hold on to yourself now. Sure the Canon knows. And Brigie will be all right in a minute.

FATHER CORR [*hysteric*]. I did it! I did it! . . . I wasn't wise like—like the Canon . . . I—I only meant, Canon—

CANON [*not unkindly*]. Father Corr, you will control your emotion.

FATHER CORR. Y-yes, Canon.

CANON. And cease allowing it to run you into fresh idiocies.

FATHER KIRWAN. I'll take him out to the fresh air, Canon.

CANON. You will both go out to these people, and order them in my name to return instantly to their homes and their work.

FATHER CORR. Very well, Canon. [*They go out, back,* FATHER KIRWAN *assisting* FATHER CORR. *The* CANON *bends in fear over to the couch*]

CANON. Will that doctor ever come! . . . Could we do anything of ourselves? God would guide us surely.

O'FLINGSLEY [*cautiously*]. Better not. If the blood started . . .

CANON [*drawing bandages slightly*]. My God, my God, what have they done? Did she speak at all, O'Flingsley?

O'FLINGSLEY. She whispered something about the Angelus bell and you. Then she sank into this.

CANON [*huskily*]. We are all in this—this dark she lies in, only deeper than her. . . . Brigid, I am with you, the Canon, your friend. . . .

O'FLINGSLEY. There may be hope, if only that doctor is not playing golf. . . .

CANON [*wringing his hands*]. It is like that—always—stupidities lying in the way. . . . God! Hasten him! Hasten him out! . . . [*At this moment, the Angelus Bell begins ringing clearly from the Church tower outside.* BRIGID *groans, stirs weakly and moves her head. They regard her emotionally*]

O'FLINGSLEY [*softly*]. Brigid . . . it's the Canon and I.

BRIGID [*weakly*]. The man O'Flingsley. . . . [*Moving painfully*] The—the Angelus . . . the Angelus . . . and I'm not—able. . . . Canon, make me able. . . .

CANON. I am here, Brigid. But you must not speak. You are very ill, poor child.

BRIGID [*as in a dream*]. There's blood on the Master's head. . . . I felt it. . . . Then the stone came . . . with the pain in it . . . and I knew my face was like St. Brigid's then . . . torn and hurt. . . . My mouth is burnin' . . . me. . . . [*The* CANON *pours a little of his Spanish wine into a glass and brings it towards her*]

O'FLINGSLEY. The Canon is right this time, Brigid. You must lie very still and not talk till the doctor comes.

BRIGID. But how can I rest . . . and that bell ringin'. . . . The Canon knows . . . Canon! . . .

CANON. There, child! I am here with you. . . . You must take a sip of this wine to strengthen you. . . . [*She takes a few sips from the glass*]

BRIGID. Don Miguel's wine. . . . He said to the Canon, "Where there is truth there is God.". . . I wish I could rise up, and be *true* to her . . . and not false. . . . But I'm not able. . . .

CANON [*striving to hold in his emotions*]. Brigid, if you will live for me, live on as the Canon's friend, I will do what you want. I will bend for you. The Canon will bend. He will stoop. He will—believe. . . .

BRIGID [*weakly, struggling*]. C-Canon! . . . I—I want to live for that . . . I must live . . . I must show you the stone . . . and my white dress on . . . me. . . .

O'FLINGSLEY [*tenderly supporting her*]. Yes, Brigid, but not till the doctor examines you.

BRIGID [*weakly moving*]. But there is no time, Master . . . no time. . . . The Angelus will soon not be ringin'. . . .

O'FLINGSLEY. She's fighting hard as if there was something that mattered a lot.

CANON. So there is. . . . [*Emotionally*] So there is. . . .

BRIGID [*rising a little, painfully*]. Make me able, Canon. I want to keep faith with her. I want her to see me face like hers. . . . I want to be a white rose in her mouth . . . not a smut of soot brushed away. . . . [*She rises still more—only her eyes and brow and hair visible and glowing above the bandages*] I want to see your face stooped, Canon, in the way she said . . . and the love of the little things in it. . . . I want to dip me fingers in the new water, and to say what she told me, "Mary of the Gael, show us the way . . . through the dark.". . . [*For a moment her face is poised eloquently. The Angelus bell ceases. She suddenly collapses back, and lies still. The* CANON *buries his face in his hands.* O'FLINGSLEY *stifles a sob*]

CANON [*shakingly*]. Tell me, O'Flingsley. No, no. Don't—don't say it. . . .

O'FLINGSLEY [*simply*]. It's one of the things must be said, Canon. She's dead. . . .

CANON. God . . . God . . . Have I blundered? [O'FLINGSLEY *takes up a coverlet to draw it over* BRIGID'*s face, but the* CANON *pathetically intervenes, childishly*] No, no. Let—let *me*, O'Flingsley. . . . Let *me*.

O'FLINGSLEY [*slowly*]. Let both of us. . . . [*Terribly*] It will be—worthy of us. . . . [*Together they draw the coverlet over* BRIGID'*s face. Their eyes meet fully for the first time, and hold each other over* BRIGID'*s body. Then slowly each moves slowly back in different directions*]

CANON [*huskily, as* O'FLINGSLEY *nears the door*]. No, no. . . . Do not leave me, O'Flingsley. . . . I am alone. . . .

O'FLINGSLEY [*turning slowly*]. I must. [*Very low*]. We must work this out. . . . Innocent blood. . . .

CANON [*hands to face, shakingly*]. Am I just an embittered old man . . . living here with shades too glorious to forget? [*For a moment,* O'FLINGSLEY *regards him from the doorway, his face a study—in mingled hate, pity and respect. He turns slowly and goes out. A moment passes. The* CANON *sits down heavily. He lifts heavy weary eyes to the couch and the empty room*]

CANON [*his head down again, slowly*]. I am not well. . . .

**SLOW CURTAIN**

# EYE-WITNESS

## *Ridgely Torrence* (*1925*)

Down by the railroad in a green valley
By dancing water, there he stayed awhile
Singing, and three men with him, listeners,
All tramps, all homeless reapers of the wind,

Motionless now and while the song went on     5
Transfigured into images thronged with visions;
There with the late light of the sunset on them
And on clear water spinning from a spring

Through little cones of sand dancing and fading,
Close beside pine woods where a hermit-thrush                                    10
Cast, when love dazzled him, shadows of music
That lengthened, fluting, through the singer's pauses
While the sure earth rolled eastward bringing stars
Over the singer and the men that listened
There by the roadside, understanding all.                                        15
A train went by but nothing seemed to be changed
Some eye at a car window must have flashed
From the plush world inside the glassy Pullman,
Carelessly bearing off the scene for ever,
With idle wonder what the men were doing,                                        20
Seeing they were so strangely fixed, and seeing
Torn papers from their smeary, dreary meal
Spread on the ground with old tomato cans
Muddy with dregs of lukewarm chicory,
Neglected while they listened to the song.                                       25
And while he sang the singer's face was lifted,
And the sky shook down a soft light upon him
Out of its branches where like fruits there were
Many beautiful stars and planets moving,
With lands upon them, rising from their seas,                                    30
Glorious lands with glittering sands upon them,
With soils of gold and magic mould for seeding,

The shining loam of lands afoam with gardens
On mightier stars with giant rains and suns
There in the heavens; but on none of all                                         35
Was there ground better than he stood upon:
There was no world there in the sky above him
Deeper in promise than the earth beneath him
Whose dust had flowered up in him the singer
And three men understanding every word.                                          40

### The Tramp Sings:

I will sing, I will go, and never ask me why.
I was born a rover and a passer-by.

I seem to myself like water and sky,
A river and a rover and a passer-by.

But in the winter three years back      45
We lit us a night fire by the track,

And the snow came up and the fire it flew
And we couldn't find the warming room for two.

One had to suffer, so I left him the fire
And I went to the weather from my heart's desire,                               50

It was night on the line, it was no more fire,
But the zero whistle through the icy wire.

As I went suffering through the snow
Something like a shadow came moving slow.

I went up to it and I said a word;      55
Something flew above it like a kind of bird.

I leaned in closer and I saw a face;
A light went round me but I kept my
place.

My heart went open like an apple
sliced;                                    59
I saw my Saviour and I saw my Christ.

Well, you may not read it in a book,
But it takes a gentle Saviour to give a
gentle look.

I looked in his eyes and I read the
news;
His heart was having the railroad
blues.

Oh, the railroad blues will cost you
dear,                                      65
Keeps you moving on for something
that you don't see here.

We stood and whispered in a kind of
moon;
The line was looking like May and
June.

I found he was a roamer and a journey
man,
Looking for a lodging since the night
began.                                     70

He went to the doors but he didn't
have the pay,
He went to the windows, then he
went away.

Says: "We'll walk together and we'll
both be fed."
Says: "I will give you the 'other'
bread."

Oh, the bread he gave and without
money!                                     75
O drink, O fire, O burning honey!

It went all through me like a shining
storm:
I saw inside me, it was light and
warm.

I saw deep under and I saw above,
I saw the stars weighed down with
love.                                      80

They sang that love to burning birth,
They poured that music to the earth.

I heard the stars sing low like mothers.
He said: "Now look, and help feed
others."                                   84

I looked around, and as close as touch
Was everybody that suffered much.

They reached out, there was darkness
only;
They could not see us, they were
lonely.

I saw the hearts that deaths took hold
of,
With the wounds bare that were not
told of;                                   90

Hearts with things in them making
gashes;
Hearts that were choked with their
dreams' ashes;

Women in front of the rolled-back
air,
Looking at their breasts and nothing
there;

Good men wasting and trapped in
hells;                                     95
Hurt lads shivering with the fare-
thee-wells.

I saw them as if something bound
them;
I stood there but my heart went round
them.

I begged him not to let me see them
  wasted.
Says: "Tell them then what you have
  tasted."                                    100

I told him I was weak as a rained-on
  bee;
Told him I was lost.—Says: "Lean on
  me."

Something happened then I could not
  tell,
But I knew I had the water for every
  hell.

Any other thing it was no use bringing;                                        105
They needed what the stars were
  singing,

What the whole sky sang like waves
  of light,
The tune that it danced to, day and
  night.

Oh, I listened to the sky for the tune
  to come;
The song seemed easy, but I stood
  there dumb.                                 110

The stars could feel me reaching
  through them;
They let down light and drew me to
  them.

I stood in the sky in a light like day,
Drinking in the word that all things
  say

Where the worlds hang growing in
  clustered shapes                            115
Dripping the music like wine from
  grapes.

With "Love, Love, Love," above the
  pain,
—The vinelike song with its winelike
  rain.

Through heaven under heaven the
  song takes root
Of the turning, burning, deathless
  fruit.                                      120

I came to the earth and the pain so
  near me,
I tried that song but they couldn't
  hear me.

I went down into the ground to grow
A seed for a song that would make
  men know.

Into the ground from my Roamer's
  light,                                      125
I went; he watched me sink to night.

Deep in the ground from my human
  grieving,
His pain ploughed in me to believing.

Oh, he took earth's pain to be his
  bride,
While the heart of life sang in his side.

For I felt that pain, I took its kiss,    131
My heart broke into dust with his.

Then sudden through the earth I
  found life springing;
The dust men trampled on was singing.

Deep in my dust I felt its tones;         135
The roots of beauty went round my
  bones.

I stirred, I rose like a flame, like a
  river,
I stood on the line, I could sing for
  ever.

Love had pierced into my human
  sheathing,
Song came out of me simple as breathing.                                        140

A freight came by, the line grew
   colder.
He laid his hand upon my shoulder.

Says, "Don't stay on the line such
   nights,"
And led me by the hand to the station
   lights.

I asked him in front of the station-
   house wall              145
If he had lodging. Says: "None at
   all."

I pointed to my heart and looked in
   his face.—
"Here,—if you haven't got a better
   place."

He looked and he said: "Oh, we still
   must roam
But if you'll keep it open, well, I'll
   call it 'home.' "          150

The thrush now slept whose pillow
   was his wing.
So the song ended and the four re-
   mained
Still in the faint starshine that silvered
   them,
While the low sound went on of
   broken water
Out of the spring and through the
   darkness flowing       155
Over a stone that held it from the sea.
Whether the men spoke after could
   not be told,
A mist from the ground so veiled
   them, but they waited
A little longer till the moon came up;
Then on the gilded track leading to
   the mountains,      160
Against the moon they faded in com-
   mon gold
And earth bore East with all toward
   the new morning.

# THE DIVINE IMAGE
### *William Blake* (*1789*)

To Mercy, Pity, Peace, and Love
All pray in their distress;
And to these virtues of delight
Return their thankfulness.

For Mercy, Pity, Peace, and Love   5
Is God, our Father dear,
And Mercy, Pity, Peace, and Love
Is man, His child and care.

For Mercy has a human heart,
Pity a human face,      10
And Love, the human form divine,
And Peace, the human dress.

Then every man, of every clime,
That prays in his distress,
Prays to the human form divine,   15
Love, Mercy, Pity, Peace.

And all must love the human form,
In heathen, Turk, or Jew;
Where Mercy, Love, and Pity dwell
There God is dwelling too.     20

# THE TIGER
### *William Blake* (*1794*)

Tiger! Tiger! burning bright
In the forests of the night,
What immortal hand or eye
Could frame thy fearful symmetry?

In what distant deeps or skies   5
Burnt the fire of thine eyes?
On what wings dare he aspire?
What the hand dare seize the fire?

And what shoulder, and what art,
Could twist the sinews of thy heart?
And when thy heart began to beat,   11
What dread hand? and what dread
   **feet?**

What the hammer? what the chain?
In what furnace was thy brain?
What the anvil? what dread grasp  15
Dare its deadly terrors clasp?

When the stars threw down their
   spears,
And watered heaven with their tears,

Did he smile his work to see?
Did he who made the Lamb make
   thee?  20

Tiger! Tiger! burning bright
In the forests of the night,
What immortal hand or eye
Dare frame thy fearful symmetry?

## THE LAMB

### *William Blake*  (*1789*)

Little Lamb, who made thee?
Dost thou know who made thee?
Gave thee life, and bid thee feed,
By the stream and o'er the mead;
Gave thee clothing of delight,  5
Softest clothing, woolly, bright;
Gave thee such a tender voice,
Making all the vales rejoice?
   Little Lamb, who made thee?
   Dost thou know who made thee?  10

Little Lamb, I'll tell thee,
Little Lamb, I'll tell thee:
He is calléd by thy name,
For He calls Himself a Lamb,
He is meek, and He is mild;  15
He became a little child.
I a child, and thou a lamb,
We are calléd by His name.
   Little Lamb, God bless thee!
   Little Lamb, God bless thee!  20

## THE HOUND OF HEAVEN

### *Francis Thompson*  (*1891*)

I fled Him, down the nights and down the days;
   I fled Him, down the arches of the years;
   I fled Him, down the labyrinthine ways
      Of my own mind; and in the mist of tears
I hid from Him, and under running laughter.  5
      Up vistaed hopes I sped;
      And shot, precipitated,
Adown Titanic glooms of chasmèd fears,
   From those strong Feet that followed, followed after.
      But with unhurrying chase,  10
      And unperturbèd pace,
Deliberate speed, majestic instancy,
      They beat—and a Voice beat
      More instant than the Feet—
"All things betray thee, who betrayest Me."  15

      I pleaded, outlaw-wise,
By many a hearted casement, curtained red,
   Trellised with intertwining charities;

(For, though I knew His love Who followèd,
    Yet was I sore adread 20
Lest, having Him, I must have naught beside)
But, if one little casement parted wide,
    The gust of His approach would clash it to.
Fear wist not to evade, as Love wist to pursue.
Across the margent of the world I fled, 25
    And troubled the gold gateways of the stars,
      Smiting for shelter on their clangèd bars;
        Fretted to dulcet jars
And silvern chatter the pale ports o' the moon.
I said to dawn: Be sudden—to eve: Be soon; 30
    With thy young skiey blossoms heap me over
      From this tremendous Lover!
Float thy vague veil about me, lest He see!
    I tempted all His servitors, but to find
My own betrayal in their constancy, 35
In faith to Him their fickleness to me,
    Their traitorous trueness, and their loyal deceit.
To all swift things for swiftness did I sue;
    Clung to the whistling mane of every wind.
      But whether they swept, smoothly fleet, 40
    The long savannahs of the blue;
      Or whether, Thunder-driven,
      They clanged his chariot 'thwart a heaven,
Plashy with flying lightnings round the spurn o' their feet:—
    Fear wist not to evade as Love wist to pursue. 45
      Still with unhurrying chase,
      And unperturbèd pace,
    Deliberate speed, majestic instancy,
      Came on the following Feet,
      And a Voice above their beat— 50
    "Naught shelters thee, who wilt not shelter Me."

I sought no more that, after which I strayed,
    In face of man or maid;
But still within the little children's eyes
    Seems something, something that replies, 55
*They* at least are for me, surely for me!
I turned me to them very wistfully;
But, just as their young eyes grew sudden fair
    With dawning answers there,
Their angel plucked them from me by the hair. 60
"Come then, ye other children, Nature's—share
With me" (said I) "your delicate fellowship;
    Let me greet you lip to lip,
    Let me twine with your caresses,
      Wantoning 65

With our Lady-Mother's vagrant tresses,
   Banqueting
With her in her wind-walled palace,
Underneath her azured daïs,
Quaffing, as your taintless way is,                              70
   From a chalice
Lucent-weeping out of the dayspring."
   So it was done:
I in their delicate fellowship was one—
Drew the bolt of Nature's secrecies.                             75
I knew all the swift importings
   On the wilful face of skies;
   I knew how the clouds arise
   Spumèd of the wild sea-snortings;
     All that's born or dies                      80
   Rose and drooped with—made them shapers
Of mine own moods, or wailful or divine—
   With them joyed and was bereaven.
   I was heavy with the even,
   When she lit her glimmering tapers            85
   Round the day's dead sanctities.
   I laughed in the morning's eyes.
I triumphed and I saddened with all weather,
   Heaven and I wept together,
And its sweet tears were salt with mortal mine;                 90
Against the red throb of its sunset-heart
   I laid my own to beat,
   And share commingling heat;
But not by that, by that, was eased my human smart.
In vain my tears were wet on Heaven's grey cheek.               95
For ah! we know not what each other says,
   These things and I; in sound *I* speak—
*Their* sound is but their stir, they speak by silences.
Nature, poor stepdame, cannot slake my drouth;
   Let her, if she would owe me,                  100
Drop yon blue bosom-veil of sky, and show me
   The breasts o' her tenderness:
Never did any milk of hers once bless
   My thirsting mouth.
   Nigh and nigh draws the chase,               105
   With unperturbèd pace,
   Deliberate speed, majestic instancy;
   And past those noisèd Feet
   A voice comes yet more fleet—
"Lo! naught contents thee, who content'st not Me."              110

Naked I wait Thy love's uplifted stroke!
My harness piece by piece Thou hast hewn from me,

And smitten me to my knee;
   I am defenceless utterly,
   I slept, methinks, and woke,                                      115
And, slowly gazing, find me stripped in sleep.
In the rash lustihead of my young powers,
   I shook the pillaring hours
And pulled my life upon me; grimed with smears,
I stand amid the dust o' the mounded years—                                120
My mangled youth lies dead beneath the heap.
My days have crackled and gone up in smoke,
Have puffed and burst as sun-starts on a stream.
   Yea, faileth now even dream
The dreamer, and the lute the lutanist;                                     125
Even the linked fantasies, in whose blossomy twist
I swung the earth a trinket at my wrist,
Are yielding; cords of all too weak account
For earth with heavy griefs so overplussed.
   Ah! is Thy love indeed                                          130
A weed, albeit an amaranthine weed,
Suffering no flowers except its own to mount?
   Ah! must—
   Designer infinite!—
Ah! must Thou char the wood ere Thou canst limn with it?                    135
My freshness spent its wavering shower i' the dust;
And now my heart is as a broken fount,
Wherein tear-drippings stagnate, spilt down ever
   From the dank thoughts that shiver
Upon the sighful branches of my mind.                                       140
   Such is; what is to be?
The pulp so bitter, how shall taste the rind?
I dimly guess what Time in mists confounds;
Yet ever and anon a trumpet sounds
From the hid battlements of Eternity,                                       145
Those shaken mists a space unsettle, then
Round the half-glimpsèd turrets slowly wash again;
   But not ere him who summoneth
   I first have seen, enwound
With glooming robes purpureal, cypress-crowned;                             150
His name I know, and what his trumpet saith.
Whether man's heart or life it be which yields
   Thee harvest, must Thy harvest fields
   Be dunged with rotten death?
     Now of that long pursuit                                155
     Comes on at hand the bruit;
That Voice is round me like a bursting sea:
   "And is thy earth so marred,
   Shattered in shard on shard?
Lo, all things fly thee, for thou fliest Me!                                160

"Strange, piteous, futile thing!
Wherefore should any set thee love apart?
Seeing none but I makes much of naught" (He said),
"And human love needs human meriting:
        How hast thou merited—                              165
Of all man's clotted clay the dingiest clot?
        Alack, thou knowest not
How little worthy of any love thou art!
Whom wilt thou find to love ignoble thee,
        Save Me, save only Me?                              170
All which I took from thee I did but take,
        Not for thy harms,
But just that thou might'st seek it in My arms.
        All which thy child's mistake
Fancies as lost, I have stored for thee at home:           175
        Rise, clasp My hand, and come!"

        Halts by me that footfall:
        Is my gloom, after all,
Shade of His hand, outstretched caressingly?
        "Ah, fondest, blindest, weakest,                    180
        I am He Whom thou seekest!
Thou dravest love from thee, who dravest Me."


# THE PULLEY

## *George Herbert* (*1633*)

When God at first made Man,
Having a glass of blessings standing
        by—
"Let us," said he, "pour on him all we
        can;
Let the world's riches, which dis-
        perséd lie,
Contract into a span."                              5

So strength first made a way;
Then beauty flowed, then wisdom,
        honor, pleasure.
When almost all was out, God made a
        stay,
Perceiving that, alone of all his treas-
        ure,
Rest in the bottom lay.                             10

"For if I should," said he,
"Bestow this jewel also on my crea-
        ture,
He would adore my gifts instead of
        me,
And rest in nature, not the God of
        nature;
So both should losers be.                           15

"Yet let him keep the rest,
But keep them with repining restless-
        ness;
Let him be rich and weary, that at
        least,
If goodness lead him not, yet weari-
        ness
May toss him to my breast."            20

## THE COLLAR

*George Herbert*  (*1633*)

I struck the board, and cried, "No
    more;
  I will abroad!
What! shall I ever sigh and pine?
My lines and life are free; free as the
    road,
  Loose as the wind, as large as store.
    Shall I be still in suit?   6
Have I no harvest but a thorn
To let me blood, and not restore
What I have lost with cordial fruit?
    Sure there was wine   10
Before my sighs did dry it; there
    was corn
  Before my tears did drown it;
Is the year only lost to me?
Have I no bays to crown it,
No flowers, no garlands gay? all
    blasted,   15
  All wasted?
Not so, my heart; but there is fruit,
  And thou hast hands.
Recover all thy sigh-blown age

On double pleasures; leave thy cold
    dispute   20
Of what is fit and not; forsake thy
    cage,
  Thy rope of sands
Which petty thoughts have made;
    and made to thee
Good cable, to enforce and draw,
  And be thy law,   25
While thou didst wink and wouldst
    not see
  Away! take heed;
  I will abroad.
Call in thy death's-head there; tie up
    thy fears.
  He that forbears   30
To suit and serve his need
  Deserves his load."
But as I raved, and grew more fierce
    and wild
  At every word,
Methought I heard one calling,
    "Child";   35
  And I replied, "My Lord."


## A HYMN TO GOD THE FATHER

*John Donne*  (*1633*)

Wilt thou forgive that sin where I begun,
  Which was my sin, though it were done before?
Wilt thou forgive that sin through which I run,
  And do run still, though still I do deplore?
When thou hast done, thou hast not done;   5
    For I have more.


Wilt thou forgive that sin which I have won
  Others to sin, and made my sins their door?
Wilt thou forgive that sin which I did shun
  A year or two, but wallowed in a score?   10
When thou hast done, thou hast not done;
    For I have more.

I have a sin of fear, that when I've spun
    My last thread, I shall perish on the shore;
But swear by thyself that at my death thy Son                    15
    Shall shine as he shines now and heretofore;
And having done that, thou hast done;
    I fear no more.


## GOD'S GRANDEUR

*Gerard Manley Hopkins*   (*1918*)

The world is charged with the grandeur of God.
It will flame out, like shining from shook foil;
It gathers to a greatness, like the ooze of oil
Crushed.  Why do men then now not reck his rod?
Generations have trod, have trod, have trod;                    5
And all is seared with trade; bleared, smeared with toil;
And wears man's smudge and shares man's smell—the soil
Is bare now, nor can foot feel, being shod.
And for all this, nature is never spent;
There lives the dearest freshness deep down things;            10
And though the last lights off the black West went
Oh, morning, at the brown brink eastward, springs—
Because the Holy Ghost over the bent
World broods with warm breast and with ah! bright wings.


## JUSTUS QUIDEM TU ES . . .

*Gerard Manley Hopkins*   (*1918*)

Thou art indeed just, Lord, if I contend
With thee; but, sir, so what I plead is just.
Why do sinners' ways prosper? and why must
Disappointment all I endeavour end?
    Wert thou my enemy, O thou my friend,                    5
How would thou worse, I wonder, than thou dost
Defeat, thwart me?  Oh, the sots and thralls of lust
Do in spare hours more thrive than I that spend,
Sir, life upon thy cause.  See, banks and brakes
Now, leavèd how thick! lacèd they are again                    10
With fretty chervil, look, and fresh wind shakes
Them; birds build—but not I build; no, but strain,
Time's eunuch, and not breed one work that wakes.
Mine, O thou Lord of life, send my roots rain.

# THE PREACHER
## *DuBose Heyward*  (*1931*)

In the red church with checkered window-panes,
That squats among its cluttered graves, and stains
The laurelled clearing with its ugly blot,
He preached his God on Sunday, while the hot
Thin mountain air vibrated to the sound      5
Of hotter threats, and in from miles around,
Threading still trails through rhododendron gloom,
Came silent groups to fill his house of doom.

Raw-boned and thunder-voiced, with brandished fist,
He shouted of an errant egotist      10
Swift to avenge a wrong, carrying hate
Beyond the grave, hurling a dire fate
On all who failed to follow his decree.
Until his God emerged, the Deity
Behind the mountain feud—the iron code      15
Of eye for eye was his.  Slowly there showed,
Behind impassive faces, sullen fear
Of the all-seeing Foe they worshipped there.

Wednesday the freshet came; and Pigeon Creek,
That threads the laurel blossoms on a streak      20
Of morning sunshine, dropped its slender song,
Drew one deep breath, then lifting with a long
Slow shudder, hurtled like a tawny beast,
Froth-lipped and baying, oceanward and east.
Where the trail leads from church to Garvin's house,      25
Tom Garvin's boy was driving up the cows.
A vaulting seethe of water, trees, and foam
Lunged for the bank, then curved and tumbled home,
On yellow chaos, and the sky's hard slate,
For one swift heart-beat, beauty, slim and straight,      30
Swung sharply upward, crumpled, hung and fell:
There may have been a cry—no one could tell.

That night, ten miles away, the preacher heard.
The first stream took his horse and rig; the third
Hurled him a mile down stream, and gashed his head.      35
A sallow morning light lay on the bed
At Garvin's when he staggered through the door
And closed it very softly on the roar
Of hungry water.  Slowly silence grew
And spread—and suddenly the watchers knew      40
There was a God, and He was very kind.
While the grim, silent man, with eyes gone blind,
Gathered the broken form that never stirred
Into his bleeding arms—and said no word.

## BALLAD OF THE GOODLY FERE

### (SIMON ZELOTES SPEAKETH IT SOMEWHILE AFTER THE CRUCIFIXION)

*Ezra Pound* (*1910*)

Ha' we lost the goodliest fere o' all
For the priests and the gallows tree?
Aye lover he was of browny men,
O' ships and the open sea.
When they came wi' a host to take
Our Man          5

His smile was good to see;
"First let these go!" quo' our Goodly Fere,
"Or I'll see you damned," says he.

Aye, he sent us out through the crossed high spears,
And the scorn of his laugh rang free,          10
"Why took ye not me when I walked about
Alone in the town?" says he.

Oh, we drunk his "Hale" in the good red wine
When we last made company;
No capon priest was the Goodly Fere          15
But a man o' men was he.

I ha' seen him drive a hundred men
Wi' a bundle o' cords swung free,
That they took the high and holy house
For their pawn and treasury.          20

They'll no' get him a' in a book I think,
Though they write it cunningly;
No mouse of the scrolls was the Goodly Fere
But aye loved the open sea.

If they think they ha' snared our Goodly Fere          25
They are fools to the last degree.

"I'll go to the feast," quo' our Goodly Fere,
"Though I go to the gallows tree."

"Ye ha' seen me heal the lame and blind,
And wake the dead," says he;          30
"Ye shall see one thing to master all:
'Tis how a brave man dies on the tree."

A son of God was the Goodly Fere
That bade us his brothers be.
I ha' seen him cow a thousand men.          35
I have seen him upon the tree.

He cried no cry when they drave the nails
And the blood gushed hot and free;
The hounds of the crimson sky gave tongue
But never a cry cried he.          40

I ha' seen him cow a thousand men
On the hills o' Galilee;
They whined as he walked out calm between,
Wi' his eyes like the grey o' the sea.

Like the sea that brooks no voyaging          45
With the winds unleashed and free,
Like the sea that he cowed at Genseret
Wi' twey words spoke' suddenly.

A master of men was the Goodly Fere,
A mate of the wind and sea;          50
If they think they ha' slain our Goodly Fere
They are fools eternally.

I ha' seen him eat o' the honey-comb
Sin' they nailed him to the tree.

## NO COWARD SOUL IS MINE

### *Emily Brontë  (1850)*

No coward soul is mine,
No trembler in the world's storm-
    troubled sphere;
I see Heaven's glories shine,
And faith shines equal, arming me
    from fear.

O God within my breast,          5
Almighty, ever-present Deity!
Life—that in me has rest,
As I—undying Life—have power in
    Thee!

Vain are the thousand creeds
That move men's hearts—unutter-
    ably vain;                      10
Worthless as withered weeds,
Or idlest froth amid the boundless
    main,

To waken doubt in one
Holding so fast by Thine infinity;

So surely anchored on          15
The steadfast rock of immortality.

With wide-embracing love
Thy spirit animates eternal years,
    Pervades and broods above,
Changes, sustains, dissolves, creates,
    and rears.                      20

Though earth and man were
    gone,
And suns and universes ceased to be,
    And Thou were left alone,
Every existence would exist in Thee.

There is not room for Death,   25
Nor atom that his might could render
    void;
Thou—Thou art Being and
    Breath,
And what Thou art may never be
    destroyed.

## DAREST THOU NOW, O SOUL

### (*From* Passage to India)

### *Walt Whitman  (1855)*

Darest thou now, O soul,
Walk out with me toward the unknown region,
Where neither ground is for the feet nor any path to follow?

No map there, nor guide,
Nor voice sounding, nor touch of human hand,          5
Nor face with blooming flesh, nor lips, nor eyes, are in that land.

I know it not, O soul,
Nor dost thou, all is a blank before us,
All waits undream'd of in that region, that inaccessible land.
Till when the ties loosen,          10
All but the ties eternal, Time and Space,
Nor darkness, gravitation, sense, nor any bounds bound us.

Then we burst forth, we float,
In Time and Space, O soul, prepared for them,
Equal, equipt at last (O joy! O fruit of all!), them to fulfil, O Soul.   15

## INSIDE OF KING'S COLLEGE CHAPEL, CAMBRIDGE

*William Wordsworth* (1822)

Tax not the royal Saint with vain expense,
With ill-matched aims the Architect
　who planned—
Albeit laboring for a scanty band
Of white robed Scholars only—this
　immense
And glorious Work of fine intelligence!　　　　　　　　　　　　　5
Give all thou canst; high Heaven rejects the lore
Of nicely-calculated less or more;
So deemed the man who fashioned
　for the sense
These lofty pillars, spread that
　branching roof
Self-poised, and scooped into ten
　thousand cells,　　　　　　　　　10
Where light and shade repose, where
　music dwells
Lingering—and wandering on as
　loath to die;
Like thoughts whose very sweetness
　yieldeth proof
That they were born for immortality.　　　　　　　　　　　　　15

## IT IS A BEAUTEOUS EVENING, CALM AND FREE

*William Wordsworth* (1802)

It is a beauteous evening, calm and
　free,
The holy time is quiet as a Nun
Breathless with adoration; the broad
　sun
Is sinking down in its tranquillity;
The gentleness of heaven broods o'er
　the Sea:　　　　　　　　　　　5
Listen! the mighty Being is awake,

And doth with his eternal motion
　make
A sound like thunder—everlastingly.
Dear Child! dear Girl! that walkest
　with me here,
If thou appear untouched by solemn
　thought,　　　　　　　　　　10
Thy nature is not therefore less
　divine:
Thou liest in Abraham's bosom all
　the year,
And worship'st at the Temple's inner
　shrine,
God being with thee when we know
　it not.

## GOD-FORGOTTEN

*Thomas Hardy* (1901)

I towered far, and lo! I stood within
The presence of the Lord Most High,
Sent thither by the sons of Earth, to
　win
　　Some answer to their cry.

—"The Earth, sayest thou? The Human race?
By Me created? Sad its lot?
Nay: I have no remembrance of such
　place:
　　Such world I fashioned not."—

—"O Lord, forgive me when I say
Thou spakest the word and made it
　all."—　　　　　　　　　　　10
"The Earth of men—let me bethink
　me . . . Yea!
　　I dimly do recall.

"Some tiny sphere I built long back
(Mid millions of such shapes of mine)
So named . . . It perished, surely—
　not a wrack　　　　　　　　　15
　　Remaining, or a sign?

"It lost my interest from the first,
My aims therefor succeeding ill;
Haply it died of doing as it durst?"—
　　"Lord, it existeth still."—　　20

"Dark, then, its life! For not a cry
Of aught it bears do I now hear;
Of its own act the threads were snapt
　　whereby
　　Its plaints had reached mine ear.

"It used to ask for gifts of good,　　25
Till came its severance, self-entailed,
When sudden silence on that side en-
　　sued,
　　And has till now prevailed.

"All other orbs have kept in touch;
Their voicings reach me speedily:　30
Thy people took upon them over-
　　much
　　In sundering them from me!

"And it is strange—though sad
　　enough—
Earth's race should think that one
　　whose call
Frames, daily, shining spheres of flaw-
　　less stuff　　35
　　Must heed their tainted ball! . . .

"But sayest it is by pangs distraught,
And strife, and silent suffering?—

Sore grieved am I that injury should
　　be wrought
　　Even on so poor a thing!　　40

"Thou shouldst have learnt that *Not
　　to Mend*
For Me could mean but *Not to Know:*
Hence, Messengers! and straightway
　　put an end
　　To what men undergo." . . .

Homing at dawn, I thought to see　45
One of the Messengers standing by.
—Oh, childish thought! . . . Yet
　　often it comes to me
　　When trouble hovers nigh.

## THE CONCLUSION

### Sir Walter Raleigh　(*1618*)

Even such is time, that takes in trust
　　Our youth, our joys, our all we
　　　have,
And pays us but with earth and dust;
　　Who, in the dark and silent grave,
When we have wandered all our
　　ways,　　5
Shuts up the story of our days;
But from this earth, this grave, this
　　dust,
My God shall raise me up, I trust!

# THE GOOD LIFE

Wʜᴀᴛ sᴏʀᴛ of life is most likely to make me happy? What goal should I set as the end of all my striving? What work will give me the deepest and most permanent satisfaction? These are questions which everyone asks before he decides upon a career or determines what aspects of his personality he would like to strengthen and which of his interests he wishes to develop.

It is very hard to think calmly about such matters in the turmoil of the modern world. Its speed, its uproar, its instability create an atmosphere in which it is almost impossible to find the leisure and quiet necessary for taking stock of one's deepest needs and dearest ambitions. Doing something for its own sake often becomes the end of existence, and speed in the process seems to enhance its value. But to drive a motor car through England or France at sixty miles an hour is only exhilarating folly if we go so fast that we become acquainted with no landscapes, no towns, no people on the way. To be able to shoot up to the thirty-fifth floor of a skyscraper in an express elevator is a feat of no importance unless one does something of use to others or of pleasure to oneself when he reaches the top. Our mechanical marvels of speed and efficiency often serve merely to obscure the difference between the machinery of life and life itself. They may lead us to substitute the mere accumulation of money or the attainment of physical comfort for more genuinely satisfying ends.

Fortunately no individual needs to enter blindly upon his quest for the good life. During the ages man's tireless pursuit of happiness has shown him what attitudes of mind and what activities are most sure to give him durable satisfaction. A few of the answers which he has found appear in the following pages. No one of them is likely to prove a sovereign remedy for the spiritual uneasiness of any individual. At certain moments we may feel with Mr. Barbellion that joyous sensations will awaken in us the most perfect delight. To bathe in a woodland brook while birds sing and the water ripples and eddies deliciously over mossy stones may now and then seem very Heaven. In other moods we may think the highest good is to sit in idleness gazing into a log fire or to watch from a window one motor car follow another along a gray winding road. Yet in more serious moments we know that we must build our lives on a sounder basis of happiness than mere sensations can afford, however thrilling or soothing they may be.

Matthew Arnold asks us to see life steadily and to see it whole—to seek an harmonious expansion of all of our powers. The advice is sound, but it is difficult to translate it into a specific program for any one person. It is hard for a man even partially to understand himself and harder still for him to discover what are the deepest needs of his nature and how they can be satisfied. But he can learn through his reading what have been regarded as the most suitable ends of human effort. He will find that the sages have held up for admiration many different and incompatible ideals. Physical well-being, power, riches, work congenial to one's nature, love, intelligent social intercourse, service to one's fellows, devotion to duty, heroic acceptance of inevitable disappointment, pain, and bereavement, a sound philosophy, religious surety—each one of these values has been set up as a justifiable end of human endeavor.

Yet no one of them can serve any man as the goal of all of his striving at every stage of his career. Each one of us must discover a combination of ideals that will most completely liberate his nature. It is easier to allow one's personality to become part of the mechanism of some social machine or to accept some ready-made system of ideas. To lose one's self in the prescribed theories of a religious or political cult, or in the exacting demands of our jobs or professions, may give one a sense of security. We may thus be less terrified by the swift incalculable change in events. But it is of first importance that we should realize that we cannot live a good life unless we free ourselves from the routine of our jobs, our social habits, and our traditional attitudes long enough to define the vital problem to ourselves. Then we can spend the rest of our lives seeking its solution. We shall, of course, never find one that will completely satisfy us, for no one ever fully realizes an ideal. But if we can only feel that we continue to approach the remote goals which we have set for ourselves, then we shall live what the philosophers call the "good life."

## ENJOYING LIFE
### *W. N. P. Barbellion* (*1920*)

### I

W<small>HEN</small> I awoke, a glance toward the window told me that outside it had already happened—the sun was up! humming along through a cloudless sky full of bees and skylarks. I shut my eyes and buried my nose in the pillow, awake sufficiently to realize that another great day had dawned for me while I slept.

I lay still for a moment in luxurious anticipation and listened to a tiny joy, singing within like the voice of a girl in the distance, until at last great waves of happiness roared through my heart like sea horses. I jumped out of bed, flung on my dressing-gown, and went off across the meadow to bathe in the stream. Into the water I plunged, and struggled and kicked with a sensuous delight in its coldness and in every contraction of a muscle, glad to be nude and clean and cool among the dragon flies and trout. I clambered to a rock in midstream, on which I rested in a moment of expansion, relaxed in every tissue.

The current rocked one foot in the water, and the sun made every cell in my body vibrate. Upstream, a dipper sang—and surely nothing but happiness could ever enter life again! Neither the past nor the future existed for me any more, but only the glorious and all-absorbing present. I put my whole being into the immediate ticking hour with its sixty minutes of precious life, and catching each pearl drop as it fell, said, "Now my happiness is complete, and now, and now." I lay thus for I know not how long, centuries perhaps, for down in the silent well of our existence time is not reckoned by the clock, nor our abiding joy in idle, obstinate words. Then I rubbed down with a hard towel—how I loved my cool, pink skin!—and stood a moment in the shade of the pine trees, still unembarrassed by a single demoralizing garment. I was free, immaculate, untouched by anything coarser than the soft morning air around and the moss in the turf that supported the soles of my feet.

In the afternoon, I strode over the hills in a spirit of burning exultation. The moors rolled to the sea infinitely far, and the sea to the horizon infinitely wide. I opened both arms and tried to embrace the immensity of that wind-swept space through sheer love of it. The wind roared past my ears and through my hair. Overhead a herring gull made use of the air currents and soared on motionless wings. Verily, the flight of a gull is as magnificent as the Andes! No other being save myself was in sight. If I had chanced to meet someone I should have greeted him with the question that was stinging the tip of my tongue, "What does it all mean and what do you think?" And he, of course, after a moment's puzzled reflection, would have answered: "It means nout, tho' I think us could do with a change of Government." But so excited as to be heedless of his reply, I should have followed up, in the grand manner, with: "Whence do we come and whither do we go?" or "Tell me where have you lived, what countries have you seen? Which is your favorite mountain? Do you like thunderstorms or sunsets best? How many times have you been in love, and what about God?"

At night, I turned homeward, flushed and excited with the day's life, going to bed unwillingly at last and even depressed because the day was at an end and I must needs put myself into a state of unconsciousness while the earth itself is never asleep, but always spins along amid the stars with its precious human freightage. To lose a single minute of conscious life in sleep seemed a real loss!

## II

I like all things which are swift or immense—lightning, Popocatepetl, London, Roosevelt!

So, anyhow, I like to think in periods of ebullience when wind and sun beat down upon the face and the blood races along the arteries. We live in an age of hustle and speed. We sweep from one end of the country to the other by rail, 'plane, and motor, and the quidnunc querulously complains, "Too much rushing about nowadays and too little thinking." Yet does he think we ought to remain at home, arranging the cosmos with Lotze or William James, while Hamel gets into an aeroplane on the neighboring heath and shows us how to loop the loop? Must I be improving my mind with socio-logical ruminations while the herring fleet is ready to take me out to the deep sea? The speed, ferocity, and dash of the London street, full of cars and strenuous, sleek, top-hatted gentlemen and raddled women, is most exhilarat-ing. Londoners must enjoy a perpetual exhilaration. Like mountain air, I suspect that the stinks of petrol and horse dung get into the blood. There may be a little mountain sickness at first, but the system soon adapts itself. On the first day of my arrival in London, as the train moved over the roofs of the squalid tenements in the environs of Waterloo and round about the great dome of St. Paul's, its cross reaching up into the sky like a great symbolic X, I kept thinking to myself that here was the greatest city in the world, and that here again was I, in it—one of its five millions of inhabitants. I said so to myself aloud and whistled low. Already I was in love with London's dirt and grandeur, and by the time I had reached the Strand, I plunged like a man who cannot swim. After all, only Shakespeare could stand on the top of Mont Blanc and not lose his spiritual equilibrium.

## III

But it is not always possible to be living on the heights. And life in the plains is often equally furious. We may climb to peaks in Darien without ever leaving our armchairs. We may be swimming the Hellespont as we light a cigarette. Some of the tiniest outward incidents in life, in appearance as harmless as cricket balls, may be actually as explosive as bombs. That little, scarcely audible thing, a kiss, may shatter the fortress of the heart with the force of a fifteen-inch gun. A melody in music, one of Bach's fugues or the Unfinished Symphony of Schubert, may, in a few bars, create a *bouleverse-ment,* sweep us out into the high seas past all our usual anchorages, and leave us there alone to struggle with a new destiny. And who cannot recall—some there be, I think, who, with delightful preciosity, collect them in the mem-ory—those silent, instantaneous flashes of collusion with beauty, of which even the memory so electrifies the emotions that no mental analysis of them is ever made. The intellect is knocked out in the first round. We can simply catalogue them without comment—for example, a girl leaping and running into the sea to bathe; those blue butterflies and thyme flowers which Richard Jefferies loved with an almost feminine tenderness; the nude body of a child of four; a young, red-topped larch cone; a certain smile; a pressure of the hand; an unresolved inflection of a voice.

## IV

Life pursues me like a fury. Everywhere, at all times, I am feeling, think-ing, hoping, hating, loving, cheering. It is impossible to escape.

I once sought refuge in a deserted country churchyard, where the gravestones stood higgledy-piggledy among the long grass, their inscriptions almost obliterated by moss and time. "Here," said I, "it will be cold and lifeless and I can rest." I wanted to be miserable, dull, and unresponsive. With difficulty I read an inscription expressing the sorrow of a father and mother in 1701 for the loss of their beautiful daughter, Joan, aged 21. I read others, but the most pathetic barely amused me. I was satisfactorily indifferent. These people, I said sardonically, had lived and suffered so long ago that even their sorrows were petrified. Parents' grief in 1701 is simply a piece of palæontology. So I passed on, content to be unmolested, thinking I had escaped. But beside the old graves were a few recent ones with fresh flowers upon them; across the road in the schoolroom the children began to sing, and up at the farm, I then recalled, the old folk, Mr. and Mrs. Brooks, were waiting for the call—all of them beneath the shadow of the church tower whose clock-face watched the generations come and go and come again to lie beneath the shadow of the yews. I saw the procession of human life, generation after generation, pass through the village down through the ages, and though all had been silent before, I heard now the roar of existence sweeping through the churchyard as loudly as in Piccadilly.

I jumped from peak to peak of thought, from human life on the planet to the planet itself; the earth fell away from my feet, and far below was the round world whole, a sphere among other spheres in the planetary system bound up by the laws of evolution and motion. As I hung aloft at so great a height and in an atmosphere so cold and rare, I shivered at the immensity of the universe of which I formed a part; for the moment a colossal stage-fright seized me; I longed to cease to be, to vanish in complete self-annihilation. But only for a moment; then, gathering the forces of the soul as every man must and does at times of crisis, I leaped upon the rear of the great occasion before it was too late, crying: The world is a ship, on an unknown and dangerous commission. But I for my part, as a silly ship-boy, will stand on the ratlines and cheer. I left the churchyard almost hilarious!

## V

"Dans littérature," said M. Taine, "j'aime tout." I would shake his hand for saying that and add: "In life, monsieur, as well." All things attract me equally. I cannot concentrate. I am ready to do anything, go anywhere, think anything, read anything. Wherever I hitch my wagon I am confident of an adventurous ride. Somebody says, "Come and hear some Wagner." I am ready to go. Another, "I say, they are going to ring the bull"—and who wants to complete his masterpiece or count his money when they are going to ring the bull? I will go with you to Norway, Switzerland, Jericho, Timbuctoo. Talk to me about the Rosicrucians or the stomach of a flea and I will listen to you. Tell me that the Chelsea power station is as beautiful as the Parthenon at Athens and I'll believe you. Everything is beautiful, even the ugly

—why did Whistler paint the squalor of the London streets, or Brangwyn the gloom of a steam crane? To subscribe to any one particular profession, mode of life, doctrine, philosophy, opinion, or enthusiasm, is to cut one's self off from all the rest. I subscribe to all. With the whole world before you, beware lest the machinery of education seizes hold of the equipotential of your youth and grinds you out the finished product! You were a human being to start with; now, you are only a soldier, sailor, tinker, tailor. Leonardo da Vinci, racked with frustrate passion after the universal, is reported to have declared that only to do one thing and only to know one thing was a disgrace, no less. "We should not be able to say of a man, 'He is a mathematician,' or a preacher,' or 'eloquent'; but that he is 'a gentleman.' That universal quality alone pleases me."

"The works of man don't interest me much," an enthusiast in natural history once said to me; "I prefer the works of God." Unctuous wretch! He was one of those forlorn creatures with a carefully ordered mind, his information and opinions written out in indelible ink and pigeonholed for easy reference. He had never shrunk to realize all he did not know—he knew all the things worth knowing. He never shuddered to reflect upon the limitations of a single point of view—other folk were simply wrong. He was scarcely one to understand the magnanimous phrase of the French, "Tout comprendre c'est tout pardonner." Other folk were either good or bad.

## VI

Perhaps too great an enthusiasm exhausts the spirit. Love kills. I know it. The love of one's art or profession, passion for another's soul, for one's children, sap the life-blood and hurry us on to the grave. I know a man who killed himself with a passion for dragon flies—a passion ending in debauchery; and debauchery of books, lust of knowledge, is as fatal as any other kind.

I know it. But I don't care. Your minatory forefinger is of no avail. Already I am too far gone. Those days are ancient history now when I endured the torture of an attempt to reclaim myself. I even reduced myself to so little as a grain a day by reading Kant and talking to entomologists. But no permanent cure was ever effected.

Once, I recall, I sat down to study zoölogy, because I thought it would be sober and dull. How foolish! Rousseau said he cooled his brain by dissecting a moss. But I know of few more blood-curdling achievements than the thoroughly successful completion of a difficult dissection.

Then I immersed myself in old books and forgotten learning. I had the idea that a big enough tumulus of dust and parchments over my head would be a big enough stopper for the joy of life. I became an habitué of the British Museum reading room, and rummaged among the dead books, as Lord Rosebery calls them, but only to find that they were buried alive. Any unfortunate devil received the cataract of superlatives I poured upon him at the discovery of some lively memoirs of 1601. One of my favorite books became the *Encyclopædia Britannica*. I read its learned articles till my eyes ached and my head swam. The sight of those huge tomes made me tremble with a lover's impatience. I could have wept in thinking of all the facts I should never know and of all those I had forgotten! I grew to love facts and learning with the same passion as I had loved life. My enthusiasm was not quenched. It was only diverted.

I tried to laugh myself out of it. But it was no use being cynical. For I found that no fact, no piece of information about this world, is greater or less than another, but that all are equal as the angels. So with the utmost serious-ness I looked up any word I thought upon—pins, nutmegs, wallaby (it's a terrible game!) and gorged. I winced at nothing. I rejected nothing. I raked over even the filth, determined that no nastiness should escape my mind: I studied syphilis and politics, parasitology and crime, and, like Sir Thomas Browne, soon discovered that I could digest a salad gathered in a churchyard as easily as one in a garden.

## VII

I have long since given up the idea of hiding away from life in a museum or a library. Life seeks you out wherever you are. For the diarist, the most com-monplace things of daily life are of absorbing interest. Each day the diarist finds himself born into a world as strange and beautiful as the dead world of the day before. The diarist lives on the globe for all the world as if he lodged on the slopes of a mountain, and unlike most mountain dwellers, he never loses his sense of awe at his situation. Life is vivid to him. "And so to bed," writes Mr. Secretary Pepys, a hundred times in his diary; and we may be sure that each time he joined Mrs. Pepys beneath the coverlet he felt that the moment which marked the end of his wonderful day was one deserving care-ful record.

A man shut up in a dark room can still be living a tense and eager life. Cut off from sight and sound, he still can sit in his chair and listen to the beatings of his own heart—that wonderful muscle inside the cage of the thorax, work-ing and moving like some independent entity, some *other person*, upon whom the favor of our daily life depends. The human body, what a wonderful mechanism it is! It never ceases to astonish me that anyone, on waking up in this world and finding himself in possession of a body—his only bit of real property—should be satisfied when he has clothed and fed it. One would think that the infant's first articulated request would be for a primer of physiology.

I have often wondered how a beautiful woman regards her body. The loveliness which I must seek outside myself sleeps on "the ivories of her pure members." She carries the incommunicable secret in herself, in the texture of her own skin, and the contour of her own breasts. She is guardian of the hidden treasure which fills the flowers and lives in the sunset. How must it be to possess so burning a secret hidden even to the possessor? What must she think on looking into the glass?

I look into the glass, and am baffled by the intolerable strangeness that that face is mine, that I am I, that my name is Barbellion. It is easy, too fatally easy, to continue exploring the recesses of one's own life and mind day by day, making fresh discoveries, opening up new tracts, and on occasion getting a sight of blue mountain ranges in the distance whither we endeavor to arrive.

## VIII

Life is beautiful and strange. Too beautiful, too strange. I sometimes envy those folk whom I see daily accepting life without question or wonderment as a homely fireside affair—except of course for some unusual places like the Niagara Falls, only to be visited on a holiday, or for some unpleasant tragedies they read about in the newspapers. It would be useless to put to them the ultimate and staggering question why anything exists at all—"Why not sheer negation?"—to the folk who find their circumstances so dull that they have to play with bat and ball to fend off ennui, who are always in search of what is known as a "pastime," or who invite children to stay with them "to keep them alive," as they explain, as if there were not enough weeping, wondering, and laughing to be done in this blessed world to keep us all alive and throbbing! Life has ceased to be an intoxication for them. It is just a mild illusion, in which they attend to the slugs in the strawberry beds and get in that extra hundredweight of coal, accepting the bountiful flow of still, calm, happy days as their due and, like spoiled children, feeling bored with them. Yet confront these dormice with a slice of life and they will blink and scamper off. Show them a woman suckling a baby or a dirty man drinking beer, and they will raise their eyebrows or blench. There is no limit to their fear of living. They are nervous of their appetites and instincts; they will not eat themselves into a bilious attack nor smoke themselves into a weak heart. They fear either to love or to hate unreservedly. Men like Baudelaire and Villon terrify them, liner disasters and earthquakes send them trembling to their knees and books of devotion. They will not brazen life out. Let them come out of their houses and seek courage in the thunder of the surf on the seashore, or amid the tall majestic columns of the strong Scots pines, whose lower branches spread down and outward graciously like friendly hands to frightened children. How many times have I sought sanctuary among the tall Scots pines!

## IX

Courage, I know, is necessary. Let us pray for courage, if we are to regard without flinching our amazing situation on this island planet where we are marooned. Amid the island's noise and rapture, struggle, and vicissitude, we must wrestle with the forces of nature for our happiness. True happiness is the spoil of conquest seized out of the clutches of furious life. We must pay for it with a price. That which is given away contains no value. Tall cliffs, a dancing sea, and the sun glorious perhaps. Yes, but simple enjoyment of that kind is a Pyrrhic victory. The real victor must exult in the menace of two hundred feet of sheer, perpendicular rock surface; and when he bathes, remember that the sea has talons, and that the glorious sun itself, what is it? A globe of incandescent heat, compared with which the blast furnaces of Sheffield are only warm, and around which our earth ever keeps on its dizzy mothlike circle.

I am far from believing that the world is a paradise of sea bathing and horse exercise, as R. L. S. said. That is a piece of typical Stevensonian bravura. It is a rare gymnasium, to be sure; but it is also a blood-spattered abattoir, a theatre of pain, an anabasis of travail, a Calvary and a Crucifixion. Therein lies its extraordinary fascination—in those strange antitheses of comedy and tragedy, joy and sorrow, beauty and ugliness. It is the sock one day and the buskin the next. Marriage sheet and shroud are inextricably interwoven. Like a beautiful and terrible mistress, the world holds me its devoted slave. She flouts me, but I love her still. She is cruel, but still I love her. My love for her is a guilty love—for the voluptuous curves of the Devonshire moors, for the bland benignity of the sun smiling alike on the just and on the unjust, for the sea which washes in a beautiful shell or a corpse with the same meditative indifference.

There are many things I ought to scowl upon. But I cannot. The spell is too great. I surprise myself sometimes with my callous exuberation at the triumph of brute force, at some of the grotesque melodramas engineered by Fate—for, in spite of Thomas Hardy and Greek tragedy, Fate is often but a sorry artist—at the splendid hypocrisy of many persons even in high places, or when I learn that a whole army has been "cut to pieces." I rub my hands, murmuring in ironical delight, "It is simply colossal." Marlowe, I believe, drew Barabbas out of sheer love of his wickedness. Shakespeare surely exulted in the unspeakable tragedy of King Lear.

I have been too long now in love with this wicked old earth to wish to change one jot or one tittle of it. I am loath to surrender even the Putumayo atrocities. Let me have Crippen as well as Father Damien, Heliogabalus as well as Marcus Aurelius. Liars and vagabonds are the salt of the earth. Who wants Benvenuto Cellini to tell the truth? What missionary spirit feels tempted to reclaim Aretino or Laurence Sterne? The man who wrote of "the pitiful end" of Marlowe, killed in a tavern brawl, bores me with his peevishness. It is silly to repine because Keats died young or because Poe drank himself to death. This kind of jejune lament from the people who live in garden cities soon becomes very monotonous indeed. Tragedy and comedy, I thought we were all agreed, are the warp and woof of life, and if we have agreed to accept life and accept it fully, let us stand by our compact and whoop like cowboys on the plains. Who wants to be pampered with divine or miraculous intervention? We are too proud. Let the world run on. We can manage. If you suffer, at least you live, said Balzac. So Heine and Schubert out of their great sorrows wrote their little songs, and out of Amiel's life of wasted opportunity came the *Journal*, to give the lie to those who do not hold it to be as much a triumph to fail as to succeed, to despair as to win through with joy.

## AN APOLOGY FOR IDLERS

### *Robert Louis Stevenson* (*1881*)

BOSWELL: We grow weary when idle.
JOHNSON: That is, sir, because others being busy, we want company; but if we were all idle, there would be no growing weary; we should all entertain one another.

JUST now, when every one is bound, under pain of a decree in absence convicting them of *lèse*-respectability, to enter on some lucrative profession, and labor therein with something not far short of enthusiasm, a cry from the opposite party who are content when they have enough, and like to look on and enjoy in the meanwhile, savors a little of bravado and gasconade. And yet this should not be. Idleness so called, which does not consist in doing nothing, but in doing a great deal not recognized in the dogmatic formularies of the ruling class, has as good a right to state its position as industry itself. It is admitted that the presence of people who refuse to enter in the great handicap race for sixpenny pieces, is at once an insult and a disenchantment for those who do. A fine fellow (as we see so many) takes his determination, votes for the sixpences, and in the emphatic Americanism, "goes for" them. And while such an one is plowing distressfully up the road, it is not hard to understand his resentment, when he perceives cool persons in the meadows by the wayside, lying with a handkerchief over their ears and a glass at their elbow. Alexander is touched in a very delicate place by the disregard of Diogenes. Where was the glory of having taken Rome for these tumultuous barbarians, who poured into the Senate house, and found the Fathers sitting silent and unmoved by their success? It is a sore thing to have labored along and scaled the arduous hilltops, and when all is done, find humanity indifferent to your achievement. Hence physicists condemn the unphysical; financiers have only a superficial toleration for those who know little of stocks; literary persons despise the unlettered; and people of all pursuits combine to disparage those who have none.

But though this is one difficulty of the subject, it is not the greatest. You could not be put in prison for speaking against industry, but you can be sent to Coventry for speaking like a fool. The greatest difficulty with most subjects is to do them well; therefore, please to remember this is an apology. It is certain that much may be judiciously argued in favor of diligence; only there is something to be said against it, and that is what, on the present occasion, I have to say. To state one argument is not necessarily to be deaf to all others, and that a man has written a book of travels in Montenegro, is no reason why he should never have been to Richmond.

It is surely beyond a doubt that people should be a good deal idle in youth. For though here and there a Lord Macaulay may escape from school honors with all his wits about him, most boys pay so dear for their medals that they never afterward have a shot in their locker, and begin the world bankrupt. And the same holds true during all the time a lad is educating himself, or suffering others to educate him. It must have been a very foolish old gentleman who addressed Johnson at Oxford in these words: "Young man, ply your book diligently now, and acquire a stock of knowledge; for when years come upon you, you will find that poring upon books will be but an irksome task." The old gentleman seems to have been unaware that many other things besides reading grow irksome, and not a few become impossible, by the time a man has to use spectacles and cannot walk without a stick. Books are good enough in their own way, but they are a mighty bloodless substitute for life. It seems a pity to sit, like the Lady of Shalott, peering into a mirror, with your back turned on all the bustle and glamour of reality. And if a man reads very hard, as the old anecdote reminds us, he will have little time for thoughts.

If you look back on your own education, I am sure it will not be the full, vivid, instructive hours of truantry that you regret; you would rather cancel some lack-luster periods between sleep and waking in the class. For my own part, I have attended a good many lectures in my time. I still remember that the spinning of a top is a case of Kinetic Stability. I still remember that Emphyteusis is not a disease, nor Stillicide a crime. But though I would not willingly part with such scraps of science, I do not set the same store by them as by certain other odds and ends that I came by in the open street while I was playing truant. This is not the moment to dilate on that mighty place of education, which was the favorite school of Dickens and of Balzac, and turns out yearly many inglorious masters in the Science of the Aspects of Life. Suffice it to say this: if a lad does not learn in the streets, it is because he has no faculty of learning. Nor is the truant always in the streets, for if he prefers, he may go out by the gardened suburbs into the country. He may pitch on some tuft of lilacs over a burn, and smoke innumerable pipes to the tune of the water on the stones. A bird will sing in the thicket. And there he may fall into a vein of kindly thought, and see things in a new perspective. Why, if this be not education, what is? We may conceive Mr. Worldly Wiseman accosting such an one, and the conversation that should thereupon ensue:

"How now, young fellow, what dost thou here?"

"Truly, sir, I take mine ease."

"Is not this the hour of the class? and should'st thou not be plying thy Book with diligence, to the end thou mayest obtain knowledge?"

"Nay, but thus also I follow after Learning, by your leave."

"Learning, quotha! After what fashion, I pray thee? Is it mathematics?"

"No, to be sure."

"Is it metaphysics?"

"Nor that."

"Is it some language?"

"Nay, it is no language."

"Is it a trade?"

"Nor a trade neither."

"Why, then, what is't?"

"Indeed, sir, as a time may soon come for me to go upon Pilgrimage, I am desirous to note what is commonly done by persons in my case, and where are the ugliest Sloughs and Thickets on the Road; as also, what manner of Staff is of the best service. Moreover, I lie here, by this water, to learn by root-of-heart a lesson which my master teaches me to call Peace, or Contentment."

Hereupon Mr. Worldly Wiseman was much commoved with passion, and shaking his cane with a very threatful countenance, broke forth upon this wise: "Learning, quotha!" said he; "I would have all such rogues scourged by the Hangman!"

And so he would go his way, ruffling out his cravat with a crackle of starch, like a turkey when it spread its feathers.

Now this, of Mr. Wiseman's, is the common opinion. A fact is not called a fact, but a piece of gossip, if it does not fall into one of your scholastic categories. An inquiry must be in some acknowledged direction, with a name to go by; or else you are not inquiring at all, only lounging; and the workhouse is too good for you. It is supposed that all knowledge is at the bottom of a well, or the far end of a telescope. Sainte-Beuve, as he grew older, came to regard all experience as a single great book, in which to study for a few years ere we go hence; and it seemed all one to him whether you should read in Chapter xx, which is the differential calculus, or in Chapter xxxix, which is hearing the band play in the gardens. As a matter of fact, an intelligent person, looking out of his eyes and hearkening in his ears, with a smile on his face all the time, will get more true education than many another in a life of heroic vigils. There is certainly some chill and arid knowledge to be found upon the summits of formal and laborious science; but it is all round about you, and for the trouble of looking, that you will acquire the warm and palpitating facts of life. While others are filling their memory with a lumber of words, one-half of which they will forget before the week be out, your truant may learn some really useful art: to play the fiddle, to know a good cigar, or to speak with ease and opportunity to all varieties of men. Many who have "plied their book diligently," and know all about some one branch or another of accepted lore, come out of the study with an ancient and owl-like demeanor, and prove dry, stockish, and dyspeptic in all the better and brighter parts of life. Many make a large fortune, who remain underbred and pathetically stupid to the last. And meantime there goes the idler, who began life along with them—by your leave, a different picture. He has had time to take care of his health and his spirits; he has been a great deal in the open air, which is the most salutary of all things for both body and mind; and if he has never read the great Book in very recondite places, he has dipped into it and skimmed it over to excellent purpose. Might not the student afford some Hebrew roots, and the business man some of his half-crowns, for a share of the idler's knowledge of life at large, and Art of Living? Nay, and the idler has another and more important quality than these. I mean his wisdom. He who has much looked on at the childish satisfaction of other people in their hobbies, will regard his own with only a very ironical indulgence. He will not be heard among the dogmatists. He will have a great and cool allowance for all sorts of people and opinions. If he finds no out-of-the-way truths, he will identify himself with no very burning falsehood. His way takes him along a by-road, not much frequented, but very even and pleasant, which is called Commonplace Lane, and leads to the Belvedere of Common-sense. Thence he shall command an agreeable, if no very noble prospect; and while others behold the East and West, the Devil and the Sunrise, he will be contentedly aware of a sort of morning hour upon all sublunary things, with an army of shadows running speedily and in many different directions into the great daylight of Eternity. The shadows and the generations, the shrill doctors and the plangent wars, go by into ultimate silence and emptiness; but underneath all this, a man may see, out of the Belvedere windows, much green and peaceful landscape; many firelit parlors; good people laughing, drinking, and making love as they did before the Flood or the French Revolution; and the old shepherd telling his tale under the hawthorn.

Extreme *busyness*, whether at school or college, kirk or market, is a symptom of deficient vitality; and a faculty for idleness implies a catholic appetite and a strong sense of personal identity. There is a sort of dead-alive, hackneyed people about, who are scarcely conscious of living except in the exercise of some conventional occupation. Bring these fellows into the country, or set them aboard ship, and you will see how they pine for their desk or their study. They have no curiosity; they cannot give themselves over to random provocations; they do not take pleasure in the exercise of their faculties for its own sake; and unless Necessity lays about them with a stick, they will even stand still. It is no good speaking to such folk: they *cannot* be idle, their nature is not generous enough; and they pass those hours in a sort of coma, which are not dedicated to furious moiling in the gold-mill. When they do not require to go to the office, when they are not hungry and have no mind to drink, the whole breathing world is a blank to them. If they have to wait an hour or so for a train, they fall into a stupid trance with their eyes open. To see them, you would suppose there was nothing to look at and no one to speak with; you would imagine they were paralyzed or alienated; and yet very possibly they are hard workers in their own way, and have good eyesight for a flaw in a deed or a turn of the market. They have been to school and college, but all the time they had their eye on the medal; they have gone about in the world and mixed with clever people, but all the time they were thinking of their own affairs. As if a man's soul were not too small to begin with, they have dwarfed and narrowed theirs by a life of all work and no play; until here they are at forty, with a listless attention, a mind vacant of all material of amusement, and not one thought to rub against another while they wait for the train. Before he was breeched, he might have clambered on the boxes; when he was twenty, he would have stared at the girls; but now the pipe is smoked out, the snuffbox empty, and my gentleman sits bolt upright upon a bench, with lamentable eyes. This does not appeal to me as being Success in Life.

But it is not only the person himself who suffers from his busy habits, but his wife and children, his friends and relations, and down to the very people he sits with in a railway carriage or an omnibus. Perpetual devotion to what a man calls his business is only to be sustained by perpetual neglect of many other things. And it is not by any means certain that man's business is the most important thing he has to do. To an impartial estimate it will seem clear that many of the wisest, most virtuous, and most beneficent parts that are to be played upon the Theater of Life are filled by gratuitous performers, and pass, among the world at large, as phases of idleness. For in that Theater, not only the walking gentlemen, singing chambermaids, and diligent fiddlers in the orchestra, but those who look on and clap their hands from the benches, do really play a part and fulfil important offices towards the general result. You are no doubt very dependent on the care of your lawyer and stockbroker, of the guards and signalmen who convey you rapidly from place to place, and the policemen who walk the streets for your protection; but is there not a thought of gratitude in your heart for certain other benefactors who set you smiling when they fall in your way, or season your dinner with good company? Colonel Newcome helped to lose his friend's money; Fred Bayham had an ugly trick of borrowing shirts; and yet they were better people to fall among than Mr. Barnes. And though Falstaff was neither sober nor very honest, I think I could name one or two long-faced Barabbases whom the world could better have done without. Hazlitt mentions that he was more sensible of obligation to Northcote, who had never done him anything he could call a service, than to his whole circle of ostentatious friends; for he thought a good companion emphatically the greatest benefactor. I know there are people in the world who cannot feel grateful unless the favor has been done them at the cost of pain and difficulty. But this is a churlish disposition. A man may send you six sheets of letter-paper covered with the most entertaining gossip, or you may pass half an hour pleasantly, perhaps profitably, over an article of his; do you think the service would be greater, if he had made the manuscript in his heart's blood, like a compact with the devil? Do you really fancy you should be more beholden to your correspondent, if he had been damning you all the while for your importunity? Pleasures are more beneficial than duties because, like the quality of mercy, they are not strained, and they are twice blest. There must always be two to a kiss, and there may be a score in a jest; but wherever there is an element of sacrifice, the favor is conferred with pain, and, among generous people, received with confusion. There is no duty we so much underrate as the duty of being happy. By being happy, we sow anonymous benefits upon the world, which remain unknown even to ourselves, or when they are disclosed, surprise nobody so much as the benefactor. The other day, a ragged, barefoot boy ran down the street after a marble, with so jolly an air that he set every one he passed into a good-humor; one of these persons, who had been delivered from more than usually black thoughts, stopped the little fellow and gave him some money with this remark: "You see what sometimes comes of looking pleased." If he had looked pleased before, he had now to look both pleased and mystified. For my part, I justify this encouragement of smiling rather than tearful children; I do not wish to pay for tears anywhere but upon the stage; but I am prepared to deal largely in the opposite commodity. A happy man or woman is a better thing to find than a five-pound note. He or she is a radiating focus of good-will; and their entrance into a room is as though another candle had been lighted. We need not care whether they could prove the forty-seventh proposition; they do a better thing than that, they practically demonstrate the great Theorem of the Livableness of Life. Consequently, if a person cannot be happy without remaining idle, idle he should remain. It is a revolutionary precept; but thanks to hunger and the workhouse, one not easily to be abused; and within practical limits, it is one of the most incontestable truths in the whole Body of Morality. Look at one of your industrious fellows for a moment, I beseech you. He sows hurry and reaps indigestion; he puts a vast deal of activity out to interest, and receives a large measure of nervous derangement in return. Either he absents himself entirely from all fellowship, and lives a recluse in a garret, with carpet slippers and a leaden inkpot; or he comes among people swiftly and bitterly, in a contraction of his whole nervous system, to discharge some temper before he returns to work. I do not care how much or how well he works, this fellow is an evil feature in other people's lives. They would be happier if he were dead. They could easier do without his services in the Circumlocution Office, than they can tolerate his fractious spirits. He poisons life at the well-head. It is better to be beggared out of hand by a scapegrace nephew, than daily hag-ridden by a peevish uncle.

And what, in God's name, is all this pother about? For what cause do they embitter their own and other people's lives? That a man should publish three or thirty articles a year, that he should finish or not finish his great allegorical picture, are questions of little interest to the world. The ranks of life are full; and although a thousand fall, there are always some to go into the breach. When they told Joan of Arc she should be at home minding women's work, she answered there were plenty to spin and wash. And so, even with your own rare gifts! When nature is "so careless of the single life," why should we coddle ourselves into the fancy that our own is of exceptional importance? Suppose Shakespeare had been knocked on the head some dark night in Sir Thomas Lucy's preserves, the world would have wagged on better or worse, the pitcher gone to the well, the scythe to the corn, and the student to his book; and no one been any the wiser of the loss. There are not many works extant, if you look the alternative all over, which are worth the price of a pound of tobacco to a man of limited means. This is a sobering reflection for the proudest of our earthly vanities. Even a tobacconist may, upon consideration, find no great cause for personal vainglory in the phrase; for although tobacco is an admirable sedative, the qualities necessary for retailing it are neither rare nor precious in themselves. Alas and alas! you may take it how you will, but the services of no single individual are indispensable. Atlas was just a gentleman with a protracted nightmare! And yet you see merchants who go and labor themselves into a great fortune and hence into the bankruptcy court; scribblers who keep scribbling at little articles until their temper is a cross to all who come about them, as though Pharaoh should set the Israelites to make a pin instead of a pyramid; and fine young men who work themselves into a decline, and are driven off in a hearse with white plumes upon it. Would you not suppose these persons had been whispered, by the Master of the Ceremonies, the promise of some momentous destiny? and that this lukewarm bullet on which they play their farces was the bull's eye and center-point of all the universe? And yet it is not so. The ends for which they gave away their priceless youth, for all they know, may be chimerical or hurtful; the glory and riches they expect may never come, or may find them indifferent; and they and the world they inhabit are so inconsiderable that the mind freezes at the thought.

# WHERE I LIVED, AND WHAT I LIVED FOR

## *Henry David Thoreau* (*1854*)

At a certain season of our life we are accustomed to consider every spot as the possible site of a house. I have thus surveyed the country on every side within a dozen miles of where I live. In imagination I have bought all the farms in succession, for all were to be bought, and I knew their price. I walked over each farmer's premises, tasted his wild apples, discoursed on husbandry with him, took his farm at his price, at any price, mortgaging it to him in my mind; even put a higher price on it,—took everything but a deed of it,—took his word for his deed, for I dearly love to talk,—cultivated it, and him too to some extent, I trust, and withdrew when I had enjoyed it long enough, leaving him to carry it on. This experience entitled me to be regarded as a sort of real-estate broker by my friends. Wherever I sat, there I might live, and the landscape radiated from me accordingly. What is a house but a *sedes*, a seat?—better if a country seat. I discovered many a site for a house not likely to be soon improved, which some might have thought too far from the village, but to my eyes the village was too far from it. Well, there I might live, I said; and there I did live, for an hour, a summer and a winter life; saw how I could let the years run off, buffet the winter through, and see the spring come in. The future inhabitants of this region, wherever they may place their houses, may be sure that they have been anticipated. An afternoon sufficed to lay out the land into orchard, woodlot, and pasture, and to decide what fine oaks or pines should be left to stand before the door, and whence each blasted tree could be seen to the best advantage; and then I let it lie, fallow perchance, for a man is rich in proportion to the number of things which he can afford to let alone.

My imagination carried me so far that I even had the refusal of several farms—the refusal was all I wanted,—but I never got my fingers burned by actual possession. The nearest that I came to actual possession was when I bought the Hollowell place, and had begun to sort my seeds, and collected materials with which to make a wheelbarrow to carry it on or off with; but before the owner gave me a deed of it, his wife—every man has such a wife—changed her mind and wished to keep it, and he offered me ten dollars to release him. Now, to speak the truth, I had but ten cents in the world, and it surpassed my arithmetic to tell, if I was that man who had ten cents, or who had a farm, or ten dollars, or all together. However, I let him keep the ten dollars and the farm too, for I had carried it far enough; or rather, to be generous, I sold him the farm for just what I gave for it, and, as he was not a rich man, made him a present of ten dollars, and still had my ten cents, and seeds, and materials for a wheelbarrow left. I found thus that I had been a rich man without any damage to my poverty. But I retained the landscape, and have since annually carried off what it yielded without a wheelbarrow. With respect to landscapes,—

> "I am monarch of all I *survey*,
> My right there is none to dispute."

I have frequently seen a poet withdraw, having enjoyed the most valuable part of a farm, while the crusty farmer supposed that he had got a few wild apples only. Why, the owner does not know it for many years when a poet has put his farm in rhyme, the most admirable kind of invisible fence, has fairly impounded it, milked it, skimmed it, and got all the cream, and left the farmer only the skimmed milk.

The real attractions of the Hollowell farm, to me, were: its complete retirement, being about two miles from the village, half a mile from the nearest neighbor, and separated from the highway by a broad field; its bounding on the river, which the owner said protected it by its fogs from frosts in the spring, though that was nothing to me; the gray color and ruinous state of the house and barn, and the dilapidated fences, which put such an interval between me and the last occupant; the hollow and lichen-covered apple trees, gnawed by rabbits, showing what kind of neighbors I should have; but above all, the recollection I had of it from my earliest voyages up the river, when the house was concealed behind a dense grove of red maples, through which I heard the house-dog bark. I was in haste to buy it, before the proprietor finished getting out some rocks, cutting down the hollow apple trees, and grubbing up some young birches which had sprung up in the pasture, or, in short, had made any more of his improvements. To enjoy these advantages I was ready to carry it on; like Atlas, to take the world on my shoulders,—I have never heard what compensation he received for that—and do all those things which had no other motive or excuse but that I might pay for it and be unmolested in my possession of it; for I knew all the while that it would yield the most abundant crop of the kind I wanted if I could only afford to let it alone. But it turned out as I have said.

All that I could say, then, with respect to farming on a large scale (I have always cultivated a garden), was, that I had had my seeds ready. Many think that seeds improve with age. I have no doubt that time discriminates between the good and the bad; and when at last I shall plant, I shall be less likely to be disappointed. But I would say to my fellows, once for all, as long as possible live free and uncommitted. It makes but little difference whether you are committed to a farm or the county jail.

Old Cato, whose *De Re Rustica* is my "Cultivator," says, and the only translation I have seen makes sheer nonsense of the passage, "When you think of getting a farm, turn it thus in your mind, not to buy greedily, nor spare your pains to look at it, and do not think it enough to go round it once. The oftener you go there the more it will please you, if it is good." I think I shall not buy greedily, but go round and round it as long as I live, and be buried in it first, that it may please me the more at last.

The present was my next experiment of this kind, which I purpose to describe more at length; for convenience, putting the experience of two years into one. As I have said, I do not propose to write an ode to dejection, but to brag as lustily as chanticleer in the morning, standing on his roost, if only to wake my neighbors up.

When first I took up my abode in the woods, that is, began to spend my nights as well as days there, which, by accident, was on Independence Day, on the 4th of July, 1845, my house was not finished for winter, but was merely a defense against the rain, without plastering or chimney, the walls being of rough weather-stained boards, with wide chinks, which made it cool at night. The upright white hewn studs and freshly planed door and window-casings gave it a clean and airy look, especially in the morning, when its timbers were saturated with dew, so that I fancied that by noon some sweet gum would exude from them. To my imagination it retained throughout the day more or less of this auroral character, reminding me of a certain house on a mountain which I had visited the year before. This was an airy, an unplastered cabin, fit to entertain a traveling god, and where a goddess might trail her garments. The winds which passed over my dwelling were such as sweep over the ridges of mountains, bearing the broken strains, or celestial parts only, of terrestrial music. The morning wind forever blows, the poem of creation is uninterrupted; but few are the ears that hear it. Olympus is but the outside of the earth everywhere.

The only house I had been the owner of before, if I except a boat, was a tent, which I used occasionally when making excursions in the summer, and this is still rolled up in my garret; but the boat, after passing from hand to hand, has gone down the stream of time. With this more substantial shelter about me, I had made some progress toward settling in the world. This frame, so slightly clad, was a sort of crystallization around me, and reacted on the builder. It was suggestive somewhat as a picture in outlines. I did not need to go outdoors to take the air, for the atmosphere within had lost none of its freshness. It was not so much within doors as behind a door where I sat, even in the rainiest weather. The Harivansa says, "An abode without birds is like a meat without seasoning." Such was not my abode, for I found myself suddenly neighbor to the birds; not by having imprisoned one, but having caged myself near them. I was not only nearer to some of those which commonly frequent the garden and the orchard, but to those wilder and more thrilling songsters of the forest which never, or rarely, serenade a villager,— the wood-thrush, the veery, the scarlet tanager, the field-sparrow, the whippoorwill, and many others.

I was seated by the shore of a small pond, about a mile and a half south of the village of Concord and somewhat higher than it, in the midst of an extensive wood between that town and Lincoln, and about two miles south of that our only field known to fame, Concord battle-ground; but I was so low in the woods that the opposite shore, half a mile off, like the rest, covered with wood, was my most distant horizon. For the first week, whenever I looked out on the pond, it impressed me like a tarn high up on the one side of a mountain, its bottom far above the surface of other lakes, and, as the sun arose, I saw it throwing off its nightly clothing of mist, and here and there, by degrees, its soft ripples or its smooth reflecting surface was revealed, while the mists, like ghosts, were stealthily withdrawing in every direction into the woods, as at the breaking up of some nocturnal conventicle. The very dew seemed to hang upon the trees later into the day than usual, as on the sides of mountains.

This small lake was of most value as a neighbor in the intervals of a gentle rainstorm in August, when, both air and water being perfectly still, but the sky overcast, mid-afternoon had all the serenity of evening, and the wood-thrush sang around, and was heard from shore to shore. A lake like this is never smoother than at such a time; and the clear portion of the air above it being shallow and darkened by clouds, the water, full of light and reflections, becomes a lower heaven itself so much the more important. From a hill-top near by, where the wood had been recently cut off, there was a pleasing vista southward across the pond, through a wide indentation in the hills which form the shore there, where their opposite sides sloping toward each other suggested a stream flowing out in that direction through a wooded valley, but stream there was none. That way I looked between and over the near green hills to some distant and higher ones in the horizon, tinged with blue. Indeed, by standing on tiptoe I could catch a glimpse of some of the peaks of the still bluer and more distant mountain ranges in the northwest, those true-blue coins from heaven's own mint, and also of some portion of the village. But in other directions, even from this point, I could not see over or beyond the woods which surrounded me. It is well to have some water in your neighborhood, to give buoyancy to and float the earth. One value even of the smallest well is, that when you look into it you see that earth is not continent, but insular. This is as important as that it keeps butter cool. When I looked across the pond from this peak toward the Sudbury meadows, which in time of flood I distinguished elevated perhaps by a mirage in their seething valley, like a coin in a basin, all the earth beyond the pond appeared like a thin crust insulated and floated even by this small sheet of intervening water, and I was reminded that this on which I dwelt was but *dry land*.

Though the view from my door was still more contracted, I did not feel crowded or confined in the least. There was pasture enough for my imagination. The low shrub-oak plateau to which the opposite shore arose, stretched away toward the prairies of the West and the steppes of Tartary, affording ample room for all the roving families of men. "There are none happy in the world but beings who enjoy freely a vast horizon," said Damondara, when his herds required new and larger pastures.

Both place and time were changed, and I dwelt nearer to those parts of the universe and to those eras in history which had most attracted me. Where I lived was as far off as many a region viewed nightly by astronomers. We are wont to imagine rare and delectable places in some remote and more celestial corner of the system, behind the constellation of Cassiopeia's Chair, far from noise and disturbance. I discovered that my house actually had its site in such a withdrawn, but forever new and unprofaned, part of the universe. If it were worth the while to settle in those parts near to the Pleiades or the Hyades, to Aldebaran or Altair, then I was really there, or at an equal remoteness from the life which I had left behind, dwindled and twinkling with as fine a ray to my nearest neighbor, and to be seen only in moonless nights by him. Such was that part of creation where I had squatted—

> "There was a shepherd that did live,
>     And held his thoughts as high
> As were the mounts whereon his flocks
>     Did hourly feed him by."

What should we think of the shepherd's life if his flocks always wandered to higher pastures than his thoughts?

Every morning was a cheerful invitation to make my life of equal simplicity, and I may say innocence, with Nature herself. I have been as sincere a worshiper of Aurora as the Greeks. I got up early and bathed in the pond: that was a religious exercise, and one of the best things which I did. They say that characters were engraven on the bathing tub of king Tching-thang to this effect: "Renew thyself completely each day; do it again, and again, and forever again." I can understand that. Morning brings back the heroic ages. I was as much affected by the faint hum of a mosquito making its invisible and unimaginable tour through my apartment at earliest dawn, when I was sitting with door and windows open, as I could be by any trumpet that ever sang of fame. It was Homer's requiem; itself an Iliad and Odyssey in the air, singing its own wrath and wanderings. There was something cosmical about it; a standing advertisement, till forbidden, of the everlasting vigor and fertility of the world. The morning, which is the most memorable season of the day, is the awakening hour. Then there is least somnolence in us; and for an hour, at least, some part of us awakes which slumbers all the rest of the day and night. Little is to be expected of that day, if it can be called a day, to which we are not awakened by our Genius, but by the mechanical nudgings of some servitor, are not awakened by our own newly acquired force and aspirations from within, accompanied by the undulations of celestial music, instead of factory bells, and a fragrance filling the air—to a higher life than we fell asleep from; and thus the darkness bear its fruit, and prove itself to be good, no less than the light. That man who does not believe that each day contains an earlier, more sacred, and auroral hour than he has yet profaned, has despaired of life, and is pursuing a descending and darkening way. After a partial cessation of his sensuous life, the soul of man, or its organs, rather, are reinvigorated each day, and his Genius tries again what noble life it can make. All memorable events, I should say, transpire in morning time and in a morning atmosphere. The Vedas say, "All intelligences awake with the morning." Poetry and art, and the fairest and most memorable of the actions of men, date from such an hour. All poets and heroes, like Memnon, are the children of Aurora, and emit their music at sunrise. To him whose elastic and vigorous thought keeps pace with the sun, the day is a perpetual morning. It matters not what the clocks say or the attitudes and labors of men. Morning is when I am awake and there is a dawn in me. Moral reform is the effort to throw off sleep. Why is it that men give so poor an account of their day if they have not been slumbering? They are not such poor calculators. If they had not been overcome with drowsiness they would have performed something. The millions are awake enough for physical labor; but only one in a million is awake enough for effective intellectual exertion, only one in a hundred millions to a poetic or divine life. To be awake is to be alive. I have never yet met a man who was quite awake. How could I have looked him in the face?

We must learn to reawaken and keep ourselves awake, not by mechanical aids, but by an infinite expectation of the dawn, which does not forsake us in our soundest sleep. I know of no more encouraging fact than the unquestionable ability of man to elevate his life by a conscious endeavor. It is something to be able to paint a particular picture, or to carve a statue, and so to make a few objects beautiful; but it is far more glorious to carve and paint the very atmosphere and medium through which we look, which morally we can do. To affect the quality of the day, that is the highest of arts. Every man is tasked to make his life, even in its details, worthy of the contemplation of his most elevated and critical hour. If we refused, or rather used up, such paltry information as we get, the oracles would distinctly inform us how this might be done.

I went to the woods because I wished to live deliberately, to front only the essential facts of life, and see if I could not learn what it had to teach, and not, when I came to die, discover that I had not lived. I did not wish to live what was not life, living is so dear; nor did I wish to practice resignation, unless it was quite necessary. I wanted to live deep and suck out all the marrow of life, to live so sturdily and Spartan-like as to put to rout all that was not life, to cut a broad swath and shave close, to drive life into a corner, and reduce it to its lowest terms, and, if it proved to be mean, why then to get the whole and genuine meanness of it, and publish its meanness to the world; or if it were sublime, to know it by experience, and be able to give a true account of it in my next excursion. For most men, it appears to me, are in a strange uncertainty about it, whether it is of the devil or of God, and have *somewhat hastily* concluded that it is the chief end of man here to "glorify God and enjoy Him forever."

Still we live meanly, like ants; though the fable tells us that we were long ago changed into men; like pygmies we fight with cranes; it is error upon error, and clout upon clout, and our best virtue has for its occasion a superfluous and evitable wretchedness. Our life is frittered away by detail. An honest man has hardly need to count more than his ten fingers, or in extreme cases he may add his ten toes, and lump the rest. Simplicity, simplicity, simplicity! I say, let your affairs be as two or three, and not a hundred or a thousand; instead of a million count half a dozen, and keep your accounts on your thumb nail. In the midst of this chopping sea of civilized life, such are the clouds and storms and quicksands and thousand-and-one items to be allowed for, that a man has to live, if he would not founder and go to the bottom and not make his port at all, by dead reckoning, and he must be a great calculator indeed who succeeds. Simplify, simplify. Instead of three meals a day, if it be necessary eat but one; instead of a hundred dishes, five, and reduce other things in proportion. Our life is like a German Confederacy, made up of petty states, with its boundary forever fluctuating, so that even a German cannot tell you how it is bounded at any moment. The nation itself, with all its so-called internal improvements, which by the way, are all external and superficial, is just such an unwieldy and overgrown establishment, cluttered with furniture and tripped up by its own traps, ruined by luxury and heedless expense, by want of calculation and a worthy aim, as the million households in the land; and the only cure for it as for them is in a rigid economy, a stern and more than Spartan simplicity of life and elevation of purpose. It lives too fast. Men think that it is essential that the *Nation* have commerce, and export ice, and talk through a telegraph, and ride thirty miles an hour, without a doubt, whether *they* do or not; but whether we should live like baboons or like men, is a little uncertain. If we do not get out sleepers, and forge rails, and devote days and nights to the work, but go to tinkering upon our *lives* to improve *them*, who will build railroads? And if railroads are not built, how shall we get to heaven in season? But if we stay at home and mind our business, who will want railroads? We do not ride on the railroad; it rides upon us. Did you ever think what those sleepers are that underlie the railroad? Each one is a man, an Irishman, or a Yankee man. The rails are laid on them, and they are covered with sand, and the cars run smoothly over them. They are sound sleepers, I assure you. And every few years a new lot is laid down and run over; so that, if some have the pleasure of riding on a rail, others have the misfortune to be ridden upon. And when they run over a man that is walking in his sleep, a supernumerary sleeper in the wrong position, and wake him up, they suddenly stop the cars, and make a hue and cry about it, as if this were an exception. I am glad to know that it takes a gang of men for every five miles to keep the sleepers down and level in their beds as it is, for this is a sign that they may sometime get up again.

Why should we live with such hurry and waste of life? We are determined to be starved before we are hungry. Men say that a stitch in time saves nine, and so they take a thousand stitches to-day to save nine to-morrow. As for *work*, we haven't any of any consequence. We have the Saint Vitus' dance, and cannot possibly keep our heads still. If I should only give a few pulls at the parish bell-rope, as for a fire, that is, without setting the bell, there is hardly a man on his farm in the outskirts of Concord, notwithstanding that press of engagements which was his excuse so many times this morning, nor a boy, nor a woman, I might almost say, but would forsake all and follow that sound, not mainly to save property from the flames, but, if we will confess the truth, much more to see it burn, since burn it must, and we, be it known, did not set it on fire,—or to see it put out, and have a hand in it, if that is done as handsomely; yes, even if it were the parish church itself. Hardly a man takes a half-hour's nap after dinner, but when he wakes he holds up his head and asks, "What's the news?" as if the rest of mankind had stood his sentinels. Some give directions to be waked every half-hour, doubtless for no other purpose; and then to pay for it, they tell what they have dreamed. After a night's sleep the news is as indispensable as the breakfast. "Pray, tell me anything new that has happened to a man anywhere on this globe,"—and he reads it over his coffee and rolls, that a man has had his eyes gouged out this morning on the Wachito River; never dreaming the while that he lives in the dark unfathomed mammoth cave of this world, and has but the rudiment of an eye himself.

For my part, I could easily do without the post office. I think that there are very few important communications made through it. To speak critically, I never received more than one or two letters in my life—I wrote this some years ago—that were worth the postage. The penny-post is, commonly, an institution through which you seriously offer a man that penny for his thoughts which is so often safely offered in jest. And I am sure that I never read any memorable news in a newspaper. If we read of one man robbed, or murdered, or killed by accident, or one house burned, or one vessel wrecked, or one steamboat blown up, or one cow run over on the Western Railroad, or one mad dog killed, or one lot of grasshoppers in the winter,—we never need read of another. One is enough. If you are acquainted with the principle, what do you care for a myriad instances and applications? To a philosopher all *news,* as it is called, is gossip, and they who edit and read it are old women over their tea. Yet not a few are greedy after this gossip. There was such a rush, as I hear, the other day at one of the offices to learn the foreign news by the last arrival, that several large squares of plate glass belonging to the establishment were broken by the pressure,—news which I seriously think a ready wit might write a twelve-month or twelve years beforehand with sufficient accuracy. As for Spain, for instance, if you know how to throw in Don Carlos and the Infanta, and Don Pedro and Seville and Granada, from time to time in the right proportions,—they may have changed the names a little since I saw the papers,—and serve up a bullfight when other entertainments fail, it will be true to the letter, and give us as good an idea of the exact state or ruin of things in Spain as the most succinct and lucid reports under this head in the newspapers: and as for England, almost the last significant scrap of news from that quarter was the Revolution of 1649; and if you have learned the history of her crops for an average year, you never need attend to that thing again, unless your speculations are of a merely pecuniary character. If one may judge who rarely looks into the newspapers, nothing new does ever happen in foreign parts, a French revolution not excepted.

What news! how much more important to know what that is which was never old! "Kieou-he-yu (great dignitary of the state of Wei) sent a man to Khoung-tseu to know his news. Khoung-tseu caused the messenger to be seated near him, and questioned him in these terms: 'What is your master doing?' The messenger answered with respect: 'My master desires to diminish the number of his faults, but he cannot come to the end of them.' The messenger being gone, the philosopher remarked: What a worthy messenger! What a worthy messenger!" The preacher, instead of vexing the ears of drowsy farmers on their day of rest at the end of the week,—for Sunday is the fit conclusion of an ill-spent week, and not the fresh and brave beginning of a new one,—with this one other draggle-tail of a sermon, should shout with thundering voice,—"Pause! Avast! Why so seeming fast, but deadly slow?"

Shams and delusions are esteemed for soundest truths, while reality is fabulous. If men would steadily observe realities only, and not allow themselves to be deluded, life, to compare it with such things as we know, would be like a fairy tale and the Arabian Nights' Entertainments. If we respected only what is inevitable and has a right to be, music and poetry would resound along the streets. When we are unhurried and wise, we perceive that only great and worthy things have any permanent and absolute existence,—that petty fears and petty pleasures are but the shadow of the reality. This is always exhilarating and sublime. By closing the eyes and slumbering, and consenting to be deceived by shows, men establish and confirm their daily life of routine and habit everywhere, which still is built on purely illusory foundations. Children, who play life, discern its true law and relations more clearly than men, who fail to live it worthily, but who think that they are wiser by experience, that is, by failure. I have read in a Hindu book, that "there was a king's son, who, being expelled in infancy from his native city, was brought up by a forester, and, growing up to maturity in that state, imagined himself to belong to the barbarous race with which he lived. One of his father's ministers having discovered him, revealed to him what he was, and the misconception of his character was removed, and he knew himself to be a prince. So soul," continues the Hindu philosopher, "from the circumstances in which it is placed, mistakes its own character, until the truth is revealed to it by some holy teacher, and then it knows itself to be *Brahma*." I perceive that we inhabitants of New England live this mean life that we do because our vision does not penetrate the surface of things. We think that that *is* which *appears* to be. If a man should walk through this town and see only the reality, where, think you, would the "Mill-dam" go to? If he should give us an account of the realities he beheld there, we should not recognize the place in his description. Look at a meeting-house, or a court-house, or a jail, or a shop, or a dwelling-house, and say what that thing really is before a true gaze, and they would all go to pieces in your account of them. Men esteem truth remote, in the outskirts of the system, behind the farthest star, before Adam and after the last man. In eternity there is indeed something true and sublime. But all these times and places and occasions are now and here. God himself culminates in the present moment, and will never be more divine in the lapse of all the ages. And we are enabled to apprehend at all what is sublime and noble only by the perpetual instilling and drenching of the reality that surrounds us. The universe constantly and obediently answers to our conceptions; whether we travel fast or slow, the track is laid for us. Let us spend our lives in conceiving then. The poet or the artist never yet had so fair and noble a design but some of his posterity at least could accomplish it.

Let us spend one day as deliberately as Nature, and not be thrown off the track by every nutshell and mosquito's wing that falls on the rails. Let us rise early and fast, or break fast, gently and without perturbation; let company come and let company go, let the bells ring and the children cry,—determined to make a day of it. Why should we knock under and go with the stream?

Let us not be upset and overwhelmed in that terrible rapid and whirlpool called a dinner, situated in the meridian shallows. Weather this danger and you are safe, for the rest of the way is downhill. With unrelaxed nerves, with morning vigor, sail by it, looking another way, tied to the mast like Ulysses. If the engine whistles, let it whistle till it is hoarse for its pains. If the bell rings, why should we run? We will consider what kind of music they are like. Let us settle ourselves, and work and wedge our feet downward through the mud and slush of opinion, and prejudice, and tradition, and delusion, and appearance, that alluvion which covers the globe, through Paris and London, through New York and Boston and Concord, through church and state, through poetry and philosophy and religion, till we come to a hard bottom and rocks in place, which we can call *reality*, and say, This is, and no mistake; and then begin, having a *point d'appui*, below freshet and frost and fire, a place where you might found a wall or a state, or set a lamp-post safely, or perhaps a gauge, not a Nilometer, but a Realometer, that future ages might know how deep a freshet of shams and appearances had gathered from time to time. If you stand right fronting and face to face to a fact, you will see the sun glimmer on both its surfaces, as if it were a scimeter, and feel its sweet edge dividing you through the heart and marrow, and so you will happily conclude your mortal career. Be it life or death, we crave only reality. If we are really dying, let us hear the rattle in our throats and feel cold in the extremities; if we are alive, let us go about our business.

Time is but the stream I go a-fishing in. I drink at it; but while I drink I see the sandy bottom and detect how shallow it is. Its thin current slides away, but eternity remains. I would drink deeper; fish in the sky, whose bottom is pebbly with stars. I cannot count one. I know not the first letter of the alphabet. I have always been regretting that I was not as wise as the day I was born. The intellect is a cleaver; it discerns and rifts its way into the secret of things. I do not wish to be any more busy with my hands than is necessary. My head is hands and feet. I feel all my best faculties concentrated in it. My instinct tells me that my head is an organ for burrowing, as some creatures use their snout and forepaws, and with it I would mine and burrow my way through these hills. I think that the richest vein is somewhere hereabouts; so by the divining rod and thin rising vapors I judge; and here I will begin to mine.

## SWEETNESS AND LIGHT

### (*From* Culture and Anarchy)

### Matthew Arnold (*1867*)

THE disparagers of culture make its motive curiosity; sometimes, indeed, they make its motive mere exclusiveness and vanity. The culture which is supposed to plume itself on a smattering of Greek and Latin is a culture which is begotten by nothing so intellectual as curiosity; it is valued either out of sheer vanity and ignorance or else as an engine of social and class distinction, separating its holder, like a badge or title, from other people who have not got it. No serious man would call this *culture*, or attach any value to it, as culture, at all. To find the real ground for the very different estimate which serious people will set upon culture, we must find some motive for culture in the terms of which may lie a real ambiguity; and such a motive the word *curiosity* gives us.

I have before now pointed out that we English do not, like the foreigners, use this word in a good sense as well as in a bad sense. With us the word is always used in a somewhat disapproving sense. A liberal and intelligent eagerness about the things of the mind may be meant by a foreigner when he speaks of curiosity, but with us the word always conveys a certain notion of frivolous and unedifying activity. In the *Quarterly Review*, some little time ago, was an estimate of the celebrated French critic, M. Sainte-Beuve, and a very inadequate estimate it in my judgment was. And its inadequacy consisted chiefly in this: that in our English way it left out of sight the double sense really involved in the word *curiosity*, thinking enough was said to stamp M. Sainte-Beuve with blame if it was said that he was impelled in his operations as a critic by curiosity, and omitting either to perceive that M. Sainte-Beuve himself, and many other people with him, would consider that this was praiseworthy and not blameworthy, or to point out why it ought really to be accounted worthy of blame and not of praise. For, as there is a curiosity about intellectual matters which is futile, and merely a disease, so there is certainly a curiosity,—a desire after the things of the mind simply for their own sakes and for the pleasure of seeing them as they are,—which is, in an intelligent being, natural and laudable. Nay, and the very desire to see things as they are implies a balance and regulation of mind which is not often attained without fruitful effort, and which is the very opposite of the blind and diseased impulse of mind which is what we mean to blame when we blame curiosity. Montesquieu says: "The first motive which ought to impel us to study is the desire to augment the excellence of our nature, and to render an intelligent being yet more intelligent." This is the true ground to assign for the genuine scientific passion, however manifested, and for culture, viewed simply as a fruit of this passion; and it is a worthy ground, even though we let the term *curiosity* stand to describe it.

But there is of culture another view, in which not solely the scientific passion, the sheer desire to see things as they are, natural and proper in an intelligent being, appears as the ground of it. There is a view in which all the love of our neighbour, the impulses towards action, help, and beneficence, the desire for removing human error, clearing human confusion, and diminishing human misery, the noble aspiration to leave the world better and happier than we found it,—motives eminently such as are called social,—come in as part of the grounds of culture, and the main and preëminent part. Culture is then properly described not as having its origin in curiosity, but as having its origin in the love of perfection; it is *a study of perfection*. It moves by the force, not merely or primarily of the scientific passion for pure knowledge, but also of the moral and social passion for doing good. As, in the first view of it, we took for its worthy motto Montesquieu's words: "To render an intelligent being yet more intelligent!" so, in the second view of it, there is no better motto which it can have than these words of Bishop Wilson: "To make reason and the will of God prevail!"

Only, whereas the passion for doing good is apt to be overhasty in determining what reason and the will of God say, because its turn is for acting rather than thinking and it wants to be beginning to act; and whereas it is apt to take its own conceptions, which proceed from its own state of development and share in all the imperfections and immaturities of this, for a basis of action; what distinguishes culture is, that it is possessed by the scientific passion as well as by the passion of doing good; that it demands worthy notions of reason and the will of God, and does not readily suffer its own crude conceptions to substitute themselves for them. And knowing that no action or institution can be salutary and stable which is not based on reason and the will of God, it is not so bent on acting and instituting, even with the great aim of diminishing human error and misery ever before its thoughts, but that it can remember that acting and instituting are of little use, unless we know how and what we ought to act and to institute.

This culture is more interesting and more far-reaching than that other, which is founded solely on the scientific passion for knowing. But it needs times of faith and ardour, times when the intellectual horizon is opening and widening all around us, to flourish in. And is not the close and bounded intellectual horizon within which we have long lived and moved now lifting up, and are not new lights finding free passage to shine in upon us? For a long time there was no passage for them to make their way in upon us, and then it was of no use to think of adapting the world's action to them. Where was the hope of making reason and the will of God prevail among people who had a routine which they had christened reason and the will of God, in which they were inextricably bound, and beyond which they had no power of looking? But now the iron force of adhesion to the old routine—social, political, religious—has wonderfully yielded; the iron force of exclusion of all which is new has wonderfully yielded. The danger now is, not that people should obstinately refuse to allow anything but their old routine to pass for reason and the will of God, but either that they should allow some novelty or other to pass for these too easily, or else that they should underrate the importance of them altogether, and think it enough to follow action for its own sake, without troubling themselves to make reason and the will of God prevail therein. Now, then, is the moment for culture to be of service, culture which believes in making reason and the will of God prevail, believes in perfection, is the study and pursuit of perfection, and is no longer debarred by a rigid invincible exclusion of whatever is new, from getting acceptance for its ideas, simply because they are new.

The moment this view of culture is seized, the moment it is regarded not solely as the endeavour to see things as they are, to draw towards a knowledge of the universal order which seems to be intended and aimed at in the world, and which it is a man's happiness to go along with or his misery to go counter to,—to learn, in short, the will of God,—the moment, I say, culture is considered not merely as the endeavour to *see* and *learn* this, but as the endeavour, also, to make it *prevail*, the moral, social, and beneficent character of culture becomes manifest. The mere endeavour to see and learn the truth for our own personal satisfaction is indeed a commencement for making it prevail, a preparing the way for this, which always serves this, and is wrongly, therefore, stamped with blame absolutely in itself and not only in its caricature and degeneration. But perhaps it has got stamped with blame, and disparaged with the dubious title of curiosity, because in comparison with this wider endeavour of such great and plain utility it looks selfish, petty, and unprofitable.

And religion, the greatest and most important of the efforts by which the human race has manifested its impulse to perfect itself,—religion, that voice of the deepest human experience,—does not only enjoin and sanction the aim which is the great aim of culture, the aim of setting ourselves to ascertain what perfection is and to make it prevail; but also, in determining generally in what human perfection consists, religion comes to a conclusion identical with that which culture—culture seeking the determination of this question through *all* the voices of human experience which have been heard upon it, of art, science, poetry, philosophy, history, as well as of religion, in order to give a greater fulness and certainty to its solution—likewise reaches. Religion says: *The kingdom of God is within you;* and culture, in like manner, places human perfection in an *internal* condition, in the growth and predominance of our humanity proper, as distinguished from our animality. It places it in the ever-increasing efficacy and in the general harmonious expansion of those gifts of thought and feeling, which make the peculiar dignity, wealth, and happiness of human nature. As I have said on a former occasion: "It is in making endless additions to itself, in the endless expansion of its powers, in endless growth in wisdom and beauty, that the spirit of the human race finds its ideal. To reach this ideal, culture is an indispensable aid, and that is the true value of culture." Not a having and a resting, but a growing and a becoming, is the character of perfection as culture conceives it; and here, too, it coincides with religion.

And because men are all members of one great whole, and the sympathy which is in human nature will not allow one member to be indifferent to the rest or to have a perfect welfare independent of the rest, the expansion of our humanity, to suit the idea of perfection which culture forms, must be a *general* expansion. Perfection, as culture conceives it, is not possible while the individual remains isolated. The individual is required, under pain of being stunted and enfeebled in his own development if he disobeys, to carry others along with him in his march towards perfection, to be continually doing all he can to enlarge and increase the volume of the human stream sweeping thitherward. And here, once more, culture lays on us the same obligation as religion, which says, as Bishop Wilson has admirably put it, that "to promote the kingdom of God is to increase and hasten one's own happiness."

But, finally, perfection—as culture from a thorough disinterested study of human nature and human experience learns to conceive it—is a harmonious expansion of *all* the powers which make the beauty and worth of human nature, and is not consistent with the over-development of any one power at the expense of the rest. Here culture goes beyond religion, as religion is generally conceived by us.

If culture, then, is a study of perfection, and of harmonious perfection, general perfection, and perfection which consists in becoming something rather than in having something, in an inward condition of the mind and spirit, not in an outward set of circumstances,—it is clear that culture, instead of being the frivolous and useless thing which Mr. Bright, and Mr. Frederic Harrison, and many other Liberals are apt to call it, has a very important function to fulfil for mankind. And this function is particularly important in our modern world, of which the whole civilization is, to a much greater degree than the civilization of Greece and Rome, mechanical and external, and tends constantly to become more so. But above all in our own country has culture a weighty part to perform, because here that mechanical character, which civilization tends to take everywhere, is shown in the most eminent degree. Indeed nearly all the characters of perfection, as culture teaches us to fix them, meet in this country with some powerful tendency which thwarts them and sets them at defiance. The idea of perfection as an *inward* condition of the mind and spirit is at variance with the mechanical and material civilization in esteem with us, and nowhere, as I have said, so much in esteem as with us. The idea of perfection as a *general* expansion of the human family is at variance with our strong individualism, our hatred of all limits to the unrestrained swing of the individual's personality, our maxim of "every man for himself." Above all, the idea of perfection as a *harmonious* expansion of human nature is at variance with our want of flexibility, with our inaptitude for seeing more than one side of a thing, with our intense energetic absorption in the particular pursuit we happen to be following. So culture has a rough task to achieve in this country. Its preachers have, and are likely long to have, a hard time of it, and they will much oftener be regarded, for a great while to come, as elegant or spurious Jeremiahs than as friends and benefactors. That, however, will not prevent their doing in the end good service if they persevere. And, meanwhile, the mode of action they have to pursue, and the sort of habits they must fight against, ought to be made quite clear for every one to see, who may be willing to look at the matter attentively and dispassionately.

Faith in machinery is, I said, our besetting danger; often in machinery most absurdly disproportioned to the end which this machinery, if it is to do any good at all, is to serve; but always in machinery, as if it had a value in and for itself. What is freedom but machinery? what is population but machinery? what is coal but machinery? what are railroads but machinery? what is wealth but machinery? what are, even, religious organizations but machinery? Now almost every voice in England is accustomed to speak of these things as if they were precious ends in themselves, and therefore had some of the characters of perfection indisputably joined to them. I have before now noticed Mr. Roebuck's stock argument for proving the greatness and happiness of England as she is, and for quite stopping the mouths of all gainsayers. Mr. Roebuck is never weary of reiterating this argument of his, so I do not know why I should be weary of noticing it. "May not every man in England say what he likes?"—Mr. Roebuck perpetually asks; and that, he thinks, is quite sufficient, and when every man may say what he likes, our aspirations ought to be satisfied. But the aspirations of culture, which is the study of perfection, are not satisfied, unless what men say, when they may say what they like, is worth saying,—has good in it, and more good than bad. In the same way the *Times*, replying to some foreign strictures on the dress, looks, and behaviour of the English abroad, urges that the English ideal is that every one should be free to do and to look just as he likes. But culture indefatigably tries, not to make what each raw person may like the rule by which he fashions himself, but to draw ever nearer to a sense of what is indeed beautiful, graceful, and becoming, and to get the raw person to like that.

And in the same way with respect to railroads and coal. Every one must have observed the strange language current during the late discussions as to the possible failure of our supplies of coal. Our coal, thousands of people were saying, is the real basis of our national greatness; if our coal runs short, there is an end of the greatness of England. But what is greatness?—culture makes us ask. Greatness is a spiritual condition worthy to excite love, interest, and admiration; and the outward proof of possessing greatness is that we excite love, interest, and admiration. If England were swallowed up by the sea to-morrow, which of the two, a hundred years hence, would most excite the love, interest, and admiration of mankind,—would most, therefore, show the evidences of having possessed greatness,—the England of the last twenty years, or the England of Elizabeth, of a time of splendid spiritual effort, but when our coal, and our industrial operations depending on coal, were very little developed? Well, then, what an unsound habit of mind it must be which makes us talk of things like coal or iron as constituting the greatness of England, and how salutary a friend is culture, bent on seeing things as they are, and thus dissipating delusions of this kind and fixing standards of perfection that are real!

Wealth, again, that end to which our prodigious works for material advantage are directed,—the commonest of commonplaces tells us how men are always apt to regard wealth as a precious end in itself; and certainly they have never been so apt thus to regard it as they are in England at the present time. Never did people believe anything more firmly than nine Englishmen out of ten at the present day believe that our greatness and welfare are proved by our being so very rich. Now, the use of culture is that it helps us, by means of its spiritual standard of perfection, to regard wealth as but machinery, and not only to say as a matter of words that we regard wealth as but machinery, but really to perceive and feel that it is so. If it were not for this purging effect wrought upon our minds by culture, the whole world, the future as well as the present, would inevitably belong to the Philistines. The people who believe most that our greatness and welfare are proved by our being very rich, and who most give their lives and thoughts to becoming rich, are just the very people whom we call Philistines. Culture says: "Consider these people, then, their way of life, their habits, their manners, the very tones of their voices: look at them attentively; observe the literature they read, the things which give them pleasure, the words which come forth out of their mouths, the thoughts which make the furniture of their minds; would any amount of wealth be worth having with the condition that one was to become just like these people by having it?" And thus culture begets a dissatisfaction which is of the highest possible value in stemming the common tide of men's thoughts in a wealthy and industrial community, and which saves the future, as one may hope, from being vulgarized, even if it cannot save the present.

Population, again, and bodily health and vigour, are things which are nowhere treated in such an unintelligent, misleading, exaggerated way as in England. Both are really machinery; yet how many people all around us do we see rest in them and fail to look beyond them! Why, one has heard people, fresh from reading certain articles of the *Times* on the Registrar-General's returns of marriages and births in this country, who would talk of our large English families in quite a solemn strain, as if they had something in itself beautiful, elevating, and meritorious in them; as if the British Philistine would have only to present himself before the Great Judge with his twelve children, in order to be received among the sheep as a matter of right!

But bodily health and vigour, it may be said, are not to be classed with wealth and population as mere machinery; they have a more real and essential value. True; but only as they are more intimately connected with a perfect spiritual condition than wealth or population are. The moment we disjoin them from the idea of a perfect spiritual condition, and pursue them, as we do pursue them, for their own sake and as ends in themselves, our worship of them becomes as mere worship of machinery, as our worship of wealth or population, and as unintelligent and vulgarizing a worship as that is. Every one with anything like an adequate idea of human perfection has distinctly marked this subordination to higher and spiritual ends of the cultivation of bodily vigour and activity. "Bodily exercise profiteth little; but godliness is profitable unto all things," says the author of the Epistle to Timothy. And the utilitarian Franklin says just as explicitly:—"Eat and drink such an exact quantity as suits the constitution of thy body, *in reference to the services of*

*the mind.*" But the point of view of culture, keeping the mark of human perfection simply and broadly in view, and not assigning to this perfection, as
religion or utilitarianism assigns to it, a special and limited character, this point
of view, I say, of culture is best given by these words of Epictetus: "It is a sign
of ἀφυΐα," says he,—that is, of a nature not finely tempered,—"to give yourselves up to things which relate to the body; to make, for instance, a great
fuss about exercise, a great fuss about eating, a great fuss about drinking, a
great fuss about walking, a great fuss about riding. All these things ought to
be done merely by the way: the formation of the spirit and chararacter must
be our real concern." This is admirable; and, indeed, the Greek word εὐφυΐα,
a finely tempered nature, gives exactly the notion of perfection as culture
brings us to conceive it: a harmonious perfection, a perfection in which the
characters of beauty and intelligence are both present, which unites "the two
noblest of things,"—as Swift, who of one of the two, at any rate, had himself
all too little, most happily calls them in his *Battle of the Books*,—"the two
noblest of things, *sweetness and light.*" The εὐφυής is the man who tends
towards sweetness and light; the ἀφυής, on the other hand, is our Philistine.
The immense spiritual significance of the Greeks is due to their having been
inspired with this central and happy idea of the essential character of human
perfection; and Mr. Bright's misconception of culture, as a smattering of
Greek and Latin, comes itself, after all, from this wonderful significance of
the Greeks having affected the very machinery of our education, and is in
itself a kind of homage to it.

In thus making sweetness and light to be characters of perfection, culture
is of like spirit with poetry, follows one law with poetry. Far more than on
our freedom, our population, and our industrialism, many amongst us rely
upon our religious organizations to save us. I have called religion a yet more
important manifestation of human nature than poetry, because it has worked
on a broader scale for perfection, and with greater masses of men. But the
idea of beauty and of a human nature perfect on all its sides, which is the
dominant idea of poetry, is a true and invaluable idea, though it has not yet
had the success that the idea of conquering the obvious faults of our animality,
and of a human nature perfect on the moral side,—which is the dominant idea
of religion,—has been enabled to have; and it is destined, adding to itself the
religious idea of a devout energy, to transform and govern the other.

The best art and poetry of the Greeks, in which religion and poetry are
one, in which the idea of beauty and of a human nature perfect on all sides
adds to itself a religious and devout energy, and works in the strength of that,
is on this account of such surpassing interest and instructiveness for us, though
it was—as, having regard to the human race in general, and, indeed, having
regard to the Greeks themselves, we must own—a premature attempt, an
attempt which for success needed the moral and religious fibre in humanity to
be more braced and developed than it had yet been. But Greece did not err
in having the idea of beauty, harmony, and complete human perfection, so

present and paramount. It is impossible to have this idea too present and paramount; only, the moral fibre must be braced too. And we, because we have braced the moral fibre, are not on that account in the right way, if at the same time the idea of beauty, harmony, and complete human perfection, is wanting or misapprehended amongst us; and evidently it *is* wanting or mis-apprehended at present. And when we rely as we do on our religious organizations, which in themselves do not and cannot give us this idea, and think we have done enough if we make them spread and prevail, then, I say, we fall into our common fault of overvaluing machinery. . . .

The pursuit of perfection, then, is the pursuit of sweetness and light. He who works for sweetness and light, works to make reason and the will of God prevail. He who works for machinery, he who works for hatred, works only for confusion. Culture looks beyond machinery, culture hates hatred; culture has one great passion, the passion for sweetness and light. It has one even yet greater!—the passion for making them *prevail*. It is not satisfied till we *all* come to a perfect man; it knows that the sweetness and light of the few must be imperfect until the raw and unkindled masses of humanity are touched with sweetness and light. If I have not shrunk from saying that we must work for sweetness and light, so neither have I shrunk from saying that we must have a broad basis, must have sweetness and light for as many as possible. Again and again I have insisted how those are the happy moments of humanity, how those are the marking epochs of a people's life, how those are the flowering times for literature and art and all the creative power of genius, when there is a *national* glow of life and thought, when the whole of society is in the fullest measure permeated by thought, sensible to beauty, intelligent and alive. Only it must be *real* thought and *real* beauty; *real* sweetness and *real* light. Plenty of people will try to give the masses, as they call them, an intellectual food prepared and adapted in the way they think proper for the actual condition of the masses. The ordinary popular literature is an example of this way of working on the masses. Plenty of people will try to indoctrinate the masses with the set of ideas and judgments constituting the creed of their own profession or party. Our religious and political organizations give an example of this way of working on the masses. I condemn neither way: but culture works differently. It does not try to teach down to the level of inferior classes; it does not try to win them for this or that sect of its own, with ready-made judgments and watchwords. It seeks to do away with classes; to make the best that has been thought and known in the world current everywhere; to make all men live in an atmosphere of sweetness and light, where they may use ideas, as it uses them itself, freely,—nourished, and not bound by them.

This is the *social idea;* and the men of culture are the true apostles of equality. The great men of culture are those who have had a passion for diffusing, for making prevail, for carrying from one end of society to the other, the best knowledge, the best ideas of their time; who have laboured to divest knowledge of all that was harsh, uncouth, difficult, abstract, professional, exclusive; to humanize it, to make it efficient outside the clique of the cultivated and learned, yet still remaining the *best* knowledge and thought of the time, and a true source, therefore, of sweetness and light. Such a man was Abelard in the Middle Ages, in spite of all his imperfections; and thence the boundless emotion and enthusiasm which Abelard excited. Such were Lessing and Herder in Germany, at the end of the last century; and their services to Germany were in this way inestimably precious. Generations will pass, and literary monuments will accumulate, and works far more perfect than the works of Lessing and Herder will be produced in Germany; and yet the names of these two men will fill a German with a reverence and enthusiasm such as the names of the most gifted masters will hardly awaken. And why? Because they *humanized* knowledge; because they broadened the basis of life and intelligence; because they worked powerfully to diffuse sweetness and light, to make reason and the will of God prevail. With Saint Augustine they said: "Let us not leave thee alone to make in the secret of thy knowledge, as thou didst before the creation of the firmament, the division of light from darkness; let the children of thy spirit, placed in their firmament, make their light shine upon the earth, mark the division of night and day, and announce the revolution of the times; for the old order is passed, and the new arises; the night is spent, the day is come forth; and thou shalt crown the year with thy blessing, when thou shalt send forth labourers into thy harvest sown by other hands than theirs; when thou shalt send forth new labourers to new seed-times, whereof the harvest shall be not yet."

## SWEETNESS AND LIGHT—SIXTY YEARS AFTER

### *James Truslow Adams* (*1929*)

### I

THROUGHOUT life we always, I think, maintain a peculiar interest in the men and books that deeply influenced our earliest and most formative years. No later work, however influential or revolutionary in our thought, ever attains to quite the same intensity of reality as those which helped to stir our minds in boyhood, when the whole world was opening before us, when thought was the great adventure, and when prophets commanded whole-souled homage. As it chanced, my own first decade was that which is generally accepted as the turning point between the old and the new worlds of thought. In America the Civil War was scarcely less recent, in Europe the pregnant Franco-Prussian War was more so, than is the Great War to-day. Carlyle died when I was three, Darwin when I was four, John Richard Green and Karl Marx when I was five, Matthew Arnold and Sir Henry Maine when I was ten, Browning when I was eleven, and Cardinal Newman and Tennyson a few years later. Dickens was but eight years gone when I was born, and Thomas Huxley and John Ruskin were writing when I was in college.

I have barely to-day touched my half-century, yet these names sound like a long-bygone age. In my boyhood, however, when I was keen on every new intellectual trail, their works were not classics or "required reading," but living voices to which I listened with the same sense of contemporaneity with which to-day we read Eddington or Harvey Robinson, Einstein, O'Neill, or Aldous Huxley. The life, however, which has embraced both Darwin and Einstein, Thomas and Aldous Huxley, has straddled, as it were, two eras in thought and civilization. A straddle is generally considered to be neither a dignified nor a determined position, but if it entails certain discomforts it also offers certain advantages, certain piquancies of comparison. Just as a man who knows only one country cannot be considered to know even that, so a man who knows only one era cannot savor its peculiarities with the same biting relish as one who has been a wider traveler in time.

Time, however, in a busy life is apt to pass imperceptibly, and I confess that it was with a good deal of a shock that I happened to note the other day, when engaged in the scholar's equivalent of big-game hunting, the glancing over of secondhand-book catalogues, that Matthew Arnold's most influential work, *Culture and Anarchy*, was published just sixty years ago. I had the sudden sense of being caught in the swift current of a river. I walked to my study window to look out and ponder.

In these present years of wanderings, my windows open on many scenes in many countries in the course of a twelvemonth, but at the moment my study overlooks Kensington Gardens, in which Arnold wrote one of his well-known poems:—

> I, on men's impious uproar hurl'd,
> Think often, as I hear them rave,
> That peace has left the upper world,
> And now keeps only in the grave.

If Arnold found "impious uproar" in 1869, the very mid-year of the Victorian reign, what would he find, I wondered, in 1929? What change, if any, would he feel called upon to make to-day in his philosophy, and how has the world moved with reference to it in those sixty years gone? Dickens, Darwin, Huxley, Green, Maine, and some of the others have conquered. The world has moved in the directions indicated by them. How about Arnold, who seemed to the cultured youth of the late-Victorian period perhaps the greatest prophet of them all?

One recalls his simple and singularly lucid prognosis and prescription for his own age, an age that to us now looking back seems itself singularly lucid and simple. One has to recall, however, a fact easily forgotten, that every age has its own "uproar." We have to be in it to hear it. Getting into an "age" is a good deal like getting into a railroad train. As we see it first approaching, far down the track, it seems very peaceful. There is no sound, no tremor, only the ease of swift motion. It is only when we are traveling in it ourselves that we feel the jolts and jars, hear the whistle shriek, the brakes grind, the roar of the wheels, and the babel of unedifying conversation in the club smoker.

Even, however, if we are justified in conceding to our self-esteem that we have raised a good deal more of an uproar than was confusing the ears of Arnold, and that there may be more raving now than there was in 1869, it is to misconceive his philosophy to think of him as having given a simple solution for the problems of a simple age. His age was by no means as easy-gliding as the distant railroad train, by no means as stodgy and unstirred as the Georgian retrospect among the younger generation would make out. Arnold's doctrine, in spite of its emphasis on "sweetness and light," in spite of its being the mid-Victorian equivalent of "highbrow," was not intended for the scholar cloistered in an ivory tower, but for the man of action in the turmoil of a transition era.

That doctrine may easily be condensed to two chief points—the eternal contest between Hebraism and Hellenism, and the mediating function of culture, of "sweetness and light." The final aim of both Hebraism and Hellenism Arnold found to be the same, man's perfection or salvation, in spite of the fact that they approach the problem by utterly diverse routes. Hebraism lays the whole stress on doing, on the importance of the *act*, on religion, on strictness of conscience. On the other hand, Hellenism stresses knowing rather than doing, the whole rather than a part, spontaneity of consciousness. The "uppermost idea with Hellenism is to see things as they really are; the uppermost idea with Hebraism is conduct and obedience." Ideas of action and conduct fill the space of the Hebraist's mind. "He is zealous to do battle for them and affirm them, for in affirming them he affirms himself, and that is what we all like." The Hellenist, on the other hand, tries to apprehend the whole of life, to let no part of it slip, to stress no part to the exclusion of the others. He insists upon a flexible activity of mind, and so attains to that clearness and radiancy of vision, that intelligence and tolerance, which Arnold called "sweetness and light." Nothing, he states, can do away with the ineffaceable difference between these two approaches to the problems of life.

Both of these disciplines, as we may call them, Arnold saw were necessary for the development of man. If the tendency of unimpeded Hellenism was toward rather a weakening of the moral fibre, that of Hebraism was no less inevitably toward an extreme hardening and narrowing of man's whole nature. Man's only salvation from swinging helplessly between these two poles was to be found in culture, which should not be a mere dilettante toying with art, but a disinterested aiming to see things as they really are, the effort to cultivate the best in all sides of man's nature. I do not think it has ever been noted that, whether Arnold was aware of it or not, his doctrine was exactly that of Kant, who in his philosophy placed the æsthetic consciousness at the centre to mediate between reason and will. Feeling, however, that in his own time the whole tendency was to stress the Hebraic side, the side of unthinking action, Arnold stressed the other, the side of "sweetness and light," and throughout his life in one form and another preached his doctrine of the saving grace of a mediating and all-embracing culture.

## II

Amid the complete confusion of our present-day social, intellectual, and spiritual life it is certainly not necessary to bring out in any great detail the evidence that Arnold, unlike some of the more fortunate Victorian leaders of thought, did not point in the direction in which the world was immediately to move. Thanks largely to America, where the forces of the modern world have had their freest sphere of influence, Hebraism has conquered Hellenism with an appalling completeness for the time being.

Arnold clearly saw and constantly preached the essential difference between the machinery of life and life itself. It was not that he merely questioned the utility of physical machinery, although it is easy enough to do so. We may well ask, for example, in what lies the great advantage of being able to travel thrice as fast as our grandparents if, arrived at our destination, we do not know how to occupy the time "saved" to as great advantage as they did? It was rather that Arnold saw all the institutional life of our time as machinery—our state constitutions, our churches, universities, libraries, and organizations of every sort. All these he found, of course, essential to life, but merely the tools of life, valuable only for their results, and not for themselves.

In this respect we have obviously gone directly counter to his teaching. We have come to worship our social machinery as an end in itself. Not only is every possible activity organized, which perhaps is to some extent unavoidable in our great modern masses of population, but, what surely is avoidable, we have come to lay more stress on the machinery than on the product, on the means than on the end.

Perhaps we may consider the five great educative influences for the life of the spirit to be one's daily toil, social intercourse, travel, education in its more technical sense, and religion. What of these to-day?

One's daily toil has always of course had for a main object the earning of a living, but it should have in addition an interest in itself. It is a mistake to think that such an interest can be aroused only by intellectual and not by manual work, but, in order that it should be, the worker must feel that he is creating something which he can see grow and develop as a result of his toil. In this respect there was never before, perhaps, a period in which work had less spiritual value for most people than it has to-day. The worker himself has been lost in the complicated machinery of production, and in our worship of efficiency the machinery has come to be considered somehow such a desirable good in itself as to warrant any sacrifice in its name.

Social intercourse in the same way has succumbed to the machinery ostensibly provided for it. Clubs and organizations of all sorts for bringing people together are legion, but conversation has almost as completely disappeared as has letter writing between friends. We are so busy and wearied in rushing from one meeting to another that our minds themselves have almost entirely ceased to meet. It is not only in the hurry of great cities that there is no longer opportunity for friendly communion. For the inhabitants of innumerable Main Streets throughout the country, Monday night is for Grange, Tuesday the Red Men or Daughters of Pocahontas, Wednesday the Junior Mechanics or the Eastern Star, Thursday the Masons, Friday the Lions, Saturday the Rotary, to mention only a few of the provisions for social intercourse that have ended by destroying all real intercourse itself. There is no genuine depth or value to such gatherings—merely a sense of physical proximity to one's kind. For the life of the spirit they are utterly useless.

Travel, again, as its means have become multiplied and more accessible to all, has largely ceased to have the educational value it once had. Because one can make two hundred miles a day in a motor, people make it. Because one can cross to Europe and pass through half a dozen countries and back in a month, people do it. Let it not be thought that I am exaggerating. Ask any number of people what sort of motor trip they had, and all too frequently the answer will be, "Fine! We did a hundred and eighty miles the first day, two hundred the second, and so on. No trouble. We were gone only two weeks, and covered nearly twenty-five hundred miles!"

An excellent guidebook to London, lying before me on my desk as I write, tells how one may see the city in one day. In the morning one is to go to the National Gallery, the National Portrait Gallery, Houses of Parliament, Westminster Abbey, London Museum, St. James's Park, and four other places. One is to lunch near Piccadilly. In the afternoon one goes to the Royal Academy, Wallace Collection, British Museum, St. Paul's Cathedral, the Law Courts, and drives through two parks and three important thoroughfares. If the traveler intends to remain overnight, the guide continues, he should visit the Embankment and attend a theatre.

This is not a joke. It is intended as a serious guide for 1929 travelers in search, presumably, of education and culture. Comment would be superfluous, but it is evident that the end of travel, the broadening of our minds, the development of our natures, has become lost to sight in the mere machinery of travel—that is, the physical transporting of our bodies from place to place.

Is not the same transfer of stress on, and interest in, the end to the mere means shown daily in our educational and religious systems? If one drops in to see a clergyman and inquire about his work, is not one, nine times out of ten, immediately shown over the "plant"—the new parish house, the gymnasium and the swimming pool, the men's clubroom—or offered statistics? If one goes to a college, one is shown with pride the new "J. Jefferson Jones" dormitory or the "Simeon Smith" laboratory, or the new stadium or business college building. If we turn to the teaching from desk or pulpit, we find the same immersion in the machinery of life rather than in life itself. The body, the "plant," is superb, but one too often looks in vain for the spirit of either Christ or culture.

Is not the reason for all this the fact that in taking the road that Arnold pointed out would surely lead to destruction, to anarchy, we have lost, with the loss of Hellenism, the power to see life steadily and see it whole? We see only parts, the physical part, the machinery part, and have failed to see the end of all these things, the full rounded life of the spirit for the growth of which alone these other things have any validity or value. Of what possible use is a machine, whether it be a dynamo or a university, unless it is to produce something of essential value for human life? Why waste that life on tending machines that produce nothing? Why travel sixty miles an hour if one sees nothing of the landscape, towns, or people on the way? Why go to five picture galleries, two museums, and two cathedrals in a day if one adds nothing to one's spiritual impressions—as one cannot—by doing so?

## III

In seeking the reason of Arnold's failure more to influence his time and ours, I think we may trace it to the extraordinarily rapid increase in the influence of one force in the modern world to which he paid curiously scant attention—science, with its offshoot, modern business theory and practice. It is true that Arnold stood only at the threshold of the changes that science was to bring. In *Culture and Anarchy*, at least, he, in striking contrast to Tennyson, seemed wholly oblivious of the dangers threatening from a new quarter.

Science, which from one standpoint may almost be considered a traitor in the Hellenistic camp, would seem to have deflected the world toward Hebraism in two ways. In the first place, through the products of applied science, and business, it has provided man with an infinity of things of all sorts. Whatever may be the ultimate result, the dream that control over the forces of nature would at once make life easier for man and increase his leisure for the things of the spirit has to a great extent been proved wrong. It is true that in very many cases the mere physical labor entailed in an occupation has been lightened by the new inventions. On the other hand, however, man has been overwhelmed by the very multiplicity and variety of his new goods. These new goods differ in one marked respect from the old range. The old goods, such as enjoying the beauty of nature, reading, expressing one's self in one's work, "making things," playing music, conversing intelligently, looking at pictures or statues, studying, friendship, love, social intercourse, could all be had for little or no money, in civilized communities. The new goods, however, those provided by applied science and business, can only be had in exchange for money.

The consequence is that whoever turns from the old goods to the new at once increases enormously his need for money, and the financial pressure upon the individual becomes so great as in most cases to result in his complete absorption in providing the mere means for living, the accumulating of the things that belong to the machinery of life. So far from increasing the leisure for thought, feeling, and emotion, not only has the time for leisure been greatly decreased, but with the abnormal condition of exhausting one's energies in preparation to live and enjoy, instead of actually living, comes an abnormal mental condition which finds relief only in an excitable activity instead of a normal savoring and enjoyment of existence.

Aside from the new inventions, such as motors, aeroplanes, and so on, of which the prime object is speed, the pressure of modern life due to science and business working hand in hand has greatly increased the whole tempo of life. We used to measure the hours. Now we live by the second hand. The spirit, however, cannot be hurried. We may get more quickly to the Grand Central and the 4:50 by the subway, but not to Heaven. Quiet and time are essential for the fruits of the spirit, whatever a Burbank may do with bulbs. I think it was Daniel Webster who once said that the most valuable thoughts he had ever had came to him while jogging on his nag from place to place on his court circuit. No such deep reflections could come to a modern judge covering the same distance in a tenth of the time at sixty miles an hour in a high-powered car. It has recently been well said of our age that it is "restless, wide-ranging, enjoying pleasure and novelty, but moving in space rather than in time, dwelling on the surface rather than in the depth of things." These characteristics we can trace, I think, clearly enough to that applied science that disturbed Arnold so slightly.

In another and equally important way science has deflected us from that Hellenistic attitude which, in one of Arnold's definitions, is the effort to see things as they really are. To do this is precisely what, until almost the present day, science has claimed for itself, and what even to-day most people think it does. The now deeply ingrained belief that not only has science a peculiar validity, but it gives us the entire truth regarding all aspects of the universe, has acted as a corrosive upon a very large part of the content of culture and the things that have contributed to man's highest life—literature, art, and religion. Much of all this has come to seem mere moonshine fancies when contrasted with the "facts" of science, of which not only the validity, but the completeness, is not to be questioned whatever happens to any side of man's nature or whatever in that nature they leave unaccounted for.

A whole vast range of beliefs and values that were essentially human were wiped off the slate in the name of science. It is needless to catalogue them. The Hellenistic effort to see life steadily and see it whole on the human plane was replaced by an effort to follow a dance of atoms on the scientific plane. Human values became an irrelevant phantasmagoria. The universe was reduced to pure act. In place of the old dangerous error at the upper end of the Hellenistic scale of "art for art's sake," we reached the no less dangerous one at the lower end of the Hebraic, the "act for the act's sake." Hebraism, always more potent among the mass of men than Hellenism, has thus found itself since Arnold's day strengthened to a remarkable degree in both the practical and the theoretical spheres. Not only have the Hebraistic battalions been heavily reënforced, but in science, in the eyes of the public, they have apparently gained a recruit from the Hellenistic camp. The whole scene has shifted since Arnold. And yet was he not right? Is not culture, in its best and broadest sense, our only salvation? Can the present materialistic welter of confusion, if unchecked, lead eventually to anything but that anarchy that formed the half of Arnold's title for his work? If so, what of the future?

## IV

It seems to me that our civilization may take either of two courses. The first may be indicated by a suggestion made to Arnold by an American sixty years ago. This was that "we should for the future call industrialism culture, and the industrialists the men of culture"; and then of course, as Arnold ironically adds, "there can be no longer any misapprehension about their true character; and besides the pleasure of being wealthy and comfortable, they will have authentic recognition as vessels of sweetness and light." We must confess that to a great extent our leaders in religion and education have seem-ingly chosen to follow this suggestion in their teaching of the American people. The Christian spirit has got so mixed up with "drives" and gym-nasiums, and culture with cost accounting and business English, that it takes a wise young man indeed to disentangle them in the face of the strenuous and muddle-headed efforts of his elders.

In many directions at present, however, we are getting suggestions which are not put forward by business men, clerics, or professional educators, and which for that reason, and because they are clothed in a semiscientific lan-guage, may claim more consideration from many. Thus a few weeks ago the noted French architect, Le Corbusier, speaking of bridges, steamships, and other engineering works, said they once provoked æsthetically a "violent antagonistic feeling. They were deemed ugly. Yet these works to-day are acclaimed as admirable. A miracle has been accomplished, a spiritual revolu-tion—'the spirit of the age becoming conscious of itself.'" Others suggest that art is an affair of the whole organism and that the art of any age is intri-cately bound up with the nervous organization of the people of the age. Others, again, hold that the essence of art is one thing and the form another, and that for the future the essence may be permanently passing from pictures, poems, and statues to engineering works.

There is no reason why an engineering work or any other utilitarian one should not be beautiful. They frequently have been in the past, from kitchen pots to bridges. But one cannot help the feeling, in reading such suggestions as that the age is becoming conscious of itself in the sense of admiring its own works, that their authors are unconsciously engaged less in finding new beauty than in condoning our lack of it, though the suggestions are worth pondering. A friend of mine claims not only that a finely made carpenter's tool has a beauty of form of its own, which is true, but that he can get as much pleasure out of studying it as he can out of a Rembrandt. Our race has behind it a long history and a far longer development. From the days of the Quaternary epoch in Europe we have been making both pictures and tools, but it has remained for our own epoch to claim that a tool, however beautifully made, has the same spiritual value as a picture. It is true that the populace of Athens enjoyed spending its leisure in listening intelligently to a play by Æschylus, Sophocles, or Euripides, whereas the populace to-day prefers the horseplay or sentimental slush of the movies, but I do not think the way out of the difficulty is to say that watching a slice of pie jump across the screen or kisses in a close-up is as culturally or æsthetically valuable as the unrolling of fate in Greek drama.

The fact would seem to be that for the time we have lost our scale of æsthetic values, because we have lost our scale of values for the whole of life itself. An age which cares only for the speed of its locomotion and nothing for its purpose or destination is not likely to distinguish between a gasoline station and the Parthenon. We obviously cannot have a scale of values unless we consider the whole of life, consider all the possibilities of man's nature, and reckon one against the other; unless we attain to that perfection which Arnold considered the end of culture—which is "an harmonious expansion of *all* the powers which make the beauty and worth of human nature, and is not consistent with the over-development of any one power at the expense of the rest."

## V

Of course, the anarchy suggested by Arnold as the final outcome of a democracy devoted to a philosophy of doing, not of being, of action rather than of thought, of developing only one side of man's nature at the expense of all the rest, is not impossible. It has overtaken mankind many times before, and in our busy lives immersed in intense activity we need not believe that what has been can never be again. We cannot rely too blindly upon a moderate distribution of baby bonds, savings deposits, and a share or two of stocks among the populace. It is conceivable, in a civilization based on tensions between its members, resulting from trying to secure each for himself the largest share of material goods possible, that as the gap between salary or wage earners and billionaire proprietors increases it may some day, in an economic debacle, prove too wide to be bridged even by a baby bond.

On the whole, however, I do not think this is the direction in which we are going to travel, though I trust to neither the applied scientist nor the business man to divert us from it, useful as are the functions which each otherwise performs. It seems to me, however, that there are not a few signs in the social heavens that the times are changing and that Arnold's doctrine may come into its own at last.

For one thing, the constant stream of self-criticism that arises from the vocal and more thinking part of the American people at present, morbid as it may seem from one point of view, does indicate a deep dissatisfaction with life as it is now being lived by us. There is a widespread feeling that there is something radically wrong with that life, which feeling appears to centre in the demand that we should have more scope for the development of our own individuality, that we should somehow, vaguely as people may yet apprehend it, have a chance to *be* something rather than eternally to be *doing* something, whether for ourselves, posterity, or the Lions Club. In many households this is taking the form of refusing any longer to be dragooned by advertising and high-powered salesmanship into buying every new device that promises even the least contribution to amusement or efficiency. The very activity of the inventor and the business man may itself help in time to bring about our salvation.

For a while we lost our heads. The novel goods offered by the wonders of applied science have been like the glass beads and red cloth offered to savages. We have bestirred ourselves to unwonted exertions in order to get something to trade for them. But we are not savages. We have a long cultural history behind us. We have deep in us desires and cravings that cannot permanently be satisfied with beads and cloth; and there is a limit beyond which we cannot and will not work. If in the future applied science spawns out purchasable goods which business offers us at a rapidly accelerating rate, we shall, instead of trying to have every new thing that comes along, begin to exercise choice. Once we have discovered that among such a multiplicity of objects choice is inevitable from all standpoints, such as capacity or willingness to work, room space, or even time to enjoy them, we shall become more individual, use our minds again, and once more take pleasure in expressing our own personalities. In trying to choose, in deciding what we really want, we shall discover that a great many things worth having are those that do not cost anything to speak of, such as reading, making our own music, conversation, and other old-fashioned things of the mind. Once the strike is on against working to the limit in order to buy to the limit, we shall begin once more to try to see life steadily and see it whole. With the dawn of that day, the pendulum will begin to swing again toward Hellenism.

Intellectually, also, I believe the way will be made easier by a better understanding both among scientists and among the public of just what scientific truth is as an interpretation of the whole of the universe. That understanding, as I have recently said elsewhere, is making rapid headway among many leading scientists, although the public may be long in following their lead. Once, however, the way is open for the reinstatement, not only in a human world but in the universe, of the purely human *values*, the door toward Hellenism will be swung wide. We shall once more see life whole after a dark night of the spirit.

In that day Matthew, or some new Arnold with more contemporaneity of reference and style, will become our prophet, for as I turn from his works to glance at the books on my shelves on economics, sociology, psychology, and science, with their sprinkling of Freuds, Watsons, and Heaven knows how many other "modern" voices, I cannot see that there is, after all, any saner doctrine being preached to-day for the salvation of society or the inner peace of the individual than that preached by the apostle of culture sixty years ago. That doctrine is simply that if democracy is to be saved from anarchy it must be permeated through with "sweetness and light," understood as intelligence and tolerance; that this can be attained only by culture, and not by ceaseless economic activity; and that, eventually, people will not consider that life worth living or that society worth saving which does not allow them to live normally and fully with all sides of their being.

Arnold believed his doctrine worth fighting for through a lifetime. It is assuredly worth fighting for to-day, with far better chances of success, as I see them, from the probable trend of thought and history in the next sixty years than in those which Arnold faced. But if our leaders—our clergy, our educators, our industrial captains, our statesmen, and our writers—continue to preach the contrary one, that our satisfaction and salvation are to be found in *busyness* and things and a unilateral warping of our nature, then Arnold will indeed have been a prophet, for the second half of his title and thesis will have come to pass.

## WAKE UP AND LIVE, EH?

### *James Thurber* (*1936*)

Now Mrs. Dorothea Brande has written a book and Simon & Schuster have published it, with the grim purpose in mind of getting me and all the other wool-gatherers mentally organized so that, in a world which is going to pieces, we can be right up on our toes. I have no doubt that the book, which is called "Wake Up and Live!," will sell some two hundred thousand copies, because there are at least that many people in the United States who want to face the final crack-up in the pink of mental condition. I am not one of these. I don't want a copy of the book; in fact, I don't need one. I have got the gist of the idea of "Wake Up and Live!" from reading an advertisement for it in the Sunday *Times* book section. The writer of the ad said that Mrs. Brande in her inspirational volume suggests "twelve specific disciplines," and he names these, in abbreviated form. I'll take them up in order and show why it is no use for Mrs. Brande to try to save me if these disciplines are all she has to offer:

"1. Spend one hour a day without speaking except in answer to direct questions."

No hour of the day goes by that I am not in some minor difficulty which could easily become major if I did not shout for help. Just a few hours ago, for example, I found myself in a dilemma that has become rather familiar about my house: I had got tied up in a typewriter ribbon. The whole thing had come unwound from the spool and was wound around me. What started as an unfortunate slip of the hand slowly grew into an enormous involvement. To have gone a whole hour waiting for someone to show up and ask me a question could not conceivably have improved my mind. Two minutes of silence now and then is all right, but that is as far as I will go.

"2. Think one hour a day about one subject exclusively."

Such as what, for example? At forty-two, I have spent a great many hours thinking about all sorts of subjects, and there is not one of them that I want to go back to for a whole solid hour. I can pretty well cover as much of any subject as I want to in fifteen minutes. Sometimes in six. Furthermore, it would be impossible for me, or for Mrs. Brande, or for Simon & Schuster to think for an hour exclusively on one subject. What is known as "psychological association" would be bound to come into the thing. For instance, let us say that I decide to think for a solid hour about General Grant's horse (as good a subject as any at a time when practically all subjects are in an unsettled state). The fact that it is General Grant's horse would remind me of General Grant's beard and that would remind me of Charles Evans Hughes and that would remind me of the NRA. And so it would go. If I resolutely went back to General Grant's horse again, I would, by association, begin thinking about General Lee's horse, which was a much more famous horse, a horse named Traveller. I doubt if Mrs. Brande even knows the name of General Grant's horse, much less enough about it to keep her mind occupied for sixty minutes. I mean sixty minutes of real constructive thinking that would get her somewhere. Sixty minutes of thinking of any kind is bound to lead to confusion and unhappiness.

"3. Write a letter without using the first person singular."

What for? To whom? About what? All I could possibly think of to write would be a letter to a little boy telling him how to build a rabbit hutch, and I don't know how to build a rabbit hutch very well. I never knew a little boy who couldn't tell me more about building a rabbit hutch than I could tell him. Nobody in my family was ever good at building rabbit hutches, although a lot of us raised rabbits. I have sometimes wondered how we managed it. I remember the time that my father offered to help me and my two brothers build a rabbit hutch out of planks and close-meshed chicken wire. Somehow or other he got inside of the cage after the wire had been put up around the sides and over the top, and he began to monkey with the stout door. I don't know exactly what happened, but he shut the door and it latched securely and he was locked in with the rabbits. The place was a shambles before he got out, because nobody was home at the time and he couldn't get his hand through the wire to unlatch the door. He had his derby on in the hutch all during his captivity and that added to his discomfiture. I remember, too, that we boys (we were not yet in our teens) didn't at first know what the word "hutch" meant, but we had got hold of a pamphlet on the subject, which my brother Herman read with great care. One sentence in the pamphlet read, "The rabbits' hutches should be cleaned thoroughly once a week." It was this admonition which caused my brother one day to get each of the astonished rabbits down in turn and wash its haunches thoroughly with soap and water.

No, I do not think that anybody can write a letter without using the first person singular. Even if it could be done, I see no reason to do it.

"4. Talk for fifteen minutes without using the first person."

No can do. No going to *try* to do, either. You can't teach an old egoist new persons.

"5. Write a letter in a placid, successful tone, sticking to facts about yourself."

Now we're getting somewhere, except that nothing is more stuffy and conceited-sounding than a "placid, successful tone." The way to write about yourself is to let yourself go. Build it up, exaggerate, make yourself out a person of importance. Fantasy is the food for the mind, not facts. Are we going to wake up and live or are we going to sit around writing factual letters in a placid, successful tone?

"6. Pause before you enter any crowded room and consider your relations with the people in it."

Now, Mrs. Brande, if I did that there would be only about one out of every thirty-two crowded rooms I approached that I would ever enter. I always shut my mind and plunge into a crowded room as if it were a cold bath. That gives me and everybody in the room a clean break, a fresh starting point. There is no good in rehashing a lot of old relations with people. The longer I paused outside a crowded room and thought about my relations with the people in it, the more inclined I would be to go back to the checkroom and get my hat and coat and go home. That's the best place for a person, anyway—home.

"7. Keep a new acquaintance talking exclusively about himself."

And then tiptoe quietly away. He'll never notice the difference.

"8. Talk exclusively about yourself for fifteen minutes."

And see what happens.

"9. Eliminate the phrases 'I mean' and 'As a matter of fact' from your conversation."

Okie-dokie.

"10. Plan to live two hours a day according to a rigid time schedule."

Well, I usually wake up at nine in the morning and lie there till eleven, if that would do. Of course, I could *plan* to do a lot of different things over a period of two hours, but if I actually started out to accomplish them I would instantly begin to worry about whether I was going to come out on the dot in the end and I wouldn't do any of them right. It would be like waiting for the pistol shot during the last quarter of a close football game. This rule seems to me to be devised simply to make men irritable and jumpy.

"11. Set yourself twelve instructions on pieces of paper, shuffle them, and follow the one you draw. Here are a few samples: 'Go twelve hours without food.' 'Stay up all night and work.' 'Say nothing all day except in answer to questions.' "

In that going twelve hours without food, do you mean I can have drinks? Because if I can have drinks, I can do it easily. As for staying up all night and working, I know all about that: that simply turns night into day and day into night. I once got myself into such a state staying up all night that I was always having orange juice and boiled eggs at twilight and was just ready for lunch after everybody else had gone to bed. I had to go away to a sanitarium to get turned around. As for saying nothing all day except in answer to questions, what am I to do if a genial colleague comes into my office and says, "I think your mother is one of the nicest people I ever met" or "I was thinking about giving you that twenty dollars you lent me"? Do I just stare at him and walk out of the room? I lose enough friends, and money, the way it is.

"12. Say 'Yes' to every reasonable request made of you in the course of one day."

All right, start making some. I can't think of a single one offhand. The word "reasonable" has taken a terrible tossing around in my life—both personal and business. If you mean watering the geraniums, I'll do that. If you mean walking around Central Park with you for the fresh air and exercise, you are crazy.

Has anybody got any more sets of specific disciplines? If anybody has, they've got to be pretty easy ones if I am going to wake up and live. It's mighty comfortable dozing here and waiting for the end.

## WHAT I BELIEVE
### Lewis Mumford   (1931)

BETWEEN one's conscious philosophy and the faith that one lives by there is a greater or smaller gap, as the first becomes more deeply integrated with one's nature, and as the second rises to completer expression. In a harmonious life, the intellectual formula and the inner impetus would be one; but such harmony is far to seek. There are professed Christians, perhaps honest in their intellectual convictions, who have never had a single natural impulse to live in charity and peace. In *Androcles and the Lion,* Bernard Shaw confronted one of these creatures with the temptation to exercise his physical strength in combat and overthrew in a moment all his dearly prized beliefs: the powerful Ferrovius had a conscious philosophy which neither emerged from nor properly disciplined the man that he was; the discrepancy was too great, the points of contact too infrequent. The result of holding such a system is either perpetual conflict or perpetual hypocrisy.

Within the norms of society, every man must find his own living philosophy. This is more than the sum of one's beliefs, judgments, standards, axioms, put together in an orderly system: it is rather a resolution of one's abstract plan of living with the circumstances and emergencies of actual existence. An adequate philosophy ought to bring together one's scheme of living, one's conscious reflections, and the inner go of the self. While it faces the evils of existence, it should recognize and consciously multiply the goods. What are these goods? Where are they to be found, and how are they to be embodied?

Most of the ethical philosophies of the past have sought to isolate the goods of life and to make one or another of them supreme: they have looked upon pleasure or efficiency or duty or sacrifice or imperturbability or self-annihilation or decorum as the chief end of a disciplined and cultivated spirit. Since no one goes through the world unhurt, and since violence and injustice have often had the upper hand, they have sometimes sought by a system of supernatural bookkeeping to redress the evils of earthly existence in another sphere; but to seek pleasure or immortality or happiness has been the common goal of these faiths—if not now, then hereafter.

There is no sanction in my philosophy for any single set of ends or goals. The fact that sunshine is beneficial to the body does not make the Sahara an ideal place to live in; and no single principle will produce an harmonious and well-balanced life. Values emerge from life at all its levels: there is virtue, as Plato saw, in the good shoemaker, just as much as there is in the philosophic guardians of the Republic; and just as a well-organized state would destroy the foundations of its existence if all its members became philosophers, which is very much what happened in our American Brook Farm experiment, so no particular function or good can gather exhaustively to itself all the possibilities of existence. To despise the animal basis of life, to seek value only at the level of conscious intelligence and rational effort, is ultimately to lose one's sense of cosmic relationships; and without this sense a noble consciousness of human destiny, higher and wider than any merely human institution, has never arisen.

Instead of framing our philosophy around an abstract end, and reproaching the universe because it appears indifferent to the particular goal we have erected, it would be wiser to begin with the nature of life itself, and to observe at what point one good or another does in fact emerge from it.

One knows life, not as a fact in the raw, but only as one is born into human society and uses the tools and instruments society has developed through history: words, symbols, grammar, logic, science, art. One finds oneself within a human world of values; and only as a result of persistent inquiry and experiment does one reach such a useful concept as that of a physical universe, considered as self-existent and apart from these values. Logically, one may begin with an abstract system of space-time relations, or with the conception of a lifeless physical universe of matter in motion, and one may build up a succession of steps culminating in human consciousness and value; but in actuality, it is with the complete tissue of experience that one begins, and only by steadily sloughing off personality, myth, human relevance can one descend to a universe from which one has voluntarily abstracted oneself.

This orientation is important. If it is correct, values are not accidental to experience, nor are they merely ornaments added to the brutal body of existence, as in a bad piece of architecture, without affecting either the function or the design: values are, on the contrary, present from the beginning, and they exercise a determining influence over every stage of life and thought.

If the physical universe does not, as a separate concept, imply life and value, it is nevertheless true that human value implies the physical universe: hence the preoccupation with the stars and with cosmic destiny that pervades almost every religion, even that austere and attenuated form associated with modern positive science. The vague stir within us, which we associate with the beat of our hearts and the expansion of our lungs, requires for sustenance a whole solar system, merely to maintain such elementary relations as the heat of our blood. Similarly, the crudest social existence implies the effort of untold generations of men to differentiate foods from poisons, invent tools, devise shelters, create symbols, signs, and gestures, and build up a body of communicable experience.

Individualism in the sense of isolation is merely a spatial illusion. The more self-sufficient an individual seems to be, the more sure it is that, like Thoreau at Walden Pond, he carries a whole society in his bosom. This fact applies equally to nations. Both physically and spiritually we are members one of another; and we have never been anything else, although the callosities of ignorance and egotism have sometimes made us insensitive to this condition. This sense of cosmic interdependence is both one's ultimate intuition about the universe, and the most direct key to its practical activities: for the cosmic sense probably grew originally out of the realities of social life itself, the oneness of the tribe, of parent and child, of husband and wife. Without this sense, man is a defiant atom, awaiting annihilation—a cruel joke in a mirthless world.

Life begins then with a tissue of inherited values. Only by hard effort and experiment does one reach the matter-of-fact plane: indeed, the sense of a neutral world, untouched by man's efforts, indifferent to his activities, obdurate to wish and supplication, is one of the supreme triumphs of his imagination, and in itself represents a fresh human value.

Thought, social relations, biological activities, cosmic backgrounds—all call for a system of manifold coöperations, and the finer life becomes, the more complicated is this network, and the more highly conscious must one become of one's relations within it. Goethe once put the case admirably in a conversation with Eckermann: "People are always talking about originality; but what do they mean? As soon as we are born, the world begins to work upon us, and keeps on to the end. What can we call ours, except energy, strength, will? If I could give an account of what I owe to great predecessors and contemporaries, there would be but a small remainder." The person who fancies he has made his own career, or the inventor who believes he has the sole right to his invention, or the philosopher who announces a completely new system of thought, is merely ignorant of his sources. Darwin formulated his *Origin of Species* with the sense of having made a unique personal discovery; before he was finished the similar hypothesis of another young naturalist, Wallace, was brought to his attention; by the time he published his second edition, he had at last become aware that a whole literature on evolution had preceded his announcement. The individual contribution, the work of any single generation, is infinitesimal: the power and glory belong to human society at large, and are the long result of time.

This is the philosophic justification for communism. Since it coincides with the practical reason for communism—namely, that every human being requires approximately the same share of air, water, clothing, food, shelter, and the prevailing material culture, with small differences to allow for climate and occupation—the political institutions of society should be arranged to establish this minimum basis of life. Differentiation and preference and special incentive should be taken into account only after the security and continuity of life itself is assured. This is my fundamental political faith: it corresponds roughly to Plato's. Necessarily, the task of organizing a basic communism is not an easy one, particularly in an industrial world where so many steps intervene between the land and the raw resources of nature and the ultimate products that must be made available. While special societies like monasteries and armies have often achieved a rough measure of communism, the real difficulty is to apply the method to the community at large and still preserve those delicate volitions and intense individual interests which are an incentive to creative activity.

One of the first moves in this direction is to alter by example and education the current scheme of values. In our present Western societies, with the exception of Soviet Russia, pecuniary prestige and property interests come first; life, and the values derived from actual living, exist on sufferance, or are scourged out of existence. Love, art, poetry, disinterested thought, the free use of the imagination, the pursuit of non-utilitarian activities and the enjoyment of non-consumable goods—all these things do not come within the dominant pecuniary scale of values, and are falsified and belittled by any such association. Yet a life that does not enter into their realm is a life that has never fully come to flower: the means and instruments of daily activity, which are sanctified by the existence of these deeper values, are bereft of even their proper significance by being condemned to serve as substitutes for the whole.

While a basic economic communism, which would extend to the whole community the decent practices of the household, seems to me a necessary measure of justice and practical statesmanship, one need not therefore hold, with an older school of revolutionary thinkers, that the evils of life are entirely the work of an ominous capitalist class, or that they are entirely economic in origin and would be abolished under a more humane régime.

On the contrary, I have no more notion of abolishing evil than I have of abolishing shadow in a world of light. Fourier's belief that the ocean itself under a harmonized social order might turn into lemonade, and Spencer's picture of the future society as a sort of polite eternal Sunday afternoon, are merely exhibitions, as it were, of an unfathomable shallowness. Evil and good are phases in the process of growth; and who shall say which is the better teacher? Illness, error, defeat, frustration, disintegration, malicious accident, all these elements are as much in the process of life as waste, nutrition, and repair. The very forces which, if triumphant, would destroy life are needful to season experience and deepen understanding. The virtuous man aims, not at the abstract condition of goodness, but at a life abundant: his success lies, not in escaping evil, as the Brahmin avoids taking life by having even the insects swept out of his path, but by turning it to the account of the vital process itself.

Observing the role of evil, the greater religions of the past have celebrated almost solely the negative aspects of existence: they have confronted death and extinction in all their forms, and have been concerned above all with the relief of the ailing and the release of the transgressor. In reaction against the superstitious element in these religions, one must not commit the opposite error of ignoring the function of evil in the vital economy. The goods of life have large capacities for mischief: who has not observed the charity that poisons the giver, and the brotherhood that is based upon hatred of the outsider? In fact, nothing needs such constant watching and revision as the practice of the virtues: before one realizes it, as Emerson pointed out in *Uriel*, goods become evils. But similarly, the evils of life have a large capacity for good; and the mature person knows that they must be faced, embraced, assimilated; that to shun them or innocently hope to eliminate them altogether is to cling to an existence that is both false to reality and essentially lacking in perspective and depth. Like arsenic, evil is a tonic in grains and a poison in ounces. The real problem of evil, the problem that justifies every assault upon war and poverty and disease, is to reduce it to amounts that can be spiritually assimilated.

This doctrine is just the opposite of certain "optimistic" life-denying attitudes and habits of mind that have become popular during the last three centuries: particularly, the notion that comfort, safety, the absence of physical disease are the greatest blessings of civilization, and that as they increase evil will be automatically abolished. The fallacy of this view lies in the fact that comfort and safety are not absolute qualities, but are capable of defeating life quite as thoroughly as hardship and disease and uncertainty; and the notion that every other human interest, religion, art, friendship, love, must be subordinated to the production of increasing amounts of comforts and luxuries is merely one of the dark superstitions of our money-bent utilitarian society. By accepting this superstition as an essential modern creed, the utilitarian has turned an elementary condition of existence, the necessity for providing for the physical basis of life, into an end. Avaricious of power and riches and goods, he has summoned to his aid the resources of modern science and technology. As a result, we are oriented to "things," and have every sort of possession except self-possession. By putting business before every other manifestation of life, our mechanical and financial civilization has forgotten the chief business of life, namely, growth, reproduction, development. It pays infinite attention to the incubator—and it forgets the egg.

Now, the end of all practical activity is culture: a maturing mind, a ripening character, an increasing sense of mastery and fulfillment, a higher integration of all one's powers in a social personality, a larger capacity for intellectual interests and emotional enjoyments, for more complex and subtle states of mind. In part, the interests of culture are served directly by participation in workaday activity, and in part, they emerge from it and independently preside over it. Arrested personalities look back, perhaps, with regret to some temporary fulfillment in youth, as Mark Twain looked back to the happy adventures of Huckleberry Finn; whereas developing personalities accept, without impatience or regret, the next stage in their growth; and by the time they are men, they have no difficulty in putting away childish things.

Growth and culture imply both activity and periods of leisure sufficient to absorb the results of this activity, using it to enrich art and manners and personality. The Athenians were quite right in believing that the final goods of life could not be achieved by anyone who was forced to spend the entire day in some spiritually deadening or physically exhausting task in the shop or on the farm; but it is equally true that the spiritual life itself suffers by complete divorce from the vivid experiences and the salutary restraints of practical activity, and though the Athenians in some measure retained their hold on the fundamental manual and operative realities by participating in sport and war, it is perhaps no accident that their most original mind was a stone-cutter by trade, and the son of a midwife. A society that gives to one class all the opportunities of leisure, and to another all the burdens of work, dooms both classes to a partial spiritual sterility: for one of the main tasks of life is to keep the inner world and the outer, the spiritual and the practical, in constant and rhythmically related activity.

The practical moral to be drawn from this is that servile labor—even if it produces necessities—should be minimized to the utmost, and that leisure must be distributed more universally in the form of a shorter working day, instead of being permitted to exist as the penalizing burden of "unemployment." Without leisure, there can be neither art nor science nor fine conversation, nor any ceremonious performance of the offices of love and friendship. If our Machine Age has any promise for culture, it is not in the actual multiplication of motor cars and vacuum cleaners, but in the potential creation of leisure. But so long as "comfort" and not life is our standard, the Machine Age will remain impotent.

Our higher activities are curbed in society by the present alternations of excessive toil and short periods of sodden release. The fact that the majority of people go to the theater or the concert hall, for example, at the end of a long working day explains in good part the quality of the drama they demand: in a state of physical fatigue, they are unable to face the intense experiences that the great composers and dramatists call forth: they are jaded, and they need stimuli, or they are irritated, and they need sedatives. Except for an occasional musical festival for the leisured, like those at Salzburg or Glastonbury or Bethlehem, there has been little opportunity in our civilization to experience art under conditions which permit sensitive enjoyment, to say nothing of complete rapture. In this respect the traditional religions with their days of rest devoted to contemplation, and their seasonal festivals, were far more favorable to the finer culture of the mind. The effect of leisure in our machine-ridden society is merely to promote other forms of purely consumptive activity; such as the ritualistic vacuity of motoring, or equally banal forms of sport and show.

What applies to the contemplative arts applies equally to the arts of action: the dance, gymnastics, above all, perhaps, to sexual intercourse. Without leisure, freshness, energy, they lose their inner impetus, and must be excited to activity by the rivalry of athletic matches, by the negative stimulus of ill-health, or by preliminary bouts of strong liquor. Yet all these arts are quite as central to life as the most beneficent instrumental activity. In so far as many primitive communities have maintained the arts of action in a more consistent and whole-hearted way than our Western civilization, we need not boast too loudly about our advantages; for our progress has not been unmixed with lapses and regressions in matters that are much more important to our welfare than the production of cheap pig iron.

Instead of the one-sided practical activity fostered by the ideals of the utilitarians, and abetted by our modern technology, with its intense specialization, I believe in a rounded, symmetrical development of both the human personality and the community itself. Economics would play a part in that development, but it would not dominate it. That specialization leads inevitably to efficiency is a specious argument; for as there is, in Ruskin's words, no wealth but life, so there is no efficiency except that which furthers life. Moreover, this argument takes no account of the mountains of useless arid work that are accumulated under our present habit of specialization; and it gives to this practice the sole credit for gains that are due to quite another technique, namely, coöperative intercourse and association.

The metaphysical case against specialization is even more overwhelming. We live in a world where no single event exists by itself; but, on the contrary, where every event is originally conditioned by its environment. If one attempts to deal with any little segment in isolation, one is dealing with a temporary abstraction. One begins, indeed, to learn a little about the things that are closest to one's interest only when one has traced out their interrelationships with that which may, apparently, lie far beyond. While abstract,

analytical thinking is one of the great achievements of the race, it is misleading
and mischievous unless it takes place in a synthetic environment. The habit
of substituting abstractions for the situation as a whole is responsible, for
example, for our habit of placing economic needs ahead of esthetic and
spiritual ones, whereas it should be plain that they are indissolubly connected
from the first moment of infancy when the baby taking milk at the breast
responds equally to the esthetic stimulus of the lullaby; and it is only by a
systematic and brutal miseducation that these interrelated needs can be
sundered. That we have actually achieved this divorce during the last century
is only a proof of the overwhelming power of the educational process when
it is reënforced by the customs and preoccupations of society at large.

How are we to achieve synthesis in thought and synergy in action? Shall
we heap together in a vast mechanical accumulation all our specialist researches, in the fashion of an encyclopedia? Shall we boil down all knowledge
and practice into popular outlines? No: the result of such an arithmetical
addition would merely be another specialism. While a schematic synthesis is
a necessary help to orderly thinking, the place to achieve synthesis primarily
is in living itself, in encompassing all the activities that make a full life. This
does not mean that we are to disperse ourselves, like the proverbial rolling
stone, in a series of inconsecutive and nonrelated occupations: it means,
rather, that once we have found a central purpose and point of view in our
own life, we should subject ourselves to every activity that is necessary for a
full experience and a complete understanding of life—knowing at first hand
both manual toil and esthetic ecstasy, periods of hard routine and periods of
adventure, intellectual concentration and the animal relaxation, strict discipline and random activity. We must explore our environment in space and
time, and selectively reconstitute its chaotic elements in a related pattern—
taking possession of the historic heritage of culture by reëducation, and react-
ing upon the cities and landscapes and industries we have surveyed by replanning them for actual functions and humane ends. Both reëducation and
replanning begin at home: a social program that lacks a form of individual
discipline is a hollow shell. This form of discovery is ultimately self-dis-
covery; and through coöperative action, it becomes self-fulfillment.

Such a complete mode of living must inevitably carry over into each special situation: only a vicious system of miseducation can prevent it. By
ceasing to live in isolated compartments, one avoids the delusive habit of treating the world in this manner, and one approaches each event with an intuition
of its wholeness—as not primarily physical or biological or economic or
esthetic, but as all of these things together in a certain unique, emergent combination. Temporarily, as a practical convenience, one will not be afraid of
using the method of analysis to the utmost; but, weighing, measuring, de-
composing, one will still be aware of the organic whole in space and time
with which one started, and to which, enriched by the processes of analysis
and specialized activity, one must ultimately return.

In so far as we fall short of completeness and symmetry in our daily life, we must be doubly aware of the unconscious distortions and falsifications that follow from such a condition. The conceptions of purity and chastity and biological fulfillment, formed by abstemious saints driven grudgingly to admit that it is better to marry than to burn, have very little relevance or efficacy in guiding the rest of the race in the joys and duties of family life; and in general, the intensification of the spiritual life which follows from complete abstention from the normal routine of the mass of mankind, has frequently erected for society goals and duties that arise properly only from such spiritual concentration—and without it work mischief. The peace achievable in solitude gives small clue to the proper guidance of the ego in social situations of strife and rivalry. A living philosophy must face life and society in their complex wholeness; it must avoid those deceptive simplifications which derive from the conscious or unconscious renunciation of the whole.

My faith, for its full consummation, must be embodied in a community; for a well-integrated life is impossible unless the social relations that condition and develop it respond to its needs. How shall I describe such a community? This life does not exist in the past, although every civilization in its best moments gives more than a hint of it, and plenty of guarantee against its being fantastic and beyond reach. Symbolically, this rounded and interrelated life has been expressed in certain works of art, such as *Moby Dick, War and Peace, The Magic Mountain;* and if one were founding a church, instead of summoning up one's intuition of life, one would include in the calendar of saints a Plato, a Blake, a Goethe, a Whitman. Though among men of science this faith has cohered more slowly, partly because the pattern of research has been set by a purely analytical seventeenth century physics, it gets its rational support from science to-day, and would include men like A. N. Whitehead, J. S. Haldane, J. A. Thomson, L. J. Henderson, Jennings, and Wheeler.

For me, the confirmation of my intuitions came through acquaintance with Patrick Geddes, whose long life spans the service of many sciences, from biology to sociology, and many types of activity, from that of the speculative philosopher to the planner of cities. Geddes showed that a conception of life, unified at the center and ramifying in many interrelations and comprehensions at the periphery, could be rationally lived; that it had not been outmoded by the age of specialization but was actually a mode that might, through its superior vitality and efficiency, supplant this age; that one could practice in one's own person in the germ a type of thinking and feeling and acting which might ultimately be embodied, with fuller, deeper effect, in the whole community; that even on the crude test of survival, a life that was organically grounded and pursued with a little courage and audacity, had perhaps a better chance than the narrow goals and diminished possibilities of our dominant civilization. My utopia is such a life, writ large.

To be alive, to act, to contemplate, to embody significance and value, to become fully human—these ends are difficult of achievement; and they are all the more so at a time like the present when the whole weight of our civilization is thrown in the opposite direction and, as Spengler has profoundly demonstrated, tends towards forms of sterility and death. But these goals are none the worse for being difficult; and even if the battle were doomed to be lost, one would remember that the path of salvation lies not in the victory, but as Krishna tells Arjuna, in the acceptance of battle. "Not tame and gentle bliss, but disaster, heroically encountered, is man's true happy ending"; and in this spirit one can face with equanimity both life itself, and its tragic and ambiguous rewards.

## LINCOLN AT 37

(*From* The Prairie Years)

*Carl Sandburg* (*1926*)

THE thirty-seven-year-old son of Thomas Lincoln and Nancy Hanks Lincoln had changed with a changing western world. His feet had worn deerskin moccasins as a boy; they were put into rawhide boots when he was full-grown; now he had them in dressed calf leather. His head-cover was a coon-skin cap when he was a boy, and all men and boys wore the raccoon tail as a high headpiece; floating down the Mississippi to New Orleans he wore a black felt hat from an eastern factory and it held the post-office mail of New Salem; now he was a prominent politician and lawyer wearing a tall, stiff, silk hat known as a "stovepipe," also called a "plug hat."

In this "stovepipe" hat he carried letters, newspaper clippings, deeds, mortgages, checks, receipts. Once he apologized to a client for not replying to a letter; he had bought a new hat and in cleaning out the old hat he missed this particular letter. The silk stovepipe hat was nearly a foot high, with a brim only an inch or so in width; it was a high, lean, longish hat and it made Lincoln look higher, leaner, more longish.

As he had gone along farther in law practice and politics, he had taken more care of his looks. His first partner, John T. Stuart, was one of the handsomest figures and best-dressed men in Springfield; and Lincoln had to take Stuart's place once in a courthouse near Springfield, handling a case for a client; when Lincoln introduced himself as the man sent by Stuart to take Stuart's place, the client, an Englishman accustomed to wigs and gowns in a courtroom, refused to take Lincoln as his lawyer, snorted with disgust, and hired another lawyer.

And though Lincoln had begun wearing broadcloth and white shirts with a white collar and black silk cravat, and a suggestion of sideburns coming down three-fourths the length of his ears, he was still known as one of the carelessly dressed men of Springfield, along with Stephen Logan, who wore unbleached cotton shirts and had sat two years as a circuit-court judge wearing an unbleached cotton shirt with no cravat or stock.

The loose bones of Lincoln were hard to fit with neat clothes; and, once on, they were hard to keep neat; trousers go baggy at the knees of a story-teller who has the habit, at the end of a story, where the main laugh comes in, of putting his arms around his knees, raising his knees to his chin, and rocking to and fro. Those who spoke of his looks often mentioned his trousers creeping to the ankles and higher, his rumpled hair, his wrinkled vest. When he wasn't away making speeches, electioneering or practicing law on the circuit, he cut kindling wood, tended to the cordwood for the stoves in the house, milked the cow, gave her a few forks of hay and changed her straw bedding every day.

He analyzed the tariff, the national banks, the public lands, and the annexation of Texas, while pailing a cow. One evening he went to where his cow was pastured with other cows, and as he told it: "I found the calves all together and away from the cows, and I didn't know my calf well enough to distinguish her from the others. Still, I picked out one that I thought was mine. Presently that identical calf went and sucked my cow and then I knew it was mine."

He looked like a farmer, it was often said; he seemed to have come from prairies and barns rather than city streets and barber shops; and in his own way he admitted and acknowledged it; he told voters from the stump that it was only a few years since he had worn buckskin breeches and they shrank in the rain and crept to his knees, leaving the skin blue and bare. The very words that came off his lips in tangled important discussions among lawyers had a wilderness air and a log-cabin smack. The way he pronounced the word "idea" was more like "idee," the word "really" more like a drawled Kentucky "ra-a-ly."

As he strode or shambled into a gathering of men, he stood out as a special figure for men to look at; it was a little as though he had come farther on harder roads and therefore had longer legs for the traveling; and a little as though he had been where life is stripped to its naked facts and it would be useless for him to try to put on certain pretenses of civilization. He may have figured out for himself about how far he could go and find it easy and healthy and comfortable for him to be in speech and looks the Indiana cornhusker and the Mississippi River flatboatman. The manners of a gentleman and a scholar dropped off him sometimes like a cloak, and his speech was that of a farmer who works his own farm, or a lawyer who pails a cow morning and evening and might refer to it incidentally in polite company or in a public address. He was not embarrassed, and nobody else was embarrassed, when at the Bowling Green funeral he had stood up and, instead of delivering a formal funeral address on the character of the deceased, had shaken with grief and put a handkerchief to his face and wept tears, and motioned to the body-bearers to take his dead friend away.

There was a natural grace to it; funerals should be so conducted; a man who loves a dead man should stand up and try to speak and find himself overwhelmed with grief so that instead of speaking he smothers his face in a handkerchief and weeps. This was the eloquence of naked fact beyond which there is no eloquence.

At the death of a great friend he could weep without shame, lone and inevitable; at a petty campaign lie alluding to his aristocratic relatives visiting him, he could laugh and say that only one had made a visit and he was arrested for stealing a jew's-harp. He could be immensely solemn, tenderly grave, quizzically humorous, and flatly comic. As he strode or shambled into a gathering of men, he stood out as a special figure to look at; some of the range of his feeling, the gamut of the solemn and comic, was registered in the angles of his body, in the sweeping lengths of extra long arms and legs, in the panther slouch of running and throwing muscles, in the wiry, rawbone frame that seemed to have been at home once handling an ax in tall timber, with the silent silhouette of an eagle watching.

Standing, Lincoln loomed tall with his six feet, four inches of height; sitting in a chair he looked no taller than other men, except that his knees rose higher than the level of the seat of the chair. Seated on a low chair or bench he seemed to be crouching. The shoulders were stooped and rounded, the head bent forward and turned downward; shirt-collars were a loose fit; an Adam's apple stood out on a scrawny neck; his voice was a tenor that carried song-tunes poorly but had clear and appealing modulations in his speeches; in rare moments of excitement it rose to a startling and unforgettable falsetto tone that carried every syllable with unmistakable meaning. In the stoop of his shoulders and the forward bend of his head there was a grace and familiarity so that it was easy for shorter people to look up into his face and talk with him.

The mouth and eyes, and the facial muscles running back from the mouth and eyes, masked a thousand shades of meaning. In hours of melancholy, when poisons of dejection drugged him, the underlip and its muscles dropped; his friends felt either that he then was a sick man with a disorder of bile and secretions or else that his thoughts roamed in farther and darker caverns than ordinary men ventured into. Ordinarily there was a fresh, gracious calm; it was a grave, sad calm, perhaps gloomy, but strong with foundations resting on substrata of granite; a mouth shaped with depths of hope that its fixed resolves would be kept and held. And between this solemn mouth of Lincoln and at the other end of the gamut, his comic mouth, there was the play of a thousand shades of meaning. Besides being tragedian, he was comedian. Across the mask of his dark gravity could come a light-ray of the quizzical, the puzzled. This could spread into the beginning of a smile and then spread farther into wrinkles and wreaths of laughter that lit the whole face into a glow; and it was of the quality of his highest laughter that it traveled through his whole frame, currents of it vitalizing his toes.

A fine chiseling of lines on the upper lip seemed to be some continuation of the bridge of the nose, forming a feature that ended in a dimple at the point of the chin. The nose was large; if it had been a trifle larger he would have been called big-nosed; it was a nose for breathing deep sustained breaths of air, a strong shapely nose, granitic with resolve and patience. Two deepening wrinkles started from the sides of the right and left nostrils and ran down the outer rims of the upper lip; farther out on the two cheeks were deepening wrinkles that had been long crude dimples when he was a boy; hours of toil, pain, and laughter were deepening these wrinkles. From the sides of the nose, angular cheek-bones branched right and left toward the large ears, forming a base for magnificently constructed eye-sockets. Bushy black eyebrows shaded the sockets where the eyeballs rested with gray transformers of action, thought, laughter. Shaded into the gray of his eyes was a tinting of hazel. In his eyes as nowhere else was registered the shifting light of his moods; their language ran from rapid twinkles of darting hazel that won the hearts of children on to a fixed baffling gray that the shrewdest lawyers and politicians could not read, to find there an intention he wanted to hide.

The thatch of coarse hair on the head was black when seen from a distance, but close up it had a brownish, rough, sandy tint. He had been known to comb it, parting it far on the right side, and slicking it down so that it looked groomed by a somewhat particular man; but most of the time it was loose and rumpled. The comb might have parted it either on the far right or on the far left side; he wasn't particular.

Throughout his life as a grown man he was holding to the hacked-out slants of body that his father had in mind in the younger days when his frame stretched upward in a rapid, uneven growth, and his father said he looked like he needed a carpenter's plane put to him. In those days they had called him "Long Shanks"; and as a grown man his long shanks were a dominant feature of his physical presence. Yet it was true that men and women as varied as Stephen T. Logan and Hannah Armstrong felt about him something elusive, glancing, elfin, off and beyond all that was told by the gaunt, rambling lines of his physical structure. The eyes, the laughter, the play of words, a scrutinizing, drawling poise, curves that came and went with the tricks of sun-showers and rainbows—he gave out echoes and values. A cherishing of true testimonies ran out from his face and form. All he could do for Bowling Green was to weep; the words had not been made that could tell what he wanted to say in that hour. As the day came near for his marriage to the brilliant, fashionable daughter of a Kentucky bank president, he held odds even by writing an old friend—also of hacked-out and slanted structure—the plain, old, dependable, silent, truth-telling John Hanks who could not write his own name: "I hope you will come over; be sure to be on deck by early candlelight." The lizard story might be a rehearsal of a comic pantomime with two players having a line each to speak; and still further it might be a portentous allegory in democratic and religious behavior and words.

When he had bought his house at Eighth and Jackson streets from Rev. Charles Dresser there was a mortgage of $900 on it. And in the deed of title from Dresser to Lincoln this $900 mortgage wasn't mentioned. He trusted Dresser, took a chance on losing $900, just on the personal assurance of the preacher who had married him. And the money was later paid in full.

It was natural that Abraham Lincoln was many things to many people; some believed him a cunning, designing lawyer and politician who coldly figured all his moves in advance; some believed him a sad, odd, awkward man trying to find a niche in life where his hacked-out frame could have peace and comfort; some believed him a superb human struggler with solemn and comic echoes and values far off and beyond the leashes and bonds that held him to earth and law and politics.

In his own mind he did not divide people into good people and bad people. As he walked from his own home close to the cornfields near the city limits of Springfield and met people on his way to the courthouse and the post office, and as he watched the two-legged figures on their many errands or, forgetting their errands, moving around the public square, he saw good mixed in the bad and bad mixed in the good.

In his own mind he made the note: "The true rule in determining to embrace or reject anything, is not whether it have any evil in it, but whether it have more of evil than of good. There are few things wholly evil or wholly good. Almost everything is an inseparable compound of the two; so that our best judgment of the preponderance between them is continually demanded."

## ALMOST THIRTY

### *John Reed* (*1936*)

I AM twenty-nine years old, and I know that this is the end of a part of my life, the end of youth. Sometimes it seems to me the end of the world's youth too; certainly the Great War has done something to us all. But it is also the beginning of a new phase of life; and the world we live in is so full of swift change and color and meaning that I can hardly keep from imagining the splendid and terrible possibilities of the time to come. The last ten years I've gone up and down the earth drinking in experience, fighting and loving, seeing and hearing and testing things. I've traveled all over Europe, and to the borders of the East, and down in Mexico, having adventures; seeing men killed and broken, victorious and laughing, men with visions and men with a sense of humor. I've watched civilization change and broaden and sweeten in my lifetime; and I've watched it wither and crumble in the red blast of war. And war I have seen, too, in the trenches, with the armies. I'm not quite sick of seeing yet, but soon I will be—I know that. My future life will not be what it has been. And so I want to stop a minute, and look back, and get my bearings.

A great deal of my boyhood was illness and physical weakness, and I was never really well until my sixteenth year. The beginning of my remembered life was a turmoil of imaginings—formless perceptions of beauty, which broke forth in voluminous verses, sensations of fear, of tenderness, of pain. Then came a period of intense emotion, in which I endowed certain girls with the attributes of Guinevere, and had a vision of Galahad and the Sangraal in the sky over the school football field; a furious energy drove me to all kinds of bodily and mental exercise, without any particular direction—except that I felt sure I was going to be a great poet and novelist. After that I was increasingly active and restless, more ambitious of place and power, less exalted, scattering myself in a hundred different directions; life became a beloved moving picture, thought about only in brilliant flashes, conceived as emotion and sensation. And now, almost thirty, some of that old superabundant vitality is gone, and with it the all-sufficient joy of mere living. A good many of my beliefs have got twisted by the Great War. I am weakened by a serious operation. Some things I think I have settled, but in other ways I am back where I started—a turmoil of imaginings.

I must find myself again. Some men seem to get their direction early, to grow naturally and with little change to the thing they are to be. I have no idea what I shall be or do one month from now. Whenever I have tried to become some one thing, I have failed; it is only by drifting with the wind that I have found myself, and plunged joyously into a new role. I have discovered that I am only happy when I'm working hard at something I like. I never stuck long at anything I didn't like, and now I couldn't if I wanted to; on the other hand, there are very few things I don't get some fun out of, if only the novelty of experience. I love people, except the well fed smug, and am interested in all new things and all the beautiful old things they do. I love beauty and chance and change, but less now in the external world and more in my mind. I suppose I'll always be a Romanticist.

From the very beginning my excitable imagination fed on fantasy. I still remember my grandfather's house, where I was born—a lordly gray mansion modeled on a French chateau, with its immense park, its formal gardens, lawns, stables, greenhouses and glass grape-arbor, the tame deer among the trees. All that remains to me of my grandfather is his majestic height, his long slim fingers and the polished courtesy of his manners. He had come around the Horn in a sailing ship when the West Coast was the wild frontier, made his pile and lived with Russian lavishness. Portland was less than thirty years old, a little town carved out of the Oregon forests, with streets deep in mud and the wilderness coming down close around it. Through this my grandfather drove his blooded horses to his smart carriages, imported from the East —and from Europe—with liveried coachmen and footmen on the box. The lawn terrace below the house was surrounded on three sides by great fir trees, up whose sides ran gas-pipes grown over with bark; on summer evenings canvas was laid on the turf, and people danced, illuminated by flaming jets of gas which seemed to spout from the trees. There was something fantastic in all that.

Then we were poor, living in a little house down in the town, with a crowd of gay young people around my gay young father and mother. My head was full of fairy stories and tales of giants, witches and dragons, and I invented a monster called Hormuz, who lived in the woods behind the town and devoured little children—with which I terrified the small boys and girls of the neighborhood and incidentally myself. Almost all the servants in those days were Chinese, who stayed for years, at last getting to be almost members of the family. They brought ghosts and superstitions into the house, and the tang of bloody feuds among themselves, idols and foods and drinks, strange customs and ceremonies; half-affectionate, half-contemptuous, wholly inde-pendent, and withal outlandish, they have left me a memory of pig-tails and gongs and fluttering red paper. And there was my uncle, a romantic figure who played at coffee-planting in Central America, mixed in revolutions, and sometimes blew in, tanned and bearded and speaking "spigotty" like a *mes-tizo*. Once the tale ran that he had helped to lead a revolution that captured Guatemala for a few brief days, and was made Secretary of State; the first thing he did was to appropriate the funds of the National Treasury to give a grand state ball, and then he declared war on the German Empire—because he had flunked his German course in college. Later he went out to the Philip-pines as a volunteer in the Spanish War—and the tale of how he was made King of Guam is still told with shouts of mirth by the veterans of the Second Oregon.

My mother, who has always encouraged me in the things I wanted to do, taught me to read. I don't know when that was, but I remember the orgy of books I plunged into. History was my passion, kings strutting about and the armored ranks of men-at-arms clashing forward in close ranks against a hail of cloth-yard shafts; but I was equally enamored of Mark Twain, and Bill Nye, and Blackmore's *Lorna Doone*, and Webster's Unabridged Dictionary, and *The Arabian Nights*, and the *Tales of the Round Table*. What I didn't understand, my imagination interpreted. At the age of nine I began to write a Comic History of the United States—after Bill Nye—and I think it was then I made up my mind to be a writer.

About that time we moved to an apartment hotel, and I went to school. Those first few years of school stimulated my ambition to learn; but since then the curricula of schools and colleges have meant little to me. I've always been an indifferent student, to say the least, except when some subject like elementary chemistry, or English poetry, or composition caught my imagina-tion—or the personality of some great teacher, like Professor Copeland of Harvard. Why should I have been interested in the stupid education of our time? We take young soaring imaginations, consumed with curiosity about the life they see all around, and feed them with dead technique: the flawless purity of Washington, Lincoln's humdrum chivalry, our dull and virtuous history and England's honest glory; Addison's graceful style as an essayist, Goldsmith celebrating the rural clergy of the eighteenth century, Dr. Johnson at his most vapid, and George Eliot's *Silas Marner*, Macaulay, and the sonorous oratings of Edmund Burke; and in Latin Caesar's Gallic guide-book, and Cicero's mouthings about Roman politics. And the teachers! Men and women—usually women—whose chief qualification is that they can plough steadily through a dull round of dates, acts, half-truths and rules for style, without questioning, without interpreting and without seeing how ridiculously unlike the world their teachings are. I have forgotten most of it, forced on me before I was ready; what I do know came mostly from books I had the curiosity to read outside school hours. And many fine things I have had to force myself to explore again, because school once spoiled them for me.

But in going to school I first entered the world of my fellows, and the social experience meant more and more to me until it almost crowded out the study side altogether. I can still see the school playground full of running and shouting and clamoring boys, and feel as I felt then when they stopped here and there to look at me, a new boy, with curious and insolent eyes. I was small though, and not very well, and at the beginning I didn't mix much with them. . . . But after school was out there were great doings, which were too exciting to keep out of. The town was divided into districts, ruled over by gangs of boys in a constant state of fierce warfare. I belonged to the Four-teenth Street gang, whose chief was a tall, curly-headed Irish boy who lived across the street—he is now a policeman. My best friend could make sounds like a bugle, and he was trumpeter. Standing in the middle of the street he would blow, and in a minute boys would come swarming to him, tearing up lawns and making mud-balls as they came. Then we'd go running and shout-ing up the hill to give battle to the Montgomery Street gang, or beat off their attack. . . . And there were the wooded hills behind the town, where Indians and bears and outlaws might be lurking to be trailed by our scouts and Robin Hoods.

Both my mother's parents and my father came from upper New York State, and when I was ten years old my mother and my brother and I went East to visit them. We spent a summer month at Plymouth, Massachusetts, visited New York (I still remember the awful summer heat, the vermin in our boarding-house and the steam-engines on the Elevated), and were in Wash-ington when the "Maine" blew up and the first volunteers left for the Spanish War.

Then I was back in Portland, in a new house, settling into the life of school and play. We had a theatre in our attic, where we acted our own plays, and we built scenic railways in the yard, and log cabins in the woods back of town. I had a number of highly colored schemes for getting adventure and wealth at the same time. For instance, I once began to dig a tunnel from our house to school, about a mile away; we were going to steal two sheep and hide them in the tunnel, and these two sheep were going to have children, and so on, until a large flock had gathered—then we'd sell them. My brother and I had a pony, and we went on camping trips back in the woods, and sailing and swimming and camping up the Willamette River. I began to write poetry, too, and read voraciously everything I could get hold of, from Edwin Arnold's *Light of Asia* and Marie Corelli, to Scott and Stevenson and Sir Thomas Malory.

But with all this I wasn't entirely happy. I was often ill. Outside of a few friends, I wasn't a success with the boys. I hadn't strength or fight enough to be good at athletics—except swimming, which I have always loved; and I was a good deal of a physical coward. I would sneak out over the back fence to avoid boys who were "laying" for me, or who I thought were "laying" for me. Sometimes I fought, when I couldn't help myself, and sometimes even won; but I preferred to be called a coward than fight. I hated pain. My imagination conjured up horrible things that would happen to me, and I simply ran away. One time, when I was on the editorial board of the school paper, a boy I was afraid of warned me not to publish a joking paragraph I had written about him—and I didn't. . . . My way to school lay through a sort of slum district, called Goose Hollow, peopled with brutal Irish boys, many of whom grew up to be prizefighters and baseball stars. I was literally frightened out of my senses when I went through Goose Hollow. Once a Goose Hollowite made me promise to give him a nickel if he didn't hit me, and walked up to my house with me while I got it for him. . . . The strange thing was that when I was cornered, and fought, even a licking wasn't a hundredth as bad as I thought it would be; but I never learned anything from that —the next time I ran away just the same, and suffered the most ghastly pangs of fear.

I wasn't much good at the things other boys were, and their codes of honor and conduct didn't hold me. They felt it, too, and had a sort of good-natured contempt for me. I was neither one thing nor the other, neither altogether coward nor brave, neither manly nor sissified, neither ashamed nor unashamed. I think that is why my impression of my boyhood is an unhappy one, and why I have so few close friends in Portland, and why I don't want ever again to live there.

It must have disappointed my father that I was like that, though he never said much about it. He was a great fighter, one of the first of the little band of political insurgents who were afterwards, as the Progressive party, to give expression to the new social conscience of the American middle class. His terrible slashing wit, his fine scorn of stupidity and cowardice and littleness, made him many enemies, who never dared attack him to his face, but fought him secretly, and were glad when he died. As United States Marshal under Roosevelt, it was he who, with Francis J. Heney and Lincoln Steffens, smashed the Oregon Land Fraud Ring; which was a brave thing to do in Oregon then. I remember him and Heney in the Marshal's office guying William J. Burns, the detective on the case, for his Hawkshaw make-up and his ridiculous melodramatics. In 1910 a man came around to browbeat my father into contributing to the Republican campaign fund, and he kicked the collector down the courthouse stairs—and was removed from the marshalship by President Taft. Afterward he ran for Congress, but lost out by a slim margin, mainly because he came East to see me graduated from college instead of stumping the state.

When I was sixteen I went East to a New Jersey boarding school, and then to Harvard College, and afterward to Europe for a year's travel, and my brother followed me through college. We never knew until later how much our mother and father denied themselves that we might go, and how he poured out his life that we might live like rich men's sons. He and mother always gave us more than we asked, in freedom and understanding as well as material things. And on the day my brother graduated from college, he broke under the terrible effort, and died a few weeks later. It has always seemed to me bitter irony that he couldn't have lived to see my little success. He was always more like a wise, kind friend than a father.

Boarding school, I think, meant more to me than anything in my boyhood Among these strange boys I came as a stranger, and I soon found out that they were willing to accept me at my own value. I was in fine health. The ordered life of the community interested me; I was impressed by its traditional customs and dignities, school patriotism, and the sense of a long settled and established civilization, so different from the raw, pretentious West. My stories and verses were published in the school paper; I played football, and ran the quarter-mile, with very good average success; I had a fight or two, and stuck it out. There were perilous adventures, too, when a few of us stole down the fire escapes at night and went to country dances, slipping back to bed in the dormitory at dawn. With the school social butterflies, I "fussed" girls in the town, and was not laughed at. Busy, happy, with lots of friends, I expanded into self-confidence. So without trying I found myself; and since then I have never been very much afraid of men.

## II

In 1906 I went up to Harvard almost alone, knowing hardly a soul in the University. My college class entered over seven hundred strong, and for the first three months it seemed to me, going around to lectures and meetings, as if every one of the seven hundred had friends but me. I was thrilled with the immensity of Harvard, its infinite opportunities, its august history and traditions—but desperately lonely. I didn't know which way to turn, how to meet people. Fellows passed me in the Yard, shouting gayly to one another; I saw parties off to Boston Saturday night, whooping and yelling on the back platform of the street car, and they passed hilariously singing under my window in the early dawn. Athletes and musicians and writers and statesmen were emerging from the ranks of the class. The freshman clubs were forming.

And I was out of it all. I "went out" for the college papers, and tried to make the freshman crew, even staying in Cambridge vacations to go down to the empty boat-house and plug away at the machines—and was the last man kicked off the squad before they went to New London. I got to know many fellows to nod to, and a very few intimately; but most of my friends were whirled off and up into prominence, and came to see me no more. One of them said he'd room with me sophomore year—but he was tipped off that I wasn't "the right sort" and openly drew away from me. And I, too, hurt a boy who was my friend. He was a Jew, a shy, rather melancholy person. We were always together, we two outsiders. I became irritated and morbid about it—it seemed I would never be part of the rich splendor of college life with him around—so I drew away from him. . . . It hurt him very much, and it taught me better. Since then he has forgiven it, and done wonderful things for me, and we are friends.

My second year was better. I was elected an editor of two of the papers, and knew more fellows. The fortunate and splendid youths, the aristocrats who filled the clubs and dominated college society, didn't seem so attractive. In two open contests, the trial for editor of the college daily paper and that for assistant manager of the varsity crew, I qualified easily for election; but the aristocrats blackballed me. However, that mattered less. During my freshman year I used to *pray* to be liked, to have friends, to be popular with the crowd. Now I had friends, plenty of them; and I have found that when I am working hard at something I love, friends come without my trying, and stay; and fear goes, and that sense of being lost which is so horrible.

From that time on I never felt out of it. I was never popular with the aristocrats; I was never elected to any clubs but one, and that one largely because of a dearth of members who could write lyrics for the annual show. But I was on the papers, was elected president of the Cosmopolitan Club, where forty-three nationalities met, became manager of the Musical Clubs, captain of the water-polo team, and an officer in many undergraduate activities. As song-leader of the cheering section, I had the supreme blissful sensation of swaying two thousand voices in great crashing choruses during the big football games. The more I met the college aristocrats, the more their cold, cruel stupidity repelled me. I began to pity them for their lack of imagination, and the narrowness of their glittering lives—clubs, athletics, society. College is like the world; outside there is the same class of people, dull and sated and blind.

Harvard University under President Eliot was unique. Individualism was carried to the point where a man who came for a good time could get through and graduate without having learned anything; but on the other hand, anyone could find there anything he wanted from all the world's store of learning. The undergraduates were practically free from control; they could live pretty much where they pleased, and do as they pleased—so long as they attended lectures. There was no attempt made by the authorities to weld the student body together, or to enforce any kind of uniformity. Some men came with allowances of fifteen thousand dollars a year pocket money, with automobiles and servants, living in gorgeous suites in palatial apartment houses; others in the same class starved in attic bedrooms.

All sorts of strange characters, of every race and mind, poets, philosophers, cranks of every twist, were in our class. The very hugeness of it prevented any one man from knowing more than a few of his classmates, though I managed to make the acquaintance of about five hundred of them. The aristocrats controlled the places of pride and power, except when a democratic revolution, such as occurred in my senior year, swept them off their feet; but they were so exclusive that most of the real life went on outside their ranks—and all the intellectual life of the student body. So many fine men were outside the charmed circle that, unlike most colleges, there was no disgrace in not being a "club man." What is known as "college spirit" was not very powerful; no odium attached to those who didn't go to football games and cheer. There was talk of the world, and daring thought, and intellectual insurgency; heresy has always been a Harvard and a New England tradition. Students themselves criticized the faculty for not educating them, attacked the sacred institution of intercollegiate athletics, sneered at undergraduate clubs so holy that no one dared mention their names. No matter what you were or what you did—at Harvard you could find your kind. It wasn't a breeder for masses of mediocrely educated young men equipped with "business" psychology; out of each class came a few creative minds, a few scholars, a few "gentlemen" with insolent manners, and a ruck of nobodies. . . . Things have changed now. I liked Harvard better then.

Toward the end of my college course two influences came into my life, which had a good deal to do with shaping me. One was contact with Professor Copeland, who, under the pretense of teaching English composition, has stimulated generations of men to find color and strength and beauty in books and in the world, and to express it again. The other was what I call, for lack of a better name, the manifestation of the modern spirit. Some men, notably Walter Lippmann, had been reading and thinking and talking about politics and economics, not as dry theoretical studies, but as live forces acting on the world, on the University even. They formed the Socialist Club, to study and discuss all modern social and economic theories, and began to experiment with the community in which they lived.

Under their stimulus the college political clubs, which had formerly been quadrennial mushroom growths for the purpose of drinking beer, parading and burning red fire, took on a new significance. The Club drew up a platform for the Socialist Party in the city elections. It had social legislation introduced into the Massachusetts Legislature. Its members wrote articles in the college papers challenging undergraduate ideals, and muckraked the University for not paying its servants living wages, and so forth. Out of the agitation sprang the Harvard Men's League for Women's Suffrage, the Single

Tax Club, an Anarchist group. The faculty was petitioned for a course in socialism. Prominent radicals were invited to Cambridge to lecture. An open forum was started, to debate college matters and the issues of the day. The result of this movement upon the undergraduate world was potent. All over the place radicals sprang up, in music, painting, poetry, the theatre. The more serious college papers took a socialistic, or at least progressive tinge. Of course all this made no ostensible difference in the look of Harvard society, and probably the clubmen and the athletes, who represented us to the world, never even heard of it. But it made me, and many others, realize that there was something going on in the dull outside world more thrilling than college activities, and turned our attention to the writings of men like H. G. Wells and Graham Wallas, wrenching us away from the Oscar Wildean dilettantism that had possessed undergraduate littérateurs for generations.

After college Waldo Peirce and I went abroad as "bull-pushers" on a cattle-boat, for a year's happy-go-lucky wandering. Waldo rebelled at the smells and the ship's company, and jumped overboard off Boston Light, swimming back to shore and later taking the *Lusitania* to Liverpool; meanwhile, I was arrested for his murder, clapped in irons and brought before an Admiralty court at Manchester, where Waldo turned up in the nick of time. I tramped down across England alone, working on farms and sleeping in haymows, meeting Peirce in London again. Then we hoofed it to Dover and tried to stow away on a Channel steamer for France—and got arrested in Calais, of course. Separating, we went through northern France on foot, to Rouen and Paris, and started on a wild automobile trip through Touraine to the Spanish border, and across; and I proceeded into Spain alone, having adventures. I spent the winter in Paris, with excursions around the country, letting it soak in. Then I came home to America to settle down and make my living.

Lincoln Steffens recommended me for a job on *The American Magazine*, where I stayed three years, reading manuscripts and writing stories and verses. More than any other man Lincoln Steffens has influenced my mind. I met him first while I was at Harvard, where he came loving youth, full of understanding, with the breath of the world clinging to him. I was afraid of him then—afraid of his wisdom, his seriousness, and we didn't talk. But when I came back from France I told him what I had seen and done, and he asked me what I wanted to do. I said I didn't know, except that I wanted to write. Steffens looked at me with that lovely smile: "You can do anything you want to," he said; and I believed him. Since then I have gone to him with my difficulties and troubles, and he has always listened while I solved them myself in the warmth of his understanding. Being with Steffens is to me like flashes of clear light; it is as if I see him, and myself, and the world, with new eyes. I tell him what I see and think, and it comes back to me beautiful, full of meaning. He does not judge or advise—he simply makes everything clear. There are two men who give me confidence in myself, who make me want to work, and to do nothing unworthy—Copeland and Steffens.

New York was an enchanted city to me. It was on an infinitely grander scale than Harvard. Everything was to be found there—it satisfied me utterly. I wandered about the streets, from the soaring imperial towers of down-town, along the East River docks, smelling of spices and the clipper ships of the past, through the swarming East Side—alien towns within towns—where the smoky flare of miles of clamorous pushcarts made a splendor of shabby streets; coming upon sudden shrill markets, dripping blood and fish-scales in the light of torches, the big Jewish women bawling their wares under the roaring great bridges; thrilling to the ebb and flow of human tides sweeping to work and back, west and east, south and north. I knew Chinatown, and Little Italy, and the quarter of the Syrians; the marionette theatre, Sharkey's and McSorley's saloons, the Bowery lodging houses and the places where the tramps gathered in winter; the Haymarket, the German Village, and all the dives of the Tenderloin. I spent all one summer night on top of a pier of the Williamsburg Bridge; I slept another night in a basket of squid in the Fulton Market, where the red and green and gold sea things glisten in the blue light of the sputtering arcs. The girls that walk the streets were friends of mine, and the drunken sailors off ships new-come from the world's end, and the Spanish longshoremen down on West Street.

I found wonderful obscure restaurants, where the foods of the whole world could be found. I knew how to get dope; where to go to hire a man to kill an enemy; what to do to get into gambling rooms, and secret dance halls. I knew well the parks, and streets of palaces, the theatres and hotels; the ugly growth of the city spreading like a disease, the decrepit places whence life was ebbing, and the squares and streets where an old, beautiful leisurely existence was drowned in the mounting roar of the slums. I knew Washington Square, and the artists and writers, the near-Bohemians, the radicals. I went to gangsters' balls at Tammany Hall, on excursions of the Tim Sullivan Association, to Coney Island on hot summer nights. . . . Within a block of my house was all the adventure of the world; within a mile was every foreign country.

In New York I first loved, and I first wrote of the things I saw, with a fierce joy of creation—and knew at last that I could write. There I got my first perceptions of the life of my time. The city and its people were an open book to me; everything had its story, dramatic, full of ironic tragedy and terrible humor. There I first saw that reality transcended all the fine poetic inventions of fastidiousness and medievalism. I was not happy or well long away from New York . . . I am not now, for that matter; but I cannot live continually in its heart any more. In the city I have no time for much but sensation and experience; but now I want some time of quiet, and leisure for thought, so I can extract from the richness of my life something beautiful and strong. I am living now in the country, within an hour of town, so I can go down occasionally and plunge into the sea of people, the roaring and the lights—and then come back here to write of it, in the quiet hills, in sunshine and clean wind.

During this time I read a good deal of radical literature, attended meetings of all sorts, met socialists, anarchists, single-taxers, labor-leaders, and besides, all the hair-splitting Utopians and petty doctrine-mongers who cling to skirts of Change. They interested me, so many different human types; and the livingness of theories which could dominate men and women captivated my imagination. On the whole, ideas alone didn't mean much to me. I had to see. In my rambles about the city I couldn't help but observe the ugliness of poverty and all its train of evil, the cruel inequality between rich people who had too many motor cars and poor people who didn't have enough to eat. It didn't come to me from books that the workers produced all the wealth of the world, which went to those who did not earn it.

The Lawrence strike of the textile workers had just ended, and the I.W.W. dominated the social and industrial horizon like a portent of the rising of the oppressed. That strike brought home to me hard the knowledge that the manufacturers get all they can out of labor, pay as little as they must, and permit the existence of great masses of the miserable unemployed in order to keep wages down; that the forces of the State are on the side of property against the propertyless. Our Socialist Party seemed to me duller than religion, and almost as little in touch with labor. The Paterson strike broke out. I met Bill Haywood, Elizabeth Gurley Flynn, Tresca and the other leaders; they attracted me. I liked their understanding of the workers, their revolutionary thought, the boldness of their dream, the way immense crowds of people took fire and came alive under their leadership. Here was drama, change, democracy on the march and visible—a war of the people. I went to Paterson to watch it, was mistaken for a striker while walking the public street, beaten by the police and jailed without any charge. In the jail I talked with exultant men who had blithely defied the lawless brutality of the city government and gone to prison laughing and singing. There were horrors in that jail too; men and boys shut up for months without trial, men going mad and dying, bestial cruelty and disease and filth—and all for the poor. When I came out I helped to organize the Pageant of the Paterson Strike, in Madison Square Garden, New York, drilling a thousand men and women in Paterson and bringing them across New Jersey to act out, before an immensely moved audience of twenty thousand people, the wretchedness of their lives and the glory of their revolt.

Since then I have seen and reported many strikes, most of them desperate struggles for the bare necessities of life; and all I have witnessed only confirms my first idea of the class struggle and its inevitability. I wish with all my heart that the proletariat would rise and take their rights—I don't see how else they will get them. Political relief is so slow to come, and year by year the opportunities of peaceful protest and lawful action are curtailed. But I am not sure any more that the working class is capable of revolution, peaceful or otherwise; the workers are so divided and bitterly hostile to each other, so badly led, so blind to their class interest. The War has been a terrible shatterer of faith in economic and political idealism. And yet I cannot give up the idea that out of democracy will be born the new world—richer, braver, freer, more beautiful. As for me, I don't know what I can do to help—I don't know yet. All I know is that my happiness is built on the misery of other people, that I eat because others go hungry, that I am clothed when other people go almost naked through the frozen cities in winter; and that fact poisons me, disturbs my serenity, makes me write propaganda when I would rather play—though not so much as it once did.

I quit my job to work on the Pageant, and when it was all over I went to pieces nervously, and friends took me abroad for the summer. The strike was starved and lost, the men went back to work dispirited and disillusioned, and the leaders, too, broke down under the long strain of the fight. The I.W.W. itself seemed smashed—indeed it has never recovered its old prestige. I got diphtheria in Italy, and came back to New York weak and despondent. For six months I did almost nothing. And then, through the interest of Lincoln Steffens, *The Metropolitan Magazine* asked me to go to Mexico as a war correspondent, and I knew that I must do it.

Villa had just captured Chihuahua when I got to the border, and was getting ready to move on Torreon. I made straight for Chihuahua, and there got a chance to accompany an American mining man down into the mountains of Durango. Hearing that an old half-bandit, half-general was moving to the front, I cut loose and joined him, riding with a wild troop of Mexican cavalry two weeks across the desert, seeing battle at close range, in which my companions were defeated and killed, and fleeing for my life across the desert. I joined Villa then in his march on Torreon, and was in at the fall of that stronghold.

Altogether I was four months with the Constitutionalist armies in Mexico. When I first crossed the border deadliest fear gripped me. I was afraid of death, of mutilation, of a strange land and strange people whose speech and thought I did not know. But a terrible curiosity urged me on; I felt I *had to know* how I would act under fire, how I would get along with these primitive folks at war. And I discovered that bullets are not very terrifying, that the fear of death is not such a great thing, and that the Mexicans are wonderfully congenial. That four months of riding hundreds of miles across the blazing plains, sleeping on the ground with the *hombres*, dancing and carousing in looted haciendas all night after an all-day ride, being with them intimately in play, in battle, was perhaps the most satisfactory period of my life. I made good with these wild fighting men, and with myself. I loved them and I loved the life. I found myself again. I wrote better than I have ever written.

Then came the European War, to which I went as correspondent, spending a year and a half traveling in all the belligerent countries and on the front of five nations in battle. In Europe I found none of the spontaneity, none of the idealism of the Mexican revolution. It was a war of the workshops, and the trenches were factories turning out ruin—ruin of the spirit as well as of the body, the real and only death. Everything had halted but the engines of hate and destruction. European life, that flashed so many vital facets, ran in one channel, and runs in it now. There seems to me little to choose between the sides; both are horrible to me. The whole Great War is to me just a stoppage of the life and ferment of human evolution. I am waiting, waiting for it all to end, for life to resume so I can find my work.

In thinking it over, I find little in my thirty years that I can hold to. I haven't any God and don't want one; faith is only another word for finding oneself. In my life as in most lives, I guess, love plays a tremendous part. I've had love affairs, passionate happiness, wretched maladjustments; hurt deeply and been deeply hurt. But at last I have found my friend and lover, thrilling and satisfying, closer to me than anyone has ever been. And now I don't care what comes.

# THE DEVIL AND DANIEL WEBSTER
## *Stephen Vincent Benét   (1936)*

Iт's a story they tell in the border country, where Massachusetts joins Vermont and New Hampshire.

Yes, Dan'l Webster's dead—or, at least, they buried him. But every time there's a thunderstorm around Marshfield, they say you can hear his rolling voice in the hollows of the sky. And they say that if you go to his grave and speak loud and clear, "Dan'l Webster—Dan'l Webster!" the ground'll begin to shiver and the trees begin to shake. And after a while you'll hear a deep voice saying, "Neighbor, how stands the Union?" Then you better answer the Union stands as she stood, rock-bottomed and copper-sheathed, one and indivisible, or he's liable to rear right out of the ground. At least, that's what I was told when I was a youngster.

You see, for a while, he was the biggest man in the country. He never got to be President, but he was the biggest man. There were thousands that trusted in him right next to God Almighty, and they told stories about him and all the things that belonged to him that were like the stories of patriarchs and such. They said, when he stood up to speak, stars and stripes came right out in the sky, and once he spoke against a river and made it sink into the ground. They said, when he walked the woods with his fishing rod, Killall, the trout would jump out of the streams right into his pockets, for they knew it was no use putting up a fight against him; and, when he argued a case, he could turn on the harps of the blessed and the shaking of the earth underground. That was the kind of man he was, and his big farm up at Marshfield was suitable to him. The chickens he raised were all white meat down through the drumsticks, the cows were tended like children, and the big ram he called

Goliath had horns with a curl like a morning-glory vine and could butt through an iron door. But Dan'l wasn't one of your gentlemen farmers; he knew all the ways of the land, and he'd be up by candlelight to see that the chores got done. A man with a mouth like a mastiff, a brow like a mountain and eyes like burning anthracite—that was Dan'l Webster in his prime. And the biggest case he argued never got written down in the books, for he argued it against the devil, nip and tuck and no holds barred. And this is the way I used to hear it told.

There was a man named Jabez Stone, lived at Cross Corners, New Hampshire. He wasn't a bad man to start with, but he was an unlucky man. If he planted corn, he got borers; if he planted potatoes, he got blight. He had good-enough land, but it didn't prosper him; he had a decent wife and children, but the more children he had, the less there was to feed them. If stones cropped up in his neighbor's field, boulders boiled up in his; if he had a horse with the spavins, he'd trade it for one with the staggers and give something extra. There's some folks bound to be like that, apparently. But one day Jabez Stone got sick of the whole business.

He'd been plowing that morning and he'd just broke the plowshare on a rock that he could have sworn hadn't been there yesterday. And, as he stood looking at the plowshare, the off horse began to cough—that ropy kind of cough that means sickness and horse doctors. There were two children down with the measles, his wife was ailing, and he had a whitlow on his thumb. It was about the last straw for Jabez Stone. "I vow," he said, and he looked around him kind of desperate—"I vow it's enough to make a man want to sell his soul to the devil! And I would, too, for two cents!"

Then he felt a kind of queerness come over him at having said what he'd said; though, naturally, being a New Hampshireman, he wouldn't take it back. But, all the same, when it got to be evening and, as far as he could see, no notice had been taken, he felt relieved in his mind, for he was a religious man. But notice is always taken, sooner or later, just like the Good Book says. And, sure enough, next day, about suppertime, a soft-spoken, dark-dressed stranger drove up in a handsome buggy and asked for Jabez Stone.

Well, Jabez told his family it was a lawyer, come to see him about a legacy. But he knew who it was. He didn't like the looks of the stranger, nor the way he smiled with his teeth. They were white teeth, and plentiful— some say they were filed to a point, but I wouldn't vouch for that. And he didn't like it when the dog took one look at the stranger and ran away howling, with his tail between his legs. But having passed his word, more or less, he stuck to it, and they went out behind the barn and made their bargain. Jabez Stone had to prick his finger to sign, and the stranger lent him a silver pin. The wound healed clean, but it left a little white scar.

After that, all of a sudden, things began to pick up and prosper for Jabez Stone. His cows got fat and his horses sleek, his crops were the envy of the neighborhood, and lightning might strike all over the valley, but it wouldn't strike his barn. Pretty soon, he was one of the prosperous people of the country; they asked him to stand for selectman, and he stood for it; there began to be talk of running him for state senate. All in all, you might say the Stone family was as happy and contented as cats in a dairy. And so they were, except for Jabez Stone.

He'd been contented enough, the first few years. It's a great thing when bad luck turns; it drives most other things out of your head. True, every now and then, especially in rainy weather, the little white scar on his finger would give him a twinge. And once a year, punctual as clockwork, the stranger with the handsome buggy would come driving by. But the sixth year, the stranger lighted, and, after that, his peace was over for Jabez Stone.

The stranger came up through the lower field, switching his boots with a cane—they were handsome black boots, but Jabez Stone never liked the look of them, particularly the toes. And, after he'd passed the time of day, he said, "Well, Mr. Stone, you're a hummer! It's a very pretty property you've got here, Mr. Stone."

"Well, some might favor it and others might not," said Jabez Stone, for he was a New Hampshireman.

"Oh, no need to decry your industry!" said the stranger, very easy, showing his teeth in a smile. "After all, we know what's been done, and it's been according to contract and specifications. So when—ahem—the mortgage falls due next year, you shouldn't have any regrets."

"Speaking of that mortgage, mister," said Jabez Stone, and he looked around for help to the earth and the sky, "I'm beginning to have one or two doubts about it."

"Doubts?" said the stranger, not quite so pleasantly.

"Why, yes," said Jabez Stone. "This being the U. S. A. and me always having been a religious man." He cleared his throat and got bolder. "Yes, sir," he said, "I'm beginning to have considerable doubts as to that mortgage holding in court."

"There's courts and courts," said the stranger, clicking his teeth. "Still, we might as well have a look at the original document." And he hauled out a big black pocketbook, full of papers. "Sherwin, Slater, Stevens, Stone," he muttered. "I, Jabez Stone, for a term of seven years—Oh, it's quite in order, I think."

But Jabez Stone wasn't listening, for he saw something else flutter out of the black pocketbook. It was something that looked like a moth, but it wasn't a moth. And as Jabez Stone stared at it, it seemed to speak to him in a small sort of piping voice, terrible small and thin, but terrible human.

"Neighbor Stone!" it squeaked. "Neighbor Stone! Help me! For God's sake, help me!"

But before Jabez Stone could stir hand or foot, the stranger whipped out a big bandanna handkerchief, caught the creature in it, just like a butterfly, and started tying up the ends of the bandanna.

"Sorry for the interruption," he said. "As I was saying—"

But Jabez Stone was shaking all over like a scared horse.

"That's Miser Stevens' voice!" he said, in a croak. "And you've got him in your handkerchief!"

The stranger looked a little embarrassed.

"Yes, I really should have transferred him to the collecting box," he said with a simper, "but there were some rather unusual specimens there and I didn't want them crowded. Well, well, these little contretemps will occur."

"I don't know what you mean by contertan," said Jabez Stone, "but that was Miser Stevens' voice! And he ain't dead! You can't tell me he is! He was just as spry and mean as a woodchuck, Tuesday!"

"In the midst of life—" said the stranger, kind of pious. "Listen!" Then a bell began to toll in the valley and Jabez Stone listened, with the sweat running down his face. For he knew it was tolled for Miser Stevens and that he was dead.

"These long-standing accounts," said the stranger with a sigh; "one really hates to close them. But business is business."

He still had the bandanna in his hand, and Jabez Stone felt sick as he saw the cloth struggle and flutter.

"Are they all as small as that?" he asked hoarsely.

"Small?" said the stranger. "Oh, I see what you mean. Why, they vary." He measured Jabez Stone with his eyes, and his teeth showed. "Don't worry, Mr. Stone," he said. "You'll go with a very good grade. I wouldn't trust you outside the collecting box. Now, a man like Dan'l Webster, of course—well, we'd have to build a special box for him, and even at that, I imagine the wing spread would astonish you. He'd certainly be a prize. I wish we could see our way clear to him. But, in your case, as I was saying—"

"Put that handkerchief away!" said Jabez Stone, and he began to beg and to pray. But the best he could get at the end was a three years' extension, with conditions.

But till you make a bargain like that, you've got no idea of how fast four years can run. By the last months of those years, Jabez Stone's known all over the state and there's talk of running him for governor—and it's dust and ashes in his mouth. For every day, when he gets up, he thinks, "There's one more night gone," and every night when he lies down, he thinks of the black pocketbook and the soul of Miser Stevens, and it makes him sick at heart. Till, finally, he can't bear it any longer, and, in the last days of the last year, he hitches up his horse and drives off to see Dan'l Webster. For Dan'l was born in New Hampshire, only a few miles from Cross Corners, and it's well known that he has a particular soft spot for old neighbors.

It was early in the morning when he got to Marshfield, but Dan'l was up already, talking Latin to the farm hands and wrestling with the ram, Goliath, and trying out a new trotter and working up speeches to make against John C.

Calhoun. But when he heard a New Hampshireman had come to see him, he dropped everything else he was doing, for that was Dan'l's way. He gave Jabez Stone a breakfast that five men couldn't eat, went into the living history of every man and woman in Cross Corners, and finally asked him how he could serve him.

Jabez Stone allowed that it was a kind of mortgage case.

"Well, I haven't pleaded a mortgage case in a long time, and I don't generally plead now, except before the Supreme Court," said Dan'l, "but if I can, I'll help you."

"Then I've got hope for the first time in ten years," said Jabez Stone, and told him the details.

Dan'l walked up and down as he listened, hands behind his back, now and then asking a question, now and then plunging his eyes at the floor, as if they'd bore through it like gimlets. When Jabez Stone had finished, Dan'l puffed out his cheeks and blew. Then he turned to Jabe Stone and a smile broke over his face like the sunrise over Monadnock.

"You've certainly given yourself the devil's own row to hoe, Neighbor Stone," he said, "but I'll take your case."

"You'll take it?" said Jabez Stone, hardly daring to believe.

"Yes," said Dan'l Webster. "I've got about seventy-five other things to do and the Missouri Compromise to straighten out, but I'll take your case. For if two New Hampshiremen aren't a match for the devil, we might as well give the country back to the Indians."

Then he shook Jabez Stone by the hand and said, "Did you come down here in a hurry?"

"Well, I admit I made time," said Jabez Stone.

"You'll go back faster," said Dan'l Webster, and he told 'em to hitch up Constitution and Constellation to the carriage. They were matched grays with one white forefoot, and they stepped like greased lightning.

Well, I won't describe how excited and pleased the whole Stone family was to have the great Dan'l Webster for a guest, when they finally got there. Jabez Stone had lost his hat on the way, blown off when they overtook a wind, but he didn't take much account of that. But after supper he sent the family off to bed, for he had most particular business with Mr. Webster. Mrs. Stone wanted them to sit in the front parlor, but Dan'l Webster knew front parlors and said he preferred the kitchen. So it was there they sat, waiting for the stranger, with a jug on the table between them and a bright fire on the hearth—the stranger being scheduled to show up on the stroke of midnight, according to specification.

Well, most men wouldn't have asked for better company than Dan'l Webster and a jug. But with every tick of the clock Jabez Stone got sadder and sadder. His eyes roved round, and though he sampled the jug you could see he couldn't taste it. Finally, on the stroke of 11:30 he reached over and grabbed Dan'l Webster by the arm.

"Mr. Webster, Mr. Webster!" he said, and his voice was shaking with fear and a desperate courage. "For God's sake, Mr. Webster, harness your horses and get away from this place while you can!"

"You've brought me a long way, neighbor, to tell me you don't like my company," said Dan'l Webster, quite peaceable, pulling at the jug.

. "Miserable wretch that I am!" groaned Jabez Stone. "I've brought you a devilish way, and now I see my folly. Let him take me if he wills. I don't hanker after it, I must say, but I can stand it. But you're the Union's stay and New Hampshire's pride! He mustn't get you, Mr. Webster! He mustn't get you!"

Dan'l Webster looked at the distracted man, all gray and shaking in the firelight, and laid a hand on his shoulder.

"I'm obliged to you, Neighbor Stone," he said gently. "It's kindly thought of. But there's a jug on the table and a case in hand. And I never left a jug or a case half finished in my life." And just at that moment there was a sharp rap on the door.

"Ah," said Dan'l Webster, very coolly, "I thought your clock was a trifle slow, Neighbor Stone." He stepped to the door and opened it. "Come in!" he said.

The stranger came in—very dark and tall he looked in the firelight. He was carrying a box under his arm—a black, japanned box with little air holes in the lid. At the sight of the box, Jabez Stone gave a low cry and shrank into a corner of the room.

"Mr. Webster, I presume," said the stranger, very polite, but with his eyes glowing like a fox's deep in the woods.

"Attorney of record for Jabez Stone," said Dan'l Webster, but his eyes were glowing too. "Might I ask your name?"

"I've gone by a good many," said the stranger carelessly. "Perhaps Scratch will do for the evening. I'm often called that in these regions."

Then he sat down at the table and poured himself a drink from the jug. The liquor was cold in the jug, but it came steaming into the glass.

"And now," said the stranger, smiling and showing his teeth, "I shall call upon you, as a law-abiding citizen, to assist me in taking possession of my property."

Well, with that the argument began—and it went hot and heavy. At first, Jabez Stone had a flicker of hope, but when he saw Dan'l Webster being forced back at point after point, he just sat scrunched in his corner, with his eyes on that japanned box. For there wasn't any doubt as to the deed or the signature—that was the worst of it. Dan'l Webster twisted and turned and thumped his fist on the table, but he couldn't get away from that. He offered to compromise the case; the stranger wouldn't hear of it. He pointed out the property had increased in value, and state senators ought to be worth more; the stranger stuck to the letter of the law. He was a great lawyer, Dan'l Webster, but we know who's the King of Lawyers, as the Good Book tells us, and it seemed as if, for the first time, Dan'l Webster had met his match.

Finally, the stranger yawned a little. "Your spirited efforts on behalf of your client do you credit, Mr. Webster," he said, "but if you have no more arguments to adduce, I'm rather pressed for time—" and Jabez Stone shuddered.

Dan'l Webster's brow looked dark as a thundercloud. "Pressed or not, you shall not have this man!" he thundered. "Mr. Stone is an American citizen, and no American citizen may be forced into the service of a foreign prince. We fought England for that in '12 and we'll fight all hell for it again!"

"Foreign?" said the stranger. "And who calls me a foreigner?"

"Well, I never yet heard of the dev—of your claiming American citizenship," said Dan'l Webster with surprise.

"And who with better right?" said the stranger, with one of his terrible smiles. "When the first wrong was done to the first Indian, I was there. When the first slaver put out for the Congo, I stood on her deck. Am I not in your books and stories and beliefs, from the first settlements on? Am I not spoken of, still, in every church in New England? 'Tis true the North claims me for a Southerner, and South for a Northerner, but I am neither. I am merely an honest American like yourself—and of the best descent—for, to tell the truth, Mr. Webster, though I don't like to boast of it, my name is older in this country than yours."

"Aha!" said Dan'l Webster, with the veins standing out in his forehead. "Then I stand on the Constitution! I demand a trial for my client!"

"The case is hardly one for an ordinary court," said the stranger, his eyes flickering. "And, indeed, the lateness of the hour—"

"Let it be any court you choose, so it is an American judge and an American jury!" said Dan'l Webster in his pride. "Let it be the quick or the dead; I'll abide the issue!"

"You have said it," said the stranger, and pointed his finger at the door. And with that, and all of a sudden, there was a rushing of wind outside and a noise of footsteps. They came, clear and distinct, through the night. And yet, they were not like the footsteps of living men.

"In God's name, who comes by so late?" cried Jabez Stone, in an ague of fear.

"The jury Mr. Webster demands," said the stranger, sipping at his boiling glass. "You must pardon the rough appearance of one or two; they will have come a long way."

And with that the fire burned blue and the door blew open and twelve men entered, one by one.

If Jabez Stone had been sick with terror before, he was blind with terror now. For there was Walter Butler, the loyalist, who spread fire and horror through the Mohawk Valley in the times of the Revolution; and there was Simon Girty, the renegade, who saw white men burned at the stake and whooped with the Indians to see them burn. His eyes were green, like a catamount's, and the stains on his hunting shirt did not come from the blood of the deer. King Philip was there, wild and proud as he had been in life, with the great gash in his head that gave him his death wound, and cruel Governor Dale, who broke men on the wheel. There was Morton of Merry Mount, who so vexed the Plymouth Colony, with his flushed, loose, handsome face and his hate of the godly. There was Teach, the bloody pirate, with his black beard curling on his breast. The Reverend John Smeet, with his strangler's hands and his Geneva gown, walked as daintily as he had to the gallows. The red print of the rope was still around his neck, but he carried a perfumed handkerchief in one hand. One and all, they came into the room with the fires of hell still upon them, and the stranger named their names and their deeds as they came, till the tale of twelve was told. Yet the stranger had told the truth—they had all played a part in America.

"Are you satisfied with the jury, Mr. Webster?" said the stranger mock-ingly, when they had taken their places.

The sweat stood upon Dan'l Webster's brow, but his voice was clear .

"Quite satisfied," he said. "Though I miss General Arnold from the company."

"Benedict Arnold is engaged upon other business," said the stranger, with a glower. "Ah, you asked for a justice, I believe."

He pointed his finger once more, and a tall man, soberly clad in Puritan garb, with the burning gaze of the fanatic, stalked into the room and took his judge's place.

"Justice Hathorne is a jurist of experience," said the stranger. "He pre-sided at certain witch trials once held in Salem. There were others who repented of the business later, but not he."

"Repent of such notable wonders and undertakings?" said the stern old justice. "Nay, hang them—hang them all!" And he muttered to himself in a way that struck ice into the soul of Jabez Stone.

Then the trial began, and, as you might expect, it didn't look anyways good for the defense. And Jabez Stone didn't make much of a witness in his own behalf. He took one look at Simon Girty and screeched, and they had to put him back in his corner in a kind of swoon.

It didn't halt the trial, though; the trial went on, as trials do. Dan'l Web-ster had faced some hard juries and hanging judges in his time, but this was the hardest he'd ever faced, and he knew it. They sat there with a kind of glitter in their eyes, and the stranger's smooth voice went on and on. Every time he'd raise an objection, it'd be "Objection sustained," but whenever Dan'l objected, it'd be "Objection denied." Well, you couldn't expect fair play from a fellow like this Mr. Scratch.

It got to Dan'l in the end, and he began to heat, like iron in the forge. When he got up to speak he was going to flay that stranger with every trick known to the law, and the judge and jury too. He didn't care if it was con-tempt of court or what would happen to him for it. He didn't care any more what happened to Jabez Stone. He just got madder and madder, thinking of what he'd say. And yet, curiously enough, the more he thought about it, the less he was able to arrange his speech in his mind.

Till, finally, it was time for him to get up on his feet, and he did so, all ready to bust out with lightnings and denunciations. But before he started he looked over the judge and jury for a moment, such being his custom. And he noticed the glitter in their eyes was twice as strong as before, and they all leaned forward. Like hounds just before they get the fox, they looked, and the blue mist of evil in the room thickened as he watched them. Then he saw what he'd been about to do, and he wiped his forehead, as a man might who's just escaped falling into a pit in the dark.

For it was him they'd come for, not only Jabez Stone. He read it in the glitter of their eyes and in the way the stranger hid his mouth with one hand. And if he fought them with their own weapons, he'd fall into their power; he knew that, though he couldn't have told you how. It was his own anger and horror that burned in their eyes, and he'd have to wipe that out or the case was lost. He stood there for a moment, his black eyes burning like anthracite. And then he began to speak.

He started off in a low voice, though you could hear every word. They say he could call on the harps of the blessed when he chose. And this was just as simple and easy as a man could talk. But he didn't start out by condemning or reviling. He was talking about the things that make a country a country, and a man a man.

And he began with the simple things that everybody's known and felt—the freshness of a fine morning when you're young, and the taste of food when you're hungry, and the new day that's every day when you're a child. He took them up and he turned them in his hands. They were good things for any man. But without freedom, they sickened. And when he talked of those enslaved, and the sorrows of slavery, his voice got like a big bell. He talked of the early days of America and the men who had made those days. It wasn't a spread-eagle speech, but he made you see it. He admitted all the wrong that had ever been done. But he showed how, out of the wrong and the right, the suffering and the starvations, something new had come. And everybody had played a part in it, even the traitors.

Then he turned to Jabez Stone and showed him as he was—an ordinary man who'd had hard luck, and wanted to change it. And, because he'd wanted to change it, now he was going to be punished for all eternity. And yet there was good in Jabez Stone, and he showed that good. He was hard and mean, in some ways, but he was a man. There was sadness in being a man, but it was a proud thing too. And he showed what the pride of it was till you couldn't help feeling it. Yes, even in hell, if a man was a man, you'd know it. And he wasn't pleading for any one person any more, though his voice rang like an organ. He was telling the story and the failures and the endless journey of mankind. They got tricked and trapped and bamboozled, but it was a great journey. And no demon that was ever foaled could know the inwardness of it—it took a man to do that.

The fire began to die on the hearth and the wind before morning to blow. The light was getting gray in the room when Dan'l Webster finished. And his words came back at the end to New Hampshire ground, and the one spot of land that each man loves and clings to. He painted a picture of that, and to each one of that jury he spoke of things long forgotten. For his voice could search the heart, and that was his gift and his strength. And to one, his voice was like the forest and its secrecy, and to another like the sea and the storms of the sea; and one heard the cry of his lost nation in it, and another saw a little harmless scene he hadn't remembered for years. But each saw something. And when Dan'l Webster finished he didn't know whether or not he'd saved Jabez Stone. But he knew he'd done a miracle. For the glitter was gone from the eyes of judge and jury, and, for the moment, they were men again, and knew they were men.

"The defense rests," said Dan'l Webster, and stood there like a mountain. His ears were still ringing with his speech, and he didn't hear anything else till he heard Judge Hathorne say, "The jury will retire to consider its verdict."

Walter Butler rose in his place and his face had a dark, gay pride on it.

"The jury has considered its verdict," he said, and looked the stranger full in the eye. "We find for the defendant, Jabez Stone."

With that, the smile left the stranger's face, but Walter Butler did not flinch.

"Perhaps 'tis not strictly in accordance with the evidence," he said, "but even the damned may salute the eloquence of Mr. Webster."

With that, the long crow of a rooster split the gray morning sky, and judge and jury were gone from the room like a puff of smoke and as if they had never been there. The stranger turned to Dan'l Webster, smiling wryly. "Major Butler was always a bold man," he said. "I had not thought him quite so bold. Nevertheless, my congratulations, as between two gentlemen."

"I'll have that paper first, if you please," said Dan'l Webster, and he took it and tore it into four pieces. It was queerly warm to the touch. "And now," he said, "I'll have you!" and his hand came down like a bear trap on the stranger's arm. For he knew that once you bested anybody like Mr. Scratch in fair fight, his power on you was gone. And he could see that Mr. Scratch knew it too.

The stranger twisted and wriggled, but he couldn't get out of that grip. "Come, come, Mr. Webster," he said, smiling palely. "This sort of thing is ridic—ouch!—is ridiculous. If you're worried about the costs of the case, naturally, I'd be glad to pay—"

"And so you shall!" said Dan'l Webster, shaking him till his teeth rattled. "For you'll sit right down at that table and draw up a document, promising never to bother Jabez Stone nor his heirs or assigns nor any other New Hampshireman till doomsday! For any hades we want to raise in this state, we can raise ourselves, without assistance from strangers."

"Ouch!" said the stranger. "Ouch! Well, they never did run very big to the barrel, but—ouch!—I agree!"

So he sat down and drew up the document. But Dan'l Webster kept his hand on his coat collar all the time.

"And, now, may I go?" said the stranger, quite humble, when Dan'l'd seen the document was in proper and legal form.

"Go?" said Dan'l, giving him another shake. "I'm still trying to figure out what I'll do with you. For you've settled the costs of the case, but you haven't settled with me. I think I'll take you back to Marshfield," he said, kind of reflective. "I've got a ram there named Goliath that can butt through an iron door. I'd kind of like to turn you loose in his field and see what he'd do."

Well, with that the stranger began to beg and to plead. And he begged and he pled so humble that finally Dan'l, who was naturally kindhearted, agreed to let him go. The stranger seemed terrible grateful for that and said, just to show they were friends, he'd tell Dan'l's fortune before leaving. So Dan'l agreed to that, though he didn't take much stock in fortune-tellers ordinarily.

But, naturally the stranger was a little different. Well, he pried and he peered at the lines in Dan'l's hands. And he told him one thing and another that was quite remarkable. But they were all in the past.

"Yes, all that's true, and it happened," said Dan'l Webster. "But what's to come in the future?"

The stranger grinned, kind of happily, and shook his head. "The future's not as you think it," he said. "It's dark. You have a great ambition, Mr. Webster."

"I have," said Dan'l firmly, for everybody knew he wanted to be President.

"It seems almost within your grasp," said the stranger, "but you will not attain it. Lesser men will be made President and you will be passed over."

"And, if I am, I'll still be Daniel Webster," said Dan'l. "Say on."

"You have two strong sons," said the stranger, shaking his head. "You look to found a line. But each will die in war and neither reach greatness."

"Live or die, they are still my sons," said Dan'l Webster. "Say on."

"You have made great speeches," said the stranger. "You will make more."

"Ah," said Dan'l Webster.

"But the last great speech you make will turn many of your own against you," said the stranger. "They will call you Ichabod; they will call you by other names. Even in New England some will say you have turned your coat and sold your country, and their voices will be loud against you till you die."

"So it is an honest speech, it does not matter what men say," said Dan'l Webster. Then he looked at the stranger and their glances locked.

"One question," he said. "I have fought for the Union all my life. Will I see that fight won against those who would tear it apart?"

"Not while you live," said the stranger, grimly, "But it will be won. And after you are dead, there are thousands who will fight for your cause, because of words that you spoke."

"Why, then, you long-barreled, slab-sided, lantern-jawed, fortune-telling note shaver!" said Dan'l Webster, with a great roar of laughter, "be off with you to your own place before I put my mark on you! For, by the thirteen original colonies, I'd go to the Pit itself to save the Union!"

And with that he drew back his foot for a kick that would have stunned a horse. It was only the tip of his shoe that caught the stranger, but he went flying out of the door with his collecting box under his arm.

"And now," said Dan'l Webster, seeing Jabez Stone beginning to rouse from his swoon, "Let's see what's left in the jug, for it's dry work talking all night. I hope there's pie for breakfast, Neighbor Stone."

But they say that whenever the devil comes near Marshfield, even now, he gives it a wide berth. And he hasn't been seen in the state of New Hampshire from that day to this. I'm not talking about Massachusetts or Vermont.

## THE BET

### *Anton Chekhov*  (*1888*)

### I

It was a dark autumn night. The old banker was walking up and down his study and remembering how, fifteen years before, he had given a party one autumn evening. There had been many clever men there, and there had been interesting conversations. Among other things they had talked of capital punishment. The majority of the guests, among whom were many journalists and intellectual men, disapproved of the death penalty. They considered that form of punishment out of date, immoral, and unsuitable for Christian states. In the opinion of some of them the death penalty ought to be replaced everywhere by imprisonment for life.

"I don't agree with you," said their host the banker. "I have not tried either the death penalty or imprisonment for life, but if one may judge *a priori*, the death penalty is more moral and more humane than imprisonment for life. Capital punishment kills a man at once, but lifelong imprisonment kills him slowly. Which executioner is the more humane, he who kills you in a few minutes or he who drags the life out of you in the course of many years?"

"Both are equally immoral," observed one of the guests, "for they both have the same object—to take away life. The State is not God. It has not the right to take away what it cannot restore when it wants to."

Among the guests was a young lawyer, a young man of five-and-twenty. When he was asked his opinion, he said:

"The death sentence and the life sentence are equally immoral, but if I had to choose between the death penalty and imprisonment for life, I would certainly choose the second. To live anyhow is better than not at all."

A lively discussion arose. The banker, who was younger and more nervous in those days, was suddenly carried away by excitement; he struck the table with his fist and shouted at the young man:

"It's not true! I'll bet you two millions you wouldn't stay in solitary confinement for five years."

"If you mean that in earnest," said the young man, "I'll take the bet, but I would stay not five but fifteen years."

"Fifteen? Done!" cried the banker. "Gentlemen, I stake two millions!"

"Agreed! You stake your millions and I stake my freedom!" said the young man.

And this wild, senseless bet was carried out! The banker, spoilt and frivolous, with millions beyond his reckoning, was delighted at the bet. At supper he made fun of the young man, and said:

"Think better of it, young man, while there is still time. To me two millions are a trifle, but you are losing three or four of the best years of your life. I say three or four, because you won't stay longer. Don't forget either, you unhappy man, that voluntary confinement is a great deal harder to bear than compulsory. The thought that you have the right to step out in liberty at any moment will poison your whole existence in prison. I am sorry for you."

And now the banker, walking to and fro, remembered all this, and asked himself: "What was the object of that bet? What is the good of that man's losing fifteen years of his life and my throwing away two millions? Can it prove that the death penalty is better or worse than imprisonment for life? No, no. It was all nonsensical and meaningless. On my part it was the caprice of a pampered man, and on his part simple greed for money. . . ."

Then he remembered what followed that evening. It was decided that the young man should spend the years of his captivity under the strictest supervision in one of the lodges in the banker's garden. It was agreed that for fifteen years he should not be free to cross the threshold of the lodge, to see human beings, to hear the human voice, or to receive letters and newspapers. He was allowed to have a music instrument and books, and was allowed to write letters, to drink wine, and to smoke. By the terms of the agreement, the only relations he could have with the outer world were by a little window made purposely for that object. He might have anything he wanted—books, music, wine, and so on—in any quantity he desired by writing an order, but could only receive them through the window. The agreement provided for every detail and every trifle that would make his imprisonment strictly solitary, and bound the young man to stay there *exactly* fifteen years, beginning from twelve o'clock of November 14, 1870, and ending at twelve o'clock of November 14, 1885. The slightest attempt on his part to break the conditions, if only two minutes before the end, released the banker from the obligation to pay him two millions.

For the first year of his confinement, as far as one could judge from his brief notes, the prisoner suffered severely from loneliness and depression. The sounds of the piano could be heard continually day and night from his lodge. He refused wine and tobacco. Wine, he wrote, excites the desires, and desires are the worst foes of the prisoner; and besides, nothing could be more dreary than drinking good wine and seeing no one. And tobacco spoilt the air of his room. In the first year the books he sent for were principally of a light character; novels with a complicated love plot, sensational and fantastic stories, and so on.

In the second year the piano was silent in the lodge, and the prisoner asked only for the classics. In the fifth year music was audible again, and the prisoner asked for wine. Those who watched him through the window said that all that year he spent doing nothing but eating and drinking and lying on his bed, frequently yawning and angrily talking to himself. He did not read books. Sometimes at night he would sit down to write; he would spend hours writing, and in the morning tear up all that he had written. More than once he could be heard crying.

In the second half of the sixth year the prisoner began zealously studying languages, philosophy, and history. He threw himself eagerly into these studies—so much so that the banker had enough to do to get him the books he ordered. In the course of four years some six hundred volumes were procured at his request. It was during this period that the banker received the following letter from his prisoner:

"My dear Jailer, I write you these lines in six languages. Show them to people who know the languages. Let them read them. If they find not one mistake I implore you to fire a shot in the garden. That shot will show me that my efforts have not been thrown away. The geniuses of all ages and of all lands speak different languages, but the same flame burns in them all. Oh, if you only knew what unearthly happiness my soul feels now from being able to understand them!" The prisoner's desire was fulfilled. The banker ordered two shots to be fired in the garden.

Then after the tenth year, the prisoner sat immovably at the table and read nothing but the Gospel. It seemed strange to the banker that a man who in four years had mastered six hundred learned volumes should waste nearly a year over one thin book easy of comprehension. Theology and histories of religion followed the Gospels.

In the last two years of his confinement the prisoner read an immense quantity of books quite indiscriminately. At one time he was busy with the natural sciences, then he would ask for Byron or Shakespeare. There were notes in which he demanded at the same time books on chemistry, and a manual of medicine, and a novel, and some treatise on philosophy or theology. His reading suggested a man swimming in the sea among the wreckage of his ship, and trying to save his life by greedily clutching first at one spar and then at another.

## II

The old banker remembered all this, and thought:

"To-morrow at twelve o'clock he will regain his freedom. By our agreement I ought to pay him two millions. If I do pay him, it is all over with me: I shall be utterly ruined."

Fifteen years before, his millions had been beyond his reckoning; now he was afraid to ask himself which were greater, his debts or his assets. Desperate gambling on the Stock Exchange, wild speculation, and the excitability which he could not get over even in advancing years, had by degrees led to the decline of his fortune, and the proud, fearless, self-confident millionaire had become a banker of middling rank, trembling at every rise and fall in his investments. "Cursed bet!" muttered the old man, clutching his head in despair. "Why didn't the man die? He is only forty now. He will take my last penny from me, he will marry, will enjoy life, will gamble on the Exchange; while I shall look at him with envy like a beggar, and hear from him every day the same sentence: 'I am indebted to you for the happiness of my life, let me help you!' No, it is too much! The one means of being saved from bankruptcy and disgrace is the death of that man!"

It struck three o'clock, the banker listened; everyone was asleep in the house, and nothing could be heard outside but the rustling of the chilled trees. Trying to make no noise, he took from a fireproof safe the key of the door which had not been opened for fifteen years, put on his overcoat, and went out of the house.

It was dark and cold in the garden. Rain was falling. A damp cutting wind was racing about the garden, howling and giving the trees no rest. The banker strained his eyes, but could see neither the earth nor the white statues, nor the lodge, nor the trees. Going to the spot where the lodge stood, he twice called the watchman. No answer followed. Evidently the watchman had sought shelter from the weather, and was now asleep somewhere either in the kitchen or in the greenhouse.

"If I had the pluck to carry out my intention," thought the old man, "suspicion would fall first upon the watchman."

He felt in the darkness for the steps and the door, and went into the entry of the lodge. Then he groped his way into a little passage and lighted a match. There was not a soul there. There was a bedstead with no bedding on it, and in the corner there was a dark cast-iron stove. The seals on the door leading to the prisoner's rooms were intact.

When the match went out the old man, trembling with emotion, peeped through the little window. A candle was burning dimly in the prisoner's room. He was sitting at the table. Nothing could be seen but his back, the hair on his head, and his hands. Open books were lying on the table, on the two easy-chairs, and on the carpet near the table.

Five minutes passed and the prisoner did not once stir. Fifteen years' imprisonment had taught him to sit still. The banker tapped at the window with his finger, and the prisoner made no movement whatever in response. Then the banker cautiously broke the seals off the door and put the key in the keyhole. The rusty lock gave a grating sound and the door creaked. The banker expected to hear at once footsteps and a cry of astonishment, but three minutes passed and it was as quiet as ever in the room. He made up his mind to go in.

At the table a man unlike ordinary people was sitting motionless. He was a skeleton with the skin drawn tight over his bones, with long curls like a woman's, and a shaggy beard. His face was yellow with an earthy tint in it, his cheeks were hollow, his back long and narrow, and the hand on which his shaggy head was propped was so thin and delicate that it was dreadful to look at it. His hair was already streaked with silver, and seeing his emaciated, aged-looking face, no one would have believed that he was only forty. He was asleep. . . . In front of his bowed head there lay on the table a sheet of paper on which there was something written in fine handwriting.

"Poor creature!" thought the banker, "he is asleep and most likely dreaming of the millions. And I have only to take this half-dead man, throw him on the bed, stifle him a little with the pillow, and the most conscientious expert would find no sign of a violent death. But let us first read what he has written here. . . ."

The banker took the page from the table and read as follows:

"To-morrow at twelve o'clock I regain my freedom and the right to associate with other men, but before I leave this room and see the sunshine, I think it necessary to say a few words to you. With a clear conscience I tell you, as before God, who beholds me, that I despise freedom and life and health, and all that in your books is called the good things of the world.

"For fifteen years I have been intently studying earthly life. It is true I have not seen the earth nor men, but in your books I have drunk fragrant wine, I have sung songs, I have hunted stags and wild boars in the forests, have loved women. . . . Beauties as ethereal as clouds, created by the magic of your poets and geniuses, have visited me at night, and have whispered in my ears wonderful tales that have set my brain in a whirl. In your books I have climbed to the peaks of Elbruz and Mont Blanc, and from there I have seen the sun rise and have watched it at evening flood the sky, the ocean, and the mountain-tops with gold and crimson. I have watched from there the lightning flashing over my head and cleaving the storm-clouds. I have seen green forests, fields, rivers, lakes, towns. I have heard the singing of the sirens, and the strains of the shepherds' pipes; I have touched the wings of comely devils who flew down to converse with me of God. . . . In your books I have flung myself into the bottomless pit, performed miracles, slain, burned towns, preached new religions, conquered whole king-doms. . . .

"Your books have given me wisdom. All that the unresting thought of man has created in the ages is compressed into a small compass in my brain. I know that I am wiser than all of you.

"And I despise your books, I despise wisdom and the blessings of this world. It is all worthless, fleeting, illusory, and deceptive, like a mirage. You may be proud, wise, and fine, but death will wipe you off the face of the earth as though you were no more than mice burrowing under the floor, and your posterity, your history, your immortal geniuses will burn or freeze together with the earthly globe.

"You have lost your reason and taken the wrong path. You have taken lies for truth, and hideousness for beauty. You would marvel if, owing to strange events of some sorts, frogs and lizards suddenly grew on apple and orange trees instead of fruit, or if roses began to smell like a sweating horse; so I marvel at you who exchange heaven for earth. I don't want to understand you.

"To prove to you in action how I despise all that you live by, I renounce the two millions of which I once dreamed as of paradise and which now I despise. To deprive myself of the right to the money I shall go out from here five hours before the time fixed, and so break the compact. . . ."

When the banker had read this he laid the page on the table, kissed the strange man on the head, and went out of the lodge, weeping. At no other time, even when he had lost heavily on the Stock Exchange, had he felt so great a contempt for himself. When he got home he lay on his bed, but his tears and emotion kept him for hours from sleeping.

Next morning the watchmen ran in with pale faces, and told him they had seen the man who lived in the lodge climb out of the window into the garden, go to the gate, and disappear. The banker went at once with the servants to the lodge and made sure of the flight of his prisoner. To avoid arousing unnecessary talk, he took from the table the writing in which the millions were renounced, and when he got home locked it up in the fireproof safe.

## HIS AUTUMN–COLORED FACE

### *Jesse Stuart* (*1938*)

His autumn-colored face and eagle eyes
Look on toward more darkened hills of space;
He stands a gaunt man under windy skies.
His sons have fallen to the softer race
Of those who fear to till the rugged lands;                    5
They've taken to clean pages of sweet books
And fear to blister their soft dainty hands—
They fear some day they'll have their father's looks.

He now surveys the winter's waves of weeds
That lie dark-beaten on the rugged slope;                10
He plans to turn them under for soil needs—
A better corn-crop is his next year's hope.
His far-off eagle eyes survey his dreams
When snows cap high-hills and the world is dead
And ice has spanned the little mountain streams,        15
His cattle will have corn, his family, bread.

## NONSENSE RHYME

### *Elinor Wylie* (*1929*)

Whatever's good or bad or both
Is surely better than the none;
There's grace in either love or loathe;
Sunlight, or freckles on the sun.

The worst and best are both inclined 5
To snap like vixens at the truth;
But, O, beware the middle mind
That purrs and never shows a tooth!

Beware the smooth ambiguous smile
That never pulls the lips apart;        10

Salt of pure and pepper of vile
Must season the extremer heart.

A pinch of fair, a pinch of foul.
And bad and good make best of all;
Beware the moderated soul              15
That climbs no fractional inch to fall.

Reason's a rabbit in a hutch,
And ecstasy's a were-wolf ghost;
But, O, beware the nothing-much
And welcome madness and the
    most!                              20

## A PRAYER FOR MY DAUGHTER

### *William Butler Yeats* (*1921*)

Once more the storm is howling, and
    half hid
Under this cradle-hood and coverlid
My child sleeps on. There is no ob-
    stacle
But Gregory's wood and one bare
    hill
Whereby the haystack- and roof-
    levelling wind,                    5
Bred on the Atlantic, can be stayed;
And for an hour I have walked and
    prayed
Because of the great gloom that is in
    my mind.

I have walked and prayed for this
    young child an hour
And heard the sea-wind scream upon
    the tower,                         10
And under the arches of the bridge,
    and scream
In the elms above the flooded stream;
Imagining in excited reverie
That the future years had come,
Dancing to a frenzied drum,           15
Out of the murderous innocence of
    the sea.

May she be granted beauty and yet
not
Beauty to make a stranger's eye dis-
traught,
Or hers before a looking-glass, for
such,                                          20
Being made beautiful overmuch,
Consider beauty a sufficient end,
Lose natural kindness and maybe
The heart-revealing intimacy
That chooses right, and never find a
friend.

Helen being chosen found life flat
and dull                                       25
And later had much trouble from a
fool,
While that great Queen, that rose out
of the spray,
Being fatherless could have her way
Yet chose a bandy-leggèd smith for
man.
It's certain that fine women eat        30
A crazy salad with their meat
Whereby the Horn of Plenty is un-
done.

In courtesy I'd have her chiefly
learned;
Hearts are not had as a gift but hearts
are earned
By those that are not entirely beauti-
ful;                                           35
Yet many, that have played the fool
For beauty's very self, has charm
made wise,
And many a poor man that has roved,
Loved and thought himself beloved,
From a glad kindness cannot take his
eyes.                                          40

May she become a flourishing hidden
tree
That all her thoughts may like the
linnet be,
And have no business but dispensing
round
Their magnanimities of sound.

Nor but in merriment begin a chase,
Nor but in merriment a quarrel.   46
O may she live like some green laurel
Rooted in one dear perpetual place.

My mind, because the minds that I
have loved,
The sort of beauty that I have ap-
proved,                                        50
Prosper but little, has dried up of
late,
Yet knows that to be choked with
hate
May well be of all evil chances chief.
If there's no hatred in a mind
Assault and battery of the wind        55
Can never tear the linnet from the
leaf.

An intellectual hatred is the worst,
So let her think opinions are accursed.
Have I not seen the loveliest woman
born
Out of the mouth of Plenty's horn, 60
Because of her opinionated mind
Barter that horn and every good
By quiet natures understood
For an old bellows full of angry wind?

Considering that, all hatred driven
hence,                                         65
The soul recovers radical innocence
And learns at last that it is self-delight-
ing,
Self-appeasing, self-affrighting,
And that its own sweet will is Heav-
en's will;
She can, though every face should
scowl                                          70
And every windy quarter howl
Or every bellows burst, be happy
still.

And may her bridegroom bring her
to a house
Where all's accustomed, ceremonious;

For arrogance and hatred are the
  wares                 75
Peddled in the thoroughfares.
How but in custom and in ceremony

Are innocence and beauty born?
Ceremony's a name for the rich horn,
And custom for the spreading laurel
  tree.                  80

# FLAMMONDE

## *Edwin Arlington Robinson* (*1916*)

The man Flammonde, from God
  knows where,
With firm address and foreign air,
With news of nations in his talk
And something royal in his walk,
With glint of iron in his eyes,     5
But never doubt, nor yet surprise,
Appeared, and stayed, and held his
  head
As one of kings accredited.

Erect, with his alert repose
About him, and about his clothes,   10
He pictured all tradition hears
Of what we owe to fifty years.
His cleansing heritage of taste
Paraded neither want nor waste;
And what he needed for his fee   15
To live, he borrowed graciously.

He never told us what he was,
Or what mischance, or other cause,
Had banished him from better days
To play the Prince of Castaways.   20
Meanwhile he played surpassing well
A part, for most, unplayable;
In fine, one pauses, half afraid
To say for certain that he played.

For that, one may as well forego   25
Conviction as to yes or no;
Nor can I say just how intense
Would then have been the difference
To several, who, having striven
In vain to get what he was given,   30
Would see the stranger taken on
By friends not easy to be won.

Moreover, many a malcontent
He soothed and found munificent;

His courtesy beguiled and foiled   35
Suspicion that his years were soiled;
His mien distinguished any crowd,
His credit strengthened when he
  bowed;
And women, young and old, were
  fond
Of looking at the man Flammonde.  40

There was a woman in our town
On whom the fashion was to frown;
But while our talk renewed the tinge
Of a long-faded scarlet fringe,
The man Flammonde saw none of
  that,            45
And what he saw we wondered at—
That none of us, in her distress,
Could hide or find our littleness.

There was a boy that all agreed
Had shut within him the rare seed  50
Of learning. We could understand,
But none of us could lift a hand.
The man Flammonde appraised the
  youth,
And told a few of us the truth;
And thereby, for a little gold,   55
A flowered future was unrolled.

There were two citizens who fought
For years and years, and over nought;
They made life awkward for their
  friends,
And shortened their own dividends.
The man Flammonde said what was
  wrong           61
Should be made right; nor was it
  long
Before they were again in line,
And had each other in to dine.

And these I mention are but four 65
Of many out of many more.
So much for them. But what of him—
So firm in every look and limb?
What small satanic sort of kink
Was in his brain? What broken link
Withheld him from the destinies 71
That came so near to being his?

What was he, when we came to sift
His meaning, and to note the drift
Of incommunicable ways, 75
That make us ponder while we praise?
Why was it that his charm revealed
Somehow the surface of a shield?
What was it that we never caught? '
What was he, and what was he not? 80

How much it was of him we met
We cannot ever know; nor yet
Shall all he gave us quite atone
For what was his, and his alone;
Nor need we now, since he knew best,
Nourish an ethical unrest— 86
Rarely at once will nature give
The power to be Flammonde and live.

We cannot know how much we learn
From those who never will return, 90
Until a flash of unforeseen
Remembrance falls on what has been.
We've each a darkening hill to climb;
And this is why, from time to time
In Tilbury Town, we look beyond 95
Horizons for the man Flammonde.

## RESOLVE

*William Ellery Leonard*   (*1928*)

There is an end. The fever and the pain,
The craving unto life with that far hope
Of mornings and of twilights, seen by two,
Shall torture me no more. The nightly stars
Beam downward and the sun and moon arise                    5
And pass o'er earth with all its snows and grass
And towers and scattered graves, and seeds are blown
And pestilence with winds, and there be tears
For sorrow, smiles for joy. The Eternal Law
Works in all regions, bringing light and dark.              10
It works in me. It makes in me an end
Even of the woe which it before had wrought,
And leads me to the springs beyond the mount,
Beyond all populous cities, where each man
Must flee when all is lost, and in myself                    15
I find at last the rod which strikes the rocks
Of living waters.

                    I have garnered long
O'er many lands, in many books. I own
Old trees and castles, cataracts and heights,               20
And orient cities dusk along the Nile,
Old fountains, marbles, pictures, red and gold,
From blue Valdarno, and old meters too
From Scio, Delphi, Mantua down the South,

From northern Weimar and the Avon stream,                    25
And folksongs of the Alp and Apennine
And German rivers. Lo, I own the dream
Of Plato and the hardiness of Kant.
I have all wealth within me; I will look.

And I have that within me which shall build            30
Even from the fragments of dead hopes a house
Where I may dwell as I grow more a god.

## BE STILL, MY SOUL

(*From* The Shropshire Lad)

*A. E. Housman*   (*1896*)

Be still, my soul, be still; the arms you bear are brittle,
  Earth and high heaven are fixed of old and founded strong.
Think rather—call to thought, if now you grieve a little,
  The days when we had rest, O soul, for they were long.

Men loved unkindness then, but lightless in the quarry        5
  I slept and saw not; tears fell down, I did not mourn;
Sweat ran and blood sprang out and I was never sorry.
  Then it was well with me, in days ere I was born.

Now, and I muse for why and never find the reason,
  I pace the earth, and drink the air, and feel the sun.       10
Be still, be still, my soul; it is but for a season;
  Let us endure an hour and see injustice done.

Aye, look—high heaven and earth ail from the prime foundation;
  All thoughts to rive the heart are here, and all are vain:
Horror and scorn and hate and fear and indignation—           15
  Oh, why did I awake? when shall I sleep again?

## LAUGH AND BE MERRY

*John Masefield*   (*1910*)

Laugh and be merry; remember, better the world with a song,
Better the world with a blow in the teeth of a wrong.
Laugh, for the time is brief, a thread the length of a span,
Laugh and be proud to belong to the old proud pageant of man.

Laugh and be merry; remember, in olden time,                  5
God made heaven and earth, for joy He took in a rime,
Made them, and filled them full with the strong red wine of His mirth,
The splendid joy of the stars, the joy of the earth.

So we must laugh and drink from the deep blue cup of the sky,
Join the jubilant song of the great stars sweeping by,                       10
Laugh, and battle, and work, and drink of the wine outpoured
In the dear green earth, the sign of the joy of the Lord.

Laugh and be merry together, like brothers akin,
Guesting awhile in the rooms of a beautiful inn,
Glad till the dancing stops, and the lilt of the music ends.                 15
Laugh till the game is played; and be you merry, my friends.


## MY MIND TO ME A KINGDOM IS

### *Sir Edward Dyer*   (*1588*)

My mind to me a kingdom is;
  Such present joys therein I find
That it excels all other bliss
  That earth affords or grows by
    kind.
Though much I want which most
    would have,                                    5
Yet still my mind forbids to crave.

No princely pomp, no wealthy store,
  No force to win the victory,
No wily wit to salve a sore,
  No shape to feed a loving eye;       10
To none of these I yield as thrall—
For why? My mind doth serve for
    all.

I see how plenty surfeits oft,
  And hasty climbers soon do fall;
I see that those which are aloft       15
  Mishap doth threaten most of all;
They get with toil, they keep with
    fear—
Such cares my mind could never bear.

Content to live, this is my stay;
  I seek no more than may suffice;    20
I press to bear no haughty sway;
  Look, what I lack my mind sup-
    plies.
Lo, thus I triumph like a king,
Content with that my mind doth
    bring.

Some have too much, yet still do
    crave;                                         25
  I little have, and seek no more.
They are but poor, though much
    they have,
  And I am rich with little store.
They poor, I rich; they beg, I give;
They lack, I leave; they pine, I live. 30

I laugh not at another's loss;
  I grudge not at another's pain;
No worldly waves my mind can toss;
  My state at one doth still remain.
I fear no foe, I fawn no friend;          35
I loathe not life, nor dread my end.

Some weigh their pleasure by their
    lust,
  Their wisdom by their rage of will;
Their treasure is their only trust;
  A cloakéd craft their store of skill.
But all the pleasure that I find        41
Is to maintain a quiet mind.

My wealth is health and perfect ease;
  My conscience clear my chief de-
    fense;
I neither seek by bribes to please,     45
  Nor by deceit to breed offense.
Thus do I live; thus will I die;
Would all did so as well as I!

## LIFE OF THE MIND, 1935

### *Genevieve Taggard* (*1935*)

*The words in the books are not true*
*If they do not act in you.*

Fret fools the days away,
Best-sellers for their food,
And bad philosophy,                    5
Fret fools.
      But we,
We dare not read for long.
We snatch our thought, our song,
As soldiers do their meat.
Necessity to eat,                      10
Necessity to act,
And act aright, renews
The mind's link with the arm.
Imperative to choose,
Imperative to do,                      15
Our time's dynamic form.

Once we were students—then
Grave faces hours pored
Over the activity stored—
The energy of great men.                20

That time must come again.
If not for us, for those
We will to endow once more
With the tested word-in-deed.
Poetry and the great prose              25
Born in a like uproar
Where someone had to bleed.

The battle of the mind,
Tranquillity, too, the kind
Quick teacher's face, the jest,         30
Keen argument with a friend,
That sport and the sweet zest,—
All fall, must fall, behind.
That time is at an end.

Now action like a sword.                35
Now to redeem the word.
Now blood for stubborn proof
No one may cut apart
Word from the living deed,
Or live this life aloof.                40
Fear is a flimsy creed.
*"I believe with all my heart."*
In the one way to believe:
*"This thing is good—I give*
*My living to see it live."*            45

Bleak thought and a bastard art,
How easy to relinquish both!
So to be wise, so learned
If never more returned
To temporary peace.                     50
So not to die of sloth
Or live best-sellers' ease.
But to stand upon our oath.

## ON MAN'S POWERS

### (*From* An Essay on Man)

### *Alexander Pope* (*1734*)

Know then thyself, presume not God to scan,
The proper study of mankind is man.
Placed on this isthmus of a middle state,
A being darkly wise, and rudely great:
With too much knowledge for the sceptic side,    5
With too much weakness for the stoic's pride,
He hangs between, in doubt to act or rest;
In doubt to deem himself a god or beast;

In doubt his mind or body to prefer;
Born but to die, and reasoning but to err;                       10
Alike in ignorance, his reason such,
Whether he thinks too little or too much:
Chaos of thought and passion, all confused;
Still by himself abused or disabused;
Created half to rise, and half to fall;                          15
Great lord of all things, yet a prey to all;
Sole judge of truth, in endless error hurled:
The glory, jest, and riddle of the world!
    Go, wondrous creature! mount where science guides,
Go, measure earth, weigh air, and state the tides;              20
Instruct the planets in what orbs to run,
Correct old Time, and regulate the sun;
Go, soar with Plato to the empyreal sphere,
To the first good, first perfect, and first fair;
Or tread the mazy round his followers trod,                     25
And quitting sense call imitating God;
As eastern priests in giddy circles run,
And turn their heads to imitate the sun.
Go, teach Eternal Wisdom how to rule—
Then drop into thyself, and be a fool!                          30

## ULYSSES

### *Alfred, Lord Tennyson* (*1842*)

It little profits that an idle king,
By this still hearth, among these barren crags,
Matched with an agéd wife, I mete and dole
Unequal laws unto a savage race,
That hoard, and sleep, and feed, and know not me.               5
I cannot rest from travel; I will drink
Life to the lees. All times I have enjoyed
Greatly, have suffered greatly, both with those
That loved me, and alone; on shore, and when
Through scudding drifts the rainy Hyades                        10
Vexed the dim sea. I am become a name;
For always roaming with a hungry heart
Much have I seen and known,—cities of men
And manners, climates, councils, governments,
Myself not least, but honored of them all,—                     15
And drunk delight of battle with my peers,
Far on the ringing plains of windy Troy.
I am a part of all that I have met;
Yet all experience is an arch wherethrough
Gleams that untraveled world whose margin fades                 20
For ever and for ever when I move.

How dull it is to pause, to make an end,
To rust unburnished, not to shine in use!
As though to breathe were life! Life piled on life
Were all too little, and of one to me     25
Little remains; but every hour is saved
From that eternal silence, something more,
A bringer of new things; and vile it were
For some three suns to store and hoard myself,
And this gray spirit yearning in desire     30
To follow knowledge like a sinking star,
Beyond the utmost bound of human thought.

     This is my son, mine own Telemachus,
To whom I leave the scepter and the isle,—
Well-loved of me, discerning to fulfil     35
This labor, by slow prudence to make mild
A rugged people, and through soft degrees
Subdue them to the useful and the good.
Most blameless is he, centered in the sphere
Of common duties, decent not to fail     40
In offices of tenderness, and pay
Meet adoration to my household gods,
When I am gone. He works his work, I mine.

     There lies the port; the vessel puffs her sail;
There gloom the dark, broad seas. My mariners,     45
Souls that have toiled, and wrought, and thought with me,—
That ever with a frolic welcome took
The thunder and the sunshine, and opposed
Free hearts, free foreheads,—you and I are old;
Old age hath yet his honor and his toil.     50
Death closes all; but something ere the end,
Some work of noble note, may yet be done,
Not unbecoming men that strove with Gods.
The lights begin to twinkle from the rocks;
The long day wanes; the slow moon climbs; the deep     55
Moans round with many voices. Come, my friends.
'Tis not too late to seek a newer world.
Push off, and sitting well in order smite
The sounding furrows; for my purpose holds
To sail beyond the sunset, and the baths     60
Of all the western stars, until I die.
It may be that the gulfs will wash us down;
It may be that we shall touch the Happy Isles,
And see the great Achilles, whom we knew.
Though much is taken, much abides; and though     65
We are not now that strength which in old days
Moved earth and heaven, that which we are, we are,—
One equal temper of heroic hearts,
Made weak by time and fate, but strong in will
To strive, to seek, to find, and not to yield.     70

## TO THE VIRGINS, TO MAKE MUCH OF TIME

*Robert Herrick* (*1648*)

Gather ye rose-buds while ye may,
  Old time is still a flying,
And this same flower that smiles to-
    day,
  To-morrow will be dying.

The glorious lamp of Heaven, the
    sun,              5
  The higher he's a getting,
The sooner will his race be run,
  And nearer he's to setting.

That age is best which is the first,
  When youth a n d b l o o d are
    warmer;         10
But being spent, the worse, and worst
  Times still succeed the former.

Then be not coy, but use your time,
  And while ye may, go marry;
For having lost but once your prime
  You may forever tarry.     16

## RABBI BEN EZRA

*Robert Browning* (*1864*)

Grow old along with me!
The best is yet to be,
The last of life, for which the first was
    made:
Our times are in His hand
Who saith "A whole I planned,    5
Youth shows but half; trust God: see
  all, nor be afraid!"

Not that, amassing flowers,
Youth sighed "Which rose make ours,
Which lily leave and then as best re-
    call?"
Not that, admiring stars,     10
It yearned "Nor Jove, nor Mars;
Mine be some figured flame which
  blends, transcends them all!"

Not for such hopes and fears
Annulling youth's brief years,
Do I remonstrate: folly wide the
    mark!       15
Rather I prize the doubt
Low kinds exist without,
Finished and finite clods, untroubled
  by a spark.

Poor vaunt of life indeed,
Were man but formed to feed    20
On joy, to solely seek and find and
    feast:
Such feasting ended, then
As sure an end to men;
Irks care the crop-full bird? Frets
  doubt the maw-crammed beast?

Rejoice we are allied     25
To That which doth provide
And not partake, effect and not re-
    ceive!
A spark disturbs our clod;
Nearer we hold of God
Who gives, than of His tribes that
  take, I must believe.     30

Then, welcome each rebuff
That turns earth's smoothness rough,
Each sting that bids nor sit nor stand
  but go!
Be our joys three-parts pain!
Strive, and hold cheap the strain;   35
Learn, nor account the pang; dare,
  never grudge the throe!

For thence,—a paradox
Which comforts while it mocks,—
Shall life succeed in that it seems to
    fail:
What I aspired to be,     40
And was not, comforts me:
A brute I might have been, but would
  not sink i' the scale.

What is he but a brute
Whose flesh hath soul to suit,
Whose spirit works lest arms and legs
  want play?     45

To man, propose this test—
Thy body at its best,
How far can that project thy soul on
    its lone way?

Yet gifts should prove their use:
I own the Past profuse     50
Of power each side, perfection every
    turn:
Eyes, ears took in their dole,
Brain treasured up the whole;
Should not the heart beat once "How
    good to live and learn?"

Not once beat "Praise be Thine!     55
I see the whole design,
I, who saw Power, see now Love per-
    fect too:
Perfect I call Thy plan:
Thanks that I was a man!
Maker, remake, complete,—I trust
    what Thou shalt do!"     60

For pleasant is this flesh;
Our soul in its rose-mesh
Pulled ever to the earth, still yearns
    for rest:
Would we some prize might hold
To match those manifold     65
Possessions of the brute,—gain most,
    as we did best!

Let us not always say
"Spite of this flesh to-day
I strove, made head, gained ground
    upon the whole!"
As the bird wings and sings,     70
Let us cry "All good things
Are ours, nor soul helps flesh more,
    now, than flesh helps soul!"

Therefore I summon age
To grant youth's heritage,
Life's struggle having so far reached
    its term:     75
Thence shall I pass, approved
A man, for aye removed
From the developed brute; a God
    though in the germ.

And I shall thereupon
Take rest, ere I be gone     80
Once more on my adventure brave
    and new:
Fearless and unperplexed,
When I wage battle next,
What weapons to select, what armour
    to indue.

Youth ended, I shall try     85
My gain or loss thereby;
Be the fire ashes, what survives is gold:
And I shall weigh the same,
Give life its praise or blame:
Young, all lay in dispute; I shall
    know, being old.     90

For note, when evening shuts,
A certain moment cuts
The deed off, calls the glory from the
    grey:
A whisper from the west
Shoots—"Add this to the rest,     95
Take it and try its worth: here dies
    another day."

So, still within this life,
Though lifted o'er its strife,
Let me discern, compare, pronounce
    at last,
"This rage was right i' the main,     100
That acquiescence vain:
The Future I may face now I have
    proved the Past."

For more is not reserved
To man, with soul just nerved
To act to-morrow what he learns to-
    day:     105
Here, work enough to watch
The Master work, and catch
Hints of the proper craft, tricks of
    the tool's true play.

As it was better, youth
Should strive, through acts uncouth,
Toward making, than repose on
    aught found made;     111

So, better, age, exempt
From strife, should know, than tempt
Further.  Thou waitedst age; wait
    death nor be afraid!

Enough now, if the Right          115
And Good and Infinite
Be named here, as thou callest thy
    hand thine own,
With knowledge absolute,
Subject to no dispute
From fools that crowded youth, nor
    let thee feel alone.          120

Be there, for once and all,
Severed great minds from small,
Announced to each his station in the
    Past!
Was I, the world arraigned,
Were they, my soul disdained,          125
Right?  Let age speak the truth and
    give us peace at last!

Now, who shall arbitrate?
Ten men love what I hate,
Shun what I follow, slight what I re-
    ceive;
Ten, who in ears and eyes          130
Match me: we all surmise,
They, this thing, and I, that: whom
    shall my soul believe?

Not on the vulgar mass
Called "work," must sentence pass,
Things done, that took the eye and
    had the price;          135
O'er which, from level stand,
The low world laid its hand,
Found straightway to its mind, could
    value in a trice:

But all, the world's coarse thumb
And finger failed to plumb,          140
So passed in making up the main ac-
    count;
All instincts immature,
All purposes unsure,
That weighed not as his work, yet
    swelled the man's amount:

Thoughts hardly to be packed          145
Into a narrow act,
Fancies that broke through language
    and escaped;
All I could never be,
All, men ignored in me,
This, I was worth to God, whose
    wheel the pitcher shaped.          150

Ay, note that Potter's wheel,
That metaphor! and feel
Why time spins fast, why passive lies
    our clay,—
Thou, to whom fools propound,
When the wine makes its round,          155
"Since life fleets, all is change; the
    Past gone, seize to-day!"

Fool!  All that is, at all,
Lasts ever, past recall;
Earth changes, but thy soul and God
    stand sure:
What entered into thee,          160
*That* was, is, and shall be:
Time's wheel runs back or stops;
    Potter and clay endure.

He fixed thee mid this dance
Of plastic circumstance,
This Present, thou, forsooth, wouldst
    fain arrest:          165
Machinery just meant
To give thy soul its bent,
Try thee and turn thee forth, suffi-
    ciently impressed.

What though the earlier grooves
Which ran the laughing loves          170
Around thy base, no longer pause and
    press?
What though, about thy rim,
Skull-things in order grim
Grow out, in graver mood, obey the
    sterner stress?

Look not thou down but up! 175
To uses of a cup,
The festal board, lamp's flash and
    trumpet's peal,
The new wine's foaming flow,
The Master's lips aglow!
Thou, heaven's consummate cup,
    what needst thou with earth's
    wheel? 180

But I need, now as then,
Thee, God, who mouldest men;
And since, not even while the whirl
    was worst,

Did I,—to the wheel of life
With shapes and colours rife, 185
Bound dizzily,—mistake my end, to
    slake Thy thirst:

So, take and use Thy work!
Amend what flaws may lurk,
What strain o' the stuff, what warp-
    ings past the aim!
My times be in Thy hand! 190
Perfect the cup as planned!
Let age approve of youth, and death
    complete the same!

## CHARACTER OF THE HAPPY WARRIOR

*William Wordsworth* (*1807*)

Who is the happy Warrior? Who is he
That every man in arms should wish to be?
—It is the generous spirit, who, when brought
Among the task of real life, hath wrought
Upon the plan that pleased his boyish thought; 5
Whose high endeavors are an inward light
That makes the path before him always bright;
Who, with a natural instinct to discern
What knowledge can perform, is diligent to learn;
Abides by this resolve, and stops not there, 10
But makes his moral being his prime care;
Who, doomed to go in company with pain
And fear and bloodshed, miserable train!
Turns his necessity to glorious gain;
In face of these doth exercise a power 15
Which is our human nature's highest dower;
Controls them and subdues, transmutes, bereaves
Of their bad influence, and their good receives;
By objects, which might force the soul to abate
Her feeling, rendered more compassionate; 20
Is placable—because occasions rise
So often that demand such sacrifice;
More skilful in self-knowledge, even more pure,
As tempted more; more able to endure,
As more exposed to suffering and distress; 25
Thence, also, more alive to tenderness.
—'Tis he whose law is reason; who depends
Upon that law as on the best of friends;

Whence, in a state where men are tempted still
To evil for a guard against worse ill,                              30
And what in quality or act is best
Doth seldom on a right foundation rest,
He labors good on good to fix, and owes
To virtue every triumph that he knows;
—Who, if he rise to station of command,              35
Rises by open means; and there will stand
On honorable terms, or else retire,
And in himself possess his own desire;
Who comprehends his trust, and to the same
Keeps faithful with a singleness of aim;              40
And therefore does not stoop, nor lie in wait
For wealth or honors or for worldly state;
Whom they must follow; on whose head must fall,
Like showers of manna, if they come at all;
Whose powers shed round him in the common strife,    45
Or mild concerns of ordinary life,
A constant influence, a peculiar grace;
But who, if he be called upon to face
Some awful moment to which Heaven has joined
Great issues, good or bad for human kind,             50
Is happy as a lover; and attired
With sudden brightness, like a man inspired;
And, through the heat of conflict, keeps the law
In calmness made, and sees what he foresaw;
Or if an unexpected call succeed,                     55
Come when it will, is equal to the need.
—He who, though thus endued as with a sense
And faculty for storm and turbulence,
Is yet a soul whose master-bias leans
To home-felt pleasures and to gentle scenes;         60
Sweet images! which, wheresoe'er he be,
Are at his heart; and such fidelity
It is his darling passion to approve;
More brave for this, that he hath much to love.
'Tis, finally, the man, who, lifted high,            65
Conspicuous object in a nation's eye,
Or left unthought-of in obscurity—
Who, with a toward or untoward lot,
Prosperous or adverse, to his wish or not—
Plays, in the many games of life, that one           70
Where what he most doth value must be won;
Whom neither shape of danger can dismay,
Nor thought of tender happiness betray;
Who, not content that former worth stand fast,
Looks forward, persevering to the last,              75
From well to better, daily self-surpassed;

Who, whether praise of him must walk the earth
Forever, and to noble deeds give birth,
Or he must fall to sleep without his fame,
And leave a dead, unprofitable name—            80
Finds comfort in himself and in his cause;
And, while the mortal mist is gathering, draws
His breath in confidence of Heaven's applause—
This is the happy Warrior; this is he
That every man in arms should wish to be.        85

## LONDON, 1802

### *William Wordsworth* (*1802*)

Milton! thou should'st be living at this hour;
England hath need of thee. She is a fen
Of stagnant waters; altar, sword, and pen
Fireside, the heroic wealth of hall and bower,
Have forfeited their ancient English dower       5
Of inward happiness. We are selfish men;
Oh! raise us up, return to us again,
And give us manners, virtue, freedom, power.
Thy soul was like a star, and dwelt apart.
Thou hadst a voice whose sound was like the sea.  10
Pure as the naked heavens, majestic, free,
So didst thou travel on life's common way,
In cheerful godliness; and yet thy heart
The lowliest duties on herself did lay.

## TO CYRIACK SKINNER

### *John Milton* (*1635*)

Cyriack, this three years' day these eyes, though clear
To outward view, of blemish or of spot,
Bereft of light, their seeing have forgot;
Nor to their idle orbs doth sight appear
Of sun or moon or star throughout the year,       5
Or man or woman. Yet I argue not
Against Heaven's hand or will, nor bate a jot
Of heart or hope, but still bear up and steer
Right onward. What supports me, dost thou ask?
The conscience, friend, to have lost them overplied  10
In liberty's defense, my noble task,
Of which all Europe talks from side to side.
This thought might lead me through the world's vain mask
Content, though blind, had I no better guide.

## ON HIS BLINDNESS

### *John Milton* *(1655)*

When I consider how my light is
 spent
  Ere half my days in this dark world
  and wide,
  And that one talent which is death
  to hide
  Lodged with me useless, though
  my soul more bent
To serve therewith my Maker, and
  present                                    5
  My true account, lest He return-
  ing, chide,
  "Doth God exact day-labor, light
  denied?"
  I fondly ask. But Patience, to pre-
  vent
That murmur, soon replies, "God
  doth not need
  Either man's work or his own gifts.
  Who best                                   10
  Bear his mild yoke, they serve him
  best. His state
Is kingly: thousands at his bidding
  speed,
  And post o'er land and ocean with-
  out rest;
  They also serve who only stand and
  wait."

## DOVER BEACH

### *Matthew Arnold* *(1867)*

The sea is calm to-night.
The tide is full, the moon lies fair
Upon the straits;—on the French
  coast the light
Gleams and is gone; the cliffs of Eng-
  land stand,
Glimmering and vast, out in the tran-
  quil bay.                                   5
Come to the window, sweet is the
  night-air!
Only, from the long line of spray

Where the sea meets the moon-
  blanch'd land
Listen! you hear the grating roar
Of pebbles which the waves draw
  back, and fling                            10
At their return, up the high strand,
Begin, and cease, and then again be-
  gin,
With tremulous cadence slow, and
  bring
The eternal note of sadness in.

Sophocles long ago                           15
Heard it on the Ægean, and it
  brought
Into his mind the turbid ebb and flow
Of human misery; we
Find also in the sound a thought,
Hearing it by this distant northern
  sea.                                       20
The sea of faith
Was once, too, at the full, and round
  earth's shore
Lay like the folds of a bright girdle
  furl'd.
But now I only hear
Its melancholy, long, withdrawing
  roar,                                      25
Retreating to the breath
Of the night-wind down the vast
  edges drear
And naked shingles of the world.

Ah, love, let us be true
To one another! for the world, which
  seems                                      30
To lie before us like a land of dreams,
So various, so beautiful, so new,
Hath really neither joy, nor love,
  nor light,
Nor certitude, nor peace, nor help
  for pain;
And we are here as on a darkling
  plain                                      35
Swept with confused alarms of strug-
  gle and flight
Where ignorant armies clash by
  night.

## "DOVER BEACH"—A NOTE TO THAT POEM
### *Archibald MacLeish* (*1936*)

The wave withdrawing
Withers with seaward rustle of flimsy water
Sucking the sand down: dragging at empty shells:
The roil after it settling: too smooth: smothered . . .

After forty a man's a fool to wait in the           5
Sea's face for the full force and the roaring of
Surf to come over him: droves of careening water.
After forty the tug's out and the salt and the
Sea follow it: less sound and violence:
Nevertheless the ebb has its own beauty—           10
Shells sand and all and the whispering rustle.
There's earth in it then and the bubbles of foam gone.

Moreover—and this too has its lovely uses—
It's the outward wave that spills the inward forward
Tripping the proud piled mute virginal           15
Mountain of water in wallowing welter of light and
Sound enough—thunder for miles back: it's a fine and a
Wild smother to vanish in: pulling down—
Tripping with outward ebb the urgent inward.

Speaking alone for myself it's the steep hill and the           20
Toppling lift of the young men I am toward now—
Waiting for that as the wave for the next wave.
Let them go over us all I say with the thunder of
What's to be next in the world. It's we will be under it!

## SPEECH TO THE DETRACTORS
### *Archibald MacLeish* (*1936*)

What should a man do but love excellence
Whether of earth or art
Whether the hare's leap or the heart's recklessness?

What honor has any man but with eagerness
Valuing wasteless things           5
To praise the great and speak the unpraise meagerly?

Because the heroes with the swords have vanished
Leaving us nearer by
Actual life and the more human manhood—

Because the common face: the anonymous figure:                              10
The nameless and mortal man:
Is our time's birth to bear and to be big with—

Because the captains and the kings are dust—
Need we deny our hearts
Their natural duty and the thing they *must* do?                            15

Not to the wearers of wreaths but those who bring them
Coming with heaped-up arms
Is fame the noble and ennobling thing.

Bequeathers of praise the unnamed numberless peoples
Leave on the lasting earth                                                   20
Not fame but their hearts' love of fame for keeping.

They raise not alone memorial monuments:
Outlasting these
They raise their need to render greatness honor.

The ignorant and rabble rain erases                                         25
Dates and the dead man's kind.
It leaves the blindness of the stones that praised him.

Why then must this time of ours be envious?
Why must the great man now—
Sealed from the mouths of worms—be sucked by men's mouths?                  30

Refusing ribbons that the rest have clowned for—
Dying and wishing peace—
The best are eaten by the envy round them.

When Lawrence died the hate was at his bier.
Fearing there might have lived                                              35
A man really noble: really superior—

Fearing that worth had lived and had been modest—
Men of envious minds
Ate with venom his new buried body.

We cheat ourselves in cheating worth of wonder.                            40
Not the unwitting dead
But we who leave the praise unsaid are plundered.

## SONG OF THE OPEN ROAD
### *Walt Whitman* (*1855*)

#### I

Afoot and light-hearted, I take to the open road,
Healthy, free, the world before me,
The long brown path before me, leading wherever I choose.

Henceforth I ask not good-fortune—I myself am good-fortune;
Henceforth I whimper no more, postpone no more, need nothing,          5
Strong and content, I travel the open road.

The earth—that is sufficient;
I do not want the constellations any nearer;
I know they are very well where they are;
I know they suffice for those who belong to them. . . .          10

#### II

You road I enter upon and look around! I believe you are not all that is here;
I believe that much unseen is also here. . . .

#### III

You air that serves me with breath to speak!
You objects that call from diffusion my meanings, and give them shape!
You light that wraps me and all things in delicate equable showers!          15
You paths worn in the irregular hollows by the roadsides!
I think you are latent with unseen existences—you are so dear to me.

You flagg'd walks of the cities! you strong curbs at the edges!
You ferries! you planks and posts of wharves! you timber-lined sides! you
    distant ships!
You rows of houses! you window-pierc'd facades! you roofs! . . .          20

From all that has been near you, I believe you have imparted to yourselves, and
    now would impart the same secretly to me;
From the living and the dead I think you have peopled your impassive surfaces,
    and the spirits thereof would be evident and amicable with me.

#### V

From this hour freedom!
From this hour I ordain myself loos'd of limits and imaginary lines,
Going where I list, my own master, total and absolute,          25
Listening to others, and considering well what they say,
Pausing, searching, receiving, contemplating,
Gently, but with undeniable will, divesting myself of the holds that would
    hold me.

I inhale great draughts of space;
The east and the west are mine, and the north and the south are mine . . .          30

**VI**

. . . Now I see the secret of the making of the best persons,
It is to grow in the open air, and to eat and sleep with the earth. . . .

**IX**

Allons! whoever you are, come travel with me!
Traveling with me, you find what never tires.

The earth never tires;                                                    35
The earth is rude, silent, incomprehensible at first—Nature is rude and incom-
    prehensible at first;
Be not discouraged—keep on—there are divine things, well envelop'd;
I swear to you there are divine things, more beautiful than words can tell.

Allons! we must not stop here!
However sweet these laid-up stores—however convenient this dwelling, we
    cannot remain here;                                                   40
However shelter'd this port, and however calm these waters, we must not
    anchor here;
However welcome the hospitality that surrounds us, we are permitted to
    receive it but a little while.

**XI**

Listen! I will be honest with you;
I do not offer the old smooth prizes, but offer rough new prizes:
These are the days that must happen to you:                               45

You shall not heap up what is call'd riches,
You shall scatter with lavish hand all that you earn or achieve,
You but arrive at the city to which you were destin'd—you hardly settle
    yourself to satisfaction, before you are call'd by an irresistible call to
    depart,
You shall be treated to the ironical smiles and mockings of those who remain
    behind you;
What beckonings of love you receive, you shall only answer with passionate
    kisses of parting,                                                    50
You shall not allow the hold of those who spread their reach'd hands toward
    you.

**XII**

Allons! after the GREAT COMPANIONS! and to belong to them!
They too are on the road! they are the swift and majestic men! they are the
    greatest women. . . .

**XIV**

The Soul travels;
The body does not travel as much as the soul;                            55
The body has just as great a work as the soul, and parts away at last for the
    journeys of the soul.

All parts away for the progress of souls;
All religion, all solid things, arts, governments,—all that was or is apparent
    upon this globe or any globe, falls into riches and corners before the
    procession of Souls along the grand roads of the universe.

Of the progress of the souls of men and women along the grand roads of the
    universe, all other progress is the needed emblem and sustenance. . . .

### XV

Allons! whoever you are! come forth!                                              60
You must not stay sleeping and dallying there in the house, though you built
    it, or though it has been built for you.

Allons! out of the dark confinement!
It is useless to protest—I know all, and expose it.

Behold, through you as bad as the rest,
Through the laughter, dancing, dining, supping, of people,                       65
Inside of dresses and ornaments, inside of those wash'd and trimm'd faces,
Behold a secret silent loathing and despair. . . .

### XVII

Allons! the road is before us!
It is safe—I have tried it—my own feet have tried it well:

Allons! be not detain'd!                                                          70
Let the paper remain on the desk unwritten, and the book on the shelf
    unopen'd!
Let the tools remain in the workshop! let the money remain unearn'd!
Let the school stand! mind not the cry of the teacher!
Let the preacher preach in his pulpit! let the lawyer plead in the court, and
    the judge expound the law.

Mon enfant! I give you my hand!                                                   75
I give you my love, more precious than money,
I give you myself, before preaching or law;
Will you give me yourself? will you come travel with me?
Shall we stick by each other as long as we live?

Notes for
Reading and Writing

Biographical Notes

# NOTES FOR READING AND WRITING

## THE WORLD OF THE SENSES AND NATURE

1. Trace the steps by which Arnold Bennett shows the connection between the observation of individuals—or events—and the complete understanding of them in relation to their total background, their past, present, and future. Illustrate from your reading the truth or falsity of this statement from *Seeing Life:* "An ugly deed—such as a deed of cruelty—takes on artistic beauty when its origin and hence its fitness in the general scheme begins to be comprehended." *Suggestions for writing:* In a taxi (bus, street car, or train); First impressions revised; Observations on my way to class; The character of a street; "Every street is a mirror, an illustration, an exposition, an explanation of the human beings who live in it"; A crowd gathers; Looking without seeing; Coma; The feminine instinct; Prigs and other futile souls; The charity which signs cheques; The trouble of understanding; We are insular; A room of one's own; Gloomy preoccupations; The hinterland of consciousness; Learning the whole truth from the face; A plain face; A name has contented you; Veils; Watching the procession; Introducing myself against my background.

2. Apply the criteria of Bennett to the subject matter of *Young Writer Remembering Chicago*, showing how the writer has pointed the relations between individuals and groups. Discuss the use of sensuous descriptive detail in building up the total impression of *Young Writer Remembering Chicago*. Comment on the differences in theme and mood through the four sections of the sketch; the means of achieving unity. *Suggestions for writing:* The hurly-burly season; Panhandle boys; A booster for my city; Freshman remembering his home town; Youth does not always win; Heroes; Bucking the wind; I am sorry.

3. In what respects does the account of the Baer-Louis fight fulfill the requirements of Bennett for "seeing life," interpreting the individual in relation to his background, and suggesting the social relationships involved in the situation? *Suggestions for writing:* Ringside seats; The champion; Rooters I have known; An athletic contest.

4. Compare *Young Writer Remembering Chicago* with Stevenson's *Walking Tours* in subject matter, style, and mood. What differences might you assume in experience and social background of the two writers? Verify your conclusions by consulting biographical data and report on them. Summarize the physical joys of the walk for Stevenson. What other values does he

find? Why does he criticize business men? How might his criticism be justified in the modern scheme of things? *Suggestions for writing:* Sinking into oneself; What the busy man misses; Pleasure trips into the land of thought; A walking tour; My favorite companion on a walk; From a train window; The temperate walker; As the freak takes you; If the millennium were to arrive; A definition of happiness; Social heresy; Empty words.

5. Discuss the farm pictured by Mark Twain as an ideal background for a growing boy. What methods does he use to achieve variety? *Suggestions for writing:* I can remember; My first day at school; A childhood hero; A stranger in the family; My phantasy world; Books that colored my childhood; The farm early in the morning; Night in the country.

6. In the selection from *Swann's Way*, Proust illustrates the psychological process by which all that has ever been a part of our experience may be recalled through association. Compare Proust's ideas with those of Münsterberg, who presents the social implications of this psychological truth. *Suggestions for writing:* Strands of memory; The spell is broken; How I learned to concentrate; Distractions; I testify; Can one be objective? My memory fails me; Mental color blindness. Test the validity of Münsterberg's argument by having several members of the class attempt an accurate written report of an episode they have all witnessed and compare the results. Compare these objective reports with one in which the writer is emotionally concerned (perhaps through relationship to one of the persons involved). Compare several newspaper accounts of an accident, a public meeting, a fight, or a strike. What kinds of material take on different aspects in the several accounts, and how do you explain the variations? Write an accurate, detailed description in class of some person or place you think you know intimately. Check your accuracy by further observations and rewrite the sketch. Try to analyze further the reasons for any inaccuracies in the first sketch.

7. Where would you place the responsibility for Paul's tragedy? Discuss his family relationships and social and economic forces as they contributed to the shaping of his personality. Analyze the various means which Paul employs to escape from reality. How do you explain his arrogant manner before the faculty group? Discuss the story as it is a severe indictment of our educational system and of the values cherished on Cordelia Street. What change do you note in Paul's escapes from reality after he is taken out of school and forbidden entrance to the theater and the opera house? Analyze Paul's interest in art. To what extent is it an interest in art for its own sake? *Suggestions for writing:* A non-conformist in my class; The ban of suspension; Before the faculty; Private worlds; Listening to a symphony; An orgy of living; On having someone held up to one as a model; Making believe.

8. What light does the selection from *Typhoon* throw on Conrad's view of man and nature? How does he give personality to natural forces? Study the descriptive effects, noting especially the appeal to various senses and the force given by the verbs of action.

9. What is Rupert Brooke's purpose in paying tribute to the things he has loved? Compare the things he praises with those in Keats's *Proem to Endymion*. Refute or establish the thesis that for Brooke beauty is found solely in things; for Keats, in the effect of things on the spirit. Discuss the philosophical implications of this problem. How does Keats's poem answer the idea expressed by Brooke that "nothing remains"? Discuss the appropriateness of the images in Fletcher's *Down the Mississippi*. Select your favorite pictures. In the two poems of Gibson sense impressions serve as a point of departure for what reflections? Which of the two poems is the more vivid for you and why?

10. Summarize the argument of Herrick for the eager pursuit of sensuous delight. Comment on the effectiveness of the final note of tragedy in this joyous poem. Compare the mood and theme of *To His Coy Mistress* and *Corinna's Going A-Maying*. In what respect is MacLeish's *You, Andrew Marvell* an answer to, or continuation of, Marvell's poem? What is the common denominator with regard to form and to attitude toward life in all of these poems?

11. Summarize the arguments presented by the mariners in *The Lotos-Eaters* for the life of sensuous ease as opposed to the life of courageous action urged by their leader, Ulysses. For further development of this philosophy see the poem, *Ulysses*, in the section, *The Good Life*. Present concretely your own argument for either point of view, or record a conversation or debate in which you present the opposing philosophies. Trace the relation between the images, the lyric effects, and the thought of Tennyson's *Lotos-Eaters*.

12. Study the relation between the philosophic passages and the illustrative incidents in the selection from *The Prelude*. What does Wordsworth mean when he refers to himself as "fostered alike by beauty and by fear"? Note the appeal to concrete sense experiences. Try writing a sketch in which you describe a similar moment of keen sensuous delight and suggest its relation to your growing personality. What view of the means by which nature forms the mind is presented in *Expostulation and Reply* and *The Tables Turned*? In what way are the "tables turned"? How does Wordsworth extend his personal philosophy of the value of contact with nature to a criticism of society? In relation to his central thought, what is the significance of his wish to be a pagan?

13. Discuss the relation between the philosophy, mood, and sense experience in *Birches*. Compare the treatment of a boy's sports, and their relation to character, in Frost and in Wordsworth.

14. Show how the speaker in *Up at a Villa—Down in the City* reveals himself as a much more limited person in his response to life than the speaker in *Give Me the Splendid Silent Sun*. What evidence can you present from Browning's poem to show that the poet does not share the indifference to nature expressed by the Italian "person of quality"? Write an informal debate on the relative delights of town and country.

15. Some modern poets, perhaps influenced by new concepts of science,

fail to find in nature the restorative power and joy which earlier poets discovered. Trace this theme through Arnold's *In Harmony with Nature,* Taggard's *Try Tropic,* and Spender's *I Hear the Cries of Evening.* Supplementary poems more specifically expressing this idea may be found in the poems listed under science. Write a paper based on your study of this note in poetry, relating it to your own feelings concerning nature. In an essay by Aldous Huxley, *Wordsworth in the Tropics,* you will find a suggestive refutation of the idea that nature can afford moral guidance and emotional solace.

16. Compare the farm boy in Sandburg's *Prairie* with the youth in *Young Writer Remembering Chicago.* In what way might the two be considered representative of social changes which have taken place within the last twenty years? Can the farmer today face the future as confidently as Sandburg's son of the prairie? Discuss the problem in an essay. An interesting study might be made in a paper comparing the theme, mood, and style of Sandburg's *Prairie* with Whitman's *Pioneers! O Pioneers!* in the section on *The World of Tomorrow.*

## Suggestions for Further Reading

ESSAYS AND CRITICAL MATERIAL

Eastman, Max, *The Enjoyment of Poetry* (Chapters I and II)
Emerson, Ralph Waldo, *Nature*
Grayson, David, *Essays in Contentment*
Machen, Arthur, *The Hill of Dreams*
Pater, Walter, *Marius the Epicurean; The Renaissance* (conclusion)
Powys, John Cowper, *The Meaning of Culture*
Wilde, Oscar, *The Picture of Dorian Gray*
Wilkinson, Marguerite, *New Voices* ("Nature in Contemporary Poetry")

TRAVEL AND NATURE WRITINGS

Akeley, C., *In Brightest Africa*
Beebe, William, *Galopagos, World's End; Jungle Peace*
Ellis, Havelock, *The Soul of Spain*
Hemingway, Ernest, *The Green Hills of Africa*

Peattie, Donald Culross, *Singing in the Wilderness; An Almanac for Moderns; Green Laurels; A Prairie Grove*
Sanderson, I., *Animal Treasure*
Muir, John, *Yosemite*
Thoreau, Henry David, *Walden; A Week on the Concord and Merrimack Rivers*

BIOGRAPHIES, JOURNALS, AND LETTERS

Gissing, George, *The Private Papers of Henry Ryecroft*
Keats, John, *Letters*
Rourke, Constance, *Audubon*
Wordsworth, Dorothy, *Journals*

FICTION

Hudson, W. H., *Green Mansions; Far Away and Long Ago*
Huxley, Aldous, *Point Counterpoint*
Powys, John Cowper, *Wolf Solent*
Wolfe, Thomas, *Look Homeward Angel; Of Time and the River*

## PERSONAL RELATIONSHIPS

1. Evaluate in the light of your own experience the criticism that Steffens makes of his own up-bringing and his methods of rearing his son. An interesting report might be given on Steffens' relationship with his father and his

son by reference to his autobiography and his letters. Steffens suggests in his autobiography that his true education was a process of unlearning. How is this idea reflected in the essay? Study the early chapters of the autobiography and the later letters for material that may throw further light on this concept. *Suggestions for writing:* If I had been my father; My father's son (or daughter); Hints on bringing up children; On bringing up my parents; Things I have had to unlearn; "I think so, but I don't know"; Punishment enough; The tragedy of this comedy; We'll forget it now; Whoppers; Grown-ups say it's so; Indirect inheritance; They don't understand a fellow; Family traits; Letting off steam.

2. Find details in Lamb's life which throw light on the mood and the subject matter of *Dream Children*. Discuss the relationship of rhetorical devices to the mood of the essay. How does Lamb reveal a knowledge of child psychology in his portraits of the children? Compare his psychology with that of Steffens.

3. What support does Pearl Buck's analysis lend to the argument of Krutch that love has ceased to be a value? Make a study of a modern novelist, such as Hemingway, Dos Passos, Joyce, Aldous Huxley, or Lewis, testing the validity of Krutch's argument in your analysis. What other forces in modern life might Krutch have brought to bear on his thesis? Does he over-emphasize the place of literature in the life of the average man? *Suggestions for writing:* On falling in love; Something that Krutch (or Buck) overlooked; Educating women; He's just like a boy!; A home vs. a career; No woman has a man's chance; A masculine bugaboo; The double standard; If I want dates; Dutch treat; Men are like that; Women are like that; Beautiful but dumb.

4. Compare the strictness of Ruskin's nineteenth-century rearing with the freedom from restraint demanded by psychologists and educators for the development of the child of today. How fairly does Ruskin estimate his gains and losses in this atmosphere of restraint? What clue do you find to his difficulty in making emotional adjustments in maturity and his eventual mental breakdown? Note especially his statement, "On the whole, I had nothing animate to care for but myself, some nests of ants, which the gardener would never leave undisturbed for me, and a-sociable bird or two." *Suggestions for writing:* My parents take me to college; Forbidden fruit; Two types of home life; Advantages and disadvantages of Ruskin's up-bringing; My first contact with the Bible; The child-centered home or school; On learning the difference between right and wrong; The value of obedience.

5. Compare the implied relation of father and son in *The Father* with that in *The Fly*. Discuss self-love as the motivating force of the two fathers and contrast the implications in the conclusions. How does the author of *The Father* achieve remarkable concentration of effect and at the same time suggestiveness in this brief masterpiece? What is the role of the priest? Write a character sketch of the father. Comment on the relation of the end of this

story to the beginning. Are you prepared for this conclusion? By what means?

6. Twenty-five years ago in popular fiction, the theme of *Boy in the Summer Sun,* the breaking up of a love affair, was usually treated as the occasion for a dramatic scene or an exhibition of emotionalism. What social and economic aspects of our life today might be responsible for a change in treatment? Do you think that this story is representative of the reactions that your contemporaries might make to a similar situation? Read Rupert Brooke's poem *When Love Has Changed to Kindliness.* How does the fact that love has changed to kindliness alter the nature of the emotion?

7. *David, I've Told Them* was written by a girl of college age. How valid a picture is it of college romance? What are the foundations for the love, and what do you think of the chances for its permanence? Consider the narrative method. What advantages and disadvantages does the letter form offer here? Show how the point of view here expressed and the political interests of the two young people support the conclusions of the Fortune study of *Youth in College. Suggestions for writing:* Social conflicts in college; What makes for true compatibility?; Breaking down social barriers; What will they say?; The trade and barter system of romance; Why can't we be honest with each other?

8. What methods of characterization does Mr. Steinbeck use to emphasize the incompatibility of wife and husband in *The Chrysanthemums?* At what point are you given a clue to the real motive of the stranger? Discuss the ironic contrast between the stranger's real motive and the woman's interpretation of it. What is the relation between her desire to see the fight and her disillusioning experience? How does the line, "Each man kills the thing he loves" relate to the character of the woman? *Suggestions for writing:* Saturday night celebration; Clashes in personality; On revealing myself to a stranger; Making things grow; Thwarted creative impulses; Artistic creations in everyday life; Opportunities for creative expression in my community.

9. What is the dramatic role of Mr. Pim? Could the action of the play have been as effectively presented without him? Why is he made no more of a character in the play? How are you made aware of the conflict in temperament and ideas between Olivia and George? To what extent is this the real problem of the play? Discuss the relation between Olivia and George as a foil for that between Dinah and Brian. Trace the conflict between genuine emotions and social attitudes as it is reflected in the reactions of George. Analyze your reaction to him. Is Brian's attitude typical of that of modern youth? Why is the revelation at the end of Act II not a solution of the problem of the play? Study the dialogue in the first part of Act III in which Olivia manipulates the situation in such a way as to turn George's arguments against him. Why does Olivia not reveal to her husband Mr. Pim's final announcement? *Suggestions for writing:* Breaking the news; "And they call that art nowadays!"; "I never heard of such nonsense!"; If my parents could choose my wife (or husband); Keeping up appearances; "I can't think what

young people are coming to nowadays!"; A defense of George; Olivia's strategies; My Aunt Julia; If Mr. Telworthy had lived; Nobody need know; A comparison of the divergent views of marriage in the play.

10. Show how by understatement Millay's *Love Is Not All* really builds a strong case for her love. Compare her sonnet with Donne's *The Indifferent* and *Sonnet 116* of Shakespeare. Make a critical study of Edna St. Vincent Millay using as a point of departure her support or repudiation of Krutch's theory in *The Life and Death of a Value.*

11. Wordsworth said of Shakespeare's sonnets, "With this same key Shakespeare unlocked his heart." Browning replied, "Then, the less Shakespeare he." Read more of Shakespeare's sonnets and draw your own conclusions on the problem of whether or not Shakespeare herein reveals his personal emotions. Study the function of the concluding couplets in Shakespeare's sonnets. Write sentence summaries of the central thought of each sonnet.

12. In studying Browning's treatment of the theme of personal relationships analyze the two phases of his treatment: Love as a creative force; Love as a destructive force. Read some of the letters of the Brownings for light thrown on this problem. Select the details by which Browning gives us insight into the character of the speaker in *My Last Duchess.* How does the lover in *The Last Ride Together* illustrate the theme of Blake's *The Clod and the Pebble?* How does he reconcile himself to his failure as a lover? Compare the mood and ideas of this poem with those of Rukeyser's *Effort at Speech Between Two People.* Why does the latter poem seem more real to us today? Summarize the excuses which Andrea del Sarto offers for his failure to achieve a place with the greatest artists. Does Browning accept Andrea's conclusions or does he present them as rationalizations concealing the truth? What evidence can you bring to bear on this problem? Look up Vasari's account of Andrea del Sarto in his *Lives of the Painters* to discover what support Browning had for his characterizations of Andrea and his wife. *Suggestions for writing:* Heard over the tea cups; On not saying what I mean; Portrait of myself in an uncongenial setting; The egotist in love; A defense of the duke in *My Last Duchess;* Behind the scenes; Love is not enough; Clashes with my family; The role of my mother (or father) in shaping my character; An effort at speech between two people; Self-revelations; Alone in the crowd; First choice; A dramatic conversation; The last ride together.

13. Analyze the character of Prufrock, attempting to discover why his relationships with other people leave him with a sense of overwhelming loneliness and frustration. In what lines do you find the most explicit clues to his character? Find evidence that he is criticizing not only himself but his entire social milieu. What details suggest the social background? What figures and descriptive details suggest the influence of a machine age? Read Engle's *Poetry in a Machine Age* in the next section for helpful suggestions. How might modern theories of science throw light on the lines: "I should have been a pair of ragged claws scuttling across the floors of silent seas"?

Find instances in T. S. Eliot of the linking of the intense and trivial, the beautiful and ugly, the elevated and the banal. It has been said that Eliot writes in the spirit of Browning but with far different intention. Test the validity of this statement by a study of the poems and personalities of both authors. *Suggestions for writing:* Myself when I am old; On measuring out my life with coffee spoons; Conversations over the tea table; Half deserted streets; Restless nights; A tedious argument; Preparing a face to meet the faces that you meet; Indecisions; I am not Prince Hamlet; A bit obtuse; Almost the fool; I grow old; I am not a prophet; Do I dare?; Time to turn back; I was afraid; Visitors in an art gallery.

14. Comment on the significance of each of the nouns in the title, *Satires of Circumstance.* Discuss the element of satire and the role played by chance or circumstance in each of the selections. If you have read one of Hardy's novels, discuss these same elements in the larger work.

15. How does *Boy and Father* illustrate the associative process described by Proust?

16. Blake, Burns, Wordsworth, Byron, Keats, and Shelley are all called "romantic poets." What qualities do you find that they have in common? What differences? Compare Wordsworth's *She Was a Phantom of Delight* with Byron's *She Walks in Beauty* for theme and mood. Discover what you can of the usual treatment of women in the poetry of these two men.

17. Write an essay considering one of these problems: the relationship between Fanny Brawne and Keats as reflected in their letters and in Keats's poetry; a comparison of the values which Shakespeare found in love with those sought by D. G. Rosetti; the treatment of love by a modern woman poet: Millay, Parker, Teasdale, Taggard, Moore, Tietjens or Wylie; the treatment of love by a nineteenth-century woman poet: Mrs. Browning, Christina Rossetti, Emily Brontë, or Emily Dickinson; the relationship between Shelley's treatment of love in his poetry and his actual experience (See Maurois' *Ariel* and Shelley's *Epipsychidion*); the treatment of love by one of the following poets: E. A. Robinson, W. E. Leonard, Robert Frost, E. L. Masters, W. B. Yeats, Rupert Brooke, or Archibald MacLeish.

## Suggestions for Further Reading

ESSAYS, CRITICISM AND LETTERS

Cicero, *Friendship*
Collins, Joseph, *The Doctor Looks at Love and Life*
Dell, Floyd, *Love in the Machine Age*
Emerson, Ralph Waldo, *Essays (Friendship)*
Freud, Sigmund, *The Basic Writings of Sigmund Freud*
Montaigne, *Friendship*
*Letters of G. B. Shaw and Ellen Terry*

DRAMA

Aeschylus, *Agamemnon*
Anderson, Maxwell, *Elizabeth the Queen*
Barrie, James, *Dear Brutus; The Admirable Crichton*
Behrman, Max, *End of Summer*
Besier, Rudolf, *The Barretts of Wimpole Street*
Chekhov, Anton, *The Cherry Orchard*
Dryden, John, *All for Love*
Euripides, *Medea*

Franken, Rose, *Another Language*

Gale, Zona, *Miss Lulu Bett*

Glaspell, Susan, *Alison's House; Trifles*

Goldsmith, Oliver, *She Stoops to Conquer*

Hellman, Lillian, *The Little Foxes*

Howard, Sidney, *The Silver Cord*

Ibsen, Henrik, *Hedda Gabbler; A Doll's House*

Kelly, George, *Craig's Wife*

Millay, Edna St. Vincent, *The King's Henchman*

Milne, A. A., *The Dover Road*

Molnar, Ferenc, *Liliom*

Moody, William Vaughn, *The Great Divide*

O'Neill, Eugene, *Strange Interlude; Mourning Becomes Electra; Ile; Anna Christie; Ah, Wilderness!*

Pirandello, Luigi, *As You Desire Me*

Shakespeare, William, *Romeo and Juliet; Othello; King Lear; Anthony and Cleopatra*

Sheridan, Richard, *The Rivals*

Sophocles, *Antigone*

Strindberg, August, *The Father*

Wilder, Thornton, *Our Town*

Yeats, William Butler, *Deirdre*

FICTION

Anderson, Sherwood, *Winesburg, Ohio*

Austen, Jane, *Pride and Prejudice*

Bennett, Arnold, *The Old Wives' Tale*

Bromfield, Louis, *Possession*

Brontë, Charlotte, *Jane Eyre*

Brontë, Emily, *Wuthering Heights*

Butler, Samuel, *The Way of All Flesh*

Cather, Willa, *The Lost Lady*

Chekhov, Anton, *Love, and Other Stories*

de la Roche, Mazo, *Jalna; Whiteoaks of Jalna*

Eliot, George, *The Mill on the Floss*

Fielding, Henry, *Tom Jones*

Flaubert, Gustave, *Madame Bovary*

Galsworthy, John, *The Forsyte Saga*

Glasgow, Ellen, *The Romantic Comedians; They Stooped to Folly*

Hardy, Thomas, *Tess of the D'Urbervilles; The Mayor of Casterbridge*

Hemingway, Ernest, *The Sun Also Rises*

Hergesheimer, Joseph, *Cytherea*

Huxley, Aldous, *Point Counterpoint*

James, Henry, *The Ambassadors*

Lagerlöf, Selma, *The Ring of the Löwenskold's*

Lawrence, D. H., *Women in Love; Sons and Lovers*

Mann, Thomas, *Buddenbrooks; Joseph in Egypt*

Maurois, André, *The Family Circle*

Meredith, George, *The Ordeal of Richard Feverel*

Morgan, Charles, *The Fountain*

Proust, Marcel, *The Remembrance of Things Past*

Richardson, Samuel, *Pamela*

Richardson, Dorothy, *Pilgrimage*

Rolland, Romain, *The Soul Enchanted*

Suckow, Ruth, *The Folks*

Swinnerton, Frank, *Nocturne*

Thackeray, William M., *Vanity Fair*

Thomas, Dorothy, *The Home Place*

Undset, Sigrid, *Kristin Lavransdatter*

Van Etten, Winifred, *I Am the Fox*

Walpole, Hugh, *The Duchess of Wrexe; The Cathedral*

Wescott, Glenway, *The Grandmothers*

Wilder, Thornton, *The Bridge of San Luis Rey*

Wolfe, Thomas, *The Web and the Rock*

Woolf, Virginia, *The Waves; Jacob's Room*

## THE ARTS

1. It may be said that the author of *The Plain Reader* takes neither the "art for art's sake" position nor the stand that art should have a moral or social purpose. Define clearly her middle-of-the-road position. Support or refute, by reference to your own reading, Anatole France's suggestion that it will depend upon the reader "whether the book be dull or brilliant, hot with passion or cold as ice." *Suggestions for writing:* If all the good people were clever; If all the clever people were good; The business of living beautifully; A cultured person; An exclusive cult for exclusive people; The froth of

personalities; Does human nature remain unchanged?; A good hater; A sentimentalist; Gusto for life; Inspired common sense; Life's mockeries.

2. In the preface to *The Nigger of the Narcissus*, what distinction is
drawn between the word, *wisdom*, which is the result of the work of scientists
and thinkers, and the word, *truth*, as it is the means of the writer's rendering
"justice to the visible universe"? What is the relation of art to the senses?
Show how Conrad's practice in the selection which you read from *Typhoon*
demonstrates his aesthetic theory. Art, according to Conrad, both speaks to
our already existing "invincible conviction of solidarity" and it awakens "that
feeling of unavoidable solidarity." How is this dual function of art established by Conrad?

3. Of what did Farrell's "education in living" consist, and how did it
become a part of his novel? Compare his essay, *A Novelist Begins*, with
Conrad's preface to *The Nigger of the Narcissus* and determine the differences in social background, purpose, and method of the two writers. *Suggestion for writing:* Burning bridges; Defending myself from myself; A nobody;
Miserable grains of experience; At loggerheads; My spiritual godfathers;
Spiritual poverty; A social ritual.

4. How does Mark Van Doren limit the meaning of the term *sensitiveness*
in his definition of the poet? How does this limitation limit also his interpretation of Wordsworth's analysis? According to Wordsworth, what characteristics possessed by the ordinary man does the poet share in an intensified form?
Read Day Lewis's *Hope for Poetry* and the entire Preface to the *Lyrical
Ballads* of Wordsworth and suggest how the social and political changes of
the last decades may have helped to make some of the theories of Day Lewis
a verification of certain ideas advanced by Wordsworth. What distinctions
does Wordsworth make between the poet and the man of science? In the
light of Engle's *Poetry in a Machine Age* discuss how modern poets have
attempted "to carry sensation into the midst of the objects of science" and
to make science a "genuine inmate of the household of man." How do the
poems in the following section, *The World of Science*, illustrate this attempt
of modern poets? Select specific figures derived from the realm of science
and show how they put on "a form of flesh and blood." How does Van Doren
destroy the common conception of the "sensitive poet"? How fair is he in his
assertion that Wordsworth created considerable confusion in his picture of
the poet as a man with a "peculiar mind which enables him to plumb the
world's appearances"?

5. Outline Engle's analysis of the influences of modern machinery, psychology, and sociology on poetry today. This essay suggests many interesting problems for further investigation: A study of the relation between
mood and verse in MacLeish's *Conquistador;* The relation of mood and verse
and the sources of imagery in *John Brown's Body;* the use of machine imagery
in *Smoke and Steel*, or in the poems of Auden, Day Lewis, Spender, and

MacLeish; "Anything that affects the lives of men is fit subject for poetry." Support or challenge this conviction of Engle's by making a study of the themes of a group of modern poets; The influence of psychology on the poetry of one of the following: Lawrence, Joyce, Aiken, Hardy, Masters, Millay, MacLeish, Jeffers, Robinson; Shelley's use of contemporary social and political material; A study of one or more of the social poets in this volume to illustrate Engle's ideas regarding the passing from individual to social consciousness.

6. John Holmes says of the poet, "By his passionately scrupulous examination of one moment he can re-create it as it is and let it go. Nothing is ever lost, no experience is ever in vain." Consider this idea in relation to MacLeish's *"Not Marble Nor the Gilded Monuments"*; in relation to Slesinger's *A Life in the Day of a Writer*.

7. Katharine Cornell says, "Every part must mirror something of the actor himself, just as every book, every painting, every piece of music, reflects something of its creator." Discuss the relation of this idea to the older tradition of the theater that acting is a mimetic art in which the actor loses his own identity. What is the relation of the emotion of the actor to the emotion of the character he portrays? Criticize the acting in a recent movie or play you have seen with reference to Miss Cornell's theories.

8. Why may the motion picture be more effective than other agencies in the process of true democratization? The story of the dust bowl has been the theme of a number of recent books. Compare *The Grapes of Wrath* by Steinbeck with Carey McWilliams' *Factories in the Field*. Which, in your opinion, would have the greater influence on people? Analyze your reactions in relation to the main argument of *Much Could Be Done*. If you have seen any pictures such as those described here, write a criticism of one, showing why it was, or was not, effective artistically. Consider its effect on your mental and emotional attitudes toward the subject treated. *Suggestions for writing:* A criticism of *The March of Time;* Recent pictures which present social themes; Propaganda in the movies; The dreams that guide us; Pictures as moving blueprints of possibilities; An hour of reality in the movies; Recent technical achievements of Hollywood; A successful screen adaptation of a novel; Should the movies afford more than escape?; Russian films.

9. Maxwell Anderson holds that the heart of the artist's message is that "men are not essentially as they are, but as they imagine themselves to be." Find support for this idea in the following poems of Browning: *Abt Vogler, Rabbi Ben Ezra, Fra Lippo Lippi, Andrea del Sarto.* Write a paper presenting your conclusions. How does Maxwell Anderson establish his conviction that the scientist reinforces the faith of prophet and artist? Show why Anderson's insistence on the need for a personal, national, and racial faith must not be confused with a creed such as that of the Nazis. What sort of world does he envision? *Suggestions for writing:* "If the time arrives when our young men

and women lose their extravagant faith in the dollar and turn to the arts we may then become a great nation"; Are we awakening to an interest in the arts in America?; The artist and his public; The arts and the workingman; Art in the home; Should the arts have a more prominent place in the curriculum?; My experience in the realm of the arts; The little theater as a social force; Radio, the arts, and the public. There are no selections here which treat of architecture or sculpture. If your interest lies in one of these media, read a number of articles in this field and make a report on your findings.

10. Discuss the ways in which Leonardo may be considered the "matchless composite of all that the Renaissance contributed to civilization." On the other hand, why was he a "lonely figure in the center of culture"? There has been of late almost more interest in Leonardo as man of science than as artist. Summarize his contributions to science. What relationship do you see between the artist and the scientist in Leonardo? Study the Mona Lisa and write your interpretation of her character. Refer to Pater's famous description of "La Gioconda" (Mona Lisa) in *The Renaissance*.

11. Mr. Gilman says that with few exceptions the greatest creative artists have been religious—not in the narrow and doctrinal sense of the word, but in the free and ultimate sense. Discuss this idea in relation to the central thought of Maxwell Anderson in his *The Arts as Motive Power*. How does Mr. Gilman relate the genuine music lover to the musician? Discuss the relationship between the insatiable gardener, or one who has an intense love for any creative activity, and Gilman's presentation of the character of the music lover or artist. Compare the character in Steinbeck's *The Chrysanthemums* with Gilman's picture of the artist gardener. *Suggestions for writing:* The music lover and the radio; Music as a background; The orchestra conductor; Mad about music; What music means to me; Jitterbugs; On listening to a symphony.

12. In the *Lord of Marutea* how is the character of Herr Müller built up before he appears on the scene? How do you account for the rapid changes in mood, the apparent inconsistencies of action in this character? Show how the musician transferred his individual creative urges to the molding of the artistic response in others. Have you ever observed a similar transference, perhaps in a teacher of music? Trace the temperamental conflict between Herr Müller's love of music, his love of his people, and his violent temper, and discuss the tragic resolution of this conflict. *Suggestions for writing:* The dictator at home; A lovable tyrant; A tragedy of thwarted talent; The music lover.

13. What conflicting forces within and without impinge upon the writer's consciousness in *A Life in the Day of a Writer*? What is the relationship of the title of the story to the author's theory of art? O'Brien, who placed this story in his collection of the best short stories of 1936, suggests that Miss Slesinger's "notable gift is her ability to use the stream of con-

sciousness technique to reflect poignantly that curious insulation of modern metropolitan man and woman divided between inward aspiration and chromium-plated outward event. She can register for us better than any other writer I know the continuous bombardment of petty and irrelevant experience upon the soul of modern man. Her characters all dance in *Heartbreak House* with fixed smiles on their faces concealing the tragedy within." Discuss the implications of this criticism by direct reference to the story.

14. What view of the poet and his mission does Robinson express? Investigate the facts of his life to throw light on his meaning when he says: "The gold I miss for dreaming is all yours." Write a characterization of Robinson, man and poet, embodying your discoveries.

15. In Dauber's yearning to paint the sea "from the inside," Masefield probably expresses his own desire to paint the life of the sea realistically as a poet. Study some of his sea poems, relating them to his own experience on the sea.

16. What is the significance of the duality of the artist's nature suggested in *A Musical Instrument*? Can you illustrate the theme by reference to the lives of poets or artists?

17. Trace the argument of Genevieve Taggard for the superiority of music to speech. Of what does this activity become a symbol for her? If you have ever been a part of a choric or orchestral group, analyze your feelings in an essay.

18. What does Spender's poem, *Without that once clear aim*, suggest to you about the problems of the poet in the contemporary world? Study other poems of Spender to discover whether poetry is really no more to him than "wings away." What is the idea of the poet's function expressed in *I think continually of those who were truly great*?

19. What new themes for the poetry of a new world does Muriel Rukeyser outline in *Notes for a Poem*? Read in her *U.S.1* to discover how she uses "factual timbers" in building her social poems. Refer again to Engle's *Poetry in a Machine Age* and try to establish a point of view regarding the problem of propaganda and art. Write a critical paper using the *Suggestions for further reading* as a guide.

20. In the sonnet from which MacLeish takes his title, Shakespeare proudly boasts of the immortality his verse imparts to his loved one. Why does Mac-Leish reject the usual idealization of a beautiful woman? How does he succeed, nevertheless, in building up a climactic picture in which "Beauty is truth"? Show how Keats, by a succession of images, arrives at the same conclusion that "Beauty is truth."

21. How does Shelley attest to the permanence of art as a means of achieving immortality of the human passions? Compare *To the Stone Cutters* and *Ozymandias* as tributes to the permanence of art.

## Suggestions for Further Reading

ESSAYS AND CRITICISM

Austin, Mary, *The American Rhythm*

Cabell, James Branch, *Beyond Life*

Cheney, Sheldon, *The Theatre*

Craven, Thomas, *Modern Art*

Day Lewis, Cecil, *A Hope for Poetry*

Dewey, John, *Art as Experience*

Eastman, Max, *The Enjoyment of Poetry*

Eliot, Thomas Stearns, *The Literary Mind*

Ellis, Havelock, *The Dance of Life*

Faure, Elie, *History of Art*

Hart, Henry (ed.), *The Writer in a Changing World; The American Writers' Congress*

Hearn, Lafcadio, *Appreciation of Poetry*

Housman, A. E., *The Name and Nature of Poetry*

Krutch, Joseph Wood, *Experience and Art*

Lewisohn, Ludwig, *Expression in America; The Permanent Horizon*

Lowes, John L., *Convention and Revolt in Poetry*

Maurois, André, *Mape: The World of Illusion*

Mearns, Hugh, *Creative Youth*

Monroe, Harriet, *Poets and Their Art*

Mumford, Lewis, *Sticks and Stones*

Pound, Ezra, *The A.B.C. of Reading; Instigations*

Powys, John Cowper, *The Meaning of Culture* (Chapters II, III, IV)

Seldes, Gilbert, *The Seven Lively Arts*

Spaeth, Sigmund, *Stories Behind the World's Great Music*

Spender, Stephen, *The Destructive Element*

Van Loon, Hendrik, *The Arts*

Wilde, Oscar, *Intentions*

Wilkinson, Marguerite, *The Way of the Makers*

Wilson, Edmund, *Axel's Castle*

Woolf, Virginia, *The Common Reader; The Second Common Reader*

Wright, Frank Lloyd, *Architecture and Modern Life*

Wrinn, Mary J., *The Hollow Reed*

AUTOBIOGRAPHY, BIOGRAPHY, JOURNALS, LETTERS

Anderson, Sherwood, *The Story Teller's Story*

Bowen, C. D., and Von Meck, B., *Beloved Friend*

Cellini, Benvenuto, *Autobiography*

Coward, Noel, *Present Indicative*

Craven, Thomas, *Men of Art*

Gilman, Lawrence, *Toscanini*

Glaspell, Susan, *The Road to the Temple*

Keats, John, *Letters*

Kreymborg, Alfred, *Troubadour*

Le Gallienne, Eva, *At Thirty-Three*

Mansfield, Katharine, *Letters and Journals*

Nijinsky, Romola, *Life of Nijinsky*

Scudder, Janet, *Modelling My Life*

Stone, Irving, *Lust for Life*

Vallentin, Antonina, *Leonardo da Vinci*

da Vinci, Leonardo, *Notebooks*

Yeats, William Butler, *Autobiography*

FICTION

Cather, Willa, *The Song of the Lark*

Freeman, Joseph (ed.), *An Anthology of Proletarian Literature*

Galsworthy, John, *A Novelist's Allegory; Castles in Spain*

Hawthorne, Nathaniel, *Drowne's Wooden Image; The Artist of the Beautiful*

Joyce, James, *A Portrait of the Artist as a Young Man*

Mann, Thomas, *Stories of Three Decades* ("Tonio Krueger," "Death in Venice," "Child Prodigy")

Morgan, Charles, *Sparkenbroke*

Rolland, Romain, *Jean Christophe*

Woolf, Virginia, *Orlando*

## THE WORLD OF SCIENCE

1. What are the principles underlying the struggle for existence as outlined by Darwin? Discuss the following topics: causes of struggle; causes which check the tendency of the species to increase; the relation of structure to competition; the relation of environment to the struggle.

2. In what does the superiority of man to other animals lie, according to

Bradley? What is the relationship between this superiority and the struggle for physical survival? What physical attributes has man lost in the process of evolution from lower planes of life? If man is to fail as a beast, what evidence does Bradley find in history that he may yet triumph as a god? What does he see as the great problem of the future? What is his suggested method for approaching it? *Suggestions for writing:* "Only fools and charlatans have panaceas for the varied distempers of humanity"; Man the grub of a butterfly.

3. What criticism of nineteenth-century culture does Ruskin introduce as preliminary to his attack on science? What is the relation of the introduction to the main argument? How do the contradictions he sees compare with those noted by Bradley in *Is Man an Absurdity*? See if you can extend to the practical modern world his criticism that we have violated the three material things, air, water, earth. What movements today attempt to control man's use of these things? Report on one of these topics: soil erosion and measures to preserve and restore the soil; control of smoke in cities; control of water supplies; flood control; new irrigation projects; forestry and the water supply. Study Ruskin's definition of the three immaterial, useful things to determine whether they are sufficiently inclusive. Do you agree with Ruskin that we have destroyed these values? *Suggestions for writing:* A modern exhibit as an evidence of public taste; Ruskin as a botanist; What would Ruskin say of us today?; A defense of the machine; Iron servants vs. human servants; The modern workman and the machine; Report on Ruskin's Guild of St. George, the experiment he proposes at the end of this letter to workmen in 1871. Discuss the practicability of his plan in the world of today.

4. Trace the steps in the probable evolution of the physical world as Mr. Eddington describes it. What accident in the solar system seems to be responsible for our earth? Explain what Eddington means by the terms Mechanists and Vitalists in relation to the story of evolution. Analyze the effect upon you of this suggestive picture of vast evolutionary processes. Does it induce an attitude of wonder, scepticism, a sense of man's importance, his insignificance?

5. We shall encounter many criticisms of the machine in its effects on man. What does *The Man with a Tractor* suggest as to the potentiality of the machine for increasing the joys of living? What does the essay suggest as to the changing position of man in relation to nature?

6. Explain Harding's analysis of the contradiction between our evaluation of science today and the place given to the scientist by an obsolete economic system. What further illustrations of this contradiction can you find for an oral or written report? *Suggestions for writing:* We educate people to do, not to be; To work for the joy of working; The gods of things as they are; Science offers new frontiers; The public loses.

7. Why does Mr. Hooton call his first apology *defensive*, the other *penitential*? Summarize the physical adaptations that man has made in his evolu-

tion from his early ancestors. Explain: "Some doubting Thomases among our ape critics may regard as futile man's attempt to correlate with superior intelligence that vast malignancy which surmounts his spinal cord." Show how the three divisions under *Apology for Man's Behavior* illustrate the above comment. What illustrations can you bring to bear on the statement: "Language erects more barriers than bridges"? What defense can you offer against Mr. Hooton's charge that man's lack of judgment in controlling natural resources would disgust critics of higher intelligence? How would you answer his implied criticism of our regard for the weak, sickly, and constitutionally unfit in our society? Do you think Mr. Hooton takes sufficiently into account the role of education in a democracy? Write an answer to his Apology in which you present the case for man from any point of view which interests you. *Suggestions for writing:* Man as a talking animal; Do we dislike those who speak another language?; Man's use of natural resources as a means of destruction; Have we learned to control water power?; The denudation of our forests; Causes of soil erosion; Man is an economic fool; Children as economic parasites; Should medical skill be devoted to preservation of the "unfit"?; Who determines the "unfit"?; The old-age problem today. The concluding questions in the essay may well present interesting problems for long research papers.

8. In what sense has chemistry "wrecked" the farm? The authors of the essay believe that the farmer can no longer be "an independent entrepreneur." What role may the farmer of the future play? Do you think that his best solution lies in his becoming "an adjunct to industry and dependent on its swift changes and its highly competitive markets," or in unionization of farmers, or in some kind of collective farming? What do we mean by synthetic products? Do most buyers still think synthetic products inferior to the natural product? *Suggestions for writing:* Growing food in test tubes; How the A.A.A. helped the farmers in my community; "Triple-A Plowed Under"; Future Farmers of America; My idea of a model farm; My experiences in a 4-H Club.

9. Show how the achievements of science make possible the sort of mass hypnotism that Calverton describes. Refer to several texts on psychology to test the validity of Calverton's presentation of the power of suggestion. Read about the Orson Welles radio presentation of *An Attack from Mars* and consider the results as illustrative of Calverton's thesis. *Suggestions for writing:* Hitler, Mussolini, and mass hypnotism; The Munich pact, a result of mass hypnotism; Medicine and the use of hypnotic suggestion; Should the radio be censored?; Methods of propaganda and the press; A study of *It Can't Happen Here* for illustrations of Calverton's thesis; What the power of suggestion did to me; How President Roosevelt uses the power of suggestion; Billboard hypnotism.

10. Summarize the difficulties which confronted the Curies as they undertook their great experiment. Write character analyses of these two scientists,

attempting to distinguish their individual qualities. Comment on the inter-
weaving of narrative and descriptive detail throughout this account. What
does each contribute? Show how the whole achieves a unity of impression
that approaches the short story.

11. How does Dr. Gottlieb in *Arrowsmith* lend support to the argument
of Mr. Harding regarding the scientist in commercial research?

12. In *No More of the Moon* a modern poet renounces an age-old subject
of poetry. Why? It would be interesting to make a collection of poems
about the moon to discover what poets have formerly felt and expressed on
this subject. Does the scientific approach to nature necessarily destroy the
possibility of an aesthetic or emotional approach?

13. Compare the idea in Sandburg's *Prayers of Steel* with the conclusion of
*John Brown's Body*. How does Sandburg, in his symbolism, also suggest
hope for a united world?

14. Study *The Express* and *The Landscape near an Aerodrome* in relation
to Engle's study, *Poetry in a Machine Age*. Comment on the effectiveness of
the imagery and its symbolism in a short paper.

15. Compare the lines from Tennyson which show the influence of the
theory of evolution with those of Aldous Huxley. What significance do you
find in the fact that Huxley is the grandson of T. H. Huxley, Darwin's
"bulldog"?

## Suggestions for Further Reading

ESSAYS, CRITICISM, AND BIOGRAPHY

Adler, Mortimer, *What Man Has Made of Men*

Beers, Clifford, *A Mind That Found Itself*

Boas, George, "In Defense of Machines," *Harper's*, June, 1932

Bridgman, Percy Williams, "The New Vision of Science," *Harper's*, Mar., 1929

Carrel, Alexis, *Man the Unknown*

Compton, A. H., "Can Science Point the Way?" *Forum*, May, 1937

Curie, Eve, *The Life of Madame Curie*

De Kruif, Paul, *Hunger Fighters; Microbe Hunters; Why Keep Them Alive?*

Eddington, A. S., *The Nature of the Physical World*

Einstein, Albert, and Infeld, L., *The Evolution of Physics*

Haldane, J. B. S., *Possible Worlds*

Hogben, Lancelot, *Mathematics for the Millions; Science for the Citizen*

Hooton, E. A., "An Anthropologist Looks at Medicine," *Science*, Mar. 20, 1936

Huxley, Thomas Henry, *The Method of Scientific Investigation*

Jeans, Sir James, *The Mysterious Universe*

Menninger, Karl, *The Human Mind; Man Against Himself*

Millikan, Robert A., *Science and Life*

Seabrook, William, *Asylum*

Slosson, E. E., *Creative Chemistry*

Sullivan, J. W. N., *Science*

Ward, Henshaw, "Science Has Not Gone Mystical," *Atlantic Monthly*, Aug., 1933

Whitehead, Alfred N., *Science and the Modern World*

## THE APPEAL OF RELIGION

1. How valid a criticism of the church today is presented in Miss Newton's
essay? To what extent does she speak for all of youth, and to what extent
for only a limited group? Discuss her criticism of the attitude of the church

toward the realities of the modern world. What has she overlooked in her consideration of the duties of the church? Do you think that the church should assume the various responsibilities which she suggested? *Suggestions for writing:* What the church means to me: My criticism of the church; Why I go (or do not go) to church; The church as a social center; The church should (or should not) take a stand on social problems; An answer to Miss Newton; The church challenges youth (See *Scribner's* for September, 1936); A religious cult; Mr. Chesterton answers Miss Newton.

2. In the light of your reading of Darwin, evaluate Chesterton's criticism of the popular social application of Darwinism. In what way does reliance on science fail to take the place of religion in our world? What does Chesterton see as the individual and social effects of scepticism? Can you find specific evidences of the return to religion heralded by Chesterton?

3. What criticisms of the church does Addison imply in his sketch of Sir Roger? Comment on the effectiveness of his method. It might be interesting to attempt a comparison of Sir Roger and Clarence Day's father. If you know anyone who holds a prominent position in your church or community, present him in a specific situation, in such a way as to reveal his character and at the same time to suggest your own point of view. *Suggestions for writing:* God and my father (or mother); Pillars of respectability; Arguing with God.

4. What does Russell suggest as the first step in finding a solution to the problem of adjustment to the world in which we live? How adequate to the problem which he presents does his solution seem to you? Discuss his tragic view of life in relation to Krutch's definition of tragedy. What contemporary events attest to the truth of this statement: "The worship of Force, to which Carlyle and Nietzsche and the creed of Militarism have accustomed us, is the result of failure to maintain our own ideals against a hostile universe; it is itself a prostrate submission to evil, a sacrifice of our best to Moloch"? Trace Newman's argument for the superiority of faith to science and logic. How does he suggest that the study of nature may lead one to religious faith?

5. Relate Russell's conviction that the past has mystical power to that of Proust in the tea-drinking episode. To what extent is *A Free Man's Worship* a renunciation of life; to what extent is it an affirmation?

6. Analyze the various attitudes toward religion represented by the Canon, Brigid, O'Flingsley, and the two curates in *Shadow and Substance*. In what two characters does the external conflict of the play center? What is the nature of the conflict within these characters? What is the role of Brigid in relation to the conflict, internal and external? Discuss the means by which the author makes her a somewhat convincing character in the modern world. Do you feel that he intends us to accept her visions as reality, symbol, or mental hallucination? Are the visions of Brigid as important to the theme and the action of the play as her purely human qualities? What is your conclusion as to the values the author of the play considers most important in religion, in life? What is the significance of the title *Shadow and Sub-*

*stance* in relation to the theme and characters? Do you consider the play a tragedy? How should you conclude it?

7. List illustrations of the qualities of God expressed in the image of animals in the two poems of Blake. Why should Blake's definition of the qualities of God seem revolutionary in his day and yet be generally acceptable today?

8. What is the poet of *The Hound of Heaven* searching for, and where does he look in vain? What view of nature do you find in this poem? Study the imagery and comment on its symbolism. How does the movement of the verse suggest pursuit?

9. Compare the religious doubts suggested in *The Collar, Hymn to God the Father,* and the sonnet of G. M. Hopkins. Compare the religious attitude of these poets with that of Thompson in *The Hound of Heaven.*

10. Comment on *The Preacher* as an exposition of the idea that God is a God of love rather than a God of wrath. Write a characterization of a preacher whom you know.

11. Compare the Brontë and Whitman selections as they suggest the role the individual must play in achieving an affirmative view of life.

12. Relate the theme of *It Is a Beauteous Evening* to other poems in which Wordsworth suggests the divinity of childhood.

13. Relate the philosophy of *God-Forgotten* to Hardy's *Satires of Circumstance* and to any novel of his that you have read.

14. Evaluate in your own mind the theistic, mystic, and agnostic approaches to religion which you have encountered in this section. Write a critical paper defending the point of view most convincing to you. Consult the bibliography for suggestive material. Write an autobiographical essay tracing the development of your religious convictions.

## Suggestions for Further Reading

ESSAYS AND CRITICAL MATERIAL

Adams, Henry, *The Education of Henry Adams*
Arnold, Matthew, *Hebraism and Hellenism*
Durant, Will, *Transition*
Ellis, Havelock, *The Dance of Life* (Chapter on religion)
Edman, Irwin, *The Contemporary and His Soul; Richard Kane Looks at Life*
Emerson, Ralph Waldo, *Essays* ("The Over-Soul")
Fosdick, Harry Emerson, *Adventurous Religion; As I See Religion*
Holmes, John Haynes, *Rethinking Religion*
Huxley, Aldous, *Ends and Means*
James, William, *Varieties of Religious Experience*
Kagawa, Toyohiko, *Meditations*

Kempis, Thomas à, *Imitation of Christ*
Link, Henry C., *The Return to Religion*
Maritain, Jacques, *True Humanism*
Pater, Walter, *Marius the Epicurean*
Powys, John Cowper, *The Meaning of Culture*
Santayana, George, *Interpretations of Poetry and Religion*
Scudder, Vida, *The Life of the Spirit in the Modern English Poets*
Van Doren, Carl, *Why I am an Unbeliever*
Wilson, S. L., *The Theology of Modern Literature*

BIOGRAPHY AND AUTOBIOGRAPHY

Caine, Hall, *Life of Christ*
Leonard, William Ellery, *The Poet of Galilee*

Papini, G., *The Life of Christ*
Renan, Ernest, *The Life of Jesus*
St. Augustine, *Confessions*
Twain, Mark, *Joan of Arc*
Wesley, John, *Journals*
Woolman, John, *Journal and Essays*

FICTION

Asch, Sholem, *Salvation*
Böjer, Johann, *The Great Hunger; The New Temple*
Butler, Samuel, *The Way of All Flesh*
Dostoevski, Feodor, *The Brothers Karamazov*
Eliot, George, *Adam Bede; Romola*
France, Anatole, *The Procurator of Judea*
Hauptmann, Gerhardt, *The Fool in Christ*
Huxley, Aldous, *Eyeless in Gaza*
Lagerlöf, Selma, *Jerusalem; The Holy City; Christ Legends*
Lewis, Sinclair, *Elmer Gantry*
Rølvaag, Ole, *Their Father's God*
Tolstoi, Leo, *Resurrection*
Undset, Sigrid, *The Burning Bush*

Voltaire, *Candide*
White, Helen C., *Not Built With Hands; A Watch in the Night*
Wilder, Thornton, *Heaven's My Destination*

DRAMA

Anonymous, *Everyman*
Connelly, Marc, *The Green Pastures*
Ferris, Walter, *Death Takes a Holiday*
Galsworthy, John, *Escape*
Goethe, Johann Wolfgang von, *Faust*
Ibsen, Henrik, *The Lady from the Sea*
Kennedy, Charles R., *The Servant in the House*
Maeterlinck, Maurice, *Sister Beatrice*
Marlowe, Christopher, *The Tragical History of Doctor Faustus*
Moody, William Vaughn, *The Masque of Judgment*
O'Neill, Eugene, *Days Without End*
Shaw, George Bernard, *Saint Joan*
Wilder, Thornton, *Our Town*
Yeats, William Butler, *The Hour Glass*

## THE GOOD LIFE

1. What concrete illustrations does Barbellion offer in support of his thesis that "no fact, no piece of information about this world, is greater or less than another, but that all are equal as the angels"? To what extent does this conviction lead him to the well-balanced life, to what extent to a life of excesses? Discuss the relative components of romanticism and realism, of selfishness and altruism, in his view of life. *Suggestions for writing:* While I slept; A tiny joy; Human freightage; Looping the loop; Living on the heights; Wherever I hitch my wagon; Beauty in the ugly; Hiding away from life; And so to bed; A slice of life; Sanctuaries; Bravura; Strange antitheses; Devoted slave; Things I ought to scowl upon.

2. Sum up Stevenson's arguments which give support to the thesis that "extreme *busyness*, whether at school or college, kirk or market, is a symptom of deficient vitality, and a faculty for idleness implies a catholic appetite and a strong sense of personal identity." *Suggestions for writing:* A defense of busyness; We grow weary when idle; Peering into a mirror; Little time for thoughts; Hours of truantry; Lack-luster periods; Odds and ends; Arid knowledge; The art of living; By-roads; Success in life; Luke-warm; Vanities; A recluse I know.

3. Interpret the character and view of life of Thoreau by considering the following key statements in relation to their context: "A man is rich in proportion to the number of things which he can afford to let alone"; "I never

got my fingers burned by actual possession"; "I would say to my fellows, once for all, as long as possible live free and uncommitted"; "Olympus is but the outside of the earth everywhere"; "Little is to be expected of that day, if it can be called a day, to which we are not awakened by our Genius . . ."; "To him whose elastic and vigorous thought keeps pace with the sun, the day is a perpetual morning"; "Every man is tasked to make his life, even in its details, worthy of the contemplation of his most elevated and critical hour"; "We think that that *is* which *appears* to be"; "Be it life or death, we crave only reality"; "My head is hands and feet. I feel all my best faculties concentrated in it." *Suggestions for writing:* At any price; Words and deeds; I take the world on my shoulders; Shams and delusions; Reading the newspaper; Letter writing; Greedy after gossip.

4. On what scientific basis does Arnold ground his requirements for culture? What have culture and religion in common? Where do they differ? What does Arnold include under the term *machinery*? Study each factor to determine in what way it is only machinery. How are the men of culture truly "apostles of equality"? What does Mr. Adams find applicable to the problems of our day in Arnold's definition of culture? Consider his illustrations of the even greater need of the twentieth century to distinguish between the machinery of life and life itself. Are his criticisms of our age valid ones?

5. Justify or challenge the point of view which Mr. Thurber takes concerning *Wake Up and Live*. Analyze the sources and method of his humor. What is the difference between fashioning one's life in accordance with precepts such as Mrs. Brande's and the quest for "the good life"? *Suggestions for writing:* Wake up and live; The pink of mental condition; In a dilemma; Let yourself go; Saying yes (or no).

6. Mr. Mumford says that a living philosophy is "more than the sum of one's beliefs, judgments, standards, axioms, put together in an orderly system; it is rather a resolution of one's abstract plan of living with the circumstances and emergencies of actual existence." To what extent does his philosophy approximate this definition? Compare his conclusions with those of Bertrand Russell. What are the essential distinctions between his way of life and that of Stevenson and Barbellion?

7. What qualities of Lincoln noted by Sandburg might illustrate Wordsworth's *The Happy Warrior*? What physical characteristics which Sandburg introduces are especially significant in suggesting character? Find illustrations of the effective use of contrast in descriptive detail and traits of character. Would Arnold accept Lincoln as a man truly representative of culture?

8. John Reed's *Almost Thirty* treats of his quest for certainty rather than of any achievement of it. What circumstances in his background and training contributed to his restlessness and uncertainty? What values does he affirm? *Suggestions for writing:* Testing things; Looking back; Drifting; Feeding on

fantasy; The orgy of books; Apartment hotel; In our attic; How to meet people; Full of meaning.

9. See what you can discover about the life of Daniel Webster which would lend support to Mr. Benét's characterization of him. Do you find any evidence of the truth of the devil's prophecy? Comment on the suitability of the informal narrative style to the elements of folklore and superstition, to the story, and to its homely realism in portrayal of the Yankee character and the New England setting. What comparisons might be made between the philosophy of life expressed by Daniel Webster in his speech and some of the ideas in Barbellions' *Enjoying Life*; in Russell's *A Free Man's Worship*? What elements of social criticism do you find in addition to the personal philosophy? *Suggestions for writing:* An explanation of the change in Daniel Webster; Daniel Webster's idea of the good life; "The things that make a country a country"; A personal interview with the devil.

10. What view of the "good life" does *The Bet* exemplify? What other views does it challenge? Do you find the lawyer's conclusions as to true and false values in life convincing? Explain your position in a brief paper. Comment on the effectiveness of the narrative method here, noting the shifts in time, the use of sensuous descriptive detail, means of concentration, use of conversation, handling of climax, and irony. *Suggestions for writing:* Write a conclusion to the story as you would have it, or follow the life of the lawyer after this experience. Imagine a conversation in which the banker tells his story the next morning.

11. What two ideals of the best way of life are contrasted in Stuart's *His Autumn-Colored Face*? Compare the picture of Ulysses and his son in Tennyson's poem.

12. Although Elinor Wylie calls her poem a *Nonsense Rhyme*, what rather serious contrasting views of life does the mocking title veil? *Suggestions for writing:* The middle mind; The smooth ambiguous smile; The enthusiast; All or nothing.

13. Why does Yeats not covet great beauty for his daughter? Summarize and evaluate the good things he wishes for her. What is his view of the "opinionated" woman? Compare the woman he admires with the man in Wordsworth's *Happy Warrior*. An interesting report might be given comparing another poet's wishes for his son in *Frost at Midnight* by Coleridge. *Suggestions for writing:* The calamity of beauty; The power of a "glad kindness"; The art of quarreling in merriment; A wish for my son (or daughter).

14. What is the anomaly in the character of Flammonde and what clue to its solution can you suggest? *Suggestions for writing:* I have known Flammonde; A contrast between *Richard Cory* (also by Robinson) and *Flammonde;* Broken links of destiny; A flash of unforeseen remembrance; We look beyond horizons.

15. Which of the attitudes toward life do you find more acceptable, that

of Housman or that of Masefield? Write a character sketch in which you present a possible speaker for either philosophy or a conversation between the two.

16. The rewards, responsibilities, and limitations of the intellectual life form the dominant theme of Dyer, Taggard, and Pope. Analyze these specific elements as represented in the three poems; comment on what the poems have in common and how they differ. To what extent do these authors consider that the life of the mind must also be a life of action? Compare the thought in the passage from Pope with the famous speech of Hamlet beginning "What a piece of work is man."

17. Study the balance between the life of thought and the life of action in *Ulysses* and *The Happy Warrior*. To what extent might the story of Ulysses, the adventurer, be considered a fable of the aspiring mind eager for new experience? What is the effect of the background of the sea in this poem? How does the introduction of Telemachus accentuate the main theme? Contrast the philosophy of Ulysses in this poem with that of his men as presented in *The Lotos-Eaters*. Read in Homer's *Odyssey* to see if you can find support for this characterization of Ulysses (Odysseus) and write an essay on your discoveries.

18. In what way might *Rabbi Ben Ezra* be considered an answer to the philosophy of Herrick's *To the Virgins*? Why is youth considered best in Herrick's poem, age in Browning's? Can you find in Browning's poem praise of the complete life, embodying physical, intellectual, and spiritual values? Trace each theme through the successive stanzas. *Suggestions for writing:* My mind a kingdom; Glory, jest and riddle; Proper study of mankind; Rising by open means; Where ignorant armies clash; The eternal note of sadness; Youth against age; Envy of the great is the key to the debunking biography; The best is yet to be; I prize the doubt; Success in failure.

19. How are the claims of the life of action and intellect united in *Speech to the Detractors*? How are the claims of the common man and the hero reconciled?

20. That the renunciation of personal desires and ambitions for public duty represents for Milton an aspect of the "good life" is suggested in his two sonnets. Relate the theme to the facts of his life in a brief investigative paper.

21. Study the symbolism of the sea as representative of modern life in *Dover Beach*. What is the quest of the speaker here, and what is his answer? Comment on MacLeish's poem as an answer to Arnold's. Which do you consider the more affirmative and hopeful assertion of life's values?

22. Compare the theme of *Ulysses* with *Song of the Open Road*. What does Whitman add that is not evident in Tennyson? In your own words summarize the joys of the full life praised by Whitman. Does he omit anything you consider important? Read Emerson's *Self-Reliance* for possible influences of his thought on Whitman. Write a paper on your discoveries. Compare this poem with Whitman's *Pioneers! O Pioneers!*

## Suggestions for Further Reading

### ESSAYS AND CRITICISM

Aurelius, Marcus, *Meditations*

Brooks, Van Wyck, "High Brow" and "Low Brow" (*America's Coming of Age*)

Durant, Will, *The Story of Philosophy; Transition*

Einstein, Albert, and others, *Living Philosophies*

Ellis, Havelock, *The Dance of Life*

Fadiman, Clifton (ed.), *I Believe*

Huxley, Aldous, *Proper Studies*

Krutch, Joseph W., *The Modern Temper*

Plato, *The Apology of Socrates*

Powys, John Cowper, *The Philosophy of Solitude*

Russell, Bertrand, *Education and the Good Life*

Steele, Richard, "A Fine Gentleman" (*The Guardian*, Apr. 20, 1713)

### FICTION AND DRAMA

Addison, Joseph, *The Vision of Mirza*

Allen, Hervey, *Anthony Adverse*

Cabell, James Branch, *Jurgen*

Cather, Willa, *Death Comes for the Archbishop*

Dostoevski, Feodor, *Crime and Punishment*

Fisher, Dorothy Canfield, *The Brimming Cup*

Galsworthy, John, *Quality*

Goethe, Johann Wolfgang von, *Faust*

Howells, William Dean, *The Rise of Silas Lapham*

Ibsen, Henrik, *Peer Gynt*

James, Henry, *The American; A Portrait of a Lady*

Johnson, Samuel, *Rasselas; The Voyage of Life*

Joyce, James, *Ulysses*

Mann, Thomas, *The Magic Mountain*

Maugham, Somerset, *Of Human Bondage*

Pater, Walter, *Marius the Epicurean*

Proust, Marcel, *The Remembrance of Things Past*

Rolland, Romain, *Jean Christophe*

Santayana, George, *The Last Puritan*

Sinclair, May, *Mary Olivier*

Swift, Jonathan, "The Voyage to the Houyhnhnms" (*Gulliver's Travels*)

Walpole, Hugh, *Fortitude; The Dark Forest*

Wassermann, Jacob, *The World's Illusion*

Wharton, Edith, *The Age of Innocence*

## THE ROLE OF EDUCATION

1. To what extent do the editors of *Fortune* lend support to the Emersonian figure likening the undergraduate to "four snakes gliding up and down a hollow for no purpose that I could see—not to eat, not for love, but only gliding . . ."? To what extent do their conclusions seem contradictory to those of Emerson? Read a college novel of the post-war period and one of your own era and write a comparative study. Bring evidence to bear on the truth or falsity of the more controversial generalizations regarding college youth of today. *Suggestions for writing:* Compulsory chapel; Scholastic eye-openers; On the varsity squad; Best sellers on the campus; Outguessing the professor; Campus snobbery; Human paving stones; Crusades for tomorrow; Campus smoothies; The cult of hobbies; As the world wags, so wags the undergraduate; Intellectual doldrums; Milquetoasts on the campus; The college daily; The rah-rah stage; The jazz age has passed; Heeling the paper; Mental vacuums; Only gliding; The personal equation.

2. "The teacher may imitate the drill sergeant or follow the example of Socrates." Discuss the implications of Mr. Beard's statement as it applies to education in Germany. Refer to Erica Mann's *School for Barbarians* and to

Hitler's *Mein Kampf* for further information regarding Nazi educational administration. The purge of professors led to the establishment of the "university in exile" in this country. Find out what you can of its contribution to democratic education. Analyze the relationship of Nazi education to the state. Investigate educational policies in England, France, Russia, or Sweden and evaluate them in a paper.

3. Consider Emerson's definition of the scholar as "man thinking" in relation to *Education under the Nazis*. Summarize Mr. Jones' conclusions with respect to the American universities' approximation to the Emersonian ideal. Read about one of the educational experiments being conducted in the United States: The program at Iowa recommended by Norman Foerster; The University of Chicago plan; Commonwealth College; Antioch College; Bennington College; Sarah Lawrence College. Write a critical paper analyzing its purposes and methods and evaluating them. Why have the social studies tended to supersede the humanities in so far as student interest is concerned? What constructive suggestions does Mr. Jones offer for restoring the humanities to their earlier position of prominence? *Suggestions for writing:* One hundred per cent Americans; A liberal education; First things first; Airy abstractions; The humanely educated man; In a vacuum; The student accepts on faith; "Give me insight into today, and you may have the antique and future worlds."

4. Analyze the individual and social objectives held for education by Cardinal Newman. Evaluate the criticism sometimes made of Newman's educated man that he would be too self-effacing to be capable of adjustment to the aggressive twentieth century. Do you think the qualities outlined by Newman would, or would not, be desirable today? Compare the ideas of Huxley and Cardinal Newman, attempting to discover where they agree and where they differ. What do you think would be Newman's criticism of Huxley's educated man? Huxley's, of Newman's educated man? Do you see any inconsistency in the development of Huxley's analogy when he describes the hidden player as always fair, just and patient? How do you reconcile this with his statement that "Nature's discipline is not even a word and a blow, and the blow first; but the blow without the word"? *Suggestions for writing:* Knowing the rules of the game; A lesson nature taught me; A university is not the place for a genius; On knowing when to trifle and when to be serious; The tactful person; Dale Carnegie and Cardinal Newman.

5. What view of the relation between liberty and education is held up by the leaders of St. John's College? Do you think it true of modern education that the "side shows are putting the main tent out of business"? In what sense is the liberal "experimental" plan of St. John's not really new? On what view of human life is this educational philosophy grounded? Do you think that it fails to take into consideration any important aspects of modern life? Draw up your arguments for or against such a plan. Do you agree with its sponsor that this program of education is best for the many in a democracy as well as

for the few? Explain your position. Can you justify this plan with regard to its attack on the system of electives? If you think of books not on this list which you believe invaluable as teachers, justify your selections. What do you think of the relative neglect of contemporary writers? Evaluate a recent book according to the five rules for a great book laid down at St. John's. Do these rules omit anything you consider important? *Suggestions for writing:* "Things have changed; men have not"; What education is best for the masses in a democracy?; The educator as nurse or physician; Selecting the educational pill that looks easiest to swallow; The failure of charm-school education; "The average professor is as stale as a stone"; How I should teach Shakespeare; A book that changed my mind; American classics I should list; "A great book raises questions about the great themes in human thought"; The failure of American liberalism; The end of education is to develop men who think for themselves. Look up President Hutchins' book, *No Friendly Voice,* and some of his magazine articles on education and prepare a report or paper on his educational theories. Look up the criticism of his views by John Dewey or Alfred North Whitehead.

6. What events in contemporary society lead the professor in the *Midwifery of Ideas* to say that we must re-examine our familiar dualities, virtue-toil, vice-idleness? What does he mean by a workable bourgeoise ideology? Relate the *Midwifery of Ideas* to the Emersonian ideal of education set forth in *The American Scholar Once More.* What direction does Mr. Bishop's irony take, and how is it pointed?

7. What is the educational significance of the reverie periods at Curtiss College? Discuss the relative values of a *College for One* by evolving your own concept of the purpose of an education. *Suggestions for writing:* Pleasant chit-chat; Day dreamers; A keen sense of the ridiculous; The ritual of modern pedagogy; Ultra-modern; Social contacts; The value of competition with one's fellows; Books as teachers.

8. What did Lincoln Steffens expect to find at college, and what did he find? Compare his conclusions with those of John Reed in the section, *The Good Life.* What support can you find in your own experience for his conclusions in regard to the absence of intellectual curiosity, on the one hand, and established knowledge on the other? Discuss the implications of Steffens' statement: "With all their knowledge they knew no essential truth." Write your critical reaction to the paragraph in Steffens, beginning "Nothing is done. Everything in the world remains to be done or done over." *Suggestions for writing:* Memorable or immemorable teachers; Examination questions for the professor to answer; Knowledge in compartments; The unknown is the province of the student; Overthrowing academic idols; On getting by; A battle of wits; Systems of mind-fixing.

9. Discuss the motivating force behind, and the nature of, Miss Strong's "compensation" in high school. How does the picture of Miss Strong's contemporaries in *The Tools for Life* differ from the conclusions of the editors

of *Fortune* in their picture of youth today? How does the author's experience as editor supplement her formal education? What is the significance of her experience on the Midway following her defense of her thesis? Discuss this paradox presented by Miss Strong: that the very elements of personal efficiency which education taught her were to her evidence of the failure of her education. *Suggestions for writing:* Tools for life; Beating the others; Too young to go to dances; I wasn't popular; Routes out of loneliness; Killing time; Giving the teacher what he wants; Making a little learning seem much; Rationalizing; Losing caste; Working one's way; I save my face; I was converted; Planning the school day; Private worlds; Protecting youth; Developing self-reliance.

10. What has the school of Mr. Gradgrind in common with that described by Wordsworth in *The Prelude?* What tendencies in modern education as you know it might be compared with the educational theories of Gradgrind? What are the chief differences? *Suggestions for writing:* Measuring parcels of human nature; On giving the expected answer; Education as the acquisition of facts; School teacher—factory model, 1940; "If he had only learnt a little less, how infinitely better he might have been taught much more"; On being a model child.

11. Summarize the differences in educational theory represented by Mr. Clegg and Mr. Minnow. How real is this conflict in the world of today? If you have known either a Mr. Clegg or a Mr. Minnow write a sketch presenting him as vividly as you can. Imagine the scene between Mr. Clegg and Mr. Minnow the next morning and present it through dialogue.

12. How does the introductory presentation of Knute Axelbrod prepare you for the action of the story? By what concrete means are you made aware of the contrast between Axelbrod's dream of college life and the reality he finds? How valid are Lewis's sketches of various types of students? How does he suggest that the people at Yale do not differ essentially from the natives of Joralemon? What have both groups in common in their attitude toward one who does not conform to their accepted standards? Explain why the conclusion of the story does or does not present a logical resolution of Knute's inner conflict. *Suggestions for writing:* A nonconformist in my town (or college); The student who earns his way; The campus dilettante; The person I might have been; Escaping for a night.

13. What criticism of the teaching of English does Robert Hillyer make? What suggestions for an approach to literature? What is his attitude toward the student? Do you think that Hillyer and Yeats are agreed in their attitude toward scholars and teachers? What is the common basis for the criticism of education in each poem? *Suggestions for writing:* Literature as archeology; "Learning and life are too far wrenched apart"; "What is the use of knowing the evil in the world?"; On thinking what other people think; The price of truth.

14. Miss Taggard quotes Engels in the last lines of her poem. What are

the implications for society in general, and for education in particular, of such a view of human nature? Defend or challenge the theory that human nature can be changed.

15. What is the quest of Arnold's scholar who flees from college halls? What criticism of modern life do you find in this poem? Do you think it is as valid today as when Arnold wrote the poem in the late nineteenth century? *Suggestions for writing:* An imaginary conversation between the scholar and the gypsies; A defense of the scholar gypsy; The scholar gypsy as an escapist.

16. Why is Browning's grammarian to be buried on the mountain top? How does the poet make the scholar's task heroic? What was the quest of the Renaissance scholar, and what does the world owe him? What view of the whole of human life is here presented? What is the relation of knowledge to this philosophy? Do you know any people today who pursue knowledge with this "sacred thirst"? Write a character sketch of such a person. To what problems would he be most likely to devote his powers?

17. In the selection from *The Prelude* Wordsworth contrasts the products of two different methods of education, that of the formal system and that of nature. Do you find any similarity between his Boy of Winander and Arnold's Scholar Gypsy? How is criticism of the formal system of education suggestive of tendencies today? What does he suggest as to the value of myths and fairy tales? What is nature's method of forming the child's mind? *Suggestions for writing:* A modern progressive school I know; Does the modern elementary school produce child prigs?; The influence of fairy stories on my childhood; Wishing caps and invisible coats.

18. What tendencies among "progressive" schools is Miss McGinley satirizing in her poem? *Suggestions for writing:* Problem children and problem parents; I develop *me;* Complexes I have (or don't have); A square peg in a round hole; Anti-social attitudes.

19. What would be Seth Compton's attitude toward censorship of a book such as *Grapes of Wrath*? Present an argument supporting or refuting his point of view. In what way might Seth Compton be said to carry on the philosophy of Gibbon and Milton as represented in Hardy's *Lausanne*?

## Suggestions for Further Reading

Essays and Criticism

Emerson, Ralph Waldo, *The American Scholar*

Flexner, Abraham, *Universities: American, English, German*

Foerster, Norman, *The Function of the State University*

Hutchins, Robert Maynard, *The Higher Learning in America*

Mann, Erika, *School for Barbarians*

Martin, Everett Dean, *The Meaning of a Liberal Education*

Meiklejohn, Alexander, *The Experimental College*

Newman, John Henry, *The Idea of a University*

Schopenhauer, Arthur, *On Thinking for Oneself*

## IDEAS OF LIBERTY AND DEMOCRACY

1. What proofs does Miss Kirchwey offer that democracy needs to be fought for? What further evidence can you bring to bear from your own reading or experience? Investigate and report on the work of one of the following organizations to determine the nature of their efforts to preserve democracy: The Hollywood Anti-Nazi League; The American League for Peace and Democracy; The American Student Union; The Civil Liberties Union; The American Youth Congress, and any similar groups active in your community.

2. In what situation does Mr. Lippmann find the real reasons for the suppression of individual liberty in the dictator countries? How does he define private property, and what limits would he place upon it? How does he propose to effect a balance between the plutocratic and the proletarian groups in society? What are some of the specific measures by which he would meet the problem of a country which no longer has a frontier for expansion? Summarize his arguments for extension of a system of public works. What does he mean by "free collectivism," and how does it differ from "laissez-faire"? Evaluate his arguments for faith in a society grounded upon the independence of a large middle class? What factors do you think Mr. Lippmann neglects in his analysis? Write a defense or refutation of his point of view.

3. What are the components of the modern democratic idea as Mr. Freeman surveys it? Trace its evolution. Make a special study of the relation of Wordsworth to the French Revolution, his early sympathy and his later disillusion. On what foundation does Freeman believe any real democracy must be built? What new factors does Mr. Freeman see as making possible the existence of a genuine democracy?

4. Since the idea of democracy is under fire at the present time, it is interesting to review Carlyle's criticism of it in 1850. Why does he distrust democracy and prefer a strong central power? What is to be the basis of choice of a ruler? If Carlyle were living today, do you think he would be a defender of fascism? What qualities has his ruler that are not to be found in fascist dictators of the present? Compare as symbols Carlyle's "old crazy dwelling"; Blind leaders of the blind; Kings and Sham-Kings; Roast goose with

apple sauce for the working man (cf. "a chicken in every pot"); Anarchy plus a street constable; The privilege of governing vs. the privilege of being governed. Can democracy find the best men as leaders?

5. Explain why the workman under both the Greek and the Assyrian systems was a slave. How was slavery abolished in the medieval Christian system? What is Ruskin's argument for the superiority of the imperfect over the perfect? How is this theory related to his evaluation of the individual? What is the relation of the machine to his doctrine of individualism? On the basis of your reading of history evaluate his praise of the freedom of the medieval worker. Comment on his statement: "Men may be beaten, chained, tormented, yoked like cattle, slaughtered like summer flies, and yet remain in one sense, in the best sense, free."

6. Trace the history of social legislation in the last thirty-five years, following the leads of *The Diary of a Worrier*. Write an investigative paper on one of the following topics to determine conditions preceding and following legislation: Child labor; Women in industry; Income taxes; Property taxes; Workman's compensation; Federal Reserve Act; Federal Trade Commission; The Clayton Act; Old age pensions; The work of Justice Brandeis in the Supreme Court; The Woman Suffrage Amendment; Public Works projects; The A.F. of L. and C.I.O.; Unemployment insurance.

7. Analyze the forces in his personal life which led Mr. Laski to his acceptance of the Marxian philosophy. Report on the fundamentals of Marxism. A careful study of the *Communist Manifesto* written by Marx and Engels is suggested as the basis of your report. Report on the Boston Police Strike to which Mr. Laski refers. What do you think of the stand taken by President Lowell? By Mr. Laski? Can you think of any recent parallels? In the light of your interpretation of the idea of liberty, explain what Mr. Laski means when he says, "I came back from America convinced that liberty has no meaning save in the context of equality, and that equality also has no meaning unless the instruments of production are socially owned." Why did he come to the conclusion that he could not hope for real social justice through the "slow permeation of economic relationships by the democratic principle"? How does he explain the relation between capitalism and war? What specific suggestions does he make for the future if we are to avoid the dangers of fascism? *Suggestions for writing:* The relation of the university to its social environment; Shaw and the Fabian society; Sidney and Beatrice Webb; Oxford and the radical movement today; Eugene Debs; My social philosophy, and how it developed; The recent history of the British Labor Party; Why the League of Nations failed.

8. Why does the Liberal in Mr. Becker's debate refuse to accept Russia as proof of the validity of the Marxian doctrine? What arguments does he present for his refusal to accept the evidence of the past as basis for prophecies of the future? In what direction does the Communist look for human development to take place after the establishment of a classless society? Evaluate his

reasoning. How does the Communist explain the Marxian statement: "By acting on the external world man changes his own nature"? Can you bring any evidence to bear on this point from recent educational and sociological studies on the relation between the individual and his environment? How valid is the theory that "as men acquire knowledge of the influences that determine their acts, this knowledge becomes a new influence that enables them to act differently"? Evaluate this idea in relation to the aims of education. What is the dilemma of the Marxian philosophy which the Liberal points out? Why does he refuse to join the Communists even though he shares their dream of justice for the masses? How does he believe that the economic system of capitalism may be preserved and yet adapted to the needs of a changing world? Which argument seems to you the most convincingly carried out? Write a paper evaluating the conclusions of either Liberal or Communist. An interesting study of the liberal is made in Spender's *The Trial of a Judge*. See if you can find any similarities between the Judge and the Liberal of this essay. *Suggestions for writing:* The classless society in poetry; We do not profit by experience; Must we choose?; "A plague on both your houses"; A professor is "a man who thinks otherwise."

9. Relate the convictions expressed in the essay, *Wasteland*, to the title of Mr. Lerner's new book, *It Is Later Than You Think*. What justification does the author offer for calling liberalism a "never-never land"? What is meant by a "preoccupation not with life but with its symbols, its myths, its language"? What hope does the author hold out for man's triumph over hostile forces? Compare the implications of the definition of tragedy which he presents with those suggested by Russell, Mumford, and Maxwell Anderson. *Suggestions for writing:* The problem of values; The tired liberal; Accent of the martyr; The plague of doubt; Scoffers; Strange and false gods; Psychological barriers; The bursting point; Short-lived beliefs; Men of good will; Opportunists; The middle way; Grace under pressure; Unsuspected heroism; Sublimating the brute in us; Habit patterns; Uprooted.

10. Discuss Milton's famous judgment, "I cannot praise a fugitive and cloistered virtue, unexercised and unbreathed, that never sallies out and sees her adversary, but slinks out of the race, where that immortal garland is to be run for, not without dust and heat" with relation to recent instances of censorship at home and abroad. Write a critical paper defending or challenging Milton's point of view.

11. The problem of the citizen torn between two national loyalties, each representing different ideas of the relation of individual liberty to the interests of the state, is a common one today. Discuss the method of handling this problem in *If This Be Treason*. Note how the author keeps interest focused on the human being and yet gives us insight into differences in national ideals and their effects on the individual. Do you find any portions of the story which fail to contribute to the development of character or situation?

12. On what qualities of man do Wordsworth, Byron, and Shelley base

their faith in the eventual triumph of liberty? Supplement Byron's *Sonnet on Chillon* by reading *The Prisoner of Chillon*, which tells the story of Bonnivard.

13. Consider the two poems of Tennyson as representative expressions of the English idea of freedom. What meaning is implicit in both poems?

14. Discover Swinburne's definition of freedom. On the basis of your knowledge of Whitman can you state why this poem is addressed to him?

## Suggestions for Further Reading

ESSAYS AND CRITICISM

Adams, James Truslow, *The Epic of America*

Antin, Mary, *The Promised Land*

Ascoli, M., and Feiler, A., *Fascism for Whom?*

Beard, Charles and Mary, *The Rise of American Civilization*

Chase, Stuart, *Men and Machines; Rich Land, Poor Land*

Childs, Marquis, *This Is Democracy: Collective Bargaining in Scandinavia*

Counts, George S., *The Prospects of American Democracy*

Dodd, Martha, *Through Embassy Eyes*

Freeman, Joseph, *An American Testament*

Gedye, G. E. R., *Betrayal in Central Europe*

Holmes, O. W., *The Dissenting Opinions of Justice Holmes*

Lamont, Corliss, *You Might Like Socialism*

Lerner, Max, *It Is Later Than You Think*

Magil, A. B., and Stevens, Henry, *The Peril of Fascism*

Mann, Erika and Klaus, *Escape to Life*

Mann, Thomas, *The Coming Victory of Democracy*

Martin, Everett Dean, *Liberty*

Russell, Bertrand, *Power: A New Social Analysis*

Schuman, Frederick, *Europe on the Eve*

Seldes, Gilbert, *You Can't Print That! Lords of the Press*

Silone, Ignazio, *The School for Dictators*

Snow, Edgar, *Red Star Over China*

Strachey, John, *The Coming Struggle for Power; Hope in America*

Thomas, Norman, *As I See It*

Van Paassen, P., *Days of Our Years*

Waln, Nora, *Reaching for the Stars*

FICTION

Bottome, Phyllis, *Mortal Storm*

Canfield, Dorothy, *Seasoned Timber*

Lewis, Sinclair, *It Can't Happen Here*

Sinclair, Upton, *The Brass Check*

Taylor, K., *Address Unknown*

## THE STRUGGLE FOR JUSTICE

1. To build your background for understanding of the chapter from *The Grapes of Wrath* you might read an article by Avis Carlson, *Dust Blowing,* in *Harper's Magazine* for July, 1935. Other books contributing to an understanding of this problem are Erskine Caldwell's *You Have Seen Their Faces,* Carey McWilliams' *Factories in the Field,* and *The Collapse of Cotton Tenancy* by C. S. Johnson, R. Embree, and W. W. Alexander. What effects does Mr. Steinbeck achieve with his lyrical-narrative style? Compare the picture of the man on the tractor with that of Mr. Mayo in the section on The World of Science. What do you think the truer picture of the effect on man of the mechanization of his labor? To what extent are both pictures colored emotionally by the attitude of the author? What has Steinbeck's man on the tractor in common with the tenant he supplants? *Suggestions for*

*writing:* A tenant farmer I know; "Caught in something larger than themselves"; A study of the Missouri eviction of tenant farmers in 1939; What makes ownership?; The thrill of controlling a machine; If I were a farmer; Times are changed; Passing the buck.

2. By what means are you made aware of the intense sympathy which Swift feels for the poor Irish tenants? Should you characterize him as misanthrope or humanitarian? How does he make the reader feel that the present treatment of these people is in reality no less cruel than that which he ironically proposes? What is the effect on the reader of social satire such as Swift's?

3. Consider the poets mentioned by Hatcher in *The Second Lost Generation* whom you have read in this anthology. Determine how far they "have turned away from a preoccupation with their own personal Hamlets to make poetry of the bitter facts of living in a poverty-bludgeoned world." What elements of hope do you find in even the gloomiest writing which Hatcher analyzes? *Suggestions for writing:* Are we a lost generation?; A disrupted world; Damaged spirits; Saved from the wreckage; There is much that needs to be done; The ivory tower; Inheritors of a marshland. Read one of the novelists or dramatists mentioned in this essay and write a criticism determining how representative is his picture of the youth of today.

4. Analyze the conflict, the motivating forces, the characterization, style, and mood of *The Disinherited*. Consider the relationship of the youth with his father, as it bears on the outcome of the story.

5. *595 F.O.B.* represents aspects of modern industrial life: the speed up, the stretch out, the union, the labor spy. Interview a factory owner and a factory workman, and, if possible, visit a factory. Evaluate this story in the light of what you learn from your independent investigation. If you have worked in a factory, how far does your experience and observation coincide with Corey's picture? Read articles for and against unionization and write a critical paper presenting your own convictions on the matter.

6. H. G. Wells said of Miss Gellhorn's stories, "There is no propaganda in this book, not a passage of exhortation, no effort to sharpen or barb the point, and yet I do not think it will be easy to read it through and not feel a new strength of resolve, to learn, to work, for such a willful reorganization of human life as will make these stories at last seem like an incredible nightmare of misery in the history of mankind. Today, alas! they are all too credible." Discuss this story from three points of view: the element of propaganda, the effect on the reader, the credibility of this character and situation in the world as you know it. Discuss *Man on the Road* from the same points of view.

7. To what extent do the characters of Miriamne, Mio, the judge, and the Rabbi fulfill Krutch's definition of tragedy: the outward failure of the principal personage is compensated for by the dignity and greatness of his character. To what extent do social and economic forces motivate the tragedy?

In what sense are Mio and Miriamne "star-crossed lovers"? *Winterset* has been called "Shakespeare in shirt sleeves." Read *Romeo and Juliet* or *Hamlet* to determine the reason for this epithet. As a basis of comparison consider the theme, motivating forces, characterization, resolution of plot, and the blank verse. Prepare a bibliography which will include such source materials as the court proceedings for the Sacco-Vanzetti trial, newspaper accounts of it, and the letters of Sacco and Vanzetti. After reading a substantial number of documents, write a critical paper showing how Anderson has molded an unorganized "slice of life" into a complete and unified art form. Or you might prefer to examine the events of the trial to arrive at a decision of your own regarding the justice of the conclusion. How does Miss Vorse's portrait of Sacco compare with Mio's analysis of his father? You will find the Sacco-Vanzetti case treated also in Millay's *Justice Denied in Massachusetts*.

8. Show how Shakespeare sums up in a brief sonnet many of the social wrongs existent today. In what does he find solace and desire to live?

9. Blake's *The Little Black Boy*, and Wordsworth's *Toussaint L'Ouverture* both deal with the colored race. Analyze the particular quality of the race suggested in each poem. Which author do you find most hopeful of an eventual solution of the race problem, and what is the nature of his solution?

10. Intense pity for the poor marks the poems of Horace Gregory and Stephen Spender. What specific aspects of our contemporary social problems are suggested in each of these poems?

11. What social evils does Crabbe condemn? How many of these have been eradicated today? Read Goldsmith's *Deserted Village* or Masters' *Spoon River Anthology* as the basis for a comparative study with Crabbe. Consider the respective settings, descriptive words, characterizations, and social criticism.

12. Comment on Burns's poem as one that presents hope for the eventual triumph of justice and love.

13. *Suggestions for reports:*

    a. Compare *Through Streets Where Crooked Wicklow Flows* with Coleridge's *The Rime of the Ancient Mariner* in theme and mood, central figure, natural imagery, and conclusion.

    b. Burns as a critic of his own age.

    c. The negro and the arts.

    d. A report on Langston Hughes' *The Ways of White Folks*.

    e. Race prejudice as a theme in drama; for example, *Wingless Victory* by Maxwell Anderson; *All God's Chillun* by O'Neill; *In Abraham's Bosom* by Paul Green.

    f. Report on *John Brown's Body* by Stephen Vincent Benét.

    g. Silicosis victims in the United States.

## Suggestions for Further Reading

ESSAYS AND CRITICISM

Addams, Jane, *Twenty Years at Hull House*
Ehrman, H., *The Untried Case*
Linn, James Weber, *Jane Addams*
McWilliams, Carey, *Factories in the Field*
Reed, John, *Ten Days That Shook the World*
Riis, Jacob, *The Making of an American*
Wald, Lillian, *Windows on Henry Street*
Washington, Booker T., *Up from Slavery*
Veblen, Thorstein, *The Theory of the Leisure Class*

FICTION

Asch, Sholem, *Three Cities*
Bentley, Phyllis, *Inheritance*
Cantwell, Robert, *The Land of Plenty*
Caldwell, Erskine, *God's Little Acre*
Dickens, Charles, *Oliver Twist; Hard Times; David Copperfield*
Disraeli, Benjamin, *Sybil*
di Donato, Pietro, *Christ in Concrete*
Dos Passos, John, *U.S.A.*
Dreiser, Theodore, *An American Tragedy*
Fallada, Hans, *Little Man, What Now?*
Gorki, Maxim, *Bystander*
Hamsun, Knut, *The Growth of the Soil; Hunger*
Hardy, Thomas, *Tess of the D'Urbervilles; Jude the Obscure*

Huxley, Aldous, *Eyeless in Gaza*
Kingsley, Charles, *Alton Locke; Yeast*
Lumpkin, Grace, *To Make My Bread*
Malraux, André, *Man's Fate; Man's Hope*
Norris, Frank, *The Pit; The Octopus*
Silone, Ignazio, *Bread and Wine*
Sinclair, Upton, *The Jungle; Little Steel*
Slesinger, Tess, *The Unpossessed*
Steinbeck, John, *Of Mice and Men; In Dubious Battle; Tortilla Flat; The Grapes of Wrath*
Wright, R., *Uncle Tom's Children*

DRAMA

Anderson, Maxwell, *The Wingless Victory*
Caldwell, Erskine, *Tobacco Road*
Galsworthy, John, *Justice; Strife; The Silver Box; Loyalties*
Glaspell, Susan, *The Inheritors*
Green, Paul, *In Abraham's Bosom; Johnny Johnson*
Hauptmann, Gerhardt, *The Weavers*
Kingsley, Sidney, *Dead End*
Odets, Clifford, *Golden Boy; Paradise Lost; Till the Day I Die; Waiting for Lefty*
O'Neill, Eugene, *The Hairy Ape*
Rice, Elmer, *Street Scene; We, the People*
Riggs, Lynn, *Russet Mantle*
Sherwood, Robert, *The Petrified Forest*
Spender, Stephen, *The Trial of a Judge*

## WAR AND PEACE

1. Discuss the causes of war suggested by Gulliver in relation to modern economic, political, and psychological theory. Compare the tone and method of Swift's satire with that in *Gulliver's Grandson*. Find out what details you can of the historical facts on which the latter is based. Write a satirical sketch of some local, national, or international event of interest to you.

2. One often hears as a reason for the continuance of war that "it's human nature to fight, and human nature never changes." Criticize this aphorism in the light of Mr. Zilboorg's essay. The author believes, as do most modern psychologists, that our aggressive impulses can be directed into socially acceptable channels. What means does he suggest for thus directing them? What hope does he give the reader that war may finally be eradicated? Do you agree that the doctor should merely "treat those wounded in battle," not try to prevent the battle? *Suggestions for writing:* Harnessing my emotions; How I learned to control my temper; On knocking oneself out; The

audience at a prize fight; Fighting disease (or injustice, or ignorance) rather than my fellow men; A hero of peace.

3. How does Mr. Kolnai show that pro-fascist and pacifist elements in the democracies may unite to bring about the victory of fascism? Show how the distinction between various attitudes toward peace painted by Mr. Kolnai is the same as that made by Mrs. Browning in *Casa Guidi Windows*. What does he mean when he says that "it is not war but peace which seals the doom of liberal civilization"? Why does he believe that it is impossible to combat fascism by means of a pacifistic and compromising attitude? In the light of recent events evaluate his arguments.

4. Summarize the points on which Mr. Russell agrees and disagrees with his opponent, Mr. Kolnai. In so far as you are able, evaluate his arguments. How does Mr. Russell support his statement that "war can still settle problems but it can only settle them the wrong way?" What inconsistencies does he point out in the attitudes of America toward Munich?

5. According to Mr. Borchard what factors have led to a retreat from representative government and concentration of power in the executive? What threats to the maintenance of a true American democracy does Mr. Borchard see at the present time? Trace briefly the traditional American foreign policy of non-intervention from the time of the colonies. What fallacies does Mr. Borchard point out in the idea of collective security? Summarize his fundamental objections to the Geneva system. See what arguments you can find in its defense and write an answer to Mr. Borchard. In the light of recent world events what do you think the author means when he says: "A supposed political division between dictatorships and democracies is false"?

6. Show how the *Old Man at the Bridge* achieves effectiveness through indirectness, irony, and understatement. The emphasis on the plight of the animals, for instance, accentuates the human tragedy. What is the effect of the insistence on the self-dependence and ingenuity of the cat; of the remark "I am without politics"; of the quietness and simplicity of the writing? Find other examples of this typical Hemingway technique. Write a critical paper on the problem of portraying human emotion. *Other Suggestions for writing:* The cat who walked by himself (see Kipling's story of that title); On being kept by a cat (see Elmer Davis's essay of that name); Man and his animals; Old age.

7. In *No More Peace!* what two types of character prominent in the world today are represented by St. Francis and Napoleon? What opposing views of the motivation of mankind do they represent? Discover the contemporary counterparts—types, not individuals—of Noah, David, Samuel, Laban, Sarah, Lot, the Little Man, the Fat Man, Jacob, Rachel and Cain. Explain the satire on dictators in the rise of Cain to power and the methods he employs. In relation to the theme of the play comment on this statement: "People believe things not because they're true, but because they want to believe

them." In the light of Byron's statement, "And if I laugh 'tis that I may not weep," comment on the comic treatment of a tragic theme by a man who was himself a German exile. What issues in the contemporary world does this satire enable you to see more clearly? Comment on the most effective instances of irony in this play. What hope for the future is set forth in the conclusion?

8. In what sense is Chaplin's film *The Great Dictator* the comic treatment of a tragic theme? What aspects of it have led to the belief that it is part of the propaganda to induce America to fight Hitler?

9. What contrasts between fundamental values in human life and the conditions imposed upon men do you find in the poems of Hardy?

10. The horror of war, its tragic waste, is portrayed in *Aftermath*, *Dreamers*, and *Strange Meeting* by men who have participated in it. What is the effect of contrasting details introduced in this group of poems? Study the effect of contrasting ideas and images. Note the use of harsh sounds.

11. What support can you bring to bear on Lindsay's imaginary picture of Lincoln from your knowledge of him? What are the social implications of the phrases, "the league of sober folk, the Worker's Earth"? *Suggestions for writing:* If Abraham Lincoln were President today; "Too many peasants fight, they know not why"; A criticism of the treatment of Lincoln in a movie or play you have seen such as *Young Mr. Lincoln, Prologue to Glory, Abe Lincoln in Illinois,* or Drinkwater's *Abraham Lincoln.*

12. The long poem, *Casa Guidi Windows*, named for the house of the Brownings in Venice, voices Mrs. Browning's hopes for the cause of liberty in Italy in the 19th century. How might it be considered a comment on the world of today? *Suggestions for writing:* Peace exalted for the ends of trade; "I love no peace which is not fellowship"; "A peace that sits beside a hearth in self-commended mood"; "Peace which is no counterfeit."

## Suggestions for Further Reading

ESSAYS AND CRITICISM

Allen, Frederick, *Only Yesterday*

Fortune, editors of, *Arms and the Man* (Mar., 1934)

Fosdick, Harry Emerson, *The Unknown Soldier; A Christian Conscience About War*

Hankey, Donald, *A Student in Arms*

Huxley, Aldous, *Ends and Means*

Krutch, Joseph Wood, *Was Europe a Success?*

Millis, Walter, *The Road to War*

Page, Kirby, *Must We Go to War?*

Sheean, Vincent, *Not Peace but a Sword*

Strachey, John, *The Coming Struggle for Power*

Woolf, Virginia, *Three Guineas*

FICTION

Crane, Stephen, *The Red Badge of Courage*

Cummings, E. E., *The Enormous Room*

Dos Passos, John, *One Man's Initiation; Three Soldiers*

Euripides, *The Trojan Women*

Hemingway, Ernest, *A Farewell to Arms; The Fifth Column and the First Forty-Nine Stories*

March, William, *Company K*

Remarque, Erich, *All Quiet on the Western Front; The Road Back*

Wells, H. G., *War Between the Worlds*

Zweig, Stefan, *The Case of Sergeant Grischa*

AUTOBIOGRAPHY

Brittain, Vera, *Testament of Youth*

DRAMA

Aristophanes, *Lysistrata*

Capek, Karel, *The Power and the Glory,*
    *R. U. R.*

Green, Paul, *Johnny Johnson*

Shaw, George Bernard, *Arms and the Man*

Shaw, Irwin, *Bury the Dead*

Sheriff, Robert, *Journey's End*

Sherwood, Robert, *Idiot's Delight; The
    Road to Rome*

Stallings, L., and Anderson, M., *What Price
    Glory?*

## THE WORLD OF TOMORROW

1. Explain how the inhabitants of More's *Utopia* take care of the problems of idleness, production, occupations of women, the working day, leisure time, building, public works, and government. Would it be well for any of the regulations of this ideal commonwealth to become a part of our social order? Have any been adopted?

2. Contrast the emphasis of Bacon in *The New Atlantis* with that of More. Recalling that Bacon was writing before the advent of modern science, what seems to you especially remarkable about his kingdom?

3. Although Mr. Chase presents a "private utopia," his vision has universal implications in its portrayal of an ideal community. Note especially the way in which he constantly ties the good of the individual with that of the group. Wherein do you find his utopia practicable, wherein too visionary? Any one of Mr. Chase's list of things to avoid or things to enjoy might be expanded into a theme of personal reaction. Try your hand at one or two of these topics.

4. In the light of your experience in group living in a dormitory or fraternity house, test the claims of Mr. Preston for the collective life. What limitations does he impose on the size and character of the group for whom such a scheme as the one he describes is possible? *Suggestions for writing:* A criticism or defense of Mr. Preston's "Collectiva"; What do I live by?; On facing myself; The average American party; The cult of personality.

5. Enumerate some of the inventions and discoveries which have made "the new age and the new man." Distinguish between "pure science" and the science of the engineer. In what way may the engineer be said to be typical of the "new man"? What are the chief problems which confront him in the world of today? To what extent are they problems for all of us to solve? What are the principal resources which engineering offers to the world? Explain the relation between the new plenty and leisure. What is the responsibility of the engineer and of the average man in relation to the new possibilities of leisure? Explain the author's relation of the gifts of engineering to the ideas of Goodness, Beauty, and Truth. What must be the relation of the capitalist to the world now made possible by modern engineering? What does Mr. Flanders see as the highest social service the individual can render? What can you add to his list of engineering feats that have introduced a new beauty into life? What would Ruskin have thought of the proposals made by Mr. Flanders? Make a comparative study of their ideas. Why does this age hold

forth greater promise of general achievement and human happiness than an age such as the fifth century in Italy or the eighteenth century in England? Why does Mr. Flanders believe that the literature of personal experience must now be supplanted by that of social experience? Do you think the two are necessarily hostile to each other? After you have finished reading the literature in this book, answer this question in the light of your own experience. Read *Berkeley Square*, a play in which a youth who idealizes the 18th century, finds out the truth about it. *Suggestions for writing:* A study of some specific feat of engineering which interests you; A factory I have visited (coal-mine or cotton-mill, etc.); Alice in Wonderland visits a modern city; New frontiers for the engineer; There can be plenty for all; A four-day week; Education for leisure; The earning of money as a social service; The limitations of "charity"; Usefulness and beauty may be united; Nostalgia for the past; I prefer to look ahead, not backward.

6. On what view of human nature does Thomas Mann base his hope for a better world? What is the role of the artist in his scheme of things? What evidence can you offer that Thomas Mann would approve of Blake's theme in the *Stanzas from Milton*?

7. What elements of satire on our world as it is do you find in *Brave New World*? What are the methods of satire employed here? What support does modern psychology lend to the illusion of reality in the situation? Refer again to Erika Mann's *School for Barbarians* for illustration of a modern application of psychology to the education of children for the state. *Suggestions for writing:* How I was conditioned to like (or dislike) the country, city, school, a person, food, etc.; A world without parents; Developing class consciousness; The trials of being superior; If we were all alike.

8. Julian West, the hero of *Looking Backward*, fell asleep in 1887 and awakened in Boston one hundred years later to find a new world. What does he discover about the system of distribution of goods? What plans recently proposed or attempted does the method suggest to you? Upon what view of human nature is this system grounded? Does it seem to you a valid one? To what extent may our modern system of trade be said to be an education in self-seeking at the expense of others? What arguments can you present in its defense? Evaluate the statement: "The lust of honor even in your sordid day notoriously impelled men to more desperate effort than the love of money could." Base your conclusions on studies of a number of men who have achieved recognition today. *Suggestions for writing:* Is ours a system in which the interests of every individual are antagonistic to those of every other?; A world without wages; All men who do their best are equally successful; Men will not work without the motive of material gain; Joys of a shopping tour; The burden of shopping; On being induced to buy what I do not want; *Looking Backward* as a criticism of modern life.

9. What criticism of conventional ideas of success is involved in the Grand Lama's picture of Shangri-La? What are the positive values asserted

here? To what extent do they represent a mere escape philosophy, and to what extent are they values upon which a civilization could be built? In the light of the world situation today, what can you say of this picture: "He foresaw a time when men, exultant in the technique of homicide, would rage so hotly over the world that every precious thing would be in danger, every book and picture and harmony, every treasure garnered through two millenniums"? What suggestions can you offer for the preservation of the world's cultural heritage? To what extent is the cultivation of the attitude of passionlessness and moderation an adequate answer? In the light of recent scientific discoveries, to what extent is the achievement of longevity in Shangri-La within the realm of possibility? *Suggestions for writing:* My Shangri-La; A criticism of Shangri-La as a utopia; We are slaves of time; If I could live to be a hundred; How can the world be re-built?; The burning of the books; The new dark ages; While the storm rages; A new world stirring in the ruins.

10. Although Morris was not himself an "idle singer," but one who worked earnestly for a better and more beautiful world, in *An Apology* he presents the point of view of the escapist from the problems of reality. Contrast this attitude with that of many of the modern social poets here represented. By this time you have formulated your ideas of the relation of the artist to the social order. Write a critical paper presenting your conclusions.

11. What is the "rising tide" of W. R. Benét's poem, and on what is his hope based?

12. It will be interesting to apply the theories on modern social poetry expressed in Engle's *Poetry in a Machine Age* with his poem, *Epilogue at the Core of Earth*. You may wish to read his entire volume, *Break the Heart's Anger*, for further light on his handling of the social theme and his use of imagery drawn from the modern world of men and machines. Compare the reasons for hope found in Sandburg, Engle, MacLeish, Spender, Day Lewis and Gregory.

13. In what respects may Whitman's prophecy be said to have been fulfilled? In what ways was he mistaken? What lines seem to you still prophetic of coming events? To what elements does he refer as the "perform'd America, and Europe"; to what as the "unperform'd, more gigantic than ever"?

14. Shelley's nineteenth-century vision of a liberated humanity is the vision of our social poets today. Compare the final chorus of Day Lewis with that from Shelley's *Hellas*. If from his personal emotions and his universal sympathies, his criticism of his own age and his dream of a new day, the literary artist could always create an *Ode to the West Wind*, there would be no conflict between the claims of propaganda and art. Comment on the truth or limitations of this statement by a study of the purpose of Shelley; and of the thought, the personal emotion, and the imagery of the ode. The concluding lines of *Prometheus Unbound* suggest that hope for the world is finally centered in the character of the individual. What further support for this idea

have you found in the social poets? In what way might it be true that, as Shelley said, the poets are the "unacknowledged legislators of the world"?

## Suggestions for Further Reading

Bacon, Francis, *The New Atlantis*

Bellamy, Edward, *Looking Backward*

Butler, Samuel, *Erewhon; Erewhon Revisited*

Hilton, James, *Lost Horizon*

Howells, William Dean, *A Traveller from Altruria*

Huxley, Aldous, *Brave New World*

Lyons, Eugene, *Assignment in Utopia*

More, Thomas, *Utopia*

Morris, William, *News from Nowhere*

Mumford, Lewis, *The Story of Utopias*

Plato, *The Republic*

Soule, George, *A Planned Society*

*The Nation,* 1927—Series of articles on Utopias by Edna Ferber, Sinclair Lewis, C. A. Finger, H. L. Mencken, *et al.*

Webb, Sidney, and Beatrice, *Soviet Communism: A New Civilization?*

Wells, H. G., *A Modern Utopia*

Williams, Albert Rhys, *The Soviets*

# BIOGRAPHICAL NOTES

JAMES TRUSLOW ADAMS (1878–    ), born in Brooklyn, New York, is an American historian and critic of our contemporary civilization. Among his books are *The Founding of New England, The Epic of America,* and *Our Business Civilization.*

JOSEPH ADDISON (1672–1718) was an English essayist, playwright, poet, and statesman, associated with Steele on *The Tatler* and *The Spectator,* to which they contributed essays on manners and morals which have become models of the familiar essay form. For perfection of his style, Dr. Johnson advised the writer to give his days and nights to the study of Addison.

MAXWELL ANDERSON (1888–    ), after serving many years as a professor and journalist, has devoted himself to writing. Among his best known plays are *Winterset, Both Your Houses, Mary of Scotland, Elizabeth the Queen, The Wingless Victory,* and *Key Largo.*

MATTHEW ARNOLD (1822–1888), poet, educator, and literary critic, expresses the emotional and intellectual conflict of one caught between two worlds, "one dead, the other powerless to be born." An Oxford fellow, for thirty years an inspector of schools, he had moments of vagrancy, such as those recorded in *The Scholar Gipsy,* when he revolted against academic tradition and conformity. As a critic of his era, he is remembered for his advocacy of "sweetness and light" as opposed to materialism or "Philistinism."

FRANCIS BACON (1561–1626) is famous as essayist, philosopher, statesman, and scientist. *The New Atlantis,* a philosophical romance, presents Bacon's ideal commonwealth, which is centered about a college for interpreting nature and producing great works for the benefit of man. He wished to extend and organize man's knowledge through systematic observation and experiment.

W. N. P. BARBELLION (1890–1917) was the son of a newspaper reporter in a small Devonshire town. At the age of 13 he started his diary *The Journal of a Disappointed Man,* in which he records his fight with disease, poverty, and all the stupidities of the world.

HAMILTON BASSO (1904–    ), born in New Orleans, worked on several New Orleans newspapers. He has lived in the mountains of North Carolina and in Aiken, South Carolina, where he gained the ideas and impressions contained in his novel, *Cinnamon Seed.* He has written two other novels, *In Their Own Image* and *Courthouse Square* and a biography, *Beauregard: The Great Creole.*

CHARLES BEARD (1874–    ) is generally regarded as one of our finest American historians. His primary interest lies in the economic interpretation of American history and institutions. He served many years as a professor at Columbia University and has written *The Rise of American Civilization* and *America in Midpassage* (in collaboration with his wife, Mary Beard), and edited *Wither Mankind?*

CARL BECKER (1873–    ), born in Iowa, is a member of the American Academy of Arts and Sciences. Among his published works are *Beginnings of the American People, Eve of the Revolution, The Heavenly City of the Eighteenth Century Philosophers, Progress and Power*, and *Every Man His Own Historian.*

EDWARD BELLAMY (1850–1898), born at Chicopee Falls, Massachusetts, was an editorial writer for the *New York Evening Post* early in his career. In 1888 he caught the public attention with *Looking Backward, 2000–1887*, in which he set forth his vision of a technocratic society. In 1897 Bellamy published *Equality*, a sequel to *Looking Backward.*

STEPHEN VINCENT BENÉT (1898–    ) is notable as a short story writer and poet. Among his published works are *John Brown's Body*, which won the Pulitzer prize in 1928, *Ballads and Poems* and several volumes of short stories.

WILLIAM ROSE BENÉT (1886–    ), born at Fort Hamilton, New York Harbor, was associate editor of the *Century Magazine* from 1910 to 1917. With Henry Seidel Canby and Christopher Morley, Benét started the *Literary Review* of the *New York Evening Post* in 1920, and in 1924 this group organized the *Saturday Review of Literature.* His earliest published works are *Merchants from Cathay, Falconer of God, and Other Poems, Great White Wall, Burglar of the Zodiac, and Other Poems, Perpetual Light, A Memorial* and *Moons of Grandeur.*

ARNOLD BENNETT (1867–1931), an Englishman, was a lawyer and editor, as well as a man of letters. Among his published works are *The Old Wives' Tale, Hilda Lessways, Books and Persons, Things That Have Interested Me*, and *The Savour of Life.*

MORRIS BISHOP (1893–    ), is a professor of Romance languages at Cornell University. He is the author of a number of books and has contributed frequently to the *New Yorker* and the *Saturday Review of Literature.*

BJÖRNSTJERNE BJÖRNSON (1832–1910), a Norwegian novelist, dramatist, and poet, was also a revolutionary leader and social reformer. His name lives in the literature of Europe by virtue of his realistic studies of heredity and other social problems and is immortal in his own country by virtue of his noble and patriotic lyric verse.

WILLIAM BLAKE (1757–1827) was an English mystical poet and artist whose revolutionary ideas have been more influential on later writers than on his contemporaries. He anticipates Freud in his subtle psychology, and modern social poets in his vision of an era of brotherhood and love. *Songs of Innocence* and *Songs of Experience* present opposing states of the human soul with a simplicity that is really extreme subtlety. Many of his poems are protests against social evils.

BRUCE BLIVEN (1889–    ), born at Emmetsburg, Iowa, was chief editorial writer (1919), managing editor (1920–22), and associate editor (1922–23) of *The New York Globe.* He has been editor in chief of the *New Republic* since 1923.

EDWIN BORCHARD (1884–    ), is professor of International Law at Yale University.

JOHN HODGDON BRADLEY (1898–    ), a professor since 1929 at the University of Southern California, is also a geologist and author. Among his published works are *The Earth and Its History, Parade of the Living, Autobiography of Earth*, and *Patterns of Survival.*

EMILY BRONTË (1818–1848), one of three sisters to contribute to the literature of the Victorian Age, is chiefly known for her powerful novel, *Wuthering Heights*. She was the only member of her family to write notable poetry as well as fiction.

RUPERT BROOKE (1887–1915), an English poet, is chiefly notable for his poems on war, love, and the beauties of the English countryside. A member of the British Mediterranean Expeditionary Force, he died in Gallipoli and was buried there in 1915.

ELIZABETH BARRETT BROWNING (1806–1861) was an English poet, wife of Robert Browning, for whom she wrote her *Sonnets from the Portuguese*. *Casa Guidi Windows*, concerned with Italian political events, expresses her love of freedom and her conviction that nations as well as men must ground their lives on ideals of moral integrity.

ROBERT BROWNING (1812–1889) wrote a number of long poems and poetic dramas, but he is best known for his concentrated dramatic monologues in which a character reveals himself at a significant moment. His is an affirmative philosophy of life, reflecting the poet's own intellectual vigor and zest for living.

PEARL BUCK (1892–   ), a Nobel prize winner in 1938 in recognition of her novel, *The Good Earth*, has written also *Sons, A House Divided, The Exile, The Mother*, and *Fighting Angel*.

ROBERT BURNS (1759–1796), Scotch poet, is recognized as one of the greatest love poets and song writers of all time. Himself a man of humble birth, he had a deep sympathy with the poor, a passionate love of liberty, and a hatred of injustice and hypocrisy, all of which find expression in his ballads and satires.

LORD BYRON (George Gordon Byron) (1788–1824) has exerted great influence on poetry because of the vigor of his narrative, the grandeur of his style, and the power of his satire. It is perhaps as the poet of the epic satire, *Don Juan*, ridiculing British hypocrisy and exposing social corruption, that he will have his most enduring fame. He was a life-long devotee of liberty and died in Greece where he had gone to defend Greek freedom.

V. F. CALVERTON (1900–   ), is an editor, writer, and lecturer. He was founder and editor of *The Modern Quarterly*, now *The Modern Monthly*. Some of his works are *Sex Expression in Literature, The Liberation of American Literature, The Passing of the Gods*, and *The New Ground of Criticism*.

THOMAS CARLYLE (1785–1881) was born in Scotland and educated at the University of Edinburgh. Dismissing law, divinity, and school teaching after attempting a career in each of these fields, he turned to the career of writing in London, as a social pamphleteer, literary critic, and historian. He became one of the most powerful literary and social critics of his age and a prophet of ours. At the heart of his criticism in such works as *Past and Present* and *Latter Day Pamphlets* is his distrust of the ideas of democracy and laissez-faire, his exaltation of the spiritual values of the middle ages, and his worship of great men (*On Heroes, Hero Worship, and the Heroic in History*).

PAUL VINCENT CARROLL (1900–   ), born in Ireland, saw the Abbey theatre as the spiritual rebirth of the Irish people. His *Shadow and Substance* won the award of the New York Drama Critics' Circle for the 1938 season's best importation. A more recent work is *The White Steed*.

WILLA CATHER (1876–    ), formerly an editor of *McClure's Magazine*, is one of America's most highly regarded writers of fiction. Her best known works are *Death Comes for the Archbishop*, *Shadows on the Rock*, *Obscure Destinies*, *The Song of the Lark*, *O Pioneers* and *The Professor's House*.

STUART CHASE (1888–    ) as a public accountant exposed the exploitation of the American people by business interests during the War. Continuing to be a critic of social conditions in the United States, he has written *The Tragedy of Waste*, *Men and Machines*, and *The Economy of Abundance*.

ANTON CHEKHOV (1860–1904), great Russian short story writer, was the son of a freed serf in South Russia. Educated for medicine at the University of Moscow, he never practised except once during a cholera plague. His highly concentrated and powerful stories have exerted great influence on the modern short story. They are marked by irony, compassion for suffering and poverty, and emotional restraint. He also wrote a number of plays including *The Cherry Orchard*, *Uncle Vanya*, and *Three Sisters*.

G. K. CHESTERTON (1874–1936) is a well known English essayist, novelist, dramatist, and poet. Among his published works are *Orthodoxy*, *Heretics*, *What Is Wrong with the World*, *What I Saw in America*, and *The Everlasting Man*.

HAROLD F. CLARK is a professor at Teachers College, Columbia University, and author of *The Cost of Government and the Support of Education*, *The Effect of Population on the Ability to Support Schools*, and *Economic Effects of Education*.

JOSEPH CONRAD (1857–1924), an English novelist of Polish parentage, was a sailor as well as a writer of novels about the sea. Among his most significant novels are *Almayer's Folly*, *The Nigger of the Narcissus*, *Lord Jim*, *Typhoon*, and *Nostromo*.

GEORGE COREY has had a diversity of experience as bell hop, assembler in a Ford factory, cabin boy, dock hand, dentist, journalist, and teacher of oral surgery at the Shantung Christian University. He has written several unproduced plays and occasional printed articles. *$595 F. O. B.* is his first published story.

GEORGE CRABBE (1750–1832), an English poet, is interesting to us chiefly as one of the first to treat realistically in verse the relation between the sordid surroundings of the poor and their lives and characters. In its vivid sketches of types and case histories, *The Village* anticipates what Edgar Lee Masters has done in his *Spoon River Anthology*.

THOMAS CRAVEN (1889–    ), one of our finest interpreters of art, has been a pioneer in bringing art into the consciousness of the American public. He is author of *Men of Art*, *Modern Art*, and the editor of *A Treasury of American Prints*.

EVE CURIE (1904–    ), daughter of the late Marie Curie, discoverer of radium, has recently received public attention through her lectures and especially through her biography of her mother, *The Life of Marie Curie*.

PHILIP CURTISS is a frequent contributor to leading periodicals. He is also author of the following books: *Between Two Worlds*, *Wanted—A Fool*, *Mummers in Mufti*, and *The Gay Conspirators*.

CHARLES DARWIN (1809–1882) arrived at his theory of the "survival of the fittest" after long years of collecting data and specimens. The entire first edition of *On the Origin of Species by Means of Natural Selection* was exhausted on the first day of publication.

CLARENCE DAY (1874–1935) was one of our most popular humorists. He was author of *This Simian World*, a fine satire on the human race, and *Life With Father*, which has been very successfully dramatized.

CHARLES DICKENS (1812–1870) was an English humanitarian novelist who devoted his talents to the portrayal of evil conditions in English schools, factories, work-houses, and prisons. In *Hard Times* he presents the squalor and misery of a factory town and satirizes the type of education which stresses mere acquisition of facts and deadens the emotions and the imagination.

JOHN DONNE (1572–1631) has been a distinct influence on many modern poets because of the subtle intellectual themes, the powerful metaphysical imagery, and the cynicism of mood which characterize his verse. He treats love in a mocking, flippant manner in one lyric, and in the next, he exalts and dignifies it. Later as Dean of St. Paul's he was famed for his sermons which inspired terror by their vivid and powerful pictures of death.

ELIZABETH DREW resides at Cambridge, England, and lectures at the university. She is the author of *The Modern Novel, Jane Welsh and Jane Carlyle, Discovering Poetry,* and *The Enjoyment of Literature.*

SIR EDWARD DYER (1550–1607), a member of a sixteenth-century association of scholars and poets, was interested in the union of scholarship and poetry, an ideal held by many of his contemporaries.

ARTHUR STANLEY EDDINGTON (1882–    ), a professor of astronomy at Cambridge University and director of the observatory there, is one of the most eminent of our scientists today. He is author of *The Nature of the Physical World, Science and the Unseen World, The Expanding Universe,* and *New Pathways in Science.*

T. S. ELIOT (1888–    ), born in Missouri and educated at Harvard and the Sorbonne, has lived most of his life in England. He has been a bank clerk, teacher, lecturer, and editor. His influence both as critic and poet has been extensive, and in both fields he reflects his Anglo-Catholicism, classicism, and his royalist sympathies. Among his works are *Poems 1909–1935, The Sacred Wood,* a collection of essays, *Murder in the Cathedral,* and *The Waste Land.*

PAUL ENGLE (1910–    ) is a young Iowa poet who won recently a Rhodes Scholarship for study at Oxford. He is now teaching at the University of Iowa. His poetry, concerned primarily with a criticism of social institutions and social change, carries on the tradition of Whitman and Sandburg. His two volumes of poetry are *American Song* and *Break the Heart's Anger.*

MORTON EUSTIS is a member of the editorial staff of *Theatre Arts Monthly* and author of *B'way, Inc.*

ERNESTINE EVANS (1889–    ) is a free lance writer and newspaper correspondent. She was Balkan correspondent for the London *Times* in 1915, and has been feature editor of the *Christian Science Monitor.* She is author of *The Frescoes of Diego Rivera.*

JAMES T. FARRELL (1904–    ) was educated at a parochial school on Chicago's South Side and at the University of Chicago. His novel, *Studs Lonigan,* admittedly reflects his own early experiences and his broad social sympathies.

RALPH E. FLANDERS (1880–    ), an engineer and industrialist, was a member of the Industrial Advisory Board of the N. R. A. He has written *Taming Our Machines* and numerous technical papers.

JOHN GOULD FLETCHER (1886–     ) is a poet and essayist of distinction. He is known chiefly for his association with the early Imagists. Among his books are *Irradiations—Sand and Spray, Japanese Prints, Paul Gauguin: His Life and Art, The Two Frontiers,* and *XXIV Elegies.*

JOSEPH FREEMAN (1897–     ), born in a Ukrainian village of Russia, and educated at Columbia University, has been one of the editors of *The New Masses.* Among his publications are *The Soviet Worker, Voices of October* and *An American Testament.*

ROBERT FROST (1875–     ), born in San Francisco, has spent most of his life on a farm in New England. His poetry treats sympathetically New England country life and the lives of simple people. Among his books are *A Boy's Will, North of Boston, Mountain Interval, New Hampshire,* and *West-Running Brook.*

MARTHA GELLHORN has written for *Collier's* and *Scribner's* and has published a book of short stories, *The Trouble I've Seen.*

WILFRED GIBSON (1878–     ) is an English poet whose work has shifted from a Tennysonian sentimentality to a realistic portrayal of the lives of common men, farmers, tramps, soldiers, berry-pickers, stone-cutters. His collected poems were published in 1926.

LAWRENCE GILMAN (1878–1939) was born at Flushing, Long Island. He was musical critic of the *New York Tribune* and also musical and literary critic of the *North American Review.* He was author of *The Music of Tomorrow, A Guide to Debussy's Pelléas and Mélisande,* and *Nature in Music.*

HORACE GREGORY (1898–     ), born in Milwaukee, Wisconsin, went to New York in 1923 and contributed formal verse to *Vanity Fair, The Nation,* and *Books.* His books of poetry include *Chelsea Rooming House, No Retreat, Phoenix in Broadcloth,* and *Chorus for Survival.* He is on the faculty of Sarah Lawrence College.

WILLIAM HARLAN HALE is a graduate of Yale where, with Selden Rodman, he caused quite a furor by the publication of *The Harkness Hoot.* He is the author of *Challenge to Defeat: Modern Man in Goethe's World and Spengler's Century.*

JAMES NORMAN HALL (1887–     ) has had varied experience as special agent for the Society for the Prevention of Cruelty to Children, army officer, editor, traveler, and magazine writer. His publications are *On the Stream of Travel, Mid-Pacific, Flying with Chaucer,* and with Charles Nordhoff he wrote *Mutiny on the Bounty, Men Against the Sea,* and *Pitcairn's Island.*

ALBERT HALPER (1904–     ) grew up in a slum district near the railroad tracks in Chicago. He has been order-picker in a mail-order house, factory hand, office worker, salesman, jewelry clerk, agent for a tobacco company, shipping clerk in an electrotype foundry, and mail sorter in a post office. Since 1928 he has been drifting around but writing steadily. His stories and sketches have appeared in *The Dial, Harper's Magazine, The American Mercury,* and *The New Republic.* Among his books are *Union Square,* a Literary Guild choice in 1933, *On the Shore,* and *The Foundry.*

T. SWANN HARDING is a Maryland scientist and philosopher who contributes frequently to leading magazines.

THOMAS HARDY (1840–1928), distinguished novelist and poet, earned his living at the outset of his career as an architect. Both his novels and his poetry reflect his awareness of the tragic in life, his sense of the irony involved in human relationships, and his fearless facing of the grimmer aspects of life.

HARLAN HATCHER (1899–    ) is a professor of English at Ohio State University. He is author of *The Versification of Robert Browning, Tunnel Hill: a Novel,* and essays in *The Bookman, The English Journal* and the *Saturday Review of Literature.*

ERNEST HEMINGWAY (1898–    ) is a journalist, novelist, and essayist whose work reflects the post-war disillusionment. Among his works are *Men Without Women, The Sun Also Rises, A Farewell to Arms, Death in the Afternoon, To Have and Have Not,* and *The Fifth Column and the First Forty-nine Stories.*

GEORGE HERBERT (1593–1633) was educated at Cambridge, where he was university orator. Of a prominent noble family, himself a man of great brilliance, he took holy orders and devoted himself to a small country parish at Bemerton. His poems were posthumously published. They reflect the conflict between worldly and spiritual desires and the victory of the spirit.

ROBERT HERRICK (1591–1674) was an English clergyman who wrote exquisite poetry in a pagan mood celebrating the joys of love and life, urging the delights of the senses and expressing the beauties of rural life and the charm of folk customs. His short poems are noted for perfection of their form, their fancy, and zest for living.

DU BOSE HEYWARD (1885–    ) is an American poet, novelist, and playwright whose life in the south and observation of negroes on the Charleston waterfront have given him the material for the sympathetic portraits of colored people found in his novels, *Porgy* and *Mamba's Daughters,* both of which were later dramatized.

ROBERT HILLYER (1895–    ), born in East Orange, New Jersey, published his first book of poetry in the year of his graduation from Harvard. After the World War he joined the faculty of Harvard as instructor in English. In 1920 he brought out two poetic volumes, *The Five Books of Youth* and *Alchemy: A Symphonic Poem.* He has also written *The Seventh Hill, The Gates of the Campus,* and *Letter to Robert Frost and Other Poems.*

JAMES HILTON (1900–    ), educated at Cambridge, includes travel and mountain climbing among his recreations. Among his publications are *And Now Goodbye* (1931), *Knight Without Armour* (1933), *Lost Horizon* (1933), *Goodbye, Mr. Chips* (1934), and *We Are Not Alone* (1937).

EARNEST A. HOOTON (1887–    ), born in Clemansville, Wisconsin, is a professor at Harvard and the author of *Ancient Inhabitants of the Canary Islands, The Indians of Pecos* and *Up from the Ape.*

GERARD MANLEY HOPKINS (1844–1889) became a convert to Catholicism and later a Jesuit priest. Little of his verse was printed or known during his lifetime, but in 1918 Robert Bridges published his poetry in book form. Nature and religious themes were his chief concern, and to these he gave expression in original and noteworthy forms.

A. E. HOUSMAN (1859–1936), born in Shropshire, England, was professor of Latin at University College, London, and edited Juvenal, Manillius and Lucan. His first volume was *A Shropshire Lad* (1896). His second volume, *Last Poems,* was published almost thirty years later.

ALDOUS HUXLEY (1894–    ), the third son of Leonard Huxley (eldest son and biographer of Thomas Henry Huxley) and Julia Arnold (niece of Matthew Arnold and sister of Mrs. Humphry Ward), was educated at Eton and Oxford. He has been a prolific writer. Some of his novels are *Crome Yellow, Antic Hay, Barren Leaves, Point Counterpoint, Eyeless in Gaza,* and *After Many a Summer Dies the Swan.* He has also written many volumes of essays, including *Do What You Will, Brief Candles, Proper Studies,* and *Ends and Means.* Mr. Huxley is now living in Hollywood, California.

THOMAS HENRY HUXLEY (1825–1895) was known as "Darwin's bull-dog" for his vigorous defense of Darwinian theory and his popularization of science in his lectures to laboring men and students. More than any other individual he is responsible for the great emphasis given the sciences in the school curriculum today. He served as a surgeon in the British navy and was for thirty-two years a professor of natural history at the Royal School of Mines.

ROBINSON JEFFERS (1887–    ) lives in Carmel, California, where he writes his poetry in a tower studio he built with his own hands of ocean boulders. Reserved and self-sufficient, he has devoted himself to poetry which reflects his knowledge of the strange depths of human personality and his acceptance of the tragedy of life. Among his books are *Cawdor, The Women at Point Sur, The Roan Stallion,* and *Selected Poems.*

MARY JONATHAN is the pseudonym of a recent Smith College graduate whose story, *David, I've Told Them,* appeared in *Story* magazine.

HOWARD MUMFORD JONES (1892–    ) is a professor of English at Harvard University and literary editor of the *Boston Evening Transcript.* His contributions to periodicals are numerous.

JOHN KEATS (1795–1821), expresses in his poetry both sensuous beauty and the truth it reveals. His life was tragically shadowed by consumption, which caused his early death, but his name is one of the glories of English poetry, not "writ in water" as he feared.

FREDA KIRCHWEY (1885–    ), born in Lake Placid, New York, was a reporter on the *Morning Telegraph* and on the editorial staff of *Every Week.* She has been with *The Nation* since 1918, as managing editor, literary editor, and publisher and owner since 1937.

AUREL KOLNAI is the author of *The War Against the West* and a frequent contributor to *The Nation.*

JOSEPH WOOD KRUTCH (1893–    ), a professor at Columbia University and formerly an editor of *The Nation,* has become widely known not only for his dramatic criticism but for his general criticism of the arts and of contemporary life. Among his books are *Experience and Art, Edgar Allan Poe: A Study in Genius, The Modern Temper, Was Europe a Success?, The American Drama Since 1918.*

CHARLES LAMB (1775–1834) was perhaps the greatest of all English familiar essayists, certainly the best loved for the pathos and geniality, the wistfulness and philosophical understanding, and the mellow literary charm of his varied commentaries on life, published as *Essays of Elia* (1823 and 1833). He ranked high also for his literary criticism, chiefly of the Elizabethan drama, and for his personal letters.

HAROLD LASKI (1893–    ) has been a professor at Harvard University and has lectured at Yale University, Amherst College, and The New School for Social Research. Since 1926 he has been on the faculty of the University of London. He has written for many liberal periodicals both in this country and in England. Some of his books are *Liberty in the Modern State, Democracy in Crisis, A Grammar of Politics,* and *The Rise of Liberalism.*

WILLIAM ELLERY LEONARD is a professor of English at the University of Wisconsin. He is distinguished not only as a philologist but as the author of several volumes of poetry and an autobiographical study, *Locomotive God.*

MAX LERNER (1902–    ), born in Russia, has been until recently an editor of *The Nation.* He now contributes regularly to *The New Republic* and *The Nation* and is a professor of political science at Williams College. His last books are *It Is Later Than You Think* and *Ideas Are Weapons.*

C. DAY LEWIS (1904–    ), born in Ireland and educated at Oxford, is a poet and critic interested primarily in social themes. His works are *Collected Poems (1929–1933), A Hope for Poetry,* and *A Time to Dance.*

SINCLAIR LEWIS (1885–    ), born in Sauk Center, Minnesota, was Nobel prize winner in literature in 1930. His principal novels are *Main Street, Babbitt, Arrowsmith, Dodsworth,* and *It Can't Happen Here.*

VACHEL LINDSAY (1897–1931), born in Springfield, Illinois, devoted his life to poetry and lecturing. His books are *General Booth Enters Heaven and Other Poems, The Congo and Other Poems,* and *Collected Poems.*

WALTER LIPPMANN (1889–    ) is widely known as a journalist, editor, and author. His columns have been syndicated in newspapers all over the United States. Among his books are *A Preface to Politics, A Preface to Morals, Public Opinion, The Method of Freedom, The Good Society,* and *The New Imperative.*

ARCHIBALD MacLEISH (1892–    ), a lawyer in Boston before he retired to devote himself to literature, was one of the editors of *Fortune Magazine.* He is now head of the Library of Congress in Washington. Some of his best known works are *Conquistador* (Pulitzer prize poem), *Frescoes for Mr. Rockefeller's City, Union Pacific—A Ballet, Panic, The Fall of the City* and *Public Speech.*

PHYLLIS McGINLEY is a frequent contributor to *The New Yorker.*

ALBERT MALTZ (1908–    ), born in Brooklyn, New York, studied playwrighting at Yale with George Pierce Baker. With George Sklar he wrote *Merry-Go-Round* to arouse intelligent indignation against the New York Tammany machine. Later the pair wrote *Peace on Earth,* an anti-war collaboration, and *Black Pit,* a tale of a West Virginia coal-miner. The best of Maltz' three one-act plays, *Private Hicks,* won first prize in The New Theater League contest in 1935.

THOMAS MANN (1875–    ), now a lecturer at Princeton University, is an exile from Germany. In 1929 he was awarded the Nobel prize in literature. His best known books are *The Magic Mountain, Death in Venice, Buddenbrooks, Joseph in Egypt,* and *The Coming Victory of Democracy.*

KATHARINE MANSFIELD (1888–1923), British short story writer and critic, was born in Wellington, New Zealand. She married John Middleton Murry in 1913 and became associated with him in editing a literary magazine called *Rhythm,* contributing short stories regularly. Some of her short story collections are *Bliss, The Garden Party, The Dove's Nest,* and *The Aloe.* Her criticism is to be found in *Novels and Novelists* and her *Journal.*

ANDREW MARVELL (1621–1678) was a poet, satirist and politician in the time of Charles I, Cromwell, and Charles II. He served as secretary to Milton in 1657. The intellectual subtlety and richness of imagery of *To His Coy Mistress* have made it influential on later poets as they consider the inevitable passing of love and beauty.

JOHN MASEFIELD (1878–    ) was born in Ludbury, Herefordshire, England. After serving for three years on a merchant ship and working at odd jobs for several years in New York City, he discovered he was a poet. Among his works are *The Everlasting Mercy, Reynard the Fox, Midsummer Night,* and *The Coming of Christ.*

EDGAR LEE MASTERS (1869–    ), born in Garnett, Kansas, was admitted to the bar in 1891. Among his publications are *Spoon River Anthology, The Great Valley, Domesday Book, The New Spoon River, The Tale of Chicago, Vachel Lindsay, Poems of People,* and *Mark Twain.*

MILTON S. MAYER is a Chicago journalist who has a part-time connection with the University of Chicago. He contributes frequently to leading periodicals.

MORROW MAYO (1897–    ) has been an American newspaper man and a contributor to such periodicals as *The New Republic, The Nation, The Atlantic Monthly,* and *Harper's Magazine.*

EDNA ST. VINCENT MILLAY (1892–    ) was born in Rockland, Maine. One of her finest poems, *Renascence,* was written before she was nineteen. She won the Pulitzer prize for poetry in 1922 and wrote the libretto for *The King's Henchman* which was performed in New York in 1927. Some of her publications are *The Harp-Weaver and Other Poems* (1923), *The Buck in the Snow and Other Poems* (1928), *Fatal Interview* (1931), *Wine from these Grapes* (1934), and *Conversation at Midnight* (1937).

A. A. MILNE (1882–    ) was educated at Cambridge and was assistant editor of *Punch* from 1906 to 1914. Some of his publications are *When We Were Very Young, Winnie-the-Pooh, Two People,* and *Peace with Honour.* Among his plays are *Mr. Pim Passes By, Michael and Mary,* and *Gentleman Unknown.*

JOHN MILTON (1608–1674), England's greatest epic poet, devoted nearly twenty of his best years to the cause of liberty, as political pamphleteer and Foreign Secretary under the Commonwealth government. This work is considered responsible for his loss of eye-sight. The *Areopagitica* (1644) remains one of the finest defenses of freedom of thought and expression. Placed high among English poets for his sonnets and his shorter poems, such as *Lycidas, L'Allegro,* and *Il Penseroso,* Milton is honored especially as the poet of the great epic of man's fall, *Paradise Lost.*

JONATHAN MITCHELL (1895–    ) was born in Portland, Maine. He was a reporter on the *New York World* from 1921 to 1929 and London and Paris correspondent from 1926 to 1928. He is a contributing editor to *The New Republic* and is the author of *Goosesteps to Peace.*

SIR THOMAS MORE (1478–1535) was an English author, scholar, judge, and statesman whose picture of an ideal commonwealth in the *Utopia* (1515) has influenced all subsequent visions of a world approaching perfection. His ideas on religious toleration, education, war, economic planning, and other problems seem strangely modern, some of them anticipating reforms still desired but unrealized.

WILLIAM MORRIS (1834–1896), English poet and romanticist in prose, was by no means merely the "idle singer of an empty day," for he busied himself with the designing and manufacturing of beautiful textiles, stained glass windows, furniture, and book printing, as well as with propaganda for a socialist order of society. His *Dream of John Ball* (1888) and *News from Nowhere* (1891) are the best known of his social criticisms and visions; *The Earthly Paradise* (1868–70) illustrates his power of story telling in Chaucerian verse.

LEWIS MUMFORD (1895–    ) is a critic of art and of society. Among his publications are *The Story of Utopias, Herman Melville, Technics and Civilization*, and *The Culture of Cities*.

HUGO MÜNSTERBERG (1863–    ), born at Danzig, became in 1892 professor of psychology at Harvard. Among his more important works are *Psychology and Life* (1899), *American Traits from the Point of View of a German* (1901), *Psychology and Crime* (1908), and *On the Witness Stand*.

JOHN HENRY NEWMAN (Cardinal Newman) (1801–1890) was an English author, an Anglican and later Catholic divine, and founder of the Oxford Movement. His conversion from Anglicanism to the Church of Rome he defended with sincerity and simplicity in his spiritual autobiography, *Apologia pro Vita Sua*. *The Idea of a University* was a series of lectures concerning the founding of a Catholic University in Dublin to be devoted to study of the humanities and to moral training.

JOSEPHINE K. NEWTON, born in Cedar Rapids, Iowa, was educated as a young girl in London where her father, a minister, was located during the War, and later at Vassar College. She has done feature syndicate writing and has contributed occasionally to magazines.

WILFRED OWEN (1893–1918) was born in England and died in his attempt, as commander of the Artists' Rifles, O. T. C., to get his men across the Lambre Canal. Much of his poetry was written while he was convalescing from injuries sustained at the front.

JO PAGANO is a Californian who knows the foreign population intimately. He has contributed to popular magazines.

WAYNE PARRISH, formerly on the staff of the *New York Herald Tribune*, is a professor of economics.

ALEXANDER POPE (1688–1744) holds his place among the great English poets chiefly because of the perfection of his heroic couplet and the keenness and polish of his satiric verse. His *Essay of Man* is a long philosophic poem dealing with man's relation to himself, to society, and to the universe. His physical deformity and his ill-health are probably responsible for the bitterness of his personal satires, his constant quarrels with his friends, his pettiness and vindictiveness.

EZRA POUND (1885–    ) was born in Hailey, Idaho. He traveled extensively in Europe and settled in London where he occupied himself for more than ten years with translating, lecturing on the arts, writing poetry, and contributing to the *Fortnightly Review, The Dial*, and *Poetry*. Since then he has traveled widely and written several volumes of prose and poetry.

JOHN HYDE PRESTON is a contemporary writer now living in Connecticut. He has written two historical volumes, *Gentleman Rebel and Revolution—1776*, and a novel, *Portrait of a Woman*.

MARCEL PROUST (1871–1922), generally regarded as one of the most notable of modern novelists, was born in Paris. His *Remembrance of Things Past*, a monumental work of many volumes, has been considered one of the greatest works of all time.

SIR WALTER RALEIGH (1552–1618) represents the Renaissance type of versatile individual, poet, historian, essayist, courtier, soldier, explorer, statesman. *Even Such Is Time* was probably written on the night before his execution following the failure of his Spanish expedition. His unfinished *History of the World*, written in prison, 1604–1614, reflects the vast ambition of this Elizabethan courtier and man of letters.

JOHN REED (1887–1920), born at Portland, Oregon, was called by Upton Sinclair "the playboy of the social revolution." He worked on the *American Magazine*, became managing editor of *The Masses* and when Villa's revolt broke out in Mexico, he reported for the *World* and sent graphic sketches to *Metropolitan*. After the Russian revolution he wrote his most famed book, *Ten Days that Shook the World*.

EDWIN ARLINGTON ROBINSON (1869–1935), born in Head Tide, Maine, spent most of his summers at the MacDowell Colony, Peterboro, New Hampshire, where much of his work was written. In addition to *Tristram* and his *Collected Poems*, some of his most significant works are *The Man Against the Sky*, *Cavender's House*, and *The Glory of the Nightingales*. Three times he was a Pulitzer prize winner.

LEONARD Q. ROSS (1908–    ) is the pseudonym of Leo Rosten, who was educated at the University of Chicago and has been a teacher and research worker. He has written *The Education of Hyman Kaplan*, *The Washington Correspondents*, and *The Strangest Places*.

CHRISTINA ROSSETTI (1830–1894) was the sister of Dante Gabriel Rossetti. Her poetry is marked by exquisite melody and perfection of form in her treatment of her favorite themes, love and religious ecstasy.

DANTE GABRIEL ROSSETTI (1828–1882), was a Pre-Raphaelite poet and painter whose work is marked by its fusion of passion and mystical tone. The union of body and soul is the chief theme of his sonnet sequence, *The House of Life* (1870–1881), inspired mainly by his love for Elizabeth Siddall, his wife.

MURIEL RUKEYSER, a native New Yorker, was selected for her *Theory of Flight* as winner in the "Yale Series of Younger Poets" contest. She has been on the staff of *New Theatre* and contributes to left wing publications.

JOHN RUSKIN (1819–1900) was one of the most vigorous 19th century critics of our industrial civilization. In *Crown of Wild Olive* (1866) and in *Fors Clavigera* (1871–1884) we find some of his keenest social criticism. He was noted also as a critic of art and a defender of the Pre-Raphaelites. In *Praeterita* (1885–1889), his unfinished autobiography, we gain some understanding of the rigid family discipline which was possibly responsible for the lack of balance in his later emotional life.

BERTRAND RUSSELL (1872–    ), born at Trelleck, was appointed lecturer at Trinity College at Cambridge in 1910. His first important book was *The Principles of Mathematics*. He and his wife started a famous nursery school which has been a success in every way except financially. He is now a roving professor in the United States. Among his works are *The Problems of Philosophy*, *Mysticism and Logic*, *Marriage and Morals*, and *The Conquest of Happiness*.

CARL SANDBURG (1878–    ) has won recognition as a vigorous poet and critic of American life in his *Chicago Poems, Smoke and Steel, The People, Yes,* and more recently as a biographer of Lincoln in his monumental study, *Abraham Lincoln: The War Years,* which completes his earlier volumes, *Abraham Lincoln: The Prairie Years.*

SIEGFRIED SASSOON (1886–    ) is chiefly known for his poetry showing the horror and ruthlessness of war. Some of the titles of his publications are *The Old Huntsman, Counter-Attack, Picture Show, Satirical Poems, The Heart's Journey,* and *Vigils.*

MARK SCHORER is a young Wisconsin writer whose short stories have appeared from time to time in *Story Magazine.*

WILLIAM SHAKESPEARE (1564–1616), poet, dramatist, and actor, has contributed richly to the sonnets of our language both conventional and original themes. He varied the classic Italian sonnet form of octave and sestet by using a new form of three quatrains and a couplet. His sonnets are universally accepted as among the finest in English literature.

PERCY BYSSHE SHELLEY (1792–1822) was a rebel against conventional authority from the days of his Eton school boy opposition to the "fagging system" and his expulsion from Oxford for a tract on *The Necessity of Atheism* to his elopement with Harriet Westbrook to save her from parental tyranny, his later elopement with Mary Godwin, and his early death in Italy, where he was living a virtual exile from an English society whose hypocritical codes he had flaunted. His poetry lives among the finest expressions of revolutionary ardor and hope for the eventual brotherhood of man.

TESS SLESINGER (1905–    ) has traveled extensively, worked on New York newspapers, and written short stories for *Story, The American Mercury, Vanity Fair,* and *Forum.* She is principally concerned with portrayal in fictional form of the problems of intellectuals in a changing society, the theme of her novel, *The Unpossessed.*

ROBERT SOUTHEY (1774–1843) was an English poet and poet-laureate, closely associated with Wordsworth and Coleridge. A brother-in-law of Coleridge, he was interested in the Pantisocratic scheme for an ideal state on the banks of the Susquehanna. Although he was rated highly in his time, only a few of his ballads and shorter poems can be read with pleasure today.

STEPHEN SPENDER (1909–    ) is one of the group of young Oxford poets who have devoted themselves largely to criticisms of the present social order. In addition to his *Poems* (1936) he has written a verse play, *Trial of a Judge,* and a critical study, *The Destructive Element.*

LINCOLN STEFFENS (1866–1936) was a newspaper man and editor of *McClure's Magazine* from 1902 to 1906, associate editor of *American Magazine* and *Everybody's Magazine* from 1906 to 1911. He first attracted wide attention for his exposé of political and civic corruption in the United States (*The Shame of the Cities,* 1904). *The Autobiography of Lincoln Steffens* is recognized as a masterpiece of personal analysis and social criticism.

JOHN STEINBECK (1900–    ) is a California writer whose experiences as newspaper man, ranch hand, carpenter's helper, painter's apprentice, and laborer make him a valid critic of American life. His interest in the psychopathic is especially evident in *Of Mice and Men* (1937); his novels, *In Dubious Battle*

(1936) and *The Grapes of Wrath* (1939), have given us memorable pictures of the problems of America's laboring classes.

ROBERT LOUIS STEVENSON (1850–1894) is a romantic novelist, short story writer, and essayist whose life of physical suffering and mental conflicts is in contrast to the gay, zestful mood of most of his writings. Many of his most delightful essays reveal the joy of an adventurous spirit in travel and in strange places, which he constantly views as scenes for colorful actions.

ANNA LOUISE STRONG (1885–    ), born at Friend, Nebraska, is an expert in exhibition work especially in connection with child welfare. She was the founder and magazine editor of the *Moscow News*, the first English language paper published in Russia. Among the magazines to which she has contributed are *Collier's*, *Harper's*, *Atlantic Monthly*, *Asia*, and *Survey*. Some of her books are *Psychology of Prayer*, *History of the Seattle General Strike*, *China's Millions*, *I Change Worlds*, and *Spain in Arms*.

JESSE STUART (1908–    ) was born at Riverton, Kentucky, the scene of many of the stories of his book, *Head O' W-Hollow*, and celebrated in the sonnets which appeared in his *Man with a Bull-Tongue Plow*. The story of his Kentucky boyhood and background is found in his latest book, *Beyond Dark Hills*. Much of his work is found today in *The Yale Review*, *Scribner's*, *Harper's*, *Story Magazine* and *Esquire*.

SIR JOHN SUCKLING (1609–1642) was one of the most famous of the so-called Cavalier poets at the court of King Charles I. He fought for his king in the civil war and died in exile. He is best known for his short love lyrics. .

JONATHAN SWIFT (1667–1745) is generally acknowledged to be the greatest English satirist in prose. With savage irony he probes beneath appearances and exposes harsh realities. His hatred of sham and oppression find vent in *Gulliver's Travels* (1726) in which he has written a tale delighting children and shocking and challenging adults by bitter satire on human vices and follies.

ALGERNON CHARLES SWINBURNE (1837–1901) has been called "the greatest lyric poet that ever wrote in the English tongue when skill and virtuosity are considered." His poetry is pervaded by his enthusiasm for freedom, individual, political and religious. *To Walt Whitman—In America* appeared in 1871 in his volume *Songs Before Sunrise*, exalting the cause of Italian freedom.

GENEVIEVE TAGGARD (1894–    ) has had a wide experience of American life, from California to New York. Her work includes social criticism and poems in subtle metaphysical vein (*Calling Western Union*, 1936, and *Collected Poems*, 1938). She is now on the faculty of Sarah Lawrence College.

ALFRED, LORD TENNYSON (1809–1892) is considered the most representative poet of the Victorian era in the faith which finally resolves his doubts, in his acceptance of the new science and the age of industrialism as bringing human progress, and in the conservatism, which made him an acceptable poet-laureate. Valued in his own day for his ideas, he lives today rather for the felicity of his diction and his skill in handling lyric forms. *Locksley Hall* (1842) expresses his earlier moods of bitter personal feeling and social criticism.

FRANCIS THOMPSON (1859–1907) was an English poet of Catholic faith who united religious mysticism with power of vivid imagery and intense feeling.

HENRY DAVID THOREAU (1817–1862) was a member of the Concord group, a graduate of Harvard, and an ardent non-conformist in his social and political ideals. Determined to assert his individual freedom from bonds of society, he lived alone at Walden Pond from 1845 to 1847. *Walden* (1854) is the record of this experience, interspersed with delightful descriptions, philosophical digressions, and reflections of his colorful personality.

JAMES THURBER (1894–   ), a well known humorist, contributes both pen and ink drawings and literary sketches to *The New Yorker.* Among his published works are *My Life and Hard Times* and *Let Your Mind Alone.*

ERNST TOLLER (1893–1939), born at Samochin in German Poland, was imprisoned for five years after the revolution in Bavaria. His books were burned in Germany, and he was deprived of citizenship. Among his better known plays are *Machine-Wreckers, Man and the Masses,* and *Hinkemann.*

RIDGELY TORRENCE (1875–   ), born at Xenia, Ohio, was editor of *The Critic* (1903); associate editor of *The Cosmopolitan* (1905–1907); and poetry editor of *The New Republic* (1920–1934). He is the author of *The House of a Hundred Lights, Abelard and Heloise* (poetic drama), *The Undefended Line* (play) and *Plays for a Negro Theatre.*

MARK TWAIN (Samuel Clemens) (1835–1910), first of American humorists, was born in Hannibal, Missouri, a river town he has immortalized as background of Tom Sawyer and Huckleberry Finn. *Innocents Abroad* (1869) is the result of his European travels and brought him recognition abroad as well as at home. He excels in power to tell a swift moving, realistic, and humorous tale, bringing to bear his vivid impressions of the varied life he has known.

MARK VAN DOREN (1894–   ) is a professor in the English Department at Columbia University. He is known also as poet, critic, and associate editor of *The Nation.*

MARY HEATON VORSE, for many years a contributor to magazines, has long been interested in the struggle of the working class. She has written *The Autobiography of an Elderly Woman, Growing Up, Men and Steel, Second Cabin, Strike—A Novel of Gastonia,* and *A Footnote to Folly.*

WALT WHITMAN (1819–1892) has exerted a great liberalizing effect on American poetry and American life. His *Leaves of Grass,* first published in 1855, startled the country with its freedom from conventions of theme and form, but it was not until rather late in life that he was taken seriously as a great original poet, the first to be genuinely American. He attacks American complacence and the hypocritical aspects of our democracy, setting forth a vision of real brotherhood based on recognition of man's humane and divine nature.

WILLIAM WORDSWORTH (1770–1850), English poet, was early influenced by the French Revolution to embrace liberal principles, but on his disillusionment with France and England following the Revolution, he became conservative. As poet of nature and man he ranks high, and he was most influential in bringing about, with Coleridge, a revolution in the diction and subject matter of poetry. He advocated use of the "very language" of men in treating themes from rustic and humble life.

ELINOR WYLIE (1885–1928) began writing poetry as a very young girl. *Nets to Catch the Wind* appeared in 1921, and after her marriage to poet and critic, William Rose Benét (1923), she turned to writing novels. She is the author of

*Jennifer Lorn* and *The Orphan Angel*, an imaginative romance about Shelley. Her work is noted for its exquisite precision and delicacy.

WILLIAM BUTLER YEATS (1865–1939) was leader and greatest poet of the Irish Literary Renaissance which has given us rich treatments in prose, poetry, and drama of Irish folk lore and history, as well as expressions of Irish nationalist feeling. His *Collected Poems*, published in 1933, represent a passing from the poetry of sheer lyric artistry and imagination to poetry of social criticism and intellectual subtlety. Among his best known plays are *Deirdre, The Hour Glass, Cathleen Ni Hoolihan.*

GREGORY ZILBOORG (1890–    ), born in Kiev, Russia, is author of *The Passing of the Old Order in Europe* and *The Medical Man and the Witch During the Renaissance.* Editor and founder of the *Psychoanalytic Quarterly*, he has also contributed medical articles to the *N. Y. S. Journal of Medicine*, the *American Journal of Obstetrics and Gynecology*, the *Journal of Nervous and Mental Diseases*, and many others.

# INDEX OF AUTHORS